T0138913

HANDBOOK OF
NATURAL
LANGUAGE
PROCESSING

SECOND EDITION

Chapman & Hall/CRC
Machine Learning & Pattern Recognition Series

SERIES EDITORS

Ralf Herbrich and Thore Graepel
Microsoft Research Ltd.
Cambridge, UK

AIMS AND SCOPE

This series reflects the latest advances and applications in machine learning and pattern recognition through the publication of a broad range of reference works, textbooks, and handbooks. The inclusion of concrete examples, applications, and methods is highly encouraged. The scope of the series includes, but is not limited to, titles in the areas of machine learning, pattern recognition, computational intelligence, robotics, computational/statistical learning theory, natural language processing, computer vision, game AI, game theory, neural networks, computational neuroscience, and other relevant topics, such as machine learning applied to bioinformatics or cognitive science, which might be proposed by potential contributors.

PUBLISHED TITLES

MACHINE LEARNING: An Algorithmic Perspective
Stephen Marsland

HANDBOOK OF NATURAL LANGUAGE PROCESSING,
Second Edition
Nitin Indurkhya and Fred J. Damerau

Chapman & Hall/CRC
Machine Learning & Pattern Recognition Series

HANDBOOK OF
NATURAL
LANGUAGE
PROCESSING

SECOND EDITION

Edited by
NITIN INDURKHYA
FRED J. DAMERAU

CRC Press
Taylor & Francis Group
Boca Raton   London   New York

CRC Press is an imprint of the
Taylor & Francis Group, an **informa** business

A CHAPMAN & HALL BOOK

Chapman & Hall/CRC
Taylor & Francis Group
6000 Broken Sound Parkway NW, Suite 300
Boca Raton, FL 33487-2742

© 2010 by Taylor and Francis Group, LLC
Chapman & Hall/CRC is an imprint of Taylor & Francis Group, an Informa business

No claim to original U.S. Government works

Printed in the United States of America on acid-free paper
10 9 8 7 6 5 4 3 2 1

International Standard Book Number: 978-1-4200-8592-1 (Hardback)

This book contains information obtained from authentic and highly regarded sources. Reasonable efforts have been made to publish reliable data and information, but the author and publisher cannot assume responsibility for the validity of all materials or the consequences of their use. The authors and publishers have attempted to trace the copyright holders of all material reproduced in this publication and apologize to copyright holders if permission to publish in this form has not been obtained. If any copyright material has not been acknowledged please write and let us know so we may rectify in any future reprint.

Except as permitted under U.S. Copyright Law, no part of this book may be reprinted, reproduced, transmitted, or utilized in any form by any electronic, mechanical, or other means, now known or hereafter invented, including photocopying, microfilming, and recording, or in any information storage or retrieval system, without written permission from the publishers.

For permission to photocopy or use material electronically from this work, please access www.copyright.com (http://www.copyright.com/) or contact the Copyright Clearance Center, Inc. (CCC), 222 Rosewood Drive, Danvers, MA 01923, 978-750-8400. CCC is a not-for-profit organization that provides licenses and registration for a variety of users. For organizations that have been granted a photocopy license by the CCC, a separate system of payment has been arranged.

Trademark Notice: Product or corporate names may be trademarks or registered trademarks, and are used only for identification and explanation without intent to infringe.

Library of Congress Cataloging-in-Publication Data

Handbook of natural language processing / [edited by] Nitin Indurkhya and Fred J. Damerau.
       p. cm. -- (Chapman & Hall/CRC machine learning & pattern recognition)
    Includes bibliographical references and index.
    ISBN 978-1-4200-8592-1 (alk. paper)
    1. Natural language processing (Computer science)--Handbooks, manuals, etc. I. Indurkhya, Nitin.
II. Damerau, Frederick J. (Frederick Jacob), 1931-

QA76.9.N38H363 2010
006.3'5--dc22   2009049507

Visit the Taylor & Francis Web site at
http://www.taylorandfrancis.com

and the CRC Press Web site at
http://www.crcpress.com

To Fred Damerau
born December 25, 1931; died January 27, 2009

Some enduring publications:

Damerau, F. 1964. A technique for computer detection and correction of spelling errors. *Commun. ACM* 7, 3 (Mar. 1964), 171–176.

Damerau, F. 1971. *Markov Models and Linguistic Theory: An Experimental Study of a Model for English*. The Hague, the Netherlands: Mouton.

Damerau, F. 1985. Problems and some solutions in customization of natural language database front ends. *ACM Trans. Inf. Syst.* 3, 2 (Apr. 1985), 165–184.

Apté, C., Damerau, F., and Weiss, S. 1994. Automated learning of decision rules for text categorization. *ACM Trans. Inf. Syst.* 12, 3 (Jul. 1994), 233–251.

Weiss, S., Indurkhya, N., Zhang, T., and Damerau, F. 2005. *Text Mining: Predictive Methods for Analyzing Unstructured Information*. New York: Springer.

Contents

PART I   Classical Approaches

PART II   Empirical and Statistical Approaches

PART III Applications

List of Figures

List of Tables

Editors

Nitin Indurkhya is on the faculty at the School of Computer Science and Engineering, University of New South Wales, Sydney, Australia, and also teaches online courses on natural language processing and text mining at statistics.com. He is also the founder and president of Data-Miner Pty. Ltd., an Australian company that specializes in education, training, and consultation for data/text analytics and human language technologies. He is a coauthor (with Weiss, Zhang, and Damerau) of *Text Mining*, published by Springer in 2005, and a coauthor (with Weiss) of *Predictive Data Mining*, published by Morgan Kaufmann in 1997.

Fred Damerau passed away recently. He was a researcher at IBM's Thomas J. Watson Research Center, Yorktown Heights, New York, Research Staff Linguistics Group, where he worked on machine learning approaches to natural language processing. He is a coauthor (with Weiss, Indurkhya, and Zhang) of *Text Mining* as well as of numerous papers in computational linguistics, information retrieval, and like fields.

Keh-Yih Su, Behavior Design Corporation, Hsinchu, Taiwan
Ellen Voorhees, National Institute of Standards and Technology, Gaithersburg, Maryland
Bonnie Webber, University of Edinburgh, Edinburgh, United Kingdom
Theresa Wilson, University of Edinburgh, Edinburgh, United Kingdom

Board of Reviewers

Sophia Ananiadou, University of Manchester, Manchester, United Kingdom
Douglas E. Appelt, SRI International, Menlo Park, California
Nathalie Aussenac-Gilles, IRIT-CNRS, Toulouse, France
John Bateman, University of Bremen, Bremen, Germany
Steven Bird, University of Melbourne, Melbourne, Australia
Francis Bond, Nanyang Technological University, Singapore
Giuseppe Carenini, University of British Columbia, Vancouver, Canada
John Carroll, University of Sussex, Brighton, United Kingdom
Eugene Charniak, Brown University, Providence, Rhode Island
Ken Church, Johns Hopkins University, Baltimore, Maryland
Stephen Clark, University of Cambridge, Cambridge, United Kingdom
Robert Dale, Macquarie University, Sydney, Australia
Gaël Dias, Universidade da Beira Interior, Covilhã, Portugal
Jason Eisner, Johns Hopkins University, Baltimore, Maryland
Roger Evans, University of Brighton, Brighton, United Kingdom
Randy Fish, Messiah College, Grantham, Pennsylvania
Bob Futrelle, Northeastern University, Boston, Massachusetts
Gerald Gazdar, University of Sussex, Bringhton, United Kingdom
Andrew Hardie, Lancaster University, Lancaster, United Kingdom
David Hawking, Funnelback, Canberra, Australia
John Henderson, MITRE Corporation, Bedford, Massachusetts
Eduard Hovy, ISI-USC, Arlington, California
Adam Kilgariff, Lexical Computing Ltd., Bringhton, United Kingdom
Richard Kittredge, CoGenTex Inc., Ithaca, New York
Kevin Knight, ISI-USC, Arlington, California
Greg Kondrak, University of Alberta, Edmonton, Canada
Alon Lavie, Carnegie Mellon University, Pittsburgh, Pennsylvania
Haizhou Li, Institute for Infocomm Research, Singapore
Chin-Yew Lin, Microsoft Research Asia, Beijing, China
Anke Lüdeling, Humboldt-Universität zu Berlin, Berlin, Germany
Adam Meyers, New York University, New York, New York
Ray Mooney, University of Texas at Austin, Austin, Texas
Mark-Jan Nederhof, University of St Andrews, St Andrews, United Kingdom
Adwait Ratnaparkhi, Yahoo!, Santa Clara, California
Salim Roukos, IBM Corporation, Yorktown Heights, New York
Donia Scott, Open University, Milton Keynes, United Kingdom

Keh-Yih Su, Behavior Design Corporation, Hsinchu, Taiwan
Ellen Voorhees, National Institute of Standards and Technology, Gaithersburg, Maryland
Bonnie Webber, University of Edinburgh, Edinburgh, United Kingdom
Theresa Wilson, University of Edinburgh, Edinburgh, United Kingdom

Contributors

Anne Abeillé
Laboratoire LLF
Université Paris 7 and CNRS
Paris, France

Timothy Baldwin
Department of Computer
  Science and Software
  Engineering
University of Melbourne
Melbourne, Victoria, Australia

Paul Buitelaar
Natural Language Processing
  Unit
Digital Enterprise Research
  Institute
National University of Ireland
Galway, Ireland

Rudi L. Cilibrasi
Centrum Wiskunde &
  Informatica
Amsterdam, the Netherlands

Philipp Cimiano
Web Information Systems
Delft University of Technology
Delft, the Netherlands

K. Bretonnel Cohen
Center for Computational
  Pharmacology
School of Medicine
University of Colorado Denver
Aurora, Colorado

Robert Dale
Department of Computing
Faculty of Science
Macquarie University
Sydney, New South Wales,
  Australia

Li Deng
Microsoft Research
Microsoft Corporation
Redmond, Washington

Barbara Di Eugenio
Department of Computer
  Science
University of Illinois at Chicago
Chicago, Illinois

Pascale Fung
Department of Electronic and
  Computer Engineering
The Hong Kong University of
  Science and Technology
Clear Water Bay, Hong Kong

Eric Gaussier
Laboratoire d'informatique de
  Grenoble
Université Joseph Fourier
Grenoble, France

Cliff Goddard
School of Behavioural,
  Cognitive and Social Sciences
University of New England
Armidale, New South Wales,
  Australia

Nancy L. Green
Department of Computer
  Science
University of North Carolina
  Greensboro
Greensboro, North Carolina

Tunga Güngör
Department of Computer
  Engineering
Boğaziçi University
Istanbul, Turkey

Jan Hajič
Faculty of Mathematics and
  Physics
Institute of Formal and Applied
  Linguistics
Charles University
Prague, Czech Republic

Eva Hajičová
Faculty of Mathematics and
  Physics
Institute of Formal and Applied
  Linguistics
Charles University
Prague, Czech Republic

Andrew Hippisley
Department of English
College of Arts and Sciences
University of Kentucky
Lexington, Kentucky

Jerry R. Hobbs
Information Sciences Institute
University of Southern
    California
Los Angeles, California

Xuedong Huang
Microsoft Corporation
Redmond, Washington

Abraham Ittycheriah
IBM Corporation
Armonk, New York

Su Nam Kim
Department of Computer
    Science and Software
    Engineering
University of Melbourne
Melbourne, Victoria, Australia

Bing Liu
Department of Computer
    Science
University of Illinois at Chicago
Chicago, Illinois

Peter Ljunglöf
Department of Philosophy,
    Linguistics and Theory of
    Science
University of Gothenburg
Gothenburg, Sweden

David D. McDonald
BBN Technologies
Cambridge, Massachusetts

Jiří Mírovský
Faculty of Mathematics and
    Physics
Institute of Formal and Applied
    Linguistics
Charles University
Prague, Czech Republic

Diego Mollá-Aliod
Faculty of Science
Department of Computing
Macquarie University
Sydney, New South Wales,
    Australia

Joakim Nivre
Department of Linguistics and
    Philology
Uppsala University
Uppsala, Sweden

David D. Palmer
Advanced Technology Group
Autonomy Virage
Cambridge, Massachusetts

Ellen Riloff
School of Computing
University of Utah
Salt Lake City, Utah

Jacques Savoy
Department of Computer
    Science
University of Neuchatel
Neuchatel, Switzerland

Andrea C. Schalley
School of Languages and
    Linguistics
Griffith University
Brisbane, Queensland, Australia

Zdeňka Urešová
Institute of Formal and Applied
    Linguistics
Faculty of Mathematics and
    Physics
Charles University
Prague, Czech Republic

José-Luis Vicedo
Departamento de Lenguajes y
    Sistemas Informáticos
Universidad de Alicante
Alicante, Spain

Paul M.B. Vitányi
Centrum Wiskunde &
    Informatica
Amsterdam, the Netherlands

Johanna Völker
Institute of Applied Informatics
    and Formal Description
    Methods
University of Karlsruhe
Karlsruhe, Germany

Leo Wanner
Institució Catalana de Recerca i
    Estudis Avançats
and
Universitat Pompeu Fabra
Barcelona, Spain

Mats Wirén
Department of Linguistics
Stockholm University
Stockholm, Sweden

Dekai Wu
Department of Computer
    Science and Engineering
The Hong Kong University of
    Science and Technology
Clear Water Bay, Hong Kong

Richard Xiao
Department of English and
    History
Edge Hill University
Lancashire, United Kingdom

David Yarowsky
Department of Computer
    Science
Johns Hopkins University
Baltimore, Maryland

Tong Zhang
Department of Statistics
Rutgers, The State University of
    New Jersey
Piscataway, New Jersey

Preface

As the title of this book suggests, it is an update of the first edition of the *Handbook of Natural Language Processing* which was edited by Robert Dale, Hermann Moisl, and Harold Somers and published in the year 2000. The vigorous growth of new methods in Natural Language Processing (henceforth, NLP) since then, strongly suggested that a revision was needed. This handbook is a result of that effort.

From the first edition's preface, the following extracts lay out its focus, and distinguish it from other books within the field:

- *Throughout, the emphasis is on practical tools and techniques for implementable systems.*
- *The handbook takes NLP to be exclusively concerned with the design and implementation of effective natural language input and output components for computational systems.*
- *This handbook is aimed at language-engineering professionals.*

For continuity, the focus and general structure has been retained and this edition too focuses strongly on the *how* of the techniques rather than the *what*. The emphasis is on practical tools for implementable systems. Such a focus also continues to distinguish the handbook from recently published handbooks on Computational Linguistics.

Besides the focus on practical issues in NLP, there are two other noteworthy features of this handbook:

- **Multilingual Scope:** Since the handbook is for practitioners, many of whom are very interested in developing systems for their own languages, most chapters in this handbook discuss the relevance/deployment of methods to many different languages. This should make the handbook more appealing to international readers.
- **Companion Wiki:** In fields, such as NLP, that grow rapidly with significant new directions emerging every year, it is important to consider how a reference book can remain relevant for a reasonable period of time. To address this concern, a companion wiki is integrated with this handbook. The wiki not only contains static links as in traditional websites, but also supplementary material. Registered users can add/modify content.

Consistent with the update theme, several contributors to the first edition were invited to redo their chapters for this edition. In cases where they were unable to do so, they were invited to serve as reviewers. Even though the contributors are well-known experts, all chapters were peer-reviewed. The review process was amiable and constructive. Contributors knew their reviewers and were often in close contact with them during the writing process. The final responsibility for the contents of each chapter lies with its authors.

In this handbook, the original structure of three sections has been retained but somewhat modified in scope. The first section keeps its focus on classical techniques. While these are primarily symbolic, early empirical approaches are also considered. The first chapter in this section, by Robert Dale, one of the editors of the first edition, gives an overview. The second section acknowledges the emergence and dominance of statistical approaches in NLP. Entire books have been written on these methods, some by the contributors themselves. By having up-to-date chapters in one section, the material is made more accessible to readers. The third section focuses on applications of NLP techniques, with each chapter describing a class of applications. Such an organization has resulted in a handbook that clearly has its roots in the first edition, but looks towards the future by incorporating many recent and emerging developments.

It is worth emphasizing that this is a handbook, not a textbook, nor an encyclopedia. A textbook would have more pedagogical material, such as exercises. An encyclopedia would aim to be more comprehensive. A handbook typically aims to be a ready reference providing quick access to key concepts and ideas. The reader is not required to read chapters in sequence to understand them. Some topics are covered in greater detail and depth elsewhere. This handbook does not intend to replace such resources. The individual chapters strive to strike a balance between in-depth analysis and breadth of coverage while keeping the content accessible to the target audience. Most chapters are 25–30 pages. Chapters may refer to other chapters for additional details, but in the interests of readability and for notational purposes, some repetition is unavoidable. Thus, many chapters can be read without reference to others. This will be helpful for the reader who wants to quickly gain an understanding of a specific subarea. While standalone chapters are in the spirit of a handbook, the ordering of chapters does follow a progression of ideas. For example, the applications are carefully ordered to begin with well-known ones such as Chinese Machine Translation and end with exciting cutting-edge applications in biomedical text mining and sentiment analysis.

Audience

The handbook aims to cater to the needs of NLP practitioners and language-engineering professionals in academia as well as in industry. It will also appeal to graduate students and upper-level undergraduates seeking to do graduate studies in NLP. The reader should likely have or will be pursuing a degree in linguistics, computer science, or computer engineering. A double degree is not required, but basic background in both linguistics and computing is expected. Some of the chapters, particularly in the second section, may require mathematical maturity. Some others can be read and understood by anyone with a sufficient scientific bend. The prototypical reader is interested in the practical aspects of building NLP systems and may also be interested in working with languages other than English.

Companion Wiki

An important feature of this handbook is the companion wiki:
http://handbookofnlp.cse.unsw.edu.au
It is an integral part of the handbook. Besides pointers to online resources, it also includes supplementary information for many chapters. The wiki will be actively maintained and will help keep the handbook relevant for a long time. Readers are encouraged to contribute to it by registering their interest with the appropriate chapter authors.

Acknowledgments

My experience of working on this handbook was very enjoyable. Part of the reason was that it put me in touch with a number of remarkable individuals. With over 80 contributors and reviewers, this handbook has been a huge community effort. Writing readable and useful chapters for a handbook is not an easy task. I thank the contributors for their efforts. The reviewers have done an outstanding job of giving extensive and constructive feedback in spite of their busy schedules. I also thank the editors of the first edition, many elements of which we used in this edition as well. Special thanks to Robert Dale for his thoughtful advice and suggestions. At the publisher's editorial office, Randi Cohen has been extremely supportive and dependable and I could not have managed without her help. Thanks, Randi. The anonymous reviewers of the book proposal made many insightful comments that helped us with the design. I lived and worked in several places during the preparation of this handbook. I was working in Brasil when I received the initial invitation to take on this project and thank my friends in Amazonas and the Nordeste for their love and affection. I also lived in Singapore for a short time and thank the School of Computer Engineering, Nanyang Technological University, for its support. The School of Computer Science and Engineering in UNSW, Sydney, Australia is my home base and provides me with an outstanding work environment. The handbook's wiki is hosted there as well. Fred Damerau, my co-editor, passed away early this year. I feel honoured to have collaborated with him on several projects including this one. I dedicate the handbook to him.

Nitin Indurkhya
Australia and Brasil
Southern Autumn, 2009

I

Classical Approaches

I

Classical Approaches

1

Classical Approaches to Natural Language Processing

Robert Dale
Macquarie University

1.1 Context

The first edition of this handbook appeared in 2000, but the project that resulted in that volume in fact began 4 years earlier, in mid-1996. When Hermann Moisl, Harold Somers, and I started planning the content of the book, the field of natural language processing was less than 10 years into what some might call its "statistical revolution." It was still early enough that there were occasional signs of friction between some of the "old guard," who hung on to the symbolic approaches to natural language processing that they had grown up with, and the "young turks," with their new-fangled statistical processing techniques, which just kept gaining ground. Some in the old guard would give talks pointing out that there were problems in natural language processing that were beyond the reach of statistical or corpus-based methods; meanwhile, the occasional young turk could be heard muttering a variation on Fred Jelinek's 1988 statement that "whenever I fire a linguist my system performance improves." Then there were those with an eye to a future peaceful coexistence that promised jobs for all, arguing that we needed to develop hybrid techniques and applications that integrated the best properties of both the symbolic approaches and the statistical approaches.

At the time, we saw the handbook as being one way of helping to catalog the constituent tools and techniques that might play a role in such hybrid enterprises. So, in the first edition of the handbook, we adopted a tripartite structure, with the 38 book chapters being fairly evenly segregated into Symbolic Approaches to NLP, Empirical Approaches to NLP, and NLP based on Artificial Neural Networks. The editors of the present edition have renamed the Symbolic Approaches to NLP part as Classical Approaches: that name change surely says something about the way in which things have developed over the last 10 years or so. In the various conferences and journals in our field, papers that make use of statistical techniques now very significantly outnumber those that do not. The number of chapters in the present edition of the handbook that focus on these "classical" approaches is half the number that focus on the empirical and statistical approaches. But these changes should not be taken as an indication that the earlier-established approaches are somehow less relevant; in fact, the reality is quite the opposite, as

3

the incorporation of linguistic knowledge into statistical processing becomes more and more common. Those who argue for the study of the classics in the more traditional sense of that word make great claims for the value of such study: it encourages the questioning of cultural assumptions, allows one to appreciate different cultures and value systems, promotes creative thinking, and helps one to understand the development of ideas. That is just as true in natural language processing as it is in the study of Greek literature.

So, in the spirit of all those virtues that surely no one would question, this part of the handbook provides thoughtful and reflective overviews of a number of areas of natural language processing that are in some sense foundational. They represent areas of research and technological development that have been around for some time; long enough to benefit from hindsight and a measured and more objective assessment than is possible for work that is more recent. This introduction comments briefly on each of these chapters as a way of setting the scene for this part of the handbook as a whole.

1.2 The Classical Toolkit

Traditionally, work in natural language processing has tended to view the process of language analysis as being decomposable into a number of stages, mirroring the theoretical linguistic distinctions drawn between SYNTAX, SEMANTICS, and PRAGMATICS. The simple view is that the sentences of a text are first analyzed in terms of their syntax; this provides an order and structure that is more amenable to an analysis in terms of semantics, or literal meaning; and this is followed by a stage of pragmatic analysis whereby the meaning of the utterance or text in context is determined. This last stage is often seen as being concerned with DISCOURSE, whereas the previous two are generally concerned with sentential matters. This attempt at a correlation between a stratificational distinction (syntax, semantics, and pragmatics) and a distinction in terms of granularity (sentence versus discourse) sometimes causes some confusion in thinking about the issues involved in natural language processing; and it is widely recognized that in real terms it is not so easy to separate the processing of language neatly into boxes corresponding to each of the strata. However, such a separation serves as a useful pedagogic aid, and also constitutes the basis for architectural models that make the task of natural language analysis more manageable from a software engineering point of view.

Nonetheless, the tripartite distinction into syntax, semantics, and pragmatics only serves at best as a starting point when we consider the processing of real natural language texts. A finer-grained decomposition of the process is useful when we take into account the current state of the art in combination with the need to deal with real language data; this is reflected in Figure 1.1.

We identify here the stage of tokenization and sentence segmentation as a crucial first step. Natural language text is generally not made up of the short, neat, well-formed, and well-delimited sentences we find in textbooks; and for languages such as Chinese, Japanese, or Thai, which do not share the apparently easy space-delimited tokenization we might believe to be a property of languages like English, the ability to address issues of tokenization is essential to getting off the ground at all. We also treat lexical analysis as a separate step in the process. To some degree this finer-grained decomposition reflects our current state of knowledge about language processing: we know quite a lot about general techniques for tokenization, lexical analysis, and syntactic analysis, but much less about semantics and discourse-level processing. But it also reflects the

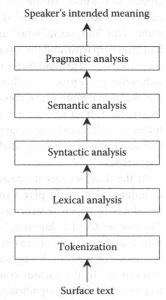

FIGURE 1.1 The stages of analysis in processing natural language.

fact that the known is the surface text, and anything deeper is a representational abstraction that is harder to pin down; so it is not so surprising that we have better-developed techniques at the more concrete end of the processing spectrum.

Of course, natural language analysis is only one-half of the story. We also have to consider natural language generation, where we are concerned with mapping from some (typically nonlinguistic) internal representation to a surface text. In the history of the field so far, there has been much less work on natural language generation than there has been on natural language analysis. One sometimes hears the suggestion that this is because natural language generation is easier, so that there is less to be said. This is far from the truth: there are a great many complexities to be addressed in generating fluent and coherent multi-sentential texts from an underlying source of information. A more likely reason for the relative lack of work in generation is precisely the correlate of the observation made at the end of the previous paragraph: it is relatively straightforward to build theories around the processing of something known (such as a sequence of words), but much harder when the input to the process is more or less left to the imagination. This is the question that causes researchers in natural language generation to wake in the middle of the night in a cold sweat: what does generation start from? Much work in generation is concerned with addressing these questions head-on; work in natural language understanding may eventually see benefit in taking generation's starting point as its end goal.

1.2.1 Text Preprocessing

As we have already noted, not all languages deliver text in the form of words neatly delimited by spaces. Languages such as Chinese, Japanese, and Thai require first that a segmentation process be applied, analogous to the segmentation process that must first be applied to a continuous speech stream in order to identify the words that make up an utterance. As Palmer demonstrates in his chapter, there are significant segmentation and tokenization issues in apparently easier-to-segment languages—such as English—too. Fundamentally, the issue here is that of what constitutes a word; as Palmer shows, there is no easy answer here. This chapter also looks at the problem of sentence segmentation: since so much work in natural language processing views the sentence as the unit of analysis, clearly it is of crucial importance to ensure that, given a text, we can break it into sentence-sized pieces. This turns out not to be so trivial either. Palmer offers a catalog of tips and techniques that will be useful to anyone faced with dealing with real raw text as the input to an analysis process, and provides a healthy reminder that these problems have tended to be idealized away in much earlier, laboratory-based work in natural language processing.

1.2.2 Lexical Analysis

The previous chapter addressed the problem of breaking a stream of input text into the words and sentences that will be subject to subsequent processing. The words, of course, are not atomic, and are themselves open to further analysis. Here we enter the realms of computational morphology, the focus of Andrew Hippisley's chapter. By taking words apart, we can uncover information that will be useful at later stages of processing. The combinatorics also mean that decomposing words into their parts, and maintaining rules for how combinations are formed, is much more efficient in terms of storage space than would be the case if we simply listed every word as an atomic element in a huge inventory. And, once more returning to our concern with the handling of real texts, there will always be words missing from any such inventory; morphological processing can go some way toward handling such unrecognized words. Hippisley provides a wide-ranging and detailed review of the techniques that can be used to carry out morphological processing, drawing on examples from languages other than English to demonstrate the need for sophisticated processing methods; along the way he provides some background in the relevant theoretical aspects of phonology and morphology.

1.2.3 Syntactic Parsing

A presupposition in most work in natural language processing is that the basic unit of meaning analysis is the sentence: a sentence expresses a proposition, an idea, or a thought, and says something about some real or imaginary world. Extracting the meaning from a sentence is thus a key issue. Sentences are not, however, just linear sequences of words, and so it is widely recognized that to carry out this task requires an analysis of each sentence, which determines its structure in one way or another. In NLP approaches based on generative linguistics, this is generally taken to involve the determining of the syntactic or grammatical structure of each sentence. In their chapter, Ljunglöf and Wirén present a range of techniques that can be used to achieve this end. This area is probably the most well established in the field of NLP, enabling the authors here to provide an inventory of basic concepts in parsing, followed by a detailed catalog of parsing techniques that have been explored in the literature.

1.2.4 Semantic Analysis

Identifying the underlying syntactic structure of a sequence of words is only one step in determining the meaning of a sentence; it provides a structured object that is more amenable to further manipulation and subsequent interpretation. It is these subsequent steps that derive a meaning for the sentence in question. Goddard and Schalley's chapter turns to these deeper issues. It is here that we begin to reach the bounds of what has so far been scaled up from theoretical work to practical application. As pointed out earlier in this introduction, the semantics of natural language have been less studied than syntactic issues, and so the techniques described here are not yet developed to the extent that they can easily be applied in a broad-coverage fashion.

After setting the scene by reviewing a range of existing approaches to semantic interpretation, Goddard and Schalley provide a detailed exposition of Natural Semantic Metalanguage, an approach to semantics that is likely to be new to many working in natural language processing. They end by cataloging some of the challenges to be faced if we are to develop truly broad coverage semantic analyses.

1.2.5 Natural Language Generation

At the end of the day, determining the meaning of an utterance is only really one-half of the story of natural language processing: in many situations, a response then needs to be generated, either in natural language alone or in combination with other modalities. For many of today's applications, what is required here is rather trivial and can be handled by means of canned responses; increasingly, however, we are seeing natural language generation techniques applied in the context of more sophisticated back-end systems, where the need to be able to custom-create fluent multi-sentential texts on demand becomes a priority. The generation-oriented chapters in the Applications part bear testimony to the scope here.

In his chapter, David McDonald provides a far-reaching survey of work in the field of natural language generation. McDonald begins by lucidly characterizing the differences between natural language analysis and natural language generation. He goes on to show what can be achieved using natural language generation techniques, drawing examples from systems developed over the last 35 years. The bulk of the chapter is then concerned with laying out a picture of the component processes and representations required in order to generate fluent multi-sentential or multi-paragraph texts, built around the now-standard distinction between text planning and linguistic realization.

1.3 Conclusions

Early research into machine translation was underway in both U.K. and U.S. universities in the mid-1950s, and the first annual meeting of the Association for Computational Linguistics was in 1963; so, depending on how you count, the field of natural language processing has either passed or is fast approaching its 50th birthday. A lot has been achieved in this time. This part of the handbook provides a consolidated summary of the outcomes of significant research agendas that have shaped the field and the issues it chooses to address. An awareness and understanding of this work is essential for any modern-day practitioner of natural language processing; as George Santayana put it over a 100 years ago, "Those who cannot remember the past are condemned to repeat it."

One aspect of computational work not represented here is the body of research that focuses on discourse and pragmatics. As noted earlier, it is in these areas that our understanding is still very much weaker than in areas such as morphology and syntax. It is probably also the case that there is currently less work going on here than there was in the past: there is a sense in which the shift to statistically based work restarted investigations of language processing from the ground up, and current approaches have many intermediate problems to tackle before they reach the concerns that were once the focus of "the discourse community." There is no doubt that these issues will resurface; but right now, the bulk of attention is focused on dealing with syntax and semantics.* When most problems here have been solved, we can expect to see a renewed interest in discourse-level phenomena and pragmatics, and at that point the time will be ripe for another edition of this handbook that puts classical approaches to discourse back on the table as a source of ideas and inspiration. Meanwhile, a good survey of various approaches can be found in Jurafsky and Martin (2008).

Reference

Jurafsky, D. and Martin, J. H., 2008, *Speech and Language Processing: An Introduction to Natural Language Processing, Speech Recognition, and Computational Linguistics*, 2nd edition. Prentice-Hall, Upper Saddle River, NJ.

---

* A notable exception is the considerable body of work on text summarization that has developed over the last 10 years.

2

Text Preprocessing

David D. Palmer
Autonomy Virage

2.1 Introduction

In the linguistic analysis of a digital natural language text, it is necessary to clearly define the characters, words, and sentences in any document. Defining these units presents different challenges depending on the language being processed and the source of the documents, and the task is not trivial, especially when considering the variety of human languages and writing systems. Natural languages contain inherent ambiguities, and writing systems often amplify ambiguities as well as generate additional ambiguities. Much of the challenge of Natural Language Processing (NLP) involves resolving these ambiguities. Early work in NLP focused on a small number of well-formed corpora in a small number of languages, but significant advances have been made in recent years by using large and diverse corpora from a wide range of sources, including a vast and ever-growing supply of dynamically generated text from the Internet. This explosion in corpus size and variety has necessitated techniques for automatically harvesting and preparing text corpora for NLP tasks.

In this chapter, we discuss the challenges posed by **text preprocessing**, the task of converting a raw text file, essentially a sequence of digital bits, into a well-defined sequence of linguistically meaningful units: at the lowest level characters representing the individual graphemes in a language's written system, words consisting of one or more characters, and sentences consisting of one or more words. Text preprocessing is an essential part of any NLP system, since the characters, words, and sentences identified at this stage are the fundamental units passed to all further processing stages, from analysis and tagging components, such as morphological analyzers and part-of-speech taggers, through applications, such as information retrieval and machine translation systems.

Text preprocessing can be divided into two stages: document triage and text segmentation. **Document triage** is the process of converting a set of digital files into well-defined text documents. For early corpora, this was a slow, manual process, and these early corpora were rarely more than a few million words.

In contrast, current corpora harvested from the Internet can encompass billions of words *each day*, which requires a fully automated document triage process. This process can involve several steps, depending on the origin of the files being processed. First, in order for any natural language document to be machine readable, its characters must be represented in a character encoding, in which one or more bytes in a file maps to a known character. **Character encoding identification** determines the character encoding (or encodings) for any file and optionally converts between encodings. Second, in order to know what language-specific algorithms to apply to a document, **language identification** determines the natural language for a document; this step is closely linked to, but not uniquely determined by, the character encoding. Finally, **text sectioning** identifies the actual content within a file while discarding undesirable elements, such as images, tables, headers, links, and HTML formatting. The output of the document triage stage is a well-defined text corpus, organized by language, suitable for text segmentation and further analysis.

Text segmentation is the process of converting a well-defined text corpus into its component words and sentences. **Word segmentation** breaks up the sequence of characters in a text by locating the **word boundaries**, the points where one word ends and another begins. For computational linguistics purposes, the words thus identified are frequently referred to as **tokens**, and word segmentation is also known as **tokenization**. **Text normalization** is a related step that involves merging different written forms of a token into a canonical normalized form; for example, a document may contain the equivalent tokens "Mr.", "Mr", "mister", and "Mister" that would all be normalized to a single form.

Sentence segmentation is the process of determining the longer processing units consisting of one or more words. This task involves identifying **sentence boundaries** between words in different sentences. Since most written languages have punctuation marks that occur at sentence boundaries, sentence segmentation is frequently referred to as **sentence boundary detection**, **sentence boundary disambiguation**, or **sentence boundary recognition**. All these terms refer to the same task: determining how a text should be divided into sentences for further processing.

In practice, sentence and word segmentation cannot be performed successfully independent from one another. For example, an essential subtask in both word and sentence segmentation for most European languages is identifying abbreviations, because a period can be used to mark an abbreviation as well as to mark the end of a sentence. In the case of a period marking an abbreviation, the period is usually considered a part of the abbreviation token, whereas a period at the end of a sentence is usually considered a token in and of itself. In the case of an abbreviation at the end of a sentence, the period marks *both* the abbreviation and the sentence boundary.

This chapter provides an introduction to text preprocessing in a variety of languages and writing systems. We begin in Section 2.2 with a discussion of the challenges posed by text preprocessing, and emphasize the document triage issues that must be considered before implementing a tokenization or sentence segmentation algorithm. The section describes the dependencies on the language being processed and the character set in which the language is encoded. It also discusses the dependency on the application that uses the output of the segmentation and the dependency on the characteristics of the specific corpus being processed.

In Section 2.3, we introduce some common techniques currently used for tokenization. The first part of the section focuses on issues that arise in tokenizing and normalizing languages in which words are separated by whitespace. The second part of the section discusses tokenization techniques in languages where no such whitespace word boundaries exist. In Section 2.4, we discuss the problem of sentence segmentation and introduce some common techniques currently used to identify sentence boundaries in texts.

2.2 Challenges of Text Preprocessing

There are many issues that arise in text preprocessing that need to be addressed when designing NLP systems, and many can be addressed as part of document triage in preparing a corpus for analysis.

The type of writing system used for a language is the most important factor for determining the best approach to text preprocessing. Writing systems can be **logographic**, where a large number (often thousands) of individual symbols represent words. In contrast, writing systems can be **syllabic**, in which individual symbols represent syllables, or **alphabetic**, in which individual symbols (more or less) represent sounds; unlike logographic systems, syllabic and alphabetic systems typically have fewer than 100 symbols. According to Comrie et al. (1996), the majority of all written languages use an alphabetic or syllabic system. However, in practice, no modern writing system employs symbols of only one kind, so no natural language writing system can be classified as purely logographic, syllabic, or alphabetic. Even English, with its relatively simple writing system based on the Roman alphabet, utilizes logographic symbols including Arabic numerals (0–9), currency symbols ($, £), and other symbols (%, &, #). English is nevertheless predominately alphabetic, and most other writing systems are comprised of symbols which are mainly of one type.

In this section, we discuss the essential document triage steps, and we emphasize the main types of dependencies that must be addressed in developing algorithms for text segmentation: **character-set dependence** (Section 2.2.1), **language dependence** (Section 2.2.2), **corpus dependence** (Section 2.2.3), and **application dependence** (Section 2.2.4).

2.2.1 Character-Set Dependence

At its lowest level, a computer-based text or document is merely a sequence of digital bits in a file. The first essential task is to interpret these bits as characters of a writing system of a natural language.

2.2.1.1 About Character Sets

Historically, interpreting digital text files was trivial, since nearly all texts were encoded in the **7-bit character set** ASCII, which allowed only 128 (2^7) characters and included only the Roman (or Latin) alphabet and essential characters for writing English. This limitation required the "asciification" or "romanization" of many texts, in which ASCII equivalents were defined for characters not defined in the character set. An example of this asciification is the adaptation of many European languages containing umlauts and accents, in which the umlauts are replaced by a double quotation mark or the letter 'e' and accents are denoted by a single quotation mark or even a number code. In this system, the German word *über* would be written as *u"ber* or *ueber*, and the French word *déjà* would be written as *de'ja'* or *de1ja2*. Languages that do not use the roman alphabet, such as Russian and Arabic, required much more elaborate romanization systems, usually based on a phonetic mapping of the source characters to the roman characters. The Pinyin transliteration of Chinese writing is another example of asciification of a more complex writing system. These adaptations are still common due to the widespread familiarity with the roman characters; in addition, some computer applications are still limited to this 7-bit encoding.

Eight-bit character sets can encode 256 (2^8) characters using a single 8-bit byte, but most of these 8-bit sets reserve the first 128 characters for the original ASCII characters. Eight-bit encodings exist for all common alphabetic and some syllabic writing systems; for example, the ISO-8859 series of 10+ character sets contains encoding definitions for most European characters, including separate ISO-8859 sets for the Cyrillic and Greek alphabets. However, since all 8-bit character sets are limited to exactly the same 256 byte codes (decimal 0–255), this results in a large number of overlapping character sets for encoding characters in different languages.

Writing systems with larger character sets, such as those of written Chinese and Japanese, which have several thousand distinct characters, require multiple bytes to encode a single character. A **two-byte character set** can represent 65,536 (2^{16}) distinct characters, since 2 bytes contain 16 bits. Determining individual characters in two-byte character sets involves grouping pairs of bytes representing a single character. This process can be complicated by the tokenization equivalent of code-switching, in which characters from many different writing systems occur within the same text. It is very common in digital texts to encounter multiple writing systems and thus multiple encodings, or as discussed previously, character encodings that include other encodings as subsets. In Chinese and Japanese texts, single-byte letters, spaces, punctuation marks (e.g., periods, quotation marks, and parentheses), and Arabic numerals (0–9) are commonly interspersed with 2-byte Chinese and Japanese characters. Such texts also frequently contain ASCII headers. Multiple encodings also exist for these character sets; for example, the Chinese character set is represented in two widely used encodings, Big-5 for the complex-form (traditional) character set and GB for the simple-form (simplified) set, with several minor variants of these sets also commonly found.

The **Unicode 5.0 standard** (Unicode Consortium 2006) seeks to eliminate this character set ambiguity by specifying a Universal Character Set that includes over 100,000 distinct coded characters derived from over 75 supported scripts representing all the writing systems commonly used today. The Unicode standard is most commonly implemented in the **UTF-8 variable-length character encoding**, in which each character is represented by a 1 to 4 byte encoding. In the UTF-8 encoding, ASCII characters require 1 byte, most other characters included in ISO-8859 character encodings and other alphabetic systems require 2 bytes, and all other characters, including Chinese, Japanese, and Korean, require 3 bytes (and very rarely 4 bytes). The Unicode standard and its implementation in UTF-8 allow for the encoding of all supported characters with no overlap or confusion between conflicting byte ranges, and it is rapidly replacing older character encoding sets for multilingual applications.

2.2.1.2 Character Encoding Identification and Its Impact on Tokenization

Despite the growing use of Unicode, the fact that the same range of numeric values can represent different characters in different encodings can be a problem for tokenization. For example, English or Spanish are both normally stored in the common 8-bit encoding Latin-1 (or ISO-8859-1). An English or Spanish tokenizer would need to be aware that bytes in the (decimal) range 161–191 in Latin-1 represent punctuation marks and other symbols (such as '¡', '¿', '£', and '©'). Tokenization rules would then be required to handle each symbol (and thus its byte code) appropriately for that language. However, this same byte range in UTF-8 represents the second (or third or fourth) byte of a multi-byte sequence and is meaningless by itself; an English or Spanish tokenizer for UTF-8 would thus need to model multi-byte character sequences explicitly. Furthermore, the same byte range in ISO-8859-5, a common Russian encoding, contains Cyrillic characters; in KOI8-R, another Russian encoding, the range contains a *different set* of Cyrillic characters. Tokenizers thus must be targeted to a specific language in a specific encoding.

Tokenization is unavoidably linked to the underlying character encoding of the text being processed, and character encoding identification is an essential first step. While the header of a digital document may contain information regarding its character encoding, this information is not always present or even reliable, in which case the encoding must be determined automatically.

A character encoding identification algorithm must first explicitly model the known encoding systems, in order to know in what byte ranges to look for valid characters as well as which byte ranges are unlikely to appear frequently in that encoding. The algorithm then analyzes the bytes in a file to construct a profile of which byte ranges are represented in the file. Next, the algorithm compares the patterns of bytes found in the file to the expected byte ranges from the known encodings and decides which encoding best fits the data.

Russian encodings provide a good example of the different byte ranges encountered for a given language. In the ISO-8859-5 encoding for Russian texts, the capital Cyrillic letters are in the (hexadecimal) range B0-CF (and are listed in the traditional Cyrillic alphabetical order); the lowercase letters are in the range D0-EF. In contrast, in the KOI8-R encoding, the capital letters are E0-FF (and are listed in pseudo-Roman order); the lowercase letters are C0-DF. In Unicode, Cyrillic characters require two bytes, and the capital letters are in the range 0410 (the byte 04 followed by the byte 10) through 042F; the lowercase letters are in the range 0430-045F. A character encoding identification algorithm seeking to determine the encoding of a given Russian text would examine the bytes contained in the file to determine the byte ranges present. The hex byte 04 is a rare control character in ISO-8859-5 and in KOI8-R but would comprise nearly half the bytes in a Unicode Russian file. Similarly, a file in ISO-8859-5 would likely contain many bytes in the range B0-BF but few in F0-FF, while a file in KOI8-R would contain few in B0-BF and many in F0-FF. Using these simple heuristics to analyze the byte distribution in a file should allow for straightforward encoding identification for Russian texts.

Note that, due to the overlap between existing character encodings, even with a high-quality character encoding classifier, it may be impossible to determine the character encoding. For example, since most character encodings reserve the first 128 characters for the ASCII characters, a document that contains only these 128 characters could be any of the ISO-8859 encodings or even UTF-8.

2.2.2 Language Dependence

2.2.2.1 Impact of Writing System on Text Segmentation

In addition to the variety of symbol types (logographic, syllabic, or alphabetic) used in writing systems, there is a range of orthographic conventions used in written languages to denote the boundaries between linguistic units such as syllables, words, or sentences. In many written Amharic texts, for example, both word and sentence boundaries are explicitly marked, while in written Thai texts neither is marked. In the latter case, where no boundaries are explicitly indicated in the written language, written Thai is similar to spoken language, where there are no explicit boundaries and few cues to indicate segments at any level. Between the two extremes are languages that mark boundaries to different degrees. English employs whitespace between most words and punctuation marks at sentence boundaries, but neither feature is sufficient to segment the text completely and unambiguously. Tibetan and Vietnamese both explicitly mark syllable boundaries, either through layout or by punctuation, but neither marks word boundaries. Written Chinese and Japanese have adopted punctuation marks for sentence boundaries, but neither denotes word boundaries.

In this chapter, we provide general techniques applicable to a variety of different writing systems. Since many segmentation issues are language-specific, we will also highlight the challenges faced by robust, broad-coverage tokenization efforts. For a very thorough description of the various writing systems employed to represent natural languages, including detailed examples of all languages and features discussed in this chapter, we recommend Daniels and Bright (1996).

2.2.2.2 Language Identification

The wide range of writing systems used by the languages of the world result in language-specific as well as orthography-specific features that must be taken into account for successful text segmentation. An important step in the document triage stage is thus to identify the language of each document or document section, since some documents are multilingual at the section level or even paragraph level.

For languages with a unique alphabet not used by any other languages, such as Greek or Hebrew, language identification is determined by character set identification. Similarly, character set identification can be used to narrow the task of language identification to a smaller number of languages that all share many characters, such as Arabic vs. Persian, Russian vs. Ukrainian, or Norwegian vs. Swedish. The byte range distribution used to determine character set identification can further be used to identify bytes, and thus characters, that are predominant in one of the remaining candidate languages, if the languages do not share exactly the same characters. For example, while Arabic and Persian both use the Arabic alphabet, the Persian language uses several supplemental characters that do not appear in Arabic. For more difficult cases, such as European languages that use exactly the same character set but with different frequencies, final identification can be performed by training models of byte/character distributions in each of the languages. A basic but very effective algorithm for this would sort the bytes in a file by frequency count and use the sorted list as a signature vector for comparison via an n-gram or vector distance model.

2.2.3 Corpus Dependence

Early NLP systems rarely addressed the problem of robustness, and they normally could process only well-formed input conforming to their hand-built grammars. The increasing availability of large corpora in multiple languages that encompass a wide range of data types (e.g., newswire texts, email messages, closed captioning data, Internet news pages, and weblogs) has required the development of robust NLP approaches, as these corpora frequently contain misspellings, erratic punctuation and spacing, and other irregular features. It has become increasingly clear that algorithms which rely on input texts to be well-formed are much less successful on these different types of texts.

Similarly, algorithms that expect a corpus to follow a set of conventions for a written language are frequently not robust enough to handle a variety of corpora, especially those harvested from the Internet. It is notoriously difficult to prescribe rules governing the use of a written language; it is even more difficult to get people to "follow the rules." This is in large part due to the nature of written language, in which the conventions are not always in line with actual usage and are subject to frequent change. So while punctuation roughly corresponds to the use of suprasegmental features in spoken language, reliance on well-formed sentences delimited by predictable punctuation can be very problematic. In many corpora, traditional prescriptive rules are commonly ignored. This fact is particularly important to our discussion of both word and sentence segmentation, which to a large degree depends on the regularity of spacing and punctuation. Most existing segmentation algorithms for natural languages are both language-specific and corpus-dependent, developed to handle the predictable ambiguities in a well-formed text. Depending on the origin and purpose of a text, capitalization and punctuation rules may be followed very closely (as in most works of literature), erratically (as in various newspaper texts), or not at all (as in email messages and personal Web pages). Corpora automatically harvested from the Internet can be especially ill-formed, such as Example (1), an actual posting to a Usenet newsgroup, which shows the erratic use of capitalization and punctuation, "creative" spelling, and domain-specific terminology inherent in such texts.

> (1) *ive just loaded pcl onto my akcl. when i do an 'in- package' to load pcl, ill get the prompt but im not able to use functions like defclass, etc... is there womething basic im missing or am i just left hanging, twisting in the breeze?*

Many digital text files, such as those harvested from the Internet, contain large regions of text that are undesirable for the NLP application processing the file. For example, Web pages can contain headers, images, advertisements, site navigation links, browser scripts, search engine optimization terms, and other markup, little of which is considered actual *content*. Robust text segmentation algorithms designed for use with such corpora must therefore have the capability to handle the range of irregularities, which distinguish these texts from well-formed corpora. A key task in the document triage stage for such files is text sectioning, in which extraneous text is removed. The sectioning and cleaning of Web pages has recently become the focus of Cleaneval, "a shared task and competitive evaluation on the topic of cleaning arbitrary Web pages, with the goal of preparing Web data for use as a corpus for linguistic and language technology research and development." (Baroni et al. 2008)

2.2.4 Application Dependence

Although word and sentence segmentation are necessary, in reality, there is no absolute definition for what constitutes a word or a sentence. Both are relatively arbitrary distinctions that vary greatly across written languages. However, for the purposes of computational linguistics we need to define exactly what we need for further processing; in most cases, the language and task at hand determine the necessary conventions. For example, the English words *I am* are frequently contracted to *I'm*, and a tokenizer frequently expands the contraction to recover the essential grammatical features of the pronoun and the verb. A tokenizer that does not expand this contraction to the component words would pass the single token *I'm* to later processing stages. Unless these processors, which may include morphological analyzers, part-of-speech taggers, lexical lookup routines, or parsers, are aware of both the contracted and uncontracted forms, the token may be treated as an unknown word.

Another example of the dependence of tokenization output on later processing stages is the treatment of the English possessive *'s* in various tagged corpora.* In the Brown corpus (Francis and Kucera 1982), the word *governor's* is considered one token and is tagged as a possessive noun. In the Susanne corpus (Sampson 1995), on the other hand, the same word is treated as two tokens, *governor* and *'s*, tagged singular noun and possessive, respectively.

Examples such as the above are usually addressed during tokenization by normalizing the text to meet the requirements of the applications. For example, language modeling for automatic speech recognition requires that the tokens be represented in a form similar to how they are spoken (and thus input to the speech recognizer). For example, the written token $300 would be spoken as "three hundred dollars," and the text normalization would convert the original to the desired three tokens. Other applications may require that this and all other monetary amounts be converted to a single token such as "MONETARY_TOKEN."

In languages such as Chinese, which do not contain white space between any words, a wide range of word segmentation conventions are currently in use. Different segmentation standards have a significant impact on applications such as information retrieval and text-to-speech synthesis, as discussed in Wu (2003). Task-oriented Chinese segmentation has received a great deal of attention in the MT community (Chang et al. 2008; Ma and Way 2009; Zhang et al. 2008).

The tasks of word and sentence segmentation overlap with the techniques discussed in many other chapters in this handbook, in particular the chapters on Lexical Analysis, Corpus Creation, and Multiword Expressions, as well as practical applications discussed in other chapters.

2.3 Tokenization

Section 2.2 discussed the many challenges inherent in segmenting freely occurring text. In this section, we focus on the specific technical issues that arise in tokenization.

Tokenization is well-established and well-understood for artificial languages such as programming languages.[†] However, such artificial languages can be strictly defined to eliminate lexical and structural ambiguities; we do not have this luxury with natural languages, in which the same character can serve many different purposes and in which the syntax is not strictly defined. Many factors can affect the difficulty of tokenizing a particular natural language. One fundamental difference exists between tokenization approaches for **space-delimited** languages and approaches for **unsegmented** languages. In space-delimited languages, such as most European languages, some word boundaries are indicated by the insertion of whitespace. The character sequences delimited are not necessarily the tokens required for further processing, due both to the ambiguous nature of the writing systems and to the range of tokenization conventions required by different applications. In unsegmented languages, such as Chinese and Thai, words are written in succession with no indication of word boundaries. The tokenization of unsegmented languages therefore requires additional lexical and morphological information.

In both unsegmented and space-delimited languages, the specific challenges posed by tokenization are largely dependent on both the writing system (logographic, syllabic, or alphabetic, as discussed in Section 2.2.2) and the typographical structure of the words. There are three main categories into which word structures can be placed,[‡] and each category exists in both unsegmented and space-delimited writing systems. The morphology of words in a language can be **isolating**, where words do not divide into smaller units; **agglutinating** (or **agglutinative**), where words divide into smaller units (morphemes) with clear

* This example is taken from Grefenstette and Tapanainen (1994).
† For a thorough introduction to the basic techniques of tokenization in programming languages, see Aho et al. (1986).
‡ This classification comes from Comrie et al. (1996) and Crystal (1987).

boundaries between the morphemes; or **inflectional**, where the boundaries between morphemes are not clear and where the component morphemes can express more than one grammatical meaning. While individual languages show tendencies toward one specific type (e.g., Mandarin Chinese is predominantly isolating, Japanese is strongly agglutinative, and Latin is largely inflectional), most languages exhibit traces of all three. A fourth typological classification frequently studied by linguists, **polysynthetic**, can be considered an extreme case of agglutinative, where several morphemes are put together to form complex words that can function as a whole sentence. Chukchi and Inuktitut are examples of polysynthetic languages, and some research in machine translation has focused on a Nunavut Hansards parallel corpus of Inuktitut and English (Martin et al. 2003).

Since the techniques used in tokenizing space-delimited languages are very different from those used in tokenizing unsegmented languages, we discuss the techniques separately in Sections 2.3.1 and 2.3.2, respectively.

2.3.1 Tokenization in Space-Delimited Languages

In many alphabetic writing systems, including those that use the Latin alphabet, words are separated by whitespace. Yet even in a well-formed corpus of sentences, there are many issues to resolve in tokenization. Most tokenization ambiguity exists among uses of punctuation marks, such as periods, commas, quotation marks, apostrophes, and hyphens, since the same punctuation mark can serve many different functions in a single sentence, let alone a single text. Consider example sentence (3) from the *Wall Street Journal* (1988).

> (3) *Clairson International Corp. said it expects to report a net loss for its second quarter ended March 26 and doesn't expect to meet analysts' profit estimates of $3.9 to $4 million, or 76 cents a share to 79 cents a share, for its year ending Sept. 24.*

This sentence has several items of interest that are common for Latinate, alphabetic, space-delimited languages. First, it uses periods in three different ways: within numbers as a decimal point (*$3.9*), to mark abbreviations (*Corp.* and *Sept.*), and to mark the end of the sentence, in which case the period following the number *24* is not a decimal point. The sentence uses apostrophes in two ways: to mark the genitive case (where the apostrophe denotes possession) in *analysts'* and to show contractions (places where letters have been left out of words) in *doesn't*. The tokenizer must thus be aware of the uses of punctuation marks and be able to determine when a punctuation mark is part of another token and when it is a separate token.

In addition to resolving these cases, we must make tokenization decisions about a phrase such as *76 cents a share*, which on the surface consists of four tokens. However, when used adjectivally such as in the phrase *a 76-cents-a-share dividend*, it is normally hyphenated and appears as one. The semantic content is the same despite the orthographic differences, so it makes sense to treat the two identically, as the same number of tokens. Similarly, we must decide whether to treat the phrase *$3.9 to $4 million* differently than if it had been written as *3.9 to 4 million dollars* or *$3,900,000 to $4,000,000*. Note also that the semantics of numbers can be dependent on both the genre and the application; in scientific literature, for example, the numbers 3.9, 3.90, and 3.900 have different significant digits and are not semantically equivalent. We discuss these ambiguities and other issues in the following sections.

A logical initial tokenization of a space-delimited language would be to consider as a separate token any sequence of characters preceded and followed by space. This successfully tokenizes words that are a sequence of alphabetic characters, but does not take into account punctuation characters. In many cases, characters such as commas, semicolons, and periods should be treated as separate tokens, although they are not preceded by whitespace (such as the case with the comma after *$4 million* in Example (3)). Additionally, many texts contain certain classes of character sequences which should be filtered out before actual tokenization; these include existing markup and headers (including HTML markup), extra whitespace, and extraneous control characters.

2.3.1.1 Tokenizing Punctuation

While punctuation characters are usually treated as separate tokens, there are many cases when they should be "attached" to another token. The specific cases vary from one language to the next, and the specific treatment of the punctuation characters needs to be enumerated within the tokenizer for each language. In this section, we give examples of English tokenization.

Abbreviations are used in written language to denote the shortened form of a word. In many cases, abbreviations are written as a sequence of characters terminated with a period. When an abbreviation occurs at the end of a sentence, a single period marks both the abbreviation and the sentence boundary. For this reason, recognizing abbreviations is essential for both tokenization and sentence segmentation. Compiling a list of abbreviations can help in recognizing them, but abbreviations are productive, and it is not possible to compile an exhaustive list of all abbreviations in any language. Additionally, many abbreviations can also occur as words elsewhere in a text (e.g., the word *Mass* is also the abbreviation for *Massachusetts*). An abbreviation can also represent several different words, as is the case for *St.* which can stand for *Saint*, *Street*, or *State*. However, as *Saint* it is less likely to occur at a sentence boundary than as *Street*, or *State*. Examples (4) and (5) from the *Wall Street Journal* (1991 and 1987 respectively) demonstrate the difficulties produced by such ambiguous cases, where the same abbreviation can represent different words and can occur both within and at the end of a sentence.

(4) *The contemporary viewer may simply ogle the vast wooded vistas rising up from the Saguenay River and Lac St. Jean, standing in for the St. Lawrence River.*

(5) *The firm said it plans to sublease its current headquarters at 55 Water St. A spokesman declined to elaborate.*

Recognizing an abbreviation is thus not sufficient for complete tokenization, and the appropriate definition for an abbreviation can be ambiguous, as discussed in Park and Byrd (2001). We address abbreviations at sentence boundaries fully in Section 2.4.2.

Quotation marks and apostrophes (" " ' ') are a major source of tokenization ambiguity. In most cases, single and double quotes indicate a quoted passage, and the extent of the tokenization decision is to determine whether they open or close the passage. In many character sets, single quote and apostrophe are the same character, and it is therefore not always possible to immediately determine if the single quotation mark closes a quoted passage, or serves another purpose as an apostrophe. In addition, as discussed in Section 2.2.1, quotation marks are also commonly used when "romanizing" writing systems, in which umlauts are replaced by a double quotation mark and accents are denoted by a single quotation mark or an apostrophe.

The apostrophe is a very ambiguous character. In English, the main uses of apostrophes are to mark the genitive form of a noun, to mark contractions, and to mark certain plural forms. In the genitive case, some applications require a separate token while some require a single token, as discussed in Section 2.2.4. How to treat the genitive case is important, since in other languages, the possessive form of a word is not marked with an apostrophe and cannot be as readily recognized. In German, for example, the possessive form of a noun is usually formed by adding the letter *s* to the word, without an apostrophe, as in *Peters Kopf* (*Peter's head*). However, in modern (informal) usage in German, *Peter's Kopf* would also be common; the apostrophe is also frequently omitted in modern (informal) English such that *Peters head* is a possible construction. Furthermore, in English, *'s* can serve as a contraction for the verb *is*, as in *he's, it's, she's,* and *Peter's head and shoulders above the rest*. It also occurs in the plural form of some words, such as *I.D.'s* or *1980's*, although the apostrophe is also frequently omitted from such plurals. The tokenization decision in these cases is context dependent and is closely tied to syntactic analysis.

In the case of apostrophe as contraction, tokenization may require the expansion of the word to eliminate the apostrophe, but the cases where this is necessary are very language-dependent. The English contraction *I'm* could be tokenized as the two words *I am*, and *we've* could become *we have*. Written French contains a completely different set of contractions, including contracted articles (*l'homme, c'etait*), as well as contracted pronouns (*j'ai, je l'ai*) and other forms such as *n'y, qu'ils, d'ailleurs,* and *aujourd'hui*. Clearly, recognizing the contractions to expand requires knowledge of the language, and the specific contractions to expand, as well as the expanded forms, must be enumerated. All other word-internal apostrophes are treated as a part of the token and not expanded, which allows the proper tokenization of multiply-contracted words such as *fo'c's'le* (forecastle) and *Pudd'n'head* (Puddinghead) as single words. In addition, since contractions are not always demarcated with apostrophes, as in the French *du*, which is a contraction of *de le*, or the Spanish *del*, contraction of *de el*, other words to expand must also be listed in the tokenizer.

2.3.1.2 Multi-Part Words

To different degrees, many written languages contain space-delimited words composed of multiple units, each expressing a particular grammatical meaning. For example, the single Turkish word *çöplüklerim-izdekilerdenmiydi* means "was it from those that were in our garbage cans?"* This type of construction is particularly common in strongly agglutinative languages such as Swahili, Quechua, and most Altaic languages. It is also common in languages such as German, where noun–noun (*Lebensversicherung*, life insurance), adverb–noun (*Nichtraucher*, nonsmoker), and preposition–noun (*Nachkriegszeit*, postwar period) compounding are all possible. In fact, though it is not an agglutinative language, German compounding can be quite complex, as in *Feuerundlebensversicherung* (fire and life insurance) or *Kundenzufriedenheitsabfragen* (customer satisfaction survey).

To some extent, agglutinating constructions are present in nearly all languages, though this compounding can be marked by hyphenation, in which the use of hyphens can create a single word with multiple grammatical parts. In English, it is commonly used to create single-token words like *end-of-line* as well as multi-token words like *Boston-based*. As with the apostrophe, the use of the hyphen is not uniform; for example, hyphen usage varies greatly between British and American English, as well as between different languages. However, as with the case of apostrophes as contractions, many common language-specific uses of hyphens can be enumerated in the tokenizer.

Many languages use the hyphen to create essential grammatical structures. In French, for example, hyphenated compounds such as *va-t-il* (will it?), *c'est-à-dire* (that is to say), and *celui-ci* (it) need to be expanded during tokenization, in order to recover necessary grammatical features of the sentence. In these cases, the tokenizer needs to contain an enumerated list of structures to be expanded, as with the contractions discussed above.

Another tokenization difficulty involving hyphens stems from the practice, common in traditional typesetting, of using hyphens at the ends of lines to break a word too long to include on one line. Such end-of-line hyphens can thus occur within words that are not normally hyphenated. Removing these hyphens is necessary during tokenization, yet it is difficult to distinguish between such incidental hyphenation and cases where naturally hyphenated words happen to occur at a line break. In an attempt to dehyphenate the artificial cases, it is possible to incorrectly remove necessary hyphens. Grefenstette and Tapanainen (1994) found that nearly 5% of the end-of-line hyphens in an English corpus were word-internal hyphens, which happened to also occur as end-of-line hyphens.

In tokenizing multi-part words, such as hyphenated or agglutinative words, whitespace does not provide much useful information to further processing stages. In such cases, the problem of tokenization is very closely related both to tokenization in unsegmented languages, discussed in Section 2.3.2, and to morphological analysis, discussed in Chapter 3 of this handbook.

2.3.1.3 Multiword Expressions

Spacing conventions in written languages do not always correspond to the desired tokenization for NLP applications, and the resulting multiword expressions are an important consideration in the tokenization stage. A later chapter of this handbook addresses Multiword Expressions in full detail, so we touch briefly in this section on some of the tokenization issues raised by multiword expressions.

---

* This example is from Hankamer (1986).

For example, the three-word English expression *in spite of* is, for all intents and purposes, equivalent to the single word *despite*, and both could be treated as a single token. Similarly, many common English expressions, such as *au pair*, *de facto*, and *joie de vivre*, consist of foreign loan words that can be treated as a single token.

Multiword numerical expressions are also commonly identified in the tokenization stage. Numbers are ubiquitous in all types of texts in every language, but their representation in the text can vary greatly. For most applications, sequences of digits and certain types of numerical expressions, such as dates and times, money expressions, and percents, can be treated as a single token. Several examples of such phrases can be seen in Example (3) above: *March 26*, *$3.9 to $4 million*, and *Sept. 24* could each be treated as a single token. Similarly, phrases such as *76 cents a share* and *$3-a-share* convey roughly the same meaning, despite the difference in hyphenation, and the tokenizer should normalize the two phrases to the same number of tokens (either one or four). Tokenizing numeric expressions requires the knowledge of the syntax of such expressions, since numerical expressions are written differently in different languages. Even within a language or in languages as similar as English and French, major differences exist in the syntax of numeric expressions, in addition to the obvious vocabulary differences. For example, the English date *November 18, 1989* could alternately appear in English texts as any number of variations, such as *Nov. 18, 1989*, *18 November 1989*, *11/18/89* or *18/11/89*. These examples underscore the importance of text normalization during the tokenization process, such that dates, times, monetary expressions, and all other numeric phrases can be converted into a form that is consistent with the processing required by the NLP application.

Closely related to hyphenation, the treatment of multiword expressions is highly language-dependent and application-dependent, but can easily be handled in the tokenization stage if necessary. We need to be careful, however, when combining words into a single token. The phrase *no one*, along with *noone* and *no-one*, is a commonly encountered English equivalent for *nobody*, and should normally be treated as a single token. However, in a context such as *No one man can do it alone*, it needs to be treated as two words. The same is true of the two-word phrase *can not*, which is not always equivalent to the single word *cannot* or the contraction *can't*.* In such cases, it is safer to allow a later process (such as a parser) to make the decision.

2.3.2 Tokenization in Unsegmented Languages

The nature of the tokenization task in unsegmented languages like Chinese, Japanese, and Thai is fundamentally different from tokenization in space-delimited languages like English. The lack of any spaces between words necessitates a more informed approach than simple lexical analysis. The specific approach to word segmentation for a particular unsegmented language is further limited by the writing system and orthography of the language, and a single general approach has not been developed. In Section 2.3.2.1, we describe some algorithms, which have been applied to the problem to obtain an initial approximation for a variety of languages. In Sections 2.3.2.2 and 2.3.2.3, we give details of some successful approaches to Chinese and Japanese segmentation, and in Section 2.3.2.4, we describe some approaches, which have been applied to languages with unsegmented alphabetic or syllabic writing systems.

2.3.2.1 Common Approaches

An extensive word list combined with an informed segmentation algorithm can help to achieve a certain degree of accuracy in word segmentation, but the greatest barrier to accurate word segmentation is in recognizing unknown (or out-of-vocabulary) words, words not in the lexicon of the segmenter. This problem is dependent both on the source of the lexicon as well as the correspondence (in vocabulary) between the text in question and the lexicon; for example, Wu and Fung (1994) reported that segmentation

---

* For example, consider the following sentence: "Why is my soda can not where I left it?"

accuracy in Chinese is significantly higher when the lexicon is constructed using the same type of corpus as the corpus on which it is tested.

Another obstacle to high-accuracy word segmentation is the fact that there are no widely accepted guidelines as to what constitutes a word, and there is therefore no agreement on how to "correctly" segment a text in an unsegmented language. Native speakers of a language do not always agree about the "correct" segmentation, and the same text could be segmented into several very different (and equally correct) sets of words by different native speakers. A simple example from English would be the hyphenated phrase *Boston-based*. If asked to "segment" this phrase into words, some native English speakers might say *Boston-based* is a single word and some might say *Boston* and *based* are two separate words; in this latter case there might also be disagreement about whether the hyphen "belongs" to one of the two words (and to which one) or whether it is a "word" by itself. Disagreement by native speakers of Chinese is much more prevalent; in fact, Sproat et al. (1996) give empirical results showing that native speakers of Chinese agree on the correct segmentation in fewer than 70% of the cases. Such ambiguity in the definition of what constitutes a word makes it difficult to evaluate segmentation algorithms that follow different conventions, since it is nearly impossible to construct a "gold standard" against which to directly compare results.

A simple word segmentation algorithm consists of considering each character to be a distinct word. This is practical for Chinese because the average word length is very short (usually between one and two characters, depending on the corpus*) and actual words can be recognized with this algorithm. Although it does not assist in tasks such as parsing, part-of-speech tagging, or text-to-speech systems (see Sproat et al. 1996), the character-as-word segmentation algorithm is very common in Chinese information retrieval, a task in which the words in a text play a major role in indexing and where incorrect segmentation can hurt system performance.

A very common approach to word segmentation is to use a variation of the *maximum matching algorithm*, frequently referred to as the *greedy algorithm*. The greedy algorithm starts at the first character in a text and, using a word list for the language being segmented, attempts to find the longest word in the list starting with that character. If a word is found, the maximum-matching algorithm marks a boundary at the end of the longest word, then begins the same longest match search starting at the character following the match. If no match is found in the word list, the greedy algorithm simply segments that character as a word (as in the character-as-word algorithm above) and begins the search starting at the next character. A variation of the greedy algorithm segments a sequence of unmatched characters as a single word; this variant is more likely to be successful in writing systems with longer average word lengths. In this manner, an initial segmentation can be obtained that is more informed than a simple character-as-word approach. The success of this algorithm is largely dependent on the word list.

As a demonstration of the application of the character-as-word and greedy algorithms, consider an example of artificially "desegmented" English, in which all the white space has been removed. The desegmented version of the phrase *the table down there* would thus be *thetabledownthere*. Applying the character-as-word algorithm would result in the useless sequence of tokens *t h e t a b l e d o w n t h e r e*, which is why this algorithm only makes sense for languages with short average word length, such as Chinese. Applying the greedy algorithm with a "perfect" word list containing all known English words would first identify the word *theta*, since that is the longest sequence of letters starting at the initial *t*, which forms an actual word. Starting at the *b* following *theta*, the algorithm would then identify *bled* as the maximum match. Continuing in this manner, *thetabledownthere* would be segmented by the greedy algorithm as *theta bled own there*.

A variant of the maximum matching algorithm is the *reverse maximum matching* algorithm, in which the matching proceeds from the end of the string of characters, rather than the beginning. In the example above, *thetabledownthere* would be correctly segmented as *the table down there* by the reverse maximum matching algorithm. Greedy matching from the beginning and the end of the string of characters enables an

---

* As many as 95% of Chinese words consist of one or two characters, according to Fung and Wu (1994).

algorithm such as *forward-backward matching*, in which the results are compared and the segmentation optimized based on the two results. In addition to simple greedy matching, it is possible to encode language-specific heuristics to refine the matching as it progresses.

2.3.2.2 Chinese Segmentation

The Chinese writing system consists of several thousand characters known as *Hanzi*, with a word consisting of one or more characters. In this section, we provide a few examples of previous approaches to Chinese word segmentation, but a detailed treatment is beyond the scope of this chapter. Much of our summary is taken from Sproat et al. (1996) and Sproat and Shih (2001). For a comprehensive summary of early work in Chinese segmentation, we also recommend Wu and Tseng (1993).

Most previous work in Chinese segmentation falls into one of the three categories: statistical approaches, lexical rule-based approaches, and hybrid approaches that use both statistical and lexical information. Statistical approaches use data such as the mutual information between characters, compiled from a training corpus, to determine which characters are most likely to form words. Lexical approaches use manually encoded features about the language, such as syntactic and semantic information, common phrasal structures, and morphological rules, in order to refine the segmentation. The hybrid approaches combine information from both statistical and lexical sources.

Sproat et al. (1996) describe such a hybrid approach that uses a weighted finite-state transducer to identify both dictionary entries as well as unknown words derived by productive lexical processes. Palmer (1997) also describes a hybrid statistical-lexical approach in which the segmentation is incrementally improved by a trainable sequence of transformation rules; Hockenmaier and Brew (1998) describe a similar approach. Teahan et al. (2000) describe a novel approach based on adaptive language models similar to those used in text compression. Gao et al. (2005) describe an adaptive segmentation algorithm that allows for rapid retraining for new genres or segmentation standards and which does not assume a universal segmentation standard.

One of the significant challenges in comparing segmentation algorithms is the range in segmentation standards, and thus the lack of a common evaluation corpus, which would enable the direct comparison of algorithms. In response to this challenge, Chinese word segmentation has been the focus of several organized evaluations in recent years. The "First International Chinese Word Segmentation Bakeoff" in 2003 (Sproat and Emerson 2003), and several others since, have built on similar evaluations within China to encourage a direct comparison of segmentation methods. These evaluations have helped to develop consistent standards both for segmentation and for evaluation, and they have made significant contributions by cleaning up inconsistencies within existing corpora.

2.3.2.3 Japanese Segmentation

The Japanese writing system incorporates alphabetic, syllabic and logographic symbols. Modern Japanese texts, for example, frequently consist of many different writing systems: Kanji (Chinese Hanzi symbols), hiragana (a syllabary for grammatical markers and for words of Japanese origin), katakana (a syllabary for words of foreign origin), romanji (words written in the Roman alphabet), Arabic numerals, and various punctuation symbols. In some ways, the multiple character sets make tokenization easier, as transitions between character sets give valuable information about word boundaries. However, character set transitions are not enough, since a single word may contain characters from multiple character sets, such as inflected verbs, which can contain a Kanji base and hiragana inflectional ending. Company names also frequently contain a mix of Kanji and romanji. For these reasons, most previous approaches to Japanese segmentation, such as the popular JUMAN (Matsumoto and Nagao 1994) and Chasen programs (Matsumoto et al. 1997), rely on manually derived morphological analysis rules.

To some extent, Japanese can be segmented using the same statistical techniques developed for Chinese. For example, Nagata (1994) describes an algorithm for Japanese segmentation similar to that used for Chinese segmentation by Sproat et al. (1996). More recently, Ando and Lee (2003) developed an unsupervised statistical segmentation method based on n-gram counts in Kanji sequences that produces high performance on long Kanji sequences.

2.3.2.4 Unsegmented Alphabetic and Syllabic Languages

Common unsegmented alphabetic and syllabic languages are Thai, Balinese, Javanese, and Khmer. While such writing systems have fewer characters than Chinese and Japanese, they also have longer words; localized optimization is thus not as practical as in Chinese or Japanese segmentation. The richer morphology of such languages often allows initial segmentations based on lists of words, names, and affixes, usually using some variation of the maximum matching algorithm. Successful high-accuracy segmentation requires a thorough knowledge of the lexical and morphological features of the language. An early discussion of Thai segmentation can be found in Kawtrakul et al. (1996), describing a robust rule-based Thai segmenter and morphological analyzer. Meknavin et al. (1997) use lexical and collocational features automatically derived using machine learning to select an optimal segmentation from an n-best maximum matching set. Aroonmanakun (2002) uses a statistical Thai segmentation approach, which first seeks to segment the Thai text into syllables. Syllables are then merged into words based on a trained model of syllable collocation.

2.4 Sentence Segmentation

Sentences in most written languages are delimited by punctuation marks, yet the specific usage rules for punctuation are not always coherently defined. Even when a strict set of rules exists, the adherence to the rules can vary dramatically based on the origin of the text source and the type of text. Additionally, in different languages, sentences and subsentences are frequently delimited by different punctuation marks. Successful sentence segmentation for a given language thus requires an understanding of the various uses of punctuation characters in that language. In most languages, the problem of sentence segmentation reduces to disambiguating all instances of punctuation characters that may delimit sentences. The scope of this problem varies greatly by language, as does the number of different punctuation marks that need to be considered.

Written languages that do not use many punctuation marks present a very difficult challenge in recognizing sentence boundaries. Thai, for one, does not use a period (or any other punctuation mark) to mark sentence boundaries. A space is sometimes used at sentence breaks, but very often the space is indistinguishable from the carriage return, or there is no separation between sentences. Spaces are sometimes also used to separate phrases or clauses, where commas would be used in English, but this is also unreliable. In cases such as written Thai where punctuation gives no reliable information about sentence boundaries, locating sentence boundaries is best treated as a special class of locating word boundaries.

Even languages with relatively rich punctuation systems like English present surprising problems. Recognizing boundaries in such a written language involves determining the roles of all punctuation marks, which can denote sentence boundaries: periods, question marks, exclamation points, and sometimes semicolons, colons, dashes, and commas. In large document collections, each of these punctuation marks can serve several different purposes in addition to marking sentence boundaries. A period, for example, can denote a decimal point or a thousands marker, an abbreviation, the end of a sentence, or even an abbreviation at the end of a sentence. Ellipsis (a series of periods (...)) can occur both within sentences and at sentence boundaries. Exclamation points and question marks can occur at the end of a sentence, but also within quotation marks or parentheses (really!) or even (albeit infrequently) within a word, such as in the Internet company *Yahoo!* and the language name *!Xũ*. However, conventions for the use of these two punctuation marks also vary by language; in Spanish, both can be unambiguously recognized as sentence delimiters by the presence of '¡' or '¿' at the start of the sentence. In this section, we introduce the challenges posed by the range of corpora available and the variety of techniques that have been successfully applied to this problem and discuss their advantages and disadvantages.

2.4.1 Sentence Boundary Punctuation

Just as the definition of what constitutes a sentence is rather arbitrary, the use of certain punctuation marks to separate sentences depends largely on an author's adherence to changeable and frequently ignored conventions. In most NLP applications, the only sentence boundary punctuation marks considered are the period, question mark, and exclamation point, and the definition of sentence is limited to the *text-sentence* (as defined by Nunberg 1990), which begins with a capital letter and ends in a full stop. However, grammatical sentences can be delimited by many other punctuation marks, and restricting sentence boundary punctuation to these three can cause an application to overlook many meaningful sentences or can unnecessarily complicate processing by allowing only longer, complex sentences. Consider Examples (6) and (7), two English sentences that convey exactly the same meaning; yet, by the traditional definitions, the first would be classified as two sentences, the second as just one. The semicolon in Example (7) could likewise be replaced by a comma or a dash, retain the same meaning, but still be considered a single sentence. Replacing the semicolon with a colon is also possible, though the resulting meaning would be slightly different.

> (6) *Here is a sentence. Here is another.*

> (7) *Here is a sentence; here is another.*

The distinction is particularly important for an application like part-of-speech tagging. Many taggers seek to optimize a tag sequence for a sentence, with the locations of sentence boundaries being provided to the tagger at the outset. The optimal sequence will usually be different depending on the definition of sentence boundary and how the tagger treats "sentence-internal" punctuation.

For an even more striking example of the problem of restricting sentence boundary punctuation, consider Example (8), from Lewis Carroll's *Alice in Wonderland*, in which .!? are completely inadequate for segmenting the meaningful units of the passage:

> (8) *There was nothing so VERY remarkable in that; nor did Alice think it so VERY much out of the way to hear the Rabbit say to itself, 'Oh dear! Oh dear! I shall be late!' (when she thought it over afterwards, it occurred to her that she ought to have wondered at this, but at the time it all seemed quite natural); but when the Rabbit actually TOOK A WATCH OUT OF ITS WAISTCOAT-POCKET, and looked at it, and then hurried on, Alice started to her feet, for it flashed across her mind that she had never before seen a rabbit with either a waistcoat-pocket, or a watch to take out of it, and burning with curiosity, she ran across the field after it, and fortunately was just in time to see it pop down a large rabbit-hole under the hedge.*

This example contains a single period at the end and three exclamation points within a quoted passage. However, if the semicolon and comma were allowed to end sentences, the example could be decomposed into as many as ten grammatical sentences. This decomposition could greatly assist in nearly all NLP tasks, since long sentences are more likely to produce (and compound) errors of analysis. For example, parsers consistently have difficulty with sentences longer than 15–25 words, and it is highly unlikely that any parser could ever successfully analyze this example in its entirety.

In addition to determining which punctuation marks delimit sentences, the sentence in parentheses as well as the quoted sentences *'Oh dear! Oh dear! I shall be late!'* suggest the possibility of a further decomposition of the sentence boundary problem into types of sentence boundaries, one of which would be "embedded sentence boundary." Treating embedded sentences and their punctuation differently could assist in the processing of the entire text-sentence. Of course, multiple levels of embedding would be possible, as in Example (9), taken from *Watership Down* by Richard Adams. In this example, the main sentence contains an embedded sentence (delimited by dashes), and this embedded sentence also contains an embedded quoted sentence.

> (9) *The holes certainly were rough - "Just right for a lot of vagabonds like us," said Bigwig - but the exhausted and those who wander in strange country are not particular about their quarters.*

It should be clear from these examples that true sentence segmentation, including treatment of embedded sentences, can only be achieved through an approach, which integrates segmentation with parsing. Unfortunately, there has been little research in integrating the two; in fact, little research in computational linguistics has focused on the role of punctuation in written language.* With the availability of a wide range of corpora and the resulting need for robust approaches to NLP, the problem of sentence segmentation has recently received a lot of attention. Unfortunately, nearly all published research in this area has focused on the problem of sentence boundary detection in a small set of European languages, and all this work has focused exclusively on disambiguating the occurrences of period, exclamation point, and question mark. A great deal of recent work has focused on trainable approaches to sentence segmentation, which we discuss in Section 2.4.4. These new methods, which can be adapted to different languages and different text genres, should make a tighter coupling of sentence segmentation and parsing possible. While the remainder of this chapter focuses on published work that deals with the segmentation of a text into text-sentences, which represent the majority of sentences encountered in most text corpora, the above discussion of sentence punctuation indicates that the application of trainable techniques to broader problems may be possible. It is also important to note that this chapter focuses on disambiguation of punctuation in text and thus does not address the related problem of the *insertion* of punctuation and other structural events into automatic speech recognition transcripts of spoken language.

2.4.2 The Importance of Context

In any attempt to disambiguate the various uses of punctuation marks, whether in text-sentences or embedded sentences, some amount of the context in which the punctuation occurs is essential. In many cases, the essential context can be limited to the character immediately following the punctuation mark. When analyzing well-formed English documents, for example, it is tempting to believe that sentence boundary detection is simply a matter of finding a period followed by one or more spaces followed by a word beginning with a capital letter, perhaps also with quotation marks before or after the space. Indeed, in some corpora (e.g., literary texts) this single period-space-capital (or period-quote-space-capital) pattern accounts for almost all sentence boundaries. In *The Call of the Wild* by Jack London, for example, which has 1640 periods as sentence boundaries, this single rule correctly identifies 1608 boundaries (98%) (Bayer et al. 1998). However, the results are different in journalistic texts such as the *Wall Street Journal* (*WSJ*). In a small corpus of the *WSJ* from 1989 that has 16,466 periods as sentence boundaries, this simple rule would detect only 14,562 (88.4%) while producing 2900 **false positives**, placing a boundary where one does not exist.

Most of the errors resulting from this simple rule are cases where the period occurs immediately after an abbreviation. Expanding the context to consider whether the word preceding the period is a known abbreviation is thus a logical step. This improved abbreviation-period-space-capital rule can produce mixed results, since the use of abbreviations in a text depends on the particular text and text genre. The new rule improves performance on *The Call of the Wild* to 98.4% by eliminating five false positives (previously introduced by the phrase "St. Bernard" within a sentence). On the *WSJ* corpus, this new rule also eliminates all but 283 of the false positives introduced by the first rule. However, this rule also introduces 713 **false negatives**, erasing boundaries where they were previously correctly placed, yet still improving the overall score. Recognizing an abbreviation is therefore not sufficient to disambiguate the period, because we also must determine if the abbreviation occurs at the end of a sentence.

---

* A notable exception is Nunberg (1990).

The difficulty of disambiguating abbreviation-periods can vary depending on the corpus. Liberman and Church (Liberman and Church 1992) report that 47% of the periods in a *Wall Street Journal* corpus denote abbreviations, compared to only 10% in the Brown corpus (Francis and Kucera 1982), as reported by Riley (1989). In contrast, Müller et al. (1980) reports abbreviation-period statistics ranging from 54.7% to 92.8% within a corpus of English scientific abstracts. Such a range of figures suggests the need for a more informed treatment of the context that considers more than just the word preceding or following the punctuation mark. In difficult cases, such as an abbreviation which can occur at the end of a sentence, three or more words preceding and following must be considered. This is the case in the following examples of "garden path sentence boundaries," the first consisting of a single sentence, the other of two sentences.

(10) *Two high-ranking positions were filled Friday by Penn St. University President Graham Spanier.*

(11) *Two high-ranking positions were filled Friday at Penn St. University President Graham Spanier announced the appointments.*

Many contextual factors have been shown to assist sentence segmentation in difficult cases. These contextual factors include

- **Case distinctions**—In languages and corpora where both uppercase and lowercase letters are consistently used, whether a word is capitalized provides information about sentence boundaries.
- **Part of speech**—Palmer and Hearst (1997) showed that the parts of speech of the words within three tokens of the punctuation mark can assist in sentence segmentation. Their results indicate that even an estimate of the *possible* parts of speech can produce good results.
- **Word length**—Riley (1989) used the length of the words before and after a period as one contextual feature.
- **Lexical endings**—Müller et al. (1980) used morphological analysis to recognize suffixes and thereby filter out words which were not likely to be abbreviations. The analysis made it possible to identify words that were not otherwise present in the extensive word lists used to identify abbreviations.
- **Prefixes and suffixes**—Reynar and Ratnaparkhi (1997) used both prefixes and suffixes of the words surrounding the punctuation mark as one contextual feature.
- **Abbreviation classes**—Riley (1989) and Reynar and Ratnaparkhi (1997) further divided abbreviations into categories such as titles (which are not likely to occur at a sentence boundary) and corporate designators (which are more likely to occur at a boundary).
- **Internal punctuation**—Kiss and Strunk (2006) used the presence of periods within a token as a feature.
- **Proper nouns**—Mikheev (2002) used the presence of a proper noun to the right of a period as a feature.

2.4.3 Traditional Rule-Based Approaches

The success of the few simple rules described in the previous section is a major reason sentence segmentation has been frequently overlooked or idealized away. In well-behaved corpora, simple rules relying on regular punctuation, spacing, and capitalization can be quickly written, and are usually quite successful. Traditionally, the method widely used for determining sentence boundaries is a regular grammar, usually with limited lookahead. More elaborate implementations include extensive word lists and exception lists to attempt to recognize abbreviations and proper nouns. Such systems are usually developed specifically for a text corpus in a single language and rely on special language-specific word lists; as a result they are not portable to other natural languages without repeating the effort of compiling extensive lists and rewriting rules. Although the regular grammar approach can be successful, it requires a large manual effort to compile the individual rules used to recognize the sentence boundaries. Nevertheless, since rule-based sentence segmentation algorithms can be very successful when an application does deal with well-behaved corpora, we provide a description of these techniques.

An example of a very successful regular-expression-based sentence segmentation algorithm is the text segmentation stage of the Alembic information extraction system (Aberdeen et al. 1995), which was created using the lexical scanner generator flex (Nicol 1993). The Alembic system uses flex in a preprocess pipeline to perform tokenization and sentence segmentation at the same time. Various modules in the pipeline attempt to classify all instances of punctuation marks by identifying periods in numbers, date and time expressions, and abbreviations. The preprocess utilizes a list of 75 abbreviations and a series of over 100 hand-crafted rules and was developed over the course of more than six staff months. The Alembic system alone achieved a very high accuracy rate (99.1%) on a large *Wall Street Journal* corpus. However, the performance was improved when integrated with the trainable system Satz, described in Palmer and Hearst (1997), and summarized later in this chapter. In this hybrid system, the rule-based Alembic system was used to disambiguate the relatively unambiguous cases, while Satz was used to disambiguate difficult cases such as the five abbreviations *Co.*, *Corp.*, *Ltd.*, *Inc.*, and *U.S.*, which frequently occur in English texts both within sentences and at sentence boundaries. The hybrid system achieved an accuracy of 99.5%, higher than either of the two component systems alone.

2.4.4 Robustness and Trainability

Throughout this chapter we have emphasized the need for robustness in NLP systems, and sentence segmentation is no exception. The traditional rule-based systems, which rely on features such as spacing and capitalization, will not be as successful when processing texts where these features are not present, such as in Example (1) above. Similarly, some important kinds of text consist solely of uppercase letters; closed captioning (CC) data is an example of such a corpus. In addition to being uppercase-only, CC data also has erratic spelling and punctuation, as can be seen from the following example of CC data from CNN:

> (12) *THIS IS A DESPERATE ATTEMPT BY THE REPUBLICANS TO SPIN THEIR STORY THAT NOTHING SEAR WHYOUS – SERIOUS HAS BEEN DONE AND TRY TO SAVE THE SPEAKER'S SPEAKERSHIP AND THIS HAS BEEN A SERIOUS PROBLEM FOR THE SPEAKER, HE DID NOT TELL THE TRUTH TO THE COMMITTEE, NUMBER ONE.*

The limitations of manually crafted rule-based approaches suggest the need for trainable approaches to sentence segmentation, in order to allow for variations between languages, applications, and genres. Trainable methods provide a means for addressing the problem of embedded sentence boundaries discussed earlier, as well as the capability of processing a range of corpora and the problems they present, such as erratic spacing, spelling errors, single-case, and OCR errors.

For each punctuation mark to be disambiguated, a typical trainable sentence segmentation algorithm will automatically encode the context using some or all of the features described above. A set of training data, in which the sentence boundaries have been manually labeled, is then used to train a machine learning algorithm to recognize the salient features in the context. As we describe below, machine learning algorithms that have been used in trainable sentence segmentation systems have included neural networks, decision trees, and maximum entropy calculation.

2.4.5 Trainable Algorithms

One of the first published works describing a trainable sentence segmentation algorithm was Riley (1989). The method described used regression trees (Breiman et al. 1984) to classify periods according to contextual features describing the single word preceding and following the period. These contextual features included word length, punctuation after the period, abbreviation class, case of the word, and the probability of the word occurring at beginning or end of a sentence. Riley's method was trained using 25 million words from the AP newswire, and he reported an accuracy of 99.8% when tested on the Brown corpus.

Palmer and Hearst (1997) developed a sentence segmentation system called Satz, which used a machine learning algorithm to disambiguate all occurrences of periods, exclamation points, and question marks. The system defined a contextual feature array for three words preceding and three words following the punctuation mark; the feature array encoded the context as the parts of speech, which can be attributed to each word in the context. Using the lexical feature arrays, both a neural network and a decision tree were trained to disambiguate the punctuation marks, and achieved a high accuracy rate (98%–99%) on a large corpus from the *Wall Street Journal*. They also demonstrated the algorithm, which was trainable in as little as one minute and required less than 1000 sentences of training data, to be rapidly ported to new languages. They adapted the system to French and German, in each case achieving a very high accuracy. Additionally, they demonstrated the trainable method to be extremely robust, as it was able to successfully disambiguate single-case texts and OCR data.

Reynar and Ratnaparkhi (1997) described a trainable approach to identify English sentence boundaries using a statistical maximum entropy model. The system used a system of contextual templates, which encoded one word of context preceding and following the punctuation mark, using such features as prefixes, suffixes, and abbreviation class. They also reported success in inducing an abbreviation list from the training data for use in the disambiguation. The algorithm, trained in less than 30 min on 40,000 manually annotated sentences, achieved a high accuracy rate (98%+) on the same test corpus used by Palmer and Hearst (1997), without requiring specific lexical information, word lists, or any domain-specific information. Though they only reported results on English, they indicated that the ease of trainability should allow the algorithm to be used with other Roman-alphabet languages, given adequate training data.

Mikheev (2002) developed a high-performing sentence segmentation algorithm that jointly identifies abbreviations, proper names, and sentence boundaries. The algorithm casts the sentence segmentation problem as one of disambiguating abbreviations to the left of a period and proper names to the right. While using unsupervised training methods, the algorithm encodes a great deal of manual information regarding abbreviation structure and length. The algorithm also relies heavily on consistent capitalization in order to identify proper names.

Kiss and Strunk (2006) developed a largely unsupervised approach to sentence boundary detection that focuses primarily on identifying abbreviations. The algorithm encodes manual heuristics for abbreviation detection into a statistical model that first identifies abbreviations and then disambiguates sentence boundaries. The approach is essentially language independent, and they report results for a large number of European languages.

Trainable sentence segmentation algorithms such as these are clearly necessary for enabling robust processing of a variety of texts and languages. Algorithms that offer rapid training while requiring small amounts of training data allow systems to be retargeted in hours or minutes to new text genres and languages. This adaptation can take into account the reality that good segmentation is task dependent. For example, in parallel corpus construction and processing, the segmentation needs to be consistent in both the source and target language corpus, even if that consistency comes at the expense of theoretical accuracy in either language.

2.5 Conclusion

The problem of text preprocessing was largely overlooked or idealized away in early NLP systems; tokenization and sentence segmentation were frequently dismissed as uninteresting. This was possible because most systems were designed to process small, monolingual texts that had already been manually selected, triaged, and preprocessed. When processing texts in a single language with predictable orthographic conventions, it was possible to create and maintain hand-built algorithms to perform tokenization and sentence segmentation. However, the recent explosion in availability of large unrestricted corpora in many different languages, and the resultant demand for tools to process such corpora, has forced researchers to examine the many challenges posed by processing unrestricted texts. The result has been a move toward developing robust algorithms, which do not depend on the well-formedness of the texts being processed. Many of the hand-built techniques have been replaced by trainable corpus-based approaches, which use machine learning to improve their performance.

The move toward trainable robust segmentation systems has enabled research on a much broader range of corpora in many languages. Since errors at the text segmentation stage directly affect all later processing stages, it is essential to completely understand and address the issues involved in document triage, tokenization, and sentence segmentation and how they impact further processing. Many of these issues are language-dependent: the complexity of tokenization and sentence segmentation and the specific implementation decisions depend largely on the language being processed and the characteristics of its writing system. For a corpus in a particular language, the corpus characteristics and the application requirements also affect the design and implementation of tokenization and sentence segmentation algorithms. In most cases, since text segmentation is not the primary objective of NLP systems, it cannot be thought of as simply an independent "preprocessing" step, but rather must be tightly integrated with the design and implementation of all other stages of the system.

References

Aberdeen, J., J. Burger, D. Day, L. Hirschman, P. Robinson, and M. Vilain (1995). MITRE: Description of the Alembic system used for MUC-6. In *Proceedings of the Sixth Message Understanding Conference (MUC-6)*, Columbia, MD.

Aho, A. V., R. Sethi, and J. D. Ullman (1986). *Compilers, Principles, Techniques, and Tools*. Reading, MA: Addison-Wesley Publishing Company.

Ando, R. K. and L. Lee (2003). Mostly-unsupervised statistical segmentation of Japanese Kanji sequences. *Journal of Natural Language Engineering 9*, 127–149.

Aroonmanakun, W. (2002). Collocation and Thai word segmentation. In *Proceedings of SNLP-COCOSDA2002*, Bangkok, Thailand.

Baroni, M., F. Chantree, A. Kilgarriff, and S. Sharoff (2008). Cleaneval: A competition for cleaning web pages. In *Proceedings of the Sixth Language Resources and Evaluation Conference (LREC 2008)*, Marrakech, Morocco.

Bayer, S., J. Aberdeen, J. Burger, L. Hirschman, D. Palmer, and M. Vilain (1998). Theoretical and computational linguistics: Toward a mutual understanding. In J. Lawler and H. A. Dry (Eds.), *Using Computers in Linguistics*. London, U.K.: Routledge.

Breiman, L., J. H. Friedman, R. Olshen, and C. J. Stone (1984). *Classification and Regression Trees*. Belmont, CA: Wadsworth International Group.

Chang, P.-C., M. Galley, and C. D. Manning (2008). Optimizing Chinese word segmentation for machine translation performance. In *Proceedings of the Third Workshop on Statistical Machine Translation*, Columbus, OH, pp. 224–232.

Comrie, B., S. Matthews, and M. Polinsky (1996). *The Atlas of Languages*. London, U.K.: Quarto Inc.

Crystal, D. (1987). *The Cambridge Encyclopedia of Language*. Cambridge, U.K.: Cambridge University Press.

Daniels, P. T. and W. Bright (1996). *The World's Writing Systems*. New York: Oxford University Press.

Francis, W. N. and H. Kucera (1982). *Frequency Analysis of English Usage*. New York: Houghton Mifflin Co.

Fung, P. and D. Wu (1994). Statistical augmentation of a Chinese machine-readable dictionary. In *Proceedings of Second Workshop on Very Large Corpora (WVLC-94)*, Kyoto, Japan.

Gao, J., M. Li, A. Wu, and C.-N. Huang (2005). Chinese word segmentation and named entity recognition: A pragmatic approach. *Computational Linguistics 31*(4), 531–574.

Grefenstette, G. and P. Tapanainen (1994). What is a word, What is a sentence? Problems of Tokenization. In *The 3rd International Conference on Computational Lexicography (COMPLEX 1994)*, Budapest, Hungary.

Hankamer, J. (1986). Finite state morphology and left to right phonology. In *Proceedings of the Fifth West Coast Conference on Formal Linguistics*, Stanford, CA.

Hockenmaier, J. and C. Brew (1998). Error driven segmentation of Chinese. *Communications of COLIPS 8*(1), 69–84.

Kawtrakul, A., C. Thumkanon, T. Jamjanya, P. Muangyunnan, K. Poolwan, and Y. Inagaki (1996). A gradual refinement model for a robust Thai morphological analyzer. In *Proceedings of COLING96*, Copenhagen, Denmark.

Kiss, T. and J. Strunk (2006). Unsupervised multilingual sentence boundary detection. *Computational Linguistics 32*(4), 485–525.

Liberman, M. Y. and K. W. Church (1992). Text analysis and word pronunciation in text-to-speech synthesis. In S. Furui and M. M. Sondhi (Eds.), *Advances in Speech Signal Processing*, pp. 791–831. New York: Marcel Dekker, Inc.

Ma, Y. and A. Way (2009). Bilingually motivated domain-adapted word segmentation for statistical machine translation. In *Proceedings of the 12th Conference of the European Chapter of the ACL (EACL 2009)*, Athens, Greece, pp. 549–557.

Martin, J., H. Johnson, B. Farley, and A. Maclachlan (2003). Aligning and using an english-inuktitut parallel corpus. In *Proceedings of the HLT-NAACL 2003 Workshop on Building and Using Parallel Texts Data Driven: Machine Translation and Beyond*, Edmonton, Canada, pp. 115–118.

Matsumoto, Y. and M. Nagao (1994). Improvements of Japanese morphological analyzer JUMAN. In *Proceedings of the International Workshop on Sharable Natural Language Resources*, Nara, Japan.

Matsumoto, Y., A. Kitauchi, T. Yamashita, Y. Hirano, O. Imaichi, and T. Imamura (1997). Japanese morphological analysis system ChaSen manual. Technical Report NAIST-IS-TR97007, Nara Institute of Science and Technology, Nara, Japan (in Japanese).

Meknavin, S., P. Charoenpornsawat, and B. Kijsirikul (1997). Feature-based Thai word segmentation. In *Proceedings of the Natural Language Processing Pacific Rim Symposium 1997 (NLPRS97)*, Phuket, Thailand.

Mikheev, A. (2002). Periods, capitalized words, etc. *Computational Linguistics 28*(3), 289–318.

Müller, H., V. Amerl, and G. Natalis (1980). Worterkennungsverfahren als Grundlage einer Universalmethode zur automatischen Segmentierung von Texten in Sätze. Ein Verfahren zur maschinellen Satzgrenzenbestimmung im Englischen. *Sprache und Datenverarbeitung 1*.

Nagata, M. (1994). A stochastic Japanese morphological analyzer using a Forward-DP backward A* n-best search algorithm. In *Proceedings of COLING94*, Kyoto, Japan.

Nicol, G. T. (1993). *Flex—The Lexical Scanner Generator*. Cambridge, MA: The Free Software Foundation.

Nunberg, G. (1990). *The Linguistics of Punctuation*. C.S.L.I. Lecture Notes, Number 18. Stanford, CA: Center for the Study of Language and Information.

Palmer, D. D. (1997). A trainable rule-based algorithm for word segmentation. In *Proceedings of the 35th Annual Meeting of the Association for Computational Linguistics (ACL97)*, Madrid, Spain.

Palmer, D. D. and M. A. Hearst (1997). Adaptive multilingual sentence boundary disambiguation. *Computational Linguistics 23*(2), 241–67.

Park, Y. and R. J. Byrd (2001). Hybrid text mining for finding abbreviations and their definitions. In *Proceedings of the 2001 Conference on Empirical Methods in Natural Language Processing*, Pittsburgh, PA.

Reynar, J. C. and A. Ratnaparkhi (1997). A maximum entropy approach to identifying sentence boundaries. In *Proceedings of the Fifth ACL Conference on Applied Natural Language Processing*, Washington, DC.

Riley, M. D. (1989). Some applications of tree-based modelling to speech and language indexing. In *Proceedings of the DARPA Speech and Natural Language Workshop*, San Mateo, CA, pp. 339–352. Morgan Kaufmann.

Sampson, G. R. (1995). *English for the Computer*. Oxford, U.K.: Oxford University Press.

Sproat, R. and T. Emerson (2003). The first international Chinese word segmentation bakeoff. In *Proceedings of the Second SigHan Workshop on Chinese Language Processing*, Sapporo, Japan.

Sproat, R. and C. Shih (2001). Corpus-based methods in Chinese morphology and phonology. Technical Report, Linguistic Society of America Summer Institute, Santa Barbara, CA.

Sproat, R. W., C. Shih, W. Gale, and N. Chang (1996). A stochastic finite-state word-segmentation algorithm for Chinese. *Computational Linguistics 22*(3), 377–404.

Teahan, W.J., Y. Wen, R. McNab, and I. H. Witten (2000). A compression-based algorithm for Chinese word segmentation. *Computational Linguistics 26*(3), 375–393.

Unicode Consortium (2006). *The Unicode Standard, Version 5.0*. Boston, MA: Addison-Wesley.

Wu, A. (2003). Customizable segmentation of morphologically derived words in Chinese. *International Journal of Computational Linguistics and Chinese Language Processing 8*(1), 1–27.

Wu, D. and P. Fung (1994). Improving Chinese tokenization with linguistic filters on statistical lexical acquisition. In *Proceedings of the Fourth ACL Conference on Applied Natural Language Processing*, Stuttgart, Germany.

Wu, Z. and G. Tseng (1993). Chinese text segmentation for text retrieval: Achievements and problems. *Journal of the American Society for Information Science 44*(9), 532–542.

Zhang, R., K. Yasuda, and E. Sumita (2008). Improved statistical machine translation by multiple Chinese word segmentation. In *Proceedings of the Third Workshop on Statistical Machine Translation*, Columbus, OH, pp. 216–223.

3

Lexical Analysis

Andrew Hippisley
University of Kentucky

3.1 Introduction

Words are the building blocks of natural language texts. As a proportion of a text's words are morphologically complex, it makes sense for text-oriented applications to register a word's structure. This chapter is about the techniques and mechanism for performing text analysis at the level of the word, *lexical analysis*. A word can be thought of in two ways, either as a string in running text, for example, the verb *delivers*; or as a more abstract object that is the cover term for a set of strings. So the verb DELIVER names the set {*delivers, deliver, delivering, delivered*}. A basic task of lexical analysis is to relate *morphological variants* to their *lemma* that lies in a lemma dictionary bundled up with its invariant semantic and syntactic information. Lemmatization is used in different ways depending on the task of the natural language processing (NLP) system. In machine translation (MT), the lexical semantics of word strings can be accessed via the lemma dictionary. In transfer models, it can be used as part of the source language linguistic analysis to yield the morphosyntactic representation of strings that can occupy certain positions in syntactic trees, the result of syntactic analyses. This requires that lemmas are furnished not only with semantic but also with morphosyntactic information. So *delivers* is referenced by the item DELIVER + {3rd, Sg, Present}. In what follows we will see how the mapping between *deliver* and DELIVER, and the substring *s* and {3rd, Sg, Present} can be elegantly handled using finite state transducers (FSTs).

We can think of the mapping of string to lemma as only one side of lexical analysis, the parsing side. The other side is mapping from the lemma to a string, morphological generation. Staying with our MT example, once we have marphosyntactically analyzed a string in the source language, we can then use the resulting information to generate the equivalent morphologically complex string in the target language. Translation at this level amounts to accessing the morphological rule of the target language that introduces the particular set of features found from the source language parse. In information retrieval (IR), parsing and generation serve different purposes. For the automatic creation of a list of key terms, it makes sense to notionally collapse morphological variants under one lemma. This is achieved in practice during *stemming*, a text preprocessing operation where morphologically complex strings are identified, decomposed into invariant stem (= lemma's canonical form) and affixes, and the affixes are then deleted. The result is texts as search objects that consist of stems only so that they can be searched via a lemma list. Morphological generation also plays a role in IR, not at the preprocessing stage but as part of query matching. Given that a lemma has invariant semantics, finding an occurrence of one of its morphological variants satisfies the semantic demands of a search. In languages with rich morphology it is more economical to use rules to generate the search terms than list them. Moreover, since morphology is used to create new words through derivation, a text that uses a newly coined word would not be missed if the string was one of many outputs of a productive morphological rule operating over a given lemma. Spelling dictionaries also make use of morphological generation for the same reason, to account for both listed and 'potential' words. Yet another application of lexical analysis is text preprocessing for syntactic analysis where parsing a string into morphosyntactic categories and subcategories furnishes the string with POS tags for the input of a syntactic parse. Finally tokenization, the segmentation of strings into word forms, is an important preprocessing task required for languages without word boundaries such as Chinese since a morphological parse of the strings reveals morphological boundaries, including words boundaries.

It is important from the start to lay out three main issues that any lexical analysis has to confront in some way. First, as we have shown, lexical analysis may be used for generation or parsing. Ideally, the mechanism used for parsing should be available for generation, so that a system has the flexibility to go both ways. Most lexical analysis is performed using FSTs, as we will see. One of the reasons is that FSTs provide a trivial means from flipping from parsing (analysis) to generation. Any alternative to FST lexical analysis should at least demonstrate it has this same flexibility. Two further issues concern the linguistic objects of lexical analysis, morphologically complex words. The notion that they are structures consisting of an invariant stem encoding the meaning and syntactic category of a word, joined together with an affix that encodes grammatical properties such as number, person, tense, etc is actually quite idealistic. For some languages, this approach takes you a long way, for example, Kazakh, Finnish, and Turkish. But it needs refinement for the languages more often associated with large NLP applications such as English, French, German, and Russian.

One of the reasons that this is a somewhat idealized view of morphology is that morphosyntactic properties do not have to be associated with an affix. Compare, for example, the string *looked* which is analyzed as LOOK+{Past} with *sang*, also a simple past. How do you get from the string *sang* to the lemma SING+{Past, Simple}? There is no affix but instead an alternation in the canonical stem's vowel. A related problem is that the affix may be associated with more than one property set: *looked* may correspond to either LOOK+{Past, Simple} or LOOK+{Past, Participle}. How do you know which *looked* you have encountered? The second problem is that in the context of a particular affix, the stem is not guaranteed to be invariant, in other words equivalent to the canonical stem. Again not straying beyond English, the string associated with the lemma FLY+{Noun, Plural} is not *flys but flies. At some level the parser needs to know that *flie* is part of the FLY lemma, not some as yet unrecorded FLIE lemma; moreover this variant form of the stem is constrained to a particular context, combination with the suffix −s. A further complication is changes to the canonical affix. If we propose that −s is the (orthographic) plural affix in English we have to account for the occasions when it appears in a text as −es, for example, in *foxes*.

In what follows we will see how lexical analysis models factor in the way a language assigns structure to words. Morphologists recognize three main approaches to word structure, first discussed in detail in Hockett (1958) but also in many recent textbooks, for example, Booij (2007: 116–117). All three approaches find their way into the assumptions that underlie a given model. An item and arrangement approach (I&A) views analysis as computing the information conveyed by a word's stem morpheme with that of its affix morpheme. Finite state morphology (FSM) incorporates this view using FSTs. This works well for the 'ideal' situation outlined above: *looked* is a stem plus a suffix, and information that the word conveys is simply a matter of computing the information conveyed by both morphemes. Item and process approaches (I&P) account for the kind of stem and affix variation that can happen inside a complex word, for example, *sing* becomes *sang* when it is past tense, and a vowel is added to the suffix −*s* when attached *fox*. The emphasis is on possible phonological processes that are associated with affixation (or other morphological operations), what is known as *morphonology*. Finally, in word and paradigm approaches (W&P), a lemma is associated with a table, or paradigm, that associates a morphological variant of the lemma with a morphosyntactic property set. So *looked* occupies the cell in the paradigm that contains the pairing of LOOK with {Past, Simple}. And by the same token *sang* occupies the equivalent cell in the SING paradigm. Meaning is derived from the definition of the cell, not the meaning of stem plus meaning of suffix, hence no special status is given to affixes.

FSTs have been used to handle *morphonology*, expressed as spelling variation in a text, and *morphotactics*, how stems and affixes combine, and how the meaning behind the combination can be computed. We begin with FSTs for morphonology, the historic starting point for FSM. This leaves us clear to look at lexical analysis as morphology proper. We divide this into two main parts, the model that assumes the I&A approach using FSTs (Section 3.3) and the alternative W&P model (Section 3.5). Section 3.4 is a brief overview of the types of 'difficult' morphology that the paradigm-based approaches are designed to handle but which FSM using the I&A approach can negotiate with some success too.

3.2 Finite State Morphonology

Phonology plays an important role in morphological analysis, as affixation is the addition of phonological segments to a stem. This is phonology as *exponent* of some property set. But there is another 'exponent-less' way in which phonology is involved, a kind of phonology of morpheme boundaries. This area of linguistics is known as *morphophonology* or *morphonology*: "the area of linguistics that deals with the relations and interaction of morphology with phonology" (Aronoff and Fudeman 2005: 240). Morpheme boundary phonology may or may not be reflected in the orthography. For example, in Russian word final voiced obstruents become voiceless—but they are spelled as if they stay as they are, unvoiced. A good example of morphonology in English is plural affixation. The plural affix can be pronounced in three different ways, depending on the stem it attaches to: as /z/ in *flags*, as /əz/ in *glasses* and as /s/ in *cats*. But only the /əz/ alternation is consequential because it shows up as a variant of orthographic −*s*. Note that text to speech processing has to pay closer attention to morphonology since it has to handle the two different pronunciations of orthographic −*s*, and for the Russian situation it has to handle the word final devoicing rule. For lexical analysis to cope with morphological alternations, the system has to provide a means of mapping the 'basic' form with its orthographic variant. As the variation is (largely) determined by context, the mapping can be rule governed. For example, the suffix −*s* you get in a plural word shows up as −*es* (the mapping) when the stem it attaches to ends in a −*s*- (specification of the environment). As we saw in the previous section, stems can also have variants. For *flie* we need a way of mapping it to basic *fly*, and a statement that we do this every time we see this string with a −*s* suffix. Note that this is an example of orthographic variation with no phonological correlate (*flie* and *fly* are pronounced the same).

The favored model for handling morphonology in the orthography, or morphology-based orthographic spelling variation, is a specific type of finite state machine known as a finite state transducer (FST). It is assumed that the reader is familiar with finite state automata. Imagine a finite state transition network (FSTN) which takes two tapes as input, and transitions are licensed not by arcs notated with a single symbol but a pair of symbols. The regular language that the machine represents is the *relation* between the language that draws from one set of symbols and the language that draws from the set of symbols it is paired with. An FST that defines the relation between underlying *glass^s* (where ^ marks a morpheme boundary) and surface *glasses* is given in Figure 3.1.

Transition from one state to another is licensed by a specific correspondence between symbols belonging to two tapes. Underlying, more abstract representations are conventionally the upper tape. The colon

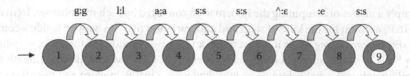

FIGURE 3.1   A spelling rule FST for *glasses*.

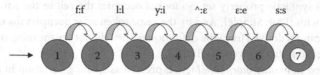

FIGURE 3.2   A spelling rule FST for *flies*.

between symbols labeling the arcs declares the correspondence. The analysis of the surface string into its canonical morphemes is simply reading the lower language symbol and printing its upper language correspondent. And generation is the inverse. Morpheme boundaries do not have surface representations; they are deleted in generation by allowing the alphabet of the lower language to include the empty string symbol ε. This correspondence of ^ to ε labels the transition from State 6 to State 7. The string *glasses* is an example of *insertion*-based orthographic variation where a character has to be inserted between stem and suffix. Since ε can also belong to the upper language its correspondence with lower language *e* provides for the insertion (State 7 to State 8). In a similar vein, an FST can encode the relation between underlying *fly^s* and surface *flies* (Figure 3.2). This is a combination of *substitution* based variation (the symbol *y* is substituted by *i*) and insertion based variation, if we treat the presence of *e* as the same as in the *glasses* example. Variation takes place both in the stem and in the suffix.

A practical demonstration of an FST treatment of English orthographic variation, i.e., spelling rules helps to show these points. To do this we will use the lexical knowledge representation language DATR (Evans and Gazdar 1996). DATR notation for FSTs is a good expository choice since its syntax is particularly transparent, and has been shown to define FSTs in an economical way (Evans and Gazdar 1996: 191–193).* And as we will be using DATR anyway when we discuss an alternative to finite state–based lexical analysis, it makes sense to keep with the same notation throughout. But the reader should note that there are alternative FST notations for lexical analysis, for example, in Koskenniemi (1983), Beesley and Karttunen (2003), and Sproat (1997). DATR expresses the value for some attribute, or a set of attributes, as an association of the value with a path at some node. A DATR definition is given in (3.1).

$$(3.1) \qquad \texttt{State\_n:}$$
$$\texttt{<g> == g.}$$

Basically, (3.1) says that at a particular node, `State_n`, the attribute `<g>` has the value g. Nodes are in (initial) upper case, attribute sets are paths of one or more atoms delimited by angle brackets. We could think of (3.1) as a trivial single state FST that takes an input string g, represented by an attribute path, and generates the output string g, represented by the value. DATR values do not need to be explicitly stated, they can be *inherited* via another path. And values do not need to be simple; they can be a combination of atom(s) plus inheriting path(s). Imagine you are building a transducer to transliterate words in the Cyrillic alphabet into their Roman alphabet equivalents. For example, you want the FST to capture the proper name Саша transliterated as Sasha. So we would have `<C> == S, <a> == a`. For ш we need two glyphs and to get them we could associate `<ш>` with the complex value s`<h>`, and somewhere else provide the equation `<h> == h`. So `<ш> == s <h>` implies `<ш> == s h`. We will

---

* Gibbon (1987) is an FST account of tone morphonology in Tem and Baule, African languages spoken in Togo and the Ivory Coast. In a later demonstration, Gibbon showed how DATR could be used to considerably reduce the number of states needed to describe the same problem (Gibbon 1989).

see the importance of including a path as part of the value to get (3.1) to look more like a more serious transducer that maps *glass^s* to *glasses*. This is given in (3.2).

```
(3.2)    Glasses_FST:
                    <g> == g <>
                    <l> == l <>
                    <a> == a <>
                    <s> == s <>
                    <s> == s <>
                    <^> == e <>
                    <s> == s <>
                    <> ==.
```

The input string is the path <g l a s s ^ s>. The path <g> that we see in the second line of (3.2) is in fact the *leading subpath* of this path. The leading subpath expresses the first symbol of the input string. It is associated with the atom g, a symbol of the output string. So far, we have modeled a transition from the initial state to another state, and transduced g to g. Further transitions are by means of the <> and this needs careful explanation. In DATR, any extensions of a subpath on the left of an equation are automatically transferred to a path on the right of the equation. So the extensions of <g> are transferred into the path <> as <l a s s ^ s>. This path then needs to be evaluated by linking it to a path on the left hand side. The path <l> in the third line is suitable because it is the leading subpath of this new path. As we can see the value associated with <l> is the atom l, so another symbol has been consumed on the input string and a corresponding symbol printed onto the output string. The extensions of <l a s s ^ s> fill the path <> on the right side. To take stock: at this point the evaluation of <g l a s s ^ s> is g l together with the extended path <a s s ^ s>. As we continue down the equation list the leading subpaths are always the next attribute atom in the input string path, and this path is given the equivalent value atom. But something more interesting happens when we get to the point where the leading subpath is <^>. Here a nonequivalent value atom is given, the atom e. This of course expresses the *e* insertion that is the essence of the spelling rule. The deletion of the ^ is represented very straightforwardly as saying nothing about it, i.e., no transduction. Finally, the equation at the bottom of the list functions to associate any subpath not already specified, expressed as <>, with a null value. Suppose we represent input strings with an end of word boundary #, so we have the lexical entry <g l a s s ^ e s #>. Through the course of the evaluation <#> will ultimately be treated as a leading subpath. As this path is not explicitly stated anywhere else at the node, it is implied by <>. So <> == is interpreted as the automatic deletion of any substring for which there is no explicit mapping statement. This equation also expresses the morphologically simple input string <g l a s s #> mapping to g l a s s. The theorem, expressing input and output string correspondences licensed by the FST in (3.2) is given in (3.3).

```
(3.3)    <g l a s s #> = g l a s s
         <g l a s s ^ s #> = g l a s s e s
```

The FST in (3.2) is very useful for a single word in the English language but says nothing about other words, such *class:classes*, *mass:masses*, or *fox:foxes*. Nor does it provide for 'regular' plurals such as *cat:cats*. FSTs are set up to manage the regular situation as well as problems that are general to entire classes. To do this, symbols can be replaced by *symbol classes*. (3.4) replaces (3.3) by using a symbol class represented by the expression $abc, an abbreviatory variable ranging over the 26 lower case alphabetic characters used in English orthography (see Evans and Gazdar 1996: 192–193 for the DATR FST on which this is based).

```
(3.4)    Glasses&Classes:
                    <$abc> == $abc <>
                    <^> == e <>
                    <> == .
```

For an input string consisting of a stem composed of alphabetic symbols, the first equation takes this string represented as a path and associates whatever character denotes its leading subpath with the equivalent character as an atomic value. Equivalence is due to the fact that $abc is a bound variable. If the string is the path <g l a s s ^ s #> then the leading subpath <g> is associated with the atomic value g; by the same token for the string <c a t ^ s> the subpath <c> would be associated with c. The extension of this path fills <> on the right hand side as in (3.2), and just in case the new leading subpath belongs to $abc, it will be evaluated as <$abc> == &abc <>. This represents a self-loop, a transition whose source and destination state is the same. In case we hit a morpheme boundary, i.e., we get to the point where the leading subpath is <^>, then as in (3.2) the value given is e. Whatever appears after the morpheme boundary is the new leading subpath. And since it is <s>, the plural affix, it belongs to $abc so through <$abc> == $abc <> will map to s. As before, the # will be deleted through <> == since this symbol does not belong to $abc.

Whereas (3.2) undergeneralizes, we now have an FST in (3.4) which overgeneralizes. If the input is <c a t ^ s> the output will be incorrect c a t e s. A morphonological rule or spelling rule (the orthographic counterpart) has to say not only (a) what changes from one level representation to another, and (b) where in the string the change takes place but also (c) under what circumstances. The *context* of e insertion is an s followed by the symbol sequence ^s. But if we want to widen the context so that *foxes* is included in the rule, then the rule needs to specify e insertion when not just s but also x is followed by ^ s. We can think of this as a class of contexts, a subset of the stem symbol class above. Figure 3.3 is a graphical representation of a transition labeled by the symbol class of all stem characters, and another transition labeled by the class of just those symbols providing the left context for the spelling rule.

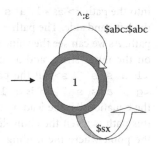

FIGURE 3.3 An FST with symbol classes.

Our (final)FST for the −*es* spelling rule in English is given in (3.5) with its theorem in (3.6). The context of e insertion is expressed by the variable $sx (left context) followed by the morpheme boundary symbol (right context). As 'regular' input strings such as <c a t ^ s>, <d o g ^ s>, <c h a i r ^ s> do not have pre-morpheme boundary s or x they avoid the path leading to e insertion.

(3.5)   Es_Spelling_Rule:
          <$abc> == $abc <>
          <$sx ^> == $sx e <>
          <^> == <>
          <> ==

(3.6)   <g l a s s #> = g l a s s.
         <g l a s s ^ s #> = g l a s s e s.
         <f o x #> = f o x.
         <f o x ^ s> = f o x e s.
         <c a t #> = c a t.
         <c a t ^ s #> = c a t s.

A final comment on the spelling rule FST is in order. In (3.5) how do we ensure that the subpath <x> for <f o x ^ s> will not be evaluated by the first equation since x belongs to $abc as well as $sx? In other words, how do we 'look ahead' to see if the next symbol on the input string is a ^ ? In DATR, look ahead is captured by the 'longest path wins' principle so that any extension of a subpath takes precedence over the subpath. As <x ^> is an extension of <x>, the <x ^> path 'wins' and gets evaluated, i.e., it overrides the shorter path and its value. We look more closely at this principle when we use DATR to represent default inheritance hierarchies in Section 5.

3.2.1 Closing Remarks on Finite State Morphonology

Morphonological alternations at first glance seem marginal to word structure, or morphology 'proper.' In the previous discussion, we have barely mentioned a morphosyntactic feature. But their importance in lexical analysis should not be overlooked. On the one hand, text processors have to somehow handle orthographic variation. And on the other, it was earlier attempts at computationally modeling theoretical accounts of phonological and morphonological variations that suggested FSTs were the most efficient means of doing this. Kaplan and Kay in the 1980s, belatedly published as Kaplan and Kay (1994), demonstrated that the (morph)phonological rules for English proposed by Chomsky and Halle (1968) could be modeled in FSTs. Their work was taken up by Koskenniemi (1983) who used FSTs for the morphonology of Finnish, which went beyond proof of concept and was used in a large-scale text-processing application. Indeed Koskenniemi's Two-Level Morphology model is the real starting point for finite state–based analysis. Its motivation was to map the underlying lexical (= lemma) representation to the surface representation without the need to consult an intermediary level. Indeed, intermediary levels can be handled by cascading FSTs so that the output of FST1 is the input of FST2, and the output of FST2 is in the input of FST3. But then the ordering becomes crucial for getting the facts right. Koskenniemi had the FSTs operate in parallel. An FST requires a particular context that could be an underlying or surface symbol (class) and specifies a particular mapping between underlying and surface strings. It thus acts as a constraint on the mapping of underlying and surface representations, and the specific environment of this mapping. All FSTs simultaneously scan both underlying and surface strings. A mapping is accepted by all the FSTs that do not specify a constraint. For it to work the underlying and surface strings have to be equal length, so the mapping is one to one. One rule maps underlying y to surface i provided that a surface e comes next; so the context is the surface string. The other is sensitive to the underlying string where it ensures a surface e appears whenever y precedes the morpheme boundary, shown in (3.6).

(3.6)

f	l	y	0	^	s
f	l	i	e	0	s

Koskenniemi's model launched FST-based morphology because, as Karttunen (2007: 457) observes, it was "the first practical model in the history of computational linguistics for analysis of morphologically complex languages." Despite its title, the framework was essentially for morphonology rather than morphology proper, as noted in an early review (Gazdar 1985: 599). Nonetheless, FST morphonology paved the way for FST morphology proper which we now discuss.

3.3 Finite State Morphology

In the previous section we showed how lexical analysis has to account for surface variation of a canonical string. But the canonical string with morpheme boundaries is itself the lower string of its associated lemma. For example, *fox's* has the higher-level representation as the (annotated) lemma *fox+noun^plural*. FSTs are used to translate between these two levels to model what we could think of as morphology 'proper.' To briefly highlight the issues in FSM let us consider an example from Turkish with a morphosyntactic translation, or interlinear gloss, as well as a standard translation.

(3.7)   gör-mü-yor-du-k
          see-NEG-PROGR-PAST-1PL
          'We weren't seeing' (Mel'čuk 2006: 299)

In Turkish, the morphological components of a word are neatly divisible into stem and contiguous affixes where each affix is an exponent of a particular morphosyntactic property. Lexical analysis treats the interlinear gloss (second line) as the lemma and maps it onto a morphologically decomposed string. The language of the upper, or lexical, language contains symbols for morphosyntactic features. The ordering of the morphemes is important: Negation precedes Aspect which precedes Tense which in turn precedes Subject Agreement information. For a correct mapping, the FST must encode morpheme ordering, or *morphotactics*. This is classic I&A morphological analysis. As in the previous section, we can demonstrate with an FST for English notated in DATR (3.8). English does not match Turkish for richness in inflectional morphology but does better in derivational morphology. The lexical entries for the derivational family *industry, industrial, industrialize, industrialization* are given in (3.8b).

```
(3.8)    DERIVATION:
           <$abc> == $abc <>
           <+noun> == Noun_Stem:<>.
         Noun_Stem:
           <> == \#
           <^ +adj> == ^ a l Adj_Stem:<>.
         Adj_Stem:
           <> == \#
           <^ +vb> == ^ i z e Verb_Stem:<>.
         Verb_Stem:
           <> == \#
           <^ +noun> == ^ a t i on <>.

(3.8b)   <i n d u s t r y +noun>
         <i n d u s t r y +noun ^ +adj>
         <i n d u s t r y +noun ^ +adj ^ +vb>
         <i n d u s t r y +noun ^ +adj ^ +vb ^ +noun>.
```

The FST maps the lemma lexical entries in (3.8b) to their corresponding (intermediary) forms, the noun *industry#*, the adjective *industry^al#*, the verb *industry^al^ize#*, and the noun *industry^al^ize^ation#*. As in the morphonological demonstration in the previous section, the trivial alphabetical mapping is performed through a variable expressing a symbol class and path extensions for arc transitioning. The first difference is a path with a morphosyntactic feature as its attribute, <+noun> showing that in this FST we have lemmas and features as input. We see that this feature licenses the transition to another set of states gathered round the node Noun_Stem. In FSM, lemmas are classified according to features such as POS to enable appropriate affix selection, and hence capture the morphotactics of the language. Three nodes representing three stem classes are associated with the three affixes *–al, -ize, -ation*. For ^ a l to be a possible affix value the evaluation must be at the Noun_Stem node. Once the affix is assigned, further evaluation must be continued at a specified node, here Adj_Stem. This is because the continuation to *–al* affixation is severely restricted in English. We can think of the specified 'continuation' node as representing a *continuation class*, a list of just those affixes that can come after *–al*. In this way, a lemma is guided through the network, outputting an affix and being shepherded to the subnetwork where the next affix will be available. So (3.8) accounts for *industy^al^ize^ation#* but fails for **industry^ation^al^ize#* or **industy-ize-al-ation#*. It also accounts for *industry#* and *industy^al^ize#* by means of the equation <> == \ # at each continuation class node. Note that # is a reserved symbol in DATR, hence the need for escape \.

Let us quickly step through the FST to see how it does the mapping <i n d u s t r y +noun ^ +adj ^ +vb> = i n d u s t r y ^ a l ^ i z e #. The first path at DERIVATION maps the entire stem of the lemma to its surface form, in the manner described for the spelling rule FST. After this, the leading subpath is <+noun>; the path extensions are passed over to the node Noun_Stem. The first line at Noun_Stem covers the morphologically simple <i n d u s t r y +noun>. For this string, there is no further path to extend, i.e., no morphological boundaries, and transduction amounts to appending to the output string the word boundary symbol. Similar provision is made at all nodes just in case the derivation stops there. If, however, the lemma is annotated as being morphologically complex, and specifically as representing adjectival derivation, <^ +adj>, the output is a morpheme boundary plus –*al* affix (second line at the Adj_Stem node). At this point the path can be extended as <^ +vb> in the case of derivative *industrialize* or *industrialization*, or not in the case of *industrial*. With no extensions, evaluation will be through <> == \# yielding i n d u s t r y ^ a l #. Otherwise an extension with leading subpath <^ + vb> outputs suffix ^ i z e and is then passed onto the node Verb_Stem for further evaluation. As there is no new subpath the end of word boundary is appended to the output string value. But if the input path happened to extend this path any further evaluation would have to be at Verb_Stem, e.g., adding the affix –*ation*.

3.3.1 Disjunctive Affixes, Inflectional Classes, and Exceptionality

Affix continuation classes are important for getting the morphotactics right but they also allow for more than one affix to be associated with the same morphosyntactic feature set. This is very common in inflectionally rich languages such as Russian, French, Spanish, and German. To illustrate, consider the paradigm of the Russian word *karta* 'map.' I am giving the forms in their transliterated versions for expository reasons, so it should be understood that *karta* is the transliteration of карта. Note the suffix used for the genitive plural —Ø. This denotes a 'zero affix,' i.e., the word is just the stem *kart* (or карт) in a genitive plural context.

(3.9)   Karta

	Singular	Plural
Nominative	*kart-a*	*kart-y*
Accusative	*kart-u*	*kart-y*
Genitive	*kart-y*	*kart-Ø*
Dative	*kart-e*	*kart-am*
Instrumental	*kart-oj*	*kart-ami*
Locative	*kart-e*	*kart-ax*

The FST in (3.10) maps lexical entries such as <k a r t +noun ^ sg nom> to its corresponding surface form k a r t ^ a #.

(3.10)   RUSSIAN:
           <$abc> == $abc <>
           <+noun> == Noun_Stem:<>.
     Noun_Stem:
        <> == \#
        <^ sg nom> == ^ a <>
        <^ sg acc> == ^ u <>
        <^ sg gen> == ^ y <>
        <^ sg dat> == ^ e <>
        <^ sg inst> == ^ o j <>
        <^ sg loc> == ^ e <>
        <^ pl nom> == ^ y <>
        <^ pl acc> == ^ y <>
        <^ pl gen> == ^ 0 <>
        <^ pl dat> == ^ am <>
        <^ pl inst> == ^ a m i <>
        <^ pl loc> == ^ a x <>.

This FST accounts for *any* Russian noun. But this makes it too powerful as not all nouns share the inflectional pattern of *karta*. For example, *zakon* 'law' has a different way of forming the genitive

TABLE 3.1 Russian Inflectional Classes

	I	II	III	IV
	Zakon	Karta	Rukopis'	Boloto
		Singular		
Nom	zakon-ø	kart-a	rukopis'-ø	bolot-o
Acc	zakon-ø	kart-u	rukopis'-ø	bolot-o
Gen	zakon-a	kart-y	rukopis-i	bolot-a
Dat	zakon-u	kart-e	rukopis-i	bolot-u
Inst	zakon-om	kart-oj	rukopis-ju	bolot-om
Loc	zakon-e	kart-e	rukopis-i	bolot-e
		Plural		
Nom	zakon-y	kart-y	rukopis-i	bolot-a
Acc	zakon-y	kart-y	rukopis-i	bolot-a
Gen	zakon-ov	kart-ø	rukopis-ej	bolot-ø
Dat	zukon-am	kart-am	rukopis-jam	bolot-am
Inst	zakon-ami	kart-ami	rúkopis-jami	bolot-ami
Loc	zakon-ax	kart-ax	rukopis-jax	bolot-ax

singular: it affixes −*a* to the stem and not −*y* (*zakon-a*). And *bolot-o* 'swamp' differs in its nominative singular. Finally *rukopis'* 'manuscript' has a distinct dative singular *rukopisi*. Because of these and other distinctions, Russian can be thought of as having four major inflectional patterns, or *inflectional classes*, that are shown in Table 3.1.

To handle situations where there is a *choice* of affix corresponding to a given morphosyntactic property set, an FST encodes subclasses of stems belonging to the same POS class. (3.11) is a modified version of the FST in (3.10) that incorporates inflectional classes as sets of disjunctive affixes. For reasons of space, only two classes are represented. Sample lexical entries are given in (3.12).

```
(3.11)    RUSSIAN_2:
              <$abc> == $abc <>
              <+noun> == Noun_Stem:<>.
          Noun_Stem:
              < 1 > == Stem_1:<>
              < 2 > == Stem_2:<>
              < 3 > == Stem_3:<>
              < 4 > == Stem_4:<>.
          Stem_1:
              <> == \#
              <^ sg nom> == ^ 0 <>
              <^ sg acc> == ^ 0 <>
              <^ sg gen> == ^ a <>
              <^ sg dat> == ^ u <>
              <^ sg inst> == ^ o m <>
              <^ sg loc> == ^ e <>
              <^ pl nom> == ^ y <>
              <^ pl acc> == ^ y <>
              <^ pl gen> == ^ o v <>
              <^ pl dat> == ^ a m <>
              <^ pl inst> == ^ a m i <>
              <^ pl loc> == ^ a x <>.
```

```
                    Stem_2:
                       <> == \#
                       <^ sg nom> == ^ a <>
                       <^ sg acc> == ^ u <>
                       <^ sg gen> == ^ y <>
                       <^ sg dat> == ^ e <>
                       <^ sg inst> == ^ o j <>
                       <^ sg loc> == ^ e <>
                       <^ pl nom> == ^ y <>
                       <^ pl acc> == ^ y <>
                       <^ pl gen> == ^ 0 <>
                       <^ pl dat> == ^ am <>
                       <^ pl inst> == ^ a m i <>
                       <^ pl loc> == ^ a x <>.
```

(3.12) `<k a r t +noun 2 ^ sg nom>`
`<k a r t +noun 2 ^ sg acc>`
`<z a k o n +noun 1 ^ sg nom>`
`<z a k o n +noun 1 ^ sg acc>`

What is different about the partial lexicon in (3.12) is that stems are annotated for stem class (1, 2, 3, 4) as well as POS. The node Noun_Stem assigns stems to appropriate stem class nodes for affixation. Each of the four stem class nodes maps a given morphosyntactic feature sequence to an affix. In this way, separate affixes that map to a single feature set do not compete as they are distributed across the stem class nodes. Even English has something like inflectional classes. There are several ways of forming a past participle: suffix *–ed* as in 'have looked,' suffix *–en* as in 'have given,' and no affix (-Ø) as in 'have put.' An English verb FST would encode this arrangement as subclasses of stems, as in the more elaborate Russian example.

Classifying stems also allows for a fairly straightforward treatment of exceptionality. For example, the Class I noun *soldat* is exceptional in that its genitive plural is not *soldat-ov* as predicted by its pattern, but *soldat-Ø*'soldier.' This is the genitive plural you expect for a Class 2 noun (see Table 3.1). To handle this we annotate *soldat* lexical entries as Class 1 for all forms *except* the genitive plural, where it is annotated as Class 2. This is shown in (3.13) where a small subset of the lemmas are given.

(3.13) `<s o l d a t +noun 1 ^ sg nom>`
`<s o l d a t +noun 1 ^ sg gen>`
`<s o l d a t +noun 1 ^ pl nom>`
`<s o l d a t +noun 2 ^ pl gen>`

Another type of exception is represented by *pal'to* 'overcoat.' What is exceptional about this item is that it does not combine with any inflectional affixes, i.e., it is an indeclinable noun. There are a number of such items in Russian. An FST assigns them their own class and maps all lexical representations to the same affixless surface form, as shown in (3.14).

(3.14) Stem_5:
`<> == \#.`

Our last type of exception is what is called a *pluralia tantum* word, such as *scissors* in English, or *trousers*, where there is no morphological singular form. The Russian for 'trousers' is also pluralia tantum: *brjuk-i*. We provide a node in the FST that carries any input string singular features to a node labeled for input plural features. This is shown in (3.15) as the path `<^ sg>` inheriting from another path at another node, i.e., `<^ pl>` at Stem_2. This is because *brjuki* shares plural affixes with other Class 2 nouns.

(3.15)   Stem_6:
              <> == \#
              <^ sg> == Stem_2:<^ pl>.

FSTs for lexical analysis are based on I&A style morphology that assumes a straightforward mapping of feature to affix. Affix rivalry of the kind exemplified by Russian upsets this mapping since more than one affix is available for one feature. But by incorporating stem classes and continuation affix classes they can handle such cases and thereby operate over languages with inflectional classes. The subclassification of stems also provides FSM with a way of incorporating exceptional morphological behavior.

3.3.2 Further Remarks on Finite State Lexical Analysis

FSTs can be combined in various ways to encode larger fragments of a language's word structure grammar. Through *union* an FST for, say Russian nouns, can be joined with another FST for Russian verbs. We have already mentioned that FSTs can be cascaded such that the output of FST1 is the input to FST2. This operation is known as *composition*. The FSTs for morphology proper take lemmas as input and give morphologically decomposed string as output. These strings are then the input of morphonological/spelling rules FSTs that are sensitive to morpheme boundaries, i.e., where the symbols ^ and # define contexts for a given rule as we saw with the English plural spelling rule. So, for example, the lemma <k a r t + noun ^ sg nom> maps on to an intermediate level of representation k a r t ^ a #. Another transducer takes this as input path k a r t ^ a # and maps it onto the surface form k a r t a, stripping away the morpheme boundaries and performing any other (morphonological) adjustments. Intermediate levels of representation are dispensed with altogether if the series of transducers is *composed* into a single transducer, as detailed in Roark and Sproat (2007) where <x, y> representing the upper and lower tape of transducer 1 and <y, z> the upper and lower tapes of transducer 2 are composed into a single transducer T as <x, z>, i.e., intermediary <y, z> is implied. As we saw in the previous section, Two-Level Morphology does not compose the morphonological FSTs but intersects them. There is no intermediary level of representation because the FSTs operate orthogonally to a simple finite state automaton representing lexical entries in their lexical (lemma) forms.

Finite state approaches have dominated lexical analysis from Koskenniemi's (1983) implementation of a substantial fragment of Finnish morphology. In the morphology chapters of computational linguistics textbooks the finite state approach takes centre stage, for example, Dale et al. (2000), Mitkov (2004), and Jurafsky and Martin (2007), where it takes center stage for two chapters. In Roark and Sproat (2007) computational morphology *is* FSM. From our demonstration it is not hard to see why this is the case. Implementations of FSTNs are relatively straightforward and extremely efficient, and FSTs provide the simultaneous modeling of morphological generation and analysis. They also have an impressive track record in large-scale multilingual projects, such as the Multext Project (Armstrong 1996) for corpus analysis of many languages including Czech, Bulgarian, Swedish, Slovenian, and Swahili. More recent two-level systems include Ui Dhonnchadha et al. (2003) for Irish, Pretorius and Bosch (2003) for Zulu, and Yona and Wintner (2007) for Hebrew. Finite state morphological environments have been created for users to build their own models, for example, Sproat's (1997) *lex tools* and more recently Beesley and Karttunen's (2003) *xerox finites state tools*. The interested reader should consult the accompanying Web site for this chapter for further details of these environments, as well as DATR style FSTs.

3.4 "Difficult" Morphology and Lexical Analysis

So far we have seen lexical analysis as morphological analysis where there are two assumptions being made about morphologically complex word: (1) one morphosyntactic feature set, such as 'Singular Nominative,' maps onto one *exponent*, for example, a suffix or a prefix; and (2) the exponent itself is identifiable as a sequence of symbols lying contiguous to the stem, either on its left (as a prefix) or its right (as a suffix). But in many languages neither (1) nor (2) necessarily hold. As NLP systems are increasingly multilingual, it becomes more and more important to explore the challenges other languages pose for finite state models, which are ideally suited to handle data that conform to assumptions (1) and (2). In this section, we look at various sets of examples that do not conform to a neat I&A analysis. There are sometimes ways around these difficult cases, as we saw with the Russian case where stem classes were used to handle multiple affixes being associated with a single feature. But our discussion will lead to an alternative to I&A analysis that finite state models entail. As we will see in Section 3.5, the alternative W&P approach appears to offer a much more natural account of word structure when it includes the difficult cases.

3.4.1 Isomorphism Problems

It turns out that few languages have a morphological system that can be described as one feature (or feature set) expressed as one morpheme, the exponent of that feature. In other words, *isomorphism* turns out not to be the common situation. In Section 3.3, I carefully chose Turkish to illustrate FSTs for morphology proper because Turkish seems to be isomorphic, a property of agglutinative languages. At the same time derivational morphology tends to be more isomorphic than inflection, hence an English derivational example. But even agglutinative languages can display non-isomorphic behavior in their inflection (3.16) is the past tense set of forms for the verb 'to be' (Haspelmath 2002: 33).

(3.16)	ol-i-n	'I was'
	ol-i-t	'you (singular) were'
	ol-i	'he/she was'
	ol-i-mme	'we were'
	ol-i-tte	'you (plural) were'
	ol-i-vat	'they were'

A lexical entry for 'I was' would be `<o l +verb ^ past ^ 1stSg>` mapping to `o l ^ i ^ n #`. Similarly for 'we were,' `<o l +verb ^ past ^ 1stSPL>` maps to `o l ^ i ^ mme #`. But what about 'he/she was'? In this case there is no exponent for the feature set '3rd Person Singular' to map onto; we have lost isomorphism. But in a sense we had already lost it since for all forms in (3.16) we are really mapping a *combination* of features to a single exponent: a Number feature (plural) and a Person feature (1st) map to the single exponent *-mme*, etc. Of course the way out is to use a symbol on the lexical string that describes a feature combination. This is what we did with the Russian examples in Section 3.3.2 to avoid the difficulty, and it is implicit in the Finnish data above. But back to the problem we started with: where there is a 'missing' element on the surface string we can use a Ø a 'zero affix,' for the upper string feature symbol to map to. Indeed, in Tables 3.1 and 3.2 I used Ø to represent the morphological complexity of some Russian word-forms. So the Russian FST maps the lemma `<z a k o n +noun ^ sg ^ nom>` onto `z a k o n ^ Ø #`. To get rid of the Ø, a morphophonological FST can use empty transitions in the same way it does to delete morpheme boundaries. Variations of this problem can be met with variations of the solution. The French adverb 'slowly' is *lentement* where *lent-* is the stem and *–ment* expresses 'adverb.' This leaves the middle *–e-* without anything to map onto. The mapping is one upper string symbol to two lower string symbols. The solution is to squeeze in a zero feature, or 'empty morpheme' between the stem and the 'adverb' feature: `<l e n t ^ Ø ^ adverb>`. The converse, two features with a single exponent, is collapsing the two features into a feature set, as we discussed. The alternative is to place zeros on the lower string: `<o l +verb Past ^ 1stPerson ^ Singular>` maps to `<o l ^ i ^ m m e ^ Ø #`. But then the choice of what feature has the zero affix is arbitrary.

Finally, we can think of the competition of exponents for a particular feature as a similar kind of isomorphism problem: one feature, several exponents. In Section 3.3.1, we showed how Russian has inflectional classes, where nouns are grouped according to the choice of suffix they make for a given

TABLE 3.2   Russian Inflectional Classes

	I Zakon	II Karta	III Rukopis'	IV Boloto
		Singular		
Nom	zakon-ø	kart-a	rukopis'-ø	bolot-o
Acc	zakon-ø	kart-u	rukopis'-ø	bolot-o
Gen	zakon-a	kart-y	rukopis-i	bolot-a
Dat	zakon-u	kart-e	rukopis-i	bolot-u
Inst	zakon-om	kart-oj	rukopis-ju	bolot-om
Loc	zakon-e	kart-e	rukopis-i	bolot-e
		Plural		
Nom	zakon-y	kart-y	rukopis-i	bolot-a
Acc	zakon-y	kart-y	rukopis-i	bolot-a
Gen	zakon-ov	kart-ø	rukopis-ej	bolot-ø
Dat	zakon-am	kart-am	rukopis-jam	bolot-am
Inst	zakon-ami	kart-ami	rúkopis-jami	bolot-ami
Loc	zakon-ax	kart-ax	rukopis-jax	bolot-ax

feature. To handle this we used affix classes together with stem classes such that different stem classes were licensed to navigate over different parts of the network where the appropriate affixes are stored.

3.4.2 Contiguity Problems

As well as isomorphism, I&A approaches rely on contiguity: the exponent of a feature should be found at the left or right edge of the stem of the lower string, mirroring the position of the feature relative to the stem on the upper lexical string. But one does not need to look far to find examples of 'noncontiguous' morphology. In Section 3.1, I discussed the potential problem of *sang*, past tense of *sing*. This is an example of a feature mapping onto an exponent, which is really the change we make to the stem's vowel. How can an FST map the correct lower string to the upper string <s i n g ^ past>? To account for the feature *not* mapping onto an affix, it can use the Ø as we did (extensively) with the isomorphism problems above. This then leaves the vowel alternation as the exponent of the feature. One way is to target the stem vowel so that lexical i maps onto surface a; and allow navigation through the subnetwork just for those items that behave this way (*sing/sang, ring/rang, spin/span*). This is represented in (3.17). Lexical entries for regular *cook* and irregular *sing* and *ring* are given in (3.18).

```
(3.17)    Ablaut_FST:
              <$abc> == $abc <>
              <s i n g ^ past> == Past_Stem
              <r i n g ^ past> == Past_Stem
              <^ present> == ^ 0 <>
              <^ past> == ^ e d <>
              <> == \#.
          Past_Stem:
              <$abc> == $abc <>
              <$vow> == a <>
              <^ past> == ^ 0 <>
              <> == \#.

(3.18)    <s i n g ^ present>    <s i n g ^ past>
          <r i n g ^ present>    <r i n g ^ past>
          <c o o k ^ present>    <c o o k ^ past>
```

The first node provides for the trivial stem string mappings required by regular non-ablauting verbs. The fourth equation expresses lexical 'present' mapping to Ø (where no account is taken of −s affixation for '3rd person singular'). The fifth equation handles regular past formation in *-ed*, as in *cooked*. But just in case the path to evaluate is `<s i n g ^ past>` or `<r i n g ^ past>`, an extra node is provided for the evaluation, the node `Past_Stem`. At this node, the symbol class for all stem characters is used to perform the normal upper to lower stem mapping, as in previous DATR examples. The difference is that there is a new symbol class expressed as the variable $vow, ranging over vowels that alternate with *a* in the past. The path equation `<$vow> == a <>` takes the vowel in the stem and maps it to a, the vowel alternation that is the exponent of 'past.' Any other character belonging to the input (stem) string maps onto itself on the lower string (through `<$abc> == $abc <>`). Finally `<^ past> == ^ 0 <>` represents the fact that for this class of verbs the zero affix is used as exponent of 'past.' The theorem is given in (3.19).

```
(3.19)    <s i n g ^ present> = s i n g ^ 0 #.
          <s i n g ^ past> = s a n g ^ 0 #.
          <r i n g ^ present> = r i n g ^ 0 #.
          <r i n g ^ past> = r a n g ^ 0 #.
          <c o o k ^ present> = c o o k ^ 0 #.
          <c o o k ^ past> = c o o k ^ e d #.
```

Another example of noncontiguous morphology is *infixation*, where an affix attaches not to the right or left edges but within the stem itself. (3.20) is an infixation example from Tagolog, a language spoken in the Philippines with nearly sixteen million speakers worldwide (*Ethnologue*). The data are from Mel'čuk (2006: 300).

```
(3.20)              Sulat 'write'   Patay 'kill'
        ACTIVE      s-um-ulat       p-um-atay
        PASSIVE     s-in-ulat       p-in-atay
```

A way of handling infixation with FSTs is to add an intermediary level of representation, as outlined in Roark and Sproat (2007: 29–31, 39–40). A first transducer maps the location of the affixation to an 'anchor' symbol within the stem. A second transducer operates over intermediate representations and maps the anchor with either `^ in ^` or `^ um ^` depending on the voice feature (Active or Passive). Note that features need to be preserved from the lexical to intermediate levels. This is because the only difference between the two string types is the anchor; and as it is an affix it needs boundaries, and as it is an infix the boundaries need to be on both left and right. This is important in case there are any morphonological consequences to the infixation. This approach informs the DATR transducers in (3.21) and (3.23).

```
(3.21)    Itermediate_FST:
              <$features> == $features <>
              <$abc> == $abc <>
              <^ $abc $vow> == ^ $abc & $vow <>
              <> == .
```

```
(3.22)    <active ^ s u l a t>   <passive ^ s u l a t>
          <active ^ p a t a y>   <passive ^ p a t a y>
```

As feature annotations are needed in the output string, we need a symbol class for them, expressed as the variable $ features; then identity mapping is treated as in the previous FSTs. The second equation is the (by now) familiar trivial stem character mapping. Note that lexical entries come with features to the left of the canonical stem (3.22). The third equation in (3.21) represents the way the FST targets the first character followed by the first vowel of a stem. The right hand side expresses the transduction: the boundary symbol is preserved, as is the first letter of the stem and the first vowel of the stem. But at the same time a symbol & is inserted between them. This is our anchor. The output of the transducer is therefore: active ^ s & u l a t, and passive ^ s & u l a t. These strings are then the input to a second transducer in (3.23) by recasting them as paths.

```
(3.23)    Infixation_FST:
              <active ^> == Active:<>
              <passive ^> == Passive:<>.
          Active:
              <$abc> == $abc <>
              <& > == ^ um ^ <>
              <> == \#.
          Passive:
              <$abc> == $abc <>
              <& > == ^ in ^ <>
              <> == \#.
```

Here the feature symbols are used to decode the anchor &. Paths beginning <active ^> are evaluated at the Active node, and paths beginning <passive ^> at the Passive node. The first line at each node maps stem letters to themselves in the normal way. The second line maps & to a boundary delimited um at the Active node and in at the Passive node. End of word boundaries are inserted when there is no more path to extend, as previously. The theorem is given in (3.24).

```
(3.24)    <active ^ s & u l a t> = s ^ um ^ u l a t #
          <passive ^ s & u l a t> = s ^ in ^ u l a t #
```

Our final example of noncontiguous morphology is where the root is interrupted, and at the same time so is the exponent: "where affixes interrupt roots and are interrupted by elements of roots themselves." (Mel'čuk 2006: 300). Mel'čuk uses the term 'transfixation' but in the FST literature this type is usually called 'root and template,' 'root and pattern,' or simply 'non-concatenative' morphology. In Arabic, the root for 'draw' is the consonant template, or skeleton, *r-s-m*. The exponent is the flesh. For 'active perfect,' the exponent is the vowel series *-a-a-*, for 'passive perfect,' there is another exponent *–u-i-*. So *rasam(a)* 'he has drawn,' and *rusim(a)* 'it has been drawn' (where the bracketed *–a* is the more normal suffix exponent): the root is interrupter and interrupted, as is the exponent. Another way of thinking about situations of this sort is to have different *tiers* of structural information. Booij (2007: 37) gives a Modern Hebrew example. The root of the verb grow is the consonant series *g-d-l*. The root occupies one tier. The formal distinction between the word 'grow' *gadal* and its nominalization 'growth' *gdila* is expressed by a pattern of consonants and vowels occupying separate tiers. This is represented in (3.25).

(3.25)

gadal

Tier 1		a		a	
Tier 2	C	V	C	V	C
Tier 3	g		d		l

gdila

Tier 1			i		a
Tier 2	C	C	V	C	V
Tier 3	g	d		l	

There are therefore three separate pieces of surface information: the root (consonants) as tier 3 information, the exponent (vowels) as tier 1, and the instruction for how they interleave as tier 2. How is this modeled as finite state machine? A method reported in Kiraz (2000) for Arabic and widely discussed in the FSM literature is to have an *n*- tape FST where $n > 1$. Each tier has representation on one of several lower tapes. Another tape is also provided for concomitant prefixation or suffixation. Rather ingeniously, a noncontiguous problem is turned into a contiguous one so that it can receive a contiguous solution. Roark and Sproat (2007) propose a family of transducers for different CV patterns (where V is specified) and the morphosyntactic information they express. The union of these transducers is composed with a transducer that maps the root consonants to the Cs. The intermediate level involving the pattern disappears.

3.5 Paradigm-Based Lexical Analysis

The various morphological forms of Russian *karta* in (3.9) were presented in such a way that we could associate form and meaning difference among the word-forms by consulting the cell in the table, the place where case and number information intersect with word-form. The presentation of a lexeme's word-forms as a *paradigm* provides an alternative way of capturing word structure that does not rely on either isomorphism or contiguity. For this reason, the W&P approach has been adopted by the main stream of morphological theorists with the view that "paradigms are essential to the very definition of a language's inflectional system" (Stewart and Stump 2007: 386). A suitable representation language that has been used extensively for paradigm-based morphology is the lexical knowledge representation language DATR, which up until now we have used to demonstrate finite state models. In this section, we will outline some of the advantages of paradigm-based morphology. To do this we will need to slightly extend our discussion of the DATR formalism to incorporate the idea of *inheritance* and *defaults*.

3.5.1 Paradigmatic Relations and Generalization

The FSM demonstrations above have been used to capture properties not only about single lexical items but whole classes of items. In this way, lexical analysis goes beyond simple listing and attempts generalizations. It may be helpful at this point to summarize how generalizations have been captured. Using symbol classes, FSTs can assign stems and affixes to categories, and encode operations over these categories. In this way, they capture classes of environments and changes for morphophonological rules, and morpheme orderings that hold for classes of items, as well as selections when there is a choice of affixes for a given feature. But there are other generalizations that are properties of paradigmatic organization itself, what we could think of as *paradigmatic relations*. To illustrate let us look again at the Russian inflectional class paradigms introduced earlier in Table 3.1, and presented again here as Table 3.3.

TABLE 3.3 Russian Inflectional Classes

	I Zakon	II Karta	III Rukopis'	IV Boloto
Singular				
Nom	zakon-ø	kart-a	rukopis'-ø	bolot-o
Acc	zakon-ø	kart-u	rukopis'-ø	bolot-o
Gen	zakon-a	kart-y	rukopis-i	bolot-a
Dat	zakon-u	kart-e	rukopis-i	bolot-u
Inst	zakon-om	kart-oj	rukopis-ju	bolot-om
Loc	zakon-e	kart-e	rukopis-i	bolot-e
Plural				
Nom	zakon-y	kart-y	rukopis-i	bolot-a
Acc	zakon-y	kart-y	rukopis-i	bolot-a
Gen	zakon-ov	kart-ø	rukopis-ej	bolot-ø
Dat	zakon-am	kart-am	rukopis-jam	bolot-am
Inst	zakon-ami	kart-ami	rúkopis-jami	bolot-ami
Loc	zakon-ax	kart-ax	rukopis-jax	bolot-ax

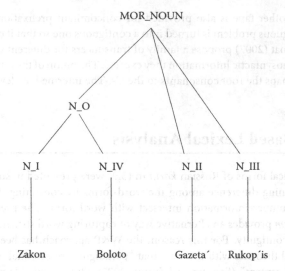

FIGURE 3.4   Russian nouns classes as an inheritance hierarchy (based on Corbett, C.G. and Fraser, N.M., Network Morphology: A DATR account of Russian inflectional morphology. In Katamba, F.X. (ed), pp. 364–396. 2003).

One might expect that each class would have a unique set of forms to set them apart from the other class. So looking horizontally across a particular cell pausing at, say, the intersection of Instrumental and Singular, there would be four different values, i.e., four different ways of forming a Russian singular instrumental noun. Rather surprisingly, this does not happen here: for Class 1 the suffix *–om* is used, for Class II *–oj*, for Class III *–ju*, but Class IV does the same as Class I. Even more surprising is that there is not a single cell where a four-way distinction is made. Another expectation is that within a class, each cell would be different from the other, so, for example, forming a nominative singular is different from a nominative plural. While there is a tendency for *vertical* distinctions across cells, it is only a tendency. So for Class II, dative singular is in *–e*, but so is locative singular. In fact, in the world's languages it is very rare to see fully horizontal and fully vertical distinctions. Recent work by Corbett explores what he calls 'canonical inflectional classes' and shows that the departures from the canon are the norm, so canonicity does not correlate with frequency (Corbett 2009). Paradigm-based lexical analysis takes the departures from the canon as the starting point. It then attempts to capture departures by treating them as *horizontal relations* and *vertical relations*, as well as a combination of the two. So an identical instrumental singular for Classes I and IV is a relation between these classes at the level of this cell. And in Class II there is a relationship between the dative and locative singular. To capture these and other paradigmatic relations in Russian, the inflectional classes in Table 3.2 can be given an alternative presentation as a hierarchy of nodes down which are inherited instructions for forming morphologically complex words (Figure 3.4).

Horizontal relations are expressed as inheritance of two daughter nodes from a mother node. The node N_O stores the fact about the instrumental singular, and both Classes I and IV, represented as N_I and N_IV, inherit it. They also inherit genitive singular, dative singular, and locative singular. This captures the insight of Russian linguists that these two classes are really versions of each other, for example, Timberlake (2004: 132–141) labels them 1a and 1b. Consulting Table 3.2, we see that all classes in the plural form the dative, instrumental, and locative in the same way. The way these are formed should therefore be stated at the root node MOR_NOUN and from there inherited by all classes. In the hierarchy, leaf nodes are the lexical entries themselves, each a daughter of an appropriate inflectional class node. The DATR representation of the lexical entry Karta and the node form that it inherits is given in (3.25). The ellipsis '....' indicates here and elsewhere that the node contains more equations, and is not part of the DATR language.

(3.25) Karta:
        `<mor> == N_II`
        `<stem> == kart.`
    N_II:
        `<mor sg nom> == "<stem>" ^a`
        `<mor sg acc> == "<stem>" ^u`
        `<mor sg dat> == "<stem>" ^e`
        `<mor sg loc> == "<stem>" ^e`
    ....

The first equation expresses that the `Karta` node inherits path value equations from the `N_II` node. Recall that in DATR a subpath implies any extension of itself. So the path `<mor>` implies any path that is an extension of `<mor>` including `<mor sg nom>`, `<mor sg acc>`, `<mor sg dat>`, `<mor sg loc>`, etc. These are all paths that are specified with values at `N_II`. So the first equation in (3.25) is equivalent to the equations in (3.26). But we want these facts to be inherited by `Karta` rather than being explicitly stated at `Karta` to capture the fact that they are shared by other (Class II) nouns.

(3.26) Karta:
        `<mor sg nom> == "<stem>" ^a`
        `<mor sg acc> == "<stem>" ^u`
        `<mor sg dat> == "<stem>" ^e`
        `<mor sg loc> == "<stem>" ^e`
    ....

The value of these paths at `N_II` is complex: the concatenation of the value of another path and an exponent. The value of the other path is the string expressing a lexical entry's stem. In fact, this represents how paradigm-based approaches model word structure: the formal *realization* of a set of morphosyntactic features by a rule operating over stems. The value of `"<stem>"` depends on what lexical entry is the object of the morphological query. If it is `Karta`, then it is the value for the path `<stem>` at the node `Karta` (3.25). The quoted path notation means that inheritance is set to the context of the initial query, here the node `Karta`, and is not altered even if the evaluation of `<stem>` is possible locally. So we could imagine a node (3.27) similar to (3.25) `N_II` but adding an eccentric local fact about itself, namely that Class II nouns always have *zakon* as their stem, no matter what their real stem is.

(3.27) N_II:
        `<mor sg nom> == "<stem>" ^a`
        `<stem> == zakon`
    ....

Nonetheless, the value of `<mor sg nom>` will not involve altering the initial context of `<stem>` to the local context. By quoting `<stem>` the value will be kart^a and not zakon^a. There are equally occasions where local inheritance of paths is precisely what is needed. Equation 3.25 fails to capture the vertical relation that for Class II nouns the dative singular and the locative singular are the same. Local inheritance expresses this relation, shown in (3.28).

(3.28) N_II:
        `<mor sg dat> == "<stem>" ^e`
        `<mor sg loc> == <mor sg dat>`
    ....

The path `<mor sg loc>` locally inherits from `<mor sg dat>`, so that both paths have the value kart^e where `Karta` is the query lexical entry.

Horizontal relations are captured by hierarchical relations. (3.29) is the partial hierarchy involving
MOR_NOUN, N_O, N_I and N_IV.

(3.29)   MOR_NOUN:
                   <mor pl loc> == "<stem>" ax
                   <mor sg dat> == "<stem>" e
                   ...
           N_O:
                   <> == MOR_NOUN
                   <mor sg gen> == "<stem>" a
                   <mor sg dat> == "<stem>" u
                   <mor sg inst > == "<stem>" om
                   <mor sg loc > == "<stem>" e.
           N_IV:
                   <> == N_O
                   <mor sg nom > == "<stem>" o
                   <mor pl nom > == "<stem>" a
                   ...
           N_I:
                   <> == N_O
                   <mor sg nom > == "<stem>"
                   <mor pl nom > == "<stem>" y
                   ...

Facts about cells that are shared by inflectional classes are stated as path: value equations gathered at
MOR_NOUN. These include instructions for forming the locative singular and the locative plural. Facts
that are shared only by Classes I and IV are stored at an intermediary node N_O: the genitive, dative,
instrumental, and locative singular. Nodes for Classes I and IV inherit from this node, and via this node
they inherit the wider generalizations stated at the hierarchy's root node. The passing of information
down the hierarchy is through the empty path <>, which is the leading subpath of every path that is not
defined at the local node. So at N_I the empty path implies <mor gen sg> at its mother node N_O
but *not* <mor sg nom> because this path is already defined at N_I.

From Figure 3.4, we can observe a special type of relation that is at once vertical and horizontal. In the
plural, the accusative is the same as the nominative in Class I, but this same vertical relation extends to all
the other classes: they all have an accusative/nominative identity in the plural. To capture this we store
the vertical relation at the root node so that all inflectional class nodes can inherit it (3.30).

(3.30)   MOR_NOUN:
                   <mor pl acc > == "<mor pl nom >".
                   ...

It needs to be clear from (3.30) that what is being hierarchically inherited is not an exponent of a feature
set but a way of getting the exponent. The quoted path at the right hand side expresses that the nominative
plural value depends on the global context, i.e., what noun is being queried: if it is a Class I noun it will
be stem plus *−y*, and if it is a Class IV noun it will be stem plus *−a*. These will therefore be the respective
values for Class I and Class IV accusative singular forms. In other words, the horizontal relation being
captured is the vertical relation that the accusative and nominative plural for a given class is the same,
although in principle the value itself may be different for each class.

3.5.2 The Role of Defaults

Interestingly the identity of accusative with nominative is not restricted to the plural. From Figure 3.4 we see that for Classes I, III, and IV the singular accusative is identical to the nominative but Class II has separate exponents. If inheritance from MOR_NOUN is interpreted as default inheritance then (3.31) captures a strong tendency for the accusative and nominative to be the same. The bound variable $num ranges over sg and pl atoms.

(3.31)   MOR_NOUN

<mor $num acc > == "<mor $num nom>"

...

This vertical relation does not, however, extend to Class II which has a unique accusative singular exponent. Class II inherits facts from MOR_NOUN, as any other class does. But it needs to override the fact about the accusative singular (3.32).

(3.32)   N_II:

<> == MOR_NOUN

<mor sg nom> == "<stem>" a

<mor sg acc> == "<stem>" u

...

A path implies any extension of itself, but the value associated with the implied path is by default and can be overridden by an explicitly stated extended path. In (3.32) the empty path implies all of its extensions and their values held at MOR_NOUN, including <mor sg acc> == <mor sg nom>. But because <mor sg acc> is stated locally at N_II, the explicitly stated local evaluation overrides the (implied) inherited one. In similar vein we can capture the locative singular in –*e* as a generalization over all classes *except* Class III (see Table 3.2) by stating <mor sg loc> == "<stem>" e at the root node, but also stating <mor sg loc> == "<stem>" i at the node N_III.

Defaults also allow for a straightforward account of exceptional or semi-regular lexical entries. In Section 3.3.1, I gave several examples from Russian to show how exceptionality could be captured in FSM. Let us briefly consider their treatment in a paradigm-based approach. Recall that the item *soldat* 'soldier' is a regular Class 1 noun in every respect except for the way it forms its genitive plural. Instead of **soldatov* it is simply *soldat*. As in the FSM account, it can be assigned Class II status just for its genitive plural by overriding the default for its class, and inheriting the default from another class.

(3.33)   Soldat:

<mor> == N_I

<stem> == soldat

<mor pl gen> == N_II.

The other example was a pluralia tantum noun, *brjuki* 'trousers.' Here the singular had plural morphology. This is simply a matter of overriding the inheritance of <mor sg> paths from N_II with the equation <mor sg> == <mor pl>. Of course <mor pl> and its extensions will be inherited from the mother node in the same way it is for all other Class II nouns.

(3.34)   Brjuki:

<mor> == N_II

<stem> == brjuk

<mor sg> == <mor pl>.

Finally, indeclinable *pal'to* can be specified as inheriting from a fifth class that generalizes over all indeclinables. It is not *pal'to* that does the overriding but the class itself. All extensions of <mor> are overridden and assigned the value of the lexical entry's stem alone, with no exponent.

(3.35)   N_V:
                    <> == MOR_NOUN
                    <mor> == "<stem>".

3.5.3 Paradigm-Based Accounts of Difficult Morphology

In Section 3.4, we described 'difficult' morphology as instances where isomorphism, one feature (set) mapping to one exponent, breaks down. The Russian demonstration of the paradigm-based approach has run into this almost without noticing. We have already seen how more than one feature can map onto a single exponent. First, an exponent is a value associated with an attribute path that defines *sets* of features: Number and Case in our running example of Russian. Second, the whole idea behind vertical relations is that two different feature sets can map onto a single exponent: the −*e* suffix maps onto two feature sets for Class II nouns, the singular dative and the singular locative, similarly the accusative and nominative mapping onto a single exponent for all but Class II. This is handled by setting one attribute path to inherit from another attribute path. In paradigm-based morphology, this is known as a *rule of referral* (Stump 1993, 2001: 52–57). Then the reverse problem of more than exponent realizing a singe feature (set) is handled through the stipulation of inflectional classes, so that affixes for the same feature are not in competition. Finally, a feature that does not map onto any exponent we treat as *zero exponence* rather than a zero affix. For example, the genitive plural of a Russian Class II noun is the stem plus nothing. The attribute path is associated with the query lexical entry's stem, and nothing more.

(3.36)   N_II
                    <> == MOR_NOUN
                    <mor pl gen> == "<stem>"
                    ...

In paradigm-based accounts, a stem of a word in a given cell of a particular set of features is in contrast with stems of the same word in different cells. Morphological structure is then the computation of what makes the stem contrastive together with the feature content of the cell. For this reason, affixation is not given any special status: contrast could be through ablaut, stress shift, or zero exponence as shown above since it also can mark a contrast: by having no exponence, the genitive plural is opposed to all other cells since they do have an exponent. Noncontiguous morphology does not pose a problem for paradigm-based approaches, as Stump (2001) demonstrates. The exponent a rule introduces does not have to target stem edges (affixation) but can target any part of the stem: for example, *sing* has the past tense form *sang*. Cahill and Gazdar (1999) handle ablaut morphological operations of this kind in German plural nouns by defining stems as syllable sequences where the syllable itself has internal structure: an onset consonant, vowel, and a coda consonant. The target of the rule is definable as stem-internal, the syllable vowel. With an inheritance hierarchy, ablaut operations are captured as semi-regular by drawing together items with the similar ablaut patterns under a node that houses the non-concatenative rule: which part of the syllable is modified, and how it is modified. Many nouns undergo ablaut and simultaneously use regular suffixation, for example, *Mann* 'man' has plural *Männer*. The hierarchical arrangement allows for a less regular ablaut together with inheritance of the more regular suffixation rule, -*er* added to the right edge of stem, i.e., after the coda of rightmost syllable. Default inheritance coupled with realization rules simultaneously captures multiple exponence, semi-regularity, and nonlinear morphology.

In more recent work, Cahill (2007) used the same 'syllable-based morphology' approach for root-and-pattern morphological description that we discussed in Section 3.4 with reference to Hebrew. The claim is that with inheritance hierarchies, defaults and the syllable as a unit of description, Arabic verb morphology lies more or less within the same problem (and solution) space as German (and English) ablaut cases. A morphologically complex verb such as *kutib* has the default structural description: <mor word> == "<agr prefix>" "<tense prefix>" "<ph root form>" "<agr suffix>". Each quoted path expresses the value of an exponent inferable from the organization of the network. These exponents can appear as prefixes and suffixes, which are by default null. But an exponent can be a systematic internal modification of the root: `"<ph root form>"`. Just as for German, the root (or stem) is syllable defined, and more specifically as a series of consonants, e.g., *k t b* 'write.' In syllable terms, these are (by default) the onset of the first (logical order) syllable and the onset and coda of the second. The vowels that occupy nucleus positions of the two syllables can vary and these variations are exponents of tense and mood. So one possible perfect passive form is *kutib* that contrasts with perfect passive *katab*. There are many such root alternations and associated morphosyntactic property sets. To capture similarities and differences, they are organized into default inheritance hierarchies.

This is necessarily an oversimplified characterization of the complexity that Cahill's account captures, but the important point is that defaults and W&P morphology can combine to give elegant accounts of noncontiguous morphology. In Soudi et al. (2007), the collection of computational Arabic morphology papers where Cahill's work appears, it is significant that most of the symbolic accounts are lexeme-based and make use of inheritance; two are DATR theories. Finkel and Stump (2007) is another root-and-pattern account, this time of Hebrew. It also is W&P morphology with default inheritance hierarchies. Its implementation is in KATR, a DATR with 'enhancements,' including a mechanism for expressing morphosyntactic features as unordered members of sets as well as ordered lists to better generalize the Hebrew data. Kiraz (2008) and Sproat (2007) note that Arabic computational morphology has been neglected; this is because "root-and-pattern morphology defies a straightforward implementation in terms of morpheme concatenation" (Sproat 2007: vii). Cahill (2007), and Finkel and Stump (2007) offer an alternative W&P approach, which suggests that perhaps Arabic is not really "specifically engineered to maximize the difficulties for automatic processing."

3.5.4 Further Remarks on Paradigm-Based Approaches

Many computational models of paradigm-based morphological analysis are represented in the DATR lexical knowledge representation language. These include analyses of major languages, for example, Russian in Corbett and Fraser (2003), the paper which the W&P demonstration in this chapter is based on, and more recently in Brown and Hippisley (forthcoming); also Spanish (Moreno-Sandoval and Goñi-Menoyo 2002), Arabic as we have seen (Cahill 2007), German (Cahill and Gazder 1999, Kilbury 2001), Polish (Brown 1998), as well as lesser known languages, for example, Dalabon (Evans et al. 2000), Mayali (Evans et al. 2002), Dhaasanac (Baerman et al. 2005: Chapter 5), and Arapesh (Fraser and Corbett 1997). The paradigm-based theory Network Morphology (Corbett and Fraser 2003, Brown and Hippisley forthcoming) is formalized in DATR. The most well articulated paradigm-based theory is Paradigm Function Morphology (Stump 2001, 2006), and DATR has also been used to represent Paradigm Function Morphology descriptions (Gazdar 1992). DATR's mechanism for encoding default inference is central to Network Morphology and Paradigm Function Morphology. Defaults are used in other theoretical work on the lexicon as part of the overall system of language. For example, HPSG (Pollard and Sag 1994, Sag et al. 2003), uses inheritance hierarchies to capture shared information; inheritance *by default* is used for specifically lexical descriptions in some HPSG descriptions, for example, Krieger and Nerbonne (1992) and more recently Bonami and Boyé (2006).*

We close this section with a comment about DATR. Throughout our discussion of FSM and the paradigm-based alternative, we have used DATR as the demonstration language. But it is important to note that DATR theories are 'one way' as they start with the lexical representation and generate the

---

* HPSG has been ambivalent over the incorporation of defaults for lexical information but Bonami and Boyé (2006) are quite clear about its importance:

  In the absence of an explicit alternative, we take it that the use of defaults is the only known way to model regularity in an HPSG implementation of the stem space.

  The latest HPSG textbook appears to endorse defaults for the lexicon (Sag et al. 2003: 229–236).

surface representation; they do not start with the surface representation and parse out the lexical string. In and of itself, this restriction has not hampered a discussion of the major lexical analysis issues, which is the motivation for using DATR in this chapter but it is important to bear in mind this aspect of DATR. There are ways round this practical restriction. For example, a DATR theory could be compiled into a database so that its theorem is presented as a surface string to lexical string look up table. Earlier work has experimented with extending DATR implementations to provide inference in reverse. Langer (1994) proposes an implementation of DATR that allows for 'reverse queries,' or inference operating in reverse. Standardly, the query is a specific node/path/value combination, for example, `Karta:<mor nom sg>`. The value is what is inferred by this combination. By treating a DATR description as being analogous to a context free phrase structure grammar (CF-PSG), with left hand sides as nonterminal symbols, which rewrite as right hand sides that include nonterminal and terminal symbols, reverse query can be tackled as a CF-PSG bottom-up parsing problem. You start with the value string (`kart^a`) and discover how it has been inferred (`Karta:<mor nom sg>`). Finally, a DATR description could be used to generate the pairing of lexical string to surface string, and these pairings could then be the input to an FST inducer to perform analysis. For example, Gildea and Jurafsky (1995, 1996) use an augmented version of Oncina et al.'s (1993) OSTIA algorithm (Onward Subsequential Transducer Inference Algorithm) to induce phonological rule FSTs. More recently, Carlson (2005) reports on promising results of an experiment inducing FSTs from paradigms of Finnish inflectional morphology in Prolog.

3.6 Concluding Remarks

If the building blocks of natural language texts are words, then words are important units of information, and language-based applications should include some mechanism for registering their structural properties. Finite state techniques have long been used to provide such a mechanism because of their computational efficiency, and their invertibility: they can be used both to generate morphologically complex forms from underlying representations, and parse morphologically complex forms into underlying representations. The linguistic capital of the FSM is an I&A model of word structure. Though many languages, including English, contain morphologically complex objects that resist an I&A analysis, FSM handles these situations by recasting these problems as I&A problems: isomorphism is retained trough empty transitions, collecting features into symbol sets, and introducing stem classes and affix classes. For nonlinear morphology, infixation, and root-and-template, the problem is recast as a linear one and addressed accordingly. FSM can capture morphological generalization, exceptionality, and the organization of complex words into inflectional classes. An alternative to FSM is an approach based on paradigmatic organization where word structure is computed by the stem's place in a cell in a paradigm, the unique clustering of morphologically meaningful elements, and some phonologically contrasting element, not necessarily an affix, and feasibly nothing. W&P approaches appear to offer a better account of what I have called difficult morphology. They also get at the heart of morphological generalization.

Both approaches to lexical analysis are strongly rule based. This puts lexical analysis at odds with most fields of NLP, including computational syntax where statistics plays an increasingly important role. But Roark and Sproat (2007: 116–117) observe that hand-written rules can take you a long way in a morphologically complex language; at the same time ambiguity does not play such a major role in morphological analysis as it does in statistical analysis where there can be very many candidate parse trees for a single surface sentence. That is not to say that ambiguity is not a problem in lexical analysis: given the prominence we have attached to inflectional classes in this chapter, it is not hard to find situations where a surface string has more than one structure. This is the case for all vertical relations, discussed in the previous section. In Russian, the string *karte* can be parsed as a dative or locative, for example. A worse case is *rukopisi*. Consulting Table 3.2 you can see that this form could be a genitive, dative, or locative singular; or nominative or accusative plural. Roark and Sproat go on to note that resolving these ambiguities requires too broad a context for probability information to be meaningful. That is not to say that morphological analysis does not benefit from statistical methods. Roark and Sproat give as examples Goldsmith (2001), a method for inducing from corpora morphonological alternations of a given lemma (Goldsmith 2001), and Yarowski and Wicentowski (2001), who use pairings of morphological variants to induce morphological analyzers.

It should be noted that the important place of lexical/morphological analysis in a text-based NLP system is not without question. In IR, there is a view that symbolic, rule-based models are difficult to accommodate within a strongly statistically oriented system, and the symbolic statistical disconnect is hard to resolve. Furthermore, there is evidence that morphological analysis does not greatly improve performance: indeed stemming can lower precision rates (Tzoukerman et al. 2003). A rather strong position is taken in Church (2005), which amounts to leaving out morphological analysis altogether. His paper catalogues the IR community's repeated disappointments with morphological analysis packages, primarily due to the fact that morphological relatedness does not always equate with semantic relatedness: for example, *awful* has nothing to do with *awe*. He concludes that simple listing is preferable to attempting lexical analysis. One response is that inflectional morphologically complex words are more transparent than derivational, so less likely to be semantically disconnected from related forms. Another is that Church's focus is English which is morphologically poor anyway, whereas with other major languages such as Russian, Arabic, and Spanish listing may not be complete, and will certainly be highly redundant.

Lexical analysis is in fact increasingly important as NLP reaches beyond English to other languages, many of which have rich morphological systems. The main lexical analysis model is FSM that has a good track record for large-scale systems, English as well as multilingual. The paradigm-based model is favored by linguists as an elegant way of describing morphologically complex objects. Languages like DATR can provide a computable lexical knowledge representation of paradigm-based theories. Communities working within the two frameworks can benefit from one another. Kay (2004) observes that early language-based systems were deliberately based on scientific principles, i.e., linguistic theory. At the same time, giving theoretical claims some computational robustness led to advances in linguistic theory. The fact that many DATR theories choose to implement the morphonological variation component of their descriptions as FSTs shows the intrinsic value of FSM to morphology as a whole. The fact that there is a growing awareness of the paradigm-based model within the FSM community, for example, Roark and Sproat (2007) and Karttunen (2003) have implementations of Paradigm Function Morphology accounts in FSTs, may lead to an increasing awareness of the role paradigm relations play in morphological analysis, which may lead to enhancements in conventional FST lexical analysis. Langer (1994) gives two measures of adequacy of lexical representation: declarative expressiveness and accessing strategy. While a DATR formalized W&P theory delivers on the first, FSM by virtue of generation and parsing scores well on the second. Lexical analysis can only benefit with high scores in both.

Acknowledgments

I am extremely grateful to Roger Evans and Gerald Gazdar for their excellent comments on an earlier draft of the chapter which I have tried to take full advantage of. Any errors I take full responsibility for. I would also like to thank Nitin Indurkhya for his commitment to this project and his gentle encouragement throughout the process.

References

Armstrong, S. 1996. Multext: Multilingual text tools and corpora. In: Feldweg, H. and Hinrichs, W. (eds). *Lexikon und Text*. Tübingen, Germany: Niemeyer.

Aronoff, M. and Fudeman, K. 2005. *What is Morphology?* Oxford, U.K.: Blackwell.

Arpe, A. et al. (eds). 2005. *Inquiries into Words, Constraints and Contexts (Festschrift in Honour of Kimmo Koskenniemi on his 60th Birthday)*. Saarijärvi, Finland: Gummerus.

Baerman, M., Brown, D., and Corbett, G.G. 2005. *The Syntax-Morphology Interface: A Study of Syncretism*. Cambridge, U.K.: Cambridge University Press.

Beesley, K. and Karttunen, L. 2003. *Finite State Morphology*. Stanford, CA: CSLI.

Bonami, O. and Boyé, G. 2006. Deriving inflectional irregularity. In: Müller, S. (ed). *Proceedings of the HPSG06 Conference*. Stanford, CA: CSLI.

Booij, G. 2007. *The Grammar of Words*. Oxford, U.K.: Oxford University Press.

Brown, D. and Hippisley, A. Under review. *Default Morphology*. Cambridge: Cambridge University Press.

Brown, D. 1998. Defining 'subgender': Virile and devirilized nouns in Polish. *Lingua* 104 (3–4). 187–233.

Cahill, L. 2007. A syllable-based account of Arabic morphology. In: Soudi, A. (eds). pp. 45–66.

Cahill, L. and Gazdar, G. 1999. German noun inflection. *Journal of Linguistics* 35 (1). 1–42.

Carlson, L. 2005. Inducing a morphological transducer from inflectional paradigms. In: Arpe et al. (eds). pp. 18–24.

Chomsky, N. and Halle, M. 1968. *The Sound Pattern of English*. New York: Harper & Row.

Church, K.W. 2005. The DDI approach to morphology. In Arpe et al. (eds). pp. 25–34.

Corbett, G.G. 2009. Canonical inflection classes. In: Montermini, F., Boyé, G. and Tseng, J. (eds). *Selected Proceedings of the Sixth Decembrettes: Morphology in Bordeaux*, Somerville, MA: Cascadilla Proceedings Project. www.lingref.com, document #2231, pp. 1–11.

Corbett, G.G. and Fraser, N.M. 2003. Network morphology: A DATR account of Russian inflectional morphology. In: Katamba, F.X. (ed). pp. 364–396.

Dale, R., Moisl, H., and Somers, H. (eds). 2000. *Handbook of Natural Language Processing*. New York: Marcel Dekker.

Evans, N., Brown, D., and Corbett, G.G. 2000. Dalabon pronominal prefixes and the typology of syncretism: A network morphology analysis. In: Booij, G. and van Marle, J. (eds). *Yearbook of Morphology 2000*. Dordrecht, the Netherlands: Kluwer. pp. 187–231.

Evans, N., Brown, D., and Corbett, G.G. 2002. The semantics of gender in Mayali: Partially parallel systems and formal implementation. *Language* 78 (1). 111–155.

Evans, R. and Gazdar, G. 1996. DATR: A language for lexical knowledge representation. *Computational Linguistics* 22. 167–216.

Finkel, R. and Stump, G. 2007. A default inheritance hierarchy for computing Hebrew verb morphology. *Literary and Linguistics Computing* 22 (2). 117–136.

Fraser, N. and Corbett, G.G. 1997. Defaults in Arapesh. *Lingua* 103 (1). 25–57.

Gazdar, G. 1985. Review article: Finite State Morphology. *Linguistics* 23. 597–607.

Gazdar, G. 1992. Paradigm-function morphology in DATR. In: Cahill, L. and Coates, R. (eds). *Sussex Papers in General and Computational Linguistics*. Brighton: University of Sussex, CSRP 239. pp. 43–53.

Gibbon, D. 1987. Finite state processing of tone systems. *Proceedings of the Third Conference, European ACL*, Morristown, NJ: ACL. pp. 291–297.

Gibbon, D. 1989. 'tones.dtr'. Located at ftp://ftp.informatics.sussex.ac.uk/pub/nlp/DATR/dtrfiles/tones.dtr

Gildea, D. and Jurafsky, D. 1995. Automatic induction of finite state transducers for single phonological rules. *ACL* 33. 95–102.

Gildea, D. and Jurafsky, D. 1996. Learning bias and phonological rule induction. *Computational Linguistics* 22 (4). 497–530.

Goldsmith, J. 2001. Unsupervised acquisition of the morphology of a natural language. *Computational Linguistics* 27 (2). 153–198.

Haspelmath, M. 2002. *Understanding Morphology*. Oxford, U.K.: Oxford University Press.

Hockett, C. 1958. Two models of grammatical description. In: Joos, M. (ed). *Readings in Linguistics*. Chicago, IL: University of Chicago Press.

Jurafsky, D. and Martin, J.H. 2007. *Speech and Language Processing*. Upper Saddle River, NJ: Pearson/Prentice Hall.

Kaplan, R.M. and Kay, M. 1994. Regular models of phonological rule systems. *Computational Linguistics* 20. 331–378.

Karttunen, L. 2003. Computing with realizational morphology. In: Gelbukh, A. (ed). *CICLing 2003 Lecture Notes in Computer Science 2588*. Berlin, Germany: Springer-Verlag. pp. 205–216.

Karttunen, L. 2007. Word play. *Computational Linguistics* 33 (4). 443–467.

Katamba, F.X. (ed). 2003. *Morphology: Critical Concepts in Linguistics, VI: Morphology: Its Place in the Wider Context*. London, U.K.: Routledge.

Kay, M. 2004. Introduction to Mitkov (ed.). xvii–xx.

Kiraz, G.A. 2000. Multitiered nonlinear morphology using multitape finite automata. *Computational Linguistics* 26 (1). 77–105.

Kiraz, G. 2008. Book review of *Arabic Computational Morphology: Knowledge-Based and Empirical Methods*. *Computational Linguistics* 34 (3). 459–462.

Koskenniemi, K. 1983. *Two-Level Morphology: A General Computational Model for Word-Form Recognition and Production*. Publication 11, Department of General Linguistics, Helsinki, Finland: University of Helsinki.

Krieger, H.U. and Nerbonne, J. 1992. Feature-based inheritance networks for computational lexicons. In: Briscoe, E., de Paiva, V., and Copestake, A. (eds). *Inheritance, Defaults and the Lexicon*. Cambridge, U.K.: Cambridge University Press. pp. 90–136.

Kilbury, J. 2001. German noun inflection revisited. *Journal of Linguistics* 37 (2). 339–353.

Langer, H. 1994. Reverse queries in DATR. *COLING-94*. Morristown, NJ: ACL. pp. 1089–1095.

Mel'čuk. I. 2006. *Aspects of the Theory of Morphology*. Trends in Linguistics 146. Berlin/New York: Mouton de Gruyter.

Mitkov, R. (ed). 2004. *The Oxford Handbook of Computational Linguistics*. Oxford, U.K.: Oxford University Press.

Moreno-Sandoval, A. and Goñi-Menoyo, J.M. 2002. Spanish inflectional morphology in DATR. *Journal of Logic, Language and Information*. 11 (1). 79–105.

Oncina, J., Garcia, P., and Vidal, P. 1993. Learning subsequential transducers for pattern recognition tasks. *IEEE Transactions on Pattern Analysis and Machine Intelligence* 15. 448–458.

Pollard, C. and Sag, I.A. 1994. *Head-Driven Phrase Structure Grammar*. Chicago, IL: University of Chicago Press.

Pretorius, L. and Bosch, S.E. 2003. Finite-sate morphology: An analyzer for Zulu. *Machine Translation* 18 (3). 195–216.

Roark, B. and Sproat, R. 2007. *Computational Approaches to Syntax*. Oxford, U.K.: Oxford University Press.

Sag, I., Wasow, T., and Bender, E.M. (eds). 2003. *Syntactic Theory: A Formal Introduction*. Stanford, CA: CSLI.

Soudi, A. et al. (eds). 2007. *Arabic Computational Morphology: Knowledge-Based and Empirical Methods*. Dordrecht: Springer.

Sproat, R. 1997. *Multilingual Text to Speech Synthesis: The Bell Labs Approach*. Dordrecht, the Netherlands: Kluwer.

Sproat, R. 2000. Lexical analysis. In Dale, R. et al. (eds). pp. 37–58.

Sproat, R. 2007. Preface. In: Soudi, A. et al (eds). *Arabic Computational Morphology: Knowledge-Based and Empirical Methods*. Dordrecht, the Netherlands: Springer. pp. vii–viii.

Stewart, T. and Stump, G. 2007. Paradigm function morphology and the morphology-syntax interface. In: Ramchand, G. and Reiss, C. (eds). *Linguistic Interfaces*. Oxford, U.K.: Oxford University Press. pp. 383–421.

Stump, G. 2001. *Inflectional Morphology*. Cambridge, U.K.: Cambridge University Press.

Stump, G. 1993. On rules of referral. *Language* 69. 449–79.

Stump, G. 2006. Heteroclisis and paradigm linkage. *Language* 82, 279–322.

Timberlake, A.A. 2004. *A Reference Grammar of Russian*. Cambridge, U.K.: Cambridge University Press.

Tzoukermann, E., Klavans, J., and Strzalkowski, T. 2003. Information retrieval. In: Mitkov (ed.) 529–544.

Ui Dhonnchadha, E., Nic Phaidin, C., and van Genabith, J. 2003. Design, implementation and evaluation of an inflectional morphology finite-state transducer for Irish. *Machine Translation* 18 (3). 173–193.

Yarowski, D. and Wicentowski, R. 2001. Minimally supervised morphological analysis by multimodal alignment. *Proceedings of the 38th ACL*. Morristown, NJ: ACL. pp. 207–216.

Yona, S. and Wintner, S. 2007. A finite-state morphological grammar of Hebrew. *Natural Language Engineering* 14. 173–190.

4

Syntactic Parsing

Peter Ljunglöf
University of Gothenburg

Mats Wirén
Stockholm University

4.1 Introduction

This chapter presents basic techniques for grammar-driven natural language parsing, that is, analyzing a string of words (typically a sentence) to determine its structural description according to a formal grammar. In most circumstances, this is not a goal in itself but rather an intermediary step for the purpose of further processing, such as the assignment of a meaning to the sentence. To this end, the desired output of grammar-driven parsing is typically a hierarchical, syntactic structure suitable for semantic interpretation (the topic of Chapter 5). The string of words constituting the input will usually have been processed in separate phases of tokenization (Chapter 2) and lexical analysis (Chapter 3), which is hence not part of parsing proper.

To get a grasp of the fundamental problems discussed here, it is instructive to consider the ways in which parsers for natural languages differ from parsers for computer languages (for a related discussion, see Steedman 1983, Karttunen and Zwicky 1985). One such difference concerns the power of the grammar formalisms used—the *generative capacity*. Computer languages are usually designed so as to permit encoding by unambiguous grammars and parsing in linear time of the length of the input. To this end, carefully restricted subclasses of context-free grammar (CFG) are used, with the syntactic specification of ALGOL 60 (Backus et al. 1963) as a historical exemplar. In contrast, natural languages are typically taken to require more powerful devices, as first argued by Chomsky (1956).* One of the strongest cases for expressive power has been the occurrence of long-distance dependencies, as in English *wh*-questions:

$$\text{Who did you sell the car to \_\_?} \tag{4.1}$$

$$\text{Who do you think that you sold the car to \_\_?} \tag{4.2}$$

$$\text{Who do you think that he suspects that you sold the car to \_\_?} \tag{4.3}$$

In (4.1) through (4.3) it is held that the noun phrase "who" is displaced from its canonical position (indicated by "__") as indirect object of "sell." Since there is no clear limit as to how much material may be embedded between the two ends, as suggested by (4.2) and (4.3), linguists generally take the position that these dependencies might hold at unbounded distance. Although phenomena like this have at times provided motivation to move far beyond context-free power, several formalisms have also been developed with the intent of making minimal increases to expressive power (see Section 4.2.4). A key reason for this is to try to retain efficient parsability, that is, parsing in polynomial time of the length of the input. Additionally, for the purpose of determining the expressive power needed for linguistic formalisms, *strong generative capacity* (the structural descriptions assigned by the grammar) is usually considered more relevant than *weak generative capacity* (the sets of strings generated); compare Chomsky (1965, pp. 60–61) and Joshi (1997).

A second difference concerns the extreme structural *ambiguity* of natural language. At any point in a pass through a sentence, there will typically be several grammar rules that might apply. A classic example is the following:

$$\text{Put the block in the box on the table} \tag{4.4}$$

Assuming that "put" subcategorizes for two objects, there are two possible analyses of (4.4):

$$\text{Put the block [in the box on the table]} \tag{4.5}$$

$$\text{Put [the block in the box] on the table} \tag{4.6}$$

If we add another prepositional phrase ("in the kitchen"), we get five analyses; if we add yet another, we get 14, and so on. Other examples of the same phenomenon are conjuncts and nominal compounding. As discussed in detail by Church and Patil (1982), "every-way ambiguous" constructions of this kind have a number of analyses that grows exponentially with the number of added components. Even though only one of them may be appropriate in a given context, the purpose of a general grammar might be to capture what is possible in *any* context. As a result of this, even the process of just returning all the possible analyses would lead to a combinatorial explosion. Thus, much of the work on parsing—hence, much of the following exposition—deals somehow or the other with ways in which the potentially enormous search spaces can be efficiently handled, and how the most appropriate analysis can be selected (*disambiguation*). The latter problem also leads naturally to extensions of grammar-driven parsing with statistical inference, as dealt with in Chapter 11.

A third difference stems from the fact that natural language data are inherently *noisy*, both because of errors (under some conception of "error") and because of the ever persisting incompleteness of lexicon and grammar relative to the unlimited number of possible utterances which constitute the language. In contrast, a computer language has a complete syntax specification, which means that by definition all correct input strings are parsable. In natural language parsing, it is notoriously difficult to distinguish

---

* For a background on formal grammars and formal-language theory, see Hopcroft et al. (2006).

whether a failure to produce a parsing result is due to an error in the input or to the lack of coverage of the grammar, also because a natural language by its nature has no precise delimitation. Thus, input not licensed by the grammar may well be perfectly adequate according to native speakers of the language. Moreover, input containing errors may still carry useful bits of information that might be desirable to try to recover. *Robustness* refers to the ability of always producing *some* result in response to such input (Menzel 1995).

The rest of this chapter is organized as follows. Section 4.2 gives a background on grammar formalisms and basic concepts in natural language parsing, and also introduces a small CFG that is used in examples throughout. Section 4.3 presents a basic tabular algorithm for parsing with CFG, the Cocke–Kasami–Younger algorithm. Section 4.4 then describes the main approaches to tabular parsing in an abstract way, in the form of "parsing as deduction," again using CFG. Section 4.5 discusses some implementational issues in relation to this abstract framework. Section 4.6 then goes on to describing LR parsing, and its nondeterministic generalization GLR parsing. Section 4.7 introduces a simple form of constraint-based grammar and describes tabular parsing using this kind of grammar formalism. Section 4.8 discusses in some further depth the three main challenges in natural language parsing that have been touched upon in this introductory section—robustness, disambiguation, and efficiency. Finally, Section 4.9 provides some brief historical notes on parsing relative to where we stand today.

4.2 Background

This section introduces grammar formalisms, primarily CFGs, and basic parsing concepts, which will be used in the rest of this chapter.

4.2.1 Context-Free Grammars

Ever since its introduction by Chomsky (1956), CFG has been the most influential grammar formalism for describing language syntax. This is not because CFG has been generally adopted as such for linguistic description, but rather because most grammar formalisms are derived from or can somehow be related to CFG. For this reason, CFG is often used as a base formalism when parsing algorithms are described.

The standard way of defining a CFG is as a tuple $G = \langle \Sigma, N, S, R \rangle$, where Σ and N are disjoint finite sets of *terminal* and *nonterminal* symbols, respectively, and $S \in N$ is the *start symbol*. The nonterminals are also called *categories*, and the set $V = N \cup \Sigma$ contains the symbols of the grammar. R is a finite set of *production rules* of the form $A \to \alpha$, where $A \in N$ is a nonterminal and $\alpha \in V^*$ is a sequence of symbols.

We use capital letters $A, B, C, \ldots$ for nonterminals, lower-case letters $s, t, w, \ldots$ for terminal symbols, and uppercase $X, Y, Z, \ldots$ for general symbols (elements in V). Greek letters $\alpha, \beta, \gamma, \ldots$ will be used for sequences of symbols, and we write ϵ for the empty sequence.

The rewriting relation $\Rightarrow$ is defined by $\alpha B \gamma \Rightarrow \alpha \beta \gamma$ if and only if $B \to \beta$. A *phrase* is a sequence of terminals $\beta \in \Sigma^*$ such that $A \Rightarrow \cdots \Rightarrow \beta$ for some $A \in N$. Accordingly, the term *phrase-structure grammar* is sometimes used for grammars with at least context-free power. The sequence of rule expansions is called a *derivation* of β from A. A (*grammatical*) *sentence* is a phrase that can be derived from the start symbol S. The *string language* $L(G)$ accepted by G is the set of sentences of G.

Some algorithms only work for particular *normal forms* of CFGs:

- In Section 4.3 we will use grammars in *Chomsky normal form* (CNF). A grammar is in CNF when each rule is either (*i*) a unary terminal rule of the form $A \to w$, or (*ii*) a binary nonterminal rule of the form $A \to BC$. It is always possible to transform a grammar into CNF such that it accepts

$$
\begin{aligned}
S &\rightarrow \text{NP} \quad \text{VP} & \text{Det} &\rightarrow a \mid an \mid the \\
\text{NP} &\rightarrow \text{Det} \quad \text{NBar} & \text{Adj} &\rightarrow old \\
\text{NBar} &\rightarrow \text{Adj} \quad \text{Noun} & \text{Noun} &\rightarrow man \mid men \mid ship \mid ships \\
\text{NBar} &\rightarrow \text{Noun} & \text{Verb} &\rightarrow man \mid mans \\
\text{NBar} &\rightarrow \text{Adj} \\
\text{VP} &\rightarrow \text{Verb} \\
\text{VP} &\rightarrow \text{Verb} \quad \text{NP}
\end{aligned}
$$

FIGURE 4.1 Example grammar.

the same language.* However, the transformation can change the structure of the grammar quite radically; e.g., if the original grammar has n rules, the transformed version may in the worst case have $O(n^2)$ rules (Hopcroft et al. 2006).

- We can relax this normal form by allowing (*iii*) unary nonterminal rules of the form $A \rightarrow B$. The transformation to this form is much simpler, and the transformed grammar is structurally closer; e.g., the transformed grammar will have only $O(n)$ rules. This relaxed variant of CNF is also used in Section 4.3.
- In Section 4.4 we relax the normal form even further, such that each rule is either (*i*) a unary terminal rule of the form $A \rightarrow w$, or (*ii*) a nonempty nonterminal rule of the form $A \rightarrow B_1 \cdots B_d$ ($d > 0$).
- In Section 4.6, the only restriction is that the rules are nonempty.

We will not describe how transformations are carried out here, but refer to any standard textbook on formal languages, such as Hopcroft et al. (2006).

4.2.2 Example Grammar

Throughout this chapter we will make use of a single (toy) grammar in our running examples. The grammar is shown in Figure 4.1, and is on CNF relaxed according to the first relaxation condition above. Thus it only contains unary and binary nonterminal rules, and unary terminal rules. The right-hand sides of the terminal rules correspond to *lexical items*, whereas the left-hand sides are *preterminal* (or *part-of-speech*) symbols. In practice, lexical analysis is often carried out in a phase distinct from parsing (as described in Chapter 3); the preterminals then take the role of terminals during parsing. The example grammar is lexically ambiguous, since the word "man" can be a noun as well as a verb. Hence, the *garden path* sentence "the old man a ship," as well as the more intuitive "the old men man a ship," can be recognized using this grammar.

4.2.3 Syntax Trees

The standard way to represent the syntactic structure of a grammatical sentence is as a *syntax tree*, or a parse tree, which is a representation of all the steps in the derivation of the sentence from the root node. This means that each internal node in the tree represents an application of a grammar rule. The syntax tree of the example sentence "the old man a ship" is shown in Figure 4.2. Note that the tree is drawn upside-down, with the root of the tree at the top and the leaves at the bottom.

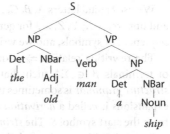

FIGURE 4.2 Syntax tree of the sentence "the old man a ship."

---

* Formally, only grammars that do not accept the empty string can be transformed into CNF, but from a practical point of view we can disregard this, as we are not interested in empty string languages.

Another representation, which is commonly used in running text, is as a *bracketed* sentence, where the brackets are labeled with nonterminals:

[s [NP [Det *the*] [NBar [Adj *old*]]] [VP [Verb *man*] [NP [Det *a*] [NBar [Noun *ship*]]]]]

4.2.4 Other Grammar Formalisms

In practice, pure CFG is not widely used for developing natural language grammars (though grammar-based language modeling in speech recognition is one such case; see Chapter 15). One reason for this is that CFG is not expressive enough—it cannot describe all peculiarities of natural language, e.g., Swiss–German or Dutch scrambling (Shieber 1985a), or Scandinavian long-distance dependencies (Kaplan and Zaenen 1995). But the main practical reason is that it is difficult to use; e.g., agreement, inflection, and other common phenomena are complicated to describe using CFG.

The example grammar in Figure 4.1 is overgenerating—it recognizes both the noun phrases "a men" and "an man," as well as the sentence "the men mans a ship." However, to make the grammar syntactically correct, we must duplicate the categories Noun, Det, and NP into singular and plural versions. All grammar rules involving these categories must be duplicated too. And if the language is, e.g., German, then Det and Noun have to be inflected on number (SING/PLUR), gender (FEM/NEUTR/MASC) and, case (NOM/ACC/DAT/GEN).

Ever since the late 1970s, a number of extensions to CFGs have emerged, with different properties. Some of these formalisms, for example, Regulus and Generalized Phrase-Structure Grammar (GPSG), are context-free-equivalent, meaning that grammars can be compiled to an equivalent CFG which then can be used for parsing. Other formalisms, such as Head-driven Phrase-Structure Grammar (HPSG) and Lexical-Functional Grammar (LFG), have more expressive power, but their similarities with CFG can still be exploited when designing tailor-made parsing algorithms.

There are also several grammar formalisms (e.g., categorial grammar, TAG, dependency grammar) that have not been designed as extensions of CFG, but have other pedigrees. However, most of them have been shown later to be equivalent to CFG or some CFG extension. This equivalence can then be exploited when designing parsing algorithms for these formalisms.

Mildly Context-Sensitive Grammars

According to Chomsky's hierarchy of grammar formalisms (Chomsky 1959), the next major step after context-free grammar is *context-sensitive grammar*. Unfortunately, this step is substantial; arguably, context-sensitive grammars can express an unnecessarily large class of languages, with the drawback that parsing is no longer polynomial in the length of the input. Joshi (1985) suggested the notion of *mild context-sensitivity* to capture the precise formal power needed for defining natural languages. Roughly, a grammar formalism is regarded as mildly context-sensitive (MCS) if it can express some linguistically motivated non-context-free constructs (multiple agreement, crossed agreement, and duplication), and can be parsed in polynomial time with respect to the length of the input.

Among the most restricted MCS formalisms are Tree-Adjoining Grammar (TAG; Joshi et al. 1975, Joshi and Schabes 1997) and Combinatory Categorial Grammar (CCG; Steedman 1985, 1986), which are equivalent to each other (Vijay-Shanker and Weir 1994). Extending these formalisms we obtain a hierarchy of MCS grammar formalisms, with an upper bound in the form of Linear Context-Free Rewriting Systems (LCFRS; Vijay-Shanker et al. 1987), Multiple Context-Free Grammar (MCFG; Seki et al. 1991), and Range Concatenation Grammar (RCG; Boullier 2004), among others.

Constraint-Based Formalisms

A key characteristic of constraint-based grammars is the use of feature terms (sets of attribute–value pairs) for the description of linguistic units, rather than atomic categories as in CFG. Feature terms are partial (underspecified) in the sense that new information may be added as long as it is compatible with old information. Regulus (Rayner et al. 2006) and GPSG (Gazdar et al. 1985) are examples of constraint-based formalisms that are context-free-equivalent, whereas HPSG (Pollard and Sag 1994) and LFG (Bresnan 2001) are strict extensions of CFG. Not only CFG can be augmented with feature terms—constraint-based variants of, e.g., TAG and dependency grammars also exist. Constraint-based grammars are further discussed in Section 4.7.

Immediate Dominance/Linear Precedence

When describing languages with a relatively free word order, such as Latin, Finnish, or Russian, it can be fruitful to separate *immediate dominance* (ID; the parent–child relation) from *linear precedence* (LP; the linear order between the children) within phrases. The first formalism to make use of the ID/LP distinction was GPSG (Gazdar et al. 1985), and it has also been used in HPSG and other recent grammar formalisms. The main problem with ID/LP formalisms is that parsing can become very expensive. Some work has therefore been done to devise ID/LP formalizations that are easier to parse (Nederhof and Satta 2004a; Daniels and Meurers 2004).

Head Grammars

Some linguistic theories make use of the notion of the syntactic *head* of a phrase; e.g., the head of a verb phrase could be argued to be the main verb, whereas the head of a noun phrase could be the main noun. The simplest head grammar formalism is obtained by marking one right-hand side symbol in each context-free rule; more advanced formalisms include HPSG. The head information can, e.g., be used for driving the parser by trying to find the head first and then its arguments (Kay 1989).

Lexicalized Grammars

The nonterminals in a CFG do not depend on the lexical words at the surface level. This is a standard problem for *PP attachment*—which noun phrase or verb phrase constituent a specific prepositional phrase should be attached to. For example, considering a sentence beginning with "I bought a book...," it is clear that a following PP "... with my credit card" should be attached to the verb "bought," whereas the PP "... with an interesting title" should attach to the noun "book." To be able to express such lexical syntactic preferences, CFGs and other formalisms can be lexicalized in different ways (Joshi and Schabes 1997, Eisner and Satta 1999, Eisner 2000).

Dependency Grammars

In contrast to constituent-based formalisms, *dependency grammar* lacks phrasal nodes; instead the structure consists of lexical elements linked by binary dependency relations (Tesnière 1959, Nivre 2006). A dependency structure is a directed acyclic graph between the words in the surface sentence, where the edges are labeled with syntactic functions (such as SUBJ, OBJ, MOD, etc.). Apart from this basic idea, the dependency grammar tradition constitutes a diverse family of different formalisms that can impose different constraints on the dependency relation (such as allowing or disallowing crossing edges), and incorporate different extensions (such as feature terms).

Type-Theoretical Grammars

Some formalisms are based on dependent type theory utilizing the Curry–Howard isomorphism between propositions and types. These formalisms include ALE (Carpenter 1992), Grammatical Framework (Ranta 1994, 2004, Ljunglöf 2004), and Abstract Categorial Grammar (de Groote 2001).

4.2.5 Basic Concepts in Parsing

A *recognizer* is a procedure that determines whether or not an input sentence is grammatical according to the grammar (including the lexicon). A *parser* is a recognizer that produces associated structural analyses according to the grammar (in our case, parse trees or feature terms). A *robust parser* attempts to produce useful output, such as a partial analysis, even if the input is not covered by the grammar (see Section 4.8.1).

We can think of a grammar as inducing a search space consisting of a set of states representing stages of successive grammar-rule rewritings and a set of transitions between these states. When analyzing a sentence, the parser (recognizer) must rewrite the grammar rules in some sequence. A sequence that connects the state S, the string consisting of just the start category of the grammar, and a state consisting of exactly the string of input words, is called a *derivation*. Each state in the sequence then consists of a string over V^* and is called a *sentential form*. If such a sequence exists, the sentence is said to be grammatical according to the grammar.

Parsers can be classified along several dimensions according to the ways in which they carry out derivations. One such dimension concerns rule invocation: In a *top-down* derivation, each sentential form is produced from its predecessor by replacing one nonterminal symbol A by a string of terminal or nonterminal symbols $X_1 \cdots X_d$, where $A \rightarrow X_1 \cdots X_d$ is a grammar rule. Conversely, in a *bottom-up* derivation, each sentential form is produced by replacing $X_1 \cdots X_d$ with A given the same grammar rule, thus successively applying rules in the reverse direction.

Another dimension concerns the way in which the parser deals with ambiguity, in particular, whether the process is *deterministic* or *nondeterministic*. In the former case, only a single, irrevocable choice may be made when the parser is faced with local ambiguity. This choice is typically based on some form of lookahead or systematic preference.

A third dimension concerns whether parsing proceeds from left to right (strictly speaking front to back) through the input or in some other order, for example, inside-out from the right-hand-side heads.

4.3 The Cocke–Kasami–Younger Algorithm

The Cocke–Kasami–Younger (CKY, sometimes written CYK) algorithm, first described in the 1960s (Kasami 1965, Younger 1967), is one of the simplest context-free parsing algorithms. A reason for its simplicity is that it only works for grammars in CNF.

The CKY algorithm builds an upper triangular matrix T, where each cell $T_{i,j}$ ($0 \le i < j \le n$) is a set of nonterminals. The meaning of the statement $A \in T_{i,j}$ is that A spans the input words $w_{i+1} \cdots w_j$, or written more formally, $A \Rightarrow^* w_{i+1} \cdots w_j$.

CKY is a purely bottom-up algorithm consisting of two parts. First we build the lexical cells $T_{i-1,i}$ for the input word w_i by applying the lexical grammar rules, then the nonlexical cells $T_{i,k}$ ($i < k - 1$) are filled by applying the binary grammar rules:

$$T_{i-1,i} = \{ A \mid A \rightarrow w_i \}$$
$$T_{i,k} = \{ A \mid A \rightarrow B\,C, \; i < j < k, \; B \in T_{i,j}, \; C \in T_{j,k} \}$$

The sentence is recognized by the algorithm if $S \in T_{0,n}$, where S is the start symbol of the grammar.

To make the algorithm less abstract, we note that all cells $T_{i,j}$ and $T_{j,k}$ ($i < j < k$) must already be known when building the cell $T_{i,k}$. This means that we have to be careful when designing the i and k loops, so that smaller spans are calculated before larger spans.

One solution is to start by looping over the end node k, and then loop over the start node i in the *reverse* direction. The pseudo-code is as follows:

procedure CKY(T, $w_1 \cdots w_n$)
    $T_{i,j} := \emptyset$ **for all** $0 \le i, j \le n$
    for $i := 1$ **to** n **do**
        for all lexical rules $A \rightarrow w$ **do**
            if $w = w_i$ **then** add A to $T_{i-1,i}$

    for $k := 2$ **to** n **do**
        for $i := k - 2$ **downto** 0 **do**
            for $j := i + 1$ **to** $k - 1$ **do**
                for all binary rules $A \to B\,C$ **do**
                    if $B \in T_{i,j}$ and $C \in T_{j,k}$ **then** add A to $T_{i,k}$

But there are also several alternative possibilities for how to encode the loops in the CKY algorithm; e.g., instead of letting the outer k loop range over end positions, we could equally well let it range over span lengths. We have to keep in mind, however, that smaller spans must be calculated before larger spans.

As already mentioned, the CKY algorithm can only handle grammars in CNF. Furthermore, converting a grammar to CNF is a bit complicated, and can make the resulting grammar much larger, as mentioned in Section 4.2.1. Instead we will show how to modify the CKY algorithm directly to handle unary grammar rules and longer right-hand sides.

4.3.1 Handling Unary Rules

The CKY algorithm can only handle grammars with rules of the form $A \to w_i$ and $A \to B\,C$. Unfortunately most practical grammars also contain lots of unary rules of the form $A \to B$. There are two possible ways to solve this problem. Either we transform the grammar into CNF, or we modify the CKY algorithm.

If $B \in T_{i,k}$ and there is a unary rule $A \to B$, then we should also add A to $T_{i,k}$. Furthermore, the unary rules can be applied after the binary rules, since binary rules only apply to smaller phrases. Unfortunately, we cannot simply loop over each unary rule $A \to B$ to test if $B \in T_{i,k}$. The reason for this is that we cannot possibly know in which order the unary rules will be applied, which means that we cannot know in which order we have to select the unary rules $A \to B$. Instead we need to add the *reflexive, transitive closure* UNARY-CLOSURE$(B) = \{A \mid A \Rightarrow^* B\}$ for each $B \in T_{i,k}$. Since there are only a finite number of nonterminals, UNARY-CLOSURE() can be precompiled from the grammar into an efficient lookup table.

Now, the only thing we have to do is to map UNARY-CLOSURE() onto $T_{i,k}$ within the k and i loops, and after the j loop (as well as onto $T_{i-1,i}$ after the lexical rules have been applied). The final pseudo-code for the extended CKY algorithm is as follows:

    procedure UNARY-CKY$(T, w_1 \cdots w_n)$
        $T_{i,j} := \emptyset$ **for all** $0 \le i,j \le n$
        for $i := 1$ **to** n **do**
            for all lexical rules $A \to w$ **do**
                if $w = w_i$ **then** add A to $T_{i-1,i}$
            for all $B \in T_{i-1,i}$ **do**
                add UNARY-CLOSURE(B) to $T_{i-1,i}$
        for $k := 2$ **to** n **do**
            for $i := k - 2$ **downto** 0 **do**
                for $j := i + 1$ **to** $k - 1$ **do**
                    for all binary rules $A \to B\,C$ **do**
                        if $B \in T_{i,j}$ and $C \in T_{j,k}$ **then** add A to $T_{i,k}$
                for all $B \in T_{i,k}$ **do**
                  add UNARY-CLOSURE(B) to $T_{i,k}$

4.3.2 Example Session

The final CKY matrix after parsing the example sentence "the old man a ship" is shown in Figure 4.3. In the initial lexical pass, the cells in the first diagonal are filled. For example, the cell $T_{2,3}$ is initialized to {Noun,Verb}, after which UNARY-CLOSURE() adds NBar and VP to it.

	1	2	3	4	5
0	Det	NP	NP, S		S
	the	Adj, NBar	NBar		
1		*old*	Noun, Verb, NBar, VP		VP
2			*man*	Det	NP
3				*a*	Noun, NBar
4					*ship*

FIGURE 4.3 CKY matrix after parsing the sentence "the old man a ship."

Then other cells are filled from left to right, bottom up. For example, when filling the cell $T_{0,3}$, we have already filled $T_{0,2}$ and $T_{1,3}$. Now, since Det $\in T_{0,1}$ and NBar $\in T_{1,3}$, and there is a rule NP $\to$ Det NBar, NP is added to $T_{0,3}$. And since NP $\in T_{0,2}$, VP $\in T_{2,3}$, and S $\to$ NP VP, the algorithm adds S to $T_{0,3}$.

4.3.3 Handling Long Right-Hand Sides

To handle longer right-hand sides (RHS), there are several possibilities. A straightforward solution is to add a new inner loop for each RHS length. This means that, e.g., ternary rules will be handled by the following loop inside the k, i, and j nested loops:

> **for** $k, i, j := \ldots$ **do**
>   **for all** binary rules $\ldots$ **do** $\ldots$
>   **for** $j' := j + 1$ to $k - 1$ **do**
>   **for all** ternary rules $A \to B\,C\,D$ **do**
>   **if** $B \in T_{i,j}$ and $C \in T_{j,j'}$ and $D \in T_{j',k}$ **then**
>   add A to $T_{i,k}$

To handle even longer rules we need to add new inner loops inside the j' loop. And for each nested loop, the parsing time increases. In fact, the worst case complexity is $O(n^{d+1})$, where d is the length of the longest right-hand side. This is discussed further in Section 4.8.3.

A more general solution is to replace each long rule $A \to B_1 \cdots B_d$ ($d > 2$) by the $d - 1$ binary rules $A \to B_1 X_2$, $X_2 \to B_2 X_3$, $\ldots$, $X_{d-1} \to B_{d-1} B_d$, where each $X_i = \langle B_i \cdots B_n \rangle$ is a new nonterminal. After this transformation the grammar only contains unary and binary rules, which can be handled by the extended CKY algorithm.

Another variant of the binary transform is to do the RHS transformations implicitly during parsing. This gives rise to the well-known chart parsing algorithms that we introduce in Section 4.4.

4.4 Parsing as Deduction

In this section we will use a general framework for describing parsing algorithms in a high-level manner. The framework is called *deductive parsing*, and was introduced by Pereira and Warren (1983); a related framework introduced later was the *parsing schemata* of Sikkel (1998). Parsing in this sense can be seen as "a deductive process in which rules of inference are used to derive statements about the grammatical status of strings from other such statements" (Shieber et al. 1995).

4.4.1 Deduction Systems

The statements in a deduction system are called *items*, and are represented by formulae in some formal language. The inference rules and axioms are written in natural deduction style and can have side conditions mentioning, e.g., grammar rules. The inference rules and axioms are rule schemata; in other words, they contain metavariables to be instantiated by appropriate terms when the rule is invoked. The set of items built in the deductive process is sometimes called a *chart*.

The general form of an inference rule is

$$\frac{e_1 \quad \cdots \quad e_n}{e} \phi$$

where $e, e_1, \ldots, e_n$ are items and ϕ is a side condition. If there are no antecedents (i.e., $n = 0$), the rule is called an *axiom*. The meaning of an inference rule is that whenever we have derived the items $e_1, \ldots, e_n$, and the condition ϕ holds, we can also derive the item e. The inference rules are applied until no more items can be added. It does not make any difference in which order the rules are applied—the final chart is the reflexive, transitive closure of the inference rules. However, one important constraint is that the system is terminating, which is the case if the number of possible items is finite.

4.4.2 The CKY Algorithm

As a first example, we describe the extended CKY algorithm from Section 4.3.1 as a deduction system. The items are of the form $[\,i, k : A\,]$, corresponding to a nonterminal symbol A spanning the input words $w_{i+1} \cdots w_k$. This is equivalent to the statement $A \in T_{i,k}$ in Section 4.3. We need three inference rules, of which one is an axiom.

Combine

$$\frac{[i,j : B] \quad [j,k : C]}{[\,i,k : A\,]} \quad A \to B\,C \tag{4.7}$$

If there is a B spanning the input positions $i - j$, and a C spanning $j - k$, and there is a binary rule $A \to B\,C$, we know that A will span the input positions $i - k$.

Unary Closure

$$\frac{[i,k : B]}{[\,i,k : A\,]} \quad A \to B \tag{4.8}$$

If we have a B spanning $i - k$, and there is a rule $A \to B$, then we also know that there is an A spanning $i - k$.

Scan

$$\frac{}{[\,i-1, i : A\,]} \quad A \to w_i \tag{4.9}$$

Finally we need an axiom adding an item for each matching lexical rule.

Note that we do not have to say anything about the order in which the inference rules should be applied, as was the case when we presented the CKY algorithm in Section 4.3.

4.4.3 Chart Parsing

The CKY algorithm uses a bottom-up parsing strategy, which means that it starts by recognizing the lexical nonterminals, i.e., the nonterminals that occur as left-hand sides in unary terminal rules. Then the algorithm recognizes the parents of the lexical nonterminals, and so on until it reaches the starting symbol.

A disadvantage of CKY is that it only works on restricted grammars. General CFGs have to be converted, which is not a difficult problem, but can be awkward. The parse results also have to be back-translated into the original form. Because of this, one often implements more general parsing strategies instead.

In the following we give examples of some well-known parsing algorithms for CFGs. First we give a very simple algorithm, and then two refinements; Kilbury's bottom-up algorithm (Leiss 1990), and Earley's top-down algorithm (Earley 1970). The algorithms are slightly modified for presentational purposes, but their essence is still the same.

Parse Items

Parse items are of the form $[\,i, j : A \rightarrow \alpha \cdot \beta\,]$ where $A \rightarrow \alpha\beta$ is a context-free rule, and $0 \leq i \leq j \leq n$ are positions in the input string. The meaning is that α has been recognized spanning $i - j$; i.e., $\alpha \Rightarrow^* w_{i+1} \cdots w_j$. If β is empty, the item is called *passive*. Apart from the logical meaning, the item also states that it is searching for β to span the positions j and k (for some k). The goal of the parsing process is to deduce an item representing that the starting category is found spanning the whole input string; such an item can be written $[\,0, n : S \rightarrow \alpha \cdot\,]$ in our notation.

To simplify presentation, we will assume that all grammars are of the relaxed normal form presented in Section 4.2.1, where each rule is either lexical $A \rightarrow w$ or nonempty $A \rightarrow B_1 \cdots B_d$. To extend the algorithms to cope with general grammars constitutes no serious problem.

The Simplest Chart Parsing Algorithm

Our first context-free chart parsing algorithm consists of three inference rules. The first two, Combine and Scan, remain the same in all our chart parsing variants; while the third, Predict, is very simple and will be improved upon later. The algorithm is also presented by Sikkel and Nijholt (1997), who call it *bottom-up Earley* parsing.

Combine

$$\frac{[\,i, j : A \rightarrow \alpha \cdot B\beta\,] \quad [\,j, k : B \rightarrow \gamma \cdot\,]}{[\,i, k : A \rightarrow \alpha B \cdot \beta\,]} \tag{4.10}$$

The basis for all chart parsing algorithms is *the fundamental rule*; saying that if there is an active item looking for a category B spanning $i - j$, and there is a passive item for B spanning $j - k$, then the dot in the active item can be moved forward, and the new item will span the positions $i - k$.

Scan

$$\frac{}{[\,i - 1, i : A \rightarrow w_i \cdot\,]} \; A \rightarrow w_i \tag{4.11}$$

This is similar to the scanning axiom of the CKY algorithm.

Predict

$$\frac{}{[\,i, i : A \rightarrow \cdot \beta\,]} \; A \rightarrow \beta \tag{4.12}$$

This axiom takes care of introducing active items; each rule in the grammar is added as an active item spanning $i - i$ for any possible input position $0 \leq i \leq n$.

The main problem with this algorithm is that prediction is "blind"; active items are introduced for every rule in the grammar, at all possible input positions. Only very few of these items will be used in later inferences, which means that prediction infers a lot of useless items. The solution is to make prediction an inference rule instead of an axiom, so that an item is only predicted if it is potentially useful for already existing items.

In the rest of this section we introduce two basic prediction strategies, *bottom-up* and *top-down*.

4.4.4 Bottom-Up Left-Corner Parsing

The basic idea with bottom-up parsing is that we predict a grammar rule only when its first symbol has already been found. Kilbury's variant of bottom-up parsing (Leiss 1990) moves the dot in the new item forward one step. Since the first symbol in the right-hand side is called the left corner, the algorithm is sometimes called *bottom-up left-corner parsing* (Sikkel 1998).

Bottom-Up Predict

$$\frac{[\,i,k:B \to \gamma\cdot\,]}{[\,i,k:A \to B\cdot\beta\,]}\ A \to B\beta \qquad (4.13)$$

Bottom-up prediction is like Combine for the first symbol on the right-hand side in a rule. If we have found a B spanning $i - k$, and there is a rule $A \to B\beta$, we can draw the conclusion that $A \to B\cdot\beta$ will span $i - k$.

Note that this algorithm does not work for grammars with ϵ-rules; there is no way an empty rule can be predicted. There are two possible ways ϵ-rules can be handled: (1) either convert the grammar to an equivalent ϵ-free grammar; or (2) add extra inference rules to handle ϵ-rules.

4.4.5 Top-Down Earley-Style Parsing

Earley prediction (Earley 1970) works in a top-down fashion; meaning that we start by stating that we want to find an S starting in position 0, and then move downward in the presumptive syntactic structure until we reach the lexical tokens.

Top-Down Predict

$$\frac{[\,i,k:B \to \gamma\cdot A\alpha\,]}{[\,k,k:A \to \cdot\beta\,]}\ A \to \beta \qquad (4.14)$$

If there is an item looking for an A beginning in position k, and there is a grammar rule for A, we can add that rule as an empty active item starting and ending in k.

Initial Predict

$$\frac{}{[\,0,0:S \to \cdot\beta\,]}\ S \to \beta \qquad (4.15)$$

Top-down prediction needs an active item to be triggered, so we need some way of starting the inference process. This is done by adding an active item for each rule of the starting category S, starting and ending in 0.

4.4.6 Example Session

The final charts after bottom-up and top-down parsing of the example sentence "the old man a ship" are shown in Figures 4.4 and 4.5. This is a standard way of visualizing a chart, as a graph where the items are drawn as edges between the input positions. In the figures, the dotted and grayed-out edges correspond

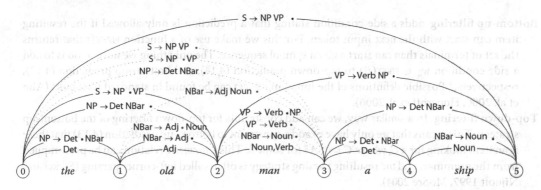

FIGURE 4.4 Final chart after bottom-up parsing of the sentence "the old man a ship." The dotted edges are inferred but useless.

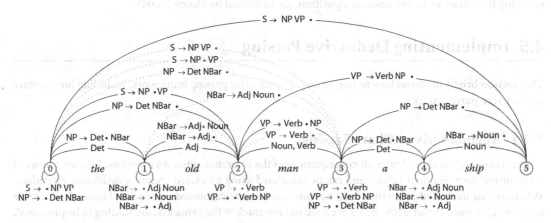

FIGURE 4.5 Final chart after top-down parsing of the sentence "the old man a ship." The dotted edges are inferred but useless.

to useless items, i.e., items that are not used in any derivation of the final S item spanning the whole sentence.

The bottom-up chart contains the useless item [2, 3 : NBar → Noun·], which the top-down chart does not contain. One the other hand, the top-down chart contains a lot of useless cyclic predictions. This suggests that both bottom-up and top-down parsing have their advantages and disadvantages, and that combining the strategies could be the way to go. This leads us directly into the next section about dynamic filtering.

4.4.7 Dynamic Filtering

Both the bottom-up and the top-down algorithms have disadvantages. Bottom-up prediction has no idea of what the final goal of parsing is, which means that it predicts items which will not be used in any derivation from the top node. Top-down prediction on the other hand never looks at the input words, which means that it predicts items that can never start with the next input word.

Note that these useless items do not make the algorithms incorrect in any way; they only decrease parsing efficiency. There are several ways the basic algorithms can be optimized; the standard optimizations are by adding top-down and/or bottom-up *dynamic filtering* to the prediction rules.

Bottom-up filtering adds a side condition stating that a prediction is only allowed if the resulting item can start with the next input token. For this we make use of a function FIRST() that returns the set of terminals than can start a given symbol sequence. The only thing we have to do is to add a side condition $w_k \in$ FIRST(β) to top-down prediction (4.14), and bottom-up prediction (4.13), respectively.* Possible defintions of the function FIRST() can be found in standard textbooks (Aho et al. 2006, Hopcroft et al. 2006).

Top-down filtering In a similar way, we can add constraints for top-down filtering of the bottom-up strategy. This means that we only have to add a constraint to bottom-up prediction (4.13) that there is an item looking for a C, where $C \Rightarrow^* A\delta$ for some δ. This *left-corner* relation can be precompiled from the grammar, and the resulting parsing strategy is often called left-corner parsing (Sikkel and Nijholt 1997, Moore 2004).

Furthermore, both bottom-up and top-down filterings can be added as side-conditions to bottom-up prediction (4.13). Further optimizations in this direction, such as introducing special predict items and realizing the parser as an incremental algorithm, are discussed by Moore (2004).

4.5 Implementing Deductive Parsing

This section briefly discusses how to implement the deductive parsing framework, including how to store and retrieve parse results.

4.5.1 Agenda-Driven Chart Parsing

A deduction engine should infer all consequences of the inference rules. As mentioned above, the set of all resulting items is called a *chart*, and can be calculated using a forward-chaining deduction procedure. Whenever an item is added to the chart, its consequences are calculated and added. However, since one item can give rise to several new items, we need to keep track of the items that are waiting to be processed. New items are thus added to a separate agenda that is used for bookkeeping.

The idea is as follows: First we add all possible consequences of the axioms to the agenda. Then we remove one item e from the agenda, add it to the chart, and add all possible inferences that are trigged by e to the agenda. This second step is repeated until the agenda is empty.

Regarding efficiency, the bottleneck of the algorithm is searching the chart for items matching the inference rule. Because of this, the chart needs to be indexed for efficient antecedent lookup. Exactly what indexes are needed depend on the inference rules and will not be discussed here. For a thorough discussion about implementation issues, see Shieber et al. (1995).

4.5.2 Storing and Retrieving Parse Results

The set of syntactic analyses (or *parse trees*) for a given string is called a *parse forest*. The size of this set can be exponential in the length of the string, as mentioned in the introduction section. A classical example is a grammar for PP attachment containing the rules NP → NP PP and PP → Prep NP. In some pathological cases (i.e., when the grammar is cyclic), there might even be an infinite number of trees. The polynomial parse time complexity stems from the fact that the parse forest can be compactly stored in polynomial space.

A parse forest can be represented as a CFG recognizing the language consisting of only the input string (Bar-Hillel et al. 1964). The forest can then be further investigated to remove useless nodes, increase sharing, and reduce space complexity (Billot and Lang 1989).

---

* There is nothing that prevents us from adding a bottom-up filter to the combine rule (4.10) either. However, this filter is seldom used in practice.

Retrieving a single parse tree from a (suitably reduced) forest is efficient, but the problem is to decide which tree is the best one. We do not want to examine exponentially many trees, but instead we want a clever procedure for directly finding the best tree. This is the problem of disambiguation, which is discussed in Section 4.8.2 and in Chapter 11.

4.6 LR Parsing

Instead of using the grammar directly, we can precompile it into a form that makes parsing more efficient. One of the most common strategies is LR parsing, which was introduced by Knuth (1965). It is mostly used for deterministic parsing of formal languages such as programming languages, but was extended to nondeterministic languages by Lang (1974) and Tomita (1985, 1987).

One of the main ideas of LR parsing is to handle a number of grammar rules simultaneously by merging common subparts of their right-hand sides, rather than attempting one rule at a time. An LR parser compiles the grammar into a finite automaton, augmented with *reductions* for capturing the nesting of nonterminals in a syntactic structure, making it a kind of push-down automaton (PDA). The automaton is called an LR automaton, or an LR table.

4.6.1 The LR(0) Table

LR automata can be constructed in several different ways. The simplest construction is the LR(0) table, which uses no *lookahead* when it constructs its states. In practice, most LR algorithms use SLR(1) or LALR(1) tables, which utilize a lookahead of one input symbol. Details of how to construct these automata are, e.g., given by Aho et al. (2006). Our LR(0) construction is similar to the one by Nederhof and Satta (2004b).

States

The states in an LR table are sets of dotted rules $A \to \alpha \cdot \beta$. The meaning of being in a state is that any of the dotted rules in the state can be the correct one, but we have not decided yet.

To build an LR(0) table we do the following. First we have to define the function PREDICT-CLOSURE(q), which is the smallest set such that:

- $q \subseteq$ PREDICT-CLOSURE(q), and
- if $(A \to \alpha \cdot B\beta) \in$ PREDICT-CLOSURE(q),
  then $(B \to \cdot\gamma) \in$ PREDICT-CLOSURE(q) for all $B \to \gamma$

Transitions

Transitions between states are defined by the function GOTO, taking a grammar symbol as argument. The function is defined as

$$\text{GOTO}(q, X) = \text{PREDICT-CLOSURE}(\{A \to \alpha X \cdot \beta \mid A \to \alpha \cdot X\beta \in q\})$$

The idea is that all dotted rules $A \to \alpha \cdot X\beta$ will survive to the next state, with the dot moved forward one step. To this the closure of all top-down predictions are added. The initial state q_{init} of the LR table contains predictions of all S rules:

$$q_{\text{init}} = \text{PREDICT-CLOSURE}(\{ S \to \cdot\gamma \mid S \to \gamma \})$$

We also need a special final state q_{final} that is reachable from the initial state by the dummy transition GOTO(q_{final}, S). Figure 4.6 contains the resulting LR(0) table of the example grammar in Figure 4.1. The reducible states, marked with a thicker border in the figure, are the states that contain passive dotted rules, i.e., rules of the form $A \to \alpha \cdot$. For simplicity we have not included the lexical rules in the LR table.

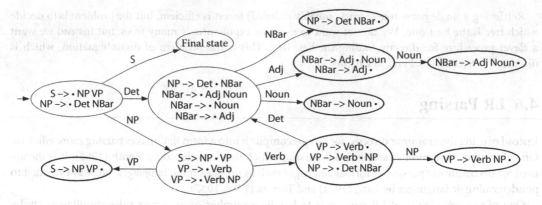

FIGURE 4.6 Example LR(0) table for the grammar in Figure 4.1.

4.6.2 Deterministic LR Parsing

An LR parser is a shift-reduce parser (Aho et al. 2006) that uses the transitions of the LR table to push states onto a stack. When the parser is in a reducible state, containing a rule $B \rightarrow \beta\cdot$, it pops $|\beta|$ states off the stack and shifts to a new state by the symbol B.

In our setting we do not use LR states directly, but instead LR states indexed by input position, which we write as $\sigma = q@i$. An LR stack $\omega = \sigma_1 \cdots \sigma_n$ is a sequence of indexed LR states. There are three basic operations:*

$$\text{TOP}(\omega) = \sigma \quad (\text{where } \omega = \omega'\sigma)$$

$$\text{POP}(\omega) = \omega' \quad (\text{where } \omega = \omega'\sigma)$$

$$\text{PUSH}(\omega, \sigma) = \omega\sigma$$

The parser starts with a stack containing only the initial state in position 0. Then it shifts the next input symbol, and pushes the new state onto the stack. Note the difference with traversing a finite automaton; we do not forget the previous state, but instead push the new state on top. This way we know how to go backward in the automaton, which we cannot do in a finite automaton.

After shifting, we try to reduce the stack as often as possible, and then we shift the next input token, reduce and continue until the input is exhausted. The parsing has succeeded if we end up with q_{final} as the top state in the stack.

> **function** LR($w_1 \cdots w_n$)
>
> $\omega := (q_{\text{init}}@0)$
> **for** $i := 1$ **to** n **do**
> $\quad \omega := \text{REDUCE}(\text{SHIFT}(\omega, w_i@i))$
> **if** $\text{TOP}(\omega) = q_{\text{final}}@n$ **then** success **else** failure

Shifting a Symbol

To shift a symbol X onto the stack ω, we follow the edge labeled X from the current state $\text{TOP}(\omega)$, and push the new state onto the stack:

---

* We will abuse the function $\text{TOP}(\omega)$ by sometimes letting it denote the indexed state $q@i$ and sometimes the LR state q. Furthermore we will write POP^n for n applications of POP.

function SHIFT($\omega, X@i$)
  $\sigma_{\text{next}} := \text{GOTO}(\text{TOP}(\omega), X) \ @ \ i$
  return PUSH($\omega, \sigma_{\text{next}}$)

Reducing the Stack

When the top state of the stack contains a rule $A \rightarrow B_1 \cdots B_d\cdot$, the nonterminal A has been recognized. The only way to reach that state is from a state containing the rule $A \rightarrow B_1 \cdots B_{d-1}\cdot B_d$, which in turn is reached from a state containing $A \rightarrow B_1 \cdots B_{d-2}\cdot B_{d-1}B_d$, and so on d steps back in the stack. This state, d steps back, contains the predicted rule $A \rightarrow \cdot B_1 \cdots B_d$. But there is only one way this rule could have been added to the state—as a prediction from a rule $C \rightarrow \alpha \cdot A\beta$. So, if we remove d states from the stack (getting the popped stack ω_{red}), we reach a state that has an A transition.* And since we started this paragraph by knowing that A was just recognized, we can shift the popped stack ω_{red}. This whole sequence (popping the stack and then shifting) is called a *reduction*.

However, it is not guaranteed that we can stop here. It is possible that we, after shifting A onto the popped stack, enter a new reducible state, and we can do the whole thing again. This is done until there are no more possible reductions:

function REDUCE(ω)
  $q_{\text{top}}@i := \text{TOP}(\omega)$
  if $(A \rightarrow B_1 \cdots B_d\cdot) \in q_{\text{top}}$ **then**
    $\omega_{\text{red}} := \text{POP}^d(\omega)$
    return REDUCE(SHIFT($\omega_{\text{red}}, A@i$))
  else
    return ω

Ungrammaticality and Ambiguities

The LR automaton can only handle grammatically correct input. If the input is ungrammatical, we might end up in a state where we can neither reduce nor shift. In this case we have to stop parsing and report an error.

The automaton could also contain nondeterministic choices, even on unambiguous grammars. Thus we might enter a state where it is possible to both shift and reduce at the same time (or reduce in two different ways). In deterministic LR parsing this is called a shift/reduce (or reduce/reduce) conflict, which is considered to be a problem in the grammar. However, since natural language grammars are inherently ambiguous, we have to change the algorithm to handle these cases.

4.6.3 Generalized LR Parsing

To handle nondeterminism, the top-level LR algorithm does not have to be changed much, and only small changes have to be made on the shift and reduce functions. Conceptually, we can think of a "stack" for nondeterministic LR parsing as a set Ω of ordinary stacks ω, which we reduce and shift in parallel. When reducing the stack set, we perform all possible reductions on the elements and take the union of the results. This means that the number of stacks increases, but (hopefully) some of these stacks will be lost when shifting.

The top-level parsing function LR remains as before, with the slight modification that the initial stack set is the singleton set $\{(q_{\text{init}})\}$, and that the final stack set should contain some stack whose top state is $q_{\text{final}}@n$.

---

* Note that if A is the starting symbol S, and $\text{TOP}(\omega_{\text{red}})$ is the initial state $q_{\text{init}}@0$, then there will in fact *not* be any rule $C \rightarrow \alpha \cdot S\beta$ in that state. But in this case there is a dummy transition to the final state q_{final}, so we can still shift over S.

Using a Set of Stacks

The basic stack operations POP and PUSH are straightforward to generalize to sets:

$$\text{POP}(\Omega) = \{\omega \mid \omega\sigma \in \Omega\}$$

$$\text{PUSH}(\Omega, \sigma) = \{\omega\sigma \mid \omega \in \Omega\}$$

However, there is one problem when trying to obtain the TOP state—since there are several stacks, there can be several different top states. And the TOP operation cannot simply return an unstructured set of states, since we have to know which stacks correspond to which top state. Our solution is to introduce an operation TOP-PARTITION that returns a *partition* of the set of stacks, where all stacks in each part have the same unique top state. The simplest definition is to just make each stack a part of its own, TOP-PARTITION$(\Omega) = \{\{\omega\} \mid \omega \in \Omega\}$, but there are several other possible definitions. Now we can define the TOP operation to simply return the top state of any stack in the set, since it will be unique.

$$\text{TOP}(\Omega) = \sigma \quad (\text{where } \omega\sigma \in \Omega)$$

Shifting

The difference compared to deterministic shift is that we loop over the stack partitions, and shift each partition in parallel, returning the union of the results:

function SHIFT$(\Omega, X@i)$
    $\Omega' := \emptyset$
    for all $\omega_{\text{part}} \in$ TOP-PARTITION(Ω) **do**
        $\sigma_{\text{next}} :=$ GOTO(TOP$(\omega_{\text{part}}), X) @ i$
        add PUSH$(\omega_{\text{part}}, \sigma_{\text{next}})$ to Ω'
    return Ω'

Reduction

Nondeterministic reduction also loops over the partition, and does reduction on each part separately, taking the union of the results. Also note that the original set of stacks is included in the final reduction result, since it is always possible that some stack has finished reducing and should shift next.

function REDUCE(Ω)
    for all $\omega_{\text{part}} \in$ TOP-PARTITION(Ω) **do**
        $q_{\text{top}}@i :=$ TOP(ω_{part})
        for all $(A \rightarrow B_1 \cdots B_d\cdot) \in q_{\text{top}}$ **do**
            $\omega_{\text{red}} :=$ POP$^d(\omega_{\text{part}})$
            add REDUCE(SHIFT$(\omega_{\text{red}}, A@i))$ to Ω
    return Ω

Grammars with Empty Productions

The GLR algorithm as it is described in this chapter cannot correctly handle all grammars with ϵ-rules. This is a well-known problem for GLR parsers, and there are two main solutions. One possibility is of course to transform the grammar into ϵ-free form (Hopcroft et al. 2006). Another possibility is to modify the GLR algorithm, possibly together with a modified LR table (Nozohoor-Farshi 1991, Nederhof and Sarbo 1996, Aycock et al. 2001, Aycock and Horspool 2002, Scott and Johnstone 2006, Scott et al. 2007).

4.6.4 Optimized GLR Parsing

Each stack that survives in the previous set-based algorithm corresponds to a possible parse tree. But since there can be exponentially many parse trees, this means that the algorithm is exponential in the length of the input.

The problem is the data structure—a set of stacks does not take into account that parallel stacks often have several parts in common. Tomita (1985, 1988) suggested to store a set of stacks as a directed acyclic graph (calling it a *graph-structured stack*), which together with suitable algorithms make GLR parsing polynomial in the length of the input.

The only things we have to do is to reimplement the five operations POP, PUSH, TOP-PARTITION, TOP, and (∪); the functions LR, SHIFT, and REDUCE all stay the same. We represent a graph-structured stack as a pair $G : T$, where G is a directed graph over indexed states, and T is a subset of the nodes in G that constitute the current stack tops. Assuming that the graph is represented by a set of directed edges $\sigma' \mapsto \sigma$, the operations can be implemented as follows:

$$\text{POP}(G : T) = G : \{ \sigma' \mid \sigma \in T, \sigma' \mapsto \sigma \in G \}$$

$$\text{PUSH}(G : T, \sigma) = \big(G \cup \{ \sigma' \mapsto \sigma \mid \sigma' \in T \}\big) : \{\sigma\}$$

$$\text{TOP-PARTITION}(G : T) = \{ G : \{\sigma\} \mid \sigma \in T \}$$

$$\text{TOP}(G : \{\sigma\}) = \sigma$$

$$(G_1 : T_1) \cup (G_2 : T_2) = (G_1 \cup G_2) : (T_1 \cup T_2)$$

The initial stack in the top-level LR function is still conceptually a singleton set, but will be encoded as a graph-structured stack $\emptyset : \{q_{\text{init}}@0\}$. Note that for the graph-structured version to be correct, we need the LR states to be indexed. Otherwise the graph will merge all nodes having the same LR state, regardless of where in the input it is recognized.

The graph-structured stack operations never remove edges from the graph, only add new edges. This means that it is possible to implement GLR parsing using a global graph, where the only thing that is passed around is the set T of stack tops.

Tabular GLR Parsing

The astute reader might have noticed the similarity between the graph-structured stack and the chart in Section 4.5: The graph (chart) is a global set of edges (items), to which edges (items) are added during parsing, but never removed. It should therefore be possible to reformulate GLR parsing as a tabular algorithm. For this we need two inference rules, corresponding to SHIFT and REDUCE, and one axiom corresponding to the initial stack. This tabular GLR algorithm is described by Nederhof and Satta (2004b).

4.7 Constraint-Based Grammars

This section introduces a simple form of constraint-based grammar, or unification grammar, which for more than two decades has constituted a widely adopted class of formalisms in computational linguistics.

4.7.1 Overview

A key characteristic of constraint-based formalisms is the use of feature terms (sets of attribute–value pairs) for the description of linguistic units, rather than atomic categories as in CFGs. Feature terms can be nested: their values can be either atomic symbols or feature terms. Furthermore, they are partial (underspecified) in the sense that new information may be added as long as it is compatible with old information. The operation for merging and checking compatibility of feature constraints is usually formalized as *unification*. Some formalisms, such as PATR (Shieber et al. 1983, Shieber 1986) and Regulus (Rayner et al. 2006), are restricted to simple unification (of conjunctive terms), while others such as LFG (Kaplan and Bresnan 1982) and HPSG (Pollard and Sag 1994) allow disjunctive terms, sets, type hierarchies, or other extensions. In sum, feature terms have proved to be an extremely versatile and powerful device for linguistic description. One example of this is unbounded dependency, as illustrated by examples (4.1)–(4.3) in Section 4.1, which can be handled entirely within the feature system by the technique of gap threading (Karttunen 1986).

Several constraint-based formalisms are phrase-structure-based in the sense that each rule is factored in a phrase-structure backbone and a set of constraints that specify conditions on the feature terms associated with the rule (e.g., PATR, Regulus, CLE, HPSG, LFG, and TAG, though the latter uses certain tree-building operations instead of rules). Analogously, when parsers for constraint-based formalisms are built, the starting-point is often a phrase-structure parser that is augmented to handle feature terms. This is also the approach we shall follow here.

4.7.2 Unification

We make use of a constraint-based formalism with a context-free backbone and restricted to simple unification (of conjunctive terms), thus corresponding to PATR (Shieber et al. 1983, Shieber 1986). A grammar rule in this formalism can be seen as an ordered pair of a production $X_0 \rightarrow X_1 \cdots X_d$ and a set of equational constraints over the feature terms of types $X_0, \ldots, X_d$. A simple example of a rule, encoding agreement between the determiner and the noun in a noun phrase, is the following:

$$X_0 \rightarrow X_1 \; X_2$$

$$\langle X_0 \; category \rangle = \text{NP}$$

$$\langle X_1 \; category \rangle = \text{Det}$$

$$\langle X_2 \; category \rangle = \text{Noun}$$

$$\langle X_1 \; agreement \rangle = \langle X_2 \; agreement \rangle$$

Any such rule description can be represented as a phrase-structure rule where the symbols consist of feature terms. Below is a feature term rule corresponding to the previous rule (where $\boxed{1}$ indicates identity between the associated elements):

$$\left[category : \text{NP} \right] \rightarrow \begin{bmatrix} category : & \text{Det} \\ agreement : \boxed{1} \end{bmatrix} \begin{bmatrix} category : & \text{Noun} \\ agreement : \boxed{1} \end{bmatrix}$$

The basic operation on feature terms is *unification*, which determines if two terms are compatible by merging them to the most general term compatible with both. As an example, the unification $A \sqcup B$ of the terms $A = \left[agreement : \left[number : \text{plural} \right] \right]$ and $B = \left[agreement : \left[gender : \text{neutr} \right] \right]$ succeeds with the result:

$$A \sqcup B = \left[agreement : \begin{bmatrix} gender : & \text{neutr} \\ number : & \text{plural} \end{bmatrix} \right]$$

However, neither A nor $A \sqcup B$ can be unified with

$$C = \left[agreement : \left[number : \text{singular} \right] \right]$$

since the atomic values plural and singular are distinct. The semantics of feature terms including the unification algorithm is described by Pereira and Shieber (1984), Kasper and Rounds (1986), and Shieber

(1992). The unification of feature terms is an extension of Robinson's unification algorithm for first-order terms (Robinson 1965). More advanced grammar formalisms such as HPSG and LFG use further extensions of feature terms, such as type hierarchies and disjunction.

4.7.3 Tabular Parsing with Unification

Basically, the tabular parsers in Section 4.4 as well as the GLR parsers in Section 4.6 can be adapted to constraint-based grammar by letting the symbols in the grammar rules be feature terms instead of atomic nonterminal symbols (Shieber 1985b, Tomita 1987, Nakazawa 1991, Samuelsson 1994). For example, an item in tabular parsing then still has the form $[\, i, j : A \rightarrow \alpha \cdot \beta \,]$, where A is a feature term and α, β are sequences of feature terms.

A problem in tabular parsing with constraint-based grammar as opposed to CFG is that the item-redundancy test involves comparing complex feature terms instead of testing for equality between atomic symbols. For this reason, we need to make sure that no previously added item *subsumes* a new item to be added (Shieber 1985a, Pereira and Shieber 1987). Informally, an item e subsumes another item e' if e contains a subset of the information in e'. Since the input positions i, j are always fully instantiated, this amounts to checking if the feature terms in the dotted rule of e subsumes the corresponding feature terms in e'. The rationale for using this test is that we are only interested in adding edges that are less specific than the old ones, since everything we could do with a more specific edge, we can also do with a more general one.

The algorithm for implementing the deduction engine, presented in Section 4.5.1, only needs minor modifications to work on unification-based grammars: (1) instead of checking that the new item e is contained in the chart, we check that there is an item in the chart that subsumes e, and (2) instead of testing whether two items e_j and e'_j matches, we try to perform the unification $e_j \sqcup e'_j$.

However, subsumption testing is not always sufficient for correct and efficient tabular parsing, since tabular CFG-based parsers are not fully specified in the order in which ambiguities are discovered (Lavie and Rosé 2004). Unification grammars may contain rules that lead to the prediction of ever more specific feature terms that do not subsume each other, thereby resulting in infinite sequences of predictions. This kind of problem occurs in natural language grammars when keeping lists of, say, subcategorized constituents or gaps to be found. In logic programming, the *occurs check* is used for circumventing a corresponding circularity problem. In constraint-based grammar, Shieber (1985b) introduced the notion of *restriction* for the same purpose. A restrictor removes those portions of a feature term that could potentially lead to non-termination. This is in general done by replacing those portions with free (newly instantiated) variables, which typically removes some coreference. The purpose of restriction is to ensure that terms to be predicted are only instantiated to a certain depth, such that terms will eventually subsume each other.

4.8 Issues in Parsing

In the light of the previous exposition, this section reexamines the three fundamental challenges of parsing discussed in Section 4.1.

4.8.1 Robustness

Robustness can be seen as the ability to deal with input that somehow does not conform to what is normally expected (Menzel 1995). In grammar-driven parsing, it is natural to take "expected" input to correspond to those strings that are in the formal language $L(G)$ generated by the grammar G. However, as discussed in Section 4.1, a natural language parser will always be exposed to some amount of input that is not in $L(G)$. One source of this problem is *undergeneration*, which is caused by a lack of coverage of G relative to the natural language L. Another problem is that the input may contain errors; in other words, that it may be *ill-formed* (though the distinction between well-formed and ill-formed input is by no means clear-cut). But regardless of why the input is not in $L(G)$, it is usually desirable to try to recover as much meaningful information from it as possible, rather than returning no result at all. This is the problem of *robustness*, whose basic notion is to always return *some* analysis of the input. In a stronger sense, robustness means that small deviations from the expected input will only cause small impairments of the parse result, whereas large deviations may cause large impairments. Hence, robustness in this stronger sense amounts to *graceful degradation*.

Clearly, robustness requires methods that sacrifice something from the traditional ideal of recovering complete and exact parses using a linguistically motivated grammar. To avoid the situation where the parser can only stop and report failure in analyzing the input, one option is to *relax* some of the grammatical constraints in such a way that a (potentially) ungrammatical sentence obtains a complete analysis (Jensen and Heidorn 1983, Mellish 1989). Put differently, by relaxing some constraints, a certain amount of *overgeneration* is achieved relative to the original grammar, and this is then hopefully sufficient to account for the input. The key problem of this approach is that, as the number of errors grows, the number of relaxation alternatives that are compatible with analyses of the whole input may explode, and that the search for a best solution is therefore very difficult to control.

One can then instead focus on the design of the *grammar*, making it less rich in the hope that this will allow for processing that is less brittle. The amount of information contained in the structural representations yielded by the parser is usually referred to as a distinction between *deep parsing* and *shallow parsing* (somewhat misleadingly, as this distinction does not necessarily refer to different parsing methods per se, but rather to the syntactic representations used). Deep parsing systems typically capture long-distance dependencies or predicate–argument relations directly, as in LFG, HPSG, or CCG (compare Section 4.2.4). In contrast, shallow parsing makes use of more skeletal representations. An example of this is Constraint Grammar (Karlsson et al. 1995). This works by first assigning all possible part-of-speech and syntactic labels to all words. It then applies pattern-matching rules (constraints) to disambiguate the labels, thereby reducing the number of parses. The result constitutes a dependency structure in the sense that it only provides relations between words, and may be ambiguous in that the identities of dependents are not fully specified.

A distinction which is sometimes used more or less synonymously with deep and shallow parsing is that between *full parsing* and *partial parsing*. Strictly speaking, however, this distinction refers to the degree of completeness of the analysis with respect to a given target representation. Thus, partial parsing is often used to denote an initial, surface-oriented analysis ("almost parsing"), in which certain decisions, such as attachments, are left for subsequent processing. A radical form of partial parsing is *chunk parsing* (Abney 1991, 1997), which amounts to finding boundaries between basic elements, such as non-recursive clauses or low-level phrases, and analyzing each of these elements using a finite-state grammar. Higher-level analysis is then left for processing by other means. One of the earliest approaches to partial parsing was *Fidditch* (Hindle 1989, 1994). A key idea of this approach is to leave constituents whose roles cannot be determined unattached, thereby always providing exactly one analysis for any given sentence. Another approach is *supertagging*, introduced by Bangalore and Joshi (1999) for the LTAG formalism as a means to reduce ambiguity by associating lexical items with rich descriptions (supertags) that impose complex constraints in a local context, but again without itself deriving a syntactic analysis. Supertagging has also been successfully applied within the CCG formalism (Clark and Curran 2004).

A second option is to sacrifice completeness with respect to covering the entire *input*, by parsing only fragments that are well-formed according to the grammar. This is sometimes referred to as *skip parsing*. Partial parsing is a means to achieve this, since leaving a fragment unattached may just as well be seen as a way of skipping that fragment. A particularly important case for skip parsing is noisy input, such as written text containing errors or output from a speech recognizer. (A word error rate around 20%–40% is by no means unusual in recognition of spontaneous speech; see Chapter 15.) For the parsing of spoken language in conversational systems, it has long been commonplace to use pattern-matching rules that trigger on domain-dependent subsets of the input (Ward 1989, Jackson et al. 1991, Boye and Wirén 2008). Other approaches have attempted to render deep parsing methods robust, usually by trying to connect the maximal subset of the original input that is covered by the grammar. For example, GLR* (Lavie 1996, Lavie and Tomita 1996), an extension of GLR (Section 4.6.3), can parse all subsets of the input that are licensed by the grammar by being able to skip over any words. Since many parsable subsets of the original input must then be analyzed, the amount of ambiguity is greatly exacerbated. To control the search space, GLR* makes use of statistical disambiguation similar to a method proposed by Carroll (1993) and Briscoe and Carroll (1993), where probabilities are associated directly with the actions in the pre-compiled LR parsing table (a method that in turn is an instance of the conditional history-based models discussed in Chapter 11). Other approaches in which subsets of the input can be parsed are Rosé and Lavie (2001), van Noord et al. (1999), and Kasper et al. (1999).

A third option is to sacrifice the traditional notion of *constructive parsing*, that is, analyzing sentences by building syntactic representations imposed by the rules of a grammar. Instead one can use *eliminative parsing*, which works by initially setting up a maximal set of conditions, and then gradually reducing analyses that are illegal according to a given set of constraints, until only legal analyses remain. Thus, parsing is here viewed as a constraint satisfaction problem (or, put differently, as disambiguation), in which the set of constraints guiding the process corresponds to the grammar. Examples of this kind of approach are Constraint Grammar (Karlsson et al. 1995) and the system of Foth and Menzel (2005).

4.8.2 Disambiguation

The dual problem of undergeneration is that the parser produces superfluous analyses, for example, in the form of *massive ambiguity*, as illustrated in Section 4.1. Ultimately, we would like not just *some* analysis (robustness), but rather *exactly one* (disambiguation). Although not all information needed for disambiguation (such as contextual constraints) may be available during parsing, some pruning of the search space is usually possible and desirable. The parser may then pass on the n best analyses, if not a single one, to the next level of processing. A related problem, and yet another source of superfluous analyses, is that the grammar might be incomplete not only in the sense of undergeneration, but also by licensing constructions that do not belong to the natural language L. This problem is known as *overgeneration* or *leakage*, by reference to Sapir's famous statement that "[a]ll grammars leak" (Sapir 1921, p. 39).

A basic observation is that, although a general grammar will allow a large number of analyses of almost any nontrivial sentence, most of these analyses will be extremely implausible in the context of a particular domain. A simple approach that was pursued early on was then to code a new, specialized *semantic grammar* for each domain Burton 1976, Hendrix et al. 1978).* A more advanced alternative is to tune the parser and/or grammar for each new domain. Grishman et al. (1984), Samuelsson and Rayner (1991), and Rayner et al. (2000) make use of a method known as *grammar specialization*, which takes advantage of actual rule usage in a particular domain. This method is based on the observation that, in a given domain, certain groups of grammar rules tend to combine frequently in some ways but not in others. On the basis of a sufficiently large corpus parsed by the original grammar, it is then possible to identify common combinations of rules of a (unification) grammar and to collapse them into single "macro" rules. The result is a specialized grammar, which, compared to the original grammar, has a larger number of rules but a simpler structure, reducing ambiguity and allowing very fast processing using an LR parser. Another possibility is to use a hybrid method to rank a set of analyses according to their likelihood in the domain, based on data from supervised training (Rayner et al. 2000, Toutanova et al. 2002). Clearly, disambiguation leads naturally in one way or another to the application of statistical inference; for a systematic exposition of this, we refer to Chapter 11.

---

* Note that this early approach can be seen as a text-oriented and less robust variant of the domain-dependent pattern-matching systems of Ward (1989) and others aimed at spoken language, referred to in Section 4.8.1.

4.8.3 Efficiency

Theoretical Time Complexity

The worst-case time complexity for parsing with CFG is cubic, $O(n^3)$, in the length of the input sentence. This can most easily be seen for the algorithm CKY() in Section 4.3. The main part consists of three nested loops, all ranging over $O(n)$ input positions, giving cubic time complexity. This is not changed by the UNARY-CKY() algorithm. However, if we add inner loops for handling long right-hand sides, as discussed in Section 4.3.3, the complexity increases to $O(n^{d+1})$, where d is the length of the longest right-hand side in the grammar.

The time complexities of the tabular algorithms in Section 4.4 are also cubic, since using dotted rules constitutes an implicit transformation of the grammar into binary form. In general, assuming that we have a decent implementation of the deduction engine, the time complexity of a deductive algorithm is the complexity of the most complex inference rule. In our case this is the combine rule (4.10), which contains three variables i, j, k ranging over $O(n)$ input positions.

The worst-case time complexity of the optimized GLR algorithm, as formulated in Section 4.6.4, is $O(n^{d+1})$. This is because reduction pops the stack d times, for a rule with right-hand side length d. By binarizing the stack reductions it is possible to obtain cubic time complexity for GLR parsing (Kipps 1991, Nederhof and Satta 1996, Scott et al. 2007).

If the CFG is lexicalized, as mentioned in Section 4.2.4, the time complexity of parsing becomes $O(n^5)$ rather than cubic. The reason for this is that the cubic parsing complexity also depends on the grammar size, which for a bilexical CFG depends quadratically on the size of the lexicon. And after filtering out the grammar rules that do not have a realization in the input sentence, we obtain a complexity of $O(n^2)$ (for the grammar size) multiplied by $O(n^3)$ (for context-free parsing). Eisner and Satta (1999) and Eisner (2000) provide an $O(n^4)$ algorithm for bilexical CFG, and an $O(n^3)$ algorithm for a common restricted class of lexicalized grammars.

Valiant (1975) showed that it is possible to transform the CKY algorithm into the problem of Boolean matrix multiplication (BMM), for which there are sub-cubic algorithms. Currently, the best BMM algorithm is approximately $O(n^{2.376})$ (Coppersmith and Winograd 1990). However, these sub-cubic algorithms all involve large constants making them inefficient in practice. Furthermore, since BMM can be reduced to context-free parsing (Lee 2002), there is not much hope in finding practical parsing algorithms with sub-cubic time complexity.

As mentioned in Section 4.2.4, MCS grammar formalisms all have polynomial parse time complexity. More specifically, TAG and CCG have $O(n^6)$ time complexity (Vijay-Shanker and Weir 1993), whereas for LCFRS, MCFG, and RCG the exponent depends on the complexity of the grammar (Satta 1992).

In general, adding feature terms and unification to a phrase-structure backbone makes the resulting formalism undecidable. In practice, however, conditions are often placed on the phrase-structure back-bone and/or possible feature terms to reduce complexity (Kaplan and Bresnan 1982, p. 266; Pereira and Warren 1983, p. 142), sometimes even to the effect of retaining polynomial parsability (Joshi 1997). For a general exposition of computational complexity in connection with linguistic theories, see Barton et al. (1987).

Practical Efficiency

The complexity results above represent theoretical worst cases, which in actual practice may occur only under very special circumstances. Hence, to assess the practical behavior of parsing algorithms, empirical evaluations are more informative. As an illustration of this, in a comparison of three unification-based parsers using a wide-coverage grammar of English, Carroll (1993) found parsing times for exponential-time algorithms to be approximately quadratic in the length of the input for sentence lengths of 1–30 words.

Early work on empirical parser evaluation, such as Pratt (1975), Slocum (1981), Tomita (1985), Wirén (1987) and Billot and Lang (1989), focused on the behavior of specific algorithms. However, reliable comparisons require that the same grammars and test data are used across different evaluations. Increasingly, the availability of common infrastructure in the form of grammars, treebanks, and test suites has facilitated this, as illustrated by Carroll (1994), van Noord (1997), Oepen et al. (2000), Oepen and Carroll (2002), and Kaplan et al. (2004), among others. A more difficult problem is that reliable comparisons also require that parsing times can be normalized across different implementations and computing platforms. One way of trying to handle this complication would be to have standard implementations of reference algorithms in all implementation languages of interest, as suggested by Moore (2000).

4.9 Historical Notes and Outlook

With the exception of machine translation, parsing is probably the area with the longest history in natural language processing. Victor Yngve has been credited with describing the first method for parsing, conceived of as one component of a system for machine translation, and proceeding bottom-up (Yngve 1955). Subsequently, top-down algorithms were provided by, among others, Kuno and Oettinger (1962). Another early approach was the Transformation and Discourse Analysis Project (TDAP) of Zellig Harris 1958–1959, which in effect used cascades of finite-state automata for parsing (Harris 1962; Joshi and Hopely 1996).

During the next decade, the focus shifted to parsing algorithms for context-free grammar. In 1960, John Cocke invented the core dynamic-programming parser that was independently generalized and formalized by Kasami (1965) and Younger (1967), thus evolving into the CKY algorithm. This allowed for parsing in cubic time with grammars in CNF. Although Cocke's original algorithm was never published, it remains a highly significant achievement in the history of parsing (for sources to this, see Hays 1966 and Kay 1999). In 1968, Earley then presented the first algorithm for parsing with general CFG in no worse than cubic time (Earley 1970). In independent work, Kay (1967, 1973, 1986) and Kaplan (1973) generalized Cocke's algorithm into what they coined chart parsing. A key idea of this is to view tabular parsing algorithms as instances of a general algorithm schema, with specific parsing algorithms arising from different instantiations of inference rules and the agenda (see also Thompson 1981, 1983, Wirén 1987).

However, with the growing dominance of Transformational Grammar, particularly with the *Aspects* ("Standard Theory") model introduced by Chomsky (1965), there was a diminished interest in context-free phrase-structure grammar. On the other hand, Transformational Grammar was not itself amenable to parsing in any straightforward way. The main reason for this was the inherent directionality of the transformational component, in the sense that it maps from deep structure to surface word string.

A solution to this problem was the development of Augmented Transition Networks (ATNs), which started in the late 1960s and which became the dominating framework for natural language processing during the 1970s (Woods et al. 1972, Woods 1970, 1973). Basically, the appeal of the ATN was that it constituted a formalism of the same power as Transformational Grammar, but one whose operational claims could be clearly stated, and which provided an elegant (albeit procedural) way of linking the surface structure encoded by the network path with the deep structure built up in registers.

Beginning around 1975, there was a revival of interest in phrase-structure grammars (Joshi et al. 1975, Joshi 1985), later augmented with complex features whose values were typically matched using unification (Shieber 1986). One reason for this revival was that some of the earlier arguments against the use of CFG had been refuted, resulting in several systematically restricted formalisms (see Section 4.2.4). Another reason was a movement toward declarative (constraint-based) grammar formalisms that typically used a phrase-structure backbone, and whose parsability and formal properties could be rigorously analyzed. This allowed parsing to be formulated in ways that abstracted from implementational detail, as demonstrated most elegantly in the parsing-as-deduction paradigm (Pereira and Warren 1983).

Another development during this time was the generalization of Knuth's deterministic LR parsing algorithm (Knuth 1965) to handling nondeterminism (ambiguous CFGs), leading to the notion of GLR parsing (Lang 1974, Tomita 1985). Eventually, the relation of this framework to tabular (chart) parsing was also illuminated (Nederhof and Satta 1996, 2004b). Finally, in contrast to the work based on phrase-structure grammar, there was a renewed interest in more restricted and performance-oriented notions of parsing, such as finite-state parsing (Church 1980, Ejerhed 1988) and deterministic parsing (Marcus 1980, Shieber 1983).

In the late 1980s and during the 1990s, two interrelated developments were particularly apparent: on the one hand, an interest in robust parsing, motivated by an increased involvement with unrestricted text and spontaneous speech (see Section 4.8.1), and on the other hand the revival of empiricism, leading to statistics-based methods being applied both on their own and in combination with grammar-driven parsing (see Chapter 11). These developments have continued during the first decade in the new millenium, along with a gradual closing of the divide between grammar-driven and statistical methods (Nivre 2002, Baldwin et al. 2007).

In sum, grammar-driven parsing is one of the oldest areas within natural language processing, and one whose methods continue to be a key component of much of what is carried out in the field. Grammar-driven approaches are essential when the goal is to achieve the precision and rigor of deep parsing, or when annotated corpora for supervised statistical approaches are unavailable. The latter situation holds both for the majority of the world's languages and frequently when systems are to be engineered for new application domains. But also in shallow and partial parsing, some of the most successful systems in terms of accuracy and efficiency are rule based. However, the best performing broad-coverage parsers for theoretical frameworks such as CCG, HPSG, LFG, TAG, and dependency grammar increasingly use statistical components for preprocessing (e.g., tagging) and/or postprocessing (by ranking competing analyses for the purpose of disambiguation). Thus, although grammar-driven approaches remain a basic framework for syntactic parsing, it appears that we can continue to look forward to an increasingly symbiotic relationship between grammar-driven and statistical methods.

Acknowledgments

We want to thank the reviewers, Alon Lavie and Mark-Jan Nederhof, for detailed and constructive comments on an earlier version of this chapter. We also want to thank Joakim Nivre for helpful comments and for discussions about the organization of the two parsing chapters (Chapters 4 and 11).

References

Abney, S. (1991). Parsing by chunks. In R. Berwick, S. Abney, and C. Tenny (Eds.), *Principle-Based Parsing*, pp. 257–278. Kluwer Academic Publishers, Dordrecht, the Netherlands.

Abney, S. (1997). Part-of-speech tagging and partial parsing. In S. Young and G. Bloothooft (Eds.), *Corpus-Based Methods in Language and Speech Processing*, pp. 118–136. Kluwer Academic Publishers, Dordrecht, the Netherlands.

Aho, A., M. Lam, R. Sethi, and J. Ullman (2006). *Compilers: Principles, Techniques, and Tools* (2nd ed.). Addison-Wesley, Reading, MA.

Aycock, J. and N. Horspool (2002). Practical Earley parsing. *The Computer Journal* 45(6), 620–630.

Aycock, J., N. Horspool, J. Janoušek, and B. Melichar (2001). Even faster generalized LR parsing. *Acta Informatica* 37(9), 633–651.

Backus, J. W., F. L. Bauer, J. Green, C. Katz, J. Mccarthy, A. J. Perlis, H. Rutishauser, K. Samelson, B. Vauquois, J. H. Wegstein, A. van Wijngaarden, and M. Woodger (1963). Revised report on the algorithm language ALGOL 60. *Communications of the ACM* 6(1), 1–17.

Baldwin, T., M. Dras, J. Hockenmaier, T. H. King, and G. van Noord (2007). The impact of deep linguistic processing on parsing technology. In *Proceedings of the 10th International Conference on Parsing Technologies, IWPT'07*, Prague, Czech Republic, pp. 36–38.

Bangalore, S. and A. K. Joshi (1999). Supertagging: An approach to almost parsing. *Computational Linguistics 25*(2), 237–265.

Bar-Hillel, Y., M. Perles, and E. Shamir (1964). On formal properties of simple phrase structure grammars. In Y. Bar-Hillel (Ed.), *Language and Information: Selected Essays on Their Theory and Application*, Chapter 9, pp. 116–150. Addison-Wesley, Reading, MA.

Barton, G. E., R. C. Berwick, and E. S. Ristad (1987). *Computational Complexity and Natural Language*. MIT Press, Cambridge, MA.

Billot, S. and B. Lang (1989). The structure of shared forests in ambiguous parsing. In *Proceedings of the 27th Annual Meeting of the Association for Computational Linguistics, ACL'89*, Vancouver, Canada, pp. 143–151.

Boullier, P. (2004). Range concatenation grammars. In H. Bunt, J. Carroll, and G. Satta (Eds.), *New Developments in Parsing Technology*, pp. 269–289. Kluwer Academic Publishers, Dordrecht, the Netherlands.

Boye, J. and M. Wirén (2008). Robust parsing and spoken negotiative dialogue with databases. *Natural Language Engineering 14*(3), 289–312.

Bresnan, J. (2001). *Lexical-Functional Syntax*. Blackwell, Oxford, U.K.

Briscoe, T. and J. Carroll (1993). Generalized probabilistic LR parsing of natural language (corpora) with unification-based grammars. *Computational Linguistics 19*(1), 25–59.

Burton, R. R. (1976). Semantic grammar: An engineering technique for constructing natural language understanding systems. BBN Report 3453, Bolt, Beranek, and Newman, Inc., Cambridge, MA.

Carpenter, B. (1992). *The Logic of Typed Feature Structures*. Cambridge University Press, New York.

Carroll, J. (1993). Practical unification-based parsing of natural language. PhD thesis, University of Cambridge, Cambridge, U.K. Computer Laboratory Technical Report 314.

Carroll, J. (1994). Relating complexity to practical performance in parsing with wide-coverage unification grammars. In *Proceedings of the 32nd Annual Meeting of the Association for Computational Linguistics, ACL'94*, Las Cruces, NM, pp. 287–294.

Chomsky, N. (1956). Three models for the description of language. *IRE Transactions on Information Theory 2*(3), 113–124.

Chomsky, N. (1959). On certain formal properties of grammars. *Information and Control 2*(2), 137–167.

Chomsky, N. (1965). *Aspects of the Theory of Syntax*. MIT Press, Cambridge, MA.

Church, K. W. (1980). On memory limitations in natural language processing. Report MIT/LCS/TM-216, Massachusetts Institute of Technology, Cambridge, MA.

Church, K. W. and R. Patil (1982). Coping with syntactic ambiguity or how to put the block in the box on the table. *Computational Linguistics 8*(3–4), 139–149.

Clark, S. and J. R. Curran (2004). The importance of supertagging for wide-coverage CCG parsing. In *Proceedings of the 20th International Conference on Computational Linguistics, COLING'04*, Geneva, Switzerland.

Coppersmith, D. and S. Winograd (1990). Matrix multiplication via arithmetic progressions. *Journal of Symbolic Computation 9*(3), 251–280.

Daniels, M. W. and D. Meurers (2004). A grammar formalism and parser for linearization-based HPSG. In *Proceedings of the 20th International Conference on Computational Linguistics, COLING'04*, Geneva, Switzerland, pp. 169–175.

de Groote, P. (2001). Towards abstract categorial grammars. In *Proceedings of the 39th Annual Meeting of the Association for Computational Linguistics, ACL'01*, Toulouse, France.

Earley, J. (1970). An efficient context-free parsing algorithm. *Communications of the ACM 13*(2), 94–102.

Eisner, J. (2000). Bilexical grammars and their cubic-time parsing algorithms. In H. Bunt and A. Nijholt (Eds.), *New Developments in Natural Language Parsing*. Kluwer Academic Publishers, Dordrecht, the Netherlands.

Eisner, J. and G. Satta (1999). Efficient parsing for bilexical context-free grammars and head automaton grammars. In *Proceedings of the 37th Annual Meeting of the Association for Computational Linguistics, ACL'99*, pp. 457–464.

Ejerhed, E. (1988). Finding clauses in unrestricted text by finitary and stochastic methods. In *Proceedings of the Second Conference on Applied Natural Language Processing*, Austin, TX, pp. 219–227.

Foth, K. and W. Menzel (2005). Robust parsing with weighted constraints. *Natural Language Engineering 11*(1), 1–25.

Gazdar, G., E. Klein, G. Pullum, and I. Sag (1985). *Generalized Phrase Structure Grammar*. Basil Blackwell, Oxford, U.K.

Grishman, R., N. T. Nhan, E. Marsh, and L. Hirschman (1984). Automated determination of sublanguage syntactic usage. In *Proceedings of the 10th International Conference on Computational Linguistics and 22nd Annual Meeting of the Association for Computational Linguistics, COLING-ACL'84*, Stanford, CA, pp. 96–100.

Harris, Z. S. (1962). *String Analysis of Sentence Structure*. Mouton, Hague, the Netherlands.

Hays, D. G. (1966). Parsing. In D. G. Hays (Ed.), *Readings in Automatic Language Processing*, pp. 73–82. American Elsevier Publishing Company, New York.

Hendrix, G. G., E. D. Sacerdoti, and D. Sagalowicz (1978). Developing a natural language interface to complex data. *ACM Transactions on Database Systems 3*(2), 105–147.

Hindle, D. (1989). Acquiring disambiguation rules from text. In *Proceedings of the 27th Annual Meeting of the Association for Computational Linguistics, ACL'89*, Vancouver, Canada, pp. 118–125.

Hindle, D. (1994). A parser for text corpora. In A. Zampolli (Ed.), *Computational Approaches to the Lexicon*. Oxford University Press, New York.

Hopcroft, J., R. Motwani, and J. Ullman (2006). *Introduction to Automata Theory, Languages, and Computation* (3rd ed.). Addison-Wesley, Boston, MA.

Jackson, E., D. Appelt, J. Bear, R. Moore, and A. Podlozny (1991). A template matcher for robust NL interpretation. In *Proceedings of the Workshop on Speech and Natural Language, HLT'91*, Pacific Grove, CA, pp. 190–194.

Jensen, K. and G. E. Heidorn (1983). The fitted parse: 100% parsing capability in a syntactic grammar of English. In *Proceedings of the First Conference on Applied Natural Language Processing*, Santa Monica, CA, pp. 93–98.

Joshi, A. K. (1997). Parsing techniques. In R. Cole, J. Mariani, H. Uszkoreit, A. Zaenen, and V. Zue (Eds.), *Survey of the State of the Art in Human Language Technology*, pp. 351–356. Cambridge University Press, Cambridge, MA.

Joshi, A. K. (1985). How much context-sensitivity is necessary for characterizing structural descriptions – tree adjoining grammars. In D. Dowty, L. Karttunen, and A. Zwicky (Eds.), *Natural Language Processing: Psycholinguistic, Computational and Theoretical Perspectives*, pp. 206–250. Cambridge University Press, New York.

Joshi, A. K. and P. Hopely (1996). A parser from antiquity: An early application of finite state transducers to natural language parsing. *Natural Language Engineering 2*(4), 291–294.

Joshi, A. K., L. S. Levy, and M. Takahashi (1975). Tree adjunct grammars. *Journal of Computer and System Sciences 10*(1), 136–163.

Joshi, A. K. and Y. Schabes (1997). Tree-adjoining grammars. In G. Rozenberg and A. Salomaa (Eds.), *Handbook of Formal Languages. Vol 3: Beyond Words*, Chapter 2, pp. 69–123. Springer-Verlag, Berlin.

Kaplan, R. and J. Bresnan (1982). Lexical-functional grammar: A formal system for grammatical representation. In J. Bresnan (Ed.), *The Mental Representation of Grammatical Relations*, pp. 173–281. MIT Press, Cambridge, MA.

Kaplan, R. M. (1973). A general syntactic processor. In R. Rustin (Ed.), *Natural Language Processing*, pp. 193–241. Algorithmics Press, New York.

Kaplan, R. M., S. Riezler, T. H. King, J. T. Maxwell III, A. Vasserman, and R. S. Crouch (2004). Speed and accuracy in shallow and deep stochastic parsing. In *Proceedings of Human Language Technology Conference of the North American Chapter of the Association for Computational Linguistics, HLT-NAACL'04*, Boston, MA, pp. 97–104.

Kaplan, R. M. and A. Zaenen (1995). Long-distance dependencies, constituent structure, and functional uncertainty. In R. M. Kaplan, M. Dalrymple, J. T. Maxwell, and A. Zaenen (Eds.), *Formal Issues in Lexical-Functional Grammar*, Chapter 3, pp. 137–165. CSLI Publications, Stanford, CA.

Karlsson, F., A. Voutilainen, J. Heikkilä, and A. Anttila (Eds.) (1995). *Constraint Grammar. A Language-Independent System for Parsing Unrestricted Text*. Mouton de Gruyter, Berlin, Germany.

Karttunen, L. (1986). D-PATR: A development environment for unification-based grammars. In *Proceedings of 11th International Conference on Computational Linguistics, COLING'86*, Bonn, Germany.

Karttunen, L. and A. M. Zwicky (1985). Introduction. In D. Dowty, L. Karttunen, and A. Zwicky (Eds.), *Natural Language Processing: Psycholinguistic, Computational and Theoretical Perspectives*, pp. 1–25. Cambridge University Press, New York.

Kasami, T. (1965). An efficient recognition and syntax algorithm for context-free languages. Technical Report AFCLR-65-758, Air Force Cambridge Research Laboratory, Bedford, MA.

Kasper, R. T. and W. C. Rounds (1986). A logical semantics for feature structures. In *Proceedings of the 24th Annual Meeting of the Association for Computational Linguistics, ACL'86*, New York, pp. 257–266.

Kasper, W., B. Kiefer, H. U. Krieger, C. J. Rupp, and K. L. Worm (1999). Charting the depths of robust speech parsing. In *Proceedings of the 37th Annual Meeting of the Association for Computational Linguistics, ACL'99*, College Park, MD, pp. 405–412.

Kay, M. (1967). Experiments with a powerful parser. In *Proceedings of the Second International Conference on Computational Linguistics [2ème conférence internationale sur le traitement automatique des langues], COLING'67*, Grenoble, France.

Kay, M. (1973). The MIND system. In R. Rustin (Ed.), *Natural Language Processing*, pp. 155–188. Algorithmics Press, New York.

Kay, M. (1986). Algorithm schemata and data structures in syntactic processing. In B. Grosz, K. S. Jones, and B. L. Webber (Eds.), *Readings in Natural Language Processing*, pp. 35–70, Morgan Kaufmann Publishers, Los Altos, CA. Originally published as Report CSL-80-12, Xerox PARC, Palo Alto, CA, 1980.

Kay, M. (1989). Head-driven parsing. In *Proceedings of the First International Workshop on Parsing Technologies, IWPT'89*, Pittsburgh, PA.

Kay, M. (1999). Chart translation. In *Proceedings of the MT Summit VII*, Singapore, pp. 9–14.

Kipps, J. R. (1991). GLR parsing in time $O(n^3)$. In M. Tomita (Ed.), *Generalized LR Parsing*, Chapter 4, pp. 43–59. Kluwer Academic Publishers, Boston, MA.

Knuth, D. E. (1965). On the translation of languages from left to right. *Information and Control 8*, 607–639.

Kuno, S. and A. G. Oettinger (1962). Multiple-path syntactic analyzer. In *Proceedings of the IFIP Congress*, Munich, Germany, pp. 306–312.

Lang, B. (1974). Deterministic techniques for efficient non-deterministic parsers. In J. Loeckx (Ed.), *Proceedings of the Second Colloquium on Automata, Languages and Programming*, Saarbrücken, Germany, Volume 14 of *LNCS*, pp. 255–269. Springer-Verlag, London, U.K.

Lavie, A. (1996). GLR*: A robust parser for spontaneously spoken language. In *Proceedings of the ESSLLI'96 Workshop on Robust Parsing*, Prague, Czech Republic.

Lavie, A. and C. P. Rosé (2004). Optimal ambiguity packing in context-free parsers with interleaved unification. In H. Bunt, J. Carroll, and G. Satta (Eds.), *New Developments in Parsing Technology*, pp. 307–321. Kluwer Academic Publishers, Dordrecht, the Netherlands.

Lavie, A. and M. Tomita (1996). GLR*—an efficient noise-skipping parsing algorithm for context-free grammars. In H. Bunt and M. Tomita (Eds.), *Recent Advances in Parsing Technology*, Chapter 10, pp. 183–200. Kluwer Academic Publishers, Dordrecht, the Netherlands.

Lee, L. (2002). Fast context-free grammar parsing requires fast Boolean matrix multiplication. *Journal of the ACM 49*(1), 1–15.

Leiss, H. (1990). On Kilbury's modification of Earley's algorithm. *ACM Transactions on Programming Language and Systems 12*(4), 610–640.

Ljunglöf, P. (2004). Expressivity and complexity of the grammatical framework. PhD thesis, University of Gothenburg and Chalmers University of Technology, Gothenburg, Sweden.

Marcus, M. P. (1980). *A Theory of Syntactic Recognition for Natural Language*. MIT Press, Cambridge, MA.

Mellish, C. S. (1989). Some chart-based techniques for parsing ill-formed input. In *Proceedings of the 27th Annual Meeting of the Association for Computational Linguistics, ACL'89*, Vancouver, Canada, pp. 102–109.

Menzel, W. (1995). Robust processing of natural language. In *Proceedings of the 19th Annual German Conference on Artificial Intelligence*, Bielefeld, Germany.

Moore, R. C. (2000). Time as a measure of parsing efficiency. In *Proceedings of the COLING'00 Workshop on Efficiency in Large-Scale Parsing Systems*, Luxembourg.

Moore, R. C. (2004). Improved left-corner chart parsing for large context-free grammars. In H. Bunt, J. Carroll, and G. Satta (Eds.), *New Developments in Parsing Technology*, pp. 185–201. Kluwer Academic Publishers, Dordrecht, the Netherlands.

Nakazawa, T. (1991). An extended LR parsing algorithm for grammars using feature-based syntactic categories. In *Proceedings of the Fifth Conference of the European Chapter of the Association for Computational Linguistics, EACL'91*, Berlin, Germany.

Nederhof, M.-J. and J. Sarbo (1996). Increasing the applicability of LR parsing. In H. Bunt and M. Tomita (Eds.), *Recent Advances in Parsing Technology*, pp. 35–58. Kluwer Academic Publishers, Dordrecht, the Netherlands.

Nederhof, M.-J. and G. Satta (1996). Efficient tabular LR parsing. In *Proceedings of the 34th Annual Meeting of the Association for Computational Linguistics, ACL'96*, Santa Cruz, CA, pp. 239–246.

Nederhof, M.-J. and G. Satta (2004a). IDL-expressions: A formalism for representing and parsing finite languages in natural language processing. *Journal of Artificial Intelligence Research 21*, 287–317.

Nederhof, M.-J. and G. Satta (2004b). Tabular parsing. In C. Martin-Vide, V. Mitrana, and G. Paun (Eds.), *Formal Languages and Applications*, Volume 148 of *Studies in Fuzziness and Soft Computing*, pp. 529–549. Springer-Verlag, Berlin, Germany.

Nivre, J. (2002). On statistical methods in natural language processing. In J. Bubenko, Jr. and B. Wangler (Eds.), *Promote IT: Second Conference for the Promotion of Research in IT at New Universities and University Colleges in Sweden*, pp. 684–694, University of Skövde.

Nivre, J. (2006). *Inductive Dependency Parsing*. Springer-Verlag, New York.

Nozohoor-Farshi, R. (1991). GLR parsing for ε-grammars. In M. Tomita (Ed.), *Generalized LR Parsing*. Kluwer Academic Publishers, Boston, MA.

Oepen, S. and J. Carroll (2002). Efficient parsing for unification-based grammars. In H. U. D. Flickinger, S. Oepen and J.-I. Tsujii (Eds.), *Collaborative Language Engineering: A Case Study in Efficient Grammar-based Processing*, pp. 195–225. CSLI Publications, Stanford, CA.

Oepen, S., D. Flickinger, H. Uszkoreit, and J.-I. Tsujii (2000). Introduction to this special issue. *Natural Language Engineering 6*(1), 1–14.

Pereira, F. C. N. and S. M. Shieber (1984). The semantics of grammar formalisms seen as computer languages. In *Proceedings of the 10th International Conference on Computational Linguistics, COLING'84*, Stanford, CA, pp. 123–129.

Pereira, F. C. N. and S. M. Shieber (1987). *Prolog and Natural-Language Analysis*, Volume 4 of *CSLI Lecture Notes*. CSLI Publications, Stanford, CA. Reissued in 2002 by Microtome Publishing.

Pereira, F. C. N. and D. H. D. Warren (1983). Parsing as deduction. In *Proceedings of the 21st Annual Meeting of the Association for Computational Linguistics, ACL'83*, Cambridge, MA, pp. 137–144.

Pollard, C. and I. Sag (1994). *Head-Driven Phrase Structure Grammar*. University of Chicago Press, Chicago, IL.

Pratt, V. R. (1975). LINGOL – a progress report. In *Proceedings of the Fourth International Joint Conference on Artificial Intelligence*, Tbilisi, Georgia, USSR, pp. 422–428.

Ranta, A. (1994). *Type-Theoretical Grammar*. Oxford University Press, Oxford, U.K.

Ranta, A. (2004). Grammatical framework, a type-theoretical grammar formalism. *Journal of Functional Programming 14*(2), 145–189.

Rayner, M., D. Carter, P. Bouillon, V. Digalakis, and M. Wirén (2000). *The Spoken Language Translator*. Cambridge University Press, Cambridge, U.K.

Rayner, M., B. A. Hockey, and P. Bouillon (2006). *Putting Linguistics into Speech Recognition: The Regulus Grammar Compiler*. CSLI Publications, Stanford, CA.

Robinson, J. A. (1965). A machine-oriented logic based on the resolution principle. *Journal of the ACM 12*(1), 23–49.

Rosé, C. P. and A. Lavie (2001). Balancing robustness and efficiency in unification-augmented context-free parsers for large practical applications. In J.-C. Junqua and G. van Noord (Eds.), *Robustness in Language and Speech Technology*. Kluwer Academic Publishers, Dordrecht, the Netherlands.

Samuelsson, C. (1994). Notes on LR parser design. In *Proceedings of the 15th International Conference on Computational Linguistics*, Kyoto, Japan, pp. 386–390.

Samuelsson, C. and M. Rayner (1991). Quantitative evaluation of explanation-based learning as an optimization tool for a large-scale natural language system. In *Proceedings of the 12th International Joint Conference on Artificial Intelligence*, Sydney, Australia, pp. 609–615.

Sapir, E. (1921). *Language: An Introduction to the Study of Speech*. Harcourt Brace & Co. Orlando, FL.

Satta, G. (1992). Recognition of linear context-free rewriting systems. In *Proceedings of the 30th Annual Meeting of the Association for Computational Linguistics, ACL'92*, Newark, DE, pp. 89–95.

Scott, E. and A. Johnstone (2006). Right nulled GLR parsers. *ACM Transactions on Programming Languages and Systems 28*(4), 577–618.

Scott, E., A. Johnstone, and R. Economopoulos (2007). BRNGLR: A cubic Tomita-style GLR parsing algorithm. *Acta Informatica 44*(6), 427–461.

Seki, H., T. Matsumara, M. Fujii, and T. Kasami (1991). On multiple context-free grammars. *Theoretical Computer Science 88*, 191–229.

Shieber, S. M. (1983). Sentence disambiguation by a shift-reduce parsing technique. In *Proceedings of the 21st Annual Meeting of the Association for Computational Linguistics, ACL'83*, Cambridge, MA, pp. 113–118.

Shieber, S. M. (1985a). Evidence against the context-freeness of natural language. *Linguistics and Philosophy 8*(3), 333–343.

Shieber, S. M. (1985b). Using restriction to extend parsing algorithms for complex-feature-based formalisms. In *Proceedings of the 23rd Annual Meeting of the Association for Computational Linguistics, ACL'85*, Chicago, IL, pp. 145–152.

Shieber, S. M. (1986). *An Introduction to Unification-based Approaches to Grammar*. Volume 4 of CSLI Lecture Notes. University of Chicago Press, Chicago, IL.

Shieber, S. M. (1992). *Constraint-Based Grammar Formalisms*. MIT Press, Cambridge, MA.

Shieber, S. M., Y. Schabes, and F. C. N. Pereira (1995). Principles and implementation of deductive parsing. *Journal of Logic Programming 24*(1–2), 3–36.

Shieber, S. M., H. Uszkoreit, F. C. N. Pereira, J. J. Robinson, and M. Tyson (1983). The formalism and implementation of PATR-II. In B. J. Grosz and M. E. Stickel (Eds.), *Research on Interactive Acquisition and Use of Knowledge*, Final Report, SRI project number 1894, pp. 39–79. SRI International, Melano Park, CA.

Sikkel, K. (1998). Parsing schemata and correctness of parsing algorithms. *Theoretical Computer Science 199*, 87–103.

Sikkel, K. and A. Nijholt (1997). Parsing of context-free languages. In G. Rozenberg and A. Salomaa (Eds.), *The Handbook of Formal Languages*, Volume II, pp. 61–100. Springer-Verlag, Berlin, Germany.

Slocum, J. (1981). A practical comparison of parsing strategies. In *Proceedings of the 19th Annual Meeting of the Association for Computational Linguistics, ACL'81*, Stanford, CA, pp. 1–6.

Steedman, M. (1985). Dependency and coordination in the grammar of Dutch and English. *Language 61*, 523–568.

Steedman, M. (1986). Combinators and grammars. In R. Oehrle, E. Bach, and D. Wheeler (Eds.), *Categorial Grammars and Natural Language Structures*, pp. 417–442. Foris Publications, Dordrecht, the Netherlands.

Steedman, M. J. (1983). Natural and unnatural language processing. In K. Sparck Jones and Y. Wilks (Eds.), *Automatic Natural Language Parsing*, pp. 132–140. Ellis Horwood, Chichester, U.K.

Tesnière, L. (1959). *Éléments de Syntaxe Structurale*. Libraire C. Klincksieck, Paris, France.

Thompson, H. S. (1981). Chart parsing and rule schemata in GPSG. In *Proceedings of the 19th Annual Meeting of the Association for Computational Linguistics, ACL'81*, Stanford, CA, pp. 167–172.

Thompson, H. S. (1983). MCHART: A flexible, modular chart parsing system. In *Proceedings of the Third National Conference on Artificial Intelligence*, Washington, DC, pp. 408–410.

Tomita, M. (1985). *Efficient Parsing for Natural Language*. Kluwer Academic Publishers, Norwell, MA.

Tomita, M. (1987). An efficient augmented context-free parsing algorithm. *Computational Linguistics 13*(1–2), 31–46.

Tomita, M. (1988). Graph-structured stack and natural language parsing. In *Proceedings of the 26th Annual Meeting of the Association for Computational Linguistics, ACL'88*, University of New York at Buffalo, Buffalo, NY.

Toutanova, K., C. D. Manning, S. M. Shieber, D. Flickinger, and S. Oepen (2002). Parse disambiguation for a rich HPSG grammar. In *Proceedings of the First Workshop on Treebanks and Linguistic Theories*, Sozopol, Bulgaria, pp. 253–263.

Valiant, L. (1975). General context-free recognition in less than cubic time. *Journal of Computer and Systems Sciences 10*(2), 308–315.

van Noord, G. (1997). An efficient implementation of the head-corner parser. *Computational Linguistics 23*(3), 425–456.

van Noord, G., G. Bouma, R. Koeling, and M.-J. Nederhof (1999). Robust grammatical analysis for spoken dialogue systems. *Natural Language Engineering 5*(1), 45–93.

Vijay-Shanker, K. and D. Weir (1993). Parsing some constrained grammar formalisms. *Computational Linguistics 19*(4), 591–636.

Vijay-Shanker, K. and D. Weir (1994). The equivalence of four extensions of context-free grammars. *Mathematical Systems Theory 27*(6), 511–546.

Vijay-Shanker, K., D. Weir, and A. K. Joshi (1987). Characterizing structural descriptions produced by various grammatical formalisms. In *Proceedings of the 25th Annual Meeting of the Association for Computational Linguistics, ACL'87*, Stanford, CA.

Ward, W. (1989). Understanding spontaneous speech. In *Proceedings of the Workshop on Speech and Natural Language, HLT '89*, Philadelphia, PA, pp. 137–141.

Wirén, M. (1987). A comparison of rule-invocation strategies in context-free chart parsing. In *Proceedings of the Third Conference of the European Chapter of the Association for Computational Linguistics EACL'87*, Copenhagen, Denmark.

Woods, W. A. (1970). Transition network grammars for natural language analysis. *Communications of the ACM 13*(10), 591–606.

Woods, W. A. (1973). An experimental parsing system for transition network grammars. In R. Rustin (Ed.), *Natural Language Processing*, pp. 111–154. Algorithmics Press, New York.

Woods, W. A., R. M. Kaplan, and B. Nash-Webber (1972). The lunar sciences natural language information system: final report. BBN Report 2378, Bolt, Beranek, and Newman, Inc., Cambridge, MA.

Yngve, V. H. (1955). Syntax and the problem of multiple meaning. In W. N. Locke and A. D. Booth (Eds.), *Machine Translation of Languages*, pp. 208–226. MIT Press, Cambridge, MA.

Younger, D. H. (1967). Recognition of context-free languages in time n^3. *Information and Control 10*(2), 189–208.

5

Semantic Analysis

Cliff Goddard
University of New England

Andrea C. Schalley
Griffith University

A classic NLP interpretation of semantic analysis was provided by Poesio (2000) in the first edition of the *Handbook of Natural Language Processing*:

> The ultimate goal, for humans as well as natural language-processing (NLP) systems, is to under-
> stand the utterance—which, depending on the circumstances, may mean incorporating information
> provided by the utterance into one's own knowledge base or, more in general performing some
> action in response to it. 'Understanding' an utterance is a complex process, that depends on the
> results of parsing, as well as on lexical information, context, and commonsense reasoning... (Poesio
> 2000: 93).

For extended texts, specific NLP applications of semantic analysis may include information retrieval, information extraction, text summarization, data-mining, and machine translation and translation aids. Semantic analysis is also pertinent for much shorter texts, right down to the single word level, for example, in understanding user queries and matching user requirements to available data. Semantic analysis is also of high relevance in efforts to improve Web ontologies and knowledge representation systems.

Two important themes form the grounding for the discussion in this chapter. First, there is great value in conducting semantic analysis, as far as possible, in such a way as to reflect the cognitive reality of ordinary speakers. This makes it easier to model the intuitions of native speakers and to simulate their inferencing processes, and it facilitates human–computer interactions via querying processes, and the like. Second, there is concern over to what extent it will be possible to achieve comparability, and, more ambitiously, interoperability, between different systems of semantic description. For both reasons, it is highly desirable if semantic analyses can be conducted in terms of intuitive representations, be it in simple ordinary language or by way of other intuitively accessible representations.

5.1 Basic Concepts and Issues in Natural Language Semantics

In general linguistics, semantic analysis refers to analyzing the meanings of words, fixed expressions, whole sentences, and utterances in context. In practice, this means translating original expressions into some kind of semantic metalanguage. The major theoretical issues in semantic analysis therefore turn on the nature of the metalanguage or equivalent representational system (see Section 5.2). Many approaches under the influence of philosophical logic have restricted themselves to truth-conditional meaning, but such analyses are too narrow to enable a comprehensive account of ordinary language use or to enable many practically required applications, especially those involving human–computer interfacing or naïve reasoning by ordinary users. Unfortunately, there is even less consensus in the field of linguistic semantics than in other subfields of linguistics, such as syntax, morphology, and phonology. NLP practitioners interested in semantic analysis nevertheless need to become familiar with standard concepts and procedures in semantics and lexicology. The following is a tutorial introduction. It will provide the reader with foundational knowledge on linguistic semantics. It is not intended to give an overview of applications within computational linguistics or to introduce hands-on methods, but rather aims to provide basic theoretical background and references necessary for further study, as well as three case studies.

There is a traditional division made between lexical semantics, which concerns itself with the meanings of words and fixed word combinations, and supralexical (combinational, or compositional) semantics, which concerns itself with the meanings of the indefinitely large number of word combinations—phrases and sentences—allowable under the grammar. While there is some obvious appeal and validity to this division, it is increasingly recognized that word-level semantics and grammatical semantics interact and interpenetrate in various ways. Many linguists now prefer to speak of lexicogrammar, rather than to maintain a strict lexicon-grammar distinction. In part, this is because it is evident that the combinatorial potential of words is largely determined by their meanings, in part because it is clear that many grammatical constructions have construction-specific meanings; for example, the construction *to have a VP* (*to have a drink, a swim*, etc.) has meaning components additional to those belonging to the words involved (Wierzbicka 1982; Goldberg 1995; Goddard 2000; Fried and Östman 2004). Despite the artificiality of rigidly separating lexical semantics from other domains of semantic analysis, lexical semantics remains the locus of many of the hard problems, especially in crosslinguistic contexts. Partly this is because lexical semantics has received relatively little attention in syntax-driven models of language or in formal (logic-based) semantics.

It is widely recognized that the overriding problems in semantic analysis are how to avoid circularity and how to avoid infinite regress. Most approaches concur that the solution is to ground the analysis in a terminal set of primitive elements, but they differ on the nature of the primitives (are they elements of natural language or creations of the analyst? are they of a structural-procedural nature or more encompassing than this? are they language-specific or universal?). Approaches also differ on the extent to which they envisage that semantic analysis can be precise and exhaustive (how fine-grained can one expect a semantic analysis to be? are semantic analyses expected to be complete or can they be underspecified? if the latter, how exactly are the missing details to be filled in?).

A major divide in semantic theory turns on the question of whether it is possible to draw a strict line between semantic content, in the sense of content encoded in the lexicogrammar, and general encyclopedic knowledge. Whatever one's position on this issue, it is universally acknowledged that ordinary language use involves a more or less seamless integration of linguistic knowledge, cultural conventions, and real-world knowledge.

In general terms, the primary evidence for linguistic semantics comes from native speaker interpretations of the use of linguistic expressions in context (including their entailments and implications), from naturalistic observation of language in use, and from the distribution of linguistic expressions, that is, patterns of usage, collocation, and frequency, discoverable using the techniques of corpus linguistics (see Chapter 7).

One frequently identified requirement for semantic analysis in NLP goes under the heading of ambiguity resolution. From a machine point of view, many human utterances are open to multiple interpretations, because words may have more than one meaning (lexical ambiguity), or because certain words, such as quantifiers, modals, or negative operators may apply to different stretches of text (scopal ambiguity), or because the intended reference of pronouns or other referring expressions may be unclear (referential ambiguity).

In relation to lexical ambiguities, it is usual to distinguish between homonymy (different words with the same form, either in sound or writing, for example, *light* (vs. *dark*) and *light* (vs. *heavy*), *son* and *sun*, and polysemy (different senses of the same word, for example, the several senses of the words *hot* and *see*). Both phenomena are problematical for NLP, but polysemy poses greater problems, because the meaning differences concerned, and the associated syntactic and other formal differences, are typically more subtle. Mishandling of polysemy is a common failing of semantic analysis: both the positing of false polysemy and failure to recognize real polysemy (Wierzbicka 1996: Chap. 9; Goddard 2000). The former problem is very common in conventional dictionaries, including Collins Cobuild and Longman, and also in WordNet. The latter is more common in theoretical semantics, where theorists are often reluctant to face up to the complexities of lexical meanings. Further problems for lexical semantics are posed by the widespread existence of figurative expressions and/or multi-word units (fixed expressions such as *by and large*, *be carried away*, or *kick the bucket*), whose meanings are not predictable from the meanings of the individual words taken separately.

5.2 Theories and Approaches to Semantic Representation

Various theories and approaches to semantic representation can be roughly ranged along two dimensions: (1) formal vs. cognitive and (2) compositional vs. lexical. Formal theories have been strongly advocated since the late 1960s (e.g., Montague 1973, 1974; Cann 1994; Lappin 1997; Portner and Partee 2002; Gutiérrez-Rexach 2003), while cognitive approaches have become popular in the last three decades (e.g., Fauconnier 1985; Johnson 1987; Lakoff 1987; Langacker 1987, 1990, 1991; Jackendoff 1990, 2002; Wierzbicka 1988, 1992, 1996; Talmy 2000; Geeraerts 2002; Croft and Cruse 2003; Cruse 2004), driven also by influences from cognitive science and psychology. Compositional semantics is concerned with the bottom-up construction of meaning, starting with the lexical items, whose meanings are generally treated as given, that is, are left unanalyzed. Lexical semantics, on the other hand, aims at precisely analyzing the meanings of lexical items, either by analyzing their internal structure and content (decompositional approaches) or by representing their relations to other elements in the lexicon (relational approaches, see Section 5.3).

This section surveys some of the theories and approaches, though due to limitations of space this can only be done in a cursory fashion. Several approaches will have to remain unmentioned here, but the interested reader is referred to the accompanying wiki for an expanded reading list. We will start with a formal-compositional approach and move toward more cognitive-lexical approaches.

5.2.1 Logical Approaches

Logical approaches to meaning generally address problems in compositionality, on the assumption (the so-called *principle of compositionality*, attributed to Frege) that the meanings of supralexical expressions are determined by the meanings of their parts and the way in which those parts are combined.

There is no universal logic that covers all aspects of linguistic meaning and characterizes all valid arguments or relationships between the meanings of linguistic expressions (Gamut 1991 Vol. I: 7). Different logical systems have been and are being developed for linguistic semantics and NLP. The most well known and widespread is predicate logic, in which properties of sets of objects can be expressed via predicates, logical connectives, and quantifiers. This is done by providing a "syntax" (i.e., a specification how the elements of the logical language can be combined to form well-formed logical expressions) and a "semantics" (an interpretation of the logical expressions, a specification of what these expressions mean within the logical system). Examples of predicate logic representations are given in (1b) and (2b), which represent the semantic interpretation or meaning of the sentences in (1a) and (2a), respectively. In these formulae, x is a 'variable,' k a 'term' (denoting a particular object or entity), **politician, mortal, like,** etc. are predicates (of different arity), ∧, → are 'connectives,' and ∃, ∀ are the existential quantifier and universal quantifier, respectively. Negation can also be expressed in predicate logic, using the symbol ¬ or a variant.

(1) a. *Some politicians are mortal.*
    b. $\exists x\,(\mathbf{politician}(x) \wedge \mathbf{mortal}(x))$
       [There is an x (at least one) so that x is a politician and x is mortal.]
(2) a. *All Australian students like Kevin Rudd.*
    b. $\forall x\,((\mathbf{student}(x) \wedge \mathbf{Australian}(x)) \rightarrow \mathbf{like}(x, k))$
       [For all x with x being a student and Australian, x likes Kevin Rudd.]

Notice that, as mentioned, there is no analysis of the meanings of the predicates, which correspond to the lexical items in the original sentences, for example, *politician, mortal, student,* etc. Notice also the "constructed" and somewhat artificial sounding character of the example sentences concerned, which is typical of much work in the logical tradition.

Predicate logic also includes a specification of valid conclusions or inferences that can be drawn: a proof theory comprises inference rules whose operation determines which sentences must be true given that some other sentences are true (Poesio 2000). The best known example of such an inference rule is the rule of *modus ponens*: If P is the case and P → Q is the case, then Q is the case (cf. (3)):

(3) a. Modus ponens:
       (i) P (premise)
       (ii) P → Q (premise)
       (iii) Q (conclusion)
    b. (i) *Conrad is tired*   (P: **tired**(c))
       (ii) *Whenever Conrad is tired, he sleeps*   (P: **tired**(c), Q: **sleep**(c), P → Q)
       (iii) *Conrad sleeps*   (Q: **sleep**(c))

In the interpretation of sentences in formal semantics, the meaning of a sentence is often equated with its truth conditions, that is, the conditions under which the sentence is true. This has led to an application of model theory (Dowty et al. 1981) to natural language semantics. The logical language is interpreted in a way that for the logical statements general truth conditions are formulated, which result in concrete truth values under concrete models (or possible worlds). An alternative approach to truth-conditional and possible world semantics is situation semantics (Barwise and Perry 1983), in which situations rather than truth values are assigned to sentences as referents.

Although sometimes presented as a general-purpose theory of knowledge, predicate logic is not powerful enough to represent the intricacies of semantic meaning and is fundamentally different from human reasoning (Poesio 2000). It has nevertheless found application in logic programming, which in turn has been successfully applied in linguistic semantics (e.g., Lambalgen and Hamm 2005). For detailed introductions to logic formalisms, including lambda calculus and typed logical approaches,* see Gamut (1991) and Blackburn and Bos (2005). Amongst other things, lambda calculus provides a way of converting open formulae (those containing free variables) into complex one-place predicates to allow their use as predicates in other formulae. For instance, in **student**(x) ∧ **Australian**(x) the variable x is

---

* Types are assigned to expression parts, allowing the computation of the overall expression's type. This allows the well-formedness of a sentence to be checked. If α is an expression of type <m, n>, and β is an expression of type m, then the application of α to β, α(β), will have the type n. In linguistic semantics, variables and terms are generally assigned the type e ('entity'), and formulae the type t ('truth value'). Then one-place predicates have the type <e, t>: The application of the one-place predicate **sleep** to the term c (*Conrad*) yields the type t formula **sleep**(c).

not bound. The lambda operator λ converts this open formula into a complex one-place predicate: λx (**student**(x) ∧ **Australian**(x)), which is read as "those x for which it is the case that they are a student and Australian."

5.2.2 Discourse Representation Theory

Discourse representation theory (DRT) was developed in the early 1980s by Kamp (1981) (cf. Kamp and Reyle 1993; Blackburn and Bos 1999; van Eijck 2006; Geurts and Beaver 2008) in order to capture the semantics of discourses or texts, that is, coherent sequences of sentences or utterances, as opposed to isolated sentences or utterances. The basic idea is that as a discourse or text unfolds the hearer builds up a mental representation (represented by a so-called discourse representation structure, DRS), and that every incoming sentence prompts additions to this representation. It is thus a dynamic approach to natural language semantics (as it is in the similar, independently developed File Change Semantics (Heim 1982, 1983)).

DRT formally requires the following components (Geurts and Beaver 2008): (1) a formal definition of the representation language, consisting of (a) a recursive definition of the set of all well-formed DRSs, and (b) a model-theoretic semantics for the members of this set; and (2) a construction procedure specifying how a DRS is to be extended when new information becomes available.

A DRS consists of a universe of so-called discourse referents (these represent the objects under discussion in the discourse), and conditions applying to these discourse referents (these encode the information that has been accumulated on the discourse referents and are given in first-order predicate logic). A simple example is given in (4). As (4) shows, a DRS is presented in a graphical format, as a rectangle with two compartments. The discourse referents are listed in the upper compartment and the conditions are given in the lower compartment. The two discourse referents in the example (x and y) denote *a man* and *he*, respectively. In the example, *a man* and *he* are anaphorically linked through the condition y = x, that is, the pronoun *he* refers back to *a man*. The linking itself is achieved as part of the construction procedure referred to above.

(4) *A man sleeps. He snores.*

x, y
man (x)
sleep (x)
y = x
snore (y)

Recursiveness is an important feature. DRSs can comprise conditions that contain other DRSs. An example is given in (5). Notice that according to native speaker intuition this sequence is anomalous: though on the face of it *every man* is a singular noun-phrase, the pronoun *he* cannot refer back to it.

(5) *Every man sleeps. He snores.*

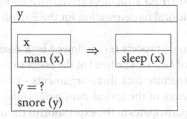

In the DRT representation, the quantification in the first sentence of (5) results in an if-then condition: if x is a man, then x sleeps. This condition is expressed through a conditional (A ⇒ B) involving two DRSs. This results in x being declared at a lower level than y, namely, in the nested DRS that is part of the conditional, which means that x is not an accessible discourse referent for y, and hence that *every man* cannot be an antecedent for *he*, in correspondence with native speaker intuition.

The DRT approach is well suited to dealing with indefinite noun phrases (and the question of when to introduce a new discourse referent, cf. also Karttunen 1976), presupposition, quantification, tense, and anaphora resolution. Discourse Representation Theory is thus seen as having "enabled perspicuous treatments of a range of natural language phenomena that have proved recalcitrant over many years" (Geurts and Beaver 2008) to formal approaches. In addition, inference systems have been developed (Saurer 1993; Kamp and Reyle 1996) and implementations employing Prolog (Blackburn and Bos 1999, 2005). Extensions of DRT have also been developed. For the purposes of NLP, the most relevant is Segmented Discourse Representation Theory (SDRT; Asher 1993; Asher and Lascarides 2003). It combines the insights of DRT and dynamic semantics on anaphora with a theory of discourse structure in which each clause plays one or more rhetorical functions within the discourse and entertains rhetorical relations to other clauses, such as "explanation," "elaboration," "narration," and "contrast."

5.2.3 Pustejovsky's Generative Lexicon

Another dynamic view of semantics, but focusing on lexical items, is Pustejovsky's (1991a,b, 1995, 2001) Generative Lexicon theory. He states: "our aim is to provide an adequate description of how our language expressions have content, and how this content appears to undergo continuous modification and modulation in new contexts" (Pustejovsky 2001: 52).

Pustejovsky posits that within particular contexts, lexical items assume different senses. For example, the adjective *good* is understood differently in the following four contexts: (a) *a good umbrella* (an umbrella that guards well against rain), (b) *a good meal* (a meal that is delicious or nourishing), (c) *a good teacher* (a teacher who educates well), (d) *a good movie* (a movie that is entertaining or thought provoking). He develops "the idea of a lexicon in which senses [of words/lexical items, CG/AS] in context can be flexibly derived on the basis of a rich multilevel representation and generative devices" (Behrens 1998: 108). This lexicon is characterized as a computational system, with the multilevel representation involving at least the following four levels (Pustejovsky 1995: 61):

1. *Argument structure*: Specification of number and type of logical arguments and how they are realized syntactically.
2. *Event structure*: Definition of the event type of a lexical item and a phrase. The event type sorts include states, processes, and transitions; sub-event structuring is possible.
3. *Qualia structure*: Modes of explanation, comprising qualia (singular: quale) of four kinds: *constitutive* (what an object is made of), *formal* (what an object is—that which distinguishes it within a larger domain), *telic* (what the purpose or function of an object is), and *agentive* (how the object came into being, factors involved in its origin or coming about).
4. *Lexical Inheritance Structure*: Identification of how a lexical structure is related to other structures in the lexicon and its contribution to the global organization of a lexicon.

The multilevel representation is given in a structure similar to HPSG structures (Head Driven Phrase Structure Grammar; Pollard and Sag 1994). An example of the lexical representation for the English verb *build* is given in Figure 5.1 (Pustejovsky 1995: 82).

The event structure shows that *build* is analyzed as involving a process (e_1) followed by a resultant state (e_2) and ordered by the relation "exhaustive ordered part of ($<_\alpha$)." The head of the event structure, and hence foregrounded, is the process e_1. The argument structure lists three arguments—two true arguments (ARG$_1$, ARG$_2$) that are syntactically realized parameters of the lexical item *build* (*John built a house*), and one default argument (D-ARG$_1$), a parameter that participates in the expression of the qualia but is not necessarily expressed syntactically (*John built a house out of bricks*). For the arguments, their characteristics are being noted in that their ontological restriction and qualia are listed: ARG$_1$, for instance, is restricted to arguments that are animate individuals and of a physical nature, while ARG$_2$ is—also a physical object—an artifact and made out of D-ARG$_1$ (as the cross-reference via the boxed number '3'

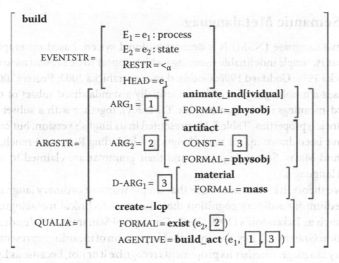

FIGURE 5.1 The lexical representation for the English verb *build*. (From Pustejovsky, J., *The Generative Lexicon*, MIT Press, Cambridge, MA, 1995, 92. With permission.)

indicates). The qualia structure outlines that *build* is overall a **create** eventity (event or similar entity, cf. Zaefferer 2002), and that what is created comes about by a **build_act**—a process (e_1) performed by ARG$_1$ ('1') and using D-ARG$_1$ ('3'). The result is the **exist** resultant state (e_2) of ARG$_2$. Notice that expressions such as **create, build_act, physobj** (physical object), etc., are taken as givens, that is, they are not analyzed, although they are embedded in inheritance structures.

The generative devices in Pustejovsky's system connect the levels of representation with the aim of providing the compositional interpretation of the lexical elements in context. They include those listed below (Pustejovsky 1995: 61–62). For further details and a formalization of the generative devices, see Pustejovsky (1995, esp. Chap. 7).

1. *Type coercion*: A lexically governed type shifting; a semantic operation that converts an argument to the type which is expected by a function, where it would otherwise result in a type error (Pustejovsky 1995: 111). For example, if *want* is assumed to have a proposition as an argument, the non-propositional argument *a beer* in *Mary wants a beer* is coerced into a propositional type (on the basis of the telic quale of *beer drinking*); hence, *Mary wants a beer* amounts to 'Mary wants to drink a beer.'

2. *Selective binding*: A lexical item operates specifically on the substructure of a phrase, without changing the overall type in the composition—an adjective can modify a particular aspect of noun qualia structure it is in composition with. For example, *a good knife* describes a knife in which the cutting is good (i.e., which cuts well): the adjective *good* functions as an event predicate and is able to selectively modify the event description in the telic quale of the noun (which is cutting).

3. *Co-composition*: Multiple elements within a phrase behave as functors, generating new non-lexicalized senses for the words in composition—the argument qualia structure can modify the semantic type of the predicate. For example, *bake* is generally analyzed as having a change of state meaning (as in *bake potatoes*), but in *bake a cake*, the meaning of the predicate *bake* is modified into a creation meaning. This is because the agentive quale of the cake "makes reference to the very process within which it is embedded in this phrase" (Pustejovsky 1995: 123), namely, the baking.

The Generative Lexicon has a different focus from the logic-inspired approaches to semantics. It does not aim principally at capturing or explaining phenomena such as quantification, anaphora, or presupposition. It is geared towards a detailed, decompositional lexical approach to linguistic semantics, while at the same time providing devices that allow for the computing of compositional meaning in context.

5.2.4 Natural Semantic Metalanguage

Natural semantic metalanguage (NSM) is a decompositional system based on empirically established semantic primes, that is, simple indefinable meanings which appear to be present as word-meanings in all languages (Wierzbicka 1996; Goddard 1998; Goddard and Wierzbicka 2002; Peeters 2006; Goddard 2008). The NSM system uses a metalanguage, which is essentially a standardized subset of natural language: a small subset of word-meanings (63 in number, see Table 5.1), together with a subset of their associated syntactic (combinatorial) properties. Table 5.1 is presented in its English version, but comparable tables of semantic primes have been drawn up for many languages, including Russian, French, Spanish, Chinese, Japanese, Korean, and Malay. Semantic primes and their grammar are claimed to represent a kind of "intersection" of all languages.

NSM is a cognitive theory. Its adherents argue that simple words of ordinary language provide a better representational medium for ordinary cognition than the more technical metalanguages used by other cognitive theories, such as Jackendoff's (1990, 2002) Conceptual Semantics or Wunderlich's (1996, 1997) Lexical Decomposition Grammar. They also argue that any system of meaning representation is necessarily grounded in ordinary language, whether its proponents recognize it or not, because as Lyons (1977: 12) put it: "any formalism is parasitic upon the ordinary everyday use of language, in that it must be understood intuitively on the basis of ordinary language." In relation to crosslinguistic semantics, NSM theorists charge that other cognitivist approaches typically incur "terminological ethnocentrism" (Goddard 2002, 2006; Wierzbicka 2009a), that is, the imposition of inauthentic nonnative categories, because they usually treat the language-specific categories of English as if they represent objective language-independent categories.

The formal mode of meaning representation in the NSM approach is the semantic explication. This is a reductive paraphrase, that is, an attempt to say in other words what a speaker is saying when he or she utters the expression being explicated. Unlike other decompositional systems, reductive paraphrase attempts to capture an insider perspective—with its sometimes naïve first-person quality, rather than the sophisticated outsider perspective of an expert linguist, logician, etc. Originating with Wierzbicka (1972),

TABLE 5.1   Semantic Primes, Grouped into Related Categories

I, YOU, SOMEONE, SOMETHING/THING, PEOPLE, BODY	Substantives
KIND, PART	Relational substantives
THIS, THE SAME, OTHER/ELSE	Determiners
ONE, TWO, SOME, ALL, MUCH/MANY	Quantifiers
GOOD, BAD	Evaluators
BIG, SMALL	Descriptors
KNOW, THINK, WANT, FEEL, SEE, HEAR	Mental predicates
SAY, WORDS, TRUE	Speech
DO, HAPPEN, MOVE, TOUCH	Actions, events, movement, contact
BE (SOMEWHERE), THERE IS, HAVE, BE (SOMEONE/SOMETHING)	Location, existence, possession, specification
LIVE, DIE	Life and death
WHEN/TIME, NOW, BEFORE, AFTER, A LONG TIME, A SHORT TIME, FOR SOME TIME, MOMENT	Time
WHERE/PLACE, HERE, ABOVE, BELOW, FAR, NEAR, SIDE, INSIDE	Space
NOT, MAYBE, CAN, BECAUSE, IF	Logical concepts
VERY, MORE	Intensifier, augmentor
LIKE/WAY	Similarity

Notes: Primes exist as the meanings of lexical units (not at the level of lexemes). Exponents of primes may be words, bound morphemes, or phrasemes. They can be formally complex. They can have combinatorial variants (allolexes). Each prime has well-specified syntactic (combinatorial) properties.

the NSM system has been developed and refined over some 35 years. There is a large body of descriptive empirical work in the framework, with hundreds of published explications. Some lexicon areas that have been explored in great depth are emotions and other mental states, speech-acts, causatives, cultural values, natural kind words, concrete objects, physical activity verbs, and discourse particles. The approach also has been extensively applied to grammatical semantics and pragmatics, but it is not possible to cover these aspects here. Though the NSM approach is arguably the best developed theory of lexical semantics on the contemporary scene, it so far has had minimal application to NLP. (Exceptions include Andrews (2006) on semantic composition for NSM using glue-logic, cf. Dalrymple (2001: 217–254); and Francesco Zamblera's ongoing work on a PROLOG-based parser-generator for NSM. For more information, refer to this chapter's section in the accompanying wiki.)

A simple example of an NSM explication is given in [A] for the English verb *to break*, in one of its several senses. The explication applies only to the sense of the word found in examples like *to break a stick* (*an egg, a lightbulb, a vase, a model plane*). Its successive components indicate action, concurrent effect, aspect, and a result ('this thing was not one thing anymore'); the final "subjective" component indicates that the result is seen as irreversible. Interestingly, many languages—including Chinese, Malay, and Lao—lack a comparably broad verb that subsumes many different manners of "breaking" (Majid and Bowerman 2007).

[A]   Semantic explication for *Someone X broke something Y*

a.   someone X did something to something Y
b.   because of this, something happened to this something Y at the same time
c.   it happened in one moment
d.   because of this, afterwards this thing was not one thing anymore
e.   people can think about it like this: "it can't be one thing anymore"

NSM researchers recognize that for many words in the concrete vocabulary, it is not possible to produce plausible explications directly in terms of semantic primes alone (Wierzbicka 1991; Goddard 2007, 2008). Rather, the explications typically require a combination of semantic primes and certain complex lexical meanings known in NSM theory as "semantic molecules." Though ultimately decomposable into combinations of primes, semantic molecules function as building blocks in the structure of other, yet more complex concepts. For example, explications for *sparrow* and *eagle* must include 'bird [M]' as a semantic molecule; explications for *walk* and *run* must include 'feet [M]' and 'ground [M].' (In NSM explications, semantic molecules are marked as such by the notation [M].) The concept of semantic molecules is similar to that of intermediate-level concepts in the semantic practice of the Moscow School (Apresjan 1992, 2000; Wanner 1996, 2007), but with the constraint that they must be meanings of lexical units in the language concerned. Semantic molecules can be nested, one within the other, creating chains of semantic dependency. Up to four levels of nesting are attested. Some semantic molecules appear to be universal or near-universal, but many are clearly language- and culture-specific. Semantic molecules vary in their degree of productivity and in how widely they range across the lexicon.

NSM researchers estimate there to be about 150–250 productive semantic molecules in English. They are drawn from at least the following categories (examples given are non-exhaustive): (a) parts of the body: 'hands,' 'mouth,' 'legs'; (b) physical descriptors: 'long,' 'round,' 'flat,' 'hard,' 'sharp,' 'straight'; (c) activities and actions: 'eat,' 'drink,' 'sit,' 'kill,' 'pick up,' 'fight with'; (d) expressive/communicative actions: 'laugh,' 'sing,' 'write,' 'read'; (e) topological terms: 'edges,' 'hole'; (f) life-form words: 'creature,' 'animal,' 'bird,' 'fish,' 'tree'; (g) environment: 'ground,' 'sky,' 'sun,' 'water,' 'fire,' 'day,' 'night'; (h) materials: 'wood,' 'stone,' 'metal,' 'glass,' 'paper'; (i) mechanical parts and technology: 'wheel,' 'pipe,' 'wire,' 'engine,' 'electricity,' 'machine'; (j) transport: 'car,' 'train,' 'boat,' 'plane'; (k) social categories and kin roles: 'men,' 'women,' 'children,' 'mother,' 'father'; (l) important cultural concepts: 'money,' 'book,' 'color,' 'number,' 'God.' All of these posited semantic molecules, it must be emphasized, can ultimately be explicated, without circularity, into the fundamental underlying metalanguage of semantic primes.

The concept of semantic molecules leads to new ways of understanding semantic complexity in the lexicon, quite different to anything envisaged in other cognitive or generative approaches to lexical semantics, and very different to structuralist and logic-based approaches. Many lexical semantic structures appear to have a kind of "gangly and lumpy" quality—lengthy strings of simple semantic primes interspersed with semantically dense molecules (for examples, see Section 5.4). Semantic molecules enable a great compression of semantic complexity, but at the same time this complexity is disguised by its being encapsulated and telescoped into lexical units embedded one in the other, like a set of Russian dolls.

5.2.5 Object-Oriented Semantics

Object-oriented semantics is a new field in linguistic semantics. Although it is rather restricted in its semantic application domains so far—mainly applied to the representation of verbal meaning—it promises to become relevant for NLP applications in the future, and due to the large body of research in computer science a wealth of resources is already available for object-oriented systems in general. There is some overlap with Pustejovsky's ideas, as he himself observes:

> When we combine the qualia structure of a NP with the argument structure of a verb, we begin to see a richer notion of compositionality emerging, one that looks very much like object-oriented approaches to programming. (Pustejovsky 1991a: 427)

The basic motive behind deploying the computational object-oriented paradigm to linguistic semantics is, however, its intuitive accessibility. The human cognitive system centers around entities and what they are like, how they are related to each other, what happens to them and what they do, and how they interact with one another. This corresponds to the object-oriented approach, in which the concept of "object" is central, whose characteristics, relations to other entities, behavior, and interactions are modeled in a rigorous way. This correspondence between object-orientation and cognitive organization strongly suggests the application of object-orientation for the representational task at hand.

Schalley (2004a,b) introduces a decompositional representational framework for verbal semantics, the Unified Eventity Representation (UER). It is based on the Unified Modeling Language (UML; cf. Object Management Group 1997–2009), the standard formalism for object-oriented software design and analysis. The UER adopts the graphical nature of the UML as well as the UML's general architecture. UER diagrams are composed of well-defined graphical modeling elements that represent conceptual categories. Conceptual containments, attachments, and relations are thus expressed by graphical entailments, attachments, and relations.

The lexical representation is much more detailed than in the Generative Lexicon, and the graphical modeling elements highlight the internal structure of verbal meaning. An example is given in Figure 5.2 (Schalley 2004b: 787).

The modeling of the transitive *wake up* (as in *Mary woke up her husband*), dubbed **wake_up_2** in Figure 5.2, contains a detailed modeling of the "static structure" of verbal meaning (primarily of the participants in the wake up eventity, their characteristics, and roles) and of the "dynamic structure" (what is happening to the participants in the wake up eventity? which states and transitions do the participants undergo? how do they interact?). Roughly, there is an instigating actor x (either a volitional agent or an non-volitional effector) who/which does something that causes (triggers) a change of state in the animate patient undergoer y, so that y is in the passive state of being awake as a result. A detailed interpretation of the diagrammatic representation, in particular a definition of the diagrammatic modeling elements, can be found in Schalley (2004a).

Work is underway on supralexical semantics and the development of an object-oriented discourse representation system. The ability to model verbal meanings in fine detail is an important prerequisite for such an enterprise, as verbs are the central elements of supralexical expressions. The eventity structure underlying verbal meaning constitutes a scaffolding for utterance interpretation, which is instantiated

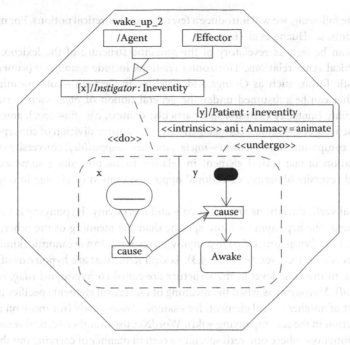

FIGURE 5.2 UER diagrammatic modeling for transitive verb *wake up*. (Schalley 2004b: 787, cf. Schalley 2004a: 76)

and contextually completed in the situation. The type-instance dichotomy of object-oriented systems is expected to reflect this perfectly. While the modeling of lexical meaning is a task for the type level, the representation of utterance meaning is a task for the instance or user objects layer.

5.3 Relational Issues in Lexical Semantics

Linguistic expressions are not isolated, but are interrelated in many ways. In this section, we focus on relational issues in lexical semantics.

5.3.1 Sense Relations and Ontologies

Sense relations—semantic relations between lexical elements—form the basis for word nets, such as the electronic lexical database WordNet (Fellbaum 1998a,b) and similar approaches for languages other than English, for example, the multilingual lexical database EuroWordNet (Vossen 1998, 2001). The large number of NLP applications drawing on WordNet—in areas such as information retrieval and extraction (including audio and video retrieval and the improvement of internet search technology), disambiguation, document structuring and categorization (cf., e.g., Fellbaum 1998b; Morato et al. 2004; Huang et al. in press), to mention a few—show that there is a high demand for information on lexical relations and linguistically informed ontologies. Although a rather new field, the interface between ontologies and linguistic structure is becoming a vibrant and influential area in knowledge representation and NLP (cf. Chapter 24; Schalley and Zaefferer 2007), also due to increasingly popular research on Semantic Web and similar areas.* In the following, we will introduce a few relevant theoretical notions. For more information on resources and tools, see Huang et al. (in press).

Sense relations can be seen as revelatory of the semantic structure of the lexicon. There are both horizontal and vertical sense relations. Horizontal relations include *synonymy* (sameness of meaning of different linguistic forms, such as *Orange* and *Apfelsine* in German—both meaning 'orange') and various relations that can be subsumed under the general notion of *opposition* (Cruse 1986). These include incompatibility (mutually exclusive in a particular context, e.g., *fin—foot*), antonymy (gradable, directionally opposed, e.g., *big—small*), complementarity (exhaustive division of conceptual domain into mutually exclusive compartments, e.g., *aunt—uncle, possible—impossible*), conversity (static directional opposites: specification of one lexical element in relation to another along some axis, for example, *above—below*), and reversity (dynamic directional opposites: motion or change in opposite ways, e.g., *ascend—descend*).

The two principal vertical relations are hyponymy and meronymy. Hyponymy is when the meaning of one lexical element, the hyponym, is more specific than the meaning of the other, the hyperonym (e.g., *dog—animal*). It is often assumed that hyponymy corresponds to a taxonomic (kind of) relationship, but this assumption is incorrect (see Section 5.4.3). Lexical items that are hyponyms of the same lexical element and belong to the same level in the structure are called co-hyponyms (*dog, cat, horse* are co-hyponyms of *animal*). Meronymy is when the meaning of one lexical element specifies that its referent is 'part of' the referent of another lexical element, for example, *hand—body* (for more on meronymy, refer to this chapter's section in the accompanying wiki). WordNet uses another vertical sense relation for the verbal lexicon: troponymy—where one verb specifies a certain manner of carrying out the action referred to by the other verb, such as in *amble—walk* or *shelve—put*.

It should be emphasized that when talking about sense relations we are talking about meaning relations between lexical items. These relations have to be distinguished from ontological relations, notwithstanding that there is a close link between the two: "sense relations are relations between words (in a reading) based on ontological relations between the concepts that constitute the meanings of these words (in that reading)" (Nickles et al. 2007: 37). Ontologies can be conceived of as networks of cross-connected conceptualizations, with the relations holding between those conceptualizations being ontological relations. (This, admittedly, is a very broad definition, which in principle allows any conceptual relation to be subsumed under the label "ontological relation.") Ontological relations might exist without being reflected in a language's lexicon. An example is the concept PUT, for which there is no German lexical coding. Instead, German uses *stellen, setzen, legen, stecken*, which all involve an actor displaying a behavior that causes an exponent to move into a goal location (*Er stellte das Buch ins Regal* 'He put the book on the shelf'). But they all include additional information on the orientation or position of the motion exponent in the goal location: upright (*stellen*), sitting (*setzen*), horizontal (*legen*), or partially fitting into an aperture (*stecken*). Although the respective concepts are all subordinate concepts of PUT and they thus all entertain an ontological relation to PUT, there are no sense relations in German corresponding to these ontological relations, as there is no lexical item available to express the superordinate concept PUT. Unfortunately, the distinction between lexical and ontological relations is often not clearly drawn, neither in linguistics nor in NLP and AI. The most obvious case in point is that WordNet, which was devised as a lexical resource and built on the basis of sense relations, is often treated and discussed as if it were an ontology at the same time (Fellbaum 2007: 420).

Ontologies—particularly upper-level and domain ontologies—have been developed and employed in AI and knowledge representation (e.g., Sowa 2000), and more generally in computer science, for some time. In computational linguistics, there is accordingly a branch which systematically takes advantage

---

* The Semantic Web is conceived of as an extension of the World Wide Web, which aims to provide conceptual descriptions and structured information on documents, in an effort to make the knowledge contained in these documents understandable by machines. Means to achieve this include semantic tagging and the use of specifically designed standards and tools such as the Resource Description Framework (RDF), Web Ontology Language (OWL), and Extensible Markup Language (XML). For more information and pointers to references, refer to this chapter's section in the accompanying wiki.

of ontologies in the AI sense (also see Chapter 24). One of the most extensive works in this area is Nirenburg and Raskin's (2004) *Ontological Semantics*. Their ontology lists definitions of concepts for describing the meanings of lexical items of natural languages, but also for specifying the meanings of the text-meaning representations that serve as part of an interlingua for machine translation (Nickles et al. 2007). Application domains also include information extraction, question answering, human–computer dialog systems, and text summarization.

> Ontological semantics is a theory of meaning in natural language and an approach to natural language processing (NLP) which uses a constructed world model, or ontology, as the central resource for extracting and representing meaning of natural language texts, reasoning about knowledge derived from texts as well as generating natural language texts based on representations of their meaning. The architecture of an archetypal implementation of ontological semantics comprises, at the most coarse-grain level of description:
>
> - a set of static knowledge sources, namely, an **ontology**, a **fact database**, a **lexicon** connecting an ontology with a natural language and an **onomasticon**, a lexicon of names (one lexicon and one onomasticon are needed for each language);
> - **knowledge representation languages** for specifying meaning structures, ontologies, and lexicons; and
> - a set of processing modules, at the least, a semantic **analyzer** and a semantic **text generator**. (Nirenburg and Raskin 2004: 10)

In linguistics proper, ontology-based approaches are only just becoming an explicit focus of research. In addition to ontological relations underlying sense relations and hence impacting on lexical structure, it has recently been recognized that there are many more areas of semantic research that need to take language ontologies into account. Several examples, including lexical semantics, classifiers, word classes, anaphora resolution, and the grammar of coordination, can be found in Nickles et al. (2007: 37–38).

5.3.2 Roles

While ontological relations are stable conceptual relations, there are also situation-specific relations. For example, an instance of an eventity such as German *setzen über* ('cross a waterbody,' 'leap across an obstacle') requires a specification of its participants. Who is crossing or leaping across what? What are they deploying to do so? What is important in the relational context is that such participant specifications include the role they play in the eventity they partake in. In semantics, these roles are referred to as semantic roles, thematic roles, or predicate-argument relations (Van Valin 2004). Semantic roles are important for the linking of the arguments to their syntactic realizations (e.g., a patient participant is realized in English as a direct object of an active voice sentence), in addition to their value in describing and representing semantics. We will not focus on the linking of arguments in the following, the interested reader may want to consult, for instance, Dowty (1991), Goldberg (1995), Van Valin and LaPolla (1997), Van Valin (1999), and Bowerman and Brown (2008).

The number and definition of semantic roles are still subject to controversial discussions. Initiated by Gruber (1965) and Fillmore (1968), there have been two opposing trends in linguistics with regard to semantic roles. Localistic approaches, descending from Gruber, work with a small number of concrete, spatial relationships, such as *goal* and *source*, which they see as the foundation for other, more abstract roles. For example, an experiencer, intentional agent, or originating location would all be assigned the source role. Non-localistic approaches, descending from Fillmore, work with a much larger number of roles, which can be tailored to specific verbal subclasses. The FrameNet project (Ruppenhofer et al. 2006),

TABLE 5.2 Semantic Roles and Their Conventional Definitions

Role	Description
agent	a wilful, purposeful instigator of an action or event
effector	the doer of an action, which may or may not be wilful or purposeful
experiencer	a sentient being that experiences internal states, such as perceivers, cognizers, and emoters
instrument	a normally inanimate entity manipulated by an agent in carrying out an action
force	somewhat like an instrument, but it cannot be manipulated
patient	a thing that is in a state or condition, or undergoes a change of state or condition
theme	a thing which is located or is undergoing a change of location (motion)
benefactive	the participant for whose benefit some action is performed
recipient	someone who gets something (recipients are always animate or some kind of quasi-animate entity)
goal	destination, which is similar to recipient, except that it is often inanimate
source	the point of origin of a state of affairs
location	a place or a spatial locus of a state of affairs
path	a route

Source: Van Valin, R.D. and LaPolla, R.J., *Syntax: Structure, Meaning and Function*, Cambridge University Press, Cambridge, U.K., 1997, 85–89.

for example, which is based on Fillmore's frame semantics, uses a very large number of semantic roles (so-called frame elements), which are defined separately for each frame:

> Although something as straightforward as 'Agent' will in one frame have very much in common with the 'Agent' in another unrelated frame — based on what we all agree to be true about agents — it is also true that the Agent role in each frame is operating within a unique context.
>
> For example, the Agent in the Accomplishment frame, besides exerting his conscious will, is specifically involved in achieving a particular Goal that requires some amount of time and effort; in the Adjusting frame, this Agent is controlling Parts to bring about some effect. These facts about these Agents and their contexts are defined by the frame, but it is not possible to completely divorce these facts from the semantics of the 'do-er,' called an Agent for convention and convenience's sake. In other words, we could just as easily call him the Accomplisher or the Adjuster.*

Austere and abstract localism, on the one hand, and the FrameNet approach, on the other, represent extremes on a spectrum. In practice, most linguists nowadays tend to employ a set of a dozen or so semantic roles, regarding them as somewhat fuzzy, prototypical notions rather than fixed absolute categories. Van Valin and LaPolla (1997) give the non-exhaustive list shown in Table 5.2. Nevertheless, there is no consensus on which prototypical role notions are to be included and how they should be defined. Much is left to intuition and interpretation.

Furthermore, although a set of prototypical role notions seems desirable, such a list would not suffice to model all eventities. To return to the example of *setzen über* (Schalley 2004a: 315–322), it clearly involves an agent (the wilful purposive instigator), an instrument (the entity manipulated by the agent to carry out the action), and a location or ground (the place or locus where the leaping or crossing occurs). Yet, as mentioned above, the ground also needs to be an obstacle that has to be overcome, and therefore an eventity-related characteristic needs to be added to the ground specification. In other words, if semantic roles are specified using prototypical role notions, some mechanism needs to be provided to allow for additional specifications on the role of a participant. The UER system (Section 2.5) provides such mechanisms by defining prototypical participant roles in participant class specifications, and allowing additional characteristics to be expressed via attributes. In FrameNet, the Core Frame Elements can

---

* This quotation is taken from FrameNet FAQs, 'Are Frame Elements unique across frames?'; <http://framenet. icsi.berkeley.edu/index.php?option=com_content&task=view&id=19038&Itemid=49>. We have taken the liberty of correcting a number of typographical errors.

be further defined using 'semantic types' (STs). "For example, in the Chatting frame, the Interlocutor definitions take the ST 'Human,' thereby excluding non-human agents as Core participants in the frame."*

Not all systems accept the existence of semantic roles as independent entities, either in an absolute or prototypical sense. In the NSM system, the relevant generalizations are seen to emerge from top-level components of the meaning structures of individual verbs. At this level, many verbs are based on the semantic primes DO, HAPPEN, and WANT, the first two of which have several alternative valency frames. Rather than saying that complex physical activity verbs like *cut, chop, dig,* and *grind* involve an agent, a patient, and an instrument, for example, in the NSM system these verbs are analyzed as sharing the top-level components (lexico-syntactic frame) shown in (6a) below. Likewise, verbs of bodily locomotion like *walk, run,* and *swim* are assigned the frame in (6b) (Goddard and Wierzbicka 2009). Additional specifications on the nature of the participants or their roles can be spelt out later in the explication.

(6a) NSM lexico-syntactic frame for complex physical activities

i.   someone X was doing something to something Y with something else Z for some time
ii.   because of this, something was happening at the same time to this something Y, as this someone
      wanted

(6b) NSM lexico-syntactic frame for bodily locomotion

i.   someone X was doing something somewhere with parts of his/her body for some time
ii.   because of this, this someone's body was moving at the same time in this place, as this someone
      wanted

Another approach that considers semantic roles not to be independent entities is Jackendoff's (1990, 2002) Conceptual Semantics. Jackendoff (1990: 127) explicitly identifies semantic roles as the argument slots of abstract basic predicates.

5.4 Fine-Grained Lexical-Semantic Analysis: Three Case Studies

In this section, we present three case studies of fine-grained lexical-semantic analysis. The framework is the NSM method (Section 5.2.4), but to a considerable extent the findings can be repackaged into different models.

5.4.1 Emotional Meanings: "Sadness" and "Worry" in English and Chinese

Formal semantics has had little to say about the meanings of emotion words, but words like these are of great importance to social cognition and communication in ordinary language use. They may be of special importance to NLP applications connected with social networking and with machine–human interaction, but they differ markedly in their semantics from language to language. In this section, we will illustrate with contrastive examples from English and Chinese.

Consider first the difference between English *sad* and *unhappy.* Conventional dictionaries may make them seem virtually synonymous, but this does not tally with the intuitions of native speakers or with the evidence of usage. There are contexts in which one could use one word but not the other, as shown in (7), or where the choice of one word or the other would lead to different implications, as suggested by the examples in (8) (Wierzbicka 1999: 60–63, 84–85).

---

* FrameNet FAQs, 'Are Frame Elements unique across frames?'; <http://framenet.icsi.berkeley.edu/index.php?option=com_content&task=view&id=19038&Itemid=49>. It should be noted that the attribute 'human' is not, strictly speaking, a role characteristic, but rather a selectional restriction on the participants. Although important in semantic representation, selectional restrictions should, for the sake of precise semantic modeling, be kept separate from role characterizations.

(7) *I miss you a lot at work . . .. I feel so sad (*unhappy) about what's happening to you* [said to a colleague in hospital who is dying of cancer].

(8a) *I was feeling unhappy at work* [suggests dissatisfaction].

(8b) *I was feeling sad at work* [suggests depression, sorrow, etc.].

NSM explications for emotion meanings work by linking a feeling (usually a good feeling or a bad feeling) with a prototypical cognitive scenario which serves as a kind of reference situation. Explication [B] below is for the expression *feel sad*. Notice that the content of the scenario, in section (b) of the explication, is given in the first-person. It involves awareness that 'something bad happened' (not necessarily to me), which I didn't want to happen but am prepared to accept, in the sense of recognizing that I can't do anything about it (an attitude akin to resignation). Explication [B] is compatible with the wide range of use of *sad*; for example, that I may feel *sad* on hearing that my friend's dog has died or when thinking about some bickering in my workplace. *Unhappy* has a more personal character than *sad*: one feels *unhappy* because of bad things that have happened to one personally, things that one did not want to happen. The attitude is not exactly active, but it is not passive either. It suggests something like dissatisfaction, rather than resignation. These properties are modeled in explication [C]. Notice that there is an extra final component (c), saying that the experiencer actually had thoughts like those identified in the cognitive scenario. In other words, feeling *unhappy* implies a more cognitively active state than feeling *sad*. (While one can say *I feel sad, I don't know why*, it would be a little odd to say *I feel unhappy, I don't know why*.)

[B] Semantic explication for *Someone X felt sad*

a.   someone X felt something bad
     like someone can feel when they think like this:
b.   "I know that something bad happened
         I don't want things like this to happen
         I can't think like this: I will do something because of it now
         I know that I can't do anything"

[C] Semantic explication for *Someone X felt unhappy*

a.   someone X felt something bad
     like someone can feel when they think like this:
b.   "some bad things happened to me
         I wanted things like this not to happen to me
         I can't not think about it"
c.   this someone felt something like this, because this someone thought like this

For speakers of English, states of mind like 'feeling sad' and 'feeling unhappy' may seem so natural that one could assume they would have matching words in all languages, but this is very far from being the case. Ye (2001) shows that Chinese lacks a precise equivalent to English "sadness" (cf. Russell and Yik 1996). One possible match would be *ai*, but this is strongly linked with mourning (hence, closer to English *sorrow*). The two other candidates are *bei* and *chou* (tone markings omitted), but each differs significantly from English *sad*. *Bei* is more intense and has a tragic, fatalist tone, suggesting powerlessness before the laws of nature, the inevitability of ageing and death, etc. *Chou* lacks this existential gravitas and is a more common everyday word than *bei*, but *chou* is at least as close to English *worried*, as it is to *sad*. *Chou* is focused on the experiencer's present situation. One experiences this feeling when confronting a personal predicament that is forced on one by the circumstances, "leaving the experiencer caught in a dilemma—wanting to overcome a difficult situation, yet not finding a solution" (Ye 2001: 379). The experiencer, moreover, cannot stop thinking about it, creating a link with English *preoccupied*. Ye (2001) proposes the following explications (slightly modified):

[D] Semantic explication for *Someone X felt* bei [Chinese]

a. someone X felt something very bad
      like someone can feel when they think like this:
b.   "something bad happened now
      I know that after this good things will not happen anymore
      I don't want things like this to happen
      I want to do something if I can
      I know that I can't do anything
            because I know that no one can do anything when things like this happen"
c. this someone felt something like this, because this someone thought like this

[E] Semantic explication for *Someone X felt* chou [Chinese]

a. someone X felt something bad
      like someone can feel when they think like this:
b.   "something bad is happening to me
      before this, I did not think that this would happen to me
      I don't want things like this to happen to me
      because of this, I want to do something if I can
      I don't know what I can do
      I can't not think about this all the time"
c. this someone felt something like this, because this someone thought like this

It seems clear that Chinese bei and chou have no close equivalents in English, and conversely, that *sad* and *unhappy* have no close equivalents in Chinese. Similar demonstrations of semantic nonequivalence could be adduced for many other languages and for many other areas of the mental states lexicon (Russell 1991; Goddard 1996a; Wierzbicka 1999, 2004; Harkins and Wierzbicka 2001; Enfield and Wierzbicka 2002; Schalley and Khlentzos 2007).

5.4.2 Ethnogeographical Categories: "Rivers" and "Creeks"

Words for landforms and landscape features—like English *desert*, *mountain*, and *river*—might seem an unlikely domain for complex lexical semantics or for extensive crosslinguistic variation, since it seems at first blush that their referents are objective physical entities. But things are not that simple. Unlike as in the biological world, where to a large extent a structure of kinds (species) is "given" by nature, the demarcation between different categories of geophysical referents is often far from clear-cut (compare *mountain* and *hill*, *river* and *stream*, *lake* and *pond*). Languages differ considerably in the nature of the distinctions they recognize (Burenhult and Levinson 2008). Sometimes these differences are related to the nature of the landforms themselves, but categorization of the landscape also has a human dimension. It reflects anthropocentric concerns, and these concerns can vary with the culture as well as with the physical world.

The problem has been noted by researchers in geospatial data information systems, as well as by geographers and linguists (Mark and Turk 2003, 2004). Some have called for the creation of a new field of study into naïve geography: "a set of theories that provide the basis for designing future geographic information systems (GIS) that follow human intuition and are, therefore, easily accessible to a large range of users" (Egenhofer and Mark 1995). From a computational point of view, questions like the following arise (Scharl 2007; Oosterom and Zlatanova 2008; Stock 2008): What is the optimal ontology for geospatial databases? What set of place categories or semantic descriptions should be used to annotate and index them? How can querying systems be implemented that will be responsive to the expectations of user communities with different native languages? How can interoperability be achieved between heterogeneous Web services and data sets in the geographic domain? Is it possible to devise systems for extracting and compiling geographical information from Web-based documents, for example, online news reports?

We now report on lexical-semantic analysis of geographical categories being undertaken by Bromhead (2008), taking our examples from "elongated" hydrological features. Explication [F] for English *river* claims that a *river* is conceptualized as 'a place of one kind': a place with a lot of water, a long, big place that can be a potential barrier at times (components (b)–(e)). The water, furthermore, is constantly moving and can be thought of as, so to speak, traveling from a distant source to a destination far away (components (f) and (g)).

[F] Semantic explication for *a river*

a. a place of one kind
b. there is a lot of water [M] in places of this kind
c. places of this kind are long [M] places
d. places of this kind are big places
e. because it is like this, at many times when someone is on one side of a place of this kind, if this
         someone wants to be on the other side, this someone can't be on the other side after a short time
f. the water [M] in places of this kind is moving at all times
g. when someone is somewhere on one side of a place of this kind, this someone can think like this:
         "some time before this, this water [M] was in a place far from here
         some time after this, this water [M] will be in another place far from here"

The comparable explication for *stream* is distinguished from that of *river* in terms of the smaller size of the place and lesser quantity of water (not only moving, but moving quickly), and also by lacking components corresponding to (e) and (g) above. These intuitively plausible differences correlate with collocational preferences of the two words; for example, the acceptability contrast between expressions like *great river* and *?great stream*, and the much higher frequency of *little stream*, as compared with *little river*.

In Australian English, the word *creek* is extremely common, and like *stream* it refers to a smaller water feature than a *river*. What then is the difference between *creek* and *stream*? The major differences are connected with the fact that in the world's driest continent the water flow in most watercourses is not reliable. Typically the water level in a *creek* fluctuates a lot and, in times of drought may dry up entirely. Consistent with this, collocations of the word *creek* with expressions like *dries up* and *dried up* are quite common. Likewise, the expression *creekbed* is common, referring to the dry surface (not to the bottom of a full creek, as does the comparable form *riverbed*). Consider explication [G]. For *creek*, both the presence of water in the said location and its movement is qualified by 'at many times.' The variability of the water level is implied by the additional component (c).

[G] Semantic explication for *a creek* [Australian English]

a. a place of one kind
b. at many times there is water [M] in parts of places of this kind
c. at some times there is water [M] in all parts of places of this kind
d. places of this kind are long [M] places
e. places of this kind are not big places
f. at many times the water [M] in places of this kind is moving

Consider now the word *karu* from the Central Australian Aboriginal language Yankunytjatjara. In Central Australia, a *karu* is usually dry, and as such would be normally referred to in English as a *creekbed*, but *karu* makes no distinction between what English describes differently as either a *creek* or a *creekbed*. As Mark et al. (2007: 8) observe: "in arid and semi-arid regions, the distinction between topographic and hydrological features quite literally dries up." Some naturally occurring examples of *karu* (cf. Goddard 1996b) are as follows:

(9a) *Ka karungka uṟu puḻka ukalingangi.* 'There was a lot of water flowing in the *karu*.'

(9b) *Apaṟa tjuṯa ngaṟala waṉaṉi karungka.* 'River gums line the *karu*.'

(9c) *Haast's Bluff-ala ngayulu iṯingaringu, karungka, manta tjulangka.* 'I was born at Haast's Bluff, in the *karu*, where the ground is soft.'

Explication [H] contains several components that are the same or similar to those in English *creek*, but there are significant differences. Water is said to be present only 'at some times,' and, more dramatically, there is a description of what the ground is like in a *karu*, that is, lower than the surroundings and distinctively soft. A final component adds the detail, very salient in the traditional desert lifestyle, that water is often to be found below the ground in a *karu* (it can be obtained by digging in a so-called soakage).

[H] Semantic explication for *karu* ('creekbed, creek') [Yankunytjatjara]

a. a place of one kind
b. at some times there is water [M] in places of this kind
c. places of this kind are long [M] places
d. the ground [M] in a place of this kind is below the ground [M] on both sides of a place of this kind
e. it is not like the ground [M] in other places, it is soft [M]
f. when there is water [M] in places of this kind, at some times this water [M] is moving
g. at many times there is water [M] in some places below the ground [M] in places of this kind

Semantic analysis along similar lines can be used to spell out the different conceptualizations behind terms for all sorts of landscape (and seascape) features. As well as providing plausible semantic structures that can be linked with collocational and other linguistic evidence, such explications offer a potential solution to another problem that has sometimes been identified for landscape features, namely, the existence of a certain indeterminacy and overlap in the referential ranges of related words. Going back to *river, stream,* and *creek,* for example, the explications account for why certain physical referents can be open to being described by any of these three terms. The difference is not necessarily a matter of physical dimensions, but can be determined by how the user is thinking about the referent at the time.

5.4.3 Functional Macro-Categories

Functional macro-category words, also called collective nouns (e.g., Mihatsch 2007), pose interesting semantic challenges in themselves, not least because they tend to vary across languages to a much greater extent than do true taxonomic words. In addition, their semantics have a direct relevance to the architecture of semantic networks: semantic networks are typically organized in a hierarchical fashion, with classificatory relationships indicated by the "is-a" relation, which is often assumed to correspond essentially to 'is a kind of.' Higher level nodes are typically labeled indifferently with either taxonomic or with functional macro-category words. To put it another way, the "is-a" relationship sometimes corresponds to a genuine taxonomic one and sometimes does not, leading to inconsistent results and mismatches with the intuitions of ordinary speakers (Brachman 1983; cf. Wisniewski et al. 1996; Cruse 2002; Veres and Sampson 2005). In this section, we will concentrate on English and discuss the semantic differences between three types of classificatory relationships that can be exemplified as shown in Table 5.3.

TABLE 5.3 Three Different Types of Classificatory Relationships in English

True Taxonomic Category Words	"Plural-Mostly" Functional Macro-Category Words	Singular-Only Functional-Collective Macro-Category Words
birds—sparrow, wren, eagle, …	*vegetables—carrots, peas, celery, …*	*furniture—table, chair, bed, …*
fish—trout, tuna, bream, …	*herbs—basil, oregano, rosemary, …*	*cutlery—knife, fork, spoon, …*
animal—dog, cat, horse, …	*cosmetics—lipstick, powder, mascara, …*	*jewelry—ring, earring, necklace, …*

The relationships illustrated in the left-hand column of Table 5.3 are genuinely taxonomic. For example, *birds* are 'living things of one kind' and this kind is understood to have various sub-kinds. The meaning of the words *sparrow*, *wren*, and *eagle*, for example, all contain the semantic molecule 'bird [M].' The relationships exemplified in the other two columns are quite different, both semantically and in their grammatical behavior. Though words like *vegetables* and *furniture* may express classification in a broad sense, it is not in terms of a taxonomic hierarchy. Words like *vegetables*, *herbs*, *cosmetics*, *furniture*, *cutlery*, and *jewelry* do not designate 'things of one kind,' but 'things of many kinds' unified by factors such as shared functions, contiguity, and similar origins (Wierzbicka 1985, esp. Chap. 4, pp. 258–354; Goddard 2009).*

"Plural-mostly" functional macro-category words (e.g., *vegetables*, *cosmetics*, *herbs*, *cereals*, *drugs*) are so called because they occur predominantly in the plural, other than when they are bare stems in compounds, for example, *vegetable soup*, *cosmetic surgery*. Singular occurrences are mostly in predicate position with the indefinite article *a*, in a generic construction, for example, *Spinach is a green vegetable*; while singulars with the definite article are rare and anomalous (*?the vegetable, ?the cosmetic*). Their most distinctive semantic property is that when counting the referents of "plural-mostly" functional categories, such as vegetables, cosmetics, etc., one counts not individual items but kinds. For example, *There were only two vegetables on the plate* means 'only vegetables of two kinds.'

A semantic explication for *vegetables* is given in [I]. As mentioned, it begins with the component 'things of many kinds.' Component (b) is an exemplar component, mentioning several of the most salient kinds (cf. Battig and Montague 1969; Rosch 1973; Rosch et al. 1976), which, needless to say, are highly culture-specific. Component (c) sets out the salient properties shared by the various kinds, presented not as inherent properties but in terms of how people think about them—as edible items requiring some preparation (cooking, peeling, washing, etc.), that come from things that people cultivate and that grow close to the ground. They are not (thought of as) sweet. Component (d) says that these shared construals allow people to see things of these different kinds as 'like things of one kind.' This makes the macro-category "quasi-taxonomic." The semantic structure of other "plural-mostly" macro-category words, such as *herbs*, *cereals*, *cosmetics*, and *drugs* follow the same basic template.

[I] Semantic explication for *vegetables*

a. things of many kinds
b. carrots [M] are things of one of these kinds, peas [M] are things of one of these kinds
c. people can think about things of all these kinds like this:
    – people can eat [M] things of these kinds, if someone does some things to them beforehand
    – before people can eat [M] things of this kind, they are parts of some other things
    – people do things in some places because they want these things to grow [M] in these places
    – when things of these kinds grow [M] in a place, they are near the ground [M]
    – things of this kind are not sweet [M]
d. because people can think about things of all these kinds like this, people can think that they are like things of one kind

Singular-only functional-collective category words (e.g., *furniture*, *cutlery*, *clothing*, *crockery*, *jewelry*) are invariably singular in form (**furnitures*, **clothings*, etc.), but, unlike normal singular nouns, they cannot take an indefinite singular article or the word *one* (**a/one furniture*, **a/one clothing*). A distinctive property is that they are generally compatible with the *item(s) of X* or *piece(s) of X* construction. Although grammatically singular, these nouns can be objects of verbs that imply a multiplex object, for example, *laying out the cutlery*, *re-arranging the furniture*, *sorting through the clothing*. Many are compatible with

---

* The source of the confusion is no doubt the assumption that set inclusion (a referential, extensionalist relationship) equates to a 'kind of' relationship (an intensional, conceptual relationship), but this assumption is flawed. Every policeman, for example, is somebody's son, but it doesn't follow that a policeman is conceptualized as a 'kind of son' (Wierzbicka 1985: 259).

phrases like *a collection of X, a range of X* or *a set of X*. Words like *furniture, cutlery, clothing, crockery*, and the like, tend to imply "unity of place," that is, they designate things of different kinds that are expected to be used in heterogeneous groups of items all put in the same place.

A sample explication is given in [J]. As with other functional macro-category explications, it begins with 'things of many kinds,' followed by a component stating the most salient exemplar kinds (in the case of *furniture*: tables and chairs). Next comes a set of shared properties, including location in people's homes (and other similar places), serving the purpose, roughly speaking, of bodily comfort and convenience. There is also a "moveability" component. On account of these shared properties, it is claimed, when things of these different kinds are in the one place, people can think that they are 'like one thing.' This semantic property is linked with singular number status of words of this type. Other singular-only functional macro-category words, such as *cutlery, crockery, clothing*, and *jewelry*, follow the same basic semantic template.

[J] Semantic explication for *furniture*

a. things of many kinds
b. tables [M] are things of one of these kinds, chairs [M] are things of one these kinds
c. people can think about things of all these kinds like this:
   - there are many things of these kinds in people's homes [M]
   - there are many things of these kinds in other places where people want to be for some time
   - these things are like parts of these places
   - people want things of these kinds to be in these places because they don't want to feel something bad in their bodies when they do some things in these places for some time
   - if something of one of these kinds is somewhere in a place at some time, at another time it can be somewhere else in this place if this someone wants it
d. because people can think about things of all these kinds like this, when things of these kinds are in one place, people can think that they are like one thing

If the semantic analyses in [I] and [J] are correct in their main outlines, in order to be faithful to human cognitive organization, it is problematical to use functional macro-categories as higher level nodes in semantic networks, as if they were taxonomic categories. They could be more appropriately used as attribute features, though it has to be borne in mind that such categories are highly variable across languages.

5.5 Prospectus and "Hard Problems"

Despite declining "syntacticocentrism" (Jackendoff 2002: 107–111), semantics—especially lexical semantics—remains the poor cousin of linguistics. There are relatively few specialists, especially with additional crosslinguistic or NLP expertise.

The complexity of lexical semantics and the extent of lexical-semantic differences across languages have been vastly underestimated by most NLP practitioners and, for that matter, by most linguists. To some extent, this underestimation is due to the tendency of twentieth century work to concentrate on truth-conditional and referentialist approaches to meaning. Though there are in fact considerable divergences between languages in words that refer to concrete physical phenomena (including biological species), the extent of differences is much greater in relation to more cultural, more subjective words—words whose meanings are, so to speak, creatures of the mind. Such meanings are crucial to ordinary social cognition and to ordinary language use and interpretation. To mention two more categories, there are culture-specific social ideals, such as Japanese *wa* and Chinese *xiào*, usually clumsily rendered into English as "unity, harmony" and as "filial piety," respectively (Ho 1996; Wierzbicka 1997: 248–254; Goddard 2005: 84–88); and there are culture-specific social categories, such as English *friend*, Russian *drug* 'trusted friend,' Chinese *zìjǐrén* 'insider, one of us' and *wàirén* 'outsider' (Wierzbicka 1997: 32–84; Ye 2004).

Another significant problem are abstract nouns such as English *rights, security, dialogue, trauma,* and *experience,* which lack exact equivalents in many of the world's languages (Wierzbicka 2006, 2009b).

Despite the tremendous advances in computational power and improvements in corpus linguistics, the prospectus is not particularly good for next-generation NLP applications that would depend on high-detail semantic analysis; for example, in information extraction from unstructured text (see Chapter 21), machine translation, and the Semantic Web. Many common semantic phenomena are likely to remain computationally intractable for the foreseeable future. Rough-and-ready semantic processing (partial text understanding), especially in restricted domains and/or in restricted "sublanguages" offer more promising prospects but we have to be realistic about what is achievable, even with next-generation technologies.

A particular problem is that standard resources such as WordNet and GlobalWordNet cannot support fine-grained semantic analysis even for English, let alone for other major languages of the world. Major controlled vocabulary dictionaries such as Collins Cobuild have their uses, but they too are not adequate to the task (Hoelter 1999; Guenthner 2008). Though corpus techniques and other computational tools are providing valuable new resources and heuristics, there are no quick and easy automatic methods for generating detailed lexical-semantic analyses. They must be hand built by experienced human analysts and it will be a long time before even a decent fragment of "ordinary English" (to speak with Montague 1973) has been adequately analyzed.

It might be a practical proposition to specify moderately sized controlled auxiliary languages, such as, in the case of English, Formalized English and Frame-CG (cf. Martin 2002) or an improved "Globish" (Nerrière 2004), and to hand build complete semantically analyzed lexicogrammars for them. But such auxiliary languages would be radically constrained compared with their ordinary unconstrained counterparts.

Above all, if progress is to be made, researchers in NLP and linguistic semantics must give serious consideration to the question of standards, which play a prominent role in computer science. It would not be possible, or even desirable, to standardize working methods among all the multifarious research groups and communities involved, but there needs to be some collective attention to the problem of ensuring the longevity and comparability of research results and interoperability of systems. The enduring presence of the predicate calculus (despite its inadequacies) is largely a testimony to the value of widely known and understood notations. We venture to suggest that intuitive systems such as those based on reductive paraphrase in natural language (for verbal representation) and/or on industry-wide standards such as UML (for object-oriented representation) offer the best potential to meet this need.

Acknowledgments

We are grateful to Bonnie Webber, Nitin Indurkhya, and Csaba Verés for comments on an earlier version of this chapter. This research was supported by the Australian Research Council.

References

Andrews, A. D. 2006. Semantic composition for NSM, using LFG + glue. In *Selected Papers from the 2005 Conference of the Australian Linguistics Society,* Melbourne, Australia, K. Allan (ed.). http://www.als.asn.au

Apresjan, J. D. 1992. *Lexical Semantics: User's Guide to Contemporary Russian Vocabulary.* Ann Arbor, MI: Karoma. [Orig. published 1974 as *Leksiceskaja Semantika—Sinonimeceskie Sredstva Jazyka.* Moskva, Russia: Nauka.]

Apresjan, J. D. 2000. *Systematic Lexicography* (Trans. K. Windle). Oxford, U.K.: Oxford University Press.

Asher, N. 1993. *Reference to Abstract Objects in Discourse.* Dordrecht, the Netherlands: Kluwer.

Asher, N. and A. Lascarides 2003. *Logics of Conversation.* Cambridge, U.K.: Cambridge University Press.

Barwise, J. and J. Perry. 1983. *Situations and Attitudes.* Cambridge, MA: MIT Press.

Battig, W. F. and W. E. Montague. 1969. Category norms for verbal items in 56 categories: A replication and extension of the Connecticut category norms. *Journal of Experimental Psychology Monograph* 80(3):1–46.

Behrens, L. 1998. Polysemy as a problem of representation—'representation' as a problem of polysemy. Review article on: James Pustejovsky. *The Generative Lexicon. Lexicology* 4(1):105–154.

Blackburn, P. and J. Bos. 1999. *Working with Discourse Representation Theory: An Advanced Course in Computational Semantics.* Stanford, CA: CSLI Press. Manuscript. http://homepages. inf.ed.ac.uk/jbos/comsem/book2.html

Blackburn, P. and J. Bos. 2005. *Representation and Inference for Natural Language: A First Course in Computational Semantics.* Stanford, CA: CSLI Press.

Bowerman, M. and P. Brown (eds.). 2008. *Crosslinguistic Perspectives on Argument Structure.* New York, NY/London, U.K.: Taylor & Francis.

Brachman, R. 1983. What IS-A is and isn't: An analysis of taxonomic links in semantic networks. *IEEE Computer* 16(10):30–36.

Bromhead, H. 2008. Ethnogeographical classification in Australia. *Paper presented at the 2008 Annual Meeting of the Australian Linguistics Society.* Sydney, Australia, July 3, 2008.

Burenhult, N. and S. C. Levinson (eds.). 2008. Language and landscape: A cross-linguistic perspective (Special Issue). *Language Sciences* 30(2/3):135–150.

Cann, R. 1994. *Formal Semantics. An Introduction.* Cambridge, U.K.: Cambridge University Press.

Croft, W. and D. A. Cruse. 2003. *Cognitive Linguistics.* Cambridge, U.K.: Cambridge University Press.

Cruse, D. A. 1986. *Lexical Semantics.* Cambridge, U.K.: Cambridge University Press.

Cruse, D. A. 2002. Hyponymy and its varieties. In *The Semantics of Relationships: An Interdisciplinary Perspective*, R. Green, C. A. Bean, and S. H. Myaeng (eds.), pp. 3–21. Dordrecht, the Netherlands: Kluwer.

Cruse, D. A. 2004. *Meaning in Language: An Introduction to Semantics and Pragmatics*, 2nd edn. Oxford, U.K.: Oxford University Press.

Dalrymple, M. 2001. *Lexical Functional Grammar.* San Diego, CA: Academic Press.

Dowty, D. R. 1991. Thematic proto-roles and argument selection. *Language* 67(3):547–619.

Dowty, D. R., R. E. Wall, and S. Peters. 1981. *Introduction to Montague Semantics.* Dordrecht, the Netherlands: Reidel.

Egenhofer, M. J. and D. M. Mark. 1995. Naïve geography. In *Spatial Information Theory: A Theoretical Basis for GIS.* In *Proceedings of the International Conference COSIT'95, Semmering, Austria, September 21–23, 1995*, A. Frank and W. Kuhn (eds.). *Lecture Notes in Computer Science* 988:1–15. Berlin, Germany: Springer-Verlag.

van Eijck, J. 2006. Discourse representation theory. In *Encyclopedia of Language and Linguistics*, 2nd edn, Vol. 3, K. Brown (ed.), pp. 660–669. Oxford, U.K.: Elsevier.

Enfield, N. J., and A. Wierzbicka (eds.). 2002. The body in the description of emotion (Special Issue). *Pragmatics and Cognition* 10(1).

Fauconnier, G. 1985. *Mental Spaces.* Cambridge, MA: MIT Press.

Fellbaum, C. 1998a. A semantic network of English: The mother of all WordNets. In *EuroWordNet: A Multilingual Database with Lexical Semantic Networks*, P. Vossen (ed.), pp. 209–220. Dordrecht, the Netherlands: Kluwer.

Fellbaum, C. (ed.). 1998b. *WordNet: An Electronic Lexical Database.* Cambridge, MA: MIT Press.

Fellbaum, C. 2007. The ontological loneliness of verb phrase idioms. In *Ontolinguistics: How Ontological Status Shapes the Linguistic Coding of Concepts*, A. C. Schalley and D. Zaefferer (eds.), pp. 419–434. Berlin, Germany: Mouton de Gruyter.

Fillmore, C. J. 1968. The case for case. In *Universals in Linguistic Theory*, E. Bach and R. T. Harms (eds.), pp. 1–88. New York, NY: Holt, Rinehart & Winston.

Fried, M. and J.-O. Östman. 2004. Construction grammar. A thumbnail sketch. In *Construction Grammar in Cross-Language Perspective*, M. Fried and J.-O. Östman (eds.), pp. 11–86. Amsterdam, the Netherlands: Benjamins.

Gamut, L. T. F. 1991. *Logic, Language and Meaning*, 2 Vols. Chicago, IL/London, U.K.: University of Chicago Press.

Geeraerts, D. 2002. Conceptual approaches III: Prototype theory. In *Lexikologie/Lexicology. Ein internationales Handbuch zur Natur und Struktur von Wörtern und Wortschätzen. [An International Handbook on the Nature and Structure of Words and Vocabularies]*, Vol. I., D. A. Cruse, F. Hundsnurscher, M. Job, and P. R. Lutzeier (eds.), pp. 284–291. Berlin, Germany: Mouton de Gruyter.

Geurts, B. and D. I. Beaver. 2008. Discourse representation theory. In *The Stanford Encyclopedia of Philosophy* (Winter 2008 Edition), E. N. Zalta (ed.), Stanford University, Stanford, CA. http://plato.stanford.edu/archives/win2008/entries/discourse-representation-theory/

Goddard, C. 1996a. The "social emotions" of Malay (Bahasa Melayu). *Ethos* 24(3):426–464.

Goddard, C. 1996b. *Pitjantjatjara/Yankunytjatjara to English Dictionary*, revised 2nd edn. Alice Springs, Australia: Institute for Aboriginal Development.

Goddard, C. 1998. *Semantic Analysis: A Practical Introduction*. Oxford, U.K.: Oxford University Press.

Goddard, C. 2000. Polysemy: A problem of definition. In *Polysemy and Ambiguity. Theoretical and Applied Approaches*, Y. Ravin and C. Leacock (eds.), pp. 129–151. Oxford, U.K.: Oxford University Press.

Goddard, C. 2002. Overcoming terminological ethnocentrism. *IIAS Newsletter* 27:28 (International Institute for Asian Studies, Leiden, The Netherlands). http://www.iias.nl/nl/27/IIAS_NL27_28.pdf

Goddard, C. 2005. *The Languages of East and Southeast Asia: An Introduction*. Oxford, U.K.: Oxford University Press.

Goddard, C. 2006. Ethnopragmatics: A new paradigm. In *Ethnopragmatics: Understanding Discourse in Cultural Context*, C. Goddard (ed.), pp. 1–30. Berlin, Germany: Mouton de Gruyter.

Goddard, C. 2007. Semantic molecules. In *Selected Papers of the 2006 Annual Meeting of the Australian Linguistic Society*, I. Mushin and M. Laughren (eds.), Brisbane, Australia. http://www.als.asn.au

Goddard, C. 2009. Vegetables, furniture, weapons: Functional macro-categories in the English lexicon. *Paper Presented at the 2009 Annual Meeting of the Australian Linguistics Society*, Melbourne, Australia, July 9–11, 2009.

Goddard, C. (ed.) 2008. *Cross-Linguistic Semantics*. Amsterdam, the Netherlands: John Benjamins.

Goddard, C. and A. Wierzbicka. 2009. Contrastive semantics of physical activity verbs: 'Cutting' and 'chopping' in English, Polish, and Japanese. *Language Sciences* 31:60–96.

Goddard, C. and A. Wierzbicka (eds.). 2002. *Meaning and Universal Grammar—Theory and Empirical Findings*, 2 Vols. Amsterdam, the Netherlands: John Benjamins.

Goldberg, A. 1995. *Constructions: A Construction Grammar Approach to Argument Structure*. Chicago, IL: University of Chicago Press.

Gruber, J. S. 1965. Studies in lexical relations. PhD thesis, Massachusetts Institute of Technology, Cambridge, MA.

Guenthner, F. 2008. *Electronic Dictionaries, Tagsets and Tagging*. Munich, Germany: Lincom.

Gutiérrez-Rexach, J. (ed.). 2003. *Semantics. Critical Concepts in Linguistics*, 6 Vols. London, U.K.: Routledge.

Harkins, J. and A. Wierzbicka (eds.). 2001. *Emotions in Crosslinguistic Perspective*. Berlin, Germany: Mouton de Gruyter.

Heim, I. 1982. The semantics of definite and indefinite noun phrases. PhD thesis, University of Massachusetts, Amherst, MA.

Heim, I. 1983. File change semantics and the familiarity theory of definiteness. In *Meaning, Use and Interpretation of Language*, R. Bäuerle, C. Schwarze, and A. von Stechow (eds.), pp. 164–189. Berlin, Germany: Walter de Gruyter. [Reprinted in Gutiérrez-Rexach (2003) Vol. III, pp. 108–135].

Ho, D. Y. F. 1996. Filial piety and its psychological consequences. In *The Handbook of Chinese Psychology*, M. H. Bond (ed.), pp. 155–165. Hong Kong, China: Oxford University Press.

Hoelter, M. 1999. *Lexical-Semantic Information in Head-Driven Phrase Structure Grammar and Natural Language Processing*. Munich, Germany: Lincom.

Huang, C.-R., N. Calzolari, A. Gangemi, A. Lenci, A. Oltramari, and L. Prévot (eds.). In press. *Ontology and the Lexicon: A Natural Language Processing Perspective*. Cambridge, U.K.: Cambridge University Press.

Jackendoff, R. 1990. *Semantic Structures*. Cambridge, MA: MIT Press.

Jackendoff, R. 2002. *Foundations of Language: Brain, Meaning, Grammar, Evolution*. Oxford, U.K.: Oxford University Press.

Johnson, M. 1987. *The Body in the Mind: The Bodily Basis of Meaning, Imagination, and Reason*. Chicago, IL: University of Chicago Press.

Kamp, H. 1981. A theory of truth and semantic representation. In *Formal Methods in the Study of Language*, J. Groenendijk, T. Janssen, and M. Stokhof (eds.), pp. 277–322. Amsterdam, the Netherlands: Mathematical Centre. [Reprinted in Portner and Partee (eds.) (2002), pp. 189–222; Reprinted in Gutiérrez-Rexach (ed.) (2003) Vol. VI, pp. 158–196].

Kamp, H. and U. Reyle. 1993. *From Discourse to Logic: Introduction to Modeltheoretic Semantics of Natural Language, Formal Logic and Discourse Representation Theory*. Dordrecht, the Netherlands: Kluwer.

Kamp, H. and U. Reyle. 1996. A calculus for first order discourse representation structures. *Journal of Logic, Language, and Information* 5(3/4):297–348.

Karttunen, L. 1976. Discourse referents. In *Syntax and Semantics 7*, J. McCawley (ed.), pp. 363–385. New York, NY: Academic Press.

Lakoff, G. 1987. *Women, Fire and Dangerous Things. What Categories Reveal about the Mind*. Chicago, IL: Chicago University Press.

van Lambalgen, M. and F. Hamm. 2005. *The Proper Treatment of Events*. Malden, MA: Blackwell.

Langacker, R. W. 1987. *Foundations of Cognitive Grammar, Vol. 1: Theoretical Prerequisites*. Stanford, CA: Stanford University Press.

Langacker, R. W. 1990. *Concept, Image, and Symbol. The Cognitive Basis of Grammar*. Berlin, Germany: Mouton de Gruyter.

Langacker, R. W. 1991. *Foundations of Cognitive Grammar, Vol. 2: Descriptive Application*. Stanford, CA: Stanford University Press.

Lappin, S. (ed.). 1997. *The Handbook of Contemporary Semantic Theory*. Oxford, U.K.: Blackwell.

Lyons, J. 1977. *Semantics*. Cambridge, U.K.: Cambridge University Press.

Majid, A. and M. Bowerman (eds.). 2007. "Cutting and breaking" events—A cross-linguistic perspective (Special Issue). *Cognitive Linguistics* 18(2).

Mark, D. M. and A. G. Turk. 2003. Landscape categories in Yindjibarndi: Ontology, environment, and language. In *Spatial Information Theory: Foundations of Geographic Information Science. Proceedings of the International Conference COSIT 2003*, Kartause Ittingen, Switzerland, September 24–28, 2003, W. Kuhn, M. Worboys, and S. Timpf (eds.). *Lecture Notes in Computer Science* 2825:28–45. Berlin, Germany: Springer-Verlag.

Mark, D. M. and A. G. Turk. 2004. Ethnophysiography and the ontology of landscape. In *Proceedings of GIScience*, Adelphi, MD, October 20–23, 2004, pp. 152–155.

Mark, D. M., A. G. Turk, and D. Stea. 2007. Progress on Yindjibarndi Ethnophysiography. In *Spatial Information Theory. Proceedings of the International Conference COSIT 2007*, Melbourne, Australia,

September 19–23, 2007, S. Winter, M. Duckham, and L. Kulik (eds.). *Lecture Notes in Computer Science* 4736:1–19. Berlin, Germany: Springer-Verlag.

Martin, P. 2002. Knowledge representation in CGLF, CGIF, KIF, Frame-CG, and Formalized English. In *Conceptual Structures: Integration and Interfaces. Proceedings of the 10th International Conference on Conceptual Structures, ICSS 2002*, Borovets, Bulgaria, July 15–19, 2002, U. Priss, D. Corbett, and G. Angelova (eds.). *Lecture Notes in Artificial Intelligence* 2393:77–91. Berlin, Germany: Springer-Verlag.

Mihatsch, W. 2007. Taxonomic and meronomic superordinates with nominal coding. In *Ontolinguistics: How Ontological Status Shapes the Linguistic Coding of Concepts*, A. C. Schalley and D. Zaefferer (eds.), pp. 359–377. Berlin, Germany: Mouton de Gruyter.

Montague, R. 1973. The proper treatment of quantification in ordinary English. In *Approaches to Natural Language. Proceedings of the 1970 Stanford Workshop on Grammar and Semantics*, J. Hintikka, J. M. E. Moravcsik, and P. Suppes (eds.), pp. 221–242. Dordrecht, the Netherlands: Reidel. [Reprinted in Montague (1974), pp. 247–270; Reprinted in Portner and Partee (eds.) (2002), pp. 17–34; Reprinted in Gutiérrez-Rexach (ed.) (2003) Vol. I, pp. 225–244].

Montague, R. 1974. *Formal Philosophy: Selected Papers of Richard Montague*, ed. and with an intr. by R. H. Thomason. New Haven, CT: Yale University Press.

Morato, J., M. Á. Marzal, J. Lloréns, and J. Moreiro. 2004. WordNet applications. In *GWC 2004: Proceedings of the Second International WordNet Conference*, P. Sojka, K. Pala, P. Smrž, C. Fellbaum, and P. Vossen (eds.), pp. 270–278. Brno, Czech Republic: Masaryk University.

Nerrière, J.-P. 2004. *Don't Speak English, Parlez Globish*. Paris, France: Eyrolles.

Nickles, M., A. Pease, A. C. Schalley, and D. Zaefferer. 2007. Ontologies across disciplines. In *Ontolinguistics: How Ontological Status Shapes the Linguistic Coding of Concepts*, A. C. Schalley and D. Zaefferer (eds.), pp. 23–67. Berlin, Germany: Mouton de Gruyter.

Nirenburg, S. and V. Raskin. 2004. *Ontological Semantics*. Cambridge, MA: MIT Press.

Object Management Group (1997–2009). *Unified Modeling Language. UML Resource Page.* http://www.uml.org

Oosterom, P. van and S. Zlatanova (eds.). 2008. *Creating Spatial Information Infrastructures: Towards the Spatial Semantic Web*. Boca Raton, FL: CRC Press.

Peeters, B. (ed.). 2006. *Semantic Primes and Universal Grammar: Empirical Evidence from the Romance Languages*. Amsterdam, the Netherlands: John Benjamins.

Poesio, M. 2000. Semantic analysis. In *Handbook of Natural Language Processing*, R. Dale, H. Moisl, and H. Somers (eds.), pp. 93–122. New York, NY/Basel, Switzerland: Marcel Dekker.

Pollard, C. and I. A. Sag 1994. *Head-Driven Phrase Structure Grammar*. Chicago, IL/Stanford, CA: University of Chicago Press and CSLI.

Portner, P. and B. H. Partee (eds.). 2002. *Formal Semantics: The Essential Readings*. Oxford, U.K.: Blackwell.

Pustejovsky, J. 1991a. The generative lexicon. *Computational Linguistics* 17(4):409–441.

Pustejovsky, J. 1991b. The syntax of event structure. *Cognition* 41:47–81.

Pustejovsky, J. 1995. *The Generative Lexicon*. Cambridge, MA: MIT Press.

Pustejovsky, J. 2001. Generativity and explanation in semantics: A reply to Fodor and Lepore. In *The Language of Word Meaning*, P. Bouillon and F. Busa (eds.), pp. 51–74. Cambridge, U.K.: Cambridge University Press.

Rosch, E. H. 1973. On the internal structures of perceptual and semantic categories. In *Cognitive Development and the Acquisition of Language*, T. E. Moore (ed.), pp. 111–144. New York, NY: Academic Press.

Rosch, E., C. B. Mervis, W. D. Gray, D. M. Johnson, and P. Boynes-Braem. 1976. Basic objects in natural categories. *Cognitive Psychology* 8:382–439.

Ruppenhofer, J., M. Ellsworth, M. R. L. Petruck, C. R. Johnson, and J. Scheffczyk. 2006. *FrameNet II: Extended Theory and Practice*. http://framenet.icsi.berkeley.edu./book/book.pdf

Russell, J. A. 1991. Culture and the categorization of emotion. *Psychological Bulletin* 110:426–450.

Russell, J. A. and M. Yik. 1996. Emotion among the Chinese. In *Handbook of Chinese Psychology*, M. H. Bond (ed.), pp. 166–188. Hong Kong, China: Oxford University Press.

Saurer, W. 1993. A natural deduction system for discourse representation theory. *Journal of Philosophical Logic* 22(3):249–302.

Schalley, A. C. 2004a. *Cognitive Modeling and Verbal Semantics. A Representational Framework Based on UML*. Berlin, Germany/New York, NY: Mouton de Gruyter.

Schalley, A. C. 2004b. Representing verbal semantics with diagrams. An adaptation of the UML for lexical semantics. In *Proceedings of the 20th International Conference on Computational Linguistics (COLING)*, Geneva, Switzerland, Vol. II, pp. 785–791. Geneva, Switzerland: Association for Computational Linguistics.

Schalley, A. C. and D. Khlentzos (eds.). 2007. *Mental States. Volume 2: Language and Cognitive Structure*. Amsterdam, the Netherlands: John Benjamins.

Schalley, A. C. and D. Zaefferer (eds.). 2007. *Ontolinguistics: How Ontological Status Shapes the Linguistic Coding of Concepts*. Berlin, Germany: Mouton de Gruyter.

Scharl, A. 2007. Towards the geospatial web: Media platforms for managing geotagged knowledge repositories. In *The Geospatial Web—How Geo-Browsers, Social Software and the Web 2.0 are Shaping the Network Society*, A. Scharl and K. Tochtermann (eds.), pp. 3–14. London, U.K.: Springer-Verlag.

Sowa, J. 2000. *Knowledge Representation. Logical, Philosophical, and Computational Foundations*. Pacific Grove, CA: Brooks/Cole.

Stock, K. 2008. Determining semantic similarity of behaviour using natural semantic metalanguage to match user objectives to available web services. *Transactions in GIS* 12(6):733–755.

Talmy, L. 2000. *Toward a Cognitive Semantics*. 2 Vols. Cambridge, MA: MIT Press.

Van Valin, R. D. 1999. Generalised semantic roles and the syntax-semantics interface. In *Empirical Issues in Formal Syntax and Semantics 2*, F. Corblin, C. Dobrovie-Sorin, and J.-M. Marandin (eds.), pp. 373–389. The Hague, the Netherlands: Thesus. Available at http://linguistics.buffalo.edu/people/faculty/vanvalin/rrg/vanvalin_papers/gensemroles.pdf

Van Valin, R. D. 2004. Semantic macroroles in Role and Reference Grammar. In *Semantische Rollen*, R. Kailuweit and M. Hummel (eds.), pp. 62–82. Tübingen, Germany: Narr.

Van Valin, R. D., and R. J. LaPolla. 1997. *Syntax: Structure, Meaning and Function*. Cambridge, U.K.: Cambridge University Press.

Veres, C. and J. Sampson. 2005. Ontology and taxonomy: Why "is-a" still isn't just "is-a." In *Proceedings of the 2005 International Conference on e-Business, Enterprise Information Systems, e-Government, and Outsourcing*, Las Vegas, NV, June 20–23, 2005, H. R. Arabnia (ed.), pp. 174–186. Las Vegas, NV: CSREA Press.

Vossen, P. 2001. Condensed meaning in EuroWordNet. In *The Language of Word Meaning*, P. Bouillon and F. Busa (eds.), pp. 363–383. Cambridge, U.K.: Cambridge University Press.

Vossen, P. (ed.). 1998. *EuroWordNet: A Multilingual Database With Lexical Semantic Networks*. Dordrecht, the Netherlands: Kluwer. [Reprinted from *Computers and the Humanities* 32(2/3)]

Wanner, L. (ed.). 1996. *Lexical Functions in Lexicography and Natural Language Processing*. Amsterdam, the Netherlands: John Benjamins.

Wanner, L. (ed.). 2007. *Selected Lexical and Grammatical Issues in Meaning-Text Theory: In Honour of Igor Mel'čuk*. Amsterdam, the Netherlands: John Benjamins.

Wierzbicka, A. 1972. *Semantic Primitives*. Frankfurt, Germany: Athenäum.

Wierzbicka, A. 1982. Why can you *have a drink* when you can't **have an eat*? *Language* 58(4):753–799.

Wierzbicka, A. 1985. *Lexicography and Conceptual Analysis*. Ann Arbor, MI: Karoma.

Wierzbicka, A. 1988. *The Semantics of Grammar*. Amsterdam, the Netherlands: John Benjamins.

Wierzbicka, A. 1991. Semantic complexity: Conceptual primitives and the principle of substitutability. *Theoretical Linguistics* 17(1/2/3):75–97.

Wierzbicka, A. 1992. *Semantics, Culture and Cognition: Universal Human Concepts in Culture-Specific Configurations.* Oxford, U.K.: Oxford University Press.

Wierzbicka, A. 1996. *Semantics: Primes and Universals.* Oxford, U.K.: Oxford University Press.

Wierzbicka, A. 1997. *Understanding Cultures Through Their Key Words: English, Russian, Polish, German and Japanese.* Oxford, U.K.: Oxford University Press.

Wierzbicka, A. 1999. *Emotions across Languages and Cultures.* Cambridge, U.K.: Cambridge University Press.

Wierzbicka, A. 2004. 'Happiness' in cross-linguistic and cross-cultural perspective. *Daedalus* Spring 2004, 133(2):34–43.

Wierzbicka, A. 2006. *English: Meaning and Culture.* New York, NY: Oxford University Press.

Wierzbicka, A. 2009a. Overcoming anglocentrism in emotion research. *Emotion Review* 1:24–30.

Wierzbicka, A. 2009b. *Experience, Evidence, and Sense: The Hidden Cultural Legacy of English.* New York, NY: Oxford University Press.

Wisniewski, E. J., M. Imai, and L. Casey. 1996. On the equivalence of superordinate concepts. *Cognition* 60:269–298.

Wunderlich, D. 1996. Models of lexical decomposition. In *Lexical Structures and Language Use. Proceedings of the International Conference on Lexicology and Lexical Semantics*, Vol. 1, *Plenary Lectures and Session Papers*, E. Weigand and F. Hundsnurscher (eds.). pp. 169–183. Tübingen, Germany: Niemeyer.

Wunderlich, D. 1997. Cause and the structure of verbs. *Linguistic Inquiry* 28(1):27–68.

Ye, Z. 2001. An inquiry into "sadness" in Chinese. In *Emotions in Crosslinguistic Perspective*, J. Harkins and A. Wierzbicka (eds.), pp. 359–404. Berlin, Germany: Mouton de Gruyter.

Ye, Z. 2004. Chinese categorization of interpersonal relationships and the cultural logic of Chinese social categories: An indigenous perspective. *Intercultural Pragmatics* 1(2):211–230.

Zaefferer, D. 2002. Polysemy, polyvalence, and linking mismatches. The concept of RAIN and its codings in English, German, Italian, and Spanish. *DELTA—Documentação de Estudos em Lingüística Téorica e Aplicada* 18(spe):27–56.

6

Natural Language Generation

David D. McDonald
BBN Technologies

6.1 Introduction

Natural language generation (NLG) is the process by which thought is rendered into language. It has been studied by philosophers, neurologists, psycholinguists, child psychologists, and linguists. Here, we examine what generation is to those who look at it from a computational perspective: people in the fields of artificial intelligence and computational linguistics.

From this viewpoint, the 'generator'—the equivalent of a person with something to say—is a computer program. Its work begins with the initial intention to communicate, and then on to determining the content of what will be said, selecting the wording and rhetorical organization and fitting it to a grammar, through to formatting the words of a written text or establishing the prosody of speech. Today, what a generator produces can range from a single word or phrase given in answer to a question or as label on a diagram, through multi-sentence remarks and questions within a dialog, and on to multipage explanations and beyond depending on the capacity and goals of the program it is working for—the machine 'speaker' with something to say—and the demands and particulars of the context.

Modulo a number of caveats discussed later, the process of generation is usually divided into three parts, often implemented as three separate programs: (1) identifying the goals of the utterance, (2) planning how the goals may be achieved by evaluating the situation and available communicative resources, and (3) realizing the plans as a text.

Generation has been part of computational linguistics for as long as the field has existed, though it only became a substantial subfield in the 1980s. It appeared first in the 1950s as a minor aspect of machine translation. In the 1960s, random sentence generators were developed, often for use as grammar checkers. The 1970s saw the first cases of dynamically generating the motivated utterances of an artificial speaker: composing answers to questions put to database query programs and providing simple explanations for expert systems. That period also saw the first theoretically important generation systems. These systems reasoned, introspected, appreciated the conventions of discourse, and used sophisticated models of grammar. The texts they produced, while small in number, remain among the most fluent in the literature. By the beginning of the 1980s, generation had emerged as a field of its own, with unique concerns and issues.

6.1.1 Generation Compared to Comprehension

To understand those issues, it will be useful to compare generation with its far more studied and sophisticated cousin, natural language comprehension. Even after 40 years, generation is often misunderstood as a simple variation on comprehension—a tendency that should be dispelled. Generation must be seen as a problem of construction and planning, not analysis.

As a process, generation has its own basis of organization, a fact that follows directly from intrinsic differences in information flow. The processing in language comprehension typically follows the traditional stages of a linguistic analysis: phonology, morphology, syntax, semantics, pragmatics/discourse; moving gradually from the text to the intentions behind it. In comprehension, the 'known' is the wording of the text (and possibly its intonation). From the wording, the comprehension process constructs and deduces the propositional content conveyed by the text and the probable intentions of the speaker in producing it. The primary process involves scanning the words of the text in sequence, during which the form of the text gradually unfolds. The need to scan imposes a methodology based on the management of multiple hypotheses and predictions that feed a representation that must be expanded dynamically. Major problems are caused by ambiguity (one form can convey a range of alternative meanings), and by under-specification (the audience gets more information from inferences based on the situation than is conveyed by the actual text). In addition, mismatches in the speaker's and audience's model of the situation (and especially of each other) lead to unintended inferences.

Generation has the opposite information flow: from intentions to text, content to form. What is already known and what must be discovered is quite different from comprehension, and this has many implications. The known is the generator's awareness of its speaker's intentions and mood, its plans, and the content and structure of any text the generator has already produced. Coupled with a model of the audience, the situation, and the discourse, this information provides the basis for making choices among the alternative wordings and constructions that the language provides—the primary effort in deliberately constructing a text.

Most generation systems do produce texts sequentially from left to right, but only after having made decisions top-down for the content and form of the text as a whole. Ambiguity in a generator's knowledge is not possible (indeed one of the problems is to notice that an ambiguity has inadvertently been introduced into the text). Rather than under-specification, a generator's problem is how to choose how to signal its intended inferences from an oversupply of possibilities along with that what information should be omitted and what must be included.

With its opposite flow of information, it would be reasonable to assume that the generation process can be organized like the comprehension process but with the stages in opposite order, and to a certain extent this is true: pragmatics (goal selection) typically precedes consideration of discourse structure and coherence, which usually precede semantic matters such as the fitting of concepts to words. In turn, the syntactic context of a word must be fixed before the precise morphological and suprasegmental form it should take can be known. However, we should avoid taking this as the driving force in a generator's design, since to emphasize the ordering of representational levels derived from theoretical linguistics would be to miss generation's special character, namely, that generation is above all a planning process. Generation entails realizing goals in the presence of constraints and dealing with the implications of limitations on resources.*

This being said, the consensus among people who have studied both is that generation is the more difficult of the two. What a person needs to know in order to develop a computer program that produces fluent text is either trivial (the text is entered directly into the code, perhaps with some parameters, and produced as is—virtually every commercial program in wide use that produces text uses this 'template' method) or else it is quite difficult because one has to work out a significant number of techniques and facts about language that other areas of language research have never considered. It is probably no accident that for most of its history advances in NLG have only come through the work of graduate students on their PhD theses.

This also goes a long way toward explaining why so little work has been done on generation as compared with comprehension. At a general meeting, papers on parsing will outnumber those on generation by easily five to one or more. Instead, most work on generation is reported at the international workshops on generation, which have been held nearly every year since 1983.

6.1.2 Computers Are Dumb

Two other difficulties with doing research on generation should be cited before moving on. One just alluded to is the relative stupidity of computer programs, and with it the lack of any practical need for natural language generation as those in the field view it—templates will do just fine. We have seen this with the popular success of programs such as Alice (Wallace), perhaps the best known of the chatterbots that use a large set of stimulus-response rules and clever script writing to simulate an intelligent agent while in fact having virtually no comprehension of what they are saying or what is said to them—a line of work that goes back to Weizenbaum's Eliza (1966).

People who study generation tend more to be scientists than engineers and are trying to understand the human capacity to use language—with all its subtleties of nuance, and the complexity, even arbitrariness, of its motivations. Computers, on the other hand, do not think very subtle thoughts. The authors of their programs, even artificial intelligence programs, inevitably leave out the rationales and goals behind the instructions for their behavior, and with very few exceptions,[†] computer programs do not have any emotional or even rhetorical attitudes toward the people who are using them. Without the richness of information, perspective, and intention that humans bring to what they say, computers have no basis for making the decisions that go into natural utterances. It does not make sense to include a natural language generator in one's system if there is nothing for it to do.

6.1.3 The Problem of the Source

The other difficulty is ultimately more serious and is in large part responsible for the relative lack of sophistication in the field as compared with other language processing disciplines. This is the problem of

---

* Examples of limited resources include the expressive capacity of the syntactic and lexical devices a given language happens to have, or the limited space available in a sentence or a figure title given the prose style that has been chosen.

† The exceptions are programs deliberately written to entertain or interact with people. The animated characters developed at Zoesis Inc. are a prime example (Loyall et al. 2004) as is the work of Mateas and Stern (2002) on Facade that uses the same technology. While less emotionally grounded, the synthetic characters developed at the USC Institute for Creative Technologies such as their Iraqi Tutor or Mission Rehearsal Exercise are also rich enough to know what to say and why; see, e.g., Traum et al. (2007) or Swartout et al. (2006).

the source. We know virtually nothing about what a generation system should start from if it is to speak as well as people do.

Even when approached as a problem in artificial intelligence rather then human psycholinguistics, this lack of a definitive and well-understood starting point remains a problem, since unlike the situation with automated chess players or the expert systems that control factories, we know next to nothing about how our only examples of effective natural language generators—people—go about the business of producing an utterance.

In language comprehension the source is obvious; we all know what a written text or an acoustic signal is. In generation, the source is a 'state of mind' inside a speaker with 'intentions' acting in a 'situation'—all terms of art with very slippery meanings. Studying it from a computational perspective, as we are here, we presume that this state of mind has a representation, but there are dozens of formal (consistently implementable) representations used within the Artificial Intelligence (AI) community that have (what we assume is) the necessary expressive power, with no a priori reason to expect one to be better than another as the mental source of an utterance. Worse yet is the lack of consistency between research groups in their choice of primitive terms and relations—does the representation of a meal bottom-out with 'eat,' or must that notion necessarily be expanded into a manner, a result, and a time period, with 'eat' just a runtime abstraction.

The lack of a consistent answer to the question of the generator's source has been at the heart of the problem of how to make research on generation intelligible and engaging for the rest of the computational linguistics community, and it has complicated efforts to evaluate alternative treatments even for people in the field. As a result, the ever-increasing effort at comparative evaluation has focused on isolated subproblems such as the generation of referring expressions.

6.2 Examples of Generated Texts: From Complex to Simple and Back Again

If we look at the development of natural language generation in terms of the sorts of texts different systems have produced, we encounter something of a paradox. As the field advanced, the texts got simpler. Only in the last decade have most generation systems begun to produce texts with the sophistication and fluency that was present in the systems of the early 1970s.

6.2.1 Complex

One dramatic example that developed during the earliest period is John Clippinger's program Erma (1977), which modeled an actual psychoanalytic patient talking to her therapist. It emulated one paragraph of speech by the patient excerpted from extensive transcripts of her conversations. The effort was joint work by Clippinger in his 1974 PhD thesis and Richard Brown in his Bachelor's thesis (1974).

The paragraph was the result of a computationally complex model of the patient's thought processes: from the first identification of a goal, through planning, criticism, and replanning of how to express it, and finally linguistic realization. Clippinger and Brown's program had a multiprocessing capability—it could continue to think and plan while talking. This allowed them to develop a model of 'restart' phenomena in generation, including the motivation behind fillers like "*uh*" or dubitatives like "*you know*." Text segments shown below in parenthesis are what Erma was planning to say before it cut itself off and restarted. In other respects, this is an actual paragraph from a transcript of the patient reproduced in every detail, but from a first principles model of thought and generation.

> *You know for some reason I just thought about the bill and payment again. (You shouldn't give me a*
> *bill.) <Uh> I was thinking that I (shouldn't be given a bill) of asking you whether it wouldn't be all*

right for you not to give me a bill. That is, I usually by (the end of the month know the amount of the bill), well, I immediately thought of the objections to this, but my idea was that I would simply count up the number of hours and give you a check at the end of the month.

There has yet to be another program in the literature that can even begin to approach the human-like quality of this text.* On the other hand Erma only ever produced that one text and some parameter-driven variations, and neither Brown's multilevel, resumable, interrupt-driven computational architecture nor Clippinger's rich set of thinking, critiquing, and linguistic modules were ever followed up by other people.

6.2.2 Simple

By the end of the decade of the 1970s, generation began to be recognized as a field with shared assumptions and not just the work of scattered individuals. It also began to attract the attention of the research-funding community, a mixed blessing perhaps, since while the additional resources now allowed work on generation to be pursued by research teams instead of isolated graduate students, the need to conform to the expectations of other groups—particularly in the choice of source representation and conceptual vocabulary—substantially limits the creative options. Probably as a direct result, the focus of the work during the 1980s moved within the generator, and the representations and architecture of the speaker became a black box behind an impenetrable wall.

Nevertheless, the greatly increased number of people working in the field led to many important developments. If the texts that the various groups' systems produced were not of the highest quality, this was offset by increased systematicity in the techniques in use, and a markedly greater understanding of some of the specific issues in generation. Among these were the following:

- The implications of separating the processing of a generator into distinct modules and levels of representation, especially in regard to which operations (lexical choice, linear ordering, and such) took place at which level
- The use of pronouns and other forms of subsequent reference
- The possibilities and techniques for 'aggregating' minimal propositions to form syntactically complex texts
- The relationship between how lexical choice is done and the choice of representation used in the source

Here is an example of text produced by systems developed in the late 1980s—a generator that is not at least this fluent today would be well behind the state of the art. This is from Marie Meteer's Spokesman system (1992), and set in a military domain; the text shown here is an excerpt from a page-long generated operations order (OPORD). Notice the use of simple formatting elements.

2. MISSION
10th Corps defend in assigned sector to defeat the 8th Combined Arms Army.

3. EXECUTION
a. 52d Mechanized Division
(1) Conduct covering force operations along avenues B and C to defeat the lead regiments of the first tactical echelon in the CFA in assigned sector.

A text like this will never win any prizes for literature, but unlike its hand-crafted predecessors of the 1970s, it can be produced mechanically from any comparable input without any human intervention or fine tuning.

---

* One notable early exception was in Richard Gabriel's thesis (1981, 1986) where he seamlessly wove three machine generated paragraphs describing a procedure that were indistinguishable from the rest. Today we also see mundane report and web pages that are mixtures of generations from first principles (from a semantic model) and frozen templates selected by people that are hard tell from the 'real thing.'

The source OPORD for this text was a battle order data structure that was automatically constructed by a simulation system that was part of SIMNET (Cosby 1999) that fought virtual battles in detail against human troops in tank simulators—an excellent source of material for a generator to work with.

6.2.3 Today

Now, as we near the end of the first decade of the twenty-first century, we have reached a point where a well designed and linguistically sophisticated system can achieve the fluency of the special-purpose systems of the 1970s, but will operate on a better understood theoretical base. As an example of this, consider Jacques Robin's Streak (1993, 1996). It operates within a sublanguage, in this case the language of sports: it writes short summaries of basketball games. Like all news reporting, this genre is characterized by information-dense, syntactically rich summary texts, texts that remain challenging to the best of systems. With Streak, Robin has appreciated the extensive references to historical information in these texts, and his experience has important implications for how to approach the production of summaries of all sorts.

Technically, Streak is a system based on revision. It begins by producing a representation of the simple facts that will provide anchors for later extensions. Here is an example of what it could start from (Robin 1996: 206).

Dallas, TX—Charles Barkley scored 42 points Sunday as the Phoenix Suns defeated the Dallas Mavericks 123–97.

This initial text is then modified as salient historical or ancillary information about this game and the players' past records is considered. Here is the final form.

Dallas, TX—Charles Barkley tied a season high with 42 points and Danny Ainge came off the bench to add 21 Sunday as the Phoenix Suns handed the Dallas Mavericks their league worst 13th straight home defeat 123–97.

Notice what has happened. Initial forms have been progressively replaced with phrases that carry more information: "*scored N points*" has become "*tied a season high with N points.*" Syntactic formulations have been changed ("*defeat X*" has become "*hand X(a) defeat*"), where the new choice is able to carry information that the original could not (the noun form of "*defeat*" can be modified by "*their league worst*" and "*Nth straight home*"). This is sophisticated linguistic reasoning that has been matched by only a few earlier systems.

Given the rich architectures available in generation systems today, the production of detailed, if mundane, information derived directly from an application program has become almost a cookbook operation in the sense that practitioners of the art can readily engineer a system with these abilities in a relatively short period of time. Much of what makes these modern generators effective is that they are applied to very specific domains, domains where the corpus of text can be described as belonging to a 'sublanguage' (see, e.g., Kittredge and Lehrberger 1982). That is to say, they restrict themselves to a specialized area of discourse with a very focused audience and stipulated content, thereby reducing the options for word choice and syntactic style to a manageable set. In particular, museum exhibits have been a very profitable area for NLG because they provide a natural setting for tailoring text to appreciate what exhibits people have already heard about. The ILEX system, for example, focused on ordering issues and the dynamic generation of text in Web pages (e.g., O'Donnell et al. 2001 or Dale et al. 1998).

6.3 The Components of a Generator

To produce a text in the computational paradigm, there has to be a program with something to say—we can call this 'the application' or 'the speaker.' And there must be a program with the competence to render the application's intentions into fluent prose appropriate to the situation—what we will call 'the generator'—which is the natural language generation system proper.

Given that the task is to engineer the production of text or speech for a purpose—emulating what people do and/or making it available to machines—then both of these components, the speaker and the generator, are necessary. Studying the language side of the process without anchoring the work with respect to the conceptual models and intentional structures of an application may be appropriate for theoretical linguistics or the study of grammar algorithms, but not for language generation. Indeed, some of the most exciting work comes from projects where the generator is only a small part.*

As described earlier, the very earliest work on sophisticated language production interleaved the functions of the speaker and the generator into a single system. Today, there will invariably be three or four components (if not a dozen) dividing the work amongst themselves according to a myriad of different criteria. We will discuss the philosophies governing these criteria later.

6.3.1 Components and Levels of Representation

Given the point of view we adopt in this chapter, we will say that generation starts in the mind of the speaker (the execution states of the computer program) as it acts upon an intention to say something—to achieve some goal through the use of language: to express feelings, to gossip, to assemble a pamphlet on how to stop smoking (Reiter et al. 2003).

6.3.1.1 Tasks

Regardless of the approach taken, generation proper involves at least four tasks.

a. Information must be *selected* for inclusion in the utterance.
   Depending on how this information is reified into representational units (a property of the speaker's mental model), parts of the units may have to be omitted, other units added in by default, and perspectives taken on the units to reflect the speaker's attitude toward them.
b. The information must be given a *textual organization*.
   It must be ordered, both sequentially and in terms of linguistic relations such as modification or subordination. The coherence relationships among the units of the information must be reflected in this organization so that the reasons why the information was included will be apparent to the audience.
c. *Linguistic resources* must be chosen to support the information's realization.
   Ultimately these resources will come down to choices of particular words, idioms, syntactic constructions, productive morphological variations, etc., but the form they take at the first moment that they are associated with the selected information will vary greatly between approaches. (Note that to choose a resource is not ipso facto to simultaneously deploy it in its final form—a fact that is not always appreciated.)
d. The selected and organized resources must be *realized* as an actual text and written out or spoken.
   This stage can itself involve several levels of representation and interleaved processes.

6.3.1.2 Coarse Components

These four tasks are usually divided among three components as listed below. The first two are often spoken of as deciding 'what to say,' the third deciding 'how to say it.'

---

* See for example the integration of generation into dynamically produced movies that act as tour guides in the Peach system (Callaway et al. 2005, Stock and Zancanaro 2007).

1. The application program or 'speaker.'

   It does the thinking and maintains a model of the situation. Its goals are what initiate the process, and it is its representation of concepts and the world that supplies the source on which the other components operate.

2. A text planner.

   It selects (or receives) units from the application and organizes them to create a structure for the utterance as a text by employing some knowledge of rhetoric. It appreciates the conventions for signaling information flow in a linguistic medium: what information is new to the interlocutors, what is old; what items are in focus; and whether there has been a shift in topic.

3. A linguistic component.

   It realizes the planner's output as an utterance. In its traditional form during the 1970s and early 1980s it supplied all of the grammatical knowledge used in the generator. Today this knowledge is likely to be more evenly distributed throughout the system. This component's task is to adapt (and possibly to select) linguistic forms to fit their grammatical contexts and to orchestrate their composition. This process leads, possibly incrementally, to a surface structure for the utterance, which is then read out to produce the grammatically and morphologically appropriate wording for the utterance.

How these roughly drawn components interact is a matter of considerable debate and no little amount of confusion, as no two research groups are likely to agree on precisely what kinds of knowledge or processing appear in a given component or where its boundaries should lie. There have been attempts to standardize the process, most notably the RAGS project (see, e.g., Cahill et al. 1999), but to date they have failed to gain any traction.

One camp, making an analogy to the apparent abilities of people, holds that the process is monotonic and indelible. A completely opposite camp extensively revises its (abstract) draft texts. Some groups organize the components as a pipeline; others use blackboards. Nothing conclusive about the relative merits of these alternatives can be said today. We continue to be in a period where the best advice is to let a 1000 flowers bloom.

6.3.1.3 Representational Levels

There are necessarily one or more intermediate levels between the source and the text simply because the production of an utterance is a serial process extended in time. Most decisions will influence several parts of the utterance at once, and consequently cannot possibly be acted upon at the moment they are made. Without some representation of the results of these decisions there would be no mechanism for remembering them and utterances would be incoherent.

The consensus favors at least three representational levels, roughly the output of each of the components. In the first or 'earliest' level, the information units of the application that are relevant to the text planner form a *message* level—the source from which the later components operate. Depending on the system, this level can consist of anything from an unorganized heap of minimal propositions or RDF to an elaborate typed structure with annotations about the relevance and purposes of its parts.

All systems include one or more levels of *surface syntactic structure*. These encode the phrase structure of the text and the grammatical relations among its constituents. Morphological specialization of word stems and the introduction of punctuation or capitalization are typically done as this level is read out and the utterance uttered. Common formalisms at this level include systemic networks, tree-adjoining and categorial grammar, and functional unification, though practically every linguistic theory of grammar that has ever been developed has been used for generation at one time or another. Nearly all of today's generation systems express their utterances as written texts—characters printed on a computer screen or printed out as a pamphlet—rather than as speech. Consequently generators seldom include an explicit level of phonological form and intonation.*

In between the message and the surface structure is a level (or levels) of representation at which a system can reason about linguistic options without simultaneously being committed to syntactic details that are irrelevant to the problem at hand. Instead, abstract linguistic structures are combined with generalizations of the concepts in the speaker's domain-specific model and sophisticated concepts from lexical semantics. The level is variously called *text structure, deep syntax, abstract syntactic structure,* and the like. In some designs, it will employ rhetorical categories such as elaboration or temporal location. Alternatively it may be based on abstract linguistic concepts such as the matrix–adjunct distinction. It is usually organized as trees of constituents with a layout roughly parallel to that of the final text. The leaves of these trees may be direct mappings of units from the application or may be semantic structures specific to that level.

6.4 Approaches to Text Planning

Even though the classic conception of the division of labor in generation between a text planner and a linguistic component—where the latter is the sole repository of the generator's knowledge of language—was probably never really true in practice and is certainly not true today, it remains an effective expository device. In this section, we consider text planning in a relatively pure form, concentrating on the techniques for determining the content of the utterance and its large-scale (supra-sentential) organization.

It is useful in this context to consider a distinction put forward by the psycholinguist Willem Levelt (1989), between 'macro' and 'micro' planning.

- *Macro-planning* refers to the process(es) that choose the speech acts, establish the content, determine how the situation dictates perspectives, and so on.
- *Micro-planning* is a cover term for a group of phenomena: determining the detailed (sentence-internal) organization of the utterance, considering whether to use pronouns, looking at alternative ways to group information into phrases, noting the focus and information structure that must apply, and other such relatively fine-grained tasks. These, along with lexical choice, are precisely the set of tasks that fall into this nebulous middle ground that is motivating so much of today's work.

6.4.1 The Function of the Speaker

From the generator's perspective, the function of the application that it is working for is to set the scene. Since it takes no overtly linguistic actions beyond initiating the process, we are not inclined to think of the application program as a part of the generator proper. Nevertheless, the influence it wields in defining the situation and the semantic model from which the generator works is so strong that it must be designed in concert with the generator if high-quality results are to be achieved. This is the reason why we often speak of the application as the 'speaker,' emphasizing the linguistic influences on its design and its tight integration with the generator.

The speaker establishes what content is potentially relevant. It maintains an attitude toward its audience (as a tutor, reference guide, commentator, executive summarizer, copywriter, etc.). It has a history of past transactions. It is the component with the model of the present state and its physical or conceptual context. The speaker deploys a representation of what it knows, and this implicitly determines the nature and the expressive potential of the 'units' of speaker stuff that the generator works from to produce the

---

* Again, the exceptions are systems that are specifically designed to talk with people, particularly multi-modal systems that combine speech with gesture. The work by Justine Cassell on Rea (2000) is a prime example. The need to coordinate (animated) gesture with the production of the speech down to the syllable motivates a level representing coordinated action plans.

utterance (the source). We can collectively characterize all of this as the 'situation' in which the generation of the utterance takes place, in the sense of Barwise and Perry (1983) (see also Devlin 1991).

In the simplest case, the application consists of just a passive data base of items and propositions. and the situation is a selected subset of those propositions (the 'relevant data') that has been selected through some means, often by following the thread of a set of identifiers chosen in response to a question from the user.

In some cases, the situation is a body of raw data and the job of speaker is to make sense of it in linguistically communicable terms before any significant work can be done by the other components. The literature includes several important systems of this sort. Probably the most thoroughly documented is the Ana system developed by Karen Kukich (1986), where the input is a set of time points giving the values of stock indexes and trading volumes during the course of a day.

When the speaker is a commentator, the situation can evolve from moment to moment in actual real time. The SOCCER system (Andre et al. 1988) did commentary for football games that were being displayed on the user's screen. This led to some interesting problems in how large a chunk of information could reasonably be generated at a time, since too small a chunk would fail to see the larger intentions behind a sequence of individual passes and interceptions, while too large a chunk would take so long to utter that the commentator would fall behind the action.

One of the crucial tasks that must often be performed at the juncture between the application and the generator is enriching the information that the application supplies so that it will use the concepts that a person would expect even if the application had not needed them. We can see an example of this in one of the earliest, and still among the most accomplished generation systems, Anthony Davey's Proteus (1974).

Proteus played games of tic-tac-toe (noughts and crosses) and provided commentary on the results. Here is an example of what it produced:

> The game started with my taking a corner, and you took an adjacent one. I threatened you by taking the middle of the edge opposite that and adjacent to the one which I had just taken but you blocked it and threatened me. I blocked your diagonal and forked you. If you had blocked mine, you would have forked me, but you took the middle of the edge opposite of the corner which I took first and the one which you had just taken and so I won by completing my diagonal.

Proteus began with a list of the moves in the game it had just played. In this sample text, the list was the following. Moves are notated against a numbered grid; square one is the upper left corner. Proteus (P) is playing its author (D).

P:1 D:3 P:4 D:7 P:5 D:6 P:9

One is tempted to call this list of moves the 'message' that Proteus's text-planning component has been tasked by its application (the game player) to render into English—and it is what actually crosses the interface between them—but consider what this putative message leaves out when compared with the ultimate text: where are the concepts of move and countermove or the concept of a fork? The game playing program did not need to think in those terms to carry out its task and performed perfectly well without them, but if they were not in the text we would never for a moment think that the sequence was a game of tic-tac-toe.

Davey was able to get texts of this complexity and naturalness only because he imbued Proteus with a rich conceptual model of the game, and consequently could have it use terms like 'block' or 'threat' with assurance. Like most instances where exceptionally fluent texts have been produced, Davey was able to get this sort of performance from Proteus because he had the opportunity to develop the thinking part of the system as well its linguistic aspects, and consequently could insure that the speaker supplied rich perspectives and intentions for the generator to work with.

This, unfortunately, is quite a common state of affairs in the relationship between a generator and its speaker. The speaker, as an application program carrying out a task, has a pragmatically complete but conceptually impoverished model of what it wants to relate to its audience. Concepts that must be explicit in the text are implicit but unrepresented in the application's code and it remains to the generator (Proteus in this case) to make up the difference. Undoubtedly the concepts were present in the mind of the application's human programmer, but leaving them out makes the task easier to program and rarely limits the application's abilities. The problem of most generators is in effect how to convert water to wine, compensating in the generator for limitations in the application (McDonald and Meteer 1988).

6.4.2 Desiderata for Text Planning

The tasks of a text planner are many and varied. They include the following:

- Construing the speaker's situation in realizable terms given the available vocabulary and syntactic resources, an especially important task when the source is raw data. For example, precisely what points of the compass make the wind "*easterly*" (Bourbeau et al. 1990, Reiter et al. 2005)
- Determining the information to include in the utterance and whether it should be stated explicitly or left for inference
- Distributing the information into sentences and giving it an organization that reflects the intended rhetorical force, as well as the appropriate conceptual coherence and textual cohesion given the prior discourse

Since a text has both a literal and a rhetorical content, not to mention reflections of the speaker's affect and emotions, the determination of what the text is to say requires not only a specification of its propositions, statements, references, etc., but also a specification of how these elements are to be related to each other as parts of a single coherent text (what is evidence, what is a digression) and of how they are structured as a presentation to the audience to which the utterance is addressed. This presentation information establishes what is thematic, where the shifts in perspective are, how new information fits within the context established by the text that preceded it, and so on.

How to establish the simple, literal information content of the text is well understood, and a number of different techniques have been extensively discussed in the literature. How to establish the rhetorical content of the text, however, is only beginning to be explored, and in the past was done implicitly or by rote by directly coding it into the program. There have been some experiments in deliberate rhetorical planning, notably by Hovy (1990) and DiMarco and Hirst (1993). The specification and expression of affect is only just beginning to be explored, prompted by the ever increasing use of 'language enabled' synthetic characters in games, for example, Mateas and Stern (2003), and avatar-based man–machine interaction, for example, Piwek et al. (2005) or Streit et al. (2006).

6.4.3 Pushing vs. Pulling

To begin our examination of the major techniques in text planning, we need to consider how the text planner and speaker are connected. The interface between the two is based on one of two logical possibilities: 'pushing' or 'pulling.'

The application can push units of content to the text planner, in effect telling the text planner what to say and leaving it the job of organizing the units into a text with the desired style and rhetorical effect. Alternatively, the application can be passive, taking no part in the generation process, and the text planner will pull units from it. In this scenario, the speaker is assumed to have no intentions and only the simplest ongoing state (often it is a database). All of the work is then done on the generator's side of the fence.

Text planners that pull content from the application establish the organization of the text hand in glove with its content, using models of possible texts and their rhetorical structure as the basis of their actions. Their assessment of the situation determines which model they will use. Speakers that push content to the text planner typically use their own representation of the situation directly as the content source. At the time of writing, the pull school of thought has dominated new, theoretically interesting work in text planning, while virtually all practical systems are based on simple push applications or highly stylized, fixed 'schema'-based pull planners.

6.4.4 Planning by Progressive Refinement of the Speaker's Message

This technique—often called 'direct replacement'—is easy to design and implement, and is by far the most mature approach of those we will cover. In its simplest form, it amounts to little more than is done by ordinary database report generators or mail-merge programs when they make substitutions for variables in fixed strings of text. In its sophisticated forms, which invariably incorporate multiple levels of representation and complex abstractions, it has produced some of the most fluent and flexible texts in the field. Three systems discussed earlier did their text planning using progressive refinement: Proteus, Erma, and Spokesman.

Progressive refinement is a push technique. It starts with a data structure already present in the application and then it gradually transforms that data into a text. The semantic coherence of the final text follows from the underlying semantic coherence that is present in the data structure that the application passes to the generator as its message.

The essence of progressive refinement is to have the text planner add additional information on top of the basic skeleton provided by the application. We can see a good example of this in Davey's Proteus system, where in this case the skeleton is the sequence of moves. The ordering of the moves must still be respected in the final text because Proteus is a commentator and the sequence of events described in a text is implicitly understood as reflecting a sequence in the world. Proteus only departs from the ordering when it serves a useful rhetorical purpose, as in the example text where it describes the alternative events that could have occurred if its opponent had made a different move early on.

On top of the skeleton, Proteus looks for opportunities to group moves into compound complex sentences by viewing the sequence of moves in terms of the concepts of tic-tac-toe. For example, it looks for pairs of forced moves (i.e., a blocking move to counter a move that had set up two in a row). It also looks for moves with strategically important consequences (a move creating a fork). For each semantically significant pattern that it knows how to recognize, Proteus has one or more text organization patterns that can express it. For example, the pattern 'high-level action followed by literal statement of the move' might yield "*I threatened you by taking the middle of the edge opposite that.*" Alternatively, Proteus could have used 'literal move followed by its high-level consequence' pattern: "*I took the middle of the opposite edge, threatening you.*"

The choice of realization is left up to a *specialist*, which takes into account as much information as the designer of the system, Davey in this case, knows how to bring to bear. Similarly, a specialist is employed to elaborate on the skeleton when larger scale strategic phenomena occur. In the case of a fork, this prompts the additional rhetorical task of explaining what the other player might have done to avoid the fork.

Proteus' techniques are an example of the standard design for a progressive refinement text planner: start with a skeletal data structure that is a rough approximation of the final text's organization using information provided by the speaker directly from its internal model of the situation. The structure then goes through some number of successive steps of processing and re-representation as its elements are incrementally transformed or mapped to structures that are closer and closer to a surface text, becoming progressively less domain oriented and more linguistic at each step. The Streak system described earlier follows the same design, replacing simple syntactic and lexical forms with more complex ones with a greater capacity to carry content.

Control is usually vested in the structure itself, using what is known as *data-directed control*. Each element of the data is associated with a specialist or an instance of some standard mapping which takes charge of assembling the counterpart of the element within the next layer of representation. The whole process is often organized into a pipeline where processing can be going on at multiple representational levels simultaneously as the text is produced in its natural left to right order as it would unfold if being spoken by a person.

A systematic problem with progressive refinement follows directly from its strengths, namely, that its input data structure, the source of its content and control structure, is also a straightjacket. While it provides a ready and effective organization for the text, the structure does not provide any vantage point from which to deviate from that organization even if that would be more effective rhetorically. This remains a serious problem with the approach, and is part of the motivation behind the types of text planners we will look at next.

6.4.5 Planning Using Rhetorical Operators

The next text-planning technique that we will look at can be loosely called 'formal planning using rhetorical operators.' It is a pull technique that operates over a pool of relevant data that has been identified within the application. The chunks in the pool are typically full propositions—the equivalents of single simple clauses if they were realized in isolation.

This technique assumes that there is no useful organization to the propositions in the pool, or, alternatively, that such organization as is there is orthogonal to the discourse purpose at hand, and should be ignored. Instead, the mechanisms of the text planner look for matches between the items in the relevant data pool and the planner's abstract patterns, and select and organize the items accordingly.

Three design elements come together in the practice of operator-based text planning, all of which have their roots in work done in the later 1970s:

- The use of formal means–ends reasoning techniques adapted from the robot-action planning literature
- A conception of how communication could be formalized that derives from speech-act theory and specific work done at the University of Toronto
- Theories of the large-scale 'grammar' of discourse structure

Means–ends analysis, especially as elaborated in the work by Sacerdoti (1977), is the backbone of the technique. It provides a control structure that does a top-down, hierarchical expansion of goals. Each goal is expanded through the application of a set of operators that instantiate a sequence of subgoals that will achieve it. This process of matching operators to goals terminates in propositions that can directly realize the actions dictated by terminal subgoals. These propositions become the leaves of a tree-structured text plan, with the goals as the nonterminals and the operators as the rules of derivation that give the tree its shape.

6.4.6 Text Schemas

The third text-planning technique we describe is the use of preconstructed, fixed networks that are referred to as 'schemas' following the coinage of the person who first articulated this approach, Kathy McKeown (1985). Schemas are a pull technique. They make selections from a pool of relevant data provided by the application according to matches with patterns maintained by the system's planning knowledge—just like an operator-based planner. The difference is that the choice of (the equivalent of the) operators is fixed rather than actively planned. Means–ends analysis-based systems assemble a sequence of operators dynamically as the planning is underway. A schema-based system comes to the problem with the entire sequence already in hand.

Given that characterization of schemas, it would be easy to see them as nothing more than compiled plans, and one can imagine how such a compiler might work if a means–ends planner were given feedback about the effectiveness of its plans and could choose to reify it's particularly effective ones (though no one has ever done this). However, that would miss a important fact about system design that it is often simpler and just as effective to simply write down a plan by rote rather than to attempt to develop a theory of the knowledge of context and communicative effectiveness that would be deployed in the development of the plan and from that attempt to construct a plan from first principles, which is essentially what the means–ends approach to text planning does. It is no accident that schema-based systems (and even more so progressive refinement systems) have historically produced longer and more interesting texts than means–ends systems.

Schemas are usually implemented as transition networks, where a unit of information is selected from the pool as each arc is traversed. The major arcs between nodes tend to correspond to chains of common object references between units: cause followed by effect, sequences of events that are traced step by step through time, and so on. Self loops returning back to the same node dictate the addition of attributes to an object, side effects of an action, etc.

The choice of what schema to use is a function of the overall goal. McKeown's original system, for example, dispatched on a three-way choice between defining an object, describing it, or distinguishing it from another type of object. Once the goal is determined, the relevant knowledge pool is separated out from the other parts of the reference knowledge base and the selected schema is applied. Navigation through the schema's network is then a matter of what units or chains of units are actually present in the pool in combination with the tests that the arcs apply.

Given a close fit between the design of the knowledge base and the details of the schema, the resulting texts can be quite good. Such faults as they have are largely the result of weakness in other parts of the generator and not in its content-selection criteria. Experience has shown that basic schemas can be readily abstracted and ported to other domains (McKeown et al. 1990). Schemas do have the weakness when compared to systems with explicit operators and dynamic planning that, when used in interactive dialogs, do not naturally provide the kinds of information that is needed for recognizing the source of problems, which makes it difficult to revise any utterances that are initially not understood (Moore and Swartout 1991, Paris 1991). But, for most of the applications to which generation systems are put, schemas are a simple and easily elaborated technique that is probably the design of choice whenever the needs of the system or nature of the speaker's model make it unreasonable to use progressive refinement.

6.5 The Linguistic Component

In this section, we look at the core issues in the most mature and well defined of all the processes in natural language generation, the application of a grammar to produce a final text from the elements that were decided upon by the earlier processing. This is the one area in the whole field where we find true instances of what software engineers would call properly modular components: bodies of code and representations with well-defined interfaces that can be (and have been) shared between widely varying development groups.

6.5.1 Surface Realization Components

To reflect the narrow scope (but high proficiency) of these components, I refer to them here as surface realization components. 'Surface' (as opposed to deep) because what they are charged with doing is producing the final syntactic and lexical structure of the text—what linguists in the Chomskian tradition would call a surface structure; and 'realization' because what they do never involves planning or decision making: They are in effect carrying out the orders of the earlier components, rendering (realizing) their decisions into the shape that they must take to be proper texts in the target language.

The job of a surface realization component is to take the output of the text planner, render it into a form that can be conformed (in a theory-specific way) to a grammar, and then apply the grammar to arrive at the final text as a syntactically structured sequence of words, which are read out to become the output of the generator as a whole. The relationships between the units of the plan are mapped to syntactic relationships. They are organized into constituents and given a linear ordering. The content words are given grammatically appropriate morphological realizations. Function words ("*to*," "*of*," "*has*," and such) are added as the grammar dictates.

6.5.2 Relationship to Linguistic Theory

Practically without exception, every modern realization component is an implementation of one of the recognized grammatical formalisms of theoretical linguistics. It is also not an exaggeration to say that virtually every formalism in the alphabet soup of alternatives that is modern linguistics has been used as the basis of some realizer in some project somewhere.

The grammatical theories provide systems of rules, sets of principles, systems of constraints, and, especially, a rich set of representations, which, along with a lexicon (not a trivial part in today's theories), attempt to define the space of possible texts and text fragments in the target natural language. The designers of the realization components devise ways of interpreting these theoretical constructs and notations into effective machinery for constructing texts that conform to these systems.

It is important to note that all grammars are woefully incomplete when it comes to providing accounts (or even descriptions) of the actual range of texts that people produce, and no generator within the present state of the art is going to produce a text that is not explicitly in the competence of the surface grammar is it using. Generation is in a better situation in this respect than comprehension is, however. As a constructive discipline, we at least have the capability of extending our grammars whenever we can determine a motive (by the text planner) and a description (in terms of the grammar) for some new construction. As designers, we can also choose whether to use a construct or not, leaving out everything that is problematic. Comprehension systems on the other hand, must attempt to read the texts they happen to be confronted with and so will inevitably be faced at almost every turn with constructs beyond the competence of their grammar.

6.5.3 Chunk Size

One of the side effects of adopting the grammatical formalisms of the theoretical linguistics community is that every realization component generates a complete sentence at a time, with a few notable exceptions.*
Furthermore this choice of 'chunk size' becomes an architectural necessity, not a freely chosen option. As implementations of established theories of grammar, realizers must adopt the same scope over linguistic properties as their parent theories do; anything larger or smaller would be undefined.

The requirement that the input to most surface realization components specify the content of an entire sentence at a time has a profound effect on the planners that must produce these specifications. Given a set of propositions to be communicated, the designer of a planner working in this paradigm is more likely to think in terms of a succession of sentences rather than trying to interleave one proposition within the realization of another (although some of this may be accomplished by aggregation or revision). Such lockstep treatments can be especially confining when higher order propositions are to be communicated. For example, the natural realization of such a proposition might be adding "*only*" inside the sentence that realizes its argument, yet the full-sentence-at-a-time paradigm makes this exceedingly difficult to appreciate as a possibility let alone carry out.

6.5.4 Assembling vs. Navigating

Grammars, and with them the processing architectures of their realization components, fall into two camps.

---

* The Mumble-86 realizer (Meteer et al. 1987), when it was used as part of Jeff Conklin's Genaro system (Conklin and McDonald 1982) determined sentence length and composition dynamically according to a "weight" calculated from the character of the constructions it contained and began the populate the next sentence once a threshold parameter had been exceeded. This was possible because Mumble is based on lexicalized Tree Adjoining Grammar, where the grammar chunks can be as small as a single word.

- The grammar provides a set of relatively small structural elements and constraints on their combination.
- The grammar is a single complex network or descriptive device that defines all the possible output texts in a single abstract structure (or in several structures, one for each major constituent type that it defines: clause, noun phrase, thematic organization, and so on).

When the grammar consists of a set of combinable elements, the task of the realization component is to select from this set and assemble them into a composite representation from which the text is then read out. When the grammar is a single structure, the task is to navigate through the structure, accumulating and refining the basis for the final text along the way and producing it all at once when the process has finished.

Assembly-style systems can produce their texts incrementally by selecting elements from the early parts of the text first, and can thereby have a natural representation of 'what has already been said' which is a valuable resource for making decisions about whether to use pronouns and other position-based judgments. Navigation-based systems, because they can see the whole text at once as it emerges, can allow constraints from what will be the later parts of the text to effect realization decisions in earlier parts, but they can find it difficult, even impossible, to make certain position-based judgments.

Among the small-element linguistic formalisms that have been used in generation we have conventional production rule rewrite systems, CCG, Segment Grammar, and Tree Adjoining Grammar (TAG). Among the single-structure formalisms, we have Systemic Grammar and any theory that uses feature structures, for example, HPSG and LFG. We look at two of these in detail because of their influence within the community.

6.5.5 Systemic Grammars

Understanding and representing the context into which the elements of an utterance are fit and the role of the context in their selection is a central part of the development of a grammar. It is especially important when the perspective that the grammarian takes is a functional rather than a structural one—the viewpoint adopted in Systemic Grammar. A structural perspective emphasizes the elements out of which language is built (constituents, lexemes, prosodics, etc.). A functional perspective turns this on its head and asks what is the spectrum of alternative purposes that a text can serve (its 'communicative potential'). Does it introduce a new object which will be the center of the rest of the discourse? Is it reinforcing that object's prominence? Is it shifting the focus to something else? Does it question? Enjoin? Persuade? The multitude of goals that a text and its elements can serve provides the basis for a paradigmatic (alternative based) rather than a structural (form based) view of language.

The Systemic Functional Grammar (SFG) view of language originated in the early work of Michael Halliday (1967, 1985) and Halliday and Matthiessen (2004) and has a wide following today. It has always been a natural choice for work in language generation (Davey's Proteus system was based on it) because much of what a generator must do is to choose among the alternative constructions that the language provides based on the context and the purpose they are to serve—something that a systemic grammar represents directly.

A systemic grammar is written as a specialized kind of decision tree: 'If this choice is made, then this set of alternatives becomes relevant; if a different choice is made, those alternatives can be ignored, but this other set must now be addressed.' Sets of (typically disjunctive) alternatives are grouped into 'systems' (hence "systemic grammar") and connected by links from the prior choice(s) that made them relevant to the other systems that they in turn make relevant. These systems are described in a natural and compelling graphic notation of vertical bars listing each system and lines connecting them to other systems. (The Nigel systemic grammar, developed at ISI (Matthiessen 1983), required an entire office wall for its presentation using this notation.)

In a computational treatment of SFG for language generation, each system of alternative choices has an associated decision criteria. In the early stages of development, these criteria are often left to human intervention so as to exercise the grammar and test the range of constructions it can motivate (e.g., Fawcett 1981). In the work at ISI, this evolved into what was called 'inquiry semantics,' where each system had an associated set of predicates that would test the situation in the speaker's model and makes its choices accordingly. This makes it in effect a 'pull' system for surface realization; something that in other publications has been called *grammar-driven* control as opposed to the *message-driven* approach of a system like Mumble (see McDonald et al. 1987).

As the Nigel grammar grew into the Penman system (Penman Natural Language Group 1989) and gained a wide following in the late 1980s and early 1990s, the control of the decision making and the data that fed it moved from the grammar's input specification and into the speaker's knowledge base. At the heart of the knowledge base—the taxonomic lattice that categorizes all of the types of objects that the speaker could talk about and defines their basic properties—an upper structure was developed (Bateman 1997, Bateman et al. 1995). This set of categories and properties was defined in such a way as to be able to provide the answers needed to navigate through the system network. Objects in application knowledge bases built in terms of this upper structure (by specializing its categories) are assured an interpretation in terms of the predicates that the systemic grammar needs because these are provided implicitly through the location of the objects in the taxonomy.

Mechanically, the process of generating a text using a systemic grammar consists of walking through the set of systems from the initial choice (which for a speech act might be whether it constitutes a statement, a question, or a command) through to its leaves, following several simultaneous paths through the system network until it has been completely traversed. Several parallel paths because in the analyses adopted by systemicists, the final shape of a text is dictated by three independent kinds of information: *experiential*, focusing on content; *interpersonal*, focusing on the interaction and stance toward the audience; and *textual*, focusing on form and stylistics.

As the network is traversed, a set of features that describe the text are accumulated. These may be used to 'preselect' some of the options at a lower 'strata' in the accumulating text, as for example when the structure of an embedded clause is determined by the traversal of the network that determines the functional organization of its parent clause. The features describing the subordinate's function are passed through what will likely be a recursive instantiation of the network that was traversed to form the parent, and they serve to fix the selection in key systems, for example, dictating that the clause should appear without an actor, for example, as a prepositionally marked gerund: "*You blocked me by taking the corner opposite mine.*"

The actual text takes shape by projecting the lexical realizations of the elements of the input specification onto selected positions in a large grid of possible positions as dictated by the features selected from the network. The words may be given by the final stages of the system network (as systemicists say: 'lexis as most delicate grammar') or as part of the input specification.

6.5.6 Functional Unification Grammars

Having a functional or purpose-oriented perspective in a grammar is largely a matter of the grammar's content, not its architecture. What sets functional approaches to realization apart from structural approaches is the choice of terminology and distinctions, the indirect relationship to syntactic surface structure, and, when embedded in a realization component, the nature of its interface to the earlier text-planning components. Functional realizers are concerned with purposes, not contents. Just as a functional perspective can be implemented in a system network, it can be implemented in an annotated TAG (Yang et al. 1991) or, in what we will turn to now, in a unification grammar.

A unification grammar is also traversed, but this is less obvious since the traversal is done by the built-in unification process and is not something that its developers actively consider. (Except for reasons of efficiency, the early systems were notoriously slow because nondeterminism led to a vast amount of backtracking; as machines have gotten faster and the algorithms have been improved, this is no longer a problem.)

The term 'unification grammar' emphasizes the realization mechanism used in this technique, namely merging the component's input with the grammar to produce a fully specified, functionally annotated surface structure from which the words of the text are then read out. The merging is done using a particular form of unification; a thorough introduction can be found in McKeown (1985). In order to be merged with the grammar, the input must be represented in the same terms; it is often referred to as a 'deep' syntactic structure.

Unification is not the primary design element in these systems however, it just happened to be the control paradigm that was in vogue when the innovative data structure of these grammars—feature structures—was introduced by linguists as a reaction against the pure phrase structure approaches of the time (the late 1970s). Feature structures (FS) are much looser formalisms than unadorned phrase structures; they consist of sets of multilevel attribute-value pairs. A typical FS will incorporate information from (at least) three levels simultaneously: meaning, (surface) form, and lexical identities. FS allow general principles of linguistic structure to be stated more freely and with greater attention to the interaction between these levels than had been possible before.

The adaption of feature-structure-based grammars to generation was begun by Martin Kay (1984), who developed the idea of focusing on functional relationships in these systems—functional in the same sense as it is employed in systemic grammar, with the same attendant appeal to people working in generation who wanted to experiment with the feature-structure notation.

Kay's notion of a 'functional' unification grammar (FUG) was first deployed by Appelt (1985), and then adopted by McKeown. McKeown's students, particularly Michael Elhadad, made the greatest strides in making the formalism efficient. He developed the FUF system, which is now widely used (Elhadad 1991, Elhadad and Robin 1996). Elhadad also took the step of explicitly adopting the grammatical analysis and point of view of systemic grammarians, demonstrating quite effectively that grammars and the representations that embody them are separate aspects of system design.

6.6 The Cutting Edge

There has been a great deal of technical development in the last decade. For example, we have new surface realizers such as Mathew Stone's SPUD (Stone et al. 2001) that works at the semantic and syntactic level simultaneously, or Michael White's work based on the CCG grammar formalism (White and Baldridge 2003). Template-based realizers have also made a comeback (e.g., McRoy et al. 2003). And perhaps most of all there has been an massive influx of machine-learning-based machinery into the generation as there has in the rest of computational linguistics (see, e.g., Langkilde and Knight 1998, Bangalore and Rambow 2000).

However, for the most part these developments are just giving us better (or just alternative) ways of doing the things we already know how to do. In this final section I want to instead briefly describe two systems that are breaking entirely new ground.

6.6.1 Story Generation

The subject matter, or genre, of nearly all work is expository, providing explanations or simply conveying information. But much if not most of human talk is based on telling stories. Around the turn of the millennium Charles Callaway developed the StoryBook system (2002), which deployed the organizing principles of a rich model of narrative and the full panoply of generation facilities* to generate variations on the story of Little Red Riding Hood. Here is an excerpt.

---

* A narrative organizer that segmented and structured a the element of provided by the narrative planner, did lexical choice and maintained a discourse history; a sentence planner; a revision component; and a surface realizer (based on FUF) that knows how to format prose with embedded dialog.

Once upon a time a woodman and his wife lived in a pretty cottage on the borders of a great forest. They had one little daughter, a sweet child, who was a favorite with everyone. She was the joy of her mother's heart. To please her, the good woman made her a little scarlet cloak and hood. She looked so pretty in it that everyone called her Little Red Riding Hood.

StoryBook begins its substantive work at the start of the microplanning phase of generation after the content of could be said has been established and organized into a narrative stream by a simple FSA acting in lieu of a real narrative planner. The excerpt of this stream below draws on an ontology of concepts and relations that provides the raw material for the microlevel narrative planner.

```
(... ;; "once upon a time there was a woodman and his
(actor-property exist-being woodman001)
(refinement and-along-with woodman001 wife001)
(refinement belonging-to woodman001 wife001)
(specification exist-being process-step-type once-upon-a-time) ...)
```

Notice how lexical and 'close to the surface' the terms in this micro-planner input are. This permits the revision facilities in StoryBook to know enough about the individual abstract elements of the text to readily formulate highly composed prose.

6.6.2 Personality-Sensitive Generation

Remarkably few generation systems have been developed where the speaker could be said to have a particular personality. Clippinger and Brown's Erma certainly did, albeit at the cost of an intense, one-off programming effort. Eduard Hovy's Pauline (1990) was the first to show how this could be done systematically albeit just for exposition. First of all there must be a large number of relevant 'units' of content that could be included or ignored or systematically left to inference according to the desired level detail or choice of perspective. Second and more important is the use of a multilevel 'standoff' architecture whereby pragmatic notions ('use high style,' 'be brief') are progressively reinterpreted through one or more level of description as features that a generator can actually attend to (e.g., word choice, sentence length, clause complexity).

The currently most thorough and impressive treatment of personality in generation is François Mairesse and Marilyn Walker's Personage system (2007, 2008). Here are two generated examples in the domain of restaurant recommendation, one with a low extroversion rating and then one with a high rating.*

> 5 (2.83) Right, I mean, Le Marais is the only restaurant that is any good.
> 3 (6.0) I am sure you would like Le Marais, you know. The atmosphere is acceptable, the servers are nice and it's a french, kosher and steak house place. Actually, the food is good, even if its price is 44 dollars.

Personage is based on modeling the correlation of a substantial number of language variables (e.g., verbosity, repetition, filled pauses, stuttering) with personality as characterized by the Big Five personality traits. This model then drives a statistical microplanner (Stent et al. 2004) whose output is passed through a surface realizer based on Mel'cuk's *Meaning Text Theory of Language* (Lavoie and Rambow 1998). (Yet another example is the frequently eclectic combinations of theories and techniques that characterize work in computational linguistics because of the people doing the work and the accidents of history of who they studied with.)

---

* Utterance numbers and 1–7 extraversion ranking from Mairesse and Walker (2007, p. 496).

6.7 Conclusions

This chapter has covered the basic issues and perspectives that have governed work on natural language generation. With the benefit of hindsight it has tried to identify the axes that distinguish the different tacks people have taken during the last 40 years: does the speaker intentionally 'push' directives to the text planner, or does the planner 'pull' data out of a passive data base; does surface realization consist of 'assembling' a set of components or of 'navigating' through one large structure?

Given this past, what can we say about the future? One thing we can be reasonably sure of is that there will be relatively little work done on surface realization. People working on speech or doing computational psycholinguistics may see the need for new architectures at this level, and the advent of a new style of linguistic theory may prompt someone to apply it to generation; but most groups will elect to see realization as a solved problem—a complete module that they can ftp from a collaborating site.

By that same token, the linguistic sophistication and ready availability of the mature realizers (Penman, FUF) will mean that the field will no longer sustain abstract work in text planning; all planners will have to actually produce text, preferably pages of it, and that text should be of high quality. Toy output that neglects to properly use pronouns or is redundant and awkward will no longer be acceptable.

The most important scientific achievement to look toward in the course of the next 10 years is the emergence of a coherent consensus architecture for the presently muddled 'middle ground' of microplanning. Sitting between the point at which generation begins, where we have a strong working knowledge of how to fashion and deploy schemas, plan operators, and the like to select what is to be said and give it a coarse organization, and the point at which generation ends, where we have sophisticated, off-the-shelf surface realization components that one can use with only minimal personal knowledge of linguistics, we presently have a grab bag of phenomena that no two projects deal with in the same way (if they handle them at all).

In this middle ground lies the problem of where to use pronouns and other such reduced types of 'subsequent reference'; the problem of how to select the best words to use ('lexical choice') and to pick among alternative paraphrases; and the problem how to collapse the set of propositions that the planner selects, each of which might be its own sentence if generated individually, into fluent complex sentences that are free of redundancy and fit the system's stylistic goals (aggregation).

At this point, about all that is held in common in the community are the names of these problems and what their effects are in the final texts. That at least provides a common ground for comparing the proposals and systems that have emerged, but the actual alternatives in the literature tend to be so far apart in the particulars of their treatments that there are few possibilities for one group to build on the results of another.

To take just one example, it is entirely possible that aggregation—the present term of art in generation for how to achieve what others what others call 'cohesion' (Halliday and Hasan 1976) or just 'fluency'—is not a coherent notion. Consider that for aggregation to occur there must be separate, independent things to be aggregated. It might turn out that this is an artifact of the architecture of today's popular text planners and not at all a natural kind, that is, something that is handled with the same procedures and at the same points in the processing for all the different instances of it that we see in real texts.

Whatever the outcome of such questions, we can be sure that they will be pursued vigorously by an ever-burgeoning number of people. The special interest group on generation (SIGGEN) has over 400 members, the largest of all the special interest groups under the umbrella of the Association for Computational Linguistics (ACL). The field is international in scope, with major research sites from Australia to Israel.

There is much challenging work remaining to be done that will keep those of us who work in this field engaged for years, more likely decades to come. Whether the breakthroughs will come from traditional grant funded research or from the studios and basements of game makers and entrepreneurs is impossible to say. Whatever the future, this is the best part of the natural language problem in which to work.

References

Andre, E., G. Herzog, and T. Rist (1988) On the simultaneous interpretation of real world image sequences and the natural language description: The system SOCCER, *Proceedings of the Eighth ECAI*, Munich, Germany, pp. 449–454.

Appelt, D. (1985) *Planning English Sentences*, Cambridge University Press, Cambridge, U.K.

Bangalore, S. and O. Rambow (2000) Exploiting a probabilistic hierarchical model for generation, *Proceedings of the Eighteenth Conference on Computational Linguistics (COLING)*, Saarbrucken, Germany, pp. 42–48.

Barwise, J. and J. Perry (1983) *Situations and Attitudes*, MIT Press, Cambridge, MA.

Bateman, J.A. (1997) Enabling technology for multilingual natural language: The KPML development environment, *Journal of Natural Language Engineering*, 3(1):15–55.

Bateman, J.A., R. Henschel, and F. Rinaldi (1995) Generalized upper model 2.1: Documentation. Technical Report, GMD/Institute für Integrierte Publikations- und Informationssysteme, Darmstadt, Germany.

Becker, J. (1975) The phrasal lexicon, *Proceedings of the TINLAP-I*, Cambridge, MA, ACM, pp. 60–64; also available as BBN Report 3081.

Bourbeau. L., D. Carcagno, E. Goldberg, R. Kittredge, and A. Polguère (1990) Bilingual generation of weather forecasts in an operations environment, *COLING*, Helsinki, Finland.

Brown, R. (1974) Use of multiple-body interrupts in discourse generation, Bachelor's thesis, Department of Electrical Engineering and Computer Science, MIT, Cambridge, MA.

Cahill, L., C. Doran, R. Evans, C. Mellish, D. Paiva, M.R.D. Scott, and N. Tipper (1999) In search of a reference architecture for NLP systems, *Proceedings of the European Workshop on Natural Language Generation*, Toulouse, France.

Callaway, C., E. Not, A. Novello, C. Rocchi, O. Sock, and M. Zancanaro (2005) Automatic cinematography and multilingual NLG for generating video documentaries, *Artificial Intelligence*, 16(5): 57–89.

Cassell, J., T. Bickmore, L. Campbell, H. Vilhjalmsson, and H. Yan (2000) Human conversation as a system framework: Designing embodied conversational agents, In J. Cassel, J. Sullivan, S. Prevost, and E. Churchill (eds.), *Embodied Conversational Agents*, MIT Press, Cambridge, MA.

Clippinger, J. (1977) *Meaning and Discourse: A Computer Model of Psychoanalytic Speech and Cognition*, Johns Hopkins University Press, Baltimore, MA.

Conklin E.J. and D. McDonald (1982) Salience: The key to selection in deep generation, *Proceedings of the ACL-82*, University of Toronto, Toronto, ON, pp. 129–135.

Cosby, N. (1999) SIMNET—An insider's perspective, *Simulation Technology* 2(1), http://www.sisostds.org/webletter/siso/iss_39/arg_202.htm, sampled 11/08.

Dale, R., C. Mellish, and M. Zock (1990) *Current Research in Natural Language Generation*, Academic Press, Boston, MA.

Dale, R., J. Oberlander, and M. Milosavljevic (1998) Integrating natural language and hypertext to produce dynamic documents, *Interacting with Computers*, 11(2):109–135.

Davey, A. (1978) *Discourse Production*, Edinburgh University Press, Edinburgh, U.K.

De Smedt, K. (1990) Incremental sentence generation, Technical Report 90-01, Nijmegen Institute for Cognition Research and Information Technology, Nijmegen, the Netherlands.

Devlin, K. (1991) *Logic and Information*, Cambridge University Press, Cambridge, U.K.

DiMarco, C. and G. Hirst (1993) A computational theory of goal-directed style in syntax, *Computational Linguistics*, 19(3):451–499.

Elhadad, M. (1991) FUF: The universal unifier user manual (v5), Technical Report CUCS-038-91, Department of Computer Science, Columbia University, New York.

Elhadad, M. and J. Robin (1996) An overview of SURGE: A reusable comprehensive syntactic realization component, Technical Report 96-03, Department of Mathematics and Computer Science, Ben Gurion University, Beer Sheva, Israel.

Fawcett, R. (1981) Generating a sentence in systemic functional grammar, In M.A.K. Halliday and J.R. Martin (eds.), *Readings in Systemic Linguistics*, Batsford, London, U.K.

Feiner, S. and K. McKeown (1991) Automating the generation of coordinated multimedia explanations, *IEEE Computer*, 24(10):33–40.

Gabriel, R.P. (1981) An organization of programs in fluid domains, PhD thesis, Stanford; available as Stanford Artificial Intelligence Memo 342 (STAN-CA-81-856, 1981).

Gabriel, R.P. (1986) Deliberate writing, In D.D. McDonald and L. Bolc (eds.), *Natural Language Generation Systems*, Springer-Verlag, New York, pp. 1–46.

Geldof, S. (1996) Hyper-text generation from databases on the Internet, *Proceedings of the Second International Workshop on Applications of Natural Language to Information Systems, NLDB*, Amsterdam, the Netherlands, pp. 102–114, IOS Press.

Green, S.J. and C. DiMarco (1996) Stylistic decision-making in natural language generation, In A. Givanni and M. Zock (eds.), *Trends in Natural Language Generation: An Artificial Intelligence Perspective, Lecture Notes in Artificial Intelligence*, 1036, Springer-Verlag, Berlin, Germany, pp. 125–143.

Halliday, M.A.K. (1967) Notes on transitivity and theme in English Parts 1, 2, & 3, *Journal of Linguistics* 3.1, 3.2, 3.3: 37–81, 199–244, 179–215.

Halliday, M.A.K. (1985) *An Introduction to Functional Grammar*, Edward Arnold, London, U.K.

Halliday, M.A.K. and R. Hasan (1976) *Cohesion in English*, Longman, London, U.K.

Halliday, M.A.K. and C.M.I.M. Matthiessen (2004) *An Introduction to Functional Grammar*, Edward Arnold, London, U.K.

Hovy, E. (1990) Pragmatics and natural language generation, *Artificial Intelligence* 43:153–197.

Kay, M. (1984) Functional unification grammar: A formalism for machine translation, *Proceedings of COLING-84*, Stanford, CA, pp. 75–78 ACL.

Kittredge, R. and J. Lehrberger (1982) *Sublanguage: Studies of Language in Restricted Semantic Domains*, de Gruyter, Berlin, Germany.

Kukich, K. (1988) Fluency in natural language reports, In D.D. McDonald and L. Bolc (eds.), *Natural Language Generation Systems*, Springer-Verlag, New York, pp. 280–312.

Langkilde, I. and K. Knight (1998) Generation that exploits corpus-based statistical knowledge, *Proceedings of the ACL*, Montreal, Canada, pp. 704–710.

Lavoie, B. and O. Rambow (1998) A fast and portable realizer for text generation systems, *Proceedings of the ANLP*, Washington, DC, ACL.

Levelt, W.J.M. (1989) *Speaking*, MIT Press, Cambridge, MA.

Loyall, A.B., W.S.N. Reilly, J. Bates and P. Weyhrauch (2004) System for authoring highly interactive, personality-rich interactive characters, *Eurographics/ACM SIGGRAPH Symposium on Computer Animation*, Grenoble, France.

Mairesse, F. and M. Walker (2007) PERSONAGE: Personality generation for dialogue, *Proceedings of the Forty Fifth Annual Meeting of the Association for Computational Linguistics*, ACL, pp. 496–503.

Mairesse, F. and M. Walker (2008) Trainable generation of big-five personality styles through data-driven parameter estimation, *Proceedings of the Forty Sixth Annual Meeting of the Association for Computational Linguistics*, ACL, pp. 165–173.

Mateas, M. and A. Stern (2002) A behavior language for story-based believable agents, *IEEE Intelligent Systems*, 17(4):39–47.

Mateas, M. and A. Stern (2003) Façade: An experiment in building a fully-realized interactive drama, *Game Developers Conference, Game Design Track*, San Francisco, CA.

Matthiessen, C.M.I.M. (1983) Systemic grammar in computation: The Nigel case, *Proceedings of the First Annual Conference of the European Chapter of the Association for Computational Linguistics*, Pisa, Italy.

McDonald, D. and M. Meteer (1988) From water to wine: Generating natural language text from today's application programs, *Proceedings of the Second Conference on Applied Natural Language Processing (ACL)*, Austin, TX, pp. 41–48.

McDonald, D., M. Meteer, and J. Pustejovsky (1987) Factors contributing to efficiency in natural language generation, In G. Kempen (ed), *Natural Language Generation*, Martinus Nijhoff Publishers, Dordrecht, pp. 159–182.

McKeown, K.R. (1985) *Text Generation*, Cambridge University Press, Cambridge, U.K.

McKeown, K.R., M. Elhadad, Y. Fukumoto, J. Lim, C. Lombardi, J. Robin, and F. Smadja (1990) Natural language generation in COMET, In Dale et al., pp. 103–140.

McRoy, S., S. Channarukul, and S. Ali (2003) An augmented template-based approach to text realization, *Natural Language Engineering*, 9(4):381–420.

Meteer, M. (1992) *Expressibility and the Problem of Efficient Text Planning*, Pinter, London, U.K.

Meteer, M., D. McDonald, S. Anderson, D. Forster, L. Gay, A. Huettner, and P. Sibun (1987) Mumble-86: Design and Implementation, Technical Report 87–87, Department of Computer and Information Science, University of Massachusetts at Amherst, Amherst, MA.

Moore, J.D. and W.R. Swartout (1991) A reactive approach to explanation: Taking the user's feedback into account, In Paris et al., pp. 3–48.

O'Donnell, M., C. Mellish, J. Oberlander, and A. Knott (2001) ILEX: An architecture for a dynamic hypertext generation system, *Natural Language Engineering*, 7(3):225–250.

Paris, C.L. (1991) Generation and explanation: Building an explanation facility for the explainable expert systems framework, In C.L. Paris, W.R. Swartout, and W.C. Mann (eds.), *Natural Language Generation in Artificial Intelligence and Computational Linguistics*, Kluwer Academic, Boston, MA, pp. 49–82.

Penman Natural Language Group (1989) The Penman Documentation, USC Information Sciences Institute, Los Angeles, CA.

Piwek, P., J. Masthoff, and M. Bergenstråle (2005) Reference and gestures in dialog generation: Three studies with embodied conversational agents, *AISP'05: Proceedings of the Joint Symposium on Virtual Social Agents*, Hatfield, U.K., pp. 53–60.

Reiter, E., R. Robertson, and L.M. Osman (2003) Lessons from a failure: Generated tailored smoking cession letters, *Artificial Intelligence*, 144:41–58.

Reiter, E., A. Gatt, J. Hunter, S. Sripada, J. Hunter, J. Yu, and I. Davy (2005) Choosing words in computer generated weather forecasts, *Artificial Intelligence*, 167(1–2):137–169.

Robin, J. (1993) A revision-based generation architecture for reporting facts in their historical context, In H. Horacek and M. Zock (eds.), *New Concepts in Natural Language Generation: Planning, Realization, and Systems*, Pinter, London, U.K., pp. 238–268.

Robin, J. (1996) Evaluating the portability of revision rules for incremental summary generation, *Proceedings of the 34th Annual Meeting of the ACL*, Santa Cruz, CA, pp. 205–214.

Sacerdoti, E. (1977) *A Structure for Plans and Behavior*, North-Holland, Amsterdam, the Netherlands.

Stent, A., R. Prasad, and M. Walker (2004) Trainable sentence planning for complex information presentation in spoken dialog systems, *Proceedings of the 42nd Annual Meeting of the ACL*, Barcelona, Spain.

Stock, O. and M. Zancanaro (2007) *PEACH: Intelligent Interfaces for Museum Visits*, Springer-Verlag, Berlin, Germany.

Stone, M., C. Doran, B. Webber, T. Bleam, and M. Palmer (2001) Microplanning with communicative intentions: The SPUD system. Rutgers TR 65, distributed on arxiv.org.

Streit, M., A. Batliner and T. Portele (2006) Emotional analysis and emotional-handling subdialogs, In W. Wahlster (ed), *Smartkom: Foundations of Multimodal Dialogue Systems*, Springer, Berlin, Germany.

Swartout, W., J. Gratch, R. Hill, E. Hovy, S. Marsella, J. Rickel, and D. Traum (2006) Toward virtual humans, *AI Magazine*, 27(2):96–108.

Traum, D., A. Roque, A. Leuski, P. Georgiou, J. Gerten, B. Martinovski, S. Narayanan, S. Robinson, and A. Vaswani (2007) Hassan: A virtual human for tactical questioning, *Proceedings of the Eighth SIGdial Workshop on Discourse and Dialog*, Antwerp, Belgium, pp. 71–74.

Wallace, R.S. www.alicebot.org, see also en.wikipedia.org/wiki/A.L.I.C.E.

Weizenbaum, J. (1966) ELIZA—A computer program for the study of natural language communication between man and machine, *Communications of the ACM*, 9(1):36–45.

Wilcock, G. (1998) Approaches to surface realization with HPSG, *Ninth International Workshop on Natural Language Generation*, Niagara-on-the-Lake, Canada, pp. 218–227.

Wilensky, R. (1976) Using plans to understand natural language, *Proceedings of the Annual Meeting of the Association for Computing Machinery*, Houston, TX.

Winograd, T. (1972). *Understanding Natural Language*, Academic Press, New York.

White, M. and J. Baldridge. (2003) Adapting chart realization to CCG, *Proceedings of the Ninth European Workshop on Natural Language Generation*, Toulouse, France.

Yang, G., K.F. McCoy, and K. Vijay-Shanker (1991) From functional specification to syntactic structure: Systemic grammar and tree-adjoining grammar, *Computational Intelligence*, 7(4):207–219.

II
Empirical and Statistical Approaches

7

Corpus Creation

Richard Xiao
Edge Hill University

7.1 Introduction

A corpus can be defined as a collection of machine-readable authentic texts (including transcripts of spoken data) that is sampled to be representative of a particular natural language or language variety (McEnery et al. 2006: 5), though "representativeness" is a fluid concept (see Section 7.3). Corpora play an essential role in natural language processing (NLP) research as well as a wide range of linguistic investigations. They provide a material basis and a test bed for building NLP systems. On the other hand, NLP research has contributed substantially to corpus development (see Dipper 2008 for a discussion of the relationship between corpus linguistics and computational linguistics), especially in corpus annotation, for example, part-of-speech tagging (see Chapter 10), syntactic parsing (see Chapters 8 and 11), semantic tagging (see Chapters 5 and 14), as well as the alignment of parallel corpora (see Chapter 16).

There are thousands of corpora in the world, but most of them are created for specific research projects and are not publicly available. Xiao (2008) provides a comprehensive survey of a wide range of well-known and influential corpora in English and many other languages, while a survey of corpora for less-studied languages can be found in Ostler (2008). Since corpus creation is an activity that takes time and costs money, it is certainly desirable for readers to use such ready-made corpora to carry out their work. Unfortunately, however, this is not always feasible or possible. As a corpus is always designed for a particular purpose, the usefulness of a ready-made corpus must be judged with regard to the purpose to which a user intends to put it. Consequently, while there are many corpora readily available, it is often the case that readers will find that they are not able to address their research questions using ready-made corpora. In such circumstances, one must build one's own corpus. This chapter covers principal considerations involved in creating such DIY ("do-it-yourself") corpora as well as the issues that come up in major corpus creation projects.

This chapter discusses core issues in corpus creation such as corpus size, representativeness, balance and sampling, data capture and copyright, markup and annotation, as well as peripheral issues such as multilingual and multimodal corpora.

7.2 Corpus Size

One must be clear about one's research question (or questions) when planning to build a DIY corpus. This helps you to determine what material you will need to collect. For example, if you wish to compare British English and American English, you will need to collect spoken and/or written data produced by native speakers of the two regional varieties of English; if you are interested in how Chinese speakers acquire French as a second language, you will then need to collect the French data produced by Chinese learners to create a learner corpus; if you are interested in how the English language has evolved over centuries, you will need to collect samples of English produced in different historical periods to build a historical or diachronic corpus. Readers are reminded, though, that many corpora of these kinds are now already available (see Xiao 2008 for a recent survey). Having developed an understanding of the type of data you need to collect, and having made sure that no ready-made corpus of such material exists, one needs to find a source of data. Assuming that the data can be found, one then has to address the question of corpus size.

How large a corpus do you need? There is no easy answer to this question. The size of the corpus needed depends upon the purpose for which it is intended as well as a number of practical considerations. In the early 1960s, when the processing power and storage capacity of computers were quite limited, a one-million-word corpus such as the Brown corpus (i.e., the Brown University Standard Corpus of Present-day American English, see Kučera and Francis 1967) appeared to be as large a corpus as one could reasonably build. With the increase in computer power and the availability of machine-readable texts, however, a corpus of this size is no longer considered large, and in comparison with today's giant corpora like the 100-million-word British National Corpus (BNC, see Aston and Burnard 1998) and the 524-million-word Bank of English (BoE, Collins 2007) it appears somewhat small. An interesting discussion of corpus size and design can be found in Keller and Lapata (2003), who compare similarities and differences in the frequencies for bigrams (i.e., two-word clusters) obtained from the BNC and the Web.

The availability of suitable data, especially in machine-readable form, seriously affects corpus size. In building a *balanced* corpus according to fixed proportions (see Section 7.3), for example, the lack of data for one text type may accordingly restrict the size of the samples of other text types taken. This is especially the case for parallel corpora, as it is common for the availability of translations to be unbalanced across text types for many languages. For example, it will be much easier to find Chinese translations of English news stories than English translations of Chinese literary texts. While it is often possible to transfer paper-based texts into electronic form using OCR (optical character recognition) software, the process costs time and money and is error-prone. Hence, the availability of machine-readable data is often the main limiting factor in corpus creation.

Another factor that potentially limits the size of a DIY corpus is copyright (see Section 7.4 for further discussion). Unless the proposed corpus contains entirely out-of-date or copyright-free data, simply gathering available data and using it in a freely available corpus may expose the corpus creator to legal action. When one seeks copyright clearance, one can face frustration—the construction of the corpus is your priority, not the copyright holder's. They may simply ignore you. Their silence cannot be taken as consent. Copyright clearance in building a large corpus necessitates much effort, trouble, and frustration.

No matter how important legal considerations may seem, one should not lose sight of the paramount importance of the research question. This question controls all of your corpus-building decisions, including the decision regarding corpus size. Even if the conditions discussed above allow for a large corpus, it does not mean that a large corpus is what you want. First, the size of the corpus needed to explore a research question is dependent on the frequency and distribution of the linguistic features under consideration in that corpus (cf. McEnery and Wilson 2001: 80). As Leech (1991: 8–29) observes, size is not all-important. Small corpora may contain sufficient examples of frequent linguistic features. To study features such as the number of present and past tense verbs in English, for example, a sample of 1000 words may prove sufficient (Biber 1993). Second, small specialized corpora serve a very different yet important purpose from large multi-million-word corpora (Shimazumi and Berber-Sardinha 1996). It is understandable that corpora for lexical studies are much larger than those for grammatical studies, because when studying lexis one is interested in the frequency of the distribution of a word (see Baroni 2009 for a discussion of distributions in text), which can be modeled as contrasting with all others of the same category (cf. Santos 1996:11). In contrast, corpora employed in quantitative studies of grammatical devices can be relatively small (cf. Biber 1988; Givon 1995), because the syntactic freezing point is fairly low (Hakulinen et al. 1980: 104). Third, corpora that need extensive manual annotation (e.g., pragmatic annotation) are necessarily small. Fourth, many corpus tools set a ceiling on the number of concordances that can be extracted, for example, WordSmith version 3.0 can extract a maximum of 16,868 concordances (versions 4.0 and 5.0 do not have this limit). This makes it inconvenient for a frequent linguistic feature to be extracted from a very large corpus. Even if this can be done, few researchers can obtain useful information from hundreds of thousands of concordances (cf. Hunston 2002: 25). The data extracted defies manual analysis by a sole researcher by virtue of the sheer volume of examples discovered. Of course, I do not mean that DIY corpora must necessarily be small. A corpus small enough to produce only a dozen concordances of a linguistic feature under consideration will not be able to provide a reliable basis for quantification, though it may act as a spur to qualitative research.

It is important to note, however, that corpus size is an issue of ongoing debate in corpus creation. Some corpus linguists have argued that size matters (e.g., Krishnamurthy 2000; Sinclair 2004; Granath 2007). Large corpora are certainly of advantage in lexicography and in the study of infrequent linguistic structures (e.g., Keller and Lapata 2003). Also, NLP and language engineering can have different requirements for corpora from those used in linguistic research as discussed above. Corpora used in NLP and language engineering tend to be domain- or genre-specific specialized corpora (e.g., those composed of newspapers or telephone-based transactional dialogues), data for which are often easier to collect in large amounts than for balanced corpora. Furthermore, larger corpora are more reliable in statistical modeling, which is essential in natural language processing and language engineering. In a word, the point I wish to make is that the optimum size of a corpus is determined by the research question the corpus is intended to address as well as practical considerations.

7.3 Balance, Representativeness, and Sampling

One of the commonly accepted defining features of a corpus, which distinguishes a corpus from an archive (i.e., a random collection of texts), is *representativeness*. A corpus is designed to represent a particular language or language variety whereas an archive is not. What does representativeness mean in corpus linguistics? According to Leech (1991: 27), a corpus is thought to be representative of the language variety it is supposed to represent if the findings based on its contents can be generalized to the said language variety. Biber (1993: 243) defines representativeness from the viewpoint of how this quality is achieved: "Representativeness refers to the extent to which a sample includes the full range of variability in a population." A corpus is essentially a sample of a language or language variety (i.e., population). Sampling is entailed in the creation of virtually any corpus of a living language. In this respect, the representativeness of most corpora is to a great extent determined by two factors: the range of *genres*, *domains*, and *media* included in a corpus (i.e., *balance*) and how the text chunks for each genre are selected (i.e., *sampling*).

The criteria used to select texts for inclusion in a corpus are principally external to the texts themselves and dependent upon the intended use for the corpus (Aston and Burnard 1998: 23). The distinction between external and internal criteria corresponds to Biber's (1993: 243) situational vs. linguistic perspectives. External criteria are defined situationally irrespective of the distribution of linguistic features whereas internal criteria are defined linguistically, taking into account the distribution of such features. Internal criteria have sometimes been proposed as a measure of corpus representativeness (e.g., Otlogetswe 2004). In my view, it is problematic; indeed it is circular, to use internal criteria such as the distribution of words or grammatical features as the primary parameters for the selection of corpus data. A corpus is typically designed to study linguistic distributions. If the distribution of linguistic features is predetermined when the corpus is designed, there is no point in analyzing such a corpus to discover naturally occurring linguistic feature distributions. The corpus has been skewed by design. As such, I agree with Sinclair (2005) when he says that the texts or parts of texts to be included in a corpus should be selected according to external criteria so that their linguistic characteristics are, initially at least, independent of the selection process. This view is also shared by many other scholars including Atkins et al. (1992: 5–6) and Biber (1993: 256). Yet, once a corpus is created by using external criteria, the results of corpus analysis can be used as feedback to improve the representativeness of the corpus. In Biber's (1993: 256) words, "the compilation of a representative corpus should proceed in a cyclical fashion."

In addition to text selection criteria, Hunston (2002: 30) suggests that another aspect of representativeness is change over time: "Any corpus that is not regularly updated rapidly becomes unrepresentative." The relevance of permanence in corpus design actually depends on how we view a corpus, that is, whether a corpus should be viewed as a static or dynamic language model. The static view typically applies to a *sample corpus* whereas a dynamic view applies to a *monitor corpus*. A monitor corpus is primarily designed to track changes from different periods (cf. Hunston 2002: 16). It is particularly useful in tracking relatively rapid language change, such as the development and the life cycle of neologisms. Monitor corpora are constantly (e.g., annually, monthly, or even daily) supplemented with fresh material and keep increasing in size. For example, the Bank of English (BoE) has increased in size progressively since its inception in the 1980s (Hunston 2002: 15) and is around 524 million words at present. In contrast, a sample corpus is designed to represent a static snapshot of a particular language variety at a particular time. Static sample corpora, if resampled, may also allow the study of slower paced language change over time. For example, the LOB (Lancaster-Oslo-Bergen Corpus of British English, Johansson et al. 1978) and Brown corpora are supposed to represent written British and American English in the early 1960s; and their recent updates, Freiberg-LOB (FLOB, see Hundt et al. 1998) and Freiberg-Brown (Frown, see Hundt et al. 1999) corpora, represent written British and American English in the early 1990s respectively. Sample corpora such as these make it possible to track language change over the intervening three decades.

In addition to the distinction between sample and monitor corpora, representativeness has different meanings for *general* and *specialized* corpora. Corpora of the first type typically serve as a basis for an overall description of a language or language variety. The BNC corpus, for example, is supposed to represent modern British English as a whole. In contrast, a specialized corpus tends to be specific to a particular domain (e.g., medicine or law) or genre (e.g., newspaper text or academic prose). For a general corpus, it is understandable that it should cover, proportionally, as many text types as possible so that the corpus is maximally representative of the language or language variety it is supposed to represent. Even a specialized corpus, for example, one dealing with telephone calls to an operator service should be balanced by including within it a wide range of types of operator conversations (e.g., line fault, request for an engineer call out, number check, etc.) between a range of operators and customers (cf. McEnery et al. 2001) so that it can be claimed to represent this variety of language.

While both general and specialized corpora should be representative of a language or language variety, they have different criteria for representativeness. The representativeness of a general corpus depends heavily on sampling from a broad range of genres whereas the representativeness of a specialized corpus, at the lexical level at least, can be measured by the degree of *closure* (McEnery and Wilson 2001: 166) or *saturation* (Belica 1996: 61–74) of the corpus. Closure/saturation for a particular linguistic feature (e.g., size of lexicon) of a variety of language (e.g., computer manuals) means that the feature appears to be finite or is subject to very limited variation beyond a certain point. To measure the saturation of a corpus, the corpus is first divided into segments of equal size based on its tokens. The corpus is said to be saturated at the lexical level if each addition of a new segment yields approximately the same number of new lexical items as the previous segment, that is, when the curve of lexical growth is asymptotic, or flattening out. The notion of saturation is claimed to be superior to such concepts as balance for its measurability (Teubert 2000). It should be noted, however, that saturation is only concerned with lexical features. While it may be possible to adapt saturation to measure features other than lexical growth, there have been few attempts to do this to date (though see McEnery and Wilson 2001: 176–183 for a study of part-of-speech and sentence type closure).

It appears, then, that the representativeness of a corpus, especially a general corpus, depends primarily on how balanced the corpus is; in other words, the range of text categories included in the corpus. As with representativeness, the acceptable balance of a corpus is determined by its intended uses. Hence, a general corpus that contains both written and spoken data (e.g., the BNC) is balanced; so are written corpora such as Brown and LOB, and spoken corpora such as the Cambridge Nottingham Corpus of Discourse in English (CANCODE). A balanced corpus usually covers a wide range of text categories that are supposed to be representative of the language or language variety under consideration. These text categories are typically sampled proportionally for inclusion in a corpus so that "it offers a manageably small scale model of the linguistic material which the corpus builders wish to study" (Atkins et al. 1992: 6).

Balance appears to be a more important issue for a static sample corpus than for a dynamic monitor corpus. As corpora of the latter type are updated frequently, it is usually "impossible to maintain a corpus that also includes text of many different types, as some of them are just too expensive or time consuming to collect on a regular basis" (Hunston 2002: 30–31). The builders of monitor corpora appear to feel that balance has become less of a priority—sheer size seems to have become the basis of the corpus's authority, under the implicit and arguably unwarranted assumption that a corpus will in effect balance itself when it reaches a substantial size.

While balance and representativeness are important considerations in corpus design, they depend on the research question and the ease with which data can be captured and thus must be interpreted in relative terms. In other words, a corpus should only be as representative as possible of the language variety under consideration. For example, if one wants a corpus that is representative of general English, a corpus representative of newspapers will not do; if one wants a corpus representative of newspapers, a corpus representative of *The Times* will not do. Corpus balance and representativeness are fluid concepts that link directly to research questions. The research question one has in mind when building (or thinking of using) a corpus defines the required balance and representativeness. Any claim of corpus balance is largely an act of faith rather than a statement of fact as, at present, there is no reliable scientific measure of corpus balance. Rather the notion relies heavily on intuition and best estimates. Another argument supporting a loose interpretation of balance and representativeness is that these notions *per se* are open to question (cf. Hunston 2002: 28–30). To achieve corpus representativeness along the lines of the Brown corpus model one must know how often each genre is used by the language community in the *sampling period*. Yet it is unrealistic to determine the correlation of language production and reception in various genres (cf. Hausser 1999: 291; Hunston 2002: 29). The only solution to this problem is to treat corpus-based findings with caution. It is advisable to base your claims on your corpus and avoid unreasonable generalizations. Likewise, conclusions drawn from a particular corpus must be treated as deductions rather than facts (cf. also Hunston 2002: 23). With that said, however, I entirely agree with Atkins et al. (1992: 6), who comment that:

> It would be short-sighted indeed to wait until one can scientifically balance a corpus before starting to use one, and hasty to dismiss the results of corpus analysis as "unreliable" or "irrelevant" because the corpus used cannot be proved to be 'balanced.'

Given that language is infinite whereas a corpus is finite in size, *sampling* is unavoidable in corpus creation. Unsurprisingly, corpus representativeness and balance are closely associated with sampling. Given that we cannot exhaustively describe natural language, we need to sample it in order to achieve a level of balance and representativeness that matches our research question. Having decided that sampling is inevitable, there are important decisions that must be made about how to sample so that the resulting corpus is as balanced and representative as practically possible.

As noted earlier, with few exceptions, a corpus is typically a sample of a much larger *population*. A sample is assumed to be representative if what we find for the sample also holds for the general population (cf. Manning and Schütze 1999: 119). In the statistical sense, samples are scaled down versions of a larger population (cf. Váradi 2000). The aim of sampling theory "is to secure a sample which, subject to limitations of size, will reproduce the characteristics of the population, especially those of immediate interest, as closely as possible" (Yates 1965: 9).

In order to obtain a representative sample from a population, the first concern to be addressed is to define *the sampling unit* and the boundaries of the population. For written text, for example, a sampling unit may be a book, a periodical, or a newspaper. The population is the assembly of all sampling units while the list of sampling units is referred to as a *sampling frame*. The population from which samples for the pioneering Brown corpus were drawn, for instance, was all written English text published in the United States in 1961 while its sampling frame was a list of the collection of books and periodicals in the Brown University Library and the Providence Athenaeum. For the LOB corpus, the target population was all written English text published in the United Kingdom in 1961 while its sampling frame included the *British National Bibliography Cumulated Subject Index* 1960–1964 for books and *Willing's Press Guide* 1961 for periodicals.

In corpus design, a population can be defined in terms of language production, language reception, or language as a product. The first two designs are basically demographically oriented as they use the demographic distribution (e.g., age, sex, social class) of the individuals who produce/receive language data to define the population while the last design is organized around text category/genre of language data. As noted earlier, the Brown and LOB corpora were created using the criterion of language as a product while the BNC defines the population primarily on the basis of both language production and reception. However, it can be notoriously difficult to define a population or construct a sampling frame, particularly for spoken language, for which there are no ready-made sampling frames in the form of catalogues or bibliographies.

Once the target population and the sampling frame are defined, different sampling techniques can be applied to choose a sample that is as representative as possible of the population. A basic sampling method is *simple random sampling*. With this method, all sampling units within the sampling frame are numbered and the sample is chosen by use of a table of random numbers. As the chance of an item being chosen correlates positively with its frequency in the population, simple random sampling may generate a sample that does not include relatively rare items in the population, even though they can be of interest to researchers. One solution to this problem is *stratified random sampling*, which first divides the whole population into relatively homogeneous groups (so-called strata) and then samples each stratum at random (see Evert 2006 for a discussion of random sampling in corpus creation). In the Brown and LOB corpora, for example, the target population for each corpus was first grouped into 15 text categories such as news reportage, academic prose, and different types of fiction; samples were then drawn from each text category. Demographic sampling, which first categorizes sampling units in the population on the basis of speaker/writer age, sex and social class, is also a type of stratified sampling. Biber (1993) observes that a stratified sample is never less representative than a simple random sample.

A further decision to be made in sampling relates to *sample size*. For example, with written language, should we sample full texts (i.e., whole documents) or text chunks? If text chunks are to be sampled, should we sample text initial, middle, or end chunks? Full text samples are certainly useful in text linguistics, yet they may potentially constitute a challenge in dealing with vexatious copyright issues. Also, given its finite overall size, the coverage of a corpus including full texts may not be as balanced as a corpus including text segments of constant size. As a result, "the peculiarity of an individual style or topic may occasionally show through into the generalities" (Sinclair 1991: 19). Aston and Burnard (1998: 22) argue that the notion of "completeness" may sometimes be "inappropriate or problematic." As such, unless a corpus is created to study such features as textual organization, or copyright holders have granted you permission to use full texts, it is advisable to sample text segments. According to Biber (1993: 252), frequent linguistic features are quite stable in their distributions and hence short text chunks (e.g., 2000 running words) are usually sufficient for the study of such features while rare features are more varied in their distribution and thus require larger samples (Baroni 2009). In selecting samples to be included in a corpus, however, attention must also be paid to ensure that text initial, middle, and end samples are balanced.

Another sampling issue, which particularly relates to stratified sampling, is the proportion and the number of samples for each text category. The numbers of samples across text categories should be proportional to their frequencies and/or weights in the target population in order for the resulting corpus to be considered as representative. Nevertheless, it has been observed that, as with defining a target population, such proportions can be difficult to determine objectively (cf. Hunston 2002: 28–30). Furthermore, the criteria used to classify texts into different categories or genres are often dependent on intuitions. As such, the representativeness of a corpus, as noted, should be viewed as a statement of belief rather than fact. In the Brown corpus, for example, a panel of experts determined the ratios between the 15 text categories. As for the number of samples required for each category, Biber (1993) demonstrates that ten 2000-word samples are typically sufficient.

The above discussion suggests that in creating a balanced, representative corpus, stratified random sampling is to be preferred over simple random sampling while different sampling methods should be used to select different types of data. For written texts, a text typology established on the basis of external criteria is highly relevant while for spoken data demographic sampling is appropriate. However, context-governed sampling must complement samples obtained from demographic sampling so that some contextually governed linguistic variations can be included in the resulting corpus.

7.4 Data Capture and Copyright

For pragmatic reasons noted in Section 7.2, electronic data is preferred over paper-based material in building DIY corpora. The World Wide Web (WWW) is an important source of machine-readable data for many languages. For example, digital text archives mounted on the Web such as Oxford Text Archive (http://ota.ahds.ac.uk/) and Project Gutenberg (http://www.gutenberg.org/catalog/) as well as the digital collections of some university libraries (e.g., http://lib.virginia.edu/digital/collections/text/, http://onlinebooks.library.upenn.edu/) provide large amounts of publicly accessible electronic texts.

The web pages on the Internet normally use Hypertext Markup Language (i.e., HTML) to enable browsers like Internet Explorer or Netscape to display them properly. While the tags (included in angled brackets) are typically hidden when a text is displayed in a browser, they do exist in the source file of a web page. Hence, an important step in building DIY corpora using web pages is tidying up the downloaded data by converting web pages to plain text, or to some desired format, for example, XML (see Section 7.5). In this section, I will introduce some useful tools to help readers to download data from the Internet and clean up the downloaded data by removing or converting HTML tags. These tools are either freeware or commercial products available at affordable prices.

While it is possible to download data page by page, which is rather time consuming, there are a number of tools that facilitate downloading all of the web pages on a selected Web site in one go (e.g., Grab-a-Site or HTTrack), or more usefully, downloading related web pages (e.g., containing certain key words) at one go. The WordSmith Tools (versions 4.0 and 5.0), for example, incorporates the WebGetter function that helps users to build DIY corpora. WebGetter downloads related Web pages with the help of a search engine (Scott 2003: 87). Users can specify the minimum file length or word number (small files may contain only links to a couple of pictures and nothing much else), required language and, optionally, required words. Web pages that satisfy the requirements are downloaded simultaneously (cf. Scott 2003: 88–89). The WebGetter function, however, does not remove the HTML markup or convert it to XML. The downloaded data needs to be tidied up using other tools before they can be loaded into a concordancer or further annotated.

Another tool worth mentioning is the freeware Multilingual Corpus Toolkit (MLCT, see Piao et al. 2002). The MLCT runs in Java Runtime Environment (JRE) version 1.4 or above, which is freely available on the Internet. In addition to many other functions needed for multilingual language processing (e.g., markup, part-of-speech tagging, and concordancing), the system can be used to extract texts from the Internet. Once a web page is downloaded, it is cleaned up. One weakness of the program is that it can only download one web page at a time. Yet this weakness is compensated for by another utility that converts all of the web pages in a file folder (e.g., the web pages downloaded using the Webgetter function of WordSmith version 4.0) to a desired text format in one go. Another attraction of the MLCT is that it can mark up textual structure (e.g., paragraphs and sentences) automatically.

Finally, the BootCaT Toolkit provides a suite of utilities that allow the user to bootstrap specialized corpora and terms from the Web on the basis of a small set of terms as input (Baroni and Bernardini 2004). Readers interested in the Web as corpus can refer to Kilgarriff and Grefenstette (2003), Baroni and Bernardini (2006), and Hundt et al. (2007), and refer to Keller and Lapata (2003) for a comparison of the frequencies obtained from the Web and a balanced corpus such as the BNC.

A major issue in data collection is copyright. While it is possible to use copyright-free material in corpus creation, such data are usually old and a corpus consisting entirely of such data is not useful if one wishes to study contemporary English, for example. Such corpora are even less useful in NLP research, which tends to focus on current language use. Simply using copyrighted material in a corpus without the permission of the copyright holders may cause unnecessary trouble. In terms of purposes, corpora are typically of two types: for commercial purposes or for non-profit-making academic research. It is clearly unethical and illegal to use the data of other copyright holders to make money solely for oneself. Creators of commercial corpora usually reach an agreement with copyright holders as to how the profit will be shared. Publishers as copyright holders are also usually willing to contribute their data to a corpus-building project if they can benefit from the resulting corpus (e.g., the British National Corpus, the Longman Corpus Network, and the Cambridge International Corpus).

In creating DIY corpora for use in non-profit-making research, you might think that you need not worry about copyright if you are not selling your corpus to make a profit. Sadly, this is not the case. Copyright holders may still take you to the court. They may, for example, suffer a loss of profit because your use of their material diminishes their ability to sell it: why buy a book when you can read it for free in a corpus (cf. also Amsler 2002)? Copyright issues in corpus creation are complex and unavoidable. While corpus linguists have brought them up periodically for discussion, there is as yet no satisfactory solution to the issue of copyright in corpus creation.

The situation is complicated further by variation in copyright law internationally. According to the copyright law of EU countries, the term of copyright for published works in which the author owns the copyright is the author's lifetime plus 70 years. Under U.S. law, the term of copyright is the author's lifetime plus 50 years; but for works published before 1978, the copyright term is 75 years if the author renewed the copyright after 28 years.

One is able to make some use of copyrighted text without getting clearance, however. Under the convention of "fair dealing" in copyright law, permission need not be sought for short extracts not exceeding 400 words from prose (or a total of 800 words in a series of extracts, none exceeding 300 words); a citation from a poem should not exceed 40 lines or one quarter of the poem. So one can resort to using small samples to build perfectly legal DIY corpora on the grounds of fair usage. But the sizes of such samples are so small as to jeopardize any claim of balance or representativeness.

I maintain that the fair use doctrine as it applies to citations in published works should operate differently when it applies to corpus creation so as to allow corpus creators to build corpora quickly and legally. The limited reproduction of copyrighted works, for instance, in chunks of 3000 words or one-third of the whole text (whichever is shorter) should be protected under fair use for non-profit-making research and educational purposes. A position statement along these lines has been proposed by the corpus using community articulating the point of view that distributing minimal citations of copyrighted texts and allowing the public indirect access to privately held collections of copyrighted texts for statistical purposes are a necessary part of corpus linguistics research and should be inherently protected as fair use, particularly in non-profit-making research contexts (see Cooper 2003). This aim is not a legal reality yet, however. It will undoubtedly take time for a balance between copyright and fair use for corpus building to develop.

So, what does one do about copyright? My general advice is: if you are in doubt, seek permission. It is usually easier to obtain permission for samples than for full texts, and easier for smaller samples than for larger ones. If you show that you are acting in good faith, and only small samples will be used in non-profit-making research, copyright holders are typically pleased to grant you permission. If some do refuse, you remember it is their right to do so and move on to try other copyright holders until you have enough data.

It appears easier to seek copyright clearance for Web pages on the Internet than for material collected from printed publications. It has been claimed (Spoor 1996: 67) that a vast majority of the documents published on the Internet are not protected by copyright, and that many authors of texts are happy to be able to reach as many people as possible. However, readers should bear in mind that this may not be the case. For example, Cornish (1999: 141) argues that probably all material available on the Web is copyrighted, and that digital publications should be treated the same way as printed works.

Copyright law is generally formulated to prevent someone from making money from selling intellectual property belonging to other people. Unless you are making money using the intellectual property of other people, or you are somehow causing a loss of income to them, it is quite unlikely that copyright problems will arise when building a corpus. Yet copyright law is in its infancy. Different countries have different rules, and it has been argued that with reference to corpora and copyright there is very little which is obviously legal or illegal (cf. Kilgarriff 2002). My final word of advice is: proceed with caution.

7.5 Corpus Markup and Annotation

Data collected using a sampling frame as discussed in Section 7.3 forms a raw corpus. Yet such data typically needs to be processed before use. For example, spoken data needs to be transcribed from audio/video recordings; written texts may need to be rendered machine readable, if they are not already, by keyboarding or OCR scanning. Beyond this basic processing, however, lies another form of preparatory work—corpus markup. In addition, in order to extract linguistic information from a corpus, such information must first of all be encoded in the corpus, a process that is technically known as "corpus annotation."

Corpus markup is a system of standard codes inserted into a document stored in electronic form to provide information about the text itself (i.e., text metadata) and govern formatting, printing or other processing (i.e., structural organization). While metadata markup can be embedded in the same document or stored in a separate but linked document (see below for further discussion of embedding vs. stand-alone annotation), structural markup has to be embedded in the text. Both types of markups are important in corpus creation for at least three reasons. First, the corpus data basically consists of samples of used language. This means that these examples of linguistic usage are taken out of the context in which they originally occurred and their contextual information is lost. Burnard (2002) compares such out-of-context examples to a laboratory specimen and argues that contextual information (i.e., metadata or "data about data") is needed to restore the context and to enable us to relate the specimen to its original habitat. In corpus creation, therefore, it is important to recover as much contextual information as practically possible to alleviate or compensate for such a loss. Second, while it is possible to group texts and/or transcripts of similar quality together and name these files consistently (e.g., as happens with the LOB and Brown corpora), filenames can provide only a tiny amount of extra-textual information (e.g., text types for written data and sociolinguistic variables of speakers for spoken data) and no textual information (e.g., paragraph/sentence boundaries and speech turns) at all. Yet such data are of great interest to linguists as well as NLP researchers and thus should be encoded, separately from the corpus data *per se*, in a corpus. Markup adds value to a corpus and allows for a broader range of research questions to be addressed as a result. Finally, preprocessing written texts, and particularly transcribing spoken data, also involves markup. For example, in written data, when graphics/tables are removed from the original texts, placeholders must be inserted to indicate the locations and types of omissions; quotations in foreign languages should also be marked up. In spoken data, pausing and paralinguistic features such as laughter need to be marked up. Corpus markup is also needed to insert editorial comments, which are sometimes necessary in preprocessing written texts and transcribing spoken data. What is done in corpus markup has a clear parallel in existing linguistic transcription practices. Markup is essential in corpus creation.

Having established that markup is important in corpus creation, we can now move on to discuss markup schemes. It goes without saying that extra-textual and textual information should be kept separate from the corpus data (texts or transcripts) proper. Yet there are different schemes one may use to achieve this goal. One of the earliest markup schemes was COCOA. COCOA references consist of a set of attribute names and values enclosed in angled brackets, as in <A WILLIAM SHAKESPEARE>, where A (author) is the attribute name and WILLIAM SHAKESPEARE is the attribute value. COCOA references, however, only encode a limited set of features such as authors, titles, and dates (cf. McEnery and Wilson 2001: 35). Recently, a number of more ambitious metadata markup schemes have been proposed, including for example, the Dublin Core Metadata Initiative (DCMI, see Dekkers and Weibel 2003), the Open Language Archives Community (OLAC, see Bird and Simons 2000), the ISLE Metadata Initiative (IMDI, see Wittenburg et al. 2002), the Text Encoding Initiative (TEI, see Sperberg-McQueen and Burnard 2002), and the Corpus Encoding Standard (CES, see Ide and Priest-Dorman 2000). DCMI provides 15 elements used primarily to describe authored Web resources. OLAC is an extension of DCMI, which introduces refinements to narrow down the semantic scope of DCMI elements and adds an extra element to describe the language(s) covered by the resource. IMDI applies to multimedia corpora (see Section 7.7) and lexical resources as well. From even this brief review it should be clear that there is currently no widely agreed standard way of representing metadata, though all of the current schemes do share many features and similarities. Possibly the most influential schemes in corpus building are TEI and CES, hence I will discuss both of these in some detail here.

The Text Encoding Initiative (TEI) was sponsored by three major academic associations concerned with humanities computing: the Association for Computational Linguistics (ACL), the Association for Literary and Linguistic Computing (ALLC), and the Association for Computers and the Humanities (ACH). The aim of the TEI guidelines is to facilitate data exchange by standardizing the markup or encoding of information stored in electronic form. In TEI, each individual text (referred to as "document") consists of two parts: header (typically providing text metadata) and body (i.e., the text itself), which are in turn composed of different "elements." In a TEI header (tagged as <teiHeader>), for example, there are four principal elements (see Burnard 2002):

- A file description (tagged as <fileDesc>) containing a full bibliographic description of an electronic file.
- An encoding description (tagged as <encodingDesc>), which describes the relationship between an electronic text and the source or sources from which it was derived.
- A text profile (tagged as <profileDesc>), containing a detailed description of non-bibliographic aspects of a text, specifically the languages and sublanguages used, the situation in which it was produced, the participants and their setting.
- A revision history (tagged as <revisionDesc>), which records the changes that have been made to a file.

Each element may contain embedded sub-elements at different levels. Of these, however, only <fileDesc> is required to be TEI-compliant; all of the others are optional. Hence, a TEI header can be very complex, or it can be very simple, depending upon the document and the degree of bibliographic control sought. The body part of a TEI document is also conceived as being composed of elements. In this case, an element can be any unit of text, for example, chapter, paragraph, sentence, or word. Formal markup in the body (i.e., structural markup) is by far rarer than in the header (for metadata markup). It is primarily used to encode textual structures such as paragraphs and sentences. Note that the TEI scheme applies to both the markup of metadata and textual structure as well as the annotation of interpretative linguistic analysis.

The TEI scheme can be expressed using a number of different formal languages. The first editions used the Standard Generalized Markup Language (SGML); the more recent editions (i.e., TEI P4, 2002 and

TEI P5, 2007) can be expressed in the Extensible Markup Language (XML). SGML and XML are very similar, both defining a representation scheme for texts in electronic form, which is device and system independent. SGML is a very powerful markup language, but associated with this power is complexity. XML is a simplified subset of SGML intended to make SGML easy enough for use on the Web. Hence, while all XML documents are valid SGML documents, the reverse is not true. Nevertheless, there are some important surface differences between the two markup languages. End tags can optionally be left out in SGML but they cannot in XML. An attribute name (i.e., generic identifier) in SGML may or may not be case sensitive, but it is always case sensitive in XML. Unless it contains spaces or digits, an attribute value in SGML may be given without double (or single) quotes whereas quotes are mandatory in XML.

As the TEI guidelines are expressly designed to be applicable across a broad range of applications and disciplines, treating not only textual phenomena, they are designed for maximum generality and flexibility (cf. Ide 1998). As such, about 500 elements are predefined in the TEI guidelines. While these elements make TEI very powerful and suitable for the general purpose encoding of electronic texts, they also add complexity to the scheme. In contrast, the Corpus Encoding Standard (CES) is designed specifically for the encoding of language corpora. CES is described as "simplified" TEI in that it includes only the subset of the TEI tagset relevant to corpus-based work. While it simplifies the TEI specifications, CES also extends the TEI guidelines by adding new elements not covered in TEI, specifying the precise values for some attributes, marking required/recommended/optional elements, and explicating detailed semantics for elements relevant to language engineering (e.g., sentence, word, etc.) (cf. Ide 1998).

CES covers three principal types of markups: (1) document-wide markup, which uses more or less the same tags as for TEI to provide a bibliographic description of the document, encoding description, etc.; (2) gross structural markup, which encodes structural units of text (such as volume, chapter, etc.) down to the level of paragraph (but also including footnotes, titles, headings, tables, figures, etc.) and specifies normalization to recommended character sets and entities; (3) markup for sub-paragraph structures, including sentences, quotations, word abbreviations, names, dates, terms and cited words, etc. (see Ide 1998).

CES specifies a minimal encoding level that corpora must achieve to be considered standardized in terms of descriptive representation as well as general architecture. Three levels of text standardization are specified in CES: (1) the metalanguage level, (2) the syntactic level, and (3) the semantic level. Standardization at the metalanguage level regulates the form of the syntactic rules and the basic mechanisms of markup schemes. Users can use a TEI-compliant Document Type Definition (DTD) to define tag names as well as "document models" that specify the relations among tags. As texts may still have different document structures and markups even with the same metalanguage specifications, standardization at the syntactic level specifies precise tag names and syntactic rules for using the tags. It also provides constraints on content. However, the data sender and the data receiver can interpret even the same tag names differently. For example, a <title> element may be intended by the data sender to indicate the name of a book while the data receiver is under no obligation to interpret it as such, because the element can also show a person's rank, honor, and occupation, etc. This is why standardization at the semantic level is useful. In CES, the <h.title> element only refers to the name of a document. CES seeks to standardize at the semantic level for those elements most relevant to language engineering applications, in particular, linguistic elements. The three levels of standardization are designed to achieve the goal of universal document interchange. Like the TEI scheme, CES not only applies to corpus markup, it also covers encoding conventions for the linguistic annotation of text and speech, currently including morpho-syntactic tagging (i.e., part-of-speech tagging, see Chapter 10) and parallel text alignment in parallel corpora (see Chapter 16).

CES was developed and recommended by the Expert Advisory Groups on Language Engineering Standards (EAGLES) as a TEI-compliant application of SGML that could serve as a widely accepted set of encoding standards for corpus-based work. CES is available in both SGML and XML versions. The XML version, referred to as XCES, has also developed support for additional types of annotation and resources, including discourse/dialogue, lexicons, and speech (Ide et al. 2000). On the other hand, while metalanguages such as SGML and XML usually follow the system of attribute names laid out in implementation standards such as TEI and CES, this may not be necessarily the case.

Closely related to corpus markup is annotation, but the two are different. As annotation is so important in corpus creation and NLP research that specific types of annotation merit in-depth discussions in separate chapters (e.g., Chapters 8, 10, and 14), here I will only discuss annotation briefly. Corpus annotation can be defined as the process of "adding such interpretative, linguistic information to an electronic corpus of spoken and/or written language data" (Leech 1997: 2). While annotation defined in a broad sense may refer to the encoding of both textual/contextual information and interpretative linguistic analysis, as shown by the conflation of the two often found in the literature, the term is used in a narrow sense here, referring solely to the encoding of linguistic analyses such as part-of-speech tagging and syntactic parsing in a corpus text.

Corpus annotation, as used in a narrow sense, is fundamentally distinct from markup, though the distinction is not accepted by all and the two terms are sometimes used interchangeably in the literature. Corpus markup provides relatively objectively verifiable information regarding the components of a corpus and the textual structure of each text. In contrast, corpus annotation is concerned with interpretative linguistic information. "By calling annotation 'interpretative,' we signal that annotation is, at least in some degree, the product of the human mind's understanding of the text" (Leech 1997: 2). For example, the part of speech of a word may be ambiguous and hence is more readily defined as corpus annotation than corpus markup. On the other hand, the sex of a speaker or writer is normally objectively verifiable and as such is a matter of markup, not annotation.

Corpus annotation can be undertaken at different levels and may take various forms. For example, at the phonological level, corpora can be annotated for syllable boundaries (phonetic/phonemic annotation) or prosodic features (prosodic annotation); at the morphological level corpora can be annotated in terms of prefixes, suffixes and stems (morphological annotation); at the lexical level, corpora can be annotated for parts-of-speech (POS tagging), lemmas (lemmatization), and semantic fields (semantic annotation); at the syntactic level, corpora can be annotated with syntactic analysis (parsing, treebanking, or bracketing); at the discoursal level, corpora can be annotated to show anaphoric relations (coreference annotation), pragmatic information like speech acts (pragmatic annotation) or stylistic features such as speech and thought presentation (stylistic annotation). Of these the most widespread type of annotation is part-of-speech tagging (see Chapter 10), which has been successfully applied to many languages; syntactic parsing is also developing rapidly (see Chapters 8 and 11) while some types of annotation (e.g., discoursal and pragmatic annotations) are presently relatively undeveloped.

I have so far assumed that the process of annotation leads to information being mixed in the original corpus text or so-called base document when it is applied to a corpus (i.e., the annotation becomes so-called embedded annotation). However, the Corpus Encoding Standard recommends the use of "stand-alone annotation," whereby the annotation information is retained in separate SGML/XML documents (with different Document Type Definitions) and linked to the original and other annotation documents in hypertext format. In contrast to embedded annotation, stand-alone annotation has a number of advantages (Ide 1998):

- It provides control over the distribution of base documents for legal purposes.
- It enables annotation to be performed on base documents that cannot easily be altered (e.g., they are read-only).
- It avoids the creation of potentially unwieldy documents.
- It allows multiple overlapping hierarchies.
- It allows for alternative annotation schemes to be applied to the same data (e.g., different POS tagsets).
- It enables new annotation levels to be added without causing problems for existing levels of annotation or search tools.
- It allows annotation at one level to be changed without affecting other levels.

Stand-alone annotation is in principle ideal and is certainly technically feasible (see Thompson and McKelvie 1997). It may also represent the future standard for certain types of annotation. In addition, the stand-alone architecture can facilitate multilevel or multilayer annotations as well (see Dipper 2005). Presently, however, there are two problems associated with stand-alone annotation. The first issue is related to the complexity of corpus annotation. As noted earlier, annotation may have multiple forms in a corpus. While some of these readily allow for the separation of annotation codes from base documents (e.g., lemmatization, part-of-speech tagging, and semantic annotation), others may involve much more complexity in establishing links between codes and annotated items (e.g., coreference and stylistic annotations). Even if such links can be established, they are usually prone to error. The second issue is purely practical. As far as I am aware, the currently available corpus exploration tools, including the latest versions of WordSmith (versions 4.0 and 5.0) and Xaira (Burnard and Todd 2003), have all been designed for use with embedded annotation. Stand-alone annotation, while appealing, is only useful when appropriate search tools are available for use on stand-alone annotated corpora.

7.6 Multilingual Corpora

I have so far assumed in this chapter that a corpus only involves one language. Corpora of this kind are monolingual. But there are also corpora that cover more than one language, which are referred to as multilingual corpora. In this section, I will shift my focus to the multilingual dimension of corpus creation.

With ever increasing international exchange and accelerated globalization, translation and contrastive studies are more popular than ever. As part of this new wave of research on translation and contrastive studies, multilingual corpora such as parallel and comparable corpora are playing an increasingly prominent role. As Aijmer and Altenberg (1996: 12) observe, parallel and comparable corpora "offer specific uses and possibilities" for contrastive and translation studies:

- They give new insights into the languages compared—insights that are not likely to be gained from the study of monolingual corpora.
- They can be used for a range of comparative purposes and increase our knowledge of language-specific, typological and cultural differences, as well as of universal features.
- They illuminate differences between source texts and translations, and between native and nonnative texts.
- They can be used for a number of practical applications, for example, in lexicography, language teaching, and translation.

In addition to these benefits of multilingual resources in linguistic research, we can also add to the list the fact that aligned parallel corpora are indispensable to the development of NLP applications such as computer-aided translation and machine translation (see Chapters 17 and 18) and multilingual information retrieval and extraction (see Chapters 19 and 21).

A multilingual corpus involves texts of more than one language. As corpora that cover two languages are conventionally known as "bilingual," multilingual corpora, in a narrow sense, must involve more than two languages, though "multilingual" and "bilingual" are often used interchangeably in the literature, and also in this chapter. A multilingual corpus can be a parallel corpus, or a comparable corpus. Given that corpora involving more than one language are a relatively new phenomenon, with most related research hailing from the early 1990s, it is unsurprising to discover that there is some confusion surrounding the terminology used in relation to these corpora.

It can be said that terminological confusion in multilingual corpora centers on two terms: "parallel" and "comparable." For some scholars (e.g., Aijmer and Altenberg 1996; Granger 1996: 38), corpora composed of source texts in one language and their translations in another language (or other languages) are "translation corpora" while those comprising different components sampled from different native languages using comparable sampling techniques are called "parallel corpora." For others (e.g., Baker 1993: 248, 1995, 1999; Barlow 1995, 2000: 110; Hunston 2002: 15; McEnery and Wilson 1996: 57; McEnery et al. 2006), corpora of the first type are labeled "parallel" while those of the latter type are comparable corpora. As argued in McEnery and Xiao (2007a: 19–20), while different criteria can be used to define different types of corpora, they must be used consistently and logically. For example, we can say that a corpus is monolingual, bilingual, or multilingual if we take the number of languages involved as the criterion for definition. We can also say that a corpus is a translation or a non-translation corpus if the criterion of corpus content is used. But if we choose to define corpus types by the criterion of corpus form, we must use the terminology consistently. Then we can say a corpus is parallel if the corpus contains source texts and translations in parallel, or it is a comparable corpus if its components or subcorpora are comparable by applying the same sampling frame. It is illogical, however, to refer to corpora of the first type as translation corpora by the criterion of content while referring to corpora of the latter type as comparable corpora by the criterion of form.

Additionally, a parallel corpus, in my terms, can be either unidirectional (e.g., from English into Chinese or from Chinese into English alone), or bidirectional (e.g., containing both English source texts with their Chinese translations as well as Chinese source texts with their English translations), or multidirectional (e.g., the same piece of text with its Chinese, English, French, Russian, and Arabic versions). In this sense, texts that are produced simultaneously in different languages (e.g., UN regulations) also belong to the category of parallel corpora. A parallel corpus must be aligned at a certain level (for instances, at document, paragraph, sentence, or word level) in order to be useful. The automatic alignment of parallel corpora is not a trivial task for some language pairs, though alignment is generally very reliable for many closely related European language pairs (cf. McEnery et al. 2006: 50–51; see Chapter 16 for further discussion).

Another complication in terminology involves a corpus that is composed of different variants of the same language. This is particularly relevant to translation studies because it is a very common practice in this research area to compare a corpus of translated texts—that I call a "translational corpus"—and a corpus consisting of comparably sampled non-translated texts in the same language (see Xiao and Yue 2009). They form a monolingual comparable corpus. To us, a multilingual comparable corpus samples different native languages, with its comparability lying in the matching or comparable sampling techniques, similar balance (i.e., coverage of genres and domains) and representativeness, and similar sampling period (see Section 7.3). By my definition, corpora containing different regional varieties of the same language (e.g., the International Corpus of English, ICE) are not comparable corpora because all corpora, as a resource for linguistic research, have "always been pre-eminently suited for comparative studies" (Aarts 1998: ix), either intralingually or interlingually. The Brown, LOB, Frown, and FLOB corpora are also used typically for comparing language varieties synchronically and diachronically. Corpora such as these can be labeled as "comparative corpora." They are not "comparable corpora" as suggested in the literature (e.g., Hunston 2002: 15).

Having clarified some terminological confusion in multilingual corpus research, it is worth pointing out the distinctions discussed here are purely for the sake of clarification. In reality, there are multilingual corpora that are a mixture of parallel and comparable corpora. For example, in spite of its name, the English–Norwegian Parallel Corpus (ENPC) can be considered as a combination of a parallel and comparable corpus. I will not discuss the state of the art of multilingual corpus research here. Interested readers are advised to refer to McEnery and Xiao (2007b).

Multilingual corpora often involve a writing system that relies heavily on non-ASCII characters. Character encoding is rarely an issue in corpus creation for alphabetical languages (e.g., English) that use ASCII characters. However, even languages that use a small number of accented Latin characters may have encountered encoding problems. For monolingual corpora of many other languages that use different writing systems, especially for multilingual corpora that contain a wide range of writing systems, encoding is all the more important if one wants to display the corpus properly or facilitate data interchange. For example, Chinese can be encoded using GB2312 (Simplified Chinese), Big5 (Traditional Chinese), or Unicode (UTF-8, UTF-7 or UTF-16). Both GB2312 and Big5 are 2-byte encoding systems that require language-specific operating systems or language-support packs if the Chinese characters encoded are to be displayed properly. Language specific encoding systems such as these make data interchange problematic. It is also quite impossible to display a document containing both simplified and traditional Chinese characters using these encoding systems. As McEnery et al. (2000) note, the main difficulty in building a multilingual corpus of Asian languages is the need to standardize the language data into a single character set. Unicode is recommended as a solution to this problem (see McEnery and Xiao 2005). Unicode is truly multilingual in that it can display characters from a very large number of writing systems. From the Unicode Standard version 1.1 onward, Unicode is fully compatible with ISO 10646-1 (UCS). The combination of Unicode and XML is a general trend in corpus creation (see Xiao et al. 2004). As such, it is to be welcomed.

7.7 Multimodal Corpora

The corpora discussed so far in this chapter, whether spoken or written, have been assumed to be text-based; that is, spoken language is treated as if it is written. In this text-based approach to corpus creation, audio/video recordings of spoken data are transcribed, with the transcript possibly also including varying levels of details of spoken features (e.g., turn overlaps) and paralinguistic features (e.g., laughter). Corpus analysis is then usually undertaken on the textual transcript without reference to the original recording unless one is engaged in prosodic or phonetic research.

As noted in Section 7.5, a corpus is essentially a collection of samples of used language, which have been likened to a laboratory specimen out of its original habitat (Burnard 2005). While corpus markup can help to restore some contextual information, a large part of such information is lost, especially in transcripts of video clips. As Kress and van Leeuwen (2006: 41) observe, "a spoken text is never just verbal, but also visual combining with modes such as facial expressions, gesture, posture and other forms of self-presentation," the latter of which cannot be captured and transcribed easily, if at all. Consequently, "even the most detailed, faithful and sympathetic transcription cannot hope to capture" spoken language (Carter 2004: 26). As such, there has recently been an increasing interest in multimodal corpora. In this kind of corpora, annotated transcripts are aligned with digital audio/video clips with the help of time stamps, which not only renders the corpus searchable with the help of transcripts but also allows the user to access the segments of recordings corresponding to the search results. There are a number of existing multimodal corpora including, for example, the Nottingham Multi-Modal Corpus (NMMC, see Adolphs and Carter 2007), the Singapore Corpus of Research in Education (SCoRE, see Hong 2005), Padova Multimedia English Corpus (see Ackerley and Coccetta 2007), and the Spoken Chinese Corpus of Situated Discourse (SCCSD, see Gu 2002).

Multimodal corpora and multimodal concordancers are still in their infancy (Baldry 2006: 188). They are technically more challenging to develop than purely text-based corpora and corpus tools. However, given the special values of such corpora, and the advances of technologies (e.g., those that help to track and annotate gestures), multimodal corpora will become more common and more widely used in the near future.

7.8 Conclusions

This chapter has focused on corpus creation, covering the major factors that must be taken into account in this process. I have discussed both core issues relating to corpus design (e.g., corpus size, representativeness, and balance) as well as corpus processing (e.g., data collection, markup, and annotation), and peripheral issues such as multilingual and multimodal corpora.

One important reason for using corpora is to extract linguistic information present in those corpora. But it is often the case that in order to extract such information from a corpus, a linguistic analysis must first be encoded in the corpus. Such annotation adds value to a corpus in that it considerably extends the range of research questions that a corpus can readily address. In this chapter, I have discussed corpus annotation in very general terms. The chapter that follows will explore annotation in greater depth.

References

Aarts, J. (1998) Introduction. In S. Johansson and S. Oksefjell (eds.), *Corpora and Cross-Linguistic Research*, pp. ix–xiv. Amsterdam, the Netherlands: Rodopi.

Ackerley, K. and Coccetta, F. (2007) Enriching language learning through a multimedia corpus. *ReCALL* 19(3): 351–370.

Adolphs, S. and Carter, R. (2007) Beyond the word: New challenges in analyzing corpora of spoken English. *European Journal of English Studies* 11(2): 133–146.

Aijmer, K. and Altenberg, B. (1996) Introduction. In K. Aijmer, B. Altenberg and M. Johansson (eds.), Language in contrast. *Papers from Symposium on Text-Based Cross-Linguistic Studies, Lund, Sweden, March 1994*, pp. 10–16. Lund, Sweden: Lund University Press.

Amsler, R. (2002) Legal aspects of corpora compiling. In *Corpora List Archive on 1st October 2002*. URL: http://helmer.hit.uib.no/corpora/2002-3/0256.html.

Aston, G. and Burnard, L. (1998) *The BNC Handbook*. Edinburgh, U.K.: Edinburgh University Press.

Atkins, S., Clear, J., and Ostler, N. (1992) Corpus design criteria. *Literary and Linguistic Computing* 7(1): 1–16.

Baker, M. (1993) Corpus linguistics and translation studies: Implications and applications. In M. Baker, G. Francis, and E. Tognini-Bonelli (eds.), *Text and Technology: In Honour of John Sinclair*, pp. 233–352. Amsterdam, the Netherlands: Benjamins.

Baker, M. (1995) Corpora in translation studies: An overview and some suggestions for future research. *Target* 7: 223–243.

Baker, M. (1999) The role of corpora in investigating the linguistic behaviour of professional translators. *International Journal of Corpus Linguistics* 4: 281–298.

Baldry, A. P. (2006) The role of multimodal concordancers in multimodal corpus linguistics. In T. D. Royce and W. L. Bowcher (eds.), *New Directions in the Analysis of Multimodal Discourse*, pp. 173–214. London, U.K.: Routledge.

Barlow, M. (1995) *A Guide to ParaConc*. Huston, TX: Athelstan.

Barlow, M. (2000) Parallel texts and language teaching. In S. Botley, A. McEnery, and A. Wilson (eds.), *Multilingual Corpora in Teaching and Research*, pp. 106–115. Amsterdam, the Netherlands: Rodopi.

Baroni, M. (2009) Distributions in text. In A. Lüdeling and M. Kytö (eds.), *Corpus Linguistics: An International Handbook* (Vol. 2), pp. 803–822. Berlin, Germany: Mouton de Gruyter.

Baroni, M. and Bernardini, S. (2004) BootCaT: Bootstrapping corpora and terms from the Web. In M. Lino, M. Xavier, F. Ferreire, R. Costa, and R. Silva (eds.), *Proceedings of the Fourth International Conference on Language Resources and Evaluation (LREC) 2004*, Lisbon, Portugal, May 24–30, 2004.

Baroni, M. and Bernardini, S. (eds.). (2006) *Wacky! Working Papers on the Web as Corpus*. Bologna, Italy: GEDIT.

Belica, C. (1996) Analysis of temporal change in corpora. *International Journal of Corpus Linguistics* 1(1): 61–74.

Biber, D. (1988) *Variation Across Speech and Writing*. Cambridge, U.K.: Cambridge University Press.

Biber, D. (1993) Representativeness in corpus design. *Literary and Linguistic Computing* 8(4): 243–257.

Bird, S. and Simons, G. (2000) *White Paper on Establishing an Infrastructure for Open Language Archiving*. URL: http://www.language-archives.org/docs/white-paper.html.

Burnard, L. (2002) *Validation Manual for Written Language Resources*. URL: http://www.oucs.ox.ac.uk/rts/elra/D1.xml.

Burnard, L. (2005) Metadata for corpus work. In M. Wynne (ed.), *Developing Linguistic Corpora: A Guide to Good Practice*, pp. 30–46. Oxford, U.K.: AHDS.

Burnard, L. and Todd, T. (2003) Xara: An XML aware tool for corpus searching. In D. Archer, P. Rayson, A. Wilson, and A. McEnery (eds.), *Proceedings of Corpus Linguistics 2003*, Lancaster, U.K., pp. 142–144. Lancaster, U.K.: Lancaster University.

Carter, R. (2004) Grammar and spoken English. In C. Coffin, A. Hewings, and K. O'Halloran (eds.), *Applying English Grammar: Corpus and Functional Approaches*, pp. 25–39. London, U.K.: Arnold.

Collins (2007) *Collins English Dictionary* (9th ed.). Toronto, Canada: HarperCollins.

Cooper, D. (2003) Legal aspects of corpora compiling. In *Corpora List Archive on 19th June 2003*. URL: http://helmer.aksis.uib.no/corpora/2003-1/0596.html.

Cornish, G. P. (1999) *Copyright: Interpreting the Law for Libraries, Archives and Information Services* (3rd ed.). London, U.K.: Library Association Publishing.

Dekkers, M. and Weibel, S. (2003) State of the Dublin core metadata initiative. *D-Lib Magazine* 9(4). URL: http://www.dlib.org/dlib/april03/weibel/04weibel.html.

Dipper, S. (2005) XML-based stand-off representation and exploitation of multi-level linguistic annotation. In *Proceedings of Berliner XML Tage 2005 (BXML 2005)*, Berlin, Germany, pp. 39–50.

Dipper, S. (2008) Theory-driven and corpus-driven computational linguistics, and the use of corpora. In A. Ludeling and M. Kyto (eds.), *Corpus Linguistics: An International Handbook* (Vol. 1), pp. 68–96. Berlin, Germany: Mouton de Gruyter.

Evert, S. (2006) How random is a corpus? The library metaphor. *Zeitschrift für Anglistik und Amerikanistik* 54(2): 177–190.

Givon, T. (1995) *Functionalism and Grammar*. Amsterdam, the Netherlands: John Benjamins.

Granath, S. (2007) Size matters—Or thus can meaningful structures be revealed in large corpora. In R. Facchinetti (ed.), *Corpus Linguistics 25 Years On*, pp. 169–185. Amsterdam, the Netherlands: Rodopi.

Granger, S. (1996) From CA to CIA and back: An integrated approach to computerized bilingual and learner corpora. In K. Aijmer, B. Altenberg, and M. Johansson (eds.), *Language in contrast. Symposium on Text-based Cross-linguistic Studies, Lund, Sweden, March 1994*, pp. 38–51. Lund, Sweden: Lund University Press.

Gu, Y. (2002) Towards an understanding of workplace discourse. In C. N. Candlin (ed.), *Research and Practice in Professional Discourse*, pp. 137–86. Hong Kong: City University of Hong Kong Press.

Hakulinen, A., Karlsson, F., and Vilkuna, M. (1980) *Suomen tekstilauseiden piirteitä: kvantitatiivinen tutkimus*. Department of General Linguistics, University of Helsinki, Helsinki, Finland, Publications No. 6.

Hausser, H. (1999) *Functions of Computational Linguistics*. Berlin, Germany: Springer-Verlag.

Hong, H. (2005) SCORE: A multimodal corpus database of education discourse in Singapore schools. In *Proceedings of Corpus Linguistics 2005*. http://www.corpus.bham.ac.uk/pclc/ScopeHong.pdf

Hundt, M., Sand, A., and Siemund, R. (1998) *Manual of Information to Accompany the Freiburg-LOB Corpus of British English ('FLOB')*. URL: http://khnt.hit.uib.no/icame/manuals/flob/INDEX.HTM.

Hundt, M., Sand, A., and Skandera, P. (1999) *Manual of Information to Accompany the Freiburg-Brown Corpus of American English ('Frown')*. URL: http://khnt.hit.uib.no/icame/manuals/frown/INDEX.HTM.

Hundt, M., Biewer, C., and Nesselhauf, N. (eds.). (2007) *Corpus Linguistics and the Web*. Amsterdam, the Netherlands: Rodopi.

Hunston, S. (2002) *Corpora in Applied Linguistics*. Cambridge, U.K.: Cambridge University Press.

Ide, N. (1998) Corpus encoding standard: SGML guidelines for encoding linguistic corpora. In *LREC-1998 Proceedings*, Granada, Spain, pp. 463–470.

Ide, N. and Priest-Dorman, G. (2000) *Corpus Encoding Standard—Document CES 1*. URL: http://www.cs.vassar.edu/CES/.

Ide, N., Patrice, B., and Romary L. (2000) XCES: An XML-based encoding standard for linguistic corpora. In *LREC-2000 Proceedings*, Athens, Greece, pp. 825–830.

Johansson, S., Leech, G., and Goodluck, H. (1978) *Manual of Information to Accompany the Lancaster-Oslo/Bergen Corpus of British English, for Use with Digital Computers.* Oslo, Norway: University of Oslo.

Keller, F. and Lapata, M. (2003) Using the Web to obtain frequencies for unseen bigrams. *Computational Linguistics* 29(3): 459–484.

Kilgarriff, A. (2002) Legal aspects of corpora compiling. In *Corpora List Archive on 1st October 2002.* URL: http://helmer.hit.uib.no/corpora/2002-3/0253.html.

Kilgarriff, A. and Grefenstette, G. (eds.). (2003) Special Issue on Web as Corpus. *Computational Linguistics* 29(3): 333–502.

Kress, G. and van Leeuwen, T. (2006) *Reading Images: The Grammar of Visual Design* (2nd ed.). London, U.K.: Routledge.

Krishnamurthy, R. (2000) Size matters: Creating dictionaries from the world's largest corpus. In *Proceedings of KOTESOL 2000: Casting the Net: Diversity in Language Learning,* Taegu, Korea, pp. 169–180.

Kučera, H. and Francis, W. (1967) *Computational Analysis of Present-Day English.* Providence, RI: Brown University Press.

Leech, G. (1991) The state of art in corpus linguistics. In K. Aijmer and B. Altenberg (eds.), *English Corpus Linguistics,* pp. 8–29. London, U.K.: Longman.

Leech, G. (1997) Introducing corpus annotation. In R. Garside, G. Leech, and A. McEnery (eds.), *Corpus Annotation,* pp. 1–18. London, U.K.: Longman.

Manning, C. and Schütze, H. (1999) *Foundations of Statistical Natural Language Processing.* Cambridge, MA: MIT Press.

McEnery, A. and Wilson, A. (1996/2001) *Corpus Linguistics* (2nd ed. 2001). Edinburgh, U.K.: Edinburgh University Press.

McEnery, A. and Xiao, R. (2005) Character encoding in corpus construction. In M. Wynne (ed.), *Developing Linguistic Corpora: A Guide to Good Practice,* pp. 47–58. Oxford, U.K.: AHDS.

McEnery, A. and Xiao, R. (2007a) Parallel and comparable corpora: What is happening? In M. Rogers and G. Anderman (eds.), *Incorporating Corpora: The Linguist and the Translator,* pp. 18–31. Clevedon, U.K.: Multilingual Matters.

McEnery, A. and Xiao, R. (2007b) Parallel and comparable corpora: The state of play. In Y. Kawaguchi, T. Takagaki, N. Tomimori, and Y. Tsuruga (eds.), *Corpus-Based Perspectives in Linguistics,* pp. 131–145. Amsterdam, the Netherlands: John Benjamins.

McEnery, A., Baker, P., Gaizauskas, R., and Cunningham, H. (2000) EMILLE: Building a corpus of South Asian languages. *Vivek: A Quarterly in Artificial Intelligence* 13(3): 23–32.

McEnery, A., Baker, P., and Cheepen, C. (2001) Lexis, indirectness and politeness in operator calls. In C. Meyer and P. Leistyna (eds.), *Corpus Analysis: Language Structure and Language Use.* Amsterdam, the Netherlands: Rodopi.

McEnery, A., Xiao, R., and Tono, Y. (2006) *Corpus-Based Language Studies: An Advanced Resource Book.* London, U.K.: Routledge.

Ostler, N. (2008) Corpora of less studied languages. In A. Ludeling and M. Kyto (eds.), *Corpus Linguistics: An International Handbook* (Vol. 1), pp. 457–484. Berlin, Germany: Mouton de Gruyter.

Otlogetswe, T. (2004) The BNC design as a model for a Setswana language corpus. In *Proceeding of the Seventh Annual CLUK Research Colloquium,* pp. 93–198. University of Birmingham, Edgbaston, U.K., January 6–7, 2004.

Piao, S., Wilson, A., and McEnery, A. (2002) A multilingual corpus toolkit. *Paper Presented at the Fourth North American Symposium on Corpus Linguistics,* Indianapolis, IN, November 1–3, 2002.

Santos, D. (1996) Tense and aspect in English and Portuguese: A contrastive semantical study. PhD thesis, Universidade Tecnica de Lisboa, Lisbon, Portugal.

Scott, M. (2003) *WordSmith Tools Manual.* URL: http://www.lexically.net/wordsmith/version4/.

Shimazumi, M. and Berber-Sardinha, A. (1996) Approaching the assessment of performance unit (APU) archive of schoolchildren's writing from the point of view of corpus linguistics. *Paper Presented at the TALC'96 Conference*, Lancaster University, Lancaster, U.K., August 11, 1996.

Sinclair, J. (1991) *Corpus Concordance Collocation*. Oxford, U.K.: Oxford University Press.

Sinclair, J. (2004) *Trust the Text: Language, Corpus and Discourse*. London, U.K.: Routledge.

Sinclair, J. (2005) Corpus and Text: Basic Principles. In M. Wynne (ed.), *Developing Linguistic Corpora: A Guide to Good Practice*, pp. 1–20. Oxford, UK: AHDS.

Sperberg-McQueen, C. M. and Burnard, L. (eds.). (2002) *TEI P4: Guidelines for Electronic Text Encoding and Interchange (XML Version)*. Oxford, U.K.: Text Encoding Initiative Consortium.

Spoor, J. (1996) The copyright approach to copying on the Internet: (Over)stretching the reproduction right? In H. Hugenholtz (ed.), *The Future of Copyright in a Digital Environment*, pp. 67–80. Dordrecht, the Netherlands: Kluwer Law International.

Teubert, W. (2000) Corpus linguistics—A partisan view. *International Journal of Corpus Linguistics* 4(1):1–16.

Thompson, H. and McKelvie, D. (1997) Hyperlink semantics for standoff markup of read-only documents. In *Proceedings of SGML Europe'97*, Barcelona, Spain, May 1997. URL: http://www.ltg.ed.ac.uk/~ht/sgmleu97.html.

Váradi, T. (2000) Corpus linguistics—linguistics or language engineering? In T. Erjavec and J. Gross (eds.), *Information Society Multi-Conference Proceedings Language Technologies*, pp. 1–5. Ljubljana, Slovenia, October 17–18, 2000.

Wittenburg, P., Peters, W., and Broeder, D. (2002) Metadata proposals for corpora and lexica. In *LREC-2002 Proceedings*, Las Palmas, Spain, pp. 1321–1326.

Xiao, R. (2008) Well-known and influential corpora. In A. Lüdeling and M. Kyto (eds.), *Corpus Linguistics: An International Handbook* (Vol. 1), pp. 383–457. Berlin, Germany: Mouton de Gruyter.

Xiao, R. and Yue, M. (2009) Using corpora in translation studies: The state of the art. In P. Baker (ed.), *Contemporary Approaches to Corpus Linguistics*, pp. 237–262. London, U.K.: Continuum.

Xiao, R., McEnery, A., Baker, P., and Hardie, A. (2004) Developing Asian language corpora: Standards and practice. In *Proceedings of the Fourth Workshop on Asian Language Resources*, Sanya, Hainan Island, pp. 1–8, March 25, 2004.

Yates, F. (1965) *Sampling Methods for Censuses and Surveys* (3rd ed.). London, U.K.: Charles Griffin and Company Limited.

8

Treebank Annotation

Eva Hajičová
Charles University

Anne Abeillé
Université Paris 7 and CNRS

Jan Hajič
Charles University

Jiří Mírovský
Charles University

Zdeňka Urešová
Charles University

8.1 Introduction

Corpus annotation, whether lexical, morphological, syntactic, semantic, or any other, brings additional linguistic information as an added value to a corpus. The annotation scenario might differ considerably among corpora, but it is always based on some formalism that represents the desired level and area of linguistic interpretation of the corpus. From the simple annotation of part-of-speech categories to the shallow syntactic annotation to semantic role labeling to the "deep," complex annotation of semantic and discourse relations, there is usually some more or less sound linguistic theory behind the design of the representation used, or at least certain principles common to several such theories.

Corpora have become popular resources for computationally minded linguists and computer science experts developing applications in Natural Language Processing (NLP). Linguists typically look for various occurrences of specific words or patterns to find examples or counterexamples within the theories they build or work with, lexicographers use corpora for creating dictionary entries by looking for evidence of use of words in various senses and contexts, computational linguists together with computer scientists and statisticians construct language models and build part-of-speech taggers, syntactic parsers and various semantic labelers to be used in applications, such as machine translation, information retrieval, information extraction, question answering and summarization systems, dialogue systems and many more. Often, annotated corpora were built by linguists who wanted to confront their theory with real-world texts.

Most of the work on annotated corpora concerns the domain of written texts, on which this chapter is focused. However, it should be acknowledged that the growing interest in the speech community to develop advanced models of spoken language has led to an increasing effort to process corpora that represent the spoken form of language. This is well documented among other things by the contributions in the special issue of the journal Speech Communication published in 2001 (Bird and Harrington 2001), in which topics such as annotation schemes, tools for creating, searching, and manipulating the annotations as well as future directions are discussed. Also, there is an increasing number of contributions at the most recent Interspeech and other speech-related conferences that tackle the topical issues of annotation of spoken language, mostly of dialogues (see e.g., already the Tübingen corpus of spontaneous Japanese dialogues reported on in Kawata and Barteles 2000). Prosody, disfluencies, and dialogue acts (such as statements, requests, etc.) have to be annotated, too.

In this chapter, after introducing types of corpus annotation and briefly mentioning unstructured morphosyntactically annotated corpora, we will focus on treebank annotation—the definition of treebanks, their properties, examples of existing treebanks, their relation to linguistic theory, and the process of annotation and quality control. We will also refer the application of treebanks, and specifically discuss searching for linguistic information in them.

8.2 Corpus Annotation Types

Annotation consists of pieces of information added to the language data. The data may have various forms—it can be audio, video, or textual data. The added information can be external, such as the author's name, the date of recording/writing, or the type of font—this type of annotation is often called "metadata." We are more interested in linguistic information, such as part of speech, clause boundary, word sense, syntactic analysis, co-reference annotation, etc.

Usually, three linguistic annotation phases (layers, or simply types) are distinguished: a morphosyntactic layer, only dealing with morphosyntactic ambiguity (and part of speech and inflectional and morphological annotation), a layer dealing with syntactic relations of different degree of depth (oriented toward constituency or dependency annotations), and a layer focused on different aspects of semantic and discourse relations such as word sense disambiguation, anaphoric relations, etc.

A morphosyntactic tag includes (part of) the following information (e.g., for the French token *la*):

- Lemma (*le*)
- Part of speech (determiner)
- Subcategory (definite)
- Inflection (feminine singular)

A syntactic tag includes (part of) the following information:

- Constituent boundaries (clause, NP, . . .)
- Grammatical function of words or constituents (Subject, Complement, Auxiliary, . . .)
- Dependencies between words or constituents (head/dependent)

A semantic tag includes, among other things, (part of) the following information:

- Word sense for ambiguous words (interest-1 (general), interest-2 (banking), . . .)
- Domain (or hyperonym)
- Pointer to the antecedent for pronouns or anaphoric elements

A discourse tag includes (part of) the following information:

- Discourse relation (cause, purpose, etc.)
- Temporal relation (simultaneity, anteriority, . . .)
- Discourse act (statement, request, . . .)

For semantic and discourse annotations, the tagset can be open (if the expected value is a segment of the text) and the annotated element does not have to be a word but a sequence of words or a whole sentence (or utterance) (cf. Craggs and Wood 2005).

A scheme of the annotation types is given in Figure 8.1.

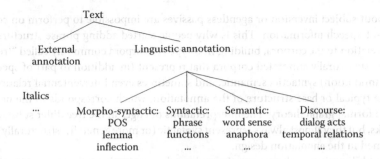

FIGURE 8.1 A scheme of annotation types (layers).

8.3 Morphosyntactic Annotation

The first morphosyntactically tagged corpora were the Brown Corpus for English (Kucera and Francis 1967) and the Lancaster-Oslo-Bergen (LOB) corpus (Johansson 1980). Corpora tagged with morphosyntactic annotation are now available for various languages: the British National Corpus for British English, the Penn Treebank (Marcus et al. 1993) for American English, PAROLE and MULTEXT corpora for various European languages (Véronis and Khouri 1995), and many others.

Morphosyntactic tagsets (the list of symbols used for categories and inflections) can vary from a dozen (Marcus et al. 1993) to several million (Oflazer et al. 2003), with diverse possibilities in between (see e.g., Hajič and Hladká 1998, Böhmová et al. 2003, Brants et al. 2003). They partly reflect the richness of the language's morphosyntax (with case or agreement systems yielding numerous features to be encoded).

In morphosyntactic annotation, information concerning the presence of so-called named entities (names of persons, organizations, locations, etc.) can be included. For example, proper names are distinguished from common names by special tags in the Penn Treebank and in the Negra Treebank, and by special lemma suffixes in the Prague Dependency Treebank (PDT). However, the annotation of named entities can also be represented independently of any morphosyntactic annotation, as it is the case with popular MUC-6 data (Message Understanding Conference focused on the named entity resolution task, Grishman and Sundheim 1996) or in Ševčíková et al. (2007), in which much richer classification of named entity types are offered (compared to what is usually stored in morphosyntactic tags).

Problematic cases are often the same across languages. Not all morphosyntactic taggers deal with compounds or idioms as such. Some sequences are ambiguous between a compound and a noncompound interpretation (e.g., *sur ce* in French can either be the compound adverb (= *at once*), or a preposition (= *on*) followed by a determiner (= *this*)). Most taggers usually prefer the compound interpretation. Unknown (or misspelled) words, foreign words, and punctuation marks can be ignored or annotated with specific tags. Proper name is often a default tag for all unknown words.

8.4 Treebanks: Syntactic, Semantic, and Discourse Annotation

8.4.1 Motivation and Definition

For simple linguistic queries, morphosyntactically annotated texts described in the previous section enable a reduction of the "noise" usually associated with answers drawn from raw texts, and they also reduce the necessity to formulate new, refined, and more complex questions. For example, when one is interested in French causatives, it is frustrating to list all the inflected forms of the verb *faire* in a simple query, and many of the answers are not relevant because they involve the homonymous noun *fait* (which is also part of a lot of compounds *en fait, de fait, du fait que*, etc.). Lemmatized tagged texts are thus helpful but inquiries about subject inversion or agentless passives are impossible to perform on corpora tagged only with parts-of-speech information. This is why people started adding phrase structure information or dependency relation to the corpora, building new types of corpora commonly called "treebanks."

Treebanks are structurally annotated corpora that represent (in addition to part of speech and other morphological annotation) syntactic, semantic, and sometimes even intersentential relations. The word *tree* refers to the typical or base structure of the annotation, which corresponds to the notion of "tree" as defined in the formal graph theory. The interpretations of edges in the tree differ substantially among various treebanks, but they almost always represent syntactic (or more generally, structurally grammatical) relations as defined in the annotation design.

Treebanks enable linguists to ask new questions, about the word order or the complexity of various types of phrases. Arnold et al. (2000), for example, use the Penn Treebank (Marcus et al. 1993) to determine which factors favor the noncanonical V PP NP order in English. One can also check psycholinguistic preferences, in the sense that a highly frequent construction can be claimed to be preferred over a less frequent one. For example, Pynte and Colonna (2000) have shown on experimental reading tests that if a sequence of two nouns is followed by a relative clause in French, the relative clause tends to attach to the first noun if it is long and to the second noun if it is short. This claim can be easily checked on a treebank, where such a correlation can be measured (cf. Abeillé et al. 2003).

The first treebanks were, for English, the IBM/Lancaster Treebank (Leech and Roger 1991), the Penn Treebank (Marcus et al. 1993), and the Susanne corpus (Sampson 1995). At present, treebanks with different degrees of complexity are available for several languages, such as Bulgarian (Simov et al. 2002), Chinese (Sinica Treebank: Chen et al. 2003, Penn Chinese Treebank: Xia et al. 2000), Czech (PDT, Böhmová et al. 2003), Dutch (van der Beek et al. 2001), several additional treebanks for English (ICE-GB: Nelson et al. 2001, Redwood Treebank: Oepen et al. 2002a,b, etc.), French (Abeillé et al. 2003), German (Negra: Brants et al. 2003), Italian (Bosco et al. 2000, Delmonte et al. 2007), Spanish (Civit and Martí 2002, Moreno et al. 2003), Swedish (Jäborg 1986), Turkish (Oflazer et al. 2003), to name just a few.[*]

8.4.2 An Example: The Penn Treebank

The Penn Treebank (Marcus et al. 1993) is currently the most cited and used treebank in the world. It originally consisted of over 4.5 million words of American English. Part of the corpus was annotated for part-of-speech information and, in addition, for skeletal syntactic structure. The POS tags (comprising 36 POS tags and 12 other tags for punctuation and currency symbols) were assigned first automatically and then revised by human annotators, and the same strategy (automatic preprocessing and manual correction) holds true for the syntactic annotation. The syntactic tagset (comprising 14 tags) was similar to that used by the Lancaster Treebank Project (Leech and Roger 1991), with one important difference: the Penn Treebank scenario allowed for addition of null elements in case of some specific cases of surface deletions (such as "understood" subject of infinitive or imperative, zero variant of *that* in subordinate clauses, trace-marked positions where an wh-element is interpreted, and marking positions where preposition is interpreted in the so-called pied-piping contexts). The reconstruction of some of these types of "null" elements was extremely important from the viewpoint of the future plans of adding predicate-argument structures (e.g., to be able to determine verb transitivity). In a later version of the Penn Treebank, functional tags have been added to the syntactic labels (such as -SBJ, -OBJ; Marcus et al. 1994). Data in the Penn Treebank are stored in separate files for different layers of annotation (morphological, syntactical) in Lisp-like format. A graphical representation of a sample tree from the Penn Treebank, representing the sentence *A few fast-food outlets are giving it a try.*, is in Figure 8.2.

---

[*] For a more comprehensive and detailed list, see http://faculty/washington.edu/fxia/treebank.htm.

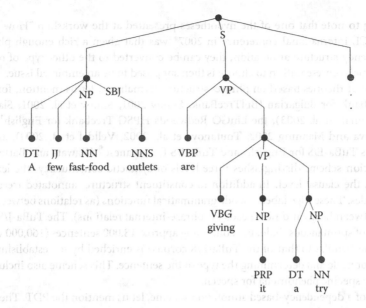

FIGURE 8.2 Example of a Penn Treebank sentence.

8.4.3 Annotation and Linguistic Theory

As already stated in the Introduction to this chapter, one of the prerequisites for achieving a reliably annotated corpus is to base the annotation scenario on a well-defined linguistic theory. This attitude has resulted in several annotation schemes based on different theoretical approaches; if these approaches are consistent, then also the annotation can be tested for its consistency. The confrontation of linguistic hypotheses with actual data leads also to checking and enriching the chosen descriptive framework.

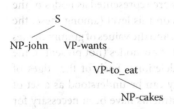

FIGURE 8.3 A simplified constituency-based tree structure for the sentence *John wants to eat cakes.*

An ongoing debate, inspired by discussions in theoretical linguistics, concerns the choice between constituency-based annotation and dependency-based annotation. As an example, let us take the English sentence *John wants to eat cakes.* In terms of constituency, a simplified structure is given in Figure 8.3: the sentence is divided into two constituents, the noun phrase NP and the verb phrase VP, the verb phrase is in turn divided into two smaller constituents, etc. In Figure 8.4, there is a simplified dependency structure for the same sentence, with the verb as the governor of the whole structure and the SUBj(ect) and OBJ(ject) depending on it; the word *cakes* depends as the OBJ(ect) on the verb *to eat.*

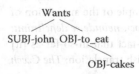

FIGURE 8.4 A simplified dependency-based tree structure for the sentence *John wants to eat cakes.*

Both types of annotations have their advantages and their drawbacks: constituents are easy to read and correspond to common grammatical knowledge (for major phrases) but they may introduce an arbitrary complexity (with more attachment nodes than needed and numerous unary phrases). Dependency links are more flexible and also correspond to common knowledge (the grammatical functions) in the sense that syntactically and semantically related nodes (words) are linked directly but consistent criteria have to be determined for the choice of the head in any group.

It is interesting to note that one of the hypotheses presented at the workshop "How to Treebank?" held at the NAACL international conference in 2007* was that given a rich enough phrase structure as well as dependency structure annotation, they can be converted to the other type of representations automatically. Which representation to choose is then supposed to be an empirical issue.

From the range of theories based on phrase–structure formalisms, let us mention, for example, the HPSG-based treebank for Bulgarian (BulTreeBank, Simov 2001, Simov et al. 2001, Slavcheva 2002), for Polish[†] (Marciniak et al. 2003), the LinGO Redwoods HPSG Treebank for English[‡] (Oepen et al. 2002a,b, Toutanova and Manning 2002, Toutanova et al., 2002, Velldal et al. 2004), and the HPSG-oriented treebanks TuBa-E/S for English[§] and TuBa-J/S for Japanese[¶] (Kawata and Barteles 2000). The TuBa-E/S annotation scheme distinguishes three levels of syntactic constituency: the lexical level, the phrasal level, and the clausal level. In addition to constituent structure, annotated trees contain edge labels between nodes. These edge labels encode grammatical functions (as relations between phrases) and the distinction between heads and non-heads (as phrase-internal relations). The TuBa-J/S is a manually annotated corpus of spontaneous dialogues containing approx. 18,000 sentences (160,000 words) and the annotation scheme (similar to that of the TuBa-E/S corpus) is enriched by the establishment of a label assigned to the root node and determining the type of the sentence. This scheme also includes additional tags to capture the specific phenomena for speech.

As an example of a dependency-based annotation scheme, let us mention the PDT. The PDT (see e.g., Hajič 1998, Böhmová et al. 2003) consists of continuous Czech texts (taken from the Czech National Corpus) analyzed on three levels of annotation (morphological, surface syntactic shape, and underlying syntactic structure). At present, the total number of documents annotated on all the three levels is 3,168, amounting to 49,442 sentences and 833,357 (occurrences of) nodes. The PDT Version 1.0 (with the annotation of the first two levels) is available on CD-ROM as well as the present Version 2.0 (with the annotation of the third, underlying level). One of the important distinctive features of the PDT annotation is the fact that in addition to the morphemic layer and to the annotation of the surface shape of the sentences the scenario includes annotation on the underlying (tectogrammatical) layer (see, e.g., Figure 8.5). The underlying sentence structure is captured in the form of a dependency tree representing (one of) the (literal) meaning(s) of a sentence. Only autosemantic words are represented as nodes of the tree, function words having indices of node labels as their counterparts on this level (among these, the functors represent the dependency relations, i.e., arguments and adjuncts, and the values of grammatemes represent morphological units such as tenses, numbers, modalities, etc.). New nodes (not present in the morphemic form of the sentence) are added to account for surface deletions. Each of the edges of the tree instantiates one type of dependency (more exactly, dependency can be understood as a set of binary relations, i.e., of arguments and adjuncts; certain technical adjustments have been necessary for including the relations of coordination, apposition, and parenthesis). In the valency frame of the head word (contained in its lexical entry), it is specified which arguments and adjuncts are obligatory with this word. Each node of the dependency tree structure is labeled not only by its underlying function (e.g., the function of an argument as Actor, Addressee, Patient, Effect, Origin, or adjuncts such as one of the types of Locatives and of Temporal modification, or Cause, Accompaniment, Manner, etc.), but also by one of the three values (c, t, f) of the attribute of information structure, namely contrastive contextually bound node, contextually bound node, and contextually non-bound node, in that order (see Hajičová and Sgall 2001, Hajičová 2002, Veselá et al. 2004). Figure 8.5 presents an example of the annotation of the Czech sentence *Česká opozice se nijak netají tím, že pokud se dostane k moci, nebude se deficitnímu rozpočtu nijak bránit.* (lit.: Czech opposition Refl. in-no-way keeps-back the-fact that in-so-far-as [it] will-come into power, [it] will-not Refl. deficit budget in-no-way oppose. English translation: *The Czech*

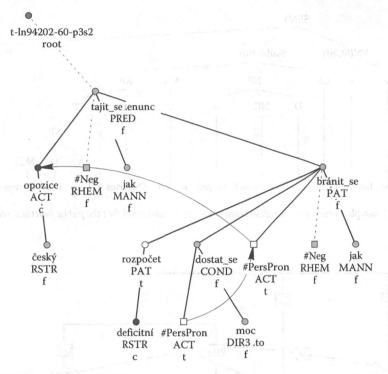

FIGURE 8.5 A sample tree from the PDT for the sentence: *Česká opozice se nijak netají tím, že pokud se dostane k moci, nebude se deficitnímu rozpočtu nijak bránit.* (lit.: Czech opposition Refl. in-no-way keeps-back the-fact that in-so-far-as [it] will-come into power, [it] will-not Refl. deficit budget in-no-way oppose. English translation: *The Czech opposition does not keep back that if they come into power, they will not oppose the deficit budget.*)

opposition does not keep back that if they come into power, they will not oppose the deficit budget.) There are three complementations of the main verb *tajit se* (keep back), namely Actor, Manner and Patient, and a negative rhematiser, and the governing verb of the dependent clause *bránit se* (oppose) depends on the main verb as its Patient and has five complementations and negation depending on it; the arrow leading from the reconstructed Actors to the node *opozice* (opposition) reflects the coreference relation. These coreference relations may, of course, cross the sentence boundary.

Another example of a treebank that includes (some kind of) dependency information is the French Treebank* with morphosyntactic and constituent annotations (more or less compatible with various syntactic frameworks) and also annotations of grammatical functions associated with major constituents which depend on a Verb or a Verbal Noun (Abeillé et al. 2003). See Figure 8.6 for a (simplified) graphical display of a sample sentence from the French Treebank.

Also the treebanks of Scandinavian languages belong to the family of dependency treebanks, see the Nordic Treebank Network,† which is related to treebanks in the Nordic countries developed in cooperation with several Scandinavian universities and including the national corpora of written and/or spoken language annotated manually or semiautomatically (see e.g., Nivre 2002 for Swedish, Bick 2003 and Kromann 2003 for Danish). Among the dependency-based treebanks the Turin University Italian Treebank should be mentioned (Bosco 2000) as well as the treebanks of Turkish (Oflazer et al. 2003), of Basque (Aduriz et al. 2003) and of Greek (Prokopidis et al. 2005).

---

* http://www.llf.cnrs.fr/Gens/Abeillé/French-Treebank-fr.php
† http://w3.msi.vxu.se/~nivre/research/nt.html

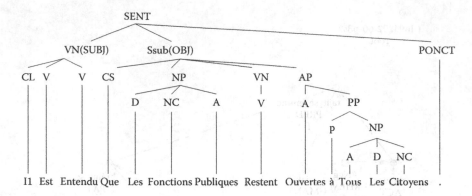

FIGURE 8.6 A sample French tree. (English translation: *It is understood that the public functions remain open to all the citizens.*)

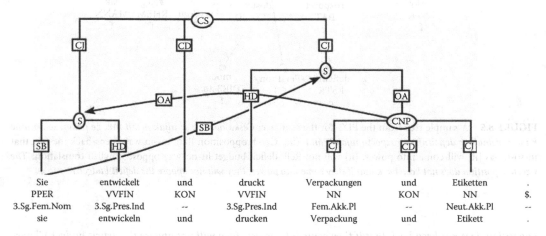

FIGURE 8.7 Example from the Tiger corpus: complex syntactic and semantic dependency annotation. (English translation: *It develops and prints packaging materials and labels.*)

A hybrid solution, chosen by some of the projects, is to maintain some constituents with dependency relations between them (cf. Brants et al. 2003, Chen et al. 2003, Kurohashi and Nagao 2003, Oflazer et al. 2003). In this case, the constituents are usually minimal phrases, called chunks, bunsetsu (Japanese), or inflection groups (Turkish). In addition to the constituent structure, annotated trees contain edge labels between nodes encoding grammatical functions and the distinction between heads and non-heads. For a typical case, see Figure 8.7, which is an example from the German Tiger Treebank (Brants et al. 2003).

The choice of annotation depends both on the availability of syntactic studies for a given language (formalized or not, theory oriented or not) and on the objective. Carroll et al. (2003) demonstrate how difficult it is to choose a reasonable annotation scheme for parser evaluation, when a variety of parsing outputs have to be matched with the annotated corpus.

8.4.4 Going Beyond the Surface Shape of the Sentence

The development of annotation schemes for large text corpora entered a new stage passing over from scenarios with tags covering phenomena "visible" or "transparent" on the surface shape of the sentence (be they of morphological or shallow syntactic character) to some kind of an underlying structure of the sentence; moreover, not only intrasentential but also intersentential relations are paid attention to. Naturally, underlying layer schemes also have to tackle ellipsis resolution, or in other words, the reconstruction of the items deleted on the surface shape of the sentences.

The urgency of deep tagging was emphasized, for example, by Uszkoreit (2004) and some interesting work in this direction is documented by the recent development of several treebanks, for example, Penn PropBank based on the Penn Treebank for English; see Kingsbury and Palmer (2002) with a related project of NomBank* the task of which is to mark the sets of arguments that co-occur with nouns in the PropBank Corpus, just as PropBank records such information for verbs (Meyers et al. 2004). The first large treebank based on a consistent account of underlying dependency relations was the tectogrammatical layer of the PDT for Czech (with the current first steps in testing the scheme for English, German, or even Arabic), see Hajičová (2002), followed by the Tiger/Negra project for German[†] (Brants et al. 2002) or the Redwood Treebank (Oepen et al. 2002). It should be noted that a common feature of all these proposals is an annotation scheme coming close to predicate argument structure. This is also a distinctive feature of the FrameNet project of semantic roles labeling (see e.g., Fillmore et al. 2002, 2003, Palmer et al. 2005) that has been originally developed for English but is being extended to other languages such as German within the SALSA project (Burchardt and Frank 2006), Bulgarian (Balabanova and Ivanova 2002), Dutch (Monachesi et al. 2007), etc. However, it should be noted that FrameNet does not link to any real-world text(s) or corpora—it only extracts relevant examples to the frames it consists of.

It is now commonly accepted in theoretical linguistics that one of the semantically relevant aspects of sentences is their information structure (topic-focus articulation). It is a great challenge for corpus annotation projects to develop a scenario that would reflect also this structuring; for a possibility, see the topic-focus annotation of the PDT (e.g., Hajičová 2003); for a rather recent attempt to annotate a spoken corpus as for the information structure, see Calhoun et al. (2005).

A related issue, the tackling of which has to go beyond the boundaries of the sentence, or, in more general terms, to take into account a broader context, is that of anaphora resolution, which means an establishment of anaphoric (coreference) links between individual referential expressions. This is a widely discussed issue in theoretical writings but the work on establishing such links in larger corpora is still rare (e.g., see adding pronoun-antecedent links in Fligelstone (1992), Tutin et al. (2000) or in the scenario of the PDT).

Considerable attention is now being paid to the analysis of intersentential relations leading to a build-up of discourse treebanks. The biggest and in a sense a pioneering comprehensive project is that of the Penn Discourse Treebank[‡] (PDTB); the first initiative to turn attention to discourse relations and discourse markers can be found in Webber and Joshi (1998) in relation to Joshi's theory of the Lexicalized Tree-Adjoining Grammar. The project has resulted in a large-scale corpus annotated with information related to discourse structure, focusing on encoding coherence relations associated with discourse connectives. The annotations include the argument structure of the connectives, basic sense distinctions for discourse connectives, and the assignment of attribution-related features for both connectives and their arguments (more recently, see e.g., Prasad et al. 2007, Miltsakaki et al. 2008, Prasad et al. 2008, Pitler et al. 2008). Senses are set up hierarchically, distinguishing four classes (Temporal, Contingency, Comparison, and Expansion); these classes are divided into several types and subtypes. The hierarchical structure helps the inter-annotator agreement. Experiments are carried out in the areas of statistics on the corpus, automatic text summarization, predicting discourse coherence, and also in automatic discourse annotation.

A similarly oriented project is that of an extension of the annotations of the PDT beyond the boundaries of sentences (see Mladová et al. 2008). The scenario is conceived of as based on the tectogrammatical annotations, making use of some of the analyses present already there (a special functor is included in the scenario for general, semantically non-distinguished intersentential relationships and also the

---

* http://nlp.cs.nyu.edu/meyers/NomBank.html
[†] http://www.ims.uni-stuttgart.de/projekte/TIGER/TIGERCorpus
[‡] http://www.seas.upenn.edu/~pdtb

intrasentential relationships of different kinds of coordination and embedded clauses are being made use of).

Another stream of semantic annotation, going often hand in hand with the deep syntactic annotations, concerns word sense disambiguation. The development of the original WordNet (Fellbaum 1998) and its language-specific derivatives gave rise to great expectations for a progress in sense disambiguation and also had a strong impact in the field of semantic lexicons. An attempt is being made to integrate the two semantic lexical resources in one of the projects of the Pisa research center, namely the ItalWordNet and the Italian SIMPLE lexicon (Roventini et al. 2002).

There is a great variety of annotation schemes focusing on some specific linguistic or extralinguistic phenomena: some of them are apparently easier to handle (such as temporal, spatial, or manner relations), some are more difficult to capture and the scenarios are still in an experimental stage (such as treatment of opinions: good/bad judgments, true/false beliefs, speech acts, presuppositions, and metaphors).

The range of these proposals only documents that there is a constant hunger for annotated corpora. However, corpus annotation is a demanding task in many aspects: it is a time consuming and a very expensive activity, and therefore ways are being investigated how to achieve a large amount of annotated data with least effort. One such possibility is being explored by Hladká (Hajičová and Hladká 2008); in her project, she aims at a design, the implementation, and the evaluation of a game-playing system as an alternative way of generating linguistic data needed by the tasks of coreference resolution, named entity recognition and document labeling. The system is designed to use the "Games with a Purpose" methodology originally proposed for image labeling and is supposed to be language independent.

8.5 The Process of Building Treebanks

In some of the first projects, corpus annotation was done from scratch entirely by humans, for example, in Sweden (Jäborg 1986), or for the Susanne corpus (Sampson 1995). Purely manual annotation is done by Marciniak et al. (2003). More often, the annotation is at least partially automated; however, automatic annotation—even if of high quality—is not always desirable since it is the human (linguistic) interpretation of a new material that is crucial to the future use of the treebank, especially for training statistical parsers and other analyzers from treebanks.

Automatic tools for corpora annotation (such as taggers, parsers, etc.—see Chapter 10 and the subsequent ones) exist for many languages, but obviously, they make mistakes. One could, in principle, run some automatic part-of-speech tagger or lemmatizer on a given corpus, and use the resulting annotation. While it might be adequate for searching, the quality of the resulting corpus is not guaranteed. In any case, the state-of-the-art automatic tools learn on manually annotated corpora so that manual annotation plays and will always play an important role in the whole process. In such corpora, annotations are devised by experienced linguists or grammarians, fully documented for the end user, and fully checked to minimize the remaining errors (introduced by a human annotator or reviewer).

Human post-checking is always necessary, be it systematic (as in the Brown Corpus for English, in the Penn Treebank or in the PDT) or partial (as in the British National Corpus). Some check all annotation levels at the same time (Brants et al. 2003, Chen et al. 2003), others check tagging and parsing information separately (Penn Treebank, Abeillé et al. 2003, Böhmová et al. 2003). Semantic information is often annotated by hand. Large-scale annotation projects typically involve dozens of human annotators, and ensuring coherence among them is a crucial matter as pointed out by Wallis (2003) for the ICE-GB project, or Brants et al. (2003) for the Negra project.

Several methods have been proposed to check the inter-annotator agreement, even for the semantic annotation and the discourse annotation that are less standardized than the morphosyntactic ones. They are based on sophisticated statistical techniques; a simple percentage agreement is insufficient because it does not discriminate how much agreement is obtained just by chance. Coefficients S (Bennett et al. 1954), π (Scott 1955), and κ (Cohen 1960) all measure the agreement between two annotators obtained above chance. The κ (kappa) coefficient is the most general and the most widely used today

$$\kappa = \frac{p(A) - p(C)}{1 - p(C)},$$

where

$p(A)$ is the percentage (or ratio) where the annotators have agreed

$p(C)$ is the probability that they agreed just by chance

In fact, the other agreement coefficients (S, π) only differ in the way they estimate the level of a chance agreement between the two annotators. Generalizations of these coefficients for more than two annotators also exist. To take the chance agreement into account, it is necessary to have prior knowledge of the distribution of the different possible annotations, which is difficult in natural language, especially for tasks such as anaphora annotation, for which there is no prior list of tags. Carletta (1996) has proposed to use a K coefficient of agreement, which takes into account annotators' biases. Krippendorff's α (Krippendorff 1980, 2004) makes it possible to differentiate degrees of disagreement, since some disagreements may be more serious than others. It is difficult to interpret values of agreement coefficients and there is a lack of consensus on it. Overall, an agreement at least 0.8 is considered to ensure high annotation quality. The number of possible tags and the number of annotators can play a crucial role in computing the agreement and sometimes a coefficient above 0.7 is good enough. Arstein and Poesio (2008) give an excellent survey of methods for measuring agreement among corpus annotators; see also (Eugenio and Glass 2004).

An attempt to propose a method for error detection and correction in corpus annotation is presented by Dickinson, first in his PhD dissertation in 2005* and then within the DECCA (Detection of Errors and Correction in Corpus Annotation[†]) project. Dickinson's method relies on the recurrence of identical strings with varying annotation to find erroneous mark-up. The method can be most readily applied to positional annotation, such as part-of-speech annotation, but can be extended to structural annotation, both for tree structures (as with syntactic annotation) and for graph structures (with syntactic annotation allowing discontinuous constituents, or crossing branches). The results indicate that errors are detected with 85% accuracy (see Dickinson 2006a,b, Boyd et al. 2007).

Most treebanks involving human validation are long and costly enterprises. In order to minimize time and cost, some new projects tend to favor merging different outputs of automatic annotation tools such as tagging with different taggers and checking only the parts with conflicts, for example, in the French Multitag project, cf. Adda et al. (1999).

Many data formats have been employed for encoding treebanks. The choice depends on the complexity of the treebank and its expected usage. Some formats can be easily read by humans—CSV (CoNLL Shared Task), simple usages of SGML (PDT 1.0), others are more easily read by computer programs—Lisp-like bracketing style (Penn Treebank, PDT 1.0), XML (PDT 2.0, French Treebank), database storage (Tiger Treebank). XML-based standards for encoding text corpora have been proposed and used, for example, XCES (Ide et al. 2000), Annotationg Graphs (Cieri and Bird 2001), or PML (Pajas and Štěpánek 2008).

8.6 Applications of Treebanks

Corpus annotation is not a self-contained task: it serves, among other things, as

1. A training and testing data resource for NLP.
2. An invaluable test for linguistic theories on which the annotation schemes are based.
3. A resource of linguistic information for the build-up of grammars and lexicons.

---

* http://ling.osu.edu/~dickinso/papers/diss/
[†] http://decca.osu.edu/index.html

The main use of treebanks is in the area of NLP, most frequently and importantly statistical parsing.* Treebanks are used as the training data for supervised machine learning (which might include the automatic extraction of grammars) and as test data for evaluating them. Recently, as corpora that combine syntactic and semantic annotation have become more widely available, parsers are also trained jointly with semantic role labelers (for different types of parsers and their evaluation, see e.g., Charniak 1993, Charniak 1996, Collins 1997, Bod 1998, Carroll 1998, Xia et al. 2000, Bod 2003, Carroll et al. 2003, Chen and Vijay-Shanker 2004, McDonald and Pereira 2006, Nivre 2006, Surdeanu et al. 2008; for a broad and comprehensive description of parsing, see Chapter 11). In essence, to find the correct analysis (the best parse) amounts to finding such a derivation tree that maximizes the probability (or "score" in general) of that derivation (usually the product of the probabilities or scores of the rules being used). For dependency trees, the situation is analogous, except that edges and their probabilities (scores) are used instead of rules. The probabilities (or scores) are estimated from the treebank during the training phase of the machine learning method used (and smoothed accordingly). Such parsers are robust—they do not fail on real corpora, as grammar-based parsers often did in the past when written manually without a proper use of scoring or probabilities. They can give just one best result, or they can provide more results, sorted according to their probability (or score).

Treebanks serve one more important purpose with regard to parsing: they are used for their evaluation. When performing such evaluation, one has to divide the corpus into a training and development part, which is used for the extraction, estimation, smoothing, and any other "tuning" of the parser's probabilities or scores; and an evaluation part, which is used only for determining the parser's accuracy after its development is completely finished. Such a division is necessary to simulate a real-world situation when the parser is applied to previously unseen data. The training/evaluation data division is typically performed several times so that the evaluation part is different for every training/evaluation experiment (called the "cross-validation" of results), to avoid biases caused by using only a single section of the treebank for evaluation.

Nevertheless, treebanks tend to be consistent in their domain, and parser performance on out-of-domain texts is usually worse than in an experiment that uses carefully simulated real-world but still in-domain evaluation data. Parser adaptation and its relation to treebank annotation is thus subject to current research. For example, the Penn Treebank's *Wall Street Journal* part, which is traditionally used as training and evaluation material for statistical parsers, comes almost exclusively from the financial domain, despite an occasional article on a new book, film or sports event; it is thus no wonder that a cross-treebank evaluation against another English treebank yields significantly worse results.[†]

The type of parser follows the treebank style (dependency parsers are trained on dependency treebanks and phrase-based treebanks are used for parsers based on context-free grammars), unless the treebank is converted first to a treebank of the other type (for a discussion how and when is such conversion possible, see Section 8.4.3).

It is also possible to merge treebanks with other annotated data, such as predicate-argument relations and valency, named entities, coreference annotation, etc. (provided they have been done on the same data). Such combined resources are very useful for applications where parsing and other types of classification are to be performed simultaneously or even jointly.[‡]

To train a system that performs well, one has to find a balance between the size of the tagset (richness of information available in the annotated corpus) and the size of the corpus (number of words or sentences annotated). Relatively good performances are obtained with a small tagset (less than 50 tags) and a large corpus (more than 1 million words). Srinivas and Joshi (1999), training a shallow parser

---

* Treebanks can also be used (and often are) for training statistical taggers, since they commonly contain part-of-speech and morphological annotation as well. For the description of tagging approaches, see Chapter 10.

† See e.g., the CoNLL-2007 and CoNLL-2009 Shared Task out-of-domain adaptation results (http://nextens.uvt.nl/depparse-wiki/AllScores and http://ufal.mff.cuni.cz/conll2009-st/results/results.php).

‡ See again the CoNLL-2008 and CoNLL-2009 Shared Task descriptions at http://barcelona.research.yahoo.net/conll2008 and http://ufal.mff.cuni.cz/conll2009-st

(called a supertagger) on the Penn Treebank, show how going from a training set of 8000 words to a training set of 1 million words improve the parser's performance from 86% (of the words with the correct syntactic structure) to 92%. The size of the various tagsets (label inventories) is determined at the treebank annotation time, but downsizing is always possible once the treebank is used as data for a particular training method.

Automatically trained statistical parsers are not the only (even if prevailing) use of treebanks.

Attempts to combine manual grammar development with semiautomatic corpus inspection and grammar rule extraction are still on. Rosén et al. (2006) notice that the manual syntactic annotation of corpora is a good empirical source for grammar development, as opposed to introspection and constructed examples, but an automatic syntactic annotation of corpora, which is fast and always consistent, requires a fully adequate grammar, which in turn should ideally be based on a corpus. The authors propose to break this seemingly vicious circle by an incremental approach that closely links grammar development and treebank construction.

As observed by Charniak (1996), treebank grammars, as a simple list of context-free rewrite rules, are often much larger than human-crafted ones (more than 10,000 rules for the Penn Treebank) and may decrease the efficiency of the parser. This is why some authors (Chen and Vijay-Shanker 2004, Xia et al. 2000) start with a linguistic model of grammar (LFG, HPSG, or TAG) that guides the type of pattern (tree-like or rule-like) to be extracted.

Other applications include text classification, word sense disambiguation, multilingual text alignment, and indexation. For text categorization, Biber (1988) works with richly annotated texts, and uses criteria such as the relative proportion of adjectives among categories (as a good discriminator for formal vs. informal speech), and the relative proportion of pronominal subjects among all subjects (as a discriminator for speech vs. written language). Malrieu and Rastier (2001) duplicate such criteria on other languages such as French.

The first corpus annotated with word senses was SemCor (Landes et al. 1998), a subset of the Brown Corpus annotated with senses from WordNet. It was developed together with (and for the purpose of) an improved WordNet (Version 1.6). New word senses identified in the data were added into the WordNet during the annotation.

In the PDT, two major word-sense-related annotation experiments took place: in 2006, a small portion of the PDT 2.0 was annotated with senses (synsets) from the Czech WordNet. The annotation proceeded word-after-word, but unlike in the case of SemCor, words that had no meaning in the Czech WordNet were skipped, that is, the annotation lexicon was not modified during the annotations. Each word was annotated individually. The other annotation took place later, and added the identification and sense-annotation of multi-word expressions in the PDT 2.0. Multi-word named entities were annotated as well. This later project was similar to the SemCor one in the handling of the annotation lexicon: the project started with a lexicon containing multi-word expressions compiled from several dictionaries, but new expressions (and meanings of existing expressions) were added as they were identified in the data.

For verb sense disambiguation, it is important to know the context of each occurrence, since it is a good guide for semantic interpretation (*can* as a modal can be distinguished from *can* as a transitive verb, etc.). For automatic word sense classification, parsed texts are also being used, for example, by Merlo and Stevenson (2001).

For text indexing or terminology extraction, too, some syntactic structure is necessary, at least for spotting the major noun phrases. Knowing that an NP is in argument position (subject or object) may make it a better candidate for indexing than NPs only occurring in adjunct phrases.

(Manually) treebanked texts are usually much smaller than raw texts. While the latter are usually available in quasi-infinite quantity (especially via various Web sites in the world as well as from established language data publishers, such as the Linguistic Data Consortium* and ELDA†), the former often require

---

* http://www.ldc.upenn.edu
† http://www.elda.org

human post-correction, without which they do not perform well enough for many languages. Some searches for individual forms or patterns may yield poor results. Another obstacle is that treebanks are not readable as such and require specific search and viewing tools. This may be why they are still more used by computational linguists than by other linguists.

It is quite understandable that together with the rapid increase of the number of languages for which annotated corpora are being developed, an agreement on some standards is felt as a priority, important also for the possibility of national or international cooperation. Among the existing standards, there are such that have been consensually agreed in multilingual initiatives such as EAGLES/ISLE, or de facto standards such as (Euro)WordNet or PAROLE/SIMPLE. The trend toward standardization brings about several important issues to be discussed. One of them is the possibility/impossibility of establishing some "theory neutral" annotation scheme. "Theory neutral," of course, does not mean "without any theoretical background"; it is our firm conviction that a reliable and meaningful scheme of annotation must be backed by a solid, empirically verified, and theoretically sound linguistic framework. "Theory neutral" may only be understood as an attempt to develop an annotation scenario on some underlying level of annotation that would be applicable to any language, or at least to languages that are typologically close to each other (see also Nivre 2003).

Another issue connected with the standardization efforts is that of the translatability of one annotation scheme to another; this feature is recently referred to as an interoperability of annotation schemes. The task is very important especially for an evaluation of annotated corpora for most different languages and its feasibility can be, for example, documented by the efforts to translate the Penn PropBank (developed from the Penn Treebank 2) argument structures into the dependency based underlying (tectogrammatical) structures of the PDT and vice versa (Žabokrtský and Kučerová 2002) and also the comparative studies carried out for these two approaches and for the UMC Lexical Database based primarily on Levin's (1993) classification of verb frames. Another attempt of a similar kind is the description of an algorithm translating the Penn Treebank into a corpus of Combinatory Categorial Grammar normal-form derivations (Hockenmeier and Steedman 2002), the tool described in Daum et al. (2004) for converting phrase treebanks to dependency trees or the discussion of the portability of methods and results over treebanks in different languages and annotation formats in Bosco and Lombardo (2006).

8.7 Searching Treebanks

The ability to search treebanks is crucial for linguists and important for computer scientists, albeit the latter use it mainly for inspecting the corpus and finding features important for building appropriate statistical models that they learn from them automatically.

Linear corpora (plain or tagged) can be very large (billions of tokens) and search tools for them have to be optimized to work with such extremely large data. Manatee/Bonito* is a client-server application that uses regular expressions and Boolean expressions to create complex queries on linearly annotated texts. The search results can be processed further to obtain frequency lists and other statistical data. The Stuttgart Corpus Workbench[†] is a collection of tools for searching plain or tagged texts. It uses a similar query language such as Manatee/Bonito and also can further process the search results.

Most corpora referred to here are static resources. A recent line of research is to develop dynamic treebanks, which are parsed corpora distributed with all annotation tools, in order to be enlarged at will by the user (cf. Oepen et al. 2002).

A treebank query language is only as good as the list of linguistic phenomena it offers to be used easily (or at all) in the searches. It has been noted (Kallmeyer 2000, Cassidy 2002, Lai and Bird 2004, Bird et al. 2006, Mírovský 2008a) that the standard XML query languages (such as XQuery that in turn builds on

---

* http://www.textforge.cz/products
[†] http://www.stanford.edu/dept/linguistics/corpora/cas-tut-cqp.html

XPath, Clark and DeRose 1999) cannot deal with some of the linguistic phenomena at all, or only in a way that is unacceptable for the users. In Bird et al. (2005), three expressive features important for linguistics queries are listed: immediate precedence, subtree scoping, and edge alignment.

Many search tools for treebanks have been developed so far. TGrep (Pito 1994) is a traditional line-based search tool developed primarily for the Penn Treebank (Marcus et al. 1993). It can be used for any treebank where each node is labeled with only one symbol—either a nonterminal or a leaf with an atomic token. Regular expressions can be used for matching node symbols. TGrep2 (Rohde 2005) is a sequel to TGrep. It is almost completely backward compatible with TGrep but brings a number of new features, such as full logical expressions on relationships and patterns, co-indexing (and handles cyclical links) and user-defined "macros." TigerSearch (Lezius 2002) is a graphically oriented search tool for the Tiger Treebank (Brants et al. 2002). The query language allows for Boolean feature-value pair expressions, immediate precedence, and immediate dominance of nodes, and on the highest level, Boolean expressions over node relations (without negation). TrEd (Pajas 2007) has primarily been used for the manual annotation of the PDT and other similar treebanks with some perl-based general search language. TrEd now contains a structured and fast, client-server, end-user-oriented extension "Tree_Query," which efficiently implements (both in online- and batch modes) most of the known linguistic query requirements on any PML-encoded corpus (Pajas and Štěpánek 2008). Netgraph (Mírovský 2008b) is a powerful, graphically oriented client-server based search tool, primarily developed also for the PDT 2.0. It uses meta-attributes, node co-indexing, and arithmetic and logical relations to express some of the necessary features that are not easily expressible by immediate relations in queries. Viqtorya (Steiner and Kallmeyer 2002) is a search tool developed for the Tübingen Treebanks (Hinrichs et al. 2000). It has a graphical interface, but without a visual depiction of the query. A first order logic without quantification is chosen as a query language, with some restrictions. Another query language developed for the Tübingen Treebanks is the Finite structure query (fsq, Kepser 2003). It uses the full first-order logic (with quantification), with LISP-like syntax.

8.8 Conclusions

Treebanking is a highly complex issue and many questions still remain to be discussed and resolved. At the 2007 NAACL workshop on treebanking mentioned earlier, the following three general topics followed by language-specific issues were discussed as being topical for the present-state-of-the-art:

1. Lessons learned from the Penn Treebank methodology. (What semantics is to be annotated? What information was missing in the underlying Penn Treebank? What information was there but represented badly? What methodology is appropriate for semantic annotation? What are the advantages of a phrase-structure and/or a dependency treebank for parsing as such and especially for semantic annotation?)
2. Grammar formalisms and transformations between formalisms (including the pros and cons for building a treebank for grammars in a particular formalism vs. building a general purpose treebank and extracting grammars from the Treebank).
3. Treebanks as training data for parsers, tackling such issues as whether a more refined tagset for parsing is preferable, which categories are useful and which are not, or what are the advantages and disadvantages of automatic preprocessing of the data to be treebanked.

Given the current state of syntactic knowledge, some annotation choices may be arbitrary. What is most important is consistency (similar cases must be handled similarly) and explicitness (a detailed documentation must accompany the annotated corpus). As noted by G. Sampson (1995), for the Susanne Corpus, the size of the documentation can be bigger than the corpus itself. Without consistency any annotated corpus becomes useless; at the same time, any annotation (except in case of a fully automatic annotation which, regretfully, seems to be far to be achieved with some reasonable richness of annotation labels and categories) involves some human intervention and as such is open for inconsistencies. Therefore, the agreement between annotators should be carefully watched and measured, in order to make the annotation guidelines more explicit and unambiguous.

Thanks to treebanks, NLP technologies such as automatic tagging, parsing, and other annotation of (mostly) written texts has made tremendous progress during the past 10–20 years. Part-of-speech tagging seems to be close to its current limits, reaching the level of human performance (as defined by the interannotator agreement). Parsing, "deep" parsing, semantic role labeling, machine translation, and other NLP technologies are still areas of vivid research and experimentation. It is expected that the findings accumulated during these experiments will influence future treebank annotation projects to serve better NLP technology needs. Similar influence might come from the theoretical side: new annotation schemes will then support, in the areas of syntax and semantics, (hopefully) more consistent, more adequate, and more explanatory linguistic theories than they do today.

Acknowledgments

The authors acknowledge the support of the Czech Ministry of Education (grants MSM-0021620838 and ME838), the Czech Grant Agency (project under the grant 405/09/0729), and the Grant Agency of Charles University in Prague (project GAUK 52408/2008). We are grateful to Barbora Vidová Hladká and Zdeněk Žabokrtský for reading and commenting upon the first draft of the chapter and for providing us with useful information and recommendations we used in the relevant places of the text, as well as to Pavel Straňák for his additions in the paragraphs on word sense disambiguation and named entities. Thanks are due to the two reviewers of the chapter Steve Bird and Adam Meyers for most helpful comments.

References

Abeillé, A., Clément, L., and F. Toussenel. 2003. Building a treebank for French. In *Treebanks: Building and Using Parsed Corpora*, ed. A. Abeillé, pp. 165–188. Dordrecht, the Netherlands: Kluwer.

Adda, G., Mariani, J., Paroubek, P., Rajman, M., and J. Lecomte. 1999. L'action GRACE d'évaluation de l'assignation de parties du discours pour le français. *Langues* 2(2): 119–129.

Aduriz, I., Aranzabe, M., Arriola, J. et al. 2003. Methodology and steps towards the construction of EPEC, a corpus of written Basque tagged at morphological and syntactic levels for the automatic processing. In *Proceedings of the Corpus Linguistics 2003 Conference*, Lancaster, U.K., eds. D. Archer, P. Rayson, A. Wilson, and T. McEnery, pp. 10–11. UCREL technical paper (16). UCREL, Lancaster University.

Arnold, J. E., Wasow, T., Losongco, A., and R. Ginstrom. 2000. Heaviness vs. newness: The effects of structural complexity and discourse status on constituent ordering, *Language* 76: 28–55.

Arstein R. and M. Poesio. 2008. Inter-coder agreement for computational LinguisticsInter-Coder agreement for computational linguistics. *Computational Linguistics* 34(4): 555–596.

Balabanova, E. and K. Ivanova. 2002. Creating a machine-readable version of Bulgarian valence dictionary (A case study of CLaRK system application). In *Proceedings of TLT 2002*, Sozopol, Bulgaria, eds. E. Hinrichs and K. Simov, pp. 1–12.

Bennett, E. M., Alpert, R., and A. C. Goldstein. 1954. Communications through limited questioning. *Public Opinion Quarterly* 18(3): 303–308.

Biber, D. 1988. *Variation Across Speech and Writing*. Cambridge, U.K.: Cambridge University Press.

Bick, E. 2003. Arboretum, a Hybrid Treebank for Danish. In *Proceedings of TLT 2003*, Växjö, Sweden, eds. J. Nivre and E. Hinrich, pp. 9–20.

Bird, S., Chen, Y., Davidson, S., Lee, H., and Y. Zheng. 2006. Designing and evaluating an XPath dialect for linguistic queries. In *Proceedings of the 22nd International Conference on Data Engineering* (*ICDE*), Atlanta, GA, pp. 52–61.

Bird, S., Chen, Y., Davidson, S., Lee, H., and Y. Zheng. 2005. Extending Xpath to support linguistic queries. In *Proceedings of the Workshop on Programming Language Technologies for XML (PLAN-X 2005)*, San Francisco, CA, pp. 35–46.

Bird, S. and J. Harrington. 2001. Editorial to the special issue of Speech Communication. *Speech Annotation and Corpus Tools* 33: 1–4.

Bod, R. 1998. *Beyond Grammar*. Stanford, CA: CSLI Publications.

Bod, R. 2003. Extracting grammars from treebanks. In *Treebanks: Building and Using Parsed Corpora*, ed. A. Abeillé, pp. 333–350. Dordrecht, the Netherlands: Kluwer.

Böhmová, A., Hajič, J., Hajičová, E., and B. Hladká. 2003. The Prague dependency treebank: A 3-level annotation scenario. In *Treebanks: Building and Using Parsed Corpora*, ed. A. Abeillé, pp. 103–128. Dordrecht, the Netherlands: Kluwer.

Bosco, C. 2000. A richer annotation schema for an Italian treebank. In *Proceedings of ESSLLI-2000 Student Session*, ed. C. Pilière, Birmingham, U.K., pp. 22–33.

Bosco, C. and V. Lombardo. 2006. Comparing linguistic information in treebank annotations. In *Proceedings of LREC 2006*, Genova, Italy, pp. 1770–1775.

Bosco, C., Lombardo, V., Vassallo, D., and L. Lesmo. 2000. Building a treebank for Italian: A data-driven annotation schema. In *Proceedings of LREC 2000*, Athens, Greece, pp. 99–105.

Boyd, A., Dickinson, M., and D. Meurers. 2007. Increasing the recall of corpus annotation error detection. In *Proceedings of TLT 2007*, Bergen, Norway, NEALT Proceedings Series, Vol. 1, pp. 19–30.

Brants, S., Dipper, S., Hansen, S., Lezius, W., and G. Smith. 2002. The TIGER treebank. In *Proceedings of TLT 2002*, Sozopol, Bulgaria, eds. Hinrichs, E. and Simov, K., pp. 24–41.

Brants, T., Skut, W., and H. Uszkoreit. 2003. Syntactic annotation of a German newspaper corpus. In *Treebanks: Building and Using Parsed Corpora*, ed. A. Abeillé, pp. 73–88. Dordrecht, the Netherlands: Kluwer.

Burchardt, A. and A. Frank. 2006. Approximating textual entailment with LFG and FrameNet frames. In *Proceedings of the Second PASCAL Recognising Textual Entailment Challenge Workshop*, Venice, Italy, ed. B. Magnini and I. Dagan, pp. 92–97.

Calhoun, S., Nissim, M., Steedman, M., and J. Brenier. 2005. A Framework for annotating information structure in discourse. In *Frontiers in Corpus Annotation II: Pie in the Sky. Proceedings of the Workshop, ACL 2005*, Ann Arbor, MI, pp. 45–52.

Carletta, J. 1996. Assessing agreement on classification tasks: The kappa statistics. *Computational Linguistics* 22(2): 249–254.

Carroll, J. 1998. Evaluation: Parsing. *ELSNews: The Newsletter of the European Network in Language and Speech* 7(3): 8.

Carroll, J., Minnen, G., and T. Briscoe. 2003. Parser evaluation with a grammatical relation annotation scheme. In *Treebanks: Building and Using Parsed Corpora*, ed. A. Abeillé, pp. 299–316. Dordrecht, the Netherlands: Kluwer.

Cassidy, S. 2002. XQuery as an annotation query language: A use case analysis. In *Proceedings of LREC 2002*, Las Palmas, Canary Islands, Spain, pp. 2055–2060.

Charniak, E. 1993. *Statistical Language Learning*. Cambridge, MA: MIT Press.

Charniak, E. 1996. Tree-bank Grammars. In *Proceedings of the 13th National Conference on Artificial Intelligence*, Menlo Park, CA, pp. 1031–1036.

Chen, J. and V. K. Shanker. 2004. Automated extraction of TAGs from the Penn Treebank. In *New Developments in Parsing Technology, Text, Speech And Language Technology*, Vol. 23, eds. H. Bunt, J. Carroll, and G. Satta, pp. 73–89. Norwell, MA: Kluwer Academic Publishers.

Chen, K., Huang, C., Chen, F., Lao, C., Chang, M., and C. Chen. 2003. Sinica treebank: Design criteria, representational issues and implementation. In *Treebanks: Building and Using Parsed Corpora*, ed. A. Abeillé, pp. 231–248. Dordrecht, the Netherlands: Kluwer.

Cieri, C. and S. Bird. 2001. Annotation graphs and servers and multi-modal resources: Infrastructure for interdisciplinary education, research and development. In *Proceedings of the ACL 2001 Workshop on Sharing Tools and Resources*, Toulouse, France, Vol. 15, pp. 23–30, July 07, 2001. *Annual Meeting of the ACL*. Association for Computational Linguistics, Morristown, NJ.

Civit, M. and M. A. Martí. 2002. Design principles for a Spanish treebank. In *Proceedings of TLT 2002*, Sozopol, Bulgaria, eds. E. Hinrichs and K. Simov, pp. 61–77.

Clark J. and S. DeRose. 1999. XML path language (XPath). http://www.w3.org/TR/xpath.

Cohen, J. 1960. A coefficient of agreement for nominal scales. *Educational and Psychological Measurement* 20(1): 37–46.

Collins, M. 1997. Three generative, lexicalized models for statistical parsing. In *Proceedings of the 35th Annual Meeting of the Association for Computational Linguistics and Eighth Conference of the European Chapter of the Association for Computational Linguistics*, Somerset, NJ, eds. P. R. Cohen and W. Wahlster, pp. 16–23.

Craggs, R. and M. M. Wood. 2005. Evaluating discourse and dialogue coding schemes. *Computational Linguistics* 31(3): 289–296.

Daum, M., Foth, K., and W. Menzel. 2004. Automatic transformation of phrase treebanks to dependency trees. In *Proceedings of LREC 2004*, Lisbon, Portugal, pp. 1149–1152.

Delmonte, R., Bristot, A., and S. Tonelli. 2007. VIT—Venice Italian treebank: Syntactic and quantitative features. In *Proceedings of TLT 2007*, Bergen, Norway, pp. 43–54.

Dickinson, M. 2006a. Rule equivalence for error detection. In *Proceedings of TLT 2006*, Prague, Czech Republic, pp. 187–198.

Dickinson, M. 2006b. From detecting errors to automatically correcting them. In *Proceedings of the 11th Conference of the European Chapter of the Association for Computational Linguistics (EACL-06)*, Trento, Italy, pp. 265–272.

Eugenio B. Di and M. Glass. 2004. The kappa statistic: A second look. *Computational Linguistics* 30(1): 95–101.

Fellbaum, C. (ed.). 1998. *WordNet: An Electronic Lexical Database*. Cambridge, MA: MIT Press.

Fillmore, C. J., Baker, C. F., and H. Sato. 2002. Seeing arguments through transparent structures. In *Proceedings of LREC 2002*, Las Palmas, Canary Islands, Spain, pp. 787–791.

Fillmore, Ch. J., Johnson, Ch. R., and M. R. L. Petruck. 2003. Background to Framenet. *International Journal of Lexicography* 16(3): 235–250.

Fligelstone, S. 1992. Developing a scheme for annotating text to show anaphoric relations. In *New Directions in English Language Corpora*, ed. G. Leitner, pp. 53–170. Berlin, Germany: Mouton de Gruyter.

Grishman, R. and B. Sundheim. 1996. Design of the MUC-6 evaluation. In *Annual Meeting of the ACL—Proceedings of a Workshop on Held at Vienna*, Vienna, VA, pp. 413–422.

Hajič, J. 1998. Building a syntactically annotated corpus: The Prague dependency treebank. In *Issues of Valency and Meaning. Studies in Honour of Jarmila Panevová*, ed. E. Hajičová, pp. 106–132. Prague, Czech Republic: Karolinum, Charles University Press.

Hajič, J. and B. Hladká. 1998. Tagging inflective languages: Prediction of morphological categories for a rich, structured tagset. In *Proceedings of the 36th Annual Meeting of the Association for Computational Linguistics and 17th International Conference on Computational Linguistics*, Montreal, QC, pp. 483–490. Montreal, QC: Association for Computational Linguistics.

Hajičová, E. 2002. Theoretical description of language as a basis of corpus annotation: The case of Prague dependency treebank. *Prague Linguistic Circle Papers* 4: 111–127.

Hajičová, E. 2003. Topic-focus articulation in the Czech national corpus. In *Language and Function: To the Memory of Jan Firbas*, ed. J. Hladký, pp. 185–194. Amsterdam, the Netherlands: John Benjamins.

Hajičová, E. and P. Sgall. 2001. Topic-focus and salience. In *Proceedings of 39th Annual Meeting of the Association for Computational linguistics*, Toulouse, France, pp. 276–281. Toulouse, France: Association for Computational Linguistics.

Hajičová, E. and B. V. Hladká. 2008. What does sentence annotation say about discourse? In *Proceedings of the 18th International Congress of Linguists*, Seoul, South Korea, Vol. 2, pp. 125–126. Seoul, South Korea: The Linguistic Society of Korea.

Hinrichs, E. W., Bartels, J., Kawata, Y., Kordoni, V., and H. Telljohann. 2000. The Tuebingen treebanks for spoken German, English, and Japanese. In *Verbmobil: Foundations of Speech-to-Speech Translation*, ed. W. Wahlster, pp. 550–574. Berlin, Germany: Springer-Verlag.

Hockenmeier, J. and M. Steedman. 2002. Acquiring compact lexicalized grammars from a cleaner treebank. In *Proceedings of LREC 2002*, Las Palmas, Spain, pp. 1974–1981.

Ide, N., Bonhomme, P., and L. Romary. 2000. XCES: An XML-based standard for linguistc corpora. In *Proceedings of LREC 2000*, Athens, Greece, pp. 825–830.

Jäborg, J. 1986. *SynTag Dokumentation. Manual för syntaggning.* Göteborgs University, Institute för språkvetenskaplig databehandling, Gothenburg: Sweden.

Johansson, S. 1980. The LOB corpus of British English texts: Presentation and comments. *ALLC Journal* 1(1): 25–36.

Kallmeyer, L. 2000. On the complexity of queries for structurally annotated linguistic data. In *Proceedings of ACIDCA'2000*, pp. 105–110. Tunisia.

Kawata, Y. and J. Barteles. 2000. *Stylebook for Japanese Treebank in Verbmobil.* Technical Report 240, Verbmobil, Eberhard-Karls-Universität, Tübingen, Germany.

Kepser, S. 2003. Finite structure query—A tool for querying syntactically annotated corpora. In *Proceedings of EACL 2003*, Budapest, Hungary, pp. 179–186.

Kingsbury, P. and M. Palmer. 2002. From TreeBank to PropBank. In *Proceedings of LREC 2002*, Las Palmas, Canary Islands, Spain, pp. 1989–1993.

Krippendorff, K. 1980. *Content Analysis: An Introduction to Its Methodology*, Chapter 12. Beverly Hills, CA: Sage.

Krippendorff, K. 2004. Reliability in content analysis: Some common misconceptions and recommendations. *Human Communication Research* 30(3): 411–433.

Kromann, M. T. 2003. The Danish dependency treebank and the DTAG treebank tool. In *Proceedings of TLT 2003*, Växjö, Sweden, pp. 217–220.

Kucera, H. and W. Francis. 1967. *Computational Analysis of Present Day American English.* Providence, RI: Brown University Press.

Kurohashi, S. and M. Nagao. 2003. Building a Japanese parsed corpus while improving the parsing system. In *Treebanks: Building and Using Parsed Corpora*, ed. A. Abeillé, pp. 249–260. Dordrecht, the Netherlands: Kluwer.

Lai, C. and S. Bird. 2004. Querying and updating treebanks: A critical survey and requirements analysis. In *Proceedings of the Australasian Language Technology Workshop*, Sydney, NSW, pp. 139–146.

Landes, S., Leacock C., and R.I. Tengi. 1998. Building semantic concordances. In *WordNet: An Electronic Lexical Database*, ed. C. Fellbaum, Cambridge, MA: MIT Press.

Leech, G. and G. Roger. 1991. Running a grammar factory, the production of syntactically analyzed corpora or "tree banks". In *English Computer Corpora*, pp. 15–32. Mouton de Gruyter, Berlin, Germany.

Levin, B. 1993. *English Verb Classes and Alternations.* Chicago IL London, U.K.: University of Chicago Press.

Lezius, W. 2002. *Ein Suchwerkzeug für syntaktisch annotierte Textkorpora.* PhD thesis IMS, University of Stuttgart, Stuttgart, Germany.

Malrieu, D. and F. Rastier. 2001. Genres et variations morpho-syntaxiques. *Traitement automatique des langues: linguistique de corpus*, ed. Daille B. and Romary R., 42(2): 547–577.

Marciniak, M., Mykowiecka, A., Przepiorkowski, A., and A. Kupsc. 2003. An HPSG-annotated test suite for polish. *Building and Using Parsed Corpora*, ed. A. Abeillé, pp. 129–146. Dordrecht, the Netherlands: Kluwer.

Marcus, M., Santorini, B., and M. A. Marcinkiewicz. 1993. Building a large annotated corpus of English: The Penn treebank. *Computational Linguistics* 19(2): 313–330.

Marcus, M., Kim, G., Marcinkiewicz, M. A. et al. 1994. The Penn treebank: Annotating predicate argument structure. In *Proceedings of the Human Language Technology Workshop*, Princeton, NJ, pp. 114–119. Princeton, NJ: Morgan Kaufmann Publishers Inc.

McDonald, R. and F. Pereira. 2006. Online learning of approximate dependency parsing algorithms. In *Proceedings of the 11th Conference of the European Chapter of the Association for Computational Linguistics: EACL 2006*, Trento, Italy, pp. 81–88.

Merlo, P. and S. Stevenson. 2001. Automatic verb classification based on statistical distribution of argument structure, *Computational Linguistics* 27(3): 373–408.

Meyers, A., Reeves, R., Macleod, C. et al. 2004. Annotating noun argument structure for NomBank. In *Proceedings of LREC 2004*, Lisbon, Portugal, pp. 803–806.

Miltsakaki, E., Robaldo, L., Lee, A., and A. Joshi. 2008. Sense annotation in the Penn discourse Treebank, *Computational Linguistics and Intelligent Text Processing. Lecture Notes in Computer Science* 4919: 275–286.

Mírovský, J. 2008a. PDT 2.0 requirements on a query language. In *Proceedings of ACL 2008*, Columbus, OH, pp. 37–45.

Mírovský, J. 2008b. Netgraph—Making searching in treebanks easy. In *Proceedings of the Third International Joint Conference on Natural Language Processing (IJCNLP 2008)*, Hyderabad, India, pp. 945–950, January 8–10, 2008.

Mladová, L., Zikánová, Š., and E. Hajičová. 2008. From sentence to discourse: Building an annotation scheme for discourse based on Prague Dependency Treebank. In *Proceedings of LREC 2008*, Marrakech, Morocco, pp. 1–7.

Monachesi, P., Stevens, G., and J. Trapman. 2007. Adding semantic role annotation to a corpus of written Dutch. In *Proceedings of the Linguistic Annotation Workshop (LAW-07)*, Prague, Czech Republic, pp. 77–84. Stroudsburg, PA: Association for Computational Linguistics.

Moreno, A., Lopez, S., and F. Sanchez. 2003. Developing a syntactic annotation scheme and tools for a Spanish Treebank. In *Treebanks: Building and Using Parsed Corpora*, ed. A. Abeillé, pp. 149–164. Dordrecht, the Netherlands: Kluwer.

Nelson, G., Wallis, S., and B. Aarts. 2001. *Exploring Natural Language: Working with the British Component of the International Corpus of English*. Amsterdam, the Netherlands: J. Benjamins.

Nivre, J. 2002. What kinds of trees grow in Swedish soil? A comparison of four annotation schemes for Swedish. In *Proceedings of TLT 2002*, Sozopol, Bulgaria, eds. Hinrichs, E. and K. Simov, pp. 123–138.

Nivre, J. 2003. Theory-supporting treebanks. In *Proceedings of the Second Workshop on Treebanks and Linguistic Theories (TLT 2003)*, Växjö University Press, Växjö, Sweden, ed. J. Nivre and E. Hinrichs, pp. 117–128.

Nivre, J. 2006. *Inductive Dependency Parsing*. Text, Speech, and Language Technology Series, eds. N. Ide and J. Véronis, Dordrecht, the Netherlands: Springer, Vol. 34, p. 216, ISBN 1-4020-4888-2.

Oepen, S., Flickinger, D., Toutanova, K., and Ch. D. Manning. 2002a. LinGO Redwoods: A rich and dynamic treebank for HPSG. In *Proceedings of TLT2002*, Sozopol, Bulgaria, pp. 139–149.

Oepen, S., Toutanova, K., Shieber, S., Manning, Ch., Flickinger, D., and T. Brants. 2002b. The LinGO Redwoods treebank: Motivation and preliminary applications. In *Proceedings of the 19th International Conference on Computational Linguistics (COLING 2002)*, Taipei, Taiwan, pp. 1253–1257.

Oflazer, K., Bilge, S., Hakkani-Tür, D. Z., and T. Gökhan. 2003. Building a Turkish treebank. In *Treebanks: Building and Using Parsed Corpora*, ed. A. Abeillé, pp. 261–277. Dordrecht, the Netherlands: Kluwer.

Pajas, P. 2007. TrEd User's manual. http://ufal.mff.cuni.cz/~pajas/tred.

Pajas, P. and J. Štěpánek. 2008: Recent advances in a feature-rich framework for treebank annotation. In *The 22nd International Conference on Computational Linguistics—Proceedings of the Conference*, pp. 673–680. The Coling 2008 Organizing Committee, Manchester, U.K., ISBN 978-1-905593-45-3.

Palmer, M., Kingsbury, P., and D. Gildea. 2005. The proposition bank: An annotated corpus of semantic roles.*Computational Linguistics* 31(1): 71–106.

Pitler, E., Raghupathy, M., Mehta, H., Nenkova, A., Lee, A., and A. Joshi. 2008. Easily identifiable discourse relations. In *Proceedings of COLING 2008: Companion Volume: Posters and Demonstrations*, Manchester, U.K.

Pito, R. 1994. TGrep Manual Page. http://www.ldc.upenn.edu/ldc/online/treebank.

Prasad, R., Dinesh, N., Lee A. et al. 2008. The Penn Discourse Treebank 2.0. In *Proceedings of LREC 2008*, Marrakech, Morocco, pp. 2961–2968.

Prasad, R., Dinesh, N., Lee, A., Joshi, A., and B. Webber. 2007. Attribution and its Annotation in the Penn Discourse TreeBank. *Traitement Automatique des Langues, Special Issue on Computational Approaches to Document and Discourse* 47(2): 43–64.

Prokopidis, P., Desypri, E., Koutsombogera, M., Papageorgiou, H., and S. Piperidin. 2005. Theoretical and practical issues in the construction of a Greek dependency treebank. In *Proceedings of TLT 2005*, Universitat de Barcelona, Barcelona, Spain, eds. M. Civit, S. Kübler, and M. A. Martí, pp. 149–160.

Pynte, J. and S. Colonna. 2000. Decoupling syntactic parsing from visual inspection: The case of relative clause attachment in French. In *Reading as a Perceptual Process*, eds. A. Kennedy, R. Radach, D. Heller, and J. Pynte, pp. 529–547. Oxford, U.K.: Elsevier.

Rohde, D. 2005. TGrep2 user manual. http://www-cgi.cs.cmu.edu/~dr/TGrep2/tgrep2.pdf.

Rosén, V., De Smedt, K., and P. Meurer. 2006. Towards a toolkit linking treebanking and grammar development. In *Proceedings of TLT 2006*, Prague, Czech Republic, pp. 55–66.

Roventini, A., Ulivieri, M., and N. Calzolari. 2002. Integrating two semantic lexicons, SIMPLE and ItalWordNet: What can we gain? In *Proceedings of LREC 2002*, Las Palmas, Canary Islands, Spain, pp. 1473–1477.

Sampson, G. 1995. *English for the Computer.* Oxford, U.K.: Oxford University Press.

Scott, W. A. 1955. Reliability of content analysis: The case of nominal scale coding. *Public Opinion Quarterly* 19(3), 321–325.

Ševčíková, M., Žabokrtský, Z., and O. Krůza. 2007. Named entities in Czech: Annotating data and developing NE tagger. In *Proceedings of the 10th International Conference on Text, Speech and Dialogue*, Pilsen, Czech Republic, pp. 188–195. *Lecture Notes In Computer Science.* Pilsen, Czech Republic: Springer.

Simov, K. 2001. Grammar extraction from an HPSG corpus. In *Proceedings of the RANLP 2001 Conference*, Tzigov Chark, Bulgaria, pp. 285–287.

Simov, K., Osenova, P., Slavcheva, M. et al. 2002. Building a linguistically interpreted corpus for Bulgarian: The Bultreebank project. In *Proceedings of LREC 2002*, Las Palmas, Canary Islands, Spain, pp. 1729–1736.

Simov, K., Popova, G., and P. Osenova. 2001. HPSG-based syntactic treebank of Bulgarian (BulTreeBank). In *Proceedings of the Corpus Linguistics 2001 Conference*, Lancaster, U.K., p. 561.

Slavcheva, M. 2002. Segmentation layers in the group of the predicate: A case study of Bulgarian within the BulTreeBank framework. In *Proceedings of TLT 2002*, Sozopol, Bulgaria, pp. 199–210.

Srinivas, B. and A. Joshi. 1999. Supertagging: An approach to almost parsing. *Computational Linguistics* 25(2): 237–266.

Steiner, I. and L. Kallmeyer. 2002. VIQTORYA—A visual tool for syntactically annotated corpora. In *Proceedings of LREC 2002*, Las Palmas, Canary Islands, Spain, pp. 1704–1711.

Surdeanu, M., Johansson, R., Meyers, A., Marquez, L., and J. Nivre. 2008. The CoNLL-2008 shared task on joint parsing of syntactic and semantic dependencies. In *Proceedings of the 12th Conference on Computational Natural Language Learning (CoNLL-2008)*, Manchester, U.K.

Toutanova, K. and Ch. D. Manning. 2002. Feature selection for a rich HPSG grammar using decision trees. In *Proceedings of the Sixth Conference on Natural Language Learning (CoNLL 2002)*, Taipei, Taiwan, pp. 1–7.

Toutanova, K., Manning, Ch. D., and S. Oepen. 2002. Parse disambiguation for a rich HPSG grammar. In *Proceedings of TLT 2002*, Sozopol, Bulgaria, pp. 253–263.

Tutin, A., Trouilleux, F., Clouzot, C., and E. Gaussier. 2000. Building a large corpus with anaphoric links in French: Some methodological issues. In *Actes de Discourse Anaphora and Reference Resolution Colloquium*, Lancaster, U.K.

Uszkoreit, H. 2004. New chances for deep linguistic processing. In *Proceedings of 19th International Conference on Computational Linguistics: COLING-2002*, Taipei, Taiwan, pp. 15–27.

van der Beek, L., Bouma, G., Malouf, R., and G. van Noord. 2001. The Alpino dependency treebank. In *Computational Linguistics in the Netherlands CLIN 2001*, pp. 8–22. Amsterdam, the Netherlands: Rodopi.

Velldal, E., Oepen, S., and D. Flickinger. 2004. Paraphrasing treebanks for stochastic realization ranking. In *Proceedings of TLT 2004*, Tuebingen, Germany, pp. 149–160.

Véronis, J. and L. Khouri. 1995. Étiquetage grammatical multilingue: le projet MULTEXT. *TAL* 36(1–2): 233–248.

Veselá, K., Havelka, J., and E. Hajičová. 2004. Annotators' agreement: The case of topic-focus articulation. In *Proceedings of LREC 2004*, Lisbon, Portugal, pp. 2191–2194.

Wallis, S. 2003. Completing parsed corpora: From correction to evolution. In *Treebanks: Building and Using Parsed Corpora*, ed. A. Abeillé, pp. 61–71. Dordrecht, the Netherlands: Kluwer.

Webber, B. and A. Joshi. 1998. Anchoring a lexicalized tree-adjoining grammar for discourse. In *Proceedings of ACL/COLING Workshop on Discourse Relations and Discourse Markers*, Montreal, QC, pp. 86–92.

Xia, F., Palmer, M., Xue, N. et al. 2000. Developing guidelines and ensuring consistency for Chinese text annotation. In *Proceedings of LREC 2000*, Athens, Greece, pp. 3–10.

Žabokrtský, Z. and I. Kučerová. 2002. Transforming Penn treebank phrase trees into (Praguian) tectogrammatical dependency trees. *The Prague Bulletin of Mathematical Linguistics* 78:77–94.

9

Fundamental Statistical Techniques

Tong Zhang
Rutgers, The State
University of New Jersey

The statistical approach to natural language processing (NLP) has become more and more important in recent years. This chapter gives an overview of some fundamental statistical techniques that have been widely used in different NLP tasks. Methods for statistical NLP mainly come from machine learning, which is a scientific discipline concerned with learning from data. That is, to extract information, discover patterns, predict missing information based on observed information, or more generally construct probabilistic models of the data. Machine learning techniques covered in this chapter can be divided into two types: supervised and unsupervised.

Supervised learning is mainly concerned with predicting missing information based on observed information. For example, predicting part of speech (POS) based on sentences. It employs statistical methods to construct a prediction rule from labeled training data. Supervised learning algorithms discussed in this chapter include naive Bayes, support vector machines (SVMs), and logistic regression. The goal of unsupervised learning is to group data into clusters. The main statistical techniques are mixture models and the expectation maximization (EM) algorithm. This chapter will also cover methods used in sequence analysis, such as hidden Markov model (HMM), conditional random field (CRF), and the Viterbi decoding algorithm.

9.1 Binary Linear Classification

The goal of binary classification is to predict an unobserved binary label $y \in \{-1, 1\}$, based on an observed input vector $x \in R^d$. A classifier $h(x)$ maps $x \in R^d$ to $\{-1, 1\}$. If it agrees with the label y, the error is zero. If it does not agree with the label y, we suffer a loss of one. That is, the classification error is defined as

$$\text{err}(h(x), y) = I(h(x) \neq y) = \begin{cases} 1 & h(x) \neq y \\ -1 & \text{otherwise,} \end{cases}$$

where $I(\cdot)$ is the set indicator function.

A commonly used method for binary classification is to learn a real-valued scoring function $f(x)$: $R^d \to R$ that induces a classification rule

$$h(x) = \begin{cases} 1 & f(x) > 0 \\ -1 & \text{otherwise.} \end{cases} \tag{9.1}$$

A commonly used scoring function is linear: $f(x) = w^T x + b$, where $w \in R^d$ and $b \in R$. A binary classification method using linear scoring function is called a linear classifier.

In supervised learning, the classifier $h(x)$, or its scoring function $f(x)$, is learned from a set of labeled examples

$$\{(x_1, y_1), \ldots, (x_n, y_n)\},$$

referred to as training data. Its performance (average classification error) should be evaluated on a separate set of labeled data called test data.

A procedure that constructs a scoring function $f(x)$ from the training data is called a learning algorithm. For example, a standard learning algorithm for linear classification is linear least squares method, which finds a weight vector $\hat{w} \in R^d$ and bias $\hat{b} \in R$ for a linear scoring function $f(x) = \hat{w}^T x + \hat{b}$ by minimizing the squared error on the training set:

$$[\hat{w}, \hat{b}] = \arg\min_{w,b} \sum_{i=1}^{n} (w^T x_i + b - y_i)^2. \tag{9.2}$$

Using linear algebra, we may write the solution of this formula in closed form as

$$\hat{w} = \left[\sum_{i=1}^{n} (x_i - \bar{x})(x_i - \bar{x})^T \right]^{-1} \sum_{i=1}^{n} (x_i - \bar{x})(y_i - \bar{y}),$$

$$\hat{b} = \bar{y} - \hat{w}^T \bar{x},$$

where

$$\bar{x} = \frac{1}{n} \sum_{i=1}^{n} x_i \quad \text{and} \quad \bar{y} = \frac{1}{n} \sum_{i=1}^{n} y_i.$$

One problem of the above formulation is that the matrix $\sum_{i=1}^{n} (x_i - \bar{x})(x_i - \bar{x})^T$ may be singular or ill-conditioned (this occurs, e.g., when n is less than the dimension of x). A standard remedy is to use the ridge regression method (Hoerl and Kennard 1970) that adds a regularization term $\lambda w^T w$ to (9.2). For convenience, we set $b = 0$:

$$\hat{w} = \arg\min_{w} \left[\frac{1}{n} \sum_{i=1}^{n} (w^T x_i y_i - 1)^2 + \lambda w^T w \right], \tag{9.3}$$

where $\lambda > 0$ is an appropriately chosen regularization parameter. The solution is given by

$$\hat{w} = \left(\sum_{i=1}^{n} x_i x_i^T + \lambda n I \right)^{-1} \left(\sum_{i=1}^{n} x_i y_i \right),$$

where I denotes the identity matrix. This method solves the ill-conditioning problem because $\sum_{i=1}^{n} x_i x_i^{\mathrm{T}} + \lambda n I$ is always non-singular.

Note that taking $b = 0$ in (9.3) does not make the resulting scoring function $f(x) = \hat{w}^{\mathrm{T}} x$ less general. To see this, one can embed all the data into a space with one more dimension with some constant A (normally, one takes $A = 1$). In this conversion, each vector $x_i = [x_{i,1}, \ldots, x_{i,d}]$ in the original space becomes the vector $x' = [x_{i,1}, \ldots, x_{i,d}, A]$ in the larger space. Therefore, the linear classifier $w^{\mathrm{T}} x + b = w'^{\mathrm{T}} x'$, where $w' = [w, b]$ is a weight vector in $(d + 1)$-dimensional space. Due to this simple change of representation, the linear scoring function with b in the original space is equivalent to a linear scoring function without b in the larger space.

The introduction of the regularization term $\lambda w^{\mathrm{T}} w$ in (9.3) makes the solution more stable. That is, a small perturbation of the observation does not significantly change the solution. This is a desirable property because the observations (both x_i and y_i) often contain noise. However, λ introduces a bias into the system because it pulls the solution $\hat{w}$ toward zero. When $\lambda \to \infty$, $\hat{w} \to 0$. Therefore, it is necessary to balance the desirable stabilization effect and the undesirable bias effect, so that the optimal trade-off can be achieved. Figure 9.1 illustrates the training error versus test error when λ changes. As λ increases, due to the bias effect, the training error always increases. However, since the solution becomes more robust to noise as λ increases, the test error will decrease first. This is because the benefit of a more stable solution is larger than the bias effect. After the optimal trade-off (the lowest test error point) is achieved, the test error becomes larger when λ increases. This is because the benefit of more stability is smaller than the increased bias.

In practice, the optimal λ can be selected using cross-validation, where we randomly split the training data into two parts: a training part and a validation part. We use only the first (training) part to compute $\hat{w}$ with different λ, and then estimate its performance on the validation part. The λ with the smallest validation error is then chosen as the optimal regularization parameter.

The decision rule (9.1) for a linear classifier $f(x) = w^{\mathrm{T}} x + b$ is defined by a decision boundary $\{x : w^{\mathrm{T}} x + b = 0\}$: on one side of this hyperplane, we predict $h(x) = 1$, and on the other side, we predict $h(x) = -1$. If the hyperplane completely separates the positive data from the negative data without error, we call it a separating hyperplane. If the data are linearly separable, then there can be more than one possible separating hyperplanes, as shown in Figure 9.2. A natural question is: What is a better separating hyperplane? One possible measure to define the quality of a separating hyperplane is through the concept of margin, which is the distance of the nearest training example to the linear decision boundary. A separating hyperplane with a larger margin is more robust to noise because training data can still be separated after a small perturbation. In Figure 9.2, the boundary represented by the solid line has a larger margin than the boundary represented by the dashed line, and thus it is the preferred classifier.

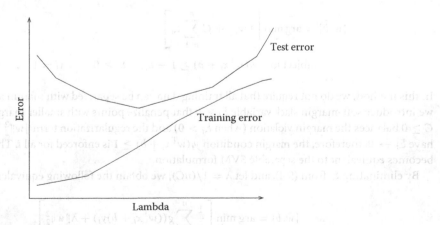

FIGURE 9.1 Effect of regularization.

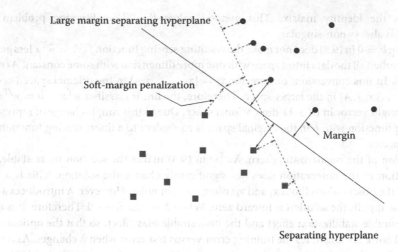

FIGURE 9.2 Margin and linear separating hyperplane.

The idea of finding an optimal separating hyperplane with largest margin leads to another popular linear classification method called support vector machine (Cortes and Vapnik 1995; Joachims 1998). If the training data are linearly separable, the method finds a separating hyperplane with largest margin defined as

$$\min_{i=1, \ldots, n} (w^T x_i + b) y_i / \|w\|_2.$$

The equivalent formulation is to minimize $\|w\|_2$ under the constraint $\min_i (w^T x_i + b) y_i \geq 1$. That is, the optimal hyperplane is the solution to

$$[\hat{w}, \hat{b}] = \arg \min_{w,b} \|w\|_2^2$$

$$\text{subject to } (w^T x_i + b) y_i \geq 1 \quad (i = 1, \ldots, n).$$

For training data that is not linearly separable, the idea of margin maximization cannot be directly applied. Instead, one considers the so-called soft-margin formulation as follows:

$$[\hat{w}, \hat{b}] = \arg \min_{w,b} \left[\|w\|_2^2 + C \sum_{i=1}^{n} \xi_i \right], \tag{9.4}$$

$$\text{subject to } y_i(w^T x_i + b) \geq 1 - \xi_i, \quad \xi_i \geq 0, \quad (i = 1, \ldots, n).$$

In this method, we do not require that all training data can be separated with margin at least one. Instead, we introduce soft-margin slack variable $\xi_i \geq 0$ that penalize points with smaller margins. The parameter $C \geq 0$ balances the margin violation (when $\xi_i > 0$) and the regularization term $\|w\|_2^2$. When $C \to \infty$, we have $\xi_i \to 0$; therefore, the margin condition $y_i(w^T x_i + b) \geq 1$ is enforced for all i. The resulting method becomes equivalent to the separable SVM formulation.

By eliminating ξ_i from (9.4), and let $\lambda = 1/(nC)$, we obtain the following equivalent formulation:

$$[\hat{w}, \hat{b}] = \arg \min_{w,b} \left[\frac{1}{n} \sum_{i=1}^{n} g((w^T x_i + b) y_i) + \lambda \|w\|_2^2 \right], \tag{9.5}$$

where

$$g(z) = \begin{cases} 1 - z & \text{if } z \leq 1, \\ 0 & \text{if } z > 0. \end{cases} \qquad (9.6)$$

This method is rather similar to the ridge regression method (9.3). The main difference is a different loss function $g(\cdot)$, which is called hinge loss in the literature. Compared to the least squares loss, the hinge loss does not penalize data points with large margin.

9.2 One-versus-All Method for Multi-Category Classification

In practice, one often encounters multi-category classification, where the goal is to predict a label $y \in \{1, \ldots, k\}$ based on an observed input x.

If we have a binary classification algorithm that can learn a scoring function $f(x)$ from training data $\{(x_i, y_i)\}_{i=1, \ldots, n}$ with $y_i \in \{-1, 1\}$, then it can also be used for multi-category classification.

A commonly used method is one-versus-all. Consider a multi-category classification problem with k classes: $y_i \in \{1, \ldots, k\}$. We may reduce it into k binary classification problems indexed by class label $\ell \in \{1, \ldots, k\}$. The ℓth problem has training data $(x_i, y_i^{(\ell)})$ $(i = 1, \ldots, n)$, where we define the binary label $y_i^{(\ell)} \in \{-1, +1\}$ as

$$y_i^{(\ell)} = \begin{cases} 1 & \text{if } y_i = \ell, \\ -1 & \text{otherwise.} \end{cases}$$

For each binary problem ℓ defined this way with training data $\{(x_i, y_i^{(\ell)})\}$, we may use a binary classification algorithm to learn a scoring function $f_\ell(x)$. For example, using linear SVM or linear least squares, we can learn a linear scoring function of the form $f_\ell(x) = w^{(\ell)}x + b^{(\ell)}$ for each ℓ. For a data point x, the higher the score $f_\ell(x)$, the more likely x belongs to class ℓ. Therefore, the classification rule for the multi-class problem is

$$h(x) = \arg \max_{\ell \in \{1, \ldots, k\}} f_\ell(x).$$

Figure 9.3 shows the decision boundary for three classes with linear scoring functions $f_\ell(x)$ $(\ell = 1, 2, 3)$. The three dashed lines represent the decision boundary $f_\ell(x) = 0$ $(\ell = 1, 2, 3)$ for the three binary problems. The three solid lines represent the decision boundary of the multi-class problem, determined by the lines $f_1(x) = f_2(x)$, $f_1(x) = f_3(x)$, and $f_2(x) = f_3(x)$, respectively.

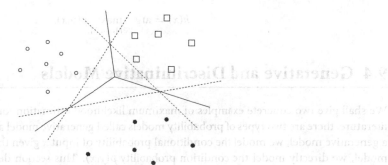

FIGURE 9.3 Multi-class linear classifier decision boundary.

9.3 Maximum Likelihood Estimation

A very general approach to machine learning is to construct a probability model of each individual data point as $p(x, y|\theta)$, where θ is the model parameter that needs to be estimated from the data. If the training data are independent, then the probability of the training data is

$$\prod_{i=1}^{n} p(x_i, y_i|\theta).$$

A commonly used statistical technique for parameter estimation is the maximum likelihood method, which finds a parameter $\hat{\theta}$ by maximizing the likelihood of the data $\{(x_1, y_1), \ldots, (x_n, y_n)\}$:

$$\hat{\theta} = \arg\max_{\theta} \prod_{i=1}^{n} p(x_i, y_i|\theta).$$

More generally, we may impose a prior $p(\theta)$ on θ, and use the penalized maximum likelihood as follows:

$$\hat{\theta} = \arg\max_{\theta} \left[p(\theta) \prod_{i=1}^{n} p(x_i, y_i|\theta) \right].$$

In the Bayesian statistics literature, this method is also called MAP (maximum a posterior) estimator. A more common way to write the estimator is to take logarithm of the right-hand side:

$$\hat{\theta} = \arg\max_{\theta} \left[\sum_{i=1}^{n} \ln p(x_i, y_i|\theta) + \ln p(\theta) \right].$$

For multi-classification problems with k classes $\{1, \ldots, k\}$, we obtain the following class conditional probability estimate:

$$p(y|x) = \frac{p(x, y|\theta)}{\sum_{\ell=1}^{k} p(x, \ell|\theta)} \quad (y = 1, \ldots, k).$$

The class conditional probability function may be regarded as a scoring function, with the following classification rule that chooses the class with the largest conditional probability:

$$h(x) = \arg\max_{y \in \{1, \ldots, k\}} p(y|x).$$

9.4 Generative and Discriminative Models

We shall give two concrete examples of maximum likelihood estimation for supervised learning. In the literature, there are two types of probability models called generative model and discriminative model. In a generative model, we model the conditional probability of input x given the label y; in a distriminative model, we directly model the condition probability $p(y|x)$. This section describes two methods: naive Bayes, a generative model, and logistic regression, a discriminative model. Both are commonly used linear classification methods.

9.4.1 Naive Bayes

The naive Bayes method starts with a generative model as in (9.7). Let $\theta = \{\theta^{(\ell)}\}_{\ell=1,\ldots,k}$ be the model parameter, where we use a different parameter $\theta^{(\ell)}$ for each class ℓ. Then we can model the data as

$$p(x, y|\theta) = p(y)p(x|y, \theta) \quad \text{and} \quad p(x|y, \theta) = p(x|\theta^{(y)}). \qquad (9.7)$$

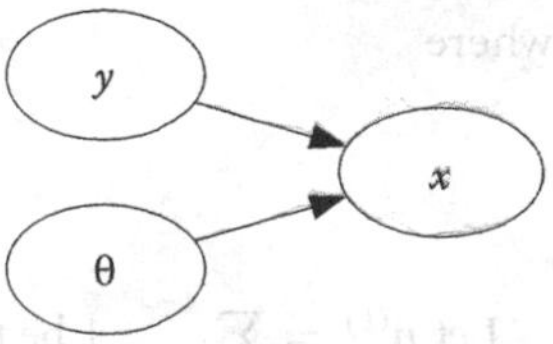

FIGURE 9.4 Graphical representation of a generative model.

This probability model can be visually represented using a graphical model as in Figure 9.4, where the arrows indicate the conditional dependency structure among the variables.

The conditional class probability is

$$p(y|x) = \frac{p(y)p(x|\theta^{(y)})}{\sum_{\ell=1}^{k} p(y = \ell)p(x|\theta^{(\ell)})}.$$

In the following, we shall describe the multinomial naive Bayes model (McCallum and Nigam 1998) for $p(x|\theta^{(y)})$, which is important in many NLP problems. In this model, the observation x represents multiple (unordered) occurrences of d possible symbols. For example, x may represent the number of word occurrences in a text document by ignoring the word order information (such a representation is often referred to as "bag of words"). Each word in the document is one of d possible symbols from a dictionary.

Specifically, each data point x_i is a d-dimensional vector $x_i = [x_{i,1}, \ldots, x_{i,d}]$ representing the number of occurrences of these d symbols: For each symbol j in the dictionary, $x_{i,j}$ is the number of occurrences of symbol j. For each class ℓ, we assume that words are independently drawn from the dictionary according to a probability distribution $\theta^{(\ell)} = [\theta_1^{(\ell)}, \ldots, \theta_d^{(\ell)}]$: that is, the symbol j occurs with probability $\theta^{(\ell)}$. Now, for a data point x_i with label $y_i = \ell$, x_i comes from a multinomial distribution:

$$p(x_i|\theta^{(\ell)}) = \prod_{j=1}^{d} (\theta_j^{(\ell)})^{x_{i,j}} p\left(\sum_{j=1}^{d} x_{i,j}\right),$$

where we make the assumption that the total number of occurrences $\sum_{j=1}^{d} x_j$ is independent of the label $y_i = \ell$. For each $y \in \{1, \ldots, k\}$, we consider the so-called Dirichlet prior for $\theta^{(y)}$ as

$$p(\theta^{(y)}) \propto \prod_{j=1}^{d} (\theta_j^{(y)})^{\lambda},$$

where $\lambda > 0$ is a tuning parameter. We may use the MAP estimator to compute $\theta^{(\ell)}$ separately for each class ℓ:

$$\hat{\theta}^{(\ell)} = \arg\max_{\theta \in R^d} \left[\left(\prod_{i:y_i=\ell} \prod_{j=1}^{d} (\theta_j)^{x_{i,j}} \right) \prod_{j=1}^{d} (\theta_j)^{\lambda} \right]$$

$$\text{subject to } \sum_{j=1}^{d} \theta_j = 1, \quad \text{and} \quad \theta_j \geq 0 \ (j = 1, \ldots, d).$$

The solution is given by

$$\hat{\theta}_j^{(\ell)} = \frac{n_j^{(\ell)}}{\sum_{j'=1}^{d} n_{j'}^{(\ell)}},$$

where

$$n_j^{(\ell)} = \lambda + \sum_{i:y_i=\ell} x_{i,j}.$$

Let $n^{(\ell)} = \sum_{i:y_i=\ell} 1$ be the number of training data with class label ℓ for each $\ell = 1, \ldots, k$, then we may estimate

$$p(y) = n^{(y)}/n.$$

With the above estimates, we obtain a scoring function

$$f_\ell(x) = \ln p(x|\theta^{(y)}) + \ln p(y) = (\hat{w}^{(\ell)})^{\mathrm{T}} x + \hat{b}^{(\ell)},$$

where

$$\hat{w}^{(\ell)} = [\ln \hat{\theta}_j^{(\ell)}]_{j=1,\ldots,d} \quad \text{and} \quad \hat{b}^{(\ell)} = \ln(n^{(\ell)}/n).$$

The conditional class probability is given by the Bayes rule:

$$p(y|x) = \frac{p(x|y)p(y)}{\sum_{\ell=1}^{k} p(x|\ell)p(\ell)} = \frac{e^{f_y(x)}}{\sum_{\ell=1}^{k} e^{f_\ell(x)}}, \tag{9.8}$$

and the corresponding classification rule is

$$h(x) = \arg \max_{\ell \in \{1, \ldots, k\}} f_\ell(x).$$

9.4.2 Logistic Regression

Naive Bayes is a generative model in which we model the conditional probability of input x given the label y. After estimating the model parameter, we may then obtain the desired class conditional probability $p(y|x)$ using the Bayes rule. A different approach is to directly model the conditional probability $p(y|x)$. Such a model is often called a discriminative model. The dependency structure is given by Figure 9.5.

Ridge regression can be interpreted as the MAP estimator for a discriminative model with Gaussian noise (note that although ridge regression can be applied to classification problems, the underlying Gaussian noise assumption is only suitable for real-valued output) and a Gaussian prior. The probability model is (with parameter $\theta = w$)

$$p(y|w, x) = N(w^{\mathrm{T}} x, \tau^2),$$

with prior on parameter

$$p(w) = N(0, \sigma^2).$$

Here, we shall simply assume that σ^2 and τ^2 are known variance parameters, and the only unknown parameter is w. The MAP estimator is

$$\hat{w} = \arg \min_w \left[\frac{1}{\tau^2} \sum_{i=1}^{n} (w^{\mathrm{T}} x_i - y_i)^2 + \frac{w^{\mathrm{T}} w}{\sigma^2} \right],$$

which is equivalent to the ridge regression method in (9.3) with $\lambda = \tau^2/\sigma^2$.

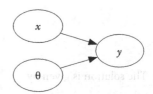

FIGURE 9.5 Graphical representation of a discriminative model.

However, for binary classification, since $y_i \in \{-1, 1\}$ is discrete, the noise $w^T x_i - y_i$ cannot be a Gaussian distribution. The standard remedy to this problem is logistic regression, which models the conditional class probability as

$$p(y = 1 | w, x) = \frac{1}{\exp(-w^T x) + 1}.$$

This means that both for $y = 1$ and $y = -1$, the likelihood is

$$p(y | w, x) = \frac{1}{\exp(-w^T xy) + 1}. \tag{9.9}$$

If we again assume a Gaussian prior $p(w) = N(0, \sigma^2)$, then the penalized maximum likelihood estimate is

$$\hat{w} = \arg \min_{w} \left[\sum_{i=1}^{n} \ln(1 + \exp(-w^T x_i y_i)) + \lambda w^T w \right], \tag{9.10}$$

where $\lambda = 1/(2\sigma^2)$. Its use in text categorization as well as numerical algorithms for solving the problem can be found in Zhang and Oles (2001).

Although binary logistic regression can be used to solve multi-class problems using the one-versus-all method described earlier, there is a direct formulation of multi-class logistic regression, which we shall describe next. Assume we have k classes, the naive Bayes method induces a probability of the form (9.8), where each function $f_\ell(x)$ is linear. Therefore, as a direct generalization of the binary logistic model in (9.9), we may consider multi-category logistic model:

$$p(y | \{w^{(\ell)}\}, x) = \frac{e^{(w^{(y)})^T x}}{\sum_{\ell=1}^{k} e^{(w^{(\ell)})^T x}}. \tag{9.11}$$

The binary logistic model is a special case of (9.11) with $w^{(1)} = w$ and $w^{(-1)} = 0$. If we further assume Gaussian priors for each $w^{(\ell)}$,

$$P(w^{(\ell)}) = N(0, \sigma^2) \quad (\ell = 1, \ldots, k),$$

then we have the following MAP estimator:

$$\{\hat{w}^{(\ell)}\} = \arg \min_{\{w^{(\ell)}\}} \left[\sum_{i=1}^{n} \left(-(w^{(y_i)})^T x_i + \ln \sum_{\ell=1}^{k} e^{(w^{(\ell)})^T x_i} \right) + \lambda \sum_{\ell=1}^{k} (w^{(\ell)})^T w^{(\ell)} \right],$$

where $\lambda = 1/(2\sigma^2)$.

Multi-class logistic regression is also referred to as the maximum entropy method (MaxEnt) (Berger et al. 1996) under the following more general form:

$$P(y | w, x) = \frac{\exp(w^T z(x, y))}{\sum_{\ell=1}^{k} \exp(w^T z(x, y))}, \tag{9.12}$$

where $z(x, y)$ is a human-constructed vector called feature vector that depends both on x and on y. Let $w = [w^{(1)}, \ldots, w^{(k)}] \in R^{kd}$, and $z(x, y) = [0, \ldots, 0, x, 0, \ldots, 0]$, where x appears only in the positions $(y - 1)d + 1$ to yd that corresponds to $w^{(y)}$. With this representation, we have $w^T z(x, y) = (w^{(y)})^T x$, and (9.11) becomes a special case of (9.12).

Although logistic regression and naive Bayes share the same conditional class probability model, a major advantage of the logistic regression method is that it does not make any assumption on how x is generated. In contrast, naive Bayes assumes that x is generated in a specific way, and uses such information to estimate the model parameters. The logistic regression approach shows that even without any assumptions on x, the conditional probability can still be reliably estimated using discriminative maximum likelihood estimation.

9.5 Mixture Model and EM

Clustering is a common unsupervised learning problem. Its goal is to group unlabeled data into clusters so that data in the same cluster are similar, while data in different clusters are dissimilar. In clustering, we only observe the input data vector x, but do not observe its cluster label y. Therefore, it is called unsupervised learning.

Clustering can also be viewed from a probabilistic modeling point of view. Assume that the data belong to k clusters. Each data point is a vector x_i, with $y_i \in \{1, \ldots, k\}$ being its corresponding (unobserved) cluster label. Each y_i takes value $\ell \in \{1, \ldots, k\}$ with probability $p(y_i = \ell | x_i)$.

The goal of clustering is to estimate $p(y_i = \ell | x_i)$. Similar to the naive Bayes approach, we start with a generative model of the following form:

$$p(x|\theta, y) = p(x|\theta^{(y)}).$$

Since y is not observed, we integrate out y to obtain

$$p(x|\theta) = \sum_{c=1}^{k} \mu_\ell p(x|\theta^{(\ell)}), \tag{9.13}$$

where $\mu_\ell = p(y = \ell)$ ($\ell = 1, \ldots, k$) are k parameters to be estimated from the data. The model in (9.13), with missing data (in this case, y) integrated out, is called a mixture model. A cluster $\ell \in \{1, \ldots, k\}$ is referred to as a mixture component.

We can interpret the data generation process in (9.13) as follows. First we pick a cluster ℓ (mixture component) from $\{1, \ldots, k\}$ with a fixed probability μ_ℓ as y_i; then we generate data points x_i according to the probability distribution $p(x_i | \theta^{(\ell)})$.

In order to obtain the cluster conditional probability $p(y = \ell | x)$, we can simple apply Bayes rule:

$$p(y|x) = \frac{\mu_y p(x|\theta^{(y)})}{\sum_{\ell=1}^{k} \mu_\ell p(x|\theta^{(\ell)})}. \tag{9.14}$$

Next we show how to estimate the model parameters $\{\theta^{(\ell)}, \mu_\ell\}$ from the data. This can be achieved using the penalized maximum likelihood method:

$$\{\hat{\theta}^{(\ell)}, \hat{\mu}_\ell\} = \arg \max_{\{\theta^{(\ell)}, \mu_\ell\}} \left[\sum_{i=1}^{n} \ln \sum_{\ell=1}^{k} \mu_\ell p(x_i|\theta^{(\ell)}) + \sum_{\ell=1}^{k} \ln p(\theta^{(\ell)}) \right]. \tag{9.15}$$

A direct optimization of (9.15) is usually difficult because the sum over the mixture components ℓ is inside the logarithm for each data point. However, for many simple models such as the naive Bayes example considered earlier, if we know the label y_i for each x_i, then the estimation becomes easier: we simply estimate the parameters using the equation

$$\{\hat{\theta}^{(\ell)}, \hat{\mu}_\ell\} = \arg \max_{\{\theta^{(\ell)}, \mu_\ell\}} \left[\sum_{i=1}^{n} \ln \mu_{y_i} p(x_i|\theta^{(y_i)}) + \sum_{\ell=1}^{k} \ln p(\theta^{(\ell)}) \right],$$

which does not have the sum inside the logarithm. For example, in the naive Bayes model, both μ_ℓ and $\theta^{(\ell)}$ can be estimated using simple counting.

The EM algorithm (Dempster et al. 1977) simplifies the mixture model estimation problem by removing the sum over ℓ inside the logarithm in (9.15). Although we do not know the true value of y_i, we can estimate the conditional probability of $y_i = \ell$ for $\ell = 1, \ldots, k$ using (9.14). This can then be used to move the sum over ℓ inside the logarithm to a sum over ℓ outside the logarithm: For each data point i, we weight each mixture component ℓ by the estimated conditional class probability $p(y_i = \ell | x_i)$. That is, we repeatedly solve the following optimization problem:

$$[\hat{\theta}^{(\ell)}_{new}, \hat{\mu}^{new}_\ell] = \arg \max_{\theta^{(\ell)}, \mu_\ell} \left[\sum_{i=1}^{n} p(y_i = \ell | x_i, \hat{\theta}_{old}, \hat{\mu}^{old}) \ln[\mu_\ell p(x_i | \theta^{(\ell)})] + \ln p(\theta^{(\ell)}) \right]$$

for $\ell = 1, \ldots, k$. Each time, we start with $[\hat{\theta}_{old}, \hat{\mu}^{old}]$ and update its value to $[\hat{\theta}_{new}, \hat{\mu}^{new}]$. Note that the solution of $\hat{\mu}^{new}_\ell$ is

$$\hat{\mu}^{new}_\ell = \frac{\sum_{i=1}^{n} p(y_i = \ell | x_i, \hat{\theta}_{old}, \hat{\mu}^{old})}{\sum_{i=1}^{n} \sum_{\ell'=1}^{k} p(y_i = \ell' | x_i, \hat{\theta}_{old}, \hat{\mu}^{old})}.$$

The algorithmic description of EM is given in Figure 9.6.

In practice, a few dozen iterations of EM often gives a satisfactory result. It is also necessary to start EM with different random initial parameters. This is to improve local optimal solutions found by the algorithm with each specific initial parameter configuration.

The EM algorithm can be used with any generative probability model including the naive Bayes model discussed earlier. Another commonly used model is Gaussian, where we assume $p(x | \theta^{(\ell)}) \propto \exp\left(-\frac{(\theta^{(\ell)} - x)^2}{2\sigma^2} \right)$. Figure 9.7 shows a two-dimensional Gaussian mixture model with two mixture components represented by the dotted circles. For simplicity, we may assume that σ^2 is known. Under this assumption, Figure 9.6 can be used to compute the mean vectors $\theta^{(\ell)}$ for the Gaussian mixture model, where the E and M steps are given by

- E step: $q_{i,y} = \mu_y \exp\left(-\frac{(x_i - \theta^{(y)})^2}{2\sigma^2} \right) / \sum_{\ell=1}^{k} \mu_\ell \exp\left(-\frac{(x_i - \theta^{(\ell)})^2}{2\sigma^2} \right)$
- M step: $\mu_\ell = \sum_{i=1}^{n} q_{i,y}/n$ and $\theta^{(\ell)} = \sum_{i=1}^{n} q_{i,\ell} x_i / \sum_{i=1}^{n} q_{i,\ell}$

Initialize $\theta^{(\ell)}$ and let $\mu_\ell = 1/k$ $(\ell = 1, \ldots, k)$
iterate
  // the E-step
  for $i = 1, \ldots, n$
    $q_{i,y} = \mu_y p(x_i | \theta^{(y)}) / \sum_{\ell=1}^{k} \mu_\ell p(x_i | \theta^{(\ell)})$ $(y = 1, \ldots, k)$
  end for
  // the M-step
  for $y = 1, \ldots, k$
    $\theta^{(y)} = \arg \max_{\bar{\theta}} \left[\sum_{i=1}^{n} q_{i,y} \ln p(x_i | \bar{\theta}) + \ln p(\bar{\theta}) \right]$
    $\mu_y = \sum_{i=1}^{n} q_{i,y}/n$
  end for
until convergence

FIGURE 9.6 EM algorithm.

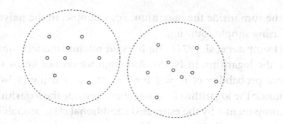

FIGURE 9.7   Gaussian mixture model with two mixture components.

9.6 Sequence Prediction Models

NLP problems involve sentences that can be regarded as sequences. For example, a sentence of n words can be represented as a sequence of n observations $\{x_1, \ldots, x_n\}$. We are often interested in predicting a sequence of hidden labels $\{y_1, \ldots, y_n\}$, one for each word. For example, in POS tagging, y_i is the POS of the word x_i.

The problem of predicting hidden labels $\{y_i\}$ given observations $\{x_i\}$ is often referred to as sequence prediction. Although this task may be regarded as a supervised learning problem, it has an extra complexity that data (x_i, y_i) in the sequence are dependent. For example, label y_i may depend on the previous label y_{i-1}. In the probabilistic modeling approach, one may construct a probability model of the whole sequence $\{(x_i, y_i)\}$, and then estimate the model parameters.

Similar to the standard supervised learning setting with independent observations, we have two types of models for sequence prediction: generative and discriminative. We shall describe both approaches in this section. For simplicity, we only consider first-order dependency where y_i only depends on y_{i-1}. Higher order dependency (e.g., y_i may depend on y_{i-2}, y_{i-3}, and so on) can be easily incorporated but requires more complicated notations. Also for simplicity, we shall ignore sentence boundaries, and just assume that the training data contain n sequential observations. In the following, we will assume that each y_i takes one of the k values in $\{1, \ldots, k\}$.

9.6.1 Hidden Markov Model

The standard generative model for sequence prediction is the HMM, illustrated in Figure 9.8. It has been used in various NLP problems, such as POS tagging (Kupiec 1992) This model assumes that each y_i depends on the previous label y_{i-1}, and x_i only depends on y_i. Since x_i depends only on y_i, if the labels are observed on the training data, we may write the likelihood mathematically as

$$p(x_i|y_i\theta) = p(x_i|\theta^{(y_i)}),$$

which is identical to (9.7).

One often uses the naive Bayes model for $p(x|\theta^{(y)})$. Because the observations x_i are independent conditioned on y_i, the parameter θ can be estimated from the training data using exactly the same method

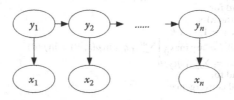

FIGURE 9.8   Graphical representation of HMM.

described in Section 9.4.1. Using the Bayes rule, the conditional probability of the label sequence $\{y_i\}$ is given by

$$p(\{y_i\}|\{x_i\}, \theta) \propto p(\{y_i\}) \prod_{i=1}^{n} p(x_i|\theta^{(y_i)}).$$

That is,

$$p(\{y_i\}|\{x_i\}, \theta) \propto \prod_{i=1}^{n} [p(x_i|\theta^{(y_i)}) p(y_i|y_{i-1})]. \qquad (9.16)$$

Similar to Section 9.4.1, the probability $p(y_i = a|y_{i-1} = b) = p(y_i = a, y_{i-1} = b)/p(y_{i-1} = b)$ can be estimated using counting. Let n_b be the number of training data with label b, and $n_{a,b}$ be the number of consecutive label pairs (y_i, y_{i-1}) with value (a, b). We can estimate the conditional probability as

$$p(y_{i-1} = b) = \frac{n_b}{n},$$

$$p(y_i = a, y_{i-1} = b) = \frac{n_{a,b}}{n},$$

$$p(y_i = a|y_{i-1} = b) = \frac{n_{a,b}}{n_b}.$$

The process of estimating the sequence $\{y_i\}$ from observation $\{x_i\}$ is often called decoding. A standard method is the maximum likelihood decoding, which finds the most likely sequence $\{\hat{y}_i\}$ based on the conditional probability model (9.16). That is,

$$[\{\hat{y}_i\}] = \arg\max_{\{y_i\}} \sum_{i=1}^{n} f(y_i, y_{i-1}), \qquad (9.17)$$

where

$$f(y_i, y_{i-1}) = \ln p(x_i|\theta^{(y_i)}) + \ln p(y_i|y_{i-1}).$$

It is not possible to enumerate all possible sequences $\{y_i\}$ and pick the largest score in (9.17) because the number of possible label sequences is k^n. However, an efficient procedure called the Viterbi decoding algorithm can be used to solve (9.17). The algorithm uses dynamic programming to track the best score up to a position j, and update the score recursively for $j = 1, \ldots, n$. Let

$$s_j(y_j) = \max_{\{y_i\}_{i=1,\ldots,j-1}} \sum_{i=1}^{j} f(y_i, y_{i-1}),$$

then it is easy to check that we have the following recursive identity:

$$s_{j+1}(y_{j+1}) = \max_{y_j \in \{1, \ldots, k\}} [s_j(y_j) + f(y_{j+1}, y_j)].$$

Therefore, $s_j(y_j)$ can be computed recursively for $j = 1, \ldots, n$. After computing $s_j(y_j)$, we may trace back $j = n, n-1, \ldots, 1$ to find the optimal sequence $\{\hat{y}_j\}$. The Viterbi algorithm that solves (9.17) is presented in Figure 9.9.

> **Initialize** $s_0(y_0) = 0$ ($y_0 = 1, \ldots, k$)
> **for** $j = 0, \ldots, n - 1$
> $s_{j+1}(y_{j+1}) = \max_{y_j \in \{1, \ldots, k\}}[s_j(y_j) + f(y_{j+1}, y_j)]$ ($y_{j+1} = 1, \ldots, k$)
> **end for**
> $\hat{y}_n = \arg\max_{y_n \in \{1, \ldots, k\}} s_n(y_n)$
> **for** $j = n - 1, \ldots, 1$
> $\hat{y}_j = \arg\max_{y_j \in \{1, \ldots, k\}}[s_j(y_j) + f(\hat{y}_{j+1}, y_j)]$
> **end for**

FIGURE 9.9   Viterbi algorithm.

9.6.2 Local Discriminative Model for Sequence Prediction

HMM is a generative model for sequence prediction. Similar to the standard supervised learning, one can also construct discriminative models for sequence prediction. In a discriminative model, in addition to the Markov dependency of y_i on y_{i-1}, we also allow an arbitrary dependency of y_i on $x_1^n = \{x_i\}_{i=1, \ldots, n}$. That is, we consider a model of the form

$$p(\{y_i\} | x_1^n, \theta) = \prod_{i=1}^{n} p(y_i | y_{i-1}, x_1^n, \theta). \tag{9.18}$$

The graphical model representation is given in Figure 9.10.

One may use logistic regression (MaxEnt) to model the conditional probability in (9.18). That is, we let $\theta = w$ and

$$p(y_i | y_{i-1}, x_1^n, \theta) = \frac{\exp(w^{\mathrm{T}} z_i(y_i, y_{i-1}, x_1^n))}{\sum_{\ell=1}^{k} \exp(w^{\mathrm{T}} z_i(y_i = \ell, y_{i-1}, x_1^n))}. \tag{9.19}$$

The vector $z_i(y_i, y_{i-1}, x_1^n)$ is a human-constructed vector called feature vector. This model has identical form as the maximum entropy model (9.12). Therefore, supervised training algorithm for logistic regression can be directly applied to train the model parameter θ. On the test data, given a sequence x_1^n, one can use the Viterbi algorithm to decode $\{y_i\}$ using the scoring function $f_\ell(y_i, y_{i-1}) = \ln p(y_i | y_{i-1}, x_1^n, \theta)$. This method has been widely used in NLP, for example, POS tagging (Ratnaparkhi 1996).

More generally, one may reduce sequence prediction into a standard prediction problem, where we simply predict the next label y_i given the previous label y_{i-1} and the observation x_1^n. One may use any classification algorithm such as SVM to solve this problem. The scoring function returned by the

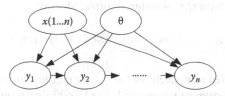

FIGURE 9.10   Graphical representation of discriminative local sequence prediction model.

underlying classifier can then be used as the scoring function for the Viterbi decoding algorithm. An example of this approach is given in Zhang et al. (2002).

9.6.3 Global Discriminative Model for Sequence Prediction

In (9.18), we decompose the conditional model of the label sequence $\{y_i\}$ using local model of the form $p(y_i|y_{i-1}, x_1^n, \theta)$ at each position i. Another approach is to treat the label sequence $y_1^n = \{y_i\}$ directly as a multi-class classification problem with k^n possible values. We can then directly apply the MaxEnt model (9.12) to this k^n-class multi-category classification problem using the following representation:

$$p(y_1^n|w, x_1^n) = \frac{e^{f(w, x_1^n, y_1^n)}}{\sum_{y_1^n} e^{f(w, x_1^n, y_1^n)}}, \tag{9.20}$$

where

$$f(w, x_1^n, y_1^n) = \sum_{i=1}^{n} w^{\mathrm{T}} z_i(y_i, y_{i-1}, x_1^n),$$

where $z_i(y_i, y_{i-1}, x_1^n)$ is a feature vector just like (9.19). While in (9.19), we model the local conditional probability $p(y_i|y_{i-1})$ that is a small fragment of the total label sequence $\{y_i\}$; in (9.20), we directly model the global label sequence.

The probability model (9.20) is called a conditional random field (Lafferty et al. 2001). The graphical model representation is given in Figure 9.11. Unlike Figure 9.10, the dependency between each y_i and y_{i-1} in Figure 9.11 is undirectional. This means that we do not directly model the conditional dependency $p(y_i|y_{i-1})$, and do not normalize the conditional probability at each point i in the maximum entropy representation of the label sequence probability.

The CRF model is more difficult to train because the normalization factor in the denominator of (9.20) has to be computed in the training phase. Although the summation is over k^n possible values of the label sequence y_1^n, similar to the Viterbi decoding algorithm, the computation can be arranged efficiently using dynamic programming. In decoding, the denominator can be ignored in the maximum likelihood solution. That is, the most likely sequence $\{\hat{y}_i\}$ is the solution of

$$\{\hat{y}_i\} = \arg \max_{y_1^n} \sum_{i=1}^{n} w^{\mathrm{T}} z_i(y_i, y_{i-1}, x_1^n). \tag{9.21}$$

The solution of this problem can be efficiently computed using the Viterbi algorithm.

More generally, global discriminative learning refers to the idea of treating sequence prediction as a multi-category classification problem with k^n classes, and a classification rule of the form (9.21). This approach can be used with some other learning algorithms such as Perceptron (Collins 2002) and large margin classifiers (Taskar et al. 2004; Tsochantaridis et al. 2005; Tillmann and Zhang 2008).

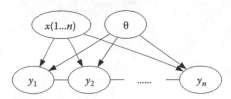

FIGURE 9.11 Graphical representation of a discriminative global sequence prediction model.

References

Berger, A., S. A. Della Pietra, and V. J. Della Pietra, A maximum entropy approach to natural language processing. *Computational Linguistics*, 22(1):39–71, 1996.

Collins, M., Discriminative training methods for hidden Markov models: Theory and experiments with perceptron algorithms. In *Proceedings of the Conference on Emperical Methods in Natural Language Modeling (EMNLP'02)*, Philadelphia, PA, pp. 1–8, July 2002.

Cortes, C. and V. N. Vapnik, Support vector networks. *Machine Learning*, 20:273–297, 1995.

Dempster, A., N. Laird, and D. Rubin, Maximum likelihood from incomplete data via the EM algorithm. *Journal of the Royal Statistical Society, Series B*, 39(1):1–38, 1977.

Hoerl, A. E. and R. W. Kennard, Ridge regression: Biased estimation for nonorthogonal problems. *Technometrics*, 12(1):55–67, 1970.

Joachims, T., Text categorization with support vector machines: Learning with many relevant features. In *European Conference on Machine Learing, ECML-98*, Berlin, Germany, pp. 137–142, 1998.

Kupiec, J., Robust part-of-speech tagging using a hidden Markov model. *Computer Speech and Language*, 6:225–242, 1992.

Lafferty, J., A. McCallum, and F. Pereira, Conditional random fields: Probabilistic models for segmenting and labeling sequence data. In *Proceedings of ICML-01*, San Francisco, CA, pp. 282–289, 2001. Morgan Kaufmann.

McCallum, A. and K. Nigam, A comparison of event models for naive Bayes text classification. In *AAAI/ICML-98 Workshop on Learning for Text Categorization*, Madison, WI, pp. 41–48, 1998.

Ratnaparkhi, A., A maximum entropy model for part-of-speech tagging. In *Proceedings of the Conference on Empirical Methods in Natural Language Processing*, Philadelphia, PA, pp. 133–142, 1996.

Taskar, B., C. Guestrin, and D. Koller, Max-margin Markov networks. In S. Thrun, L. Saul, and B. Schölkopf (editors), *Advances in Neural Information Processing Systems 16*. MIT Press, Cambridge, MA, 2004.

Tillmann, C. and T. Zhang, An online relevant set algorithm for statistical machine translation. *IEEE Transactions on Audio, Speech, and Language Processing*, 16(7):1274–1286, 2008.

Tsochantaridis, I., T. Joachims, T. Hofmann, and Y. Altun. Large margin methods for structured and interdependent output variables. *Journal of Machine Learning Research*, 6:1453–1484, 2005.

Zhang, T., F. Damerau, and D. E. Johnson, Text chunking based on a generalization of Winnow. *Journal of Machine Learning Research*, 2:615–637, 2002.

Zhang, T. and F. J. Oles, Text categorization based on regularized linear classification methods. *Information Retrieval*, 4:5–31, 2001.

10

Part-of-Speech Tagging

Tunga Güngör
Boğaziçi University

10.1 Introduction

Computer processing of natural language normally follows a sequence of steps, beginning with a phoneme- and morpheme-based analysis and stepping toward semantics and discourse analyses. Although some of the steps can be interwoven depending on the requirements of an application (e.g., doing word segmentation and part-of-speech tagging together in languages like Chinese), dividing the analysis into distinct stages adds to the modularity of the process and helps in identifying the problems peculiar to each stage more clearly. Each step aims at solving the problems at that level of processing and feeding the next level with an accurate stream of data.

One of the earliest steps within this sequence is *part-of-speech* (POS) *tagging*. It is normally a sentence-based approach and given a sentence formed of a sequence of words, POS tagging tries to label (tag) each word with its correct part of speech (also named *word category*, *word class*, or *lexical category*). This process can be regarded as a simplified form (or a subprocess) of morphological analysis. Whereas morphological analysis involves finding the internal structure of a word (root form, affixes, etc.), POS tagging only deals with assigning a POS tag to the given surface form word. This is more true for Indo-European languages, which are the mostly studied languages in the literature. Other languages such as those from Uralic or Turkic families may necessitate a more sophisticated analysis for POS tagging due to their complex morphological structures.

10.1.1 Parts of Speech

A natural question that may arise is: what are these parts of speech, or how do we specify a set of suitable parts of speech? It may be worthwhile at this point to say a few words about the origin of lexical categorization. From a linguistic point of view, the linguists mostly agree that there are three major (primary) parts of speech: noun, verb, and adjective (Pustet, 2003). Although there is some debate on the topic (e.g., the claim that the adjective–verb distinction is almost nonexistent in some languages such as the East-Asian language Mandarin or the claim that all the words in a particular category do not show the same functional/semantic behavior), this minimal set of three categories is considered universal. The usual solution to the arguable nature of this set is admitting the inconsistencies within each group and saying that in each group there are "typical members" as well as not-so-typical members (Baker, 2003). For example, eat is a prototypical instance of the verb category because it describes a "process" (a widely accepted definition for verbs), whereas hunger is a less typical instance of a verb. This judgment is supported by the fact that hunger is also related to the adjective category because of the more common adjective hungry, but there is no such correspondence for eat.

Taking the major parts of speech (noun, verb, adjective) as the basis of lexical categorization, linguistic models propose some additional categories of secondary importance (adposition, determiner, etc.) and some subcategories of primary and secondary categories (Anderson, 1997; Taylor, 2003). The subcategories either involve distinctions that are reflected in the morphosyntax (such as tense or number) or serve to capture different syntactic and semantic behavioral patterns (such as for nouns, count-noun and mass-noun). In this way, while the words in one subcategory may undergo some modifications, the others may not.

Leaving aside these linguistic considerations and their theoretical implications, people in the realm of natural language processing (NLP) approach the issue from a more practical point of view. Although the decision about the size and the contents of the *tagset* (the set of POS tags) is still linguistically oriented, the idea is providing distinct parts of speech for all classes of words having distinct grammatical behavior, rather than arriving at a classification that is in support of a particular linguistic theory. Usually the size of the tagset is large and there is a rich repertoire of tags with high discriminative power. The most frequently used corpora (for English) in the POS tagging research and the corresponding tagsets are as follows: Brown corpus (87 basic tags and special indicator tags), Lancaster-Oslo/Bergen (LOB) corpus (135 tags of which 23 are base tags), Penn Treebank and Wall Street Journal (WSJ) corpus (48 tags of which 12 are for punctuation and other symbols), and Susanne corpus (353 tags).

10.1.2 Part-of-Speech Problem

Except a few studies, nearly all of the POS tagging systems presuppose a fixed tagset. Then, the problem is, given a sentence, assigning a POS tag from the tagset to each word of the sentence. There are basically two difficulties in POS tagging:

1. *Ambiguous words.* In a sentence, obviously there exist some words for which more than one POS tag is possible. In fact, this language property makes POS tagging a real problem, otherwise the solution would be trivial. Consider the following sentence:

   We can can the can

   The three occurrences of the word can correspond to auxiliary, verb, and noun categories, respectively. When we take the whole sentence into account instead of the individual words, it is easy to determine the correct role of each word. It is easy at least for humans, but may not be so for automatic taggers. While disambiguating a particular word, humans exploit several mechanisms and information sources such as the roles of other words in the sentence, the syntactic structure of the sentence, the domain of the text, and the commonsense knowledge. The problem for computers is finding out how to handle all this information.

2. *Unknown words.* In the case of rule-based approaches to the POS tagging problem that use a set of handcrafted rules, there will clearly be some words in the input text that cannot be handled by the rules. Likewise, in statistical systems, there will be words that do not appear in the training corpus. We call such words *unknown words*. It is not desirable from a practical point of view for a tagger to adopt a closed-world assumption—considering only the words and sentences from which the rules or statistics are derived and ignoring the rest. For instance, a syntactic parser that relies on

the output of a POS tagger will encounter difficulties if the tagger cannot say anything about the unknown words. Thus, having some special mechanisms for dealing with unknown words is an important issue in the design of a tagger.

Another issue in POS tagging, which is not directly related to language properties but poses a problem for taggers, is the consistency of the tagset. Using a large tagset enables us to encode more knowledge about the morphological and morphosyntactical structures of the words, but at the same time makes it more difficult to distinguish between similar tags. Tag distinctions in some cases are so subtle that even humans may not agree on the tags of some words. For instance, an annotation experiment performed in Marcus et al. (1993) on the Penn Treebank has shown that the annotators disagree on 7.2% of the cases on the average. Building a consistent tagset is a more delicate subject for morphologically rich languages since the distinctions between different affix combinations need to be handled carefully. Thus, we can consider the inconsistencies in the tagsets as a problem that degrades the performance of taggers.

A number of studies allow some ambiguity in the output of the tagger by labeling some of the words with a set of tags (usually 2–3 tags) instead of a single tag. The reason is that, since POS tagging is seen as a preprocessing step for other higher-level processes such as named-entity recognition or syntactic parsing, it may be wiser to output a few most probable tags for some words for which we are not sure about the correct tag (e.g., both of the tags IN* and RB may have similar chances of being selected for a particular word). This decision may be left to later processing, which is more likely to decide on the correct tag by exploiting more relevant information (which is not available to the POS tagger).

The state-of-the-art in POS tagging accuracy (number of correctly tagged word tokens over all word tokens) is about 96%–97% for most Indo-European languages (English, French, etc.). Similar accuracies are obtained for other types of languages provided that the characteristics different from Indo-European languages are carefully handled by the taggers. We should note here that it is possible to obtain high accuracies using very simple methods. For example, on the WSJ corpus, tagging each word in the test data with the most likely tag for that word in the training data gives rise to accuracies around 90% (Halteren et al., 2001; Manning and Schütze, 2002). So, the sophisticated methods used in the POS tagging domain and that will be described throughout the chapter are for getting the last 10% of tagging accuracy.

On the one hand, 96%–97% accuracy may be regarded as quite a high success rate, when compared with other NLP tasks. Based on this figure, some researchers argue that we can consider POS tagging as an already-solved problem (at least for Indo-European languages). Any performance improvement above these success rates will be very small. However, on the other hand, the performances obtained with current taggers may seem insufficient and even a small improvement has the potential of significantly increasing the quality of later processing. If we suppose that a sentence in a typical English text has 20–30 words on the average, an accuracy rate of 96%–97% implies that there will be about one word erroneously tagged per sentence. Even one such word will make the job of a syntax analyzer much more difficult. For instance, a rule-based bottom-up parser begins from POS tags as the basic constituents and at each step combines a sequence of constituents into a higher-order constituent. A word with an incorrect tag will give rise to an incorrect higher-order structure and this error will probably affect the other constituents as the parser moves up in the hierarchy. Independent of the methodology used, any syntax analyzer will exhibit a similar behavior. Therefore, we may expect a continuing research effort on POS tagging.

This chapter will introduce the reader to a wide variety of methods used in POS tagging and with the solutions of the problems specific to the task. Section 10.2 defines the POS tagging problem and describes the approach common to all methods. Section 10.3 discusses in detail the main formalisms used in the

---

* In most of the examples in this chapter, we will refer to the tagset of the Penn Treebank. The tags that appear in the chapter are CD (cardinal number), DT (determiner), IN (preposition or subordinating conjunction), JJ (adjective), MD (modal verb), NN (noun, singular or mass), NNP (proper noun, singular), NNS (noun, plural), RB (adverb), TO (to), VB (verb, base form), VBD (verb, past tense), VBG (verb, gerund or present participle), VBN (verb, past participle), VBP (verb, present, non-3rd person singular), VBZ (verb, present, 3rd person singular), WDT (wh-determiner), and WP (wh-pronoun).

domain. Section 10.4 is devoted to a number of methods used less frequently by the taggers. Section 10.5 discusses the POS tagging problem for languages other than English. Section 10.6 concludes this chapter.

10.2 The General Framework

Let $W = w_1 w_2 \ldots w_n$ be a sentence having n words. The task of POS tagging is finding the set of tags $T = t_1 t_2 \ldots t_n$, where t_i corresponds to the POS tag of w_i, $1 \leq i \leq n$, as accurately as possible. In determining the correct tag sequence, we make use of the morphological and syntactic (and maybe semantic) relationships within the sentence (the *context*). The question is how a tagger encodes and uses the constraints enforced by these relationships.

The traditional answer to this question is simply limiting the context to a few words around the *target word* (the word we are trying to disambiguate), making use of the information supplied by these words and their tags, and ignoring the rest. So, if the target word is w_i, a typical context comprises w_{i-2}, t_{i-2}, w_{i-1}, t_{i-1}, and w_i. (Most studies scan the sentence from left to right and use the information on the already-tagged left context. However, there are also several studies that use both left and right contexts.) The reason for restricting the context severely is being able to cope with the exponential nature of the problem. As we will see later, adding one more word into the context increases the size of the problem (e.g., the number of parameters estimated in a statistical model) significantly.

It is obvious that long-distance dependencies between the words also play a role in determining the POS tag of a word. For instance, in the phrase

    the girls <u>can</u>...

the tag of the underlined word can is ambiguous: it may be an auxiliary (e.g., the girls can do it) or a verb (e.g., the girls can the food). However, if we use a larger context instead of only one or two previous words, the tag can be uniquely determined:

    The man who saw the girls <u>can</u>...

In spite of several such examples, it is customary to use a limited context in POS tagging and similar problems. As already mentioned, we can still get quite high success rates.

In the case of unknown words, the situation is somewhat different. One approach is again resorting to the information provided by the context words. Another approach that is more frequently used in the literature is making use of the morphology of the target word. The morphological data supplied by the word typically include the prefixes and the suffixes (more generally, a number of initial and final characters) of the word, whether the word is capitalized or not, and whether it includes a hyphen or not. For example, as an initial guess, Brill (1995a) assigns the tag proper noun to an unknown word if it is capitalized and the tag common noun otherwise. As another example, the suffix -ing for an unknown word is a strong indication for placing it in the verb category.

There are some studies in the POS tagging literature that are solely devoted to the tagging of unknown words (Mikheev, 1997; Thede, 1998; Nagata, 1999; Cucerzan and Yarowsky, 2000; Lee et al., 2002; Nakagawa and Matsumoto, 2006). Although each one uses a somewhat different technique than the others, all of them exploit the contextual and morphological information as already stated. We will not directly cover these studies explicitly in this chapter; instead, we will mention the issues relevant to unknown word handling within the explanations of tagging algorithms.

10.3 Part-of-Speech Tagging Approaches

10.3.1 Rule-Based Approaches

The earliest POS tagging systems are rule-based systems, in which a set of rules is manually constructed and then applied to a given text. Probably the first rule-based tagging system is given by Klein and Simpson (1963), which is based on a large set of handcrafted rules and a small lexicon to handle the exceptions. The initial tagging of the Brown corpus was also performed using a rule-based system, TAGGIT (Manning and Schütze, 2002). The lexicon of the system was used to constrain the possible tags of a word to those that exist in the lexicon. The rules were then used to tag the words for which the left and right context words were unambiguous. The main drawbacks of these early systems are the laborious work of manually coding the rules and the requirement of linguistic background.

10.3.1.1 Transformation-Based Learning

A pioneering work in rule-based tagging is by Brill (1995a). Instead of trying to acquire the linguistic rules manually, Brill (1995a) describes a system that learns a set of correction rules by a methodology called *transformation-based learning* (TBL). The idea is as follows: First, an initial-state annotator assigns a tag to each word in the corpus. This initial tagging may be a simple one such as choosing one of the possible tags for a word randomly, assigning the tag that is seen most often with a word in the training set, or just assuming each word as a noun (which is the most common tag). It can also be a sophisticated scheme such as using the output of another tagger. Following the initialization, the learning phase begins. By using a set of predetermined *rule templates*, the system instantiates each template with data from the corpus (thus obtaining a set of *rules*), applies temporarily each rule to the incorrectly tagged words in the corpus, and identifies the best rule that reduces most the number of errors in the corpus. This rule is added to the set of learned rules. Then the process iterates on the new corpus (formed by applying the selected rule) until none of the remaining rules reduces the error rate by more than a prespecified threshold.

The rule templates refer to a context of words and tags in a window of size seven (the target word, three words on the left, and three words on the right). Each template consists of two parts, a triggering environment (if-part) and a rewrite rule (action):

Change the tag (of the target word) from A to B if `condition`

It becomes applicable when the condition is satisfied. An example template referring to the previous tag and an example instantiation of it (i.e., a rule) for the sentence `the can rusted` are given below (`can` is the target word whose current tag is `modal`):

Change the tag from A to B if the previous tag is X
Change the tag from `modal` to `noun` if the previous tag is `determiner`

The rule states that the current tag of the target word that follows a `determiner` is `modal` but the correct tag must be `noun`. When the rule is applied to the sentence, it actually corrects one of the errors and increases its chance of being selected as the best rule.

Table 10.1 shows the rule templates used in Brill (1995a) and Figure 10.1 gives the TBL algorithm. In the algorithm, C_k refers to the training corpus at iteration k and M is the number of words in the corpus. For a rule r, r_e, r_{t_1}, and r_{t_2} correspond to the triggering environment, the left tag in the rule action, and the right tag in the rule action, respectively (i.e., "change the tag from r_{t_1} to r_{t_2} if r_e"). For a word w_i, $w_{i,e}$, $w_{i,c}$, and $w_{i,t}$ denote the environment, the current tag, and the correct tag, respectively. The function $f(e)$ is a binary function that returns 1 when the expression e evaluates to true and 0 otherwise. $C_k(r)$ is the result of applying rule r to the corpus at iteration k. R is the set of learned rules. The first statement inside the loop calculates, for each rule r, the number of times it corrects an incorrect tag and the number of times it changes a correct tag to an incorrect one, whenever its triggering environment matches the environment of the target word. Subtracting the first quantity from the second gives the amount of error reduction by

TABLE 10.1   Rule Templates Used in Transformation-Based Learning

Change the tag from A to B if

$t_{i-1} = X$	$t_{i-2} = X$ and $t_{i+1} = Y$	$w_i = X$ and $t_{i+1} = Y$
$t_{i+1} = X$	$w_{i-1} = X$	$w_i = X$
$t_{i-2} = X$	$w_{i+1} = X$	$w_{i-1} = X$ and $t_{i-1} = Y$
$t_{i+2} = X$	$w_{i-2} = X$	$w_{i-1} = X$ and $t_{i+1} = Y$
$t_{i-2} = X$ or $t_{i-1} = X$	$w_{i+2} = X$	$t_{i-1} = X$ and $w_{i+1} = Y$
$t_{i+1} = X$ or $t_{i+2} = X$	$w_{i-2} = X$ or $w_{i-1} = X$	$w_{i+1} = X$ and $t_{i+1} = Y$
$t_{i-3} = X$ or $t_{i-2} = X$ or $t_{i-1} = X$	$w_{i+1} = X$ or $w_{i+2} = X$	$w_{i-1} = X$ and $t_{i-1} = Y$ and $w_i = Z$
$t_{i+1} = X$ or $t_{i+2} = X$ or $t_{i+3} = X$	$w_{i-1} = X$ and $w_i = Y$	$w_{i-1} = X$ and $w_i = Y$ and $t_{i+1} = Z$
$t_{i-1} = X$ and $t_{i+1} = Y$	$w_i = X$ and $w_{i+1} = Y$	$t_{i-1} = X$ and $w_i = Y$ and $w_{i+1} = Z$
$t_{i-1} = X$ and $t_{i+2} = Y$	$t_{i-1} = X$ and $w_i = Y$	$w_i = X$ and $w_{i+1} = Y$ and $t_{i+1} = Z$

C_0 = training corpus labeled by initial-state annotator

$k = 0$

$R = \varnothing$

repeat

$$r_{\max} = \arg\max_r \sum_{i=1}^{M} f\left(r_e = w_{i,e} \text{ and } r_{t_1} = w_{i,c} \text{ and } r_{t_2} = w_{i,t}\right) -$$

$$\sum_{i=1}^{M} f\left(r_e = w_{i,e} \text{ and } r_{t_1} = w_{i,c} \text{ and } w_{i,c} = w_{i,t} \text{ and } r_{t_2} \neq w_{i,t}\right)$$

$C_{k+1} = C_k(r_{\max})$

$R = R \cup r_{\max}$

until (terminating condition)

FIGURE 10.1   Transformation-based learning algorithm.

this rule and we select the rule with the largest error reduction. Some example rules that were learned by the system are the following:

> Change the tag from VB to NN if one of the previous two tags is DT
> Change the tag from NN to VB if the previous tag is TO
> Change the tag from VBP to VB if one of the previous two words is n't

The unknown words are handled in a similar manner, with the following two differences: First, since no information exists for such words in the training corpus, the initial-state annotator assigns the tag proper noun if the word is capitalized and the tag common noun otherwise. Second, the templates use morphological information about the word, rather than contextual information. Two templates used by the system are given below together with example instantiations:

> Change the tag from A to B if the last character of the word is X
> Change the tag from A to B if character X appears in the word
> Change the tag from NN to NNS if the last character of the word is -s (e.g., tables)
> Change the tag from NN to CD if character. appears in the word (e.g., 10.42)

The TBL tagger was trained and tested on the WSJ corpus, which uses the Penn Treebank tagset. The system learned 447 contextual rules (for known words) and 243 rules for unknown words. The accuracy was 96.6% (97.2% for known words and 82.2% for unknown words). There are a number of advantages of TBL over some of the stochastic approaches:

- Unlike hidden Markov models, the system is quite flexible in the features that can be incorporated into the model. The rule templates can make use of any property of the words in the environment.
- Stochastic methods such as hidden Markov models and decision lists can overfit the data. However, TBL seems to be more immune from such overfitting, probably because of learning on the whole dataset at each iteration and its logic behind ordering the rules (Ramshaw and Marcus, 1994; Carberry et al., 2001).
- The output of TBL is a list of rules, which are usually easy to interpret (e.g., a determiner is most likely followed by a noun rather than a verb), instead of a huge number of probabilities as in other models.

It is also possible to use TBL in an unsupervised manner, as shown in Brill (1995b). In this case, by using a dictionary, the initial-state annotator assigns all possible tags to each word in the corpus. So, unlike the previous approach, each word will have a set of tags instead of a single tag. Then, the rules try to reduce the ambiguity by eliminating some of the tags of the ambiguous words. We no longer have rule templates that replace a tag with another tag; instead, the templates serve to reduce the set of tags to a singleton:

Change the tag from A to B if condition

where A is a set of tags and B ∈ A. We determine the most likely tag B by considering each element of A in turn, looking at each context in which this element is unambiguous, and choosing the most frequently occurring element. For example, given the following sentence and knowing that the word can (underlined) is either MD, NN, or VB,

The/DT can/MD,NN,VB is/VBZ open/JJ

we can infer the tag NN for can if the unambiguous words in the context DT _ VBZ are mostly NN. Note that the system takes advantage of the fact that many words have only one tag and thus uses the unambiguous contexts when scoring the rules at each iteration.

Some example rules learned when the system was applied to the WSJ corpus are given below:

Change the tag from {NN, VB, VBP} to VBP if the previous tag is NNS
Change the tag from {NN, VB} to VB if the previous tag is MD
Change the tag from {JJ, NNP} to JJ if the following tag is NNS

The system was tested on several corpora and it achieved accuracies up to 96.0%, which is quite a high accuracy for an unsupervised method.

10.3.1.2 Modifications to TBL and Other Rule-Based Approaches

The transformation-based learning paradigm and its success in the POS tagging problem have influenced many researchers. Following the original publication, several extensions and improvements have been proposed. One of them, named *guaranteed pre-tagging*, analyzes the effect of fixing the initial tag of those words that we already know to be correct (Mohammed and Pedersen, 2003). Unlike the standard TBL tagger, if we can identify the correct tag of a word a priori and give this information to the tagger, then the tagger initializes the word with this "pre-tag" and guarantees that it will not be changed during learning. However, this pre-tag can still be used in any contextual rule for changing the tags of other words. The rest of the process is the same as in the original algorithm. Consider the word chair (underlined) in the following sentence, with the initial tags given as shown:

Mona/NNP will/MD sit/VB in/IN the/DT pretty/RB chair/NN this/DT time/NN

The standard TBL tagger will change the tag of chair to VB due to a learned rule: "change the tag from NN to VB if the following tag is DT." Not only the word chair will be incorrectly tagged, also the initial incorrect tag of the word `pretty` will remain unchanged. However, if we have a priori information that `chair` is being used as NN in this particular context, then it can be pre-tagged and will not be affected by the mentioned rule. Moreover, the tag of `pretty` will be corrected due to the rule "change the tag from RB to JJ if the following tag is NN."

The authors developed the guaranteed pre-tagging approach during a word sense disambiguation task on Senseval-2 data. There were about 4300 words in the dataset that were manually tagged. When the standard TBL algorithm was executed to tag all the words in the dataset, the tags of about 570 of the manually tagged words (which were the correct tags) were changed. This motivated the pre-tagged version of the TBL algorithm. The manually tagged words were marked as pre-tagged and the algorithm did not allow these tags to be changed. This caused 18 more words in the context of the pre-tagged words to be correctly tagged.

The main drawback of the TBL approach is its high time complexity. During each pass through the training corpus, it forms and evaluates all possible instantiations of every suitable rule template. (We assume the original TBL algorithm as we have described here. The available version in fact contains some optimizations.) Thus, when we have a large corpus and a large set of templates, it becomes intractable. One solution to this problem is putting a limit on the number of rules (instantiations of rule templates) that are considered for incorrect taggings. The system developed by Carberry et al. (2001), named *randomized TBL*, is based on this idea: at each iteration, it examines each incorrectly tagged word, but only R (a predefined constant) of all possible template instantiations that would correct the tag are considered (randomly selected). In this way, the training time becomes independent of the number of rules.

Even with a very low value for R (e.g., $R = 1$), the randomized TBL obtains, in much less time, an accuracy very close to that of the standard TBL. This may seem interesting, but has a simple explanation. During an iteration, the standard TBL selects the best rule. This means that this rule corrects many incorrect tags in the corpus. So, although randomized TBL considers only R randomly generated rules on each instance, the probability of generating this particular rule will be high since it is applicable to many incorrect instances. Therefore, these two algorithms tend to learn the same rules at early phases of the training. In later phases, since the rules will be less applicable to the remaining instances (i.e., more specific rules), the chance of learning the same rules decreases. Even if randomized TBL cannot determine the best rule at an iteration, it can still learn a compensating rule at a later iteration.

The experiments showed the same success rates for both versions of TBL, but the training time of randomized TBL was 5–10 times better. As the corpus size decreases, the accuracy of randomized TBL becomes slightly worse than the standard TBL, but the time gain becomes more impressive.

Finite state representations have a number of desirable properties, like efficiency (using a deterministic and minimized machine) and the compactness of the representation. In Roche and Schabes (1995), it was attempted to convert the TBL POS tagging system into a finite state transducer (FST). The idea is that, after the TBL algorithm learns the rules in the training phase, the test (tagging) phase can be done much more efficiently. Given a set of rules, the FST tagger is constructed in four steps: converting each rule (contextual rule or unknown word rule) into an FST; globalizing each FST so that it can be applied to the whole input in one pass; composing all transducers into a single transducer; and determinizing the transducer.

The method takes advantage of the well-defined operations on finite state transducers—composing, determinizing, and minimizing. The lexicon, which is used by the initial-state annotator, is also converted into a finite state automaton. The experiments on the Brown corpus showed that the FST tagger runs much faster than both the TBL tagger (with the same accuracy) and their implementation of a trigram-based stochastic tagger (with a similar accuracy).

Multidimensional transformation-based learning (mTBL) is a framework where TBL is applied to more than one task jointly. Instead of learning the rules for different tasks separately, it may be beneficial to acquire them in a single learning phase. The motivation under the mTBL framework is exploiting the dependencies between the tasks and thus increasing the performance on the individual tasks. This idea was applied to POS tagging and text chunking (identification of basic phrasal structures) (Florian and

Ngai, 2001). The mTBL algorithm is similar to the TBL algorithm, except that the objective function used to select the best rule is changed as follows:

$$f(r) = \sum_{s \in corpus} \sum_{i=1}^{n} w_i^* (S_i(r(s)) - S_i(s))$$

where

r is a rule

n is the number of tasks (2, in this application)

$r(s)$ denotes the application of rule r to sample s in the corpus

$S_i(\cdot)$ is the score of task i (1: correct, 0: incorrect)

w_i is a weight assigned to task i (used to weight the tasks according to their importance).

The experiments on the WSJ corpus showed about 0.5% increase in accuracy

Below we show the rules learned in the jointly trained system and in the POS-tagging-only system for changing VBD tag to VBN. The former one learns a single rule (a more general rule), indicating that if the target word is inside a verb phrase then the tag should be VBN. However, the latter system can arrive at this decision using three rules. Since the rules are scored separately in the standard TBL tagger during learning, a more general rule in mTBL will have a better chance to capture the similar incorrect instances.

Change the tag from VBD to VBN if the target chunk is I-VP

Change the tag from VBD to VBN if one of the previous three tags is VBZ
Change the tag from VBD to VBN if the previous tag is VBD
Change the tag from VBD to VBN if one of the previous three tags is VBP

While developing a rule-based system, an important issue is determining in which order the rules should be applied. There may be several rules applicable for a particular situation and the output of the tagger may depend on in which order the rules are applied. A solution to this problem is assigning some weights (votes) to the rules according to the training data and disambiguating the text based on these votes (Tür and Oflazer, 1998). Each rule is in the following form:

$$(c_1, c_2, \ldots, c_n; v)$$

where

c_i, $1 \leq i \leq n$, is a constraint that incorporates POS and/or lexical (word form) information of the words in the context

v is the vote of the rule

Two example rule instantiations are:

([tag=MD], [tag=RB], [tag=VB]; 100)
([tag=DT, lex=that], [tag=NNS]; −100)

The first one promotes (a high positive vote) a modal followed by a verb with an intervening adverb and the second one demotes a singular determiner reading of that before a plural noun. The votes are acquired automatically from the training corpus by counting the frequencies of the patterns denoted by the constraints. As the votes are obtained, the rules are applied to the possible tag sequences of a sentence and the tag sequence that results in the maximum vote is selected. The method of applying rules to an input sentence resembles the Viterbi algorithm commonly used in stochastic taggers. The proposed method, therefore, can also be approached from a probabilistic point of view as selecting the best tag sequence among all possible taggings of a sentence.

A simple but interesting technique that is different from context-based systems is learning the rules from word endings (Grzymala-Busse and Old, 1997). This is a word-based approach (not using information from context) that considers a fixed number of characters (e.g., three) at the end of the words. A table is built from the training data that lists all word endings that appear in the corpus, accompanied with the correct POS. For instance, the sample list of four entries

   (-ine, noun) (-inc, noun) (-ing, noun) (-ing, verb)

implies noun category for -ine and -inc, but signals a conflict for -ing. The table is fed to a rule induction algorithm that learns a set of rules by taking into account the conflicting cases. The algorithm outputs a particular tag for each word ending. A preliminary experiment was done by using Roget's dictionary as the training data. The success is low as might be expected from such an information-poor approach: about 26% of the words were classified incorrectly.

10.3.2 Markov Model Approaches

The rule-based methods used for the POS tagging problem began to be replaced by stochastic models in the early 1990s. The major drawback of the oldest rule-based systems was the need to manually compile the rules, a process that requires linguistic background. Moreover, these systems are not robust in the sense that they must be partially or completely redesigned when a change in the domain or in the language occurs. Later on a new paradigm, statistical natural language processing, has emerged and offered solutions to these problems. As the field became more mature, researchers began to abandon the classical strategies and developed new statistical models.

Several people today argue that statistical POS tagging is superior to rule-based POS tagging. The main factor that enables us to use statistical methods is the availability of a rich repertoire of data sources: lexicons (may include frequency data and other statistical data), large corpora (preferably annotated), bilingual parallel corpora, and so on. By using such resources, we can learn the usage patterns of the tag sequences and make use of this information to tag new sentences. We devote the rest of this section and the next section to statistical POS tagging models.

10.3.2.1 The Model

Markov models (MMs) are probably the most studied formalisms in the POS tagging domain. Let $W = w_1 w_2 \ldots w_n$ be a sequence of words and $T = t_1 t_2 \ldots t_n$ be the corresponding POS tags. The problem is finding the optimal tag sequence corresponding to the given word sequence and can be expressed as maximizing the following conditional probability:

$$P(T|W)$$

Applying Bayes' rule, we can write

$$P(T|W) = \frac{P(W|T)P(T)}{P(W)}$$

The problem of finding the optimal tag sequence can then be stated as follows:

$$\arg\max_T P(T|W) = \arg\max_T \frac{P(W|T)P(T)}{P(W)}$$
$$= \arg\max_T P(W|T)P(T) \qquad (10.1)$$

where the $P(W)$ term was eliminated since it is the same for all T. It is impracticable to directly estimate the probabilities in Equation 10.1, therefore we need some simplifying assumptions. The first term $P(W|T)$

can be simplified by assuming that the words are independent of each other given the tag sequence (Equation 10.2) and a word only depends on its own tag (Equation 10.3):

$$P(W|T) = P(w_1 \ldots w_n|t_1 \ldots t_n)$$

$$= \prod_{i=1}^{n} P(w_i|t_1 \ldots t_n) \qquad (10.2)$$

$$= \prod_{i=1}^{n} P(w_i|t_i) \qquad (10.3)$$

The second term $P(T)$ can be simplified by using the limited horizon assumption, which states that a tag depends only on k previous tags (k is usually 1 or 2):

$$P(T) = P(t_1 \ldots t_n)$$

$$= P(t_1)P(t_2|t_1)P(t_3|t_1t_2) \ldots P(t_n|t_1 \ldots t_{n-1})$$

$$= \prod_{i=1}^{n} P(t_i|t_{i-1} \ldots t_{i-k})$$

When $k = 1$, we have a *first-order model* (*bigram model*) and when $k = 2$, we have a *second-order model* (*trigram model*). We can name $P(W|T)$ as the *lexical probability* term (it is related to the lexical forms of the words) and $P(T)$ as the *transition probability* term (it is related to the transitions between tags). Now we can restate the POS tagging problem: finding the tag sequence $T = t_1 \ldots t_n$ (among all possible tag sequences) that maximizes the lexical and transition probabilities:

$$\arg\max_T \prod_{i=1}^{n} P(w_i|t_i)P(t_i|t_{i-1} \ldots t_{i-k}) \qquad (10.4)$$

This is a hidden Markov model (HMM) since the tags (states of the model) are hidden and we can only observe the words. Having a corpus annotated with POS tags (*supervised tagging*), the training phase (estimation of the probabilities in Equation 10.4) is simple using maximum likelihood estimation:

$$P(w_i|t_i) = \frac{f(w_i, t_i)}{f(t_i)} \quad \text{and} \quad P(t_i|t_{i-1} \ldots t_{i-k}) = \frac{f(t_{i-k} \ldots, t_i)}{f(t_{i-k} \ldots t_{i-1})}$$

where

$f(w, t)$ is the number of occurrences of word w with tag t

$f(t_{l_1} \ldots t_{l_m})$ is the number of occurrences of the tag sequence $t_{l_1} \ldots t_{l_m}$

That is, we compute the relative frequencies of tag sequences and word-tag pairs from the training data. Then, in the test phase (tagging phase), given a sequence of words W, we need to determine the tag sequence that maximizes these probabilities as shown in Equation 10.4. The simplest approach may be computing Equation 10.4 for each possible tag sequence of length n and then taking the maximizing sequence. Clearly, this naive approach yields an algorithm that is exponential in the number of words. This problem can be solved more efficiently using dynamic programming techniques and a well-known dynamic programming algorithm used in POS tagging and similar tasks is the Viterbi algorithm (see Chapter 9). The Viterbi algorithm, instead of keeping track of all paths during execution, determines the optimal subpaths for each node while it traverses the network and discards the others. It is an efficient algorithm operating in linear time.

The process described above requires an annotated corpus. Though such corpora are available for well-studied languages, it is difficult to find such resources for most of the other languages. Even when an annotated corpus is available, a change of the domain (i.e., training on available annotated corpus and testing on a text from a new domain) causes a significant decrease in accuracy (e.g., Boggess et al., 1999). However, it is also possible to learn the parameters of the model without using an annotated training dataset (*unsupervised tagging*). A commonly used technique for this purpose is the expectation maximization method.

Given training data, the forward–backward algorithm, also known as the Baum–Welch algorithm, adjusts the parameter probabilities of the HMM to make the training sequence as likely as possible (Manning and Schütze, 2002). The forward–backward algorithm is a special case of the expectation maximization method. The algorithm begins with some initial probabilities for the parameters (transitions and word emissions) we are trying to estimate and calculates the probability of the training data using these probabilities. Then the algorithm iterates. At each iteration, the probabilities of the parameters that are on the paths that are traversed more by the training data are increased and the probabilities of other parameters are decreased. The probability of the training data is recalculated using this revised set of parameter probabilities. It can be shown that the probability of the training data increases at each step. The process repeats until the parameter probabilities converge. Provided that the training dataset is representative of the language, we can expect the learned model to behave well on the test data. After the parameters are estimated, the tagging phase is exactly the same as in the case of supervised tagging.

In general, it is not possible to observe all the parameters in Equation 10.4 in the training corpus for all words w_i in the language and all tags t_i in the tagset, regardless of how large the corpus is. During testing, when an unobserved term appears in a sentence, the corresponding probability and thus the probability of the whole sentence will be zero for a particular tag sequence. This is named *sparse data problem* and is a problem for all probabilistic methods. To alleviate this problem, some form of smoothing is applied. A smoothing method commonly used in POS taggers is linear interpolation, as shown below for a second-order model:

$$P(t_i|t_{i-1}t_{i-2}) \cong \lambda_1 P(t_i) + \lambda_2 P(t_i|t_{i-1}) + \lambda_3 P(t_i|t_{i-1}t_{i-2})$$

where the λ_i's are constants with $0 \leq \lambda_i \leq 1$ and $\sum_i \lambda_i = 1$. That is, unigram and bigram data are also considered in addition to the trigrams. Normally, λ_i's are estimated from a development corpus, which is distinct from the training and the test corpora. Some other popular smoothing methods are discounting and back-off, and their variations (Manning and Schütze, 2002).

10.3.2.2 HMM-Based Taggers

Although it is not entirely clear who first used MMs for the POS tagging problem, the earliest account in the literature appears to be Bahl and Mercer (1976). Another early work that popularized the idea of statistical tagging is due to Church (1988), which uses a standard MM and a simple smoothing technique. Following these works, a large number of studies based on MMs were proposed. Some of these use the standard model (the model depicted in Section 10.3.2.1) and play with a few properties (model order, smoothing, etc.) to improve the performance. Some others, on the other hand, in order to overcome the limitations posed by the standard model, try to enrich the model by making use of the context in a different manner, modifying the training algorithm, and so on.

A comprehensive analysis of the effect of using MMs for POS tagging was given in an early work by Merialdo (1994). In this work, a second-order model is used in both a supervised and an unsupervised manner. An interesting point of this study is the comparison of two different schemes in finding the optimal tag sequence of a given (test) sentence. The first one is the classical Viterbi approach as we have explained before, called "sentence level tagging" in Merialdo (1994). An alternative is "word level tagging" which, instead of maximizing over the possible tag sequences for the sentence, maximizes over the possible tags for each word:

$$\arg\max_T P(T|W) \quad \text{vs.} \quad \arg\max_{t_i} P(t_i|W)$$

This distinction was considered in Dermatas and Kokkinakis (1995) as well and none of these works observed a significant difference in accuracy under the two schemes. To the best of our knowledge, this issue was not analyzed further and later works relied on Viterbi tagging (or its variants).

Merialdo (1994) uses a form of interpolation where trigram distributions are interpolated with uniform distributions. A work that concentrates on smoothing techniques in detail is given in Sündermann and Ney (2003). It employs linear interpolation and proposes a new method for learning λ_i's that is based on the concept of training data coverage (number of distinct n-grams in the training set). It argues that using a large model order (e.g., five) accompanied with a good smoothing technique has a positive effect on the accuracy of the tagger. Another example of a sophisticated smoothing technique is given in Wang and Schuurmans (2005). The idea is exploiting the similarity between the words and putting similar words into the same cluster. Similarity is defined in terms of the left and right contexts. Then, the parameter probabilities are estimated by averaging, for a word w, over probabilities of 50 most similar words of w.

It was shown empirically in Dermatas and Kokkinakis (1995) that the distribution of the unknown words is similar to that of the less probable words (words occurring less than a threshold t, e.g., $t = 10$). Therefore, the parameters for the unknown words can be estimated from the distributions of less probable words. Several models were tested, particularly first- and second-order HMMs were compared with a simpler model, named *Markovian language model* (MLM), in which the lexical probabilities $P(W|T)$ are ignored. All the experiments were repeated on seven European languages. The study arrives at the conclusion that HMM reduces the error almost to half in comparison to the same order MLM.

A highly accurate and frequently cited (partly due to its availability) POS tagger is the TnT tagger (Brants, 2000). Though based on the standard HMM formalism, its power comes from a careful treatment of smoothing and unknown word issues. The smoothing is done by context-independent linear interpolation. The distribution of unknown words is estimated using the sequences of characters at word endings, with sequence length varying from 1 to 10. Instead of considering all the words in the training data while determining the similarity of an unknown word to other words, only the infrequent ones (occurring less than 10 times) are taken into account. This is in line with the justification in Dermatas and Kokkinakis (1995) about the similarity between unknown words and less probable words. Another interesting property is the incorporation of capitalization feature in the tagset. It was observed that the probability distributions of tags around capitalized words are different from those around lowercased words. So, each tag is accompanied with a capitalization feature (e.g., instead of VBD, VBDc and VBDc′), doubling the size of the tagset. To increase the efficiency of the tagger, beam search is used in conjunction with the Viterbi algorithm, which prunes the paths more while scanning the sentence. The TnT tagger achieves about 97% accuracy on the Penn Treebank.

Some studies attempted to change the form of Equation 10.4 in order to incorporate more context into the model. Thede and Harper (1999) change the lexical probability $P(w_i|t_i)$ to $P(w_i|t_{i-1}, t_i)$ and also use a similar formula for unknown words, $P(w_i \text{ has suffix } s|t_{i-1}, t_i)$, where the suffix length varies from 1 to 4. In a similar manner, Banko and Moore (2004) prefer the form $P(w_i|t_{i-1}, t_i, t_{i+1})$. The authors of these two works name their modified models as *full second-order HMM* and *contextualized HMM*, respectively. In Lee et al. (2000a), more context is considered by utilizing the following formulations:

$$P(T) \cong \prod_{i=1}^{n} P(t_i|t_{i-1} \ldots t_{i-K}, w_{i-1} \ldots w_{i-J})$$

$$(10.5)$$

$$P(W|T) \cong \prod_{i=1}^{n} P(w_i|t_{i-1} \ldots t_{i-L}, t_i, w_{i-1} \ldots w_{i-I})$$

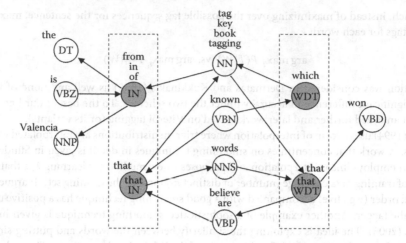

FIGURE 10.2 A part of an example HMM for the specialized word *that*. (Reprinted From Pla, F. and Molina, A., *Nat. Lang. Eng.*, 10, 167, 2004. Cambridge University Press. With permission.)

The proposed model was investigated using several different values for the parameters K, J, L, and I (between 0 and 2). In addition, the conditional distributions in Equations 10.5 were converted into joint distributions. This formulation was observed to yield more reliable estimations in such extended contexts. The experimental results obtained in all these systems showed an improvement in accuracy compared to the standard HMM.

A more sophisticated way of enriching the context is identifying a priori a set of "specialized words" and, for each such word w, splitting each state t in the HMM that emits w into two states: one state (w, t) that only emits w and another state, the original state t, that emits all the words emitted before splitting it except w (Pla and Molina, 2004). In this way, the model can distinguish among different local contexts. An example for a first-order model is given in Figure 10.2, where the dashed rectangles show the split states.

The specialized words can be selected using different strategies: words with high frequencies in the training set, words that belong to closed-class categories, or words resulting in a large number of tagging errors on a development set. The system developed uses the TnT tagger. The evaluation using different numbers of specialized words showed that the method gives better results than HMM (for all numbers of specialized words, ranging from 1 to 400), and the optimum performance was obtained with about 30 and 285 specialized words for second- and first-order models, respectively.

In addition to the classical view of considering each word and each tag in the dataset separately, there exist some studies that combine individual words/tags in some manner. In Cutting et al. (1992), each word is represented by an ambiguity class, which is the set of its possible parts of speech. In Nasr et al. (2004), the tagset is extended by adding new tags, the so-called ambiguous tags. When a word in a certain context can be tagged as $t_1, t_2, \ldots, t_k$ with probabilities that are close enough, an ambiguous tag $t_{1,2,\ldots,k}$ is created. In such cases, instead of assigning the tag with the highest score to the word in question, it seems desirable to allow some ambiguity in the output, since the tagger is not sure enough about the correct tag. For instance, the first five ambiguous tags obtained from the Brown corpus are IN-RB, DT-IN-WDT-WP, JJ-VBN, NN-VB, and JJ-NN. Success rates of about 98% were obtained with an ambiguity of 1.23 tags/word.

Variable memory Markov models (VMMM) and self-organizing Markov models (SOMM) were proposed as solutions to the POS tagging problem (Schütze and Singer, 1994; Kim et al., 2003). They aim at increasing the flexibility of the HMMs by being able to vary the size of the context as the need arises (Manning and Schütze, 2002). For instance, the VMMM can go from a state that considers the previous two tags to a state that does not use any context, then to a state that uses the previous three tags. This differs from linear interpolation smoothing which always uses a weighted average of a fixed number of *n*-grams. In both VMMM and SOMM, the structure of the model is induced from the training corpus. Kim et al. (2003) represent the MM in terms of a statistical decision tree (SDT) and give an algorithm for learning the SDT. These extended MMs yield results comparable to those of HMMs, with significant reductions in the number of parameters to be estimated.

10.3.3 Maximum Entropy Approaches

The HMM framework has two important limitations for classification tasks such as POS tagging: strong independence assumptions and poor use of contextual information. For HMM POS tagging, we usually assume that the tag of a word does not depend on previous and next words, or a word in the context does not supply any information about the tag of the target word. Furthermore, the context is usually limited to the previous one or two words. Although there exist some attempts to overcome these limitations, as we have seen in Secion 10.3.2.2, they do not allow us to use the context in any way we like.

Maximum entropy (ME) models provide us more flexibility in dealing with the context and are used as an alternative to HMMs in the domain of POS tagging. The use of the context is in fact similar to that in the TBL framework. A set of *feature templates* (in analogy to rule templates in TBL) is predefined and the system learns the discriminating features by instantiating the feature templates using the training corpus. The flexibility comes from the ability to include any template that we think useful—may be simple (target tag t_i depends on t_{i-1}) or complex (t_i depends on t_{i-1} and/or t_{i-2} and/or w_{i+1}). The features need not be independent of each other and the model exploits this advantage by using overlapping and interdependent features.

A pioneering work in ME POS tagging is Ratnaparkhi (1996, 1998). The probability model is defined over $H \times T$, where H is the set of possible contexts (histories) and T is the set of tags. Then, given $h \in H$ and $t \in T$, we can express the conditional probability in terms of a log-linear (exponential) model:

$$P(t|h) = \frac{1}{Z(h)} \prod_{j=1}^{k} \alpha_j^{f_j(t,h)}$$

where

$$Z(h) = \sum_t \prod_{j=1}^{k} \alpha_j^{f_j(t,h)}$$

$f_1, \ldots, f_k$ are the features, $\alpha_j > 0$ is the "weight" of feature f_j, and $Z(h)$ is a normalization function to ensure a true probability distribution. Each feature is binary-valued, that is, $f_j(t, h) = 0$ or 1. Thus, the probability $P(t|h)$ can be interpreted as the normalized product of the weights of the "active" features on (t, h).

The probability distribution P we seek is the one that maximizes the entropy of the distribution under some constraints:

$$\arg\max_P - \sum_{\substack{h \in H \\ t \in T}} \bar{P}(h) P(t|h) \log P(t|h)$$

subject to

$$E(f_j) = \bar{E}(f_j), \quad 1 \leq j \leq k$$

TABLE 10.2   Feature Templates Used in the Maximum Entropy Tagger

Condition	Features	
For all words w_i	$t_{i-1} = \text{X}$	and $t_i = \text{T}$
	$t_{i-2} = \text{X}$ and $t_{i-1} = \text{Y}$	and $t_i = \text{T}$
	$w_{i-1} = \text{X}$	and $t_i = \text{T}$
	$w_{i-2} = \text{X}$	and $t_i = \text{T}$
	$w_{i+1} = \text{X}$	and $t_i = \text{T}$
	$w_{i+2} = \text{X}$	and $t_i = \text{T}$
Word w_i is not a rare word	$w_i = \text{X}$	and $t_i = \text{T}$
Word w_i is a rare word	X is a prefix of w_i, $|\text{X}| \le 4$	and $t_i = \text{T}$
	X is a suffix of w_i, $|\text{X}| \le 4$	and $t_i = \text{T}$
	w_i contains number	and $t_i = \text{T}$
	w_i contains uppercase character	and $t_i = \text{T}$
	w_i contains hyphen	and $t_i = \text{T}$

Source: Ratnaparkhi, A., A maximum entropy model for part-of-speech tagging, in *EMNLP*, Brill, E. and Church, K. (eds.), ACL, Philadelphia, PA, 1996, 133–142. With permission.

where

$$E(f_j) = \sum_{i=1}^{n} \bar{P}(h_i) P(t_i|h_i) f_j(h_i, t_i)$$

$$\bar{E}(f_j) = \sum_{i=1}^{n} \bar{P}(h_i, t_i) f_j(h_i, t_i)$$

$E(f_j)$ and $\bar{E}(f_j)$ denote, respectively, the model's expectation and the observed expectation of feature f_j. $\bar{P}(h_i)$ and $\bar{P}(h_i, t_i)$ are the relative frequencies, respectively, of context h_i and the context-tag pair (h_i, t_i) in the training data. The intuition behind maximizing the entropy is that it gives us the most uncertain distribution. In other words, we do not include any information in the distribution that is not justified by the empirical evidence available to us. The parameters of the distribution P can be obtained using the generalized iterative scaling algorithm (Darroch and Ratcliff, 1972).

The feature templates used in Ratnaparkhi (1996) are shown in Table 10.2. As can be seen, the context (history) is formed of $(w_{i-2}, w_{i-1}, w_i, w_{i+1}, w_{i+2}, t_{i-2}, t_{i-1})$, although it is possible to include other data. The features for rare words (words occurring less than five times) make use of morphological clues such as affixes and capitalization. During training, for each target word w, the algorithm instantiates each feature template by using the context of w. For example, two features that can be extracted from the training corpus are shown below:

$$f_j(h_i, t_i) = \begin{cases} 1 & \text{if } t_{i-1} = \text{JJ and } t_i = \text{NN} \\ 0 & \text{else} \end{cases}$$

$$f_j(h_i, t_i) = \begin{cases} 1 & \text{if suffix } (w_{i-1}) = -\text{ing and } t_i = \text{VBG} \\ 0 & \text{else} \end{cases}$$

The features that occur rarely in the data are usually unreliable and they do not have much predictive power. The algorithm uses a simple smoothing technique and eliminates those features that appear less than a threshold (e.g., less than 10 times). There are some other studies that use more sophisticated smoothing methods, such as using a Gaussian prior on the model parameters, which improve the performance when compared with the frequency cutoff technique (Curran and Clark, 2003; Zhao et al., 2007).

In the test phase, beam search is used to find the most likely tag sequence of a sentence. If a dictionary is available, each known word is restricted to its possible tags in order to increase the efficiency. Otherwise, all tags in the tagset become candidates for the word.

Experiments on the WSJ corpus showed 96.43% accuracy. In order to observe the effect of the flexible feature selection capability of the model, the author analyzed the problematic words (words frequently mistagged) and added more specialized features into the model to better distinguish such cases. A feature about the problematic word *about* may be:

$$f_j(h_i, t_i) = \begin{cases} 1 & \text{if } w_i = \text{``about'' and } t_{i-2}t_{i-1} = \text{DT NNS and } t_i = \text{IN} \\ 0 & \text{else} \end{cases}$$

An insignificant increase was observed in the accuracy (96.49%). This 96%–97% accuracy barrier may be partly due to missing some information that is important for disambiguation or to the inconsistencies in the training corpus. In the work, this argument was also tested by repeating the experiments on more consistent portions of the corpus and the accuracy increased to 96.63%. We can thus conclude that, as mentioned by several researchers, there is some amount of noise in the corpora and this seems to prevent taggers passing beyond an accuracy limit.

It is worth noting before closing this section that there are some attempts for detecting and correcting the inconsistencies in the corpora (Květon and Oliva, 2002a,b; Dickinson and Meurers, 2003; Rocio et al., 2007). The main idea in these attempts is determining (either manually or automatically) the tag sequences that are impossible or very unlikely to occur in the language, and then replacing these sequences with the correct ones after a manual inspection. For example, in English, it is nearly impossible for a determiner to be followed by a verb. As the errors in the annotated corpora are reduced via such techniques, we can expect the POS taggers to obtain better accuracies.

10.3.3.1 Taggers Based on ME Models

The flexibility of the feature set in the ME model has been exploited in several ways by researchers. Toutanova and Manning (2000) concentrate on the problematic cases for both unknown/rare words and known words. Two new feature templates are added to handle the unknown and rare words:

- A feature activated when all the letters of a word are uppercase
- A feature activated when a word that is not at the beginning of the sentence contains an uppercase letter

In fact, these features reflect the peculiarities in the particular corpus used, the WSJ corpus. In this corpus, for instance, the distribution of words in which only the initial letter is capitalized is different from the distribution of words whose all letters are capitalized. Thus, such features need not be useful in other corpora. Similarly, in the case of known words, the most common error types are handled by using new feature templates. An example template is given below:

VBD/VBN ambiguity—a feature activated when there is *have* or *be* auxiliary form in the preceding eight positions

All these features are corpus- and language-dependent, and may not generalize easily to other situations. However, these specialized features show us the flexibility of the ME model.

Some other works that are built upon the models of Ratnaparkhi (1996) and Toutanova and Manning (2000) use bidirectional dependency networks (Toutanova et al., 2003; Tsuruoka and Tsujii, 2005). Unlike previous works, the information about the future tags is also taken into account and both left and right contexts are used simultaneously. The justification can be given by the following example:

```
will to fight ...
```

When tagging the word will, the tagger will prefer the (incorrect but most common) modal sense if only the left context (which is empty in this example) is examined. However, if the word on the right (to) is also included in the context, the fact that to is often preceded by a noun will force the correct tag for the word will. A detailed analysis of several combinations of left and right contexts reveal some useful results: the left context always carries more information than the right context, using both contexts increases the success rates, and symmetric use of the context is better than using (the same amount of) only left or right context (e.g., $t_{i-1}t_{i+1}$ is more informative than $t_{i-2}t_{i-1}$ and $t_{i+1}t_{i+2}$). Another strategy analyzed in Tsuruoka and Tsujii (2005) is called the easiest-first strategy, which, instead of tagging a sentence in left-to-right order, begins from the "easiest word" to tag and selects the easiest word among the remaining words at each step. The easiest word is defined as the word whose probability estimate is the highest. This strategy makes sense since a highly ambiguous word forced to be tagged early and tagged incorrectly will degrade the performance and it may be wiser to leave such words to the final steps where more information is available.

All methodologies used in POS tagging make the stationary assumption that the position of the target word within the sentence is irrelevant to the tagging process. However, this assumption is not always realistic. For example, when the word walk appears at the front of a sentence it usually indicates a physical exercise (corresponding to noun tag) and when it appears toward the end of a sentence it denotes an action (verb tag), as in the sentences:

```
A morning walk is a blessing for the whole day
It only takes me 20 minutes to walk to work
```

By relaxing this stationary assumption, a formalism called *nonstationary maximum entropy Markov model* (NS-MEMM), which is a generalization of the MEMM framework (McCallum et al., 2000), was proposed in Xiao et al. (2007). The model is decomposed into two component models, the *n*-gram model and the ME model:

$$P(t|h) = P(t|t')P_{\mathrm{ME}}(t|h) \qquad (10.6)$$

where t' denotes a number of previous tags (so, $P(t|t')$ corresponds to the transition probability). In order to incorporate position information into the model, sentences are divided into k bins such that the ith word of a sentence of length n takes part in (approximately) the $\lceil \frac{i}{n}k \rceil$th bin. For instance, for a 20-word sentence and $k = 4$, the first five words will be in the first bin, and so on. This additional parameter introduced into the model obviously increases the dimensionality of the model. Equation 10.6 is thus modified to include the position parameter p:

$$P(t|h,p) = P(t|t',p)P_{\mathrm{ME}}(t|h,p)$$

The experiments on three corpora showed improvement over the ME model and the MEMM. The number of bins ranged from 1 (ordinary MEMM) to 8. A significant error reduction was obtained for $k = 2$ and $k = 3$; beyond this point the behavior was less predictable.

Curran et al. (2006) employ ME tagging in a multi-tagging environment. As in other studies that preserve some ambiguity in the final tags, a word is assigned all the tags whose probabilities are within a factor of the probability of the most probable tag. To account for this, the forward–backward algorithm is adapted to the ME framework. During the test phase, a word is considered to be tagged correctly if the correct tag appears in the set of tags assigned to the word. The results on the CCGbank corpus show an accuracy of 99.7% with 1.40 tags/word.

10.4 Other Statistical and Machine Learning Approaches

There are a wide variety of learning paradigms in the machine learning literature (Alpaydın, 2004). However, the learning approaches other than the HMMs have not been used so widely for the POS tagging problem. This is probably due to the suitability of the HMM formalism to this problem and the high success rates obtained with HMMs in early studies. Nevertheless, all well-known learning paradigms have been applied to POS tagging in some degree. In this section, we list these approaches and cite a few typical studies that show how the tagging problem can be adapted to the underlying framework. The interested reader should refer to this chapter's section in the companion wiki for further details.

10.4.1 Methods and Relevant Work

- *Support vector machines.* Support vector machines (SVM) have two advantages over other models: they can easily handle high-dimensional spaces (i.e., large number of features) and they are usually more resistant to overfitting (see Nakagawa et al., 2002; Mayfield et al., 2003).

- *Neural networks.* Although neural network (NN) taggers do not in general seem to outperform the HMM taggers, they have some attractive properties. First, ambiguous tagging can be handled easily without additional computation. When the output nodes of a network correspond to the tags in the tagset, normally, given an input word and its context during the tagging phase, the output node with the highest activation is selected as the tag of the word. However, if there are several output nodes with close enough activation values, all of them can be given as candidate tags. Second, neural network taggers converge to top performances with small amounts of training data and they are suitable for languages for which large corpora are not available (see Schmid, 1994; Roth and Zelenko, 1998; Marques and Lopes, 2001; Pérez-Ortiz and Forcada, 2001; Raju et al., 2002).

- *Decision trees.* Decision trees (DT) and statistical decision trees (SDT) used in classification tasks, similar to rule-based systems, can cover more context and enable flexible feature representations, and also yield outputs easier to interpret. The most important criterion for the success of the learning algorithms based on DTs is the construction of a set of questions to be used in the decision procedure (see Black et al., 1992; Màrquez et al., 2000).

- *Finite state transducers.* Finite state machines are efficient devices that can be used in NLP tasks that require a sequential processing of inputs. In the POS tagging domain, the linguistic rules or the transitions between the tag states can be expressed in terms of finite state transducers (see Roche and Schabes, 1995; Kempe, 1997; Grāna et al., 2003; Villamil et al., 2004).

- *Genetic algorithms.* Although genetic algorithms have accuracies worse than those of HMM taggers and rule-based approaches, they can be seen as an efficient alternative in POS tagging. They reach performances near their top performances with small populations and a few iterations (see Araujo, 2002; Alba et al., 2006).

- *Fuzzy set theory.* The taggers formed using the fuzzy set theory are similar to HMM taggers, except that the lexical and transition probabilities are replaced by fuzzy membership functions. One advantage of these taggers is their high performances with small data sizes (see Kim and Kim, 1996; Kogut, 2002).

- *Machine translation ideas.* An approach used recently in the POS tagging domain and that is on a different track was inspired by the ideas used in machine translation (MT). Some of the works consider the sentences to be tagged as belonging to the source language and the corresponding tag sequences as the target language, and apply statistical machine translation techniques to find the correct "translation" of each sentence. Other works aim at discovering a mapping from the taggings in a source language (or several source languages) to the taggings in a target language. This is a useful approach when there is a shortage of annotated corpora or POS taggers for the target language (see Yarowsky et al., 2001; Fossum and Abney, 2005; Finch and Sumita, 2007; Mora and Peiró, 2007).

- *Others.* Logical programming (see Cussens, 1998; Lager and Nivre, 2001; Reiser and Riddle, 2001), dynamic Bayesian networks and cyclic dependency networks (see Peshkin et al., 2003; Reynolds and Bilmes, 2005; Tsuruoka et al., 2005), memory-based learning (see Daelemans et al., 1996), relaxation labeling (see Padró, 1996), robust risk minimization (see Ando, 2004), conditional random fields (see Lafferty et al., 2001), Markov random fields (see Jung et al., 1996), and latent semantic mapping (see Bellegarda, 2008).

It is worth mentioning here that there has also been some work on *POS induction*, a task that aims at dividing the words in a corpus into different categories such that each category corresponds to a part of speech (Schütze, 1993; Schütze, 1995; Clark, 2003; Freitag, 2004; Rapp, 2005; Portnoy and Bock, 2007). These studies mainly use clustering algorithms and rely on the distributional characteristics of the words in the text. The task of POS tagging is based on a predetermined tagset and therefore adopts the assumptions it embodies. However, this may not be appropriate always, especially when we are using texts from different genres or from different languages. So, labeling the words with tags that reflect the characteristics of the text in question may be better than trying to label with an inappropriate set of tags. In addition, POS induction has a cognitive science motivation in the sense that it aims at showing how the evidence in the linguistic data can account for language acquisition.

10.4.2 Combining Taggers

As we have seen in the previous sections, the POS tagging problem was approached using different machine learning techniques and 96%–97% accuracy seems a performance barrier for almost all of them. A question that may arise at this point is whether we can obtain better results by combining different taggers and/or models. It was observed that, although different taggers have similar performances, they usually produce different errors (Brill and Wu, 1998; Halteren et al., 2001). Based on this encouraging observation, we can benefit from using more than one tagger in such a way that each individual tagger deals with the cases where it is the best.

One way of combining taggers is using the output of one of the systems as input to the next system. An early application of this idea is given in Tapanainen and Voutilainen (1994), where a rule-based system first reduces the ambiguities in the initial tags of the words as much as possible and then an HMM-based tagger arrives at the final decision. The intuition behind this idea is that rules can resolve only some of the ambiguities but with a very high correctness and the stochastic tagger resolves all ambiguities but with a lower accuracy. The method proposed in Clark et al. (2003) is somewhat different and it investigates the effect of co-training, where two taggers are iteratively retrained on each other's output. The taggers should be sufficiently different (e.g., based on different models) for co-training to be effective. This approach is suitable in cases when there is a small amount of annotated corpora. Beginning from a seed set (annotated sentences), both of the taggers (T1 and T2) are trained initially. Then the taggers are used to tag a set of unannotated sentences. The output of T1 is added to the seed set and used to retrain T2; likewise, the output of T2 is added to the seed set to retrain T1. The process is repeated using a new set of unannotated sentences at each iteration.

The second way in combining taggers is letting each tagger to tag the same data and selecting one of the outputs according to a voting strategy. Some of the common voting strategies are given in Brill and Wu (1998); Halteren et al. (2001); Mihalcea (2003); Glass and Bangay (2005); Yonghui et al. (2006):

- *Simple voting.* The tag decided by the largest number of the taggers is selected (by using an appropriate method for breaking the ties).
- *Weighted voting* 1. The decisions of the taggers are weighted based on their general performances, that is, the higher the accuracy of a tagger, the larger its weight.
- *Weighted voting* 2. This is similar to the previous one, except that the performance on the target word (certainty of the tagger on the current situation) is used as the weight instead of the general performance.
- *Ranked voting.* This is similar to the weighted voting schemes, except that the ranks (1, 2, etc.) of the taggers are used as weights, where the best tagger is given the highest rank.

The number of taggers in the combined tagger normally ranges from two to five and they should have different structures for an effective combination. Except Glass and Bangay (2005), the mentioned studies observed an improvement in the success rates. Glass and Bangay (2005) report that the accuracies of the combined taggers are in between the accuracies of the best and the worst individual taggers, and it is not always true that increasing the number of taggers yields better results (e.g., a two-tagger combination may outperform a five-tagger combination). The discouraging results obtained in this study may be partly due to the peculiarities of the domain and the tagset used. Despite this observation, we can in general expect a performance increase by the combination of different taggers.

10.5 POS Tagging in Languages Other Than English

As in other fields of NLP, most of the research on POS tagging takes English as the language of choice. The motivation in this choice is being able to compare the proposed models (new models or variations of existing models) with previous work. The success of stochastic methods largely depends on the availability of language resources—lexicons and corpora. Beginning from 1960s, such resources have begun to be developed for the English language (e.g., Brown corpus). This availability enabled the researchers to concentrate on the modeling issue, rather than the data issue, in developing more sophisticated approaches.

However, this is not the case for other (especially non-Indo-European) languages. Until recently there was a scarcity of data sources for these languages. As new corpora begin to appear, research attempts in the NLP domain begin to increase. In addition, these languages have different morphological and syntactic characteristics than English. A naive application of a POS tagger developed with English in mind may not always work. Therefore, the peculiarities of these languages should be taken into account and the underlying framework should be adapted to these languages while developing POS taggers.

In this section, we first concentrate on two languages (that do not belong to the Indo-European family) that are widely studied in the POS tagging domain. The first one, Chinese, is typical in its word segmentation issues; the other one, Korean, is typical in its agglutinative nature. We briefly mention the characteristics of these languages from a tagging perspective. Then we explain the solutions to these issues proposed in the literature.

There are plenty of research efforts related to POS tagging of other languages. These studies range from sophisticated studies for well-known languages (e.g., Spanish, German) to those in primitive stages of development (e.g., for Vietnamese). The works in the first group follow a similar track as those for English. They exploit the main formalisms used in POS tagging and adapt these strategies to the particular languages. We have not included these works in previous parts of this chapter and instead we have mostly considered the works on English, because of being able to do a fair comparison between methodologies. The works in the second group are usually in the form of applying the well-known models to those languages.

10.5.1 Chinese

A property of the Chinese language that makes POS tagging more difficult than languages such as English is that the sentences are written without spaces between the characters. For example, two possible segmentations of the underlined part of the sentence

他俩儿谈恋爱是从头年元月开始的

are

(a) ...　是　|　从头　|　年　|　元月

　　　　V　　ADV　　TIME–CLASSIFIER　　TIME–N

(b) ...　是　|　从　|　头年　|　元月　...

　　　　V　　PREP　　TIME–N　　TIME–N

Since POS tagging depends on how the sentence is divided into words, a successful word segmentation is a prerequisite for a tagger. In some works on Chinese POS tagging, a correctly segmented word sequence is assumed as input. However, this may not always be a realistic assumption and a better approach is integrating these two tasks in such a way that any one of them may contribute to the success of the other. For instance, a particular segmentation that seems as the best one to the word segmentation component may be rejected due to its improper tagging. Another property of the Chinese language is the difference of its morphological and syntactic structures. Chinese grammar focuses on the word order rather than the morphological variations. Thus, transition information contributes more to POS tagging than morphological information. This property also indicates that unknown word processing should be somewhat different from English-like languages.

The works in Sun et al. (2006) and Zhou and Su (2003) concentrate on integrating word segmentation and POS tagging. Given a sentence, possible segmentations and all possible taggings for each segmentation are taken into account. Then the most likely path, a sequence of (word, tag) pairs, is determined using a Viterbi-like algorithm. Accuracies about 93%–95% were obtained, where it was measured in terms of both correctly identified segments and tags. Zhang and Clark (2008) formulate the word segmentation and POS tagging tasks as a single problem, take the union of the features of each task as the features of the joint system, and apply the perceptron algorithm of Collins (2002). Since the search space formed of combined (word, tag) pairs is very large, a novel multiple beam search algorithm is used, which keeps track of a list of candidate parses for each character in the sentence and thus avoids limiting the search space as in previous studies. A comparison with the two-stage (word segmentation followed by POS tagging) system showed an improvement of about 10%–15% in F-measure.

Maximum entropy framework is used in Zhao et al. (2007) and Lin and Yuan (2002). Since the performance of the ME models is sensitive to the features used, some features that take the characteristics of the language into account are included in the models. An example of an HMM-based system is given in Cao et al. (2005). Instead of using the probability distributions in the standard HMM formalism, it combines the transition and lexical probabilities as

$$\arg\max_T \prod_{i=1}^{n} P(t_i, w_i | t_{i-1}, w_{i-1})$$

and then converts into the following form to alleviate data sparseness:

$$\arg\max_T \prod_{i=1}^{n} P(t_i | t_{i-1}, w_{i-1}) P(w_i | t_{i-1}, w_{i-1}, t_i)$$

A tagger that combines rule-based and HMM-based processes in a cascaded manner is proposed in Ning et al. (2007). It first reduces the ambiguity in the initial assignment of the tags by employing a TBL-like process. Then HMM training is performed on this less ambiguous data. The accuracy results for Chinese POS tagging are around 92%–94% for open test (test data contains unknown words) and 96%–98% for closed test (no unknown words in the test data). Finally, we should mention an interesting study that is about Classical Chinese, which has some grammatical differences from Modern Chinese (Huang et al., 2002).

10.5.2 Korean

Korean, which belongs to the group of Altaic languages, is an agglutinative language and has a very productive morphology. In theory, the number of possible morphological variants of a given word can be in tens of thousands. For such languages, a word-based tagging approach does not work due to the sparse data problem. Since there exist several surface forms corresponding to a base form, the number of out-of-vocabulary words will be very large and the estimates from the corpus will not be reliable. A common solution to this problem is morpheme-based tagging: each morpheme (either a base form or an affix) is tagged separately. Thus, the problem of POS tagging changes into the problem of morphological tagging (morphological disambiguation) for agglutinative languages: we tag each morpheme separately and then combine. As an example, Figure 10.3 shows the morpheme structure of the Korean sentence na-neun hag-gyo-e gan-da (I go to school). Straight lines indicate the word boundaries, dashed lines indicate the morpheme boundaries, and the correct tagging is given by the thick lines.

The studies in Lee et al. (2000b), Lee and Rim (2004), and Kang et al. (2007) apply n-gram and HMM models to the Korean POS tagging problem. For instance, Lee et al. (2000b) propose the following morpheme-based version of the HMM model:

$$\prod_{i=1}^{u} P(c_i, p_i | c_{i-1} \ldots c_{i-K}, p_{i-1} \ldots p_{i-K}, m_{i-1} \ldots m_{i-J}) P(m_i | c_i \ldots c_{i-L}, p_i \ldots p_{i-L+1}, m_{i-1} \ldots m_{i-I})$$

(10.7)

where
   u is the number of morphemes
   c denotes a (morpheme) tag
   m is a morpheme
   p is a binary parameter (e.g., 0 and 1) differentiating transitions across a word boundary and transitions within a word

The indices K, J, L and I range from 0 to 2. In fact, Equation 10.7 is analogous to a word-based HMM equation if we regard m as word (w) and c as tag (t) (and ignore p's).

Han and Palmer (2005) and Ahn and Seo (2007) combine statistical methods with rule-based disambiguation. In Ahn and Seo (2007), different sets of rules are used to identify the idiomatic constructs and to resolve the ambiguities in highly ambiguous words. The rules eliminate some of the taggings and then an HMM executes in order to arrive at the final tag sequence. When a word is inflected in Korean, the base form of the word and/or the suffix may change their forms (by character deletion or by contraction), forming allomorphs. Before POS tagging, Han and Palmer (2005) attempt to recover the original forms of the words and the suffixes by using rule templates extracted from the corpus. Then an n-gram approach tags the given sentence in the standard way. The accuracies obtained by these works are between 94% and 97%.

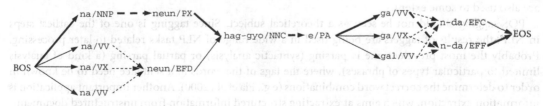

FIGURE 10.3 Morpheme structure of the sentence *na-neun hag-gyo-e gan-da*. (From Lee, D. and Rim, H., Part-of-speech tagging considering surface form for an agglutinative language, in *Proceedings of the ACL*, ACL, Barcelona, Spain, 2004. With permission.)

10.5.3 Other Languages

We can cite the following works related to POS tagging for different language families and groups. By no means we claim that the groups presented below are definite (this is a profession of linguists) nor the languages included are exhaustive. We simply mention some worth-noting studies in a wide coverage of languages. The interested readers can refer to the cited references.

- *Indo-European languages.* Spanish (Triviño-Rodriguez and Morales-Bueno, 2001; Jiménez and Morales, 2002; Carrasco and Gelbukh, 2003), Portuguese (Lopes and Jorge, 2000; Kepler and Finger, 2006), Dutch (Prins, 2004; Poel et al., 2007), Swedish (Eineborg and Lindberg, 2000), Greek (Maragoudakis et al., 2004).
- *Agglutinative and inflectional languages.* Japanese (Asahara and Matsumoto, 2000; Ma, 2002), Turkish (Altunyurt et al., 2007; Sak et al., 2007; Dinçer et al., 2008), Czech (Hajič and Hladká, 1997; Hajič, 2000; Oliva et al., 2000), Slovene (Cussens et al., 1999).
- *Semitic languages.* Arabic (Habash and Rambow, 2005; Zribi et al., 2006), Hebrew (Bar-Haim et al., 2008).
- *Tai languages.* Thai (Ma et al., 2000; Murata et al., 2002; Lu et al., 2003).
- *Other less-studied languages.* Kannada (Vikram and Urs, 2007), Afrikaans (Trushkina, 2007), Telugu (Kumar and Kumar, 2007), Urdu (Anwar et al., 2007), Uyghur (Altenbek, 2006), Kiswahili (Pauw et al., 2006), Vietnamese (Dien and Kiem, 2003), Persian (Mohseni et al., 2008), Bulgarian (Doychinova and Mihov, 2004).

10.6 Conclusion

One of the earliest steps in the processing of natural language text is POS tagging. Usually this is a sentence-based process and given a sentence formed of a sequence of words, we try to assign the correct POS tag to each word. There are basically two difficulties in POS tagging. The first one is the ambiguity in the words, meaning that most of the words in a language have more than one part of speech. The second difficulty arises from the unknown words, the words for which the tagger has no knowledge about. The classical solution to the POS tagging problem is taking the context around the target word into account and selecting the most probable tag for the word by making use of the information provided by the context words.

In this chapter, we surveyed a wide variety of techniques for the POS tagging problem. We can divide these techniques into two broad categories: rule-based methods and statistical methods. The former one was used by the early taggers that attempt to label the words by using a number of linguistic rules. Normally these rules are manually compiled, which is the major drawback of such methods. Later the rule-based systems began to be replaced by statistical systems as sufficient language resources became available. The HMM framework is the most widely used statistical approach for the POS tagging problem. This is probably due to the fact that HMM is a suitable formalism for this problem and it resulted in high success rates in early studies. However, nearly all of the other statistical and machine learning methods are also used to some extent.

POS tagging should not be seen as a theoretical subject. Since tagging is one of the earliest steps in NLP, the results of taggers are being used in a wide range of NLP tasks related to later processing. Probably the most prevalent one is parsing (syntactic analysis) or partial parsing (a kind of analysis limited to particular types of phrases), where the tags of the words in a sentence need to be known in order to determine the correct word combinations (e.g., Pla et al., 2000). Another important application is information extraction, which aims at extracting structured information from unstructured documents. Named-entity recognition, a subtask of information extraction, makes use of tagging and partial parsing in identifying the entities we are interested in and the relationships between these entities (Cardie, 1997). Information retrieval and question answering systems also make use of the outputs of taggers. The performance of such systems can be improved if they work on a phrase basis rather than treating each word individually (e.g., Cowie et al., 2000). Finally, we can cite lexical acquisition, machine translation, word-sense disambiguation, and phrase normalization as other research areas that rely on the information provided by taggers.

The state-of-the-art accuracies in POS tagging are around 96%–97% for English-like languages. For languages in other families, similar accuracies are obtained provided that the characteristics of these languages different from English are carefully handled. This seems a quite high accuracy and some researchers argue that POS tagging is an already-solved problem. However, since POS tagging serves as a preprocessing step for higher-level NLP operations, a small improvement has the potential of significantly increasing the quality of later processing. Therefore, we may expect a continuing research effort on this task.

References

Ahn, Y. and Y. Seo. 2007. Korean part-of-speech tagging using disambiguation rules for ambiguous word and statistical information. In *ICCIT*, pp. 1598–1601, Gyeongju, Republic of Korea. IEEE.

Alba, E., G. Luque, and L. Araujo. 2006. Natural language tagging with genetic algorithms. *Information Processing Letters* 100(5):173–182.

Alpaydın, E. 2004. *Introduction to Machine Learning*. MIT Press, Cambridge, MA.

Altenbek, G. 2006. Automatic morphological tagging of contemporary Uighur corpus. In *IRI*, pp. 557–560, Waikoloa Village, HI. IEEE.

Altunyurt, L., Z. Orhan, and T. Güngör. 2007. Towards combining rule-based and statistical part of speech tagging in agglutinative languages. *Computer Engineering* 1(1):66–69.

Anderson, J.M. 1997. *A Notional Theory of Syntactic Categories*. Cambridge University Press, Cambridge, U.K.

Ando, R.K. 2004. Exploiting unannotated corpora for tagging and chunking. In *ACL*, Barcelona, Spain. ACL.

Anwar, W., X. Wang, L. Li, and X. Wang. 2007. A statistical based part of speech tagger for Urdu language. In *ICMLC*, pp. 3418–3424, Hong Kong. IEEE.

Araujo, L. 2002. Part-of-speech tagging with evolutionary algorithms. In *CICLing*, ed. A. Gelbukh, pp. 230–239, Mexico. Springer.

Asahara, M. and Y. Matsumoto. 2000. Extended models and tools for high-performance part-of-speech tagger. In *COLING*, pp. 21–27, Saarbrücken, Germany. Morgan Kaufmann.

Bahl, L.R. and R.L. Mercer. 1976. Part-of-speech assignment by a statistical decision algorithm. In *ISIT*, pp. 88–89, Sweden. IEEE.

Baker, M.C. 2003. *Lexical Categories: Verbs, Nouns, and Adjectives*. Cambridge University Press, Cambridge, U.K.

Banko, M. and R.C. Moore. 2004. Part of speech tagging in context. In *COLING*, pp. 556–561, Geneva, Switzerland. ACL.

Bar-Haim, R., K. Sima'an, and Y. Winter. 2008. Part-of-speech tagging of modern Hebrew text. *Natural Language Engineering* 14(2):223–251.

Bellegarda, J.R. 2008. A novel approach to part-of-speech tagging based on latent analogy. In *ICASSP*, pp. 4685–4688, Las Vegas, NV. IEEE.

Black, E., F. Jelinek, J. Lafferty, R. Mercer, and S. Roukos. 1992. Decision tree models applied to the labeling of text with parts-of-speech. In *HLT*, pp. 117–121, New York. ACL.

Boggess, L., J.S. Hamaker, R. Duncan, L. Klimek, Y. Wu, and Y. Zeng. 1999. A comparison of part of speech taggers in the task of changing to a new domain. In *ICIIS*, pp. 574–578, Washington, DC. IEEE.

Brants, T. 2000. TnT—A statistical part-of-speech tagger. In *ANLP*, pp. 224–231, Seattle, WA.

Brill, E. 1995a. Transformation-based error-driven learning and natural language processing: A case study in part-of-speech tagging. *Computational Linguistics* 21(4):543–565.

Brill, E. 1995b. Unsupervised learning of disambiguation rules for part of speech tagging. In *Workshop on Very Large Corpora*, eds. D. Yarowsky and K. Church, pp. 1–13, Somerset, NJ. ACL.

Brill, E. and J. Wu. 1998. Classifier combination for improved lexical disambiguation. In *COLING-ACL*, pp. 191–195, Montreal, QC. ACL/Morgan Kaufmann.

Cao, H., T. Zhao, S. Li, J. Sun, and C. Zhang. 2005. Chinese pos tagging based on bilexical co-occurrences. In *ICMLC*, pp. 3766–3769, Guangzhou, China. IEEE.

Carberry, S., K. Vijay-Shanker, A. Wilson, and K. Samuel. 2001. Randomized rule selection in transformation-based learning: A comparative study. *Natural Language Engineering* 7(2):99–116.

Cardie, C. 1997. Empirical methods in information extraction. *AI Magazine* 18(4):65–79.

Carrasco, R.M. and A. Gelbukh. 2003. Evaluation of TnT tagger for Spanish. In *ENC*, pp. 18–25, Mexico. IEEE.

Church, K.W. 1988. A stochastic parts program and noun phrase parser for unrestricted text. In *ANLP*, pp. 136–143, Austin, TX.

Clark, A. 2003. Combining distributional and morphological information for part of speech induction. In *EACL*, pp. 59–66, Budapest, Hungary.

Clark, S., J.R. Curran, and M. Osborne. 2003. Bootstrapping pos taggers using unlabelled data. In *CoNLL*, pp. 49–55, Edmonton, AB.

Collins, M. 2002. Discriminative training methods for hidden Markov models: Theory and experiments with perceptron algorithms. In *EMNLP*, pp. 1–8, Philadelphia, PA. ACL.

Cowie, J., E. Ludovik, H. Molina-Salgado, S. Nirenburg, and S. Scheremetyeva. 2000. Automatic question answering. In *RIAO*, Paris, France. ACL.

Cucerzan, S. and D. Yarowsky. 2000. Language independent, minimally supervised induction of lexical probabilities. In *ACL*, Hong Kong. ACL.

Curran, J.R. and S. Clark. 2003. Investigating GIS and smoothing for maximum entropy taggers. In *EACL*, pp. 91–98, Budapest, Hungary.

Curran, J.R., S. Clark, and D. Vadas. 2006. Multi-tagging for lexicalized-grammar parsing. In *COLING/ACL*, pp. 697–704, Sydney, NSW. ACL.

Cussens, J. 1998. Using prior probabilities and density estimation for relational classification. In *ILP*, pp. 106–115, Madison, WI. Springer.

Cussens, J., S. Džeroski, and T. Erjavec. 1999. Morphosyntactic tagging of Slovene using Progol. In *ILP*, eds. S. Džeroski and P. Flach, pp. 68–79, Bled, Slovenia. Springer.

Cutting, D., J. Kupiec, J. Pedersen, and P. Sibun. 1992. A practical part-of-speech tagger. In *ANLP*, pp. 133–140, Trento, Italy.

Daelemans, W., J. Zavrel, P. Berck, and S. Gillis. 1996. MBT: A memory-based part of speech tagger-generator. In *Workshop on Very Large Corpora*, eds. E. Ejerhed and I. Dagan, pp. 14–27, Copenhagen, Denmark. ACL.

Darroch, J.N. and D. Ratcliff. 1972. Generalized iterative scaling for log-linear models. *The Annals of Mathematical Statistics* 43(5):1470–1480.

Dermatas, E. and G. Kokkinakis. 1995. Automatic stochastic tagging of natural language texts. *Computational Linguistics* 21(2):137–163.

Dickinson, M. and W.D. Meurers. 2003. Detecting errors in part-of-speech annotation. In *EACL*, pp. 107–114, Budapest, Hungary.

Dien, D. and H. Kiem. 2003. Pos-tagger for English-Vietnamese bilingual corpus. In *HLT-NAACL*, pp. 88–95, Edmonton, AB. ACL.

Dinçer, T., B. Karaoğlan, and T. Kışla. 2008. A suffix based part-of-speech tagger for Turkish. In *ITNG*, pp. 680–685, Las Vegas, NV. IEEE.

Doychinova, V. and S. Mihov. 2004. High performance part-of-speech tagging of Bulgarian. In *AIMSA*, eds. C. Bussler and D. Fensel, pp. 246–255, Varna, Bulgaria. Springer.

Eineborg, M. and N. Lindberg. 2000. ILP in part-of-speech tagging—An overview. In *LLL*, eds. J. Cussens and S. Džeroski, pp. 157–169, Lisbon, Portugal. Springer.

Finch, A. and E. Sumita. 2007. Phrase-based part-of-speech tagging. In *NLP-KE*, pp. 215–220, Beijing, China. IEEE.

Florian, R. and G. Ngai. 2001. Multidimensional transformation-based learning. In *CONLL*, pp. 1–8, Toulouse, France. ACL.

Fossum, V. and S. Abney. 2005. Automatically inducing a part-of-speech tagger by projecting from multiple source languages across aligned corpora. In *IJCNLP*, eds. R. Dale et al., pp. 862–873, Jeju Island, Republic of Korea. Springer.

Freitag, D. 2004. Toward unsupervised whole-corpus tagging. In *COLING*, pp. 357–363, Geneva, Switzerland. ACL.

Glass, K. and S. Bangay. 2005. Evaluating parts-of-speech taggers for use in a text-to-scene conversion system. In *SAICSIT*, pp. 20–28, White River, South Africa.

Grãna, J., G. Andrade, and J. Vilares. 2003. Compilation of constraint-based contextual rules for part-of-speech tagging into finite state transducers. In *CIAA*, eds. J.M. Champarnaud and D. Maurel, pp. 128–137, Santa Barbara, CA. Springer.

Grzymala-Busse, J.W. and L.J. Old. 1997. A machine learning experiment to determine part of speech from word-endings. In *ISMIS*, pp. 497–506, Charlotte, NC. Springer.

Habash, N. and O. Rambow. 2005. Arabic tokenization, part-of-speech tagging and morphological disambiguation in one fell swoop. In *ACL*, pp. 573–580, Ann Arbor, MI. ACL.

Hajič, J. 2000. Morphological tagging: Data vs. dictionaries. In *ANLP*, pp. 94–101, Seattle, WA. Morgan Kaufmann.

Hajič, J. and B. Hladká. 1997. Probabilistic and rule-based tagger of an inflective language—A comparison. In *ANLP*, pp. 111–118, Washington, DC. Morgan Kaufmann.

Halteren, H.v., J. Zavrel, and W. Daelemans. 2001. Improving accuracy in word class tagging through the combination of machine learning systems. *Computational Linguistics* 27(2):199–229.

Han, C. and M. Palmer. 2005. A morphological tagger for Korean: Statistical tagging combined with corpus-based morphological rule application. *Machine Translation* 18:275–297.

Huang, L., Y. Peng, H. Wang, and Z. Wu. 2002. Statistical part-of-speech tagging for classical Chinese. In *TSD*, eds. P. Sojka, I. Kopeček, and K. Pala, pp. 115–122, Brno, Czech Republic. Springer.

Jiménez, H. and G. Morales. 2002. Sepe: A pos tagger for Spanish. In *CICLing*, ed. A. Gelbukh, pp. 250–259, Mexico. Springer.

Jung, S., Y.C. Park, K. Choi, and Y. Kim. 1996. Markov random field based English part-of-speech tagging system. In *COLING*, pp. 236–242, Copenhagen, Denmark. ACL.

Kang, M., S. Jung, K. Park, and H. Kwon. 2007. Part-of-speech tagging using word probability based on category patterns. In *CICLing*, ed. A. Gelbukh, pp. 119–130, Mexico. Springer.

Kempe, A. 1997. Finite state transducers approximating hidden Markov models. In *EACL*, eds. P.R. Cohen and W. Wahlster, pp. 460–467, Madrid, Spain. ACL.

Kepler, F.N. and M. Finger. 2006. Comparing two Markov methods for part-of-speech tagging of Portuguese. In *IBERAMIA-SBIA*, eds. J.S. Sichman et al., pp. 482–491, Ribeirão Preto, Brazil. Springer.

Kim, J. and G.C. Kim. 1996. Fuzzy network model for part-of-speech tagging under small training data. *Natural Language Engineering* 2(2):95–110.

Kim, J., H. Rim, and J. Tsujii. 2003. Self-organizing Markov models and their application to part-of-speech tagging. In *ACL*, pp. 296–302, Sapporo, Japan. ACL.

Klein, S. and R. Simpson. 1963. A computational approach to grammatical coding of English words. *Journal of ACM* 10(3):334–347.

Kogut, D.J. 2002. Fuzzy set tagging. In *CICLing*, ed. A. Gelbukh, pp. 260–263, Mexico. Springer.

Kumar, S.S. and S.A. Kumar. 2007. Parts of speech disambiguation in Telugu. In *ICCIMA*, pp. 125–128, Sivakasi, Tamilnadu, India. IEEE.

Kvĕton, P. and K. Oliva. 2002a. Achieving an almost correct pos-tagged corpus. In *TSD*, eds. P. Sojka, I. Kopeček, and K. Pala, pp. 19–26, Brno, Czech Republic. Springer.

Kvĕton, P. and K. Oliva. 2002b. (Semi-)Automatic detection of errors in pos-tagged corpora. In *COLING*, pp. 1–7, Taipei, Taiwan. ACL.

Lafferty, J., A. McCallum, and F. Pereira. 2001. Conditional random fields: Probabilistic models for segmenting and labeling sequence data. In *ICML*, eds. C.E. Brodley and A.P. Danyluk, pp. 282–289, Williamstown, MA. Morgan Kaufmann.

Lager, T. and J. Nivre. 2001. Part of speech tagging from a logical point of view. In *LACL*, eds. P. de Groote, G. Morrill, and C. Retoré, pp. 212–227, Le Croisic, France. Springer.

Lee, D. and H. Rim. 2004. Part-of-speech tagging considering surface form for an agglutinative language. In *ACL*, Barcelona, Spain. ACL.

Lee, G.G., J. Cha, and J. Lee. 2002. Syllable-pattern-based unknown-morpheme segmentation and estimation for hybrid part-of-speech tagging of Korean. *Computational Linguistics* 28(1):53–70.

Lee, S., J. Tsujii, and H. Rim. 2000a. Part-of-speech tagging based on hidden Markov model assuming joint independence. In *ACL*, pp. 263–269, Hong Kong. ACL.

Lee, S., J. Tsujii, and H. Rim. 2000b. Hidden Markov model-based Korean part-of-speech tagging considering high agglutinativity, word-spacing, and lexical correlativity. In *ACL*, pp. 384–391, Hong Kong. ACL.

Lin, H. and C. Yuan. 2002. Chinese part of speech tagging based on maximum entropy method. In *ICMLC*, pp. 1447–1450, Beijing, China. IEEE.

Lopes, A.d.A. and A. Jorge. 2000. Combining rule-based and case-based learning for iterative part-of-speech tagging. In *EWCBR*, eds. E. Blanzieri and L. Portinale, pp. 26–36, Trento, Italy. Springer.

Lu, B., Q. Ma, M. Ichikawa, and H. Isahara. 2003. Efficient part-of-speech tagging with a min-max modular neural-network model. *Applied Intelligence* 19:65–81.

Ma, Q. 2002. Natural language processing with neural networks. In *LEC*, pp. 45–56, Hyderabad, India. IEEE.

Ma, Q., M. Murata, K. Uchimoto, and H. Isahara. 2000. Hybrid neuro and rule-based part of speech taggers. In *COLING*, pp. 509–515, Saarbrücken, Germany. Morgan Kaufmann.

Manning, C.D. and H. Schütze. 2002. *Foundations of Statistical Natural Language Processing*. 5th ed., MIT Press, Cambridge, MA.

Maragoudakis, M., T. Ganchev, and N. Fakotakis. 2004. Bayesian reinforcement for a probabilistic neural net part-of-speech tagger. In *TSD*, eds. P. Sojka, I. Kopeček, and K. Pala, pp. 137–145, Brno, Czech Republic. Springer.

Marcus, M.P., B. Santorini, and M.A. Marcinkiewicz. 1993. Building a large annotated corpus of English: The Penn treebank. *Computational Linguistics* 19(2):313–330.

Marques, N.C. and G.P. Lopes. 2001. Tagging with small training corpora. In *IDA*, eds. F. Hoffmann, D.J. Hand, N.M. Adams, D.H. Fisher, and G. Guimaraes, pp. 63–72, Cascais, Lisbon. Springer.

Màrquez, L., L. Padró, and H. Rodríguez. 2000. A machine learning approach to pos tagging. *Machine Learning* 39:59–91.

Mayfield, J., P. McNamee, C. Piatko, and C. Pearce. 2003. Lattice-based tagging using support vector machines. In *CIKM*, pp. 303–308, New Orleans, LA. ACM.

McCallum, A., D. Freitag, and F. Pereira. 2000. Maximum entropy Markov models for information extraction and segmentation. In *ICML*, pp. 591–598, Stanford, CA. Morgan Kaufmann.

Merialdo, B. 1994. Tagging English text with a probabilistic model. *Computational Linguistics* 20(2): 155–171.

Mihalcea, R. 2003. Performance analysis of a part of speech tagging task. In *CICLing*, ed. A. Gelbukh, pp. 158–167, Mexico. Springer.

Mikheev, A. 1997. Automatic rule induction for unknown-word guessing. *Computational Linguistics* 23(3):405–423.

Mohammed, S. and T. Pedersen. 2003. Guaranteed pre-tagging for the Brill tagger. In *CICLing*, ed. A. Gelbukh, pp. 148–157, Mexico. Springer.

Mohseni, M., H. Motalebi, B. Minaei-bidgoli, and M. Shokrollahi-far. 2008. A Farsi part-of-speech tagger based on Markov model. In *SAC*, pp. 1588–1589, Ceará, Brazil. ACM.

Mora, G.G. and J.A.S. Peiró. 2007. Part-of-speech tagging based on machine translation techniques. In *IbPRIA*, eds. J. Martí et al., pp. 257–264, Girona, Spain. Springer.

Murata, M., Q. Ma, and H. Isahara. 2002. Comparison of three machine-learning methods for Thai part-of-speech tagging. *ACM Transactions on Asian Language Information Processing* 1(2):145–158.

Nagata, M. 1999. A part of speech estimation method for Japanese unknown words using a statistical model of morphology and context. In *ACL*, pp. 277–284, College Park, MD.

Nakagawa, T., T. Kudo, and Y. Matsumoto. 2002. Revision learning and its application to part-of-speech tagging. In *ACL*, pp. 497–504, Philadelphia, PA. ACL.

Nakagawa, T. and Y. Matsumoto. 2006. Guessing parts-of-speech of unknown words using global information. In *CL-ACL*, pp. 705–712, Sydney, NSW. ACL.

Nasr, A., F. Béchet, and A. Volanschi. 2004. Tagging with hidden Markov models using ambiguous tags. In *COLING*, pp. 569–575, Geneva. ACL.

Ning, H., H. Yang, and Z. Li. 2007. A method integrating rule and HMM for Chinese part-of-speech tagging. In *ICIEA*, pp. 723–725, Harbin, China. IEEE.

Oliva, K., M. Hnátková, V. Petkevič, and P. Květon. 2000. The linguistic basis of a rule-based tagger for Czech. In *TSD*, eds. P. Sojka, I. Kopeček, and K. Pala, pp. 3–8, Brno, Czech Republic. Springer.

Padró, L. 1996. Pos tagging using relaxation labelling. In *COLING*, pp. 877–882, Copenhagen, Denmark.

Pauw, G., G. Schyver, and W. Wagacha. 2006. Data-driven part-of-speech tagging of Kiswahili. In *TSD*, eds. P. Sojka, I. Kopeček, and K. Pala, pp. 197–204, Brno, Czech Republic. Springer.

Pérez-Ortiz, J.A. and M.L. Forcada. 2001. Part-of-speech tagging with recurrent neural networks. In *IJCNN*, pp. 1588–1592, Washington, DC. IEEE.

Peshkin, L., A. Pfeffer, and V. Savova. 2003. Bayesian nets in syntactic categorization of novel words. In *HLT-NAACL*, pp. 79–81, Edmonton, AB. ACL.

Pla, F. and A. Molina. 2004. Improving part-of-speech tagging using lexicalized HMMs. *Natural Language Engineering* 10(2):167–189.

Pla, F., A. Molina, and N. Prieto. 2000. Tagging and chunking with bigrams. In *COLING*, pp. 614–620, Saarbrücken, Germany. ACL.

Poel, M., L. Stegeman, and R. op den Akker. 2007. A support vector machine approach to Dutch part-of-speech tagging. In *IDA*, eds. M.R. Berthold, J. Shawe-Taylor, and N. Lavrač, pp. 274–283, Ljubljana, Slovenia. Springer.

Portnoy, D. and P. Bock. 2007. Automatic extraction of the multiple semantic and syntactic categories of words. In *AIAP*, pp. 514–519, Innsbruck, Austria.

Prins, R. 2004. Beyond n in n-gram tagging. In *ACL*, Barcelona, Spain. ACL.

Pustet, R. 2003. *Copulas: Universals in the Categorization of the Lexicon*. Oxford University Press, Oxford, U.K.

Raju, S.B., P.V.S. Chandrasekhar, and M.K. Prasad. 2002. Application of multilayer perceptron network for tagging parts-of-speech. In *LEC*, pp. 57–63, Hyderabad, India. IEEE.

Ramshaw, L.A. and M.P. Marcus. 1994. Exploring the statistical derivation of transformation rule sequences for part-of-speech tagging. In *ACL*, pp. 86–95, Las Cruces, NM. ACL/Morgan Kaufmann.

Rapp, R. 2005. A practical solution to the problem of automatic part-of-speech induction from text. In *ACL*, pp. 77–80, Ann Arbor, MI. ACL.

Ratnaparkhi, A. 1996. A maximum entropy model for part-of-speech tagging. In *EMNLP*, eds. E. Brill and K. Church, pp. 133–142, Philadelphia, PA. ACL.

Ratnaparkhi, A. 1998. Maximum entropy models for natural language ambiguity resolution. PhD dissertation, University of Pennsylvania, Philadelphia, PA.

Reiser, P.G.K. and P.J. Riddle. 2001. Scaling up inductive logic programming: An evolutionary wrapper approach. *Applied Intelligence* 15:181–197.

Reynolds, S.M. and J.A. Bilmes. 2005. Part-of-speech tagging using virtual evidence and negative training. In *HLT-EMNLP*, pp. 459–466, Vancouver, BC. ACL.

Roche, E. and Y. Schabes. 1995. Deterministic part-of-speech tagging with finite-state transducers. *Computational Linguistics* 21(2):227–253.

Rocio, V., J. Silva, and G. Lopes. 2007. Detection of strange and wrong automatic part-of-speech tagging. In *EPIA*, eds. J. Neves, M. Santos, and J. Machado, pp. 683–690, Guimarães, Portugal. Springer.

Roth, D. and D. Zelenko. 1998. Part of speech tagging using a network of linear separators. In *COLING-ACL*, pp. 1136–1142, Montreal, QC. ACL/Morgan Kaufmann.

Sak, H., T. Güngör, and M. Saraçlar. 2007. Morphological disambiguation of Turkish text with perceptron algorithm. In *CICLing*, ed. A. Gelbukh, pp. 107–118, Mexico. Springer.

Schmid, H. 1994. Part-of-speech tagging with neural networks. In *COLING*, pp. 172–176, Kyoto, Japan. ACL.

Schütze, H. 1993. Part-of-speech induction from scratch. In *ACL*, pp. 251–258, Columbus, OH. ACL.

Schütze, H. 1995. Distributional part-of-speech tagging. In *EACL*, pp. 141–148, Belfield, Dublin. Morgan Kaufmann.

Schütze, H. and Y. Singer. 1994. Part-of-speech tagging using a variable memory Markov model. In *ACL*, pp. 181–187, Las Cruces, NM. ACL/Morgan Kaufmann.

Sun, M., D. Xu, B.K. Tsou, and H. Lu. 2006. An integrated approach to Chinese word segmentation and part-of-speech tagging. In *ICCPOL*, eds. Y. Matsumoto et al., pp. 299–309, Singapore. Springer.

Sündermann, D. and H. Ney. 2003. Synther—A new m-gram pos tagger. In *NLP-KE*, pp. 622–627, Beijing, China. IEEE.

Tapanainen, P. and A. Voutilainen. 1994. Tagging accurately—Don't guess if you know. In *ANLP*, pp. 47–52, Stuttgart, Germany.

Taylor, J.R. 2003. *Linguistic Categorization*. 3rd ed., Oxford University Press, Oxford, U.K.

Thede, S.M. 1998. Predicting part-of-speech information about unknown words using statistical methods. In *COLING-ACL*, pp. 1505–1507, Montreal, QC. ACM/Morgan Kaufmann.

Thede, S.M. and M.P. Harper. 1999. A second-order hidden Markov model for part-of-speech tagging. In *ACL*, pp. 175–182, College Park, MD. ACL.

Toutanova, K., D. Klein, C.D. Manning, and Y. Singer. 2003. Feature-rich part-of-speech tagging with a cyclic dependency network. In *HLT-NAACL*, pp. 252–259, Edmonton, AB. ACL.

Toutanova, K. and C.D. Manning. 2000. Enriching the knowledge sources used in a maximum entropy part-of-speech tagger. In *EMNLP/VLC*, pp. 63–70, Hong Kong.

Triviño-Rodriguez, J.L. and R. Morales-Bueno. 2001. Using multiattribute prediction suffix graphs for Spanish part-of-speech tagging. In *IDA*, eds. F. Hoffmann et al., pp. 228–237, Lisbon, Portugal. Springer.

Trushkina, J. 2007. Development of a multilingual parallel corpus and a part-of-speech tagger for Afrikaans. In *IIP III*, eds. Z. Shi, K. Shimohara, and D. Feng, pp. 453–462, New York, Springer.

Tsuruoka, Y., Y. Tateishi, J. Kim et al. 2005. Developing a robust part-of-speech tagger for biomedical text. In *PCI*, eds. P. Bozanis and E.N. Houstis, pp. 382–392, Volos, Greece. Springer.

Tsuruoka, Y. and J. Tsujii. 2005. Bidirectional inference with the easiest-first strategy for tagging sequence data. In *HLT/EMNLP*, pp. 467–474, Vancouver, BC. ACL.

Tür, G. and K. Oflazer. 1998. Tagging English by path voting constraints. In *COLING*, pp. 1277–1281, Montreal, QC. ACL.

Vikram, T.N. and S.R. Urs. 2007. Development of prototype morphological analyzer for the south Indian language of Kannada. In *ICADL*, eds. D.H.-L. Goh et al., pp. 109–116, Hanoi, Vietnam. Springer.

Villamil, E.S., M.L. Forcada, and R.C. Carrasco. 2004. Unsupervised training of a finite-state sliding-window part-of-speech tagger. In *ESTAL*, eds. J.L. Vicedo et al., pp. 454–463, Alicante, Spain. Springer.

Wang, Q.I. and D. Schuurmans. 2005. Improved estimation for unsupervised part-of-speech tagging. In *NLP-KE*, pp. 219–224, Beijing, China. IEEE.

Xiao, J., X. Wang, and B. Liu. 2007. The study of a nonstationary maximum entropy Markov model and its application on the pos-tagging task. *ACM Transactions on Asian Language Information Processing* 6(2):7:1–7:29.

Yarowsky, D., G. Ngai, and R. Wicentowski. 2001. Inducing multilingual text analysis tools via robust projection across aligned corpora. In *NAACL*, pp. 109–116, Pittsburgh, PA.

Yonghui, G., W. Baomin, L. Changyuan, and W. Bingxi. 2006. Correlation voting fusion strategy for part of speech tagging. In *ICSP*, Guilin, China. IEEE.

Zhang, Y. and S. Clark. 2008. Joint word segmentation and POS tagging using a single perceptron. In *ACL*, pp. 888–896, Columbus, OH. ACL.

Zhao, W., F. Zhao, and W. Li. 2007. A new method of the automatically marked Chinese part of speech based on Gaussian prior smoothing maximum entropy model. In *FSKD*, pp. 447–453, Hainan, China. IEEE.

Zhou, G. and J. Su. 2003. A Chinese efficient analyser integrating word segmentation, part-of-speech tagging, partial parsing and full parsing. In *SIGHAN*, pp. 78–83, Sapporo, Japan. ACL.

Zribi, C.B.O., A. Torjmen, and M.B. Ahmed. 2006. An efficient multi-agent system combining pos-taggers for Arabic texts. In *CICLing*, ed. A. Gelbukh, pp. 121–131, Mexico. Springer.

11

Statistical Parsing

Joakim Nivre
Uppsala University

This chapter describes techniques for statistical parsing, that is, methods for syntactic analysis that make use of statistical inference from samples of natural language text. The major topics covered are probabilistic context-free grammars (PCFGs), supervised parsing using generative and discriminative models, and models for unsupervised parsing.

11.1 Introduction

By *statistical parsing* we mean techniques for syntactic analysis that are based on statistical inference from samples of natural language. Statistical inference may be invoked for different aspects of the parsing process but is primarily used as a technique for disambiguation, that is, for selecting the most appropriate analysis of a sentence from a larger set of possible analyses, for example, those licensed by a formal grammar. In this way, statistical parsing methods complement and extend the classical parsing algorithms for formal grammars described in Chapter 4.

The application of statistical methods to parsing started in the 1980s, drawing on work in the area of corpus linguistics, inspired by the success of statistical speech recognition, and motivated by some of the perceived weaknesses of parsing systems rooted in the generative linguistics tradition and based solely on hand-built grammars and disambiguation heuristics. In statistical parsing, these grammars and heuristics are wholly or partially replaced by statistical models induced from corpus data. By capturing distributional tendencies in the data, these models can rank competing analyses for a sentence, which facilitates *disambiguation*, and can therefore afford to impose fewer constraints on the language accepted, which increases *robustness*. Moreover, since models can be induced automatically from data, it is relatively easy to port systems to new languages and domains, as long as representative data sets are available.

Against this, however, it must be said that most of the models currently used in statistical parsing require data in the form of syntactically annotated sentences—a *treebank*—which can turn out to be quite a severe bottleneck in itself, in some ways even more severe than the old knowledge acquisition bottleneck associated with large-scale grammar development. Since the range of languages and domains for which treebanks are available is still limited, the investigation of methods for learning from unlabeled data, particularly when adapting a system to a new domain, is therefore an important problem on the current research agenda. Nevertheless, practically all high-precision parsing systems currently available are dependent on learning from treebank data, although often in combination with hand-built grammars or other independent resources. It is the models and techniques used in those systems that are the topic of this chapter.

The rest of the chapter is structured as follows. Section 11.2 introduces a conceptual framework for characterizing statistical parsing systems in terms of syntactic representations, statistical models, and algorithms for learning and inference. Section 11.3 is devoted to the framework of PCFG, which is arguably the most important model for statistical parsing, not only because it is widely used in itself but because some of its perceived limitations have played an important role in guiding the research toward improved models, discussed in the rest of the chapter. Section 11.4 is concerned with approaches that are based on generative statistical models, of which the PCFG model is a special case, and Section 11.5 discusses methods that instead make use of conditional or discriminative models. While the techniques reviewed in Sections 11.4 and 11.5 are mostly based on supervised learning, that is, learning from sentences labeled with their correct analyses, Section 11.6 is devoted to methods that start from unlabeled data, either alone or in combination with labeled data. Finally, in Section 11.7, we summarize and conclude.

11.2 Basic Concepts and Terminology

The task of a statistical parser is to map sentences in natural language to their preferred syntactic representations, either by providing a ranked list of candidate analyses or by selecting a single optimal analysis. Since the latter case can be regarded as a special case of the former (a list of length one), we will assume without loss of generality that the output is always a ranked list. We will use $\mathcal{X}$ for the set of possible inputs, where each input $x \in \mathcal{X}$ is assumed to be a sequence of tokens $x = w_1, \ldots, w_n$, and we will use $\mathcal{Y}$ for the set of possible syntactic representations. In other words, we will assume that the input to a parser comes pre-tokenized and segmented into sentences, and we refer to Chapter 2 for the intricacies hidden in this assumption when dealing with raw text. Moreover, we will not deal directly with cases where the input does not take the form of a string, such as word-lattice parsing for speech recognition, even though many of the techniques covered in this chapter can be generalized to such cases.

11.2.1 Syntactic Representations

The set $\mathcal{Y}$ of possible syntactic representations is usually defined by a particular theoretical framework or treebank annotation scheme but normally takes the form of a complex graph or tree structure. The most common type of representation is a *constituent structure* (or *phrase structure*), where a sentence is recursively decomposed into smaller segments that are categorized according to their internal structure into *noun phrases*, *verb phrases*, etc. Constituent structures are naturally induced by context-free grammars (CFGs) (Chomsky 1956) and are assumed in many theoretical frameworks of natural language syntax, for example, Lexical Functional Grammar (LFG) (Kaplan and Bresnan 1982; Bresnan 2000), Tree Adjoining Grammar (TAG) (Joshi 1985, 1997), and Head-Driven Phrase Structure Grammar (HPSG) (Pollard and Sag 1987, 1994). They are also widely used in annotation schemes for treebanks, such as the Penn Treebank scheme for English (Marcus et al. 1993; Marcus et al. 1994), and in the adaptations of this

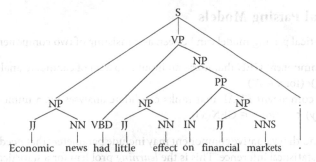

FIGURE 11.1 Constituent structure for an English sentence taken from the Penn Treebank.

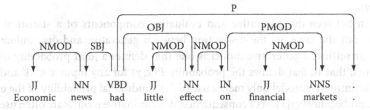

FIGURE 11.2 Dependency structure for an English sentence taken from the Penn Treebank.

scheme that have been developed for Chinese (Xue et al. 2004), Korean (Han et al. 2002), Arabic (Maamouri and Bies 2004), and Spanish (Moreno et al. 2003). Figure 11.1 shows a typical constituent structure for an English sentence, taken from the *Wall Street Journal* section of the Penn Treebank.

Another popular type of syntactic representation is a *dependency structure*, where a sentence is analyzed by connecting its words by binary asymmetrical relations called *dependencies*, and where words are categorized according to their functional role into *subject*, *object*, etc. Dependency structures are adopted in theoretical frameworks such as Functional Generative Description (Sgall et al. 1986) and Meaning-Text Theory (Mel'čuk 1988) and are used for treebank annotation especially for languages with free or flexible word order. The best known dependency treebank is the Prague Dependency Treebank of Czech (Hajič et al. 2001; Böhmová et al. 2003), but dependency-based annotation schemes have been developed also for Arabic (Hajič et al. 2004), Basque (Aduriz et al. 2003), Danish (Kromann 2003), Greek (Prokopidis et al. 2005), Russian (Boguslavsky et al. 2000), Slovene (Džeroski et al. 2006), Turkish (Oflazer et al. 2003), and other languages. Figure 11.2 shows a typical dependency representation of the same sentence as in Figure 11.1.

A third kind of syntactic representation is found in *categorial grammar*, which connects syntactic (and semantic) analysis to inference in a logical calculus. The syntactic representations used in categorial grammar are essentially proof trees, which cannot be reduced to constituency or dependency representations, although they have affinities with both. In statistical parsing, categorial grammar is mainly represented by Combinatory Categorial Grammar (CCG) (Steedman 2000), which is also the framework used in CCGbank (Hockenmaier and Steedman 2007), a reannotation of the *Wall Street Journal* section of the Penn Treebank.

In most of this chapter, we will try to abstract away from the particular representations used and concentrate on concepts of statistical parsing that cut across different frameworks, and we will make reference to different syntactic representations only when this is relevant. Thus, when we speak about assigning an analysis $y \in \mathcal{Y}$ to an input sentence $x \in \mathcal{X}$, it will be understood that the analysis is a syntactic representation as defined by the relevant framework.

11.2.2 Statistical Parsing Models

Conceptually, a statistical parsing model can be seen as consisting of two components:

1. A *generative* component GEN that maps an input x to a set of candidate analyses $\{y_1, \ldots, y_k\}$, that is, $\text{GEN}(x) \subseteq \mathcal{Y}$ (for $x \in \mathcal{X}$).
2. An *evaluative* component EVAL that ranks candidate analyses via a numerical scoring scheme, that is, $\text{EVAL}(y) \in \mathbb{R}$ (for $y \in \text{GEN}(x)$).

Both the generative and the evaluative component may include parameters that need to be estimated from empirical data using statistical inference. This is the *learning* problem for a statistical parsing model, and the data set used for estimation is called the *training set*. Learning may be *supervised* or *unsupervised*, depending on whether sentences in the training set are labeled with their correct analyses or not (cf. Chapter 9). In addition, there are *weakly supervised* learning methods, which combine the use of labeled and unlabeled data.

The distinction between the generative and evaluative components of a statistical parsing model is related to, but not the same as, the distinction between generative and discriminative models (cf. Chapter 9). In our setting, a generative model is one that defines a joint probability distribution over inputs and outputs, that is, that defines the probability $P(x, y)$ for any input $x \in \mathcal{X}$ and output $y \in \mathcal{Y}$. By contrast, a discriminative model only makes use of the conditional probability of the output given the input, that is, the probability $P(y|x)$. As a consequence, discriminative models are often used to implement the evaluative component of a complete parsing model, while generative models usually integrate the generative and evaluative components into one model. However, as we shall see in later sections, there are a number of variations possible on this basic theme.

Given that a statistical parsing model has been learned from data, we need an efficient way of constructing and ranking the candidate analyses for a given input sentence. This is the *inference* problem for a statistical parser. Inference may be *exact* or *approximate*, depending on whether or not the inference algorithm is guaranteed to find the optimal solution according to the model. We shall see that there is often a trade-off between having the advantage of a more complex model but needing to rely on approximate inference, on the one hand, and adopting a more simplistic model but being able to use exact inference, on the other.

11.2.3 Parser Evaluation

The *accuracy* of a statistical parser, that is, the degree to which it succeeds in finding the preferred analysis for an input sentence, is usually evaluated by running the parser on a sample of sentences $X = \{x_1, \ldots, x_m\}$ from a treebank, called the *test set*. Assuming that the treebank annotation y_i for each sentence $x_i \in X$ represents the preferred analysis, the *gold standard parse*, we can measure the *test set accuracy* of the parser by comparing its output $f(x_i)$ to the gold standard parse y_i, and we can use the test set accuracy to estimate the expected accuracy of the parser on sentences from the larger population represented by the test set.

The simplest way of measuring test set accuracy is to use the *exact match* metric, which simply counts the number of sentences for which the parser output is identical to the treebank annotation, that is, $f(x_i) = y_i$. This is a rather crude metric, since an error in the analysis of a single word or constituent has exactly the same impact on the result as the failure to produce any analysis whatsoever, and the most widely used evaluation metrics today are therefore based on various kinds of partial correspondence between the parser output and the gold standard parse.

For parsers that output constituent structures, the most well-known evaluation metrics are the PARSEVAL metrics (Black et al. 1991; Grishman et al. 1992), which consider the number of matching constituents between the parser output and the gold standard. For dependency structures, the closest correspondent to these metrics is the *attachment score* (Buchholz and Marsi 2006), which measures the proportion of words in a sentence that are attached to the correct head according to the gold standard. Finally, to be able to compare parsers that use different syntactic representations, several researchers have proposed evaluation schemes where both the parser output and the gold standard parse are converted into sets of more abstract dependency relations, so-called *dependency banks* (Lin 1995, 1998; Carroll et al. 1998, 2003; King et al. 2003; Forst et al. 2004).

The use of treebank data for parser evaluation is in principle independent of its use in parser development and is not limited to the evaluation of statistical parsing systems. However, the development of statistical parsers normally involves an iterative training-evaluation cycle, which makes statistical evaluation an integral part of the development. This gives rise to certain methodological issues, in particular the need to strictly separate data that are used for repeated testing during development—*development sets*—from data that are used for the evaluation of the final system—*test sets*.

It is important in this context to distinguish two different but related problems: *model selection* and *model assessment*. Model selection is the problem of estimating the performance of different models in order to choose the (approximate) best one, which can be achieved by testing on development sets or by cross-validation on the entire training set. Model assessment is the problem of estimating the expected accuracy of the finally selected model, which is what test sets are typically used for.

11.3 Probabilistic Context-Free Grammars

In the preceding section, we introduced the basic concepts and terminology that we need to characterize different models for statistical parsing, including methods for learning, inference, and evaluation. We start our exploration of these models and methods in this section by examining the framework of PCFG.

11.3.1 Basic Definitions

A PCFG is a simple extension of a CFG in which every production rule is associated with a probability (Booth and Thompson 1973). Formally, a PCFG is a quintuple $G = (\Sigma, N, S, R, D)$, where Σ is a finite set of terminal symbols, N is a finite set of nonterminal symbols (disjoint from Σ), $S \in N$ is the start symbol, R is a finite set of production rules of the form $A \rightarrow \alpha$, where $A \in N$ and $\alpha \in (\Sigma \cup N)^*$, and $D : R \rightarrow [0, 1]$ is a function that assigns a probability to each member of R (cf. Chapter 4 on context-free grammars). Figure 11.3 shows a PCFG capable of generating the sentence in Figure 11.1 with its associated parse tree. Although the actual probabilities assigned to the different rules are completely unrealistic because of the very limited coverage of the grammar, it nevertheless serves to illustrate the basic form of a PCFG.

As usual, we use $L(G)$ to denote the string language generated by G, that is, the set of strings x over the terminal alphabet Σ for which there exists a derivation $S \Rightarrow^* x$ using rules in R. In addition, we use $T(G)$ to denote the tree language generated by G, that is, the set of parse trees corresponding to valid derivations of strings in $L(G)$. Given a parse tree $y \in T(G)$, we use YIELD(y) for the terminal string in $L(G)$

S	→	NP VP.	1.00		JJ	→	Economic	0.33
VP	→	VP PP	0.33		JJ	→	little	0.33
VP	→	VBD NP	0.67		JJ	→	financial	0.33
NP	→	NP PP	0.14		NN	→	news	0.50
NP	→	JJ NN	0.57		NN	→	effect	0.50
NP	→	JJ NNS	0.29		NNS	→	markets	1.00
PP	→	IN NP	1.00		VBD	→	had	1.00
.	→	.	1.00		IN	→	on	1.00

FIGURE 11.3 PCFG for a fragment of English.

associated with y, COUNT(i, y) for the number of times that the ith production rule $r_i \in R$ is used in the derivation of y, and LHS(i) for the nonterminal symbol in the left-hand side of r_i.

The probability of a parse tree $y \in T(G)$ is defined as the product of probabilities of all rule applications in the derivation of y:

$$P(y) = \prod_{i=1}^{|R|} D(r_i)^{\text{COUNT}(i,y)} \tag{11.1}$$

This follows from basic probability theory on the assumption that the application of a rule in the derivation of a tree is independent of all other rule applications in that tree, a rather drastic independence assumption that we will come back to. Since the yield of a parse tree uniquely determines the string associated with the tree, the joint probability of a tree $y \in T(G)$ and a string $x \in L(G)$ is either 0 or equal to the probability of y, depending on whether or not the string matches the yield:

$$P(x, y) = \begin{cases} P(y) & \text{if YIELD}(y) = x \\ 0 & \text{otherwise} \end{cases} \tag{11.2}$$

It follows that the probability of a string can be obtained by summing up the probabilities of all parse trees compatible with the string:

$$P(x) = \sum_{y \in T(G):\text{YIELD}(y)=x} P(y) \tag{11.3}$$

A PCFG is *proper* if P defines a proper probability distribution over every subset of rules that have the same left-hand side $A \in N$:[*]

$$\sum_{r_i \in R:\text{LHS}(i)=A} D(r_i) = 1 \tag{11.4}$$

A PCFG is *consistent* if it defines a proper probability distribution over the set of trees that it generates

$$\sum_{y \in T(G)} P(y) = 1 \tag{11.5}$$

Consistency can also be defined in terms of the probability distribution over *strings* generated by the grammar. Given Equation 11.3, the two notions are equivalent.

11.3.2 PCFGs as Statistical Parsing Models

PCFGs have many applications in natural language processing, for example, in language modeling for speech recognition or statistical machine translation, where they can be used to model the probability distribution of a string language. In this chapter, however, we are only interested in their use as statistical parsing models, which can be conceptualized as follows:

- The set $\mathcal{X}$ of possible inputs is the set Σ^* of strings over the terminal alphabet, and the set $\mathcal{Y}$ of syntactic representations is the set of all parse trees over Σ and N.
- The generative component is the underlying CFG, that is, GEN$(x) = \{y \in T(G)|\text{YIELD}(x) = y\}$.
- The evaluative component is the probability distribution over parse trees, that is, EVAL$(y) = P(y)$.

For example, even the minimal PCFG in Figure 11.3 generates two trees for the sentence in Figure 11.1, the second of which is shown in Figure 11.4. According to the grammar, the probability of the parse tree in Figure 11.1 is 0.0000794, while the probability of the parse tree in Figure 11.4 is 0.0001871. In other

---

[*] The notion of properness is sometimes considered to be part of the definition of a PCFG, and the term *weighted* CFG (WCFG) is then used for a non-proper PCFG (Smith and Johnson 2007).

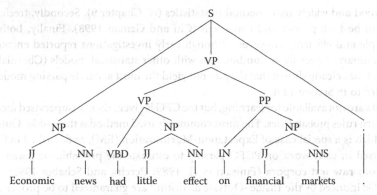

FIGURE 11.4 Alternative constituent structure for an English sentence taken from the Penn Treebank (cf. Figure 11.1).

words, using this PCFG for disambiguation, we would prefer the second analysis, which attaches the PP *on financial markets* to the verb *had*, rather than to the noun *effect*. According to the gold standard annotation in the Penn Treebank, this would not be the correct choice.

Note that the score $P(y)$ is equal to the joint probability $P(x, y)$ of the input sentence and the output tree, which means that a PCFG is a generative model (cf. Chapter 9). For evaluation in a parsing model, it may seem more natural to use the conditional probability $P(y|x)$ instead, since the sentence x is given as input to the model. The conditional probability can be derived as shown in Equation 11.6, but since the probability $P(x)$ is a constant normalizing factor, this will never change the internal ranking of analyses in GEN(x).

$$P(y|x) = \frac{P(x, y)}{\sum_{y' \in \text{GEN}(x)} P(y')} \tag{11.6}$$

11.3.3 Learning and Inference

The *learning* problem for the PCFG model can be divided into two parts: learning a CFG, $G = (\Sigma, N, S, R)$, and learning the probability assignment D for rules in R. If a preexisting CFG is used, then only the rule probabilities need to be learned. Broadly speaking, learning is either supervised or unsupervised, depending on whether it presupposes that sentences in the training set are annotated with their preferred analysis.

The simplest method for supervised learning is to extract a so-called *treebank grammar* (Charniak 1996), where the context-free grammar contains all and only the symbols and rules needed to generate the trees in the training set $Y = \{y_1, \ldots, y_m\}$, and where the probability of each rule is estimated by its relative frequency among rules with the same left-hand side:

$$D(r_i) = \frac{\sum_{j=1}^{m} \text{COUNT}(i, y_j)}{\sum_{j=1}^{m} \sum_{r_k \in R:\text{LHS}(r_k)=\text{LHS}(r_i)} \text{COUNT}(k, y_j)} \tag{11.7}$$

To give a simple example, the grammar in Figure 11.3 is in fact a treebank grammar for the treebank consisting of the two trees in Figures 11.1 and 11.4. The grammar contains exactly the rules needed to generate the two trees, and rule probabilities are estimated by the frequency of each rule relative to all the rules for the same nonterminal. Treebank grammars have a number of appealing properties. First of all, relative frequency estimation is a special case of maximum likelihood estimation (MLE), which is a well understood and widely used method in statistics (cf. Chapter 9). Secondly, treebank grammars are guaranteed to be both proper and consistent (Chi and Geman 1998). Finally, both learning and inference is simple and efficient. However, although early investigations reported encouraging results for treebank grammars, especially in combination with other statistical models (Charniak 1996, 1997), empirical research has clearly shown that they do not yield the most accurate parsing models, for reasons that we will return to in Section 11.4.

If treebank data are not available for learning, but the CFG is given, then unsupervised methods for MLE can be used to learn rules probabilities. The most commonly used method is the Inside–Outside algorithm (Baker 1979), which is a special case of Expectation-Maximization (EM), as described in Chapter 9. This algorithm was used in early work on PCFG parsing to estimate the probabilistic parameters of hand-crafted CFGs from raw text corpora (Fujisaki et al. 1989; Pereira and Schabes 1992). Like treebank grammars, PCFGs induced by the Inside–Outside algorithm are guaranteed to be proper and consistent (Sánchez and Benedí 1997; Chi and Geman 1998). We will return to unsupervised learning for statistical parsing in Section 11.6.

The *inference* problem for the PCFG model is to compute, given a specific grammar G and an input sentence x, the set GEN(x) of candidate representations and to score each candidate by the probability $P(y)$, as defined by the grammar. The first part is simply the parsing problem for CFGs, and many of the algorithms for this problem discussed in Chapter 4 have a straightforward extension that computes the probabilities of parse trees in the same process. This is true, for example, of the CKY algorithm (Ney 1991), Earley's algorithm (Stolcke 1995), and the algorithm for bilexical CFGs described in Eisner and Satta (1999) and Eisner (2000).

These algorithms are all based on dynamic programming, which makes it possible to compute the probability of a substructure at the time when it is being composed of smaller substructures and use Viterbi search to find the highest scoring analysis in $O(n^3)$ time, where n is the length of the input sentence. However, this also means that, although the model as such defines a complete ranking over all the candidate analyses in GEN(x), these parsing algorithms only compute the single best analysis. Nevertheless, the inference is exact in the sense that the analysis returned by the parser is guaranteed to be the most probable analysis according to the model. There are generalizations of this scheme that instead extract the k best analyses, for some constant k, with varying effects on time complexity (Jiménez and Marzal 2000; Charniak and Johnson 2005; Huang and Chiang 2005). A comprehensive treatment of many of the algorithms used in PCFG parsing can be found in Goodman (1999).

11.4 Generative Models

Using a simple treebank grammar of the kind described in the preceding section to rank alternative analyses generally does not lead to very high parsing accuracy. The reason is that, because of the independence assumptions built into the PCFG model, such a grammar does not capture the dependencies that are most important for disambiguation. In particular, the probability of a rule application is independent of the larger tree context in which it occurs.

This may mean, for example, that the probability with which a noun phrase is expanded into a single pronoun is constant for all structural contexts, even though it is a well-attested fact for many languages that this type of noun phrase is found more frequently in subject position than in object position. It may also mean that different verb phrase expansions (i.e., different configurations of complements and adjuncts) are generated independently of the lexical verb that functions as the syntactic head of the verb phrase, despite the fact that different verbs have different subcategorization requirements.

In addition to the lack of structural and lexical sensitivity, a problem with this model is that the children of a node are all generated in a single atomic event, which means that variants of the same structural realizations (e.g., the same complement in combination with different sets of adjuncts or even punctuation) are treated as disjoint events. Since the trees found in many treebanks tend to be rather flat, with a high average branching factor, this often leads to a very high number of distinct grammar rules with data sparseness as a consequence. In an often cited experiment, Charniak (1996) counted 10,605 rules in a treebank grammar extracted from a 300,000 word subset of the Penn Treebank, only 3,943 of which occurred more than once.

These limitations of simple treebank PCFGs have been very important in guiding research on statistical parsing during the last 10–15 years, and many of the models proposed can be seen as targeting specific weaknesses of these simple generative models. In this section, we will consider techniques based on more complex generative models, with more adequate independence assumptions. In Section 11.4.1, we will discuss approaches that abandon the generative paradigm in favor of conditional or discriminative models.

11.4.1 History-Based Models

One of the most influential approaches in statistical parsing is the use of a *history-based model*, where the derivation of a syntactic structure is modeled by a stochastic process and the different steps in the process are conditioned on events in the derivation history. The general form of such a model is the following:

$$P(y) = \prod_{i=1}^{m} P(d_i | \Phi(d_1, \ldots, d_{i-1})) \qquad (11.8)$$

where

$D = d_1, \ldots, d_m$ is a derivation of y

Φ is a function that defines which events in the history are taken into account in the model*

By way of example, let us consider one of the three generative lexicalized models proposed by Collins (1997). In these models, nonterminals have the form $A(a)$, where A is an ordinary nonterminal label (such as NP or VP) and a is a terminal corresponding to the lexical head of A. In Model 2, the expansion of a node $A(a)$ is defined as follows:

1. Choose a head child H with probability $P_h(H|A, a)$.
2. Choose left and right subcat frames, LC and RC, with probabilities $P_{lc}(LC|A, H, h)$ and $P_{rc}(RC|A, H, h)$.
3. Generate the left and right modifiers (siblings of $H(a)$) $L_1(l_1), \ldots, L_k(l_k)$ and $R_1(r_1), \ldots, R_m(r_m)$ with probabilities $P_l(L_i, l_i|A, H, h, \delta(i-1), LC)$ and $P_r(R_i, r_i|A, H, h, \delta(i-1), RC)$.

In the third step, children are generated inside-out from the head, meaning that $L_1(l_1)$ and $R_1(r_1)$ are the children closest to the head child $H(a)$. Moreover, in order to guarantee a correct probability distribution, the farthest child from the head on each side is a dummy child labeled STOP. The subcat frames LC and RC are multisets of ordinary (non-lexicalized) nonterminals, and elements of these multisets get deleted as the corresponding children are generated. The distance metric $\delta(j)$ is a function of the surface string from the head word h to the outermost edge of the jth child on the same side, which returns a vector of three features: (1) Is the string of zero length? (2) Does the string contain a verb? (3) Does the string contain 0, 1, 2, or more than 2 commas?

---

* Note that the standard PCFG model can be seen as a special case of this, for example, by letting D be a leftmost derivation of y according to the CFG and by letting $\Phi(d_1, \ldots, d_{i-1})$ be the left-hand side of the production used in d_i.

To see what this means for a concrete example, consider the following phrase, occurring as part of an analysis for *Last week Marks bought Brooks*:

$$P(S(\text{bought}) \rightarrow NP(\text{week})\ NP\text{-}C(\text{Marks})\ VP(\text{bought})) =$$

$$P_h(VP|S, \text{bought}) \times$$

$$P_{lc}(\{NP\text{-}C\}|S, VP, \text{bought}) \times$$

$$P_{rc}(\{\}|S, VP, \text{bought}) \times$$

$$\qquad\qquad\qquad\qquad\qquad\qquad\qquad\qquad\qquad\qquad\qquad (11.9)$$

$$P_l(NP\text{-}C(\text{Marks})|S, VP, \text{bought}, \langle 1,0,0\rangle, \{NP\text{-}C\}) \times$$

$$P_l(NP(\text{week})|S, VP, \text{bought}, \langle 0,0,0\rangle, \{\}) \times$$

$$P_l(STOP|S, VP, \text{bought}, \langle 0,0,0\rangle, \{\}) \times$$

$$P_r(STOP|S, VP, \text{bought}, \langle 0,0,0\rangle, \{\})$$

This phrase should be compared with the corresponding treebank PCFG, which has a single model parameter for the conditional probability of all the child nodes given the parent node.

The notion of a history-based generative model for statistical parsing was first proposed by researchers at IBM as a complement to hand-crafted grammars (Black et al. 1993). The kind of model exemplified above is sometimes referred to as *head-driven*, given the central role played by syntactic heads, and this type of model is found in many state-of-the art systems for statistical parsing using phrase structure representations (Collins 1997, 1999; Charniak 2000), dependency representations (Collins 1996; Eisner 1996), and representations from specific theoretical frameworks such as TAG (Chiang 2000), HPSG (Toutanova et al. 2002), and CCG (Hockenmaier 2003). In addition to top-down head-driven models, there are also history-based models that use derivation steps corresponding to a particular parsing algorithm, such as left-corner derivations (Henderson 2004) or transition-based dependency parsing (Titov and Henderson 2007).

Summing up, in a generative, history-based parsing model, the generative component GEN(x) is defined by a (stochastic) system of derivations that is not necessarily constrained by a formal grammar. As a consequence, the number of candidate analyses in GEN(x) is normally much larger than for a simple treebank grammar. The evaluative component EVAL(y) is a multiplicative model of the joint probability $P(x, y)$, factored into the conditional probability $P(d_i|\Phi(d_1, \ldots, d_{i-1}))$ of each derivation step d_i given relevant parts of the derivation history.

The learning problem for these models therefore consists in estimating the conditional probabilities of different derivation steps, a problem that can be solved using relative frequency estimation as described earlier for PCFGs. However, because of the added complexity of the models, the data will be much more sparse and hence the need for smoothing more pressing. The standard approach for dealing with this problem is to back off to more general events, for example, from bilexical to monolexical probabilities, and from lexical items to parts of speech. An alternative to relative frequency estimation is to use a discriminative training technique, where parameters are set to maximize the conditional probability of the output trees given the input strings, instead of the joint probability of trees and strings. The discriminative training of generative models has sometimes been shown to improve parsing accuracy (Johnson 2001; Henderson 2004).

The inference problem, although conceptually the same, is generally harder for a history-based model than for a simple treebank PCFG, which means that there is often a trade-off between accuracy in disambiguation and efficiency in processing. For example, whereas computing the most probable analysis can be done in $O(n^3)$ time with an unlexicalized PCFG, a straightforward application of the same techniques to a fully lexicalized model takes $O(n^5)$ time, although certain optimizations are possible (cf. Chapter 4). Moreover, the greatly increased number of candidate analyses due to the lack of hard grammar constraints means that, even if parsing does not become intractable in principle, the time required for an exhaustive search of the analysis space is no longer practical. In practice, most systems of this kind only apply the full probabilistic model to a subset of all possible analyses, resulting from a first pass based on an efficient approximation of the full model. This first pass is normally implemented as some kind of chart parsing with beam search, using an estimate of the final probability to prune the search space (Caraballo and Charniak 1998).

11.4.2 PCFG Transformations

Although history-based models were originally conceived as an alternative (or complement) to standard PCFGs, it has later been shown that many of the dependencies captured in history-based models can in fact be modeled in a plain PCFG, provided that suitable transformations are applied to the basic treebank grammar (Johnson 1998; Klein and Manning 2003). For example, if a nonterminal node NP with parent S is instead labeled NP^S, then the dependence on structural context noted earlier in connection with pronominal NPs can be modeled in a standard PCFG, since the grammar will have different parameters for the two rules NP^S → PRP and NP^VP → PRP. This simple technique, known as *parent annotation*, has been shown to dramatically improve the parsing accuracy achieved with a simple treebank grammar (Johnson 1998). It is illustrated in Figure 11.5, which shows a version of the tree in Figure 11.1, where all the nonterminal nodes except preterminals have been reannotated in this way.

Parent annotation is an example of the technique known as *state splitting*, which consists in splitting the coarse linguistic categories that are often found in treebank annotation into more fine-grained categories that are better suited for disambiguation. An extreme example of state splitting is the use of lexicalized categories of the form $A(a)$ that we saw earlier in connection with head-driven history-based models, where nonterminal categories are split into one distinct subcategory for each possible lexical head. Exhaustive lexicalization and the modeling of bilexical relations, that is, relations holding between two lexical heads, were initially thought to be an important explanation for the success of these models, but more recent research has called this into question by showing that these relations are rarely used by the parser and account for a very small part of the increase in accuracy compared to simple treebank grammars (Gildea 2001; Bikel 2004).

These results suggest that what is important is that coarse categories are split into finer and more discriminative subcategories, which may sometimes correspond to lexicalized categories but may also be considerably more coarse-grained. Thus, in an often cited study, Klein and Manning (2003) showed that a combination of carefully defined state splits and other grammar transformations could give almost the same level of parsing accuracy as the best lexicalized parsers at the time. More recently, models have been proposed where nonterminal categories are augmented with latent variables so that state splits can be

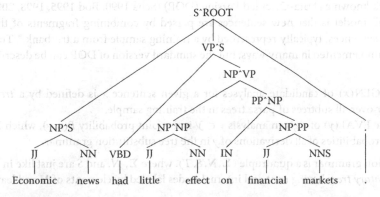

FIGURE 11.5 Constituent structure with parent annotation (cf. Figure 11.1).

learned automatically using unsupervised learning techniques such as EM (Matsuzaki et al. 2005; Prescher 2005; Dreyer and Eisner 2006; Petrov et al. 2006; Liang et al. 2007; Petrov and Klein 2007). For phrase structure parsing, these latent variable models have now achieved the same level of performance as fully lexicalized generative models (Petrov et al. 2006; Petrov and Klein 2007). An attempt to apply the same technique to dependency parsing, using PCFG transformations, did not achieve the same success (Musillo and Merlo 2008), which suggests that bilexical relations are more important in syntactic representations that lack nonterminal categories other than parts of speech.

One final type of transformation that is widely used in PCFG parsing is *markovization*, which transforms an n-ary grammar rule into a set of unary and binary rules, where each child node in the original rule is introduced in a separate rule, and where augmented nonterminals are used to encode elements of the derivation history. For example, the rule VP → VB NP PP could be transformed into

$$VP \rightarrow \langle VP{:}VB\ldots PP\rangle$$
$$\langle VP{:}VB\ldots PP\rangle \rightarrow \langle VP{:}VB\ldots NP\rangle\ PP$$
$$\langle VP{:}VB\ldots NP\rangle \rightarrow \langle VP{:}VB\rangle\ NP \tag{11.10}$$
$$\langle VP{:}VB\rangle \rightarrow VB$$

The first unary rule expands VP into a new symbol ⟨VP:VB . . . PP⟩, signifying a VP with head child VB and rightmost child PP. The second binary rule generates the PP child next to a child labeled ⟨VP:VB . . . NP⟩, representing a VP with head child VB and rightmost child NP. The third rule generates the NP child, and the fourth rule finally generates the head child VB. In this way, we can use a standard PCFG to model a head-driven stochastic process.

Grammar transformations such as markovization and state splitting make it possible to capture the essence of history-based models without formally going beyond the PCFG model. This is a distinct advantage, because it means that all the theoretical results and methods developed for PCFGs can be taken over directly. Once we have fixed the set of nonterminals and rules in the grammar, whether by ingenious hand-crafting or by learning over latent variables, we can use standard methods for learning and inference, as described earlier in Section 11.3.3. However, it is important to remember that transformations can have quite dramatic effects on the number of nonterminals and rules in the grammar, and this in turn has a negative effect on parsing efficiency. Thus, even though exact inference for a PCFG is feasible in $O(n^3 \cdot |R|)$ (where $|R|$ is the number of grammar rules), heavy pruning is often necessary to achieve reasonable efficiency in practice.

11.4.3 Data-Oriented Parsing

An alternative approach to increasing the structural sensitivity of generative models for statistical parsing is the framework known as Data-Oriented Parsing (DOP) (Scha 1990; Bod 1995, 1998, 2003). The basic idea in the DOP model is that new sentences are parsed by combining fragments of the analyses of previously seen sentences, typically represented by a training sample from a treebank.* This idea can be (and has been) implemented in many ways, but the standard version of DOP can be described as follows (Bod 1998):

- The set GEN(x) of candidate analyses for a given sentence x is defined by a *tree substitution grammar* over all subtrees of parse trees in the training sample.
- The score EVAL(y) of a given analysis $y \in \mathcal{Y}$ is the joint probability $P(x, y)$, which is equal to the sum of probabilities of all derivations of y in the tree substitution grammar.

A tree substitution grammar is a quadruple (Σ, N, S, T), where Σ, N, and S are just like in a CFG, and T is a set of *elementary trees* having root and internal nodes labeled by elements of N and leaves labeled by

---

* There are also unsupervised versions of DOP, but we will leave them until Section 11.6.

elements of $\Sigma \cup N$. Two elementary trees α and β can be combined by the substitution operation $\alpha \circ \beta$ to produce a unified tree only if the root of β has the same label as the leftmost nonterminal node in α, in which case $\alpha \circ \beta$ is the tree obtained by replacing the leftmost nonterminal node in α by β. The tree language $T(G)$ generated by a tree substitution grammar G is the set of all trees with root label S that can be derived using the substitution of elementary trees. In this way, an ordinary CFG can be thought of as a tree substitution grammar where all elementary trees have depth 1.

This kind of model has been applied to a variety of different linguistic representations, including lexical-functional representations (Bod and Kaplan 1998) and compositional semantic representations (Bonnema et al. 1997), but most of the work has been concerned with syntactic parsing using phrase structure trees. Characteristic of all these models is the fact that one and the same analysis typically has several distinct derivations in the tree substitution grammar. This means that the probability $P(x, y)$ has to be computed as a sum over all derivations d that derives y $(d \Rightarrow y)$, and the probability of a derivation d is normally taken to be the product of the probabilities of all subtrees t used in d $(t \in d)$:

$$P(x, y) = \sum_{d \Rightarrow y} \prod_{t \in d} P(t) \tag{11.11}$$

This assumes that the subtrees of a derivation are independent of each other, just as the local trees defined by production rules are independent in a PCFG derivation. The difference is that subtrees in a DOP derivation can be of arbitrary size and can therefore capture dependencies that are outside the scope of a PCFG. A consequence of the sum-of-products model is also that the most probable analysis may not be the analysis with the most probable derivation, a property that appears to be beneficial with respect to parsing accuracy but that unfortunately makes exact inference intractable.

The learning problem for the DOP model consists in estimating the probabilities of subtrees, where the most common approach has been to use relative frequency estimation, that is, setting the probability of a subtree equal to the number of times that it is seen in the training sample divided by the number of subtrees with the same root label (Bod 1995, 1998). Although this method seems to work fine in practice, it has been shown to produce a biased and inconsistent estimator (Johnson 2002), and other methods have therefore been proposed in its place (Bonnema et al. 2000; Bonnema and Scha 2003; Zollmann and Sima'an 2005).

As already noted, inference is a hard problem in the DOP model. Whereas computing the most probable *derivation* can be done in polynomial time, computing the most probable *analysis* (which requires summing over all derivations) is NP complete (Sima'an 1996a, 1999). Research on efficient parsing within the DOP framework has therefore focused on finding efficient approximations that preserve the advantage gained in disambiguation by considering several distinct derivations of the same analysis. While early work focused on a kind of randomized search strategy called Monte Carlo disambiguation (Bod 1995, 1998), the dominant strategy has now become the use of different kinds of PCFG reductions (Goodman 1996; Sima'an 1996b; Bod 2001, 2003). This again underlines the centrality of the PCFG model for generative approaches to statistical parsing.

11.5 Discriminative Models

The statistical parsing models considered in Section 11.4.3 are all generative in the sense that they model the joint probability $P(x, y)$ of the input x and output y (which in many cases is equivalent to $P(y)$). Because of this, there is often a tight integration between the system of derivations defining $GEN(x)$ and the parameters of the scoring function $EVAL(y)$. Generative models have many advantages, such as the possibility of deriving the related probabilities $P(y|x)$ and $P(x)$ through conditionalization and marginalization, which makes it possible to use the same model for both parsing and language modeling. Another attractive property is the fact that the learning problem for these models often has a clean analytical solution, such as the relative frequency estimation for PCFGs, which makes learning both simple and efficient.

The main drawback with generative models is that they force us to make rigid independence assumptions, thereby severely restricting the range of dependencies that can be taken into account for disambiguation. As we have seen Section 11.4, the search for more adequate independence assumptions has been an important driving force in research on statistical parsing, but we have also seen that more complex models inevitably makes parsing computationally harder and that we must therefore often resort to approximate algorithms. Finally, it has been pointed out that the usual approach to training a generative statistical parser maximizes a quantity—usually the joint probability of inputs and outputs in the training set—that is only indirectly related to the goal of parsing, that is, to maximize the accuracy of the parser on unseen sentences.

A discriminative model only makes use of the conditional probability $P(y|x)$ of a candidate analysis y given the input sentence x. Although this means that it is no longer possible to derive the joint probability $P(x, y)$, it has the distinct advantage that we no longer need to assume independence between features that are relevant for disambiguation and can incorporate more global features of syntactic representations. It also means that the evaluative component EVAL(y) of the parsing model is not directly tied to any particular generative component GEN(x), as long as we have some way of generating a set of candidate analyses. Finally, it means that we can train the model to maximize the probability of the output given the input or even to minimize a loss function in mapping inputs to outputs. On the downside, it must be said that these training regimes normally require the use of numerical optimization techniques, which can be computationally very intensive.

In discussing discriminative parsing models, we will make a distinction between *local* and *global* models. Local discriminative models try to maximize the probability of local decisions in the derivation of an analysis y, given the input x, hoping to find a globally optimal solution by making a sequence of locally optimal decisions. Global discriminative models instead try to maximize the probability of a complete analysis y, given the input x. As we shall see, local discriminative models can often be regarded as discriminative versions of generative models, with local decisions given by independence assumptions, while global discriminative models more fully exploit the potential of having features of arbitrary complexity.

11.5.1 Local Discriminative Models

Local discriminative models generally take the form of conditional history-based models, where the derivation of a candidate analysis y is modeled as a sequence of decisions with each decision conditioned on relevant parts of the derivation history. However, unlike their generative counterparts described in Section 11.4.1, they also include the input sentence x as a conditioning variable:

$$P(y|x) = \prod_{i=1}^{m} P(d_i|\Phi(d_1, \ldots, d_{i-1}, x))$$ (11.12)

This makes it possible to condition decisions on arbitrary properties of the input, for example, by using a lookahead such that the next k tokens of the input sentence can influence the probability of a given decision. Therefore, conditional history-based models have often been used to construct incremental and near-deterministic parsers that parse a sentence in a single left-to-right pass over the input, using beam search or some other pruning strategy to efficiently compute an approximation of the most probable analysis y given the input sentence x.

In this kind of setup, it is not strictly necessary to estimate the conditional probabilities exactly, as long as the model provides a ranking of the alternatives in terms of decreasing probability. Sometimes a distinction is therefore made between *conditional models*, where probabilities are modeled explicitly, and *discriminative models* proper, that rank alternatives without computing their probability (Jebara

2004). A special case of (purely) discriminative models are those used by deterministic parsers, such as the transition-based dependency parsers discussed below, where only the mode of the conditional distribution (i.e., the single most probable alternative) needs to be computed for each decision.

Conditional history-based models were first proposed in phrase structure parsing, as a way of introducing more structural context for disambiguation compared to standard grammar rules (Briscoe and Carroll 1993; Jelinek et al. 1994; Magerman 1995; Carroll and Briscoe 1996). Today it is generally considered that, although parsers based on such models can be implemented very efficiently to run in linear time (Ratnaparkhi 1997, 1999; Sagae and Lavie 2005, 2006a), their accuracy lags a bit behind the best-performing generative models and global discriminative models. Interestingly, the same does not seem to hold for dependency parsing, where local discriminative models are used in some of the best performing systems known as *transition-based* dependency parsers (Yamada and Matsumoto 2003; Isozaki et al. 2004; Nivre et al. 2004; Attardi 2006; Nivre 2006b; Nivre to appear). Let us briefly consider the architecture of such a system.

We begin by noting that a dependency structure of the kind depicted in Figure 11.2 can be defined as a labeled, directed tree $y = (V, A)$, where the set V of nodes is simply the set of tokens in the input sentence (indexed by their linear position in the string); A is a set of labeled, directed arcs (w_i, l, w_j), where w_i, w_j are nodes and l is a dependency label (such as SBJ, OBJ); and every node except the root node has exactly one incoming arc.

A *transition system* for dependency parsing consists of a set C of configurations, representing partial analyses of sentences, and a set D of transitions from configurations to new configurations. For every sentence $x = w_1, \ldots, w_n$, there is a unique initial configuration $c_i(x) \in C$ and a set $C_t(x) \subseteq C$ of terminal configurations, each representing a complete analysis y of x.

For example, if we let a configuration be a triple $c = (\sigma, \beta, A)$, where σ is a stack of nodes/tokens, β is a buffer of remaining input nodes/tokens, and A is a set of labeled dependency arcs, then we can define a transition system for dependency parsing as follows:

- The initial configuration $c_i(x) = ([\,], [w_1, \ldots, w_n], \emptyset)$
- The set of terminal configurations $C_t(x) = \{c \in C | c = ([w_i], [\,], A)\}$
- The set D of transitions include:
  1. Shift: $(\sigma, [w_i | \beta], A) \Rightarrow ([\sigma | w_i], \beta, A)$
  2. Right-Arc(l): $([\sigma | w_i, w_j], \beta, A) \Rightarrow ([\sigma | w_i], \beta, A \cup \{(w_i, l, w_j)\})$
  3. Left-Arc(l): $([\sigma | w_i, w_j], \beta, A) \Rightarrow ([\sigma | w_j], \beta, A \cup \{(w_j, l, w_i)\})$

The initial configuration has an empty stack, an empty arc set, and all the input tokens in the buffer. A terminal configuration has a single token on the stack and an empty buffer. The Shift transition moves the next token in the buffer onto the stack, while the Right-Arc(l) and Left-Arc(l) transitions add a dependency arc between the two top tokens on the stack and replace them by the head token of that arc. It is easy to show that, for any sentence $x = w_1, \ldots, w_n$ with a projective dependency tree y,* there is a transition sequence that builds y in exactly $2n - 1$ steps starting from $c_i(x)$. Over the years, a number of different transition systems have been proposed for dependency parsing, some of which are restricted to projective dependency trees (Kudo and Matsumoto 2002; Nivre 2003; Yamada and Matsumoto 2003), while others can also derive non-projective structures (Attardi 2006; Nivre 2006a, 2007).

Given a scoring function $S(\Phi(c), d)$, which scores possible transitions d out of a configuration c, represented by a high-dimensional feature vector $\Phi(c)$, and given a way of combining the scores of individual transitions into scores for complete sequences, parsing can be performed as search for the highest-scoring transition sequence. Different search strategies are possible, but most transition-based dependency parsers implement some form of beam search, with a fixed constant beam width k, which means that parsing can be performed in $O(n)$ time for transition systems where the length of a transition sequence is linear in the length of the sentence. In fact, many systems set k to 1, which means that parsing

---

* A dependency tree is projective iff every subtree has a contiguous yield.

is completely deterministic given the scoring function. If the scoring function $S(\Phi(c), d)$ is designed to estimate (or maximize) the conditional probability of a transition d given the configuration c, then this is a local, discriminative model. It is discriminative because the configuration c encodes properties both of the input sentence and of the transition history; and it is local because each transition d is scored in isolation.

Summing up, in statistical parsers based on local, discriminative models, the generative component $\text{GEN}(x)$ is typically defined by a derivational process, such as a transition system or a bottom-up parsing algorithm, while the evaluative component $\text{EVAL}(y)$ is essentially a model for scoring local decisions, conditioned on the input and parts of the derivation history, together with a way of combining local scores into global scores.

The learning problem for these models is to learn a scoring function for local decisions, conditioned on the input and derivation history, a problem that can be solved using many different techniques. Early history-based models for phrase structure parsing used decision tree learning (Jelinek et al. 1994; Magerman 1995), but more recently log-linear models have been the method of choice (Ratnaparkhi 1997, 1999; Sagae and Lavie 2005, 2006a). The latter method has the advantage that it gives a proper, conditional probability model, which facilitates the combination of local scores into global scores. In transition-based dependency parsing, purely discriminative approaches such as support vector machines (Kudo and Matsumoto 2002; Yamada and Matsumoto 2003; Isozaki et al. 2004; Nivre et al. 2006), perceptron learning (Ciaramita and Attardi 2007), and memory-based learning (Nivre et al. 2004; Attardi 2006) have been more popular, although log-linear models have been used in this context as well (Cheng et al. 2005; Attardi 2006).

The inference problem is to compute the optimal decision sequence, given the scoring function, a problem that is usually tackled by some kind of approximate search, such as beam search (with greedy, deterministic search as a special case). This guarantees that inference can be performed efficiently even with exponentially many derivations and a model structure that is often unsuited for dynamic programming. As already noted, parsers based on local, discriminative models can be made to run very efficiently, often in linear time, either as a theoretical worst-case (Nivre 2003; Sagae and Lavie 2005) or as an empirical average-case (Ratnaparkhi 1997, 1999).

11.5.2 Global Discriminative Models

In a local discriminative model, the score of an analysis y, given the sentence x, factors into the scores of different decisions in the derivation of y. In a global discriminative model, by contrast, no such factorization is assumed, and component scores can all be defined on the entire analysis y. This has the advantage that the model may incorporate features that capture global properties of the analysis, without being restricted to a particular history-based derivation of the analysis (whether generative or discriminative).

In a global discriminative model, a scoring function $S(x, y)$ is typically defined as the inner product of a feature vector $\mathbf{f}(x, y) = \langle f_1(x, y), \ldots, f_k(x, y) \rangle$ and a weight vector $\mathbf{w} = \langle w_1, \ldots, w_k \rangle$:

$$S(x, y) = \mathbf{f}(x, y) \cdot \mathbf{w} = \sum_{i=1}^{k} w_i \cdot f_i(x, y) \tag{11.13}$$

where each $f_i(x, y)$ is a (numerical) feature of x and y, and each w_i is a real-valued weight quantifying the tendency of feature $f_i(x, y)$ to co-occur with optimal analyses. A positive weight indicates a positive correlation, a negative weight indicates a negative correlation, and by summing up all feature–weight products we obtain a global estimate of the optimality of the analysis y for sentence x.

The main strength of this kind of model is that there are no restrictions on the kind of features that may be used, except that they must be encoded as numerical features. For example, it is perfectly straightforward to define features indicating the presence or absence of a particular substructure, such as the tree of depth 1 corresponding to a PCFG rule. In fact, we can represent the entire scoring function of the standard PCFG model by having one feature $f_i(x, y)$ for each grammar rule r_i, whose value is the number of times r_i is used in the derivation of y, and setting w_i to the log of the rule probability for r_i. The global score will then be equivalent to the log of the probability $P(x, y)$ as defined by the corresponding PCFG, in virtue of the following equivalence:

$$\log \left[\prod_{i=1}^{|R|} D(r_i)^{\text{COUNT}(i,y)} \right] = \sum_{1=1}^{|R|} \log D(r_i) \cdot \text{COUNT}(i, y) \qquad (11.14)$$

However, the main advantage of these models lies in features that go beyond the capacity of local models and capture more global properties of syntactic structures, for example, features that indicate conjunct parallelism in coordinate structures, features that encode differences in length between conjuncts, features that capture the degree of right branching in a parse tree, or features that signal the presence of "heavy" constituents of different types (Charniak and Johnson 2005). It is also possible to use features that encode the scores assigned to a particular analysis by other parsers, which means that the model can also be used as a framework for parser combination.

The learning problem for a global discriminative model is to estimate the weight vector **w**. This can be solved by setting the weights to maximize the conditional likelihood of the preferred analyses in the training data according to the following model:

$$P(y|x) = \frac{\exp\left[\mathbf{f}(x, y) \cdot \mathbf{w}\right]}{\sum_{y' \in \text{GEN}(x)} \exp\left[\mathbf{f}(x, y') \cdot \mathbf{w}\right]} \qquad (11.15)$$

The exponentiated score of analysis y for sentence x is normalized to a conditional probability by dividing it with the sum of exponentiated scores of all alternative analyses $y' \in \text{GEN}(x)$. This kind of model is usually called a log-linear model, or an exponential model. The problem of finding the optimal weights has no closed form solution, but there are a variety of numerical optimization techniques that can be used, including iterative scaling and conjugate gradient techniques, making log-linear models one of the most popular choices for global discriminative models (Johnson et al. 1999; Riezler et al. 2002; Toutanova et al. 2002; Miyao et al. 2003; Clark and Curran 2004).

An alternative approach is to use a purely discriminative learning method, which does not estimate a conditional probability distribution but simply tries to separate the preferred analyses from alternative analyses, setting the weights so that the following criterion is upheld for every sentence x with preferred analysis y in the training set:

$$y = \underset{y' \in \text{GEN}(x)}{\text{argmax}} \ \mathbf{f}(x, y') \cdot \mathbf{w} \qquad (11.16)$$

In case the set of constraints is not satisfiable, techniques such as slack variables can be used to allow some constraints to be violated with a penalty. Methods in this family include the perceptron algorithm and max-margin methods such as support vector machines, which are also widely used in the literature (Collins 2000; Collins and Duffy 2002; Taskar et al. 2004; Collins and Koo 2005; McDonald et al. 2005a). Common to all of these methods, whether conditional or discriminative, is the need to repeatedly reparse the training corpus, which makes the learning of global discriminative models computationally intensive.

The use of truly global features is an advantage from the point of view of parsing accuracy but has the drawback of making inference intractable in the general case. Since there is no restriction on the scope that features may take, it is not possible to use standard dynamic programming techniques to compute the optimal analysis. This is relevant not only at parsing time but also during learning, given the need to repeatedly reparse the training corpus during optimization.

The most common way of dealing with this problem is to use a different model to define $\text{GEN}(x)$ and to use the inference method for this base model to derive what is typically a restricted subset of all candidate analyses. This approach is especially natural in grammar-driven systems, where the base parser is used to derive the set of candidates that are compatible with the constraints of the grammar, and the global discriminative model is applied only to this subset. This methodology underlies many of the best performing broad-coverage parsers for theoretical frameworks such as LFG (Johnson et al. 1999; Riezler et al. 2002), HPSG (Toutanova et al. 2002; Miyao et al. 2003), and CCG (Clark and Curran 2004), some of which are based on hand-crafted grammars while others use theory-specific treebank grammars.

The two-level model is also commonly used in data-driven systems, where the base parser responsible for the generative component GEN(x) is typically a parser using a generative model. These parsers are known as *reranking* parsers, since the global discriminative model is used to rerank the k top candidates already ranked by the generative base parser. Applying a discriminative reranker on top of a generative base parser usually leads to a significant improvement in parsing accuracy (Collins 2000; Collins and Duffy 2002; Charniak and Johnson 2005; Collins and Koo 2005). However, it is worth noting that the single most important feature in the global discriminative model is normally the log probability assigned to an analysis by the generative base parser.

A potential problem with the standard reranking approach to discriminative parsing is that GEN(x) is usually restricted to a small subset of all possible analyses, which means that the truly optimal analysis may not even be included in the set of analyses that are considered by the discriminative model. That this is a real problem was shown in the study of Collins (2000), where 41% of the correct analyses were not included in the set of 30 best parses considered by the reranker. In order to overcome this problem, discriminative models with global inference have been proposed, either using dynamic programming and restricting the scope of features (Taskar et al. 2004) or using approximate search (Turian and Melamed 2006), but efficiency remains a problem for these methods, which do not seem to scale up to sentences of arbitrary length. A recent alternative is *forest reranking* (Huang 2008), a method that reranks a packed forest of trees, instead of complete trees, and uses approximate inference to make training tractable.

The efficiency problems associated with inference for global discriminative models are most severe for phrase structure representations and other more expressive formalisms. Dependency representations, by contrast, are more tractable in this respect, and one of the most successful approaches to dependency parsing in recent years, known as *spanning tree* parsing (or *graph-based* parsing), is based on exact inference with global, discriminative models.

The starting point for spanning tree parsing is the observation that the set GEN(x) of all dependency trees for a sentence x (given some set of dependency labels) can be compactly represented as a dense graph $G = (V, A)$, where V is the set of nodes corresponding to tokens of x, and A contains all possible labeled directed arcs (w_i, l, w_j) connecting nodes in V. Given a model for scoring dependency trees, the inference problem for dependency parsing then becomes the problem of finding the highest scoring spanning tree in G (McDonald et al. 2005b).

With suitably factored models, the optimum spanning tree can be computed in $O(n^3)$ time for projective dependency trees using Eisner's algorithm (Eisner 1996, 2000), and in $O(n^2)$ time for arbitrary dependency trees using the Chu–Liu–Edmonds algorithm (Chu and Liu 1965; Edmonds 1967). This makes global discriminative training perfectly feasible, and spanning tree parsing has become one of the dominant paradigms for statistical dependency parsing (McDonald et al. 2005a,b; McDonald and Pereira 2006; Carreras 2007). Although exact inference is only possible if features are restricted to small subgraphs (even single arcs if non-projective trees are allowed), various techniques have been developed for approximate inference with more global features (McDonald and Pereira 2006; Riedel et al. 2006; Nakagawa 2007). Moreover, using a generalization of the Chu–Liu–Edmonds algorithms to k-best parsing, it is possible to add a discriminative reranker on top of the discriminative spanning tree parser (Hall 2007).

To conclude, the common denominator of the models discussed in this section is an evaluative component where the score EVAL(y) is defined by a linear combination of weighted features that are not restricted by a particular derivation process, and where weights are learned using discriminative techniques such as conditional likelihood estimation or perceptron learning. Exact inference is intractable in general, which is why the set GEN(*x*) of candidates is often restricted to a small set generated by a grammar-driven or generative statistical parser, a set that can be searched exhaustively. Exact inference has so far been practically useful mainly in the context of graph-based dependency parsing.

11.6 Beyond Supervised Parsing

All the methods for statistical parsing discussed so far in this chapter rely on supervised learning in some form. That is, they need to have access to sentences labeled with their preferred analyses in order to estimate model parameters. As noted in the introduction, this is a serious limitation, given that there are few languages in the world for which there exist any syntactically annotated data, not to mention the wide range of domains and text types for which no labeled data are available even in well-resourced languages such as English. Consequently, the development of methods that can learn from unlabeled data, either alone or in combination with labeled data, should be of primary importance, even though it has so far played a rather marginal role in the statistical parsing community. In this final section, we will briefly review some of the existing work in this area.

11.6.1 Weakly Supervised Parsing

Weakly supervised (or semi-supervised) learning refers to techniques that use labeled data as in supervised learning but complements this with learning from unlabeled data, usually in much larger quantities than the labeled data, hence reducing the need for manual annotation to produce labeled data. The most common approach is to use the labeled data to train one or more systems that can then be used to label new data, and to retrain the systems on a combination of the original labeled data and the new, automatically labeled data. One of the key issues in the design of such a method is how to decide which automatically labeled data instances to include in the new training set.

In *co-training* (Blum and Mitchell 1998), two or more systems with complementary views of the data are used, so that each data instance is described using two different feature sets that provide different, complementary information about the instance. Ideally, the two views should be conditionally independent and each view sufficient by itself. The two systems are first trained on the labeled data and used to analyze the unlabeled data. The most confident predictions of each system on the unlabeled data are then used to iteratively construct additional labeled training data for the other system. Co-training has been applied to syntactic parsing but the results so far are rather mixed (Sarkar 2001; Steedman et al. 2003). One potential use of co-training is in domain adaptation, where systems have been trained on labeled out-of-domain data and need to be tuned using unlabeled in-domain data. In this setup, a simple variation on co-training has proven effective, where an automatically labeled instance is added to the new training set only if both systems agree on its analysis (Sagae and Tsujii 2007).

In *self-training*, one and the same system is used to label its own training data. According to the received wisdom, this scheme should be less effective than co-training, given that it does not provide two independent views of the data, and early studies of self-training for statistical parsing seemed to confirm this (Charniak 1997; Steedman et al. 2003). More recently, however, self-training has been used successfully to improve parsing accuracy on both in-domain and out-of-domain data (McClosky et al. 2006a,b, 2008). It seems that more research is needed to understand the conditions that are necessary in order for self-training to be effective (McClosky et al. 2008).

11.6.2 Unsupervised Parsing

Unsupervised parsing amounts to the induction of a statistical parsing model from raw text. Early work in this area was based on the PCFG model, trying to learn rule probabilities for a fixed-form grammar using the Inside–Outside algorithm (Baker 1979; Lari and Young 1990) but with rather limited success (Carroll and Charniak 1992; Pereira and Schabes 1992). More recent work has instead focused on models inspired by successful approaches to supervised parsing, in particular history-based models and data-oriented parsing.

As an example, let us consider the Constituent-Context Model (CCM) (Klein and Manning 2002; Klein 2005). Let $x = w_1, \ldots, w_n$ be a sentence, let y be a tree for x, and let y_{ij} be **true** if $w_i, \ldots, w_j$ is a constituent according to y and **false** otherwise. The joint probability $P(x, y)$ of a sentence x and a tree y is equivalent to $P(y)P(x|y)$, where $P(y)$ is the a priori probability of the tree (usually assumed to come from a uniform distribution), and $P(x|y)$ is modeled as follows:

$$P(x|y) = \prod_{1 \leq i < j \leq n} P(w_i, \ldots, w_j | y_{ij}) P(w_{i-1}, w_{j+1} | y_{ij}) \qquad (11.17)$$

The two conditional probabilities on the right-hand side of the equation are referred to as the *constituent* and the *context* probabilities, respectively, even though they are defined not only for constituents but for all spans of the sentence x. Using the EM algorithm to estimate the parameters of the constituent and context distributions resulted in the first model to beat the right-branching baseline when evaluated on the data set known as WSJ10, consisting of part-of-speech sequences for all sentences up to length 10 in the *Wall Street Journal* section of the Penn Treebank (Klein and Manning 2002; Klein 2005).[*] The results can be improved further by combining CCM with the dependency-based DMV model, which is inspired by the head-driven history-based models described in Section 11.4.1 (Klein and Manning 2004; Klein 2005) and further discussed below.

Another class of models that have achieved competitive results are the various unsupervised versions of the DOP model (cf. Section 11.4.3). Whereas learning in the supervised DOP model takes into account all possible subtrees of the preferred parse tree y for sentence x, learning in the unsupervised setting takes into account all possible subtrees of *all* possible parse trees of x. There are different ways to train such a model, but applying the EM algorithm to an efficient PCFG reduction (the so-called UML-DOP model) gives empirical results on a par with the combined CCM + DMV model (Bod 2007).

An alternative approach to unsupervised phrase structure parsing is the common-cover-link model (Seginer 2007), which uses a linear-time incremental parsing algorithm for a link-based representation of phrase structure and learns from very simple surface statistics. Unlike the other models discussed in this section, this model is efficient enough to learn from plain words (not part-of-speech tags) without any upper bound on sentence length. Although evaluation results are not directly comparable, the common-cover-link model appears to give competitive accuracy.

The work discussed so far has all been concerned with unsupervised phrase structure parsing, but there has also been work on inducing models for dependency parsing. Early proposals involved models that start by generating an abstract dependency tree (without words) and then populate the tree with words according to a distribution where each word is conditioned only on its head and on the direction of attachment (Yuret 1998; Paskin 2001a,b). However, a problem with this kind of model is that it tends to link words that have high mutual information regardless of whether they are plausibly syntactically related.

In order to overcome the problems of the earlier models, the DMV model mentioned earlier was proposed (Klein and Manning 2004; Klein 2005). DMV is short for Dependency Model with Valence, and the model is clearly inspired by the head-driven history-based models used in supervised parsing (cf. Section 11.4.1). In this model, a dependency (sub)tree rooted at h, denoted $T(h)$, is generated as follows:

---

[*] The right-branching baseline assigns to every sentence a strictly right-branching, binary tree. Since parse trees for English are predominantly right-branching, this constitutes a rather demanding baseline for unsupervised parsing.

$$P(T(h)) = \prod_{d \in \{l,r\}} \left[\prod_{a \in D(h,d)} P_!(\neg!|h,d,?)P_v(a|h,d)P(T(a)) \right] P_!(!|h,d,?) \qquad (11.18)$$

In this equation, d is a variable over the direction of the dependency – left (l) or right (r); $D(h, d)$ is the set of dependents of h in direction d; $P_!(!|h, d, ?)$ is the probability of stopping the generation of dependents in direction d and ? is a binary variable indicating whether any dependents have been generated or not; $P_v(a|h, d)$ is the probability of generating the dependent word a, conditioned on the head h and direction d; and $P(T(a))$ is (recursively) the probability of the subtree rooted at a.

The DMV has not only improved results for unsupervised dependency parsing but has also been combined with the CCM model to improve results for both phrase structure parsing and dependency parsing. The original work on the DMV used the EM algorithm for parameter estimation (Klein and Manning 2004; Klein 2005), but results have later been improved substantially through the use of alternative estimation methods such as contrastive estimation and structured annealing (Smith 2006).

11.7 Summary and Conclusions

In this chapter, we have tried to give an overview of the most prominent approaches to statistical parsing that are found in the field today, characterizing the different models in terms of their generative and evaluative components and discussing the problems of learning and inference that they give rise to. Overall, the field is dominated by supervised approaches that make use of generative or discriminative statistical models to rank the candidate analyses for a given input sentence. In terms of empirical accuracy, discriminative models seem to have a slight edge over generative models, especially discriminative models that incorporate global features, but it is important to remember that many discriminative parsers include the output of a generative model in their feature representations. For both generative and discriminative models, we can see a clear development toward models that take more global structure into account, which improves their capacity for disambiguation but makes parsing computationally harder. In this way, there is an inevitable trade-off between accuracy and efficiency in statistical parsing.

Parsers that learn from unlabeled data—instead of or in addition to labeled data—have so far played a marginal role in statistical parsing but are likely to become more important in the future. Developing a large-scale treebank for every new language and domain we want to parse is simply not a scalable solution, so research on methods that do not rely (only) on labeled data is a major concern for the field. Although the empirical results in terms of parsing accuracy have so far not been on a par with those for supervised approaches, results are steadily improving. Moreover, it is clear that the comparison has been biased in favor of the supervised systems, because the outputs of both systems have been compared to the kind of representations that supervised parsers learn from. One way to get around this problem is to use application-driven evaluation instead, and there are signs that in this context unsupervised approaches can already compete with supervised approaches for some applications (Bod 2007).

Finally, it is worth pointing out that this survey of statistical parsing is by no means exhaustive. We have chosen to concentrate on the types of models that have been important for driving the development of the field and that are also found in the best performing systems today, without describing any of the systems in detail. One topic that we have not touched upon at all is *system combination*, that is, techniques for improving parsing accuracy by combining several models, either at learning time or at parsing time. In fact, many of the best performing parsers available today for different types of syntactic representations do in some way involve system combination. Thus, Charniak and Johnson's reranking parser (Charniak and Johnson 2005) includes Charniak's generative parser (Charniak 2000) as a component, and there are many dependency parsers that combine several models either by voting (Zeman and Žabokrtský 2005; Sagae and Lavie 2006b; Hall 2007) or by stacking (Nivre and McDonald 2008). It is likely that system combination will remain an important technique for boosting accuracy, even if single models become increasingly more accurate by themselves in the future.

Acknowledgments

I want to thank John Carroll and Jason Eisner for valuable comments on an earlier version of this chapter. I am also grateful to Peter Ljunglöf and Mats Wirén for discussions about the organization of the two parsing chapters (Chapter 4 and this one).

References

Aduriz, I., M. J. Aranzabe, J. M. Arriola, A. Atutxa, A. Díaz de Ilarraza, A. Garmendia, and M. Oronoz (2003). Construction of a Basque dependency treebank. In *Proceedings of the Second Workshop on Treebanks and Linguistic Theories (TLT)*, Växjö, Sweden, pp. 201–204.

Attardi, G. (2006). Experiments with a multilanguage non-projective dependency parser. In *Proceedings of the 10th Conference on Computational Natural Language Learning (CoNLL)*, New York, pp. 166–170.

Baker, J. (1979). Trainable grammars for speech recognition. In *Speech Communication Papers for the 97th Meeting of the Acoustical Society of America*, Cambridge, MA, pp. 547–550.

Bikel, D. (2004). On the parameter space of generative lexicalized statistical parsing models. PhD thesis, University of Pennsylvania, Philadelphia, PA.

Black, E., S. Abney, D. Flickinger, C. Gdaniec, R. Grishman, P. Harrison, D. Hindle, R. Ingria, F. Jelinek, J. Klavans, M. Liberman, S. Roukos, B. Santorini, and T. Strzalkowski (1991). A procedure for quantitatively comparing the syntactic coverage of English grammars. In *Proceedings of the Fourth DARPA Speech and Natural Language Workshop*, Pacific Grove, CA, pp. 306–311.

Black, E., R. Garside, and G. Leech (Eds.) (1993). *Statistically-Driven Computer Grammars of English: The IBM/Lancaster Approach*. Rodopi, Amsterdam, the Netherlands.

Blum, A. and T. Mitchell (1998). Combining labeled and unlabeled data with co-training. In *Proceedings of the Workshop on Computational Learning Theory (COLT)*, Madison, WI, pp. 92–100.

Bod, R. (1995). Enriching linguistics with statistics: Performance models of natural language. PhD thesis, University of Amsterdam, Amsterdam, the Netherlands.

Bod, R. (1998). *Beyond Grammar*. CSLI Publications, Stanford, CA.

Bod, R. (2001). What is the minimal set of fragments that achieves maximal parse accuracy? In *Proceedings of the 39th Annual Meeting of the Association for Computational Linguistics (ACL)*, Toulouse, France, pp. 66–73.

Bod, R. (2003). An efficient implementation of a new DOP model. In *Proceedings of the 10th Conference of the European Chapter of the Association for Computational Linguistics (EACL)*, Budapest, Hungary, pp. 19–26.

Bod, R. (2007). Is the end of supervised parsing in sight? In *Proceedings of the 45th Annual Meeting of the Association of Computational Linguistics*, Prague, Czech Republic, pp. 400–407.

Bod, R. and R. Kaplan (1998). A probabilistic corpus-driven model for lexical-functional analysis. In *Proceedings of the 36th Annual Meeting of the Association for Computational Linguistics (ACL) and the 17th International Conference on Computational Linguistics (COLING)*, Montreal, QC, Canada, pp. 145–151.

Bod, R., R. Scha, and K. Sima'an (Eds.) (2003). *Data-Oriented Parsing*. CSLI Publications, Stanford, CA.

Boguslavsky, I., S. Grigorieva, N. Grigoriev, L. Kreidlin, and N. Frid (2000). Dependency treebank for Russian: Concept, tools, types of information. In *Proceedings of the 18th International Conference on Computational Linguistics (COLING)*, Saarbrucken, Germany, pp. 987–991.

Böhmová, A., J. Hajič, E. Hajičová, and B. Hladká (2003). The Prague Dependency Treebank: A three-level annotation scenario. In A. Abeillé (Ed.), *Treebanks: Building and Using Parsed Corpora*, Kluwer, Dordrecht, the Netherlands, pp. 103–127.

Bonnema, R. and R. Scha (2003). Reconsidering the probability model for DOP. In R. Bod, R. Scha, and K. Sima'an (Eds.), *Data-Oriented Parsing*, CSLI Publications, Stanford, CA, pp. 25–41.

Bonnema, R., R. Bod, and R. Scha (1997). A DOP model for semantic interpretation. In *Proceedings of the 35th Annual Meeting of the Association for Computational Linguistics (ACL) and the 8th Conference of the European Chapter of the Association for Computational Linguistics (EACL)*, Madrid, Spain, pp. 159–167.

Bonnema, R., P. Buying, and R. Scha (2000). Parse tree probability in data oriented parsing. In *Proceedings of the Conference on Intelligent Text Processing and Computational Linguistics*, Mexico City, Mexico, pp. 219–232.

Booth, T. L. and R. A. Thompson (1973). Applying probability measures to abstract languages. *IEEE Transactions on Computers C-22*, 442–450.

Bresnan, J. (2000). *Lexical-Functional Syntax*. Blackwell, Oxford, U.K.

Briscoe, E. and J. Carroll (1993). Generalised probabilistic LR parsing of natural language (corpora) with unification-based grammars. *Computational Linguistics 19*, 25–59.

Buchholz, S. and E. Marsi (2006). CoNLL-X shared task on multilingual dependency parsing. In *Proceedings of the 10th Conference on Computational Natural Language Learning (CoNLL)*, New York, pp. 149–164.

Caraballo, S. A. and E. Charniak (1998). New figures of merit for best-first probabilistic chart parsing. *Computational Linguistics 24*, 275–298.

Carreras, X. (2007). Experiments with a higher-order projective dependency parser. In *Proceedings of the CoNLL Shared Task of EMNLP-CoNLL 2007*, Prague, Czech Republic, pp. 957–961.

Carroll, J. and E. Briscoe (1996). Apportioning development effort in a probabilistic LR parsing system through evaluation. In *Proceedings of the Conference on Empirical Methods in Natural Language Processing (EMNLP)*, Philadelphia, PA, pp. 92–100.

Carroll, G. and E. Charniak (1992). Two experiments on learning probabilistic dependency grammars from corpora. Technical Report TR-92, Department of Computer Science, Brown University, Providence, RI.

Carroll, J., E. Briscoe, and A. Sanfilippo (1998). Parser evaluation: A survey and a new proposal. In *Proceedings of the First International Conference on Language Resources and Evaluation (LREC)*, Granda, Spain, pp. 447–454.

Carroll, J., G. Minnen, and E. Briscoe (2003). Parser evaluation using a grammatical relation annotation scheme. In A. Abeillé (Ed.), *Treebanks*, Kluwer, Dordrecht, the Netherlands, pp. 299–316.

Charniak, E. (1996). Tree-bank grammars. In *Proceedings of the 13th National Conference on Artificial Intelligence*, Portland, OR, pp. 1031–1036.

Charniak, E. (1997). Statistical parsing with a context-free grammar and word statistics. In *Proceedings of AAAI/IAAI*, Menlo Park, CA, pp. 598–603.

Charniak, E. (2000). A maximum-entropy-inspired parser. In *Proceedings of the First Meeting of the North American Chapter of the Association for Computational Linguistics (NAACL)*, Seattle, WA, pp. 132–139.

Charniak, E. and M. Johnson (2005). Coarse-to-fine *n*-best parsing and MaxEnt discriminative reranking. In *Proceedings of the 43rd Annual Meeting of the Association for Computational Linguistics (ACL)*, Ann Arbor, MI, pp. 173–180.

Cheng, Y., M. Asahara, and Y. Matsumoto (2005). Machine learning-based dependency analyzer for Chinese. In *Proceedings of International Conference on Chinese Computing (ICCC)*, Bangkok, Thailand, pp. 66–73.

Chi, Z. and S. Geman (1998). Estimation of probabilistic context-free grammars. *Computational Linguistics 24*, 299–305.

Chiang, D. (2000). Statistical parsing with an automatically-extracted tree adjoining grammar. In *Proceedings of the 38th Annual Meeting of the Association for Computational Linguistics*, Hong Kong, pp. 456–463.

Chomsky, N. (1956). Three models for the description of language. *IRE Transactions on Information Theory IT-2*, 113–124.

Chu, Y. J. and T. H. Liu (1965). On the shortest arborescence of a directed graph. *Science Sinica 14*, 1396–1400.

Ciaramita, M. and G. Attardi (2007, June). Dependency parsing with second-order feature maps and annotated semantic information. In *Proceedings of the 10th International Conference on Parsing Technologies*, Prague, Czech Republic, pp. 133–143.

Clark, S. and J. R. Curran (2004). Parsing the WSJ using CCG and log-linear models. In *Proceedings of the 42nd Annual Meeting of the Association for Computational Linguistics (ACL)*, Barcelona, Spain, pp. 104–111.

Collins, M. (1996). A new statistical parser based on bigram lexical dependencies. In *Proceedings of the 34th Annual Meeting of the Association for Computational Linguistics (ACL)*, Santa Cruz, CA, pp. 184–191.

Collins, M. (1997). Three generative, lexicalised models for statistical parsing. In *Proceedings of the 35th Annual Meeting of the Association for Computational Linguistics (ACL) and the Eighth Conference of the European Chapter of the Association for Computational Linguistics (EACL)*, Madrid, Spain, pp. 16–23.

Collins, M. (1999). Head-driven statistical models for natural language parsing. PhD thesis, University of Pennsylvania, Philadelphia, PA.

Collins, M. (2000). Discriminative reranking for natural language parsing. In *Proceedings of the 17th International Conference on Machine Learning*, Stanford, CA, pp. 175–182.

Collins, M. and N. Duffy (2002). New ranking algorithms for parsing and tagging: Kernels over discrete structures and the voted perceptron. In *Proceedings of the 40th Annual Meeting of the Association for Computational Linguistics (ACL)*, Philadelphia, PA, pp. 263–270.

Collins, M. and T. Koo (2005). Discriminative reranking for natural language parsing. *Computational Linguistics 31*, 25–71.

Curran, J. R. and S. Clark (2004). The importance of supertagging for wide-coverage CCG parsing. In *Proceedings of the 20th International Conference on Computational Linguistics (COLING)*, Geneva, Switzerland, pp. 282–288.

Dreyer, M. and J. Eisner (2006). Better informed training of latent syntactic features. In *Proceedings of the Conference on Empirical Methods in Natural Language Processing (EMNLP)*, Sydney, Australia, pp. 317–326.

Džeroski, S., T. Erjavec, N. Ledinek, P. Pajas, Z. Žabokrtsky, and A. Žele (2006). Towards a Slovene dependency treebank. In *Proceedings of the Fifth International Conference on Language Resources and Evaluation (LREC)*, Genoa, Italy.

Edmonds, J. (1967). Optimum branchings. *Journal of Research of the National Bureau of Standards 71B*, 233–240.

Eisner, J. M. (1996). Three new probabilistic models for dependency parsing: An exploration. In *Proceedings of the 16th International Conference on Computational Linguistics (COLING)*, Copenhagen, Denmark, pp. 340–345.

Eisner, J. M. (2000). Bilexical grammars and their cubic-time parsing algorithms. In H. Bunt and A. Nijholt (Eds.), *Advances in Probabilistic and Other Parsing Technologies*, Kluwer, Dordrecht, the Netherlands, pp. 29–62.

Eisner, J. and G. Satta (1999). Efficient parsing for bilexical context-free grammars and head automaton grammars. In *Proceedings of the 37th Annual Meeting of the Association for Computational Linguistics (ACL)*, College Park, MD, pp. 457–464.

Forst, M., N. Bertomeu, B. Crysmann, F. Fouvry, S. Hansen-Schirra, and V. Kordoni (2004). The TIGER dependency bank. In *Proceedings of the Fifth International Workshop on Linguistically Interpreted Corpora*, Geneva, Switzerland, pp. 31–37.

Fujisaki, T., F. Jelinek, J. Cocke, E. Black, and T. Nishino (1989). A probabilistic method for sentence disambiguation. In *Proceedings of the First International Workshop on Parsing Technologies*, Pittsburgh, PA, pp. 105–114.

Gildea, D. (2001). Corpus variation and parser performance. In *Proceedings of the Conference on Empirical Methods in Natural Language Processing (EMNLP)*, Pittsburgh, PA, pp. 167–202.

Goodman, J. (1996). Parsing algorithms and metrics. In *Proceedings of the 34th Annual Meeting of the Association for Computational Linguistics (ACL)*, Santa Cruz, CA, pp. 177–183.

Goodman, J. (1999). Semiring parsing. *Computational Linguistics 25*, 573–605.

Grishman, R., C. Macleod, and J. Sterling (1992). Evaluating parsing strategies using standardized parse files. In *Proceedings of the Third Conference on Applied Natural Language Processing (ANLP)*, Trento, Italy, pp. 156–161.

Hajič, J., B. Vidova Hladká, J. Panevová, E. Hajičová, P. Sgall, and P. Pajas (2001). Prague Dependency Treebank 1.0. LDC, 2001T10.

Hajič, J., O. Smrž, P. Zemánek, J. Šnaidauf, and E. Beška (2004). Prague Arabic Dependency Treebank: Development in data and tools. In *Proceedings of the NEMLAR International Conference on Arabic Language Resources and Tools*, Cairo, Egypt, pp. 110–117.

Hall, K. (2007). K-best spanning tree parsing. In *Proceedings of the 45th Annual Meeting of the Association for Computational Linguistics (ACL)*, Prague, Czech Republic, pp. 392–399.

Hall, J., J. Nilsson, J. Nivre, G. Eryiğit, B. Megyesi, M. Nilsson, and M. Saers (2007). Single malt or blended? A study in multilingual parser optimization. In *Proceedings of the CoNLL Shared Task of EMNLP-CoNLL 2007*, Prague, Czech Republic.

Han, C.-H., N.-R. Han, E.-S. Ko, and M. Palmer (2002). Development and evaluation of a Korean treebank and its application to NLP. In *Proceedings of the Third International Conference on Language Resources and Evaluation (LREC)*, Las Palmas, Canary Islands, Spain, pp. 1635–1642.

Henderson, J. (2004). Discriminative training of a neural network statistical parser. In *Proceedings of the 42nd Annual Meeting of the Association for Computational Linguistics (ACL)*, Barcelona, Spain, pp. 96–103.

Hockenmaier, J. (2003). Data and models for statistical parsing with combinatory categorial grammar. PhD thesis, University of Edinburgh, Edinburgh, U.K.

Hockenmaier, J. and M. Steedman (2007). CCGbank: A corpus of CCG derivations and dependency structures extracted from the Penn Treebank. *Computational Linguistics 33*, 355–396.

Huang, L. (2008). Forest reranking: Discriminative parsing with non-local features. In *Proceedings of the 46th Annual Meeting of the Association for Computational Linguistics (ACL)*, Philadelphia, PA, pp. 586–594.

Huang, L. and D. Chiang (2005). Better k-best parsing. In *Proceedings of the 9th International Workshop on Parsing Technologies (IWPT)*, Vancouver, BC, Canada.

Isozaki, H., H. Kazawa, and T. Hirao (2004). A deterministic word dependency analyzer enhanced with preference learning. In *Proceedings of the 20th International Conference on Computational Linguistics (COLING)*, Morristown, NJ, pp. 275–281.

Jebara, T. (2004). *Machine Learning: Discriminative and Generative*. Kluwer, Boston, MA.

Jelinek, F., J. Lafferty, D. M. Magerman, R. Mercer, A. Ratnaparkhi, and S. Roukos (1994). Decision tree parsing using a hidden derivation model. In *Proceedings of the ARPA Human Language Technology Workshop*, Plainsboro, NJ, pp. 272–277.

Jiménez, V. M. and A. Marzal (2000). Computation of the n best parse trees for weighted and stochastic context-free grammars. In *Proceedings of the Joint IAPR International Workshops on Advances in Pattern Recognition*, Alicante, Spain.

Johnson, M. (1998). PCFG models of linguistic tree representations. *Computational Linguistics 24*, 613–632.

Johnson, M. (2001). Joint and conditional estimation of tagging and parsing models. In *Proceedings of the 39th Annual Meeting of the Association for Computational Linguistics (ACL)*, Toulouse, France pp. 314–321.

Johnson, M. (2002). A simple pattern-matching algorithm for recovering empty nodes and their antecedents. In *Proceedings of the 40th Annual Meeting of the Association for Computational Linguistics (ACL)*, Philadelphia, PA, pp. 136–143.

Johnson, M., S. Geman, S. Canon, Z. Chi, and S. Riezler (1999). Estimators for stochastic "unification-based" grammars. In *Proceedings of the 37th Annual Meeting of the Association for Computational Linguistics (ACL)*, Morristown, NJ, pp. 535–541.

Joshi, A. (1985). How much context-sensitivity is necessary for assigning structural descriptions: Tree adjoining grammars. In D. Dowty, L. Karttunen, and A. Zwicky (Eds.), *Natural Language Processing: Psycholinguistic, Computational and Theoretical Perspectives*, Cambridge University Press, New York, pp. 206–250.

Joshi, A. K. (1997). Tree-adjoining grammars. In G. Rozenberg and A. Salomaa (Eds.), *Handbook of Formal Languages. Volume 3: Beyond Words*, Springer, Berlin, Germany, pp. 69–123.

Kaplan, R. and J. Bresnan (1982). Lexical-Functional Grammar: A formal system for grammatical representation. In J. Bresnan (Ed.), *The Mental Representation of Grammatical Relations*, MIT Press, Cambridge, MA, pp. 173–281.

King, T. H., R. Crouch, S. Riezler, M. Dalrymple, and R. M. Kaplan (2003). The PARC 700 dependency bank. In *Proceedings of the Fourth International Workshop on Linguistically Interpreted Corpora*, Budapest, Hungary, pp. 1–8.

Klein, D. (2005). The unsupervised learning of natural language structure. PhD thesis, Stanford University, Stanford, CA.

Klein, D. and C. D. Manning (2002). Conditional structure versus conditional estimation in NLP models. In *Proceedings of the Conference on Empirical Methods in Natural Language Processing (EMNLP)*, Philadelphia, PA, pp. 9–16.

Klein, D. and C. D. Manning (2003). Accurate unlexicalized parsing. In *Proceedings of the 41st Annual Meeting of the Association for Computational Linguistics (ACL)*, Stanford, CA, pp. 423–430.

Klein, D. and C. D. Manning (2004). Corpus-based induction of syntactic structure: Models of dependency and constituency. In *Proceedings of the 42nd Annual Meeting of the Association for Computational Linguistics (ACL)*, Barcelona, Spain, pp. 479–486.

Kromann, M. T. (2003). The Danish Dependency Treebank and the DTAG treebank tool. In *Proceedings of the second Workshop on Treebanks and Linguistic Theories (TLT)*, Växjö, Sweden, pp. 217–220.

Kudo, T. and Y. Matsumoto (2002). Japanese dependency analysis using cascaded chunking. In *Proceedings of the Sixth Workshop on Computational Language Learning (CoNLL)*, Taipei, Taiwan, pp. 63–69.

Lari, K. and S. S. Young (1990). The estimation of stochastic context-free grammars using the inside-outside algorithm. *Computer Speech and Language 4*, 35–56.

Liang, P., S. Petrov, M. Jordan, and D. Klein (2007). The infinite PCFG using hierarchical Dirichlet processes. In *Proceedings of the 2007 Joint Conference on Empirical Methods in Natural Language Processing and Computational Natural Language Learning (EMNLP-CoNLL)*, Prague, Czech Republic, pp. 688–697.

Lin, D. (1995). A dependency-based method for evaluating broad-coverage parsers. In *Proceedings of IJCAI-95*, Montreal, QC, Canada, pp. 1420–1425.

Lin, D. (1998). A dependency-based method for evaluating broad-coverage parsers. *Journal of Natural Language Engineering 4*, 97–114.

Maamouri, M. and A. Bies (2004). Developing an Arabic treebank: Methods, guidelines, procedures, and tools. In *Proceedings of the Workshop on Computational Approaches to Arabic Script-Based Languages*, Geneva, Switzerland, pp. 2–9.

Magerman, D. M. (1995). Statistical decision-tree models for parsing. In *Proceedings of the 33rd Annual Meeting of the Association for Computational Linguistics (ACL)*, Cambridge, MA, pp. 276–283.

Marcus, M. P., B. Santorini, and M. A. Marcinkiewicz (1993). Building a large annotated corpus of English: The Penn Treebank. *Computational Linguistics 19*, 313–330.

Marcus, M. P., B. Santorini, M. A. Marcinkiewicz, R. MacIntyre, A. Bies, M. Ferguson, K. Katz, and B. Schasberger (1994). The Penn Treebank: Annotating predicate-argument structure. In *Proceedings of the ARPA Human Language Technology Workshop*, Princeton, NJ, pp. 114–119.

Matsuzaki, T., Y. Miyao, and J. Tsujii (2005). Probabilistic CFG with latent annotations. In *Proceedings of the 43rd Annual Meeting of the Association for Computational Linguistics (ACL)*, Ann Arbor, MI, pp. 75–82.

McClosky, D., E. Charniak, and M. Johnson (2006a). Effective self-training for parsing. In *Proceedings of the Human Language Technology Conference of the NAACL, Main Conference*, New York, pp. 152–159.

McClosky, D., E. Charniak, and M. Johnson (2006b). Reranking and self-training for parser adaptation. In *Proceedings of the 21st International Conference on Computational Linguistics and the 44th Annual Meeting of the Association for Computational Linguistics*, Sydney, Australia, pp. 337–344.

McClosky, D., E. Charniak, and M. Johnson (2008). When is self-training effective for parsing? In *Proceedings of the 22nd International Conference on Computational Linguistics (COLING)*, Manchester, U.K., pp. 561–568.

McDonald, R. and F. Pereira (2006). Online learning of approximate dependency parsing algorithms. In *Proceedings of the 11th Conference of the European Chapter of the Association for Computational Linguistics (EACL)*, Philadelphia, PA, pp. 81–88.

McDonald, R., K. Crammer, and F. Pereira (2005a). Online large-margin training of dependency parsers. In *Proceedings of the 43rd Annual Meeting of the Association for Computational Linguistics (ACL)*, Ann Arbor, MI, pp. 91–98.

McDonald, R., F. Pereira, K. Ribarov, and J. Hajič (2005b). Non-projective dependency parsing using spanning tree algorithms. In *Proceedings of the Human Language Technology Conference and the Conference on Empirical Methods in Natural Language Processing (HLT/EMNLP)*, Vancouver, BC, Canada, pp. 523–530.

Mel'čuk, I. (1988). *Dependency Syntax: Theory and Practice*. State University of New York Press, New York.

Miyao, Y., T. Ninomiya, and J. Tsujii (2003). Probabilistic modeling of argument structures including non-local dependencies. In *Proceedings of the International Conference on Recent Advances in Natural Language Processing (RANLP)*, Borovets, Bulgaria, pp. 285–291.

Moreno, A., S. López, F. Sánchez, and R. Grishman (2003). Developing a Spanish treebank. In A. Abeillé (Ed.), *Treebanks: Building and Using Parsed Corpora*, pp. 149–163. Kluwer, Dordrecht, the Netherlands.

Musillo, G. and P. Merlo (2008). Unlexicalised hidden variable models of split dependency grammars. In *Proceedings of the 46th Annual Meeting of the Association for Computational Linguistics (ACL)*, Columbus, OH, pp. 213–216.

Nakagawa, T. (2007). Multilingual dependency parsing using global features. In *Proceedings of the CoNLL Shared Task of EMNLP-CoNLL 2007*, Prague, Czech Republic, pp. 952–956.

Ney, H. (1991). Dynamic programming parsing for context-free grammars in continuous speech recognition. *IEEE Transactions on Signal Processing 39*, 336–340.

Nivre, J. (2003). An efficient algorithm for projective dependency parsing. In *Proceedings of the Eighth International Workshop on Parsing Technologies (IWPT)*, Nancy, France, pp. 149–160.

Nivre, J. (2006a). Constraints on non-projective dependency graphs. In *Proceedings of the 11th Conference of the European Chapter of the Association for Computational Linguistics (EACL)*, Trento, Italy, pp. 73–80.

Nivre, J. (2006b). *Inductive Dependency Parsing*. Springer, New York.

Nivre, J. (2007). Incremental non-projective dependency parsing. In *Proceedings of Human Language Technologies: The Annual Conference of the North American Chapter of the Association for Computational Linguistics (NAACL HLT)*, Rochester, NY, pp. 396–403.

Nivre, J. (2008). Algorithms for deterministic incremental dependency parsing. *Computational Linguistics* 34, 513–553.

Nivre, J. and R. McDonald (2008). Integrating graph-based and transition-based dependency parsers. In *Proceedings of the 46th Annual Meeting of the Association for Computational Linguistics (ACL)*, Columbus, OH.

Nivre, J., J. Hall, and J. Nilsson (2004). Memory-based dependency parsing. In *Proceedings of the Eighth Conference on Computational Natural Language Learning*, Boston, MA, pp. 49–56.

Nivre, J., J. Hall, J. Nilsson, G. Eryiğit, and S. Marinov (2006). Labeled pseudo-projective dependency parsing with support vector machines. In *Proceedings of the 10th Conference on Computational Natural Language Learning (CoNLL)*, New York, pp. 221–225.

Oflazer, K., B. Say, D. Z. Hakkani-Tür, and G. Tür (2003). Building a Turkish treebank. In A. Abeillé (Ed.), *Treebanks: Building and Using Parsed Corpora*, pp. 261–277. Kluwer, Dordrecht, the Netherlands.

Paskin, M. A. (2001a). Cubic-time parsing and learning algorithms for grammatical bigram models. Technical Report UCB/CSD-01-1148, Computer Science Division, University of California, Berkeley, CA.

Paskin, M. A. (2001b). Grammatical bigrams. In *Advances in Neural Information Processing Systems (NIPS)*, Vancouver, BC, Canada, pp. 91–97.

Pereira, F. C. and Y. Schabes (1992). Inside-outside reestimation from partially bracketed corpora. In *Proceedings of the 30th Annual Meeting of the Association for Computational Linguistics (ACL)*, Newark, DE, pp. 128–135.

Petrov, S. and D. Klein (2007). Improved inference for unlexicalized parsing. In *Proceedings of Human Language Technologies: The Annual Conference of the North American Chapter of the Association for Computational Linguistics (NAACL HLT)*, New York, pp. 404–411.

Petrov, S., L. Barrett, R. Thibaux, and D. Klein (2006). Learning accurate, compact, and interpretable tree annotation. In *Proceedings of the 21st International Conference on Computational Linguistics and the 44th Annual Meeting of the Association for Computational Linguistics*, Sydney, Australia, pp. 433–440.

Pollard, C. and I. A. Sag (1987). *Information-Based Syntax and Semantics*. CSLI Publications, Stanford, CA.

Pollard, C. and I. A. Sag (1994). *Head-Driven Phrase Structure Grammar*. CSLI Publications, Stanford, CA.

Prescher, D. (2005). Head-driven PCFGs with latent-head statistics. In *Proceedings of the Ninth International Workshop on Parsing Technologies (IWPT)*, Vancouver, BC, Canada, pp. 115–124.

Prokopidis, P., E. Desypri, M. Koutsombogera, H. Papageorgiou, and S. Piperidis (2005). Theoretical and practical issues in the construction of a Greek dependency treebank. In *Proceedings of the Third Workshop on Treebanks and Linguistic Theories (TLT)*, Barcelona, Spain, pp. 149–160.

Ratnaparkhi, A. (1997). A linear observed time statistical parser based on maximum entropy models. In *Proceedings of the Conference on Empirical Methods in Natural Language Processing (EMNLP)*, Providence, RI, pp. 1–10.

Ratnaparkhi, A. (1999). Learning to parse natural language with maximum entropy models. *Machine Learning* 34, 151–175.

Riedel, S., R. Çakıcı, and I. Meza-Ruiz (2006). Multi-lingual dependency parsing with incremental integer linear programming. In *Proceedings of the 10th Conference on Computational Natural Language Learning (CoNLL)*, New York, pp. 226–230.

Riezler, S., M. H. King, R. M. Kaplan, R. Crouch, J. T. Maxwell III, and M. Johnson (2002). Parsing the Wall Street Journal using a Lexical-Functional Grammar and discriminative estimation techniques. In *Proceedings of the 40th Annual Meeting of the Association for Computational Linguistics (ACL)*, Philadelphia, PA, pp. 271–278.

Sagae, K. and A. Lavie (2005). A classifier-based parser with linear run-time complexity. In *Proceedings of the Ninth International Workshop on Parsing Technologies (IWPT)*, Vancouver, BC, Canada, pp. 125–132.

Sagae, K. and A. Lavie (2006a). A best-first probabilistic shift-reduce parser. In *Proceedings of the COLING/ACL 2006 Main Conference Poster Sessions*, Sydney, Australia, pp. 691–698.

Sagae, K. and A. Lavie (2006b). Parser combination by reparsing. In *Proceedings of the Human Language Technology Conference of the NAACL, Companion Volume: Short Papers*, New York, pp. 129–132.

Sagae, K. and J. Tsujii (2007). Dependency parsing and domain adaptation with LR models and parser ensembles. In *Proceedings of the CoNLL Shared Task of EMNLP-CoNLL 2007*, Prague, Czech Republic, pp. 1044–1050.

Sánchez, J. A. and J. M. Benedí (1997). Consistency of stochastic context-free grammars from probabilistic estimation based on growth transformations. *IEEE Transactions on Pattern Analysis and Machine Intelligence 19*, 1052–1055.

Sarkar, A. (2001). Applying co-training methods to statistical parsing. In *Proceedings of the Second Meeting of the North American Chapter of the Association for Computational Linguistics (NAACL)*, Pittsburgh, PA, pp. 175–182.

Scha, R. (1990). Taaltheorie en taaltechnologie; competence en performance [language theory and language technology; competence and performance]. In R. de Kort and G. L. J. Leerdam (Eds.), *Computertoepassingen in de Neerlandistiek*, LVVN, Almere, the Netherlands, pp. 7–22.

Seginer, Y. (2007). Fast unsupervised incremental parsing. In *Proceedings of the 45th Annual Meeting of the Association of Computational Linguistics*, Prague, Czech Republic, pp. 384–391.

Sgall, P., E. Hajičová, and J. Panevová (1986). *The Meaning of the Sentence in Its Pragmatic Aspects*. Reidel, Dordrecht, the Netherlands.

Sima'an, K. (1996a). Computational complexity of probabilistic disambiguation by means of tree grammar. In *Proceedings of the 16th International Conference on Computational Linguistics (COLING)*, Copenhagen, Denmark, pp. 1175–1180.

Sima'an, K. (1996b). An optimized algorithm for data-oriented parsing. In R. Mitkov and N. Nicolov (Eds.), *Recent Advances in Natural Language Processing. Selected Papers from RANLP '95*, John Benjamins, Amsterdam, the Netherlands, pp. 35–47.

Sima'an, K. (1999). Learning efficient disambiguation. PhD thesis, University of Amsterdam, Amsterdam, the Netherlands.

Smith, N. A. (2006). Novel estimation methods for unsupervised discovery of latent structure in natural language text. PhD thesis, Johns Hopkins University, Baltimore, MD.

Smith, N. A. and M. Johnson (2007). Weighted and probabilistic context-free grammars are equally expressive. *Computational Linguistics 33*, 477–491.

Steedman, M. (2000). *The Syntactic Process*. MIT Press, Cambridge, MA.

Steedman, M., R. Hwa, M. Osborne, and A. Sarkar (2003). Corrected co-training for statistical parsers. In *Proceedings of the International Conference on Machine Learning (ICML)*, Washington, DC, pp. 95–102.

Stolcke, A. (1995). An efficient probabilistic context-free parsing algorithm that computes prefix probabilities. *Computational Linguistics 21*, 165–202.

Taskar, B., D. Klein, M. Collins, D. Koller, and C. Manning (2004). Max-margin parsing. In *Proceedings of the Conference on Empirical Methods in Natural Language Processing (EMNLP)*, Barcelona, Spain, pp. 1–8.

Titov, I. and J. Henderson (2007). A latent variable model for generative dependency parsing. In *Proceedings of the 10th International Conference on Parsing Technologies (IWPT)*, Prague, Czech Republic, pp. 144–155.

Toutanova, K., C. D. Manning, S. M. Shieber, D. Flickinger, and S. Oepen (2002). Parse disambiguation for a rich HPSG grammar. In *Proceedings of the First Workshop on Treebanks and Linguistic Theories (TLT)*, Prague, Czech Republic, pp. 253–263.

Turian, J. and I. D. Melamed (2006). Advances in discriminative parsing. In *Proceedings of the 21st International Conference on Computational Linguistics and the 44th Annual Meeting of the Association for Computational Linguistics*, Sydney, Australia, pp. 873–880.

Xue, N., F. Xia, F.-D. Chiou, and M. Palmer (2004). The Penn Chinese Treebank: Phase structure annotation of a large corpus. *Journal of Natural Language Engineering 11*, 207–238.

Yamada, H. and Y. Matsumoto (2003). Statistical dependency analysis with support vector machines. In *Proceedings of the Eighth International Workshop on Parsing Technologies (IWPT)*, Nancy, France, pp. 195–206.

Yuret, D. (1998). Discovery of linguistic relations using lexical attraction. PhD thesis, Massachusetts Institute of Technology, Cambridge, MA.

Zeman, D. and Z. Žabokrtský (2005). Improving parsing accuracy by combining diverse dependency parsers. In *Proceedings of the Ninth International Workshop on Parsing Technologies (IWPT)*, Vancouver, BC, Canada, pp. 171–178.

Zollmann, A. and K. Sima'an (2005). A consistent and efficient estimator for data-oriented parsing. *Journal of Automata, Languages and Combinatorics 10*(2/3), 367–388.

12

Multiword Expressions

Timothy Baldwin
University of Melbourne

Su Nam Kim
University of Melbourne

12.1 Introduction

Languages are made up of words, which combine via morphosyntax to encode meaning in the form of phrases and sentences. While it may appear relatively innocuous, the question of what constitutes a "word" is a surprisingly vexed one. First, are *dog* and *dogs* two separate words, or variants of a single word? The traditional view from lexicography and linguistics is to treat them as separate inflected wordforms of the lexeme *dog*, as any difference in the syntax/semantics of the two words is predictable from the general process of noun pluralization in English. Second, what is the status of expressions like *top dog* and *dog days*? A speaker of English who knew *top*, *dog*, and *day* in isolation but had never been exposed to these two expressions would be hard put to predict the semantics of "person who is in charge" and "period of inactivity," respectively.* To be able to retrieve the semantics of these expressions, they must have lexical status of some form in the mental lexicon, which encodes their particular semantics. Expressions such as these that have surprising properties not predicted by their component words are referred to as multiword expressions (MWEs).† The focus of this chapter is the precise nature and types of MWEs, and the current state of MWE research in NLP.

---

* All glosses in this chapter are taken from WORDNET 3.0 (Fellbaum 1998).
† Terms that are largely synonymous with "multiword expression" are "multiword unit," "multiword lexical item," "phrase-ological unit," and "fixed expression"; there is also variation in the hyphenation of "multiword," with "multi-word" in common use.

Armed with our informal description of MWEs, let us first motivate this chapter with a brief overview of the range of MWEs, and complexities associated with them. We return to define MWEs formally in Section 12.2.

(1a)–(1b) include a number of MWEs, underlined.

(1)   a.   In a nutshell, the administrator can take advantage of the database's many features through a single interface.
       b.   You should also jot down the serial number of your television video.

As we can see, analogously to simple words, MWEs can occur in a wide range of lexical and syntactic configurations (e.g., nominal, verbal, and adverbial). Semantically, we can observe different effects: in some cases (e.g., *serial number* and *television video*), the component words preserve their original semantics, but the MWE encodes extra semantics (e.g., the fact that a *television video* is a single-unit device, and usually designed to be portable); in other cases (e.g., *in a nutshell*, meaning "summed up briefly"), the semantics of one or more of the component words has no obvious bearing of the semantics of the MWE.

While all of the MWE examples we have seen to date have occurred as contiguous units, this is not always the case:

(2)   a.   She likes to take a long bath for relaxation after exams.
       b.   Kim hates to put her friends out.

For example, in (2a), *long* is an internal modifier and not a component of the base MWE *take a bath*, as there is nothing surprising about the syntax of the modified MWE or the resulting semantics (cf. *take a short/leisurely/warm/mud/... bath*).

How big an issue are MWEs, though? The number of MWEs is estimated to be of the same order of magnitude as the number of simplex words in a speaker's lexicon (Jackendoff 1997; Tschichold 1998; Pauwels 2000). At the type level, therefore, MWEs are as much of an issue as simple words. Added to this, new (types of) MWE are continuously created as languages evolve (e.g., *shock and awe*, *carbon footprint*, and *credit crunch*) (Gates 1988; Tschichold 1998; Fazly et al. 2009).

Crosslingually, MWEs have been documented across a broad spectrum of the world's languages (see the companion Web site for this chapter for a detailed listing of references). In fact, MWEs are such an efficient way of providing nuance and facilitating lexical expansion with a relatively small simplex lexicon, it is highly doubtful that any language would evolve without MWEs of some description.

MWEs are broadly used to enhance fluency and understandability, or mark the register/genre of language use (Fillmore et al. 1988; Liberman and Sproat 1992; Nunberg et al. 1994; Dirven 2001). For example, MWEs can make language more or less informal/colloquial (cf. *London Underground* vs. *Tube*, and *piss off* vs. *annoy*). Regionally, MWEs vary considerably. For example, *take away* and *take out* are identical in meaning, but the former is the preferred expression in British/Australian English, while the latter is the preferred expression in American English. Other examples are *phone box* vs. *phone booth*, *lay the table* vs. *set the table*, and *no through road* vs. *not a through street*, respectively.

There is a modest body of research on modeling MWEs that has been integrated into NLP applications, for example, for the purposes of fluency, robustness, or better understanding of natural language. One area where MWEs have traditionally been used heavily (either explicitly or implicitly) is machine translation (MT), as a means of capturing subtle syntactic, semantic, and pragmatic effects in the source and target languages (Miyazaki et al. 1993; Gerber and Yang 1997; Matsuo et al. 1997; Melamed 1997). Understanding MWEs has broad utility in tasks ranging from syntactic disambiguation to conceptual (semantic) comprehension. Explicit lexicalized MWE data helps simplify the syntactic structure of sentences that include MWEs, and conversely, a lack of MWE lexical items in a precision grammar is a significant source of parse errors (Baldwin et al. 2004). Additionally, it has been shown that the accurate recognition of MWEs influences the accuracy of semantic tagging (Piao et al. 2003), and word alignment in MT can be improved through a specific handling of the syntax and semantics of MWEs (Venkatapathy and Joshi 2006).

12.2 Linguistic Properties of MWEs

We adopt the following formal definition of multiword expression, following (Sag et al. 2002):

(3) Multiword expressions (MWEs) are lexical items that: (a) can be decomposed into multiple lexemes; and (b) display lexical, syntactic, semantic, pragmatic and/or statistical idiomaticity

In languages such as English, the conventional interpretation of the requirement of decomposability into lexemes is that MWEs must in themselves be made up of multiple whitespace-delimited words. For example, *marketing manager* is potentially a MWE as it is made up of two lexemes (*marketing* and *manager*), while fused words such as *lighthouse* are conventionally not classified as MWEs.* In languages such as German, the high productivity of compound nouns such as *Kontaktlinse* "contact lens" (the concatenation of *Kontakt* "contact" and *Linse* "lens"), without whitespace delimitation, means that we tend to relax this restriction and allow for single-word MWEs. In non-segmenting languages such as Japanese and Chinese (Baldwin and Bond 2002; Xu et al. 2006), we are spared this artificial consideration. The ability to decompose an expression into multiple lexemes is still applicable, however, and leads to the conclusion, for example that *fukugō-hyōgen* "multiword expression" is a MWE (both *fukugō* "compound" and *hyōgen* "expression" are standalone lexemes), but *buchō* "department head" is *not* (*bu* "department" is a standalone lexeme, but *chō* "head" is not).

The second requirement on a MWE is for it to be idiomatic. We provide a detailed account of idiomaticity in its various manifestations in the following section.

12.2.1 Idiomaticity

In the context of MWEs, idiomaticity refers to markedness or deviation from the basic properties of the component lexemes, and applies at the lexical, syntactic, semantic, pragmatic, and/or statistical levels. A given MWE is often idiomatic at multiple levels (e.g., syntactic, semantic, and statistical in the case of *by and large*), as we return to illustrate in Section 12.2.3.

Closely related to the notion of idiomaticity is *compositionality*, which we consider to be the degree to which the features of the parts of a MWE combine to predict the features of the whole. While compositionality is often construed as applying exclusively to semantic idiomaticity (hence by "non-compositional MWE," researchers tend to mean a semantically idiomatic MWE), in practice it can apply across all the same levels as idiomaticity. Below, we present an itemized account of each subtype of idiomaticity.

12.2.1.1 Lexical Idiomaticity

Lexical idiomaticity occurs when one or more components of an MWE are not part of the conventional English lexicon. For example, *ad hoc* is lexically marked in that neither of its components (*ad* and *hoc*) are standalone English words.† Lexical idiomaticity inevitably results in syntactic and semantic idiomaticity because there is no lexical knowledge associated directly with the parts from which to predict the behavior of the MWE. As such, it is one of the most clear-cut and predictive properties of MWEhood.

12.2.1.2 Syntactic Idiomaticity

Syntactic idiomaticity occurs when the syntax of the MWE is not derived directly from that of its components (Chafe 1968; Bauer 1983; Sag et al. 2002; Katz and Postal 2004). For example, *by and large*, is syntactically idiomatic in that it is adverbial in nature, but made up of the anomalous coordination of a preposition (*by*) and an adjective (*large*). On the other hand, *take a walk* is not syntactically marked

---

* In practice, a significant subset of research on English noun compounds (see Section 12.3.1) has considered both fused and whitespace-separated expressions.
† Note that the idiomaticity is diminished if the speaker has knowledge of the Latin origins of the term. Also, while the component words do not have status as standalone lexical items, they do occur in other MWEs (e.g., *ad nauseum, post hoc*).

as it is a simple verb–object combination that is derived transparently from a transitive verb (*walk*) and a countable noun (*walk*). Syntactic idiomaticity can also occur at the constructional level, in classes of MWEs having syntactic properties that are differentiated from their component words, for example, verb particle constructions (Section 12.3.2.1) and determinerless prepositional phrases (Section 12.3.3.1).

12.2.1.3 Semantic Idiomaticity

Semantic idiomaticity is the property of the meaning of a MWE not being explicitly derivable from its parts (Chafe 1968; Bauer 1983; Sag et al. 2002; Katz and Postal 2004). For example, *middle of the road* usually signifies "non-extremism, especially in political views," which we could not readily predict from either *middle* or *road*. On the other hand, *to and fro* is not semantically marked as its semantics is fully predictable from its parts. Many cases are not as clear cut as these, however. The semantics of *blow hot and cold* ("constantly change opinion"), for example, is partially predictable from *blow* ("move" and hence "change"), but not as immediately from *hot and cold*. There are also cases where the meanings of the parts are transparently inherited but there is additional semantic content that has no overt realization. One such example is *bus driver* where, modulo the effects of word sense disambiguation (WSD), *bus* and *driver* both have their expected meanings, but there is additionally the default expectation that a *bus driver* is "one who drives a bus" and not "one who drives *like* a bus" or "an object for driving buses with," for example.

Closely related to the issue of semantic idiomaticity is the notion of figuration, that is, the property of the components of a MWE having some metaphoric (e.g., *take the bull by the horns*), hyperbolic (e.g., *not worth the paper it's printed on*), or metonymic (e.g., *lend a hand*) meaning in addition to their literal meaning (Fillmore et al. 1988; Nunberg et al. 1994). As an illustration of decomposability via metaphorical figuration, consider the English idiom *spill the beans*. Assuming a formal semantic representation of `reveal'(secret')` for the MWE, we can coerce the semantics of *spill* and *beans* into `reveal'` and `secret'`, respectively, to arrive at a figurative interpretation of the MWE semantics. A compositionality analysis would not be able to predict this regularity as these senses for *spill* and *beans* are not readily available outside this particular MWE. Predictably, MWEs vary in the immediacy of their decomposability—with *get the nod* being more transparently decomposable than *spill the beans*, for example—and not all MWEs are decomposable (cf. *kick the bucket*). We return to discuss the interaction between decomposability and syntactic flexibility in Section 12.3.2.4.

One intriguing aspect of semantic idiomaticity is that higher-usage MWEs are generally perceived to be less semantically idiomatic, or at least more readily decomposable (Keysar and Bly 1995).

12.2.1.4 Pragmatic Idiomaticity

Pragmatic idiomaticity is the condition of a MWE being associated with a fixed set of situations or a particular context (Kastovsky 1982; Jackendoff 1997; Sag et al. 2002). *Good morning* and *all aboard* are examples of pragmatic MWEs: the first is a greeting associated specifically with mornings* and the second is a command associated with the specific situation of a train station or dock, and the imminent departure of a train or ship. Pragmatically idiomatic MWEs are often ambiguous with (non-situated) literal translations; for example, *good morning* can mean "pleasant morning" (cf. *Kim had a good morning*).

12.2.1.5 Statistical Idiomaticity

Statistical idiomaticity occurs when a particular combination of words occurs with markedly high frequency, relative to the component words or alternative phrasings of the same expression (Cruse 1986; Sag et al. 2002). For example, in Table 12.1, we present an illustration of statistical idiomaticity, adapted from Cruse (1986, p. 281). The example is based on the cluster of near-synonym adjectives (*flawless*, *immaculate*, *impeccable*, and *spotless*), and their affinity to premodify a range of nouns. For a given pairing of adjective and noun, we indicate the compatibility in the form of discrete markers ("+" indicates a

---

* Which is not to say that it cannot be used ironically at other times of the day!

TABLE 12.1 Examples of Statistical Idiomaticity

	flawless	immaculate	impeccable	spotless
condition	+	−	+	+
credentials	−		+	−
hair	−	+	?	−
house	?	+	?	+
logic	+	−	+	−
timing	?	+	+	−

Note: "+" = strong lexical affinity, "?" = neutral lexical affinity, "−" = negative lexical affinity.

positive lexical affinity, "?" indicates a neutral lexical affinity, and "−" indicates a negative lexical affinity). For example, *immaculate* has a strong lexical affinity with *performance* (i.e., *immaculate performance* is a relatively common expression), whereas *spotless* has a negative affinity with *credentials* (i.e., *spotless credentials* is relatively infrequent). There may, of course, be phonological, semantic, or other grounds for particular adjective–noun combinations being more or less frequent; statistical idiomaticity is simply an observation of the relative frequency of a given combination. It is also important to note that statistical idiomaticity is a continuously graded phenomenon, and our predictions about lexical affinity in Table 12.1 are most naturally interpreted as a ranking of the propensity for each of the adjectives to occur as a pre-modifier of *record*; for example, *impeccable* and *spotless* are more probable choices than *immaculate*, which is in turn more probable than *flawless*.

Another striking case of statistical idiomaticity is with binomials such as *black and white*—as in *black and white television*—where the reverse noun ordering does not preserve the lexicalized semantics of the word combination (cf. *?white and black television*) (Benor and Levy 2006). The arbitrariness of the preferred noun order in English is poignantly illustrated by it being reversed in other languages, for example, *shirokuro* "white and black" and *blanco y negro* "white and black" in Japanese and Spanish, respectively.

Statistical idiomaticity relates closely to the notion of institutionalization (a.k.a. conventionalization), that is, a particular word combination coming to be used to refer a given object (Fernando and Flavell 1981; Bauer 1983; Nunberg et al. 1994; Sag et al. 2002). For example, *traffic light* is the conventionalized descriptor for "a visual signal to control the flow of traffic at intersections." There is no *a priori* reason why it should not instead be called a *traffic director* or *intersection regulator*, but the simple fact of the matter is that it is not referred to using either of those expressions; instead, *traffic light* was historically established as the canonical term for referring to the object. Similarly, it is an arbitrary fact of the English language that we say *many thanks* and not *several thanks*, and *salt and pepper* in preference to *pepper and salt*.* We term these anti-collocations of the respective MWEs (Pearce 2001): lexico-syntactic variants of MWEs that have unexpectedly low frequency, and in doing so, contrastively highlight the statistical idiomaticity of the target expression.[†]

12.2.2 Other Properties of MWEs

Other common properties of MWE are single-word paraphrasability, proverbiality, and prosody. Unlike idiomaticity, where some form of idiomaticity is a necessary feature of MWEs, these other properties are neither necessary nor sufficient. Prosody relates to semantic idiomaticity, while the other properties are independent of idiomaticity as described above.

---

* Which is not to say there was not grounds for the selection of the canonical form at its genesis, for example, for historical, crosslingual, or phonological reasons.

[†] The term anti-collocation originated in the context of collocation research (see Section 12.2.4). While noting the potential for confusion, we use it in the broader context of MWEs as a tool for analyzing the statistical idiomaticity of a candidate MWE relative to alternative forms of the same basic expression.

- Crosslingual variation
  There is remarkable variation in MWEs across languages (Villavicencio et al. 2004). In some cases, there is direct lexico-syntactic correspondence for a crosslingual MWE pair with similar semantics. For example, *in the red* has a direct lexico-syntactic correlate in Portuguese with the same semantics: *no vermelho*, where *no* is the contraction of *in* and *the*, *vermelho* means *red*, and both idioms are prepositional phrases (PPs). Others have identical syntax but differ lexically. For example, *in the black* corresponds to *no azul* ("in the blue") in Portuguese, with a different choice of color term (*blue* instead of *black*). More obtusely, *bring the curtain down on* corresponds to the Portuguese *botar um ponto final em* (lit. "put the final dot in"), with similar syntactic makeup but radically different lexical composition. Other MWEs again are lexically similar but syntactically differentiated. For example, *in a corner* (e.g., *The media has him in a corner*) and *encurralado* ("cornered") are semantically equivalent but realized by different constructions—a PP in English and an adjective in Portuguese.

  There are of course many MWEs that have no direct translation equivalent in a second language. For example, the Japanese MWE *zoku-giiN*, meaning "legislators championing the causes of selected industries" has no direct translation in English (Tanaka and Baldwin 2003). Equally, there are terms which are realized as MWEs in one language but single-word lexemes in another, such as *interest rate* and its Japanese equivalent *riritsu*.

- Single-word paraphrasability
  Single-word paraphrasability is the observation that significant numbers of MWEs can be paraphrased with a single word (Chafe 1968; Gibbs 1980; Fillmore et al. 1988; Liberman and Sproat 1992; Nunberg et al. 1994). While some MWEs are single-word paraphrasable (e.g., *leave out* = *omit*), others are not (e.g., *look up* = *?*). Also, MWEs with arguments can sometimes be paraphrasable (e.g., *take off clothes* = *undress*), just as non-MWEs comprised of multiple words can be single-word paraphrasable (e.g., *drop sharply* = *plummet*).

- Proverbiality
  Proverbiality is the ability of a MWE to "describe and implicitly to explain a recurrent situation of particular social interest in the virtue of its resemblance or relation to a scenario involving homely, concrete things and relations" (Nunberg et al. 1994). For example, verb particle constructions and idioms are often indicators of more informal situations (e.g., *piss off* is an informal form of *annoy*, and *drop off* is an informal form of *fall asleep*).

- Prosody
  MWEs can have distinct prosody, that is stress patterns, from compositional language (Fillmore et al. 1988; Liberman and Sproat 1992; Nunberg et al. 1994). For example, when the components do not make an equal contribution to the semantics of the whole, MWEs can be prosodically marked, for example, *soft spot* is prosodically marked (due to the stress on *soft* rather than *spot*), although *first aid* and *red herring* are not. Note that prosodic marking can equally occur with non-MWEs, such as *dental operation*.

12.2.3 Testing an Expression for MWEhood

Above, we described five different forms of idiomaticity, along with a number of other properties of MWEs. We bring these together in categorizing a selection of MWEs in Table 12.2.

Taking the example of the verb particle construction *look up* (in the sense of "seek information from," as in *Kim looked the word up in the dictionary*), we first observe that it is made up of multiple words (*look* and *up*), and thus satisfies the first requirement in our MWE definition. In terms of idiomaticity: (1) it is not lexically idiomatic, as both *look* and *up* are part of the standard English lexicon; (2) while it has peculiar syntax relative to its component words, in *up* being separable from *look*, this is a general property of transitive verb particle constructions (see Section 12.3.2.1) rather than this particular word combination,

TABLE 12.2 Classification of MWEs in Terms of Their Idiomaticity

	Lexical	Syntactic	Semantic	Pragmatic	Statistical
all aboard	−	−	−	+	+
bus driver	−	−	−	−	+
by and large	−	+	+	−	+
kick the bucket	−	−	+	−	+
look up	−	−	+	−	+
shock and awe	−	−	−	+	+
social butterfly	−	−	+	−	+
take a walk	−	−	+	−	?
to and fro	?	+	−	−	+
traffic light	−	−	+	−	+
eat chocolate	−	−	−	−	−

so it is not syntactically idiomatic; (3) it is semantically idiomatic, as the semantics of "seek information from" is not predictable from the standard semantics of *look* and *up*; (4) it is not pragmatically idiomatic, as it does not generally evoke a particular situation; and (5) it is statistically marked, as it contrasts with anti-collocations such as *see/watch up* and is a relatively frequent expression in English. That is, it is semantically and statistically idiomatic; in combination with its multiword composition, this is sufficient to classify it as a MWE.

In Table 12.2, *kick the bucket* (in the sense of "die") has only one form of idiomaticity (semantic), while all the other examples have at least two forms of idiomaticity. *Traffic light*, for example, is statistically idiomatic in that it is both a common expression in English and stands in opposition to anti-collocations such as *vehicle light/traffic lamp*, and it is semantically idiomatic in that the particular semantics of "a visual signal to control the flow of traffic" is not explicitly represented in the component words (e.g., interpretations such as "a visual signal to indicate the flow of traffic," "a device for lighting the way of traffic," or "a lamp which indicates the relative flow of data" that are predicted by the component words are not readily available). Other noteworthy claims about idiomaticity are *shock and awe* is pragmatically idiomatic because of its particular association with the commencement of the Iraq War in 2003; *take a walk* is semantically idiomatic because this sense of *take* is particular to this and other light verb constructions (see Section 12.3.2.3), and distinct from the literal sense of the verb; and *to and fro* is syntactically idiomatic because of the relative syntactic opacity of the antiquated *fro*, and (somewhat) lexically idiomatic as it is used almost exclusively in the context of *to and fro*.[†]

Table 12.2 includes one negative example: *eat chocolate*. While it satisfies the requirement for multiword decomposability (i.e., it is made up of more than one word), it clearly lacks lexical, syntactic, semantic, and pragmatic idiomaticity. We would claim that it is also not statistically idiomatic. One possible counter-argument could be that *eat* is one of the most common verbs associated with *chocolate*, but the same argument could be made for almost any foodstuff in combination with *eat*. Possible anti-collocations such as *consume chocolate* or *munch on chocolate* are also perfectly acceptable.

12.2.4 Collocations and MWEs

A common term in NLP that relates closely to our discussion of MWEs is collocation. A widely used definition for collocation is "an arbitrary and recurrent word combination" (Benson 1990), or in our terms, a statistically idiomatic MWE (esp. of high frequency). While there is considerable variation between individual researchers, collocations are often distinguished from "idioms" or "non-compositional

---

* Under the constraint that *up* is a particle; examples such as *see you up the road* occur readily, but are not considered to be anti-collocations as *up* is a (transitive) preposition.

[†] Words such as this that occur only as part of a fixed expression are known variously as cranberry words or bound words (Aronoff 1976; Moon 1998; Trawiński et al. 2008) (other examples are *tenterhooks* and *caboodle*), and the expressions that contain them are often termed cranberry expressions (e.g., *on tenterhooks* and *the whole caboodle*).

phrases" on the grounds that they are not syntactically idiomatic, and if they are semantically idiomatic, it is through a relatively transparent process of figuration or metaphor (Choueka 1988; Lin 1998; McKeown and Radev 2000; Evert 2004). Additionally, much work on collocations focuses exclusively on predetermined constructional templates (e.g., adjective–noun or verb–noun collocations). In Table 12.2, for example *social butterfly* is an uncontroversial instance of a collocation, but *look up* and *to and fro* would tend not to be classified as collocations. As such, collocations form a proper subset of MWEs.

12.2.5 A Word on Terminology and Related Fields

It is worth making mention of a number of terms that relate to MWEs.

The term idiom varies considerably in its usage, from any kind of multiword item to only those MWEs that are semantically idiomatic; even here, there are those who consider idioms to be MWEs that are *exclusively* semantically idiomatic (also sometimes termed pure idioms), and those that restrict the term to particular syntactic subtypes of semantically idiomatic MWEs (Fillmore et al. 1988; Nunberg et al. 1994; Moon 1998; Huddleston and Pullum 2002). To avoid confusion, we will avoid using this term in this chapter.

The field of terminology has a rich history of research on multiword terms, which relates closely to MWEs (Sager 1990; Justeson and Katz 1995; Frantzi et al. 2000; Kageura et al. 2004). The major difference is that terminology research is primarily interested in identifying and classifying technical terms specific to a particular domain (both MWEs and simplex lexemes) and predicting patterns of variation in those terms. It is thus broader in scope than MWEs in the sense that simple lexemes can equally be technical terms, and narrower in the sense than nontechnical MWEs are not of interest to the field.

Phraseology is another field with a rich tradition history relating to MWEs (Cowie and Howarth 1996; Cowie 2001). It originally grew out of the work of Mel'čuk and others in Russia on Meaning-Text Theory (Mel'čuk and Polguère 1987), but more recently has taken on elements from the work of Sinclair and others in the context of corpus linguistics and corpus-based lexicography (Sinclair 1991). Phraseology is primarily interested in the description and functional classification of MWEs (including "sentence-like" units, such as phrases and quotations), from a theoretical perspective.

12.3 Types of MWEs

In this section, we detail a selection of the major MWE types that have received particular attention in the MWE literature. We will tend to focus on English MWEs for expository purposes, but provide tie-ins to corresponding MWEs in other languages where possible.

12.3.1 Nominal MWEs

Nominal MWEs are one of the most common MWE types, in terms of token frequency, type frequency, and their occurrence in the world's languages (Tanaka and Baldwin 2003; Lieber and Štekauer 2009). In English, the primary type of nominal MWE is the noun compound (NC), where two or more nouns combine to form a N̄, such as *golf club* or *computer science department* (Lauer 1995; Huddleston and Pullum 2002; Sag et al. 2002); the rightmost noun in the NC is termed the head noun (i.e., *club* and *department*, respectively) and the remainder of the component(s) modifier(s) (i.e., *golf* and *computer science*, respectively).* Within NCs, there is the subset of compound nominalizations, where the head is deverbal (e.g., *investor hesitation* or *stress avoidance*). There is also the broader class of nominal MWEs

---

* In fact, the norm among Germanic languages (e.g., Danish, Dutch, German, Norwegian, and Swedish) is for NCs to be realized as a single compound word (Bauer 2001). *Solar cell*, for example, is *zonnecel* in Dutch, *Solarzelle* in German, and *solcell* in Swedish. See Section 12.2 for comments on their compatibility with our definition of MWE.

where the modifiers are not restricted to be nominal, but can also be verbs (usually present or past participles, such as *connecting flight* or *hired help*) or adjectives (e.g., *open secret*). To avoid confusion, we will term this broader set of nominal MWEs nominal compounds. In Romance languages such as Italian, there is the additional class of complex nominals that include a preposition or other marker between the nouns, such as *succo di limone* "lemon juice" and *porta a vetri* "glass door."*

One property of NCs that has put them in the spotlight of NLP research is their underspecified semantics. For example, while sharing the same head, there is little semantic commonality between *nut tree*, *clothes tree*, and *family tree*: a *nut tree* is a tree that bears edible nuts; a *clothes tree* is a piece of furniture shaped somewhat like a tree, for hanging clothes on; and a *family tree* is a graphical depiction of the genealogical history of a family (which can be shaped like a tree). In each case, the meaning of the compound relates (if at times obtusely!) to a sense of both the head and the modifier, but the precise relationship is highly varied and not represented explicitly in any way. Furthermore, while it may be possible to argue that these are all lexicalized NCs with explicit semantic representations in the mental lexicon, native speakers generally have reasonably sharp intuitions about the semantics of novel compounds. For example, a *bed tree* is most plausibly a tree that beds are made from or perhaps for sleeping in, and a *reflection tree* could be a tree for reflecting in/near or perhaps the reflected image of a tree. Similarly, context can evoke irregular interpretations of high-frequency compounds (Downing 1977; Spärck Jones 1983; Copestake and Lascarides 1997; Gagné et al. 2005). This suggests that there is a dynamic interpretation process that takes place, which complements encyclopedic information about lexicalized compounds.

One popular approach to capturing the semantics of compound nouns is via a finite set of relations. For example, *orange juice*, *steel bridge*, and *paper hat* could all be analyzed as belonging to the MAKE relation, where HEAD is made from MODIFIER. This observation has led to the development of a bewildering range of semantic relation sets of varying sizes, based on abstract relations (Vanderwende 1994; Barker and Szpakowicz 1998; Rosario and Hearst 2001; Moldovan et al. 2004; Nastase et al. 2006), direct paraphrases, for example, using prepositions or verbs (Lauer 1995; Lapata 2002; Grover et al. 2004; Nakov 2008), or various hybrids of the two (Levi 1978; Vanderwende 1994; Ó Séaghdha 2008). This style of approach has been hampered by issues including low inter-annotator agreement (especially for larger semantic relation sets), coverage over data from different domains, the impact of context on interpretation, how to deal with "fringe" instances which do not quite fit any of the relations, and how to deal with interpretational ambiguity (Downing 1977; Spärck Jones 1983; Ó Séaghdha 2008).

An additional area of interest with nominal MWEs (especially NCs) is the syntactic disambiguation of MWEs with three or more terms. For example, *glass window cleaner* can be syntactically analyzed as either *(glass (window cleaner))* (i.e., "a window cleaner made of glass," or similar) or *((glass window) cleaner)* (i.e., "a cleaner of glass windows"). Syntactic ambiguity impacts on both the semantic interpretation and the prosody of the MWE. The task of disambiguating syntactic ambiguity in nominal MWEs is called bracketing. We return to discuss the basic approaches to bracketing in Section 12.5.3.

12.3.2 Verbal MWEs

12.3.2.1 Verb-Particle Constructions

Verb-particle constructions (VPCs, also sometimes termed particle verbs or phrasal verbs) are made up of a verb and an obligatory particle, typically in the form of an intransitive preposition (e.g., *play around, take off*), but including adjectives (e.g., *cut short, band together*) and verbs (e.g., *let go, let fly*) (Bolinger 1976; Jackendoff 1997; Huddleston and Pullum 2002; McIntyre 2007). English VPCs relate closely to particle verbs (a.k.a. separable verbs) in languages such as German (Lüdeling 2001), Dutch (Booij 2002), and Estonian (Kaalep and Muischnek 2008), but the construction has its own peculiarities in each language

---

* Our use of the term complex nominal for MWEs of form N P N should not be confused with that of Levi (1978), which included NCs and nominal compounds.

that go beyond the bounds of this chapter. To avoid confusion, we will focus exclusively on English VPCs in our discussion here.

The distinguishing properties of English VPCs are:

- Transitive VPCs can occur in either the joined (e.g., *Kim put on the sweater*) or split (e.g., *Kim put the sweater on*) word order in the case that the object NP is not pronominal
- Transitive VPCs must occur in the split word order if the object NP is pronominal (e.g., *Kim polished it off* vs. **Kim polished off it*).
- Manner adverbs do not readily occur between the verb and particle, in both intransitive and transitive VPCs (e.g., *?*Kim played habitually around*, **Kim made quickly up her mind*). Note, there is a small set of degree adverbs that readily premodify particles, notably *right* (e.g., *My turn is coming right up*) and *back* (e.g., *Kim put the sweater back on*)

All of these properties are defined at the construction level and common to all VPCs, however, begging the question of where the idiomaticity comes in that allows us to define them as MWEs. The answer is, in the main, semantic and statistical idiosyncrasies. For example, the semantics of *polish* in *polish off* (e.g., *polish off dessert*, *polish off the hitman*, *polish off my homework*) is differentiated from that of the simplex lexeme. Conversely, *swallow down* (e.g., *swallow down the drink*) preserves the semantics of both *swallow* and *down* (i.e., the liquid is swallowed, and as a result goes down [the esophagus]), and is thus conventionally not considered be a MWE.

VPCs are highly frequent in English text, but the distribution is highly skewed toward a minority of the VPC types, with the majority of VPCs occurring very infrequently (Baldwin 2005a). This is bad news if we want to build a parser with full coverage, for example, as we need to capture the long tail of VPC types. Compounding the problem, the construction is highly productive. For example, the completive *up* (e.g., *eat/finish/rest/... up*) can combine productively with a large array of action verbs to form a VPC with predictable syntax and semantics, which we could never hope to exhaustively list. Having said this, there are large numbers of semantically idiomatic VPCs that need to be recorded in the lexicon if we wish to capture their semantics correctly. Even here, VPCs populate the spectrum of compositionality relative to their components (Lidner 1983; Brinton 1985; Jackendoff 2002; Bannard et al. 2003; McCarthy et al. 2003; Cook and Stevenson 2006), so while some VPCs are clear candidates for lexicalization in terms of their semantic idiomaticity (e.g., *make out*, as in *Kim made out the cheque to Sandy* or *Kim and Sandy made out*), others are semantically closer to the semantics of their component words (e.g., *check out*, *blow over*) and to some degree derivable from their component words. One approach to representing this continuum of VPC semantics is that of Bannard et al. (2003), who subclassify VPCs into four compositionality classes based on the independent semantic contribution of the verb and particle: (1) the VPC inherits its semantics from the verb and particle (i.e., is not semantically idiomatic); (2) the VPC inherits semantics from the verb only; (3) the VPC inherits semantics from the particle only; and (4) the VPC inherits semantics from neither the verb nor the particle. A second approach is to employ a one-dimensional classification of holistic VPC compositionality (e.g., in the form of a integer scale of 0 to 10 (McCarthy et al. 2003)).

12.3.2.2 Prepositional Verbs

Prepositional verbs (PVs) relate closely to VPCs in being comprised of a verb and selected preposition, with the crucial difference that the preposition is transitive (e.g., *refer to*, *look for*) (Jackendoff 1973; O'Dowd 1998; Huddleston and Pullum 2002; Baldwin 2005b; Osswald et al. 2006). English PVs occur in two basic forms: (1) fixed preposition PVs (e.g., *come across*, *grow on*), where there is a hard constraint of the verb and selected preposition being strictly adjacent; and (2) mobile preposition PVs (e.g., *refer to*, *send for*), where the selected preposition is adjacent to the verb in the canonical word order, but undergoes limited syntactic alternation. For example, mobile preposition PVs allow limited coordination of PP objects (e.g., *refer to the book and to the DVD* vs. **come across the book and across the DVD*), and the

NP object of the selected preposition can be passivised (e.g., *the book was <u>referred to</u>* vs. **I was <u>grown on</u> by the book*).

PVs are highly frequent in general text, and notoriously hard to distinguish from VPCs and simple verb–preposition combinations, for example in parsing applications.

12.3.2.3 Light-Verb Constructions

Light-verb constructions (i.e., LVCs) are made up of a verb and a noun complement, often in the indefinite singular form (Jespersen 1965; Abeillé 1988; Miyagawa 1989; Grefenstette and Tapanainen 1994; Hoshi 1994; Huddleston and Pullum 2002; Sag et al. 2002; Butt 2003; Stevenson et al. 2004). The name of the construction comes from the verb being semantically bleached or "light," in the sense that their contribution to the meaning of the LVC is relatively small in comparison with that of the noun complement. In fact, the contribution of the light verb is so slight that in many cases, the LVC can be paraphrased with the verbal form of the noun complement (e.g., *take a walk* vs. *walk* or *take a photograph* vs. *photograph*). LVCs are also sometimes termed verb-complement pairs (Tan et al. 2006) or support verb constructions (Calzolari et al. 2002).

The following are the principle light verbs in English:

- *do*, for example, *do a demo, do a drawing, do a report*
- *give*, for example, *give a wave, give a sigh, give a kiss*
- *have*, for example, *have a rest, have a drink, have pity (on)*
- *make*, for example, *make an offer, make an attempt, make a mistake*
- *take*, for example, *take a walk, take a bath, take a photograph*

There is some disagreement in the scope of the term LVC, most notably in the membership of verbs that can be considered "light." Calzolari et al. (2002), for example, argued that the definition of LVCs (or support verb constructions in their terms) should be extended to include: (1) verbs that combine with an event noun (deverbal or otherwise) where the subject is a participant in the event most closely identified with the noun (e.g., *ask a question*); and (2) verbs with subjects that belong to some scenario associated with the full understanding of the event type designated by the object noun (e.g., *keep a promise*).

Morphologically, the verb in LVCs inflects but the noun complement tends to have a fixed number and a preference for determiner type. For example, *make amends* undergoes full verbal inflection (*make/makes/made/making amends*), but the noun complement cannot be singular (e.g., **make <u>amend</u>**). Syntactically, LVCs are highly flexible, undergoing passivization (e.g., *an offer was made*), extraction (e.g., *How many offers did Kim make?*) and internal modification (e.g., *make an irresistible offer*). On the other hand, there are hard constraints on what light verbs a given noun complement can be combined with (cf. **give/do/put/take an offer*), noting that some noun complements combine with multiple light verbs (e.g., *do/give a demo*), often with different semantics (e.g., *make a call* vs. *take a call* vs. *have a call*). Also, what light verb a given noun will combine with to form an LVC is often consistent across semantically related noun clusters (e.g., *give a cry/moan/howl* vs. **take a cry/moan/howl*).

LVCs occur across a large number of the world's languages, including Japanese (Grimshaw and Mester 1988; Baldwin and Bond 2002), Korean (Ahn 1991), Hindi (Mohanan 1994), and Persian (Karimi-Doostan 1997).

12.3.2.4 Verb–Noun Idiomatic Combinations

Verb–Noun Idiomatic Combinations (VNICs, also known as VP idioms) are composed of a verb and noun in direct object position, and are (at least) semantically idiomatic (e.g., *kick the bucket, shoot the breeze*)

---

* But also note other examples where the noun complement can be either singular or plural, for example, *take a bath* vs. *take baths*.

(Nunberg et al. 1994; Fellbaum 2002; Sag et al. 2002; Fazly et al. 2009). They are a notable subclass of MWE because of their crosslingual occurrence, and high lexical and semantic variability.

VNICs (along with other semantically idiomatic MWEs) are often categorized into two groups, based on their semantic decomposability (see Section 12.2.1.3) (Nunberg et al. 1994; Riehemann 2001). With decomposable VNICs, given the interpretation of the VNIC, it is possible to associate components of the VNIC with distinct elements of the VNIC interpretation, based on semantics not immediately accessible from the component lexemes. Assuming an interpretation of *spill the beans* such as `reveal'(x,secret')`,* for example, we could analyze *spill* as having the semantics of `reveal'` and *beans* having the semantics of `secret'`, through a process of figuration. Other examples of decomposable VNICs are *pull strings* (cf. `exert'(x,influence')`) and *touch a nerve* (cf. `cause'(x,reaction')`). With non-decomposable VNICs (e.g., *get the hang (of)*, *kick the bucket*), such a semantic decomposition is not possible. The reason we make this distinction is that decomposable VNICs tend to be syntactically flexible, in a manner predicted by the nature of the semantic decomposition; non-decomposable VNICs, on the other hand, tend not to be syntactically flexible (Cruse 1986; Nunberg et al. 1994; Jackendoff 1997; Sag et al. 2002). For example, *spill the beans* can be passivized (*It's a shame the beans were spilled*) and internally modified (*AT&T spilled the Starbucks beans*), similarly to a conventional verb–direct object pair (cf. *Sandy is loved by Kim* and *Kim loves the inimitable Sandy*); this is predicted by its decomposability.

VNICs generally occur with low frequency, but are notoriously hard to distinguish from literal usages of the same word combination (e.g., *Kim made a face at the policeman* vs. *Kim made a face in pottery class*). An accurate means of disambiguation is thus important in tasks that require semantic interpretation, but generally fraught by low volumes of training data.

12.3.3 Prepositional MWEs

12.3.3.1 Determinerless-Prepositional Phrases

Determinerless prepositional phrases (PP-Ds) are MWEs that are made up of a preposition and a singular noun without a determiner (Quirk et al. 1985; Sag et al. 2002; Huddleston and Pullum 2002; Baldwin et al. 2006).

Syntactically, PP-Ds are highly diverse, and display differing levels of syntactic markedness, productivity, and modifiability (Ross 1995; Chander 1998). That is, some PP-Ds are nonproductive (e.g., *on top* vs. **on bottom*) and nonmodifiable (e.g., *on top* vs. **on table top*), whereas others are fully productive (e.g., *by car/foot/bus/...*) and highly modifiable (e.g., *at high expense*, *on summer vacation*). In fact, while some PP-Ds are optionally modifiable (e.g., *on vacation* vs. *on summer vacation*), others require modification (e.g., **at level* vs. *at eye level*, and **at expense* vs. *at company expense*) (Baldwin et al. 2006).

Syntactically marked PP-Ds can be highly productive (Ross 1995; Grishman et al. 1998). For example, *by* combines with a virtually unrestricted array of countable nouns (e.g., *by bus/car/taxi/...*) but less readily with uncountable nouns (e.g., **by information/linguistics/...*).

Semantically, PP-Ds have a certain degree of semantic markedness on the noun (Haspelmath 1997; Mimmelmann 1998; Stvan 1998; Bond 2005). For example, *in* combines with uncountable nouns that refer to a social institution (e.g., *school, church, prison* but not *information*) to form syntactically unmarked PP-Ds with marked semantics, in the sense that only the social institution sense of the noun is evoked (e.g., *in school/church/prison/...* vs. **in information*) (Baldwin et al. 2006).

PP-Ds occur with surprising frequency and cause problems during parsing and generation, in terms of achieving the right balance between over- and under-generation (Baldwin et al. 2004).

---

* i.e., `reveal'` is a 2-place predicate, with *x* binding to the subject.

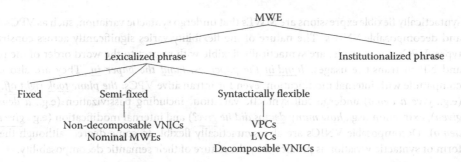

FIGURE 12.1   A classification of MWEs.

12.3.3.2 Complex Prepositions

Another common form of prepositional MWE is complex prepositions (e.g., *on top of*, *in addition to*) and other forms of complex markers (Villada Moirón 2005; Trawiński et al. 2006; Tsuchiya et al. 2006). Complex prepositions can take the form of fixed MWEs (e.g., *in addition to*) or alternatively semi-fixed MWEs, for example, optionally allowing internal modification (e.g., *with (due/particular/special/...) regard to*) or determiner insertion (e.g., *on (the) top of*).

12.4 MWE Classification

In developing a lexicon of MWEs, it is crucially important to develop a classification that captures the general properties of MWE classes, but at the same time allows for the encoding of information particular to a given MWE instance. In this section, we present a commonly used high-level classification, based particularly on the syntactic and semantic properties of MWEs outlined in Figure 12.1 (Bauer 1983; Sag et al. 2002).

The classification of MWEs into lexicalized phrases and institutionalized phrases hinges on whether the MWE is lexicalized (i.e., explicitly encoded in the lexicon), or a simple collocation (i.e., only statistically idiomatic).

Lexicalized phrases are MWEs with lexical, syntactic, semantic, or pragmatic idiomaticity. Lexicalized phrases can be further split into: fixed expressions (e.g., *ad hoc, at first*), semi-fixed expressions (e.g., *spill the beans, car dealer, Chicago White Socks*), and syntactically flexible expressions (e.g., *add up, give a demo*).

- fixed expressions are fixed strings that undergo neither morphosyntactic variation nor internal modification, often due to fossilization of what was once a compositional phrase. For example, *by and large* is not morphosyntactically modifiable (e.g., *by and larger) or internally modifiable (e.g., **by and very large*). Non-modifiable PP-Ds such as *on air* are also fixed expressions.
- semi-fixed expressions are lexically variable MWEs that have hard restrictions on word order and composition, but undergo some degree of lexical variation such as inflection (e.g., *kick/kicks/kicked/kicking the bucket* vs. **the bucket was kicked*), variation in reflexive pronouns (e.g., *in her/his/their shoes*), and determiner selection (e.g., *The Beatles* vs. *a Beatles album**). Non-decomposable VNICs (e.g., *kick the bucket, shoot the breeze*) and nominal MWEs (e.g., *attorney general, part of speech*) are also classified as semi-fixed expressions.

---

* The determiner *the* in *The Beatles* is obligatory in the case that *The Beatles* forms a noun phrase (i.e., *Beatles* can only be quantified by *the*), but in cases where *Beatles* forms a Ñ, for example, in [$_{NP}$ *a* [$_{N'}$ [$_{N'}$ *Beatles*] *album*]], the lexical item is realized without a determiner.

- syntactically flexible expressions are MWEs that undergo syntactic variation, such as VPCs, LVCs, and decomposable VNICs. The nature of the flexibility varies significantly across construction types. VPCs, for example, are syntactically flexible with respect to the word order of the particle and NP in transitive usages: *hand in the paper* vs. *hand the paper in*. They are also usually compatible with internal modification, even for intransitive VPCs: *the plane took right off*. LVCs (e.g., *give a demo*) undergo full syntactic variation, including passivization (e.g., *a demo was given*), extraction (e.g., *how many demos did he give?*) and internal modification (e.g., *give a clear demo*). Decomposable VNICs are also syntactically flexible to some degree, although the exact form of syntactic variation is predicted by the nature of their semantic decomposability.

Note that many of our MWE construction types can be assigned to a unique sub category of lexicalized phrase, namely, non-decomposable VNICs, NCs, VPCs, and LVCs. Determinerless PPs, on the other hand, cut across all three sub categories: non-modifiable PP-Ds (e.g., *at first*) are fixed expressions, PP-Ds with strict constraints on modifiability (e.g., *at level*) are semi-fixed expressions, and highly productive PP-Ds (e.g., *as president/coach/father of the bride/...*) are syntactically flexible.

The class of institutionalized phrases corresponds to MWEs that are exclusively statistically idiomatic, as described in Section 12.2.4. Examples include *salt and pepper* and *many thanks*.

12.5 Research Issues

The major NLP tasks relating to MWEs are (1) identifying and extracting MWEs from corpus data, and disambiguating their internal syntax, and (2) interpreting MWEs. Increasingly, these tasks are being pipelined with parsers and applications such as MT (Venkatapathy and Joshi 2006; Zhang et al. 2006; Blunsom 2007).

Depending on the type of MWE, the relative import of these syntactic and semantic tasks varies. For example, with NCs, the identification and extraction tasks are relatively trivial, whereas interpretation is considerably more difficult. Below, we discuss the challenges and review the key research on MWEs in NLP. For a listing of relevant resources (especially datasets and toolkits), we refer the reader to the companion Web site (http://handbookofnlp.cse.unsw.edu.au/?n_Chapter12.Chapter12).

12.5.1 Identification

Identification is the task of determining individual occurrences of MWEs in running text. The task is at the token (instance) level, such that we may identify 50 distinct occurrences of *pick up* in a given corpus. To give an example of an identification task, given the corpus fragment in (4) (taken from "The Frog Prince," a children's story), we might identify the MWEs in (4):

(4)   One fine evening a young princess put on her bonnet and clogs, and went out to take a walk by herself in a wood; ... she ran to pick it up; ...

In MWE identification, a key challenge is in differentiating between MWEs and literal usages for word combinations such as *make a face* that can occur in both usages (*Kim made a face at the policeman* [MWE] vs. *Kim made a face in pottery class* [non-MWE]). Syntactic ambiguity is also a major confounding factor, for example, in identifying VPCs in contexts such as *Have the paper in today*. For example, in the sentence *Kim signed in the room*, there is ambiguity between a VPC interpretation (*sign in* = "check in/announce arrival") and an intransitive verb + PP interpretation ("Kim performed the act of signing in the room").

MWE identification has tended to take the form of customized methods for particular MWE construction types and languages (e.g., English VPCs, LVCs, and NVICs), but there have been attempts to develop generalized techniques, as outlined below.

Perhaps the most obvious method of identifying MWEs is via a part-of-speech (POS) tagger, chunker, or parser, in the case that lexical information required to identify MWEs is contained within the parser output. For example, in the case of VPCs, there is a dedicated tag for (prepositional) particles in the Penn POS tagset, such that VPC identification can be performed simply by POS tagging a text, identifying all particle tags, and further identifying the head verb associated with each particle (e.g., by looking left for the first main verb, within a word window of fixed size) (Baldwin and Villavicencio 2002; Baldwin 2005a). Similarly, a chunker or phrase structure parser can be used to identify constructions such as NCs or VPCs (Lapata and Lascarides 2003; McCarthy et al. 2003; Kim and Baldwin to appear). This style of approach is generally not able to distinguish MWE and literal usages of a given word combination, however, as they are not differentiated in their surface syntax. Deep parsers that have lexical entries for MWEs and disambiguate to the level of lexical items are able to make this distinction, however, via supertagging or full parsing (Baldwin et al. 2004; Blunsom 2007).

Another general approach to MWE identification is to treat literal and MWE usages as different senses of a given word combination. This then allows for the application of WSD techniques to the identification problem. As with WSD research, both supervised (Patrick and Fletcher 2005; Hashimoto and Kawahara 2008) and unsupervised (Birke and Sarkar 2006; Katz and Giesbrecht 2006; Sporleder and Li 2009) approaches have been applied to the identification task. The key assumption in unsupervised approaches has been that literal usages will be contextually similar to simplex usages of the component words (e.g., *kick* and *bucket* in the case of *kick the bucket*). Mirroring the findings from WSD research, supervised methods tend to be more accurate, but have the obvious drawback that they requires large numbers of annotated literal and idiomatic instances of a given MWE to work. Unsupervised techniques are therefore more generally applicable.

A third approach, targeted particularly at semantically idiomatic MWEs, is to assume that MWEs occur: (a) in canonical forms, or (b) only in particular syntactic configurations, and do not undergo the same level of syntactic variation as literal usages. This relates to our claims in Section 12.3.2.4 relating to non-decomposable VNICs, where the prediction is that VNICs such as *kick the bucket* will not passivize or be internally modifiable. If we have a method of identifying the limits of syntactic variability of a given MWE, therefore, we can assume that any usage that falls outside these limits (e.g., *kicked a bucket*) must be literal. The problem, then, is identifying the degree of syntactic variability of a given MWE. This can be performed manually, in flagging individual MWE lexical items with predictions of what variations a given MWE can undergo (Li et al. 2003; Hashimoto et al. 2006). An alternative that alleviates the manual overhead associated with hand annotation is to use unsupervised learning to predict the "canonical" configurations for a given MWE, which can optionally be complemented with a supervised model to identify literal usages that are used in one of the canonical MWE configurations (e.g., *Kim kicked the bucket in frustration, and stormed out of the room*) (Fazly et al. 2009).

In research to date, good results have been achieved for particular MWEs, especially English VPCs. However, proposed methods have tended to rely heavily on existing resources such as parsers and hand-crafted lexical resources, and be tuned to particular MWE types.

12.5.2 Extraction

MWE extraction is a type-level task, wherein the MWE lexical items attested in a predetermined corpus are extracted out into a lexicon. For example, we may wish to know whether a given corpus provides evidence for a given verb *take* and preposition *off* combining to form a VPC (i.e., *take off*). To illustrate the difference between identification and extraction, identification would involve the determination of the individual occurrences of *take off* (e.g., each of the 240 in a given corpus), whereas extraction would involve the decision about whether *take off* occurred in the corpus or not (irrespective of the number of occurrences). Clearly there is a close connection between the two tasks, in that if we have identified one or more occurrences of a given MWE we can extract it as a MWE, and conversely, if we have extracted a given MWE, we must be able to identify at least one occurrence in the corpus.

The motivation for MWE extraction is generally lexicon development and expansion, for example, recognizing newly formed MWEs (e.g., *ring tone* or *shock and awe*) or domain-specific MWEs.

Extracting MWEs is relevant to any lexically driven application, such as grammar engineering or information extraction. Depending on the particular application, it may be necessary to additionally predict lexical properties of a given MWE, for example, its syntactic or semantic class. In addition, it is particularly important for productive MWEs or domains that are rich in technical terms (e.g., *bus speed* or *boot up* in the IT domain). MWE extraction is difficult for many of the same reasons as MWE identification, namely, syntactic flexibility and ambiguity.

There has been a strong focus on the development of general-purpose techniques for MWE extraction, particularly in the guise of collocation extraction (see Section 12.2.4). The dominating view here is that extraction can be carried out via association measures such as pointwise mutual information or the t-test, based on the analysis of the frequency of occurrence of a given word combination, often in comparison with the frequency of occurrence of the component words (Church and Hanks 1989; Smadja 1993; Frantzi et al. 2000; Evert and Krenn 2001; Pecina 2008). Association measures provide a score for each word combination, which forms the basis of a ranking of MWE candidates. Final extraction, therefore, consists of determining an appropriate cutoff in the ranking, although evaluation is often carried out over the full ranking.

Collocation extraction techniques have been applied to a wide range of extraction tasks over a number of languages, with the general finding that it is often unpredictable which association measure will work best for a given task. As a result, recent research has focused on building supervised classifiers to combine the predictions of a number of association measures, and shown that this leads to consistently superior results than any one association measure (Pecina 2008). It has also been shown that this style of approach works most effectively when combined with POS tagging or parsing, and strict filters on the type of MWE that is being extracted (e.g., ADJECTIVE–NOUN or VERB–NOUN: Justeson and Katz (1995, Pecina (2008)). It is worth noting that association measures have generally been applied to (continuous) word n-grams, or less frequently, predetermined dependency types in the output of a parser. Additionally, collocational extraction techniques tend to require a reasonable number of token occurrences of a given word combination to operate reliably, which we cannot always assume (Baldwin 2005a; Fazly 2007).

A second approach to MWE extraction, targeted specifically at semantically and statistically idiomatic MWEs, is to extend the general association measure approach to include substitution (Lin 1999; Pearce 2001; Schone and Jurafsky 2001). For example, in assessing the idiomaticity of *red tape*, explicit comparison is made with lexically related candidates generated by component word substitution, such as *yellow tape* or *red strip*. Common approaches to determining substitution candidates for a given component word are (near-)synonymy—for example, based on resources such as WORDNET—and distributional similarity.

Substitution can also be used to generate MWE candidates, and then check for their occurrence in corpus data. For example, if *clear up* is a known (compositional) VPC, it is reasonable to expect that VPCs such as *clean/tidy/unclutter/... up* are also VPCs (Villavicencio 2005). That is not to say that all of these occur as MWEs, however (c.f. **unclutter up*), so an additional check for corpus attestation is usually used in this style of approach.

A third approach, also targeted at semantically idiomatic MWEs, is to analyze the relative similarity between the context of use of a given word combination and its component words (Schone and Jurafsky 2001; Stevenson et al. 2004; Widdows and Dorow 2005). Similar to the unsupervised WSD-style approach to MWE identification (see Section 12.5.1), the underlying hypothesis is that semantically idiomatic MWEs will occur in markedly different lexical contexts to their component words. A bag of words representation is commonly used to model the combined lexical context of all usages of a given word or word combination. By interpreting this context model as a vector, it is possible to compare lexical contexts, for example, via simple cosine similarity (Widdows 2005). In order to reduce the effects of data sparseness, dimensionality reduction is often carried out over the word space prior to comparison (Schütze 1997).

The same approach has also been applied to extract LVCs, based on the assumption that the noun complements in LVCs are often deverbal (e.g., *bath, proposal, walk*), and that the distribution of nouns in PPs post-modifying noun complements in genuine LVCs (e.g., *(make a) proposal of marriage*) will be similar to that of the object of the underlying verb (e.g., *propose marriage*) (Grefenstette and Teufel 1995). Here, therefore, the assumption is that LVCs will be distributionally *similar* to the base verb form of the noun complement, whereas with the original extraction method, the assumption was that semantically idiomatic MWEs are *dissimilar* to their component words.

A fourth approach is to perform extraction on the basis of implicit identification. That is, (possibly noisy) token-level statistics can be fed into a type-level classifier to predict whether there have been genuine instances of a given MWE in the corpus. An example of this style of approach is to use POS taggers, chunkers, and parsers to identify English VPCs in different syntactic configurations, and feed the predictions of the various preprocessors into the final extraction classifier (Baldwin 2005a). Alternatively, a parser can be used to identify PPs with singular nouns, and semantically idiomatic PP-Ds extracted from among them based on distributional (dis)similarity of occurrences with and without determiners across a range of prepositions (van der Beek 2005).

A fifth approach is to use syntactic fixedness as a means of extracting MWEs, based on the assumption that semantically idiomatic MWEs undergo syntactic variation (e.g., passivization or internal modification) less readily than simple verb–noun combinations (Bannard 2007; Fazly et al. 2009).

In addition to general-purpose extraction techniques, linguistic properties of particular MWE construction types have been used in extraction. For example, the fact that a given verb–preposition combination occurs as a noun (e.g., *takeoff, clip-on*) is a strong predictor of the fact that combination occurring as a VPC (Baldwin 2005a).

One bottleneck in MWE extraction is the token frequency of the MWE candidate. With a few notable exceptions (e.g., (Baldwin 2005a; Fazly et al. 2009)), MWE research has tended to ignore low-frequency MWEs, for example, by applying a method only to word combinations that occur at least N times in a corpus.

12.5.3 Internal Syntactic Disambiguation

As part of the process of MWE identification and extraction, for some MWE types it is necessary to disambiguate the internal syntax of individual MWEs. A prominent case of this in English is NCs with three or more terms. For example, *glass window cleaner* has two possible interpretations,* corresponding to the two possible bracketings of the compound: (1) "a cleaner of glass windows" (= *[[glass window] cleaner]*), and (2) "a cleaner of windows, made of glass" (= *[glass [window cleaner]]*). In this case, the first case (of left bracketing) is the correct analysis, but *movie car chase*, for example, is right bracketing (= *(movie (car chase))*). The process of disambiguating the syntax of an NC is called bracketing.

The most common approach to bracketing is based on the statistical analysis of the components of competing analyses. In the adjacency model, for a ternary NC, *N1 N2 N3*, a comparison is made of the frequencies of the two modifier–head pairings extracted from the two analyses, namely, *N1 N2* and *N1 N3* in the left bracketing case, and *N2 N3* and *N1 N3* in the right bracketing case; as *N1 N3* is common to both, in practice, *N1 N2* is compared directly with *N2 N3*. A left bracketing analysis is selected in the case that *N1 N2* is judged to be more likely, otherwise a right bracketing analysis is selected (Marcus 1980). In the dependency model, the NC is instead decomposed into the dependency tuples of *N1 N2* and *N2 N3* in the case of left bracketing, and *N2 N3* and *N1 N3* in the case of right bracketing; once again, the dependency *N2 N3* is common to both, and can be ignored. In the instance that *N1 N2* is more likely than *N1 N3*, the model prefers a left bracketing analysis, otherwise a right bracketing analysis is selected (Lauer 1995). While the dependency model tends to outperform the adjacency model, the best-performing models take features derived from both along with various syntactic and semantic features (Nakov and Hearst 2005; Vadas and Curran 2008).

---

* More generally, for an n item NC, the number of possible interpretations is defined by the Catalan number $C_n = \frac{1}{n+1}\binom{2n}{n}$.

12.5.4 MWE Interpretation

The semantic interpretation of MWEs is usually performed in one of two ways: (1) relative to a generalized semantic inventory (compatible with both simplex words and MWEs, such as WORDNET); and (2) based on a set of semantic relations capturing semantic interplay between component words. When interpreting VPCs or lexicalized PP-Ds, for example, the former approach would be more appropriate (e.g., to capture the fact that *bow out* is synonymous with *withdraw*, both of which are troponyms of *retire*). Nominal MWEs and productive PP-Ds, on the other hand, are more amenable to interpretation by semantic relations (e.g., to capture the semantics of *apple pie* in terms of the MAKE relation, as in "pie made from apple(s)").

One common approach to MWE interpretation is via component similarity, that is, the comparison of the components of a MWE with corresponding components of annotated MWEs, or alternatively with simplex words. For example, a novel NC can be interpreted by identifying training NCs with similar modifier and head nouns (e.g., in interpreting *grape extract*, *grape* would be compared with similar modifiers, and *extract* with similar heads), as determined relative to a lexical resource or via distributional similarity. We can then extrapolate from the closely matching training NCs to predict the interpretation of the novel NC (Vanderwende 1994; Moldovan et al. 2004; Kim and Baldwin 2005; Nastase et al. 2006; Kim and Baldwin 2007b; Ó Séaghdha 2008). Alternatively, we may employ contextual similarity to compare a VPC with its simplex verb, to determine if they are sufficiently similar that the VPC can be interpreted compositionally from the verb (Baldwin et al. 2003; McCarthy et al. 2003; Cook and Stevenson 2006).

Crosslinguistic evidence can also provide valuable evidence when interpreting MWEs. For example, the analysis of what preposition is used in different Romance languages to translate a given English MWE can provide valuable insights into the range of possible interpretations for the English MWE (Girju 2009). Conversely, semantically idiomatic MWEs can be detected from parallel corpus data by identifying translation divergences in the component words lexical choice (Melamed 1997). For example, knowledge that *balance* and *sheet* are most often translated as *équilibre* and *feuille*, respectively, in French, and yet *balance sheet* is translated as *bilan* suggests that *balance sheet* is semantically idiomatic.

One popular approach to determining the underlying semantic relation associated with a MWE is to identify surface realizations or paraphrases associated with each semantic class (Lapata 2002; Grover et al. 2004; Kim and Baldwin 2006; Nicholson and Baldwin 2006; Nakov and Hearst 2008). For example, in the case of compound nominalizations, there are the two primary classes of SUBJECT and OBJECT, based on whether the modifier acts as the subject (e.g., *investor hesitation* = "investor hesitates") or object (e.g., *product replacement* = "replace (the) product") of the base verb form of the deverbal head. For a given compound nominalization and base verb form, it is possible to analyze the relative occurrence of the modifier as subject or object of the base verb, and select the interpretation that is most commonly observed (Lapata 2002; Grover et al. 2004; Nicholson and Baldwin 2006).

Another methodology that has been applied to the interpretation task with success is the analysis of the co-occurrence properties of the MWE components. For example, the semantics of particles in VPCs can be interpreted by analyzing what types of verbs can combine with a given particle (Cook and Stevenson 2006; Kim and Baldwin 2007a). Similarly, Japanese compound verbs (V-V combinations) can be interpreted by observing what set of verbs each of the component verbs combines with to form a compound verb, optionally including the semantic class of the resulting compound verb (Uchiyama et al. 2005).

One overarching assumption made in most semantic interpretation tasks is that it is possible to arrive at a compositional interpretation for each MWE via its component words. Ideally, we of course need to identify instances of semantic idiomaticity, motivating the need for methods that can model the relative compositionality or decomposability of MWEs (Lin 1999; Baldwin et al. 2003; McCarthy et al. 2003; McCarthy et al. 2007).

While there has been a healthy interest in MWE interpretation, research has suffered from a lack of agreement on semantic inventories, and the relative unavailability of annotated data. One very positive step toward redressing this situation was a shared task at SemEval-2007, on interpreting nominal MWEs in English (Girju et al. 2007), and an upcoming SemEval-2010 task on the multi-way classification of semantic relations between pairs of nominals. In practice, the SemEval-2007 task took a pair of nouns in a fixed sentential context and attempted to determine if they were interpretable using a set of semantic relations compatible with NCs. As such, the task was not specifically on NC interpretation, but NC interpretation methods could be evaluated over the dataset (Kim and Baldwin 2008; Ó Séaghdha 2008). Crucially, the task organizers chose to sidestep the controversy surrounding the precise membership of a broad-coverage set of semantic relations, and instead focused on relations where there is relatively high agreement between researchers. They additionally defused the question of interpretational overlap/ambiguity of a given nominal, by designing the task as a series of binary subtasks, where a prediction had to be made about each nominal's compatibility with a given semantic relation (ignoring whether or not it was also compatible with other relations).

12.6 Summary

MWEs are an integral part of language: vast in number and highly varied in nature. They are defined by idiomaticity at the lexical, syntactic, semantic, pragmatic, and statistical levels, and occur in a myriad of different constructions in the world's languages. In addition to providing a brief foray into the linguistic complexities of MWEs, we have detailed the key MWEs in MWE research, and outlined various approaches to the primary computational challenges associated with MWEs, namely, identification, extraction, and interpretation.

We have deliberately not provided a survey of MWE resources in this paper, choosing instead to maintain an up-to-the-moment snapshot of the field on the handbook's companion Web site. For those interested in pursuing MWE research, we recommend this as your first port of call. For readers who are interested in further reading on MWEs, we particularly recommend the following works: (Moon 1998; McKeown and Radev 2000; Cowie 2001; Sag et al. 2002; Villavicencio et al. 2005).

Acknowledgments

The chapter benefitted from detailed reviews by Francis Bond, Diarmuid Ó Séaghdha, Diana McCarthy, Paul Cook, Aline Villavicencio, and Roxana Girju.

References

Abeillé, A. (1988). Light verb constructions and extraction out of NP in a tree adjoining grammar. In *Papers of the 24th Regional Meeting of the Chicago Linguistics Society*, Chicago, IL.

Ahn, H.-D. (1991). Light verbs, VP-movement, negation and clausal structure in Korean and English. PhD thesis, University of Wisconsin-Madison, Madison, WI.

Aronoff, M. (1976). *Word Formation in Generative Grammar*. Cambridge, MA: MIT Press.

Baldwin, T. (2005a). The deep lexical acquisition of English verb-particles. *Computer Speech and Language, Special Issue on Multiword Expressions* 19(4), 398–414.

Baldwin, T. (2005b). Looking for prepositional verbs in corpus data. In *Proceedings of the Second ACL-SIGSEM Workshop on the Linguistic Dimensions of Prepositions and their Use in Computational Linguistics Formalisms and Applications*, Colchester, U.K., pp. 115–126.

Baldwin, T. and F. Bond (2002). Multiword expressions: Some problems for Japanese NLP. In *Proceedings of the Eighth Annual Meeting of the Association for Natural Language Processing (Japan)*, Keihanna, Japan, pp. 379–382.

Baldwin, T. and A. Villavicencio (2002). Extracting the unextractable: A case study on verb-particles. In *Proceedings of the Sixth Conference on Natural Language Learning (CoNLL-2002)*, Taipei, Taiwan, pp. 98–104.

Baldwin, T., C. Bannard, T. Tanaka, and D. Widdows (2003). An empirical model of multiword expression decomposability. In *Proceedings of the ACL-2003 Workshop on Multiword Expressions: Analysis, Acquisition and Treatment*, Sapporo, Japan, pp. 89–96.

Baldwin, T., E. M. Bender, D. Flickinger, A. Kim, and S. Oepen (2004). Road-testing the English Resource Grammar over the British National Corpus. In *Proceedings of the Fourth International Conference on Language Resources and Evaluation (LREC 2004)*, Lisbon, Portugal, pp. 2047–2050.

Baldwin, T., J. Beavers, L. Van Der Beek, F. Bond, D. Flickinger, and I. A. Sag (2006). In search of a systematic treatment of determinerless PPs. In P. Saint-Dizier (Ed.), *Syntax and Semantics of Prepositions*. Dordrecht, the Netherlands: Springer.

Bannard, C. (2007). A measure of syntactic flexibility for automatically identifying multiword expressions in corpora. In *Proceedings of the ACL-2007 Workshop on A Broader Perspective on Multiword Expressions*, Prague, Czech Republic, pp. 1–8.

Bannard, C., T. Baldwin, and A. Lascarides (2003). A statistical approach to the semantics of verb-particles. In *Proceedings of the ACL2003 Workshop on Multiword Expressions: Analysis, Acquisition and Treatment*, Sapporo, Japan, pp. 65–72.

Barker, K. and S. Szpakowicz (1998). Semi-automatic recognition of noun modifier relationships. In *Proceedings of the 17th International Conference on Computational Linguistics (COLING-1998)*, Montreal, Canada, pp. 96–102.

Bauer, L. (1983). *English Word-Formation*. Cambridge, U.K.: Cambridge University Press.

Bauer, L. (2001). Compounding. In M. Haspelmath (Ed.), *Language Typology and Language Universals*. The Hague, the Netherlands: Mouton de Gruyter.

Benor, S. B. and R. Levy (2006). The chicken or the egg? A probabilistic analysis of English binomials. *Language 82*(2), 233–278.

Benson, M. (1990). Collocations and general-purpose dictionaries. *International Journal of Lexicography 3*(1), 23–35.

Birke, J. and A. Sarkar (2006). A clustering approach for the nearly unsupervised recoginition of non-literal language. In *Proceedings of the 11th Conference of the EACL (EACL 2006)*, Trento, Italy, pp. 329–336.

Blunsom, P. (2007). Structured classification for multilingual natural language processing. PhD thesis, University of Melbourne, Melbourne, Australia.

Bolinger, D. (1976). *The Phrasal Verb in English*. Boston, MA: Harvard University Press.

Bond, F. (2005). *Translating the Untranslatable: A Solution to the Problem of Generating English Determiners*. CSLI Studies in Computational Linguistics. CSLI Publications, Stanford, CA.

Booij, G. (2002). Separable complex verbs in Dutch: A case of periphrastic word formation. In N. Dehé, R. Jackendoff, A. McIntyre, and S. Urban (Eds.), *Verb-Particle Explorations*, pp. 21–41. Berlin, Germany/New York: Mouton de Gruyter.

Brinton, L. (1985). Verb particles in English: Aspect or aktionsart. *Studia Linguistica 39*, 157–168.

Butt, M. (2003). The light verb jungle. In *Proceedings of the Workshop on Multi-Verb Constructions*, Trondheim, Norway, pp. 1–49.

Calzolari, N., C. Fillmore, R. Grishman, N. Ide, A. Lenci, C. MacLeod, and A. Zampolli (2002). Towards best practice for multiword expressions in computational lexicons. In *Proceedings of the Third International Conference on Language Resources and Evaluation (LREC 2002)*, Las Palmas, Canary Islands, pp. 1934–1940.

Chafe, W. L. (1968). Idiomaticity as an anomaly in the Chomskyan paradigm. *Foundations of Language 4*, 109–127.

Chander, I. (1998). Automated postediting of documents. PhD thesis, University of Southern California, Los Angeles, CA.

Choueka, Y. (1988). Looking for needles in a haystack or locating interesting collocational expressions in large textual databases. In *Proceedings of RIAO*, Cambridge, MA, pp. 609–623.

Church, K. W. and P. Hanks (1989). Word association norms, mutual information and lexicography. In *Proceedings of the 27th Annual Meeting of the Association of Computational Linguistics (ACL-1989)*, Vancouver, Canada, pp. 76–83.

Cook, P. and S. Stevenson (2006). Classifying particle semantics in English verb-particle constructions. In *Proceedings of the ACL-2006 Workshop on Multiword Expressions: Identifying and Exploiting Underlying Properties*, Sydney, Australia, pp. 45–53.

Copestake, A. and A. Lascarides (1997). Integrating symbolic and statistical representations: The lexicon pragmatics interface. In *Proceedings of the 35th Annual Meeting of the Association of Computational Linguistics and 8th Conference of the European Chapter of Association of Computational Linguistics (ACL/EACL-1997)*, Madrid, Spain, pp. 136–143.

Cowie, A. (Ed.) (2001). *Phraseology: Theory, Analysis, and Applications*. Oxford, U.K.: Oxford University Press.

Cowie, A. P. and P. A. Howarth (1996). Phraseology—A select bibliography. *International Journal of Lexicography* 9(1), 38–51.

Cruse, A. D. (1986). *Lexical Semantics*. Cambridge, U.K.: Cambridge University Press.

Dirven, R. (2001). The metaphoric in recent cognitive approaches to English phrasal verbs. *metaphorik.de 1*, 39–54.

Downing, P. (1977). On the creation and use of English compound nouns. *Language* 53(4), 810–842.

Evert, S. (2004). The statistics of word cooccurrences: Word pairs and collocations. PhD thesis, University of Stuttgart, Stuttgart, Germany.

Evert, S. and B. Krenn (2001). Methods for the qualitative evaluation of lexical association measures. In *Proceedings of the 39th Annual Meeting of the ACL and 10th Conference of the EACL (ACL-EACL 2001)*, Toulouse, France, pp. 188–195.

Fazly, A. (2007). Automatic acquisition of lexical knowledge about multiword predicates. PhD thesis, University of Toronto, Toronto, Canada.

Fazly, A., P. Cook, and S. Stevenson (2009). Unsupervised type and token identification of idiomatic expressions. *Computational Linguistics* 35(1), 61–103.

Fellbaum, C. (Ed.) (1998). *WordNet, An Electronic Lexical Database*. Cambridge, MA: MIT Press.

Fellbaum, C. (2002). VP idioms in the lexicon: Topics for research using a very large corpus. In *Proceedings of the KONVENS 2002 Conference*, Saarbrücken, Germany.

Fernando, C. and R. Flavell (1981). On idiom: Critical views and perspectives. *Exeter Linguistic Studies*; Exeter, U.K.: University of Exeter.

Fillmore, C., P. Kay, and M. C. O'Connor (1988). Regularity and idiomaticity in grammatical constructions. *Language 64*, 501–538.

Frantzi, K., S. Ananiadou, and H. Mima (2000). Automatic recognition of multi-word terms: The C-value/NC-value method. *International Journal on Digital Libraries* 3(2), 115–130.

Gagné, C. L., T. L. Spalding, and M. C. Gorrie (2005). Sentential context and the interpretation of familiar open-compounds and novel modifier-noun phrases. *Language and Speech* 28(2), 203–221.

Gates, E. (1988). *The Treatment of Multiword Lexemes in Some Current Dictionaries of English*. In *Proceedings of ZuriLEx'86*, Tübingen, Germany, pp. 99–106.

Gerber, L. and J. Yang (1997). Systran MT dictionary development. In *Proceedings of the Sixth Machine Translation Summit (MT Summit VI)*, San Diego, CA.

Gibbs, R. W. (1980). Spilling the beans on understanding and memory for idioms in conversation. *Memory and Cognition* 8(2), 149–156.

Girju, R. (2009). The syntax and semantics of prepositions in the task of automatic interpretation of nominal phrases and compounds: A cross-linguistic study. *Computational Linguistics* 35(2), 185–228.

Girju, R., P. Nakov, V. Nastase, S. Szpakowicz, P. Turney, and D. Yuret (2007). Semeval-2007 task 04: Classification of semantic relations between nominals. In *Proceedings of the Fourth International Workshop on Semantic Evaluations*, Prague, Czech Republic, pp. 13–18.

Grefenstette, G. and P. Tapanainen (1994). What is a word, what is a sentence? problems of tokenization. In *Proceedings of the Third Conference on Computational Lexicography and Text Research*, Budapest, Hungary, pp. 79–87.

Grefenstette, G. and S. Teufel (1995). A corpus-based method for automatic identification of support verbs for nominalizations. In *Proceedings of the Seventh European Chapter of Association of Computational Linguistics (EACL-1995)*, Dublin, Ireland, pp. 98–103.

Grimshaw, J. and A. Mester (1988). Light verbs and *theta*-marking. *Linguistic Inquiry* 19(2), 205–232.

Grishman, R., C. Macleod, and A. Myers (1998). *COMLEX Syntax Reference Manual*, Proteus Project, New York University, New York.

Grover, C., M. Lapata, and A. Lascarides (2004). A comparison of parsing technologies for the biomedical domain. *Journal of Natural Language Engineering* 1(1), 1–38.

Hashimoto, C. and D. Kawahara (2008). Construction of an idiom corpus and its application to idiom identification based on WSD incorporating idiom-specific features. In *Proceedings of the 2008 Conference on Empirical Methods in Natural Language Processing (EMNLP 2008)*, Honolulu, HI, pp. 992–1001.

Hashimoto, C., S. Sato, and T. Utsuro (2006). Japanese idiom recognition: Drawing a line between literal and idiomatic meanings. In *Proceedings of the COLING/ACL 2006 Interactive Poster Session*, Sydney, Australia, pp. 353–360.

Haspelmath, M. (1997). *From Space to Time in The World's Languages*. Munich, Germany: Lincorn Europa.

Hoshi, H. (1994). Passive, causive, and light verbs: A study of theta role assignment. PhD thesis, University of Connecticut, Storrs, CT.

Huddleston, R. and G. K. Pullum (2002). *The Cambridge Grammar of the English Language*. Cambridge, U.K.: Cambridge University Press.

Jackendoff, R. (1973). The base rules for prepositional phrases. In *A Festschrift for Morris Halle*, pp. 345–356. New York: Rinehart & Winston.

Jackendoff, R. (1997). *The Architecture of the Language Faculty*. Cambridge, MA: MIT Press.

Jackendoff, R. (2002). *Foundations of Language*. Oxford, U.K.: Oxford University Press.

Jespersen, O. (1965). *A Modern English Grammar on Historical Principles, Part VI, Morphology*. London, U.K.: George Allen and Unwin Ltd.

Justeson, J. S. and S. M. Katz (1995). Technical terminology: Some linguistic properties and an algorithm for identification in text. *Natural Language Engineering* 1(1), 9–27.

Kaalep, H.-J. and K. Muischnek (2008). Multi-word verbs of Estonian: A database and a corpus. In *Proceedings of the LREC 2008 Workshop: Towards a Shared Task for Multiword Expressions (MWE 2008)*, Marrakech, Morocco, pp. 23–26.

Kageura, K., B. Daille, H. Nakagawa, and L.-F. Chien (2004). Recent trends in computational terminology. *Terminology* 10(1), 1–21.

Karimi-Doostan, G. H. (1997). Light verb construction in persian. PhD thesis, University of Essex, Colchester, U.K.

Kastovsky, D. (1982). *Wortbildung und Semantik*. Dusseldorf, Germany: Bagel/Francke.

Katz, G. and E. Giesbrecht (2006). Automatic identification of non-compositional multi-word expressions using latent semantic analysis. In *Proceedings of the ACL-2006 Workshop on Multiword Expressions: Identifying and Exploiting Underlying Properties*, Sydney, Australia, pp. 28–35.

Katz, J. J. and P. M. Postal (2004). Semantic interpretation of idioms and sentences containing them. In *Quarterly Progress Report (70), MIT Research Laboratory of Electronics*, pp. 275–282. MIT Press, Cambridge, MA.

Keysar, B. and B. Bly (1995). Intuitions of the transparency of idioms: Can one keep a secret by spilling the beans? *Journal of Memory and Language 34*(1), 89–109.

Kim, S. N. and T. Baldwin (2005). Automatic interpretation of compound nouns using WordNet similarity. In *Proceedings of the Second International Joint Conference on Natural Language Processing (IJCNLP-05)*, Jeju, Korea, pp. 945–956.

Kim, S. N. and T. Baldwin (2006). Interpreting semantic relations in noun compounds via verb semantics. In *Proceedings of the COLING/ACL 2006 Interactive Poster Session*, Sydney, Australia, pp. 491–498.

Kim, S. N. and T. Baldwin (2007a). Detecting compositionality of English verb-particle constructions using semantic similarity. In *Proceedings of Conference of the Pacific Association for Computational Linguistics*, Melbourne, Australia, pp. 40–48.

Kim, S. N. and T. Baldwin (2007b). Disambiguating noun compounds. In *Proceedings of 22nd AAAI Conference on Artificial Intelligence*, Vancouver, Canada, pp. 901–906.

Kim, S. N. and T. Baldwin (2008). Benchmarking noun compound interpretation. In *Proceedings of Third International Joint Conference on Natual Language Processing (IJCNLP-2008)*, Hyderabad, India, pp. 569–576.

Kim, S. N. and T. Baldwin (to appear). How to pick out token instances of English verb-particle constructions. *Language Resources and Evaluation*.

Lapata, M. (2002). The disambiguation of nominalizations. *Computational Linguistics 28*(3), 357–388.

Lapata, M. and A. Lascarides (2003). Detecting novel compounds: The role of distributional evidence. In *Proceedings of the 11th Conference of the European Chapter for the Association of Computational Linguistics (EACL-2003)*, Budapest, Hungary, pp. 235–242.

Lauer, M. (1995). Designing statistical language learners: Experiments on noun compounds. PhD thesis, Macquarie University, Sydney, Australia.

Levi, J. (1978). *The Syntax and Semantics of Complex Nominals*. New York: Academic Press.

Li, W., X. Zhang, C. Niu, Y. Jiang, and R. K. Srihari (2003). An expert lexicon approach to identifying English phrasal verbs. In *Proceedings of the ACL2003 Workshop on Multiword Expressions: analysis, acquisition and treatment*, Sapporo, Japan, pp. 513–520.

Liberman, M. and R. Sproat (1992). The stress and structure of modified noun phrases in English. In I. A. Sag and A. Szabolcsi (Eds.), *Lexical Matters—CSLI Lecture Notes No. 24*. Stanford, CA: CSLI Publications.

Lidner, S. (1983). A lexico-semantic analysis of English verb particle constructions with OUT and UP. PhD thesis, University of Indiana at Bloomington, Bloomington, IN.

Lieber, R. and P. Štekauer (Eds.) (2009). *The Oxford Handbook of Compounding*. Oxford, U.K.: Oxford University Press.

Lin, D. (1998). Extracting collocations from text corpora. In *Proceedings of the First Workshop on Computational Terminology*, Montreal, Canada.

Lin, D. (1999). Automatic identification of non-compositional phrases. In *Proceedings of the 37th Annual Meeting of the Association for Computational Linguistics*, College Park, MD, pp. 317–324.

Lüdeling, A. (2001). *On Particle Verbs and Similar Constructions in German*. Stanford, CA: CSLI Publications.

Marcus, M. (1980). *A Theory of Syntactic Recognition for Natural Language*. Cambridge, MA: MIT Press.

Matsuo, Y., S. Shirai, A. Yokoo, and S. Ikehara (1997). Direct parse tree translation in cooperation with the transfer method. In D. Joneas and H. Somers (Eds.), *New Methods in Language Processing*, pp. 229–238. London, U.K.: UCL Press.

McCarthy, D., B. Keller, and J. Carroll (2003). Detecting a continuum of compositionality in phrasal verbs. In *Proceedings of the ACL2003 Workshop on Multiword Expressions: Analysis, Acquisition and Treatment*, Sapporo, Japan, pp. 73–80.

McCarthy, D., S. Venkatapathy, and A. Joshi (2007). Detecting compositionality of verb-object combinations using selectional preferences. In *Proceedings of the 2007 Joint Conference on Empirical Methods in Natural Language Processing and Computational Natural Language Learning (EMNLP-CoNLL)*, Prague, Czech Republic, pp. 369–379.

McIntyre, A. (2007). Particle verbs and argument structure. *Language and Linguistics Compass* 1(4), 350–367.

McKeown, K. R. and D. R. Radev (2000). Collocations. In R. Dale, H. Moisl, and H. Somers (Eds.), *A Handbook of Natural Language Processing*, Chapter 15. New York: Marcel Dekker.

Melamed, I. D. (1997). Automatic discovery of non-compositional compounds in parallel data. In *Proceedings of the Second Conference on Empirical Methods in Natural Language Processing (EMNLP-97)*, Providence, RI, pp. 97–108.

Mel'čuk, I. A. and A. Polguère (1987). A formal lexicon in the Meaning-Text Theory (or how to do lexica with words). *Computational Linguistics* 13(3–4), 261–275.

Mimmelmann, N. P. (1998). Regularity in irregularity: Article use in adpositional phrases. *Linguistic Typology* 2, 315–353.

Miyagawa, S. (1989). Light verbs and the ergative hypothesis. *Linguistic Inquiry* 20, 659–668.

Miyazaki, M., S. Ikehara, and A. Yokoo (1993). Combined word retrieval for bilingual dictionary based on the analysis of compound word. *Transactions of the Information Processing Society of Japan* 34(4), 743–754. (in Japanese).

Mohanan, T. (1994). *Argument Structure in Hindi*. Stanford, CA: CSLI Publications.

Moldovan, D., A. Badulescu, M. Tatu, D. Antohe, and R. Girju (2004). Models for the semantic classification of noun phrases. In *Proceedings of HLT-NAACL 2004: Workshop on Computational Lexical Semantics*, Boston, CA, pp. 60–67.

Moon, R. E. (1998). *Fixed Expressions and Idioms in English: A Corpus-Based Approach*. Oxford, U.K.: Oxford University Press.

Nakov, P. (2008). Noun compound interpretation using paraphrasing verbs: Feasibility study. In *Proceedings of the 13th International Conference on Artificial Intelligence: Methodology, Systems, Applications (AIMSA'08)*, Varna, Bulgaria, pp. 103–117.

Nakov, P. and M. Hearst (2005). Search engine statistics beyond the *n*-gram: Application to noun compound bracketting. In *Proceedings of the Ninth Conference on Computational Natural Language Learning (CoNLL-2005)*, Ann Arbor, MI, pp. 17–24.

Nakov, P. and M. A. Hearst (2008). Solving relational similarity problems using the web as a corpus. In *Proceedings of the 46th Annual Meeting of the ACL: HLT*, Columbus, OH, pp. 452–460.

Nastase, V., J. Sayyad-Shirabad, M. Sokolova, and S. Szpakowicz (2006). Learning noun-modifier semantic relations with corpus-based and WordNet-based features. In *Proceedings of the 21st National Conference on Artificial Intelligence (AAAI)*, Boston, MA, pp. 781–787.

Nicholson, J. and T. Baldwin (2006). Interpretation of compound nominalisations using corpus and web statistics. In *Proceedings of the COLING/ACL 2006 Workshop on Multiword Expressions: Identifying and Exploiting Underlying Properties*, Sydney, Australia, pp. 54–61.

Nunberg, G., I. A. Sag, and T. Wasow (1994). Idioms. *Language* 70, 491–538.

O'Dowd, E. M. (1998). *Prepositions and Particles in English*. Oxford, U.K.: Oxford University Press.

Ó Séaghdha, D. (2008). Learning compound noun semantics. PhD thesis, Computer Laboratory, University of Cambridge, Santa Barbara, CA.

Osswald, R., H. Helbig, and S. Hartrumpf (2006). The representation of German prepositional verbs in a semantically based computer lexicon. In *Proceedings of the Fifth International Conference on Language Resources and Evaluation (LREC 2006)*, Genoa, Italy.

Patrick, J. and J. Fletcher (2005). Classifying verb particle constructions by verb arguments. In *Proceedings of the Second ACL-SIGSEM Workshop on the Linguistic Dimensions of Prepositions and their Use in Computational Linguistics Formalisms and Applications*, Colchester, U.K., pp. 200–209.

Pauwels, P. (2000). *Put, Set, Lay, and Place: A Cognitve Linguistic Approach to Verbal Meaning*. Munich, Germany: Lincom Europa.

Pearce, D. (2001). Synonymy in collocation extraction. In *Proceedings of the NAACL 2001 Workshop on WordNet and Other Lexical Resources: Applications, Extensions and Customizations*, Pittsburgh, PA, pp. 41–46.

Pecina, P. (2008). Lexical association measures. PhD thesis, Charles University, Prague, Czech Republic.

Piao, S., P. Rayson, D. Archer, A. Wilson, and T. McEnery (2003). Extracting multiword expressions with a semantic tagger. In *Proceedings of the ACL2003 Workshop on Multiword Expressions: Analysis, Acquisition and Treatment*, Sapporo, Japan, pp. 49–56.

Quirk, R., S. Greenbaum, G. Leech, and J. Svartvik (1985). *A Comprehensive Grammar of the English Language*. London, U.K.: Longman.

Riehemann, S. (2001). A constructional approach to idioms and word formation. PhD thesis, Stanford University, Stanford, CA.

Rosario, B. and M. Hearst (2001). Classifying the semantic relations in noun compounds via a domain-specific lexical hierarchy. In *Proceedings of the Sixth Conference on Empirical Methods in Natural Language Processing (EMNLP-2001)*, Pittsburgh, PA, pp. 82–90.

Ross, H. (1995). Defective noun phrases. In *Papers of the 31st Regional Meeting of the Chicago Linguistics Society*, Chicago, IL, pp. 398–440.

Sag, I. A., T. Baldwin, F. Bond, A. Copestake, and D. Flickinger (2002). Multiword expressions: A pain in the neck for NLP. In *Proceedings of the Third International Conference on Intelligent Text Processing and Computational Linguistics (CICLing-2002)*, Mexico City, Mexico, pp. 1–15.

Sager, J. C. (1990). *A Practical Course in Terminology Processing*. Amsterdam, the Netherlands/Philadelphia, PA: John Benjamins.

Schone, P. and D. Jurafsky (2001). Is knowledge-free induction of multiword unit dictionary headwords a solved problem? In *Proceedings of the Sixth Conference on Empirical Methods in Natural Language Processing (EMNLP 2001)*, Hong Kong, China, pp. 100–108.

Schütze, H. (1997). *Ambiguity Resolution in Language Learning*. Stanford, CA: CSLI Publications.

Sinclair, J. (1991). *Corpus, Concordance, Collocation*. Oxford, U.K.: Oxford University Press.

Smadja, F. (1993). Retrieving collocations from text: Xtract. *Computational Linguistics* 19(1), 143–177.

Spärck Jones, K. (1983). *Compound Noun Interpretation Problems*. Englewood Cliffes, NJ: Prentice-Hall.

Sporleder, C. and L. Li (2009). Unsupervised recognition of literal and non-literal use of idiomatic expressions. In *Proceedings of the 12th Conference of the EACL (EACL 2009)*, Athens, Greece, pp. 754–762.

Stevenson, S., A. Fazly, and R. North (2004). Statistical measures of the semi-productivity of light verb constructions. In *Proceedings of the Second ACL Workshop on Multiword Expressions: Integrating Processing*, Barcelona, Spain, pp. 1–8.

Stvan, L. S. (1998). The semantics and pragmatics of bare singular noun phrases. PhD thesis, Northwestern University, Evanston, IL.

Tan, Y. F., M.-Y. Kan, and H. Cui (2006). Extending corpus-based identification of light verb constructions using a supervised learning framework. In *Proceedings of the EACL 2006 Workshop on Multi-Word-expressions in a multilingual context (MWEmc)*, Trento, Italy.

Tanaka, T. and T. Baldwin (2003). Noun-noun compound machine translation a feasibility study on shallow processing. In *Proceedings of the ACL 2003 Workshop on Multiword Expressions: Analysis, Acquisition and Treatment*, Sapporo, Japan, pp. 17–24.

Trawiński, B., M. Sailer, and J.-P. Soehn (2006). Combinatorial aspects of collocational prepositional phrases. In P. Saint-Dizier (Ed.), *Computational Linguistics Dimensions of Syntax and Semantics of Prepositions*. Dordrecht, the Netherlands: Kluwer Academic.

Trawiński, B., M. Sailer, J.-P. Soehn, L. Lemnitzer, and F. Richter (2008). Cranberry expressions in English and in German. In *Proceedings of the LREC 2008 Workshop: Towards a Shared Task for Multiword Expressions (MWE 2008)*, Marrakech, Morocco, pp. 35–38.

Tschichold, C. (1998). Multi-word units in natural language processing. PhD thesis, University of Basel, Basel, Switzerland.

Tsuchiya, M., T. Shime, T. Takagi, T. Utsuro, K. Uchimoto, S. Matsuyoshi, S. Sato, and S. Nakagawa (2006). Chunking Japanese compound functional expressions by machine learning. In *Proceedings of the EACL 06 Workshop on Multi-Word-expressions in a Multilingual Context*, Trento, Italy, pp. 25–32.

Uchiyama, K., T. Baldwin, and S. Ishizaki (2005). Disambiguating Japanese compound verbs. *Computer Speech and Language, Special Issue on Multiword Expressions 19*(4), 497–512.

Vadas, D. and J. R. Curran (2008). Parsing noun phrase structure with CCG. In *Proceedings of the 46th Annual Meeting of the ACL: HLT*, Columbus, OH, pp. 335–343.

van der Beek, L. (2005). The extraction of determinerless PPs. In *Proceedings of the Second ACL-SIGSEM Workshop on the Linguistic Dimensions of Prepositions and Their Use in Computational Linguistics Formalisms and Applications*, Colchester, U.K., pp. 190–199.

Vanderwende, L. (1994). Algorithm for automatic interpretation of noun sequences. In *Proceedings of the 15th Conference on Computational Linguistics*, Kyoto, Japan, pp. 782–788.

Venkatapathy, S. and A. Joshi (2006). Using information about multi-word expressions for the word-alignment task. In *Proceedings of the COLING/ACL 2006 Workshop on Multiword Expressions: Identifying and Exploiting Underlying Properties*, Sydney, Australia, pp. 53–60.

Villada Moirón, B. (2005). Data-driven identification of fixed expressions and their modifiability. PhD thesis, Alfa-Informatica, University of Groningen, Groningen, the Netherlands.

Villavicencio, A. (2005). The availability of verb-particle constructions in lexical resources: How much is enough? *Computer Speech and Language, Special Issue on Multiword Expressions 19*(4), 415–432.

Villavicencio, A., T. Baldwin, and B. Waldron (2004). A multilingual database of idioms. In *Proceedings of the Fourth International Conference on Language Resources and Evaluation (LREC 2004)*, Lisbon, Portugal, pp. 1127–1130.

Villavicencio, A., F. Bond, A. Korhonen, and D. McCarthy (2005). Introduction to the special issue on multiword expressions: Having a crack at a hard nut. *Computer Speech and Language, Special Issue on Multiword Expressions 19*(4), 365–377.

Widdows, D. (2005). *Geometry and Meaning*. Stanford, CA: CSLI Publications.

Widdows, D. and B. Dorow (2005). Automatic extraction of idioms using graph analysis and asymmetric lexicosyntactic patterns. In *Proceedings of the ACL 2004 Workshop on Deep Lexical Acquisition*, Ann Arbor, MI, pp. 48–56.

Xu, R., Q. Lu, and S. Li (2006). The design and construction of a Chinese collocation bank. In *Proceedings of the Fifth International Conference on Language Resources and Evaluation (LREC 2006)*, Genoa, Italy.

Zhang, Y., V. Kordoni, A. Villavicencio, and M. Idiart (2006). Automated multiword expression prediction for grammar engineering. In *Proceedings of the Workshop on Multiword Expressions: Identifying and Exploiting Underlying Properties*, Sydney, Australia, pp. 36–44. Association for Computational Linguistics.

13

Normalized Web Distance and Word Similarity

Paul M.B. Vitányi
Centrum Wiskunde &
Informatica

Rudi L. Cilibrasi
Centrum Wiskunde &
Informatica

13.1 Introduction

Objects can be given literally, like the literal four-letter genome of a mouse, or the literal text of *War and Peace* by Tolstoy. For simplicity, we take it that all meaning of the object is represented by the literal object itself. Objects can also be given by name, like "the four-letter genome of a mouse," or "the text of *War and Peace* by Tolstoy." There are also objects that cannot be given literally, but only by name, and that acquire their meaning from their contexts in background common knowledge in humankind, like "home" or "red."

To make computers more intelligent one would like to represent meaning in computer-digestible form. Long-term and labor-intensive efforts such as the *Cyc* project (Landauer and Dumais, 1995) and the *WordNet* project (Miller et al.) try to establish semantic relations between common objects, or, more precisely, *names* for those objects. The idea is to create a semantic web of such vast proportions that rudimentary intelligence, and knowledge about the real world, spontaneously emerge. This idea comes at the great cost of designing structures capable of manipulating knowledge, and entering high-quality contents in these structures by knowledgeable human experts. While the efforts are long running and large scale, the overall information entered is minute compared to what is available on the Internet.

The rise of the Internet has enticed millions of users to type in trillions of characters to create billions of web pages of on average low-quality contents. The sheer mass of the information about almost every conceivable topic makes it likely that extremes will cancel and the majority or average is meaningful in a low-quality approximate sense.

The goal of this chapter is to introduce the normalized web distance (NWD) method to determine the similarity between words and phrases. It is a general way to tap the amorphous low-grade knowledge available for free on the Internet, typed in by local users aiming at the personal gratification of diverse objectives, and yet globally achieving what is effectively the largest semantic electronic database in the world. Moreover, this database is available for all by using any search engine that can return aggregate page-count estimates for a large range of search-queries. In the paper (Cilibrasi and Vitányi, 2007) introducing the NWD it was called 'normalized Google distance (NGD),' but since Google does not allow computer searches anymore, we opt for the more neutral and descriptive NWD.

Previously, a compression-based method was developed to establish a universal similarity metric among objects given as finite binary strings (Bennett et al., 1998; Cilibrasi and Vitányi, 2005; Cilibrasi et al., 2004; Keogh et al., 2007; Li et al., 2001, 2004; Santos et al., 2006), which was widely reported (Delahaye, 2004; Muir, 2003; Patch, 2003) and has led to hundreds of applications in research as reported by Google Scholar. The objects can be genomes (Cilibrasi and Vitányi, 2007; Li et al., 2001, 2004), music pieces in MIDI format (Cilibrasi and Vitányi, 2007; Cilibrasi et al., 2004), computer programs in Ruby or C, pictures in simple bitmap formats, astronomical data, literature (Cilibrasi and Vitányi, 2005), time sequences such as heart rhythm data (Keogh et al., 2007; Santos et al., 2006), and so on. The method is feature free in the sense that it does not analyze the files looking for particular features; rather it analyzes all features simultaneously and determines the similarity between every pair of objects according to the most dominant shared feature. It is not parameter laden, in fact, there are no parameters to set. In the genomic context it is alignment free and much faster than alignment methods; it provides an alignment-free method such as looked for in many genomic problems.

But in the case of word similarity, we do not have the objects themselves. Rather, we have names for objects, or other words, and the crucial point is that the compression method described above analyzes the objects themselves. This precludes the comparison of abstract notions or other objects that do not lend themselves to direct analysis, like emotions, colors, Socrates, Plato, Mike Bonanno, and Albert Einstein. While the method that compares the objects themselves is particularly suited to obtain knowledge about the similarity of objects themselves, irrespective of common beliefs about such similarities, the NWD method of Cilibrasi and Vitányi (2007) uses only the name of an object (or even more simply words and phrases), and obtains knowledge about the similarity of objects (or the words and phrases), by tapping available information generated by multitudes of Web users.

In Cilibrasi and Vitányi (2007), the following example experiment determining word similarity by the NWD method is described. At that time, a Google search for "horse," returned 46,700,000 hits. The number of hits for the search term "rider" was 12,200,000. Searching for the pages where both "horse" and "rider" occur gave 2,630,000 hits, and Google indexed 8,058,044,651 web pages at the time. Using these numbers in the main formula (13.8) we derive below, with $N = 8,058,044,651$, this yields a NWD, denoted by $e_G(\cdot, \cdot)$, between the terms "horse" and "rider" as follows:

$$e_G(\text{horse}, \text{rider}) \approx 0.443.$$

We did the same calculation when Google indexed only half the number of pages: 4,285,199,774. It is instructive that the probabilities of the used search terms did not change significantly in the meantime: with half the number of pages indexed, the number of hits for "horse" was 23,700,000, for "rider" it was 6,270,000, and for "horse, rider" it was 1,180,000. The $e_G(\text{horse}, \text{rider})$ we computed in that situation was ≈ 0.460. This is in line with our contention that the relative frequencies of web pages containing search terms gives objective information about the semantic relations between the search terms.

13.2 Some Methods for Word Similarity

There is a great deal of work in cognitive psychology (Landauer and Dumais, 1997), linguistics, and computer science, about using word (or phrase) frequencies in context in text corpora to develop measures for word similarity or word association, partially surveyed in Tan et al. (2002) and Terra and Clarke (2003), going back to at least the 1960s (Lesk, 1969). Some issues in word similarity are association measures, attributed word similarity, and relational word similarity.

13.2.1 Association Measures

Association measures were the subject of Turney (2001, 2002). There the algorithm used is called PMI-IR, short for pointwise mutual information (PMI), to analyze statistical data collected by information retrieval (IR). The PMI-IR algorithm in Turney (2001), like LSA discussed in Section 13.2.4, and in fact the NWD method, which forms the core of this chapter, is based on co-occurrence of words. Assume we are given name1 and we are looking which name2 is closest related. Essentially the algorithm uses the idea that the relatedness of name2 to name1 is expressed by

$$\text{score}(\text{name2}) = \log \frac{\Pr(\text{name2 \& name1})}{\Pr(\text{name1}) \Pr(\text{name2})}.$$

Here the precise meaning of the connective "&" is subject to refinements as below. It can mean "in the same page" or "occurrences near one another in a certain window size," and so on. Since the method is looking for the maximum score one can drop the logarithm and Pr(name1) (because name1 is fixed). Thus, the formula simplifies to looking for name2 that maximizes

$$\frac{\Pr(\text{name2 \& name1})}{\Pr(\text{name2})}. \tag{13.1}$$

This leaves the question of how to compute the probabilities. This is done using a search engine and the Internet. The search engine used in the reference is Altavista, and four different probabilities are presented. Note that because we are looking at a ratio, we need only the number of hits of Altavista for a given search term.

- In the simplest case we consider co-occurrence when the two words occur in the same page:

$$\text{score}_1(\text{name2}) = \frac{\text{hits}(\text{name1 AND name2})}{\text{hits}(\text{name2})}.$$

- The next method asks if the words occur near each other:

$$\text{score}_2(\text{name2}) = \frac{\text{hits}(\text{name1 NEAR name2})}{\text{hits}(\text{name2})}.$$

Two other methods in increasing degree of sophistication are presented to refine the hits with AND, NOT, NEAR in both numerator and denominator.

Related preceding work in Brin et al. (1997) defines a notion of 'interest' to determine interesting associations in large databases. The *interest* of the association between *A* and *B* is defined exactly like (13.1) without the logarithm. This has apparently been used for data mining but not for text mining.

We continue with the results in Turney (2001). Experiments were done on synonym test questions from the Test of English as a Foreign Language (TOEFL) and 50 synonym test questions from a collection of tests for students of English as a Second Language (ESL). On both tests, the algorithm obtains a score of 74%. PMI-IR is contrasted with Latent Semantic Analysis (LSA), Section 13.2.4, which achieves a score of 64% on the same 80 TOEFL questions. Reference Turney (2001) notes that PMI-IR uses a much larger data source than LSA and PMI-IR (in all of the scores except for score₁) uses a much smaller chunk (text window examined) size than LSA. A similar application using the same method is used in Turney (2002) with some more or less evident refinements to classify 410 reviews from the Web site Epinions sampled from four different domains (reviews of automobiles, banks, movies, and travel destinations). The accuracy ranges from 84% for automobile reviews to 66% for movie reviews.

13.2.2 Attributes

Here the approach is to determine attributes as representation of words. Consider a target noun, say "horse," and this noun occurs in a sentence as "the rider rides the horse." Then we have the triple (rider, rides, horse) and the pair (rider, rides) is an attribute of the noun "horse." This approach is then coupled with an appropriate word similarity measure like the one discussed based on PMI, or another one like the cosine similarity measure in LSA as in Section 13.2.4. In fact, LSA is an example of attributional similarity of words. Good references are Ehlert (2003), Freitag et al. (2005) and Moralyiski and Dias (2007).

13.2.3 Relational Word Similarity

We cite Turney (2006): "Relational similarity is correspondence between relations, in contrast with attributional similarity, which is correspondence between attributes. When two words have a high degree of attributional similarity, we call them synonyms. When two pairs of words have a high degree of relational similarity, we say that their relations are analogous. For example, the word pair mason:stone is analogous to the pair carpenter:wood." In this context, LSA as in Section 13.2.4 measures similarity between two words but not between two relations between two pairs of words. One way to measure similarity between the relatedness of pairs of words is to score the relation between a pair of words as frequencies of features (predefined patterns in a large corpus) in vectors and then compare the closeness of the respective vectors by measuring the distance according to the Euclidean distance, the cosine between the vectors, or the logarithm of the cosine. Often a search engine such as Altavista or Google is used to determine the frequency information to build the vectors. In Turney (2006), the author introduces a new method 'latent relational analysis (LRA)' that uses a search engine, a thesaurus of synonyms, and single value decomposition or SVD. For SVD see the discussion on LSA below. LRA is an involved method, and for more details we refer the reader to the cited reference.

13.2.4 Latent Semantic Analysis

Most of the approaches have tackled synonymy detection based on the vector space model and/or probabilistic models. Obviously, there exist many other works for other semantic relations. One of the most successful is LSA (Landauer and Dumais, 1997) that has been applied in various forms in a great number of applications. The basic assumption of LSA is that "the cognitive similarity between any two words is reflected in the way they co-occur in small subsamples of the language." In particular, this is implemented by constructing a matrix with rows labeled by the d documents involved, and the columns labeled by the a attributes (words, phrases). The entries are the number of times the column attribute occurs in the row document. The entries are then processed by taking the logarithm of the entry and dividing it by the number of documents the attribute occurred in, or some other normalizing function. This results in a sparse but high-dimensional matrix A. A main feature of LSA is to reduce the dimensionality of the matrix by projecting it into an adequate subspace of lower dimension using singular value decomposition $A = UDV^{\mathrm{T}}$, where U, V are orthogonal matrices and D is a diagonal matrix. The diagonal elements $\lambda_1, \ldots, \lambda_p$ ($p = \min\{d, a\}$) satisfy $\lambda_1 \geq \cdots \geq \lambda_p$, and the closest matrix A_k of dimension $k < \mathrm{Rank}(A)$ in terms of the so-called Frobenius norm is obtained by setting $\lambda_i = 0$ for $i > k$. Using A_k corresponds to using the most important dimensions. Each attribute is now taken to correspond to a column vector in A_k, and the similarity between two attributes is usually taken to be the cosine between their two vectors.

To compare LSA to the method of using the NWD of Cilibrasi and Vitányi (2007) we treat in detail below, the documents could be the web pages, the entries in matrix A are the frequencies of a search term in each web page. This is then converted as above to obtain vectors for each search term. Subsequently, the cosine between vectors gives the similarity between the terms. LSA has been used in a plethora of applications ranging from database query systems to synonymy answering systems in TOEFL tests. Comparing LSA's performance to the NWD performance is problematic for several reasons. First, the numerical quantity measuring the semantic distance between pairs of terms cannot directly be compared, since they have quite different epistemologies. Indirect comparison could be given using the method as basis for a particular application, and comparing accuracies. However, application of LSA in terms of the Web using a search engine is computationally out of the question, because the matrix A would have 10^{10} rows, even if the search engine would report frequencies of occurrences in web pages and identify the web pages properly. One would need to retrieve the entire Web database, which is many terabytes. Moreover, each invocation of a Web search takes a significant amount of time, and we cannot automatically make more than a certain number of them per day. An alternative interpretation by considering the Web as a single document makes the matrix A above into a vector and appears to defeat the LSA process altogether. Summarizing, the basic idea of our method is similar to that of LSA in spirit. What is novel is that we can do it with selected terms over a very large document collection, whereas LSA involves matrix operations over a closed collection of limited size, and hence is not possible to apply in the Web context.

As with LSA, many other previous approaches of extracting correlations from text documents are based on text corpora that are many orders of magnitudes smaller, and that are in local storage, and on assumptions that are more refined, than what we propose here. In contrast, Bagrow and ben Avraham (2005), Cimiano and Staab (2004), and Turney (2001, 2002) and the many references cited there, use the Web and search engine page counts to identify lexico-syntactic patterns or other data. Again, the theory, aim, feature analysis, and execution are different from ours.

13.3 Background of the NWD Method

The NWD method below automatically extracts semantic relations between arbitrary objects from the Web in a manner that is feature free, up to the search engine used, and computationally feasible. This is a new direction of feature-free and parameter-free data mining. Since the method is parameter-free, it is versatile and as a consequence domain, genre, and language independent.

The main thrust in Cilibrasi and Vitányi (2007) is to develop a new theory of semantic distance between a pair of objects, based on (and unavoidably biased by) a background contents consisting of a database of documents. An example of the latter is the set of pages constituting the Internet. Another example would be the set of all ten-word phrases generated by a sliding window passing over the text in a database of web pages.

Similarity relations between pairs of objects are distilled from the documents by just using the number of documents in which the objects occur, singly and jointly. These counts may be taken with regard to location, that is, we consider a sequence of words, or without regard to location which means we use a bag of words. They may be taken with regard to multiplicity in a term frequency vector or without regard to multiplicity in a binary term vector, as the setting dictates. These decisions determine the normalization factors and feature classes that are analyzed, but do not alter substantially the structure of the algorithm. For us, the semantics of a word or phrase consists of the set of web pages returned by the query concerned. Note that this can mean that terms with different meanings have the same semantics, and that opposites such as "true" and "false" often have a similar semantics. Thus, we just discover associations between terms, suggesting a likely relationship.

As the Web grows, the semantics may become less primitive. The theoretical underpinning is based on the theory of Kolmogorov complexity (Li and Vitányi, 2008), and is in terms of coding and compression. This allows to express and prove properties of absolute relations between objects that cannot be expressed by other approaches. We start with a technical introduction outlining some notions underpinning our approach: the Kolmogorov complexity (Section 13.4), and information distance resulting in the compression-based similarity metric (Section 13.5). In Section 13.6, we give the theoretic underpinning of the NWD. In Section 13.7.1 and Section 13.7.2, we present clustering and classification experiments to validate the universality, the robustness, and the accuracy of the NWD. In Section 13.7.3, we present a toy example of translation. In Section 13.7.4, we test repetitive automatic performance of the NWD against uncontroversial semantic knowledge: We present the results of a massive randomized classification trial we conducted to gauge the accuracy of our method against the expert knowledge implemented over decades in the WordNet database. The preliminary publication in 2004 of (Cilibrasi and Vitányi, 2007) this work in the Web archive ArXiv was widely reported and discussed, for example Graham-Rowe (2005) and Slashdot (2005). The actual experimental data can be downloaded from Cilibrasi (2004). The method is implemented as an easy-to-use software tool (Cilibrasi, 2003), free for commercial and noncommercial use according to a BSD style license.

The application of the theory we develop is a method that is justified by the vastness of the Internet, the assumption that the mass of information is so diverse that the frequencies of pages returned by a good set of search engine queries averages the semantic information in such a way that one can distill a valid semantic distance between the query subjects. The method starts from scratch, is feature-free in that it uses just the Web and a search engine to supply contents, and automatically generates relative semantics between words and phrases. As noted in Bagrow and ben Avraham (2005), the returned counts can be inaccurate although linguists judge the accuracy of, for example, Google counts trustworthy enough. In Keller and Lapata (2003), (see also the many references to related research) it is shown that Web searches for rare two-word phrases correlated well with the frequency found in traditional corpora, as well as with human judgments of whether those phrases were natural. Thus, search engines on the Web are the simplest means to get the most information. The experimental evidence provided here shows that our method yields reasonable results, gauged against common sense ('colors' are different from 'numbers') and against the expert knowledge in the WordNet database.

13.4 Brief Introduction to Kolmogorov Complexity

The basis of much of the theory explored in this chapter is the Kolmogorov complexity (Kolmogorov, 1965). For an introduction and details see the textbook Li and Vitányi (2008). Here we give some intuition and notation. We assume a fixed reference universal programming system. Such a system may be a general computer language such as LISP or Ruby, and it may also be a fixed reference universal Turing machine U in a given standard enumeration of Turing machines $T_1, T_2, \ldots$ of the type such that $U(i, p) = T_i(p) < \infty$ for every index i and program p. This also involves that U started on input (i, p) and T_i started on input p both halt after a finite number of steps, which may be different in both cases and possibly unknown. Such U's have been called 'optimal' (Kolmogorov, 1965). The last choice has the advantage of being formally simple and hence easy to theoretically manipulate. But the choice makes no difference in principle, and the theory is invariant under changes among the universal programming systems, provided we stick to a particular choice. We only consider programs that are binary finite strings and such that for every Turing machine the set of programs is a prefix-free set or *prefix code*: no program is a proper prefix of another program for this Turing machine. Thus, universal programming systems are such that the associated set of programs is a prefix code—as is the case in all standard computer languages.

The *Kolmogorov complexity* $K(x)$ of a string x is the length, in bits, of a shortest computer program (there may be more than one) of the fixed reference computing system, such as a fixed optimal universal Turing machine that (without input) produces x as output. The choice of computing system changes the value of $K(x)$ by at most an additive fixed constant. Since $K(x)$ goes to infinity with x, this additive fixed constant is an ignorable quantity if we consider large x. Given the fixed reference computing system, the function K is not computable.

One way to think about the Kolmogorov complexity $K(x)$ is to view it as the length, in bits, of the ultimate compressed version from which x can be recovered by a general decompression program. Compressing x using the compressor *gzip* results in a file x_g with (for files that contain redundancies) the length $|x_g| < |x|$. Using a better compressor *bzip2* results in a file x_b with (for redundant files) usually $|x_b| < |x_g|$; using a still better compressor like *PPMZ* results in a file x_p with (for again appropriately redundant files) $|x_p| < |x_b|$. The Kolmogorov complexity $K(x)$ gives a lower bound on the ultimate length of a compressed version for every existing compressor, or compressors that are possible but not yet known: the value $K(x)$ is less or equal to the length of every effectively compressed version of x. That is, $K(x)$ gives us the ultimate value of the length of a compressed version of x (more precisely, from which version x can be reconstructed by a general purpose decompresser), and our task in designing better and better compressors is to approach this lower bound as closely as possible.

Similarly, we can define the *conditional Kolmogorov complexity* $K(x|y)$ as the length of a shortest program that computes output x given input y, and the *joint Kolmogorov complexity* $K(x, y)$ as the length of a shortest program that without input computes the pair x, y and a way to tell them apart.

Definition 13.1 *A computable rational valued function is one that can be computed by a halting program on the reference universal Turing machine. A function f with real values is upper semicomputable if there is a computable rational valued function $\phi(x, k)$ such that $\phi(x, k+1) \leq \phi(x, k)$ and $\lim_{k \to \infty} \phi(x, k) = f(x)$; it is lower semicomputable if $-f$ is upper semicomputable. We call a real valued function f computable if it is both lower semicomputable and upper semicomputable.*

It has been proved (Li and Vitányi, 2008) that the Kolmogorov complexity is the least upper semicomputable code length up to an additive constant term. Clearly, every Turing machine T_i defines an upper semicomputable code length of a source word x by $\min_q\{|q| : T_i(q) = x\}$. With U the fixed reference optimal universal Turing machine, for every i there is a constant c_i such that for every x we have $k(x) = \min_p\{|p| : U(p) = x\} \leq \min_q\{|q| : T_i(q) = x\} + c_i$.

An important identity is the *symmetry of information*

$$K(x, y) = K(x) + K(y|x) = K(y) + K(x|y), \tag{13.2}$$

which holds up to an $O(\log K(xy))$ additive term.

The following notion is crucial in the later sections. We define the *universal probability* **m** by

$$\mathbf{m}(x) = 2^{-K(x)}, \tag{13.3}$$

which satisfies $\sum_x \mathbf{m}(x) \leq 1$ by the Kraft inequality (Cover and Thomas, 1991; Kraft, 1949; Li and Vitányi, 2008) since $\{K(x) : x \in \{0, 1\}^*\}$ is the length set of a prefix code. To obtain a proper probability mass function we can concentrate the surplus probability on a new undefined element u so that $\mathbf{m}(u) = 1 - \sum_x \mathbf{m}(x)$. The universal probability mass function **m** is a form of *Occam's razor* since $\mathbf{m}(x)$ is high for simple objects x whose $K(x)$ is low such as $K(x) = O(\log |x|)$, and $\mathbf{m}(y)$ is low for complex objects y whose $K(y)$ is high such as $K(y) \geq |y|$.

It has been proven (Li and Vitányi, 2008) that **m** is the greatest lower semicomputable probability mass function up to a constant multiplicative factor. Namely, it is easy to see that **m** is a lower semicomputable probability mass function, and it turns out that for every lower semicomputable probability mass function P there is a constant c_P such that for every x we have $c_P \mathbf{m}(x) \geq P(x)$.

13.5 Information Distance

In Bennett et al. (1998), the following notion is considered: given two strings x and y, what is the length of the shortest binary program in the reference universal computing system such that the program computes output y from input x, and also output x from input y. This is called the *information distance*. It turns out that, up to a negligible logarithmic additive term, it is equal to

$$E(x, y) = \max\{K(x|y), K(y|x)\}. \tag{13.4}$$

We now discuss the important properties of E.

Definition 13.2 *A distance $D(x, y)$ is a metric if $D(x, x) = 0$ and $D(x, y) > 0$ for $x \neq y$; $D(x, y) = D(y, x)$ (symmetry); and $D(x, y) \leq D(x, z) + D(z, y)$, (triangle inequality) for all x, y, z.*

For a distance function or metric to be reasonable, it has to satisfy an additional condition, referred to as *density condition*. Intuitively this means that for every object x and positive real value d there is at most a certain finite number of objects y at distance d from x. This requirement excludes degenerate distance measures like $D(x, y) = 1$ for all $x \neq y$. Exactly how fast we want the distances of the strings y from x to go to infinity is not important, it is only a matter of scaling. For convenience, we will require the following *density conditions*:

$$\sum_{y:y \neq x} 2^{-D(x,y)} \leq 1 \text{ and } \sum_{x:x \neq y} 2^{-D(x,y)} \leq 1. \tag{13.5}$$

Finally, we allow only distance measures that are computable in some broad sense, which will not be seen as unduly restrictive. The upper semicomputability in Definition 13.1 is readily extended to two-argument functions and in the present context to distances. We require the distances we deal with to be upper semicomputable. This is reasonable: if we have more and more time to process x and y, then we may discover newer and newer similarities among them, and thus may revise our upper bound on their distance.

Definition 13.3 *An admissible distance is a total, possibly asymmetric, nonnegative function with real values on the pairs x, y of binary strings that is 0 if and only if $x = y$, is upper semicomputable, and satisfies the density requirement (13.5).*

Definition 13.4 *Consider a family $\mathcal{F}$ of two-argument real valued functions. A function f is universal for the family $\mathcal{F}$ if for every $g \in \mathcal{F}$ we have*

$$f(x, y) \leq g(x, y) + c_g,$$

where c_g is a constant that depends only on g but not on x, y and f. We say that f minorizes every $g \in \mathcal{F}$ up to an additive constant.

The following theorem is proven in Bennett et al. (1998) and Li and Vitányi (2008).

Theorem 13.1

i. E *is universal for the family of admissible distances.*
ii. E *satisfies the metric (in)equalities up to an $O(1)$ additive term.*

If two strings x and y are close according to *some* admissible distance D, then they are at least as close according to the metric E. Every feature in which we can compare two strings can be quantified in terms of a distance, and every distance can be viewed as expressing a quantification of how much of a particular feature the strings do not have in common (the feature being quantified by that distance). Therefore, the information distance is an admissible distance between two strings minorizing the *dominant* feature expressible as an admissible distance that they have in common. This means that, if we consider more than two strings, the information distance between every pair may be based on minorizing a different dominant feature.

13.5.1 Normalized Information Distance

If strings of length 1000 bits differ by 800 bits then these strings are very different. However, if two strings of 1,000,000 bits differ by 800 bits only, then they are very similar. Therefore, the information distance itself is not suitable to express true similarity. For that we must define a relative information distance: we need to normalize the information distance. Our objective is to normalize the universal information distance E in (13.4) to obtain a universal *similarity* distance. It should give a similarity with distance 0 when objects are maximally similar and distance 1 when they are maximally dissimilar. Such an approach was first proposed in Li et al. (2001) in the context of genomics-based phylogeny, and improved in Li et al. (2004) to the one we use here. Several alternative ways of normalizing the information distance do not work. It is paramount that the normalized version of the information metric is also a metric in the case we deal with literal objects that contain all their properties within. Were it not, then the relative relations between the objects would be disrupted and this could lead to anomalies, if, for instance, the triangle inequality would be violated for the normalized version. However, for nonliteral objects that have a semantic distance NWD based on hit count statistics as in Section 13.6, which is the real substance of this work, the triangle inequality will be seen not to hold.

The *normalized information distance* (NID) is defined by

$$e(x,y) = \frac{\max\{K(x|y), K(y|x)\}}{\max\{K(x), K(y)\}}. \tag{13.6}$$

Theorem 13.2

The normalized information distance $e(x,y)$ takes values in the range [0,1] and is a metric, up to ignorable discrepancies.

The theorem is proven in Li et al. (2004) and the ignorable discrepancies are additive terms $O((\log K)/K)$, where K is the maximum of the Kolmogorov complexities of strings x, x,y, or x,y,z involved in the metric (in)equalities. The NID discovers for every pair of strings the feature in which they are most similar, and expresses that similarity on a scale from 0 to 1 (0 being the same and 1 being completely different in the sense of sharing no features). It has several wonderful properties that justify its description as the most informative metric (Li et al., 2004).

13.5.2 Normalized Compression Distance

The NID $e(x,y)$, which we call 'the' similarity metric because it accounts for the dominant similarity between two objects, is not computable since the Kolmogorov complexity is not computable. First we observe that using $K(x,y) = K(xy) + O(\log \min\{K(x), K(y)\})$ and the symmetry of information (13.2) we obtain

$$\max\{K(x|y), K(y|x)\} = K(xy) - \min\{K(x), K(y)\},$$

up to an additive logarithmic term $O(\log K(xy))$, which we ignore in the sequel. In order to use the NID in practice, admittedly with a leap of faith, the approximation of the Kolmogorov complexity uses real compressors to approximate the Kolmogorov complexities $K(x), K(y), K(xy)$. A compression algorithm defines a computable function from strings to the lengths of the compressed versions of those strings. Therefore, the number of bits of the compressed version of a string is an upper bound on the Kolmogorov complexity of that string, up to an additive constant depending on the compressor but not on the string in question. This direction has yielded a very practical success of the Kolmogorov complexity. Substitute the last displayed equation in the NID of (13.6), and subsequently use a real-world compressor Z (such as *gzip, bzip2,* and *PPMZ*) to heuristically replace the Kolmogorov complexity. In this way, we obtain the distance e_Z, often called the *normalized compression distance* (NCD), defined by

$$e_Z(x, y) = \frac{Z(xy) - \min\{Z(x), Z(y)\}}{\max\{Z(x), Z(y)\}}, \tag{13.7}$$

where $Z(x)$ denotes the binary length of the compressed version of the file x, compressed with compressor Z. The distance e_Z is actually a family of distances parametrized with the compressor Z. The better Z is, the closer e_Z approaches the NID, the better the results. Since Z is computable the distance e_Z is computable. In Cilibrasi and Vitányi (2005), it is shown that under mild conditions on the compressor Z, the distance e_Z takes values in $[0, 1]$ and is a metric, up to negligible errors. One may imagine e as the limiting case e_K, where $K(x)$ denotes the number of bits in the shortest code for x from which x can be decompressed by a computable general purpose decompressor.

13.6 Word Similarity: Normalized Web Distance

Can we find an equivalent of the NID for names and abstract concepts? In Cilibrasi and Vitányi (2007), the formula (13.6) to determine word similarity from the Internet is derived. It is also proven that the distance involved is 'universal' in a precise quantified manner. The present approach follows the treatment in Li and Vitányi (2008) and obtains 'universality' in yet another manner by viewing the NWD (13.8) below as a computable approximation to the universal distribution **m** of (13.3).

Let **W** be the set of pages of the Internet, and let $x \subseteq \mathbf{W}$ be the set of pages containing the search term x. By the conditional version of (13.3) in (Li and Vitányi, 2008), which appears straightforward but is cumbersome to explain here, we have $\log 1/\mathbf{m}(\mathbf{x}|\mathbf{x} \subseteq \mathbf{W}) = K(\mathbf{x}|\mathbf{x} \subseteq \mathbf{W}) + O(1)$. This equality relates the incompressibility of the set of pages on the Web containing a given search term to its universal probability. We know that **m** is lower semicomputable since K is upper semicomputable, and **m** is not computable since K is not computable. While we cannot compute **m**, a natural heuristic is to use the distribution of x on the Web to approximate $\mathbf{m}(\mathbf{x}|\mathbf{x} \subseteq \mathbf{W})$. Let us define the probability mass function $g(x)$ to be the probability that the search term x appears in a page indexed by a given Internet search engine G, that is, the number of pages returned divided by the number N, which is the sum of the numbers of occurrences of search terms in each page, summed over all pages indexed. Then the Shannon–Fano code (Li and Vitányi, 2008) length associated with g can be set at

$$G(x) = \log \frac{1}{g(x)}.$$

Replacing $Z(x)$ by $G(x)$ in the formula in (13.7), we obtain the distance e_G, called the NWD, which we can view as yet another approximation of the NID, defined by

$$\begin{aligned} e_G(x, y) &= \frac{G(xy) - \min\{G(x), G(y)\}}{\max\{G(x), G(y)\}} \\ &= \frac{\max\{\log f(x), \log f(y)\} - \log f(x, y)}{\log N - \min\{\log f(x), \log f(y)\}}, \end{aligned} \tag{13.8}$$

where $f(x)$ is the number of pages containing x, the frequency $f(x, y)$ is the number of pages containing both x and y, and N is defined above.

Since the code G is a Shannon–Fano code for the probability mass function g it yields an on average minimal code-word length. This is not so good as an individually minimal code-word length, but is an approximation to it. Therefore, we can view the search engine G as a compressor using the Web, and $G(x)$ as the binary length of the compressed version of the set of all pages containing the search term x, given the indexed pages on the Web. The distance e_G is actually a family of distances parametrized with the search engine G.

The better a search engine G is in the sense of covering more of the Internet and returning more accurate aggregate page counts, the closer e_G approaches the NID e of (13.6), with $K(x)$ replaced by $K(\mathbf{x}|\mathbf{x} \subseteq \mathbf{W})$ and similarly the other terms, and the better the results are expected to be.

In practice, we use the page counts returned by the search engine for the frequencies and choose N. From (13.8) it is apparent that by increasing N we decrease the NWD, everything gets closer together, and by decreasing N we increase the NWD, everything gets further apart. Our experiments suggest that every reasonable value can be used as normalizing factor N, and our results seem in general insensitive to this choice. This parameter N can be adjusted as appropriate, and one can often use the number of indexed pages for N. N may be automatically scaled and defined as an arbitrary weighted sum of common search term page counts.

The better G is the more informative the results are expected to be. In Cilibrasi and Vitányi (2007) it is shown that the distance e_G is computable and is symmetric, that is, $e_G(x, y) = e_G(y, x)$. It only satisfies "half" of the identity property, namely $e_G(x, x) = 0$ for all x, but $e_G(x, y) = 0$ can hold even if $x \neq y$, for example, if the terms x and y always occur together in a web page.

The NWD also does *not* satisfy the triangle inequality $e_G(x, y) \leq e_G(x, z) + e_G(z, y)$ for all x, y, z. To see that, choose x, y, and z such that x and y never occur together, z occurs exactly on those pages on which x or y occurs, and $f(x) = f(y) = \sqrt{N}$. Then $f(x) = f(y) = f(x, z) = f(y, z) = \sqrt{N}$, $f(z) = 2\sqrt{N}$, and $f(x, y) = 0$. This yields $e_G(x, y) = \infty$ and $e_G(x, z) = e_G(z, y) = 2/\log N$, which violates the triangle inequality for all N. It follows that the NWD is not a metric.

Therefore, the liberation from lossless compression as in (13.6) to probabilities based on page counts as in (13.8) causes in certain cases the loss of metricity. But this is proper for a relative semantics. Indeed, we should view the distance e_G between two concepts as a relative semantic similarity measure between those concepts. While concept x is semantically close to concept y and concept y is semantically close to concept z, concept x can be semantically very different from concept z.

Another important property of the NWD is its *scale-invariance* under the assumption that if the number N of pages indexed by the search engine grows sufficiently large, the number of pages containing a given search term goes to a fixed fraction of N, and so does the number of pages containing conjunctions of search terms. This means that if N doubles, then so do the f-frequencies. For the NWD to give us an objective semantic relation between search terms, it needs to become stable when the number N of indexed pages grows. Some evidence that this actually happens was given in the example in Section 13.1.

The NWD can be used as a tool to investigate the meaning of terms and the relations between them as given by the Internet. This approach can be compared with the *Cyc* project (Landauer and Dumais, 1995), which tries to create artificial common sense. Cyc's knowledge base consists of hundreds of microtheories and hundreds of thousands of terms, as well as over a million hand-crafted assertions written in a formal language called CycL (Reed and Lenat, 2002). CycL is an enhanced variety of first order predicate logic. This knowledge base was created over the course of decades by paid human experts. It is therefore of extremely high quality. The Internet, on the other hand, is almost completely unstructured, and offers only a primitive query capability that is not nearly flexible enough to represent formal deduction. But what it lacks in expressiveness the Internet makes up for in size; Internet search engines have already indexed more than ten billion pages and show no signs of slowing down. Therefore, search engine databases represent the largest publicly available single corpus of aggregate statistical and indexing information so far created, and it seems that even rudimentary analysis thereof yields a variety of intriguing possibilities. It is unlikely, however, that this approach can ever achieve 100% accuracy like in principle deductive logic can, because the Internet mirrors humankind's own imperfect and varied nature. But, as we will see below, in practical terms the NWD can offer an easy way to provide results that are good enough for many applications, and which would be far too much work if not impossible to program in a deductive way.

In the following sections we present a number of applications of the NWD: the hierarchical clustering and the classification of concepts and names in a variety of domains, and finding corresponding words in different languages.

13.7 Applications and Experiments

To perform the experiments in this section, we used the *CompLearn* software tool (Cilibrasi, 2003). The same tool has been used also to construct trees representing hierarchical clusters of objects in an unsupervised way using the NCD. However, now we use the NWD.

13.7.1 Hierarchical Clustering

The method first calculates a distance matrix using the NWDs among all pairs of terms in the input list. Then it calculates a best-matching unrooted ternary tree using a novel quartet-method style heuristic based on randomized hill-climbing using a new fitness objective function optimizing the summed costs of all quartet topologies embedded in candidate trees (Cilibrasi and Vitányi, 2005). Of course, given the distance matrix one can use also standard tree-reconstruction software from biological packages such as the MOLPHY package (Adachi and Hasegawa, 1996).

However, such biological packages are based on data that are structured like rooted binary trees, and possibly do not perform well on hierarchical clustering of arbitrary natural data sets.

Colors and numbers. In the first example (Cilibrasi and Vitányi, 2007), the objects to be clustered are search terms consisting of the names of colors, numbers, and some words that are related but no color or number. The program automatically organized the colors toward one side of the tree and the numbers toward the other, as in Figure 13.1. It arranges the terms that have as only meaning a color or a number, and nothing else, on the farthest reach of the color side and the number side, respectively. It puts the more general terms black and white, and zero, one, and two, toward the center, thus indicating their more ambiguous interpretation. Also, things that were not exactly colors or numbers are also put toward the center, like the word "small." We may consider this an (admittedly very weak) example of automatic ontology creation.

English dramatists and novelists. The authors and texts used are

WILLIAM SHAKESPEARE: *A Midsummer Night's Dream; Julius Caesar; Love's Labours Lost; Romeo and Juliet.*

JONATHAN SWIFT: *The Battle of the Books; Gulliver's Travels; A Tale of a Tub; A Modest Proposal.*

OSCAR WILDE: *Lady Windermere's Fan; A Woman of No Importance; Salome; The Picture of Dorian Gray.*

The clustering is given in Figure 13.2, and to provide a feeling for the figures involved we give the associated NWD matrix in Figure 13.3. The $S(T)$ value written in Figure 13.2 gives the fidelity of the tree as a representation of the pairwise distances in the NWD matrix: $S(T) = 1$ is perfect and $S(T) = 0$ is as bad as possible (For details see Cilibrasi, 2003; Cilibrasi and Vitányi, 2005).

The question arises why we should expect this outcome. Are names of artistic objects so distinct? Yes. The point also being that the distances from every single object to all other objects are involved. The tree takes this global aspect into account and therefore disambiguates other meanings of the objects to retain the meaning that is relevant for this collection.

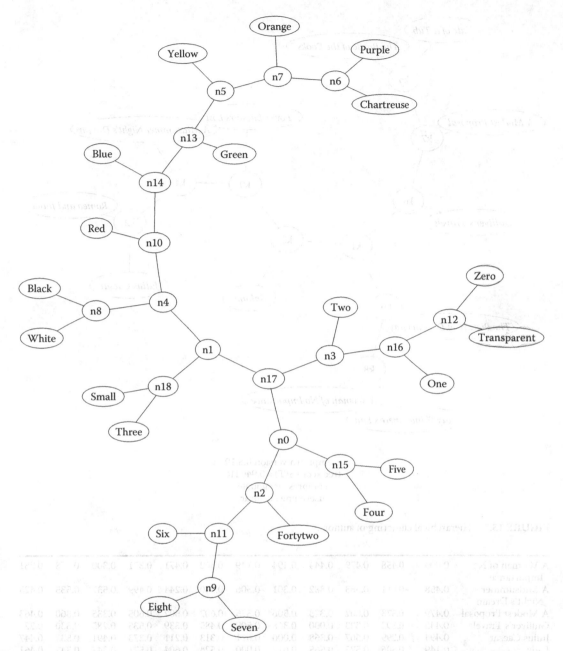

FIGURE 13.1 Colors, numbers, and other terms arranged into a tree based on the NWDs between the terms.

Is the distinguishing feature subject matter or title style? In these experiments with objects belonging to the cultural heritage it is clearly a subject matter. To stress the point we used "Julius Caesar" of Shakespeare. This term occurs on the Web overwhelmingly in other contexts and styles. Yet the collection of the other objects used, and the semantic distance toward those objects, given by the NWD formula, singled out the semantics of "Julius Caesar" relevant to this experiment. The term co-occurrence in this specific context of author discussion is not swamped by other uses of this common term because of the particular form of the NWD and the distances being pairwise. Using very common book titles this swamping effect may still arise though.

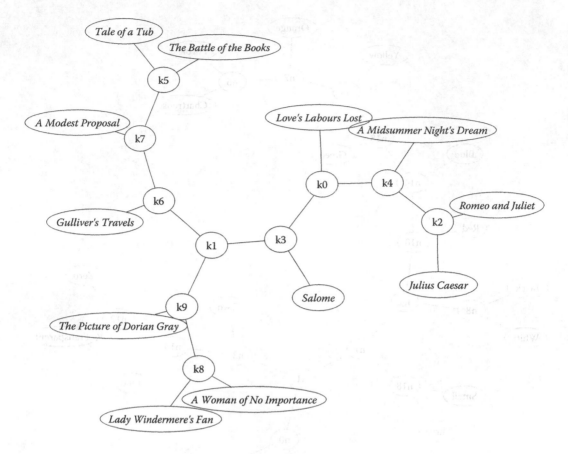

Complearn version 0.8.19
tree score S(T) = 0.940416
compressor : google
username : cilibrar

FIGURE 13.2 Hierarchical clustering of authors.

A Woman of No Importance	0.000	0.458	0.479	0.444	0.494	0.149	0.362	0.471	0.371	0.300	0.278	0.261
A Midsummer Night's Dream	0.458	−0.011	0.563	0.382	0.301	0.506	0.340	0.244	0.499	0.537	0.535	0.425
A Modest Proposal	0.479	0.573	0.002	0.323	0.506	0.575	0.607	0.502	0.605	0.335	0.360	0.463
Gulliver's Travels	0.445	0.392	0.323	0.000	0.368	0.509	0.485	0.339	0.535	0.285	0.330	0.228
Julius Caesar	0.494	0.299	0.507	0.368	0.000	0.611	0.313	0.211	0.373	0.491	0.535	0.447
Lady Windermere's Fan	0.149	0.506	0.575	0.565	0.612	0.000	0.524	0.604	0.571	0.347	0.347	0.461
Love's Labours Lost	0.363	0.332	0.607	0.486	0.313	0.525	0.000	0.351	0.549	0.514	0.462	0.513
Romeo and Juliet	0.471	0.248	0.502	0.339	0.210	0.604	0.351	0.000	0.389	0.527	0.544	0.380
Salome	0.371	0.499	0.605	0.540	0.373	0.568	0.553	0.389	0.000	0.520	0.538	0.407
Tale of a Tub	0.300	0.537	0.335	0.284	0.492	0.347	0.514	0.527	0.524	0.000	0.160	0.421
The Battle of the Books	0.278	0.535	0.359	0.330	0.533	0.347	0.462	0.544	0.541	0.160	0.000	0.373
The Picture of Dorian Gray	0.261	0.415	0.463	0.229	0.447	0.324	0.513	0.380	0.402	0.420	0.373	0.000

FIGURE 13.3 Distance matrix of pairwise NWDs.

Does the system get confused if we add more artists? Representing the NWD matrix in bifurcating trees without distortion becomes more difficult for, say, more than 25 objects (See Cilibrasi and Vitányi, 2005).

What about other subjects, such as music or sculpture? Presumably, the system will be more trustworthy if the subjects are more common on the Web.

These experiments are representative for those we have performed with the current software. We did not cherry pick the best outcomes. For example, all experiments with these three English writers, with different selections of four works of each, always yielded a tree so that we could draw a convex hull around the works of each author, without overlap.

The NWD method works independently of the alphabet, and even takes Chinese characters. In the example of Figure 13.4, several Chinese names were entered. The tree shows the separation according to concepts such as regions, political parties, people, etc. See Figure 13.5 for English translations of these names. The dotted lines with numbers between each adjacent node along the perimeter of the tree represent the NWD values between adjacent nodes in the final ordered tree. The tree is presented in such a way that the sum of these values in the entire ring is minimized. This generally results in trees that make the most sense upon initial visual inspection, converting an unordered bifurcating tree to an ordered one.

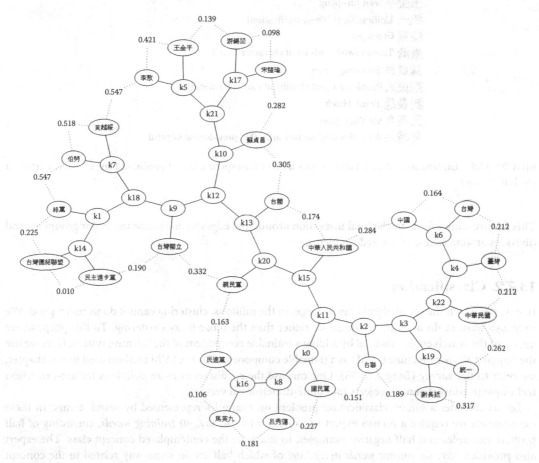

FIGURE 13.4 Names of several Chinese people, political parties, regions, and others. The nodes and *solid lines* constitute a tree constructed by a hierarchical clustering method based on the NWDs between all names. The numbers at the perimeter of the tree represent NWD values between the nodes pointed to by the *dotted lines*. For an explanation of the names, refer to Figure 13.5.

中國 China

中華人民共和國 People's Republic of China

中華民國 Republic of China

伯勞 Shirike (bird) (outgroup)

台灣 Taiwan (with simplified character "tai")

台灣團結聯盟 Taiwan solidarity union [Taiwanese political party]

台灣獨立 Taiwan independence

台獨 (abbreviation of the above)

台聯 (abbreviation of Taiwan solidarity union)

呂秀蓮 Annette Lu

國民黨 Kuomintag

宋楚瑜 James Soong

李敖 Li Ao

民主進步黨 Democratic progressive party

民進黨 (abbreviation of the above)

游錫堃 Yu Shyi–kun

王金平 Wan Jin–pyng

統一 Unification [Chinese unification]

綠黨 Green party

臺灣 Taiwan (with traditional character "tai")

蘇貞昌 Su Tseng–chang

親民黨 People first party [political party in Taiwan]

謝長廷 Frank Hsieh

馬英九 Ma Ying–jeou

黃越綏 A presidential advisor and 2008 presidential hopeful

FIGURE 13.5 Explanations of the Chinese names used in the experiment that produced Figure 13.4. (Courtesy of Dr. Kaihsu Tai.)

This feature allows for a quick visual inspection around the edges to determine the major groupings and divisions among coarse structured problems.

13.7.2 Classification

In cases in which the set of objects can be large, in the millions, clustering cannot do us much good. We may also want to do definite classification, rather than the more fuzzy clustering. To this purpose, we augment the search engine method by adding a trainable component of the learning system. Here we use the Support Vector Machine (SVM) as a trainable component. For the SVM method used in this chapter, we refer to the survey (Burges, 1998). One can use the e_G distances as an oblivious feature-extraction technique to convert generic objects into finite-dimensional vectors.

Let us consider a binary classification problem on examples represented by search terms. In these experiments we require a human expert to provide a list of, say, 40 *training words*, consisting of half positive examples and half negative examples, to illustrate the contemplated concept class. The expert also provides, say, six *anchor words* $a_1, \ldots, a_6$, of which half are in some way related to the concept under consideration. Then, we use the anchor words to convert each of the 40 training words $w_1, \ldots, w_{40}$ to six-dimensional *training vectors* $\bar{v}_1, \ldots, \bar{v}_{40}$. The entry $v_{j,i}$ of $\bar{v}_j = (v_{j,1}, \ldots, v_{j,6})$ is defined as $v_{j,i} = e_G(w_j, a_i)$ $(1 \leq j \leq 40, \ 1 \leq i \leq 6)$. The training vectors are then used to train an SVM to learn the concept, and then test words may be classified using the same anchors and trained SVM model. Finally

Training Data

Positive Training	(22 cases)			
avalanche	bomb threat	broken leg	burglary	car collision
death threat	fire	flood	gas leak	heart attack
hurricane	landslide	murder	overdose	pneumonia
rape	roof collapse	sinking ship	stroke	tornado
train wreck	trapped miners			

Negative Training	(25 cases)			
arthritis	broken dishwasher	broken toe	cat in tree	contempt of court
dandruff	delayed train	dizziness	drunkenness	enumeration
flat tire	frog	headache	leaky faucet	littering
missing dog	paper cut	practical joke	rain	roof leak
sore throat	sunset	truancy	vagrancy	vulgarity

Anchors	(6 dimensions)			
crime	happy	help	safe	urgent
wash				

Testing Results

	Positive tests	Negative tests
Positive Predictions	assault, coma, electrocution, heat stroke, homicide, looting, meningitis, robbery, suicide	menopause, prank call, pregnancy, traffic jam
Negative Predictions	sprained ankle	acne, annoying sister, campfire, desk, mayday, meal
Accuracy	15/20 = 75.00%	

FIGURE 13.6   NWD–SVM learning of "emergencies."

testing is performed using 20 examples in a balanced ensemble to yield a final accuracy. The kernel-width and error-cost parameters are automatically determined using fivefold cross validation. The LIBSVM software (Chang and Lin, 2001) was used for all SVM experiments.

Classification of "emergencies." In Figure 13.6, we trained using a list of "emergencies" as positive examples, and a list of "almost emergencies" as negative examples. The figure is self-explanatory. The accuracy on the test set is 75%.

Classification of prime numbers. In an experiment to learn prime numbers, we used the literal search terms below (digital numbers and alphabetical words) in the Google search engine.

Positive training examples: 11, 13, 17, 19, 2, 23, 29, 3, 31, 37, 41, 43, 47, 5, 53, 59, 61, 67, 7, 71, 73.

Negative training examples: 10, 12, 14, 15, 16, 18, 20, 21, 22, 24, 25, 26, 27, 28, 30, 32, 33, 34, 4, 6, 8, 9.

Anchor words: composite, number, orange, prime, record.

Unseen test examples: The numbers 101, 103, 107, 109, 79, 83, 89, 97 were correctly classified as primes. The numbers 36, 38, 40, 42, 44, 45, 46, 48, 49 were correctly classified as nonprimes. The numbers 91 and 110 were false positives, since they were incorrectly classified as primes. There were no false negatives. The accuracy on the test set is 17/19 = 89.47%. Thus, the method learns to distinguish prime numbers from nonprime numbers by example, using a search engine. This example illustrates several common features of our method that distinguish it from the strictly deductive techniques.

13.7.3 Matching the Meaning

Assume that there are five words that appear in two different matched sentences, but the permutation associating the English and Spanish words is, as yet, undetermined. Let us say, *plant, car, dance, speak, friend* versus *bailar, hablar, amigo, coche, planta*. At the outset we assume a preexisting vocabulary of eight English words with their matched Spanish translations: *tooth, diente; joy, alegria; tree, arbol; electricity, electricidad; table, tabla; money, dinero; sound, sonido; music, musica*. Can we infer the correct permutation mapping the unknown words using the preexisting vocabulary as a basis?

We start by forming an English basis matrix in which each entry is the e_G distance between the English word labeling the column and the English word labeling the row. We label the columns by the translation-known English words, and the rows by the translation-unknown English words. Next, we form a Spanish matrix with the known Spanish words labeling the columns in the same order as the known English words. But now we label the rows by choosing one of the many possible permutations of the unknown Spanish words. For every permutation, each matrix entry is the e_G distance between the Spanish words labeling the column and the row. Finally, choose the permutation with the highest positive correlation between the English basis matrix and the Spanish matrix associated with the permutation. If there is no positive correlation, report a failure to extend the vocabulary. The method inferred the correct permutation for the testing words: *plant, planta; car, coche; dance, bailar; speak, hablar; friend, amigo*.

13.7.4 Systematic Comparison with WordNet Semantics

WordNet (Miller et al.) is a semantic concordance of English. It focuses on the meaning of words by dividing them into categories. We use this as follows. A category we want to learn, the concept, is termed, say, "electrical," and represents anything that may pertain to electrical devices. The negative examples are constituted by simply everything else. This category represents a typical expansion of a node in the WordNet hierarchy. In an experiment we ran, the accuracy on this test set is 100%: It turns out that "electrical terms" are unambiguous and easy to learn and classify by our method.

The information in the WordNet database is entered over the decades by human experts and is precise. The database is an academic venture and is publicly accessible. Hence it is a good baseline against which to judge the accuracy of our method in an indirect manner. While we cannot directly compare the semantic distance, the NWD, between objects, we can indirectly judge how accurate it is by using it as basis for a learning algorithm. In particular, we investigated how well semantic categories that are learned using the NWD–SVM approach agree with the corresponding WordNet categories. For details about the structure of WordNet we refer to the official WordNet documentation available online.

We considered 100 randomly selected semantic categories from the WordNet database. For each category we executed the following sequence. First, the SVM is trained on 50 labeled training samples. The positive examples are randomly drawn from the WordNet database in the category in question. The negative examples are randomly drawn from a dictionary. While the latter examples may be false negatives, we consider the probability negligible. For every experiment we used a total of six anchors, three of which are randomly drawn from the WordNet database category in question, and three of which are drawn from the dictionary. Subsequently, every example is converted to six-dimensional vectors using NWD. The ith entry of the vector is the NWD between the ith anchor and the example concerned ($1 \leq i \leq 6$). The SVM is trained on the resulting labeled vectors. The kernel-width and error-cost parameters are automatically determined using fivefold cross validation. Finally, testing of how well the SVM has learned the classifier is performed using 20 new examples in a balanced ensemble of positive and negative examples obtained in the same way, and converted to six-dimensional vectors in the same manner, as the training examples. This results in an accuracy score of correctly classified test examples. We ran 100 experiments. The actual data are available at Cilibrasi (2004).

A histogram of agreement accuracies is shown in Figure 13.7. On average, our method turns out to agree well with the WordNet semantic concordance made by human experts. The mean of the accuracies

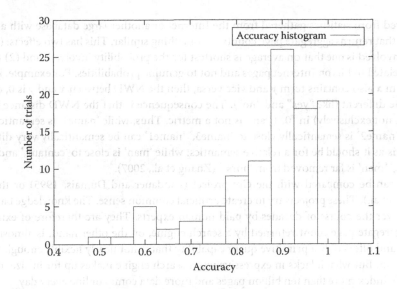

FIGURE 13.7 Histogram of accuracies over 100 trials of WordNet experiment.

of agreements is 0.8725. The variance is ≈ 0.01367, which gives a standard deviation of ≈ 0.1169. Thus, it is rare to find agreement less than 75%. The total number of Web searches involved in this randomized automatic trial is upper bounded by $100 \times 70 \times 6 \times 3 = 126,000$. A considerable savings resulted from the fact that it is simple to cache search count results for efficiency. For every new term, in computing its six-dimensional vector, the NWD computed with respect to the six anchors requires the counts for the anchors which needs to be computed only once for each experiment, the count of the new term which can be computed once, and the count of the joint occurrence of the new term and each of the six anchors, which has to be computed in each case. Altogether, this gives a total of $6 + 70 + 70 \times 6 = 496$ for every experiment, so 49,600 Web searches for the entire trial.

13.8 Conclusion

The approach in this chapter rests on the idea that *information distance* between two objects can be measured by the size of the shortest description that transforms each object into the other one. This idea is most naturally expressed mathematically using the Kolmogorov complexity. The Kolmogorov complexity, moreover, provides mathematical tools to show that such a measure is, in a proper sense, universal among all (upper semi)computable distance measures satisfying a natural density condition. These comprise most, if not all, distances one may be interested in. Since two large, very similar, objects may have the same information distance as two small, very dissimilar, objects, in terms of similarity it is the relative distance we are interested in. Hence we normalize the information metric to create a relative similarity in between 0 and 1. However, the normalized information metric is uncomputable. We approximate its Kolmogorov complexity parts by off-the-shelf compression programs (in the case of the normalized compression distance) or readily available statistics from the Internet (in case of the NWD). The outcomes are two practical distance measures for literal as well as for non-literal data that have been proved useful in numerous applications, some of which have been presented in the previous sections.

It is interesting that while the (normalized) information distance and the normalized compression distance between literal objects are metrics, this is *not* the case for the NWD between nonliteral objects like words, which is the measure of word similarity that we use here. The latter derives the code-word lengths involved from statistics gathered from the Internet or another large database with an associated search engine that returns aggregate page counts or something similar. This has two effects: (1) the code-word length involved is one that on average is shortest for the probability involved, and (2) the statistics involved are related to hits on Internet pages and not to genuine probabilities. For example, if every page containing term x also contains term y and vice versa, then the NWD between x and y is 0, even though x and y may be different (like "yes" and "no"). The consequence is that the NWD distance takes values primarily (but not exclusively) in [0, 1] and is not a metric. Thus, while 'name1' is semantically close to 'name2,' and 'name2' is semantically close to 'name3,' 'name1' can be semantically very different from 'name3.' This is as it should be for a relative semantics: while 'man' is close to 'centaur,' and 'centaur' is close to 'horse,' 'man' is far removed from 'horse' (Zhang et al., 2007).

The NWD can be compared with the *Cyc* project (Landauer and Dumais, 1995) or the WordNet project (Miller et al.). These projects try to create artificial common sense. The knowledge bases involved were created over the course of decades by paid human experts. They are therefore of extremely high quality. An aggregate page count returned by a search engine, on the other hand, is almost completely unstructured, and offers only a primitive query capability that is not nearly flexible enough to represent formal deduction. But what it lacks in expressiveness a search engine makes up for in size; many search engines already index more than ten billion pages and more data comes online every day.

References

Adachi, J. and M. Hasegawa. *MOLPHY* version 2.3: Programs for molecular phylogenetics based on maximum likelihood. Computer Science Monograph, Vol. 28. Institute of Statistical Mathematics, 1996.

Bagrow, J.P. and D. ben Avraham. On the google-fame of scientists and other populations. In AIP Conference Proceedings, Gallipoli, Italy vol. 779:1, pp. 81–89, 2005.

Bennett, C.H., P. Gács, M. Li, P.M.B. Vitányi, and W. Zurek. Information distance. *IEEE Trans. Inform. Theory*, 44(4):1407–1423, 1998.

Brin, S., R. Motwani, J. Ullman, and S. Tsur. Dynamic itemset counting and implication rules for market basket data. In *Proceedings of the ACM-SIGMOD International Conference on Management of Data*, Tucson, AZ, pp. 255–264, 1997.

Burges, C.J.C. A tutorial on support vector machines for pattern recognition. *Data Min. Knowl. Disc.*, 2(2):121–167, 1998.

Chang, C.-C. and C.-J. Lin. LIBSVM: A library for support vector machines. Software available at http://www.csie.ntu.edu.tw/cjlin/libsvm, 2001.

Cilibrasi, R.L. Complearn. http://www.complearn.org, 2003.

Cilibrasi, R.L. Automatic meaning discovery using google: 100 experiments in learning WordNet categories. See supporting material on accompanying Web page, 2004.

Cilibrasi, R.L. and P.M.B. Vitányi. Clustering by compression. *IEEE Trans. Inform. Theory*, 51(4):1523–1545, 2005.

Cilibrasi, R.L. and P.M.B. Vitányi. The Google similarity distance. *IEEE Trans. Knowl. Data Eng.*, 19(3):370–383, 2007. Preliminary version: Automatic meaning discovery using Google, http://xxx.lanl.gov/abs/cs.CL/0412098, 2007.

Cilibrasi, R.L., P.M.B. Vitányi, and R. de Wolf. Algorithmic clustering of music based on string compression. *Computer Music J.*, 28(4):49–67, 2004.

Cimiano, P. and S. Staab. Learning by Googling. *SIGKDD Explor.*, 6(2):24–33, 2004.

Cover, T.M. and J.A. Thomas. *Elements of Information Theory*. John Wiley & Sons, New York, 1991.

Delahaye, J.P. Classer musiques, langues, images, textes et genomes. *Pour La Science*, 317:98–103, March 2004.

Ehlert, E. Making accurate lexical semantic similarity judgments using word-context co-occurrence statistics. Master's thesis, 2003.

Freitag, D., M. Blume, J. Byrnes, E. Chow, S. Kapadia, R. Rohwer, and Z. Wang. New experiments in distributional representations of synonymy. In *Proceedings of the Ninth Conference on Computational Natural Language Learning*, Ann Arbor, MI, pp. 25–31, 2005.

Graham-Rowe, D. A search for meaning. *New Scientist*, p. 21, January 29, 2005.

Keller, F. and M. Lapata. Using the web to obtain frequencies for unseen bigrams. *Comput. Linguist.*, 29(3):459–484, 2003.

Keogh, E., S. Lonardi, C.A. Ratanamahatana, L. Wei, H.S. Lee, and J. Handley. Compression-based data mining of sequential data. *Data Min. Knowl. Disc.*, 14:99–129, 2007. Preliminary version: E. Keogh, S. Lonardi, and C.A. Ratanamahatana, Toward parameter-free data mining, In *Proceedings of the 10th ACM SIGKDD International Conference on Knowledge Discovery and Data Mining*, Toronto, Canada, pp. 206–215, 2004.

Kolmogorov, A.N. Three approaches to the quantitative definition of information. *Problems Inform. Transm.*, 1(1):1–7, 1965.

Kraft, L.G. A device for quantizing, grouping and coding amplitude modulated pulses. Master's thesis, Department of Electrical Engineering, MIT, Cambridge, MA, 1949.

Landauer, T. and S. Dumais. Cyc: A large-scale investment in knowledge infrastructure. *Comm. ACM*, 38(11):33–38, 1995.

Landauer T. and S. Dumais. A solution to Plato's problem: The latent semantic analysis theory of acquisition, induction and representation of knowledge. *Psychol. Rev.*, 104:211–240, 1997.

Lesk, M.E. Word-word associations in document retrieval systems. *Am. Doc.*, 20(1):27–38, 1969.

Li, M. and P.M.B. Vitányi. *An Introduction to Kolmogorov Complexity and Its Applications*, 3rd edn. Springer-Verlag, New York, 2008.

Li, M., J. Badger, X. Chen, S. Kwong, P. Kearney, and H. Zhang. An information-based sequence distance and its application to whole mitochondrial genome phylogeny. *Bioinformatics*, 17(2):149–154, 2001.

Li, M., X. Chen, X. Li, B. Ma, and P.M.B. Vitányi. The similarity metric. *IEEE Trans. Inform. Theory*, 50(12):3250–3264, 2004.

Miller, G.A. et al. A lexical database for the English language. http://www.cogsci.princeton.edu/wn.

Moralyiski, R. and G. Dias. One sense per discourse for synonym detection. In *Proceedings of the International Conference on Recent Advances in Natural Language Processing*, Borovets, Bulgaria, pp. 383–387, 2007.

Muir, H. Software to unzip identity of unknown composers. *New Scientist*, April 12, 2003.

Patch, K. Software sorts tunes. *Technology Research News*, April 23/30, 2003.

Reed, S.L. and D.B. Lenat. Mapping ontologies into cyc. In *Proceedings of the AAAI Conference 2002 Workshop on Ontologies for the Semantic Web*, Edmonton, Canada, July 2002.

Santos, C.C., J. Bernardes, P.M.B. Vitányi, and L. Antunes. Clustering fetal heart rate tracings by compression. In *Proceedings of the 19th IEEE International Symposium Computer-Based Medical Systems*, Salt Lake City, UT, pp. 685–670, 2006.

Slashdot contributers. Slashdot. From January 29, 2005: http://science.slashdot.org/article.pl?sid=05/01/29/1815242&tid=217&tid=14.

Tan, P.N., V. Kumar, and J. Srivastava. Selecting the right interestingness measure for associating patterns. In *Proceedings of the ACM-SIGKDD Conference on Knowledge Discovery and Data Mining*, Edmonton, Canada, pp. 491–502, 2002.

Terra, E. and C.L.A. Clarke. Frequency estimates for statistical word similarity measures. In *Proceedings of the HLT–NAACL*, Edmonton, Canada, pp. 244–251, 2003.

Turney, P.D. Mining the web for synonyms: Pmi-ir versus lsa on toefl. In *Proceedings of the 12th European Conference on Machine Learning*, Freiburg, Germany, pp. 491–502, 2001.

Turney, P.D. Thumbs up or thumbs down? Semantic orientation applied to unsupervised classification of reviews. In *Proceedings of the 40th Annual Meeting on Association for Computational Linguistics*, Philadelphia, PA, pp. 417–424, 2002.

Turney, P.D. Similarity of semantic relations. *Comput. Linguist.*, 32(3):379–416, 2006.

Zhang, X., Y. Hao, X. Zhu, and M. Li. Information distance from a question to an answer. In *Proceedings of the 13th ACM SIGKDD International Conference on Knowledge Discovery and Data Mining*, New York, pp. 874–883. ACM Press, 2007.

14

Word Sense Disambiguation

David Yarowsky
Johns Hopkins University

14.1 Introduction

Word sense disambiguation (WSD) is essentially a classification problem. Given a word such as *sentence* and an inventory of possible semantic tags for that word, which tag is appropriate for each individual instance of that word in context? In many implementations, these labels are major sense numbers from an online dictionary, but they may also correspond to topic or subject codes, nodes in a semantic hierarchy, a set of possible foreign language translations, or even assignment to an automatically induced sense partition. The nature of this given sense inventory substantially determines the nature and complexity of the sense disambiguation task.

Table 14.1 illustrates the task of sense disambiguation for three separate sense inventories: (a) the dictionary sense number in *Collins* COBUILD *English Dictionary* (Sinclair et al., 1987), (b) a label corresponding to an appropriate translation into Spanish, and (c) a general topic, domain, or subject-class label. Typically, only one inventory of labels would be used at a time, and in the case below, each of

315

TABLE 14.1   **Sense Tags** for the Word *Sentence* from Different Sense
Inventories

COBUILD Dictionary	Spanish Translation	Subject Class	Instance of Target Word in Context
noun-2	*sentencia*	LEGAL	...maximum *sentence* for a young offender ...
noun-2	*sentencia*	LEGAL	...minimum *sentence* of seven years in jail ...
noun-2	*sentencia*	LEGAL	...under the *sentence* of death at that time..
noun-2	*sentencia*	LEGAL	...criticize a *sentence* handed down by any...
noun-1	*frase*	LING	in the next *sentence* they say their electors
noun-1	*frase*	LING	...the second *sentence* because it is just as ...
noun-1	*frase*	LING	... the next *sentence* is a very important ...
noun-1	*frase*	LING	the second *sentence* which I think is at ...
noun-1	*frase*	LING	...said this *sentence* uttered by a former ...

the three inventories has roughly equivalent discriminating power. Sense disambiguation constitutes the assignment of the most appropriate tag from one of these inventories corresponding to the semantic meaning of the word in context. Section 14.2 discusses the implications of the sense inventory choice on this task.

The words in context surrounding each instance of *sentence* in Table 14.1 constitute the primary evidence sources with which each classification can be made. Words immediately adjacent to the target word typically exhibit the most predictive power. Other words in the same sentence, paragraph, and even entire document typically contribute weaker evidence, with predictive power decreasing roughly proportional to the distance from the target word. The nature of the syntactic relationship between potential evidence sources is also important.

Section 14.5 discusses the extraction of these contextual evidence sources and their use in supervised learning algorithms for word sense classification. Sections 14.6 and 14.7 discuss lightly supervised and unsupervised methods for sense classification and discovery when costly hand-tagged training data is unavailable or is not available in sufficient quantities for supervised learning. As a motivating precursor to these algorithm-focused sections, Section 14.3 provides a survey of applications for WSD and Section 14.8 concludes with a discussion of current research priorities in sense disambiguation.

14.2 Word Sense Inventories and Problem Characteristics

Philosophers and lexicographers have long struggled with the nature of word sense and the numerous bases over which they can be defined and delimited. Indeed Kilgarriff (1997) has argued that word "senses" do not exist independent of the meaning distinctions required of a specific task or target use. All sense "disambiguation" is relative to a particular sense inventory, and inventories can differ based on criteria including their source, granularity, hierarchical structure, and treatment of part-of-speech (POS) differences.

14.2.1 Treatment of Part of Speech

Although sense ambiguity spans POS (e.g., a sense inventory for *bank* may contain: 1, river *bank* [noun]; 2, financial *bank* [noun]; and 3, to *bank* an airplane [verb]), the large majority of sense disambiguation systems treat the resolution of POS distinctions as an initial and entirely separate tagging or parsing process (see Chapters 4, 10, and 11). The motivation for this approach is that POS ambiguity is best resolved by a class of algorithms driven by local syntactic sequence optimization having a very different character from the primarily semantic word associations that resolve within-POS ambiguities.

The remainder of this chapter follows this convention, assuming that a POS tagger including lemmatization has been run over the text first and focusing on remaining sense ambiguities within the same POS.

In many cases, the POS tags for surrounding words will also be used as additional evidence sources for the within-POS sense classifications.

14.2.2 Sources of Sense Inventories

The nature of the sense disambiguation task depends largely on the source of the sense inventory and its characteristics.

- **Dictionary-based inventories:** Much of the earliest work in sense disambiguation (e.g., Lesk, 1986; Walker and Amsler, 1986) involved the labeling of words in context with sense numbers extracted from machine-readable dictionaries. Use of such a reference standard provides the automatic benefit of the "free" classification information and example sentences in the numbered definitions, making it possible to do away with hand-tagged training data altogether. Dictionary-based sense inventories tend to encourage hierarchical classification methods and support relatively fine levels of sense granularity.

- **Concept hierarchies (e.g., WordNet):** One of the most popular standard sense inventories in recent corpus-based work, especially on verbs, is the WordNet semantic concept hierarchy (Miller, 1990). Each "sense number" corresponds to a node in this hierarchy, with the BIRD sense of *crane* embedded in a concept-path from HERON-LIKE-BIRDS through BIRD to the concept LIVING-THING and PHYSICAL-ENTITY. This inventory supports extensive use of class-based inheritance and selectional restriction (e.g., Resnik, 1993). Despite concerns regarding excessively fine-grained and occasionally redundant sense distinctions, WordNet-based sense inventories have formed the basis of most recent WSD evaluation frameworks (see Section 14.5.1), and are utilized in state-of-the-art open-source disambiguation libraries (Pedersen, 2009).

- **Domain tags/subject codes (e.g., LDOCE):** The online version of the *Longman Dictionary of Contemporary English* (Procter et al., 1978) assigns general domain or subject codes (such as *EC* for economic/financial usages, and *EG* for engineering usages) to many, but not all, word senses. In the cases where sense differences correspond to domain differences, LDOCE subject codes can serve as sense labels (e.g., Guthrie et al., 1991; Cowie et al., 1992), although coverage is limited for non-domain-specific senses. Subject codes from hierarchically organized thesauri such as *Roget's 4th International* (Chapman, 1977) can also serve as sense labels (as in Yarowsky (1992)), as can subject field codes linked to WordNet (Magnini and Cavaglia, 2000).

- **Multilingual translation distinctions:** Sense distinctions often correspond to translation differences in a foreign language, and as shown in the example of *sentence* in Table 14.1, these translations (such as the Spanish *frase* and *sentencia*) can be used as effective sense tags. Parallel polysemy across related languages may reduce the discriminating power of such sense labels (as discussed in Section 14.3.2), but this problem is reduced by using translation labels from a more distantly related language family. The advantages of such a sense inventory are that (a) it supports relatively direct application to machine translation (MT), and (b) sense-tagged training data can be automatically extracted for such a sense inventory from parallel bilingual corpora (as in Gale et al. (1992a)). WSD systems trained on parallel corpora have achieved top performance in Senseval all-words tasks (Ng et al., 2003).

- **Ad hoc and specialized inventories:** In many experimental studies with a small example set of polysemous words, the sense inventories are often defined by hand to reflect the sense ambiguity present in the data. In other cases, the sense inventory may be chosen to support a particular application (such as a specialized meaning resolution in information extraction systems).

- **Artificial sense ambiguities ("Pseudo-words"):** *Pseudo-words*, proposed by Gale et al. (1992d), are artificial ambiguities created by replacing all occurrences of two monosemous words in a corpus (such as *guerilla* and *reptile*) with one joint word (e.g., *guerilla-reptile*). The task of deciding which original word was intended for each occurrence of the joint word is largely equivalent to determining which "sense" was intended for each occurrence of a polysemous word. The problem is not entirely unnatural, as there could well exist a language where the concepts *guerilla* and *reptile* are indeed represented by the same word due to some historical-linguistic phenomenon. Selecting between these two meanings would naturally constitute WSD in that language. This approach offers the important benefit that potentially unlimited training and test data are available and that sense ambiguities of varying degrees of subtlety can be created on demand by using word pairs of the desired degree of semantic similarity, topic distribution, and frequency.

- **Automatically induced sense inventories:** Finally, as discussed in Section 14.7, work in unsupervised sense disambiguation has utilized automatically induced semantic clusters as effective sense labels (e.g., Schütze, 1992, 1998; Pantel and Lin, 2002). Although these clusters may be aligned with more traditional inventories such as dictionary sense numbers, they can also function without such a mapping, especially if they are used for secondary applications like information retrieval where the effective sense partition (rather than the choice of label) is most important.

14.2.3 Granularity of Sense Partitions

Sense disambiguation can be performed at various levels of subtlety. Major meaning differences called *homographs* often correspond to different historical derivations converging on the same orthographic representation. For example, the homographs (in Roman numerals) for the English word *bank*, as shown in Table 14.2, entered English through the French *banque*, Anglo-Saxon *benc* and French *banc*, respectively. More subtle distinctions such as between the (I.1) financial bank and (I.2) general repository sense of bank typically evolved through later usage, and often correspond to quite clearly distinct meanings that are likely translated into different words in a foreign language. Still more subtle distinctions, such as between the (1.1a) general institution and (1.1b) physical building senses of financial bank, are often difficult for human judges to resolve through context (e.g., *He owns the bank on the corner*), and often exhibit parallel polysemy in other languages.

The necessary level of granularity clearly depends on the application. Frequently, the target granularity comes directly from the sense inventory (e.g., whatever level of distinction is represented in the system's online dictionary). In other cases, the chosen level of granularity derives from the needs of the target application: those meaning distinctions that correspond to translation differences are appropriate for MT, while only homograph distinctions that result in pronunciation differences (e.g., /baes/ vs. /beIs/ for the word *bass*) may be of relevance to a text-to-speech synthesis application.

Such granularity issues often arise in the problem of evaluating sense disambiguation systems, and how much penalty to assign to errors of varying subtlety. One reasonable approach is to generate a penalty matrix for misclassification sensitive to the functional semantic distance between any two sense/subsenses of a word. Such a matrix can be derived automatically from hierarchical distance in a sense tree, as shown in Table 14.2.

TABLE 14.2 Example of Pairwise Semantic Distance between the Word Senses of *Bank*, Derived from a Sample Hierarchical Sense Inventory

I *Bank*—REPOSITORY						
I.1 Financial Bank		I.1a	I.1b	I.2	II.1	II.2	III
I.1a—an institution							
I.1b—a building	I.1a	0	1	2	4	4	4
I.2 General Supply/Reserve	I.1b	1	0	2	4	4	4
	I.2	2	2	0	4	4	4
II *Bank*—GEOGRAPHICAL	II.1	4	4	4	0	1	4
II.1 Shoreline	II.2	4	4	4	1	0	4
II.2 Ridge/Embankment	III	4	4	4	4	4	0
III *Bank*—ARRAY/GROUP/ROW							

Such a penalty matrix can also be based on confusability or functional distance within an application (e.g., in a speech-synthesis application, only those sense-distinction errors corresponding to pronunciation differences would be penalized). Such distances can also be based on psycholinguistic data, such as experimentally derived estimates of similarity or confusability (Miller and Charles, 1991; Resnik, 1995).

In this framework, rather than computing system accuracy with a Boolean match/no-match weighting of classification errors between subsenses (however subtle the difference), a more sensitive weighted accuracy measure capturing the relative seriousness of misclassification errors can be defined as follows:

$$WeightedAccuracy = \frac{1}{N} \sum_{i=1}^{N} \text{distance}(cs_i, as_i)$$

where distance(cs_i, as_i) is the normalized pairwise penalty or cost of misclassification between an assigned sense (as_i) and correct sense (cs_i) over all N test examples (Resnik and Yarowsky, 1999).

If the sense disambiguation system assigns a probability distribution to the different sense/subsense options, rather than a hard boolean assignment, the weighted accuracy can be defined as follows:

$$WeightedAccuracy = \frac{1}{N} \sum_{i=1}^{N} \sum_{j=1}^{S_i} \text{distance}(cs_i, s_j) \times P_A(s_j | w_i, \text{context}_i)$$

where for any test example i of word w_i having senses s_i, the probability mass assigned by the classifier to incorrect senses is weighted by the communicative distance or cost of that misclassification. Similar cross-entropy-based measures can be used as well.

14.2.4 Hierarchical vs. Flat Sense Partitions

Another issue in sense disambiguation is that many sense inventories only represent a flat partition of senses, with no representation of relative semantic similarity through hierarchical structure. Furthermore, flat partitions offer no natural label for underspecification or generalization for use when full subsense resolution cannot be made. When available, such hierarchical sense/subsense inventories can support top-down hierarchical sense classifiers such as in Section 14.7, and can contribute to the evaluation of partial correctness in evaluation.

14.2.5 Idioms and Specialized Collocational Meanings

A special case of fine granularity sense inventories is the need to handle idiomatic usages or cases where a specialized sense of a word derives almost exclusively from a single collocation. *Think tank* and *tank top* (an article of clothing) are examples. Although these can in most cases be traced historically to one of the major senses (e.g., CONTAINER *tank* in the two foregoing examples), these are often inadequate labels and the inclusion of these idiomatic examples in training data for the major sense can impede machine learning. Thus, the inclusion of such specialized, collocation-specific senses in the inventory is often well justified.

14.2.6 Regular Polysemy

The term *regular polysemy* refers to standard, relatively subtle variations of usage or aspect that apply systematically to classes of words, such as physical objects. For example, the word *room* can refer to a physical entity (e.g., "The room was painted red.") or the space it encloses (e.g., "A strong odor filled the room."). The nouns *cup* and *box* exhibit similar ambiguities. This class of ambiguity is often treated as part of a larger theory of compositional semantics (as in Pustejovsky (1995)).

14.2.7 Related Problems

Several additional classes of meaning distinctions may potentially be considered as word sense ambiguities. These include *named entity disambiguation* (such as deciding whether *Madison* is a U.S. president, city in Wisconsin, or a corporation) and the expansion of ambiguous abbreviations and acronyms (such as deciding whether *IRA* is the Irish Republican Army or Individual Retirement Account). Although these share many properties and utilized approaches with traditional WSD, the ambiguity instances here are unbounded and dynamic in scope, and these tasks have their own distinct literature (e.g., Pakhomov, 2002).

14.3 Applications of Word Sense Disambiguation

Sense disambiguation tends not to be considered a primary application in its own right, but rather is an intermediate annotation step that is utilized in several end-user applications.

14.3.1 Applications in Information Retrieval

The application of WSD to information retrieval (IR) has had mixed success. One of the goals in IR is to map the words in a document or in a query to a set of *terms* that capture the semantic content of the text. When multiple morphological variants of a word carry similar semantic content (e.g., *computing/ computer*), stemming is used to map these words to a single term (e.g., COMPUT). However, when a single word conveys two or more possible meanings (e.g., *tank*), it may be useful to map that word into separate distinct terms (e.g., TANK-1 ["vehicle"] and TANK-2 ["container"]) based on context.

The actual effectiveness of high-accuracy WSD on bottom-line IR performance is unclear. Krovetz and Croft (1992) and Krovetz (1997) argue that WSD *does* contribute to the effective separation of relevant and nonrelevant documents, and even a small domain-specific document collection exhibits a significant degree of lexical ambiguity (over 40% of the query words in one collection).

In contrast, Sanderson (1994) and Voorhees (1993) present a more pessimistic perspective on the helpfulness of WSD to IR. Their experiments indicate that in full IR applications, WSD offers very limited additional improvement in performance, and much of this was due to resolving POS distinctions (*sink* [a verb] vs. *sink* [a bathroom object]). Although Schütze and Pedersen (1995) concur that dictionary-based sense labels have limited contribution to IR, they found that automatically induced sense clusters (see Section 14.7) are useful, as the clusters directly characterize different contextual distributions.

A reasonable explanation of the above results is that the similar disambiguating clues used for sense tagging (e.g., *Panzer* and *infantry* with *tank* selecting for the military vehicle sense of *tank*) are also used directly by IR algorithms (e.g., *Panzer*, *tank*, and *infantry* together indicate relevance for military queries). The additional knowledge that *tank* is sense-1 is to a large extent simply echoing the same contextual information already available to the IR system in the remainder of the sentence. Thus, sense tagging should be more productive for IR in the cases of ambiguities resolved through a single collocation rather than the full sentence context (e.g., *think tank* ≠ CONTAINER), and for added discriminating power in short queries (e.g., *tank-1 procurement policy* vs. just *tank procurement policy*).

14.3.2 Applications in Machine Translation

It should be clear from Section 14.1 that lexical translation choice in MT is similar to word sense tagging. There are substantial divergences, however.

In some cases (such as when all four major senses of the English word *interest* translate into French as *intérêt*), the target language exhibits parallel ambiguities with the source and full-sense resolution is not necessary for appropriate translation choice. In other cases, a given sense of a word in English may correspond to multiple similar words in the target language that mean essentially the same thing, but have different preferred or licensed collocational contexts in the target language. For example, *sentencia* and *condena* are both viable Spanish translations for the LEGAL (noun) sense of the English word *sentence*. However, *condena* rather than *sentencia* would be preferred when associated with a duration (e.g., *life sentence*). Selection between such variants is largely an optimization problem in the target language.

Nevertheless, monolingual sense disambiguation algorithms may be utilized productively in MT systems once the mapping between source-language word senses and corresponding target-language translations has been established. This is clearly the case in interlingual MT systems, where source-language sense disambiguation algorithms can help serve as the lexical semantic component in the analysis phase. Brown et al. (1991) have also utilized monolingual sense disambiguation in their statistical transfer-based MT approach, estimating a probability distribution across corresponding translation variants and using monolingual language models to select the optimal target word sequence given these weighted options.

Carpuat and Wu (2005) have raised doubts about the efficacy of WSD for MT using monolingual lexicographically based sense inventories, but have shown (in Carpuat and Wu (2007)) that WSD using a sense inventory based on actual translation ambiguities can improve end-to-end Chinese–English MT. Others (including Chan et al. (2007a)) have further shown the contribution of some form of sense disambiguation to MT.

14.3.3 Other Applications

Sense disambiguation procedures may also have commercial applications as intelligent dictionaries, thesauri, and grammar checkers. Students looking for definitions of or synonyms for unfamiliar words are often confused by or misuse the definitions/synonyms for contextually inappropriate senses. Once the correct sense has been identified for the currently highlighted word in context, an intelligent dictionary/thesaurus would list only the definition(s) and synonym(s) appropriate for the actual document context.

Some search engines have improved their user experience by clustering their output based on the senses of the word(s) in the query. For example, a search-engine query of *java* benefits from having results about the programming language segregated from those referring to the coffee and Indonesian island senses.

A somewhat indirect application is that the algorithms developed for classical sense disambiguation may also be productively applied to related lexical ambiguity resolution problems exhibiting similar problem characteristics. One such closely related application is accent and diacritic restoration (such as *cote*→ *côte* in French), studied using a supervised sense-tagging algorithm in Yarowsky (1994).

14.4 Early Approaches to Sense Disambiguation

WSD is one of the oldest problems in natural language processing (NLP). It was recognized as a distinct task as early as 1955, in the work of Yngve (1955) and later Bar-Hillel (1960). The target application for this work was MT, which was of strong interest at the time.

14.4.1 Bar-Hillel: An Early Perspective on WSD

To appreciate some of the complexity and potential of the sense disambiguation task, it is instructive to consider Bar-Hillel's early assessment of the problem. Bar-Hillel felt that sense disambiguation was a key bottleneck for progress in MT, one that ultimately led him and others to conclude that the problem of general MT was intractable given current, and even foreseeable, computational resources. He used the now famous example of the polysemous word *pen* as motivation for this conclusion:

Little John was looking for his toy box. Finally he found it.
The box was in the **pen**. John was very happy.

In his analysis of the feasibility of MT, Bar-Hillel (1960) argued that even this relatively simple sense ambiguity could not be resolved by electronic computer, either current or imaginable:

> Assume, for simplicity's sake, that *pen* in English has only the following two meanings: (1) a certain writing utensil, (2) an enclosure where small children can play. I now claim that no existing or imaginable program will enable an electronic computer to determine that the word *pen* in the given sentence within the given context has the second of the above meanings, whereas every reader with a sufficient knowledge of English will do this "automatically." (Bar-Hillel, 1960)

Such sentiments helped cause Bar-Hillel to abandon the NLP field. Although one can appreciate Bar-Hillel's arguments given their historical context, the following counter-observations are warranted.

Bar-Hillel's example was chosen to illustrate where selectional restrictions fail to disambiguate: both an enclosure *pen* and a writing *pen* have internal space and hence admit the use of the preposition *in*. Apparently more complex analysis regarding the relative size of toy boxes and writing pens is necessary to rule out the second interpretation.

What Bar-Hillel did not seem to appreciate at the time was the power of associational proclivities rather than hard selectional constraints. One almost never refers to what is *in* a writing pen (except in the case of *ink*, which is a nearly unambiguous indicator of writing pens by itself), while it is very common to refer to what is *in* an enclosure pen. Although the trigram *in the pen* does not *categorically* rule out either interpretation, *probabilistically* it is very strongly the indicative of the enclosure sense and would be very effective in disambiguating this example even without additional supporting evidence.

Thus, while this example does illustrate the limitations of selectional constraints and the infeasible complexity of full pragmatic inference, it actually represents a reasonably good example of where simple collocational patterns in a probabilistic framework may be successful.

14.4.2 Early AI Systems: Word Experts

After a lull in NLP research following the 1966 ALPAC report, semantic analysis closely paralleled the development of artificial intelligence (AI) techniques and tended to be embedded in larger systems such as Winograd's Blocks World (1972) and LUNAR (Woods et al., 1972). Word sense ambiguity was not generally considered as a separate problem, and indeed did not arise very frequently given the general monosemy of words in restricted domains.

Wilks (1975) was one of the first to focus extensively on the discrete problem of sense disambiguation. His model of preference semantics was based primarily on selectional restrictions in a Schankian framework, and was targeted at the task of MT. Wilks developed frame-based semantic templates of the form

```
policeman    → ((folk sour)((((notgood man)obje)pick)(subj man)))
interrogates → ((man subj)((man obje)(tell force)))
crook        → (((((notgood act) obje)do)(subj man))
crook        → ((((((this beast)obje)force)(subj man))poss)(line
             thing))
```

which were used to analyze sentences such as "The policeman interrogates the crook" by finding the maximally consistent combination of templates.

Small and Rieger (1982) proposed a radically lexicalized form of language processing using the complex interaction of "word experts" for parsing and semantic analysis. These experts included both selectional constraints and hand-tailored procedural rules, and were focused on multiply ambiguous sentences such as "The man eating peaches throws out a pit."

Hirst (1987) followed a more general word-expert-based approach, with rules based primarily on selectional constraints with backoff to more general templates for increased coverage. Hirst's approach also focused on the dynamic interaction of these experts in a marker-passing mechanism called "polaroid words."

Cottrell (1989) addressed similar concerns regarding multiply conflicting ambiguities (e.g., "Bob threw a ball for charity") in a connectionist framework, addressing the psycholinguistic correlates of his system's convergence behavior.

14.4.3 Dictionary-Based Methods

To overcome the daunting task of generating hand-built rules for the entire lexicon, many researchers have turned to information extracted from existing dictionaries. This work became practical in the late 1980s with the availability of several large scale dictionaries in machine-readable format.

Lesk (1986) was one of the first to implement such an approach, using overlap between definitions in *Oxford's Advanced Learner's Dictionary of Current English* to resolve word senses. The word *cone* in *pine cone* was identified as a "fruit of certain evergreen trees" (sense 3), by overlap of both the words "evergreen" and "tree" in one of the definitions of *pine*. Such models of strict overlap clearly suffer from sparse data problems, as dictionary definitions tend to be brief; without augmentation or class-based generalizations, they do not capture nearly the range of collocational information necessary for broad coverage.

Another fertile line of dictionary-based work used the semantic subject codes such as in the online version of Longman's LDOCE (see Section 14.2). These codes, such as *EC* for economic/financial usages and *AU* for automotive usages, label specialized, domain-specific senses of words. Walker and Amsler (1986) estimated the most appropriate subject code for words like *bank* having multiple specialized domains, by summing up dominant presence of subject codes for other words in context. Guthrie et al. (1991) enriched this model by searching for the globally optimum classifications in the cases of multiple-ambiguities, using simulated annealing to facilitate search. Veronis and Ide (1990) pursued a connectionist approach using co-occurrences of specialized subject codes from *Collins English Dictionary*.

14.4.4 Kelly and Stone: An Early Corpus-Based Approach

Interestingly, perhaps the earliest corpus-based approach to WSD emerged in the 1975 work of Kelly and Stone, nearly 15 years before data-driven methods for WSD became popular in the 1990s. For each member of a target vocabulary of 1815 words, Kelly and Stone developed a flowchart of simple rules based on a potential set of patterns in the target context. These included the morphology of the polysemous word and collocations within a ± 4 word window, either for exact word matches, POS, or one of 16 hand-labeled semantic categories found in context.

Kelly and Stone's work was particularly remarkable for 1975 in that they based their disambiguation procedures on empirical evidence derived from a 500,000 word text corpus rather than their own intuitions. Although they did not use this corpus for automatic rule induction, their hand-built rule sets were clearly sensitive to and directly inspired by patterns observed in sorted KWIC (key word in context) concordances. As an engineering approach, this data-driven but hand-tailored method has much to recommend it even today.

14.5 Supervised Approaches to Sense Disambiguation

Corpus-based sense disambiguation algorithms can be viewed as falling on a spectrum between fully *supervised* techniques and fully *unsupervised* techniques, often for the purposes of *sense discovery*. In general, supervised WSD algorithms derive their classification rules and/or statistical models directly or predominantly from sense-labeled training examples of polysemous words in context. Often hundreds of labeled training examples per word sense are necessary for adequate classifier learning, and shortages of training data are a primary bottleneck for supervised approaches. In contrast, unsupervised WSD algorithms do not require this direct sense-tagged training data, and in their purest form induce sense partitions from strictly untagged training examples. Many such approaches do make use of a secondary knowledge source, such as the WordNet semantic concept hierarchy to help bootstrap structure from raw data. Such methods can arguably be considered unsupervised as they are based on existing independent knowledge sources with no direct supervision of the phenomenon to be learned. This distinction warrants further discussion, however, and the term *minimally supervised* shall be used here to refer to this class of algorithms.

14.5.1 Training Data for Supervised WSD Algorithms

Several collections of hand-annotated data sets have been created with polysemous words in context labeled with the appropriate sense for each instance in both system training and evaluation. Early supervised work in WSD was trained on small sense-tagged data sets, including 2094 instances of *line* in context (Leacock et al., 1993a,b) and 2269 instances of *interest* in context (Bruce and Wiebe, 1994). Gale et al. (1992a) based their work on 17,138 instances of 6 polysemous English words (*duty*, *drug*, *land*, *language*, *position*, and *sentence*), annotated by their corresponding French translation in bilingual text. The first simultaneous multi-site evaluation, SenseEval-1 (Kilgarriff and Palmer, 2000), expanded coverage to 36 trainable English polysemous words from the Oxford Hector inventory. This was expanded considerably in the Senseval-2 framework (Edmonds and Kilgarriff, 2002), with evaluation data from 9 languages, including an English lexical sample task containing 12,939 instances of 73 lemmas using the WordNet sense inventory (Section 14.2). The WordNet sense inventory has also been used to annotate over 200,000 consecutive words in the SEMCOR semantic concordance (Miller et al., 1993). Vocabulary coverage is wide and balanced, while the number of examples per polysemous word is somewhat limited. The DSO corpus (Ng and Lee, 1996) has addressed this sparsity issue by annotating over 1,000 examples each for 191 relatively frequent and polysemous English words (121 nouns and 70 verbs), with a total of 193,000 annotated word instances in the *Brown Corpus* and *Wall Street Journal*. Senseval-3 (Mihalcea et al., 2004) expanded coverage to 14 tasks and 12,000 annotated examples from the Open Mind Word Expert corpus (Chklovski and Mihalcea, 2002), utilizing nonexpert volunteer annotators across the Web at significant cost to inter-annotator agreement rates (67% vs. 85.5% in Senseval-2). The follow-on community-wide evaluation framework (SemEval, 2007) has further expanded to specialized tasks and associated data sets focusing on such specialized topics as WSD of prepositions, Web people disambiguation, new languages, and target tasks, and using bilingual parallel text for annotating evaluation data. The OntoNotes project (Hovy et al., 2006), utilizing a coarser variant of the WordNet inventory for higher inter-annotator agreement rates, has released over 1 million words of continuously sense-annotated newswire, broadcast news, broadcast conversation, and Web data in English, Chinese, and Arabic, some of which are parallel bilingual sources to facilitate MT research, with observed empirical contributions to WSD (Zhong et al., 2008). The OntoNotes corpus also has the advantage of being annotated with a full-parse and propositional (PropBank) structure, so many sense distinctions based on argument structure can be derived in part from these additional syntactic annotations.

It is useful to visualize sense-tagged data as a table of tagged words in context (typically the surrounding sentence or ±50 words), from which specialized classification features can be extracted. For example, the polysemous word *plant*, exhibiting a manufacturing plant and living plant sense, has contexts illustrated in Table 14.3.

TABLE 14.3   Example of the Sense-Tagged Word *Plant* in Context

Sense Tag	Instance of Polysemous Word in Context
MANUFACT	...from the Toshiba *plant* located in...
MANUFACT	...union threatened *plant* closures...
MANUFACT	...chloride monomer *plant*, which is...
LIVING	...with animal and *plant* tissues can be...
LIVING	...Golgi apparatus of *plant* and animal cell..
LIVING	...the molecules in *plant* tissue from the...

14.5.2 Features for WSD Algorithms

Relevant features typically exploited by supervised WSD algorithms include, but are not limited to, the surrounding raw words, lemmas (word roots), and POS tags, often itemized by relative position and/or syntactic relationship, but in some models represented as a position-independent bag of words. An example of such feature extraction from the foregoing data is shown in Table 14.4.

Once these different features are extracted from the data, it is possible to compute the frequency distribution of the sense tags for each feature pattern. Table 14.5 illustrates this for several different feature types, with $f(M)$ indicating the frequency of the feature pattern as the manufacturing sense of *plant*, and $f(L)$ gives the frequency of the living sense of *plant* for this feature pattern. These raw statistics will drive almost all of the classification algorithms discussed below.

Note that word order and syntactic relationship can be of crucial importance for the predictive power of word associations. The word *open* occurs within $\pm k$ words of *plant* with almost equal likelihood of both senses, but when *plant* is the direct object of *open* it exclusively means the manufacturing sense. The word *pesticide* immediately to the left of *plant* indicates the manufacturing sense, but in any other position the distribution in the data is 6 to 0 in favor of the living sense. This would suggest that there are strong advantages for algorithms that model collocations and syntactic relationships carefully, rather than treating contexts strictly as unordered bags of words.

Several studies have been conducted assessing the relative contributions of diverse features for WSD. Gale et al. (1992c) and Yarowsky (1993) have empirically observed, for example, that wide-context, unordered bag-of-word or topic-indicating features contribute most to noun disambiguation, especially for coarser senses, while verb and adjective disambiguation rely more heavily on local syntactic and collocational features and selectional preference features. Optimal context window sizes are also quite sensitive to target-word POS, with words in context up to 10,000 words away still able to provide marginally useful information to the sense classification of polysemous nouns. Polysemous verbs depend much more exclusively on features in their current sentence. Stevenson and Wilks (2001), Lee and Ng (2002), and Agirre and Stevenson (2007) provide a very detailed cross-study analysis of the relative contribution of diverse knowledge sources, ranging from subcategorization and argument structure to LDOCE topical

TABLE 14.4   Example of Basic Feature Extraction for the Example Instances of *Plant* in Table 14.3

	Relative Position-2			Relative Position-1			0	+1
SenseTag	Class	Word	POS	Class	Lemma	POS	Word	Word
MANUFCT		the	DET	CORP	Toshiba	NP	plant	located
MANUFCT	BUSN	union	NN		threaten	VBD	plant	closures
MANUFCT	CHEM	chloride	NN	CHEM	monomer	NN	plant	,
LIVING	ZOOL	animal	NN		and	CON	plant	tissues
LIVING		apparatus	NN		of	PREP	plant	and
LIVING	CHEM	molecules	NNS		in	PREP	plant	tissue

TABLE 14.5 Frequency Distribution of Various Features Used to Distinguish the Two Senses of *Plant*

Feature Type	Feature Pattern	$f(M)$	$f(L)$	Majority Sense
WORD +1	plant *growth*	0	244	LIVING
WORD +1	plant *height*	0	183	LIVING
LEMMA +1	plant *size/N*	7	32	LIVING
LEMMA +1	plant *closure/N*	27	0	MANUFACT
WORD −1	*assembly* plant	161	0	MANUFACT
WORD −1	*nuclear* plant	144	0	MANUFACT
WORD −1	*pesticide* plant	9	0	MANUFACT
WORD −1	*tropical* plant	0	6	LIVING
POS +1	plant <NOUN>	561	2491	LIVING
POS −1	<NOUN> plant	896	419	MANUFACT
WORD $\pm k$	*car* within $\pm k$ words	86	0	MANUFACT
WORD $\pm k$	*union* within $\pm k$ words	87	0	MANUFACT
WORD $\pm k$	*job* within $\pm k$ words	47	0	MANUFACT
WORD $\pm k$	*pesticide* $\pm k$ words	9	6	MANUFACT
WORD $\pm k$	*open* within $\pm k$ words	20	21	LIVING
WORD $\pm k$	*flower* within $\pm k$ words	0	42	LIVING
Verb/Obj	*close/V*, Obj=plant	45	0	MANUFACT
Verb/Obj	*open/V*, Obj=plant	10	0	MANUFACT
Verb/Obj	*water/V*, Obj=plant	0	7	LIVING

domain codes. The former performs best in isolation on verbs while the latter on nouns, and all tested features yield marginally productive improvements on all POS. WSD is also sensitive to the morphology of the target polysemous word, with sense distributions for a word such as *interest* differing substantially between the word's singular and plural form. Ng and Lee (1996), Stevenson (2003), Wu and Palmer (1994), McCarthy et al. (2002), Chen and Palmer (2005), and others have further demonstrated the effectiveness of combining rich knowledge sources, especially including verb frame and selectional preference features.

14.5.3 Supervised WSD Algorithms

Once WSD has been reduced to a classification task based on a rich set of discrete features per word instance, as described in Section 14.5.1, essentially all generic machine learning classification algorithms are applicable. Most supervised WSD research has been either an application of existing machine learning algorithms to WSD, or in rare cases broadly applicable algorithmic innovations/refinements which happened to use WSD as their first target case. Progress (and relative comparative performance gains) in supervised WSD tends to mirror those in machine learning in general. Early supervised work focused on decision trees (Brown et al., 1991), naive Bayes models (Gale et al., 1992a), cosine-similarity-based vector models (Leacock et al., 1993a,b), and decision lists (Yarowsky, 1994), with Bruce and Wiebe (1994) and Pedersen and Bruce (1997) employing early graphical models. Ng and Lee (1996) achieved empirical success with k-nearest-neighbor algorithms. More recently, approaches using AdaBoost (Escudero et al., 2000) and support vector machines (SVMs) (Lee and Ng, 2002) have achieved top performance in recent comparative evaluations. Although the utilized feature spaces have varied considerably, for the most part, these are generic machine learning implementations and thus the reader is referred to the overview of machine learning methods by Zhang in Chapter 10 for descriptions of these general algorithms and background references.

Several comparative studies of relative machine learning algorithm performance on WSD have been insightful, including Leacock et al. (1993a,b) and Mooney (1996). Most comprehensively, Márquez et al.

(2007) have performed a rigorous comparative evaluation of supervised algorithms on the DSO corpus. They observed that generic decision lists were similar in overall performance to naive Bayes, although with quite different per-instance behavior, suggesting the merit of including both in classifier combination. A k-NN algorithm outperformed both, with SVMs and AdaBoost yielding similar overall performance on top. SVMs perform best with relatively few (<60) training exemplars per sense while AdaBoost performs best on training data with more than 60 exemplars per sense. All algorithms tended to perform poorly when ported between distinct corpora. Yarowsky and Florian (2002) studied relative system performance across a diverse space of training and data conditions on four languages using Senseval-2 data. With respect to use of features, they observed that aggregative algorithms (such as naive Bayes) tend to perform well using large sets of wide context or bag-of-words features, while discriminative algorithms (e.g., decision trees and decision lists) tend to perform well using smaller sets of highly descriminative features, such as local collocations or syntactic constraints. They also observed that discriminative models perform well when the majority-sense prior probability is high, when sense entropy is high, and in cases of increased training-test data divergence. Agglomerative models tend to do better in the space of sparser training data, increased number of senses, and increased noise in training data. As had been observed previously by Martínez et al. (2002), decision lists perform particularly well relative to other algorithms on the high-precision subset of data on which they are most confident. Finally, it was observed that performance variation due to the training set sizes and the inclusion and exclusion of a rich diversity of feature types tends to exceed that due to algorithm variation, suggesting that the field may be better served by research into improved feature spaces and the more efficient acquisition of training data rather than in efforts to fine tune the underlying classification algorithms.

Given the substantial observed variation in algorithm behavior and accuracy on different individual words, ambiguity types, and data conditions, it is not surprising that classifier combination (such as weighted voting or score and rank combinations) over the output of numerous diverse algorithms has been shown to be an empirical win (e.g., Brody et al., 2006). The top-performing systems on the Senseval-2 and Senseval-3 lexical sample tasks (Yarowsky et al. (2001) and Agirre et al. (2005), respectively) both have employed extensive classifier combination.

14.6 Lightly Supervised Approaches to WSD

Although there have been recent improvements in the availability of sense-tagged training data, insufficient quantities exist for many words and finer grained sense distinctions. Little or no anno-tated sense-tagged training data exists for most languages on the planet. Fortunately, a wide range of techniques in "lightly," "weakly," or "minimally" supervised learning have been developed, offering the potential to overcome the knowledge acquisition bottleneck slowing progress in this field.

14.6.1 WSD via Word-Class Disambiguation

One way to limit the amount of necessary training data is to recast WSD as word-*class* disambiguation, significantly reducing model dimensionality. Consider the disambiguation of the word *crane*, which can be a BIRD or MACHINE. If we are able to build a detector for these word classes in context, as in Table 14.6, then it is sufficient to ask which of the possible valid word classes of *crane* is most likely in a given context, or more generally:

$$P(\text{Sense}_i|\text{Context}) = \sum_{j=1}^{N} P(\text{Sense}_i|\text{Class}_j) \times P(\text{Class}_j|\text{Context})$$

TABLE 14.6 Example of Class-Based Context Detectors for *bird* and *machine*

the engine of the **crane** *was damaged*	*flocks of* **cranes** *nested in the swamp*
P(MACHINE|*context*) = .650	P(MACHINE|*context*) = .002
P(BIRD|*context*) = .007	P(BIRD|*context*) = .370
P(MINERAL|*context*) = .005	P(MINERAL|*context*) = .004
Best sense/class label: MACHINE	Best sense/class label: BIRD

It is not even necessary to have manually annotated training data of these word classes in context, only a list of potential class members. Because the majority of words on a classlist tend to be monosemous, it is sufficient to assume that all listed instances of the class belong to the class, even for the case of secondary senses of polysemous words. For example, given a list of BIRDs including heron, grebe, pelican, hawk, seagull, etc. and MACHINEs including jackhammer, drill, tractor, bulldozer, etc., it is possible to build a Bayesian classifier (or other wide-context, redundant-feature classifier) by training on *all* instances of these classes in an unannotated corpus, without removing or annotating the polysemous words such as *hawk* or *eagle*. Although non-bird examples such as congressional *hawks* and golfing *eagles* are part of the training data for the aggregate context models and thus are introduced into the aggregate context models, this noise is tolerable because (a) their numbers are modest, (b) secondary senses tend to be distributed uniformly across many different topic areas, while (c) the common contextual properties of the class (e.g., eggs/nests/feeding/migration, etc.) are focused and exhibit adequate signal-to-noise ratio.

Because word class labels can serve as word sense labels, and because word class detectors can be trained effectively on somewhat noisy polysemous data, as long as a class inventory is available where class members are primarily monosemous and share common properties, accurate sense disambiguation can be achieved without sense-tagged training data. This algorithm, developed in Yarowsky (1992), achieved 92% mean accuracy on a test set of 12 polysemous words using Roget's thesaurus as the primary sense inventory and topic-sensitive Bayesian classifiers as the primary class detection algorithm.

14.6.2 WSD via Monosemous Relatives

A variant of the preceding Yarowsky (1992) algorithm uses only the single closest monosemous member of a word's class (ideally a near synonym) as training proxy for a polysemous word. For example, the words *heron* and *derrick* alone may serve as close monosemous stand-ins for the BIRD and MACHINE senses of *crane*, respectively. A classifier trained on the instances of *heron* and *derrick* in an unannotated corpus will likely capture many of the contextual indicators for the two senses of *crane*, as in the class-based algorithm, but with the advantage that they are a more finely tailored match for the senses of *crane* than the generic centroid of all BIRDs and MACHINEs, at the cost of substantially shrinking the available training set size and requiring one disambiguation model for every sense of every word rather than one model for every O(1000) word classes. This monosemous relative model was developed by Mihalcea (2002) and Agirre and Martínez (2004), and works best when reasonably close monosemous relatives or near synonyms are available. It also requires that the closest relatives be somehow identifiable, either via the sense inventory structure or via empirically observed context similarity. Further refinements, such as proposed by Martínez et al. (2008), use larger nearby sets of potentially polysemous relatives, with their model contribution weighted by their distance from the target senses and perhaps iteratively filtered of their false secondary senses.

14.6.3 Hierarchical Class Models Using Selectional Restriction

Similar class-based models can be applied to the problem of resolving noun and verb senses through selectional restriction and selectional preference. Resnik (1993, 1997) has defined selectional preference as an probabilistic distribution over a concept hierarchy, such as WordNet. Consider the parent (hypernym) classes for the following words in WordNet:

gin	$\rightarrow$	<BEVERAGE, DEVICE, GAME>
vodka	$\rightarrow$	<BEVERAGE>
coffee	$\rightarrow$	<BEVERAGE, TREE, SEED, COLOR>
pint	$\rightarrow$	<VOLUME_UNIT>
cup	$\rightarrow$	<VOLUME_UNIT, VESSEL, TROPHY>

Resnik has extracted a large set of verb–object pairs from a parsed corpus (e.g., drink(vodka), drink(gin), drink(pint), play(gin), etc.). He then computed statistics on the common objects of the verb drink, the WordNet classes of these objects, their parent classes, and so forth. At any level of generality, he can express the likelihood of $P(\text{WORDNET\_CLASS}|drink)$, where $P(\text{BEVERAGE}|drink)$ is based on the frequency of members of the class BEVERAGE as objects of the word *drink*. In the case of polysemous words, such as *gin*, partial credit is uniformly assigned to each of the class options (e.g., $P(\text{BEVERAGE}|drink)$, $P(\text{DEVICE}|drink)$, and $P(\text{GAME}|drink)$). As in the case of Yarowsky's class models in Section 14.6.1, the noise introduced by this spurious polysemy will be tolerable, and $P(\text{BEVERAGE}|drink)$ and $P(\text{VOLUME\_UNIT}|drink)$ will be the two most likely object classes observed in a corpus, even under the partial weighting scheme for spurious secondary senses. Thus, like in Section 14.4.3, the class label of any individual verb–object pair (e.g., *drink(gin)*) can be resolved as the most likely of *gin*'s WordNet class to be drunk, given the probabilistic model of selectional preference. Similarly, as $P(\text{VOLUME\_UNIT}|drink)$ is higher than $P(\text{TROPHY}|drink)$, the correct sense of *drink(cup)* is also selected.

Similarly, verb senses in Resnik's framework can be defined as the most likely WordNet class of the verb's object. Drink(cup) is also correctly assigned the sense corresponding to drink(VOLUME_UNIT) rather than drink(TROPHY). Collectively, Resnik's work clearly demonstrates the ability for raw corpus co-occurrence statistics combined with an existing hierarchical class-based lexicon to identify the underlying semantic "signal" in the noise of polysemy.

14.6.4 Graph-Based Algorithms for WSD

Graph-based algorithms utilizing techniques such as random walks over dictionary networks have sought to identify additional lexical indicators of a word's sense directly from transitive associations in the graph topology, without the need for annotated corpora (e.g., Navigli (2006); Agirre and Soroa (2008); Navigli and Lapata (2007) and Klapaftis and Manandhar (2008)) by using variants of algorithms such as PageRank (Mihalcea et al., 2004). While efficient for extracting probabilistic models from unweighted lexical graph structures, these models are to some extent constrained by the size and availability of exploitable WordNets or other lexical knowledge bases in their target language.

14.6.5 Iterative Bootstrapping Algorithms

Hearst (1991) proposed an early application of bootstrapping based on relatively small hand-tagged data sets used in supervised sense tagging. Like Schütze (1992) and Zernik (1991), Hearst used a term-vector representation of contexts and cosine similarity measure to assign new test contexts to the most similar vector centroid computed from her tagged training examples. She later augmented the existing centroids with additional untagged vectors, assigned to their closest labeled centroid, with the goal of alleviating some of the sparse data problems in the original tagged training data. Classifiers using these augmented training sets performed nearly the same as those using the purely hand-tagged data, and in some cases the presence of the additional sentences hurt performance.

Yarowsky (1995) proposed an algorithm for multi-pass iterative bootstrapping from different types of small seed data for each target word sense. These seed configurations included information as basic as just the two sense labels (e.g., MANUFACTURING and LIVING for the word *plant*), as well as other experiments using dictionary definitions and a small set of hand-labeled collocations as minimal seed data. A key component of this work was the process by which this very small seed data was reliably and robustly expanded to eventually tag all instances of the word in a corpus.

The driving engine for this procedure were two empirically studied properties: (a) polysemous words strongly tend to exhibit only one sense per collocation (Yarowsky, 1993) and (b) polysemous words strongly tend to exhibit only one sense within a given discourse (Gale et al., 1992b).

In these studies, *collocation* was defined as an arbitrary association or juxtaposition of words, with the effects measured sensitive to syntactic relationship and distance between the two words, as well as factors such as the part of speech of the words. Yarowsky (1993) observed that for collocations with a polysemous word (such as *plant*) when in adjacent collocation with another noun (e.g., *plant closure*), on average 98% of the instances of a given collocation refer to the same word sense. As collocational distance increases to 20 words (e.g., *flower* occurring within 20 words of *plant*), over 80% of the instances of a given collocation refer to the same sense. Verbs and adjectives tend to have more localized collocational predictive reliability, while noun collocations even 100 words distant still strongly tend to select the same sense.

In a separate study (Yarowsky, 1995), it was observed that for a sample set of 12 polysemous nouns and verbs, on average 50.1% of the instances of each polysemous word occurred in a discourse with another instance of the same word. Of those discourses with two or more occurrences of the polysemous word, the probability that any randomly chosen instance of the polysemous word would have the same sense as another randomly chosen instance of the same word was measured at 99.8% for the sample set of words. Clearly, the one-sense-per-discourse tendency holds with high accuracy, and can be exploited for approximately half of the instances of polysemous words in the corpus.

Together, the strong one-sense-per-discourse and one-sense-per-collocation tendencies can be jointly exploited in an iterative bootstrapping framework. This is illustrated graphically in Figure 14.1. The algorithm begins with as few as two seed collocations that are indicative of the target senses. Examples of the word *plant* that contain the seed collocations are initially labeled as A = *life* and B = *manufacturing* for

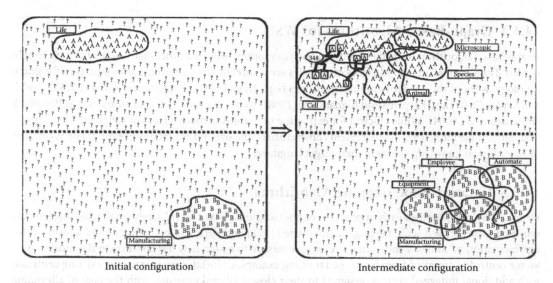

| Initial configuration | Intermediate configuration |

FIGURE 14.1   Iterative bootstrapping from two seed words for *plant*.

the two major senses of the polysemous word *plant*. The remainder of the examples of the polysemous word are initially untagged, represented graphically in Figure 14.1 as "**?**". A supervised classifier (based on decision lists in this case) is then trained on the seed sets, and applied to the residual untagged data. New collocations indicative of either sense are learned, and those classifications with confidence above a threshold are added to the next round's training set. Simulated annealing applied to this confidence threshold to help avoid overtraining. The one-sense-per-discourse tendency is also exploited as both a bridge to add new collocational examples to the training model and as effective filter or to decrement the probability of initially misclassified examples given strong evidence for the competing sense from other examples of the polysemous word in the discourse. After multiple iterations of the bootstrapping steps, the algorithm in this example converges at a partition of the example space corresponding closely to the true partition (dotted line). Mean accuracy of this algorithm starting from only two seed words was 90.6%. Starting from words in an online dictionary definition when fully using the one-sense-per-discourse model achieves 96.5%. This slightly outperforms a baseline (decision list) supervised learning algorithm *not* using discourse co-occurrence information (96.1% accuracy), indicating the power of the one-sense-per-discourse tendency to effectively guide and constrain incremental bootstrapping. Abney (2004) explores the algorithmic foundations of this algorithm in detail, while Eisner and Karakos (2005) have demonstrated substantial improvements without the need for initial seeds. Krovetz (1998) and Martínez and Agirre (2000) have provided further empirical investigations into the one-sense-per-discourse and one-sense-per-collocation properties.

14.7 Unsupervised WSD and Sense Discovery

The classic approach to "unsupervised" WSD is to automatically cluster the instances of a polysemous word in context, using some form of context or feature representation as discussed in Section 14.5.

One of the earliest such algorithms was introduced by Zernik (1991) and Schütze (1992), utilizing the framework of IR-style content vectors noted in Section 14.5.3. Just as documents can be represented as vectors $< W_1, W_2, W_3, W_4, ..., W_V >$ in V-dimensional space (where V is the vocabulary size, and W_i is a weighted function of word frequency in that document), the context surrounding a polysemous word can be similarly represented as if it were a separate document. Given a vector similarity function, context vectors may be clustered hierarchically into partitions of the vector set of high relative within-cluster similarity. The goal of unsupervised learning in this case is that the induced clusters will also correspond to word contexts exhibiting the same sense. To the extent that similar word distributions in surrounding contexts correlate with similar word sense, such a partitioning algorithm is likely to yield clusters of vectors with primarily the same sense (Figure 14.2).

Many different clustering algorithms and similarity functions may be used in this general framework. Zernik (1991) utilized bottom-up hierarchical agglomerative clustering based on cosine-similarity. Schütze (1992) utilized a top-down Bayesian algorithm Autoclass (Cheesman et al., 1988) and a partially randomized algorithm Buckshot (Cutting et al., 1992). Schütze also used singular value decomposition (Deerwester et al., 1990) to reduce the dimensionality of the vector space, using canonical discriminant analysis to optimize the weighting of dimensions in the space for maximal cluster separation. This reduced dimensionality, called word space by Schütze, helped overcome some of the sparse data problems associated with similarity measures such as cosine distance.

One significant problem with these approaches is that without at least some sense-labeled context vectors, it is difficult to map the induced clusters to a sense number in an established sense inventory that would be useful for a secondary task (such as MT). Both Zernik and Schütze used manual post-hoc alignment of clusters to word senses in their sense disambiguation experiments. Because top-level cluster partitions based purely on distributional information do not necessarily align with standard sense distinctions, Zernik and Schütze generated partitions of up to 10 separate sense clusters and manually assigned each to a fixed sense label (based on the hand-inspection of 10–20 sentences per cluster).

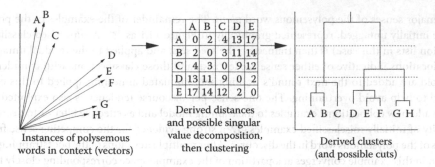

FIGURE 14.2   Illustration of vector clustering and sense partitioning.

Semi-automated post-hoc alignments are possible, if at least some information on the reference senses such as a dictionary definition is available. Without such a mapping, one cannot evaluate sense-tagging accuracy relative to an inventory, only cluster purity. Section 14.3.1 describes an application, IR, where such alignment is not necessary (only the unlabeled sense partitions are needed). It is also possible to treat this task as unsupervised *sense induction* or *sense discovery*, and use a list of distinctive words in each cluster to label the cluster. Nevertheless, for most applications, sense tagging is crucially a disambiguation task with respect to an established sense inventory tied to the application.

14.8 Conclusion

Corpus-based, statistical algorithms for sense disambiguation have demonstrated the ability to achieve respectable accuracy resolving major sense distinctions when adequate training data is available. Given the high cost and relatively limited supply of such data, current research efforts are focusing on the problems of

- Exploiting other potential sources of automatically sense-tagged training data for supervised learning, such as parallel bilingual corpora
- Improving the speed and efficiency of human annotation through active learning algorithms that dynamically guide interactive tagging sessions based on currently unsatisfied information need
- Developing algorithms that can better bootstrap from the lexical and ontological knowledge present in existing references sources such as online dictionaries, WordNet, thesauri, etc. driving minimally supervised algorithms on unannotated corpora
- Using unsupervised clustering and sense induction for applications (e.g., IR) that do not require alignment of the induced sense partitions to an existing sense inventory

Another major open challenge is the broad coverage resolution of finer-grained sense and subsense distinctions that have been underaddressed in past research. Richer feature representations that capture more refined lexical, syntactic, pragmatic, and discourse-level dependencies may be necessary, demanding improved algorithms for extracting such information from corpora and other available knowledge sources. Thus, future progress in sense disambiguation depends heavily on parallel progress in the other text-analysis tasks described in this handbook.

References

Abney, S. (2004). Understanding the Yarowsky algorithm. *Computational Linguistics*, 30(3):365–395.
Agirre, E. and P. Edmonds, eds. (2007). *Word sense disambuguation: Algorithms and applications*. Springer, New York, NY.

Agirre, E. and D. Martínez (2004). Unsupervised WSD based on automatically retrieved examples: The importance of bias. In *Proceedings of EMNLP 2004*, pp. 25–32, Barcelona, Spain.

Agirre, E. and G. Rigau (1996). Word sense disambiguation using conceptual density. In *Proceedings of COLING 1996*, pp. 16–22, Copenhagen, Denmark.

Agirre, E. and A. Soroa (2008). Using the multilingual central repository for graph-based word sense disambiguation. In *Proceedings of LREC*, pp. 1388–1392, Marrakesh, Morocco.

Agirre, E. and M. Stevenson (2007). Knowledge sources for word sense disambiguation. In E. Agirre and P. Edmonds (eds.), *Word Sense Disambiguation: Algorithms and Applications*, Springer, New York.

Agirre, E., O. Lopez de Lacalle, and D. Martínez (2005). Exploring feature spaces with SVD and unlabeled data for word sense disambiguation. In *Proceedings of RANLP*, pp. 32–38, Borovets, Bulgaria.

Bar-Hillel, Y. (1960). Automatic translation of languages. In D. Booth and R. E. Meagher (eds.), *Advances in Computers*, Academic Press, New York.

Basili, R., M. T. Pazienza, and P. Velardi (1992). Combining NLP and statistical techniques for lexical acquisition. In *Proceedings of the AAAI Fall Symposium on Probabilistic Approaches to Natural Language*, pp. 82–87, Cambridge, MA.

Basili, R., M. T. Pazienza, and P. Velardi (1994). The noisy channel and the braying donkey. In *Proceedings of the ACL Balancing Act Workshop on Combining Symbolic and Statistical Approaches to Language*, pp. 21–28, Las Cruces, NM.

Black, E. (1988). An experiment in computational discrimination of English word senses. *IBM Journal of Research and Development*, 232:185–194.

Brody, S., R. Navigli and M. Lapata (2006). Ensemble methods for unsupervised WSD. In *Proceedings of COLING-ACL06*, pp. 97–104, Sydney, Australia.

Brown, P., S. Della Pietra, V. Della Pietra, and R. Mercer (1991). Word sense disambiguation using statistical methods. In *Proceedings of ACL 1991*, pp. 264–270, Berkeley, CA.

Bruce, R. and L. Guthrie (1992). Genus disambiguation: A study in weighted preference. In *Proceedings of COLING-92*, pp. 1187–1191, Nantes, France.

Bruce, R. and J. Wiebe (1994). Word-sense disambiguation using decomposable models. In *Proceedings of ACL 1994*, pp. 139–146, Las Cruces, NM.

Carpuat, M. and D. Wu (2005). Word sense disambiguation vs. statistical machine translation. In *Proceedings of ACL 2005*, pp. 387–394, Morristown, NJ.

Carpuat, M. and D. Wu (2007). Improving statistical machine translation using word sense disambiguation. In *Proceedings of EMNLP-CoNLL07*, pp. 61–72, Prague, Czech Republic.

Chan, Y. S., H. T. Ng, and D. Chiang (2007a). Word sense disambiguation improves statistical machine translation. In *Proceedings of ACL07*, pp. 33–40, Prague, Czech Republic.

Chan, Y. S., H. T. Ng, and Z. Zhong (2007b). NUS-PT: Exploiting parallel texts for word sense disambiguation in the English all-words tasks. In *Proceedings of SemEval-2007*, pp. 253–256, Prague, Czech Republic.

Chang, J., Y. Luo, and K. Su (1992). GPSM: A generalized probabilistic semantic model for ambiguity resolution. In *Proceedings of ACL 1992*, pp. 177–184, Newark, DE.

Chapman, R. (1977). *Roget's International Thesaurus (Fourth Edition)*, Harper and Row, New York.

Cheeseman, P., M. Self, J. Kelly, W. Taylor, D. Freeman, and J. Stutz (1988). Bayesian classification. In *Proceedings of AAAI88*, pp. 607–611, St. Paul, MN.

Chen, J. and M. Palmer (2005). Towards robust high performance word sense disambiguation of English verbs using rich linguistic features. In *Proceedings of the 2nd International Joint Conference on Natural Language Processing*, pp. 933–944, Jeju Island, Korea.

Chklovski, T. and R. Mihalcea (2002). Building a sense tagged corpus with Open Mind Word Expert. In *Proceedings of the ACL 2002 Workshop on Word Sense Disambiguation: Recent Successes and Future Directions*, pp. 116–122, Philadelphia, PA.

Choueka, Y. and S. Lusignam (1985). Disambiguation by short contexts. *Computers and the Humanities*, 19:147–158.

Cottrell, G. (1989). *A Connectionist Approaches to Word Sense Disambiguation*, Pitman, London.

Cowie, J., J. Guthrie, and L. Guthrie (1992). Lexical disambiguation using simulated annealing. In *Proceedings, DARPA Speech and Natural Language Workshop*, pp. 238–242, Harriman, NY.

Cutting, D., D. Larger, J. Pedersen, and J. Tukey (1992). Scatter/gather: A cluster-based approach to browsing document collections. In *Proceedings of SIGIR92*, pp. 318–329, Copenhagen, Denmark.

Dagan, I. and A. Itai (1994). Word sense disambiguation using a second language monolingual corpus. *Computational Linguistics*, 20:563–596.

Dagan, I., A. Itai, and U. Schwall (1991). Two languages are more informative than one. In *Proceedings of ACL 1991*, pp. 130–137, Berkeley, CA.

Dang, H. T., K. Kipper, M. Palmer, and J. Rosenzweig (1998). Investigating regular sense extensions based on intersective Levin classes. In *Proceedings of Coling/ACL-98*, pp. 293–300, Montreal, CA.

Deerwester, S., S. Dumais, G. Furnas, T. Landauer, and R. Harshman (1990). Indexing by latent semantic analysis. *Journal of the American Society for Information Science*, 41(6):391–407.

Dempster, A., N. Laird, and D. Rubin (1977). Maximum likelihood from incomplete data via the EM algorithm. *Journal of the Royal Statistical Society*, 39:1–38.

Diab, M. (2003). Word sense disambiguation within a multilingual framework, PhD thesis, University of Maryland, College Park, MD.

Diab, M. and P. Resnik (2002). An unsupervised method for word sense tagging using parallel corpora. In *Proceedings of ACL 2002*, pp. 255–262, Philadelphia, PA.

Edmonds, P. and A. Kilgarriff (2002). Introduction to the special issue on evaluating word sense disambiguation systems. *Journal of Natural Language Engineering*, 8(4):279–291.

Eisner, J and D. Karakos (2005). Bootstrapping without the boot. In *Proceedings of HLT-EMNLP05*, pp. 395–402, Vancouver, BC.

Eizirik, L., V. Barbosa, and S. Mendes (1993). A Bayesian-network approach to lexical disambiguation. *Cognitive Science*, 17:257–283.

Escudero, G., L. Marquez, and G. Riagu (2000). An empirical study of the domain dependence of supervised word sense disambiguation systems. In *Proceedings of EMNLP/VLC00*, pp. 172–180, Hong Kong, China.

Firth, J. (1968). A synopsis of linguistic theory. In F.R. Palmer (ed.), *Selected Papers of J.R. Firth 1952–59*, Indiana University Press, Bloomington, IN.

Gale, W., K. Church, and D. Yarowsky (1992a). A method for disambiguating word senses in a large corpus. *Computers and the Humanities*, 26:415–439.

Gale, W., K. Church, and D. Yarowsky (1992b). One sense per discourse. In *Proceedings of the 4th DARPA Speech and Natural Language Workshop*, pp. 233–237, Harriman, NY.

Gale, W., K. Church, and D. Yarowsky (1992c). Using bilingual materials to develop word sense disambiguation methods. In *Proceedings, 4th International Conference on Theoretical and Methodological Issues in Machine Translation*, pp. 101–112, Montreal, CA.

Gale, W., K. Church, and D. Yarowsky (1992d). On evaluation of word-sense disambiguation systems. In *Proceedings of ACL 1992*, pp. 249–256, Columbus, OH.

Gale, W., K. Church, and D. Yarowsky (1994). Discrimination decisions for 100,000-dimensional spaces. In A. Zampoli, N. Calzolari, and M. Palmer (eds.), *Current Issues in Computational Linguistics: In Honour of Don Walker*, Kluwer Academic Publishers, pp. 429–450, Dordrecht, the Netherlands.

Guthrie, J., L. Guthrie, Y. Wilks, and H. Aidinejad (1991). Subject dependent co-occurrence and word sense disambiguation. In *Proceedings of ACL 1991*, pp. 146–152, Berkeley, CA.

Hearst, M. (1991). Noun homograph disambiguation using local context in large text corpora. In *Using Corpora*, University of Waterloo, Waterloo, ON.

Hirst, G. (1987). *Semantic Interpretation and the Resolution of Ambiguity*, Cambridge University Press, Cambridge, U.K.

Hovy, E., M. Marcus, M. Palmer, L. Ramshaw, and R. Weischedel (2006). OntoNotes: The 90% solution. In *Proceedings of HLT-NAACL06*, pp. 57–60, New York.

Ide, N. (2000). Cross-lingual sense determination: Can it work? *Computers and the Humanities*, 34(1-2):223–234.

Jorgensen, J. (1990). The psychological reality of word senses. *Journal of Psycholinguistic Research*, 19:167–190.

Kelly, E. and P. Stone (1975). *Computer Recognition of English Word Senses*, North-Holland, Amsterdam, the Netherlands.

Kilgarriff, A. (1992). Dictionary word sense distinctions: An enquiry into their nature. *Computers and the Humanities*, 26:365–387.

Kilgarriff, A. (1997). I don't believe in word senses. *Computers and the Humanities*, 31(2):91–113.

Kilgarriff, A. (2001). English lexical sample task description. In *Proceedings of the 2nd International Workshop on Evaluating Word Sense Disambiguation Systems*, pp. 17–20, Toulouse, France.

Kilgarriff, A. and M. Palmer (2000). Introduction to the special issue on Senseval. *Computers and the Humanities*, 34(1-2):1–13.

Klapaftis, I. and S. Manandhar (2008). Word sense induction using graphs of collocations. In *Proceedings of ECAI08*, pp. 298–302, Patras, Greece.

Kohomban, U. S. and W. S. Lee (2005). Learning semantic classes for word sense disambiguation. In *Proceedings of ACL 2005*, pp. 34–41, Ann Arbor, MI.

Krovetz, R. (1990). Lexical acquisition and information retrieval. In P.S. Jacobs (ed.), *Text-Based Intelligent Systems: Current Research in Text Analysis, Information Extraction and Retrieval*, GE Research and Development Center, Schenectady, NY, pp. 45–64.

Krovetz, R. (1997). Homonymy and polysemy in information retrieval. In *Proceedings of ACL 1997*, pp. 72–79, Madrid, Spain.

Krovetz, R. (1998). More than one sense per discourse. In *Proceedings of Senseval-1*, Sussex, U.K.

Krovetz, R. and W. Croft (1989). Word sense disambiguation using machine-readable dictionaries. In *Proceedings of the 12th Annual International ACM SIGIR Conference on Research and Development in Information Retrieval*, pp. 127–136, Cambridge, MA.

Krovetz, R. and B. Croft (1992). Lexical ambiguity and information retrieval. *ACM Trans. Information Systems*, 10(2):115–141.

Lapata, M. and F. Keller (2007). An information retrieval approach to sense ranking. In *Proceedings of HLT-NAACL07*, pp. 348–355, Rochester, NY.

Leacock, C., G. Towell, and E. Voorhees (1993). Corpus-based statistical sense resolution. In *Proceedings, ARPA Human Language Technology Workshop*, pp. 260–265, Plainsboro, NJ.

Lee, Y. K. and H. T. Ng (2002). An empirical evaluation of knowledge sources and learning algorithms for word sense disambiguation. In *Proceedings of of EMNLP02*, pp. 41–48, Philadelphia, PA.

Lesk, M. (1986). Automatic sense disambiguation: How to tell a pine cone from an ice cream cone. In *Proceeding of the 1986 SIGDOC Conference*, pp. 24–26, Toronto, ON. Association for Computing Machinery, New York.

Luk, A. (1995). Statistical sense disambiguation with relatively small corpora using dictionary definitions In *Proceedings of ACL 1995*, pp. 181–188, Cambridge, MA.

Magnini, B. and G. Cavaglia (2000). Integrating Subject Field Codes into WordNet. In *Proceedings of LREC00*, pp. 1413–1418, Athens, Greece.

Márquez, G. Escudero, D. Martinez, and G. Rigau (2007). Supervised corpus-based methods for WSD. In E. Agirre and P. Edmonds (eds.), *Word Sense Disambiguation: Algorithms and Applications*, Springer, New York.

Martínez, D. and E. Agirre (2000). One sense per collocation and genre/topic variations. In *Proceedings of EMNLP/VLC*, pp. 207–215, Hong Kong, China.

Martínez, D., E. Agirre, and L. Màrquez (2002). Syntactic features for high precision word sense disambiguation. In *Proceedings of COLING 2002*, pp. 1–7, Taipei, Taiwan.

Martínez, D., E. Agirre, and O. Lopez de Lacalle (2008). On the use of automatically acquired examples for all-nouns WSD *Journal of Artificial Intelligence Research*, 33:79–107.

Martínez, D., E. Agirre, and X. Wang (2006). Word relatives in context for word sense disambiguation. In *Proceedings of the Australasian Language Technology Workshop*, pp. 42–50, Sydney, Australia.

McCarthy, D., J. Carroll, and J. Preiss (2002). Disambiguating noun and verb senses using automatically acquired selectional preferences. In *Proceedings of SENSEVAL-2*, pp. 119–122, Toulouse, France.

McCarthy, D., R. Koeling, J. Weeds, and J. Carroll (2004). Finding predominant word senses in untagged text. In *Proceedings of ACL 2004*, pp. 279–287, Barcelona, Spain.

McKeown, K. and V. Hatzivassiloglou (1993). Augmenting lexicons automatically: Clustering semantically related adjectives. In *Proceedings, ARPA Workshop on Human Language Technology*, pp. 272–277, Plainsboro, NJ.

McRoy, S. (1992). Using multiple knowledge sources for word sense disambiguation. *Computational Linguistics*, 18(1):1–30.

Mihalcea, R. (2002). Bootstrapping large sense tagged corpora. In *Proceedings of LREC 2002*, pp. 1407–1411, Canary Islands, Spain.

Mihalcea, R. (2005). Unsupervised large-vocabulary word sense disambiguation with graph-based algorithms for sequence data labeling. In *Proceedings of HLT05*, pp. 411–418, Morristown, NJ.

Mihalcea, R. and D. Moldovan (2001). Pattern learning and active feature selection for word sense disambiguation. In *Proceedings of SENSEVAL-2*, pp. 127–130, Toulouse, France.

Mihalcea, R., T. Chklovski, and A. Killgariff (2004). The Senseval-3 English lexical sample task. In *Proceedings of ACL/SIGLEX Senseval-3*, pp. 25–28, Barcelona, Spain.

Mihalcea, R., P. Tarau, and E. Figa (2004). Pagerank on semantic networks with application to word sense disambiguation. In *Proceedings of COLING04*, pp. 1126–1132, Geneva, Switzerland.

Miller, G. (1990). WordNet: An on-line lexical database. *International Journal of Lexicography*, 3(4): 235–312.

Miller, G. and W. Charles (1991). Contextual correlates of semantic similarity. *Language and Cognitive Processes*, 6(1):1–28.

Miller, G., C. Leacock, R. Tengi, and R.Bunker (1993). A semantic concordance. In *Proceedings of the ARPA Workshop on Human Language Technology*, pp. 303–308, Plainsboro, NJ.

Mooney, R. (1996). Comparative experiments on disambiguating word senses: An illustration of the role of bias in machine learning. In *Proceedings of EMNLP*, pp. 82–91, Philadelphia, PA.

Navigli, R. (2006). Consistent validation of manual and automatic sense annotations with the aid of semantic graphs. *Computatational Linguisitics*, 32(2):273–281.

Navigli, R. and M. Lapata (2007). Graph connectivity measures for unsupervised word sense disambiguation. In *Proceedings of IJCAI*, pp. 1683–1688, Hyderabad, India.

Ng, H. T. and H. Lee (1996). Integrating multiple knowledge sources to disambiguate word sense: An exemplar-based approach. In *Proceedings of ACL 1996*, pp. 40–47, Santa Cruz, CA.

Ng, H. T., B. Wang and Y. Chan (2003). Exploiting parallel texts for word sense disambiguation: an empirical study. In *Proceedings of ACL03*, pp. 455–462, Sapporo, Japan.

Pakhomov, S. (2002). Semi-supervised maximum entropy based approach to acronym and abbreviation normalization in medical texts. In *Proceedings of ACL 2002*, pp. 160–167, Philadelphia, PA.

Palmer, M., H. Dang and C. Fellbaum (2007). Making fine-grained and coarse-grained sense distinctions, both manually and automatically. *Journal of Natural Language Engineering*, 13(2):137–163.

Pantel, P. and D. Lin (2002). Discovering word senses from text. In *Proceedings of SIGKDD'02*, pp. 613–619, Edmonton, Canada.

Pedersen, T. (2009). WordNet::SenseRelate::AllWords - A broad coverage word sense tagger that maximimizes semantic relatedness. In *Proceedings of NAACL09*, pp. 17–20, Boulder, CO.

Pedersen, T. and R. Bruce (1997). A new supervised learning algorithm for word sense disambiguation. In *Proceedings of AAAI*, pp. 604–609, Providence, RI.

Pereira, F., N. Tishby, and L. Lee (1993). Distributional clustering of English words. In *Proceedings of ACL 1993*, pp. 183–190, Columbus, OH.

Procter, P., ed. (1978). *Longman Dictionary of Contemporary English*, Longman Group Ltd., Harlow, U.K.

Pustejovsky, J. (1995). *The Generative Lexicon*, MIT Press, Cambridge, MA.

Resnik, P. (1993). Selection and information: A class-based approach to lexical relationships, PhD thesis, University of Pennsylvania, Philadelphia, PA.

Resnik, P. (1995). Using information context to evaluate sematic similarity in a taxonomy. In *Proceedings of IJCAI95*, pp 448–453, Montreal, Canada.

Resnik, P. (1997). Selectional preference and sense disambiguation. In *Proceedings of the ACL Workshop on Tagging Text with Lexical Semantics*, pp. 52–57, Washington.

Resnik, P. and D. Yarowsky (1999). Distinguishing systems and distinguishing senses: new evaluation methods for word sense disambiguation systems. *Journal of Natural Language Engineering* 5(2): 113–133.

Sanderson, M. (1994). Word sense disambiguation and information retrieval. *Proceedings of SIGIR 1994*, pp. 142–151, Dublin, Ireland.

Schütze, H. (1992). Dimensions of meaning. In *Proceedings of Supercomputing '92*, pp. 787–796, Minneapolis, MN.

Schütze, H. (1998). Automatic word sense discrimination. *Computational Linguistics*, 24(1):97–123.

Schütze, H. and J. Pedersen (1995). Information retrieval based on word senses. In *4th Annual Symposium on Document Analysis and Information Retrieval*, pp. 161–175, Las Vegas, NV.

Sinclair, J., ed. (1987). *Collins COBUILD English Language Dictionary*, Collins, London and Glasgow, U.K.

Sinha, R. and R. Mihalcea (2007). Unsupervised graphbased word sense disambiguation using measures of word semantic similarity. In *Proceedings of the IEEE International Conference on Semantic Computing*, pp. 363–369, Irvine, CA.

Small, S. and C. Rieger (1982). Parsing and comprehending with word experts (a theory and its realization). In W. Lehnert and M. Ringle (eds.), *Strategies for Natural Language Processing*, Lawrence Erlbaum Associates, Hillsdale, NJ.

Stevenson, M. (2003). *Word Sense Disambiguation: The Case for Combinations of Knowledge Sources*. CSLI Publications, Stanford, CA.

Stevenson, M. and Y. Wilks (2001). The interaction of knowledge sources in word sense disambiguation. *Computational Linguistics*, 27(3):321–349.

Veronis, J. and N. Ide (1990). Word sense disambiguation with very large neural networks extracted from machine readable dictionaries. In *Proceedings, COLING-90*, pp. 389–394, Helsinki, Finland.

Voorhees, E. (1993). Using WordNet to disambiguate word senses for text retrieval. In *Proceedings of SIGIR'93*, pp. 171–180, Pittsburgh, PA.

Walker, D. and R. Amsler (1986). The use of machine-readable dictionaries in sublanguage analysis. In R. Grishman and R. Kittredge (eds.), *Analyzing Language in Restricted Domains: Sublanguage Description and Processing*, Lawrence Erlbaum, Hillsdale, NJ, pp. 69–84.

Wang, X. and J. Carroll (2005). Word sense disambiguation using sense examples automatically acquired from a second language. In *Proceedings of HLT/EMNLP 2005*, pp. 547–554, Vancouver, BC, Canada.

Wilks, Y. (1975). A preferential, pattern-seeking semantics for natural language inference. *Artificial Intelligence*, 6:53–74.

Winograd, T. (1972). *Understanding Natural Language*. Academic Press, New York.

Woods, W., R. Kaplan, and B. Nash-Webber (1972). The lunar sciences natural language information system: Final report. *BBN Technical Report No. 2378*, Cambridge, MA.

Wu, Z. and M. Palmer (1994). Verb semantics and lexical selection. In *Proceedings of ACL 1994*, pp. 133–138, Las Cruces, NM.

Yarowsky, D. (1992). Word-Sense disambiguation using statistical models of Roget's categories trained on large corpora. In *Proceedings, COLING-92*, pp. 454–460, Nantes, France.

Yarowsky, D. (1993). One sense per collocation. In *Proceedings, ARPA Human Language Technology Workshop*, pp. 266–271, Princeton, NJ.

Yarowsky, D. (1994). Decision lists for lexical ambiguity resolution: Application to accent restoration in Spanish and French. In *Proceedings of ACL 1994*, pp. 88–97, Las Cruces, NM.

Yarowsky, D. (1995). Unsupervised word sense disambiguation rivaling supervised methods. In *Proceedings of ACL 1995*, pp. 189–196, Cambridge, MA.

Yarowsky, D. (2000). Hierarchical decision lists for word sense disambiguation. *Computers and the Humanities*, 34(2):179–186.

Yarowsky, D. and R. Florian (2002). Evaluating sense disambiguation performance across diverse parameter spaces. *Natural Language Engineering*, 8(4):293–310.

Yarowsky, D., R. Florian, S. Cucerzan, and C. Schafer (2001). The Johns Hopkins Senseval-2 system description. In *Proceedings of the Senseval-2 Workshop*, pp. 163–166, Toulouse, France.

Yngve, V. (1955). Syntax and the problem of multiple meaning. In W. Locke and D. Booth (eds.), *Machine Translation of Languages*, Wiley, New York.

Zernik, U. (1991). Train1 vs. train2: Tagging word senses in a corpus. In U. Zernik (ed.), *Lexical Acquisition: Exploiting On-Line Resources to Build a Lexicon*, Lawrence Erlbaum, Hillsdale, NJ, pp. 91–112.

Zhong, Z., H. T. Ng., and Y. S. Chan (2008). Word sense disambiguation using OntoNotes: An emprical study. In *Proceedings of EMNLP 2008*, pp. 1002–1010, Honolulu, HI.

Zhu, J. B. and E. Hovy (2007). Active learning for word sense disambiguation with methods for addressing the class imbalance problem. In *Proceedings of EMNLP/CoNLL07*, pp. 783–790, Prague, Czech Republic.

15

An Overview of Modern
Speech Recognition

Xuedong Huang and
Li Deng
Microsoft Corporation

15.1 Introduction

The task of speech recognition is to convert speech into a sequence of words by a computer program. As the most natural communication modality for humans, the ultimate dream of speech recognition is to enable people to communicate more naturally and effectively. While the long-term objective requires deep integration with many NLP components discussed in this book, there are many emerging applications that can be readily deployed with the core speech-recognition module we review in this chapter. Some of these typical applications include voice dialing, call routing, data entry and dictation, command and control, and computer-aided language learning. Most of these modern systems are typically based on statistic models such as hidden Markov models (HMMs). One reason why HMMs are popular is that their parameters can be estimated automatically from a large amount of data, and they are simple and computationally feasible.

Speech recognition is often regarded as the front-end for many NLP components discussed in this book. In practice, the speech system typically uses context-free grammar (CFG) or statistic n-grams for the same reason that HMMs are used for acoustic modeling. There are a number of excellent books that have covered the basis of speech recognition and related spoken language–processing technologies (Lee, 1988; Rabiner and Juang, 1993; Lee et al., 1996; Jelinek, 1997; Gold and Morgan, 2000; Jurafsky and Martin, 2000; Furui, 2001; Huang et al., 2001; Deng and O'Shaughnessy, 2003). In this chapter, we provide an overview in Section 15.2 of the main components in speech recognition, followed by a critical review of the historically significant developments in the field in Section 15.3. We devote Section 15.4 to speech-recognition applications, including some recent case studies. An in-depth analysis of the current state of speech recognition and detailed discussions on a number of future research directions in speech recognition are presented in Section 15.5.

15.2 Major Architectural Components

Modern speech-recognition systems have been built invariably based on statistical principles, as pioneered by the work of Baker (1975) and Jelinek (1976) and exposed in detail in Huang et al. (2001); Deng and O'Shaughnessey (2003). A source-channel mathematical model or a type of generative statistical model is often used to formulate speech-recognition problems. As illustrated in Figure 15.1, the speaker's mind decides the source word sequence $\mathbf{W}$ that is delivered through his or her text generator. The source is passed through a noisy communication channel that consists of the speaker's vocal apparatus to produce the speech waveform and the speech signal-processing component of the speech recognizer. Finally, the speech decoder aims to decode the acoustic signal $\mathbf{X}$ into a word sequence $\hat{\mathbf{W}}$, which is in ideal cases close to the original word sequence $\mathbf{W}$.

A typical, practical speech-recognition system consists of basic components shown in the dotted box of Figure 15.2. Applications interface with the decoder to obtain recognition results that may be used to adapt other components in the system. *Acoustic models* include the representation of knowledge about acoustics, phonetics, microphone and environment variability, gender and dialect differences among speakers, etc. *Language models* refer to a system's knowledge of what constitutes a possible word, what words are likely

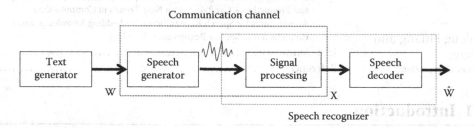

FIGURE 15.1   A source-channel model for a typical speech-recognition system.

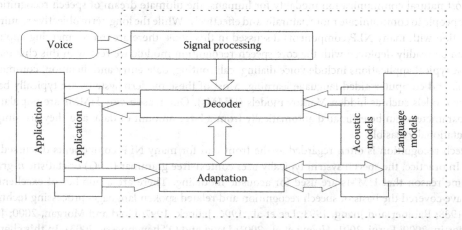

FIGURE 15.2   Basic system architecture of a speech-recognition system.

to co-occur, and in what sequence. The semantics and functions related to an operation a user may wish to perform may also be necessary for the language model. Many uncertainties exist in these areas, associated with speaker characteristics, speech style and rate, the recognition of basic speech segments, possible words, likely words, unknown words, grammatical variation, noise interference, nonnative accents, and the confidence scoring of results. A successful speech-recognition system must contend with all of these uncertainties. The acoustic uncertainty of the different accents and speaking styles of individual speakers are compounded by the lexical and grammatical complexity and variations of spoken language, which are all represented in the language model.

As shown in Figure 15.2, the speech signal is processed in the signal-processing module that extracts salient feature vectors for the decoder. The decoder uses both acoustic and language models to generate the word sequence that has the maximum posterior probability for the input feature vectors. It can also provide information needed for the adaptation component to modify either the acoustic or language models so that improved performance can be obtained.

The division of acoustic modeling and language modeling discussed above can be succinctly described by the fundamental equation of statistical speech recognition:

$$\hat{\mathbf{W}} = \arg\max_{\mathbf{w}} P(\mathbf{W}|\mathbf{A}) = \arg\max_{\mathbf{w}} \frac{P(\mathbf{W})P(\mathbf{A}|\mathbf{W})}{P(\mathbf{A})} \tag{15.1}$$

where for the given acoustic observation or feature vector sequence $\mathbf{X} = X_1 X_2 \ldots X_n$, the goal of speech recognition is to find out the corresponding word sequence $\hat{\mathbf{W}} = w_1 w_2 \ldots w_m$ that has the maximum posterior probability $P(\mathbf{W}|\mathbf{X})$ as expressed with Equation 15.1. Since the maximization of Equation 15.1 is carried out with the observation $\mathbf{X}$ fixed, the above maximization is equivalent of the maximization of the numerator:

$$\hat{\mathbf{W}} = \arg\max_{\mathbf{w}} P(\mathbf{W})P(\mathbf{X}|\mathbf{W}) \tag{15.2}$$

where $P(\mathbf{W})$ and $P(\mathbf{X}|\mathbf{W})$ constitute the probabilistic quantities computed by the language modeling and acoustic modeling components, respectively, of speech-recognition systems.

The practical challenge is how to build accurate acoustic models, $P(\mathbf{X}|\mathbf{W})$, and language models, $P(\mathbf{W})$, which can truly reflect the spoken language to be recognized. For large vocabulary speech recognition, we need to decompose a word into a subword sequence (often called pronunciation modeling), since there are a large number of words. Thus, $P(\mathbf{X}|\mathbf{W})$ is closely related to phonetic modeling. $P(\mathbf{X}|\mathbf{W})$ should take into account speaker variations, pronunciation variations, environmental variations, and context-dependent phonetic coarticulation variations. Last, but not least, any static acoustic or language model will not meet the needs of real applications. So it is vital to dynamically adapt both $P(\mathbf{W})$ and $P(\mathbf{X}|\mathbf{W})$ to maximize $P(\mathbf{W}|\mathbf{X})$ while using the spoken language systems. The decoding process of finding the best-matched word sequence, $\mathbf{W}$, to match the input speech signal, $\mathbf{X}$, in speech-recognition systems is more than a simple pattern recognition problem, since one faces a practically infinite number of word patterns to search in continuous speech recognition.

In the remainder of this section, we will provide an overview on both of $P(\mathbf{W})$ and $P(\mathbf{X}|\mathbf{W})$ components in a speech recognizer, as well as on how the maximization operation in Equation 15.2, a process known as decoding, can be carried out in practice.

15.2.1 Acoustic Models

The accuracy of automatic speech recognition remains one of the most important research challenges after years of research and development. There are a number of well-known factors that determine the accuracy of a speech-recognition system. The most noticeable ones are context variations, speaker variations, and environment variations. Acoustic modeling plays a critical role to improve the accuracy. It is not far-fetched to state that it is the central part of any speech-recognition system.

Acoustic modeling of speech typically refers to the process of establishing statistical representations for the feature vector sequences computed from the speech waveform. HMM (Baum, 1972; Baker, 1975; Jelinek, 1976) is one of the most common types of acoustic models. Other acoustic models include segmental models (Poritz, 1988; Deng, 1993; Deng et al., 1994; Ostendorf et al., 1996; Glass, 2003), super-segmental models including hidden dynamic models (Deng et al., 2006), neural networks (Lippman, 1987; Morgan et al., 2005), maximum entropy models (Gao and Kuo, 2006), and (hidden) conditional random fields (Gunawardana et al., 2005).

Acoustic modeling also encompasses "pronunciation modeling," which describes how a sequence or multi-sequences of fundamental speech units (such as phones or phonetic feature) are used to represent larger speech units such as words or phrases that are the object of speech recognition. Acoustic modeling may also include the use of feedback information from the recognizer to reshape the feature vectors of speech in achieving noise robustness in speech recognition.

In speech recognition, statistical properties of sound events are described by the acoustic model. Correspondingly, the likelihood score $p(X|W)$ in Equation 15.2 is computed based on the acoustic model. In an isolated-word speech-recognition system that has an N-word vocabulary, assuming that the acoustic model component corresponding to the ith word W_i is λ_i, then $p(X|W_i) = p(X|\lambda_i)$. In HMM-based speech recognition, it is assumed that the sequence of observed vectors corresponding to each word is generated by a Markov chain. As shown in Figure 15.3, an HMM is a finite state machine that changes state once every time frame, and at each time frame t when a state j is entered, an observation vector x_t is generated from the emitting probability distribution $b_j(x_t)$. The transition property from state i to state j is specified by the transition probability a_{ij}. Moreover, two special non-emitting states are usually used in an HMM. They include an entry state, which is reached before the speech vector generation process begins, and an exit state, which is reached when the generative process terminates. Both states are reached only once. Since they do not generate any observation, none of them has an emitting probability density.

In the HMM, the transition probability a_{ij} is the probability of entering state j given the previous state i, that is, $a_{ij} = \Pr(s(t) = j|s(t-1) = i)$, where $s(t)$ is the state index at time t. For an N-state HMM, we have,

$$\sum_{j=1}^{N} a_{ij} = 1$$

The emitting probability density $b_j(x)$ describes the distribution of the observation vectors at the state j. In continuous-density HMM (CDHMM), emitting probability density is often represented by a Gaussian mixture density:

$$b_j(x) = \sum_{m=1}^{M} c_{j,m} N(x; \mu_{jm}, \Sigma_{jm})$$

where

$N(x; \mu_{jm}, \Sigma_{jm}) = \frac{1}{(2\pi)^{\frac{D}{2}} |\Sigma_{jm}|^{\frac{1}{2}}} e^{-\frac{1}{2}(x-\mu_{jm})^T \Sigma_{jm}^{-1} (x-\mu_{jm})}$ is a multivariate Gaussian density

D is the dimension of the feature vector x

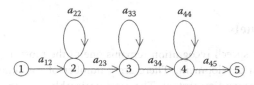

FIGURE 15.3 Illustration of a five-state left-to-right HMM. It has two non-emitting states and three emitting states. For each emitting state, the HMM is only allowed to remain at the same state or move to the next state.

c_{jm}, μ_{jm}, and Σ_{jm} are the weight, mean, and covariance of the mth Gaussian component of the mixture distribution at state j.

Generally speaking, each emitting distribution characterizes a sound event, and the distribution must be specific enough to allow discrimination between different sounds as well as robust enough to account for the variability in natural speech.

Numerous HMM training methods are developed to estimate values of the state transition probabilities and the parameters of the emitting probability densities at each state of the HMM. In early years of HMM applications to speech recognition, the EM algorithm, based on the maximum-likelihood principle, as developed in Baum (1972); Baker (1975); Jelinek (1976); Dempster et al. (1977) was typically used as the training method from the training data. The high efficiency of the EM algorithm is one crucial advantage associated with using the HMM as the acoustic model for speech recognition. The effectiveness of the EM for training HMMs was questioned in later research, resulting in a series of more effective but less efficient training algorithms, known as discriminative learning (Bahl et al., 1986; Macherey et al., 2005; Povey et al., 2005). A comprehensive and unifying review of discriminative learning methods for speech recognition can be found in He et al. (2008).

Given $\{a_{ij}\}$ and $b_j(x)$, for $i = 1, 2, \ldots, N$, $j = 1, 2, \ldots, N$, the likelihood of an observation sequence X is calculated as:

$$p(X|\lambda) = \sum_s p(X, s|\lambda) \tag{15.3}$$

where $s = s_1, s_2, \ldots, s_T$ is the HMM state sequence that generates the observation vector sequence $X = x_1, x_2, \ldots, x_T$, and the joint probability of X and the state sequence s given λ is a product of the transition probabilities and the emitting probabilities

$$p(X, s|\lambda) = \prod_{t=1}^{T} b_{s_t}(x_t) a_{s_t s_{t+1}}$$

where s_{T+1} is the non-emitting exit state.

In practice, Equation 15.3 can be approximately calculated as joint probability of the observation vector sequence X with the most possible state sequence, that is,

$$p(X|\lambda) \approx \max_s p(X, s|\lambda) \tag{15.4}$$

Although it is impractical to evaluate the quantities of Equations 15.3 and 15.4 directly due to the huge number of possible state sequences when T is large, efficient recursive algorithms exist for computing both of them. This is another crucial computational advantage, developed originally in Baum (1972); Baker (1975); Jelinek (1976), for HMMs as an acoustic model for speech recognition.

15.2.2 Language Models

The role of language modeling in speech recognition is to provide the value $P(\mathbf{W})$ in the fundamental equation of speech recognition of Equation 15.2. One type of language model is the grammar, which is a formal specification of the permissible structures for the language. The traditional, deterministic grammar gives the probability of one if the structure is permissible or of zero otherwise. The parsing technique, as discussed in Chapter 4, is the method of analyzing the sentence to see if its structure is compliant with the grammar. With the advent of bodies of text (corpora) that have had their structures hand-annotated, it is now possible to generalize the formal grammar to include accurate probabilities. Furthermore, the probabilistic relationship among a sequence of words can be directly derived and modeled from the corpora with the so-called stochastic language models, such as n-gram, avoiding the need to create broad coverage formal grammars.

Another, more common type of language model is called the stochastic language model, which plays a critical role in building a working spoken language system. We will discuss a number of important issues associated with this type of language models.

As covered earlier, a language model can be formulated as a probability distribution $P(\mathbf{W})$ over word strings $\mathbf{W}$ that reflect how frequently a string $\mathbf{W}$ occurs as a sentence. For example, for a language model describing spoken language, we might have $P(hi) = 0.01$ since perhaps one out of every 100 sentences a person speaks is *hi*. On the other hand, we would have $P(lid\ gallops\ Changsha\ pop) = 0$ since it is extremely unlikely anyone would utter such a strange string.

$P(\mathbf{W})$ can be decomposed as

$$
\begin{aligned}
P(\mathbf{W}) &= P(w_1, w_2, \ldots, w_n) \\
&= P(w_1)P(w_2|w_1)P(w_3|w_1, w_2) \cdots P(w_n|w_1, w_2, \ldots, w_{n-1}) \\
&= \prod_{i=1}^{n} P(w_i|w_1, w_2, \ldots, w_{i-1})
\end{aligned}
\tag{15.5}
$$

where $P(w_i|w_1, w_2, \ldots, w_{i-1})$ is the probability that w_i will follow given that the word sequence $w_1, w_2, \ldots, w_{i-1}$ was presented previously. In Equation 15.5, the choice of w_i thus depends on the entire past history of the input. For a vocabulary of size v there are v^{i-1} different histories and so, to specify $P(w_i|w_1, w_2, \ldots, w_{i-1})$ completely, v^i values would have to be estimated. In reality, the probabilities $P(w_i|w_1, w_2, \ldots, w_{i-1})$ are impossible to estimate for even moderate values of i, since most histories $w_1, w_2, \ldots, w_{i-1}$ are unique or have occurred only a few times. A practical solution to the above problems is to assume that $P(w_i|w_1, w_2, \ldots, w_{i-1})$ only depends on some equivalence classes. The equivalence class can be simply based on the several previous words $w_{i-N+1}, w_{i-N+2}, \ldots, w_{i-1}$. This leads to an N-gram language model. If the word depends on the previous two words, we have a *trigram*: $P(w_i|w_{i-2}, w_{i-1})$. Similarly, we can have *unigram*: $P(w_i)$, or *bigram*: $P(w_i|w_{i-1})$ language models. The trigram is particularly powerful as most words have a strong dependence on the previous two words and it can be estimated reasonably well with an attainable corpus.

In bigram models, we make the approximation that the probability of a word depends only on the identity of the immediately preceding word. To make $P(w_i|w_{i-1})$ meaningful for $i = 1$, we pad the *beginning of the sentence* with a distinguished token <s>; that is, we pretend $w_0 =$ <s>. In addition, to make the sum of the probabilities of all strings equal 1, it is necessary to place a distinguished token </s> at the *end of the sentence*. For example, to calculate $P(Mary\ loves\ that\ person)$ we would take

$$
P(Mary\ loves\ that\ person) =
$$
$$
P(Mary|\texttt{<s>})P(loves|Mary)P(that|loves)P(person|that)P(\texttt{</s>}|person)
$$

To estimate $P(w_i|w_{i-1})$, the frequency with which the word w_i occurs given that the last word is w_{i-1}, we simply count how often the sequence $P(w_i|w_{i-1})$ occurs in some text and normalize the count by the number of times w_{i-1} occurs.

In general, for a trigram model, the probability of a word depends on the two preceding words. The trigram can be estimated by observing the frequencies or counts of the word pair $C(w_{i-2}, w_{i-1})$ and triplet $C(w_{i-2}, w_{i-1}, w_i)$ as follows:

$$
P(w_i|w_{i-2}, w_{i-1}) = \frac{C(w_{i-2}, w_{i-1}, w_i)}{C(w_{i-2}, w_{i-1})}
\tag{15.6}
$$

The text available for building a model is called a training corpus. For n-gram models, the amount of training data used is typically many millions of words. The estimate of Equation 15.6 is based on the maximum likelihood principle, because this assignment of probabilities yields the trigram model that assigns the highest probability to the training data of all possible trigram models.

We sometimes refer to the value n of an n-gram model as its order. This terminology comes from the area of Markov models, of which n-gram models are an instance. In particular, an n-gram model can be interpreted as a Markov model of order $n - 1$.

Consider a small example. Let our training data Sbe comprised of the three sentences *John read her book. I read a different book. John read a book by Mulan* and let us calculate $P(John\ read\ a\ book)$ for the maximum likelihood bigram model. We have

$$P(John|<s>) = \frac{C(<s>, John)}{C(<s>)} = \frac{2}{3}$$

$$P(read|John) = \frac{C(John, read)}{C(John)} = \frac{2}{2}$$

$$P(a|read) = \frac{C(read, a)}{C(read)} = \frac{2}{3}$$

$$P(book|a) = \frac{C(a, book)}{C(a)} = \frac{1}{2}$$

$$P(</s>|book) = \frac{C(book, </s>)}{C(book)} = \frac{2}{3}$$

These trigram probabilities help us to estimate the probability for the sentence as:

$$P(John, read, a, book) = P(John|<s>)P(read|John)P(a|read)P(book|a)P(</s>|book) \tag{15.7}$$

$$\approx 0.148$$

If these three sentences are all the data we have to train our language model, the model is unlikely to generalize well to new sentences. For example, the probability for *Mulan read her book* should have a reasonable probability, but the trigram will give it a zero probability simply because we do not have a reliable estimate for $P(read|Mulan)$.

Unlike linguistics, grammaticality is not a strong constraint in the n-gram language model. Even though the string is ungrammatical, we may still assign it a high probability if n is small.

Language can be thought of as an information source whose outputs are words w_i belonging to the vocabulary of the language. The most common metric for evaluating a language model is the word recognition error rate, which requires the participation of a speech-recognition system. Alternatively, we can measure the probability that the language model assigns to test word strings without involving speech-recognition systems. This is the derivative measure of cross-entropy known as test set *perplexity*.

Given a language model that assigns probability $P(\mathbf{W})$ to a word sequence $\mathbf{W}$, we can derive a compression algorithm that encodes the text $\mathbf{W}$ using $-\log_2 P(T)$ bits. The cross-entropy $H(\mathbf{W})$ of a model $P(w_i|w_{i-n+1} \ldots w_{i-1})$ on data $\mathbf{W}$, with a sufficiently long word sequence, can be simply approximated as

$$H(\mathbf{W}) = -\frac{1}{N_W} \log_2 P(\mathbf{W}) \tag{15.8}$$

where N_W is the length of the text $\mathbf{W}$ measured in words.

The perplexity $PP(\mathbf{W})$ of a language model $P(\mathbf{W})$ is defined as the reciprocal of the (geometric) average probability assigned by the model to each word in the test set $\mathbf{W}$. This is a measure, related to cross-entropy, known as test-set perplexity:

$$PP(\mathbf{W}) = 2^{H(\mathbf{W})} \tag{15.9}$$

The perplexity can be roughly interpreted as the geometric mean of the branching factor of the text when presented to the language model. The perplexity defined in Equation 15.9 has two key parameters: a language model and a word sequence. The test-set perplexity evaluates the generalization capability of the language model. The training-set perplexity measures how the language model fits the training data, such as the likelihood. It is generally true that lower perplexity correlates with better recognition performance. This is because the perplexity is essentially a statistically weighted word branching measure on the test set. The higher the perplexity, the more branches the speech recognizer needs to consider statistically.

While the perplexity defined in Equation 15.9 is easy to calculate for the n-gram (Equation 15.5), it is slightly more complicated to compute it for a probabilistic CFG. We can first parse the word sequence and use Equation 15.5 to compute $P(\mathbf{W})$ for the test set perplexity. The perplexity can also be applied to non-stochastic models such as CFGs. We can assume they have a uniform distribution in computing $P(\mathbf{W})$.

A language with higher perplexity means the number of words branching from a previous word is larger on average. In this sense, the perplexity is an indication of the complexity of the language if we have an accurate estimate of $P(\mathbf{W})$. For a given language, the difference between the perplexity of a language model and the true perplexity of the language is an indication of the quality of the model. The perplexity of a particular language model can change dramatically in terms of the vocabulary size, the number of states or grammar rules, and the estimated probabilities. A language model with perplexity X has roughly the same difficulty as another language model in which every word can be followed by X different words with equal probabilities. Therefore, in the task of continuous digit recognition, the perplexity is 10. Clearly, lower perplexity will generally have less confusion in recognition. Typical perplexities yielded by n-gram models on English text range from about 50 to almost 1000 (corresponding to cross-entropies from about 6 to 10 bits/word), depending on the type of text. In tasks of 5000 word continuous speech recognition for the *Wall Street Journal* newspaper, the test set perplexity of the trigram grammar and the bigram grammar is reported to be about 128 and 176, respectively. In tasks of 2000 word conversational Air Travel Information System (ATIS), the test set perplexity of the word trigram model is typically less than 20.

Since perplexity does not take into account the acoustic confusability, we eventually have to measure speech-recognition accuracy. For example, if the vocabulary of a speech recognizer contains the E-set of English alphabet: B, C, D, E, G, and T, we can define a CFG that has a low perplexity value of 6. Such a low perplexity does not guarantee we will have good recognition performance, because of the intrinsic acoustic confusability of the E-set.

15.2.3 Decoding

As epitomized in the fundamental equation of speech recognition in Equation 15.2, the decoding process in a speech recognizer's operation is to find a sequence of words whose corresponding acoustic and language models best match the input feature vector sequence. Therefore, the process of such a decoding process with trained acoustic and language models is often referred to as a *search* process. Graph search algorithms have been explored extensively in the fields of artificial intelligence, operating research, and game theory, which serve as the basic foundation for the search problem in continuous speech recognition.

The complexity of a search algorithm is highly correlated to the search space, which is determined by the constraints imposed by the language models. The impact of different language models, including finite-state grammars, CFG, and n-grams are critical to decoding efficiency.

Speech recognition search is usually done with the Viterbi decoder (Viterbi, 1967; Vintsyuk, 1968; Sakoe and Chiba, 1971; Ney, 1984), or A* stack decoder (Jelinek, 1969, 1976, 1997). The reasons for choosing the Viterbi decoder involve arguments that point to speech as a left-to-right process and the efficiencies afforded by a time-synchronous process. The reasons for choosing a stack decoder involve its ability to more effectively exploit the A* criteria that holds out the hope of performing an optimal search as well as the ability to handle huge search spaces. Both algorithms have been successfully applied to various speech-recognition systems. Viterbi beam search has been the preferred method for almost all speech recognition tasks. Stack decoding, on the other hand, remains an important strategy to uncover the *n*-best and lattice structures (Schwartz and Chow, 1990).

The decoder uncovers the word sequence $\hat{\mathbf{W}} = w_1 w_2 \ldots w_m$ that has the maximum posterior probability $P(\mathbf{W}|\mathbf{X})$ for the given acoustic observation $\mathbf{X} = X_1 X_2 \ldots X_n$, according to the maximization operation described by Equation 15.2. One obvious (and brute-force) way is to search all possible word sequences and select the one with best posterior probability score. This, however, is not practically feasible.

The unit of acoustic model $P(\mathbf{X}|\mathbf{W})$ is not necessary a word model. For large-vocabulary speech-recognition systems, subword models, which include phonemes, demi-syllables, and syllables are often used. When subword models are used, the word model $P(\mathbf{X}|\mathbf{W})$ is then obtained by concatenating the subword models according to the pronunciation transcription of the words in a lexicon or dictionary.

When word models are available, speech recognition becomes a search problem. The goal for speech recognition is thus to find a sequence of word models that best describes the input waveform against the word models. As neither the number of words nor the boundary of each word or phoneme in the input waveform is known, appropriate search strategies to deal with these variable-length nonstationary patterns are extremely important.

When HMMs are used for speech-recognition systems, the states in the HMM can be expanded to form the state-search space in the search. Here, we use HMM as our speech models. Although the HMM framework is used to describe the search algorithms, the techniques discussed here can in principle be used for systems based on other modeling techniques. The HMM's state transition network is sufficiently general and it can represent the general search framework for most modeling approaches.

15.2.3.1 The Concept of State Space in Decoding

The state space in speech recognition search or decoding is an important concept, as it is a good indicator of the complexity for the search. Since the HMM representation for each word in the lexicon is fixed, the state space and its size are determined by the language models. And each language model (grammar) can be correlated to a state machine that can be expanded to form the full state space for the recognizer. The states in such a state machine are referred to as *language models states*. For simplification, we will use the concepts of state space and language model states interchangeably. The expansion of language model states to HMM states will be done implicitly. The language model states for isolated word recognition are trivial. They are just the union of the HMM states of each word. In this section, we first look at the language model states for two grammars for continuous speech recognition: Finite State Grammar (FSG) and Context Free Grammar (CFG). We then discuss a most popular decoding technique, time-synchronous beam search technique.

In general, the decoding complexity for the time-synchronous Viterbi algorithm is $O(N^2 T)$ where N is the total number states in the composite HMM and T is the length of the input observation. A full time-synchronous Viterbi search is quite efficient for moderate tasks (vocabulary ≤ 500). Most small or moderate vocabulary tasks in speech-recognition applications use an FSG. Figure 15.4 shows a simple example of an FSG, where each of the word arcs in an FSG can be expanded as a network of phoneme or other subword HMMs. The word HMMs are connected with null transitions with the grammar state. A large finite state HMM network that encodes all the legal sentences can be constructed based on the expansion procedure. The decoding process is achieved by performing the time-synchronous Viterbi search on this composite finite state HMM.

In practice, FSGs are sufficient only for simple tasks. When an FSG is made to satisfy the constraints of sharing of different sub-grammars for compactness and support for dynamic modifications, the resulting nondeterministic FSG becomes similar to CFG in terms of implementation. The CFG grammar consists of a set of productions or rules, which expand nonterminals into a sequence of terminals and nonterminals. Nonterminals in the grammar tend to refer to high-level task-specific concepts such as dates, names, and commands. The terminals are words in the vocabulary. A grammar also has a nonterminal designated as its start state. While CFG has not been widely used in the NLP community, they are one of the most widely used methods for speech recognition.

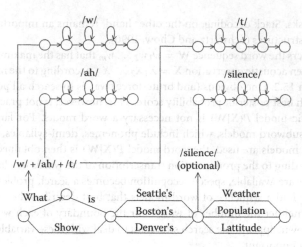

FIGURE 15.4 An illustration of how to compile a speech-recognition task with finite grammar into a composite HMM.

A CFG can be formulated with a recursive transition network (RTN). RTN allows arc labels to refer to other networks as well as words. We use Figure 15.5 to illustrate how to embed HMMs into a RTN, which represents the following CFG:

S → NP VP
NP → sam|sam davis
VP → VERB tom
VERB → likes|hates

There are three types of arcs in an RTN shown in Figure 15.5: CAT(x), PUSH(x), POP CAT(x) arc indicates x is a terminal node (which is equivalent to a word arc). Therefore, all the CAT(x) arcs can be expanded by the HMM network for x. The word HMM can again be composite HMM built from phoneme (or subword) HMMs. Similar to the finite state grammar case in Figure 15.4, all grammar states act as a state with incoming and outgoing null transitions to connect word HMMs in the CFG. During decoding, the search pursues several paths through the CFG at the same time. Associated with each of the paths is a grammar state that describes completely how the path can be extended further. When the decoder hypothesizes end of the current word of a path, it asks the CFG module to extend the path further by one word. There may be several alternative successor words for the given path. The decoder considers all the successor word possibilities. This may cause the path to be extended to generate several more paths to be considered each with its own grammar state.

Readers should note that the same word might be under consideration by the decoder in the context of different paths and grammar states at the same time. For example, there are two word arcs CAT (Sam) in Figure 15.5. Their HMM states should be considered as distinct states in the trellis because they are in completely different grammar states. Two different states in trellis also mean different paths going into these two states cannot be merged. Since these two partial paths will lead to different successive paths, the search decision needs to be postponed until the end of search. Therefore, when embedding HMM into word arc in grammar network, the HMM state will be assigned a new state identity although the HMM parameters (transition probabilities and output distributions) can still be shared across different grammar arcs.

Each path consists of a stack of production rules. Each element of the stack also contains the position within the production rule of the symbol that is currently being explored. The search graph (trellis) started from the initial state of CFG (state S). When the path needs to be extended, we look at the next

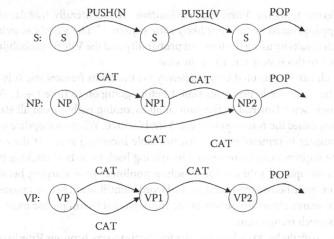

FIGURE 15.5   An simple RTN example with three types of arcs: CAT(x), PUSH(x), and POP.

arc (symbol in CFG) in the production. When the search enters a CAT(x) arc (terminal), the path gets extended with the terminal and the HMM trellis computation is performed on the CAT(x) arc to match the model x against the acoustic data. When the final state of the HMM for x is reached, the search moves on via the null transition to the destination of the CAT(x) arc. When the search enters a PUSH(x) arc, it indicates a nonterminal symbol x is encountered. In effect, the search is about to enter a subnetwork of x, the destination of the PUSH(x) arc is stored in a last in first out (LIFO) stack. When the search reaches a POP arc, the search returns to the state extracted from the top of the LIFO stack. Finally, when we reach the end of the production rule at the very bottom of the stack, we have reached an accepting state in which we have seen a complete grammatical sentence. For our decoding purpose, that is the state we want to pick as the best score at the end time frame T to obtain the search result.

The problem of connected word recognition by FSG or CFG is that the number of states increases enormously when it is applied to complex tasks and grammars. Moreover, it remains a challenge to generate such a FSG or a CFG from a large corpus, either manually or automatically. Finally, it is questionable if FSG or CFG is adequate to describe natural languages or unconstrained spontaneous languages. Instead, n-gram language models, which we described earlier in this section, are often used for natural languages or unconstrained spontaneous languages.

15.2.3.2 Time-Synchronous Viterbi Search
When HMMs are used for acoustic models, the acoustic model score (likelihood) used in search is by definition the forward probability. That is, all possible state sequences must be considered. Thus,

$$P(\mathbf{X}|\mathbf{W}) = \sum_{\text{all possibles}_0^T} P(\mathbf{X}, s_0^T|\mathbf{W})$$

where the summation is to be taken over all possible state sequences $\mathbf{S}$ with the word sequence $\mathbf{W}$ under consideration. However, under the trellis framework, more bookkeeping must be performed since we cannot add scores with different word sequence history. Since the goal of decoding is to uncover the best word sequence, we could approximate the summation with the maximum to find the best state sequence instead. We then have the following approximation:

$$\hat{\mathbf{W}} = \arg\max_{\mathbf{w}} P(\mathbf{W})P(\mathbf{X}|\mathbf{W}) \cong \arg\max_{\mathbf{w}} \left\{ P(\mathbf{W}) \max_{s_0^T} P(\mathbf{X}, s_0^T|\mathbf{W}) \right\}$$

which is often referred to as the *Viterbi approximation*. It can literally translated to "the *most likely word sequence* is approximated by the *most likely state sequence.*" The Viterbi search is then suboptimal. Although the search results by using the forward probability and the Viterbi probability could in principle be different, in practice this is very rare to be the case.

The Viterbi search can be executed very efficiently via the trellis framework. It is a time-synchronous search algorithm that completely processes time t before going on to time $t + 1$. For time t, each state is updated by the best score (instead of the sum of all incoming paths) from all states in at time $t - 1$. This is why it is often called the *time-synchronous Viterbi search*. When one update occurs, it also records the backtracking pointer to remember the most probable incoming state. At the end of the search, the most probable state sequence can be recovered by tracing back these backtracking pointers. The Viterbi algorithm provides an optimal solution for handling nonlinear time warping between HMMs and the acoustic observation, word boundary detection, and word identification in continuous speech recognition. This unified Viterbi search algorithm serves as the fundamental technique for most search algorithms in use in continuous speech recognition.

It is necessary to clarify the backtracking pointer for the time-synchronous Viterbi search for continuous word recognition. Actually, we are not interested in the optimal state sequence per se. Instead, we are only interested in the optimal word sequence Therefore, we use the backtrack pointer to just remember the word history for the current path, so the optimal word sequence can be recovered at the end of the search. To be more specific, when we reach the final state of a word, we create a history node containing the word identity and current time index and append this history node to the existing backtrack pointer. This backtrack pointer is then passed onto the successor node if it is the optimal path leading to the successor node for both intra-word and inter-word transition. The side benefit of keeping this backtrack pointer is that we no longer need to keep the entire trellis during the search. Instead, we only need space to keep two time-slices (columns) in the trellis computation (the previous time slice and the current time slice) because all the backtracking information is now kept in the backtrack pointer. This simplification is a significant benefit in the implementation of a time-synchronous Viterbi search.

The time-synchronous Viterbi search can be considered as a *breadth first search* with dynamic programming. Instead of performing a tree search algorithm, the dynamic programming principle helps to create a search graph where multiple paths leading to the same search state are merged by keeping the best path (with the minimum cost). The Viterbi trellis is a representation of the search graph. Therefore, all efficient techniques for graph search algorithms can be applied to the time-synchronous Viterbi search. Although we have so far described the trellis in an explicit fashion, where the entire search space needs to be explored before the optimal path can be found, it is not necessary to do so. When the search space contains an enormous number of states, it becomes impractical to pre-compile the composite HMM entirely and store it in the memory. It is preferable to dynamically build and allocate portions of the search space that is sufficient to search the promising paths. By using the graph search algorithm, only part of the entire Viterbi trellis is generated explicitly. By constructing the search space dynamically, the computation cost of the search is proportional only to the number of active hypotheses that is independent of the overall size of the potential search space. Therefore, dynamically generated trellis is a key to the heuristic Viterbi search for efficient large-vocabulary continuous speech recognition.

15.3 Major Historical Developments in Speech Recognition

Each of the above three components in speech-recognition technology has experienced significant historical development. In fact, the establishment of the basic statistical framework, as epitomized by the fundamental equation of speech recognition described in the preceding section in Equation 15.1 or 15.2, constitutes one major milestone in the historical development of speech recognition. In the following, we review and highlight this and other developments in the field, based partly on the recently published materials in Baker et al. (2007, 2009a,b).

In the first category of the significant historical developments in speech recognition are the establishment of the statistical paradigm, and the associated models and algorithms enabling the implementation of the paradigm. The most significant paradigm shift for speech-recognition progress has been the change from the earlier nonstatistical methods to statistical ones, especially stochastic processing with HMMs (Baker, 1975; Jelinek, 1976) introduced as an acoustic modeling component of speech recognition in the early 1970s. More than 30 years later, this methodology still remains as the predominant one. A number of models and algorithms have been efficiently incorporated within this framework. The Expectation-Maximization (EM) Algorithm and the Forward–Backward or the Baum–Welch algorithm (Baum, 1972; Dempster et al., 1977) have been the basic and principal means by which the HMMs are trained highly efficiently from data. Similarly, for the language-modeling component, N-gram language models and the variants, trained with the basic counting or EM-style techniques, have proved remarkably powerful and resilient. Beyond these basic algorithms, statistical discriminative training techniques have been developed since late 1980s based not on the likelihood for data-matching criteria but on maximum mutual information or related minimum error criteria (Bahl et al., 1986; Povey et al., 2005; He et al., 2008). And beyond the basic HMM-like acoustic models and basic N-gram-like language models, further developments include segmental models (Poritz, 1988; Deng, 1993, 1994; Ostendorf et al., 1996; Deng and Sameti, 1996; Glass, 2003), and structured speech and language models (Chelba and Jelinek, 2000; Wang et al., 2000; Deng et al., 2006). Despite continuing work in this area, however, large-scale success is yet to be demonstrated.

Another important area of algorithm development is adaptation, which is vital to accommodating a wide range of variable conditions for the channel, noise, speaker, vocabulary, accent, and recognition domain, etc. Effective adaptation algorithms enable rapid application integration, and are a key to the successful commercial deployment of speech-recognition technology. The most popular adaptation techniques include Maximum a Posteriori probability (MAP) estimation (Gauvain and Lee, 1994) and Maximum Likelihood Linear Regression (MLLR) (Leggetter and Woodland, 1995). Training can take place on the basis of small amounts of data from new tasks or domains for additional training material, as well as "one-shot" learning or "unsupervised" learning at test time (Huang and Lee, 1993). These adaptation techniques have also been generalized to train the "generic" models so that they are better able to represent the overall statistics of the full training data set, a technique called Speaker Adaptive Training or SAT (Anastasakos et al., 1997).

In the second category of the significant advancement in speech recognition is the establishment of the computational infrastructure that enables the above statistical model/algorithm developments. Moore's Law observes long-term progress in computer development, and predicts doubling the amount of computation for a given cost every 12–18 months, as well as a comparably shrinking cost of memory. These have been instrumental in enabling speech-recognition researchers to develop and evaluate complex algorithms on sufficiently large tasks in order to make realistic progress. In addition, the availability of common speech corpora for speech training, development, and evaluation, has been critical, allowing the creation of complex systems of ever-increasing capabilities. Since speech is a highly variable signal and is characterized by many parameters, large corpora become critical in modeling it well enough for automated systems to achieve proficiency. Over the years, these corpora have been created, annotated, and distributed to the worldwide community by the National Institute of Standard and Technology (NIST), the Linguistic Data Consortium (LDC), European Language Resources Association (ELRA), and other organizations. The character of the recorded speech has progressed from limited, constrained speech materials to huge amounts of progressively more realistic, spontaneous speech. The development and adoption of rigorous benchmark evaluations and standards, nurtured by NIST and others, have also been critical in developing increasingly powerful and capable systems. Many labs and researchers have benefited from the availability of common research tools such as HTK, Sphinx, CMU LM toolkit, and SRILM toolkit. Extensive research support combined with workshops, task definitions, and system evaluations sponsored by DARPA (the U.S. Department of Defense Advanced Research Projects Agency) and others have been essential to today's system developments.

Historically significant advancement of speech recognition has the third category that we call knowledge representation. This includes the development of perceptually motivated speech signal representations such as Mel-Frequency Cepstral Coefficients (MFCC) (Davis and Mermelstein, 1980) and Perceptual Linear Prediction (PLP) coefficients (Hermansky, 1990), as well as normalizations via Cepstral Mean Subtraction (CMS) (Rosenberg et al., 1994), RASTA (Hermansky and Morgan, 1994), and Vocal Tract Length Normalization (VTLN) (Eide and Gish, 1996). Architecturally, the most important development in knowledge representation has been searchable unified graph representations that allow multiple sources of knowledge to be incorporated into a common probabilistic framework. Non-compositional methods include multiple speech streams, multiple probability estimators, multiple recognition systems combined at the hypothesis level, for example, ROVER (Fiscus, 1997), and multi-pass systems with increasing constraints (bigram vs. four-gram, within word dependencies vs. cross-word, etc.). More recently, the use of multiple algorithms, applied both in parallel and sequentially has proven fruitful, as have multiple types of feature-based transformations such as heteroscedastic linear discriminant analysis (HLDA) (Kumar and Andreou, 1998), feature-space minimum phone error (fMPE) (Povey et al., 2005), and neural net-based features (Morgan et al., 2005).

The final category of major historical significant developments in speech recognition includes key decoding or search strategies that we have discussed earlier in this section. These strategies have focused on the stack decoding (A* search) (Jelinek, 1969) and the time-synchronous Viterbi search (Viterbi, 1967; Vintsyuk, 1968; Sakoe and Chiba, 1971; Ney, 1984). Without these practical decoding algorithms, large-scale continuous speech recognition would not be possible.

15.4 Speech-Recognition Applications

The ultimate impact of speech recognition depends on whether one can fully integrate the enabling technologies with applications. How to effectively integrate speech into applications often depends on the nature of the user interface and application. In discussing some general principles and guidelines in developing spoken language applications, we must look closely at designing the user interface.

A well-designed user interface entails carefully considering the particular user group of the application and delivering an application that works effectively and efficiently. As a general guideline, one needs to make sure that the interface matches the way users want to accomplish a task. One also needs to use the most appropriate modality at the appropriate time to assist users to achieve their goals. One unique challenge in speech-recognition applications is that speech recognition (as well as understanding) is imperfect. In addition, the spoken command can be ambiguous so a dialogue strategy is necessary to clarify the goal of the speaker. There are always mistakes one has to deal with. It is critical that applications employ necessary interactive error handling techniques to minimize the impact of these errors. Application developers should therefore fully understand the strengths and weaknesses of the underlying speech technologies and identify the appropriate place to use speech recognition and understanding technology effectively.

There are three broad classes of applications. (1) Cloud-based call center/IVR (Interactive Voice Response): This includes the widely used applications from Tellme's information access over the phone to Microsoft Exchange Unified Messaging. (2) PC-based dictation/command and control: There are a number of dictation applications on the PC. It is a useful tool for accessibility benefits, but not yet ready for the mainstream. (3) Device-based embedded command control: There is a wide range of devices that do not have a typical PC keyboard or mouse, and the traditional GUI application cannot be directly extended. As an example, Microsoft's Response Point blue button illustrates what speech interface can do to make the user interface much simpler. Mobile phones and automobile scenarios are also very suitable for speech applications. Because of the physical size and hands-busy and eyes-busy constraints, the traditional GUI application interaction model requires a significant modification. Ford SYNC is a

FIGURE 15.6 Ford SYNC highlights the car's speech interface—"You talk. SYNC listens."

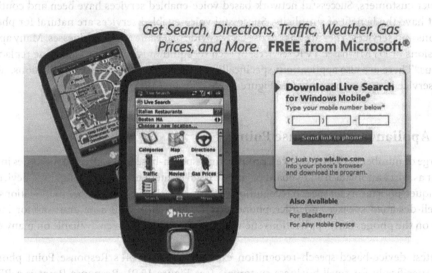

FIGURE 15.7 Bing Search highlights speech functions—just say what you're looking for!

good example on leveraging the power of speech technologies in this category (Figure 15.6). Voice search is also highly suitable for mobile phones (Figure 15.7).

Speech interface has the potential to provide a consistent and unified interaction model across these scenarios. The increased mobility of our society demanded access to information and services at anytime and anywhere. Both cloud and client-based voice-enabled applications can vastly enhance the user experience and optimize cost savings for businesses. We here in this section selectively take some examples as case studies to illustrate real-world applications and challenges.

15.4.1 IVR Applications

Given that speech recognizers make mistakes, the inconvenience to the user must be minimized. This means that careful design of human/machine interaction (e.g., the call flow) is essential in providing reliable and acceptable services. Hence, a demand for skilled user interface designers has occurred over the past decade.

Because of the increased adoption of the Web, IVR-based interaction provides a more ubiquitous but less effective information access than Web-based browsing. Because the phone is widely available, there is an important empirical principle to decide if the IVR should be deployed. If the customer can wait for more than two hours to get the information, the need to have the speech-based IVR would be less critical. This is because the Web has been very pervasive and generally provides a better user interface for customers to access the information. If the task is time sensitive, and the customer may be on the move without having the access to a PC, such IVR applications would bridge the gap and provide a complementary value. The key benefit of network-based IVR services is to provide the user with access to information independent of the user's communication device or location.

In 2005, Forrester Research published a study reporting that on average, call center human agents can cost \$5.50–\$12.00 per call and speech-enabled IVR services could reduce that down to \$0.20/call. With significantly improved natural speech applications, businesses can gain increased call completion rates and happier customers. Successful network-based voice-enabled services have been and continue to be those that have the benefit of simplicity. Successful voice-enabled services are natural for phone-based applications and services. They are easy to use and provide real value to the businesses. Many applications are extensions of DTMF-based IVR services. Speech recognition is used as a touchtone replacement for IVR menus. There are also applications specifically designed for speech-based applications. Microsoft's Tellme's service is such an example (see Figure 15.8).

15.4.2 Appliance—"Response Point"

With a large of number of diverse devices, proliferating, speech-based user interface becomes increasingly important as we cannot attach a keyboard or mouse to all of these devices. Among these devices, phones offer a unique opportunity for speech recognition as they are designed for voice communications equipped with a well-designed speaker and microphone already. Speech is such a natural way for information exchange on the phone. Early applications such as phone dialing have been available on many embedded devices.

One latest device-based speech-recognition example is Microsoft's Response Point phone system designed specifically for small business customers (see Figure 15.9). Response Point is a PBX system that runs on an embedded device without having any moving parts such as hard disk or cooling fan. It provides a comprehensive telephony solution for small business including PBX functions, unified messaging, computer telephony integration and basic IVR for finding people, location, and business hours. The key differentiation feature is a unique blue button on every Response Point phone. The blue button allows speakers to simply push the button and issue command for a wide range of communications tasks such as name dialing, transferring the call, and checking voice mails. Response Point is very simple to use, and helps to bring speech applications to the non-technological savvy customers.

15.4.3 Mobile Applications

The HMM technology has proven to be an effective method for mobile phones including dictation and name dialing. For example, Nuance offers the HMM-based speaker-independent dialer in a wide range of mobile phones. Client-based speech recognition has the benefit of low-latency.

FIGURE 15.8   Microsoft's Tellme is integrated into Windows Mobile at the network level.

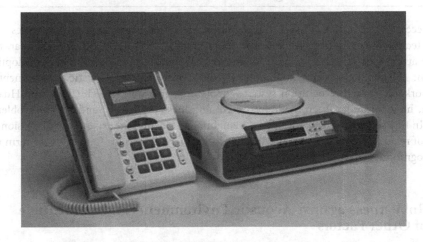

FIGURE 15.9   Microsoft's Response Point phone system designed specifically for small business customers.

Ford SYNC is a factory-installed, in-car communications and entertainment system. The system runs on most Ford, Lincoln, and Mercury vehicles. Ford SYNC allows drivers to bring nearly any mobile phone or digital media player into their vehicle and operate them using voice commands, the vehicle's steering wheel, or radio controls.

One special type of applications in the mobile environment is voice search (Wang et al., 2008). Voice search provides mobile phone users with the information they request with a spoken query. The information normally exists in a large database, and the query has to be compared with a field in the database to obtain the relevant information. The contents of the field, such as business or product names, are often unstructured text. While general voice search accuracy is not usable, structured voice search with constrained contexts have been on the market. Google Voice Local Search is now live and publicly available. Microsoft has Windows Live local search that is speech-enabled. Automated voice-based mobile search establishes a clear competitive landscape, which will likely mean a further decline in call volumes and revenues for traditional mobile directory assistance, as consumers become more aware of the availability of these free services.

Windows Live local search is a multimodal application. The widespread availability of broadband access and powerful mobile devices are fostering a new wave of human computer interfaces that support multiple modalities, thus bridging and eventually blurring the device and network voice-enabled service markets. Multimodal interfaces also solve many of today's limitations with speech applications. A picture is worth a thousand words. We believe "speech-in" and "picture-out" takes advantage of the two most natural human modalities that significantly enhance the user experience when dealing with complex applications.

As a conclusion of this section, we will see greater roles of speech recognition in the future's anytime, anywhere, and any-channel communications. The greater automation of telecommunications services, and for individuals, easier access to information and services at any time, with any device, and from anywhere, as well as in any language will be the norm. Customers will benefit from rapid and personalized information access, partly empowered by speech recognition and the related technologies. Speech recognition has just scratched the surface. But to enable this ultimate success, difficult challenges need to be overcome and intensive research is need, which is the subject of the next section.

15.5 Technical Challenges and Future Research Directions

Despite successful applications of speech recognition in the marketplace and people's lives as described above, the technology is far from being perfect and technical challenges abound. Some years ago (2003–2004), the authors of this chapter have identified two main technical challenges in adopting speech recognition: (1) making speech-recognition systems robust in noisy acoustic environments, and (2) creating workable speech-recognition systems for natural, free-style speech (Deng and Huang, 2004). Since then, huge stride has been made in overcoming these challenges, and yet the problems remain unsolved. In this section, we will address the remaining problems and expand the discussion to include a number of related and new challenges. We also discuss fertile areas for future, longer-term research in speech recognition.

15.5.1 Robustness against Acoustic Environments and a Multitude of Other Factors

As discussed in the preceding section, state-of-the-art speech recognition has been built upon a solid statistical framework after a series of successful historical developments. The statistical framework requires probabilistic models, with parameters estimated from sample speech data, which represents the variability that occurs in the natural speech data. These probabilistic models seek to recover linguistic information, such as the words or phrases uttered, from the speech signal received by microphones placed under natural acoustic environments. One key underlying challenge to speech recognition technology is the special complexity of the variability that exists in the natural speech signal. How to identify and handle a multitude of variability factors, some are related to and others are unrelated to the linguistic information being sought by the speech-recognition system, forms one principal source of technical difficulties in building successful speech-recognition systems.

One pervasive type of variability in the speech signal that is typically extraneous to the linguistic information to be decoded by speech recognizers is caused by the acoustic environment. This includes background noise, room reverberation, the channel through which the speech is acquired (such as cellular, land-line, and VoIP), overlapping speech, and Lombard or hyper-articulated speech. The acoustic environment in which the speech is captured and the communication channel through which the speech signal is transmitted prior to its processing represent significant causes of harmful variability that is responsible for the drastic degradation of system performance. Existing techniques are able to reduce variability caused by additive noise or linear distortions, as well as compensate for slowly varying linear channels (Droppo and Acero, 2008; Frey et al., 2001; Deng et al., 2004; Yu et al., 2008). However, more complex channel distortions such as reverberation or fast changing noise, as well as the Lombard effect present a significant challenge to be overcome in future research.

Another common type of speech variability that has been studied intensively is due to different speakers' characteristics. It is well known that speech characteristics vary widely among speakers due to many factors, including speaker physiology, speaker style, and accents—both regional and nonnative. The primary method currently used for making speech-recognition systems more robust to variations in speaker characteristics is to include a wide range of speakers (and speaking styles) in the training. Speaker adaptation mildly alleviates problems with new speakers within the "span" of known speaker/speaking types, but fail for new types. Further, current speech-recognition systems assume a pronunciation lexicon that models native speakers of a language and train on large amounts of speech data from various native speakers of the language. As discussed in the preceding section, a number approaches have been explored in explicit modeling of accented speech and in adaptation of native acoustic models via a moderate amount of accented speech data. Pronunciation variants have also been incorporated in the lexicon to accommodate accented speech, but except for small gains, the problem is largely unsolved. Similarly, some progress has been made for automatically detecting speaking rate from the speech signal, but such knowledge has not been exploited in speech-recognition systems, mainly due to the lack of any explicit mechanism to model speaking rate in the recognition process. Further research is needed to accommodate speaker-related variability.

The third common type of speech variability is related to language characteristics including sublanguage or dialect, vocabulary, and genre or topic of conversation. Many important aspects of speaker variability have to do with nonstandard dialects. Dialectal differences in a language can occur in all linguistic aspects: lexicon, grammar (syntax and morphology), and phonology. The vocabulary and language-use in a speech-recognition task change significantly from task to task, necessitating the estimation of new language models for each case. A primary reason language models in current speech-recognition systems are not portable across tasks even within the same language or dialect is that they lack linguistic sophistication—they cannot consistently distinguish meaningful sentences from meaningless ones, nor grammatical from ungrammatical ones. Discourse structure is not considered either, merely the local collocation of words. Another reason why language model adaptation to new domains and genre is very data intensive is the "nonparametric" nature of the current models.

The technical challenge in this area of research will entail the creation and development of systems that would be much more robust against all kinds of variability discussed above, including changes in acoustic environments, reverberation, external noise sources, and communication channels. New techniques and architectures need to be developed to enable exploring these critical issues in meaningful environments as diverse as meeting room presentations to unstructured conversations.

It is fair to say that the acoustic models used in today's speech systems have few explicit mechanisms to accommodate most of the underlying causes of variability described above. The statistical components of the model, such as Gaussian mixtures and Markov chains in the HMM, are instead burdened with implicitly modeling the variability using different mixture components and HMM states and in a frame-by-frame manner. Consequently, when the speech presented to a system deviates along one of these axes from the speech used for parameter estimation, predictions by the models become highly suspect. The performance of the technology degrades catastrophically even when the deviations are such that the intended human listener exhibits little or no difficulty in extracting the same information. The robustness of speech recognition against all these variability factors constitutes a major technical challenge in the field.

The hope for meeting this challenge lies not only in innovative architectures and techniques/algorithms that can intelligently represent explicit mechanisms for the real nature of speech variability, but perhaps more importantly, also in the ever-increasing data available to train and adapt the speech-recognition models in ways not feasible in the past.

15.5.2 Capitalizing on Data Deluge for Speech Recognition

We now have some very exciting opportunities to collect large amounts of audio data that have not previously been available. This gives rise to "data deluge." Thanks in large part to the Internet, there are now readily accessible large quantities of "everyday" speech, reflecting a variety of materials and environments previously unavailable. Other rich sources are university course lectures, seminars, and similar material, which are progressively being put online. All these materials reflect a less formal, more spontaneous, and natural form of speech than present-day systems have typically been developed to recognize. Recently emerging voice search in mobile phones has also provided a rich source of speech data, which, because of the recording of the mobile phone users' selection, can be considered as partially "labeled."

One practical benefit of working with these new speech materials is that systems will become more capable and more robust in expanding the range of speech materials that can be accurately recognized under a wide range of conditions. Much of what is learned here is also likely to be of benefit in recognizing casual "everyday" speech in non-English languages.

Over the years, the availability of both open source and commercial speech tools has been very effective in quickly bringing good quality speech processing capabilities to many labs and researchers. New Web-based tools could be made available to collect, annotate, and then process substantial quantities of speech very cost-effectively in many languages. Mustering the assistance of interested individuals on the World Wide Web (e.g., open source software, Wikipedia, etc.) could generate substantial quantities of language resources very efficiently and cost-effectively. This could be especially valuable for creating significant new capabilities for resource "impoverished" languages.

The ever-increasing amount of data, which is increasingly available to help build speech-recognition systems, presents both an opportunity and a challenge for advancing the state of the art in speech recognition. Large corpora of diverse speech will have to be compiled containing speech that carries information of the kind targeted for extraction by speech recognition. It should also exhibit large but usefully normalized extraneous deviations of the kind against which robustness is sought, such as a diverse speaker population with varying degrees of nonnative accents or different local dialects, widely varying channels and acoustic environments, diverse genre, etc.

Speech-recognition technology has barely scratched the surface in sampling the many kinds of speech, environments, and channels that people routinely experience. In fact, we currently provide to our automatic systems only a very small fraction of the amount of materials that humans utilize to acquire language. If we want our systems to be more powerful and to understand the nature of speech itself, we need to make more use of it and label more of it. Well-labeled speech corpora have been the cornerstone on which today's systems have been developed and evolved. However, most of the large quantities of data are not labeled or poorly "labeled," and labeling them accurately is costly. There is an urgent and practical need to develop high-quality active learning and unsupervised/semi-supervised learning techniques. Upon their successful development, the exploitation of unlabeled or partially labeled data becomes possible to train the models, and we can automatically (and "actively") select parts of the unlabeled data for manual labeling in a way that maximizes its utility. This need is partly related to the compilation of diverse training data discussed earlier. The range of possible combinations of channel, speaker, environment, speaking style, and domain is so large that it is unrealistic to expect transcribed or labeled speech in every configuration of conditions for training the models. However, it is feasible to simply collect raw speech in all conditions of interest. Another important reason for unsupervised learning is that the systems, like their human "baseline," will have to undergo "lifelong learning," adjusting to evolving vocabulary, channels, language use, etc.

Large amounts of speech data will enable multi-stream and multiple-module strategies for speech recognition to be developed. Robust methods are needed to identify reliable elements of the speech spectrum in a data-driven manner by employing an entire ensemble of analyses. A multiple-module approach also entails a new search strategy that treats the reliability of a module or stream in any instance as another hidden variable over which to optimize, and seeks the most likely hypothesis over all configurations of these hidden variables.

15.5.3 Self-Learning and Adaptation for Speech Recognition

State-of-the-art systems for speech recognition are based on statistical models estimated from labeled training data, such as transcribed speech, and from human-supplied knowledge, such as pronunciation dictionaries. Such built-in knowledge often becomes obsolete fairly quickly after a system is deployed in a real-world application, and significant and recurring human intervention in the form of retraining is needed to sustain the utility of the system. This is in sharp contrast with the speech facility in humans, which is constantly updated over a lifetime, routinely acquiring new vocabulary items and idiomatic expressions, as well as deftly handling previously unseen nonnative accents and regional dialects of a language. In particular, humans exhibit a remarkable aptitude for learning the sublanguage of a new domain or application without explicit supervision.

The challenge here is to create self-adaptive or self-learning techniques that will endow speech recognizers with at least a rudimentary form of the human's self-learning capability. There is a need for learning at all levels of speech and language processing to cope with changing environments, nonspeech sounds, speakers, pronunciations, dialects, accents, words, meanings, and topics, to name but a few sources of variation over the lifetime of a deployed system. Like its human counterpart, the system would engage in automatic pattern discovery, active learning, and adaptation. Research in this area must address both the learning of new models and the integration of such models into preexisting knowledge sources. Thus, an important aspect of learning is being able to discern when something has been learned and how to apply the result. Learning from multiple concurrent modalities, for example, new text and video, may also be necessary. For instance, a speech-recognition system may encounter a new proper noun in its input speech, and may need to examine contemporaneous text with matching context to determine the spelling of the name. The exploitation of unlabeled or partially labeled data would be necessary for such learning, perhaps including the automatic selection (by the system) of parts of the unlabeled data for manual labeling, in a way that maximizes its utility.

A motivation for the research direction on developing speech recognizers' self-learning capability is the growing activity in the allied field of Machine Learning. Success in this endeavor would extend the lifetime of deployed systems, and directly advance our ability to develop speech systems in new languages and domains without onerous demands of labeled speech, essentially by creating systems that automatically learn and improve over time.

One most important aspect of learning is generalization. When a small amount of test data is available to adjust speech recognizers, we call such generalization as adaptation. Adaptation and generalization capabilities enable rapid speech-recognition application integration.

Over the past three decades, the speech community has developed and refined an experimental methodology that has helped to foster steady improvements in speech technology. The approach that has worked well, and been adopted in other research communities, is to develop shared corpora, software tools, and guidelines that can be used to reduce differences between experimental setups down to the basic algorithms, so that it becomes easier to quantify fundamental improvements. Typically, these corpora are focused on a particular task. As speech technology has become more sophisticated, the scope and difficulty of these tasks has continually increased: from isolated words to continuous speech, from speaker-dependent to independent, from read to spontaneous speech, from clean to noisy, from utterance to content-based, etc. Although the complexity of such corpora has continually increased, one common property of such tasks is that they typically have a training partition that is quite similar in nature to the test data. Indeed, obtaining large quantities of training data that is closely matched to the test is perhaps the single most reliable method to improve speech-recognition performance. This strategy is quite different from the human experience however. For our entire lives, we are exposed to all kinds of speech data from uncontrolled environments, speakers, and topics, (i.e., "every day" speech). Despite this variation in our own personal training data, we are all able to create internal models of speech and language that are remarkably adept at dealing with variation in the speech chain. This ability to generalize is a key aspect of human speech processing that has not yet found its way into modern speech recognizers. Research activities on this topic should produce technology that will operate more effectively in novel circumstances, and that can generalize better from smaller amounts of data. Examples include moving from one acoustic environment to another, different tasks, languages, etc. Another research area could explore how well information gleaned from large resource languages and/or domains generalize to smaller resource languages and domains.

15.5.4 Developing Speech Recognizers beyond the Language Barrier

State-of-the-art speech recognition systems today deliver top performances by building complex acoustic and language models using a large collection of domain- and language-specific speech and text examples. This set of language resources is often not readily available for many languages. The challenge here is to create spoken language technologies that are rapidly portable. To prepare for rapid development of such spoken language systems, a new paradigm is needed to study speech and acoustic units that are more language-universal than language-specific phones. Three specific research issues need to be addressed: (1) cross-language acoustic modeling of speech and acoustic units for a new target language, (2) cross-lingual lexical modeling of word pronunciations for new language, (3) cross-lingual language modeling. By exploring correlation between these emerging languages and well-studied languages, cross-language properties (e.g., language clustering and universal acoustic modeling can be utilized to facilitate the rapid adaptation of acoustic and language models. Bootstrapping techniques are also keys to building preliminary systems from a small amount of labeled utterances first, using them to label more utterance examples in an unsupervised manner, incorporating new-labeled data into the label set, and iterating to improve the systems until they reach a comparable performance level similar to today's high-accuracy systems.

15.5.5 Detection of Unknown Events in Speech Recognition

Current ASR systems have difficulty in handling unexpected—and thus often the most information rich—lexical items. This is especially problematic in speech that contains interjections or foreign or out-of-vocabulary words, and in languages for which there is relatively little data with which to build the system's vocabulary and pronunciation lexicon. A common outcome in this situation is that high-value terms are overconfidently misrecognized as some other common and similar-sounding word. Yet, such spoken events are key to tasks such as spoken term detection and information extraction from speech. Their accurate detection is therefore of vital importance.

The challenge here is to create systems that reliably detect when they do not know a (correct) word. A clue to the occurrence of such error events is the mismatch between an analysis of a purely sensory signal unencumbered by prior knowledge, such as unconstrained phone recognition, and a word- or phrase-level hypothesis based on higher level knowledge, often encoded in a language model. A key component of this research would therefore be to develop novel confidence measures and accurate models of uncertainty based on the discrepancy between sensory evidence and *a priori* beliefs. A natural sequel to detection of such events would be to transcribe them phonetically when the system is confident that its word hypothesis is unreliable, and to devise error-correction schemes.

15.5.6 Learning from Human Speech Perception and Production

As a long-term research direction, one principal knowledge source that we can draw to benefit machine speech recognition is in the area of human speech perception, understanding, and cognition. This rich knowledge source has its basis in both psychological and physiological processes in humans. Physiological aspects of the human speech perception of most interest include cortical processing in the auditory area as well as in the associated motor area of the brain. One important principle of auditory perception is its modular organization, and recent advances in functional neuroimaging technologies provide a driving force motivating new studies toward developing the integrated knowledge of the modularly organized auditory process in an end-to-end manner. The psychological aspects of human speech perception embody the essential psychoacoustic properties that underlie auditory masking and attention. Such key properties equip human listeners with the remarkable capability of coping with cocktail party effects that no current automatic speech-recognition techniques can successfully handle. Intensive studies are needed in order for speech recognition and understanding applications to reach a new level, delivering performance comparable to humans.

Specific issues to be resolved in the study of how the human brain processes spoken (as well as written) language are the way human listeners adapt to nonnative accents and the time course over which human listeners reacquaint themselves to a language known to them. Humans have amazing capabilities to adapt to nonnative accents. Current speech-recognition systems are extremely poor in this aspect, and the improvement is expected only after we have sufficient understanding of human speech processing mechanisms. One specific issue related to human speech perception, which is linked to human speech production, is the temporal span over which speech signals are represented and modeled. One prominent weakness in current HMMs is the handicap in representing long-span temporal dependency in the acoustic feature sequence of speech, which, nevertheless, is an essential property of speech dynamics in both perception and production. The main cause of this handicap is the conditional independence assumptions inherit in the HMM formalism. The HMM framework also assumes that speech can be described as a sequence of discrete units, usually phone(me)s. In this symbolic, invariant approach, the focus is on the linguistic/phonetic information, and the incoming speech signal is normalized during preprocessing in order to remove most of the paralinguistic information. However, human speech perception experiments have shown that the paralinguistic information plays a crucial role in human speech perception.

Numerous approaches have been taken over the past dozen years to address the above weaknesses of HMMs. These approaches can be broadly classified into the following two categories. The first, parametric, structure-based approach establishes mathematical models for stochastic trajectories/segments of speech utterances using various forms of parametric characterization. The essence of such an approach is that it exploits knowledge and mechanisms of human speech perception and production so as to provide the structure of the multitiered stochastic process models. These parametric models account for the observed speech trajectory data based on the underlying mechanisms of speech coarticulation and reduction directly relevant to human speech perception, and on the relationship between speaking rate variations and the corresponding changes in the acoustic features. The second, nonparametric and template-based approach to overcoming the HMM weaknesses involves the direct exploitation of speech feature trajectories (i.e., "template") in the training data without any modeling assumptions. This newer approach is based on episodic learning as evidenced in many recent human speech perception and recognition experiments. Due to the dramatic increase of speech databases and computer storage capacity available for training, as well as the exponentially expanded computational power, nonparametric methods and episodic learning provide rich areas for future research. The essence of the template-based approach is that it captures strong dynamic segmental information about speech feature sequences in a way complimentary to the parametric, structure-based approach.

Understanding human speech perception will provide a wealth of information enabling the construction of better models (than HMMs) that reflect attributes of human auditory processing and the linguistic units used in human speech recognition. For example, to what extent may human listeners use mixed word or phrase "templates" and the constituent phonetic/phonological units in their memory to achieve relatively high-performance in speech recognition for accented speech or foreign languages (weak knowledge) and for acoustically distorted speech (weak observation)? How do human listeners use episodic learning (e.g., direct memory access) and parametric learning related to smaller phonetic units (analogous to what we are currently using for HMMs in machines) in speech recognition/understanding? Answers to these questions will benefit our design of next-generation machine speech-recognition models and algorithms.

15.5.7 Capitalizing on New Trends in Computational Architectures for Speech Recognition

Moore's law has been a dependable indicator of the increased capability for computation and storage in our computational systems for decades. The resulting effects on systems for speech recognition and understanding have been enormous, permitting the use of larger and larger training databases and recognition systems, and the incorporation of more and more detailed models of spoken language. Many of the future research directions and applications suggested in this chapter implicitly depend upon a continued advance in computational capabilities, an assumption that certainly seems justified given recent history. However, the fundamentals of this progression have recently changed. As Intel and others have noted recently, the power density on microprocessors has increased to the point that higher clock rates would begin to melt the silicon. Consequently, at this point, industry development is now focused on implementing microprocessors on multiple cores. Dual core CPUs are now very common, and four-processor and eight-processor systems are coming out. The new road maps for the semiconductor industry reflect this trend, and future speedups will come more from parallelism than from having faster individual computing elements.

For the most part, algorithm designers for speech systems have ignored investigation of such parallelism, partly because the advance of scalability has been so reliable. Future research directions and applications discussed in this chapter will require significantly more computation, and consequently researchers concerned with implementation will need to consider parallelism explicitly in their designs. This will be a significant change from the status quo. In particular, tasks such as decoding, for which extremely clever schemes to speed up single-processor performance have been developed, will require a complete rethinking of the algorithms.

15.5.8 Embedding Knowledge and Parallelism into Speech-Recognition Decoding

Decoding or search is one of the three major components in the general statistical speech-recognition architecture, as we overviewed earlier in this chapter on the conventional techniques developed including the time-synchronous Viterbi search and the stack search. These search algorithms were developed long before parallelism came into being. New search methods that explicitly exploit parallelism as a novel computational architecture may be an important research direction for speech understanding systems.

Additionally, as innovative recognition algorithms are added, there will be impact on the search component. For instance, rather than the left-to-right (and sometimes right-to-left) recognition passes that are used today, there could be advantages to either identifying islands of reliability or islands of uncertainty, and rely upon alternate knowledge sources only "locally" in the search process. The incorporation of multiple tiers of units (e.g., Deng and Sun, 1994; Sun and Deng, 2002), such as articulatory feature, sub-phone state, phone, syllable, word, and multi-word phrase, could have consequences for the search process.

Further, so-called episodic approaches to speech recognition are being investigated (Wachter et al., 2003). These approaches rely on examples of phrases, words, or other units directly, as opposed to statistical models of speech. While this seems to be a throwback to the days before the prominence of

HMMs, the idea is gaining new prominence due to the availability of larger and larger speech databases, and thus more and more examples for each modeled speech unit (Deng and Strik, 2007). One future research direction would be to learn how to best incorporate these approaches into a search that also uses statistical models, which have already proven their worth.

15.6 Summary

Speech recognition has a long history of development. It is not until the introduction of the statistical framework that the field has enjoyed steadfast progress and has opened up many practical applications. Three main components (acoustic modeling, language modeling, and decoding) discussed in this chapter can be found in most modern speech-recognition systems. Each of these components has had significant milestones in the historical developments. Beyond the set of applications discussed in this chapter, we believe other speech applications will proliferate thanks to the increased power of computing, mobile communications, and multimodal user interface, as well as to new breakthroughs and research advances in the field. Some of the fertile areas for future research discussed in Section 15.5 provide potential advances that may lead to new speech technology applications.

References

Anastasakos, T., J. McDonough, and J. Makhoul (1997). Speaker adaptive training: A maximum likelihood approach to speaker normalization, in *Proceedings of the IEEE International Conference on Acoustics, Speech, and Signal Processing*, pp. 1043–1046, Munich, Germany.

Bahl, L., P. Brown, P. de Souza, and R. Mercer (1986). Maximum mutual information estimation of hidden Markov model parameters for speech recognition, in *Proceedings of the IEEE International Conference on Acoustics, Speech, and Signal Processing*, pp. 49–52, Tokyo, Japan.

Baker, J. (1975). Stochastic modeling for automatic speech recognition, in D. R. Reddy, (ed.), *Speech Recognition*, Academic Press, New York.

Baker, J., L. Deng, J. Glass, S. Khudanpur, C.-H. Lee, and N. Morgan (2007). MINDS report: Historical development and future directions in speech recognition and understanding. http://www-nlpir.nist.gov/MINDS/FINAL/speech.web.pdf.

Baker, J., L. Deng, J. Glass, S. Khudanpur, C.-H. Lee, N. Morgan, and D. O'Shaughnessy (2009a). Updated MINDS report on speech recognition and understanding part I, *IEEE Signal Processing Magazine*, 26(3), 75–80.

Baker, J., L. Deng, J. Glass, S. Khudanpur, C.-H. Lee, N. Morgan, and D. O'Shaughnessy (2009b). Updated MINDS report on speech recognition and understanding part II, *IEEE Signal Processing Magazine*, 26(4), 78–85.

Baum, L. (1972). An inequality and associated maximization technique occurring in statistical estimation for probabilistic functions of a Markov process, *Inequalities*, III, 1–8.

Breiman, L., J. Friedman, R. Olshen, and C. Stone (1984). *Classification and Regression Trees*, Wadsworth & Brooks, Pacific Grove, CA.

Chelba C. and F. Jelinek (2000). Structured language modeling, *Computer Speech and Language*, 14, 283–332.

Davis, S. and P. Mermelstein (1980). Comparison of parametric representations for monosyllabic word recognition in continuously spoken sentences, *IEEE Transactions on Acoustics, Speech, and Signal Processing*, 28(4), 357–366.

Dempster, A., N. Laird, and D. Rubin (1977). Maximum likelihood from incomplete data via the EM algorithm, *Journal of the Royal Statistical Society*, 39(1), 1–21.

Deng, L. (1993). A stochastic model of speech incorporating hierarchical nonstationarity, *IEEE Transactions on Speech and Audio Processing*, 1(4), 471–475.

Deng, L. and X. D. Huang (2004). Challenges in adopting speech recognition, *Communications of the ACM*, 47(1), 11–13.

Deng, L. and D. O'Shaughnessy (2003). *Speech Processing—A Dynamic and Optimization-Oriented Approach*, Marcel Dekker Inc., New York.

Deng, L. and H. Sameti (1996). Transitional speech units and their representation by the regressive Markov states: Applications to speech recognition, *IEEE Transactions on Speech and Audio Processing*, 4(4), 301–306.

Deng, L. and H. Strik (2007). Structure-based and template-based automatic speech recognition— Comparing parametric and non-parametric approaches, in *Proceedings of the 8th Annual Conference of the International Speech Communication Association Interspeech*, Antwerp, Belgium.

Deng, L. and D. Sun (1994). A statistical approach to automatic speech recognition using the atomic speech units constructed from overlapping articulatory features, *Journal of the Acoustical Society of America*, 85(5), 2702–2719.

Deng, L., M. Aksmanovic, D. Sun, and J. Wu (1994). Speech recognition using hidden Markov models with polynomial regression functions as nonstationary states, *IEEE Transactions on Speech and Audio Processing*, 2, 507–520.

Deng, L., J. Droppo, and A. Acero (2004). Estimating cepstrum of speech under the presence of noise using a joint prior of static and dynamic features, *IEEE Transactions on Speech and Audio Processing*, 12(3), 218–233.

Deng, L., D. Yu, and A. Acero (2006). Structured speech modeling, *IEEE Transactions on Audio, Speech and Language Processing (Special Issue on Rich Transcription)*, 14(5), 1492–1504.

Droppo, J. and A. Acero (2008). Environmental robustness, in *Handbook of Speech Processing*, pp. 653–680, Springer-Verlag, Berlin, Germany.

Eide E. and H. Gish (1996). A parametric approach to vocal tract length normalization, in *Proceedings of the International Conference on Acoustics, Speech, and Signal Processing*, pp. 346–349, Atlanta, GA.

Fiscus, J. (1997). A post-processing system to yield reduced word error rates: Recognizer output voting error reduction (ROVER), *IEEE Automatic Speech Recognition and Understanding Workshop*, pp. 3477–3482, Santa Barbara, CA.

Frey, B., T. T. Kristjansson, L. Deng, and A. Acero (2001). ALGONQUIN—learning dynamic noise models from noisy speech for robust speech recognition, in *Proceedings of Neural Information Processing Systems*, pp. 100–107.

Furui, S. (2001). *Digital Speech Processing, Synthesis and Recognition* (2nd Ed.), Marcel Dekker Inc., New York.

Gao Y. and J. Kuo (2006). Maximum entropy direct models for speech recognition, *IEEE Transactions on Speech and Audio Processing*, 14(3), 873–881.

Gauvain, J.-L. and C.-H. Lee (1997). Maximum a posteriori estimation for multivariate Gaussian mixture observations of Markov chains, *IEEE Transactions on Speech and Audio Processing*, 7, 711–720.

Glass, J. (2003). A probabilistic framework for segment-based speech recognition, in M. Russell and J. Bilmes (eds.), *New Computational Paradigms for Acoustic Modeling in Speech Recognition*, *Computer, Speech and Language* (Special issue), 17(2–3), 137–152.

Gold, B. and N. Morgan (2000). *Speech and Audio Signal Processing*, John Wiley & Sons, New York.

Gunawardana, A. and W. Byrne (2001). Discriminative speaker adaptation with conditional maximum likelihood linear regression, *Proceedings of the EUROSPEECH*, Aalborg, Denmark.

Gunawardana, A., M. Mahajan, A. Acero, and J. C. Platt (2005). Hidden conditional random fields for phone classification, in *Proceedings of the International Conference on Speech Communication and Technology*, pp. 1117–1120.

He, X., L. Deng, C. Wu (2008). Discriminative learning in sequential pattern recognition, *IEEE Signal Processing Magazine*, 25(5), 14–36.

Hermansky, H. (1990). Perceptual linear predictive analysis of speech, *Journal of the Acoustical Society of America*, 87(4), 1738–1752.

Hermansky H. and N. Morgan (1994). RASTA processing of speech, *IEEE Transactions on Speech and Audio Processing*, 2(4), 578–589.

Huang, X. D. (2009). Leading a start-up in an enterprise: Lessons learned in creating Microsoft response point, *IEEE Signal Processing Magazine*, 26(2), 135–138.

Huang, X. D. and K.-F. Lee (1993), On speaker-independent, speaker-dependent and speaker adaptive speech recognition, *IEEE Transactions on Speech and Audio Processing*, 1(2), 150–157.

Huang, X. D., A. Acero, and H. Hon (2001). *Spoken Language Processing—A Guide to Theory, Algorithms, and System Development*, Prentice Hall, Upper Saddle River, NJ.

Jelinek, F. (1969) A fast sequential decoding algorithm using a stack, *IBM Journal of Research and Development*, 13, 675–685.

Jelinek, F. (1976). Continuous speech recognition by statistical methods, *Proceedings of the IEEE*, 64(4), 532–557.

Jelinek, F. (1997). *Statistical Methods for Speech Recognition*, MIT Press, Cambridge, MA.

Jiang, L. and X. D. Huang (1998). Vocabulary-independent word confidence measure using subword features, in *Proceedings of the International Conference on Spoken Language Processing*, pp. 401–404, Sydney, NSW.

Jurafsky D. and J. Martin (2000). *Speech and Language Processing—An Introduction to Natural Language Processing, Computational Linguistics, and Speech Recognition*, Prentice Hall, Upper Saddle River, NJ.

Kumar, N. and A. Andreou (1998). Heteroscedastic analysis and reduced rank HMMs for improved speech recognition, *Speech Communication*, 26, 283–297.

Lee, K. F. (1988). *Automatic Speech Recognition: The Development of the Sphinx Recognition System*, Springer-Verlag, Berlin, Germany.

Lee, C., F. Soong, and K. Paliwal (eds.) (1996). *Automatic Speech and Speaker Recognition—Advanced Topics*, Kluwer Academic, Norwell, MA.

Leggetter C. and P. Woodland (1995). Maximum likelihood linear regression for speaker adaptation of continuous density hidden Markov models, *Computer Speech and Language*, 9, 171–185.

Lippman, R. (1987). An introduction to computing with neural nets, *IEEE ASSP Magazine*, 4(2), 4–22.

Macherey, M., L. Haferkamp, R. Schlüter, and H. Ney (2005). Investigations on error minimizing training criteria for discriminative training in automatic speech recognition, in *Proceedings of Interspeech*, pp. 2133–2136, Lisbon, Portugal.

Morgan, N., Q. Zhu, A. Stolcke, K. Sonmez, S. Sivadas, T. Shinozaki, M. Ostendorf, P. Jain, H. Hermansky, D. Ellis, G. Doddington, B. Chen, O. Cetin, H. Bourlard, and M. Athineos (2005). Pushing the envelope—Aside, *IEEE Signal Processing Magazine*, 22, 81–88.

Ney, H. (1984). The use of a one-stage dynamic programming algorithm for connected word recognition, *IEEE Transactions on ASSP*, 32, 263–271.

Ostendorf, M., V. Digalakis, and J. Rohlicek (1996). From HMMs to segment models: A unified view of stochastic modeling for speech recognition, *IEEE Transactions on Speech and Audio Processing*, 4, 360–378.

Poritz, A. (1988). Hidden Markov models: A guided tour, in *Proceedings of the International Conference on Acoustics, Speech, and Signal Processing*, Vol. 1, pp. 1–4, Seattle, WA.

Povey, B., Kingsbury, L. Mangu, G. Saon, H. Soltau, and G. Zweig (2005). FMPE: Discriminatively trained features for speech recognition, in *Proceedings of the International Conference on Acoustics, Speech, and Signal Processing*, Philadelphia, PA.

Rabiner, L. and B. Juang (1993). *Fundamentals of Speech Recognition*, Prentice Hall, Englewood Cliffs, NJ.

Reddy, D. R. (ed.) (1975). *Speech Recognition*, Academic Press, New York.

Rosenberg, A., C. H. Lee, and F. K. Soong (1994). Cepstral channel normalization techniques for HMM-based speaker verification, in *Proceedings of the International Conference on Acoustics, Speech, and Signal Processing*, pp. 1835–1838, Adelaide, SA.

Sakoe, S. and S. Chiba (1971). A dynamic programming approach to continuous speech recognition, in *Proceedings of the 7th International Congress on Acoustics*, Vol. 3, pp. 65–69, Budapest, Hungary.

Vintsyuk, T. (1968). Speech discrimination by dynamic programming, *Kibernetika*, 4(2), 81–88.

Viterbi, A. (1967). Error bounds for convolutional codes and an asymptotically optimum decoding algorithm, in *IEEE Transactions on Information Theory*, IT-13(2), 260–269.

Schwartz, R. and Y. Chow (1990). The N-best algorithm: An efficient and exact procedure for finding the N most likely sentence hypotheses, in *Proceedings of the International Conference on Acoustics, Speech, and Signal Processing*, Albuquerque, NM.

Sun, J. and L. Deng (2002). An overlapping-feature based phonological model incorporating linguistic constraints: Applications to speech recognition, *Journal of the Acoustical Society of America*, 111(2), 1086–1101.

Vinyals, O., L. Deng, D. Yu, and A. Acero (2009) Discriminative pronunciation learning using phonetic decoder and minimum-classification-error criterion, in *Proceedings of the International Conference on Acoustics, Speech, and Signal Processing*, Taipei, Taiwan.

Wang, Y., M. Mahajan, and X. Huang (2000). A unified context-free grammar and n-gram model for spoken language processing, in *Proceedings of the International Conference on Acoustics, Speech, and Signal Processing*, Istanbul, Turkey.

Wang, Y., D. Yu, Y. Ju, and A. Acero (2008). An introduction to voice search, *IEEE Signal Processing Magazine (Special Issue on Spoken Language Technology)*, 25(3), 29–38.

Wachter, M., K. Demuynck, D. Van Compernolle, and P. Wambacq (2003). Data-driven example based continuous speech recognition, in *Proceedings of the EUROSPEECH*, pp. 1133–1136, Geneva, Switzerland.

Yaman, S., L. Deng, D. Yu, Y. Wang, and A. Acero (2008). An integrative and discriminative technique for spoken utterance classification, *IEEE Transactions on Audio, Speech, and Language Processing*, 16(6), 1207–1214.

Yu, D., L. Deng, J. Droppo, J. Wu, Y. Gong, and A. Acero (2008). Robust speech recognition using cepstral minimum-mean-square-error noise suppressor, *IEEE Transactions on Audio, Speech, and Language Processing*, 16(5), 1061–1070.

16

Alignment

Dekai Wu
The Hong Kong University of Science and Technology

16.1 Introduction

In this chapter, we discuss the work done on automatic alignment of parallel texts for various purposes. Fundamentally, an alignment algorithm accepts as input a *bitext* and produces as output a *bisegmentation* relation that identifies corresponding segments between the texts. A bitext consists of two texts that are translations of each other.* Bitext alignment fundamentally lies at the heart of all data-driven machine translation methods, and the rapid research progress on alignment since 1990 reflects the advent of statistical machine translation (SMT) and example-based machine translation (EBMT) approaches. Yet the importance of alignment extends as well to many other practical applications for translators, bilingual lexicographers, and even ordinary readers.

---

* In a "Terminological note" prefacing his book, Veronis (2000) cites Alan Melby pointing out that the alternative term *parallel text* creates an unfortunate and confusing clash with the translation theory and terminological community, who use the same term instead to mean what NLP and computational linguistics researchers typically refer to as *non-parallel corpora* or *comparable corpora*—texts in different languages from the same domain, but not necessarily translations of each other.

Automatically learned resources for MT, NLP, and humans.

Bitext alignment methods are the core of many methods for machine learning of language resources to be used by SMT or other NLP applications, as well as human translators and linguists. The side effects of alignment are often of more interest than the aligned text itself. Alignment algorithms offer the possibility of extracting various sorts of knowledge resources, such as (a) phrasal bilexicons listing word or collocation translations; (b) translation examples at the sentence, constituent, and/or phrase level; or (c) tree-structured translation patterns such as transfer rules, translation frames, or treelets. Such resources constitute a database that may be used by SMT and EBMT systems (Nagao 1984), or they may be taken as training data for further machine learning to mine deeper patterns. Alignment has also been employed to infer sentence bracketing or constituent structure as a side effect.

Biconcordances.

Historically, the first application for bitext alignment algorithms was to automate the production of the cross-indexing for bilingual concordances (Warwick and Russell 1990; Karlgren et al. 1994; Church and Hovy 1993). Such concordances are consulted by human translators to find the previous contexts in which a term, idiom, or phrase was translated, thereby helping the translator to maintain consistency with preexisting translations, which is important in government and legal documents. An additional benefit of biconcordances is a large increase in navigation ease in bitexts.

Bitext for readers.

Aligned bitexts, in addition to their use in translators' concordances, are also useful for bilingual readers and language learners.

Linked biconcordances and bilexicons.

An aligned bitext can be automatically linked with a bilexicon, providing a more effective interface for lexicographers, corpus annotators, as well as human translators. This was implemented in the BICORD system (Klavans and Tzoukermann 1990).

Translation validation.

A word-level bitext alignment system can be used within a translation checking tool that attempts to automatically flag possible errors, in the same way that spelling and style checkers operate (Macklovitch 1994). The alignment system in this case is primed to search for deceptive cognates (*faux amis*) such as *library/librarie* in English and French.

A wide variety of techniques now exist, ranging from the most simple (counting characters or words) to the more sophisticated, sometimes involving linguistic data (lexicons) that may or may not have been automatically induced themselves. Some techniques work on precisely translated parallel corpora, while others work on noisy, comparable, or nonparallel corpora. Some techniques make use of apparent morphological features, while others rely on cognates and loan-words; of particular interest is work done on languages that do not have a common writing system. Some techniques align only shallow, flat chunks, while others align compositional, hierarchical structures. The robustness and generality of different techniques have generated much discussion.

Techniques have been developed for aligning segments at various granularities: documents, paragraphs, sentences, constituents, collocations or phrases, words, and characters, as seen in the examples in Figure 16.1. In the following sections, we first discuss the general concepts underlying alignment techniques. Each of the major categories of alignment techniques are considered in turn in subsequent sections: document-structure alignment, sentence alignment, alignment for noisy bitexts, word alignment, constituent and tree alignment, and biparsing alignment.

We attempt to use a consistent notation and conceptual orientation throughout. Particularly when discussing algorithms, we stick to formal data constructs such as "token," "sequence," and "segment," rather than linguistic entities. Many algorithms for alignment are actually quite general and can often be applied at many levels of granularity. Unfortunately, this is often obscured by the use of linguistically

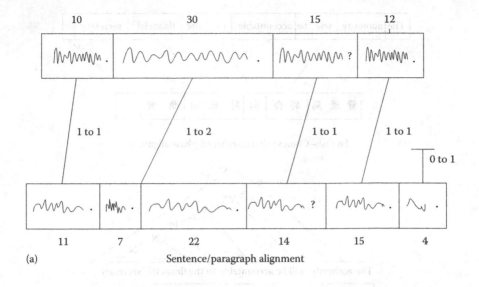

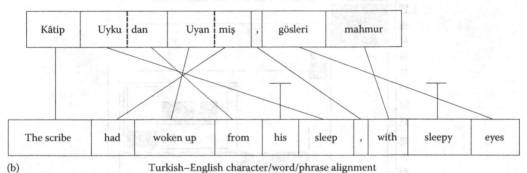

FIGURE 16.1 Alignment examples at various granularities.

loaded terms such as "word," "phrase," or "sentence." For these reasons, some techniques we discuss may appear superficially quite unlike the original works from which our descriptions were derived.

16.2 Definitions and Concepts

16.2.1 Alignment

The general problem of aligning a parallel text is, more precisely, to find its optimal parallel segmentation or *bisegmentation* under some set of constraints:

Input.
  A bitext $(\mathbf{e}, \mathbf{f})$. Assume that the vector $\mathbf{e}$ contains a sequence of T tokens $\mathbf{e}_0, \ldots, \mathbf{e}_{T-1}$ and $\mathcal{E}$ is the set $\{0, 1, 2, \ldots, T-1\}$. Similarly, the vector $\mathbf{f}$ contains a sequence of V tokens $\mathbf{f}_0, \ldots, \mathbf{f}_{V-1}$ and $\mathcal{F}$ is the set $\{0, 1, 2, \ldots, V-1\}$.* When the direction of translation is relevant, $\mathbf{f}$ is the input language (*foreign*) string, and $\mathbf{e}$ is the output language (*emitted*) string.†

---

* We use the following notational conventions: bold letters are vectors, calligraphic letters are sets, and capital (non-bold) letters are constants.
† The **e** and **f** convention dates back to early statistical MT work where the input foreign language was French and the output language emitted was English.

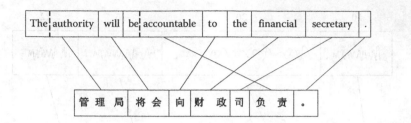

(c)   English–Chinese character/word/phase alignment

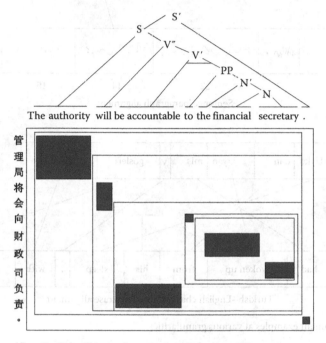

(d)   English–Chinese character/word/phase tree alignment

FIGURE 16.1 (continued)

Output.

A *bisegmentation* of the bitext, designated by a set $\mathcal{A}$ of *bisegments*, where each bisegment (p, r) *couples* an emitted segment p to a foreign segment r and often can instead more conveniently be uniquely identified by its *span pair* (s, t, u, v). Any emitted segment p has a span $\mathbf{span}(p) = (s, t)$ that bounds the passage $\mathbf{e}_{s..t}$ formed by the subsequence of tokens $\mathbf{e}_s, \ldots, \mathbf{e}_{t-1}$ where $0 \leq s \leq t \leq T$. Similarly, any foreign segment r has a span $\mathbf{span}(r) = (u, v)$, which bounds the passage $\mathbf{f}_{u..v}$ formed by the subsequence of tokens $\mathbf{f}_u, \ldots, \mathbf{f}_{v-1}$ where $0 \leq u \leq v \leq V$. Conversely, we write $p = \mathbf{seg}(s, t)$ and $r = \mathbf{seg}(u, v)$ when the span uniquely identifies a segment. Otherwise, for models that permit more than one segment to label the same span, we instead write $\mathbf{segs}(s, t)$ or $\mathbf{segs}(u, v)$ to denote the set of segments that label the span.

Note that a bisegmentation inherently defines two monolingual segmentations, on both of the monolingual texts $\mathbf{e}$ and $\mathbf{f}$.

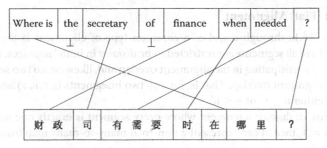

(e)   English–Chinese character/word/phase alignment

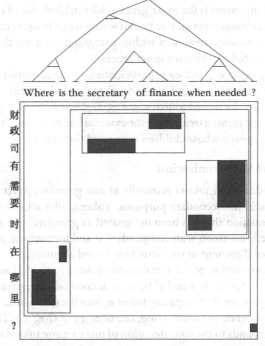

(f) English–Chinese character/word/phase tree alignment

FIGURE 16.1 (continued)

16.2.1.1 Monotonic Alignment

The term "alignment" has become something of a misnomer in computational linguistics. Technically, in an alignment the coupled passages must occur in the same order in both texts, that is, with no crossings. Many alignment techniques have their roots in speech recognition applications, where acoustic waveforms need to be aligned to transcriptions that are of course in the same order. In bitext research, the term "alignment" originally described the reasonable approximating assumption that paragraph and sentence translations always preserve the original order.

However, "word alignment" was subsequently co-opted to mean coupling of words within sentences, even when word-coupling models do not assume that order is monotonically preserved across translation. Since this permits permutations where the word segments are reordered in translation, properly speaking, such a non-monotonic "alignment" is rather a bisegmentation, which can be seen as a (partial) binary relation from the segments $e_{s..t}$ to the segments $f_{u..v}$. To avoid confusion, we will use the term *monotonic alignment* or *monotone alignment* whenever we mean "alignment" in its proper sense.

16.2.1.2 Disjoint (Flat) Alignment

As shown in Figure 16.1a through c and e, a common type of alignment is the simple, flat case of *disjoint alignment* where all segments are restricted to be *disjoint* in both languages, meaning that no two segments $e_{s..t}$ and $e_{s'..t'}$ participating in the alignment overlap and, likewise, no two segments $e_{s..t}$ and $e_{s'..t'}$ participating in the alignment overlap. That is, for any two bisegments (s, t, u, v) and (s', t', u', v'), either $s \leq t'$ or $t \leq s'$, and either $u \leq v'$ or $v \leq u'$.

In the simplest case of disjoint alignment where every segment is exactly one token long, i.e., where $t - s = 1$ and $v - u = 1$, then $\mathcal{A}$ can represent a non-total many-to-many map from $\mathcal{E}$ to $\mathcal{F}$.

16.2.1.3 Compositional (Hierarchical) Tree Alignment

Another common type of alignment is the more general, hierarchical case of *compositional alignment* or *tree alignment* where smaller bisegments may be nested within larger bisegments, as shown in Figure 16.1d and f. The simplest case is to align sentences within paragraphs that are themselves aligned. A more complex case is to couple nested constituents in sentences.

More precisely, two segments $e_{s..t}$ and $e_{s'..t'}$ participating in the alignment may be either disjoint or nested, i.e., for any two bisegments $q = (s, t, u, v)$ and $q' = (s', t', u', v')$, either q and q' are disjoint in $\mathcal{E}$ so that $s \leq t'$ or $t \leq s'$, or they are nested so that $s \leq s' \leq t' \leq t$ or $s' \leq s \leq t \leq t'$; and similarly for $\mathcal{F}$.

A compositional alignment forms a tree, where the external leaf nodes are a set of disjoint (bi)segments, and internal nodes are bisegments whose children are nested (bi)segments.

16.2.1.4 Subtokens and Subtokenization

Some models are designed to align tokens primarily at one granularity, yet the tokens can be further broken into even finer pieces for secondary purposes. Tokens, after all, are just segments at a specific level of disjoint flat segmentation that has been designated as primitive with respect to some algorithm. Subtokenization is especially common with compositional and hierarchical alignments, in applications such as paragraph/sentence alignment or tree-structured word alignment.

Intuitively, e' is a *subtokenization* of e if it refines the tokens in e into finer-grained *subtokens* (Guo 1997). More precisely, let the tokens in e and e' be both defined on some primitive alphabet Σ. Let $G(e)$ be the string generation operation that maps any token e_s into the string in Σ^* that the token represents, and assume both e and e' generate the same string, i.e., $G(e_{0..T}) = G(e'_{0..T'})$. Then e' is a subtokenization of e if every token e_s corresponds to the concatenation of one or more tokens $e'_{s'..t'}$, i.e., $G(e_s) = G(e'_{s'..t'})$.

16.2.1.5 Bijective, Injective, Partial, and Many-to-Many Alignments

When we are speaking with respect to particular *monolingual* disjoint segmentations of (both sides of) a bitext, a few other concepts are often useful.

Where the pair of monolingual segmentations comes from depends on our assumptions. In some situations, we might assume monolingual segmentations that are fixed by monolingual preprocessors such as morphological analyzers or word/phrase segmenters.

In other situations, we may instead assume whatever monolingual segmentations result from aligning a bitext. In the trivial case, we can simply assume the two monolingual segmentations that are inherently defined by the alignment's output bisegmentation. A more useful case, under compositional tree alignment, is to assume the monolingual segmentations imposed by the leaf nodes of the tree.

Whatever assumptions we use to arrive at a pair of monolingual segmentations, then, in a *1-to-1 alignment* or *bijective alignment*, every segment in each text is coupled to exactly one segment in the other text. A bijective alignment is *total*, meaning that no segment remains uncoupled. In practice, bijective alignments are almost never achievable except at the chapter/section granularity, or perhaps at the paragraph granularity for extremely tight translations. Ordinarily, we aim for a *partial alignment*, in which some segments remain uncoupled *singletons*; and/or we aim for a *many-to-many alignment*, in which segments may be coupled to multiple segments. Another often-useful approximating assumption is that the alignment is a (partial) function from a language-0 position to a language-1 position (but not necessarily vice versa). Such a relation is a *many-to-1* or *right-unique* alignment and is written $v = \mathbf{a}'(t)$. Similarly, a *1-to-many* or *left-unique* or *injective* relation is written $t = \mathbf{a}(v)$. A bijective 1-to-1 alignment is injective in both directions, i.e., both left-unique and right-unique. For convenience, we will sometimes freely switch between the set notation $\mathcal{A}$ and the function notation $\mathbf{a}(\cdot)$ to refer to the same injective alignment.

Unless we specify otherwise, "alignments" are non-monotonic, many-to-many, partial, and non-compositional.

16.2.2 Constraints and Correlations

Every alignment algorithm inputs a bitext and outputs a set of couplings. The techniques are nearly all statistical in nature, due to the need for robustness in the face of imperfect translations. Much of the variation between techniques lies in the other kinds of information—constraints and correlations—that play a role in alignment. Some alignment techniques require one or more of these as inputs, and bring them to bear on the alignment hypothesis space. Others derive or learn such kinds of information as by-products. In some cases the by-products are of sufficient quality as to be taken as outputs in their own right, as mentioned above. Important kinds of information include the following.

Bijectivity constraint

Bijectivity is the assumption that the coupling between passages is 1-to-1 (usually in the sense of partial bijective maps, which allow some passages to remain uncoupled). This assumption is inapplicable at coarser granularities than the sentence-level. However, it is sometimes useful for word-level alignment, despite being clearly inaccurate. For example, consider the case where the words within a sentence pair are being aligned (Melamed 1997). If only one word in the language-0 sentence remains uncoupled and similarly for the language-1 sentence, then the bijectivity assumption implies a preference for coupling those two words, by the process of elimination. Such benefits can easily outweigh errors caused by the inaccuracies of the assumption.

Monoticity constraint

This assumption reduces the problem of coupling bitext passages to a properly monotonic alignment problem: coupled passages occur in the same order in both sides of the bitext.

Segment constraints (disjoint and compositional)

A *segment constraint* prevents an alignment algorithm from outputting any bisegment that crosses the monolingual segment's boundaries. That is, if a segment $e_{s..t}$ is taken as a constraint, then for any bisegmentation (s', t', u', v') that forms part of an alignment, either (s, t) and (s', t') are disjoint in $\mathbf{e}$ so that $s \leq t'$ or $t \leq s'$, or they are nested so that $s \leq s' \leq t' \leq t$ or $s' \leq s \leq t \leq t'$.

Two cases of monolingual segment constraints are very common. A *disjoint segmentation* lets algorithms for disjoint (flat) alignment focus on a coarser granularity than the raw token level; for example, for sentence alignment it is usual to first break the input texts into sentence segments. On the other hand, a *compositional segmentation* of one or both of the monolingual texts can be obtained by monolingually parsing the text(s), imposing the resulting nested segments as constraints.

Bisegment constraints (anchor and slack constraints)

An anchor is a known bisegment, i.e., a pair of segments (or boundaries, in the case of zero-length segments) that is *a priori* known to be coupled, and is a hard constraint. As shown in Figure 16.2, *anchor constraints* are bisegment constraints that can be thought of as confirmed positions within the matrix that represents the alignment candidate space. The special boundary cases of the bisegments $(0, 0, 0, 0)$ and (T, T, V, V) are the *origin* and *terminus*, respectively.

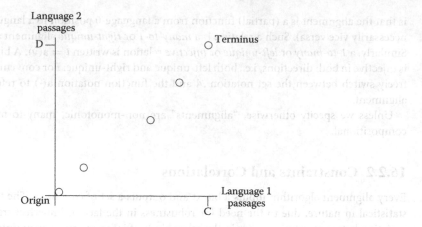

FIGURE 16.2 Anchors.

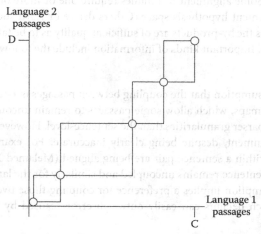

FIGURE 16.3   Slack bisegments between anchors.

When taken together with the monotonicity constraint, a set of anchors divides the problem into a set of smaller, independent alignment problems. Between any two anchors are passages whose alignment is still undetermined, but whose segment couplings must remain inside the region bounded by the anchors. As shown in Figure 16.3, the correct alignment could take any (monotonic) path through the rectangular region delimited by the anchors. We call the candidate subspace between adjacent anchors a *slack bisegment*. A set of slack bisegments can be used either as bisegment constraints (*slack constraints*), as for example described below, or to define features.

There are two common cases of anchor/slack bisegment constraints:

1. *End constraints.* Most techniques make the assumption that the origin and terminus are anchor boundaries. Some techniques also assume a coupling between the first and last *passages.*
2. *Incremental constraints.* A previous processing stage may produce an alignment of a larger passage size. If we are willing to commit to the coarser alignment, we obtain a set of anchor boundaries and/or slack bisegments.

The latter kind of anchor occurs in compositional alignment methods based on *iterative refinement* schemes, which progressively lay down anchors in a series of passes that gradually restrict

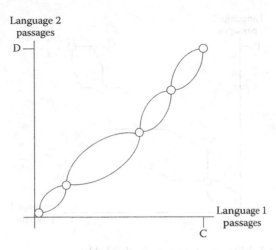

FIGURE 16.4 Banding the slack bisegments using variance.

the alignment candidate space. At the outset, candidate couplings may lie anywhere in the global (root) slack bisegment comprising the entire rectangular matrix; eventually, they are restricted to fall within many small local (leaf) slack bisegments. Each slack bisegment between adjacent anchors is a smaller alignment subproblem that can be processed independently. A variation on this scheme is *hierarchical iterative refinement*, which produces a compositional alignment by performing one pass at each level in a predefined hierarchy of token granularities. The first pass aligns segments at the coarsest token level (commonly, sections or paragraphs); this level is chosen so that the total numbers (T and V) of tokens (commonly, paragraphs or sentences) are small. Committing to the output of this stage yields a bisegmentation that is taken as the slack bisegment constraints for the next pass, which aligns segments at the next finer token level (commonly, paragraphs or sentences). This approach is taken so that the alignment subproblem corresponding to any slack bisegment has small T and V values. The alignment is refined on each pass until the sentence-level granularity is reached; at each pass, the quadratic cost is kept in check by the small number of tokens within each slack bisegment (between adjacent anchors).

Bands

A common heuristic constraint is to narrow the shape of the rectangular slack bisegments instead into *slack bands* that more closely resemble bands, as shown in Figure 16.4. We call this *banding*. Banding relies on the assumption that the correct couplings will not be displaced too far from the average, which is the diagonal between adjacent anchors. Different narrowing heuristics are possible.

One method is to model the variance assuming the displacement for each passage is independently and identically distributed. This means the standard deviation at the midpoint of a $T : V$ bitext is $O\sqrt{(T)}$ for the language-0 axis and $O\sqrt{(V)}$ for the language-1 axis. Kay and Röscheisen (1993) approximate this by using a banding function such that the maximum width of a band at its midpoint is $O\sqrt{(T)}$.*

Another method, due to Simard and Plamondon (1996), is to prune areas of the slack bisegment that are further from the rectangle's diagonal than some threshold, where the threshold is proportional to the distance between the anchors. This results in slack bands of the shape in Figure 16.5.

---

* They do not give the precise function.

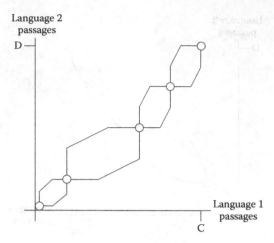

FIGURE 16.5   Banding the slack bisegments using width thresholds.

Banding has the danger of overlooking correct couplings if there are large differences in the translations. Kay and Röscheisen (1993) report a maximum displacement of 10 sentences from the diagonal, in a bitext of 255:300 sentences. However, most bitext, especially in larger collections, contains significantly more noise. The width of the band can be increased, but at significant computational expense.

Guides

A heuristic constraint we call *guiding*, due to Dagan et al. (1993), is applicable when a rough *guide* alignment already exists as the result of some earlier heuristic estimate. The preexisting alignment can be used as a guide to seek a more accurate alignment. Assuming the preexisting alignment is described by the mapping function $\mathbf{a}^0(v)$, a useful alignment range constraint is to define an allowable deviation from $\mathbf{a}^0(v)$ in terms of some distance d: a language-0 position t is a possible candidate to couple with a language-1 position v iff

$$\mathbf{a}^0(v) - d \le t \le \mathbf{a}^0(v) + d \tag{16.1}$$

This is depicted in Figure 16.6. We denote the set of $(s, s+1, t, t+1)$ couplings that meet all alignment range constraints as $\mathcal{B}$.

Alignment range constraints

Monotonicity, anchors, banding, and guiding are all special cases of alignment range constraints. There are many other possible ways to formulate restrictions on the space of allowable alignments. In general, alignment range constraints play an important role. Some alignment techniques are actually computationally infeasible without strong *a priori* alignment range constraints. Other techniques employ an iterative modification of alignment range constraints, similar to iterative refinement with anchors.

Bilexicon constraints

A bilexicon holds known translation pairs or *bilexemes*. In general, machine translation models work with phrasal bilexicons, that may contain characters, tokens, words, phrases, compounds, multi-word expressions, or collocations—particularly for non-alphabetic languages where the difference is not so clear.

The strongest lexeme-coupling constraints come from lexemes (or tokens, including punctuation) that have 1-to-1 deterministic translations. These in effect provide anchors if monotonicity is assumed. However, the rarity of such cases limits their usefulness.

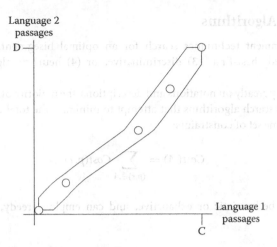

FIGURE 16.6 Guiding based on a previous rough alignment.

A bilexicon usually supplies lexical translations that are 1-to-many or many-to-many. The set of known translations can be used to cut down on the space of candidate couplings. Clearly, whatever pruning method is used must still allow for unknown word translations, since translation is not always word-by-word, and since bilexicons have imperfect coverage (especially in methods that learn a bilexicon as they perform the alignment).

A *weighted bilexicon* stores additional information about the *degree* of correlation or association in word pairs. This can be particularly clean in probabilistic alignment techniques. Various other statistical or *ad hoc* scores can also be employed.

Cognates

Cognates are word pairs with common etymological roots, for example, the bilexemes *financed:financier* or *government:gouvernement* in English and French. For alphabetic languages that share the same (or directly mappable) alphabets, it is possible to construct heuristic functions that compare the spelling of two words or passages. In the simplest case, the function returns true or false (a decision function), acting like a low-accuracy, easily constructed bilexicon with low memory requirements. Alternatively, a function that returns a score acts like a weighted bilexicon. In either case, a cognate function can be used either in place of or in addition to an alignment bilexicon.

Segment lengths

The lengths of passages at or above the sentence granularity can be strong features for determining couplings. Most reported experiments indicate that the correlation is relatively strong even for unrelated languages, if the translation is tight. This means that the utility of this feature is probably more dependent on the genre than the language pair. Segment lengths are typically measured in bytes, characters, or simple word tokenizations. Length-based methods are discussed in Section 16.3.1.

Syntactic parses

Using syntactic information from automatic parsers to improve word alignment accuracy is increasingly common, for example, as discussed in Sections 16.5 and 16.6.

Language universals

Outside of the relatively superficial features just discussed, relatively little attempt has been made to bring to bear constraints from theories about language-universal grammatical properties. One exception is discussed in Section 16.6. Language-universal constraints apply to all (or a large class) of language pairs, without making language-specific assumptions, and apply at the sentence and word granularities.

16.2.3 Classes of Algorithms

Broadly speaking, alignment techniques search for an optimal bisegmentation using (1) dynamic programming, (2) greedy best-first, (3) discriminative, or (4) heuristic algorithms for constrained optimization.

Although authors vary greatly on notations and descriptions, the majority of alignment algorithms can in fact be formulated as search algorithms that attempt to minimize the total cost of $\mathcal{A}$, the entire set of couplings, subject to some set of constraints:

$$Cost(\mathcal{A}) = \sum_{(p,r)\in\mathcal{A}} Cost(p,r) \tag{16.2}$$

Search techniques can be heuristic or exhaustive, and can employ greedy, backtracking, beam, or exhaustive strategies.

16.3 Sentence Alignment

Sentence level techniques generally adopt a restriction to monotonic alignment, and are applicable to larger units as well, such as paragraphs and sections. Taking advantage of this, hierarchical iterative refinement usually works rather well, by first aligning paragraphs, yielding biparagraphs whose internal sentences can subsequently be aligned.

Broadly speaking, sentence alignment techniques rely on sentence lengths, on lexical constraints and correlations, and/or on cognates. Other features could no doubt be used, but these approaches appear to perform well enough.

16.3.1 Length-Based Sentence Alignment

The length-based approach examines the lengths of the sentences. It is the most easily implemented technique, and performs nearly as well as lexical techniques for tightly translated corpora such as government transcripts. The overall idea is to use dynamic programming to find a minimum cost (maximum probability) alignment, assuming a simple hidden generative model that emits sentences of varying lengths. Purely length-based techniques do not examine word identities at all, and regard the bitext as nothing more than a sequence of sentences whose lengths are the only observable feature; Figure 16.7 depicts how the alignment algorithm sees the example of Figure 16.1a. The length-based approach to sentence alignment was first introduced by Gale and Church (1991a) and Brown et al. (1991), who describe essentially similar techniques; a more thorough evaluation is found in Gale and Church (1993).

This is a first example of the most common successful modeling paradigm for all sorts of alignment tasks: search for an *optimal cost alignment* that explains the bitext, assuming it was emitted by some underlying *generative model* of transduction. The generative model is usually stochastic, so the costs being minimized

Lengths of sentences in the bitext

Language 1:	10	30	15	12		
Language 2:	12	14	15	12	11	2

FIGURE 16.7 Example sentence lengths in an input bitext.

are simply weights representing negative log probabilities. In most cases, the generative models are most clearly described as *transducers* (procedural automata) or equivalent *transduction grammars** (declarative rule sets), which can be viewed in three ways:

Generation. A transducer or transduction grammar generates a *transduction*, which is a set of string translation pairs or *bistrings*, just as an ordinary (monolingual) language grammar generates a language, which is a set of strings. In the bilingual case, a transduction grammar simultaneously generates two strings (**e**, **f**) at once, which are translation pairs. The set of all bistrings that can be generated defines a relation between the input and output languages.

Recognition. A transducer or transduction grammar accepts or *biparses* all bistrings of a transduction, just as a language grammar parses or accepts all strings of a language.

Transduction. A transducer or transduction grammar translates or *transduces* foreign input strings **f** to emitted output strings **e**.

As we shall see, there is a hierarchy of equivalence classes for transductions—just as there is Chomsky's hierarchy of equivalence classes for languages. Just as in the monolingual case, there is a tradeoff between generative capacity and computational complexity: the more expressive classes of transductions are orders of magnitude more expensive to biparse and train:

MONOLINGUAL (Chomsky hierarchy)	BILINGUAL
regular or finite-state languages	regular or finite-state transductions
FSA $O(n^2)$	**FST** $O(n^4)$
or	*or*
CFG	SDTG (or synchronous CFG)
that is	*that is*
right regular or left regular	*right regular or left regular*
context-free languages	inversion transductions
CFG $O(n^3)$	**ITG** $O(n^6)$
	or
	SDTG (or synchronous CFG)
	that is
	binary or ternary or inverting
	syntax-directed transductions
	SDTG $O(n^{2n+2})$
	or
	(or synchronous CFG)

Fortunately, for length-based sentence alignment, it suffices to model one of the simplest bilingual classes—*finite-state transductions*—which can be generated by a *finite-state transducer* or *FST* as depicted in Figure 16.8, or by an equivalent *finite-state transduction grammar* or *FSTG*, written as a transduction grammar that is right regular.[†] For sentence alignment, the natural tokens that are being aligned are sentences, but for length-based models, there is a also useful subtokenization at the byte, character, or simple word level. The model emits bitext as a monotonic series of bisegments, each bisegment being a short sequence of E emitted sentence tokens in language 0 coupled with a short sequence of F foreign

---

* Also recently called "synchronous grammars."
† FSTGs may also be written in left regular form.

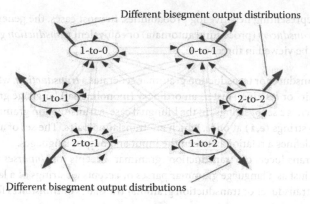

(a) FST model using transition network notation.

$$
\begin{aligned}
&\vdots \\
1\text{-to-}1 &\to [\ e_i/\epsilon\ 1\text{-to-}0\ ] && \text{for all segments of subtoken length } i \text{ in language-0} \\
1\text{-to-}1 &\to [\ \epsilon/f_j\ 0\text{-to-}1\ ] && \text{for all segments of subtoken length } j \text{ in language-1} \\
1\text{-to-}1 &\to [\ e_i/f_j\ 1\text{-to-}1\ ] && \text{for all 1-to-1 bisegments of subtoken lengths } i,j \\
1\text{-to-}1 &\to [\ e_i/f_j\ 1\text{-to-}2\ ] && \text{for all 1-to-2 bisegments of subtoken lengths } i,j \\
1\text{-to-}1 &\to [\ e_i/f_j\ 2\text{-to-}1\ ] && \text{for all 2-to-1 bisegments of subtoken lengths } i,j \\
1\text{-to-}1 &\to [\ e_i/f_j\ 2\text{-to-}2\ ] && \text{for all 2-to-2 bisegments of subtoken lengths } i,j \\
&\vdots
\end{aligned}
$$

(b) Alternative notation for the same model using FSTG transduction rule notation;
    same pattern for 1-to-0, 0-to-1, 2-to-1, 1-to-2, and 2-to-2 rules.

FIGURE 16.8 Equivalent stochastic or weighted (a) FST and (b) FSTG notations for a finite-state bisegment generation process. Note that the node transition probability distributions are often tied to be the same for all node/nonterminal types.

sentence tokens in language 1.[*] For example, Figure 16.1a shows one sequence of 1-to-1, 1-to-2, and 0-to-1 bisegments that could have generated the bitext length sequences of Figure 16.7.

Formally, we denote a transducer or transduction grammar by $G = (\mathcal{N}, \mathcal{W}_0, \mathcal{W}_1, \mathcal{R}, S)$, where $\mathcal{N}$ is a finite set of nodes (states) or nonterminals, $\mathcal{W}_0$ is a finite set of words (terminals) of language 0, $\mathcal{W}_1$ is a finite set of words (terminals) of language 1, $\mathcal{R}$ is a finite set of transduction rules (which can be written as either transition rules or rewrite rules), and $S \in \mathcal{N}$ is the start node (state) or nonterminal. The space of bisegments (terminal-pairs) $\mathcal{X} = (\mathcal{W}_0 \cup \{\epsilon\}) \times (\mathcal{W}_1 \cup \{\epsilon\})$ contains lexical translations denoted x/y and singletons denoted x/ϵ or ϵ/y, where $x \in \mathcal{W}_0$ and $y \in \mathcal{W}_1$.

Each node (state) or nonterminal represents one type of bisegment. The usual practice is to allow bisegment types representing at least the following E-to-F configurations: 0-to-1, 1-to-0, 1-to-1, 1-to-2, and 2-to-1. Allowing 2-to-2 bisegments in addition is reasonable. It can be convenient to think of these bisegment types as operations for translating language-0 passages into language-1 passages, respectively: insertion, deletion, substitution, expansion, contraction, and merger. Bisegments with three or more sentences in one language are not generally used, despite the fact that 1-to-3, 2-to-3, 3-to-3, 3-to-2, and 3-to-1 sentence translations are found in bitext once in a while. This is because alignment of such passages using only the sentence length feature is too inaccurate to make the extra parameters and computation worthwhile. Similarly, it generally suffices to ignore the state history, by tying all states so they share the same outgoing transition probability distribution, a simple multinomial distribution over the bisegment

---

[*] Brown et al. (1991) describe this FST as a single-state hidden Markov model (HMM) that emits bisegments (which they call "beads"). However, the type of bisegment must be stochastically selected each time the state is reached, and then its output probabilities must be conditioned on the bisegment type. This effectively splits the single state into separate states for each bisegment type, as described here.

types that can be estimated from a small hand-aligned corpus. Alternatively, EM can be used to estimate this distribution simultaneously with the segment length distributions.

The output distribution for each state (i.e., bisegment type) is modeled as a function of its monolingual segments' lengths as measured in subtokens (typically bytes, characters, or word subtokens). Given the bisegment type, the length $l_0 = t - s$ of its emitted segment $\mathbf{e}_{s..t}$ is determined. The length of each sentence token in the emitted segment is assumed to be independent, and to follow some distribution. This distribution is implicitly Poisson in the case of Gale and Church (1991b). In Brown et al. (1991), relative frequencies are used to estimate probabilities for short sentence lengths (up to approximately 80 simple English and French words), and the distribution for longer sentences is fit to the tail of a Poisson. Since the empirical distribution for short sentences is fairly Poisson-like,* these variations do not appear to have a significant impact.

Finally, the length $l_1 = v - u$ of the foreign segment $\mathbf{f}_{u..v}$ is determined, by assuming that its difference from the length of the emitted segment follows some distribution, usually a normal distribution. The following difference functions are used by Gale and Church (1991b) and Brown et al. (1991), respectively:

$$\delta(l_0, l_1) = \frac{(l_1 - l_0 c)}{\sqrt{l_0 s^2}} \tag{16.3}$$

$$\delta(l_0, l_1) = \log \frac{l_1}{l_0} \tag{16.4}$$

Aside from normalizing the mean and variance to one's arbitrary preference, the only decision is whether to take the logarithm of the sentence length difference, which sometimes produces a better fit to the empirical distribution.

These assumptions are sufficient to compute the probability of any bisegment. It is convenient to write a candidate bisegment as (*bisegment-type, s, u*) where its emitted segment begins with the *s*th passage in $\mathbf{e}$ and its foreign segment begins with the *u*th passage in $\mathbf{f}$ (since we assume total disjoint segmentations in both languages, t and v can be inferred). For instance, a candidate 1-to-2 bisegment that hypothesizes coupling $\mathbf{e}_{31..32}$ with $\mathbf{f}_{36..38}$ has the estimated probability $\hat{P}(1\text{-to-}2, 31, 36)$.

Given this generative model, the actual alignment algorithm relies on dynamic programming (Bellman 1957) to find the maximum probability alignment. For each bisegment, we take $Cost(p, r)$ to be its negative log probability, and we minimize Equation 16.2 subject to the constraint that the bisegmentation is bijective, and is a total cover of all sentence tokens in both languages. The recurrence has the structure of dynamic time-warping (DTW) models and is based on the fact that the probability of any sequence of bisegments can be computed by multiplying the probability of last bisegment with the total probability of all the bisegments that precede it. Let the minimum cost (maximum log probability) up to passages (t, v) be $\delta(t, v) = \log P(\mathbf{e}_{0..t}, \mathbf{f}_{0..v})$ where $0 \leq t \leq T$ and $0 \leq v \leq V$. The recurrence chooses the best configuration over the possible types of the last bisegment.

1. Initialization.

$$\delta(0, 0) = 0 \tag{16.5}$$

2. Recursion.

$$\delta(t, v) = \min \begin{cases} \delta(t, v-1) - \log \hat{P}(0\text{-to-}1, t, v-1) \\ \delta(t-1, v) - \log \hat{P}(1\text{-to-}0, t-1, v) \\ \delta(t-1, v-1) - \log \hat{P}(1\text{-to-}1, t-1, v-1) \\ \delta(t-1, v-2) - \log \hat{P}(1\text{-to-}2, t-1, v-2) \\ \delta(t-2, v-1) - \log \hat{P}(2\text{-to-}1, t-2, v-1) \\ \delta(t-2, v-2) - \log \hat{P}(2\text{-to-}2, t-2, v-2) \end{cases} \tag{16.6}$$

Note that the form of the recurrence imposes a set of slope constraints on the time warping.

---

* For example, see Figure 16.4 in Brown et al. (1991).

The most significant difference between the methods is that the Gale and Church (1991b) method measures sentence token lengths in terms of number of character subtokens, whereas the Brown et al. (1991) method uses number of simple English/French word subtokens (as determined by European language specific heuristics relying primarily on whitespace and punctuation separators). Gale and Church (1993) report that using characters instead of words, holding all other factors constant, yields higher accuracy (in their experiment, an error rate of 4.2% for characters as compared to 6.5% for words). The reasons are not immediately obvious, though Gale and Church (1993) use variance measures to argue that there is less uncertainty since the number of characters is larger (117 characters per sentence, as opposed to 17 words). However, these experiments were conducted only on English, French, and German, whose large number of cognates improve the character length correlation.

Wu (1994) showed that for a large English and Chinese government transcription bitext, where the cognate effect does not exist, the Gale and Church (1991b) method is somewhat less accurate than for English, French, and German, although it is still effective. Church et al. (1993) show that sentence lengths are well correlated for the English and Japanese AWK manuals, but do not actually align the sentences. We know of no experimental results comparing character and word length methods on non-cognate languages; the lack of such experiments is in part because of the well-known difficulties in deciding word boundaries in languages such as Chinese (Chiang et al. 1992; Lin et al. 1992; Chang and Chen 1993; Lin et al. 1993; Wu and Tseng 1993; Sproat et al. 1994; Wu and Fung 1994).

Bitexts in some language pairs may exhibit highly dissimilar sentence and clause structures, leading to very different groupings than the simple bisegments we have been considering. For example, although the sentence byte length correlations are strong in the English–Chinese government transcriptions used by Wu (1994), Xu and Tan (1996) report that the CNS English–Chinese news articles they use have very different clause and sentence groupings, and therefore suggest generalizing the bisegments to allow many-clause-to-many-clause couplings.

In general, length-based techniques perform well for tightly translated bitexts. However, they are susceptible to misalignment in the case where the bitext contains long stretches of sentences with roughly equal length, as for example in dialogues consisting of very short utterances, or in itemized lists. One possible solution is discussed in the section on lexical techniques.

The basic algorithm is $O(TV)$ in both space and time, that is, approximately quadratic in the number of segments in the bitext. This is prohibitive for reasonably large bitexts. Three basic methods for circumventing this problem are banding, the hierarchical variant of iterative refinement, and thresholding.

Banding is often a feasible approach since the true alignment paths in many kinds of bitexts lie close enough to the diagonal as to fall within reasonable bands. However, banding is not favored when the other two approaches can be used, since they make fewer assumptions about the alignment path.

Hierarchical iterative refinement appears to work well for tightly translated bitexts such as government transcripts, which are typically organized as one document or section per session. Generally, only a few passes are needed: document/section (optional), paragraph, speaker (optional), and sentence.

Thresholding techniques prune the δ matrix so that some alignment prefixes are abandoned during the dynamic programming loop. Many variants are possible. Relative thresholding is more appropriate than absolute thresholding; the effect is to prune any alignment prefix whose probability is excessively lower than the most probable alignment prefix of the same length. Beam search approaches are similar, but limit the number of "live" alignment prefixes for any given prefix length. It is also possible to define the beam in terms of a upper/lower bounded range (v^-, v^+), so that the loop iteration that computes the tth column of $\delta(t, v)$ only considers $v^- \leq v \leq v^+$. This approach is similar to banding, except that the center of the band is dynamically adjusted during the dynamic programming loop.

Thresholding can cause large warps (deletions, insertions) to be missed. Chen (1993) suggests a resynchronization method to improve the robustness of relative thresholding schemes against large warps, based on monitoring the size of the "live" prefix set during the dynamic programming loop. If this set reaches a predetermined size, indicating uncertainty as to the correct alignment prefix, the presence of a large warp is hypothesized and the alignment program switches to a resynchronization mode. In this mode, both sides of the bitext are linearly scanned forward from the current point, seeking rare words. When corresponding rare words are found in both sides, a resynchronization point is hypothesized. After collecting a set of possible resynchronization points, the best one is selected by attempting sentence alignment for some significant number of sentences following the candidate resynchronization point, taking the resulting probability as an indication of the goodness of this resynchronization point. Resynchronization can improve error rates significantly when the bitext contains large warps.

16.3.2 Lexical Sentence Alignment

The prototypical lexically based sentence alignment technique was proposed by Kay and Röscheisen (1988) in the first paper to introduce a heuristic iterative refinement solution to the bitext alignment problem.[*] The method employs banding, and has the structure shown in Algorithm 1.[†]

Algorithm 1 Lexical Sentence Align

1: Initialize the set of anchor (sentence) alignments $\mathcal{A}$
2: **repeat**
3:    Compute the (sentence alignment) candidate space by banding between each adjacent pair of anchors
4:    Collect word-similarity statistics from the candidate space
5:    Build a bilexicon containing sufficiently similar words
6:    Collect sentence-similarity statistics from the candidate space, with respect to the bilexicon
7:    Add sufficiently confident candidates to the set of alignments $\mathcal{A}$
8: **until** no new candidates were added to $\mathcal{A}$
9: **return** $\mathcal{A}$

Although this algorithm can easily be implemented in a straightforward form, its cost relative to lexicon size and bitext length is prohibitive unless the data structures and loops are optimized. In general, efficient implementations of the length-based methods are easier to build and yield comparable accuracy, so this lexical algorithm is not as commonly used.

A notable characteristic of this algorithm is that it constructs a bilexicon as a by-product. Various criteria functions for accepting a candidate bilexeme are possible, rating either the word pair's degree of correlation or its statistical significance. For the correlation between a candidate bilexeme (w, x), Kay and Röscheisen (1988) employ Dice's coefficient (van Rijsbergen 1979),

$$\frac{2N(w, x)}{N(w) + N(x)} \quad (16.7)$$

whereas Haruno and Yamazaki (1996) employ mutual information (Cover and Thomas 1991),

$$\log \frac{NN(w, x)}{N(w)N(x)} \quad (16.8)$$

For the statistical significance, Kay and Röscheisen (1988) simply use frequency, and Haruno and Yamazaki (1996) use t-score:

$$\frac{P(w, x) - P(w)P(x)}{\sqrt{P(w, x)/N}} \quad (16.9)$$

---

[*] A simplified version of the method was subsequently applied to a significantly larger corpus by Catizone et al. (1989).

[†] For the sake of clarifying the common conceptual underpinnings of different alignment techniques, our description uses different terms from Kay and Röscheisen (1988). Roughly, our $\mathcal{A}$ is the Sentence Alignment Table, our candidate space is the Alignable Sentence Table, and our bilexicon is the Word Alignment Table.

In either case, a candidate bilexeme must exceed thresholds on both correlation and significance scores to be accepted in the bilexicon.

The bilexicon can be initialized with as many pre-existing entries as desired; this may improve alignment performance significantly, depending on how accurate the initial anchors are. Even when a good pre-existing bilexicon is available, accuracy is improved by continuing to add entries statistically, rather than "freezing" the bilexicon. Haruno and Yamazaki (1996) found that combining an initial seed bilexicon (40,000 entries from a commercial machine-readable translation dictionary) with statistical augmentation significantly outperformed versions of the method that either did not employ the seed bilexicon or froze the bilexicon to the seed bilexicon entries only. Results vary greatly depending on the bitext, but show consistent significant improvement across the board. Precision and recall are consistently in the mid-90% range, up from figures in the range of 60.

With respect to applicability to non-Indo-European languages, the Haruno and Yamazaki (1996) experiments show that the algorithm is usable for Japanese–English bitexts, as long as the Japanese side is presegmented and tagged. Aside from the variations already discussed, two other modified strategies are employed. To improve the discriminativeness of the lexical features, an English–Japanese word coupling is only allowed to contribute to a sentence-similarity score when the English word occurs in only one of the candidate sentences to align to a Japanese sentence. In addition, two sets of thresholds are used for mutual information and t-score, to divide the candidate word couplings into high-confidence and low-confidence classes. The high-confidence couplings are weighted three times more heavily. This strategy attempts to limit damage from the many false translations that may be statistically acquired, but still allow the low-confidence bilexicon entries to influence the later iterations when no more discriminative leverage is available from the high-confidence entries.

It is possible to construct lexical sentence alignment techniques based on underlying generative models that probabilistically emit bisegments, similar to those used in length-based techniques. Chen (1993) describes a formulation still using bisegment types with 0-to-1, 1-to-0, 1-to-1, 1-to-2, and 2-to-1 sentence tokens, but at the same time, a subtokenization level where each bisegment is also viewed as a multiset of bilexemes. Instead of distributions that govern bisegment lengths, we have distributions governing the generation of bilexemes. Word order is ignored,* since this would be unlikely to improve accuracy significantly despite greatly worsening the computational complexity. Even with this concession, the cost of alignment would be prohibitive without a number of additional heuristics. The basic method employs the same dynamic programming recurrence as Equation 16.6, with suitable modifications to the probability terms; the quadratic cost would be unacceptable, especially since the number of bilexeme candidates per bisegment candidate is exponential in the bisegment length. Chen employs the relative thresholding heuristic, with resynchronization. The probability parameters, which are essentially the same as for the length-based methods except for the additional bilexeme probabilities, are estimated using the Viterbi approximation to EM.

Like the Kay and Röscheisen (1988) method, this method induces a bilexicon as a side effect. For the method to be able to bootstrap this bilexicon, it is important to provide a seed bilexicon initially. This can be accomplished manually, or by a rough estimation of bilexeme counts over a small manually aligned bitext. The quality of bilexicons induced in this manner has not been investigated, although related EM-based methods have been used for this purpose (see below).

The alignment precision of this method on Canadian Hansards bitext may be marginally higher than the length-based methods. Chen (1993) reports 0.4% error as compared with 0.6% for the Brown et al. (1991) method (but this includes the effect of resynchronization that was not employed by Brown et al. (1991)). Alignment recall improves by roughly 0.3%. Since the accuracy and coverage of the induced bilexicon has not been investigated, it is unclear how many distinct bilexemes are actually needed to obtain this level of performance improvement. The running time of this method is "tens of times" slower than length-based methods, despite the many heuristic search approximations.

---

* Similarly, in spirit, to IBM word alignment Model 1, discussed elsewhere.

To help reduce the running time requirements, it is possible to use a cheaper method to impose an initial set of constraints on the coupling matrix. Simard and Plamondon (1996) employ a cognate-based method within a framework similar to SIMR (discussed later) to generate a set of anchors, and then apply banding.

The *word_align* method (Dagan et al. 1993) may also be used for lexical sentence alignment, as discussed in Section 16.4.2.

16.3.3 Cognate-Based Sentence Alignment

For some language pairs like English and French, the relatively high proportion of cognates makes it possible to use cognates as the key feature for sentence alignment. Simard et al. (1992), who first proposed using cognates, manually analyzed approximately 100 English-French bisentences from the Canadian Hansards, and found that roughly 21% of the words in bisentences were cognates. In contrast, only 6% of the words in randomly chosen non-translation sentence pairs were cognates.

Cognate-based alignment can in fact be seen as a coarse approximation to lexical alignment, where the bilexemes are based on a heuristic operational definition of cognates, rather than an explicitly listed lexicon. The Simard et al. (1992) method's cognate identification heuristic considers two words w, x to be cognates if

1. w, x are identical punctuation characters;
2. w, x are identical sequences of letters and digits, with at least one digit; or
3. w, x are sequences of letters with the same four-character prefix.

This heuristic is clearly inaccurate, but still discriminates true from false sentence pairs fairly well: it considers 30% of the words in bisentences to be cognates, versus only 9% in non-translation sentence pairs.

Given such a definition, any of the lexical alignment methods could be used, simply by substituting the heuristic for lexical lookup. The techniques that require probabilities on bilexemes would require that a distribution of suitable form be imposed. Simard et al. (1992) use the dynamic programming method; however, for the cost term, they use a scoring function based on a log-likelihood ratio rather than a generative model. The score of a bisegment containing c cognates and average sentence length n is

$$- \log \left(\frac{P(c|n, t)}{P(c|n, \neg t)} \cdot P(bisegment\text{-}type) \right) \qquad (16.10)$$

The pure cognate-based method does not perform as well as the length-based methods for the Canadian Hansards. In tests on the same bitext sample, Simard et al. (1992) obtain a 2.4% error rate, where the Gale and Church (1991b) method yields a 1.8% error rate. The reason appears to be that even though the mean number of cognates differs greatly between coupled and non-coupled sentence pairs, the variance in the number of cognates is too large to separate these categories cleanly. Many true bisentences share no cognates, while many non-translation sentence pairs share several cognates by accident.

Cognate-based methods are inapplicable to language pairs such as English and Chinese, where no alphabetic matching is possible.

16.3.4 Multifeature Sentence Alignment

Higher accuracy can be obtained by combining sentence length, lexical, and/or cognate features in a single model. Since a length-based alignment algorithm requires fewer comparison tests than a lexical alignment algorithm, all other things being equal, it is preferable to employ length-based techniques when comparable accuracy can be obtained. However, as mentioned earlier, length-based techniques can misalign when the bitext contains long stretches of sentences with roughly equal length. In this case, it is possible to augment the length features with others. One method of combining features is by incorporating them into a single generative model. Alternatively, the less expensive length-based feature can be used in a first pass; afterward, the uncertain regions can be realigned using the more expensive lexical or cognate features. Uncertain regions can be identified either using low log probabilities in the dynamic programming table as indicators of uncertain regions, or using the size of the "live" prefix set during the dynamic programming loop.

The method of Wu (1994) uses a single generative model that combines sentence length with lexical (bi)subtoken features, which in their case were English words and Chinese characters. A very small translation lexicon of subtokens is chosen before alignment; to be effective, each subtoken should occur often in the bitext and should be highly discriminative, i.e., the translation of each chosen subtoken should be as close to deterministic as possible. The total set of chosen subtokens should be small; otherwise, the model degenerates into full lexical alignment with all the computational cost. The model assumes that all subtokens in a bisegment, except for those that belong to the set of chosen subtokens, are generated according to the same length distribution as in the basic length-based model. The dynamic programming algorithm is generalized to find the maximum probability alignment under this hybrid model. Significant performance improvement can typically be obtained with this method, though the degree is highly dependent upon the bitext and the bitoken vocabulary that is chosen.

Simard et al. (1992) combine sentence length with cognate features using a two-pass approach. The first pass is the Gale and Church (1991b) method which yields a 1.8% error rate. The second pass employs the cognate-based method, improving the error rate to 1.6%.

16.3.5 Comments on Sentence Alignment

Sentence alignment can be performed fairly accurately regardless of the corpus length and method used. Perhaps surprisingly, this holds even for lexicon-learning alignment methods, apparently because the decreased lexicon accuracy is offset by the increased constraints on alignable sentences.

The advantages of the length-based method are its ease of implementation and speed. Although it is sometimes argued that the asymptotic time complexity of efficiently implemented lexical methods is the same as length-based methods, even then the constant factor for would be significantly costlier than the length-based methods.

The advantages of the lexical methods are greater robustness, and the side effect of automatically extracting a lexicon.

Multifeature methods appear to offer the best combination of running time, space, accuracy, and ease of implementation for aligning sentences in tightly translated bitexts.

16.4 Character, Word, and Phrase Alignment

We now consider the case where the vectors **e** and **f** denote sentences that are sequences of lexical units or *lexemes*—character or word/phrase tokens—to be aligned (rather than documents, sections, or paragraphs that are sequences of sentence tokens, as in the preceding section).

The first new difficulty is how to define the input "word" tokens. Compared to paragraph or sentence tokens, it is significantly more slippery to define what a *word* token is. The frequently used, but simplistic, tokenization assumption that whitespace and punctuation separates "words" does not really hold even for Western European languages—as for example, in the multi-"word" words *put off, by the way, inside out, thank you, roller coaster, break a leg*, and so on. For many other major languages, the simplifying assumption is even less workable.

In Chinese, for example, which has tens of thousands of unique characters and is written without any spaces, any attempt to heuristically guess where "word" boundaries might lie is inherently highly error-prone. Premature commitment to artificial "word" boundaries significantly impacts alignment and translation accuracy, since the tokens may have been wrongly segmented to begin with. For this reason, a conservative approach is to avoid *a priori* word tokenization altogether, and assume character tokens instead.

Many simpler word alignment models in fact perform only *token alignment*, where all bisegments are one token or zero tokens long, in both languages. Other models tackle the more realistic general case of *multitoken alignment* where the lexemes being aligned may be words/phrases spanning multiple tokens.

For convenience, we will often use "word" and "lexeme" to refer generally to multitoken lexical units that may be characters, phrases, compounds, multi-word expressions, and/or collocations.

16.4.1 Monotonic Alignment for Words

For languages that share very similar constituent ordering properties, or simply to obtain a very rough word alignment as a bootstrapping step toward more sophisticated word alignments, it is possible to apply many of the techniques discussed for sentence alignment and noisy bitext alignment. For such applications, we may make the simplifying assumption that word order is more or less monotonically preserved across translation. The same dynamic programming algorithms for monotonic alignment of Section 16.3.1 can be used, for example, to perform multitoken alignment yielding bisegments that couple 0-to-1, 1-to-0, 1-to-1, 1-to-2, or 2-to-1 *lexeme* tokens.

Unless the languages are extremely similar, however, length-based features are of low accuracy. In general, useful features will be the lexical features, and for some language pairs also the cognate features.

16.4.2 Non-Monotonic Alignment for Single-Token Words

For true coupling of words (as opposed to simple linear interpolation up to the word granularity), generally speaking, we must drop the monotonicity constraint. Realistically, translating a sentence requires *permuting* (or *reordering*) its component lexemes. Motivations to move to a more accurate lexical coupling model include

Alignment accuracy.
  In principle, lexical coupling without false monotonicity assumptions leads to higher accuracy.
Sparse data.
  Smaller bitexts should be alignable, with bilexicons automatically extracted in the process. The lexical alignment models discussed above require large bitexts to ensure that the counts for good bilexemes are large enough to stand out in the noisy word-coupling hypothesis space.
Translation modeling.
  Accurate lexical coupling is necessary to bootstrap learning of structural translation patterns.

Complexity of coupling at the word level rises as a result of relaxing the monotonicity constraint. Partly for this reason, the assumption is usually made that the word coupling cannot be many-to-many. On the other hand, models that permit one-to-many couplings are feasible. The TM-Align system (Macklovitch and Hannan 1996) employs such a model, namely IBM Model 3 (Brown et al. 1988, 1990, 1993). This model incorporates a *fertility* distribution that governs the probability on the number of language-1 words generated by a language-0 word. Macklovitch and Hannan (1996) report that 68% of the words were correctly aligned. Broken down more precisely, 78% of the content words are correctly aligned, compared to only 57% of the function words.[*]

The *word_align* method (Dagan et al. 1993) employs a dynamic programming formulation similar to that discussed in Section 16.3.1, but has slope constraints that allow the coupling order to move slightly

---

[*] Although the IBM statistical translation models are all based on word alignment models, they themselves have not reported accuracy rates for word alignment.

backward as well as forward. The method does not involve any coarser (section, paragraph, sentence) segmentation of the bitexts. The output of the basic algorithm is a partial word alignment.

The method requires as input a set of alignment range constraints, to restrict the search window to a feasible size inside the dynamic programming loop. Dagan et al. (1993) employ *char_align* as a preprocessing stage to produce a rough alignment $\mathbf{a}^0(\cdot)$, and then use guiding to restrict the alignments considered by *word_align*.

An underlying stochastic channel model is assumed, similar to that of the IBM translation model (Brown et al. 1990, 1993). We assume each language-1 word is generated by a language-0 word. Insertions and deletions are permitted, as in the sentence alignment models. However we can no longer simplistically assume that bisegments describe both sides of the bitext in linear order,* since the monotonicity assumption has been dropped: the language-1 words do not necessary map to language-0 words in order. To model this, a new set of *offset probabilities* $o(k)$ are introduced. The offset k of a pair of coupled word positions t, v is defined as the deviation of the position t of the language-0 word from where it "should have been" given where v is

$$k(t, v) = t - \mathbf{a}'(v) \tag{16.11}$$

where $\mathbf{a}'(v)$ is where the language-0 word "should have been." We determine this by linear extrapolation along the slope of the diagonal, from the language-0 position $\mathbf{a}(v^-)$ corresponding to the previous language-1 word:

$$\mathbf{a}'(v) = \mathbf{a}(v^-) + (v - v^-)\frac{T}{V} \tag{16.12}$$

where v^- is the position of the most recent language-1 word to have been coupled to a language-0 word (as opposed to being an insertion). Given a language-0 string $\mathbf{w}$, the channel model generates the language-1 translation $\mathbf{x}$ with the probability

$$P(\mathbf{x}|\mathbf{w}) = \sum_{\mathbf{a}} K \prod_{v=0}^{V-1} P(x_v|w_{a(v)}) \cdot o(\mathbf{a}(v) - \mathbf{a}'(v)) \tag{16.13}$$

In theory this is computed over all possible alignments $\mathbf{a}$, but we approximate by considering only those within the alignment range constraints:†

$$P(\mathbf{x}|\mathbf{w}) = \sum_{A \subset B} K \prod_{(t,v) \in A} P(x_v|w_t) \cdot o(t - \mathbf{a}'(v)) \tag{16.14}$$

Assuming we have estimated distributions $\hat{P}(x|w)$ and $\hat{o}(k)$, the alignment algorithm searches for the most probable alignment $A*$:

$$A* = \arg \max_{A \subset B} \prod_{(t,v) \in A} P(x_v|w_t) \cdot o(t - \mathbf{a}'(v)) \tag{16.15}$$

The dynamic programming search is similar to the sentence alignment cases, except on the word granularity and with different slope constraints. It considers all values of v proceeding left-to-right through the words of the language-1 side, maintaining a hypothesis for each possible corresponding value of t. The

---

* There are no strings of "beads" as in Brown et al. (1991).
† Remember that A and $\mathbf{a}$ refer to the same alignment.

recurrence is as follows. Let $\delta(t, v)$ denote the minimum cost partial alignment up to the vth word of the language-1 side, such that the vth word is coupled to the tth position of the language-0 side.

$$\delta(t, v) = \min \begin{cases} \min_{t^- : (t^-, v^-) \subset B \wedge t^- - d \leq t \leq t^- + d} \delta(t^-, v-1) - \log \hat{P}(x_v | w_t) - \log \hat{o}(t - a'(v)) \\ \delta(t, v-1) - \log \hat{P}(x_v | \epsilon) \\ \delta(t-1, v) - \log \hat{P}(\epsilon | w_t) \end{cases} \quad (16.16)$$

$$= \min \begin{cases} \min_{t^- : (t^-, v^-) \subset B \wedge t^- - d \leq t \leq t^- + d} \delta(t^-, v-1) - \log \hat{P}(x_v | w_t) - \log \hat{o}\left(t - \left(t^- + (v - v^-)\frac{C}{D}\right)\right) \\ \delta(t, v-1) - \log \hat{P}(x_v | \epsilon) \\ \delta(t-1, v) - \log \hat{P}(\epsilon | w_t) \end{cases} \quad (16.17)$$

$$(16.18)$$

The t^- values that need to be checked are restricted to those that meet the alignment range constraints, and lie within d of t. In practice, the probabilities of word insertion and deletion, $\hat{P}(x_v | \epsilon)$ and $\hat{P}(\epsilon | w_i)$, can be approximated with small flooring constants.

The offset and bilexeme probability estimates, $\hat{o}(k)$ and $\hat{P}(x | w)$, are estimated using EM on the bitext before aligning it. The expectations can be accumulated with a dynamic programming loop of the same structure as that for alignment. An approximation that Dagan et al. (1993) make during the EM training is to use the initial rough alignment $\mathbf{a}^0(v)$ instead of $\mathbf{a}'(v)$.

An experiment performed by Dagan et al. (1993) on a small 160,000-word excerpt of the Canadian Hansards produced an alignment in which about 55% of the words were correctly aligned, 73% were within one word of the correct position, and 84% were within three words of the correct position.

Quantitative performance of *word_align* on non-alphabetic languages has not been extensively evaluated, but Church et al. (1993) align the English and Japanese AWK manuals using the technique. The Japanese text must first be segmented into words, which can lead to an incorrectly segmented text.

It is possible to use *word_align* as a lexical sentence alignment scheme, simply by post-processing its output down to the coarser sentence granularity. The output set of word couplings can be interpreted as a set of candidate anchors, of higher credibility than the usual set of possible word couplings. Using dynamic programming again, the post-processor may choose the set of sentence bisegments that maximizes the (probabilistically weighted) coverage of the candidate anchor set. However, it is not clear that the additional word-order model would significantly alter performance over a model such as that of Chen (1993).

Many single-token word alignment methods, particularly the IBM models [See Section 17.7.1] are inherently asymmetric, leading to artifacts in the alignments that can degrade translation accuracy. To compensate, *symmetrization* methods are commonly used to improve the alignments (Och and Ney 2003). IBM models are first trained in both directions, giving two different token alignments $\mathcal{A}_{ef}$ and $\mathcal{A}_{fe}$ for any sentence pair. A family of various types of symmetrization heuristics can then be applied, for example,

- Intersection: $\mathcal{A} = \mathcal{A}_{ef} \cap \mathcal{A}_{fe}$
- Union: $\mathcal{A} = \mathcal{A}_{ef} \cup \mathcal{A}_{fe}$
- Grow: Start with intersection. Iteratively extend $\mathcal{A}$ by adding token couplings (t, t, v, v) that are found in only one of $\mathcal{A}_{ef}$ or $\mathcal{A}_{fe}$, providing that neither e_t nor f_v has a coupling in $\mathcal{A}$, or the alignment (t, t, v, v) has a horizontal neighbor $(t-1, t-1, v, v)$ or $(t+1, t+1, v, v)$ or a vertical neighbor $(t, t, v-1, v-1)$ or $(t, t, v+1, v+1)$.
- Grow-diag: Same as grow, but allow diagonal neighbors as well (Koehn et al. 2003).
- Grow-diag-final-and: Same as Grow-diag but as a final step, also add non-neighbor token couplings of words that otherwise meet the requirements (Koehn et al. 2003).

A simple variant of the ITG model of Wu (1997) restricted to 1-to-1 token alignment can also be trained via EM Wu (1995d) to produce highly accurate single-token bisegmentations (Section 16.6).

```
[.... graphical examples including a complete m-to-n coupling
 plus various sparse and medium-density couplings, all attempting
 to describe exactly the same coupling of an m-token lexeme to an
 n-token lexeme ....]
```

FIGURE 16.9   Multitoken lexemes of length m and n must be coupled in awkward ways if constrained to using only 1-to-1 single-token bisegments.

16.4.3 Non-Monotonic Alignment for Multitoken Words and Phrases

The techniques of the previous section make the simplifying assumption that a word/lexeme is a single token, i.e., that bisegments couple only single tokens. When confronted with the more realistic case where an m-token lexeme needs to be coupled to an n-token lexeme, such models must resort to using some subset of the $m \times n$ possible 1-to-1 single-token couplings, as for example in Figure 16.9. Ultimately, this becomes problematic, because it forces models to make artificial, meaningless distinctions between the many arbitrary variations like those exemplified in Figure 16.9. By failing to capture straightforward sequence patterns, the 1-to-1 single-token simplification wastes probability mass on unnecessary alignment ambiguities, and creates needless computational complexity.

These problems do not arise in word alignment with m-to-n bisegments that couple multiple tokens (such as we also used for aligning sentences). Because this impacts translation quality significantly, increasingly, alignment is seen in terms of finding segmentations of multitoken words/lexemes to align. This is commonly emphasized by terms like "multi-word expression," "phrase," and "phrase alignment."

The key to multitoken alignment is to integrate the segmentation decisions into the alignment cost optimization, since the optimal coupling of segments depends on how **e** and **f** are segmented, and vice versa.

IBM Models 4 and 5 support a limited asymmetric form of 1-to-n bisegments (Brown et al. 1993), but still do not cope well with multitoken words/lexemes since they cannot occur on the **e** side.

In contrast, the general ITG model introduced by Wu (1997) fully integrates alignment and segmentation, producing multitoken m-to-n word/phrase alignments subject to compositionally structured constraints on lexeme and segment permutations, using an underlying generative model based on a stochastic transduction grammar (Section 16.6).

Generally speaking, multitoken alignment is best performed with respect to some bilexicon that enumerates possible translations for multitoken lexemes—i.e., a list of all legal bisegment types.* Thus, there are two steps to multitoken alignment: (1) induce a bilexicon, and (2) compute a minimum-cost bisegmentation of the bitext using the induced bilexicon.

In practice, very simple methods for inducing a (phrasal) bilexicon perform surprisingly well, if a good 1-to-1 token alignment is available to bootstrap from. A commonly used method is simply to take as a bilexeme every possible bisegment that is consistent with the 1-to-1 token alignment seen in training sentence pairs, up to some maximum token length. Bilexeme probabilities are estimated simply using relative frequency, and (optionally) very low-frequency bilexemes may be discarded. Although the accuracy of multitoken alignment was not directly evaluated, experimental results from Koehn et al. (2003) indicate that when evaluated on translation accuracy, this approach outperforms more complicated methods that filter out bisegments violating syntactic constituent boundaries.

On the other hand, the quality of the induced bilexicon has proven to be fairly sensitive to the quality of the initial 1-to-1 token alignment. The method of Koehn et al. (2003) employs the intersection of IBM alignments trained via EM in both directions, supplemented with the grow-diag-final-and family of heuristics discussed in Section 16.4.2. However, comparative experiments by Saers and Wu (2009) indicate that higher accuracy is obtained by using ITG alignments trained via EM and restricted to 1-to-1 token alignment.

---

* Often referred to as a *phrase table* in work on phrase-based SMT.

Given an induced bilexicon, multitoken alignment of any sentence pair can then be obtained by computing a minimum-cost bisegmentation, for example by using the dynamic programming method of the ITG biparsing model (Section 16.6) or greedy or heuristic variants.

16.5 Structure and Tree Alignment

A *structure alignment* algorithm produces an alignment between constituents (or sentence substructures) within sentence pairs of a bitext. The segments to be aligned are labeled by the nodes in the constituent analyses of the sentences; the output set $\mathcal{A}$ contains pairs of labeled segments (p, r) corresponding to the coupled nodes. All existing techniques process the bitext one bisentence at a time, so sentence alignment always precedes structure alignment. Coupled constituents may be useful in translators' concordances, but they are usually sought for use as examples in EBMT systems (Nagao 1984), phrase-based SMT systems (Koehn et al. 2003), and tree-based SMT systems like those of Wu (1997) and Chiang (2005). Alternatively, the examples constitute training data for machine learning of transfer patterns.

Tree alignment is the special case of structure alignment where the output $\mathcal{A}$ must be a strictly compositional, hierarchical alignment. (The same constraint is applicable to dependency tree models.) This means that tree alignment obeys the following:

Crossing constraint

Suppose two nodes in language-0 p_0 and p_1 correspond to two nodes in language-0 r_0 and r_1 respectively, and p_0 dominates p_1. Then r_0 must dominate r_0.

In other words, couplings between subtrees cannot cross each another, unless the subtrees' immediate parent nodes are also coupled to each other. Most of the time this simplifying assumption is accurate, and it greatly reduces the space of legal alignments and thereby the search complexity. An example is shown in Figure 16.10, where both *Security Bureau* and *police station* are potential lexical couplings to 公安局,

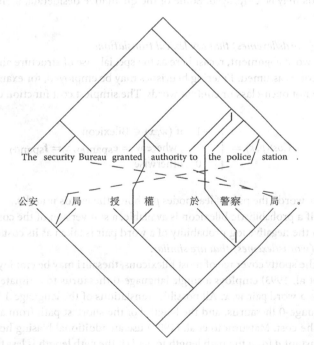

FIGURE 16.10 The crossing constraint.

but the crossing constraint rules out the dashed-line couplings because of the solid-line couplings. The crossing constraint reflects an underlying cross-linguistic hypothesis that the core arguments of frames tend to stay together over different languages. A special case of the crossing constraint is that a constituent will not be coupled to two disjoint constituents in the other language, although it may be coupled to multiple levels within a single constituent subtree.

Structure alignment is usually performed using a *parse-parse-match* strategy. Tree alignment methods require as input the constituent analysis of each side of the bitext (with the exception of the biparsing methods described later). Unfortunately, it is rarely possible to obtain bitext in which the constituent structures of both sides have been marked. However, if suitable monolingual grammars for each of the languages are available, each side can (independently) be parsed automatically, yielding a low-accuracy analysis of each sides, before the tree alignment begins. A variant on this is to supply alternative parses for each sentence, either explicitly in a list (Grishman 1994) or implicitly in a well-formed substring table (Kaji et al. 1992). Note that the parsed bitext is not parallel in the sense that corresponding sentences do not necessarily share a parallel constituent structure. It is difficult, if not impossible, to give an interpretation based on some underlying generative model.

The kind of structures that are to be coupled clearly depend on the linguistic theory under which the sides are parsed. The simplest approach is to use surface structure, which can be represented by bracketing each side of the bitext (Sadler and Vendelmans 1990; Kaji et al. 1992). Another approach was described by Matsumoto et al. (1993), who use LFG-like (Bresnan 1982) unification grammars to parse an English–Japanese bitext. For each side, this yields a set of candidate feature-structures corresponding to the constituent structures. The feature-structures are simplified to dependency trees. Structural alignment is then performed on the dependency trees, rather than the original constituent trees. (Alignment of dependency trees can be performed in essentially the same way as alignment of constituent trees.)

16.5.1 Cost Functions

Various cost functions may be employed. Some of the qualitative desiderata, along with exemplar cost functions, are as follows.

Couple leaf nodes (words/lexemes) that are lexical translations.
  This is simply word alignment, recast here as the special case of structure alignment at the leaf level. A bilexicon is assumed. Filtering heuristics may be employed, for example, to ignore any words that are not open-class or content words. The simplest cost function of this type is

$$Cost(p, r) = \begin{cases} -1 & \text{if } (w, x) \in \text{Bilexicon} \\ & \text{where } w = e_{\text{span}(p)}, x = f_{\text{span}(r)} \\ 0 & \text{otherwise} \end{cases} \quad (16.19)$$

  where, in other words, the pair of leaf nodes p, r holds the words w and x.
  Alternatively, if a probabilistic bilexicon is available, a soft version of the cost function may be used, in which the negative log probability of a word pair is taken as its cost (instead of -1).
Couple leaf nodes (words/lexemes) that are similar.
  To overcome the spotty coverage of most bilexicons, thesauri may be employed. One approach (Matsumoto et al. 1993) employs a single language-0 thesaurus to estimate the cost (dissimilarity) between a word pair w, x. All possible translations of the language-1 word x are looked up in the language-0 thesaurus, and the length l of the shortest path from any one of them to w is taken as the cost. Matsumoto et al. (1993) use an additional biasing heuristic that always subtracts a constant d from the path length to get l (if the path length is less than the d, then l is assumed to be zero).

$$Cost(p,r) = \begin{cases} -6 & \text{if } (w,x) \in \text{Bilexicon} \\ & \text{where } w = \mathbf{e}_{\text{span}(p)}, x = \mathbf{f}_{\text{span}(r)} \\ l & \text{otherwise} \end{cases} \qquad (16.20)$$

Couple internal nodes that share coupled leaf nodes (words/lexemes).

Let $\mathcal{A}_{words}$ denote the subset of $\mathcal{A}$ that deals with coupling of leaf nodes (usually this subset is precomputed in an earlier stage, according to one of the criteria above and possibly with additional constraints). Let $Keywords(p)$ be the set of leaves of p that are deemed important, for example, all the content words. The simplest cost function of this type is

$$Cost(p,r) = \begin{cases} -1 & \text{if } (w,x) \in \mathcal{A}_{words} \\ & \text{for all } w \in Keywords(p), x \in Keywords(r) \\ 0 & \text{otherwise} \end{cases} \qquad (16.21)$$

This cost function is what Kaji et al. (1992) in effect use, permitting nodes to be matched only if they share exactly the same set of coupled content words.

A softer approach is to maximize the number of shared coupled leaf nodes.

$$Cost(p,r) = \sum_{w \in Keywords(p), x \in Keywords(r)} Cost(w,x) \qquad (16.22)$$

Again, probabilistic versions of these cost functions are straightforward, if a probabilistic bilexicon is available.

Couple nodes that share as many coupled children/descendants as possible.

Similar *ad hoc* cost functions to those above can be formulated. The idea is to maximize structural isomorphism. Through the recursion, this also attempts to share as many coupled leaf nodes as possible.

16.5.2 Algorithms

Alignment still optimizes Equation 16.2, but the bisegments may now be either compositional or disjoint.

In general, constituent alignment has lower complexity than tree alignment, as there is no need to enforce the crossing constraint. Kaji et al. (1992) describe a simple bottom-up greedy strategy. Suppose that a bracketed sentence pair contains P language-0 nodes and R language-1 nodes. The algorithm simply considers all $P \times R$ possible couplings between node pairs p, r, starting with the smallest spans. Any pair whose cost is less than a preset threshold is accepted. Thus, as many pairs as possible are output, so long as they meet the threshold.

For tree alignment as opposed to constituent alignment, bottom-up greedy search is still possible but performance is likely to suffer due to the interaction of the coupling hypotheses. Crossing constraints deriving from early miscouplings can easily preclude later coupling of large constituents, even when the later coupling would be correct. For this reason, more sophisticated strategies are usually employed.

Matsumoto et al. (1993) employ a branch-and-bound search algorithm. The algorithm proceeds top-down, depth-first. It hypothesizes constituent couplings at the highest level first. For each coupling that is tried, a lower bound on its cost is estimated. The algorithm always backtracks to expand the hypothesis with the lowest expected cost. The hypothesis is expanded by further hypothesizing couplings involving the constituent's immediate children (subconstituents).

Grishman (1994) employs a beam search. Search proceeds bottom-up, hypothesizing couplings of individual words first. Only hypotheses whose cost is less than a preset threshold are retained. Each step in the search loop considers all couplings involving the next larger constituents consistent with the current set of smaller hypotheses. The costs of the larger hypotheses depend on the previously computed costs of the smaller hypotheses.

Dynamic programming search procedures can be constructed. However, the worst case complexity is exponential, since it grows with the number of permutations of constituents at any level. The procedure of Kaji et al. (1992) employs two separate well-formed substring tables as input, one for each sentence of the input sentence pair, that are computed by separate dynamic-programming chart parsing processes. However, the actual coupling procedure is greedy, as described above. A true dynamic programming approach (Wu 1995c) is described later in Section 16.6.4 on biparsing alignment (in which permutation constraints guarantee polynomial time complexity).

16.5.3 Strengths and Weaknesses of Structure and Tree Alignment Techniques

The most appropriate application of constituent alignment approaches appears to be for EBMT models. Given the same bitext, constituent alignment approaches can produce many more examples than strict tree alignment approaches (driving up recall), though many of the examples are incorrect (driving down precision). However, the nearest-neighbor tactics of EBMT models have the effect of ignoring incorrect examples most of the time, so recall is more important than precision.

Strict tree alignment approaches tend to have higher precision, since the effects of local disambiguation decisions are propagated to the larger contexts, and vice versa. For this reason, these methods appear to be more suitable for machine learning of transfer patterns.

Constituent alignment has three main weaknesses stemming from the parse-parse-match approach:

Lack of appropriate, robust, monolingual grammars.
This condition is particularly relevant for many low-resource languages. A grammar for this purpose must be robust since it must still identify constituents for the subsequent coupling process even for unanticipated or ill-formed input sentences.

Mismatch of the grammars across languages.
The best-matching constituent types between the two languages may not include the same core arguments. While grammatical differences can make this problem unavoidable, there is often a degree of arbitrariness in a grammar's chosen set of syntactic categories, particularly if the grammar is designed to be robust. The mismatch can be exacerbated when the monolingual grammars are designed independently, or under different theoretical considerations. For example, the negative results of Och et al. (2004) were widely interpreted to be due to the mismatch between independent parsers for the different languages.

Inaccurate selection between multiple possible constituent couplings.
A constituent in one sentence may have several potential couplings to the other, and the coupling heuristic may be unable to discriminate between the options.

16.6 Biparsing and ITG Tree Alignment

Bilingual parsing approaches use the same grammar to simultaneously parse both sides of a bitext (Wu 1995a). In contrast to the parse-parse-match approaches discussed in Section 16.5.3, biparsing approaches readily admit interpretations based on underlying generative *transduction grammar* models. Recall from Section 16.3.1 that a single transduction grammar governs the production of sentence pairs that are mutual translations. The most useful biparsers are the probabilistic versions, which work with stochastic transduction grammars that in fact constitute structured *bilingual language models*.

Biparsing approaches unify many of the concepts discussed above. The simplest version accepts sentence-aligned, unparsed bitext as input. The result of biparsing includes parses for both sides of the bitext, plus the alignment of the constituents.

There are several major variants of biparsing. It is possible to perform biparsing alignment *without* a linguistic grammar of either language, using the BITG technique discussed below. On the other hand, biparsing can make use of a monolingual grammar if one exists. If any *a priori* brackets on the input bitext are available, biparsing can accept them as constraints.

16.6.1 Syntax-Directed Transduction Grammars (or Synchronous CFGs)

Aside from the finite-state transductions considered in Section 16.3.1, the other major equivalence class of transductions from classic compiler theory is the class of *syntax-directed transductions*, which are transductions that can be generated by a *syntax-directed transduction grammar* or *SDTG* (Lewis and Stearns 1968; Aho and Ullman 1969,b; Aho and Ullman 1972), which have also recently been called "synchronous context-free grammars."[*]

As with the finite-state models in Section 16.3.1, formally $G = (\mathcal{N}, \mathcal{W}_0, \mathcal{W}_1, \mathcal{R}, S)$, the only difference being that the transduction rules in $\mathcal{R}$ are more expressive. The transduction rules in SDTGs superficially resemble the production rules in CFGs, except for generating terminal symbols on two streams instead of one, and allowing the right-hand-side symbols to be reordered by any permutation for language-1, as for example in $A \rightarrow a_0 a_1 a_2 a_3 :: a_1 a_3 a_0 a_2$ or simply $A \rightarrow a_0 a_1 a_2 a_3 :: 1\ 3\ 0\ 2$.

However, the similarity ends upon closer inspection. Unlike monolingual CFGs, bilingual SDTGs (or synchronous CFGS) do *not* form a single primary equivalence class. As seen in Section 16.3.1, in the Chomsky (1957) hierarchy, all CFGs form a single equivalence class, independent of the *rank*, which is the maximum number k of nonterminals in the rules' right-hand-sides. However, in the bilingual case of SDTGs, the hierarchy shatters into an infinite number of classes—for any $k > 4$, the class of SDTGs of rank k has strictly greater generative capacity than the class of SDTGs of rank $k - 1$. (The cases of $k = 2$ and $k = 3$ are suprisingly different, however, as in the discussion of ITGs below.)

In SDTGs (or synchronous CFGs), segment order variation (for words or phrases) between languages is accommodated by letting the symbols on each rule's right-hand-side appear in different order for language-0 and language-1. Any permutation of the right-hand-side symbols is allowed.

Any SDTG trivially implements the crossing constraint. This is because in the generative model, at any time the rewrite process only substitutes for a single constituent, which necessarily corresponds to contiguous spans in (both of) the sentences.

The main issue for alignment models based on transduction grammars is how much flexibility to allow. It is obvious that finite-state transductions are insufficiently expressive at a subsentential granularity, since they do not allow reordering of words and phrases across languages. SDTGs were widely used in rule-based MT, as well as example-based MT (Nagao 1984). However, computational complexity for SDTGs (or synchronous CFGs) is excessively expensive. No polynomial-time biparsing or parameter training algorithm is known for the general case, since growth in a number of possible alignments follows the number of permutations of right-hand-side symbols, which is exponential—resulting in algorithms that are $O(n^{2n+2})$, as seen in the hierachy in Section 16.3.1.

16.6.2 Inversion Transduction Grammars

In current state-of-the-art machine translation models, an intermediate equivalence class of transductions that offers a balance of generative capacity and computational complexity falling in between that of FSTGs and SDTGs (or synchronous CFGs) has become widely used, namely that of *inversion transduction grammars* or *ITGs*. Theoretical analyses and numerous empirical results have accumulated indicating a better fit of *inversion transductions* to modeling translation and alignment between many human

---

[*] The motivation for the standard term "syntax-directed" stems from the roots of SDTGs in compiler theory, where the input–output connotation of the term reflects a transduction view, but the theory of course remains compatible with the generation or recognition (biparsing) views as well. Also, "transduction" and "translation" are often used interchangeably, as are "grammar" and "schema."

language pairs, despite the fact that ITGs do not attempt to fully model so-called free word order languages and "second-order" phenomena such as raising and topicalization (Wu 1995b, 1997). Given that the polynomial-time biparsing and training algorithms for ITGs are much less expensive than for SDTGs—no more than $O(n^6)$, as seen in the hierachy in Section 16.3.1—and translation accuracy is at the same time empirically *higher* using ITGs, it is often worth accepting the restricted expressiveness of ITG constraints upon the space of permitted reordering permutations.

For ITGs the transduction rules in $\mathcal{R}$ are more expressive than in finite-state models, but less expressive than in SDTGs (or synchronous CFGs). For example, inversion transductions do not permit the permutation described by the transduction rule example in Section 16.6.1. A simple example of a permutation allowed in inversion transductions is shown in Figure 16.1c and d. However, inversion transductions are surprisingly flexible; even the extreme reordering shown in Figure 16.1e and f falls within the class.

Inversion transductions can be described in at least three equivalent ways, as follows.

ITGs are transduction grammars with only straight or inverted rules.

This means the order of right-hand-side symbols for language-1 is either the same as language-0 (*straight* orientation) or exactly the reverse (*inverted* orientation). A straight rule is written $A \rightarrow [a_0 a_1 \ldots a_{r-1}]$, and an inverted rule is written $A \rightarrow \langle a_0 a_1 \ldots a_{r-1} \rangle$, where $a_i \in \mathcal{N} \cup \mathcal{X}$ and r is the rank of the rule.*

ITGs are the closest bilingual analogue of monolingual CFGs in that any ITG can be converted to a 2-normal form—which is not true for SDTGs (or synchronous CFGs) in general. In particular, a theorem in Wu (1995c) shows that for any inversion transduction grammar G, there exists an equivalent inversion transduction grammar G' where all rules are either lexical rules or binary rank syntactic rules (analogous to Chomsky normal form for monolingual CFGs), such that every rule takes one of the following forms:

$$
\begin{aligned}
S &\rightarrow \epsilon/\epsilon \\
A &\rightarrow x/y \\
A &\rightarrow x/\epsilon \\
A &\rightarrow \epsilon/y \\
A &\rightarrow [B\,C] \\
A &\rightarrow \langle B\,C \rangle
\end{aligned}
$$

where as before x and y are segments of one or more tokens (so the bisegments are typically *phrasal*), and A, B, and C are any nonterminals. The theorem leads directly to the second characterization of ITGs.

ITGs are transduction grammars with rules of rank ≤ 2.

That is, any SDTG whose rules are all binary-branching is an ITG. The equivalence follows trivially from the fact that the only two possible permutations of a rank-2 right-hand-side are straight and inverted. This means that any SDTG (or synchronous CFG) of binary rank—having at most two nonterminals on the right-hand-side of any rule—is an ITG. (Similarly, any SDTG (or synchronous CFG) that is right regular is a FSTG.)

Thus, for example, any grammar computed by the binarization algorithm of Zhang et al. (2006) is an ITG. Similarly, any grammar induced following the hierarchical phrase-based translation method, which always yields a binary transduction grammar (Chiang 2005), is an ITG.

ITGs are transduction grammars with rules of rank ≤ 3.

It can be shown that all six possible permutations of a rank-3 right-hand-side can be generated using only straight and inverted rules in combination.

---

* This notation is a useful shorthand for the straight rule that can also be written in other forms such as $A \rightarrow a_0 a_1 \ldots a_{r-1} :: a_0 a_1 \ldots a_{r-1}$ or $A \rightarrow a_0 a_1 \ldots a_{r-1} :: 0\ 1 \ldots r-1$, and the inverted rule that can also be written in other forms such as $A \rightarrow a_0 a_1 \ldots a_{r-1} :: a_{r-1} \ldots a_1 a_0$ or $A \rightarrow a_0 a_1 \ldots a_{r-1} :: r-1 \ldots 1\ 0$.

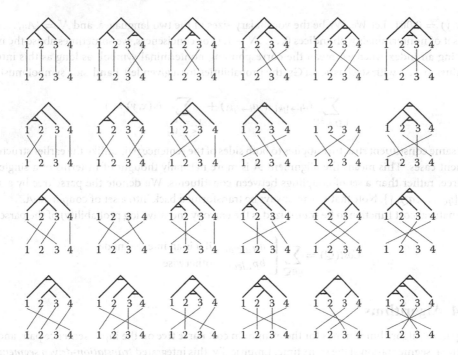

FIGURE 16.11 The 24 complete alignments of length four, with ITG parses for 22. All nonterminal and terminal labels are omitted. A horizontal bar under a parse tree node indicates an inverted rule.

The expressiveness of *ITG constraints* on reordering words, phrases, and constituents in different natural languages is not straightforward to characterize formally. Some light is shed by Figure 16.11, which enumerates how ITGs can deal with the transposition of four adjacent constituents. This case is important because the number of core arguments of a frame is normally less than four, in nearly all linguistic theories. There are 4! = 24 possible permutations of four adjacent constituents, of which 22 can be produced by combining straight and inverted rules. The remaining two permutations are highly distorted "inside-out" alignments, which are extremely rare in (correctly translated) bitext.* For more than four adjacent constituents, many permutations cannot be generated and do not appear necessary.

The *ITG hypothesis* posits a language universal, namely that the core arguments of frames, which exhibit great ordering variation between languages, are relatively few and surface in syntactic proximity. Of course, this assumption over-simplistically blends syntactic and semantic notions, but the ITG hypothesis has held true empirically to a remarkably large extent. That semantic frames for different languages share common core arguments is more plausible than syntactic frames, but ITGs depend on the tendency of syntactic arguments to correlate closely with semantics. If in particular cases this assumption does not hold, the biparsing algorithm can attempt to contain the damage by dropping some word couplings (as few as possible). For more detailed analyses see Wu (1997) and Saers and Wu (2009).

16.6.3 Cost Functions

A cost function can be derived naturally from the generative model. First a stochastic version of the ITG is created by associating a probability with each rule. Just as for ordinary monolingual parsing, probabilizing the grammar permits ambiguities to be resolved by choosing the maximum likelihood parse. For example, the probability of the rule NN $\overset{0.4}{\rightarrow}$ [A N] is $a_{\text{NN}\rightarrow[\text{A N}]} = 0.4$. The probability of a lexical rule A $\overset{0.001}{\rightarrow}$ x/y

---

* In fact, we know of no actual examples in any parallel corpus for languages that do not have free word order.

is $b_A(x, y) = 0.001$. Let W_0, W_1 be the vocabulary sizes of the two languages, and $\mathcal{N} = \{A_0, \ldots, A_{N-1}\}$ be the set of nonterminals with indices $0, \ldots, N - 1$. (For conciseness, we sometimes abuse the notation by writing an index when we mean the corresponding nonterminal symbol, as long as this introduces no confusion.) As with stochastic CFGs, the probabilities for a given left-hand-side symbol must sum to unity:

$$\sum_{1 \leq j,k \leq N} (a_{i \to [jk]} + a_{i \to \langle jk \rangle}) + \sum_{\substack{1 \leq x \leq W_0 \\ 1 \leq y \leq W_1}} b_i(x, y) = 1$$

The same constituent structure applies to both sides of the sentence pair unlike the earlier structure/tree alignment cases. This means the alignment $\mathcal{A}$ is more naturally thought of in terms of a single shared parse tree, rather than a set of couplings between constituents. We denote the parse tree by a set $\mathcal{Q}$ of nodes $\{q_0, \ldots, q_{Q-1}\}$. Note that $\mathcal{Q}$ can always be transformed back into a set of couplings $\mathcal{A}$.

The natural cost function to be minimized is the entropy (negative log probability) of the parse tree $\mathcal{Q}$:

$$Cost(\mathcal{Q}) = \sum_{q \in \mathcal{Q}} \begin{cases} a_{Rule(q)} & \text{if } q \text{ is an internal node} \\ b_{Rule(q)} & \text{otherwise} \end{cases} \tag{16.23}$$

16.6.4 Algorithms

The biparsing algorithm searches for the minimum cost parse tree on the input sentence pair, and selects the optimal segmentation at the same time. Empirically, this integrated *translation-driven segmentation* is highly effective at taking advantage of the phrasal terminals of ITGs to avoid alignment errors commonly caused by word segmenters that prematurely commit to inappropriate segmentations during preprocessing. The probabilistic cost function optimizes the overlap between the structural analysis of the two sentences. The algorithm resembles the recognition algorithm for HMMs (Viterbi 1967) and CKY parsing (Kasami 1965; Younger 1967).

Let the input English sentence be $\mathbf{e}_0, \ldots, \mathbf{e}_{T-1}$ and the corresponding input Chinese sentence be $\mathbf{f}_0, \ldots, \mathbf{f}_{V-1}$. As an abbreviation we write $\mathbf{e}_{s..t}$ for the sequence of words $\mathbf{e}_s, \mathbf{e}_{s+1}, \ldots, \mathbf{e}_{t-1}$, and similarly for $\mathbf{f}_{u..v}$; also, $\mathbf{e}_{s..s} = \epsilon$ is the empty string.

Assuming an ITG in 2-normal form, it is convenient to use the 4-tuple (s, t, u, v) to uniquely identify each node of the parse tree $q = \mathbf{seg}(s, t, u, v)$, where the substrings $\mathbf{e}_{s..t}$ and $\mathbf{f}_{u..v}$ both derive from the node q. Denote the nonterminal label on q by $\ell(q)$. Then for any node $q = \mathbf{seg}(s, t, u, v)$, define

$$\delta_q(i) = \delta_{stuv}(i) = \max_{\text{subtrees of } q} P[\text{subtree of } q, \ell(q) = i, i \overset{*}{\Rightarrow} \mathbf{e}_{s..t}/\mathbf{f}_{u..v}]$$

as the maximum probability of any derivation from i that successfully parses both $\mathbf{e}_{s..t}$ and $\mathbf{f}_{u..v}$. Then the best parse of the sentence pair has probability $\delta_{0,T,0,V}(S)$.

The algorithm computes $\delta_{0,T,0,V}(S)$ using the following recurrences. Note that optimal segmentation in both languages is integrated into the algorithm: $s..t$ and $u..v$ are spans delimiting segments of one or more tokens; if $s = t$ or $u = v$, the span length is zero, meaning that the segment is the empty string ϵ. The argmax notation is generalized to the case where maximization ranges over multiple indices, by making the argument vector-valued. Note that $[\ ]$ and $\langle \rangle$ are just constants. The condition $(S - s)(t - S) + (U - u)(v - U) \neq 0$ is a way to specify that the substring in one but not both languages may be split into an empty string ϵ and the substring itself; this ensures that the recursion terminates, but permits words that have no match in the other language to map to an ϵ instead.

1. Initialization

$$\delta_{stuv}^0(i) = b_i(\mathbf{e}_{s..t}/\mathbf{c}_{u..v}), \quad \begin{matrix} 0 \leq s \leq t \leq T \\ 0 \leq u \leq v \leq V \end{matrix} \tag{16.24}$$

2. Recursion

For all i, s, t, u, v such that $\begin{cases} 1 \leq i \leq N \\ 0 \leq s < t \leq T \\ 0 \leq u < v \leq V \\ t-s+v-u>2 \end{cases}$

$$\delta_{stuv}(i) = \max\left[\delta_{stuv}^{[]}(i), \delta_{stuv}^{\langle\rangle}(i), \delta_{stuv}^{0}(i)\right] \tag{16.25}$$

$$\theta_{stuv}(i) = \begin{cases} [] & \text{if } \delta_{stuv}^{[]}(i) > \delta_{stuv}^{\langle\rangle}(i) \text{ and } \delta_{stuv}^{[]}(i) > \delta_{stuv}^{0}(i) \\ \langle\rangle & \text{if } \delta_{stuv}^{\langle\rangle}(i) > \delta_{stuv}^{[]}(i) \text{ and } \delta_{stuv}^{\langle\rangle}(i) > \delta_{stuv}^{0}(i) \\ 0 & \text{otherwise} \end{cases} \tag{16.26}$$

where

$$\delta_{stuv}^{[]}(i) = \max_{\substack{1 \leq j \leq N \\ 1 \leq k \leq N \\ s \leq S \leq t \\ u \leq U \leq v \\ (S-s)(t-S)+(U-u)(v-U) \neq 0}} a_{i \to [jk]} \, \delta_{sSuU}(j) \, \delta_{StUv}(k) \tag{16.27}$$

$$\begin{bmatrix} \iota_{stuv}^{[]}(i) \\ \kappa_{stuv}^{[]}(i) \\ \sigma_{stuv}^{[]}(i) \\ \upsilon_{stuv}^{[]}(i) \end{bmatrix} = \operatorname*{argmax}_{\substack{1 \leq j \leq N \\ 1 \leq k \leq N \\ s \leq S \leq t \\ u \leq U \leq v \\ (S-s)(t-S)+(U-u)(v-U) \neq 0}} a_{i \to [jk]} \, \delta_{sSuU}(j) \, \delta_{StUv}(k) \tag{16.28}$$

$$\delta_{stuv}^{\langle\rangle}(i) = \max_{\substack{1 \leq j \leq N \\ 1 \leq k \leq N \\ s \leq S \leq t \\ u \leq U \leq v \\ (S-s)(t-S)+(U-u)(v-U) \neq 0}} a_{i \to \langle jk \rangle} \, \delta_{sSUv}(j) \, \delta_{StuU}(k) \tag{16.29}$$

$$\begin{bmatrix} \iota_{stuv}^{\langle\rangle}(i) \\ \kappa_{stuv}^{\langle\rangle}(i) \\ \sigma_{stuv}^{\langle\rangle}(i) \\ \upsilon_{stuv}^{\langle\rangle}(i) \end{bmatrix} = \operatorname*{argmax}_{\substack{1 \leq j \leq N \\ 1 \leq k \leq N \\ s \leq S \leq t \\ u \leq U \leq v \\ (S-s)(t-S)+(U-u)(v-U) \neq 0}} a_{i \to \langle jk \rangle} \, \delta_{sSUv}(j) \, \delta_{StuU}(k) \tag{16.30}$$

3. Reconstruction

Initialize by setting the root of the parse tree to $q_1 = (0, T, 0, V)$ and its nonterminal label to $\ell(q_1) = S$. The remaining descendants in the optimal parse tree are then given recursively for any $q = (s, t, u, v)$ by

$$\text{LEFT}(q) = \begin{cases} \text{NIL} & \text{if } t-s+v-u \leq 2 \\ \left(s, \sigma_q^{[]}(\ell(q)), u, \upsilon_q^{[]}(\ell(q))\right) & \text{if } \theta_q(\ell(q)) = [] \text{ and } t-s+v-u>2 \\ \left(s, \sigma_q^{\langle\rangle}(\ell(q)), \upsilon_q^{\langle\rangle}(\ell(q)), v\right) & \text{if } \theta_q(\ell(q)) = \langle\rangle \text{ and } t-s+v-u>2 \\ \text{NIL} & \text{otherwise} \end{cases} \tag{16.31}$$

$$\text{RIGHT}(q) = \begin{cases} \text{NIL} & \text{if } t-s+v-u \leq 2 \\ \left(\sigma_q^{[]}(\ell(q)), t, \upsilon_q^{[]}(\ell(q)), v\right) & \text{if } \theta_q(\ell(q)) = [] \text{ and } t-s+v-u>2 \\ \left(\sigma_q^{\langle\rangle}(\ell(q)), t, u, \upsilon_q^{\langle\rangle}(\ell(q))\right) & \text{if } \theta_q(\ell(q)) = \langle\rangle \text{ and } t-s+v-u>2 \\ \text{NIL} & \text{otherwise} \end{cases} \tag{16.32}$$

$$\ell(\text{LEFT}(q)) = \iota_q^{\theta_q(\ell(q))}(\ell(q)) \qquad (16.33)$$

$$\ell(\text{RIGHT}(q)) = \kappa_q^{\theta_q(\ell(q))}(\ell(q)) \qquad (16.34)$$

The time complexity of this algorithm in the general case is $\Theta(N^3 T^3 V^3)$ where N is the number of distinct nonterminals and T and V are the lengths of the two sentences. (Compare this to the case monolingual parsing, which is faster by a factor of V^3.) The complexity is acceptable for corpus analysis that does not require real-time parsing.

16.6.5 Grammars for Biparsing

Biparsing techniques may be used without a specific grammar, with a coarse grammar, or with detailed grammars.

No language-specific grammar (the BITG technique).
  In the minimal case, no language-specific grammar is used (this is particularly useful when grammars do not exist for both languages). Instead, a generic *bracketing inversion transduction grammar* or BITG is used:

A	$\xrightarrow{a_{[]}}$	$[A\ A]$	
A	$\xrightarrow{a_{\langle\rangle}}$	$\langle A\ A \rangle$	
A	$\xrightarrow{b_{ij}}$	e_i/f_j	for all i, j lexical translation pairs
A	$\xrightarrow{b_{i\epsilon}}$	e_i/ϵ	for all i language-0 vocabulary
A	$\xrightarrow{b_{\epsilon j}}$	ϵ/f_j	for all j language-1 vocabulary

This grammar is sufficient to cover the full range of word-order transpositions that can be generated under any ITG (because the 2-normal form implies that rules with rank > 2 are not needed). The unlabeled tree in Figure 16.1f is an example of a BITG biparse tree.

All probability parameters may be estimated by EM (Wu 1995d). However, in practice alignment performance is not very sensitive to the exact probabilities, and rough estimates are adequate. The b_{ij} distribution can be estimated through simpler EM-based bilexicon learning methods, as discussed later. For the two singleton rules, which permit any word in either sentence to be unmatched, a small ϵ-constant can be chosen for the probabilities $b_{i\epsilon}$ and $b_{\epsilon j}$, so that the optimal bracketing resorts to these rules only when it is otherwise impossible to match the singletons. Similarly, the parameters $a_{[]}$ and $a_{\langle\rangle}$ can be chosen to be very small relative to the b_{ij} probabilities of lexical translation pairs. The result is that the maximum-likelihood parser selects the parse tree that best meets the combined lexical translation preferences, as expressed by the b_{ij} probabilities.

BITG biparsing can be seen as being similar in spirit to *word_align*, but without positional offsets. The maximum probability word alignment is chosen, but with little or no penalty for crossed couplings, as long as they are consistent with constituent structure (even if the coupled words have large positional offsets). The assumption is that the language-universal core-arguments hypothesis modeled by ITGs is a good constraint on the space of alignments allowed. The *word_align* bias toward preferring the same word order in both languages can be imitated to a large extent by choosing $a_{\langle\rangle}$ to be slightly smaller than $a_{[]}$ and thereby giving prefering the straight orientation.

Empirically, the BITG technique is fairly sensitive to the bilexicon accuracy and coverage. This is due to the fact that a missed word coupling can adversely affect many couplings of its dominating constituents. Also, in practice, additional heuristics are useful to compensate for ambiguities that arise from the underconstrained nature of a BITG. (The extreme case is where both sides of a sentence pair have the same word order; in this case there is no evidence for any bracketing.) A number of heuristics are discussed in Wu (1997).

Coarse grammar.

Performance over the BITG technique may often be improved by introducing a small number of rules to capture frequent constituent patterns. This can be done by writing a very small grammar either for one of the languages (Wu 1995d) or for both languages simultaneously. The generic bracketing rules should still be retained, to handle all words that do not fit the constituent patterns. The labeled tree in Figure 16.1f is an example of a biparse tree with a linguistic grammar.

Detailed grammar.

A detailed monolingual grammar for one of the languages can be augmented to convert it into an ITG. A simple but effective heuristic for doing this simply mirrors each rule into straight and inverted versions (Wu and Wong 1998). This biases the constituents that will be aligned to fit the selected language, at the expense of degraded parsing of the other language. Again, the labeled tree in Figure 16.1f is an example of a biparse tree with a linguistic grammar.

16.6.6 Strengths and Weaknesses of Biparsing and ITG Tree Alignment Techniques

Biparsing models have a stronger theoretical basis for selecting alignments, as they are clearly formulated with respect to a generative bilingual language model. This permits probabilistic trading-off between the amount of information in the monolingual parses versus the lexical correspondences.

Biparsing techniques may be used with pre-bracketed bitext, just as with parse-parse-match tree alignment techniques, by including the brackets as *a priori* constraints in the dynamic programming search (Wu 1997). Performance in this case is similar, except that the ordering constraints are slightly stronger with ITGs. Otherwise, the exhaustive dynamic programming search is more reliable than the heuristic search used by tree alignment methods.

The BITG technique can be used to produce a rough bracketing of bitext where no other parsers or grammars are available. It is the only approach under circumstances where no grammar is available for one or both of the languages (thereby precluding the possibility of preparsing the sides of the bitext). Clearly it is the weakest of all the structure/tree/biparsing alignment methods in terms of parsing accuracy. The flip side is that the BITG technique infers new bracketing hypotheses, which can be used for grammar induction. In fact, Zhang and Gildea (2004) show that unsupervised BITG alignments empirically produce significantly better AER scores than a supervised tree-to-string model that depends on the output of a monolingual parser, due to the "impedance mismatch" between the syntactic structure of Chinese and English.

Similarly, if a grammar is available for only one of the languages, a biparsing approach can use just the single grammar whereas parse-parse-match techniques do not apply. The biparsing technique is also useful if two grammars are available but use very different constituent structures (as mentioned earlier, structure/tree alignment methods may be unable to come up with good constituent couplings under these circumstances).

One issue with (non-BITG) biparsing techniques is that it can be difficult and time-consuming to write a single grammar that parses both sides well. It is relatively easy to parse one side well, by using a grammar that fits one of the languages. However, the more language-specific details in the grammar, the more nonterminals it requires to keep the rules in sync with both languages. For this reason, it is important to retain backup generic rules for robustness.

To avoid the manual construction of transduction grammars, a great deal of recent research has focused on automatic methods for inducing transduction grammars—generally ITGs of one form or another, and occasionally SDTGs.* One popular approach is the *hierarchical phrase-based translation* method of Chiang (2005), which learns a highly lexicalized ITG in a binary-rank normal form with either straight rules like $A \rightarrow a_0 A_1 a_2 A_3 a_4 :: a_0 A_1 a_2 A_3 a_4$ (or simply $A \rightarrow [a_0 A_1 a_2 A_3 a_4]$) or inverted rules like $A \rightarrow a_0 A_1 a_2 A_3 a_4 :: a_4 A_3 a_2 A_1 a_0$ (or simply $A \rightarrow \langle a_0 A_1 a_2 A_3 a_4 \rangle$), where a_i is any sequence of lexical translations x/y or singletons x/ϵ or ϵ/y, and there is only one undifferentiated nonterminal category A (as in BITGs). Various other lexicalized and headed variants of ITGs—including dependency models—have also been shown to improve SMT accuracy (Alshawi et al. 2000; Cherry and Lin 2003; Zhang and Gildea 2005).

Neither biparsing, nor structure/tree alignment techniques that work on surface constituency structures, can accommodate the general case of "second-order transformations" such as raising, topicalization, wh-movement, and gapping. Such transformations can cause the surface constituency structure to lose its isomorphism with the "deep" structure's frames and core arguments. No consistent set of couplings is then possible between the surface tree structures of the two languages. For these phenomena, working on the feature-structure tree instead of the constituency tree may hold more hope.

Nevertheless, a large body of empirical research has shown that inversion transductions appear optimal for the vast majority of statistical MT models (e.g., Lu et al. 2001; Lu et al. 2002; Simard and Langlais 2003; Zhao and Vogel 2003). Zens and Ney (2003) show a significantly higher percentage of word alignments are covered under BITG constraints than under IBM constraints, for German–English (96.5% vs. 91.0%), English–German (96.9% vs. 88.1%), French–English (96.1% vs. 87.1%), and English–French (95.6% vs. 87.6%). Wu et al. (2006) find similar results for Arabic–English (96.2%) and English–Arabic (97.0%).

Furthermore, a comparison of IBM versus (Bracketing) ITG constraints on Japanese–English translation by Zens et al. (2004) found significantly higher MT accuracy measured via BLEU, NIST, WER, and PER scores.

The excellent fit of BITG reordering permutations to naturally occurring sentence translations has led to the development of automated MT evaluation metrics that correlate well with human judgment, such as invWER (Leusch et al. 2003) based on interpreting ITG constraints as a compositional block generalization of Levenshtein string edit distance, and its successor, CDER (Leusch et al. 2006).

The biparsing algorithms for ITG alignment have moreover been successfully applied to numerous other tasks including paraphrasing and textual entailment (Wu 2006) and mining parallel sentences from very nonparallel comparable corpora (Wu and Fung 2005).

For languages without explicit word boundaries, particularly Asian languages, the biparsing techniques are particularly well suited. With segmentation integrated into the biparsing algorithm, the word segmentation of the text can be chosen in tandem with choosing the bracketing and couplings, thereby selecting a segmentation that optimally fits the alignment (Wu 1995c).

16.7 Conclusion

The alignment of matching passages can be performed at various granularities: document-structure, sentence, word, or constituent. A variety of techniques are available for each granularity, with trade-offs in speed and memory requirements, accuracy, robustness to noisy bitext, ease of implementation, and suitability for unrelated and non-alphabetic languages. Sources of leverage include lexical translations, cognates, end constraints, passage lengths, syntactic parses, and assumptions about monotonicity, approximate monotonicity, and word order.

New approaches to alignment in SMT are continually being developed. Recent perspectives on the tremendous amount of research on syntax and tree-structured models can be seen, for example, in the "Syntax and Structure in Statistical Translation" (SSST) series of workshops (Wu and Chiang 2007; Chiang

---

* Recall that any SDTG (or synchronous CFG) that is binary rank, ternary rank, or only allows straight/inverted permutations is an ITG; and any SDTG that is right-regular or left-regular is an FSTG.

and Wu 2008; Wu and Chiang 2009). Heuristic association-based models are easier to implement than generative models, and can provide reasonable performance (Melamed 2000; Moore 2005a). Recently, discriminative training methods have been applied to word alignment (Callison-Burch et al. 2004; Moore 2005b; Liu et al. 2005; Klein and Taskar 2005; Fraser and Marcu 2007; Lambert et al. 2007; Ma et al. 2009); one potential advantage is to directly train model parameters to maximize some translation accuracy objective function such as BLEU (Papineni et al. 2002), rather than measures such as *alignment error rate* or *AER* (Och and Ney 2003). Empirically, AER does not necessarily correlate with translation quality (Ayan and Dorr 2006); merely improving AER can reduce translation accuracy (Liang et al. 2006) and vice versa (Vilar et al. 2006).

Alignment models are the core of all modern SMT and EBMT models. They are also tremendously useful in supporting a broad range of functionality in tools such as translators' and lexicographers' workstations, as is well surveyed in the volume edited by Veronis (2000) and the seminal ARCADE project on evaluating alignment (Veronis and Langlais 2000). Increasingly today, alignment algorithms that are faster, more accurate, and more robust are being used for automatic and semi-automatic resource acquisition, especially the extraction of phrasal translation lexicons as well as compositional and hierarchical tree-structured translation examples.

Acknowledgments

This work was supported in part by the Defense Advanced Research Projects Agency (DARPA) under GALE Contract No. HR0011-06-C-0023, and by the Hong Kong Research Grants Council (RGC) research grants RGC6083/99E, RGC6256/00E, and DAG03/04.EG09. Any opinions, findings and conclusions, or recommendations expressed in this material are those of the author(s) and do not necessarily reflect the views of the Defense Advanced Research Projects Agency.

References

Aho, Alfred V. and Jeffrey D. Ullman (1969a). Properties of syntax-directed translations. *Journal of Computer and System Sciences 3*(3), 319–334.

Aho, Alfred V. and Jeffrey D. Ullman (1969b). Syntex-directed translations and the pushdown assembler. *Journal of Computer and System Sciences 3*(1), 37–56.

Aho, Alfred V. and Jeffrey D. Ullman (1972). *The Theory of Parsing, Translation, and Compiling (Volumes 1 and 2)*. Englewood Cliffs, NJ: Prentice-Hall.

Alshawi, Hiyan, Shona Douglas, and Srinivas Bangalore (2000, Mar). Learning dependency translation models as collections of finite-state head transducers. *Computational Linguistics 26*(1), 45–60.

Ayan, Necip Fazil and Bonnie J. Dorr (2006, Jul). Going beyond AER: An extensive analysis of word alignments and their impact on MT. In *21st International Conference on Computational Linguistics and 44th Annual Meeting of the Association for Computational Linguistics (COLING-ACL'06)*, Sydney, Australia, pp. 9–16.

Bellman, Richard (1957). *Dynamic Programming*. Princeton, NJ: Princeton University Press.

Bresnan, Joan (Ed.) (1982). *The Mental Representation of Grammatical Relations*. Cambridge, MA: MIT Press.

Brown, Peter F., Jennifer C. Lai, and Robert L. Mercer (1991). Aligning sentences in parallel corpora. In *29th Annual Meeting of the Association for Computational Linguistics (ACL-91)*, Berkeley, CA, pp. 169–176.

Brown, Peter F., John Cocke, Stephen A. Della Pietra, Vincent J. Della Pietra, Frederick Jelinek, Robert L. Mercer, and Paul S. Roossin (1988, Aug). A statistical approach to language translation. In *12th International Conference on Computational Linguistics (COLING-88)*, Budapest, Hungary, pp. 71–76.

Brown, Peter F., John Cocke, Stephen A. Della Pietra, Vincent J. Della Pietra, Frederick Jelinek, John D. Lafferty, Robert L. Mercer, and Paul S. Roossin (1990, Jun). A statistical approach to machine translation. *Computational Linguistics 16*(2), 79–85.

Brown, Peter F., Stephen A. Della Pietra, Vincent J. Della Pietra, and Robert L. Mercer (1993, Jun). The mathematics of statistical machine translation: Parameter estimation. *Computational Linguistics 19*(2), 263–311.

Callison-Burch, Chris, David Talbot, and Miles Osborne (2004, Jul). Statistical machine translation with word- and sentences-aligned parallel corpora. In *42nd Annual Meeting of the Association for Computational Linguistics (ACL-04)*, Barcelona, Spain, pp. 176–183.

Catizone, Roberta, Graham Russell, and Susan Warwick (1989, Aug). Deriving translation data from bilingual texts. In Uri Zernik (Ed.), *First Lexical Acquisition Workshop*, Detroit, MI.

Chang, Chao-Huang and Cheng-Der Chen (1993, Jun). HMM-based part-of-speech tagging for Chinese corpora. In *Workshop on Very Large Corpora (WVLC)*, Columbus, OH, pp. 40–47.

Chen, Stanley F. (1993). Aligning sentences in bilingual corpora using lexical information. In *31st Annual Meeting of the Association for Computational Linguistics (ACL-93)*, Columbus, OH, pp. 9–16.

Cherry, Colin and Dekang Lin (2003, Aug). A probability model to improve word alignment. In *41st Annual Meeting of the Association for Computational Linguistics (ACL-2003)*, Sapporo, Japan, pp. 88–95.

Chiang, David (2005, Jun). A hierarchical phrase-based model for statistical machine translation. In *43rd Annual Meeting of the Association for Computational Linguistics (ACL-2005)*, Ann Arbor, MI, pp. 263–270.

Chiang, David and Dekai Wu (Eds.) (2008, Jun). In *Proceedings of SSST-2, Second Workshop on Syntax and Structure in Statistical Translation, at ACL-08:HLT*. Columbus, OH: Association for Computational Linguistics.

Chiang, Tung-Hui, Jing-Shin Chang, Ming-Yu Lin, and Keh-Yih Su (1992). Statistical models for word segmentation and unknown resolution. In *ROCLING-92*, Taipei, Taiwan, pp. 121–146.

Chomsky, Noam (1957). *Syntactic Structures*. The Hague, the Netherlands/Paris, France: Mouton.

Church, Kenneth Ward and Eduard H. Hovy (1993). Good applications for crummy machine translation. *Machine Translation 8*, 239–358.

Church, Kenneth Ward, Ido Dagan, William Gale, Pascale Fung, J. Helfman, and B. Satish (1993). Aligning parallel texts: Do methods developed for English-French generalize to Asian languages? In *Pacific Asia Conference on Formal and Computational Linguistics*, Taipei, Taiwan, pp. 1–12.

Cover, Thomas M. and Joy A. Thomas (1991). *Elements of Information Theory*. New York: Wiley.

Dagan, Ido, Kenneth Ward Church, and William A. Gale (1993, June). Robust bilingual word alignment for machine aided translation. In *Proceedings of the Workshop on Very Large Corpora*, Columbus, OH, pp. 1–8.

Fraser, Alexander and Daniel Marcu (2007, Sep). Measuring word alignment quality for statistical machine translation. *Computational Linguistics 33*(3), 293–303.

Gale, William A. and Kenneth Ward Church (1991a). A program for aligning sentences in bilingual corpora. In *29th Annual Meeting of the Association for Computational Linguistics (ACL-91)*, Berkley, CA, pp. 177–184.

Gale, William A. and Kenneth Ward Church (1991b, Feb). A program for aligning sentences in bilingual corpora. Technical Report 94, AT&T Bell Laboratories, Statistical Research, Murray Hill, NJ.

Gale, William A. and Kenneth Ward Church (1993, Mar). A program for aligning sentences in bilingual corpora. *Computational Linguistics 19*(1), 75–102.

Grishman, Ralph (1994, Aug). Iterative alignment of syntactic structures for a bilingual corpus. In *Second Annual Workshop on Very Large Corpora (WVLC-2)*, Kyoto, Japan, pp. 57–68.

Guo, Jin (1997, Dec). Critical tokenization and its properties. *Computational Linguistics 23*(4), 569–596.

Haruno, Masahiko and Takefumi Yamazaki (1996, Jun). High-performance bilingual text alignment using statistical and dictionary information. In *34th Annual Conference of the Association for Computational Linguistics (ACL-96)*, Santa Cruz, CA, pp. 131–138.

Kaji, Hiroyuki, Yuuko Kida, and Yasutsugu Morimoto (1992, Aug). Learning translation templates from bilingual text. In *14th International Conference on Computational Linguistics (COLING 92)*, Nantes, France, pp. 672–678.

Karlgren, Hans, Jussi Karlgren, Magnus Nordström, Paul Pettersson, and Bengt Wahrolén (1994, Aug). Dilemma–an instant lexicographer. In *15th International Conference on Computational Linguistics (COLING-94)*, Kyoto, Japan, pp. 82–84.

Kasami, T. (1965). An efficient recognition and syntax analysis algorithm for context-free languages. Technical Report AFCRL-65-758, Air Force Cambridge Research Laboratory, Bedford, MA.

Kay, Martin and M. Röscheisen (1988). Text-translation alignment. Technical Report P90-00143, Xerox Palo Alto Research Center, Palo Alto, CA.

Kay, Martin and M. Röscheisen (1993). Text-translation alignment. *Computational Linguistics 19*(1), 121–142.

Klavans, Judith and Evelyne Tzoukermann (1990, Aug). The BICORD system. In *13th International Conference on Computational Linguistics (COLING-90)*, Helsinki, Finland, Volume 3, pp. 174–179.

Klein, Dan and Ben Taskar (2005, Jun). Max-margin methods for nlp: Estimation, structure, and applications. In *Tutorial at ACL-05*, Ann Arbor, MI.

Koehn, Philipp, Franz Josef Och, and Daniel Marcu (2003, May). Statistical phrase-based translation. In *Human Language Technology Conference of the North American Chapter of the Association for Computational Linguistics (HLT/NAACL-2003), Companion Volume*, Edmonton, Canada, pp. 48–54.

Lambert, Patrik, Rafael E. Banchs, and Josep M. Crego (2007, Apr). Discriminative alignment training without annotated data for machine translation. In *Human Language Technologies 2007: The Conference of the North American Chapter of the Association for Computational Linguistics (NAACL-HLT 2007)*, Rochester, NY, pp. 85–88.

Leusch, Gregor, Nicola Ueffing, and Hermann Ney (2003, Sep). A novel string-to-string distance measure with applications to machine translation evaluation. In *Machine Translation Summit IX (MT Summit IX)*, New Orleans, LA.

Leusch, Gregor, Nicola Ueffing, and Hermann Ney (2006, Apr). Cder: Efficient mt evaluation using block movements. In *EACL-2006 (11th Conference of the European Chapter of the Association for Computational Linguistics)*, Trento, Italy, pp. 241–248.

Lewis, Philip M. and Richard E. Stearns (1968). Syntax-directed transduction. *Journal of the Association for Computing Machinery 15*(3), 465–488.

Liang, Percy, Ben Taskar, and Dan Klein (2006). Alignment by agreement. In *Human Language Technology Conference of the North American chapter of the Association for Computational Linguistics (HLT-NAACL 2006)*, New York, pp. 104–111.

Lin, Yi-Chung, Tung-Hui Chiang, and Keh-Yih Su (1992). Discrimination oriented probabilistic tagging. In *Proceedings of the ROCLING-92*, Taipei, Taiwan, pp. 85–96.

Lin, Ming-Yu, Tung-Hui Chiang, and Keh-Yih Su (1993). A preliminary study on unknown word problem in Chinese word segmentation. In *Proceedings of the ROCLING-93*, Taipei, Taiwan, pp. 119–141.

Liu, Yang, Qun Liu, and Shouxun Lin (2005, Jun). Log-linear models for word alignment. In *43rd Annual Meeting of the Association for Computational Linguistics (ACL-05)*, Ann Arbor, MI, pp. 459–466.

Lu, Yajuan, Sheng Li, Tiejun Zhao, and Muyun Yang (2002, Aug). Learning chinese bracketing knowledge based on a bilingual language model. In *17th International Conference on Computational Linguistics (COLING-02)*, Taipei, Taiwan.

Lu, Yajuan, Ming Zhou, Sheng Li, Changning Huang, and Tiejun Zhao (2001, Feb). Automatic translation template acquisition based on bilingual structure alignment. *Computational Linguistics and Chinese Language Processing* 6(1), 83–108.

Ma, Yanjun, Patrik Lambert, and Andy Way (2009, Jun). Tuning syntactically enhanced word alignment for statistical machine translation. In *13th Annual Conference of the European Association for Machine Translation (EAMT 2009)*, Barcelona, Spain, pp. 250–257.

Macklovitch, Elliott (1994, Oct). Using bi-textual alignment for translation validation:the transcheck system. In *First Conference of the Association for Machine Translation in the Americas (AMTA-94)*, Columbia, MD, pp. 157–168.

Macklovitch, Elliott and Marie-Louise Hannan (1996). Line 'em up: Advances in alignment technology and their impact on translation support tools. In *Second Conference of the Association for Machine Translation in the Americas (AMTA-96)*, Montreal, Canada, pp. 145–156.

Matsumoto, Yuji, Hiroyuki Ishimoto, and Takehito Utsuro (1993, Jun). Structural matching of parallel texts. In *31st Annual Meeting of the Association for Computational Linguistics (ACL-93)*, Columbus, OH, pp. 23–30.

Melamed, I. Dan (1997, Jul). A word-to-word model of translational equivalence. In *35th Annual Meeting of the Association for Computational Linguistics (ACL-97)*, Madrid, Spain, pp. 104–111.

Melamed, I. Dan (2000, Jun). Models of translational equivalence. *Computational Linguistics* 26(2), 221–249.

Moore, Robert C. (2005a). Association-based bilingual word alignment. In *Building and Using Parallel Texts: Data-Driven Machine Translation and Beyond*, Ann Arbor, MI, pp. 1–8.

Moore, Robert C. (2005b, Oct). A discriminative framework for bilingual word alignment. In *Human Language Technology Conference and Conference on Empirical Methods in Natural Language Processing (HLT/EMNLP 2005)*, Vancouver, Canada, pp. 81–88.

Nagao, Makoto (1984). A framework of a mechanical translation between Japanese and English by analogy principle. In Alick Elithorn and Ranan Banerji (Eds.), *Artificial and Human Intelligence: Edited Review Papers Presented at the International NATO Symposium on Artificial and Human Intelligence*, pp. 173–180. Amsterdam, the Netherlands: North-Holland.

Och, Franz, Daniel Gildea, Sanjeev Khudanpur, Anoop Sarkar, Kenji Yamada, Alex Fraser, Shankar Kumar, Libin Shen, David Smith, Katherine Eng, Viren Jain, Zhen Jin, and Dragomir Radev (2004, May). A smorgasbord of features for statistical machine translation. In *Human Language Technology Conference of the North American Chapter of the Association for Computational Linguistics (HLT/NAACL-2004)*, Boston, MA.

Och, Franz Josef and Hermann Ney (2003). A systematic comparison of various statistical alignment models. *Computational Linguistics* 29(1), 19–52.

Papineni, Kishore, Salim Roukos, Todd Ward, and Wei-Jing Zhu (2002, Jul). BLEU: A method for automatic evaluation of machine translations. In *40th Annual Meeting of the Association for Computational Linguistics (ACL-2002)*, Philadelphia, PA, pp. 311–318.

Sadler, Victor and Ronald Vendelmans (1990). Pilot implementation of a bilingual knowledge bank. In *13th International Conference on Computational Linguistics (COLING-90)*, Helsinki, Finland, Volume 3, pp. 449–451.

Saers, Markus and Dekai Wu (2009). Improving phrase-based translation via word alignments from stochastic inversion transduction grammars. In *Proceedings of SSST-3, Third Workshop on Syntax and Structure in Statistical Translation, at NAACL-HLT, 2009*, Boulder, CO, pp. 28–36.

Simard, Michel, George F. Foster, and Pierre Isabelle (1992). Using cognates to align sentences in bilingual corpora. In *Fourth International Conference on Theoretical and Methodological Issues in Machine Translation (TMI-92)*, Montreal, Canada, pp. 67–81.

Simard, Michel and Philippe Langlais (2003, May). Statistical translation alignment with compositionality constraints. In *HLT/NAACL-2003 Workshop on Building and Using Parallel Texts*, Edmonton, Canada.

Simard, Michel and Pierre Plamondon (1996, Oct). Bilingual sentence alignment: Balancing robustness and accuracy. In *Second Conference of the Association for Machine Translation in the Americas (AMTA-96)*, Montreal, Canada, pp. 135–144.

Sproat, Richard, Chilin Shih, William A. Gale, and Nancy Chang (1994, Jun). A stochastic word segmentation algorithm for a Mandarin text-to-speech system. In *32nd Annual Conference of the Association for Computational Linguistics (ACL-94)*, Las Cruces, NM, pp. 66–72.

van Rijsbergen, Cornelis Joost (1979). *Information Retrieval* (2nd ed.). Butterworth-Heinemann, Newton, MA.

Veronis, Jean (Ed.) (2000). *Parallel Text Processing: Alignment and Use of Translation Corpora*, Kluwer, Dordrecht, the Netherlands.

Veronis, Jean and Philippe Langlais (2000, Aug). Evaluation of parallel text alignment systems: The ARCADE project. In Jean Veronis (Ed.), *Parallel Text Processing: Alignment and Use of Translation Corpora*. Dordrecht, the Netherlands: Kluwer. ISBN 0-7923-6546-1.

Vilar, David, Maja Popovic, and Hermann Ney (2006, Nov). AER: Do we need to "improve" our alignments? In *International Workshop on Spoken Language Translation (IWSLT 2006)*, Kyoto, Japan, pp. 205–212.

Viterbi, Andrew J. (1967). Error bounds for convolutional codes and an asymptotically optimal decoding algorithm. *IEEE Transactions on Information Theory 13*, 260–269.

Warwick, Susan and Graham Russell (1990). Bilingual concordancing and bilingual lexicography. In *EURALEX-90*, Malaga, Spain.

Wu, Dekai (1994, Jun). Aligning a parallel english-chinese corpus statistically with lexical criteria. In *32nd Annual Meeting of the Association for Computational Linguistics (ACL-94)*, Las Cruces, NM, pp. 80–87.

Wu, Dekai (1995a, Jun). An algorithm for simultaneously bracketing parallel texts by aligning words. In *33rd Annual Meeting of the Association for Computational Linguistics (ACL-95)*, Cambridge, MA, pp. 244–251.

Wu, Dekai (1995b, Jul). Grammarless extraction of phrasal translation examples from parallel texts. In *Sixth International Conference on Theoretical and Methodological Issues in Machine Translation (TMI-95)*, Leuven, Belgium, pp. 354–372.

Wu, Dekai (1995c, Aug). Stochastic Inversion Transduction Grammars, with application to segmentation, bracketing, and alignment of parallel corpora. In *14th International Joint Conference on Artificial Intelligence (IJCAI-95)*, Montreal, Canada, pp. 1328–1334.

Wu, Dekai (1995d, Jun). Trainable coarse bilingual grammars for parallel text bracketing. In *Third Annual Workshop on Very Large Corpora (WVLC-3)*, Cambridge, MA, pp. 69–81.

Wu, Dekai (1997, Sep). Stochastic Inversion Transduction Grammars and bilingual parsing of parallel corpora. *Computational Linguistics 23*(3), 377–404.

Wu, Dekai (2006). Textual entailment recognition based on Inversion Transduction Grammars. In Joaquin Quiñonero Candela, Ido Dagan, Bernardo Magnini, and Florence d'Alché Buc (Eds.), *Machine Learning Challenges, Evaluating Predictive Uncertainty, Visual Object Classification and Recognizing Textual Entailment, First PASCAL Machine Learning Challenges Workshop, MLCW 2005*, Southampton, U.K., April 11–13, 2005, *Revised Selected Papers*, Volume 3944 of *Lecture Notes in Computer Science*, Southampton, U.K., pp. 299–308. Springer, Berlin.

Wu, Dekai, Marine Carpuat, and Yihai Shen (2006, Dec). Inversion Transduction Grammar coverage of Arabic-English word alignment for tree-structured statistical machine translation. In *IEEE/ACL 2006 Workshop on Spoken Language Technology (SLT 2006)*, Aruba.

Wu, Dekai and David Chiang (Eds.) (2007, Apr). *Proceedings of SSST, NAACL-HLT 2007 / AMTA Workshop on Syntax and Structure in Statistical Translation*. Rochester, New York: Association for Computational Linguistics.

Wu, Dekai and David Chiang (Eds.) (2009, Jun). *Proceedings of SSST-3, Third Workshop on Syntax and Structure in Statistical Translation, at NAACL-HLT 2009*, Boulder, CO: Association for Computational Linguistics.

Wu, Dekai and Pascale Fung (1994, Oct). Improving Chinese tokenization with linguistic filters on statistical lexical acquisition. In *Fourth Conference on Applied Natural Language Processing (ANLP-94)*, Stuttgart, Germany, pp. 180–181.

Wu, Dekai and Pascale Fung (2005, Oct). Inversion Transduction Grammar constraints for mining parallel sentences from quasi-comparable corpora. In *Second International Joint Conference on Natural Language Processing (IJCNLP 2005)*, Jeju, Korea, pp. 257–268.

Wu, Dekai and Hongsing Wong (1998, Aug). Machine translation with a stochastic grammatical channel. In *36th Annual Meeting of the Association for Computational Linguistics and 17th International Conference on Computational Linguistics (COLING-ACL'98)*, Montreal, Canada.

Wu, Zimin and Gwyneth Tseng (1993). Chinese text segmentation for text retrieval: Achievements and problems. *Journal of The American Society for Information Science 44*(9), 532–542.

Xu, Donghua and Chew Lim Tan (1996, Jun). Automatic alignment of English-Chinese bilingual texts of CNS news. In *International Conference on Chinese Computing (ICCC-96)*, Singapore, pp. 90–97.

Younger, David H. (1967). Recognition and parsing of context-free languages in time n^3. *Information and Control 10*(2), 189–208.

Zens, Richard and Hermann Ney (2003, Aug). A comparative study on reordering constraints in statistical machine translation. In *41st Annual Meeting of the Association for Computational Linguistics (ACL-2003)*, Sapporo, Japan, pp. 192–202.

Zens, Richard, Hermann Ney, Taro Watanabe, and Eiichiro Sumita (2004, Aug). Reordering constraints for phrase-based statistical machine translation. In *20th International Conference on Computational Linguistics (COLING-04)*, Geneva, Switzerland.

Zhang, Hao and Daniel Gildea (2004, Aug). Syntax-based alignment: Supervised or unsupervised? In *20th International Conference on Computational Linguistics (COLING-04)*, Geneva, Switzerland.

Zhang, Hao and Daniel Gildea (2005, Jun). Stochastic lexicalized inversion transduction grammar for alignment. In *43rd Annual Meeting of the Association for Computational Linguistics (ACL-2005)*, Ann Arbor, MI, pp. 475–482.

Zhang, Hao, Liang Huang, Daniel Gildea, and Kevin Knight (2006, Jun). Synchronous binarization for machine translation. In *Human Language Technology Conference of the North American Chapter of the Association for Computational Linguistics (HLT/NAACL-2006)*, New York, pp. 256–263. Association for Computational Linguistics.

Zhao, Bing and Stephan Vogel (2003, May). Word alignment based on bilingual bracketing. In *HLT/NAACL-2003 Workshop on Building and Using Parallel Texts*, Edmonton, Canada.

17

Statistical Machine Translation

Abraham Ittycheriah
IBM Corporation

17.1 Introduction

Human languages have evolved over a significant period of time and although initially in our journey as a species it may have been sufficient to know the local language ("mother tongue") and perhaps the language of neighboring peoples, current trends dictate that we are able to process material produced in many languages. The Web and global access allows for access of content; however, comprehending the content requires a multilingual person or for the majority of people, an automated way of rendering the content into the user's preferred language is required. Machine Translation (MT) technology fulfills this requirement. Statistical techniques (Brown et al., 1993) for MT are now pervasive.

Statistical machine translation (SMT) takes a source sequence, $S = [s_1\ s_2\ \ldots\ s_K]$, and generates a target sequence, $T^* = [t_1\ t_2\ \ldots\ t_L]$, by finding the most likely translation given by

$$T^* = \arg\max_{T \in \mathbf{T}} p(T|S). \tag{17.1}$$

SMT is then concerned with making models for $p(T|S)$ and subsequently searching the space of all target strings to find the optimal string given the source and the model. This approach shares much with speech recognition. Both are sequence prediction problems and many of the tools developed for speech recognition can be applied in SMT also. In building MT models, there are two major problems that need to be addressed:

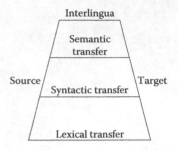

FIGURE 17.1 Machine translation transfer pyramid.

- Word Order: Translation is normally done at the sentence-level* and it might very well be that the last token in the source sentence is the key informant to the first token in the target sentence.
- Word Choice: Each source token can be represented in the target language in a variety of ways.

These two problems are not independent and the order in which we translate the source tokens directly affects which words might be used in the output sentence. As an example from an Arabic–English MT test (NIST, 2003),

> *Arabic*: Ezp AbrAhym ystqbl ms&wlA AqtSAdyA sEwdyA fy bgdAd
> *English1*: Izzet Ibrahim Meets Saudi Trade Official in Baghdad
> *English2*: Izzat Ibrahim Welcomes a Saudi Economic Official to Baghdad
> *English3*: A Saudi Arabian Economic Official is welcomed by Izzat Ibrahim to Baghdad

While the first two translations in English are official translations, the last one is rewritten as an example; here, the Romanized Arabic word "ystqbl" gives rise to the passive construction "is welcomed by." All three references essentially capture the meaning of the sentence in Arabic and the order of the translation leads to different choices for the target words.

Machine Translation can be viewed as taking the source sequence S and performing increasing amounts of analysis as suggested by the pyramid (Vauquois, 1968) shown in Figure 17.1. At the base of the pyramid, words can be transferred from the source to target language. As we go up the pyramid, the level of sophistication increases and at the very top, we have some representation of the meaning and the meaning can be cast as words in either language. In this chapter, we deal only with the first few steps and the focus will be how to represent some of the higher level analysis as features in our translation systems.

17.2 Approaches

Warren Weaver's memorandum (Weaver, 1955) clearly initiated ideas in the statistical approach to MT; however, it was the pioneering work of the IBM group (Brown et al., 1993) in the early 1990s that led to the renewed and sustained interest in the statistical approach to MT. While initial efforts in SMT were mostly word-based, as of the writing of this chapter almost all approaches use phrases as their basic unit of translation. In Addition, natural language parsers have been developed and this has led to both Syntax- and Hierarchical-based approaches.

The early measures of MT included 'Adequacy' and 'Fluency' and these utilized human evaluators and may be defined as follows.

Adequacy. Does the translation capture an adequate amount of the meaning of the sentence in the source language?

Fluency. Is the translation fluent in English?

A more detailed analysis of the evaluation of MT can be found in Hovy (1999). The first automatic metric to be adopted widely is BLEU (Papineni et al., 2002), which provides a score that correlates well with

---

* Document-level and more general features are being investigated, but have not been susccessfully applied to machine translation *yet*.

these two measures. For a test set, a few references are developed by asking independent translators to provide translations. BLEU then computes the precision of various length strings and the final score is weighted sum with a penalty if the system produces a very short translation. This penalty acts as a measure of the recall of a system. BLEU revolutionized the rate of progress of statistical systems since it made possible to run many evaluations automatically. The list of MT metrics utilized currently is quite long and entire conferences and workshops are dedicated to finding better metrics; the major alternatives are now: (a) Translation Error Rate (TER) (Snover et al., 2006), (b) METEOR (Banerjee and Lavie, 2005). Most major MT evaluations in addition to automatic methods, utilize human editors to edit the system outputs and compute TER of the system output relative to the edited string, which is termed Human-TER or HTER. For the purpose of this chapter, automatic methods of measuring MT performance gives us the ability to evaluate various features and present objective results without worrying about agreement rates of humans. The problem of human agreement has been shifted to the set of references that are developed for a set of documents and each test system can then be evaluated objectively since the set of references are common to all systems.

In Brown et al. (1993), Equation 17.1 is expanded by applying Bayes Rule and stated as the Fundamental Theorem of MT:

$$T^* = \arg\max_{T \in \mathbf{T}} p(T|S) = \arg\max_{T \in \mathbf{T}} p(S|T)p(T). \tag{17.2}$$

The motivation presented in Brown et al. (1993) was that the S at decoding time was observed and thus well-formed. This formulation allowed a decomposition into a translation model, $p(S|T)$, and a language model, $p(T)$. More recent efforts utilize a log-linear approach and model directly $p(T|S)$:

$$p(T|S) = \frac{1}{Z(S, T)} e^{\sum_i \lambda_i \phi_i(S,T)} \tag{17.3}$$

where
  ϕ_i are a set of feature functions computed over this translation
  Z is the normalizing constant

The λ_i are computed by a minimum error-rate training (Och and Ney, 2003) in systems with a few features. These features (see (Och et al., 2004) for a more complete list of features) include a language model, phrase unigram probability, Model 1 scores, etc. Note that Equation 17.2 is a just special case of Equation 17.3. These features are functions of the source sequence and the target sequence in the translation units and their context. State-of-the-art systems now employ millions of features (binary indicator functions) trained utilizing machine learning methods.

17.3 Language Models

Monolingual data collected from the Internet and other sources are available often in larger quantities than parallel data. N-gram language models (LM) trained on such monolingual data capture the preference of which words follow given some context. For example, in a sentence like "It was a sunny _," there are very few words that can fill in the blank. In terms of the above notation for MT, the LM computes

$$p(T) = \prod_{i=0}^{|T|} p(t_i|t_{i-1}, t_{i-2}, \ldots) \tag{17.4}$$

where t_i is the current word being generated. If the model is a trigram model, and we use a maximum likelihood estimate,

$$p(t_i|t_{i-1}, t_{i-2}) = \frac{C_{t_i t_{i-1} t_{i-2}}}{C_{t_{i-1} t_{i-2}}} \qquad (17.5)$$

where

$C_{t_{i-1} t_{i-2}}$ is the count of the bigram $t_{i-1} t_{i-2}$ occurring in the monolingual data

$C_{t_i t_{i-1} t_{i-2}}$ the count of the tri-gram $t_i t_{i-1} t_{i-2}$

Such estimates are too sharp and are typically smoothed (Chen, 1998). In English, the amount of data utilized in such models has grown to over one trillion words (Brants and Franz, 2006). These models tend to be very important in MT systems but they are in a sense not the essence of the subject and we will focus on the translation model in what follows.

17.4 Parallel Corpora

In previous chapters, methods have been presented to do sentence alignment and the output of such a process is a sentence aligned parallel corpus. For some language pairs in addition to the automatically aligned corpora, there are manually created translations of sentences. This type of data is often much better in quality and leads to better MT output though the cost is significantly higher and therefore in limited in quantity.

17.5 Word Alignment

Given a pair of sentences, word alignment produces a correspondence at the word level. Algorithms for word alignment have been discussed in previous chapters. An example alignment for an Arabic–English sentence pair is shown in Figure 17.2 where the Arabic has been Romanized. In this example, English words are being aligned to their Arabic informants. The Arabic sentence has been segmented following the style of the Arabic Treebank (available from the Linguistic Data Consortium as Catalog Id LDC2007E65).

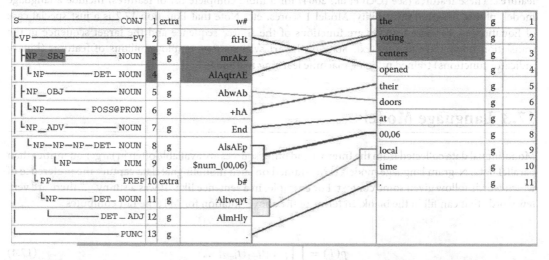

FIGURE 17.2 Arabic parse example.

The first Arabic word, "w#," has no English informant and is aligned to the *null*-cept (we utilize the string "e_0" to represent the null-cept), which is an imaginary English word that gives rise to spontaneous Arabic words. Multi-word Arabic alignments, such as those at positions 8 and 9, are done after the alignment process (Ge, 2004). The Arabic word, "mrAkz" is an example of a split alignment. Numbers are replaced by a class label (in our example, we use '$num').

17.6 Phrase Library

Once a sentence pair has been aligned at the word level, phrase pairs can be extracted and a simple set is shown in Table 17.1. Phrase pairs are extracted following the inverse projection constraint (Block, 2000), which enforces that regions are contiguous in both languages. Most phrase-based translation systems will also extract longer phrase pairs in order to capture word-reorder. For example, in addition to the phrases shown in the Table 17.1, we could add the phrase for "AbwAb + hA" and the translation "their doors." This allows a system to minimize the amount of reorder that is required in the search process to produce good translations. However, extracting such a phrase pair comes with the cost of estimating parameters for such phrase pairs. As the phrase size grows, the number of instances of such phrase pairs obeys Zipf's Law (see, e.g., (Le Quan Ha et al., 2002) who shows the behavior of longer n-grams).

TABLE 17.1 Phrase Library for Example of Figure 17.2

Source Phrase	Target Phrase
w#	e_0
ftHt	opened
mrAkz	the X centers
AlAqtrAE	voting
AbwAb	doors
+hA	their
End	at
AlsAEp $num	$num
b#	e_0
Altwqyt AlmHly	local time
.	.

17.7 Translation Models

In the original formulation of Brown et al. (1993), the source-channel model of Equation 17.2 has a component, $p(s|t)$, which involves both the source and the target languages and is named the "translation" model. We will continue to use this name but interchangeably for both that distribution as well as, $p(t|s)$. A conditional probability model can be expanded using the normal chain rule as,

$$p(S|T) = p([\ s_0 \ \ s_1 \ \ \dots \ \ s_k \ ][\ t_0 \ \ t_1 \ \ \dots \ \ t_l \ ])$$

$$= p(s_0|[\ t_0 \ \ t_1 \ \ \dots \ \ t_l \ ])p(s_1|s_0, [\ t_0 \ \ t_1 \ \ \dots \ \ t_l \ ]) \dots$$

$$= \prod_{i=0}^{k} p\left(s_i | s_0^{i-1}, t_0^l\right) \tag{17.6}$$

where we have used the notation $s_0^{i-1} = [\ s_0 \ \ s_1 \ \ \dots \ \ s_{i-1} \ ]$. The form of the model in the last step seems to indicate that the source word, s_i, is dependent on the entire target sequence. For most sentences in human languages, this is certainly not true and only a few of the target words change the probability of observing the i-th source word. This is captured in the model by introducing an alignment between the elements of the sequence (Brown et al., 1993)

$$p(S|T) = \sum_{A \in \mathcal{A}} p(S, A|T)$$

$$= \sum_{A \in \mathcal{A}} p(k|T) \prod_{i=0}^{k} p\left(a_i | a_1^{i-1}, s_0^{i-1}, k, T\right) p\left(s_i | a_1^i, s_1^{i-1}, k, T\right) \tag{17.7}$$

where

    $\mathcal{A}$ is the set of all valid alignment configurations

    a_i is an element of the configuration and its value is the target position where this source word is
        aligned to

Each of the models below makes some assumptions that allows a tractable solution. Although the equations are symmetric and certainly translation is often desired in both directions, alignment has a preferred direction. The language selected to be the "state" of the algorithms (such as Hidden Markov Models (HMM) (Vogel et al., 1996) or Maximum Entropy (MaxEnt) (Ittycheriah and Roukos, 2005)) below is usually the shorter of the two languages since this configuration allows the many to one alignments that are required by the language pair assuming that only a small portion of the words are unaligned.

17.7.1 IBM Models

The IBM models are a series of increasingly complex models that use EM to estimate the parameters of Equation 17.7. In Model 1, $p\left(a_i|a_1^{i-1}, s_0^{i-1}, k, T\right)$ is assumed to depend only on the length of the target sequence, l, and that the $p(k|T) = \varepsilon$, yielding

$$p(S|T) = \frac{\varepsilon}{(1+l)^k} \sum_{a_0=0}^{l} \sum_{a_2=0}^{l} \cdots \sum_{a_k=0}^{l} \prod_{i=1}^{k} p(s_i|t_{a_i}). \tag{17.8}$$

As shown in Brown et al. (1993), some algebraic manipulation yields

$$p(S|T) = \frac{\varepsilon}{(1+l)^k} \prod_{i=1}^{k} \sum_{j=0}^{l} p(s_i|t_j) \tag{17.9}$$

Using a Lagrange multiplier to express the constraint that the parameters must yield a probability distribution and then solving this unconstrained optimization problem gives us the Model 1 estimate for $p(s|t)$. Model 1 assumes that all alignments were equally likely and thus the order of the elements in the source and target sentence is irrelevant. Models 2 improves on this assumption by making $p(a_i|a_1^{i-1}, s_0^{i-1}, k, T)$ depend on the current position being aligned and the lengths of the source and target sequences. Models 3, 4, and 5 model the "fertility" of the generation process with increasing complexity.

While Model 4 is currently still popular as a word alignment technique due to its incorporation in the GIZA++ toolkit (Och and Ney, 2003), significant improvements have been made over such models. Nevertheless, the scoring function of Equation 17.9 is one of many features used in many phrase-based systems (Och et al., 2004). If we compare Equations 17.9 and 17.6, we see that the Model 1 score treats source words as being independent and it sums over the contributions of the target words. If the sum is replaced with a "max," we call that score the *Viterbi* Model 1 score,

$$p(S|T) = \frac{\varepsilon}{(1+l)^k} \prod_{i=1}^{k} \max_j p(s_i|t_j). \tag{17.10}$$

17.7.2 Phrase-Based Systems

The Alignment Template (AT) approach for MT (Och and Ney, 2004) was a departure from the style of the word-based generative models of IBM, and together with a training method (Och and Ney, 2002; Och, 2003) is the basis for most of the phrase-based MT systems used today. In terms of our notation from above, a sentence can be segmented into phrases as

$$[\; s_0 \quad s_1 \quad \cdots \quad s_k \;] = s_0^k = \tilde{s}_0^m$$

where $\tilde{s}_0^m$ is a contiguous segmentation of the source into m phrases, and clearly $k \geq m$. Similarly the target sentence can be segmented into a sequence of phrases,

$$[\ t_0 \quad t_1 \quad \ldots \quad t_l\ ] = t_0^l = \tilde{t}_0^n$$

and then the alignment template can be defined as

$$z_i = (\tilde{s}_i, \tilde{t}_j, a(\tilde{s}_i, \tilde{t}_j)).$$

The order of applying these alignment templates can be represented using a hidden variable, π_0^m. In this approach then, the hidden variables in the process are (a) the optimal segmentation of the source, (b) the order of applying the alignment templates. The search process yields the optimal values for these variables subject to the limits of the search.

The alignment template remembers the internal alignment of the words and this is used in the context features used in that system. Other phrase-based approaches often drop the alignment and compute the features for the phrase-pair when the phrase-pair is created. The typical features in a phrase-based system have significant overlap with Och et al. (2004) and they will be used in subsequent systems described here also. Perhaps the most attractive feature of the AT approach is the extensibility of the feature set and the ability to train parameters for arbitrary features. The maximum entropy formulation (Della Pietra et al., 1995) was suggested in Papineni et al. (1997, 1998) as a model for natural language understanding. In MT, Och and Ney (2002) utilize the GIS algorithm for training the parameters of the AT. The form of the model is given in Equation 17.3 and the training is done over sentence pairs in the training corpus. Three issues arise in the training of this model (Och and Ney, 2002):

- Normalization: The normalization Z of the exponential model requires the sum over many target sequences. Obviously, some approximation is required and in the AT system the sentences being summed over in the denominator are the very probably sentences derived from an n-best algorithm.
- Multiple-references: Unlike speech recognition and indeed many pattern recognition problems, the translation of a source sentence is ambiguous and there are many ways to render the meaning in the target language. In the AT system, the optimization criterion is modified to reflect many references.
- Reachability: Occasionally, the n-best is insufficient and the references are not in the n-best list. This problem is solved by selecting as the reference translation those that have the minimal number of word errors given the reference translations.

Despite these problems, phrase-based systems are the workhorse of SMT systems due to their simple and relatively straight forward method of extracting phrase libraries and training weights. Systems for new language pairs that have parallel corpora can be built by utilizing the GIZA++ toolkit for generating word-alignments and the open source phrase decoders such as Moses (Koehn et al., 2007).

17.7.3 Syntax-Based Systems for Machine Translation

Syntax is the study of the grammar of a language and in particular how phrases and clauses are put together. Syntax-based approaches rely on parsing the source, or the target, or in some cases both languages. Our earlier example sentence pair with both parses is shown in Figure 17.3, where the words of the sentences are shown across the bottom and the parse structure is shown as a directed graph. These parses are obtained from a statistical parser trained for each language; for English, the parser is trained on the Penn Treebank (Marcus et al., 1993) and the Arabic parser on the Arabic Treebank (Bies and Maamouri, 2008). Parsing output can be either as a Constituent Parse or a Dependency Parse. A constituent parse is a rooted tree whose leaves are the original words of the sentence. The internal nodes of the tree cover a contiguous sequence of the words in the sentence (usually called a span) and to each of these internal

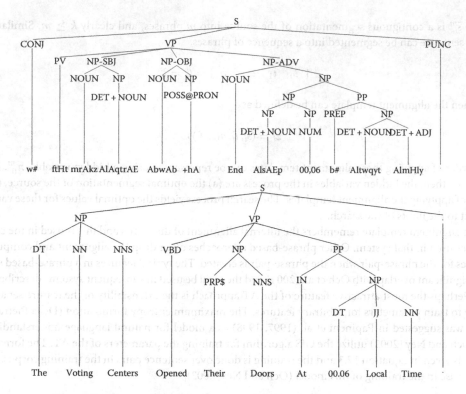

FIGURE 17.3 Source and target parse trees.

nodes is associated a label that describes the syntactic role of the words under this node. A dependency parse shows for each word in the sentence the "parent" or "head word."

Consider the English phrase "local time" and its Arabic translation "Altwqyt AlmHly"; in both languages, they have a NP node that spans just these phrases. Syntax-based systems could learn to reorder the words for the translation process by collecting these tree fragments with respect to the alignments. In Yamada and Knight (2001), a decomposition similar to the IBM models is developed for a syntax-based approach that transforms the target parse tree using the operations of insertion, reorder, and translation. An efficient graph representation of these operations allows the model to compute the required parameters. Translations often have to break the parse structure and this has been studied in Fox (2002) and a better method of obtaining rules is discussed in Galley et al. (2004). From the original MT pyramid, we might expect that syntax-based systems should be more general or at least less susceptible to sparsity caused by finite training data; however, the challenge seems to be in reducing the errors in the parses and part-of-speech taggers. Source sentences that are difficult to translate seem to also be a challenge for parsers.

17.7.3.1 Hiero

In a significant generalization of the traditional phrase-based systems, Chiang (2005) describes a system (Hiero) to handle longer range word reordering. Hiero utilizes a weighted synchronous context-free grammar (CFG) extracted automatically from a word-aligned corpus, which has rules of the form

$$X \rightarrow (\gamma, \alpha, \sim) \tag{17.11}$$

where

γ correspond to source strings including nonterminals, α to target strings and non-terminals
~ indicates that any nonterminals in the strings are aligned

These nonterminals generalize the phrases used in standard phrase-based decoders. The grammar consists of two additional glue rules:

$$S \rightarrow (S_1 X_2, S_1 X_2)$$
$$S \rightarrow (X_1, X_1)$$

where S stands for the sentence and these rules constrain the system to applying the rules monotonically. The rewrite rules, X, are constrained in this work: (a) to contain at least one lexical item, (b) to have no sequences of non-terminals, (c) at most two non-terminals. Once the set of rules are obtained, the following set of features are extracted:

1. Relative frequencies $P(\gamma|\alpha)$ and $P(\alpha|\gamma)$
2. Lexical weights $P_w(\gamma|\alpha)$ and $P_w(\alpha|\gamma)$
3. Phrase penalty (word-count penalty) that allows the system to correct for length preferences
4. Glue rule cost that allows the system to learn a weight for the preference of normal phrases versus hierarchical phrases

Weights for these features are set using a minimum error rate training algorithm (Och, 2003). The decoder is a CKY parser utilizing a beam search strategy. The features are part of standard phrase-based decoders and only the language model feature is more involved due to search strategy which produces the target string in an arbitrary order. The language model is evaluated in an on-demand fashion as the history information becomes available for the path.

Hiero provides an architecture to evaluate further refinements such as syntactic categorizations of the nonterminals and although initial experimentation with syntatic categorizations did not improve automatic metrics, the platform continues to be extended and is the subject of much ongoing research.

17.7.4 Direct Translation Models

The noisy-channel model was motivated in Brown et al. (1993) on the observation that the source sentence is well-formed and that the MT hypotheses can generate arbitrary strings which are often not well-formed. As stated before, an equivalent approach for SMT is the direct model where we combine log-linearly various models.* The AT approach described above is the first example of a direct translation model (DTM). In Ittycheriah and Roukos (2007), a second approach (DTM2) at direct models for translation is discussed. The AT approach utilizes longer phrases to capture word reordering and deletion effects. The inventory of phrases in such systems is highly redundant as shown in the example in Table 17.2, which shows a set of phrases that cover the two-word Arabic fragment "mrAkz AlAqtrAE" from our earlier example in Figure 17.2. It is rather obvious that the unigram count of a word is greater than or equal to any bigram count that involves the same word. Counts are equal only in the rare case of a completely sticky pair (perhaps "Humpty Dumpty" in English) or with words that occur very few times due to data sparseness.

In DTM2, a minimalist set of phrases are used that are prescribed by the word alignments. In contrast, Blunsom et al. (2008) discusses a global method that allows overlapping phrases. Models and methods for training such global models have been covered in Chapter 9; here, we will focus on the setup and the

---

* The SMT problem can be stated as searching for the target string that maximizes the joint model, $p(T, S)$, and either the Bayes expansion is equivalent.

TABLE 17.2 Example of Arabic–English
Blocks Showing Possible 1-n and 2-n Blocks
Ranked by Frequency. Phrase Counts Are
Given in ()

mrAkz	AlAqtrAE
centers (905)	voting (476)
centres (361)	ballot (336)
stations (284)	polling (251)
the HOLE_1 centers (73)	vote (216)
positions (71)	the ballot (92)
duty stations (38)	the voting (88)
centers, (36)	polls (68)
...	...

voting centers (109)
polling stations (84)
the voting centers (70)
vote centers (34)
the polling stations (34)
ballot centers (28)
the ballot centers (23)
the vote centers (16)
...

features used in DTM2 models. We expand Equation 17.1 as we did for the IBM translation models,

$$p(T|S) = \sum_{a \in A} p(T, a|S) \approx p(T, a^\dagger|S) \tag{17.12}$$

where a_i gives the source position generating target t_i and the target sequence alignment $a^\dagger$ is selected to be close to the maximum probability path. This alignment is typically the best path that is provided by a word alignment algorithm or alternatively, this alignment could be a human alignment for some portion of the corpus. We then expand this in terms of the target words as

$$p(T, a^\dagger|S) = p(L|S) \prod_{i=1}^{L} p(t_i, a_i | t_0^{i-1}, a_0^{i-1}, s_0^K) \tag{17.13}$$

and by defining $j = a_i - a_{i-1}$ and limiting the history of the target sequence,

$$p(T, a^\dagger|S) = p(L|S) \prod_{i=1}^{L} p(t_i, j | t_{i-2}^{i-1}, a_1^{i-1}, s_0^K) \tag{17.14}$$

The model is postulated as an exponential model:

$$p(t_i, j | t_{i-2}^{i-1}, a_1^{i-1}, s_0^K) = \frac{p_0(t_i, j|s)}{Z} \exp \sum_i \lambda_i \phi_i(t_i, j, t_{i-2}^{i-1}, a_1^{i-1}, s_0^K) \tag{17.15}$$

where
  p_0 is a prior distribution
  Z is a normalizing term
  $\phi_i(t, j, t_{i-2}^{i-1}, a_1^{i-1}, s_0^k)$ are the features of the model

Note that Z is a simple partition function here since the model is about the local production, t_i. The burden of producing the words in the correct order has been shifted to the model in contrast to the phrase library and its the features of this model that allows the system to attain good performance.

TABLE 17.3 Some Features Used in the DTM2 System

Feature Name	Function	Description
Source–Target	$\phi(s_i, t_j)$	A Model 1 type of feature; examines the lexical identites of the words.
Source–Target Bigram	$\phi(s_i, t_j, s_{i-1}, t_{j-1})$	Looks at the left bigram context of the current production.
Source–Target Trigram	$\phi(s_i, t_j, s_{i-1}, t_{j-1}, s_{i-2}, t_{j-2})$	Looks at the left trigram context of the current production.
Source–Segmentation Target	$\phi(seg(s_i), t_j)$	Looks at prefix, suffix, and stem information for Arabic; Characters for Chinese and the current target word.
Source Part of speech Target Part of speech	$\phi(pos(s_i), pos(t_j))$	Looks at the part-of-speech tags of the source and target word.
Target Part-of-speech Trigram	$\phi(pos(t_j), pos(t_{j-1}), pos(t_{j-2}))$	Looks at the part-of-speech history of the target production.
Left and Right Source Node Coverage	$\phi(cov(s_{i-1}), t_j), \phi(cov(s_{i+1}), t_j)$	Looks at whether the neighboring source words have already produced some target words.
Parse Sibling Feature	$\phi(s_i, t_j, SibNode, Cov, Orient)$	Looks at the sibling parse nodes in the source parse tree. If the sibling node is covered, then Cov $= 1$ else it is 0. Orientation indicates whether its the right sibling or the left sibling.

17.7.4.1 Features

The direct model approach shares the advantage of an extensible feature set with the AT approach. The form of the model in Equation 17.15 lends itself to solutions using a variety of machine learning techniques: Generalized Iterative Scaling (Darroch and Ratcliff, 1972), Improved Iterative Scaling (IIS) (Della Pietra et al., 1995), and a variety of conjugate gradient methods. In Ittycheriah and Roukos (2007), the IIS algorithm is utilized.

Some features utilized in the model are shown in Table 17.3. In general, the features are language neutral and the only exception is the segmentation feature that varies from characters for Chinese to prefix, suffix, and stems for most other languages.

17.8 Search Strategies

We have discussed above methods to incorporate linguistic notions as features and training strategies for MT. One final issue that remains is the *argmax* from Equation 17.1, which represents the search for the optimal string under the model $p(T|S)$. The search problem has been addressed for speech recognition (see (Jelinek, 1999) for a comprehensive summary); for phrase-based MT was developed in Tillmann and Ney (2003), shown to be NP-complete for Model 1 type decoders (Knight, 1999), and an A^* algorithm for the AT approach for MT in Och and Ney (2004). Syntax-based approaches (e.g., Chiang, 2005; Zollmann and Venugopal, 2006) utilize CKY parser (Earley, 1970) and extensions for MT. For brevity, we will sketch out the decoding strategy used in the DTM approach above but recognize that heuristic search is the subject of much ongoing research.

In DTM, a beam-search algorithm is employed that is quite similar to the AT approach. The search process proceeds from left to right in a source sentence considering a *window* of source positions at each time. A second parameter, *skip*, controls how many source positions in the window can be in an "open" state. DTM allows translations that contain a variable and this requires the state of a source position to be in one of three conditions: {open, partially covered, covered}. The output of the beam search is a lattice, which has all the hypotheses that have been explored during the search. The best hypothesis at the end can then be back-tracked to produce the translation output. Each hypothesis captures the following:

- t_i, the target production at this step.
- lm_i, the language model state.
- C_i, the coverage status (implemented as two binary coverage vectors to capture partial and covered notions).
- $partial_i$, the data required to complete a state that is in partial state: (a) an index to the next target to be produced for the partial phrase, (b) the source position that is in partial state. This information can be recovered from the above coverage status but for efficiency we store the extra data.
- $score_i$, the score of this hypothesis.
- Back-pointer to do the final trace back through the lattice.

At each extension the following steps are carried out:

- ComputeSourcePositions: This function returns a vector of source positions that should be considered for generating at this point.
- Extend: This function generates a set of hypothesis from the phrase pairs aligned to the source positions obtained in the above step. This step also computes the weighted combination of scores from (a) the translation models, (b) the language models, (c) a word-count score. The translation models include the direct model and the model 1 score (Equation 17.10) for each direction. Since the language model cost increases with the number of words produced, the word-count score encourages the system to produce longer phrases.
- Merge: Paths are merged and the best one is kept when the language model state, the coverage status, and the current production are identical.
- Prune: Paths are pruned to keep, k, hypothesis for each coverage pattern.

When all alive hypotheses have no more open source positions, the search is terminated and the best sequence is output.

17.9 Research Areas

Machine translation remains the subject of many papers at conferences in natural language processing. In terms of research, the MT pyramid seems to offer the best roadmap and methods are being sought to inject more complex information into the translation systems. Constituent and dependency parsers as well as Named Entity taggers for various languages are now available and translation systems should be able to improve their performance by incorporating these types of information into the systems. Current systems are sentence oriented and this focus has left many document-level effects unattended including (certainly not an exhaustive list): (a) pronouns (when to use them, which one to use, etc.), (b) articles (e.g., in English to determine the definiteness of a noun would require document-level analysis), and (c) tense. Algorithms and methods for more robust estimation of translation models from parallel corpora that are automatically collected is being actively pursued.

Acknowledgment

This work was partially supported by the Department of the Interior, National Business Center under contract No. NBCH2030001 and Defense Advanced Research Projects Agency under contract No. HR0011-08-C-0110. The views and findings contained in this material are those of the authors and do not necessarily reflect the position or policy of the U.S. government and no official endorsement should be inferred. This chapter owes much to the collaboration of the Statistical MT group at IBM.

References

Banerjee, S. and Lavie, A. (2005). Meteor: An automatic metric for MT evaluation with improved correlation with human judgments. In *Proceedings of Workshop on Intrinsic and Entrinsic Evaluation Measures for MT and Summarization at the 43rd Annual Meeting of the Association of Computational Linguistics (ACL-2005)*, Ann Arbor, MI, pp. 65–72.

Bies, A. and Maamouri, M. (2008). Arabic treebank morphological and syntactic annotation guidelines. http://projects.ldc.upenn.edu/ArabicTreebank

Block, H. U. (2000). Example-based incremental synchronous interpretation. In Wahlster, W., editor, *Verbmobil: Foundations of Speech-to-Speech Translation*, pages 411–417. Springer-Verlag, Berlin, Germany.

Blunsom, P., Cohn, T., and Osborne, M. (2008). A discriminative latent variable model for statistical machine translation. In *46th Annual Meeting of the ACL*, Columbus, OH.

Brants, T. and Franz, A. (2006). Web 1T 5-gram version 1. *Linguistic Data Consortium*, LDC2006T13, 2006.

Brown, P. F., Pietra, V. J. D., Pietra, S. A. D., and Mercer, R. L. (1993). The mathematics of statistical machine translation: Parameter estimation. *Computational Linguistics*, 19(2):263–311.

Chen, S. F. (1998). An empirical study of smoothing techniques for language modeling. Technical Report, Harvard University, Cambridge, MA.

Chiang, D. (2005). A hierarchical phrase-based model for statistical machine translation. In *Proceedings of the 43rd Annual Meeting of the ACL*, pp. 263–270, Ann Arbor, MI.

Darroch, J. N. and Ratcliff, D. (1972). Generalized iterative scaling for log-linear models. *The Annals of Mathematical Statistics*, 43(5):1470–1480.

Della Pietra, S., Della Pietra, V., and Lafferty, J. (1995). Inducing features of random fields. Technical Report, Department of Computer Science, Carnegie-Mellon University, Pittsburg, PA, CMU-CS-95-144.

Earley, J. (1970). An efficient context-free parsing algorithm. *Communications of the Association for Computing Machinery*, 13(2):94–102.

Fox, H. J. (2002). Phrasal cohesion and statistical machine translation. In *Proceedings of EMNLP-02*, Philadelphia, PA, pp. 304–311.

Galley, M., Hopkins, M., Knight, K., and Marcu, D. (2004). What's in a translation rule? In *HLT-NAACL*, Boston, MA, pp. 273–280.

Ge, N. (2004). Improvement in Word Alignments. *Presentation Given at DARPA/TIDES MT Workshop*, Gaithersburg, MD.

Hovy, E. (1999). Toward finely differentiated evaluation metrics for machine translation. *Proceedings of EAGLES Workshop on Standards and Evaluation*, Pisa, Italy.

Ittycheriah, A. and Roukos, S. (2005). A maximum entropy word aligner for arabic-english machine translation. In *HLT '05: Proceedings of the HLT and EMNLP*, Vancouver, Canada, pp. 89–96.

Ittycheriah, A. and Roukos, S. (2007). Direct translation model 2. In *Human Language Technologies 2007: The Conference of the NA-ACL*, Rochester, NY, pp. 57–64. Association for Computational Linguistics.

Jelinek, F. (1999). *Statistical Methods for Speech Recognition*. MIT Press, Cambridge, MA.

Knight, K. (1999). Decoding complexity in word-replacement translation models. *Computational Linguistics*, (25):607–615.

Koehn, P., Hoang, H., Birch, A., Callison-Burch, C., Federico, M., Bertoldi, N., Cowan, B., Shen, W., Moran, C., Zens, R., Dyer, C., Bojar, O., Constantin, A., and Herbst, E. (2007). Moses: Open source toolkit for statistical machine translation. In *Annual Meeting of the Association for Computational Linguistics (ACL)*, Prague, Czech Republic.

Le Quan Ha, E. I. Sicilia-Garcia, J. M., and Smith, F. J. (2002). Extension of zipf's law to words and phrases. In *COLING 2002: The 19th International Conference on Computational Linguistics*, Taipei, Taiwan, pp. 315–320.

Marcus, M. P., Marcinkiewicz, M. A., and Santorini, B. (1993). Building a large annotated corpus of English: The penn treebank. *Computational Linguistics*, 19(2):313–330.

NIST. Mt03. http://www.nist.gov/speech/tests/mt/2003/

Och, F. J. (2003). Minimum error rate training in Statistical Machine Translation. In *41st Annual Meeting of the ACL*, Sapporo, Japan, pp. 160–167.

Och, F.-J. and Ney, H. (2002). Discriminative Training and Maximum Entropy Models for Statistical Machine Translations. In *40th Annual Meeting of the ACL*, Philadelphia, PA, pp. 295–302.

Och, F. J. and Ney, H. (2003). A systematic comparison of various statistical alignment models. *Computational Linguistics*, 29(1):19–51.

Och, F. J. and Ney, H. (2004). The alignment template approach to statistical machine translation. *Computational Linguistics*, 30(4):417–449.

Och, F., Gildea, D., Khudanpur, S., Sarkar, A., Yamada, K., Fraser, A., Kumar, S., Shen, L., Smith, D., Eng, K., Jain, V., Jin, Z., and Radev, D. (2004). A smorgasbord of features for statistical machine translation. *Proceedings of the HLT-NAACL*, Boston, MA.

Papineni, K., Roukos, S., and Ward, R. T. (1997). Feature-based language understanding. In *EUROSPEECH, Rhodes, Greece*, pp. 1435–1438.

Papineni, K., Roukos, S., and Ward, R. T. (1998). Maximum likelihood and discriminative training of direct translation models. In *International Conference on Acoustics, Speech and Signal Processing*, Seattle, WA, pp. 189–192.

Papineni, K., Roukos, S., Ward, T., and Zhu, W.-J. (2002). BLEU: A method for automatic evaluation of machine translation. In *40th Annual Meeting of the ACL*, Philadelphia, PA, pp. 311–318.

Snover, M., Dorr, B., Schwartz, R., Micciulla, L., and Weischedel, R. (2006). A study of translation error rate with targeted human annotation. In *Proceedings of the Association for Machine Translation in the Americas Conference 2006*, Boston, MA, pp. 223–231.

Tillmann, C. and Ney, H. (2003). Word reordering and a dynamic programming beam search algorithm for statistical machine translation. *Computational Linguists*, 29(1):97–133.

Vauquois, B. (1968). A survey of formal grammars and algorithms for recognition and transformation in machine translation. In *IFIP Congress-68*, Edinburgh, U.K., pp. 254–260.

Vogel, S., Ney, H., and Tillmann, C. (1996). HMM Based-Word Alignment in Statistical Machine Translation. In *Proceedings of the 16th International Conference on Computational Linguistics (COLING 1996)*, pp. 836–841, Copenhagen, Denmark.

Weaver, W. (1955). *Translation. [Repr. Machine translation of languages: fourteen essays, ed. W.N. Locke and A.D. Booth]*. Technology Press of MIT, Cambridge, MA.

Yamada, K. and Knight, K. (2001). A syntax-based statistical translation model. *Proceedings of the ACL*, Toulouse, France, pp. 523–530.

Zollmann, A. and Venugopal, A. (2006). Syntax augmented machine translation via chart parsing. In *NAACL 2006—Workshop on Statistical Machine Translation*, New York. Association for Computational Linguistics.

III

Applications

18

Chinese Machine Translation

Pascale Fung
*The Hong Kong University of
Science and Technology*

18.1 Introduction

Chinese, in particular Mandarin Chinese, is currently the most spoken language in the world, with an estimated 1.2 billion primary and secondary speakers, while English ranks a distant second with 330 million native speakers, and a further 150 million secondary speakers. Among various Chinese languages, Standard Mandarin (*Putonghua/Guoyu/Huayu*) is the only official written form and is the only common official language in the four Chinese-speaking countries and regions, including the People's Republic of China, the Republic of China (commonly known as "Taiwan"), Hong Kong, Macau, and Singapore. Standard Mandarin is also one of the six official languages of the United Nations. (There are dialects within the Mandarin language family, spoken in various regions in the north and southwest of China.) Incidentally, Standard Mandarin Chinese, together with the other five official UN languages, are also ranked as the six most influential languages in the world, when judged by the total number of world speakers, the geographical influence, the economic power of countries speaking the language, and the literary and scientific use of the language. China has the fastest growing economy in the world, and is the second largest economy, after the United States, in terms of purchasing power parity GDP. Perhaps most pertinent to the topic in this chapter, China (including Hong Kong) was the biggest exporter in 2008 and is poised to become the world's biggest importer in 2010. The largest trading partners with China are (1) the European Union, (2) the United States, (3) Japan, and (4) the Association of South East Asian Nations. Consequently, for various economic, political, cultural, and humanitarian reasons, machine translation (MT) of Chinese from and into other languages is an increasingly more important application in the natural language processing (NLP) area.

Since the 1950s to the present day, the development of Chinese MT systems has paralleled that of the MT field as a whole, from rule-based systems within limited domain, to extracting and adopting examples from corpus, to statistical machine translation (SMT) approaches that appeared in the early 1990s and which evolved into the mainstream approach today. Meanwhile, the dichotomy of rule-based versus corpus-based methods has become increasingly blurred. Systems by and large adopt a less ideological approach. It is common for rule-based systems to rank rules by statistics and for statistical systems to incorporate more linguistic rules related to syntax and semantics. As such, this chapter focuses more on the discussion of the merits and relationship between rule-based and corpus-based approaches, rather than contrasting their differences.

In this chapter, we describe various approaches in Chinese MT, as pertaining to and motivated by the linguistic characteristics of the Chinese language, from words to phrases, from syntax to semantics. Section 18.2 describes the challenge in Chinese morphology and word segmentation, and the role this preprocessing part plays in MT systems. We ask the question of whether it is important to pre-segment Chinese sentences into word segments before translation. In Section 18.3 and 18.4, we turn to a comparison between two corpus-based MT approaches that handles lexical units beyond words, namely, example-based and phrase-based SMTs, and point out the commonality between the two approaches, and their relationship to syntax-based methods. Section 18.5 describes syntax-driven MT and how it is an approach motivated by the word order difference between Chinese and other languages. As Chinese is often regarded as a semantics-centered language, Section 18.6 gives an overview of semantics-driven MT approaches, ranging from the earlier interlingua and transfer-based translation methods, to the latest semantics-driven SMT algorithms. We also give an overview of some of the applications related to MT in Section 18.7, such as Chinese term translation and spoken language translation. Finally, we conclude in Section 18.8. In organizing this chapter according to the linguistic characteristics of Chinese, we aim to explain the "why" behind each approach, in addition to the "how."

18.2 Preprocessing—What Is a Chinese Word?

As there are no space delimiters between words, morphological analysis must first handle the segmentation of a sentence into words. The smallest lexical unit in Chinese is a monosyllabic character, *Hanzi*. Most characters possess meanings of their own. Words are formed from using one, two, three, or sometimes more characters. The morphological analysis of a Chinese sentence must first refer to a lexicon of words. The written Chinese characters are ideographs that look like pictures and are, in effect, evolved from ancient hieroglyphs carved onto oracles. However, most Chinese characters are composed of *both* a phonetic part and a semantic element. Over 80% of Chinese words contain one to two characters only. Since Chinese sentences are written without space as delimiters between words, compound words can be arbitrarily long. Sometimes an entire phrase is considered one word in Chinese. Chinese is often said to be a morphology-poor language. Words in Chinese for the most part do not change forms according to changes in tenses, voice, case, gender, or even number (there are, however, plural markers for personal pronouns). The character for the third person singular has three, sometimes four forms, according to gender, whether it is a person, an animal, or a deity, though these are exceptions rather than the rule in Chinese. There are few articles. Instead, Chinese rely on using additional words, word order, and sentence structure to indicate the function of a word in a sentence. Aspects and mood are indicated by the use of a few articles such as le/了, hai/, yijing/已, etc. These characteristics of Chinese morphology pose a particular challenge to translation systems that translate Chinese into another language with a different set of morphological rules. To date, word and phrase alignment accuracies of Chinese to English do not rival those between European languages, or even between Arabic and English. In particular, unlike in other languages, Chinese person names consist of a close set of family names in one or two characters, followed by an open set of first names mostly in one or two characters drawn from the entire character set. It is difficult for a translation system to discern whether a character should be trans*literated* as part of a name, or trans*lated* as a semantic unit.

Like other aspects of Chinese language processing, current Chinese word segmentation systems are mostly statistical or machine learning-based, rather than rule-based, as a result of applying techniques that have shown to perform well on English first. The increasing dominance of statistical-based approach for Chinese morphological and syntactic analyzers seems to parallel the rise of *statistical* Chinese–English MT in the last two decades.

Fung and Wu (1994; 1995) first used statistics to automatically analyze Chinese words from large corpora. They used spread, cohesion, etc., borrowed from previous work in automatic collocation extraction from English (Smadja 1992), and augmented with a few Chinese morphological rules. Fung went on to use word signature features and signal processing tools to automatically extract Chinese–English bilingual dictionaries (Fung 1996; Fung and McKeown 1997; Fung and Lo 1998). Instead of focusing on what morphological rules can cover all Chinese words, these work largely regard words (and even person names), as a bag of characters that co-occur frequently together by some measure.

Modern Chinese morphological analyzers, including segmentation and part-of-speech tagging, employ a host of methods ranging from dictionary word-based and N-gram statistics-based languages models, to using classifiers such as Maximum Entropy and Conditional Random Fields with a set of features.

It has been shown (Fung et al. 2004; Zhai et al. 2004) that syntactic parsing results are better when word segmentation, part-of-speech tagging, and final parsing are all carried out with one feature-based classifier, with unsegmented text as input, rather than using a pipeline system of segmentation, tagging, and parsing. This is due to the fact that features pertinent to the latter stages of chunking and parsing are helpful to the earlier stages of segmentation and tagging as well. Most of the earlier attempts at Chinese parsing (Wu 1995; Bikel and Chiang 2000; Xue and Converse 2002) have therefore ignored the problem of word segmentation and assumed gold-standard (i.e., hand-annotated) word boundaries, which is not realistic.

The problem of Chinese word segmentation is quite challenging, owing to the lack of a good definition for what constitutes a word in Chinese. Previous experiments involving native speakers achieved an agreement rate of only around 75% (Wu and Fung 1994; Sproat et al. 1996). Most Chinese word segmenters make use of large lexicons of manually defined words. The limitations of this method, however, are that the word lists have to be manually constructed, which is a tedious and time-consuming process. In addition, the word lists constructed are heavily dependent on the domain at hand, as words vary from domain to domain.

(Fung et al. 2004) presents a method in which a maximum entropy parser, is augmented by a transformation-based learner. The combined parser, which is purely corpus-driven, takes as input a raw, unsegmented Chinese sentence, and outputs the parse tree that best fits the sentence.

18.2.1 The Maximum Entropy Framework for Word Segmentation

Maximum entropy has been applied to many NLP tasks, part-of-speech (POS) tagging and parsing among them, achieving state-of-the-art results. Most maximum entropy parsers are close variations of (Ratnaparkhi 1998), which breaks down the parsing process into three steps: tagging, chunking, and tree building. The output of each component is piped into the next as input. Since the parser is working at the word level, a fourth component, the word segmenter, is added as an initial (preprocessing) step. Since maximum entropy models are inherently classifiers, the various subtasks are mapped to classification tasks.

The probabilistic models for all the subtask components follow the form:

$$p\left(T|W\right) = \sum_{i=0}^{n} p\left(y_i \mid x_i\right)$$

$$p\left(y_i \mid x_i\right) = \frac{1}{Z\left(x_i\right)} \exp\left(\sum_{j=0}^{m} (\lambda_i) \times f_j(x_i, y_i)\right)$$

where

$W = \{w_0, w_1, ..., w_n\}$ is the input character sequence

T is the most likely output tag sequence for the corresponding component model

The output classification for the ith sample is denoted by, y_i which are determined as a probability of the given contextual features x_i.

18.2.1.1 Word Segmentation

Unlike English and many other Western languages, Chinese (and Japanese) is not written with any characters or spaces between words. The task of word segmentation therefore attempts to word-delimit a text by inserting indicators which mark the boundaries between predefined words. The difficulty of Chinese word segmentation lies in the ambiguity of the task, as well as the fact that for any given sentence, there may be more than one valid word segmentation sequence.

Since words follow one another and do not overlap, the task of word segmentation can be easily mapped to a tagging problem in a similar way to that pioneered by Ramshaw and Marcus (1995) for English text chunking. The character that begins a word segment is tagged with a "B," while all other words are tagged with "I" to denote that they are inside a word segment. Each sample is therefore a character, and the output classification is the word segment tag {B,I} that best fits the character in that context.

18.2.1.2 Part-of-Speech Tagging

POS tagging, or simply tagging, is one of the most basic tasks in NLP. The task involves labeling each word in a sentence with a tag indicating its POS function (e.g., noun, verb, adjective, etc.). Since many words have more than one POS tag, the task of the tagger is to use lexical and syntactic features of the word to determine the most likely tag for that particular use of the word in the given sentence. The problem of POS ambiguity is especially severe for Chinese, since Chinese words lack morphological information, which is an important indicator for syntactic function.

Since POS tagging is already a classification task, no extra steps are needed to map it for classification algorithms. Each sample is naturally a word, and the output classification, the POS tag (e.g., noun, verb, adjective) is the most appropriate for that particular word instance.

18.2.1.3 Text Chunking

An intermediate step between POS tagging and full parsing is text chunking, which is the task of dividing a sentence into syntactically correlated segments called chunks, or base phrases. Unlike parse constituents, chunks are non-recursive and are usually based on superficial syntactic analysis. For example, the sentence "第七屆世界游泳錦標賽在羅馬開幕" can be chunked as

[QP第七][CLP屆][NP世界游泳錦標賽][PP在][NP羅馬][VP開幕]

where each text chunk is delimited with brackets ([. . .]) that are annotated with chunk type.

Since text chunks are non-recursive, the task of text chunking can be easily mapped to that of a word classification task (Ramshaw and Marcus 1995). Each word is tagged with information that denotes the chunk that the word is in (e.g., NP, VP, PP, etc.), as well as the position of the word within the chunk

Char	第	七	届	世	界	游	泳	锦	标	赛	在	罗	马	开	幕
Word	B	I	B	B	I	B	I	B	I	I	B	B	I	B	I
POS	OD		M	NN		NN		NN			P	NP		V V	
Chunk	B-QP		B-CLP	B-NP		I-NP		I-NP			B-PP	B-NP		B-VP	

FIGURE 18.1 Marking word segment, POS, and chunk tags for a sentence.

(i.e., begin or inside). Words that did not fit inside any chunk were classified as outside. The fact that text chunks are nonoverlapping makes it possible to deterministically map all possible sequences of text chunks to some sequence of chunk tags. A sample for the chunker component would then be a word, and the classification of its corresponding chunk tag.

As an example of the various subtasks, Figure 18.1 shows an example sentence tagged with word segment, POS and chunk tags.

18.2.2 Translation-Driven Word Segmentation

Another approach in segmentation for MT is to learn the segmentation through bilingual sentence alignment during the training stage for SMT (Wu 1997; Xu et al. 2004). These methods are described in detail in Chapter 16. In this section, we give a brief summarization of it in relation to Chinese MT.

Xu et al. (2004) trained word alignment models—IBM-1, IBM-4 (Brown et al. 1993) and Hidden Markov alignment model (Vogel et al. 1996) on an unsegmented bilingual corpus of Chinese and English. All these models give rise to different decompositions of the alignment probability $\Pr\left(f_1^J, a_1^J \mid e_1^I\right)$ where a is the alignment, f is the source word, and e the target word. Chinese characters are aligned to English words with this model. A bilingual lexicon of Chinese/English word pairs are extracted from the word aligned corpus. The Chinese text is subsequently segmented using this extracted bi-lexicon, and the translation model is retrained on the segmented corpus. They showed that translation quality suffered only slightly, at a relative 5%, when no segmentation was applied *a priori* to the Chinese character strings, compared to training on segmented text. They also showed that the segmentation result learned through alignment is compatible with the Linguistic Data Consortium (LDC) manual segmentation results. Figure 18.2 shows an example of word segmentation as a result of alignment between unsegmented Chinese character strings and English words. For example, the first two Chinese characters are aligned to "industry" and segmented as a single Chinese word.

Since these Chinese morphological analyzers are used to serve the need of MT when Chinese is the source language, it is not surprising that researchers would question the effect of different morphological analysis approaches on the final translation performance. Zhang et al. (2008) explicitly compared four

FIGURE 18.2 An example of Chinese word segmentation from alignment of Chinese characters to English words (From Xu, R. et al., The construction of a Chinese shallow treebank, in the *Third SIGHAM Workshop on Chinese Language Processing*, Barcelona, Spain, pp. 94–101).

types of Chinese word segmentation methods in terms of final translation performance and suggest two methods: a simple concatenation of training data and a feature interpolation approach in which the same types of features of translation models from various Chinese word segmentation schemes are linearly interpolated. They found such combined approaches were very effective in improving the quality of translations. Moreover, comparative experiments carried out on the GALE project data and the BTEC data using different Chinese word segmentation systems showed no significant differences between the systems in influencing Chinese–English MT performance. However, all automatic segmentation systems outperformed manual segmentation for MT (team 2008). Finally, to the question of "Do we need Chinese word segmentation for translation?," the answer seems to be "Yes, but it is best if the words are segmented in *conjunction* with translation."

18.3 Phrase-Based SMT—From Words to Phrases

In Chinese, as words are not delimited by space, there is no clear distinction between words and phrases. Consequently, all Chinese MT systems can be considered as phrase-based to some extent. The distinction between various Chinese (statistical) MT systems lie in (1) whether the segmentation of Chinese sentences are translation-driven; (2) whether sentences in the other language are translation-driven; (3) whether the system allows for multiple segmentation in the output sentence during decoding. According to these criteria, the first phrase-based SMT system was also a syntax-driven system based on the Inversion Transduction Grammar (ITG). Wu (1995), designed specifically for optimizing the segmentation in Chinese sentences in conjunction with the bracketing of both Chinese and English sentences in the translation process.

Another common approach by phrase-based SMT systems learns a phrase alignment model using a noisy channel model from parallel, translated texts. Unlike word-based SMT, multi word phrases or chunks are the basic lexical units for alignment. Phrasal boundaries and alignment can also be simultaneously learned in a single Estimation-Maximization process (Och et al. 1999). The decoding process in a true phrase-based SMT system must allow for multiple segmentations in the output sentence candidates.

In particular, open source programs such as Moses are readily available for phrase-based SMT, given training corpus in any language pairs. Moses (Koehn et al. 2007) uses a beam search algorithm for decoding phrase-based translations. It allows words to have factored representation in surface form, lemma, part of speech, morphology, etc.

The Moses system uses different approaches for learning phrasal translations (sometimes called phrase tables). Marcu and Wong (2002) introduce a phrase-based joint probability model of the simultaneous occurrence of the source and target sentence in a parallel corpus. They use expectation-maximization learning to find (1) a joint probability $\Phi(e, f)$ of phrase e and phrase f being translation equivalents; and (2) a joint distribution indicating a phrase at position i in the source is translated into one at position j in the target sentence. Och and Ney (2003) use expansion heuristics to find phrase translations from word alignment models from the two directions. Based on this, Moses starts with the intersection between the word alignment points from the source and target languages, and iteratively expand to phrasal alignments using unaligned words within the limit of the union of word alignment from both directions. Words within a legal pair of phrasal translations are only aligned to each other, never outside of the phrase boundary. Zens, Och, and Ney (2002) define the set of bilingual phrases **BP** as

$$\mathbf{BP}\left(f_1^J, e_1^J, A\right) = \left\{\left(f_j^{j+m}, e_i^{i+n}\right)\right\} : \text{ forall } (i', j') \text{ in } A : j <= j' <= j+m <-> i <= i' <= i+n$$

Venugopal et al. (2003) actually allow phrasal translations that violates word alignment constraints. Zens et al. (2002) look for a unique segmentation of the sentence pair with joint probability distributions, to yield phrasal translations. Vogel et al. (2003) suggest combining different methods for more performance gain.

More recently, the Multilingual Application Network for Olympic Services (MANOS) project (Bo et al. 2005) aimed to provide speech recognition, MT, and speech synthesis in multiple languages for the 2008 Olympic Games in Beijing. The MT system is a phrase-based translation system, using not one but four different approaches, all of them described in this chapter to extract the phrase table. The four methods they use are (1) Integrated segmentation and phrase alignment (ISA) (Zhang et al. 2003); (2) HMM word alignment model (Vogel et al. 1996); (3) GIZA++ word alignment model (Och et al. 1999), and (4) (ITG) (Wu 1997).

18.4 Example-Based MT—Translation by Analogy

The Chinese language differs from many other major languages in terms of word order and syntactic structure. Japanese, despite having borrowed a substantial amount of Chinese nouns, is not part of the Sino-Tibetan language family as Chinese is, and is unrelated to Chinese in terms of morphological reflections and syntax. Based on the assumption that languages that differ significantly in grammatical and/or lexical structure can be better handled by examples, researchers in Japan have adopted example-based machine translation (EBMT) methods for Chinese to Japanese translation.

Nagao (1984) first suggested an approach of EBMT in 1984. This approach is essentially a translation process by using analogies. In a departure from a previous belief that humans perform translation by first doing deep linguistic analysis of the source sentences. It is believed by some that, instead, humans often perform the translation task by mentally retrieving previously learned phrases, or generalizing from examples. Examples of phrase translations or examples of translation templates are retrieved from translated, bilingual texts. As such, EBMT was the first corpus-based approach in this area. Nagao (1984) proposes to dispense with deep structural analysis, and look for analogies between sentence pairs stored in the system and the sentence to be translated, in an algorithm of EBMT as follows:

1. Convert an input source sentence into a canonical sentential structure.
2. Use case grammar to parse this sentential structure.
3. Look up a dictionary to find candidate target word translations, and example phrases.
4. Use a word thesaurus to measure the similarity between the input sentential phrases and example phrases stored in the dictionary.
5. Generation of target sentential form as translations from step (4) above.
6. Generation of local phrasal structures within the constraint of step (5).

Nagao (1984) noted that steps (5) and (6) are very challenging subtasks and remained, at the time, to be solved.

Researchers at NICT, Kyoto University, University of Tokyo, Shizuoka University, and JST in Japan (Isahara et al. 2007) have been developing an example-based Japanese–Chinese MT system. Unlike earlier versions of EBMT systems, Isahara et al. (2007) employ a host of statistical tools for various stages of the system. They have been developing a parallel corpus of Chinese–Japanese on the scale of 10 million sentences as the corpus from which examples can be extracted. Examples are to be aligned using their syntactic structures, the latter obtained from statistical parsers. In the final translation system, input sentences are to be analyzed syntactically and decomposed into substructures. Example translations of these substructures will be retrieved from the database, and recombined to generate the target sentence.

Researchers at Tsinghua University and the Chinese Institute of Automation have developed an example-based Chinese–English MT system (Liu and Zong 2004). In their approach, a rule-based standard template database of 209 Chinese patterns is used in conjunction with a bilingual dictionary, thesaurus, and a sentence-aligned bilingual parallel corpus. In the translation process, sentences are divided into chunks and transformed into target chunks by looking up example templates by a set of similarity rules. Translated chunks are recombined into target sentence and a final generation phase takes into consideration tense, voice, person, and number. They point out that chunk alignment and templates should be learned automatically in future improvement of such a system.

Zhang et al. (2001) showcase the advantage of the example-based approach by adapting a shallow EBMT system to Chinese–English translation, by using nothing more than the Hong Kong Hansard parallel corpus and a bilingual dictionary/phrase book from the LDC. Their system is a shallow EBMT system that, given an input sentence, looks up the Chinese part of the parallel corpus and transforms parts of it into English by word alignment. Translations not found in the corpus are provided by the bilingual phrase book.

Perhaps aware of the relative strength and weakness of the example-based approach, researchers at the Harbin Institute of Technology (Yang et al. 2008) propose a Chinese–English EBMT system that is *domain sensitive*. Examples are extracted from word-aligned corpus. Example translations are selected through a combination of text classification techniques. Researchers at the same institute also propose using Maximum Entropy method to learn example patterns from parallel corpora (Chen et al. 2007).

Compared to other approaches in MT, example-based approach sits in between SMT using phrase tables and SMT using syntax. When example phrase translations are automatically learned from the parallel corpora of translation texts, and when example lookup becomes encoded in an implicit phrase alignment statistical model, itself learned from parallel corpora, we have migrated from example-based approach to a phrase-based SMT approach. When phrase alignment is syntactically motivated, whether formally or linguistically, such an approach is considered syntax-driven.

18.5 Syntax-Based MT—Structural Transfer

As mentioned in the above section, Chinese has little morphological variations. Consequently it depends on word order and sentence structure, rather than morphology to indicate the function of a word in a sentence. As the Chinese language possesses no tenses, no voices, no numbers (singular, plural; though there are plural markers, for example for personal pronouns), only a few articles, and no gender, it has few grammatical inflections.

Even though the Chinese language in general follows the Subject–Verb–Object word order, its syntax is far from similar to Western languages that also follow the SVO word order. For example, Chinese makes frequent use of the topic-comment construction to form sentences. A common grammatical feature, which poses a huge challenge to MT systems, is the drop of pronouns and related subject. The use of serial verb construction is also a Chinese linguistic feature that often leads to ambiguities in parsing and ultimately translation.

Given the significant difference in Chinese syntax compared to English, it is interesting, and perhaps not surprising, that syntax-based SMT was first introduced to tackle exactly this language pair (Wu 1997). As the other dominant SMT approach, the IBM SMT models, made use of a *distortion model* to tackle the word order difference between two languages. While such a distortion model works relatively well for sentence pairs in related languages such as French and English, it is largely inadequate for unrelated languages with very different syntax. The reason is that the basic IBM-style model is not able to cover distortions over longer distances. In other words, reordering *"white house"* into *"la maison blanche"* is easy, reordering one phrase from the beginning of the sentence to the end of the sentence is much harder. A better approach is called for to model the complex syntactic relationship between sentences pairs that belong to unrelated language groups such as Chinese and English.

Wu's Stochastic ITG formalism models this complex syntactic relationship between bilingual sentence pairs with a kind of synchronous context-free grammar extracted automatically from translated, parallel sentences, and is particularly well-suited to model ordering shifts between languages.

The ITG remains to be a subset of context-free (syntax-directed) transduction grammars (Lewis and Stearns 1968). The ITG, unlike simple, pure transduction grammars, allows for generation of symbols

$$
\begin{array}{rcl}
\text{S} & \rightarrow & \text{[SP Stop]} \\
\text{SP} & \rightarrow & \text{[NP VP] | [NP VV] | [NP V]} \\
\text{PP} & \rightarrow & \text{[Prep NP]} \\
\text{NP} & \rightarrow & \text{[Det NN] | [Det N] | [Pro] | [NP Conj NP]} \\
\text{NN} & \rightarrow & \text{[A N] | [NN PP]} \\
\text{VP} & \rightarrow & \text{[Aux VP] | [Aux VV] | [VV PP]} \\
\text{VV} & \rightarrow & \text{[V NP] | [Cop A]} \\
\text{Det} & \rightarrow & \text{the/ε} \\
\text{Prep} & \rightarrow & \text{to/向} \\
\text{Pro} & \rightarrow & \text{I/我 | you/你} \\
\text{N} & \rightarrow & \text{authority/管理局 | secretary/司} \\
\text{A} & \rightarrow & \text{accountable/負責 | financial/財政} \\
\text{Conj} & \rightarrow & \text{and/和} \\
\text{Aux} & \rightarrow & \text{will/將會} \\
\text{Cop} & \rightarrow & \text{be/ε} \\
\text{(a) Stop} & \rightarrow & \text{./ₒ}
\end{array}
$$

(b) VP → ⟨VV PP⟩

FIGURE 18.3 (a) A simple transduction grammar and (b) an inverted orientation production. (From Wu, D., *Comput. Linguist.*, 23, 377, 1997.)

from the right-hand-side constituents of a product rule in two directions, straight left-to-right and inverted right-to-left (Figure 18.3). This way, a bilingual sentence pair with different syntax structures can be parsed by the same set of ITG rules. If [] indicates concatenation in the straight orientation, i.e., [AB] yields (C_1, C_2) where () $C_1 = A_1 B_1$ and $C_2 = A_2 B_2$, and <> indicates the reverse, where <AB> means $C_1 = A_1 B_1$ but $C_2 = B_2 A_2$, then the following sentence pair in English and Chinese, with different syntax structure, can be generated as:

In the parse tree example in Figure 18.4, the English sentence is read in the depth-first left-to-right straight order, but for the Chinese sentence, the right sub-tree is traversed instead of the left, whenever there is a horizontal line.

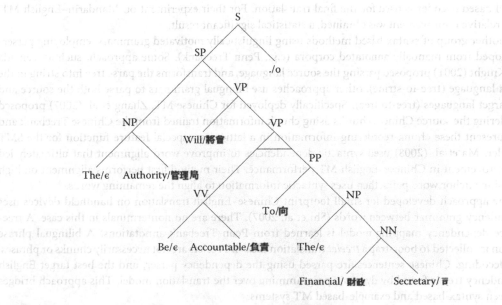

FIGURE 18.4 ITG parse tree. (From Wu, D., *Comput. Linguist.*, 23, 377, 1997.)

Wu (1997) also surveyed a number of applications of the ITG formalism, including translation-driven segmentation, word alignment, bilingual lexicon extraction, and translation-driven bi-bracketing. Wu (1995) also shows a training method based on expectation and maximization. The approach taken by this work generalizes the inside–outside algorithm to improve the likelihood of a training corpus by adjusting the grammar parameters. For details of the ITG model and its application to MT, please see Chapter 16.

Following Wu's work, there has been a steady growth in modeling tree structures in MT, not the least for Chinese MT. Some of these approaches (Chiang 2005), are formal syntax-based, deriving bilingual parses from parallel corpora without any linguistic annotations. Chiang (2005) seeks to improve the reordering power of phrase-based SMT by a hierarchical phrase model (see Figure 18.5). Like Wu (1997), this approach also (1) induces an ITG from parallel texts without any linguistic syntactic annotation, and (2) allows for entire phrases in transduction rules. Chiang (2005) uses GIZA++ word alignment tools on the training parallel corpus to obtain initial phrase pairs (Och and Ney 2004). Chiang (2005) proposes an iterative heuristic method for extracting the transduction grammar from these initial phrase pairs, using the following rules:

1. If there are multiple initial phrase pairs containing the same set of alignment points, we keep only the smallest.
2. Initial phrases are limited to a length of 10 on the French side, and rule to five (nonterminals plus terminals) on the French right-hand side.
3. In the subtraction step, f_{ji} must have length greater than one. The rationale is that little would be gained by creating a new rule that is no shorter than the original.
4. Rules can have at most two nonterminals, which simplifies the decoder implementation. Moreover, we prohibit nonterminals that are adjacent on the French side, a major cause of spurious ambiguity.
5. A rule must have at least one pair of aligned words, making translation decisions always based on some lexical evidence.

Rules numbers (4) and (5) above essentially mirror the ITG rules in Wu (1997) (see Chapter 16). From a training corpus of 7.2M words in Chinese and 9.2M words in English, they obtain 24M rules. A log-linear model based decoder is used for the final translation. For their experiment on Mandarin–English MT, 7.5% relative improvement was obtained, a statistical significant result.

Another group of syntax-based methods using linguistically motivated grammars, employing parsers developed from manually annotated corpora (e.g., Penn Treebank). Some approach, such as Yamada and Knight (2001) proposed parsing the source language, and transforms the parse tree into string in the target language (tree-to-string), other approaches use bilingual grammars to parse both the source and the target languages (tree-to-tree). Specifically deployed for Chinese MT, Zhang et al. (2007) proposed reordering the source Chinese chunks using chunk information trained from the Chinese Treebank and to represent these chunk reordering information in a lattice as a special feature function for the SMT decoder. Ma et al. (2008) used syntactic dependencies to improve word alignment that ultimately led to improvement in Chinese–English MT performance. Their method first performs alignment on high precision anchor word pairs, then uses syntactic information to align the remaining words.

One approach developed for small footprint Chinese–English translation on handheld devices uses dependency grammar between words (Shi et al. 2007). There are no nonterminals in this case. A tree-to-tree dependency mapping model is learned from Penn Treebank annotations. A bilingual phrase lexicon is collected to bootstrap a *treelet* translation model. Treelets are not necessarily chunks or phrases. For decoding, Chinese sentences are parsed using the dependency parser, and the best target English dependency tree is found by dynamic programming over the translation model. This approach bridges between syntax-based and example-based MT systems.

Rank	Chinese	English
1	。	.
3	的	the
14	在	in
23	的	's
577	$X_{\boxed{1}}$ 的 $X_{\boxed{2}}$	the $X_{\boxed{2}}$ of $X_{\boxed{1}}$
735	$X_{\boxed{1}}$ 的 $X_{\boxed{2}}$	the $X_{\boxed{2}}$ $X_{\boxed{1}}$
763	$X_{\boxed{1}}$ 之一	one of $X_{\boxed{1}}$
1201	$X_{\boxed{1}}$ 总统	president $X_{\boxed{1}}$
1240	$X_{\boxed{1}}$ 美元	\$ $X_{\boxed{1}}$
2091	今年 $X_{\boxed{1}}$	$X_{\boxed{1}}$ this year
3253	百分之 $X_{\boxed{1}}$	$X_{\boxed{1}}$ percent
10508	在 $X_{\boxed{1}}$ 下	under $X_{\boxed{1}}$
28426	在 $X_{\boxed{1}}$ 前	before $X_{\boxed{1}}$
47015	$X_{\boxed{1}}$ 的 $X_{\boxed{2}}$	the $X_{\boxed{2}}$ that $X_{\boxed{1}}$
1752457	与 $X_{\boxed{1}}$ 有 $X_{\boxed{2}}$	have $X_{\boxed{2}}$ with $X_{\boxed{1}}$

FIGURE 18.5 Example grammar rule extracted with ranks. (From Chiang, D., A hierarchical phrase-based model for statistical machine translation, In *Proceedings of the 43rd Annual Meeting on Association for Computational Linguistics*, Ann Arbor, MI, pp. 263–270. Association for Computational Linguistics, Morristown, NJ, 2005.)

One ancestor of such linguistic syntax rule-based SMT systems is what is called "transfer-based MT." Traditional transfer-based MT systems use tree structure mapping. They rely on analyzing the source and target sentences by syntactic rules and then perform a rule transfer, combined with dictionary lookup and semantic rules, to obtain the final translation. In this regard, syntax-based MT has indeed a very long history. Perhaps the first transfer-based Chinese MT system can be said to be dated to the 1950s (Zhiwei 1954) under the auspices of the Chinese National Plan the Development of Science and Technology. Experiments were performed on Russian to Chinese MT with over a vocabulary size of 2030 Russian words and 29 rules. The Chinese government continued to be the major funding source for other MT efforts in China today. Tree-based and rule-based systems use up to 1000 rules these days to translate technical domain documents into Chinese.

In the early 1990s, Su and Chang (1990) developed the ArchTran (recently renamed as BehaviorTran) system for English–Chinese translation using a combination of a rule-based approach and statistical information. Like other pioneers of SMT at the time, Su's team found that the problem of scalability of a rule-based system can be mitigated by incorporating statistics trained from large corpora. Looking back, this was probably the beginning of linguistically motivated syntax-based SMT for Chinese. Su (2005) further pointed out the advantage of linguistically motivated syntax trees in covering long distance dependencies, and urged further research into better unsupervised learning methods of such tree structures in parallel corpora.

Syntax-based MT, born out of the necessity to model Chinese–English sentence pairs, is now a mainstream approach in SMT Wu and Chiang (2009), used for other language pairs, including Arabic–English, to great success. Zollmann et al. (2008) carried out a systematic comparison of phrase-based, hierarchical, and syntax-augmented SMT in Chinese–English, Arabic–English, and Urdu–English. They found that probabilistic synchronous context-free grammar (PSCFG) models give considerable performance gain to language pairs with very different word orders, such as Chinese–English. Such gain is also consistent across small and large data scenarios. Likewise, Schwarz (Schwarz 2009) finds that hierarchical models yield significant gain for Chinese–English versus Arabic–English—four points versus one to two points in BLEU.

18.6 Semantics-Based SMT and Interlingua

The Chinese language is often described to be a semantic language, with its lack of case, tense, number, and gender morphological markers. Psycholinguistic experiments showed that there is no functional primacy of syntax over semantics in Chinese (Yu and Zhang 2008), unlike in Indo-European languages. This means humans can correctly interpret the meaning of a Chinese sentence even if there is syntax violation, but not the other way around. For example, the following single Chinese sentence can have multiple English translations, with differences in person and tense (via personal communication with BDC linguist Ms. Yu-Ling Hsu):

- 他們答應張三可以參加會議.
- They promise Zhang San that he can attend the meeting.
- They promise Zhang San that they can attend the meeting.
- They promise Zhang San that he can attend meetings.
- They promise Zhang San that they can attend the meetings.
- They promised Zhang San that he could attend the meeting.
- They promised Zhang San that they could attend the meeting.
- They promised Zhang San that he could attend the meetings.
- They promised Zhang San that they could attend the meetings.

Semantics has been believed to be the Holy Grail of MT systems since the 1950s. Translation has always been about correctly conveying the Who did What to Whom, When, Where, and Why in a sentence. Designers of interlingua systems look for a formal artificial semantic representation that can be transformed into any natural language with additional syntactic and lexical add-on rules, believing that this approach enables translation from any language to any other language possible. In reality, the continuing quest for the most suitable formal representation, be it in the form of semantic networks such as HowNet (Dong and Dong 2000), FrameNet (Baker et al. 1998), or predicate-argument structures such as Propbank, in different MT approaches, underlines the undeniable role semantics plays. As early as in the 1950s, semantic nets were invented as an "interlingua" for MT. The "semantic net" or "semantic map" that humans possess in the cognitive process is a structure of concept classes and lexicon (Illes et al. 1999) .

Su et al. (1995) adopted semantic tree mapping for MT. In their work, they use linguistically defined case labels and word senses. Given bilingual sentence pairs and their associated syntactic structure, Su et al. (1995) first perform syntactic normalization by flattening the tree structure, and then, following a step of case and word sense labeling, perform semantic normalization by extracting linguistic features such as modality and case-markers. Next, phrase or chunk mapping and transformation of the tree topology are performed to further enhance the compositionality. Finally, an unsupervised two-way training mechanism is conducted between these transformed tree pairs to automatically acquire the nondeterministic knowledge from the bilingual corpus. Su (2005) pointed out that abstracting structural mapping on the semantic level has the advantage of greater coverage than at the syntactic level (from 4.19% of directly matching syntax trees between English and Chinese, to 34.1% of matching semantic trees. If sub-trees are considered, direct semantic structure mapping is found to be above 90%). Su (2005) suggests that "[learning] semantic tree structures would be a better strategy for statistical MT systems."

In the late 1980s, the Overseas Development Agency of the Japanese government funded an ambiguous project to automatically translate between Japanese and major Asian languages, including Chinese. This project adopted an interlingua approach, with the assumption that this approach is the most efficient for translating Japanese into multiple target languages. The formal semantic structure—interlingua, is abstracted from the analysis of the source language. From there, multiple target languages can be synthesized from the interlingua. In reality, such a framework of analysis of source language, abstraction into interlingua, and synthesis of target language has met with numerous challenges at each stage.

18.6.1 Word Sense Translation

Following the emergence of various research on the task of word sense disambiguation (Yarowsky 1994, please also see Chapter 14), it was only a matter of time before it was questioned whether explicit word sense disambiguation methods can be applied to help MT. These methods look at the context words and discourse surrounding the source word and use methods ranging from boostrapping (Li et al. 2003), EM iterations (Koehn and Knight 2000; Cao and Li 2002), and the cohesive relation between the source sentence and translation candidates (Fung et al. 1999; Kikui 1999).

Fung and Chen (2006) suggest that in addition to dictionaries, bilingual frame semantics (word sense dictionary) is a useful resource for lexical selection in the translation process of a SMT system. They propose to generate a bilingual frame semantics mapping (word sense dictionary), simulating the "semantic map" in a bilingual speaker. Other questions of interest to us include how concept classes in English and Chinese break down and map to each other. They suggest that while a source word in the input sentence might have multiple translation candidates, the correct target word must have the same sense, i.e., belong to the same semantic frame. Fung and Chen (2006) designed an EM-based algorithm to automatically align FrameNet English senses to HowNet Chinese categories. They made the following assumptions:

(1) A source semantic frame is mapped to a target semantic frame if many word senses in the two frames translate to each other; and (2) a source word sense translates into a target word sense if their parent frames map to each other. By using EM, they improve the probabilities of frame mapping in $\Pr(cf \mid ef)$ and word sense translations in $\Pr(cl, cf \mid el, ef)$ iteratively: We estimate sense translations based on uniform bilingual dictionary probabilities $\Pr(cl \mid el)$ first. They obtain all word sense translations and frame mapping from the EM algorithm:

$$(cl, cf)^* = \arg\max_{(cl,cf)} \Pr(cl, cf \mid el, ef) \; \forall \, (el, ef)$$

$$cf^* = \arg\max_{cf} \Pr(cf \mid ef) \; \forall ef$$

These words and some of their sense translations are shown in Table 18.1.

TABLE 18.1 Example Word Sense Translation Output

tie.n,clothing -> 襻.n,part—部件
tie.v,cause_confinement -> 拘束.v,restrain—制止
tie.v,cognitive_connection ->聯結.v,connect—連接
make.n,type ->性質.n,attribute—屬性
make.v,building ->建造.v,build—建造
make.v,causation ->令.v,CauseToDo—使動
roll.v,body-movement ->搖動.v,wave—擺動
roll.v,mass_motion ->翻滾.v,roll—滾
roll.v,reshaping ->卷.v,FormChange—形變
feel.n,sensation ->手感.n,experience—感受
feel.v,perception_active ->覺得.v,perception—感知
feel.v,seeking ->摸.v,LookFor—尋

Fung et al. (2007) further investigated the use of bilingual semantic role labeling for MT. Semantic role labeling, or shallow semantic parsing, has been made into a fully automatic process with relative high accuracy in recent years (Gildea and Jurafsky 2002; Sun and Jurafsky 2004; Pradhan et al. 2004, 2005; Pradhan 2005; Fung et al. 2006; Fung et al. 2007; Giménez and Màrquez 2007b, 2008).

Bilingual sense dictionaries such as BiFrameNet have the potential to be applied to interlingua-based MT, as well as SMT. We can design an approach in which both source and target sentences are annotated automatically with shallow semantic parsers, similar to those described in Pradhan 2005; Fung et al. (2006); Wu and Fung (2009). BiFrameNet dictionaries can be used as the intermediate lexical semantics representation in an interlingual-based system (Dorr 1992). Or it can be used to augment the phrase table in a SMT system and help with lexical choice.

More recently, work from lexical semantics has also at long last been successfully applied to increasing SMT accuracy, in the form of techniques adapted from word sense disambiguation models (Carpuat and Dekai 2005; Chan et al. 2007; Giménez and Màrquez 2007a). (Chan et al. 2007) and Carpuat and Dekai (2005) contemporaneously showed for the first time that incorporating the predictions of a word sense disambiguation system within a typical phrase-based SMT model consistently improves translation quality. In order for word sense disambiguation or phrase sense disambiguation to be effective in improving SMT models, these work showed that sense candidates must be extracted automatically, and are not those within the manually defined Senseval set. In particular, sense candidates are defined by as *translation* candidates. Carpuat and Wu (2007) also showed that extending word sense disambiguation to phrase sense disambiguation yields statistically significant improvements over all the large tasks. They pointed out that word-based SMT architectures already handle word disambiguation intrinsically in its model, choosing a priori sense translation candidates by using lexical translation probabilities with contextual language model probabilities. To improve upon disambiguation accuracy within this framework, sense disambiguation techniques need to incorporate strong assumptions independent of what the SMT model already covers. Dedicated word sense disambiguation techniques seem to be effective because they employ a broader range of sense selection features and are more sensitive to dynamic context.

18.6.2 Semantic Role Labels

Many errors in today's SMT systems are those resulting from the confusion of semantic roles. Translation errors of this type frequently result in critical misunderstandings of the essential meaning of the original input language sentences—who did what to whom, for whom or what, how, where, when, and why. Manual inspection of the contrastive error analysis data from a state-of-the-art SMT system showed that around 20% of the error sentences produced could have been avoided if the correct predicate argument information was used (Och et al. 2003).

Semantic role confusions are errors of adequacy rather than fluency. It has often been noted that the dominance of lexically oriented, precision-based metrics such as BLEU tend to reward fluency more than adequacy. The length penalty in the BLEU metric, in particular, is only an indirect and weak indicator of adequacy. As a result, SMT work has been driven to optimize systems such that they often produce translations that contain significant role confusion errors despite reading fluently.

Can we improve translation utility via a strategy of favoring semantic adequacy slightly more—possibly at the expense of slight degradations in lexical fluency?

Shallow semantic parsing models have attained increasing levels of accuracy in recent years (Gildea and Jurafsky 2002; Sun and Jurafsky 2004; Pradhan et al. 2004, 2005; Pradhan 2005; Fung et al. 2006; Fung et al. 2007; Giménez and Màrquez 2007b, 2008). Such models, which identify semantic frames within input sentences by marking its predicates, and labeling their arguments with the semantic roles that they fill.

Evidence has begun to accumulate that semantic frames—predicates and semantic roles—tend to preserve consistency across translations better than syntactic roles do. Across Chinese and English, for example, it has been reported that approximately 84% of semantic roles are preserved consistently (Wu et al. 2006). Of these, roughly 15% do not preserve syntactic roles consistently.

Wu and Fung (2009), present a novel two-pass hybrid model that successfully applies semantic parsing technology to the challenge of improving the quality of Chinese–English SMT. The model makes use of a typical representative SMT system based on Moses, plus shallow semantic parsers for both English and Chinese.

18.6.2.1 Hybrid Two-Pass Semantic SMT

While the accuracy of shallow semantic parsers has been approaching reasonably high levels in recent years for well-studied languages such as English, and to a lesser extent, Chinese, the problem of excessive computational complexity is one of the primary challenges in adapting semantic parsing technology to the translation task.

Semantic parses, by definition, are less likely than syntactic parses to obey clearly nested hierarchical composition rules. Moreover, the semantic parses are less likely to share an exactly isomorphic structure across the input and output languages, since the raison d'etre of semantic parsing is to capture semantic frame and role regularities independent of syntactic variation—monolingually and crosslingually.

This makes it difficult to incorporate semantic parsing into SMT merely by applying the sort of dynamic programming techniques found in current syntactic and tree-structured SMT models, most of which rely on being able to factor the computation into independent computations on the sub-trees. In other words, the key computational obstacle is that the semantic parse of a larger string (or string pair, in the case of translation) is not in general strictly mechanically composable from the semantic parses of its smaller substrings (or substring pairs).

In fact, the lack of easy compositionality is the reason that today's most accurate shallow semantic parsers rely not primarily on compositional parsing techniques, but rather on ensembles of predictors that independently rate/rank a wide variety of factors supporting the role assignments given a broad sentence-wide range of context features. But while this improves semantic parsing accuracy, it poses a major obstacle for efficient tight integration into the sub-hypothesis construction and maintenance loops within SMT decoders.

To circumvent this computational obstacle, the hybrid two-pass model (Wu and Fung 2009) defers application of the non-compositional semantic parsing information until a second error-correcting pass. This imposes a division of labor between the two passes.

The first pass is performed using a conventional phrase-based SMT model. The phrase-based SMT model is assigned to the tasks of (a) providing an initial baseline hypothesis translation, and (b) fixing the lexical choice decisions. Note that the lexical choice decisions are not only at the single-word level, but are in general at the phrasal level.

The second pass takes the output of the first pass, and reorders constituent phrases corresponding to semantic predicates and arguments, seeking to maximize the crosslingual match of the semantic parse of the reordered translation to that of the original input sentence. The second pass algorithm performs the error correction shown in Algorithm 18.1.

The design decision to allow the first pass to fix all lexical choices follows an insight inspired by an empirical observation from our error analyses: the lexical choice decisions being made by today's SMT models have attained fairly reasonable levels, and are not where the major problems of adequacy lie. Rather, the ordering of arguments in relation to their predicates is often where the main failures of adequacy occur. By avoiding lexical choice variations while considering reordering hypotheses, a significantly larger amount of re-ordering can be done without further increasing computational complexity. So we sacrifice a small amount of fluency by allowing reordering without compensating lexical choice—in exchange for gaining potentially a larger amount of fluency by getting the predicate-argument structure right.

Algorithm 18.1 Algorithm for Second Pass

---

1. Apply a semantic parser for the *input* language to the input source sentence.
2. Apply a semantic parser for the *output* language to the baseline translation that was output by the first pass. Note: this also produces a shallow syntactic parse as a byproduct.
3. If the semantic frames (target predicates and their associated semantic roles) are all consistent between the input and output sentences, and are aligned to each other by the phrase alignments from the first pass, then finish immediately and output the baseline translation.
4. Segment the baseline translation by introducing segment boundaries around every constituent phrase whose shallow syntactic parse category (from step 2) was V, NP, or PP. This breaks the baseline translation into a small number of coarse chunks to consider during reordering, instead of a large number of individual words.
5. Generate a set of candidate reordered translation hypotheses by iteratively moving constituent phrases whose predicate or semantic role label was *mismatched* to the input sentence. Each new candidate generated may in turn spawn a further set of candidates (especially since moving one constituent phrase may cause another's predicate or semantic role label to change from matched to mismatched). This search is performed breadth-first to favor fewer reorderings (in case the hypothesis generation grows beyond allotted time).
6. Apply a semantic parser for the *output* language to each candidate re-ordered translation hypothesis as it is generated.
7. Return the reordered translation hypothesis with the maximum match of semantic predicates and arguments.

The model has a similar rationale for employing a reordering pass instead of re-ranking n-best lists or lattices. Oracle analysis of n-best lists and lattices show that they often focus on lexical choice alternatives rather than reordering/role variations that are more important to the semantic adequacy.

A Chinese–English experiment was conducted on the two-pass hybrid model. A phrase-based SMT baseline model was built by augmenting the open source SMT decoder Moses (Koehn et al. 2007) with additional preprocessors. English and Chinese shallow semantic parsers followed those discussed above. The model was trained on LDC newswire parallel text consisting of 3.42 million sentence pairs, containing 64.1 million English words and 56.9 million Chinese words. The English was tokenized and case-normalized; the Chinese was tokenized via a maximum-entropy model (Fung et al. 2004). The phrase-based SMT model used for the first pass achieves a BLEU score of 42.99, establishing a fairly strong baseline to begin with. In comparison, the automatically error-corrected translations that are output by the second pass achieve a BLEU score of 43.51. This represents approximately half a point improvement over the strong baseline.

An example is seen in Figure 18.6. The SMT first pass translation has an ARG0 National Development Bank of Japan in the capital market, which is badly mismatched to both the input sentence's ARG0 家行 and ARGM-LOC 在日本本市. The second pass ends up reordering the constituent phrase corresponding to the mismatched ARGM-LOC, of Japan in the capital market, to follow the PRED issued, where the new English semantic parse now assigns most of its words the correctly matched ARGM-LOC semantic role label. Similarly, samurai bonds 30 billion yen is reordered to 30 billion yen samurai bonds.

To our knowledge, this is a first result demonstrating that shallow semantic parsing can improve translation accuracy of SMT models. We note that accuracy here was measured via BLEU, and it has been widely observed that the negative impacts of semantic predicate-argument errors on the utility of the translation are underestimated by evaluation metrics based on lexical criteria such as BLEU. We conjecture that more expensive manual evaluation techniques that directly measure translation utility could even more strongly reveal improvement in role confusion errors.

FIGURE 18.6 Example, showing translations after SMT first pass and after reordering second pass.

18.7 Applications

Having overviewed the various approaches in Chinese MT, we will describe some applications in this section. We cover three such topics, namely, Chinese term and named entity translation, Chinese spoken language translation, and Chinese crosslingual information retrieval (CLIR).

18.7.1 Chinese Term and Named Entity Translation

An important component and challenging task of Chinese MT systems is the translation of special lexical items such technical terms, domain-specific terms, and named entities. Technical and domain specific terms are not often found in standard bilingual dictionaries, and are, most often than not, newly coined words. Even when such terms are found in a standard lexicon, its meaning in a particular domain is quite different from the conventional sense. For example, the verb "run" in Chinese is "跑步/paobu" in the conventional dictionary as an action, but "行/yunxing" in the computer science domain to mean the "execution of a program." Named entities include person and organization names, as well as location names. Named entities again can be rare and domain-specific. Translations of such terms into or from Chinese generally follow two strategies—that of phonetic transliteration and that of semantic translation, or a hybrid of the two. Whereas the origin of new technical and domain-specific terms, as well as certain named entities is often in English. The latter is not the sole source. Terms in biology can be from Latin or Greek, named entities can be in any possible language. Depending on the language origin of the term, phonetic transliterations are different for the same grapheme form. Japanese names written in Chinese characters (Kanji) should be transliterated into the target language according to their pronunciations in native Japanese (kun'yomi), not in Chinese. Transliterations into Chinese of French-named entities should not follow English grapheme-to-phoneme rules (e.g., Paris -> 巴黎/BĄĄ Lí).

Unlike Japanese where a distinct character set, the Katakanas, is used to indicate a borrowed word, foreign names and places are transliterated or translated into Chinese using characters from the same set. Whereas place names belong to a close set, person names can be drawn from all the languages in the world and therefore, almost an open set. The human translation of foreign names into Chinese is close to an art form, with multiple considerations to the original language of the name, its phonetic sound, the gender of the name, the convention of translation, the possible semantic connotations of the individual Chinese characters used, and last but not least, the particular Chinese target language. Whereas most written forms of Chinese in Mainland China, Taiwan, Hong Kong, and Singapore, are standard and independent of geographic regions, technical and domain specific terms, as well as named entities depend heavily on the conventions and pronunciation rules of each of these regions.

Translations and transliterations in Hong Kong follow the phonetic sound of Cantonese, the local language. Mainland China and Taiwan both use Mandarin but with different conventions in naming and spelling. Moreover, some historic foreign names have their transliterations in Shanghainese, the local language of the largest cosmopolitan city in China in the early twentieth century with heavy foreign influence. Consequently, a commonly known western name can have multiple, yet all acceptable and recognizable Chinese translations in mainland China, Hong Kong, and Taiwan. For example, the name of the actor "Arnold Schwarzenegger" is "阿諾施瓦辛格" in Mainland China and "阿諾舒華辛力加" in Hong Kong. Whereas many of the foreign names and words have long become part of the Chinese lexicon and are included in any Chinese dictionary, others still pose a challenge to MT systems.

For transliteration tasks where Chinese is the source language, the challenge lies in the identification of the source language of the particular name. For example, names in Hong Kong are transliterated into Cantonese (e.g., 曾蔭權-> Tsam Yum Kuen), those in Mainland China into Pinyin, and others in Taiwan into Wade Giles, and yet others in Singapore into the Fukian dialect. Foreign names in Chinese are even harder to transliterate as much phonetic information was lost when the name was transliterated into

Chinese in the first place (e.g., 肯特雞-> Kentucky Fried Chicken). Japanese names in Chinese characters must be transliterated into native Japanese phonetics not Pinyin (e.g., 山本喜子-> Yamamoto Akiko).

18.7.1.1 Using Parallel Corpora

Statistical methods were first proposed in the early 1990s to meet this challenge by extracting term translations from parallel, translated texts using language-independent methods (Kupiec 1993; Dagan and Church 1994; Smadja et al. 1996; Wu and Xia 1994). Indeed, commonly known named entities and their translations (e.g., 曾蔭權-> Donald Tseng Yum Kuen, the Chief Executive of Hong Kong) can be extracted from large corpora of translated news articles and official documents. Frequently used technical and domain specific terms and their translations can be extracted from domain-specific bilingual publications. Parallel corpora are available from data consortiums such as the LDC and the European Linguistic Data Association who contract professional translators to manually translate large amounts of collected texts, and form the training data for all statistical translation systems anyway. Today's SMT systems are more than adequate in learning both the segmentation and translation via word or phrase alignment models.

Certain methods have been devised to translate specifically named entities into Chinese. Noting phonetic transliteration is inadequate, due to the variety of the language source of foreign names, the gender and semantic content of some of the names, Li et al. (2007) propose an IBM4 noisy channel model to decode semantic transliterations of names in Latin script into Chinese. One approach of named entity transliteration again follows the extractive model similar to those for other term translations, from large bilingual corpora (Sproat et al. 2006).

As noted in previous Section 18.5, the formal syntax-driven ITG model (Wu 1997) counts among its applications bilingual bracketing and chunk alignment. Words and phrases within a syntactic sub-tree can be extracted, together with their translation equivalents, by using this model.

Chapter 16 contains more detailed descriptions of term extraction methods using SMT models.

18.7.1.2 Using Noisy Parallel Corpora and Nonparallel Corpora

All SMT methods require parallel corpus as training data. And these methods do not work well when the size of the parallel corpus is small, and if the parallel corpus is *noisy*, i.e., if it contains segments that only appear on one side of the bitext. When the corpus size is small, the alignment data is sparse, leading to few reliable phrasal translations. Likewise, when the corpus is noisy, the phrasal alignment model breaks down and returns many erroneous translations. Noise can arise from many sources, for example:

- Nonliteral translation
- Out-of-order translation
- Omitted sections
- Floating passages: footnotes, figures, examples, etc.
- OCR erros
- Sentence segmentation errors

Fung and McKeown (1994); Fung (1995); Fung and McKeown (1997) proposed a method, DK-vec, to perform both bilingual lexicon extraction and bitext alignment, which work well even on small and noisy corpora. In particular, their method does not assume cognate mapping between related languages such as English and French, and therefore is applicable to language pairs with different character sets.

The DK-vec method represents words in a lexical feature called the *recency vector*. Recency is defined as the number of bytes since the last occurrence of the same word token. This feature can be plotted as a type of "word signature signal," as shown in Figure 18.7.

The recency vector feature is far more robust and reliable in noisy bitexts than, say, the sentence length feature. For lexicon extraction, Dynamic Time Warping, a dynamic programming algorithm with constraints on starting point, monotonicity, length and slope, is employed to find pairs of recency vectors with the highest dynamic time warping scores.

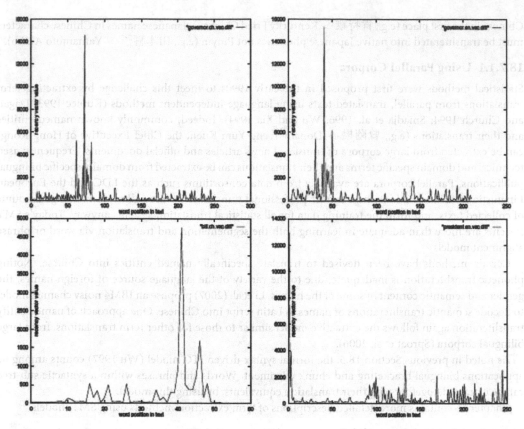

FIGURE 18.7 DK-vec signals showing similarity between *Government* in English and Chinese, contrasting with *Bill* and *President*.

Even though the DK-vec method was motivated by the objective of aligning texts with different character sets, later on this method is often used for alignment in general, and lexicon extraction in particular, from noisy parallel corpora of moderate size in many different languages. Somers and Ward (1996) report an evaluation of the front-end method for comparing DK-vecs of candidate word token pairs, upon a number of word token pairs involving English, French, German, Dutch, Spanish, and Japanese. The precision of the proposed word token pairs was found to range from 0% (English–French) to 34% (English–Japanese) to 75% (French–Spanish). Many factors apparently contribute to the variance: the size of the bitext, the human translators, the thresholds for selecting words, and so on. Chatterjee and Agrawal (2006) report new constraints on the dynamic programming part of the DK-vec method to align Hindi/ English.

We note that the full DK-vec method is invented for text alignment as well as lexicon extraction. It can also provide an initial point for EM-based word alignment methods.

However, even *noisy* parallel data are not available in all domains and the usage of some terms and named entities can be less frequent but critical. Using comparable but nonparallel multilingual data has become desirable and even necessary (Fung 1995; Rapp 1995; Kikui 1999; Fung et al. 2009).

To make use of large amounts of readily available comparable corpora is to extract bilingual terms directly from them using statistical methods (Fung 1995; Fung and Lo 1998; Zweigenbaum and Rapp 2008; Fung et al. 2009). Fung and Lo (1998) propose a method called Convec, that was applied to extracting domain-specific and new words/phrases from Chinese/English monolingual newspaper material. The

Convec method consists of constructing a context vector for each unknown term with dictionary words. The vector length is equal to the size of a known bilingual dictionary. The feature in each dimension of the vector could be simply the occurrence (1 or 0) of a known dictionary word found in the context window of the target word, or as proposed by Fung and Lo (1998) the TF/IDF of the dictionary word. The *text frequency* (TF) of a dictionary word is defined as its occurrence frequency *in the context of* the source/target word. Its *inverse document frequency* (IDF) is defined as the overall occurrence frequency of the dictionary word in the entire corpus. Vector distances, in terms of similarity measures, are computed between bilingual terms in the two languages and the highest-ranking candidate pairs are considered as translations of each other. Confidence measure is introduced to select more reliable dictionary words as seeds.

In recent years, mining parallel data from comparable corpora has shown to be beneficial to SMT systems (Zhao and Vogel 2002; Fung and Cheung 2004; Munteanu et al. 2004; Wu and Fung 2005).

These approaches are methods of mining parallel sentence pairs from segments of texts that are judged to be probable sources for them. Zhao and Vogel (2002) and Munteanu et al. (2004) both propose discovering parallel sentences from newspaper articles within the same time window (e.g., within five days) in the source and target languages. Zhao and Vogel (2002) propose to discover parallel sentences in the Xinhua Chinese–English corpus. Munteanu et al. (2004) propose to look for them from Xinhua News, Agence France Presse, BBC, etc. In both these approaches, they first select similar on-topic pairs of articles. Zhao and Vogel (2002) use a generative maximum likelihood model to iteratively extract parallel sentences and bilingual lexicon. Munteanu et al. (2004) first extract candidate parallel sentence pairs by using a word-overlap-based filter, then train a Maximum Entropy classifier on parallel sentences, and use it to determine whether a pair of extracted bilingual sentence pairs is truly parallel or not. The classifier uses a list of features including sentence length, percentage of word overlap, as well as word alignment features obtained from IBM Model 1 (Brown et al. 1993).

Fung and Cheung (2004) propose a method capable of extracting parallel sentences from far more disparate "quasi-comparable corpora" than previous "comparable corpora" methods, by exploiting bootstrapping on top of IBM Model 4 EM (Figure 18.8). They suggest the principle that text segments that are found to contain at least one pair of parallel sentences are likely to contain more of them. Step one of their method, like previous methods, uses similarity measures to find matching documents in a corpus first, and then extracts parallel sentences as well as new word translations from these documents. But unlike previous methods, they extend this with an iterative bootstrapping framework based on the principle of "find-one-get-more," which claims that documents found to contain one pair of parallel sentences must contain others even if the documents are judged to be of low similarity. They re-match documents based on extracted sentence pairs, and refine the mining process iteratively until convergence. This novel "find-one-get-more" principle allows us to add more parallel sentences from dissimilar documents, to the baseline set. Experimental results show that our proposed method is nearly 50% more effective than the baseline method without iteration. They also show that this method is effective in boosting the performance of the IBM Model 4 EM lexical learner as the latter, though stronger than Model 1 used in previous work, does not perform well on data from quasi-comparable corpus. Even though this method is applied to Arabic–English corpora, it should be easily extendable to Chinese corpora.

Wu and Fung (2005) extends this work further by finding parallel segments at both the sentential and sub-sentential chunk level by applying an ITG on parallel sentences from Fung and Cheung (2004). This approach leverages a strong language universal constraint posited by the ITG hypothesis, that can serve as a strong inductive bias for various language learning problems, resulting in both efficiency and accuracy gains.

Since monolingual technical and domain-specific data are quite abundant for Chinese and other major languages, this approach dispenses with the need for professional translators and is cost effective and efficient.

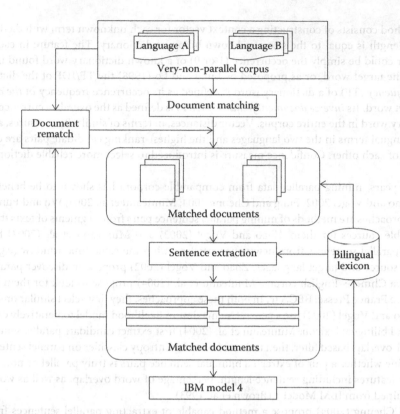

FIGURE 18.8 Parallel sentence and bilingual lexicon extraction from quasi-comparable corpora. (From Fung, P. and Cheung, P., Mining very-non-parallel corpora: Parallel sentence and lexicon extraction via bootstrapping and em, in *Proceedings of the Conference on Empirical Methods in Natural Language Processing (EMNLP 2004)*, Barcelona, Spain, pp. 57–63.)

18.7.2 Chinese Spoken Language Translation

One of the most practical applications of MT is spoken language translation for business and tourism alike. Chinese spoken language translation in the travel domain is one of the milestone tasks of the International Workshop on Spoken Language Translation (IWSLT), and within the C-Star Consortium (*see http://www.c-star.org*). Spoken language translation requires a speech recognition interface before the MT module. The decoupling and coupling of these two modules are the topic of extensive research in this area (Paulik and Waibel 2008). The challenge for this task lies in the nature of Chinese spoken language—there are many different forms of spoken languages though only one standard written form. There is as little in common between Mandarin Chinese and Cantonese than, say, between English and French. Among the 11 Sinitic languages, only one belongs to the same family as Mandarin, the standard Chinese. There are nine dialects even within this family. Consequently, even if we consider that most Chinese speakers are able to communicate in Mandarin, there are a large variety of accent differences (Fung and Liu 2007). Another central problem to spoken language translation is the recognition of named entities from Chinese speech. Chinese person name recognition is an open problem with most of the names fall into the out-of-vocabulary (OOV) category. It was first suggested in Zhai et al. (2004) that a dedicated named entity recognizer, optimizing over a wide range of acoustic and linguistic features, is effective in recognition. Practical spoken language translation in restricted domains circumvents these problems somewhat by limiting to a smaller vocabulary size and lower perplexity in the language model. Meanwhile, it has also been suggested that perhaps it is not always necessary or possible to translate entire lecture speech or meeting conversations, that it is sufficient to translate a summarization of highlights of these spoken content (Fung and Schultz 2008).

The latest research in spoken language translation include using synthetic parallel corpora from a knowledge-based MT system to enhance the training of an SMT system (Wang et al. 2008) new rescoring and re-ranking of n-best translation candidate lists, new modeling techniques, new reordering rules (He, Liu, and Lin 2008), and advanced techniques for phrase extraction from n-best list, and improved system combination using multiple SMT systems.

18.7.3 Crosslingual Information Retrieval Using Machine Translation

Crosslingual information retrieval (CLIR) means the user would input a query in language A and the system searches for relevant documents in language B. Not all CLIR systems use MT. Those CLIR systems that do use MT use it for two purposes: (1) translation of query from source to target language and (2) translation of documents from target language back to the source language. For over a decade, the National Institute of Standards and Technology (NIST) in the United States has organized a series of TextREtrieval Conferences (TREC) with the objective to advance the state-of-the-art in crosslingual IR. Such workshops produced a set of database and evaluation methods for common tasks. Crosslingual IR from Chinese was one of the major tasks. Most systems use SMT models trained from parallel corpora for this purpose. Currently, the Global Autonomous Language Exploitation (GALE) program organized by the U.S. DARPA is funding the research and development of multiple systems of speech transcription of Chinese broadcast news and broadcast conversations, MT from Chinese to English, and the distillation of the translated English documents into pertinent and consolidated information to military personnel and monolingual English-speaking analysts in response to direct or implicit requests. This program has just entered its fourth year at the time of writing. Many of the MT systems described in this chapter have been developed partially under the GALE program. For CLIR applications, the quality of document translation is of uttermost importance. As presumably the user cannot read in the target language, he or she would rely entirely on the MT output to form a view of the pertinent information. We suggest that for document translation, it might be even more important to highlight the named entities and the semantic roles. The quality of query translation, on the other hand, has more impact on precision rather than recall, as a greedy dictionary lookup method would include all possible translations of the query words and ensure that *some* of them are correct.

18.8 Conclusion and Discussion

Chinese MT, started in the 1950s, with a few hundred rules for Russian–Chinese translation, is today a cornerstone application in the MT field as a whole. Various research and commercial systems use a host of approaches with transfer rules, example-based, syntax-driven statistics, semantic-driven statistics, and ultimately system combination. Following the general evolution of MT methodologies, Chinese MT has gone evolved from transfer rule-based, example-based, to statistical methods. Today's systems are far from "pure"—rule-based systems or example-based systems all use statistical methods for extracting rules and patterns, or at least to rank them; statistical systems are enhanced by syntax, whether formal syntax or linguistic syntax, and more recently with dedicated word sense disambiguation modules and even predicate-argument semantic structures.

We highlighted two different approaches in word segmentation—a critical step when the source language is Chinese. We asked the question as to whether it is better to use word-based or character-based approach for MT and concluded that word-based or phrase-based approach gives superior performance if and only if word and phrasal boundaries are learned in conjunction with the translation model. Since it has been argued that languages with very different word orders ought to be translated by an EBMT scheme, we overviewed Chinese MT systems using EBMT and phrase-based SMT methods, respectively.

The examples and phrase tables in both methods are learned from large corpora of bilingual sentence pairs, sometimes in the order of tens of millions of sentences. Next, we examined the innovation a decade ago and the recent resurgence of syntax-driven SMT, as a form of transfer-based approach with statistical learning. Since Chinese is often translated into languages that belong to a very different family, Chinese MT must deal with mismatches in morphology, syntax, and lexical semantics. Great progress has been made in the last decade to handle such mismatches by new modeling techniques that do not make assumptions based on Indo-European languages. Approaches such as ITG-based SMT and hierarchical phrase-based SMT have shown to work particularly well in this regard. We pointed out that syntax-driven SMT was initially motivated by the large difference in word order and syntactic structure between the Chinese language and other languages. State-of-the-art results showed that, indeed, syntax-driven SMT has a larger impact on Chinese MT than, say, Arabic MT. We also showed that semantics-driven MT, with its origin in interlingua MT, is also enjoying a comeback. Statistical MT systems augmented with explicit word sense disambiguation modules or with shallow semantic parsing, have shown promising improvements in translation quality.

The translation of Chinese technical, domain-specific terms and named entities pose particular challenge due to linguistic particularity. It has been shown that, again, hybrid semantic transliteration and extractive methods are efficient, especially when they are applied to readily available, nonparallel but comparable corpora. In the near future, we expect to see more convergence between different schools of MT methodology, and between linguistically motivated and computational approaches. Further improvement still need to be made to create higher quality dictionaries, thesauri, phrase tables, with better coverage. For future work, we forsee that the translation of regional Chinese languages, even minority languages in China, will become increasing important as MT reaches the realm of practical applications. Since there is less linguistic analysis on these Chinese languages, but also little corpora available, there need be more creative synergy between linguistics and engineering. One of the current applications of MT is cross lingual information retrieval from two of the world's major languages, namely, Chinese and Arabic. Last but not least, the translation of Chinese spoken languages will face additional challenges of handling accents, regional languages, and the demands of portable platforms.

Acknowledgments

The author wishes to thank Professor Su Keh-Yih for his detailed and very helpful comments on a previous draft of this chapter, the editor Nitin Indurkhya for his useful comments and patience, Richard Schwartz and Jordan Cohen for helpful input to the chapter, to BDC linguist Ms. Yu-Ling Hsuand for her translation example, and to Li Ying for her help with the formatting. Some work described in this chapter was partly funded by Defence Advanced Research Projects (DARPA) under GALE, and by the Hong Kong Research Grants Council (RGC) under GRF 621008, 612806, RGC6256/00E, 6083/99E, and DAG 03/04.E09.

References

Baker, C., C. Fillmore, and J. Lowe (1998). FrameNet project. In *Proceedings of the Coling-ACL*, Montreal, Canada.

Bikel, D. and D. Chiang (2000). Two statistical parsing models applied to the Chinese treebank. In *Proceedings of the Second Workshop on Chinese Language Processing: Held in Conjunction with the 38th Annual Meeting of the Association for Computational Linguistics*, Volume 12, Hong Kong, pp. 1–6. Association for Computational Linguistics, Morristown, NJ.

Bo, X., Z. Chen, W. Pan, and Z. Yang (2005). Phrase-based statistical machine translation for MANOS system. In *Proceedings of the 10th Machine Translation Summit*, Phuket, Thailand, pp. 123–126.

Brown, P., V. Della Pietra, S. Della Pietra, and R. Mercer (1993). The mathematics of statistical machine translation: Parameter estimation. *Computational Linguistics 19*(2), 263–311.

Cao, Y. and H. Li (2002). Base noun phrase translation using Web data and the EM algorithm. In *Proceedings of the 19th International Conference on Computational Linguistics*, Volume 1, Taipei, Taiwan, pp. 1–7. Association for Computational Linguistics, Morristown, NJ.

Carpuat, M. and W. Dekai (2005). Word sense disambiguation vs. statistical machine translation. In *Proceedings of the 43rd Annual Meeting of the Associations for Computational Linguistics (ACL'05)*, Ann Arbor, MI, pp. 387–394.

Carpuat, M. and D. Wu (2007). How phrase sense disambiguation outperforms word sense disambiguation for statistical machine translation. In *11th Conference on Theoretical and Methodological Issues in Machine Translation*, Skovde, Sweden, pp. 43–52.

Chan, Y., H. Ng, and D. Chiang (2007). Word sense disambiguation improves statistical machine translation. In *Annual Meeting-Association for Computational Linguistics*, Prague, Czech Republic, Volume 45, pp. 33–40.

Chatterjee, N. and S. Agrawal (2006). Word alignment in English-Hindi parallel corpus using recency-vector approach: Some studies. In *Proceedings of the 21st International Conference on Computational Linguistics and the 44th Annual Meeting of the Association for Computational Linguistics*, Sydney, Australia, pp. 649–656. Association for Computational Linguistics, Morristown, NJ.

Chen, Y., M. Yang, and S. Li (2007). Maximum entropy model for example-based machine translation. *International Journal of Computer Processing of Oriental Languages, 20*(02n03), 101–113.

Chiang, D. (2005). A hierarchical phrase-based model for statistical machine translation. In *Proceedings of the 43rd Annual Meeting on Association for Computational Linguistics*, Ann Arbor, MI, pp. 263–270. Association for Computational Linguistics, Morristown, NJ.

Dagan, I. and K. Church (1994). Termight: Identifying and translating technical terminology. In *Proceedings of the Fourth Conference on Applied Natural Language Processing*, Stuttgart, Germany, pp. 34–40. Association for Computational Linguistics, Morristown, NJ.

Dong, Z. and Q. Dong (2000). HowNet Chinese-English conceptual database. Technical report, Technical Report Online Software Database, Released at ACL. http://www. keenage. com.

Dorr, B. (1992). The use of lexical semantics in interlingual machine translation. *Machine Translation 7*(3), 135–193.

Fung, P. (1995). Compiling bilingual lexicon entries from a non-parallel English-Chinese corpus. In *Proceedings of the Third Workshop on Very Large Corpora*, Bosten, MA, pp. 173–183.

Fung, P. (1996). Domain word translation by space-frequency analysis of contextlength histograms. In *Proceedings of the 1996 IEEE International Conference on Acoustics, Speech, and Signal Processing, 1996 (ICASSP-96)*, Atlanta, GA, Vol. 1.

Fung, P. and B. Chen (2006). Robust word sense translation by EM learning of frame semantics. In *Proceedings of the COLING/ACL on Main Conference Poster Sessions*, Sydney, Australia, pp. 239–246. Association for Computational Linguistics, Morristown, NJ.

Fung, P. and P. Cheung (2004). Mining very-non-parallel corpora: Parallel sentence and lexicon extraction via bootstrapping and em. In *Proceedings of the Conference on Empirical Methods in Natural Language Processing (EMNLP 2004)*, Barcelona, Spain, pp. 57–63.

Fung, P. and Y. Liu (2007). Spontaneous Mandarin speech pronunciation modeling. *Advances in Chinese Spoken Language Processing*, World Scientific Publishing Company, Singapore, p. 227.

Fung, P. and Y. Lo (1998). Translating unknown words using nonparallel, comparable texts. In *Proceedings of the 17th International Conference on Computational Linguistics and the 36th Annual Meeting of the Association for Computational Linguistics (COLING-ACL 98)*, Montreal, Quebec, Canada, pp. 414–420.

Fung, P. and K. McKeown (1994). Aligning noisy parallel corpora across language groups. In *Proceedings of Association for Machine Translation in the Americas*, Columbia, MD.

Fung, P. and K. McKeown (1997). A technical word-and term-translation aid using noisy parallel corpora across language groups. *Machine Translation 12*(1), 53–87.

Fung, P. and T. Schultz (2008). Multilingual spoken language processing. *IEEE Signal Processing Magazine 25*(3), 89–97.

Fung, P. and D. Wu (1994). Statistical augmentation of a Chinese machine-readable dictionary. *Proceedings of the Second Annual Workshop on Very Large Corpora*, Kyoto, Japan, pp. 69–85.

Fung, P. and D. Wu (1995). Coerced markov models for cross-lingual lexical-tag relations. In *The Sixth International Conference on Theoretical and Methodological Issues in Machine Translation*, Leuven, Belgium, pp. 240–255.

Fung, P., G. Ngai, Y. Yang, and B. Chen (2004). A maximum-entropy Chinese parser augmented by transformation-based learning. *ACM Transactions on Asian Language Information Processing (TALIP) 3*(2), 159–168.

Fung, P., Z. Wu, Y. Yang, and D. Wu (2007). Learning bilingual semantic frames: Shallow semantic parsing vs. semantic role projection. In *11th Conference on Theoretical and Methodological Issues in Machine Translation*, Skovde, Sweden, pp. 75.

Fung, P., L. Xiaohu, and C. Shun (1999). Mixed language query disambiguation. In *Proceedings of the 37th annual meeting of the Association for Computational Linguistics on Computational Linguistics*, College Park, MD, pp. 333–340. Association for Computational Linguistics, Morristown, NJ.

Fung, P., W. Zhaojun, Y. Yongsheng, and D. Wu (2006). Automatic learning of Chinese English semantic structure mapping. In *IEEE Spoken Language Technology Workshop, 2006*, Aruba, pp. 230–233.

Fung, P., P. Zweigenbaum, and R. Rapp (2009). In *2nd Workshop on Building and Using Comparable Corpora (BUCC 2009): From Parallel to Non-parallel Corpora*, Sunteo, Singapore.

Gildea, D. and D. Jurafsky (2002). Automatic labeling of semantic roles. *Computational Linguistics 28*(3), 245–288.

Giménez, J. and L. Màrquez (2007a). Context-aware discriminative phrase selection for SMT. In *Proceedings of WMT at ACL*, Prague, Czech Republic.

Giménez, J. and L. Màrquez (2007b). Linguistic features for automatic evaluation of heterogeneous MT systems. In *Proceedings of the ACL Workshop on Statistical Machine Translation*, Prague, Czech Republic, pp. 256–264.

Giménez, J. and L. Màrquez (2008). Discriminative phrase selection for statistical machine translation. *Learning Machine Translation*, NIPS Workshop Series. MIT Press.

He, Z., Q. Liu, and S. Lin (2008). Improving statistical machine translation using lexicalized rule selection. In *Proceedings of the 22nd International Conference on Computational Linguistics (Coling 2008)*, Manchester, U.K., pp. 321–328.

Illes, J., W. Francis, J. Desmond, J. Gabrieli, G. Glover, R. Poldrack, C. Lee, and A. Wagner (1999). Convergent cortical representation of semantic processing in bilinguals. *Brain and Language 70*(3), 347–363.

Isahara, H. et al. (2007). Development of a Japanese-Chinese machine translation system. *Proceedings of the Machine Translation Summit XI*, Copenhagen, Denmark.

Kikui, G. (1999). Resolving translation ambiguity using non-parallel bilingual corpora. In *Proceedings of ACL99 Workshop on Unsupervised Learning in Natural Language Processing*, Baltimore, MD.

Koehn, P. and K. Knight (2000). Estimating word translation probabilities from unrelated monolingual corpora using the EM algorithm. In *Proceedings of the National Conference on Artificial Intelligence*, Austin, TX, pp. 711–715. Menlo Park, CA; Cambridge, MA; London; AAAI Press; MIT Press; 1999.

Koehn, P., H. Hoang, A. Birch, C. Callison-Burch, M. Federico, N. Bertoldi, B. Cowan, W. Shen, C. Moran, R. Zens et al. (2007). Moses: Open source toolkit for statistical machine translation. In *Annual Meeting-Association for Computational Linguistics*, Prague, Czech Republic, Volume 45, pp. 2.

Kupiec, J. (1993). An algorithm for finding noun phrase correspondences in bilingual corpora. In *Proceedings of the 31st Annual Meeting of the Association for Computational Linguistics*, pp. 23–30.

Lewis, P. and R. Stearns (1968). Syntax-directed transduction, *Journal of the ACM* 15(3), 465–488.

Li, H., Y. Cao, and C. Li (2003). Using bilingual web data to mine and rank translations. *IEEE Intelligent Systems* 18(4), 54–59.

Li, H., K. Sim, J. Kuo, and M. Dong (2007). Semantic transliteration of personal names. In *Annual Meeting-Association for Computational Linguistics*, Prague, Czech Republic, Vol. 45, pp. 120.

Liu, Y. and C. Zong (2004). Example-based Chinese-English MT. In *2004 IEEE International Conference on Systems, Man and Cybernetics*, Hague, the Netherlands, Vol. 7.

Ma, Y., S. Ozdowska, Y. Sun, and A. Way (2008). Improving word alignment using syntactic dependencies. In *Proceedings of the ACL-08: HLT Second Workshop on Syntax and Structure in Statistical Translation (SSST-2)*, Columbus, OH, pp. 69–77.

Marcu, D. and W. Wong (2002). A phrase-based, joint probability model for statistical machine translation. In *Proceedings of EMNLP*, Philadelphia, PA, Vol. 2.

Munteanu, D., A. Fraser, and D. Marcu (2004). Improved machine translation performance via parallel sentence extraction from comparable corpora. In *Proceedings of the Human Language Technology and North American Association for Computational Linguistics Conference (HLT/NAACL 2004)*, Boston, MA.

Nagao, M. (1984). A framework of a mechanical translation between Japanese and English by analogy principle *Artificial and Human Intelligence*, A. Elithorn and R. Barnerji (Eds.), North-Holland, Amsterdam, the Netherlands, pp. 173–180.

Och, F. and H. Ney (2003). A systematic comparison of various statistical alignment models. *Computational Linguistics* 29(1), 19–51.

Och, F. and H. Ney (2004). The alignment template approach to statistical machine translation. *Computational Linguistics* 30(4), 417–449.

Och, F., C. Tillmann, and H. Ney (1999). Improved alignment models for statistical machine translation. In *Proceedings of the Joint SIGDAT Conference on Empirical Methods in Natural Language Processing and Very Large Corpora*, College Park, MD, pp. 20–28.

Och, F. J., D. Gildea, S. Khudanpur, A. Sarkar, K. Yamada, A. Fraser, S. Kumar et al. (2003). Final Report of Johns Hopkins 2003 Summer Workshop on Syntax for Statistical Machine Translation, Johns Hopkins University, Baltimore, MD.

Paulik, M. and A. Waibel (2008). Extracting clues from human interpreter speech for spoken language translation. In *IEEE International Conference on Acoustics, Speech and Signal Processing, 2008 (ICASSP 2008)*, Las Vegas, NV, pp. 5097–5100.

Pradhan, S. (2005). ASSERT: Automatic Statistical SEmantic Role Tagger. http://cemantix.org/assert

Pradhan, S., K. Hacioglu, V. Krugler, W. Ward, J. Martin, and D. Jurafsky (2005). Support vector learning for semantic argument classification. *Machine Learning* 60(1), 11–39.

Pradhan, S., W. Ward, K. Hacioglu, J. Martin, and D. Jurafsky (2004). Shallow semantic parsing using support vector machines. In *Proceedings of HLT/NAACL-2004*, Boston, MA.

Ramshaw, L. and M. Marcus (1995). Text chunking using transformation-based learning. In *Proceedings of the Third ACL Workshop on Very Large Corpora*, Cambridge, MA, pp. 82–94.

Rapp, R. (1995). Identifying word translations in non-parallel texts. In *Proceedings of the 33rd annual meeting on Association for Computational Linguistics*, Cambridge, MA, pp. 320–322. Association for Computational Linguistics, Morristown, NJ.

Ratnaparkhi, A. (1998). *Maximum entropy models for natural language ambiguity resolution*. PhD thesis, University of Pennsylvania, Philadelphia, PA.

Schwarz, T. (2009). *Messen und bewerten von Werkstücken mit dem digitalen Messschieber (unterweisung Feinwerkmechaniker/-in)*. GRIN Verlag.

Shi, X., Y. Chen, and J. Jia (2007). Dependency-based Chinese-English statistical machine translation. In *Proceedings of the Seventh International Conference on Intellignet Text Processing and Computational Linguistics (CICLing-2007) 4394*, Mexico City, Mexico, p. 385.

Smadja, F. (1992). Extracting collocations from text. An application: Language generation. PhD Thesis. UMI order No. GAX92-09894, Columbia University, New York, NY.

Smadja, F., K. McKeown, and V. Hatzivassiloglou (1996). Translating collocations for bilingual lexicons: A statistical approach. *Computational Linguistics* 22(1), 1–38.

Somers, H. and A. Ward (1996). Some more experiments in bilingual text alignments. In *Proceedings of the Second International Conference on New Methods in Language Methods in Language Processing*, Cambridge, MA, pp. 66–78.

Sproat, R., C. Shih, W. Gale, and N. Chang (1996). A stochastic finite-state word-segmentation algorithm for Chinese. *Computational Linguistics* 22(3), 377–404.

Sproat, R., T. Tao, and C. Zhai (2006). Named entity transliteration with comparable corpora. In *Proceedings of the 21st International Conference on Computational Linguistics and the 44th annual meeting of the Association for Computational Linguistics*, Sydney, Australia, pp. 73–80. Association for Computational Linguistics, Morristown, NJ.

Su, K. (2005). To have linguistic tree structures in statistical machine translation? In *Proceedings of 2005 IEEE International Conference on Natural Language Processing and Knowledge Engineering, 2005 (IEEE NLP-KE'05)*, Wuhan, China, pp. 3–6.

Su, K. and J. Chang (1990). Some key issues in designing MT systems. *Machine Translation* 5(4), 265–300.

Su, K., J. Chang, and Y. Hsu (1995). A corpus-based statistics-oriented two-way design for parameterized MT systems: Rationale, architecture and training issues. *Sixth Theoretical and Methodological Issues in Machine Translation (TMI-95)*, Leuven, Belgium, pp. 334–353.

Sun, H. and D. Jurafsky (2004). Shallow semantic parsing of Chinese. In *Proceedings of NAACL 2004*, Boston, MA, pp. 249–256.

Nightingale. (2008). Nightingale GALE Team Internal Communication.

Venugopal, A., S. Vogel, and A. Waibel (2003). Effective phrase translation extraction from alignment models. In *Proceedings of the 41st Annual Meeting on Association for Computational Linguistics*, Volume 1, Sparro, Japan, pp. 319–326. Association for Computational Linguistics, Morristown, NJ.

Vogel, S., H. Ney, and C. Tillmann (1996). HMM-based word alignment in statistical translation. In *Proceedings of the 16th Conference on Computational Linguistics*, Volume 2, Copenhagen, Denmark, pp. 836–841. Association for Computational Linguistics, Morristown, NJ.

Vogel, S., Y. Zhang, F. Huang, A. Tribble, A. Venugopal, B. Zhao, and A. Waibel (2003). The CMU statistical machine translation system. In *Proceedings of MT Summit*, New Orleans, LA, Vol. 9.

Wang, H., H. Wu, X. Hu, Z. Liu, J. Li, D. Ren, and Z. Niu (2008). The TCH Machine Translation System for International Workshop on Spoken Language Translation 2008 (IWSLT 2008), Honolulu, Hawaii, pp. 124–131.

Wu, D. (1995). Trainable coarse bilingual grammars for parallel text bracketing. In *Proceedings of the Third Annual Workshop on Very Large Corpora*, Cambridge, MA, pp. 69–81.

Wu, D. (1997). Stochastic inversion transduction grammars and bilingual parsing of parallel corpora. *Computational Linguistics* 23(3), 377–403.

Wu, D. and D. Chiang (2009). *Proceedings of SSST-3*, Boulder, CO.

Wu, D. and P. Fung (October, 1994). Improving Chinese tokenization with linguistic filters on statistical lexical acquisition. In *Proceedings of the Fourth Conference on Applied Natural Language Processing*, Stuttgart, Germany, pp. 13–15.

Wu, D. and P. Fung (2005). Inversion transduction grammar constraints for mining parallel sentences from quasi-comparable corpora. *Lecture notes in computer science 3651*, Jejio Island, Korea, p. 257.

Wu, D. and P. Fung (June 2009). Semantic Roles for SMT: A hybrid two-pass model. In *Proceedings of the HLT/NAACL, 2009*, Boulder, CO.

Wu, D. and X. Xia (1994). Learning an English-Chinese lexicon from a parallel corpus. In *Proceedings of the First Conference of the Association for Machine Translation in the Americas*, Columbia, MD, pp. 206–213.

Wu, D., M. Carpuat, and Y. Shen (2006). Inversion transduction grammar coverage of arabic-english word alignment for tree-structured statistical machine translation. In *IEEE Spoken Language Technology Workshop, 2006*, Aruba, pp. 234–237.

Xu, R., Q. Lu, Y. Li, and W. Li (2004). The construction of a Chinese shallow treebank. In *the Third SIGHAN Workshop on Chinese Language Processing*, Barcelona, Spain, pp. 94–101.

Xue, N. and S. Converse (2002). Combining classifiers for Chinese word segmentation. In *Proceedings of the first SIGHAN workshop on Chinese Language Processing*, Vol. 18, Taipei, Taiwan, pp. 1–7. Association for Computational Linguistics, Morristown, NJ.

Yamada, K. and K. Knight (2001). A decoder for syntax-based statistical MT. In *Proceedings of the 40th Annual Meeting on Association for Computational Linguistics*, Philadelphia, PA, pp. 303–310. Association for Computational Linguistics, Morristown, NJ.

Yang, M., H. Jiang, Z. Tiejun, S. Li, and D. Liu (2008). Domain sensitive Chinese-English example based machine translation. In *Fifth International Conference on Fuzzy Systems and Knowledge Discovery, 2008 (FSKD'08)*, Shandong, China, Vol. 2.

Yarowsky, D. (1994). Decision lists for lexical ambiguity resolution: Application to accent restoration in Spanish and French. In *Proceedings of the 32nd Annual Meeting of the Association for Computational Linguistics*. Las Cruces, NM, pp. 88-95.

Yu, J. and Y. Zhang (2008). When Chinese semantics meets failed syntax. *Neuroreport* 19(7), 745–749.

Zens, R., F. Och, and H. Ney (2002). Phrase-based statistical machine translation. In *Proceedings of the 25th Annual German Conference on AI: Advances in Artificial Intelligence (KI2002)*, Aachen, Germany, pp. 18–32.

Zhai, Y., Y. Qu, and Z. Gao (2004). Agent-based modeling for virtual organizations in grid. *Lecture Notes in Computer Science*, Springer-Verlag, Berlin, pp. 83–89.

Zhang, R., K. Yasuda, and E. Sumita (2008). Chinese word segmentation and statistical machine translation. *ACM Transactions on Speech and Language Processing* 5(2), article no. 4.

Zhang, Y., R. Brown, and R. Frederking (2001). Adapting an example-based translation system to Chinese. In *Proceedings of Human Language Technology Conference 2001*, San Diego, CA, pp. 7–10.

Zhang, Y., S. Vogel, and A. Waibel (2003). Integrated phrase segmentation and alignment algorithm for statistical machine translation. In *Proceedings of the 2003 International Conference on Natural Language Processing and Knowledge Engineering, 2003*, Beijing, China, pp. 567–573.

Zhang, Y., R. Zens, and H. Ney (2007). Chunk-level reordering of source language sentences with automatically learned rules for statistical machine translation. In *Proceedings of SSST, NAACL-HLT 2007/AMTA Workshop on Syntax and Structure in Statistical Translation*, Rochester, New York.

Zhao, B. and S. Vogel (2002). Adaptive parallel sentences mining from web bilingual news collection. In *2002 IEEE International Conference on Data Mining, 2002. ICDM 2002. Proceedings*, Maebashi City, Japan, pp. 745–748.

Zhiwei, F. (1954). The current situation and problems in machine translation. *Korea 1966*(1977), 1991.

Zollmann, A., A. Venugopal, F. Och, and J. Ponte (2008). A systematic comparison of phrase-based, hierarchical and syntax-augmented statistical MT. In *Proceedings of the 22nd International Conference on Computational Linguistics*, Manchester, U.K., pp. 1145–1152.

Zweigenbaum, P. and R. Rapp (2008). *LREC 2008 Workshop on Comparable Corpora*, Marrake, Morocco.

19

Information Retrieval

University of Neuchatel

Eric Gaussier
Université Joseph Fourier

19.1 Introduction

The Information Retrieval (IR) (Manning et al., 2008) domain can be viewed, to a certain extent, as a successful applied domain of NLP. The speed and scale of Web take-up around the world have been made possible by freely available and effective search engines. These tools are used by around 85% of Web surfers when looking for some specific information (Wolfram et al., 2001).

But what precisely is IR? We can define it in the following way: "IR deals with the representation, storage, organization of, and access to information items. These information items could be references to real documents, documents themselves, or even single paragraphs, as well as Web pages, spoken documents, images, pictures, music, video, etc." (Baeza-Yates and Ribeiro-Neto, 1999).

As for information items, we will focus mainly on documents written in the English language, but the ideas and concepts we introduce can also be applied, with some adaptations, however, to other media (music, image, picture, video) and other languages (e.g., German, Spanish, Russian, Chinese, Japanese, etc.).

One of the first and most important characteristics of IR is the fact that an IR system has to deal with imprecise and incomplete descriptions of both user needs and documents queried: in most cases, it is impossible to compute a precise and unambiguous representation for queries and documents. This contrasts with the situation for databases. In a relational table, for example, John has a wage of $1198.5 and not "almost $1200." If SQL queries cannot be ambiguous, users sending queries to Web search engines tend to write very short and ambiguous descriptions of their information needs ("Canadian recipes," "iPhone," or "Britney Spears"). Clearly, users do not describe their information needs with all the needed details, preferring the system to suggest some answers, and selecting, from these answers, the most appropriate items. The search process should be viewed more as a "trial-and-error" problem-solving approach than a direct "query-response" paradigm. Finally, and contrary to SQL-based search, the matching between the query and the information item is not deterministic: the system provides the best possible answers (best matches) by estimating their underlying probability of relevance to the submitted query.

The underlying difficulty in retrieving documents relevant to a query resides in the three aspects of all natural languages, namely, polysemy, synonymy, and, to a lesser extent, spelling errors and variations. In all natural languages, a given word may have more than one precise meaning (polysemy). Some of these senses could be related, but in other cases, the underlying meaning could vary greatly. For example, the word "bank" could be used to designate a financial institution, its building, a synonym of "rely upon" in the expression "I'm your friend, you can bank on me," or the borders of a river. The last sense is of course not related to the previous three. With the word "Java," the possible meanings are even less related (an island, coffee, a dance, a domestic fowl, a computer programming language). If this word was submitted as a query, we can understand why the search system may provide "incorrect" answers. Acronyms are also subject of such ambiguity problems as, for example, BSE (Bovine Spongiform Encephalopathy, Bombay Stock Exchange (or Boston, Beirut, Bahrain), Breast Self-Examination, Bachelor of Science in Engineering, Basic Service Element, etc.).

Polysemy corresponds to one face of a coin. Synonymy, i.e., the fact that different words or expressions can be used to refer to the same object, is the second. For example, to refer to a given car accident, we can use the following terms: "accident," "event," "incident," "situation," "problem," "difficulty," "unfortunate situation," "the subject of your last letter," "what happened last month," .... When fixing a rendezvous, we can meet in a restaurant, hotel, pizzeria, coffee shop, snack bar, café, tearoom, tea house, public house, cafeteria, inn, tavern, or simply at our favorite Starbucks. In the example below, the expressions written in italics refer to the same person. It is also interesting to note that the string "Major" does not always refer to the same person.

"*Mr Major* arrived in France today. *The Prime Minister* will meet the President tomorrow. *The Conservative leader* will then travel to Moscow where *he* will meet Mr Gorbachev. Mrs Major will join *her husband* in Russia, where *this son of a circus artist* is a relatively unknown figure." (Gal et al., 1991).

As a result of these two main problems, and as demonstrated empirically in (Furnas et al., 1987), the probability that two people use the same term to describe the same object is below 0.20. The question that then arises is to understand how a search system may operate at a reasonable performance level with such variability, a question we will address by considering the different components that make up a search system.

All search systems assume that similar words tend to correspond to similar meanings. Thus, when a query shares many terms with a document, this document is seen as an appropriate answer to the corresponding query. Search systems are thus based on a simple approach: extract words from documents and queries, compare the two sets of words, and rank the document according to this comparison (potentially using additional elements, such as PageRank [PR]). As shown by Hawking and Robertson, (2003), as the collection size increases, the achieved performance of such a process tends to increase.

Of course, different components must be described in more detail; the rest of this chapter is organized as follows: Section 19.2 outlines the main aspects of the indexing process used to build documents or query representations while Section 19.3 discusses various IR models. Section 19.4 describes the evaluation methodology used in the IR field in order to compare objectively two (or more) indexing and search strategies. Failure analysis is also described in this section. Finally, Section 19.5 presents various aspects of NLP approaches that can be used to answer some of the topic difficulties that each IR system encounters.

19.2 Indexing

Effective search systems do not work directly with the documents (or the queries). They use different techniques and strategies to represent the main semantic aspects of the documents and queries. This process is called indexing. It is described in the following two sections.

19.2.1 Indexing Dimensions

We focus here on the representation of the semantic content of the documents. External characteristics, such as the publication date, the author name, the number of pages, the book price, the edition, the publisher, the language, can be managed without real problem by a relational database system. Of course, we can use such features to conduct a search (e.g., "return all documents written by Salton"). They tend, however, to be used as filters to complement the search criteria (e.g., "best picture Oscar later than 2002" or "airplane hijacking, information in English or German").

The indexing process aims at representing the semantic content of documents (or queries) by a set of indexing features. In the most common case, these indexing units are words for documents, musical notes for music, color values for pictures, etc. If we limit ourselves to written documents, we can consider as indexing units not only single words (e.g., "language," "natural") but compound constructions ("natural language processing") or thesaurus class numbers. In the opposite direction, we can sometimes consider decompounding compound words (e.g., from "handgun," we may extract the terms "hand" and "gun," a useful feature when searching with the German language (Savoy, 2004)). Furthermore, sentences or words may be subdivided into continuous segments of n characters (n-gram indexing (McNamee and Mayfield, 2004)). Fixing $n = 4$, the phrase "white house" is represented by the following four-gram sequence: "whit," "hite," "ite h," "te ho," ..., and "ouse." Such a language-independent indexing scheme can be useful when faced with a language for which no morphological analyzers (be it traditional analyzers or stemming procedures) are readily available (e.g., the Korean language (Savoy, 2005)) or when dealing with texts containing many spelling errors (e.g., OCR-ed documents (Voorhees and Garofolo, 2005)).

After defining our indexing units, we have to answer different questions to define a complete indexing strategy. When describing a document, do we need to consider all its details or only the main aspects? In defining this exhaustivity level (completeness of the representation), one can also take into account the document importance with respect to some objectives (e.g., an in-house document may have a deeper coverage). In addition, one must fix the specificity level or the degree of accuracy applied to the selected indexing units: choose general indexing terms (e.g., "drink"), or impose the use of more specific terms ("soft drink"), or even very specific terms ("iced tea," "herbal iced tea," "Nestea"). In some cases, the indexing policy relies on a controlled vocabulary (e.g., Library of Congress Subject Headings, MeSH in the biomedical literature, or the hierarchical thesaurus associated with DMOZ*). In such cases, indexing units cannot be freely chosen, but must be present in the given authoritative list.

Traditionally, librarians have adopted a manual indexing strategy in the hope of creating a better representation of their searchable objects. Such manual indexing (Anderson and Pérez-Carballo, 2001) usually relies on the use of controlled vocabularies in order to achieve greater consistency and to improve manual indexing quality. The advantage of these authority lists is that they prescribe a uniform and invariable choice of indexing descriptors and thus help normalize orthographic variations (e.g., "Beijing" or "Peking"), lexical variants (e.g., "analyzing," "analysis") or examine equivalent terms that are synonymous in meaning. The level of generality may be represented by hierarchical relationships (e.g., "Ford" is a "car"), and related-term relationships (e.g., "see also"). However, while controlled vocabularies should increase consistency among indexers, various experiments demonstrate that different indexers tend to use different keywords when classifying the same document (Zunde and Dexter, 1969; Cleverdon, 1984). This illustrates, through yet another example, the variety of wordings human beings have at their disposal to describe the same content. It is thus important to have a certain degree of consistency between document and query representations in order to increase the chance that searchers will be able to locate the information they require (Cooper, 1969).

---

* www.dmoz.org

19.2.2 Indexing Process

Most existing IR systems nowadays rely on an automatic indexing of documents and queries. Developed from the beginning of the 1960s (Salton 1971), such an approach allows one to process the huge amounts of information available online. A simple automatic indexing algorithm is composed of four steps:

1. Structure analysis and tokenization
2. Stopword removal
3. Morphological normalization
4. Weighting

19.2.2.1 Structure Analysis and Tokenization

In this first step, documents are parsed so as to recognize their structure (title, abstract, section, para-graphs). For each relevant logical structure, the system then segments sentences into word tokens (hence the term *tokenization*). This procedure seems relatively easy but (a) the use of abbreviations may prompt the system to detect a sentence boundary where there is none, and (b) decisions must be made regarding numbers, special characters, hyphenation, and capitalization. In the expressions "don't," "I'd," "John's" do we have one, two or three tokens? In tokenizing the expression "Afro-American," do we include the hyphen, or do we consider this expression as one or two tokens? For numbers, no definite rule can be found. We can simply ignore them or include them as indexing units. An alternative is to index such entities by their type, i.e., to use the tags "date," "currency," etc. in lieu of a particular date or amount of money. Finally, uppercase letters are lowercased. Thus, the title "Export of cars from France" is viewed as the word sequence "export," "of," "cars," "from," and "france."

19.2.2.2 Stopword Removal

In a second step, very frequent word forms (such as determiners "the", prepositions "from", conjunctions "and", pronouns "you" and some verbal forms "is", etc.) appearing in a stopword list are usually removed. This removal is usually motivated by two considerations. Firstly because it allows one to base the matching between queries and documents on content bearing words only. Retrieving a document just because it contains the query words "be," "in," and "the" does not constitute an intelligent search strategy. Stopwords, also called *empty words* as they usually do not bear much meaning, represent noise in the retrieval process and actually damage retrieval performance, since they do not discriminate between relevant and nonrelevant documents. Secondly because removing stopwords allows one to reduce the storage size of the indexed collection, hopefully within the range of 30% to 50%.

Although the objectives seem clear, there is no clear and complete methodology to develop a stopword list (Fox, 1989). For example, the SMART system (Salton, 1971) has 571 words in its stopword list, while the DIALOG information services propose using only nine terms (namely, "an," "and," "by," "for," "from," "of," "the," "to," and "with"). Furthermore, some expressions, as "The Who," "and-or gates," or "vitamin A," based on words usually found in stopword list, are very useful in specifying more precisely what the user wants.

Similarly, after converting all characters into lowercase letters, some ambiguity can be introduced as, for example, with the expressions "US citizen" viewed as "us citizen" or "IT scientist" as "it scientist," as both *us* and *it* are usually considered stopwords. The strategy regarding the treatment of stopwords may thus be refined by identifying that "US" and "IT" are not pronouns in the above examples, e.g., through a part-of-speech tagging step. Commercial search engines tend to use, if any, a very short stopword list.

19.2.2.3 Morphological Normalization

As a third step, an indexing procedure uses some type of morphological normalization in an attempt to conflate word variants into the same stem or root. Stemming procedures, which aim to identify the *stem* of a word and use it in lieu of the word itself, are by far the most common morphological normalization procedures used in IR. Grouping words having the same root under the same stem (or indexing term) may increase the success rate when matching documents to a query. Such an automatic procedure may therefore be a valuable tool in enhancing retrieval effectiveness, assuming that words with the same stem refer to the same idea or concept, and must be therefore indexed under the same form. We will come back to stemming procedures and morphological analyzers in Section 19.5.1.

19.2.2.4 Weighting

As described previously, an IR system automatically segments a given sentence into words, removing the most frequent ones and stripping the suffixes to produce a set of indexing units. For example, from the sentence "In 1969, the IBM-360 computer was one of the first third generation computers," we can obtain the following indexing units: "IBM-360," "first," "third," "generat," "comput." This result corresponds to a binary indexing scheme within which each document is represented by a set of (stemmed) keywords without any weight assigned. Of course we may consider additional indexing rules as, for example, to consider only the main aspects of each document (low degree of exhaustivity). To achieve this, we can consider as indexing units only terms appearing more often than a given threshold.

Binary logical restrictions may often be too restrictive for a document and query indexing. It is not always clear whether or not a document should be indexed by a given term. Often, a more appropriate answer is neither "yes" nor "no," but rather something in between. Term weighting creates a distinction among terms and increases indexing flexibility. Thus we need to assign higher weight to more "important" features and lower weight to marginal ones. To weight appropriately each indexing unit, we may consider three components, namely, the term frequency, the document frequency, and the document length (Salton and Buckley, 1988).

First, one can assume that an indexing unit appearing more often in a document must have a higher importance in describing its semantic content. We can measure this influence by counting its term frequency (i.e., its number of occurrences within a document), a value denoted tf. Thus, if a term occurs three times in a document, its tf will be 3. Of course, one can consider other simple variants, especially when considering that the occurrence of a given term in a document is a rare event. Thus, it may be good practice to give more importance to the first occurrence than to the others. To do so, the tf component is sometimes computed as $\log(tf + 1)$ or as $0.5 + 0.5 \cdot [tf / \max(tf)]$. In this latter case, the normalization procedure is obtained by dividing tf by the maximum tf value for any term in that document.

As a second weighting component, one may consider that those terms occurring very frequently in the collection do not help us discriminate between relevant and nonrelevant documents. For example, the query "computer database" is likely to yield a very large number of articles from a collection about computer science. We meet here the notion of term frequency in the collection (i.e., the number of documents in which a term appears), a value denoted df, and called "document frequency."

More precisely, we will use the logarithm of the inverse document frequency (denoted by $idf = \log(n/df)$, with n indicating the number of documents in the collection), resulting in more weight for rare words and less weight for more frequent ones (Sparck Jones, 1972). With this component, if a term occurs in every document ($df = n$), its weight will be $\log(n/n) = 0$, and thus will be ignored. On the other hand, when a term appears in only one document ($df = 1$), its weight will reach the maximum for the collection, namely, $\log(n/1) = \log(n)$.

To integrate both components (tf and idf), we can multiply the weight corresponding to the importance of the indexing term within the document (tf) by its importance considering the whole collection (idf). We thus obtain the well-known $tf \cdot idf$ formula.

Lastly, one usually considers that the presence of a term in a shorter document provides stronger evidence than it does in a longer document. This phenomenon can be accounted for by taking into account the document length in the weighting of a term, which is usually done by comparing the length of a document to the average document length (denoted $avdl$). Different weighting schemes include the document length within their weighting formula, leading to more complex schemes as described in the next sections.

19.3 IR Models

To define an IR model, we must explain precisely how information items (documents) and queries are represented and how these representations are compared to produce a set or ranked list of retrieved items. In this section, we will start our presentation with the Boolean model, the oldest paradigm and one that is still used for some specialized applications. Section 19.3.2 describe the vector-space paradigm while different probabilistic models will be introduced in Section 19.3.3, both models corresponding to modern IR approaches, and usually achieving better retrieval effectiveness than the Boolean models.

To further improve the retrieval performance as shown in Section 19.3.4, we may consider an automatic query expansion strategy that takes different term-term relationships into account in order to expand the original query. Finally, in Section 19.3.5 we briefly introduce more advanced IR models as well as some search strategies, such as PR, based on document relationships.

19.3.1 Classical Boolean Model

The Boolean model was the first IR model developed and has a long tradition in library science (Cleverdon, 1984). Documents are represented by a set of keywords, usually obtained by manual indexing (Anderson and Pérez-Carballo, 2001) based on a controlled vocabulary. Some additional indexing terms can be provided by authors, usually by selecting some terms from an authoritative list and adding free ones. Table 19.1 shows a very small example with five indexing terms and four documents. To write a query, the user must transform his or her information need into a logical expression using the indexing terms and the Boolean operators AND, OR, and AND NOT. In order to be retrieved, a document must strictly respect the logical constraint imposed by the query. Based on our example, the query "document AND retrieval" will return the documents D_2 and D_3, while the query "search OR retrieval" will extract the documents D_2, D_3, and D_4.

Transforming an information need into a Boolean query is not always a simple task. If you are interested in cats and dogs, you may formulate the query "cat AND dog." But this logical expression imposes the presence of both terms in a document in order to be retrieved. A better formulation is "cat OR dog" allowing documents with only one of these two terms to be retrieved. The conjunctions "and" and "or" in natural languages are thus not equivalent to the corresponding logical operators. This semantic difference must be taken into account when formulating Boolean queries. Within this paradigm, however, users can formulate structured queries to express their information needs with great precision. The query "document AND retrieval" is clearly more specific than writing a broad query such as "document OR retrieval."

In order to return an answer very fast, the indexing information is not internally stored as in a matrix as depicted in Table 19.1. In fact, as the collection grows, the number of indexing terms also tends to increase

TABLE 19.1   Binary Indexing

Document	Indexing Terms				
	Linguistic	Document	Search	Compute	Retrieval
D_1	1	0	0	0	0
D_2	1	1	0	1	1
D_3	0	1	1	0	1
D_4	1	0	1	0	1

TABLE 19.2   Inverted File

Indexing Term	Sequence of Document Identifiers
Linguistic	D_1, D_2, D_4
Document	D_2, D_3
Search	D_3, D_4
Compute	D_2
Retrieval	D_2, D_3, D_4

rapidly. Therefore, it is usual to have more than tens of millions of terms for the collection containing several million documents. To verify if the documents respect the logical constraint imposed by the query, we only need to have a fast access to the document identifiers indexed under the searched keywords. To achieve this, the system stores in an "inverted file" the document numbers in which indexing terms occurs. For example, Table 19.2 shows the inverted file corresponding to Table 19.1. For the sake of clarity, we have denoted in Table 19.2 the document number with the prefix D which, of course, does not appear in reality. Various techniques have been suggested (Zobel and Moffat, 2006) to reduce storage requirements, to speed up processing, or to allow the use of phrases in queries (e.g., "New York City") as well as the use of proximity operators (e.g., through the use of the adjacency operator as in "New York" ADJ "city").

There are however major drawbacks in the Boolean model. First of all, the retrieved documents do not form a ranked list. To rank retrieved documents, a Boolean-based system has to rely on external attributes, such as the publication date, the title, etc. In principle, the ranking of the retrieved documents should reflect their degree of relevance to the submitted query. For example, considering our previous query "search OR retrieval," it seems reasonable to present first the document having both indexing terms (D_3, D_4) before items indexed only under one of them (e.g., D_2). Secondly, binary logical restrictions are often too limiting for document and query indexing. Within this model, it is not possible to specify whether a given term is essential in a user's query or just marginal. Thirdly, a Boolean search system is unable to return documents that partially match the query. As an answer to the query "document AND search," the system cannot extract document D_2, even if it is indexed under the term "document" and "retrieval," a synonym of "search". Fourthly, making the right choice of the search keywords has a real impact on the quality of the returned list. If certain terms appear in the query, the system may return a large number of documents (output overload) from which it is difficult to detect relevant ones.

In order to solve some of these problems, various attempts have been proposed to include the possibility to assign weights during the indexing of documents and/or queries (hybrid Boolean models). Moreover, this information can be used to rank retrieved documents in a sequence most likely to fulfill user intent (Savoy, 1997). However, all these approaches suffer from some logical deficiencies, and their overall performance (see Section 19.4) is lower than that of more recent IR approaches.

19.3.2 Vector-Space Models

Within this IR model (Salton, 1971; Salton and Buckley, 1988), documents and queries are indexed according to the strategies described in Section 19.2. The resulting representation is a set of weighted indexing terms. Thus, the user does not need to express his or her information needs using logical operators; a simple expression in natural language, such as "free speech on the Internet," or "Italian royal family" is enough. This model clearly provides more user-friendly access to the information.

Within the vector-space model, documents and queries are represented by vectors in a high-dimensional space in which each indexing term corresponds to one dimension. Elements of the vectors may be binary, indicating the presence or absence of the term, or fractional weights indicating the relative importance of the term in the document or query. The set of indexing terms forms an orthogonal basis (linearly independent basis vectors). We assume therefore that the indexing terms are independent of one another. For example, if the term "computer" appears in a document, this information implies nothing about the presence (or absence) of other terms such as "algorithm" or "horse." This represents, of course, a simplified assumption.

Based on a geometric intuition, the vector-space model does not have a solid and precise theory that is able to clearly justify some of its aspects. For example, to compute the degree of similarity between the document representations and the query, we can choose different formulas. If we denote by w_{ij} the weight of the indexing term t_j in the document D_i, and by w_{qj} the weight of the same term in the query Q, the similarly between this document and the query could be computed according to the inner product as follows:

$$\text{Sim}(D_i, Q) = \sum_{j=1}^{p} w_{ij} \cdot w_{qj} \tag{19.1}$$

in which p indicates the number of indexing terms included in query Q. Of course, the vector representing D_i is composed of t values with t representing the number of distinct indexing terms. However, when a term is not present in the query, its contribution to the inner product is null, and has no impact on the similarly level. We can thus restrict the computation to the p query terms.

As an alternative similarity measure, we may compute the cosine of the angle between the vectors representing D_i and Q as follows:

$$\text{Sim}(D_i, Q) = \frac{\sum_{j=1}^{p} w_{ij} \cdot w_{qj}}{\sqrt{\sum_{k=1}^{t} w_{ik}^2} \cdot \sqrt{\sum_{k=1}^{p} w_{qk}^2}} \tag{19.2}$$

In order to avoid computing all elements expressed in the previous formula at retrieval time, we may store the weights associated with each element of D_i in the inverted file. If we apply the well-known weighting scheme $tf \cdot idf$ (see Section 19.3.1), we can compute and store the weight w_{ij} of each indexing term t_j for the document D_i during the indexing as follows:

$$w_{ij} = \frac{tf_{ij} \cdot idf_j}{\sqrt{\sum_{k=1}^{t} (tf_{ik} \cdot idf_k)^2}} \tag{19.3}$$

Advanced weighting formulas have been proposed within the vector-space model leading to different formulas (Buckley et al., 1996), some being more effective than others. Moreover, various attempts have been suggested to account for term dependencies (Wong et al., 1987). Most of these attempts can be seen as transformations aiming at expanding document representation through a linear transformation $\mathbf{T}$: the vector D_i becomes $\mathbf{T} \cdot D_i$. Often, the matrix $\mathbf{T}$ represents a term–term similarity matrix, which can be defined by "compiling" some a priori given thesaurus, or by automatically building a semantic similarity matrix. In particular, the Generalized Vector-Space Model (GVSM) (Wong et al., 1987) corresponds to setting $\mathbf{T}$ to the term-document matrix (i.e., the transpose of the document-term matrix, an example is given in Table 19.1). In this case, the transformation projects the document from a term space to a dual document space. This approach can be generalized by using groups of similar documents instead of isolated documents. The Similarity Thesaurus (Qiu and Frei, 1993) is a variant of this approach that relies on a particular weighting scheme. Another interesting attempt to take into account term dependencies is the approach known as Latent Semantic Analysis (LSA).

LSA (Deerwester et al., 1990) allows the automatic derivation of semantic information (in this case a certain form of synonymy and polysemy) from a document collection through co-occurrence analysis. In particular, two terms that are synonyms of each other are likely to have the same profile (i.e., similar rows) in the term-document matrix. Such correlations are unveiled in LSA by a decomposition of the term-document matrix into singular values. More precisely, let $\mathbf{C}$ represent the term-document matrix.

Then, the singular value decomposition (SVD) of **C** aims at identifying two orthogonal matrices **U** and **V** and a diagonal matrix Σ such that

$$C = U \, \Sigma \, V^t \tag{19.4}$$

where t denotes the transpose. Assuming the eigenvalues in Σ are organized in decreasing values order, one can reduce the dimensionality by retaining only the first k columns of $\mathbf{U}(\mathbf{U_k})$, the first k rows of $\mathbf{V}(\mathbf{V_k})$, and the first k diagonal elements of $\Sigma(\Sigma_\mathbf{k})$. The matrix $\mathbf{U_k}\Sigma_\mathbf{k}\mathbf{V_k^t}$ can be shown to be the closest approximation (wrt the Frobenius norm) of **C** of rank k. Documents and queries can then be projected on the obtained latent space (via $\mathbf{U_k^t}D$) and directly compared, for example with the cosine formula, in this space. LSA has been showed to provide improvements over the standard vector-space model on several collections, however not on all. The required computing resources represent the main drawback of the LSA approach.

19.3.3 Probabilistic Models

Within the probabilistic family of models, the retrieval is viewed as a classification process. For each query, the system must form two classes: relevant and nonrelevant. Thus, for a given document D_i, one has to estimate the probability that it belongs to the relevant class (class denoted R) or to the nonrelevant one (denoted $\bar{R}$). With two classes, the decision rule is rather simple: retrieve D_i if $Prob[R|D_i] > Prob[\bar{R}|D_i]$. The main theoretical foundation of this model is given by the following principle (Robertson, 1977):

"The probability ranking principle (PRP): if a reference retrieval system's response to each request is a ranking of the documents in the collection in order of decreasing probability of usefulness to the user who submitted the request, where the probabilities are estimated as accurately as possible on the basis of whatever data has been made available to the system for this purpose, the overall effectiveness of the system to its users will be the best that is obtainable on the basis of that data."

Of course, this principle does not indicate precisely what data must be used and how to estimate the underlying probabilities. To estimate them, we need to make some assumptions. First, we assume that the relevance of a document is independent of the other documents present in the collection. Second, we assume that the number of relevant documents does not affect the relevance judgment. Both assumptions represent simplification as (a) a particular document may be a good complement to another document, relevant to the query, without being relevant alone, and (b) relevance judgments are affected by the documents already judged.

In addition, we assume for the moment that the document D_i is represented by a set of binary indexing terms. It is important to note that we do not need to compute a precise value for the underlying probabilities $Prob[R|D_i]$. What is required is to produce a ranked list of documents reflecting these values. Using the Bayes rule, we can estimate the probability that D_i belongs to the relevant class and the nonrelevant one as

$$Prob[R|D_i] = \frac{Prob[D_i|R] \cdot Prob[R]}{Prob[D_i]} \tag{19.5}$$

$$Prob[\bar{R}|D_i] = \frac{Prob[D_i|\bar{R}] \cdot Prob[\bar{R}]}{Prob[D_i]} \tag{19.6}$$

where $Prob[R]$ ($Prob[\bar{R}]$) indicates the prior probability of relevance (and of nonrelevance) of a random document (with $Prob[R] + Prob[\bar{R}] = 1$). $Prob[D_i]$ is the probability of selecting D_i. From this, we can see that the ranking order depends only on $Prob[D_i|R]$ and $Prob[D_i|\bar{R}]$ (the other factors being constant).

As described in van Rijsbergen (1979), we can assume conditional independence between terms, and thus write $Prob[D_i|R]$ as the product of the probabilities for its components (binary indexing). For a given document, we denote by p_j the probability that the document is indexed by term t_j given that the document belongs to the relevant set. Similarly, q_j is the probability that the document is indexed by term t_j given that the document belongs to the nonrelevant set. Thus we need to estimate, for each term t_j, the following two probabilities:

$$p_j = \text{Prob}[d_j = 1 \mid R] \tag{19.7}$$

$$q_j = \text{Prob}[d_j = 1 \mid \bar{R}] \tag{19.8}$$

from which we can then compute the probability of relevance (and nonrelevance) of document D_i as

$$\text{Prob}[D_i \mid R] = \prod_{j=1}^{t} p_j^{d_j} \cdot (1 - p_j)^{1-d_j} \tag{19.9}$$

$$\text{Prob}[D_i \mid \bar{R}] = \prod_{j=1}^{t} q_j^{d_j} \cdot (1 - q_j)^{1-d_j} \tag{19.10}$$

where d_j is either 1 or 0, depending on the fact that the term t_j appears or not in the representation of document D_i.

One way to estimate the underlying probabilities p_j and q_j is to model the distribution of terms according to a probability distribution such as the 2-Poisson model (Harter, 1975). In this case, we model the term distribution in the relevance class by a Poisson distribution, while the distribution over the nonrelevant class follows another Poisson distribution. These estimates can be refined based on the a set of known relevant and nonrelevant items (Robertson and Sparck Jones, 1976) for the current query (relevance feedback). For example, we can estimate the required probabilities as follows:

$$p_j = \frac{r_j}{r} \quad \text{and} \quad q_j = \frac{df_j - r_j}{n - r} \tag{19.11}$$

where

  r indicates the number of relevant documents
  r_j the number of relevant documents indexed with the term t_j
  n the number of documents in the collection
  df_j the number of documents in which the term t_j occurs

Modern probabilistic IR models take into account new variables such as term frequency, document frequency, and document length to provide useful insights regarding the probability that a given document is relevant to a query or not (e.g., the Okapi or BM25 model (Robertson et al., 2002)). Among more recent proposals, a very interesting one is DFR (*Divergence from Randomness*), proposed by Amati and van Rijsbergen (2002), which represents a general probabilistic framework within which the indexing weights w_{ij} attached to term t_j in document D_i combine two information measures as follows:

$$w_{ij} = Inf_{ij}^1 \cdot Inf_{ij}^2 = -\log_2 \left[\text{Prob}_{ij}^1(tf) \right] \cdot (1 - \text{Prob}_{ij}^2(tf)) \tag{19.12}$$

The first component measures the informative content (denoted by Inf_{ij}^1) based on the observation that in the document D_i we found tf occurrences of the term t_j. The second one measures the risk (denoted by $1 - \text{Prob}_{ij}^2(tf)$) of accepting the term t_j as a good descriptor, knowing that in document D_i there are tf occurrences of term t_j.

In the first information factor, $\text{Prob}_{ij}^1(tf)$ is the probability of observing tf occurrences of the term t_j in document D_i by pure chance. If this probability is high, term t_j may correspond to a non content-bearing word in the context of the entire collection (Harter, 1975). For the English language, these words generally correspond to determiners, such as "the," prepositions like "with," or verb forms like "is" or "have," considered as being of little or not use in describing a document's semantic content. Various nouns can also appear in numerous documents within a particular corpus (for example "computer" and "algorithm" for a computer science collection). On the other hand, if $\text{Prob}^1_{ij}(tf)$ is small (or if $-\log_2\left[\text{Prob}^1_{ij}(tf)\right]$ is high), term t_j would provide important information regarding the content of the document D_i. Several stochastic distributions can be chosen for Prob^1 (see Amati and van Rijsbergen, 2002; Clinchant and Gaussier, 2008), for example, the geometric distribution

$$\text{Prob}^1_{ij}(tf) = \left[\frac{1}{(1+\lambda_j)}\right] \cdot \left[\frac{\lambda_j}{(1+\lambda_j)}\right]^{tf} \quad \text{with} \quad \lambda_j = tc_j/n \tag{19.13}$$

where

tc_j indicates the number of the occurrences of the term t_j in the collection

n is the number of documents in the collection

The term $\text{Prob}^2_{ij}(tf)$ represents the probability of having $tf + 1$ occurrences of the term t_j, knowing that tf occurrences of this term have already been found in document D_i. This probability can be evaluated using Laplace's law of succession as $\text{Prob}^2(tf) = (tf + 1)/(tf + 2) \approx tf/(tf + 1)$, which leads, by taking into account the document length to

$$\text{Prob}^2_{ij}(tf) = \frac{tfn_{ij}}{(tfn_{ij} + 1)} \quad \text{with} \quad tfn_{ij} = tf_{ij} \cdot \log_2\left[\frac{1 + (c \cdot avdl)}{l_i}\right] \tag{19.14}$$

where

$avdl$ is the mean length of a document

l_i the length of document D_i

c a constant whose value depends on the collection

The work presented in Clinchant and Gaussier (2008) relates Laplace's law of succession to a well-known phenomenon in text modeling, namely, the one of *burstiness*, which refers to the behavior of words that tend to appear in bursts: once they appear in a document, they are much more likely to appear again. This work also shows that a single distribution can be used as the basis for Prob^1 and Prob^2.

Another interesting approach is the one known as *nonparametric probabilistic modeling*,* which is based on a statistical language model (LM) (Hiemstra, 2000). As such, probability estimates are based on the number of occurrences in document D_i and the collection C. Within this LM paradigm, various implementations and smoothing methods (Zhai and Lafferty, 2004) can be considered. We will limit ourselves here to a simple model proposed by Hiemstra (2000), and described in Equation 19.15 (Jelinek–Mercer smoothing), combining an estimate based on the document ($P[t_j|D_i]$) and one based on the collection ($P[t_j|C]$):

$$\text{Prob}[D_i|Q] = \text{Prob}[D_i] \cdot \prod_{t_j \in Q} [\lambda_j \cdot \text{Prob}[t_j|D_i] + (1 - \lambda_j) \cdot \text{Prob}[t_j|C]] \tag{19.15}$$

$$\text{Prob}[t_j|D_i] = tf_{ij}/l_i \quad \text{and} \quad \text{Prob}[t_j|C] = df_j/lc \quad \text{with} \quad lc = \sum_k df_k \tag{19.16}$$

where λ_j is a smoothing factor (constant for all indexing terms t_j, and usually fixed at 0.35) and lc an estimate of the size of the collection C. Both probability estimates $P[t_j|D_i]$ and $P[t_j|C]$ are based on a ratio,

---

* The term nonparametric is misleading here, as one can view this model as being based on a multinomial distribution. Nonparametric refers here to the fact that the number of parameters grows with the size of the collection, but this is also the case with the previous models we presented.

between tf_{ij} and the document size on the one hand, and the number of documents indexed with the term t_j and the size of the whole collection on the other hand.

Lastly, we would like to mention the risk minimization framework developed in Zhai and Lafferty (2006), which constitutes an attempt to unify several IR models into a single framework.

19.3.4 Query Expansion and Relevance Feedback

To provide better matching between user information needs and documents, various query expansion techniques have been suggested. The general principle is to expand the query using words or phrases having meanings similar or related to those appearing in the original query, either by using information from a thesaurus (see, e.g., Voorhees, 1993; Maisonnasse et al., 2008 and Section 19.5.4), or by deriving this information from the collection. To achieve this, query expansion approaches rely on (a) relationships between words, (b) term selection mechanisms, and (c) term weighting schemes. The specific answers to these three questions may vary, leading to a variety of query expansion approaches (Efthimiadis, 1996).

In the first attempt to find related search terms, we might ask the user to select additional terms to be included in an expanded query. This can be handled interactively through displaying a ranked list of retrieved items returned by the first query.

As a second strategy, Rocchio (1971) proposed taking the relevance or non-relevance of top-ranked documents into account, as indicated manually by the user. In this case, a new query would then be built automatically in the form of a linear combination of the terms included in the previous query and the terms automatically extracted from both relevant (with a positive weight) and non-relevant documents (with a negative weight). More precisely, each new query term was derived by applying the following formula:

$$ w'_{qi} = \alpha \cdot w_{qi} + \beta \cdot \sum_{j=1}^{r} w_{ij} - \gamma \cdot \sum_{j=1}^{nr} w_{ij} \qquad (19.17) $$

in which w'_{qi} denotes the weight attached to the ith query term, based on the weight of this term in the previous query (denoted by w_{qi}), and on w_{ij} the indexing term weight attached to this term in both the relevant and nonrelevant documents appearing in the top k ranks. The value r (respectively nr) indicates the number of relevant (respectively nonrelevant) documents appearing in the first k positions. The positive constants α, β, and γ are fixed empirically, usually with $\alpha \geq \beta$, and $\beta = \gamma$. Empirical studies have demonstrated that such an approach is usually quite effective.

As a third technique, Buckley et al. (1996) suggested that even without looking at them, one can assume that the top k ranked documents are relevant. Using this approach, we simply set $r = k$ and $\gamma = 0$ in Equation 19.17. This method, denoted pseudo-relevance feedback or blind-query expansion, is usually effective (at least when handling relatively large text collections).

Relevance feedback can be very effective when the results of the original query are somehow correct. In other cases, the retrieval performance may decrease. Peat and Willett (1991) provide one explanation for such poor performance. In their study they show that query terms have a greater occurrence frequency than do other terms. Query expansion approaches based on term co-occurrence data will include additional terms that also have a greater occurrence frequency in the documents. In such cases, these additional search terms will not prove effective in discriminating between relevant and nonrelevant documents. In such circumstances, the final effect on retrieval performance could be negative.

There are several works focusing on (pseudo-)relevance feedback and the best way to derive related terms from search keywords. For example, we might use large text corpora to derive various term–term relationships and apply statistical or information-based measures. For example, Qiu and Frei (1993) suggested that terms extracted from a similarity thesaurus that had been automatically built through calculating co-occurrence frequencies in the search collection could be added to a new query. The underlying effect was to add idiosyncratic terms to those found in underlying document collections, and related to query terms in accordance to the language being used. Kwok et al. (2005) suggested building an improved request by using the Web to find terms related to search keywords. Additional information about relevance feedback approaches can be found in Manning et al. (2008) and in Efthimiadis (1996).

19.3.5 Advanced Models

As we already mentioned, document and query representations are imprecise and uncertain. It has been shown that different document representations or search strategies tend to have similar overall retrieval performance, although based on different retrieved items (Turtle and Croft, 1991). This observation prompted investigations of possible enhancements to overall retrieval performance by combining different document representations (Savoy, 2004) (e.g., single terms, n-grams, phrases) or different search strategies (different vector-space and/or probabilistic implementations) (Vogt and Cottrell, 1999).

Such merging strategies, known as data fusion, tend to improve the overall performance for three reasons. First, there is a skimming process in which only the m top-ranked retrieved items from each ranked list are considered. In this case, one can combine the best answers obtained from various document representations (which retrieve various relevant items). Second, one can count on the chorus effect, by which different retrieval schemes retrieve the same item, and as such provide stronger evidence that the corresponding document is indeed relevant. Third, an opposite or dark horse effect may also play a role. A given retrieval model may provide unusually high (low) and accurate estimates regarding the relevance of a document. In this case, a combined system can return more relevant items by better accounting for those documents having a relatively high (low) score or when a relatively short (or long) result lists occurs. Such data fusion approaches however require more storage space and processing time. Weighing advantages and disadvantages of data fusion, it is unclear if it is worth deploying in a commercial system.

A second interesting research area is to propose a better estimate for prior probabilities. In the probabilistic models, we have denoted by Prob[D_i] the prior probability of document D_i which appears in different implementations (see Equation 19.5, or in the LM paradigm, see Equation 19.15). Usually, without any additional information we assume that this value is the same for all documents. On the other hand, we know that all documents are not equally important. The "80-20 rule" may apply in large document collections or IR databases, meaning that around 20% of the documents present in the collection provide the expected answer to 80% of information needs. In such situations, it may be useful to rely on user feedback to dynamically adapt the prior probability for each document.

In the Web, it is known that users have a preference for the home page of a site, a page from which they can directly buy or obtain the needed service or information (e.g., flight ticket, consult a timetable, obtain an address, reserve an hotel). If we look at the corresponding URL describing such pages (e.g., "www.apple.com," "www.easyjet.co.uk"), one immediately sees that it is composed only of the root element (sometimes with a standard file name such as "index.html" or "default.htm"). As described in Kraaij et al. (2002), we can consider this information to assign higher probability to entry pages. Such practice (used by commercial search engines) can significantly improve retrieval performance.

In addition, Web search engines usually take into account the anchor texts, i.e., the sequence of words used to indicate the presence of a hyperlink and describing, in a compact manner, the target Web page. Thus, to refer to Microsoft home page, we can collect all anchor texts written by various authors and pointing to "www.microsoft.com." All these expressions can be viewed as forming a set, manually built, of terminological variants indexing the target page (e.g., "see Microsoft," "MicroSoft," "Micro$oft," "Bill Gates' Empire," or "The $$ Empire").

Lastly, to improve existing IR models on some collections, one can consider various relationships between documents. Bibliographic references are such an example and can be viewed as a set of relationships between documents, under the assumption that the main purpose of citing earlier articles is to give credit to works (concepts, facts, models, results, methodology, etc.) the subjects of which are related to the present document (at least in the author's mind). A main advantage of bibliographic references

(Garfield, 1983) is that they are independent of a particular use of words, and even languages. Thus they do not suffer (a) from the underlying ambiguity of all natural languages, (b) from the fact that the majority of subject indexers are specialized in a given domain, whereas documents may contain information pertaining to more than one specific domain of knowledge, and (c) from the fact that terms used to describe the content of a document may become obsolete in e.g., the scientific and technological literature.

One of the bibliographic measures is *bibliographic coupling* (Kessler, 1963), which measures subject similarity on the basis of referenced documents. To define the bibliographic coupling measure between two articles, one simply counts the number of documents cited by the two papers. Another measure is the *co-citation measure*, used by (Small, 1973) to build a network of documents: for each pair of documents, one counts the number of papers that cite both. To be strongly co-cited, two documents must be cited together by a large number of papers. In this case, the underlying hypothesis is that co-citation measures the subject similarity established by an author group.

On the Web, each page typically includes hypertext links to other pages, and such links are clearly not created by chance. Based on the previous bibliographic measures, one can establish and measure an association strength between Web pages. In a similar perspective, Google uses PR (Brin and Page, 1998) as one (among others) source of information to rank retrieved Web pages. In this link-based search model, the importance assigned to each Web page is partly based on its citation pattern. More precisely, a Web page will have a higher score if many Web pages point to it. This value increases if there are documents with high scores pointing to it. The PR value of a given Web page D_i (value noted as $PR(D_i)$), having $D_1, D_2, ..., D_m$ pages pointing to it, is computed according to the following formula:

$$PR^{c+1}(D_i) = (1 - d) \cdot \frac{1}{n} + d \cdot \left[\frac{PR^c(D_1)}{C(D_1)} + \cdots + \frac{PR^c(D_m)}{C(D_m)} \right] \quad (19.18)$$

where d is a parameter (usually set to 0.85 (Brin and Page, 1998)) and $C(D_j)$ is the number of outgoing links for Web page D_j. The computation of the PR value can be done using an iterative procedure (few iterations are needed before convergence). After each iteration, each PR value is divided by the sum of all PR values. As initial values, one can set $PR(D_i)$ to $1/n$, where n indicates the number of documents in the collection.

A third link-based approach consists of HITS (Kleinberg, 1999). In this scheme, a Web page pointing to many other information sources must be viewed as a "good" hub, while a document with many Web pages pointing to it is a "good" authority. Likewise, a Web page that points to many "good" authorities is an even better hub, while a Web page pointed to by many "good" hubs is an even better authority. For Web page D_i, formulas for hub and authority scores ($H^{c+1}(D_i)$ and $A^{c+1}(D_i)$) are given, at iteration $c + 1$, by

$$A^{c+1}(D_i) = \sum_{D_j \in \text{parent}(D_i)} H^c(D_j) \quad (19.19)$$

$$H^{c+1}(D_i) = \sum_{D_j \in \text{child}(D_i)} A^c(D_j) \quad (19.20)$$

Such scores are computed for the k top-ranked documents (typical value of k is $k = 200$) retrieved by a classical search model, together with their children and parents (as given by the citation network). Hub and authority scores are updated for a few iterations, and a normalization procedure (e.g., dividing each score by the sum of all squared values) is applied after each step.

Based on these two main hyperlink-based algorithms, different variants have been suggested (Borodin et al., 2005). It is important to note, however, that using such algorithms alone to retrieve documents does not yield very interesting results, as shown in various TREC evaluation campaigns (Hawking, 2001).

This being said, their integration in a general search engine provides new, interesting functionalities (as the detection of spam Web pages, or the improvement of the rank of well-known Web pages).

More recently, several researchers have investigated the possibility of using machine learning approaches in IR. Let us assume that we have a large collection of documents, a large number of queries and relevance judgements (see Section 19.4) for these queries on the collection. We can see such judgements as a set of annotated (query, document) pairs, where the annotation takes, e.g., the value 1 if the document is relevant to the query, and −1 if it is not. Next, one can transform a given (query, document) pair into a vector that represents an example. Such a transformation needs to abstract away from the particular terms present in the query, and usually relies on a variety of features based on characteristics (Nallapati, 2004), such as

1. Number of common terms between the query and the document
2. Average inverse document frequency of the query terms present in the document
3. Width of the window in which query terms appear in the document
4. Cosine similarity between the query and the document
5. Probabilistic measure of relevance of the document
6. And, when available,
   - PR value of the document
   - number of incoming (outgoing) links

Once (query, document) pairs are seen as vectors, we end up with a standard binary classification problem, the aim of which is building a classifier that discriminates well between positive and negative examples. Once such a classifier is built, documents relevant to a new query are those documents classified in the positive class (each document of the collection is, of course, first paired to the query, the pair being then transformed, as above, into a vector which will be the input of the classifier). Many different classifiers can be used here. Because of their success in different settings, Support Vector Machines (see, e.g., Manning et al., 2008) are quite often chosen for the task.

Nallapati (2004) shows that the approach based on machine learning outperforms standard IR approaches when both the number of features used in the vector representation and the number of relevance judgements are sufficiently large. It is also possible to go beyond the framework of binary classification, and try to directly learn a ranking function, through pairwise preferences (Cao et al., 2006) or listwise preferences (Cao et al., 2007). These last two approaches outperform the one based on a direct classification of documents.

As one may have noted, the basic building block of machine learning approaches to IR is a set of relevance judgements. If some collections (as the one found in TREC for example) do have a set of associated relevant judgements, most collections do not. The situation is somewhat different for the Web and Web search engines, as Web search companies have access to clickthrough data (data recording the fact that, for a given query, a user has clicked on particular documents proposed by the search engine), which can partly be used as annotated data to develop machine learning tools (see, e.g., Joachims et al., 2007) and more recently (Scholler et al., 2008). Furthermore, it is probable that such companies try to manually develop relevance judgements in order to deploy accurate machine learning techniques. The field of research on machine learning for IR is thus very active at the time of writing this chapter, and will certainly give birth to new, interesting approaches to IR.

19.4 Evaluation and Failure Analysis

In order to know whether one search model is better than another, an evaluation methodology must be adopted. In the IR domain, this must be applied to the search process as a whole (user-in-the-loop paradigm), which means evaluation by real users with their real information needs. It would be of interest to analyze a range of characteristics such as the answer speed, its quality, the user's effort needed to write a query, the interface of the search system, the coverage of the collection, etc. All these aspects are certainly important but (a) user studies are costly, and (b) some features are hard to measure objectively. Thus traditional IR evaluation approaches are usually limited to system performance, and more particularly to the quality of the answer (retrieval effectiveness).

In this vein, to measure the retrieval performance (Buckley and Voorhees, 2005), we first need a test collection containing a set of information units (e.g., documents), and a set of topic (or query) formulations together with their relevance assessments. As described in Section 19.4.1, these corpora are usually the result of an international cooperative effort. Having such a benchmark, we can evaluate several IR models or search strategies by comparing their relative retrieval performance (measured by precision-recall values).

As shown in Section 19.4.3, even after decades of research in this field, we still need a better understanding of the reasons explaining why some topics are still hard. The analysis of some difficult queries will give us some insights on this, as well as on the ways existing IR models can be improved or designed more effectively.

19.4.1 Evaluation Campaigns

Modern IR evaluations are based on rather large test collections built during different evaluation campaigns. The oldest and best known of these campaigns is TREC* (Voorhees and Harman, 2005) (Text REtrieval Conference) established in 1992 in order to evaluate large-scale IR, to speed the transfer of technology from research labs into products and to increase the availability of appropriate evaluation methodologies. Held each year, TREC conferences have investigated retrieval techniques in different medium (written documents, Web pages, spoken documents, OCR, image, video) as well as different search tasks (*ad hoc*, interactive, routing, filtering, categorization, question/answering) or languages (English, Arabic, Chinese, Spanish, etc.).

Around the world, three other evaluation campaign series have been launched. Beginning in 1999, the NTCIR[†] conference is held every 18 months in Japan and is more oriented to problems related to Far-East languages (e.g., Japanese, traditional or simplified Chinese, Korean) used in conjunction with several search tasks (patent retrieval, Web, *ad hoc*, question/answering, summarization).

In Europe, CLEF[‡] (Peters et al., 2008) (Cross-Language Evaluation Forum) was founded to promote, study, and evaluate information access technologies using various European languages. Held each year since 2000, the CLEF campaigns have produced test collections in more than 12 languages related to different tasks (*ad hoc*, bilingual, multilingual and cross-lingual retrieval, image search, question/answering, domain-specific retrieval, etc.).

Lastly, and more recently, a campaign, called INEX,[§] was launched in order to evaluate retrieval systems in (semi-)structured collections.

Each year, these evaluation campaigns propose additional challenging tracks such as novelty (retrieval of new and unseen information items), robust (improving the performance of hard topics), spam filtering, IR on blog corpus, question/answering using Wikipedia, cross-language retrieval on audio data, multilingual Web IR, geographic-based IR (search involving spatial aspects), multimodal summarization for trend information, etc.

The user is not absent in all evaluation studies. For example, the interactive track at TREC (Dumais and Belkin, 2005) presented an interesting set of studies on various aspects of human–machine interactions. More specific experiments pertaining to cross-lingual IR systems were presented during various CLEF evaluation campaigns (Gonzalo and Oard, 2003).

---

* trec.nist.gov
† research.nii.ac.jp/ntcir
‡ www.clef-campaign.org
§ inex.is.informatik.uni-duisburg.de

One of the main objectives of these evaluation campaigns is to produce reliable test collections. To achieve this, corpora are extracted from various newspapers, news agencies, from the Web, or from other private sources (e.g., libraries, private companies). These data are preprocessed to guarantee some standardization (same encoding, homogenization of the tags, segmentation into information items).

Besides the creation and clean-up of the corpora themselves, the organizers prepare a set of topic formulations (usually 50 per year). Each of them is usually structured into three logical sections comprising a brief title (T), a one-sentence description (D) and a narrative (N) specifying the relevance assessment criteria. For example, we can find the following topic description:

<title> Oil Prices </title>
<desc> What is the current price of oil? </desc>
<narr> Only documents giving the current oil price are relevant, i.e., the price when the document was written. References to oil prices in the past or predictions for price changes in the future are not relevant. </narr>

The available topics cover various subjects (e.g., "Pesticides in Baby Food," "Whale Reserve," "Renewable Power," or "French Nuclear Tests") and may include both regional ("Swiss Initiative for the Alps") and international coverage ("Ship Collisions"). Depending on the campaigns, topics are manually translated into several languages.

After receiving the topic set, the participants have around one month to send back their answers as computed by their own search system. For each task, guidelines specify exactly the task conditions (usually by imposing that runs must be fully automatic and based only on the title and description (TD) parts of the topic formulation). After this step, the organizers may form a pool of retrieved documents for each topic. As each participant is usually allowed to send 1000 answers for each topic, the organizers take only the top n documents (e.g., $n = 100$) from each run. These documents are then presented to a human assessor who decides whether each item is relevant or not. This process is blind in the sense that the assessor only has access to a query and a set of documents.

This procedure has been applied over many years and we must recognize that the resulting judgments are a subset of true relevant set because not all documents belonging to the underlying collection were judged. However, as demonstrated by various studies, the difference is not large (Buckley and Voorhees, 2005). It is worth to note that having a large number of very different IR systems is necessary (however not sufficient) to ensure the reliability of the evaluation process. If a test collection is built with a few participants having similar search strategies, the results are questionable. Finally, the retrieval performance that can be drawn from any test collection is never absolute but only relative to the test collection in use.

19.4.2 Evaluation Measures

To measure retrieval performance (Buckley and Voorhees, 2005), we may consider that the only important aspect is to retrieve one pertinent answer. In some contexts, the answer could really be unique, or at least the number of correct answers is rather limited as, for example, when searching for a home page on the Web. In this case, the evaluation measure will be based only on the rank of the first correct answer retrieved.

For any given query, if r is the rank of the first relevant document retrieved, the query performance is computed as $1/r$. This value, called the reciprocal rank (RR), varies between 1 (the first retrieved item is relevant) and 0 (no correct response returned). It should be noted here that ranking the first relevant item in second place instead of first would seriously reduce the RR value, making it 0.5 instead of 1.

To measure the retrieval performance resulting from a set of queries, we simply compute the mean over all the queries. This value known as the mean reciprocal rank (MRR), serves as a measure of any given search engine's ability to extract one correct answer and list it among the top-ranked items. We thus believe that MRR value closely reflects the expectation of those Internet surfers who are looking for a single good response to their queries.

In IR, we usually do not want to measure a search system's ability to rank one relevant item, but to extract all relevant information from the collection. In such contexts, we assume that users want both high precision (fraction of retrieved items that are relevant) and high recall (fraction of relevant items that have been retrieved). In other words they want "the truth, the whole truth (recall), and nothing but the truth (precision)." In order to get a synthetic measure from both precision and recall, the harmonic mean between the two (known as F1 or F score (van Rijsbergen, 1979)) is sometimes used (specially in NLP tasks). Denoting the precision by P and the recall by R, the F score is defined as

TABLE 19.3 Precision–Recall Computation

Rank	System A	System B
1	NR	R 1/1
2	R 1/2	R 2/2
3	R 2/3	NR
...	NR	NR
30	R 3/30	NR
...	NR	NR
100	NR	R 3/100
AP	0.422	0.676

$$F1 = \frac{2 \cdot P \cdot R}{P + R} \tag{19.21}$$

It is however more common in IR to compute the average precision (AP) for each query by measuring the precision achieved at each relevant item extracted and then computing an overall average. Then for a given set of queries we calculate the mean average precision (MAP), which varies between 0.0 (no relevant items found) and 1.0 (all relevant items always appear at the top of the ranked list).

However, between these two values it is difficult for a user to have a meaningful and direct interpretation of a MAP value. Moreover, from a user's point of view, the value of the difference in AP achieved by two rankings is sometimes difficult to interpret. For example, in Table 19.3 we have reported the AP for a topic with three relevant items. With System A, the relevant documents appear in rank 2, 3, and 30. If we computed the AP for this query, we have a precision of 1/2 after the second document, 2/3 after the third document, and 3/30 after the 30th retrieved item given an AP of 0.422. Computing the AP for System B, we found 0.676, showing a relative improvement of 60% over ranking produced by System A.

As an alternative, we may consider that the evaluation should focus on the capability of the search system to retrieve many relevant items on the one hand, and to present them in the top-n position of the returned list. In this case, we do not attach a great importance to extracting *all* relevant items, assuming that there are too many. To evaluate the retrieval performance in such circumstances, we can compute the precision achieved after retrieving n items. On the Web, we may set this threshold to $n = 10$, corresponding to the first screen returned by a commercial search engine and then compute the precision at this point, a value denoted P@10 or Prec@10. In our previous example (see Table 19.3), both systems achieved a performance of P@10 = 0.2.

More recently, Järvelin and Kekäläinen introduced (Järvelin and Kekäläinen, 2002) a new evaluation measure called Normalized Discounted Cumulative Gain (NDCG), which is well adapted to situations where relevance judgements are graded, i.e., when they take more than just two values (relevant or not). The assumption behind NDCG is that highly relevant documents are (a) more useful when appearing earlier in the list of retrieved documents and (b) more useful than marginally relevant documents, which in turn are more useful than irrelevant documents. NDCG computes a relevance score for a list of documents through the gain brought by each document in the list discounted by the position at which the document appears. This score is then normalized relative to the optimal gain that can be achieved, yielding a score between 0 and 1 (provided the lowest value for the relevance is greater than 1). The NDCG score for the list consisting of the first k documents retrieved by an IR system is thus

$$N(k) = \overbrace{Z_k}^{\text{normalization}} \sum_{j=1}^{k} \overbrace{(2^{p(j)} - 1)}^{\text{gain}} / \underbrace{\log_2(j+1)}_{\text{position discount}} \tag{19.22}$$

where $p(j)$ corresponds to the relevance value of the document appearing at position j. With this formula, System B in Table 19.3 gets a higher score than System A on the first 10 documents as, even though they both retrieve only two documents, the position discounts for System B are lower than the ones for System A since the relevant documents are ranked higher in the list by System B.

Finally, in an effort to statistically determine whether or not a given search strategy would be better than another, we may apply different statistical tests (Conover, 1999) (Sign test, Wilcoxon signed ranks test, t-test, or using the bootstrap methodology (Savoy, 1997)). Within these tests the null hypothesis H_0 states that the two retrieval schemes produce similar MAP (or MRR) performance. This null hypothesis is accepted if the two retrieval schemes are statistically similar (i.e., yield more or less the same retrieval performance), and is rejected otherwise.

For example, the Sign test does not take the amount of difference into account, but only the fact that a search system performs better than the other. In a set of 50 topics, imagine that System A produced better MAP for 32 queries (or 32 "+"), System B was better for 16 (or 16 "–"), and for the two remaining queries both systems showed the same performance. If the null hypothesis were true, we would expect to obtain roughly the same number of "+" or "–" signs. In the current case involving 48 experiments (the two ties are ignored), we have 32 "+" and only 16 "–" signs. Accepting the null hypothesis, the probability of observing a "+" would be equal to the probability of observing a "–" (namely, 0.5). Thus, for 48 trials, the probability of observing 16 or fewer occurrences of the same sign ("+" or "–," for a two-tailed test) is only 0.0293 (see tables in Conover, 1999). With a significance level fixed at $\alpha = 5\%$, we must reject H_0, and accept the alternative hypothesis stating that there is a difference between System A and B. In such a case, the difference is said to be *statistically significant at the level* $\alpha = 0.05$.

19.4.3 Failure Analysis

Given the sound procedures described previously for both indexing (see Section 19.2) and search models (see Section 19.3), it seems *a priori* that search engines should not fail to retrieve documents queried by users, especially when those documents share many words with the query. However, unexpected and incorrect answers happen from time to time.

From a commercial IR perspective, it is important to understand the reasons why a search system fails, why customers encounter problems when searching for information. In the academic world, this aspect has been studied within several robust tracks (Voorhees, 2006). During previous evaluation campaigns, numerous topic descriptions have been created by humans and submitted to different search engines. Some of them (around 5% to 10%) have been found to be hard for almost every search paradigm, without being able to detect, *a priori*, when a query would be hard or not. Only a few studies (e.g., Buckley, 2004) tend to investigate search system failures.

To illustrate our purpose, we have extracted some topics from our participation in past evaluation campaigns. These hard queries are defined as topics having zero precision after 10 retrieved items (P@10). In an effort to explain the IR model's failure to list at least one pertinent item among the top 10, we might classify the causes into two main groups: first, system flaws (Category #1 to #3) where some advanced processing techniques may improve the performance; Second, topic intrinsic difficulties (Category #4 to #6) where a deeper understanding of user's intent and semantic analysis seems to be required.

Category 1: *Stopword list.* The way letters are normalized (or not) as well as the use of a stopword list may prevent one from finding correct answers. From the topic "Who and whom," the query representation was simply empty because the forms "who," "and," and "whom" were included in the stopword list. A similar problem might be encountered with phrases such as "IT engineer," "US citizen," or "language C." In the first two cases, the search system might fail to recognize the acronyms, treating them as the pronouns "it" or "us," which are usually included in a stopword list, along with the letter "c." This example explains why commercial IR systems may have a particular strategy for dealing with empty words.

Category 2: *Stemming.* The stemming procedure cannot always conflate all word variants into the same form or stem, as illustrated by the topic "Prehistorical Art." In this case, a light stemming approach left unchanged the search term "prehistorical." This term however does not occur in the corpus and the submitted query was therefore limited to "art." Using a more aggressive stemmer is not always the most appropriate solution. Of course, using Porter's stemmer (Porter, 1980), the IR system is able to conflate the forms "prehistorical" and "prehistoric" under the same root and to retrieve a relevant item in the top 10. However, a more aggressive stemmer may lead to overstemming with a negative impact on the search results.

Category 3: *Spelling errors.* When building topic descriptions, the organizers of the evaluation campaign usually check the spelling of each topic so that only a few, if any, of them appear in queries. They do however exist as "tartin" (instead of "tartan") or "nativityscenes" (for "nativity scenes"). The presence of proper nouns may also generate this problem (e.g., "Solzhenitsyn"). A related problem is the fact that spelling may vary across countries (e.g., "color" vs. "colour") or that several variants are acceptable ("fetus" and "foetus"). In all these cases, search systems are often unable to retrieve any pertinent items in the top of their ranked list or may ignore numerous pertinent items written using an alternate spelling. In a commercial environment, spell checking and suggestion is an essential feature for all man–machine interfaces.

Category 4: *Synonymy and language use.* The topic "Les risques du téléphone portable" ("Risks with mobile phones") illustrates how vocabulary can change across countries. For this query, the relevant documents used synonyms that are country dependent. In Switzerland, a mobile phone is usually called "natel," in Belgium "téléphone mobile," "cellulaire" in Quebec, and "portable" in France (the same problem occurs in the Chinese language with two different expressions used, one in Taiwan and another in mainland China). All IR systems included in their top 10 results certain documents covering the use of mobile phones in the mountains (and the risk of being in the mountains). Other retrieved articles simply presented certain aspects related to mobile phones (new joint ventures, new products, etc.). Other words or English expressions present similar difficulties (e.g., "film" and "movie" in the query "Films set in Scotland," or "car" and "automobile" in the query "European car industry"). In such cases, the query may include one form, and relevant documents another.

Category 5: *Missing specificity.* A fifth failure explanation is found for example in topic "Trade unions in Europe." The specific or desired meaning is not clearly specified or is too broad. This same difficulty occurs with the topics "Edouard Balladur," "Peace-keeping forces in Bosnia," "World soccer championship," or "Computer security." With all these queries, the IR system listed top-ranked articles having not one but at least two or three terms in common with the query. Placed at the top of the output list were short articles having all query terms in their title (or three out of four terms for topic "Peace-keeping"). The unspecified main purpose of the topic was clearly missing; for example, for the topic "World soccer championship" the required information was most probably the "result of the final."

Category 6: *Discrimination ability.* For example, in the topic "Chinese currency devaluation" the pertinent set must contain information about the effects of devaluation. In this case, the three relevant articles had only one or two terms in common with the query. The terms "Chinese" (also appearing in 1090 other articles) and "currency" (occurring in 2475 documents) appeared in the first relevant document. In the second, only the term "Chinese" appears to be in common with the topic's title, and in the last only the term "devaluation" (occurring also in other 552 articles). The IR system therefore found it very difficult to discriminate between relevant and nonrelevant documents, due to the fact that a lot of the latter had at least two terms in common with the query. The same difficulty arose with the topic "Wonders of ancient world" for which relevant documents describe one wonder without using explicitly the term "wonder," "ancient," or "world."

19.5 Natural Language Processing and Information Retrieval

The basic building blocks of most natural languages are words. However, the term "words" is ambiguous and we must be more precise in order to distinguish between the surface form (e.g., "horses") corresponding to tokens, and word type or lemma (entry in the dictionary, such as "horse" in our case). Moreover, the specific meaning of the term "horse" is not always an animal with four legs as in the term "horse-fly" or in expressions as "Trojan horse," "light horse," "to work like a horse," "from the horse's mouth," or "horse about."

In the design of effective IR systems, the morphological (Sproat, 1992) component plays an important role. For most search systems, and also for most human languages, the words form the basic units to build the phrases, expressions, and sentences used to transmit a precise meaning. An appropriate processing of these entities is therefore important for enhancing retrieval performance by promoting pertinent word-sense matching. In addition, the way words combine and the meanings words convey are crucial for understanding the content of a document and for representing this content accurately.

In this section, we will review some of the major relations between IR and NLP. We will do so by examining the traditional layers of Natural Language Text Processing (morphology, syntax, semantics) and see the role they play or can play in IR. Finally, we will briefly mention various applications that have direct connections with both IR and NLP.

19.5.1 Morphology

As mentioned previously, the goal of the morphological step in IR is to conflate morphological variants into the same form. In some cases, only an inflectional analysis is performed, so as to get to a lemmatized version of the original text. This step can be followed by a derivational analysis, usually relying on suffixes only, as prefixes tend to radically modify the meaning of a word (indexing the two forms "decompose" and "recompose" as the same token does not make sense from an IR point of view).

In most cases however, these two steps (inflectional and derivational analysis) are not separated, but performed in conjunction. Even though inflectional analyzers, based on electronic lexicons, exist in many languages, this is not the case for derivational analyzers, and the IR community has relied on tools that aim at identifying word stems without necessarily relying on precise morphological processes. Such tools are called *stemmers* (as mentioned in Section 19.2.2) and are described below. One can find in Hull (1996), a comparison of the use of a stemmer and a derivational lexicon for conflating words in the framework of IR.

When defining a stemming algorithm, a first approach will only remove inflectional suffixes. For English, such a procedure conflates singular and plural word forms ("car" and "cars") as well as removing the past participle ending "-ed" and the gerund or present participle ending "-ing" ("eating" and "eat").

Stemming schemes that remove only morphological inflections are termed as "light" suffix-stripping algorithms, while more sophisticated approaches have also been proposed to remove derivational suffixes (e.g., "-ment," "-ably," "-ship" in the English language). For example, Lovins (1968) is based on a list of over 260 suffixes, while Porter's algorithm (Porter, 1980) looks for about 60 suffixes. In such cases, suffix removal is also controlled through the adjunct of quantitative restrictions (e.g., "-ing" would be removed if the resulting stem had more than three letters as in "running," but not in "king") or qualitative restrictions (e.g., "-ize" would be removed if the resulting stem did not end with "e" as in "seize"). Moreover, certain *ad hoc* spelling correction rules are used to improve the conflation accuracy (e.g., "running" gives "run" and not "runn"), due to certain irregular grammar rules usually applied to facilitate easier pronunciation. Of course, one should not stem proper nouns such as "Collins" or "Hawking," at least when the system can recognize them.

Stemming schemes are usually designed to work with general text in any given language. Certain stemming procedures may also be especially designed for a specific domain (e.g., in medicine) or a given document collection, such as that of Xu and Croft (1998) who suggest developing stemming procedures using a corpus-based approach which more closely reflects the language used (including the word frequencies and other co-occurrence statistics), instead of using a set of morphological rules in which the frequency of each rule (and therefore its underlying importance) is not precisely known.

As we mentioned above, stemming procedures ignore word meanings, and thus tend to make errors. Such errors may be due to over-stemming (e.g., "general" becomes "gener," and "organization" is reduced to "organ") or under-stemming (e.g., with Porter's stemmer, the words "create" and "creation" do not conflate to the same root). Not surprisingly, the use of an online dictionary has been suggested in order to produce better conflations (Krovetz and Croft, 1992; Savoy, 1993).

The development of a morphological analyzer (be it a stemmer or a more refined tool) depends largely on the language considered. The English inflectional morphology is relatively simple. The plural form is usually denoted by adding an '-s' (with some exceptions like "foot" and "feet"). The feminine form is built using some suffixes (e.g., "actor" and "actress") and we do not have to mark the agreement between noun and adjective ("tall man," "tall women"). To build new words (derivational construction), we may add prefixes ("pay," "prepay") and/or suffixes ("bank," "banking," "banker," "bankless," "bankrupt").

For other European languages, the morphological construction can be relatively similar. In the French language, the plural is denoted as in English ("face," "faces"), while the feminine form can simply be denoted by a final '-e' ("employé," "employée") or by a suffix ("acteur," "actrice"). As in English, various suffixes are available to form new words.

For some other languages, the inflectional morphological possibilities are more numerous. In the German language, for example, we find four grammatical case endings (e.g., the genitive case by employing an '-s' or '-es' as in "Staates" (of the state), "Mannes" (of the man)). The plural form is denoted using a variety of endings such as '-en' (e.g., "Motor" and "Motoren" (engine)), '-er', '-e' (e.g., "Jahr" and "Jahre" (year)) or '-n' (e.g., "Name" and "Namen" (name)). Plural forms may also use diacritic characters (e.g., "Apfel" (apple) becomes "Äpfel") or in conjunction with a suffix (e.g., "Haus" and "Häuser" (house)). Also frequently used are the suffixes '-en' or '-n' to indicate grammatical cases or for adjectives (e.g., "... einen guten Mann" (a good man) in the accusative singular form).

The Hungarian language makes use of a greater number of grammatical cases (23 in total, although some are limited to a set of nouns or appear only in fixed and predefined forms) than does German. Each case has its own unambiguous suffix however; e.g., the noun "house" ("ház" in nominative) may appear as "házat" (accusative case), "házakat" (accusative plural case), "házamat" ("... my house") or "házamait" ("... my houses"). In this language the general construction used for nouns is as follows: 'stem' 'possessive marker' 'case' as in 'ház' + 'am' + 'at' (in which the letter 'a' is introduced to facilitate better pronunciation because "házmt" could be difficult to pronounce). Similar agglutinative aspects may be found in other languages such as Turkish, where the noun "ev" (house) may take on the form "evler" (the houses), "evlerim" (my houses), and "evlerimde" (in my houses). For these two languages at least, the automatic removing of suffixes does not present a real and complex task (Savoy, 2008; Can et al., 2008).

For the Finnish language however, it seems that the design and development of an effective stemming procedure requires a more complex morphological analysis, usually based on a dictionary. The real stemming problem with the Finnish language is that stems are often modified when suffixes are added. For example, "matto" (carpet in the nominative singular form) becomes "maton" (in the genitive singular form, with '-n' as suffix) or "mattoja" (in the partitive plural form, with '-a' as suffix). Once we remove the corresponding suffixes, we are left with three distinct stems, namely, "matto," "mato," and "matoj." Of course irregularities such as these also occur in other languages, usually helping to make the spoken language flow better, such as "submit" and "submission" in English. In Finnish however, these irregularities are more common, and thus they render the conflation of various word forms into the same stem more problematic.

Compound constructions (concatenation of two or more lexemes to form another word, e.g., handgun, worldwide) also appear in other European languages. In Italian, the plural form may alter letters within a word, for example, "capoufficio" (chief secretary) becomes "capiufficio" in its plural form. Yet, in other constructions, the stem "capo" is left unchanged (e.g., "capogiro" gives "capogiri" (dizziness) in its plural form).

In German and in most Germanic languages, compound words are widely used and are a source of additional difficulties. For example, a life insurance company employee would be "Lebensversicherungs- gesellschaftsangestellter" ("Leben" + 's' + "Versicherung" + 's' + "Gesellschaft" + 's' + "Angestellter" for life + insurance + company + employee). The augment (i.e., the letter "s" in our previous example) is not always present (e.g., "Bankangestelltenlohn" built as "Bank" + "Angestellten" + "Lohn" (salary)). Since compound construction is so widely used and can be written in different forms, it is almost impossible to build a German dictionary providing complete coverage of the language, and an automatic decompound- ing procedure is required in order to obtain an effective IR system in the German language (Savoy, 2004; Braschler and Ripplinger, 2004).

Several tools are available for identifying morphological variants in different languages. They are either based on online dictionaries and standard morphological analysis (see, e.g., http://www.xrce.xerox.com) or on stemming procedures dedicated to different languages (e.g., http://www.unine.ch/info/clef/ or http://snowball.tartarus.org).

19.5.2 Orthographic Variation and Spelling Errors

The standardization of spelling was mainly the fruit of the nineteenth century. Working with documents written previously, one encounters different spellings for a given term or proper name (e.g., Shakespeare's name appears as "Shakper," "Shakspe," "Shaksper," "Shakspere," or "Shakspeare" in his own works).

The spelling problem can be domain-specific. In the biomedical literature, it is known that several orthographic variants (Yu and Agichtein, 2003) can be found to represent a given name, generally introduced for a variety of reasons. Firstly, there are of course typographic errors and misspellings (performance errors as in "retreival" and "retrieval" or competence errors as in "ecstasy," "extasy," or "ecstacy"). Secondly, punctuation and tokenization may produce variants, mainly due to the lack of a naming convention (e.g., "Nurr77," "Nurr-77," or "Nurr 77"). Thirdly, regional variations also introduce variants (e.g., the difference between British and American English for "colour" and "color" or "grey" or "gray"). Fourthly, the transliteration of foreign names produces some differences (e.g., "Crohn" and "Krohn" or "Creutzfeld-Jakob" and "Creutzfeldt-Jacob").

The standard strategy to reduce the negative impact caused by spelling errors or orthographic variation is to relate similar (however not identical) forms in one way or another. Two main strategies can be used here: (a) compute an edit-distance between different forms (e.g., present in a dynamic dictionary) and normalize the variants with a particular form, (b) adopt an n-gram indexing strategy (n is typically set to five across a range of studies). The n-gram method has the advantage of being fast (filters have to be used to avoid comparing unrelated forms in the first approach). Moreover, this method does not require any prior linguistic knowledge and is robust to typographical errors, both in the submitted queries and documents retrieved (McNamee and Mayfield, 2004). For instance, the term "alzheimer" would be decomposed, with an overlapping five-gram approach, as: "alzhe," "lzhei," "zheim," "heime," and "eimer."

19.5.3 Syntax

Most IR systems index documents on the basis of the simple words they contain. However, there have been many attempts to make use of more complex index terms, comprising several terms, in order to get a more precise description of the content of documents. One of the first attempts, referred to as *adjacent pairs* (e.g., described in Salton et al., 1975), considered complex terms made up of two adjacent content words. Even though simple, this approach is appropriate e.g., for the English language, as it allows one to capture terminological elements consisting of *Adjective Noun* or *Noun Noun* sequences (and their combination). For other languages, such as the ones based on a composition of Romance type, i.e., in which compounds are formed through prepositions, simple regular expressions can be used over part-of-speech tags to identify terminological elements and add them to the index terms.

More generally, a syntactic analyzer can be used to identify long-distance dependencies between words, so as to improve the indexing of documents. The first works in this direction were based on "traditional" grammars, in which a complete analysis/representation of a sentence or a phrase was searched for. (Fagan, 1989) investigates, for example, the impact of a syntactic parser for noun phrases on IR performance. However, the lack of large-coverage grammars, and the difficulty of obtaining unambiguous and correct parses for many sentences effectively put a stop to this type of research at that time.

Advances in shallow (or light) parsing in the mid-1990s led to a resurgence of this type of work, as such parsers were partly defined to be general and robust. Hull et al. (1997) proposes, for example, to use a shallow parser to identify relations within and between complex noun and verb phrases. Pairs of terms thus extracted (as *Subject Verb* pairs or *Adjective Noun* pairs) are then added to simple words to provide a richer index of documents. Experiments conducted on the vector-space model showed a slight improvement on the TREC-5 collection. Similar experiments conducted on French can be found in Gaussier et al. (2000). More recently, Gao et al. (2004) proposed an extension of the language modeling approach to IR that can take into account the syntactic dependencies provided by a probabilistic parser deployed on the queried collection.

One of the major problems with the use of syntactic information is that the improvements in IR performance have been limited, and highly dependent on the queried collection. Complex terms acquired through syntactic analysis can be seen as additional information that can help refine query results and thus lead to an increase in the precision at the top of the list of retrieved documents. However, in many cases, having constituents of a compound taken independently of each other or as a whole does not change the retrieval results substantially. For example, a document indexed with the two terms *information* and *retrieval* is very likely to deal with *information retrieval*, so that the addition of this last compound does not really add any new information: all documents containing both *information* and *retrieval* will almost certainly also be indexed by *information retrieval* after a syntactic analysis phase, and the ranking will not change.

In essence, syntactic analysis provides additional indexing dimensions, but does not address the problem of the vocabulary mismatch between queries and documents. A direct way to address this problem is to resort to a semantic analysis in order to replace index terms with concepts and perform the matching between queries and documents at a more abstract level.

19.5.4 Semantics

In the absence of robust systems providing a complete semantic analysis of sentences, most work in IR and semantics have focused on lexical semantics, and the possibility to replace standard index terms with concepts or word senses. While some studies have shown that word sense disambiguation procedures can be beneficial in some cases (Sanderson, 1994; Schütze and Pedersen, 1995), the majority have tried to rely on existing semantic resources in order to index both documents and queries at the concept level. Such works have used existing semantic resources, either generic ones, as Voorhees (1993), or specialized ones for specific collections (e.g., UMLS—see below).

The usefulness of concept indexing in specific domains has been shown in several studies, mainly in the medical domain for which large-coverage thesauri and semantic networks exist. For example, the best-performing systems on text in the ImageCLEFmed task of CLEF (Maisonnasse et al., 2008; Lacoste et al., 2007) use conceptual indexing methods based on vector-space models or LMs. In the TREC genomics track, Zhou et al. (2007) used the MeSH (Medical Subject Headings) thesaurus and *Entrez* databases to select terms from medical publications. Terms in documents and queries were expanded with their variants found in these resources to achieve better indexing. They found that this strategy led to a significant improvement over standard indexing methods.

Other researchers have tried to go beyond the use of concepts by exploiting relations between them. Vintar et al. (2003) evaluates the usefulness of UMLS concepts and semantic relations in medical IR. They first extract concepts and relations from documents and queries. To select relations in a sentence, they rely on two assumptions: (1) interesting relations occur between interesting concepts; (2) relations are expressed by typical lexical markers such as verbs. However, their experiments with a vector-space model show that using both concepts and relations lower the performance obtained with concepts alone. A similar line of development has been taken on the basis of the language modeling approach to IR. The language modeling approach to IR was first proposed in Ponte and Croft (1998), and extended in Hiemstra (2000) (see Section 19.3.3). Even though smoothed unigram models have yielded good performance in IR, several studies have investigated the use of more advanced representations. Studies like (e.g., Srikanth and Srikanth (2000) or (Song and Croft, 1999)) proposed the combination of unigram models with bigram models. Others studies, e.g., Lee et al. (2006) or Gao et al. (2004), have extended the model to deal with syntactic dependencies. More recently, Maisonnasse et al. (2008) and Maisonnasse et al. (2007) have proposed a generalization of these works that can deal with semantic networks as well. In fact, any directed acyclic graph can be used to represent documents and queries.

This latter approach was applied to the medical domain, where documents are indexed at the concept level with UMLS, and where relations between concepts are added by checking whether two concepts co-occurring in the same sentence are present in the *Semantic Network* associated with UMLS. The results show that concept indexing yields a significant improvement over standard indexing in IR performance. The use of semantic relations further improves the precision of the system, namely, at the top of the list of retrieved documents, even though slightly.

What these results show is that, provided one has at his or her disposal semantic resources adapted to the collection (as is UMLS for the medical domain), then significant gains can be achieved with semantic indexing.

19.5.5 Related Applications

There are a number of applications that directly borrow models and methods from both IR and NLP. A detailed presentation of these applications is beyond the scope of this chapter, and we will just mention what we believe are the most important ones.

1. Text categorization is a good example of an application where research has been conducted in the two communities, IR and NLP (to which we should add the Machine Learning and Data Mining ones). Text categorization aims at automatically assigning new documents to existing categories. Most approaches are currently based on machine learning, where already classified documents are used to automatically learn a decision function. The way documents are represented directly derives from the vector-space model (sometimes with additional processing steps, such as named entity and term extraction) and the different weighting schemes of Section 19.3.2.

2. A second application where methods from both IR and NLP are used is document summarization, which aims at providing a summary, in a few sentences, of a document or a document collection. Current approaches focus on extracting key sentences (sometimes parts of sentences) from the document or document collection and on displaying them in an appropriate way.

3. A third application is BioNLP, which focuses on the processing of text documents in the biological domain. As for the medical domain, there exist several knowledge bases in the biological domain, which can be used to get a more accurate representation of documents. However, the kind of information searched for by biologists is complex, and one needs to deploy a whole range of technologies to be able to match the needs of biologists.

   For example, when trying to find articles relevant to an interaction between two proteins (*BRCA1* and *p53* on PubMed), simply searching for the two terms results in 733 abstracts of which a high proportion do not describe any relationship between the proteins. More precise queries, which include verbs describing interactions, such as 'interact' and 'regulate,' are often used to significantly reduce the search space. Unfortunately the information loss is unknown and the retrieved abstracts still document other relationships, for example, between *E6* and *p53*.* In this case, a tight coupling between the indexing engine, the search engine, and the natural language processing engine is needed. Interested readers are referred to Chapter 25 for a detailed presentation of the models and methods deployed in this domain.

4. The last application we would like to mention is Question/Answering, which aims at providing precise answers (as opposed to whole documents or paragraphs as is traditionally the case in IR) to questions. Most Question/Answering systems rely on a tightly coupled combination of IR and NLP techniques, leading to systems that integrate many of the existing technologies of these two domains. Here again, we refer interested readers to Chapter 20 for a detailed presentation of such systems.

19.6 Conclusion

As described in this chapter, the IR field is an extensive applied NLP domain that is able to cope successfully with search and retrieval in the huge volume of information stored on the Web—users are, on average, able to find what they are looking for. This success may however hide other challenging problems. Commercial search engines want to know more about the users and their needs to have a better knowledge of the real question behind the submitted query (what the user is really looking for). For example, a user living in Canberra who submits the query "movie tonight" is not likely to be interested in films displayed in New York City or in Washington D.C. Information about user preferences, e.g., for music, can also be exploited to re-rank retrieved items, e.g., by moving musical comedies to the top of the list. This information can play an important role in commercial advertising. From this perspective, the search system will try to complement its answer page with advertising banners that are appropriate to both the user query and preferences.

Proposing new IR models, suggesting new implementations, or adding new functionalities to existing IR models is an important and active domain in IR. There are many collections that are different from the Web. To a certain extent, commercial Web search engines provide only access to the surface Web: the deep Web is largely ignored (private collections, court decisions, patents, etc.). Within a given Web site, or a site inside an enterprise, the search function must provide an effective access to the information required (e.g., in order to allow customers to find what they want or have easy access to past e-mails).

Campaigns involving the design, implementation, and evaluation of IR systems for different languages, including both European (CLEF), and popular Asian (NTCIR) languages have already been running for a few years. Recently, the FIRE evaluation forum has been launched to study IR specialties related to the languages belonging to the Indian subcontinent. Some of these languages seem to be more difficult from an IR perspective, having, for example, a less strict spelling convention. The automatic segmentation of Chinese or Japanese sentences, the automatic decompounding of German words, or the automatic query translation represent examples of NLP problems encountered by modern IR systems.

Finally, the relationship between the IR and NLP domains tends to be strong on one hand, and multifaceted on the other. As presented in this chapter, morphology, spelling error correction, syntax, and semantics are important aspects for general or domain-specific IR systems. Moreover, IR can also be one of the steps in a complex processing chain of textual corpora. In this vein, we can mention the design and implementation of Question/Answering systems or the elaboration of opinionated IR within which the retrieved items are not related to a given topic but to personal opinions about the target. In such cases, the retrieval of textual items must be then post-processed by complex NLP system to extract short and precise answers to a question, or to define whether or not the retrieved item contains an opinion on

---

* We thank D. Hawking and T. E. McIntosh who provided us with this example.

the subject. As indicated in this chapter, the use of machine learning techniques is currently an active research area in developing IR systems with a significant NLP component.

Acknowledgments

The authors would like to thank the two reviewers of this chapter, namely, Ellen Voorhees (NIST, Washington, DC) and David Hawking (Funnelback, Canberra, Australia), for their helpful suggestions and remarks.

References

Amati, G., van Rijsbergen, C.J.: Probabilistic models of information retrieval based on measuring the divergence from randomness. *ACM—Transactions on Information Systems*, 20 (2002) 357–389.

Anderson, J.D., Pérez-Carballo, J.: The nature of indexing: How humans and machines analyze messages and texts for retrieval. *Information Processing & Management*, 37 (2001) 231–254.

Baeza-Yates, R., Ribeiro-Neto, B.: *Modern Information Retrieval*. Addison-Wesley, Reading, MA, 1999.

Borodin, A., Roberts, G.O., Rosenthal, J.S., Tsaparas, P.: Link analysis ranking: Algorithms, theory, and experiments. *ACM—Transactions on Internet Technology*, 5 (2005) 231–297.

Braschler, M., Ripplinger, B.: How effective is stemming and decompounding for German text retrieval? *IR Journal*, 7 (2004) 291–316.

Brin, S., Page, L.: The anatomy of a large-scale hypertextual web search engine. In *Proceedings of the WWW'7*, Amsterdam, the Netherlands, pp. 107–117, 1998.

Buckley, C.: Why current IR engines fail. In *Proceedings of ACM-SIGIR'2004*, Sheffield, U.K., pp. 584–585, 2004.

Buckley, C., Voorhees, E.M.: Retrieval system evaluation. In E.M. Voorhees, D.K. Harman (Eds): *TREC. Experiment and Evaluation in Information Retrieval*. MIT Press, Cambridge, MA, pp. 53–75, 2005.

Buckley, C., Singhal, A., Mitra, M., Salton, G.: New retrieval approaches using SMART. In *Proceedings of TREC-4*, NIST publication #500-236, Gaithersburg, MD, pp. 25–48, 1996.

Can, F., Kocberber, S., Balcik, E., Kaynak, C., Ocalan, H.C.: Information retrieval on Turkish texts. *Journal of the American Society for Information Science and Technology*, 59 (2008) 407–421.

Cao, Y., Xu, J., Liu, T.-Y., Li, H., Huang, Y., Hon, H.-W.: Adapting ranking SVM to document retrieval. In *Proceedings of ACM-SIGIR'2006*, Seattle, WA, pp. 186–193, 2006.

Cao, Z., Qin, T., Liu, T.-Y., Tsai, M.-F., Li, H. Learning to rank: From pairwise approach to listwise approach. In *Proceedings of ICML'2007*, Corvalis, OR, pp. 129–136, 2007.

Cleverdon, C.W.: Optimizing convenient on-line access to bibliographic databases. *Information Service & Use*, 4 (1984) 37–47.

Clinchant, S., Gaussier, E.: The BNB distribution for text modeling. In *Proceedings of ECIR'2008*, Glasgow, U.K., pp. 150–161, 2008.

Conover, W.J.: *Practical Nonparametric Statistics*. 3rd edn., John Wiley & Sons, New York, 1999.

Cooper, W.S.: Is interindexer consistency a hobgoblin? *American Documentation*, 20 (1969) 268–278.

Deerwester, S., Dumais, S.T., Furnas, G.W., Landauer, T.K., Harshman, R.: Indexing by latent semantic analysis. *Journal of the American Society for Information Science*, 41 (1990) 391–407.

Dumais, S.T., Belkin, N.J.: The TREC interactive tracks: Putting the user into search. In E.M. Voorhees, D.K. Harman (Eds): *TREC. Experiment and Evaluation in Information Retrieval*. MIT Press, Cambridge, MA, pp. 123–152, 2005.

Efthimiadis, E.N.: Query expansion. *Annual Review of Information Science and Technology*, 31 (1996) 121–187.

Fagan, J.L.: The effectiveness of a nonsyntactic approach to automatic phrase indexing for document retrieval. *Journal of the American Society for Information Science*, 40 (1989) 115–132.

Fox, C.: A stop list for general text. *ACM—SIGIR Forum*, 24 (1989) 19–21.

Furnas, G., Landauer, T.K., Gomez, L.M., Dumais, S.T.: The vocabulary problem in human-system communication. *Communications of the ACM*, 30 (1987) 964–971.

Gal, A., Lapalme, G., Saint-Dizier, P., Somers, H.: *Prolog for Natural Language Processing*. Addsion-Wesley, Reading, MA, 1991.

Gao, J., Nie, J.-Y., Wu, G., Cao, G.: Dependence language model for information retrieval. In *Proceedings of ACM-SIGIR'2004*, Sheffield, U.K., pp. 170–177, 2004.

Garfield, E.: *Citation Indexing: Its Theory and Application in Science, Technology and Humanities*. ISI Press, Philadelphia, PA, 1983.

Gaussier, E., Grefenstette, G., Hull, D., Roux, C.: Recherche d'information en français et traitement automatique des langues. *Traitement Automatique des Langues (TAL)*, 41, 473–493, 2000.

Gonzalo, J., Oard, D.W.: The CLEF 2002 interactive track. In C. Peters, M. Braschler, J. Gonzalo, M. Kluck, (Eds): *Advances in Cross-Language Information Retrieval*. LNCS 2785. Springer-Verlag, Berlin, Germany, pp. 372–382, 2003.

Harter, S.P.: A probabilistic approach to automatic keyword indexing. *Journal of the American Society for Information Science*, 26 (1975) 197–206.

Hawking, D.: Overview of the TREC-9 web track. In *Proceedings of TREC-9*, NIST Publication #500-249, Gaithersburg, MD, pp. 87–102, 2001.

Hawking, D., Robertson, S.: On collection size and retreival effectiveness. *IR Journal*, 6 (2003) 99–150.

Hiemstra, D.: Using language models for information retrieval. PhD thesis, University of Twente, the Netherlands, 2000.

Hull, D.: Stemming algorithms—A case study for detailed evaluation. *Journal of the American Society for Information Science*, 47 (1996) 70–84.

Hull, D.A., Grefenstette, G., Schültze, B.M., Gaussier, E., Schütze, H., Pedersen, J.O.: Xerox TREC-5 site report: Routing, filtering, NLP, and Spanish track. In *Proceedings of TREC-5*, NIST publication 500-238, Gaithersburg, MD, pp. 167–180, 1997.

Järvelin, K., Kekäläinen, J.: Cumulated gain-based evaluation of IR techniques. *Transaction on Information Systems*, 20 (2002) 422–446.

Joachims, T., Granka, L., Pan, B., Hembrooke, H., Gay, G.: Evaluating the accuracy of implicit feedback from clicks and query reformulations in web search. *ACM—Transactions on Information Systems*, 25 (2007) 1–26.

Kessler, M.M.: Bibliographic coupling between scientific papers. *American Documentation*, 14 (1963) 10–25.

Kleinberg, J.: Authoritative sources in a hyperlinked environment. *Journal of the ACM*, 46 (1999) 604–632.

Kraaij, W., Westerveld, T., Hiemstra, D.: The importance of prior probabilities for entry page search. In *Proceedings of ACM-SIGIR'2002*, Tempere, Finland, pp. 27–34, 2002.

Krovetz, R., Croft, B.W.: Lexical ambiguity and information retrieval. *ACM—Transactions on Information Systems*, 10 (1992) 115–141.

Kwok, K.L., Grunfield, L., Sun, H.L., Deng, P.: TREC2004 robust track experiments using PIRCS. In *Proceedings of TREC 2004*, NIST publication #500-261, Gaithersburg, MD, 2005.

Lacoste, C., Chevallet, J.P., Lim, J.-H., Wei, X., Raccoceanu, D., Le, T.H.D., Teodorescu, R., Vuillenemot, N.: Inter-media concept-based medical image indexing and retrieval with UMLS at IPAL. In C. Peters, P. Clough, F.C. Gey, J. Karlgren, B. Magnini, D.W. Oard, M. de Rijke, M. Stempfhuber (Eds): *Evaluation of Multilingual and Multi-modal Information Retrieval*. LNCS 4730. Springer-Verlag, Berlin, Germany, pp. 694–701, 2007.

Lee, C., Lee, G.G., Jang, M.G.: Dependency structure applied to language modeling for information retrieval. *ETRI Journal*, 28 (2006) 337–346.

Lovins, J.B.: Development of a stemming algorithm. *Mechanical Translation and Computational Linguistics*, 11 (1968) 22–31.

Maisonnasse, L., Gaussier, E., Chevallet, J.P.: Revisiting the dependence language model for information retrieval. In *Proceedings of ACM-SIGIR'2007*, Amsterdam, the Netherlands, pp. 695–696, 2007.

Maisonnasse, L., Gaussier, E., Chevallet, J.P.: Multiplying concept sources for graph modeling. In C. Peters, V. Jijkoun, T. Mandl, H. Müller, D.W. Oard, A. Peñas, V. Petras, D. Santos, (Eds): *Advances in Multilingual and Multimodal Information Retrieval. LNCS* 5152. Springer-Verlag, Berlin, Germany, pp. 585–592, 2008.

Manning, C.D., Raghavan, P., Schütze, H.: *Introduction to Information Retrieval*. Cambridge University Press, Cambridge, U.K., 2008.

McNamee, P., Mayfield, J.: Character n-gram tokenization for European language text retrieval. *IR Journal*, 7 (2004) 73–97.

Nallapati, R.: Discriminative models for information retrieval. In *Proceedings of ACM-SIGIR'2004*, Sheffield, U.K., pp. 64–71, 2004.

Peat, H.J., Willett, P.: The limitations of term co-occurrence data for query expansion in document retrieval systems. *Journal of the American Society for Information Science*, 42 (1991) 378–383.

Peters, C., Jijkoun, V., Mandl, T., Müller, H., Oard, D.W., Peñas, A., Petras, V., Santos, D. (Eds): *Advances in Multilingual and Multimodal Information Retrieval. LNCS* 5152. Springer-Verlag, Berlin, Germany, 2008.

Ponte, J.M., Croft, W.B.: A language modeling approach to information retrieval. In *Proceedings of ACM-SIGIR'98*, Melbourne, VIC, pp. 275–281, 1998.

Porter, M.F.: An algorithm for suffix stripping. *Program*, 14 (1980) 130–137.

Qiu, Y., Frei, H.P.: Concept based query expansion. In *Proceedings of ACM-SIGIR'93*, Pittsburgh, PA, pp. 160–169, 1993.

Robertson, S.E.: The probability ranking principle in IR. *Journal of Documentation*, 38 (1977) 294–304.

Robertson, S.E., Sparck Jones, K.: Relevance weighting of search terms. *Journal of the American Society for Information Science*, 27 (1976) 129–146.

Robertson, S.E., Walker, S., Beaulieu, M.: Experimentation as a way of life: Okapi at TREC. *Information Processing & Management*, 36 (2002) 95–108.

Rocchio, J.J.Jr.: Relevance feedback in information retrieval. In G. Salton (Ed): *The SMART Retrieval System*. Prentice-Hall Inc., Englewood Cliffs, NJ, pp. 313–323, 1971.

Salton, G. (Ed): *The SMART Retrieval System. Experiments in Automatic Document Processing*. Prentice-Hall, Englewood Cliffs, NJ, 1971.

Salton, G., Buckley, C.: Term weighting approaches in automatic text retrieval. *Information Processing & Management*, 24 (1988) 513–523.

Salton, G., Yang, C.S., Yu, C.T.: A theory of term importance in automatic text analysis. *Journal of the American Society for Information Science*, 26 (1975) 33–44.

Sanderson, M.: Word sense disambiguation and information retrieval. In *Proceedings of ACM-SIGIR'94*, Dublin, Ireland, pp. 142–151, 1994.

Savoy, J.: Stemming of French words based on grammatical category. *Journal of the American Society for Information Science*, 44 (1993) 1–9.

Savoy, J.: Ranking schemes in hybrid Boolean systems: A new approach. *Journal of the American Society for Information Science*, 48 (1997) 235–253.

Savoy, J.: Statistical inference in retrieval effectiveness evaluation. *Information Processing & Management*, 33 (1997) 495–512.

Savoy, J.: Combining multiple strategies for effective monolingual and cross-lingual retrieval. *IR Journal*, 7 (2004) 121–148.

Savoy, J.: Comparative study of monolingual and multilingual search models for use with Asian languages. *ACM—Transactions on Asian Languages Information Processing*, 4 (2005) 163–189.

Savoy, J.: Searching strategies for the Hungarian language. *Information Processing & Management*, 44 (2008) 310–324.

Scholler, F., Shokouni, M., Billerbeck, B., Turpin, A.: Using clicks as implicit judgements: Expectations versus observations. In *Proceedings of ECIR'2008*, Glasgow, U.K., pp. 28–39, 2008.

Schütze, H., Pedersen, J.O.: Information retrieval based on word senses. In *Proceedings of the 4th Annual Symposium on Document Analysis and Information Retrieval*, Las Vegas, NV, pp. 161–175, 1995.

Small, H.: Co-Citation in the scientific literature: A new measure of the relationship between two documents. *Journal of the American Society for Information Science*, 24 (1973) 265–269.

Song, F., Croft, W.B.: A general language model for information retrieval. In *Proceedings of ACM-CIKM'99*, Kensas City, MI, pp. 316–321, 1999.

Sparck Jones, K.: A statistical interpretation of term specificity and its application in retrieval. *Journal of Documentation*, 28 (1972) 11–21.

Sproat, R.: *Morphology and Computation*. MIT Press, Cambridge, MA, 1992.

Srikanth, M., Srikanth, R.: Biterm language models for document retrieval. In *Proceedings of ACM-SIGIR'2002*, Tempere, Finland, pp. 425–426, 2000.

Turtle, H., Croft, W.B.: Evaluation of an inference network-based retrieval model. *ACM - Transactions on Information Systems*, 9 (1991) 187–222.

van Rijsbergen, C.J.: *Information Retrieval*. 2nd edn., Butterworths, London, U.K., 1979.

Vintar, S., Buitelaar, P., Volk, M.: Semantic relations in concept-based cross-language medical information retrieval. In *Proceedings of the ECML/PKDD Workshop on Adaptive Text Extraction and Mining (ATEM)*, Catvat–Dubrovnik, Croatia, 2003.

Vogt, C.C., Cottrell, G.W.: Fusion via a linear combination of scores. *IR Journal*, 1 (1999) 151–173.

Voorhees, E.M.: Using WordNet™ to disambiguate word senses for text retrieval. In *Proceedings of ACM-SIGIR'93*, Pittsburgh, PA, pp. 171–180, 1993.

Voorhees, E.M.: The TREC 2005 robust track. *ACM SIGIR Forum*, 40 (2006) 41–48.

Voorhees, E.M., Garofolo, J.S.: Retrieving noisy text. In E.M. Voorhees, D.K. Harman (Eds): *TREC. Experiment and Evaluation in Information Retrieval*. MIT Press, Cambridge, MA, pp. 183–198, 2005.

Voorhees, E.M., Harman, D.K. (Eds): *TREC. Experiment and Evaluation in Information Retrieval*. MIT Press, Cambridge, MA, 2005.

Wolfram, D., Spink, A., Jansen, B.J., Saracevic, T.: Vox populi: The public searching of the web. *Journal of the American Society for Information Science and Technology*, 52 (2001) 1073–1074.

Wong, S.K.M., Ziarko, W., Raghavan, V.V.: On modelling of information retrieval concepts in vector spaces. *ACM—Transactions on Database Systems*, 12 (1987) 723–730.

Xu, J., Croft, B.W.: Corpus-based stemming using cooccurrence of word variants. *ACM—Transactions on Information Systems*, 16 (1998) 61–81.

Yu, H., Agichtein, E.: Extracting synonymous gene and protein terms from biological literature. *Bioinformatics*, 19 (2003) i340–i349.

Zhai, C., Lafferty, J.: A study of smoothing methods for language models applied to information retrieval. *ACM—Transactions on Information Systems*, 22 (2004) 179–214.

Zhai, C., Lafferty, J.: A risk minimization framework for information retrieval. *Information Processing & Management*, 42 (2006) 31–55.

Zhou, W., Yu, C., Smalheiser, N., Torvik, V., Hong, J.: Knowledge-intensive conceptual retrieval and passage extraction of biomedical literature. In *Proceedings of ACM-SIGIR'2007*, Amsterdam, the Netherlands, pp. 655–662, 2007.

Zobel, J., Moffat, A.: Inverted file for text search engines. *ACM Computing Surveys*, 38 (2006) 1–56.

Zunde, P., Dexter, M.E.: Indexing consistency and quality. *American Documentation*, 20 (1969) 259–267.

20

Question Answering

Diego Mollá-Aliod
Macquarie University

José-Luis Vicedo
Universidad de Alicante

20.1 Introduction

Describing precisely what we are talking about when we refer to Question Answering (QA) is probably not as easy as it could be expected. From a very general perspective QA can be defined as an automatic process capable of understanding questions formulated in a natural language such as English and responding exactly with the requested information.

However, this apparently simple definition turns very complex when we analyze in detail which are the characteristics and functionality an "ideal" QA system should have. This system should be able to determine the information need expressed in a question, locate the required information, extract it, and then generate an answer and present it according to the requirements expressed in the question. Moreover, this ideal system should be able to interpret questions and process documents that are written in unrestricted-domain natural languages, which would allow for a comfortable and appropriate interaction by users. Unfortunately, although research has advanced in this direction, the current state of the art remains quite far away from fulfilling all these requirements.

In the process to produce the ideal QA system, both the difficulties of the research problems encountered and a growing necessity for applications that can facilitate access to and manipulation of large quantities of information led the scientific community to simplify the requirements of ideal QA systems and concentrate its efforts on the resolution of more specialized and more manageable problems such as selecting documents based upon certain information needs (aka Information Retrieval—IR), retrieving specific information from structured data to user queries (Natural Language Interfaces to Databases— NLIDB (Androutsopoulos et al. 1995)), and finding information in large document collections as an answer to arbitrary user queries (Question Answering—QA, the focus of this chapter).

This chapter focuses on the work developed around the so-called *Open-Domain Question, Answering* where systems deal with questions posed in natural language, and answers are extracted from a very large document collection.

Interest in open-domain QA emerged from the assumption that users would prefer precise answers to their questions rather than having to inspect all the available documentation related to the search topic in order to satisfy their information needs.

As an answer to this increasing interest, two documents attempted to organize research around QA: the "Vision Statement to Guide Research in Question Answering (Q&A) and Text Summarization" (Carbonell et al. 2000) and the "Issues, Tasks and Program Structures to Roadmap Research in Question & Answering (Q&A)" (Burger et al. 2000).

The first document devised the scope and future capabilities of QA systems trying to satisfy the expectations and requirements of a wide spectrum of different potential users: from *casual users* to *professional information analysts*. While casual users ask for concrete information usually expressed in a single short phrase within a document (e.g., *How many inhabitants does China have?*), the profile for the information analysts is that of the professional consumer of information about very specialized topics. As an example, a professional police analyst who investigates the connections between two terrorist groups might pose these questions to the QA system: *Is there any connecting evidence, communication, or contact between these two terrorist groups or their best-known members?, Is there any evidence that they are planning a combined action?, And if so, when and where?*. The QA system should be able to accept questions whose answers will be based on decisions carried out by the system. In order to provide such answers, information obtained from different sources would need to be synthesized, and it should then be presented to the user in an appropriate form. Moreover, the system should be able to utilize powerful multimedia navigation tools that will allow it to check all possible information sources (answer support information, interpretations, summaries, and decisions) and to facilitate user—system interaction.

The second document defined a tight 5-year research roadmap intended to address and make possible the vision for research envisaged in the first document. It included detailed research challenges that the QA community should confront in the near future such as interactive QA, integration of information from different sources, multilingual information processing, or answer generation and presentation. This agenda was so ambitious that it would effectively solve all aspects of QA by 2005. However, most of these issues still remain unsolved.

In this chapter, we will cover the current state of the art in QA. Research in open-domain QA has mainly focused on processing questions requiring simple entities or properties as answers since time savings for these so-called *factual* or *factoid* questions are very high. Furthermore, validating answers to these questions becomes an easy task that allows defining and establishing evaluation frameworks without too much difficulty. Besides factoid questions, current QA research also addresses other kinds of questions such as definitions, procedures, relations, or opinions.

In this context, research in open-domain QA has been impulsed by fruitful collaboration between two different but complementary research fields: IR and Natural Language Processing (NLP). Not in vain, QA activity relies mainly on a combination of IR and NLP techniques trying to match a natural language query to text snippets located and extracted from huge text collections.

This chapter is intended to serve readers as a basic but up-to-date guide in their diving into the field of open-domain QA. Starting with a brief historical approach to the field, it introduces the basic principles and techniques of open-domain QA and its evaluation, and summarizes the efforts accomplished in the main research lines currently open in restricted-domain QA, Multilingual QA, and complex QA.

The work is organized as follows: Section 20.2 presents the historical context in which the research of QA technology is being developed and depicts the different directions the work on QA is following. Section 20.3 introduces the main characteristics of current QA systems and details some of the most salient methodologies used in the various stages of these systems. Section 20.4 analyzes problems related to the evaluation of these kinds of systems and reviews the progress that has been achieved as a result of the TREC evaluations and other evaluation frameworks. Section 20.5 focuses on the issues that arise from asking questions in a language and searching for answers on documents of a different language.

Section 20.6 mentions the key aspects of handling documents of restricted domains. Finally, Section 20.7 presents current main lines of research in this field.

20.2 Historical Context

Research in QA is not new. In 1965, Simmons performed the first survey of the field, reviewing the initial attempts at performing QA tasks in the English language (Simmons 1965). This survey presented and discussed the basic principles and methods of operation for a wide range of QA systems, including front-ends to structured databases and systems that attempted to find answers from ordinary English text.

Including these early attempts, research in QA has developed from two different scientific perspectives, artificial intelligence (AI) and IR.

Work in QA since the early stages of AI has led to systems that respond to questions using the knowledge encoded in databases as an information source. Obviously, these systems can only provide answers concerning the information previously encoded in the database. The benefit of this approach is that having a conceptual model of the application domain represented in the database structure allows the use of advanced techniques such as theorem proving and deep reasoning in order to address complex information needs.* LUNAR (Woods 1971) and BASEBALL (Green et al. 1961) are well-known examples of NLIDB. These interfaces understand questions expressed in natural language and retrieve the requested information by translating user questions into a series of database-understandable queries. On the other hand, QUALM (Lehnert 1977) answered questions from a knowledge base previously built from textual documents.

In the late 1990s we witnessed a surge of activity in the area from the perspective of IR, initiated by the QA track of TREC[†] in 1999 (Voorhees 2001b). Since then, increasingly powerful systems have participated in TREC and other evaluation fora such as CLEF[‡] (Vallin et al. 2005) and NTCIR[§] (Kando 2005). From this perspective, QA focuses on finding text excerpts that contain the answer within huge collections of documents. The tasks set in these conferences have molded a specific kind of QA that is easy to evaluate and that focuses on the combination of IR and NLP techniques that are generally independent of the application domain. In other words, this research focuses on text-based *open-domain QA*.

In particular, MURAX (Kupiec 1993) is considered the first open-domain QA system since it combined traditional IR techniques with shallow NLP to obtain what its author characterized as high-precision IR. Using the Grolier encyclopedia (Grolier 1990) as a document database, the MURAX system acts as an interface between a traditional IR system and the user. MURAX understands and interprets the user's questions, generates queries to an IR system for the localization of those extracts in the encyclopedia that are likely to contain the expected answers, and finally, applies basic NLP techniques (part-of-speech tagging and comparison of syntactic patterns) over these selected text fragments in order to locate and extract the expected answers.

Both AI and IR trends have developed in parallel and represent the opposite ends of a spectrum connecting what we might label as *structured knowledge-based* and *free text-based* QA. While structured knowledge-based QA systems are well adapted to applications managing complex queries in a very structured information environment, the kind of research developed in TREC, CLEF, and NTCIR is

---

* In the QA literature it is difficult to find a consensus to define what differentiates simple questions from complex questions. In the context of this chapter a question is considered to be *simple* if the answer is a piece of information that has been located and retrieved directly as it appears in the information source. On the other hand, a question is considered *complex* if its answer needs some kind of elaboration. For instance, pieces of information may come from multiple documents in different corpora and they need to be merged or possibly summarized to build the required answer.

† Text REtrieval Conference (http://trec.nist.gov/).

‡ Cross Language Evaluation Forum (http://clef.iei.pi.cnr.it/).

§ NII-NACSIS Test Collection for IR Systems (http://research.nii.ac.jp/ntcir/).

probably more well suited to broad-purpose generic applications dealing with simple factual questions such as Web-based QA.

The evolution of research in open-domain QA has been mainly directed by the TREC QA evaluations. These evaluations initially focused on factoid questions, that is, questions requiring simple facts, entities, or properties easily expressed in few words (e.g., *When did the Jurassic Period end?* or *Where is the Taj Mahal?*). Moving further, TREC evaluations have additional question types such as definition questions (*Who is Picasso?*), list questions (*What movies did James Dean appear in?*), and relationship questions that try to find relations between entities (*What is Suresh Premachandran's connection to the Tamil Tigers?*). Finally, TREC QA evaluations included the complex interactive QA task aiming at investigating how systems could interact with users with the objective of guiding them to the information they need in complex contexts.

The TREC evaluations ended in 2007 but interest in QA has fostered other evaluation fora. The Text Analysis Conference (TAC)* continues the TREC evaluations with a new track for the evaluation of QA systems with short series of opinion questions.

NTCIR and CLEF develop TREC-like QA evaluations on Asian and European languages respectively. They promote QA in languages different from English by introducing monolingual and cross-lingual tasks. For monolingual tasks, documents and questions are in the same language. In cross-lingual tasks, in contrast, documents and questions are in different languages. Although these evaluations still maintain their original orientation, existing tasks are continuously evolving and new tasks appear. Among others, it is worth to emphasize the Answer Validation Exercise (AVE) and the Question Answering over speech transcriptions (QAST) tracks at CLEF, and the Multi-lingual Opinion Analysis Task (MOAT) at NTCIR.

20.3 A Generic Question-Answering System

In this section we will describe the generic architecture of factoid question-answering systems based on free text. Most systems use the following components:

- Question analysis
- Document or passage selection
- Answer extraction

These components all work together, processing questions and documents at different levels, until the final answer is obtained. Figure 20.1 illustrates graphically the interaction and data flow between these components.

20.3.1 Question Analysis

In the question analysis module, questions posed to the system are processed to detect and extract information that might be useful to the other modules. This is carried out by two main tasks: (1) a classification of the question to determine the type of information that the question expects as answer (a date, a quantity, etc.), and (2) the selection of those elements that will allow the system to locate the documents that are likely to contain the answer. This initial process is very important since the performance of the remaining modules (and by extension, of the entire system) will depend greatly on the quality of the information extracted from the question. In fact, faulty derivation of the expected answer type is the main source of errors in current QA systems. For example, Moldovan et al. (2003, p. 143) found that 36.4% of the errors in their system was due to the wrong derivation of the expected answer type.

---

* http://www.nist.gov/tac/

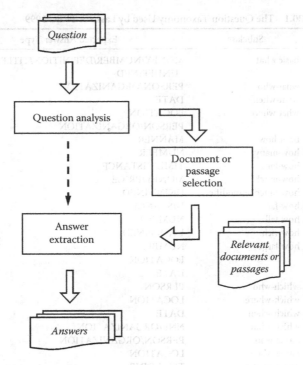

FIGURE 20.1 Generic QA system architecture.

20.3.1.1 Question Classification

An important part of question analysis is the classification of the question into categories that represent the type of answer expected. The question *In what year did Ireland elect its first female president?* seeks a date as an answer, for example, whereas the question *How far is Yaroslavl from Moscow?* seeks a distance as an answer. The classification of the answer type in some questions is complicated by the fact that there might be ambiguity in the type of expected answer. Thus, the question *How long does it take to travel from Tokyo to Niigata?* can accept either a time or a distance as an answer.

Question and answer types are categories in taxonomies. One of the first taxonomies was used in the Lasso system (Moldovan et al. 1999) and defines a two-level hierarchy of questions. Each type of question indicates a set of possible answer types (Table 20.1). Lasso's taxonomy was based on the sort of news-related domain of TREC 1999. Other systems use more complex hierarchies, such as Breck et al. (1999) who uses the taxonomy introduced by Li and Roth (2002) with a final set of over 50 answer types including types such as colors, religions, and musical instruments. The ISI taxonomy (Hovy et al. 2002) is another example of a large taxonomy with 140 different answer types, which was used by the Webclopedia QA system (Hovy et al. 2000).

The simplest method to classify questions is the use of a set of rules that map patterns of questions into question types. The patterns are expressed by means of regular expressions on the surface form. The identification of the answer type is usually performed by analyzing the interrogative terms of the question (*wh*-terms). For example, given the question *Where is the Taj Mahal?* the term *where* indicates that the question is looking for a location or a place. This approach may give acceptable results with little effort for a coarse-grained question taxonomy. Furthermore, the human-produced classification rules are easy to read by humans, thus providing help in the understanding of the classification process. However, the development of such rules can be very time-consuming when the question taxonomy is fine-grained or when very high accuracy is required. Furthermore, a change in the domain of application will typically require a new set of classification rules that need to be built almost from scratch.

TABLE 20.1 The Question Taxonomy Used by Lasso in TREC 1999

Class	Subclass	Expected Answer Type
What	basic what	MONEY/NUMBER/DEFINITION/TITLE/NNP/ UNDEFINED
	what-who	PERSON/ORGANIZATION
	what-when	DATE
	what-where	LOCATION
Who		PERSON/ORGANIZATION
How	basic how	MANNER
	how-many	NUMBER
	how-long	TIME/DISTANCE
	how-much	MONEY/PRICE
	how-much-<modifier>	UNDEFINED
	how-far	DISTANCE
	how-tall	NUMBER
	how-rich	UNDEFINED
	how-large	NUMBER
Where		LOCATION
When		DATE
Which	which-who	PERSON
	which-where	LOCATION
	which-when	DATE
	which-what	NNP/ORGANIZATION
Name	name-who	PERSON/ORGANIZATION
	name-when	LOCATION
	name-what	TITLE/NNP
Why		REASON
Whom		PERSON/ORGANIZATION

An alternative approach to question classification is the use of machine-learning techniques. With this approach, question classification is treated as a "standard" classification task that can be tackled with statistical packages of classification. Provided that there is a corpus of questions available together with annotations indicating the correct class of each question, this approach is fairly straightforward once a set of features has been identified. Thus, Li and Roth (2002, 2006) used the SNoW learning method paired with a two-level classification system that first performed a classification on a coarse-grained taxonomy and then was fine-tuned by classification on a fine-grained taxonomy. Their question taxonomy and training corpus are freely available.* An analysis of several machine-learning methods has been described by Zhang and Lee (2003). The authors compared the use of decision trees, nearest neighbors, naïve Bayes, and support vector machines (SVM). SVM obtained better results than the other methods, other things being equal.

A key step in the use of machine learning methods is the selection of features that represent the questions. Li and Roth (2002), for example, used a varied range of features including words, PoS tags, chunks (nonoverlapping phrases), named entities, head chunks (the first noun chunk in a sentence), semantically related words (words that often occur with a specific question class), and n-grams (sequences of n words). The study by Zhang and Lee (2003) incorporated features based on syntactic information. These features represented tree fragments of a syntactic tree and its sub-trees, creating a high dimensional space that was processed by SVM methods. The resulting classifier produced an accuracy of 90%, which is slightly better than their method using n-gram information (87.4%).

---

* http://l2r.cs.uiuc.edu/~cogcomp/Data/QA/QC/

20.3.1.2 Query Generation

Question-analysis also extracts the information in the question that allows the generation of queries that, processed by an IR system, will facilitate the selection of the answer-bearing text extracts from the entire document collection. These queries are commonly obtained using one of two different processes: *keyword selection* and *answer-pattern generation*.

Keyword selection consists of selecting those question terms whose appearance in a text indicates the existence of a candidate answer in the surrounding text. For the question *What country borders Spain to the north?*, the keyword group would be formed by the terms *borders*, *north*, and *Spain*.

Answer pattern generation, on the other hand, attempts a more elaborate process. In this case, queries constitute one or several combinations of question terms, in such a way that each resulting query expresses a form in which the answer might be found. The following possible queries could be derived from the previous example question: X *borders Spain to the north*, X *is the country that shares its northern border with Spain*, *The northern border of Spain is* X, . . . , where *X* refers to the expected answer. In this case, the IR system would locate verbatim text extracts that contain any of the candidate answer expressions associated with each question type (Hermjacob et al. 2002, Soubbotin and Soubbotin 2002). The generated query expressions do not need to be linguistically perfect, since they are fed to an IR system that usually treats the expressions as bags of words.

These strategies, keyword generation and answer-pattern generation, are not mutually exclusive and some approaches combine both of them. Both Brill et al. (2001) and Lin et al. (2002), for example, use very simple answer patterns that generate search queries that might or might not be linguistically accurate. Those that would not be accurate would retrieve few documents and therefore their negative impact is relatively small.

All approaches described here are able to process questions formulated in free natural language. There are also examples of systems that constrain the input language so that the questions are expressed by subsets of natural languages with a restricted vocabulary and syntax (controlled languages). Moreover, in several cases, users are required to express their queries by completing *ad hoc* templates (Buchholz and Daelemans 2001). In both cases, users' expressiveness is restricted in the service of easier and probably more accurate question interpretation.

20.3.2 Document or Passage Selection

The document or passage selection module uses part of the information extracted during the question analysis module to perform an initial selection of answer-bearing candidate texts. Given the great volume of documents these systems are expected to manage, and the limitations imposed by a reasonable response time, this task is carried out using IR or paragraph retrieval (PR) systems. According to Roberts and Gaizauskas (2004), the reason for using IR techniques instead of NLP techniques in this stage is the speed of processing. This way the system reduces the entire document database to a small subset that includes those texts that are likely to contain the required answer.

After the documents or paragraphs are extracted, a filtering component is usually introduced. This filtering component consults the expected answer type returned by the question analysis module, and filters out or penalizes those text fragments that do not contain instances of the expected answer type.

Passage-oriented approaches are preferred to document-oriented ones. A simple technique of passage retrieval consists of using a sliding window of fixed size and retrieving the most relevant paragraphs by means of traditional IR approaches.

Among the IR approaches used, ranked methods are most commonly employed, even though several authors argue that the characteristics of Boolean engines make them more suitable for QA purposes (Moldovan et al. 1999, Tellex et al. 2003).

The number of documents selected is usually predetermined and depends on the retrieval strategies applied. Although several researchers have directed their research toward minimizing the number of

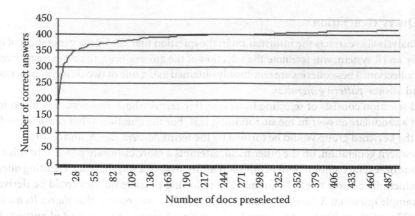

FIGURE 20.2 Number of TREC 2003 questions that have an answer in the preselected documents using TREC's search engine. The total number of questions was 413.

selected documents (Ferret et al. 2000), this issue still needs to be addressed. Figure 20.2 shows the number of questions that can be answered by the preselected documents in the study presented by Mollá (2004), who compromised on a number of 50 documents given the little improvement obtained with larger numbers of preselected documents.

Finally, since the same concepts can be expressed using different—but equivalent—terms, forms, and expressions, question keywords are usually expanded using morphological, lexical, or semantic alternations. This process permits the retrieval of text extracts that contain key concepts that are not expressed exactly as they appear in the question. Such expansion may be accomplished using statistical techniques (Yang and Chua 2002) or semantic knowledge bases such as WordNet (Vicedo 2002). As reported by Moldovan et al. (2003), this issue is very important since wrong question expansion is the second most prevalent cause of errors in the performance of QA systems.

When NLP techniques are used, they are typically incorporated at the indexing stage. For example, Chu-Carroll et al. (2002) include NE information in the index. Their system preprocesses all documents in the document collection with NE taggers and associates respective semantic classes to all the entities found. The resulting semantic classes are all indexed together with the documents, thereby facilitating the retrieval of only those document extracts containing entities whose semantic classes match the expected answer semantic classes.

A reduced number of systems incorporate word relations during the indexing stage. For example, Litkowski (2000) indexes on word pairs instead of on isolated words. More recently, Pizzato and Mollá (2008) produced an indexing system that directly incorporates word dependencies and have evaluated the use of syntactic dependency and semantic role labeling information. They observed an improvement of results when semantic role labeling information was added to the index.

20.3.3 Answer Extraction

The answer extraction module carries out a detailed analysis of the relevant texts selected by the document-selection module in order to locate and extract the answer. To achieve this, the representation of the question and the representation of relevant texts are matched against each other in order to obtain a set of candidate answers. These candidate answers are subsequently ranked according to their likelihood of correctness and they are presented to the user.

Provided that one has a named entity recognizer, the simplest method to build a list of answer candidates is to collect all the named entities appearing in the preselected passages and remove those named entities that are not compatible with the type of the expected answer. Since the answer is never explicitly said in the question, those named entities that appear in the question are removed as well.

Methods to rank the list of answer candidates are as numerous as the number of QA systems. These methods are typically a combination of the following types of methods:

Similarity: Rank higher answer candidates which are in a context that is similar to the question.
Popularity: Rank higher answer candidates that appear more frequently.
Patterns: Rank higher answer candidates that match question-specific patterns.
Answer validation: Rank higher answer candidates that have acceptable values.

20.3.3.1 Similarity with the Question

If a sentence is very similar to the question and it contains a string that is compatible with the type of the expected answer, then it is reasonable to conclude that the answer candidate is the correct answer.

To determine the similarity of two sentences one can compute the number of words in common, or one can use more complex similarity measures based on syntactic or semantic information.

To account for the possibility of variations in wording, some systems use additional linguistic resources such as WordNet (Miller 1995) and determine whether two words are related by means of synonymy or other relations.

The problem of detecting whether two sentences are similar is related to the problem of detecting paraphrases. For this reason, some systems have developed rules that encode paraphrase equivalents (Bouma et al. 2005). Other systems have developed methods to *learn* paraphrasing rules (Lin and Pantel 2001).

Other approaches compare syntactic information, taking into account the similarity between the syntactic structures of the question and the candidate-answer-bearing sentences, which is then given great weight in the final-answer-extraction process (Oard et al. 1999, Lee et al. 2001).

Some systems go deeper in the use of linguistic information and attempt to use logical forms. The university of Pisa (Attardi et al. 2002) and CLR (Litkowski 2002) systems use the concept of *semantic triples* to represent this information. A semantic triple is formed by a discourse entity, its semantic role in the text, and the term to which this entity is related. Questions and relevant sentences are represented using this notation. The answer-extraction process is accomplished by comparing and measuring the level of relation matching between the question semantic structures and the target sentences representation.

Logical form structures can be expressed as graph structures. This led Macquarie University's Center for Language Technology to compare questions and sentences by finding the minimum common subgraph of their corresponding graphs (Mollá 2006).

Although they are scarce, other systems delve even further into the natural language analysis by applying contextual analysis techniques. Such systems incorporate common world knowledge that is associated to inferential mechanisms that support the answer-extraction process. Thus, The University of Sheffield (Greenwood et al. 2002) uses logical formulae (LFs) to represent questions and candidate-answer-bearing passages and incorporates these representations in a discourse model. The discourse model is a specialization of a semantic net that encodes the common world knowledge and is enriched with the specific knowledge coded in the LFs of the question and candidate passages.

20.3.3.2 Answer Popularity

In a balanced corpus, it is reasonable to assume that the number of times a string is found as the possible answer to a given sentence is directly related to the likelihood of that string being the answer. Thus, a simple method to rank answer candidates is to count how many times they appear.

However, it is necessary to determine if two strings are actually referring to the same entity. This is what has been called *answer merging*. The task of detecting variations of an answer is related to that of the co-reference task in information extraction (MUC-6 1996, MUC-7 1998) and methods similar to those used in MUC have been applied to the task of answer merging.

A method that has gained popularity exploits the availability of increasingly large electronic data, notably via the World Wide Web. Such amount of information produces a situation of *data redundancy*, whereby the answer to a question may appear a large number of times and in various contexts. Methods of data redundancy are based on the assumption that, as the number of variations of manners to justify an answer grows, the likelihood of finding a simple justification increases. For example, Brill et al. (2001) noted that the first sentence is easier to detect than the second as containing the answer to the sentence *Who killed Abraham Lincoln?*

1. *John Wilkes Booth killed Abraham Lincoln.*
2. *John Wilkes Booth is perhaps America's most infamous assassin. He is best known for having fired the bullet that ended Abraham Lincoln's life.*

The method developed by Brill et al. (2001) exploits this principle of data redundancy to produce a system that uses very limited linguistic information and very few rules, whereas still producing results better than the average (their best run ranked ninth in TREC 2001). They achieved this by converting each question into a series of queries to the WWW, collecting snippets of text that are close to the query words, and tagging strings that appear frequently in the snippets as possible answers.

In TREC and other environments where there is a fixed document set where to search the answers, the Internet is used to carry out a parallel process of answer-search that allows the gathering of additional information in order to either expand the original question (Attardi et al. 2002, Yang and Chua 2002), or to obtain redundancy data for candidate answers and thus validate the answers that are obtained from the system document collection (Clarke et al. 2002, Chu-Carroll et al. 2002, Magnini et al. 2002). This tendency is increasing, since the experiments developed thus far have demonstrated that using the Web this way brings about a remarkable improvement in system performance.

Data redundancy becomes a key tool to find the answer in Web-based QA systems where the sheer size of the data available can compensate for its irregular quality and consistency.

20.3.3.3 Patterns that Resemble Answers

A popular method to extract the exact answer is to develop a set of patterns indicating typical ways of answering specific questions. With a number of patterns large enough, it is theoretically possible to dispense with other methods.

A system that successfully used answer patterns was developed by InsigthSoft (Soubbotin and Soubbotin 2002). The InsightSoft approach consists of the identification and construction of a series of patterns (*indicative patterns*) that depend on the question type. An indicative pattern is defined as a sequence, or certain combination, of characters, punctuation marks, spaces, digits, or words. These patterns are obtained manually by studying the expressions that are usually answers to certain types of questions. For example, the string "*Mozart (1756–1791)*" contains the answers to questions related to the dates of Mozart's birth and death. From this observation, one can build the following pattern:

"*[word with 1st letter in uppercase; parenthesis; four digits; script; four digits; parenthesis]*"

Each one of the patterns is manually assigned a certainty value. This way, the system can choose among several candidate answers, depending on the reliability level of each matched pattern to a question.

Some researchers have developed patterns based on deeper linguistic information. For example, Kwok et al. (2001) uses transformation grammars, and Jijkoun et al. (2004) combines surface patterns with syntactic patterns to extract relevant information. Mollá and Gardiner (2004) develops a small set of rules based on patterns of logical forms. A problem encountered with this method, however, was that the

TABLE 20.2 Patterns for Questions of Type
When Was NAME born?

Precision	Rule
1.0	`<NAME>( <ANSWER> - )`
0.85	`<NAME> was born on <ANSWER>,`
0.6	`<NAME> was born in <ANSWER>`
0.59	`<NAME> was born <ANSWER>`
0.53	`<ANSWER> <NAME> was born`
0.50	`- <NAME> ( <ANSWER>`
0.36	`<NAME> ( <ANSWER> -`

process of manually developing the patterns was very time-consuming. Since the patterns are dependent of the domain of the text, this approach has therefore problems of portability to other domains or genres.

Several systems have experimented with the use of *machine learning* techniques to avoid the burden of handcrafting the question-answer rules. Ravichandran and Hovy (2002) learned rules based on simple surface patterns. Given that surface patterns ignore much linguistic information, it is necessary to gather a large corpus of questions together with their answers and sentences containing the answers. To obtain such a corpus, Ravichandran and Hovy (2002) mine the Web to gather the relevant data. The general process is relatively simple and is based on the assumption that specific patterns of questions are answered with specific patterns of answers. Thus, to find sentences answering questions following the pattern *When was X born?*, a set of pairs (*X,Answer*) is gathered from known question/answer pairs, and a series of Web searches is done with these pairs. For example, a search with the terms *Gandhi* and *1869* would be done. Since the variable element in the question (*Gandhi*) is known together with the answer (*1869*), the text strings found containing these terms are converted into patterns by replacing the terms into variables. Once the patterns are found, their precision is computed by applying new Web searches, this time without the answer, and checking how often each pattern succeeds in finding the answer. By applying such method patterns like those of Table 20.2 can be learnt.

Other methods learn patterns based on deeper linguistic information. For example, Shen et al. (2005) develop a method of extracting dependency paths connecting answers with words found in the question. On a similar line, Mollá (2006) develop a method to produce graph representations of the logical contents of sentences, and then automatically learn the path between question words and their corresponding answers by applying algorithms based on graphs. This approach requires the use of a corpus annotated with the correct answers. Since the patterns learned are more precise than patterns based on surface text, the training corpus can be much smaller than the corpus used by Ravichandran and Hovy (2002).

Finally, there are systems such as the one by Hermjacob et al. (2002), who combine automatic learning techniques with a manual review of the resulting patterns.

20.3.3.4 Answer Validation

Answer validation is another method that has been used to determine if an answer candidate is a good answer. A method of answer validation that we have seen already is that of determining whether the answer is a named entity compatible with the expected answer type. But within an answer type it is possible to do more detailed validation checking. For example, negative numbers cannot be used to answer questions about distances or ages. In this section we will focus on methods of answer validation based on logic.

Methods using logic convert the question and the sentence containing the answer into logical forms that are passed on to a logic prover to determine whether the answer sentence can prove the question. These methods are an evolution of early QA systems that were entirely based on logic to find the answer to a question. For example, Green (1969) envisaged the use of techniques of resolution to find answers to a question. In Green's system, the complete information was supposed to be stored as a set of axioms such as:

1. *Smith is a man*
   MAN(Smith)
2. *Man is an animal*
   $\forall x\ MAN(x) \implies ANIMAL(x)$

The question, in turn, was converted into a proposition that needs to be proved:

- *Who is an animal?*
  ? $\exists y\ ANIMAL(y)$

To prove the question, Green proposed the use of resolution, whereby the negation of the question is introduced and the logic prover needs to find a contradiction in order to prove the question. Figure 20.3 shows the steps required to prove the above question.

Current QA systems produce the axioms automatically from the sentence containing the answer. To achieve this, expressiveness and correctness of the resulting logical forms need to be sacrificed to ensure results in short time. Thus, Harabagiu et al. (2000) and Mollá and Gardiner (2004) use flat logical forms that are inspired on Hobb's semantic notation (Hobbs et al. 1993), but without attempting to cover all the semantic nuances of sentences. Leidner et al. (2003) use an enriched form of the Discourse Representation Theory (Kamp and Reyle 1993) that combines semantic information with syntactic and sortal information, whereas still simplifying some aspects of its representation to make its production and handling computationally tractable.

The axioms need to be extended with further information that is generally assumed but rarely said explicitly in the text. This is what has been called the process of *abduction* (Hobbs et al. 1993). Figure 20.4 illustrates an example where abduction is used to prove a question (Harabagiu et al. 2000). To avoid the use of spurious data, the axioms to abduce are directly connected to the specific information of the question and answer sentence such as (Moldovan et al. 2003):

We want to prove:
1. MAN(Smith)
2. $\forall x\ \neg\ MAN(x) \vee ANIMAL(x)$
3. $\forall y\ \neg\ ANIMAL(y) \vee ANSW(y)$

From (1) and (2) we can deduce:
4. ANIMAL(Smith)

From (3) and (4) we can deduce the answer:
5. ANSW(Smith)

FIGURE 20.3   Method of resolution.

Question   *Who was the first Russian astronaut to walk in space?*
     first(x) $\wedge$ astronaut(x) $\wedge$ Russian(x) $\wedge$ space(z) $\wedge$ walk(y z x) $\wedge$ HUMAN(x)

Answer   *The broad-shouldered but paunchy Leonov, who in 1965 became the first man to walk in space, signed autographs*
     paunchy(y) $\wedge$ shouldered(e1 y x) $\wedge$ broad(x) $\wedge$ Leonov(x) $\wedge$ first(z) $\wedge$ man(z) $\wedge$ space(t) $\wedge$
     walk(e2 t z x) $\wedge$ became(e3 z u x) ... $\wedge$ HUMAN(x)

Assumption   *Leonov is a Russian astronaut*
     Leonov(x) $\wedge$ Russian(x) $\wedge$ astronaut(x)

FIGURE 20.4   An example of abduction for QA.

Linguistic information: Compound nouns, conjunctions, appositions, etc.

Named entities: Information linking instances of named entities with their named entity types

Lexical resources: WordNet glosses, lexical chains

20.3.4 Variations of the General Architecture

The general problem of building a QA system can be viewed as a problem of software engineering since the various modules need to be executed in the most efficient manner to improve speed and accuracy. There are numerous variations of the general architecture described above, but generally they are reduced to two types: introduction of feedback loops, and parallelization.

20.3.4.1 Feedback Loops

The general strategy to QA is to apply a sequence of filters to gradually reduce the amount of data. Each filter is increasingly sophisticated, until finally the last filter is able to detect and extract the exact answer. However, quite often some of the intermediate filters are either too restrictive or too lenient. If the filters are too restrictive, too many answer candidates may be filtered out. However, if the filters are too lenient, the latest filters are flooded with too much (noisy) data and they are unable to return an answer within an acceptable time frame.

By introducing feedback loops, the intermediate filters can automatically adjust their parameters and provide an optimal amount of information. This is the approach followed by Harabagiu et al. (2000), which used three feedback loops:

1. If the PR component returns a number of documents outside the range of acceptable documents, then adjust the initial document retrieval search query by deleting search terms or by introducing additional terms.
2. If the logical forms of the question and the answer sentence are not compatible (e.g., by using unification methods), then instruct the document retrieval module to include lexical alternations.
3. If the answer validation module fails to validate all answer candidates, then instruct the document retrieval module to include WordNet-based semantic alternations.

20.3.4.2 Parallelism

Given the possibility of trying alternative methods in the various modules of the general architecture, several researchers have produced systems that contain modules that work in parallel to produce information at a specific level, and then combine the outputs. For example, Brill et al. (2001) developed a system that used two independent QA systems in parallel and combined their answers in a final result that was returned to the user. The most difficult aspect of systems using parallel methods is the combination of the results of the independent modules, since their scoring systems are not necessarily compatible. Brill et al. (2001) combined the results by applying a formula whose parameters were automatically learnt.

20.4 Evaluation of QA Systems

Research into open-domain QA systems has fostered a parallel, growing interest in the development of techniques for evaluating these kinds of systems. Automatic QA evaluation has been studied from a number of different perspectives such as the use of test collections (Voorhees and Tice 2000), reading comprehension tests (Hirschman et al. 1999, Charniak et al. 2000), and the application of automatic systems that evaluate the correction of the answers returned by comparing them with human-proposed answers to the same set of questions (Breck et al. 2000).

The most important test collections currently available have been generated from the data and results of the QA evaluations developed at the TREC conferences.* Organized by the U.S. National Institute for Standards and Technology (NIST), the TREC conferences centered on various tasks related with IR. For each task, an evaluation method and a specific corpus were defined such that all the participants should provide the result of their systems on the common corpus. NIST evaluated the submissions of the participants and organized the conferences where the results were discussed.

In 1999, the TREC conference presented the first specific task for the evaluation of QA systems: *The first QA track.* For this exercise QA Track, coordinators developed an evaluation framework constituted by a test collection and evaluation metrics capable of measuring the global performance of a system.

This test collection was comprised of a collection of documents along with a set of questions. Documents consisted of 528,000 newspaper/newswire articles and they contained information on a wide variety of subjects. On the other hand, 200 test questions were finally obtained by combining a log of questions submitted to the FAQ Finder system (Burke et al. 1997) with queries developed manually by TREC assessors.

Participants were required to find the answers to the question set in the document collection and provide TREC organization with these answers to be evaluated.

To determine the correct answers, the TREC QA track used the technique of *pooling*. With this technique, all the answers returned by the systems participating and judged by human referees as correct are added to a pool of answers, together with pointers to the documents containing the answers returned by the systems. This method does not guarantee that all correct answers are found but it allows the gathering of all correct answers found by state-of-the-art systems. The resulting list of answers is later made available together with automatic evaluation scripts.

Subsequent TREC QA evaluations evolved according to the changes and additional requirements introduced in further TREC QA Tracks. These changes were mainly related to increments in the size of the document collection, the introduction of more rigid requirements for answers to be considered correct, and the amount and complexity of the proposed questions. In particular, the introduction of different types of questions in these evaluations (factual, list, definition, etc.) made necessary the development of specific evaluation techniques capable of computing the specific characteristics of each different question type.

So as to appreciate the evolution of these annual evaluations, we shall summarize each successive introduction to the test and introduce the main evaluation metrics employed. These metrics are also being used as a standard at other QA evaluation fora such as CLEF and NTCIR.

20.4.1 Evolution of the TREC QA Track

In the TREC 1999 QA track, which is the first international open-domain QA evaluation, the performance of participant systems was evaluated on 200 hand-made test questions, elaborated such that the answer to every proposed question was guaranteed to be in the document collection. For each question, the systems were expected to return a ranked list with a maximum of five possible text snippets containing the answers. There were two possible categories of answers, depending upon the maximum length permitted for the answer string (250 or 50 characters).

The TREC 2000 Conference had a considerable increase in the size of the document collection as well as in the number of questions to evaluate. At the TREC 2001 Conference the maximum length of the answer string was limited to 50 characters. In addition, the existence of a correct answer for each test question within the document collection was not guaranteed, so that the only correct answer to questions

* http://trec.nist.gov

whose answer did not exist in the documents was "no answer". This change allowed the test to evaluate the problem of answer validation. This time the questions were real questions that were gathered from the logs of search engines.

The evaluation process from TREC 1999 to TREC 2001 was similar. For each question, each participant system would return a ranked list of five passages and a pointer to the documents where the passages were found. The lists were judged by a panel of assessors appointed by NIST, who would determine whether the answer was found in the text:

> A [*document-id, answer-string*] pair was judged correct if, in the opinion of the NIST assessor, the answer-string contained an answer to the question, the answer-string was *responsive* to the question, and the document supported the answer. If the answer-string was responsive and contained a correct answer, but the document did not support the answer, the pair was judged "not supported" (except in TREC 1999 where it was marked correct). Otherwise the pair was judged incorrect. (Voorhees 2001a, p. 3)

Judging whether an answer-string was responsive to the answer was not trivial. The judges were given specific guidelines, such as: *Answer strings that contained multiple entities of the same semantic category as the correct answer but did not indicate which of those entities was the actual answer (e.g., a list of names in response to a who question) are to be judged as incorrect* (Voorhees 2001a, p. 3). But the final decision was left to the judges.

Also at TREC 2001, the *list* subtask was introduced that included questions that specified a number of answer instances to be retrieved (*Tell me three movies in which Antonio Banderas performed*).

At TREC 2002, the systems were asked only to respond with a single answer to each question and the answers needed to be *exact*, that is, the answer strings should contain only and exclusively the correct answers. The actual criteria used to judge whether an answer-string was an exact answer were very restrictive. For example, the string *the Mississippi River* was an exact answer to the question *what is the longest river in the United States?*, whereas *the river Mississippi* was not an exact answer on the grounds that the word *river* introduced additional information.

The last TREC conferences that included the QA track (from TREC 2003 to TREC 2007) integrated factoid questions, list questions, and definition questions in a main single task with the aim to encourage participants to attempt to handle all three types of questions.

As an example, we will describe here the task and evaluation method in TREC 2005. The main task consisted of a set of 75 topics, each one of which containing a list of questions. Each question could be either a factoid or a list question (tagged as such), plus an additional "other" question where the system was expected to return any additional information about the topic. Table 20.3 shows one of the topics used in the test.

By defining questions around a topic, the systems were expected to handle context and reference to common ground information such as *at the time* in question 95.4 of Table 20.3. In addition, the "*other*" question tests the ability to find information defining the topic. Each type of question was evaluated independently and the separate evaluation figures were combined to give the final performance score for the system as a whole.

TABLE 20.3 A Topic Used in TREC 2005

95	Return of Honk Kong to Chinese sovereignty	
	95.1	FACTOID	What is Hong Kong's population?
	95.2	FACTOID	When was Hong Kong returned to Chinese sovereignty?
	95.3	FACTOID	Who was the Chinese President at the time of the return?
	95.4	FACTOID	Who was the British Foreign Secretary at the time?
	95.5	LIST	What other countries formally congratulated China on the return?
	95.6	OTHER	

Differences between these evaluations were slight. Events were added as possible targets in TREC 2005, requiring that answers should be temporally compatible with the time period defined in the series. In TREC 2006, sensitivity to temporal dependencies was made explicit in the distinction between locally and globally correct answers, so that answers for questions phrased in the present tense should not only be supported by the supporting document (locally correct), but should also be the most up-to-date answer in the document collection (globally correct). The changes in TREC 2007 laid in the genre of the document collection. Instead of only newswire, the document collection also contained blogs.

20.4.2 Evaluation Metrics

Evaluation metrics employed for measuring QA systems performance have evolved continuously in order to fulfill the needs imposed mainly by the inclusion of new question types and answer restrictions in the evaluation.

The following text introduces the main evaluation metrics used by the TREC QA tracks. TREC evaluation metrics and methodology have become a standard in the field and have been adopted as a referent in other evaluation fora in QA such as CLEF, NTCIR, or TAC.

The first evaluation measure employed was the *mean reciprocal rank* (MRR). When several ranked answers are allowed, each question is scored according to the inverse of the position of the first passage that contains the correct answer. If none of the passages contain the answer, the question score is 0. The MRR was computed as the mean of the scores of all questions. This measure became a standard measure for the evaluation of QA systems.

Later, when only one answer could be returned per question, the MRR could not be used and the chosen measure was a variation of the answer accuracy called the *confidence-weighted score*. Given a list of Q questions ranked according to the confidence of the system to have found the correct answer, the confidence-weighted score was

$$\frac{1}{Q} \sum_{i=1}^{Q} \frac{\text{number correct in first } i \text{ ranks}}{i}$$

Apart from factoid questions, the inclusion of new types such as *list* and *other* questions provoked separate evaluations with different metrics for each of the question types. Systems were given a final score by combining the results obtained for each of the different types. *Factoid* questions were evaluated by their *accuracy*, that is, the percentage of questions that had a correct answer. *List* questions were evaluated using a well-known measure within the area of IR: the *F-score* combining the *recall* and *precision*. Given S target answers, N answers returned by the system, and D answers returned that belong to the target answers, recall is $R = D/S$ and precision is $P = D/N$. The measure of the question is

$$F = \frac{2 \times R \times P}{R + P}$$

To evaluate "other" questions, the judges were asked to determine a set of minimal pieces of information that should appear in the definition, the so-called information nuggets. The nuggets were classified as "vital" if they must appear in the answer, and "non-vital" if their appearance in the answer is acceptable. For example, Table 20.4 lists the vital and non-vital nuggets for the question *What is a golden parachute?* (Voorhees 2004):

All of these nuggets were searched in the answer. Again, it was the criterion of the judges to determine if a specific nugget was mentioned in the answer or not. For example, the answer string *The arrangement, which includes lucrative stock options, a hefty salary, and a "golden parachute" if Gifford is fired*, could be judged to cover nuggets 2 and 3.

The nugget recall was computed using the list of vital nuggets. Thus, if there are S_v vital nuggets and D_v of them were found by the system, the nugget recall was D_v/S_v. The nugget precision was more difficult

TABLE 20.4 Vital and Non-Vital Nuggets for the Question
What Is a Golden Parachute?

1	(vital)	Agreement between companies and top executives
2	(vital)	Provides remuneration to executives who lose jobs
3	(vital)	Remuneration is usually very generous
4	(non-vital)	Encourages execs not to resist takeover beneficial to shareholders
5	(non-vital)	Incentive for execs to join companies
6	(non-vital)	Arrangement for which IRS can impose excise tax

to compute because it is impossible to determine *all* the nuggets of information mentioned in the answer, especially if the answer is very vague. Consequently, nugget precision was estimated solely on the basis of the length of the strings returned by giving an allowance of 100 characters per nugget (vital or non-vital). Thus, if the system found D_{vnv} nuggets among the target vital and non-vital nuggets, the nugget precision was estimated with the formula:

$$1 - \frac{\text{length} - 100 \times D_{vnv}}{\text{length}}$$

The final score combined the nugget recall and precision, giving recall three times more importance than precision:

$$F(\beta = 3) = \frac{10 \times \text{precision} \times \text{recall}}{9 \times \text{precision} + \text{recall}}$$

The method consequently relies heavily on the judges' ability to define all the atomic concepts determining a definition (in practice, only those nuggets appearing in the sum of answers are required), and then to detect the information nuggets in the answer. Furthermore, the criterion to determine nugget precision is still very crude. Still, this method provides a quantitative measure that can be used to compare various systems.

20.5 Multilinguality in Question Answering

The increasing availability of information in languages other than English, the need of users to be able to manage all this information in their own language, and the social need of breaking the language barrier and enhance information access for non-English cultural areas such as Europe and Asia, have impulsed research in multilingual information systems from long ago.

In the particular case of QA, this interest promoted the organization of QA tasks in the sphere of two international Workshops traditionally devoted to research in multilingual IR the Cross-Language Evaluation Forum* (CLEF) and the NTCIR Evaluation Workshops.[†] While NTCIR organize tasks to assist in the evaluation of QA systems on Asian languages, CLEF proposes similar evaluations but focusing on a broad range of European languages.

From a general perspective, a multilingual QA system should be expected to be able to (1) understand questions formulated in various languages, (2) look for the expected information in document collections written in different languages, and (3) present answers in the user reference language.

Unfortunately, since such a system remains beyond the state of the art, the CLEF and NTCIR evaluations have limited the scope of the general multilingual problem to concentrate on more manageable tasks. These tasks are parts of a vision of a future multilingual QA system as a group of monolingual systems, each of them working on a different language. Following this schema, multilinguality is based on four main processes: (1) translating user questions to the different languages of the available document collections,

---

* http://clef-qa.itc.it
[†] http://research.nii.ac.jp/ntcir/index-en.html

TABLE 20.5 MT Translation Error
Taxonomy

Type of Translation Error	Percentage
Word-by-Word Translation	24%
Translated Sense	21%
Syntactic Structure	34%
Interrogative Particle	26%
Lexical–Syntactic Category	6%
Unknown Words	2.5%
Proper Name	12.5%

(2) running in parallel the monolingual systems integrated in the multilingual QA system, (3) selecting the final answer among the answers retrieved in the different languages, and (4) translating the final answer and its supporting text to the language of the original question.

CLEF and NTCIR evaluations have not been organized from a pure multilingual scenario. Departing from a set of languages, participants are allowed to configure their own QA scenario by selecting one language for questions (source language) and another for the document collection (target language). This way, with n different languages we can configure n^2 different subtasks depending on the selected languages. These subtasks are *monolingual* when the language of the question and the language of the text collection are the same and *cross-lingual* (or *bilingual*) when they differ. This methodology enables monolingual evaluations in different languages as well as bilingual evaluations designed to measure systems' abilities to find answers in a collection of texts in one language when questions are posed in any other language. Furthermore, it allows the development and evaluation of the independent parts that will conform in the near future a whole multilingual QA system.

The majority of QA systems dealing with multilinguality are really bilingual systems. The architecture of a bilingual system is the same of a generic QA system (presented in Section 20.3) but enhanced with a module in charge of translating the source question to the target language. For this reason, research has concentrated on translation issues and trying to develop methods and strategies capable of eliminating the effects of incorrect or nonnatural translations of the original query.

Two main strategies have been investigated namely, *question translation* and *term-by-term translation*. The former consists in translating the whole question into the target language and then performing a question analysis process in this language. On the other hand, term-by-term translation means applying question analysis over the question in the source language and then translating the information returned by this process to the modules that retrieve the answer from the target language.

The approach most widely used is *question translation* where questions are translated into the target language using general purpose machine translation (MT) tools. Systems like those by Bouma et al. (2008), Martínez-González et al. (2008), or van Zaanen and Mollá (2007) are good representatives of this approach.

Aiming at exploring why MT tools affect the performance of cross-lingual QA systems, Ferrández and Ferrández (2007) conducted an extensive study on English–Spanish cross-lingual QA. The set of 200 CLEF 2004 English questions was translated into Spanish using several online MT services. Translations were manually checked and the errors detected were organized in seven classes. Table 20.5 shows the error taxonomy along with the percentage of the translations including this error.

Word-by-Word Translation errors insert words in the translation that should not be there. Translated sense errors are produced when the MT system does not detect properly the correct sense of a polysemous word and consequently, the translation usually substitutes an important keyword by its erroneous translation. Obtaining wrong translations of proper names is very usual when using MT services. In this case, translation induces a very critical loss of information since detecting and processing correctly named entities is implicitly related with the performance of a QA system. These three errors cause a loss in precision in the passage retrieval module since the queries it receives as input will contain imprecise and noisy information.

There are also important translation errors that affect the question analysis process. In particular, errors in the translation of the syntactic structure of the question produce non-syntactically correct questions and induce errors in all the processes of the question analysis involving syntactic information. On the other hand, a wrong translation of the interrogative particle of the question causes an erroneous detection of the expected answer type.

With the goal of trying to reduce the impact of translation on the overall system performance, other approaches experimented with using different translations for the same question in order to select the best among them (Sacaleanu et al. 2008) or combine them to obtain a reformulated question (Sutcliffe et al. 2006).

Other systems opted for *term-by-term translation* approaches. In this case, questions are analyzed in the source language and their output is translated to the target language. These approaches use different linguistic resources in isolation or in combination with automatic translation. These resources include bilingual dictionaries, monolingual or multilingual lexical databases (such as WordNet* and EuroWordNet[†]), or named entity taggers among others. As an example, Tanev et al. (2006) translate the question keywords by using bilingual dictionaries and a lexical database. In order to limit the noise stemming from the different translations and to have a better cohesion, they validate the translations in a large corpus. The system described by Ferrández and Ferrández (2007) and Ferrández et al. (2007) considers more than only one translation per word by using the different synsets of each word in the Inter Lingual Index (ILI) module of EuroWordNet. This translation is combined with a special process for the translation of named entities using Wikipedia.[‡]

As reported in CLEF and NTCIR workshops, question translation remains the key issue to be investigated since systems performance loss ranges from 30% to 50% between monolingual and cross-lingual approaches. Furthermore, the efforts employed in correcting the automatic translations have improved cross-lingual QA system performance only slightly in comparison to using MT tools.

20.6 Question Answering on Restricted Domains

There has been work on the localization of QA to specific domains, some of which has been reviewed by Mollá and Vicedo (2007). Here we will simply comment on what makes restricted-domain QA something different to open QA. Based on the work by Minock (2005), the characteristics that make a good domain for QA are:

- It should be **circumscribed**. That is, it should be clear what kinds of questions are likely to be asked. For example, the domains of news and gossip are not circumscribed because they allow any kinds of questions. On the other hand, the domains of biology and technical manuals are circumscribed. Circumscribed domains should have authoritative and comprehensive resources (such as terminology dictionaries) that enable the localization to the domain.
- It should be **complex**. Otherwise a simple look-up table can replace a QA system.
- It should be **practical**. Otherwise, if there is no clear community that would want to use the QA system, there is no need to develop the QA system at all.

The most popular domains for QA are those that meet these three characteristics. Of them, the medical domain stands out. It is complex, requiring the analysis of complex and very specific questions. It is practical, since the large amount of new publications on medical aspects makes medical practitioners face

---

* http://wordnet.princeton.edu/
† http://www.illc.uva.nl/EuroWordNet/
‡ http://en.wikipedia.org/

a continuous struggle to keep up to date with new developments. Finally, it is circumscribed, with a large repository of publications that is continuously growing (MEDLINE) and a comprehensive ontology of diseases, drugs, and treatments (MeSH).

Methods used for restricted-domain QA depend heavily on the domain. Still, an issue that most domains face is that of handling the specific terminology. Good NE recognizers tuned to the specific domains and good domain-specific terminology taxonomies become essential.

20.7 Recent Trends and Related Work

The work described in this chapter has focused on factoid QA. This kind of research has been the most popular in the area of QA, but there are other kinds of QA topics and related work. The following paragraphs describe other common kinds of QA and introduce related tasks that are especially active nowadays.

Lists   Treatment of list questions was introduced in the TREC 2001 QA track and has been a constant component of the QA track until the last year the QA track was offered in TREC 2007. A list question is a question that asks for a list of facts, such as *What countries does Australia export coal to?*. Consequently most systems treated list questions in the same fashion as factoid questions. The main difference was that list questions are not forced to produce the best answer.

Two issues that arise with this kind of question are (1) the need to determine a threshold beyond which an answer is not to be returned, and (2) the need to determine when two answers are equivalent. These two issues also arise in factoid questions but they become more prominent in list questions.

Definitions   Definition questions such as *Who is Aaron Copland?* expect a list of text snippets rather than a list of facts. These questions are easy to answer if there is an encyclopedic resource that matches the topic of the question, but this is not always the case.

Web-based QA   All the methods described in this chapter can be applied to Web-based QA with minor modifications. When the corpus is the Web, a search engine is needed to gather the relevant webpages or snippets. Once the relevant text is found, the regular methods described earlier in this chapter can be applied.

The Web is an unusual corpus in that it is much larger than almost any other corpus and there is no editorial process. Due to the size of the Web, the issue of *data redundancy* becomes prominent and therefore systems operating on the Web tend to use fast and simple methods that attempt to find simple answers, and they incorporate methods of voting to select those answers that are most popular. These methods are expanded with other methods that determine the document authority in order to detect problems of misleading or contradictory answers.

Some systems take advantage of the existence of pockets of structured information on the Web. These are interfaces to databases that are accessible from the Web, such as the Movie Database with information about movies, or the CIA world factbook with geopolitical information. If the system detects a specific pattern in the question it can easily convert the question to a database query specialized to a predetermined database or databases (Lin 2002).

Textual Entailment   Research on textual entailment started with the PASCAL Recognizing Textual Entailment Challenge (Dagan et al. 2005). The challenge used pairs of texts (*text, hypothesis*), and the challenge was to determine whether the text entailed the hypothesis. Pairs of text were sourced from several applications, including QA.

Since answering questions needs a minimum understanding of questions and documents, it is argued that the relation between a question and its answer can be molded in terms of logical entailment. Textual entailment techniques are being explored with success in different processes involved in QA such as answer extraction and ranking (Harabagiu and Hickl 2006) or question analysis (Ferrández et al. 2009).

Summarization   Complex questions require the gathering of evidence from several documents and the composition of a final answer, thus employing document summarization techniques. The Document Understanding Conference DUC 2006 introduced a track that was based on summaries focused on complex questions such as the following (Dang 2006):

Describe theories concerning the causes and effects of global warming and arguments against these theories.

Systems participating in DUC 2006 used mostly summarization techniques, though there were some attempts to combine QA with summarization techniques, such as the system by Mollá and Wan (2006).

Opinions   Answering opinion questions like *What is X's opinion about Y?*, *What does X like?*, and *Who believes in Y?* has emerged as one of the main recent research interests in QA field. Although this research line is not new, the increasing availability of online opinion texts—such as blogs and newsgroups focusing on opinion topics such as social issues, political events, or product reviews—have impulsed the need of automatic tools capable of analyzing all this information mainly for commercial or political purposes.

As a consequence, the Textual Analysis Conference (TAC) has focused its 2008 QA track* on finding answers to opinion questions. This task is similar to the main QA task in TREC 2007 but question series in 2008 ask for people's opinions about a particular target and the questions are asked over blog documents.

Similar Question Finding   Similar Question Finding systems exploit the massive amount of information on the Web in the form of question and answer pairs. This information is organized in large (Q&A) where each question is associated to its corresponding answer. These archives include the FAQ archives constructed by companies for their products and the archives generated from Web services such as Yahoo Answers![†] and Live QnA,[‡] where people answer questions posed by other people.

These systems do not perform QA in the way that has been previously presented. They retrieve those questions included in the Q&A archive that are similar to new queries posed by users.

Although this area is not new—it was also known as Frequently Asked Questions Finding (FAQ Finding) (Berger et al. 2000, Burke et al. 1997)—it has strongly emerged mainly due to the popularity of these Web sites and the increasing participation of people in building those Q&A archives. Readers are referred to the publication by Jeon et al. (2005), Xue et al. (2008), and Duan et al. (2008) for additional information.

Acknowledgment

The authors would like to gratefully thank Chin-Yew Lin for his insightful comments during the review of this chapter.

---

* http://www.nist.gov/tac/tracks/2008/qa/index.html
† http://es.answers.yahoo.com/
‡ http://qna.live.com/

References

Androutsopoulos, I., G. Ritchie, and P. Thanisch (1995). Natural language interfaces to databases—An introduction. *Journal of Language Engineering* 1(1), 29–81.

Attardi, G., A. Cisternino, F. Formica, M. Simi, and A. Tommasi (2002, November). PIQASso 2002. *Eleventh Text REtrieval Conference*, Volume 500-251 of NIST Special Publications, Gaithersburg, MD. National Institute of Standards Technology.

Berger, A., R. Caruana, D. Cohn, D. Freitag, and V. Mittal (2000). Bridging the lexical chasm: Statistical approaches to answer-finding. *Proceedings of the 23rd Annual International ACM SIGIR Conference on Research and Development in Information Retrieval*, Athens, Greece, pp. 192–199.

Bouma, G., I. Fahmi, J. Mur, G. van Noord, L. van der Plas, and J. Tiedemann (2005). Linguistic knowledge and question answering. *Traitement Automatique des Langues (TAL)* 46(3), 15–39.

Bouma, G., J. Mur, G. van Noord, L. van der Plas, and J. Tiedemann (2008). Question answering with joost at CLEF 2008. *Workshop of Cross - Language Evaluation Forum (CLEF 2008)*, Aarhus, Denmark.

Breck, E., J. Burger, L. Ferro, L. Hirschman, D. House, M. Light, and I. Mani (2000). How to evaluate your question answering system every day and still get real work done. In *Proceedings of Second International Conference on Language Resources and Evaluation. LREC-2000*, Athens, Greece.

Breck, E., J. Burger, L. Ferro, D. House, M. Light, and I. Mani (1999, November). A sys called quanda. *Eighth Text REtrieval Conference*, Volume 500-246 of NIST Special Publications, Gaithersburg, MD, pp. 369–377. National Institutes of Standards and Technology.

Brill, E., J. Lin, M. Banko, and S. Dumais (2001, November). Data-intensive question answering. *Tenth Text REtrieval Conference*, Volume 500-250 of NIST Special Publications, Gaithersburg, MD. National Institute of Standards and Technology.

Buchholz, S. and W. Daelemans (2001, September). SHAPAQA: Shallow Parsing for Question Answering in the World Wide Web. In *Recent Advances in Natural Language Processing (RANLP)*, Tzigov Chark, Bulgaria.

Burger, J., C. Cardie, V. Chaudhri, R. Gaizauskas, S. Harabagiu, D. Israel, C. Jacquemin, C.-Y. Lin, S. Maiorano, G. Miller, D. Moldovan, B. Ogden, J. Prager, E. Riloff, A. Singhal, R. Shrihari, T. Strzalkowski, E. Voorhees, and R. Weishedel (2000). Issues, tasks and program structures to roadmap research in question & answering (Q&A). http://www-nlpir.nist.gov/projects/duc/papers/qa.Roadmap-paper_v2.doc.

Burke, R., K. Hammond, V. Kulyukin, S. Lytinen, N. Tomuro, and S. Schoenberg (1997). Question answering from frequently asked question files. *AI Magazine* 18(2), 57–66.

Carbonell, J., D. Harman, E. Hovy, S. Maiorano, J. Prange, and K. Sparck-Jones (2000). Vision statement to guide research in question & answering (Q&A) and text summarization. http://www-nlpir.nist.gov/projects/duc/papers/Final-Vision-Paper-v1a.doc.

Charniak, E., Y. Altun, R. Braz, B. Garrett, M. Kosmala, T. Moscovich, L. Pang, C. Pyo, Y. Sun, W. Wy, Z. Yang, S. Zeller, and L. Zorn (2000, May). Reading Comprehension Programs in a Statistical-Language-Processing Class. In *ANLP/NAACL Workshop on Reading Comprehension Tests as Evaluation for Computer-Based Language Understanding Systems*, Seattle, WA, pp. 1–5.

Chu-Carroll, J., J. Prager, C. Welty, K. Czuba, and D. Ferrucci (2002, November). A multi-strategy and multi-source approach to question answering. *Eleventh Text REtrieval Conference*, Volume 500-251 of NIST Special Publications, Gaithersburg, MD. National Institute of Standards and Technology.

Clarke, C. L., G. V. Cormack, G. Kemkes, M. Laszlo, T. R. Lynam, E. L. Terra, and P. L. Tilker (2002, November). Statistical selection of exact answers (MultiText Experiments for TREC 2002). *Eleventh Text REtrieval Conference*, Volume 500-251 of NIST Special Publications, Gaithersburg, MD. National Institute of Standards and Technology.

CLEF (2008). *Workshop of Cross-Language Evaluation Forum (CLEF 2008)*, Aarhus, Denmark.

Dagan, I., O. Glickman, and B. Magnini (2005). The pascal recognising textual entailment challenge. In *Proceedings of the PASCAL Challenges Workshop on Recognising Textual Entailment*, Southampton, U.K.

Dang, H. T. (2006). DUC 2005: Evaluation of question-focused summarization systems. In *Proceedings of the Workshop on Task-Focused Summarization and Question Answering*, Sydney, Australia, pp. 48–55. Association for Computational Linguistics.

Duan, H., Y. Cao, C.-Y. Lin, and Y. Yu (2008, June). Searching questions by identifying question topic and question focus. In *Proceedings of ACL-08: HLT*, Columbus, OH, pp. 156–164. Association for Computational Linguistics.

Ferrández, S. and A. Ferrández (2007). The negative effect of machine translation on cross-lingual question answering. *Lecture Notes in Computer Science 4394*, 494.

Ferrández, Ó., R. Izquierdo, S. Ferrández, and J. L. Vicedo (2009). Addressing ontology-based question answering with collections of user queries. *Information Processing & Management 45*(2), 175–188.

Ferrández, S., A. Toral, O. Ferrández, and A. Ferrández (2007). Applying Wikipedia's multilingual knowledge to cross–lingual question answering. In *Proceedings of the 12th International Conference on Applications of Natural Language to Information Systems*, Paris, France, pp. 352–363.

Ferret, O., B. Grau, M. Hurault-Plantet, G. Illouz, C. Jacquemin, and N. Masson (2000, November). QALC—The question answering system of LIMSI-CNRS. *Ninth Text REtrieval Conference*, Volume 500-249 of NIST Special Publication, Gaithersburg, MD, pp. 325–334. National Institute of Standards and Technology.

Green, C. (1969). Theorem-proving by resolution as a basis for question-answering systems. In B. Meltzer and D. Michie (Eds.), *Machine Intelligence*, Volume 4, Chapter 11, pp. 183–205. Edinburgh University Press, Scotland, U.K.

Green, B., A. Wolf, C. Chomsky, and K. Laugherty (1961). BASEBALL: An automatic question answerer. In *Proceedings of the Western Joint IRE-AIEE-ACM Computer Conference*, Los Angeles, CA, pp. 219–224.

Greenwood, M., I. Roberts, and R. Gaizauskas (2002, November). The University of Sheffield TREC 2002 Q&A System. *Eleventh Text REtrieval Conference*, Volume 500-251 of NIST Special Publication, Gaithersburg, MD. National Institute of Standards and Technology.

Grolier, E. P. (1990). *The Academic American Encyclopedia*. http://auth.grolier.com

Harabagiu, S. and A. Hickl (2006). Methods for using textual entailment in open-domain question answering. In *ACL-44: Proceedings of the 21st International Conference on Computational Linguistics and the 44th Annual Meeting of the Association for Computational Linguistics*, Morristown, NJ, pp. 905–912. Association for Computational Linguistics.

Harabagiu, S., D. Moldovan, M. Pasca, R. Mihalcea, M. Surdeanu, R. Bunescu, R. Gîrju, V. Rus, and P. Morarescu (2000, November). FALCON: Boosting knowledge for answer engines. *Ninth Text REtrieval Conference*, Volume 500-249 of NIST Special Publication, Gaithersburg, MD. pp. 479–488. National Institute of Standards and Technology.

Hermjacob, U., A. Echihabi, and D. Marcu (2002, November). Natural language based reformulation resource and wide exploitation for question answering. *Eleventh Text REtrieval Conference*, Volume 500-251 of NIST Special Publication, Gaithersburg, MD. National Institute of Standards and Technology.

Hirschman, L., M. Light, E. Breck, and J. Burger (1999). Deep read: A reading comprehension system. In *37th Annual Meeting of the Association for Computational Linguistics (ACL-99)*, New Brunswick, NJ, pp. 325–332.

Hobbs, J., M. Stickel, D. Appelt, and P. Martin (1993). Interpretation as abduction. *Artificial Intelligence 63*, 69–142.

Hovy, E., L. Gerber, U. Hermjacob, M. Junk, and C. Lin (2000, November). Question answering in webclopedia. *Ninth Text REtrieval Conference*, Volume 500-249 of NIST Special Publication, Gaithersburg, MD, pp. 655–664. National Institute of Standards and Technology.

Hovy, E., U. Hermjacob, and D. Ravichandran (2002). A question/answer typology with surface text patternsra. In *Proceedings of the DARPA Human Language Technology Conference (HLT)*, San Diego, CA.

Jeon, J., W. B. Croft, and J. H. Lee (2005). Finding semantically similar questions based on their answers. In *SIGIR '05: Proceedings of the 28th Annual International ACM SIGIR Conference on Research and Development in Information Retrieval*, New York, pp. 617–618. ACM.

Jijkoun, V., M. de Rijke, and J. Mur (2004). Information extraction for question answering: Improving recall through syntactic patterns. In *Proceedings of the 20th International Conference on Computational Linguistics (COLING 2004)* Geneva, Switzerland.

Kamp, H. and U. Reyle (1993). *From Discourse to Logic: Introduction to Model-Theoretic Semantics of Natural Language, Formal Logic and Discourse Representation Theory*, Volume 42 of *Studies in Linguistics and Philosophy*. New York: Springer-Verlag.

Kando, N. (2005). Overview of the fifth NTCIR workshop. In *Proceedings NTCIR 2005*, Tokyo, Japan.

Kupiec, J. (1993, June). MURAX: A robust linguistic approach for question-answering using an on-line encyclopedia. In *16th International ACM SIGIR Conference on Research and Development in Information Retrieval*, Pittsburgh, PA, pp. 181–190.

Kwok, C., O. Etzioni and S. Daniel (2001). Scaling question answering to the web. In *Proceedings of the Tenth World Wide Web Conference*, Hong Kong, China.

Lee, G., J. Seo, S. Lee, H. Jung, B. Cho, C. Lee, B. Kwak, J. Cha, D. Kim, J. An, H. Kim, and K. Kim (2001, November). SiteQ: Engineering high performance QA system using lexico-semantic pattern matching and shallow NLP. *Tenth Text REtrieval Conference*, Volume 500-250 of NIST Special Publication, Gaithersburg, MD. National Institute of Standards and Technology.

Lehnert, W. (1977). A conceptual theory of question answering. In *Proceedings of the 5th International Joint Conference on Artificial Intelligence*, Cambridge, MA, pp. 158–164.

Leidner, J. L., J. Bos, T. Dalmas, J. R. Curran, S. Clark, C. J. Bannard, B. Webber, and M. Steedman (2003). QED: The Edinburgh TREC-2003 question answering system. In E. M. Voorhees and L. P. Buckland (Eds.), *Proceedings of the TREC 2003*, Gaitersburg, MD, Number 500-255 in NIST Special Publication. NIST.

Li, X. and D. Roth (2002). Learning question classifiers. *Proceedings of the COLING 02*, Taipei, Taiwan, pp. 556–562.

Li, X. and D. Roth (2006). Learning question classifiers: The role of semantic information. *Journal of Natural Language Engineering 12*(3), 229–249.

Lin, J. (2002). The web as a resource for question answering: Perspectives and challenges. In *Proceedings of the LREC 2002*, Las Palmas, Spain, pp. 2120–2127.

Lin, D. and P. Pantel (2001). Discovery of inference rules for question-answering. *Natural Language Engineering 7*(4), 343–360.

Lin, J., A. Fernandes, B. Katz, G. Marton, and S. Tellex (2002, November). Extracting answers from the web using data annotation and knowledge mining techniques. *Eleventh Text REtrieval Conference*, Volume 500-251 of NIST Special Publication, Gaithersburg, MD. National Institute of Standards and Technology.

Litkowski, K. (2000, November). Syntactic clues and lexical resources in question answering. *Ninth Text REtrieval Conference*, Volume 500, Gaithersburg, MD, pp. 157–168.

Litkowski, K. (2002, November). Question answering using XML-tagged documents. See *The Eleventh Text REtrieval Conference*, Gaithersburg, MD, (TREC-11 (2002)).

Magnini, B., M. Negri, R. Prevete, and H. Tanev (2002, November). Mining knowledge from repeated co-occurrences: DIOGENE at TREC 2002. See TREC-11 (2002).

Martínez-González, Á., C. de Pablo-Sánchez, C. Polo-Bayo, M. T. Vicente-Díez, P. Martínez-Fernández, and J. L. Martínez-Fernández (2008). The MIRACLE team at the CLEF 2008 multilingual question answering track. See CLEF (2008).

Miller, G. (1995). Wordnet: A lexical database for english. In *Communications of the ACM 38(11)*, pp. 39–41.

Minock, M. (2005). Where are the 'killer applications' of restricted domain question answering? In *Proceedings of the IJCAI Workshop on Knowledge Reasoning in Question Answering*, Edinberg, Scotland, U.K., pp. 4.

Moldovan, D., C. Clark, S. Harabagiu, and S. Maiorano (2003). COGEX: A logic prover for question answering. In *Proceedings of the HLT-NAACL 2003*, Edmonton, Alberta, Canada, pp. 166–172.

Moldovan, D., S. Harabagiu, M. Pasca, R. Mihalcea, R. Goodrum, R. Gîrju, and V. Rus (1999, November). LASSO: A tool for surfing the answer net. *Eighth Text REtrieval Conference*, Volume 500-246 of NIST Special Publication, Gaithersburg, MD, pp. 175–184. National Institute of Standards and Technology.

Moldovan, D., M. Pasca, S. Harabagiu, and M. Surdeanu (2003, April). Performance issues and error analysis in an open-domain question answering system. *ACM Transactions on Information Systems 21(2)*, 133–154.

Mollá, D. (2004, November). Answerfinder in TREC 2003. *Twelfth Text REtrieval Conference*, Volume 500-251 of NIST Special Publication, Gaithersburg, MD. National Institute of Standards and Technology.

Mollá, D. (2006). Learning of graph-based question answering rules. In *Proceedings of the HLT/NAACL 2006 Workshop on Graph Algorithms for Natural Language Processing*, Sydney, Australia, pp. 37–44.

Mollá, D. and M. Gardiner (2004). Answerfinder—Question answering by combining lexical, syntactic and semantic information. In A. Asudeh, C. Paris, and S. Wan (Eds.), *Proceedings of the ALTW 2004*, Sydney, Australia, pp. 9–16. Macquarie University.

Mollá, D. and J. L. Vicedo (2007). Question answering in restricted domains: An overview. *Computational Linguistics 33(1)*, 41–61.

Mollá, D. and S. Wan (2006). Macquarie university at duc 2006: Question answering for summarisation. In *Proceedings DUC*, Sydney, Australia.

MUC-6 (1996). *Sixth Message Understanding Conference*, Los Altos, CA. MUC-6.

MUC-7 (1998). *Seventh Message Understanding Conference*, Washington, DC.

Oard, D. W., J. Wang, D. Lin, and I. Soboroff (1999, November). TREC-8 experiments at Maryland: CLIR, QA and routing. *Eighth Text REtrieval Conference*, Volume 500-246 of NIST Special Publication, Gaithersburg, MD, pp. 623–636. National Institute of Standards and Technology.

Pizzato, L. and D. Mollá (2008). Indexing on semantic roles for question answering. In *Proceedings of the COLING Workshop on Information Retrieval for Question Answering*, Manchester, U.K., p. 8.

Ravichandran, D. and E. Hovy (2002). Learning surface text patterns for a question answering system. In *40th Annual Meeting of the Association for Computational Linguistics (ACL-02)*, Philadelphia, PA.

Roberts, I. and R. J. Gaizauskas (2004). *Evaluating Passage Retrieval Approaches for Question Answering*, Sunderland, U.K., pp. 72–84. Lecture Notes in Computer Science. Springer.

Sacaleanu, B., G. Neumann, and C. Spurk (2008). DFKI at QA@CLEF 2008. Workshop of Cross - Language Evaluation Forum (CLEF - 2008), Aarhus, Denmark.

Shen, D., G.-J. M. Kruijff, and D. Klakow (2005). Exploring syntactic relation patterns for question answering. In R. Dale, K. -F. Wong, J. Su, and O. Y. Kwong (Eds.), *Natural Language Processing IJCNLP 2005: Second International Joint Conference*, Jeju Island, Korea, October 11–13, 2005. *Proceedings*. Springer-Verlag.

Simmons, R. F. (1965). Answering english questions: A Survey. *Communications of the ACM 1(8)*, 53–70.

Soubbotin, M. and S. Soubbotin (2002, November). Use of patterns for detection of likely answer strings: A systematic approach. *Eleventh Text REtrieval Conference*, Volume 500-251 of NIST Special Publication, Gaithersburg, MD. National Institute of Standards and Technology.

Sutcliffe, R. F. E., K. White, D. Slattery, I. Gabbay, and M. Mulcahy (2006). Cross-language French-English question answering using the DLT system at CLEF 2006. In *Workshop of Cross-Language Evaluation Forum (CLEF 2006)*, Alicante, Spain.

Tanev, H., M. Kouylekov, B. Magnini, M. Negri, and K. Simov (2006). Exploiting linguistic indices and syntactic structures for multilingual question answering: ITC-irst at CLEF 2005. *Lecture Notes in Computer Science 4022*, Toronto, Canada 390.

Tellex, S., B. Katz, J. Lin, A. Fernandes, and G. Marton (2003). Quantitavie evaluation of passage retrieval algorithms for question answering. In *SIGIR'03: Proceedings of the 26th Annual International ACM SIGIR Conference on Research and Development in Information Retrieval*, New York, pp. 41–47. ACM Press.

TREC-8 (1999, November). *Eighth Text REtrieval Conference*, Volume 500-246 of *NIST Special Publication*, Gaithersburg, MD. National Institute of Standards and Technology.

TREC-9 (2000, November). *Ninth Text REtrieval Conference*, Volume 500-249 of *NIST Special Publication*, Gaithersburg, MD. National Institute of Standards and Technology.

TREC-10 (2001, November). *Tenth Text REtrieval Conference*, Volume 500-250 of *NIST Special Publication*, Gaithersburg, MD. National Institute of Standards and Technology.

TREC-11 (2002, November). *Eleventh Text REtrieval Conference*, Volume 500-251 of *NIST Special Publication*, Gaithersburg, MD. National Institute of Standards and Technology.

TREC-12 (2004, November). *Twelfth Text REtrieval Conference*, Volume 500-255 of *NIST Special Publication*, Gaithersburg, MD. National Institute of Standards and Technology.

Vallin, A., B. Magnini, D. Giampiccolo, L. Aunimo, C. Ayache, P. Osenova, A. P. nas, M. de Rijke, B. Sacaleanu, D. Santos, and R. Sutcliffe (2005). Overview of the CLEF 2005 multilingual question answering track. In *Proceedings CLEF 2005*. Vienna, Austria, Working note.

van Zaanen, M. and D. Mollá (2007). AnswerFinder at QA@CLEF 2007. In *Workshop of Cross-Language Evaluation Forum (CLEF 2007)*, Budapest, Hungary.

Vicedo, J. L. (2002, May). SEMQA: A semantic model applied to question answering systems. PhD thesis, Departament of Languages and Information Systems. University of Alicante, Ctra. de San Vicente s/n. 03080 Alicante. España.

Voorhees, E. M. (2001a, November). Overview of the TREC 2001 question answering track. *Tenth Text REtrieval Conference*, Volume 500-250 of NIST Special Publications, Gaithersburg, MD. National Institute of Standards and Technology.

Voorhees, E. M. (2001b). The TREC question answering track. *Natural Language Engineering 7*(4), 361–378.

Voorhees, E. M. (2004, November). Overview of the TREC 2003 question answering Track. *Twelth Text REtrieval Conference*, Volume 500-255 of NIST Special Publications, Gaithersburg, MD. National Institute of Standards and Technology.

Voorhees, E. M. and D. M. Tice (2000). Building a question answering test collection. *Proceedings of the 23rd Annual International ACM SIGIR Conference on Research and Development in Information Retrieval*, Athens, Greece, pp. 200–207.

Woods, W. (1971). Progress in natural language understanding—An application to lunar geology. In *AFIPS Conference*, New York, pp. 441–450.

Xue, X., J. Jeon, and W. B. Croft (2008). Retrieval models for question and answer archives. In *SIGIR '08: Proceedings of the 31st Annual International ACM SIGIR Conference on Research and Development in Information Retrieval*, New York, pp. 475–482. ACM.

Yang, H. and T.-S. Chua (2002, November). The integration of lexical knowledge and external resources for question answering. *Eleventh Text REtrieval Conference*, Volume 500-251 of NIST Special Publication, Gaithersburg, MD. National Institute of Standards and Technology.

Zhang, D. and S. S. Lee (2003). Question classification using support vector machines. In *Proceedings of the SIGIR 03*, New York. ACM.

21

Information Extraction

Jerry R. Hobbs
University of Southern California

Ellen Riloff
University of Utah

21.1 Introduction

Information extraction (IE) is the process of scanning text for information relevant to some interest, including extracting entities, relations, and, most challenging, events—or who did what to whom, when, and where. It requires deeper analysis than keyword searches, but its aims fall short of the very hard and long-term problem of text understanding, where we seek to capture all the information in a text, along with the speaker's or writer's intention. IE represents a midpoint on this spectrum, where the aim is to capture structured information without sacrificing feasibility. IE typically focuses on surface linguistic phenomena that do not require deep inference, and it focuses on the phenomena that are most frequent in texts.

IE technology arose in response to the need for efficient processing of texts in specialized domains. Full-sentence parsers expended a lot of effort in trying to arrive at parses of long sentences that were not relevant to the domain, or that contained much irrelevant material, thereby increasing the chances for error. IE technology, by contrast, focuses on only the relevant parts of the text and ignores the rest.

Typical applications of IE systems are in gleaning business, government, or military intelligence from a large number of sources; in searches of the World Wide Web for more specific information than keywords can discriminate; for scientific literature searches; in building databases from large textual corpora; and in the curation of biomedical articles. The need for IE is well illustrated in biomedicine, where there are more than half a million articles a year, and large amounts of money are spent on curatorial activities. Similarly, in intelligence gathering, an analyst in 1990 said that reading everything she was supposed to read would be like reading *War and Peace* every day; in 1995 the same analyst said it was way beyond that.

Named entity recognition (NER) is one of the most common uses of IE technology (e.g., Bikel et al. 1999, Collins and Singer 1999, Cucerzan and Yarowsky 1999, Fleischman and Hovy 2002, Sang and Meulder 2003).

511

NER systems identify different types of proper names, such as person and company names, and sometimes special types of entities, such as dates and times, that can be easily identified using surface-level textual patterns. NER is especially important in biomedical applications, where terminology is a formidable problem. But it is important to note that IE is much more than just NER. A much more difficult and potentially much more significant capability is the recognition of events and their participants. For example, in each of the sentences

> "Microsoft acquired Powerset."
> "Powerset was acquired by Microsoft."

we would like to recognize not only that Microsoft and Powerset are company names, but also that an acquisition event took place, that the acquiring company was Microsoft, and the acquired company was Powerset.

Much of the technology in IE was developed in response to a series of evaluations and associated conferences called the Message Understanding Conference (MUC), held between 1987 and 1998.

Except for the earliest MUCs, these evaluations were based on a corpus of domain-specific texts, such as news articles on joint ventures. Participating teams were supplied with a training corpus and a template definition for the events and their roles. For joint ventures, the roles were such things as the participating companies, the joint venture company that was formed, the activity it would engage in, and the amount of money it was capitalized for. The systems were then run on a previously unseen test corpus. A system's performance was measured on recall (what percentage of the correct answers did the system get), precision (what percentage of the system's answers were correct), and F-score. The F-score is a weighted harmonic mean between recall and precision, computed by the following formula:

$$F = \frac{(\beta^2 + 1)PR}{\beta^2 P + R}$$

where

  P is precision

  R is recall

  β is a parameter encoding the relative importance of recall and precision

If $\beta = 1$, they are weighted equally. If $\beta > 1$, precision is more important; if $\beta < 1$, recall is more important.* A typical text in the joint ventures domain used in MUC-5 (July 1993) (MUC-5 Proceedings 1993) is the following:

> Bridgestone Sports Co. said Friday it has set up a joint venture in Taiwan with a local concern and a Japanese trading house to produce golf clubs to be shipped to Japan.
>
> The joint venture, Bridgestone Sports Taiwan Co., capitalized at 20 million new Taiwan dollars, will start production in January 1990 with production of 20,000 iron and "metal wood" clubs a month.

The information to be extracted from this text is shown in the following templates:

---

* When in a courtroom you promise to tell the whole truth, you are promising 100% recall. When you promise to tell nothing but the truth, you are promising 100% precision.

TIE-UP-1:
Relationship:	TIE-UP
Entities:	"Bridgestone Sports Co."
	"a local concern"
	"a Japanese trading house"
Joint Venture Company:	"Bridgestone Sports Taiwan Co."
Activity:	ACTIVITY-1
Amount:	NT$20000000

ACTIVITY-1:
Activity:	PRODUCTION
Company:	"Bridgestone Sports Taiwan Co."
Product:	"iron and 'metal wood' clubs"
Start Date:	DURING: January 1990

IE research has since been stimulated by the Automatic Content Extraction (ACE) evaluations.* The ACE evaluations have focused on identifying named entities, extracting isolated relations, and coreference resolution.

IE systems have been developed for a variety of domains, including terrorist events (MUC-4 Proceedings 1992, Soderland et al. 1995, Riloff 1996b, Chieu et al. 2003), joint ventures (MUC-5 Proceedings 1993), management succession (MUC-6 Proceedings 1995), plane crashes (MUC-7 Proceedings 1998), vehicle launches (MUC-7 Proceedings 1998), corporate acquisitions (Freitag 1998b, Freitag and McCallum 2000, Finn and Kushmerick 2004), disease outbreaks (Grishman et al. 2002, Patwardhan and Riloff 2007, Phillips and Riloff 2007), job postings (Freitag and McCallum 2000, Califf and Mooney 2003), rental ads (Soderland 1999, Ciravegna 2001), resumes (Yu et al. 2005), and seminar announcements (Freitag 1998b, Ciravegna 2001, Chieu and Ng 2002, Califf and Mooney 2003, Finn and Kushmerick 2004, Gu and Cercone 2006). There has also been a great deal of work on IE in biological and medical domains (e.g., Friedman 1986, Subramaniam et al. 2003, Ananiadou et al. 2004, Hirschman et al. 2005, Ananiadou and McNaught 2006, Yakushiji et al. 2006), which is discussed in greater depth in Chapter 25 of this book.

21.2 Diversity of IE Tasks

The MUCs led to an increased interest in the IE task and the creation of additional IE data sets. Researchers began to work on IE problems for new domains and focused on different aspects of the IE problem. In the following sections, we outline some of the fundamental distinctions that cut across different IE tasks.

21.2.1 Unstructured vs. Semi-Structured Text

Historically, most natural language processing (NLP) systems have been designed to process *unstructured text*, which consists of natural language sentences. In contrast to structured data where the semantics of the data is defined by its organization (e.g., database entries), the meaning of unstructured text depends entirely on linguistic analysis and natural language understanding. Examples of unstructured text include news stories, magazine articles, and books.[†] Figure 21.1 shows an example of a seminar announcement that is written as unstructured text.

---

* http://www.itl.nist.gov/iad/mig/tests/ace/
[†] These text forms can include some structured information as well, such as publication dates and author by-lines. But most of the text in these genres is unstructured.

> Professor John Skvoretz, U. of South Carolina, Columbia, will present a seminar entitled
> "Embedded Commitment," on Thursday, May 4th from 4-5:30 in PH 223D.

FIGURE 21.1   Example of an unstructured seminar announcement.

> Laura Petitte
> Department of Psychology
> McGill University
>
> Thursday, May 4, 1995
> 12:00 pm
> Baker Hall 355

> Name: Dr. Jeffrey D. Hermes
> Affiliation: Department of AutoImmune Diseases
> Research & Biophysical Chemistry Merck Research Laboratories
> Title: "MHC Class II: A Target for Specific Immunomodulation of the Immune
> Response"
> Host/e-mail: Robert Murphy, murph@a.crf.cmu.edu
> Date: Wednesday, May 3, 1995
> Time: 3:30 p.m.
> Place: Mellon Institute Conference Room
> Sponsor: MERCK RESEARCH LABORATORIES

FIGURE 21.2   Examples of semi-structured seminar announcements.

Semi-structured text consists of natural language that appears in a document where the physical layout of the language plays a role in its interpretation. For example, consider the seminar announcements depicted in Figure 21.2. The reader understands that the speaker is Laura Petitte, who is from the Department of Psychology at McGill University, because seminar speakers and their affiliations typically appear at the top of a seminar announcement. If McGill University had appeared below Baker Hall 355 in the announcement, then we would assume that the seminar takes place at McGill University.

Several IE data sets have been created specifically to handle domains that often include semi-structured text, such as seminar announcements, job postings, rental ads, and resumes. To accommodate semi-structured text, IE systems typically rely less on syntactic parsing and more on positional features that capture the physical layout of the words on the page.

21.2.2 Single-Document vs. Multi-Document IE

Originally, IE systems were designed to locate domain-specific information in individual documents. Given a document as input, the IE system identifies and extracts facts relevant to the domain that appear in the document. We will refer to this task as *single-document IE*.

The abundance of information available on the Web has led to the creation of new types of IE systems that seek to extract facts from the Web or other very large text collections (e.g., Brin 1998, Fleischman et al. 2003, Etzioni et al. 2005, Pasca et al. 2006, Banko et al. 2007, Pasca 2007). We will refer to this task as *multi-document IE*.

Single-document IE is fundamentally different from multi-document IE, although both types of systems may use similar techniques. One distinguishing issue is redundancy. A single-document IE system must extract domain-specific information from each document that it is given. If the system fails to find relevant information in a document, then that is an error. This task is challenging because many documents mention a fact only once, and the fact may be expressed in an unusual or complex linguistic context (e.g., one requiring inference). In contrast, multi-document IE systems can exploit the redundancy of information in its large text collection. Many facts will appear in a wide variety of contexts, so the system usually has multiple opportunities to find each piece of information. The more often a fact appears, the greater the chance that it will occur at least once in a linguistically simple context that will be straightforward for the IE system to recognize.*

Multi-document IE is sometimes referred to as "open-domain" IE because the goal is usually to acquire broad-coverage factual information, which will likely benefit many domains. In this paradigm, it does not matter where the information originated. Some open-domain IE systems, such as KnowItAll (Etzioni et al. 2005) and TextRunner (Banko et al. 2007), have addressed issues of scale to acquire large amounts of information from the Web. One of the major challenges in multi-document IE is cross-document coreference resolution: when are two documents talking about the same entities? Some researchers have tackled this problem (e.g., Bagga and Baldwin 1998, Mann and Yarowsky 2003, Gooi and Allan 2004, Niu et al. 2004, Mayfield et al. 2009), and in 2008 the ACE evaluation expanded its focus to include cross-document entity disambiguation (Strassel et al. 2008).

21.2.3 Assumptions about Incoming Documents

The IE data sets used in the MUCs consist of documents related to the domain, but not all of the documents mention a relevant event. The data sets were constructed to mimic the challenges that a real-world IE system must face, where a fundamental part of the IE task is to determine whether a document describes a relevant event, as well as to extract information about the event. In the MUC-3 through MUC-7 IE data sets, only about half of the documents describe a domain-relevant event that warrants IE.

Other IE data sets make different assumptions about the incoming documents. Many IE data sets consist only of documents that describe a relevant event. Consequently, the IE system can assume that each document contains information that should be extracted. This assumption of *relevant-only documents* allows an IE system to be more aggressive about extracting information because the texts are known to be on-topic. For example, if an IE system is given stories about bombing incidents, then it can extract the name of every person who was killed or injured and in most cases they will be victims of a bombing. If, however, irrelevant stories are also given to the system, then it must further distinguish between people who are bombing victims and people who were killed or injured in other types of events, such as robberies or car crashes.

Some IE data sets further make the assumption that each incoming document contains only one event of interest. We will refer to these as *single-event documents*. The seminar announcements, corporate acquisitions, and job postings IE data sets only contain single-event documents. In contrast, the MUC data sets and some others (e.g., rental ads and disease outbreaks) allow that a single document may describe multiple events of interest. If the IE system can assume that each incoming document describes only one relevant event, then all of the extracted information can be inserted in a single output template.[†] If multiple events are discussed in a document, then the IE system must perform discourse analysis to determine how many different events are being reported and to associate each piece of extracted information with the appropriate event template.

---

* This issue parallels the difference between single-document and multi-document question answering (QA) systems. Light et al. (2001) found that the performance of QA systems in TREC-8 was directly correlated with the number of answer opportunities available for a question.

[†] Note that coreference resolution of entities is still an issue, however. For example, a document may mention multiple victims so the IE system needs to determine whether an extracted victim refers to a previously mentioned victim or a new one.

21.3 IE with Cascaded Finite-State Transducers

Probably the most important idea that emerged in the course of the MUC evaluations was the decomposition of the IE process into a series of subproblems that can be modeled with "cascaded finite-state transducers" (Lehnert et al. 1991, 1992, Joshi 1996, Hobbs et al. 1997, Cunningham et al. 2002). A finite-state automaton reads one element at a time of a sequence of elements; each element transitions the automaton into a new state, based on the type of element it is, e.g., the part of speech of a word. Some states are designated as final, and a final state is reached when the sequence of elements matches a valid pattern. In a finite-state transducer, an output entity is constructed when final states are reached, e.g., a representation of the information in a phrase. In a cascaded finite-state transducer, there are different finite-state transducers at different stages. Earlier stages will package a string of elements into something the next stage will view as a single element.

In the typical system, the earlier stages recognize smaller linguistic objects and work in a largely domain-independent fashion. They use purely linguistic knowledge to recognize portions of the syntactic structure of a sentence that linguistic methods can determine reliably, requiring relatively little modification or augmentation as the system is moved from domain to domain. The later stages take these linguistic objects as input and find domain-dependent patterns within them. In a typical IE system, there are five levels of processing:

1. Complex Words: This includes the recognition of multiwords and proper name entities, such as people, companies, and countries.
2. Basic Phrases: Sentences are segmented into noun groups, verb groups, and particles.
3. Complex Phrases: Complex noun groups and complex verb groups are identified.
4. Domain Events: The sequence of phrases produced at Level 3 is scanned for patterns of interest to the application, and when they are found, semantic structures are built that encode the information about entities and events contained in the pattern.
5. Merging Structures: Semantic structures from different parts of the text are merged if they provide information about the same entity or event. This process is sometimes called *template generation*, and is a complex process not done by a finite-state transducer.

As we progress through the five levels, larger segments of text are analyzed and structured. In each of stages 2 through 4, the input to the finite-state transducer is the sequence of chunks constructed in the previous stage. The GATE project (Cunningham et al. 2002) is a widely used toolkit that provides many of the components needed for such an IE pipeline.

This decomposition of the natural-language problem into levels is essential to the approach. Many systems have been built to do pattern matching on strings of words. The advances in IE have depended crucially on dividing that process into separate levels for recognizing phrases and recognizing patterns among the phrases. Phrases can be recognized reliably with purely syntactic information, and they provide precisely the elements that are required for stating the patterns of interest.

Sections 21.3.1 through 21.3.5 illustrate this process on the Bridgestone Sports text.

21.3.1 Complex Words

The first level of processing identifies multiwords such as "set up," "trading house," "new Taiwan dollars," and "joint venture," and company names like "Bridgestone Sports Co." and "Bridgestone Sports Taiwan Co." The names of people and locations, dates, times, and other basic entities are also recognized at this level. Languages in general are very productive in the construction of short, multiword fixed phrases and proper names employing specialized microgrammars, and this is the level at which they are recognized.

Some names can be recognized by their internal structure. A common pattern for company names is "ProperName ProductName," as in "Acme Widgets." Others can only be recognized by means of a table.

Internal structure cannot tell us that IBM is a company and DNA is not. It is also sometimes possible to recognize the types of proper names by the context in which they occur. For example, in the following sentences:

  a. XYZ's sales
  b. Vaclav Havel, 53, president of the Czech Republic

we might not know that XYZ is a company and Vaclav Havel is a person, but the immediate context establishes that. These can be given an underspecified representation that is resolved by later stages.

21.3.2 Basic Phrases

The problem of syntactic ambiguity in natural language is AI-complete. That is, we will not have systems that reliably parse English sentences correctly until we have encoded much of the real-world knowledge that people bring to bear in their language comprehension. For example, noun phrases cannot be reliably identified because of the prepositional phrase attachment problem. However, certain syntactic constructs can be identified with reasonable reliability. One of these syntactic constructs is the noun group, which is the head noun of a noun phrase together with its determiners and other left modifiers (these are sometimes called "base NPs"). Another is what we are calling the "verb group," that is, the verb together with its auxiliaries and any intervening adverbs. Moreover, an analysis that identifies these elements gives us exactly the units we most need for subsequent domain-dependent processing. The task of identifying these simple noun and verb groups is sometimes called "syntactic chunking." The basic phrases in the first sentence of text (1) are as follows, where "Company Name" and "Location" are special kinds of noun group that would be identified by NER:

Company Name:	Bridgestone Sports Co.
Verb Group:	said
Noun Group:	Friday
Noun Group:	it
Verb Group:	had set up
Noun Group:	a joint venture
Preposition:	in
Location:	Taiwan
Preposition:	with
Noun Group:	a local concern
Conjunction:	and
Noun Group:	a Japanese trading house
Verb Group:	to produce
Noun Group:	golf clubs
Verb Group:	to be shipped
Preposition:	to
Location:	Japan

Noun groups can be recognized by a relatively simple finite-state grammar encompassing most of the complexity that can occur in English noun groups (Hobbs et al. 1992), including numbers, numerical modifiers like "approximately," other quantifiers and determiners, participles in adjectival position, comparative and superlative adjectives, conjoined adjectives, and arbitrary orderings and conjunctions of prenominal nouns and noun-like adjectives. Thus, among the noun groups that can be recognized are

  "approximately 5 kg"
  "more than 30 people"
  "the newly elected president"

"the largest leftist political force"
"a government and commercial project"

The principal ambiguities that arise in this stage are due to noun–verb ambiguities. For example, "the company names" could be a single noun group with the head noun "names," or it could be a noun group "the company" followed by the verb "names." One can use a lattice representation to encode the two analyses and resolve the ambiguity in the stage for recognizing domain events.

Verb groups (and predicate adjective constructions) can be recognized by an even simpler finite-state grammar that, in addition to chunking, also tags them as Active Voice, Passive Voice, Gerund, and Infinitive. Verbs are sometimes locally ambiguous between active and passive senses, as the verb "kidnapped" in the following two sentences:

"Several men kidnapped the mayor today."
"Several men kidnapped yesterday were released today."

These cases can be tagged as Active/Passive, and the domain-event stage can later resolve the ambiguity. Some work has also been done to train a classifier to distinguish between active voice and "reduced" passive voice constructions (Igo and Riloff 2008).

The breakdown of phrases into nominals, verbals, and particles is a linguistic universal. Whereas the precise parts of speech that occur in any language can vary widely, every language has elements that are fundamentally nominal in character, elements that are fundamentally verbal or predicative, and particles or inflectional affixes that encode relations among the other elements (Croft 1991).

21.3.3 Complex Phrases

Some complex noun groups and verb groups can be recognized reliably on the basis of domain-independent, syntactic information. For example:

- The attachment of appositives to their head noun group
  "The joint venture, Bridgestone Sports Taiwan Co.,"
- The construction of measure phrases
  "20,000 iron and 'metal wood' clubs a month"
- The attachment of "of" and "for" prepositional phrases to their head noun groups
  "production of 20,000 iron and 'metal wood' clubs a month"
- Noun group conjunction
  "a local concern and a Japanese trading house"

In the course of recognizing basic and complex phrases, domain-relevant entities and events can be recognized and the structures for these can be constructed. In the sample joint-venture text, entity structures can be constructed for the companies referred to by the phrases "Bridgestone Sports Co.," "a local concern," "a Japanese trading house," and "Bridgestone Sports Taiwan Co." Information about nationality derived from the words "local" and "Japanese" can be recorded. Corresponding to the complex noun group "The joint venture, Bridgestone Sports Taiwan Co.," the following relationship structure can be built:

Relationship:	TIE-UP
Entities:	–
Joint Venture Company:	"Bridgestone Sports Taiwan Co."
Activity:	–
Amount:	–

Corresponding to the complex noun group "production of 20,000 iron and 'metal wood' clubs a month," the following activity structure can be built up:

Activity:	PRODUCTION
Company:	–
Product:	"iron and 'metal wood' clubs"
Start Date:	–

Complex verb groups can also be recognized in this stage. Consider the following variations:

"GM *formed* a joint venture with Toyota."
"GM *announced it was forming* a joint venture with Toyota."
"GM *signed an agreement forming* a joint venture with Toyota."
"GM *announced it was signing an agreement to form* a joint venture with Toyota."

Although these sentences may differ in significance for some applications, often they would be considered equivalent in meaning. Rather than defining each of these variations, with all their syntactic variants, at the domain event level, the user should be able to define complex verb groups that share the same significance. Thus, "formed," "announced it was forming," "signed an agreement forming," and "announced it was signing an agreement to form" may all be equivalent, and once they are defined to be so, only one domain event pattern needs to be expressed. Verb group conjunction, as in

"Terrorists *kidnapped and killed* three people."

can be treated as a complex verb group as well.

21.3.4 Domain Events

The next stage is recognizing domain events, and its input is list of the basic and complex phrases recognized in the earlier stages, in the order in which they occur. Anything that was not identified as a basic or complex phrase in a previous stage can be ignored in this stage; this can be a significant source of robustness.

Identifying domain events requires a set of domain-specific patterns both to recognize phrases that correspond to an event of interest and to identify the syntactic constitutents that correspond to the event's role fillers. In early information systems, these domain-specific "extraction patterns" were defined manually. In Sections 21.4.1 and 21.4.3, we describe a variety of learning methods that have subsequently been developed to automatically generate domain-specific extraction patterns from training corpora.

The patterns for events of interest can be encoded as finite-state machines, where state transitions are effected by phrases. The state transitions are driven off the head words in the phrases. That is, each pair of relevant head word and phrase type—such as "company-NounGroup" and "formed-PassiveVerbGroup"—has an associated set of state transitions. In the sample joint-venture text, the domain event patterns

<Company/ies> <Set-up> <Joint-Venture> with <Company/ies>

and

<Produce> <Product>

would be instantiated in the first sentence, and the patterns

<Company> <Capitalized> at <Currency>

and

<Company> <Start> <Activity> in/on <Date>

in the second. These four patterns would result in the following four structures being built:

Relationship:	TIE-UP
Entities:	"Bridgestone Sports Co."
	"a local concern"
	"a Japanese trading house"
Joint Venture Company:	–
Activity:	–
Amount:	–

Activity:	PRODUCTION
Company:	–
Product:	"golf clubs"
Start Date:	–

Relationship:	TIE-UP
Entities:	–
Joint Venture Company:	"Bridgestone Sports Taiwan Co."
Activity:	–
Amount:	NT$20000000

Activity:	PRODUCTION
Company:	"Bridgestone Sports Taiwan Co."
Product:	–
Start Date:	DURING: January 1990

The third of these is an augmentation of the TIE-UP structure discovered in the complex phrase phase. Certain kinds of "pseudo-syntax" can be done at this stage, including recognizing relative clauses and conjoined verb phrases, as described in Hobbs et al. (1997).

Many subject–verb–object patterns are of course related to each other. The sentence:

"GM manufactures cars."

illustrates a general pattern for recognizing a company's activities. But the same semantic content can appear in a variety of ways, including

"Cars are manufactured by GM."
"...GM, which manufactures cars..."
"...cars, which are manufactured by GM..."
"...cars manufactured by GM..."
"GM is to manufacture cars."
"Cars are to be manufactured by GM."
"GM is a car manufacturer."

These are all systematically related to the active voice form of the sentence. Therefore, there is no reason a developer should have to specify all the variations. A simple tool would be able to generate all of the variants of the pattern from the simple active voice Subject–Verb–Object form. It would also allow adverbials to appear at appropriate points. These transformations would be executed at compile time, producing the more detailed set of patterns, so that at run time there is no loss of efficiency.

This feature is not merely a clever idea for making a system more convenient to author. It rests on the fundamental idea that underlies generative transformational grammar, but is realized in a way that does not impact the efficiency of processing.

In recent years, full-sentence parsing has improved, in large part through the use of statistical techniques. Consequently, some IE systems have begun to rely on full parsers rather than shallow parsing techniques.

21.3.5 Template Generation: Merging Structures

All the first four stages of processing operate within the bounds of single sentences. The final level of processing operates over the whole text. Its task is to see that all the information collected about a single entity, relationship, or event is combined into a unified whole. This is one of the primary ways that the problem of coreference is dealt with in IE, including both NP coreference (for entities) and event coreference. One event template is generated for each event, which coalesces all of the information associated with that event. If an input document discusses multiple events of interest, then the IE system must generate multiple event templates. Generating multiple event templates requires additional discourse analysis to (a) correctly determine how many distinct events are reported in the document, and (b) correctly assign each entity and object to the appropriate event template.

Among the criteria that need to be taken into account in determining whether two structures can be merged are the internal structure of the noun groups, nearness along some metric, and the consistency, or more generally, the compatibility of the two structures.

In the analysis of the sample joint-venture text, we have produced three activity structures. They are all consistent because they are all of type PRODUCTION and because "iron and 'metal wood' clubs" is consistent with "golf clubs." Hence, they are merged, yielding:

Activity:	PRODUCTION
Company:	"Bridgestone Sports Taiwan Co."
Product:	"iron and 'metal wood' clubs"
Start Date:	DURING: January 1990

Similarly, the two relationship structures that have been generated are consistent with each other, so they can be merged, yielding:

Relationship:	TIE-UP
Entities:	"Bridgestone Sports Co."
	"a local concern"
	"a Japanese trading house"
Joint Venture Company:	"Bridgestone Sports Taiwan Co."
Activity:	–
Amount:	NT$20000000

The entity and event coreference problems are very hard, and constitute active and important areas of research. Coreference resolution was a task in the later MUC evaluations (MUC-6 Proceedings 1995, MUC-7 Proceedings 1998), and has been a focus of the ACE evaluations. Many recent research efforts have applied machine learning techniques to the problem of coreference resolution (e.g., Dagan and Itai 1990, McCarthy and Lehnert 1995, Aone and Bennett 1996, Kehler 1997, Cardie and Wagstaff 1999, Harabagiu et al. 2001, Soon et al. 2001, Ng and Cardie 2002, Bean and Riloff 2004, McCallum and Wellner 2004, Yang et al. 2005, Haghighi and Klein 2007).

Some attempts to automate the template generation process will be discussed in Section 21.4.4.

21.4 Learning-Based Approaches to IE

As we discussed in Section 21.3, early IE systems used hand-crafted patterns and rules, often encoded in cascaded finite-state transducers. Hand-built IE systems were effective, but manually creating the patterns and rules was extremely time-consuming. For example, it was estimated that it took approximately 1500 person-hours of effort to create the patterns used by the UMass MUC-4 system (Lehnert et al. 1992, Riloff 1993).

Consequently, researchers began to use statistical techniques and machine learning algorithms to automatically create IE systems for new domains. In the following sections, we overview four types of learning-based IE methods: supervised learning of patterns and rules, supervised learning of sequential IE classifiers, weakly supervised and unsupervised learning methods for IE, and learning-based approaches for more global or discourse-oriented approaches to IE.

21.4.1 Supervised Learning of Extraction Patterns and Rules

Supervised learning methods originally promised to dramatically reduce the knowledge engineering bottleneck required to create an IE system for a new domain. Instead of painstakingly writing patterns and rules by hand, knowledge engineering could be reduced to the manual annotation of a collection of training texts. The hope was that a training set could be annotated in a matter of weeks, and nearly anyone with knowledge of the domain could do the annotation work.[*] As we will acknowledge in Section 21.4.3, manual annotation is itself a substantial endeavor, and a goal of recent research efforts is to eliminate this bottleneck as well. But supervised learning methods were an important first step toward automating the creation of IE systems.

The earliest pattern learning systems used specialized techniques, sometimes coupled with small amounts of manual effort. AutoSlog (Riloff 1993) and PALKA (Kim and Moldovan 1993) were the first IE pattern learning systems. AutoSlog (Riloff 1993, 1996a) matches a small set of syntactic templates against the text surrounding a desired extraction and creates one (or more) lexico-syntactic patterns by instantiating the templates with the corresponding words in the sentence. A "human in the loop" must then manually review the patterns to decide which ones are appropriate for the IE task. PALKA (Kim and Moldovan 1993) uses manually defined frames and keywords that are provided by a user and creates IE patterns by mapping clauses containing the keywords onto the frame's slots. The patterns are generalized based on the semantic features of the words.

Several systems use rule learning algorithms to automatically generate IE patterns from annotated text corpora. LIEP (Huffman 1996) creates candidate patterns by identifying syntactic paths that relate the role fillers in a sentence. The patterns that perform well on training examples are kept, and as learning progresses they are generalized to accommodate new training examples by creating disjunctions of terms. CRYSTAL (Soderland et al. 1995) learns extraction rules using a unification-based covering algorithm. CRYSTAL's rules are "concept node" structures that include lexical, syntactic, and semantic constraints. WHISK (Soderland 1999) was an early system that was specifically designed to be flexible enough to handle structured, semi-structured, and unstructured texts. WHISK learns regular expression rules that consist of words, semantic classes, and wildcards that match any token. $(LP)^2$ (Ciravegna 2001) induces two different kinds of IE rules: *tagging rules* to label instances as desired extractions, and *correction rules* to correct mistakes made by the tagging rules. Freitag created a rule-learning system called SRV (Freitag 1998b) and later combined it with a rote learning mechanism and a Naive Bayes classifier to explore a multi-strategy approach to IE (Freitag 1998a).

Relational learning methods have also been used to learn rule-like structures for IE (e.g., Roth and Yih 2001, Califf and Mooney 2003, Bunescu and Mooney 2004, 2007). RAPIER (Califf and Mooney 1999,

---

[*] In contrast, creating IE patterns and rules by hand typically requires computational linguists who understand how the patterns or rules will be integrated into the NLP system.

2003) uses relational learning methods to generate IE rules, where each rule has a pre-filler, filler, and post-filler component. Each component is a pattern that consists of words, POS tags, and semantic classes. Roth and Yih (2001) propose a knowledge representation language for propositional relations and create a two-stage classifier that first identifies candidate extractions and then selects the best ones. Bunescu and Mooney (2004) use Relational Markov Networks to represent dependencies and influences across entities and extractions.

IE pattern learning methods have also been developed for related applications such as question answering (Ravichandran and Hovy 2002), where the goal is to learn patterns for specific types of questions that involve relations between entities (e.g., identifying the birth year of a person).

21.4.2 Supervised Learning of Sequential Classifier Models

An alternative approach views IE as a classification problem that can be tackled using sequential learning models. Instead of using explicit patterns or rules to extract information, a machine learning classifier is trained to sequentially scan a text from left to right and label each word as an extraction or a non-extraction. A typical labeling scheme is called IOB, where each word is classified as an "I" if it is inside a desired extraction, "O" if it is outside a desired extraction, or "B" if it is the beginning of a desired extraction. The sentence below has been labeled with IOB tags corresponding to phrases that should be extracted as facts about a bombing incident.

Alleged/B guerrilla/I urban/I commandos/I launched/O two/B highpower/I bombs/I against/O a/B car/I dealership/I in/O downtown/O San/B Salvador/I this/B morning/I.

In the example above, the IOB tags indicate that five phrases should be extracted: "Alleged guerrilla urban commandos," "two highpower bombs," "a car dealership," "San Salvador," and "this morning." Note that the "B" tag is important to demarcate where one extraction begins and another one ends, particularly in the case when two extractions are adjacent. For example, if only "I" and "O" tags were used, then "San Salvador" and "this morning" would run together and appear to be a single extraction. Depending on the learning model, a different classifier may be trained for each type of information to be extracted (e.g., one classifier might be trained to identify perpetrator extractions, and another classifier may be trained to identify location extractions). Or a single classifier can be trained to produce different types of IOB tags for the different kinds of role fillers (e.g., $B_{perpetrator}$ and $B_{location}$) (Chieu and Ng 2002).

A variety of sequential classifier models have been developed using Hidden Markov Models (HMMs) (Freitag and McCallum 2000, Yu et al. 2005, Gu and Cercone 2006), Maximum Entropy Classifiers (Chieu and Ng 2002), Conditional Random Fields (Peng and McCallum 2004, Choi et al. 2005), and Support Vector Machines (SVMs) (Zelenko et al. 2003, Finn and Kushmerick 2004, Li et al. 2005, Zhao and Grishman 2005). Freitag and McCallum (2000) use HMMs and developed a method to automatically explore different structures for the HMM during the learning process. Gu and Cercone (2006) use HMMs in a two-step IE process: one HMM retrieves relevant text segments that likely contain a filler, and a second HMM identifies the words to be extracted in these text segments. Finn and Kushmerick (2004) also use a two-step IE process but in a different way: one SVM classifier identifies start and end tags for extractions, and a second SVM looks at tags that were orphaned (i.e., a start tag was found without a corresponding end tag, or vice versa) and tries to identify the missing tag. The second classifier aims to improve IE recall by producing extractions that otherwise would have been missed. Yu et al. (2005) created a cascaded model of HMMs and SVMs. In the first pass, an HMM segments resumes into blocks that represent different types of information. In the second pass, HMMs and SVMs extract information from the blocks, with different classifiers trained to extract different types of information.

Chapter 9 in this book explains how to create classifiers and sequential prediction models using supervised learning techniques.

21.4.3 Weakly Supervised and Unsupervised Approaches

Supervised learning techniques substantially reduced the manual effort required to create an IE system for a new domain. However, annotating training texts still requires a substantial investment of time, and annotating documents for IE can be deceptively complex (Riloff 1996b). Furthermore, since IE systems are domain-specific, annotated corpora cannot be reused: a new corpus must be annotated for each domain.

To further reduce the knowledge engineering required to create an IE system, several methods have been developed in recent years to learn extraction patterns using weakly supervised and unsupervised techniques. AutoSlog-TS (Riloff 1996b) is a derivative of AutoSlog that requires as input only a preclassified training corpus in which texts are identified as relevant or irrelevant with respect to the domain but are not annotated in any other way. AutoSlog-TS's learning algorithm is a two-step process. In the first step, AutoSlog's syntactic templates are applied to the training corpus exhaustively, which generates a large set of candidate extraction patterns. In the second step, the candidate patterns are ranked based on the strength of their association with the relevant texts. Ex-Disco (Yangarber et al. 2000) took this approach one step further by eliminating the need for a preclassified text corpus. Ex-Disco uses a small set of manually defined seed patterns to partition a collection of unannotated text into relevant and irrelevant sets. The pattern learning process is then embedded in a bootstrapping loop where (1) patterns are ranked based on the strength of their association with the relevant texts, (2) the best pattern(s) are selected and added to the pattern set, and (3) the corpus is re-partitioned into new relevant and irrelevant sets. Both AutoSlog-TS and Ex-Disco produce IE patterns that performed well in comparison to pattern sets used by previous IE systems. However, the ranked pattern lists produced by these systems still need to be manually reviewed.*

Stevenson and Greenwood (2005) also begin with seed patterns and use semantic similarity measures to iteratively rank and select new candidate patterns based on their similarity to the seeds. Stevenson and Greenwood use predicate-argument structures as the representation for their IE patterns, as did Surdeanu et al. (2003) and Yangarber (2003) in earlier work. Sudo et al. (2003) created an even richer *subtree model* representation for IE patterns, where an IE pattern can be an arbitrary subtree of a dependency tree. The subtree patterns are learned from relevant and irrelevant training documents. Bunescu and Mooney (2007) developed a weakly supervised method for relation extraction that uses Multiple Instance Learning (MIL) techniques with SVMs and string kernels.

Meta-bootstrapping (Riloff and Jones 1999) is a bootstrapping method that learns IE patterns and also generates noun phrases that belong to a semantic class at the same time. Given a few seed nouns that belong to a targeted semantic class, the meta-bootstrapping algorithm iteratively learns a new extraction pattern and then uses the learned pattern to hypothesize additional nouns that belong to the semantic class. The patterns learned by meta-bootstrapping are more akin to NER patterns than event role patterns, however, because they identify noun phrases that belong to general semantic classes, irrespective of any events.

Recently, Phillips and Riloff (2007) showed that bootstrapping methods can be used to learn event role patterns by exploiting *role-identifying nouns* as seeds. A role-identifying noun is a word that, by virtue of its lexical semantics, identifies the role that the noun plays with respect to an event. For example, the definition of the word *kidnapper* is the agent of a kidnapping event. By using role-identifying nouns as seeds, the Basilisk bootstrapping algorithm (Thelen and Riloff 2002) can be used to learn both event extraction patterns as well as additional role-identifying nouns.

Finally, Shinyama and Sekine (2006) have developed an approach for completely unsupervised learning of IE patterns. Given texts for a new domain, relation discovery methods are used to preemptively learn the types of relations that appear in domain-specific documents. The On-Demand Information Extraction (ODIE) system (Sekine 2006) accepts a user query for a topic, dynamically learns IE patterns for salient

---

* The human reviewer discards patterns that are not relevant to the IE task and assigns an event role to the patterns that are kept.

relations associated with the topic, and then applies the patterns to fill in a table with extracted information related to the topic.

21.4.4 Discourse-Oriented Approaches to IE

Most of the IE systems that we have discussed thus far take a relatively localized approach to IE. The IE patterns or classifiers focus only on the local context surrounding a word or phrase when making an extraction decision. Recently, some systems have begun to take a more global view of the extraction process. Gu and Cercone (2006) and Patwardhan and Riloff (2007) use classifiers to first identify the event-relevant sentences in a document and then apply an IE system to extract information from those relevant sentences.

Finkel et al. (2005) impose penalties in their learning model to enforce label consistency among extractions from different parts of a document. Maslennikov and Chua (2007) use dependency and RST-based discourse relations to connect entities in different clauses and find long-distance dependency relations.

Finally, as we discussed in Section 21.3.5, IE systems that process multiple-event documents need to generate multiple templates. Template generation for multiple events is extremely challenging, and only a few learning systems have been developed to automate this process for new domains. WRAP-UP (Soderland and Lehnert 1994) was an early supervised learning system that uses a collection of decision trees to make a series of discourse decisions to automate the template generation process. More recently, Chieu et al. (2003) developed a system called ALICE that generates complete templates for the MUC-4 terrorism domain (MUC-4 Proceedings 1992). ALICE uses a set of classifiers that identify extractions for each type of slot and a *template manager* to decide when to create a new template. The template manager uses general-purpose rules (e.g., a conflicting date will spawn a new template) as well as automatically derived "seed words" that are associated with different incident types to distinguish between events.

21.5 How Good Is Information Extraction?

Extracting information about events from free text is a challenging problem that is still far from solved. Figure 21.3 illustrates how the various MUC systems progressed from year to year. The vertical axis is precision, and the horizontal axis is recall. We have plotted the top one-third of the system scores in the small ellipse and the top two-thirds in the large ellipse.

We can see that between MUC-3 and MUC-4, the top systems moved up from the high 40s to the high 50s. The principal difference in MUC-5 is that more systems are in the high 50s. By MUC-6 the top two-thirds of the systems are all in a tight cluster with recall in the high 50s and precision in the low 60s. The principal difference between MUC-6 and MUC-7 is that in MUC-7 there were fewer participants.

This is a picture of hill-climbing, where there is a 60% barrier that determines the top of the hill. The tasks in these evaluations were somewhat different, as were the corpora, nevertheless they all seemed to exhibit a ceiling around 60% recall and precision. Although good progress has been made in automating the construction of IE systems using machine learning techniques, current state-of-the-art systems still have not broken through this 60% barrier in performance on the MUC data sets (e.g., Soderland 1999, Chieu et al. 2003, Maslennikov and Chua 2007).*

There are several possible explanations for this barrier. Detailed analysis of the performance of some of the systems revealed that the biggest source of mistakes was in entity and event coreference; more work certainly needs to be done on this. Another possibility is that 60% is what the text wears on its sleeve; the rest is implicit and requires inference and access to world knowledge.

---

* The one exception is that Maslennikov and Chua (2007) report an *F* score of 72% on a modified version of the MUC-6 corpus.

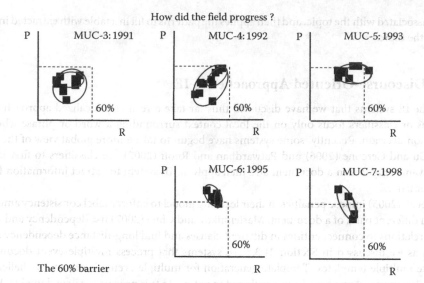

FIGURE 21.3 Chronology of MUC system performance.

Another explanation is that there is a Zipf distribution of problems that need to be solved. When we solve the more common problems, we get a big boost in performance. But we have solved all the most common problems, and now we are in the long tail of the distribution. We might take care of a dozen new problems we find in the training data, only to find that none of these problems occur in the test data, so there is no effect on measured performance. One possible solution is active learning (e.g., Lewis and Catlett 1994, Liere and Tadepalli 1997, McCallum and Nigam 1998, Thompson et al. 1999) and the automated selection of rare training examples in the tail for additional manual annotation. This could help to reduce the overall amount of training data that is required, while still adequately covering the rare cases.

A final possibility is both simple and disconcerting. Good NER systems typically recognize about 90% of the entities of interest in a text, and this is near human performance. To recognize an event and its arguments requires recognizing about four entities, and $.90^4$ is about 60%. If this is the reason for the 60% barrier, it is not clear what we can do to overcome it, short of solving the general natural language problem in a way that exploits the implicit relations among the elements of a text.

Acknowledgments

This work was supported in part by the Department of Homeland Security Grant N0014-07-1-0152. We are grateful to Doug Appelt, Ray Mooney, and Siddharth Patwardhan, who provided extremely helpful comments on an earlier draft of this chapter.

References

Ananiadou, S. and J. McNaught (Eds.) (2006). *Text Mining for Biology and Biomedicine.* Artech House, Inc., Norwood, MA.

Ananiadou, S., C. Friedman, and J. Tsujii (2004). Introduction: Named entity recognition in biomedicine. *Journal of Biomedical Informatics* 37(6).

Aone, C. and S. W. Bennett (1996). Applying machine learning to anaphora resolution. In S. Wermter, E. Riloff, and G. Scheler (Eds.), *Connectionist, Statistical, and Symbolic Approaches to Learning for Natural Language Processing*, pp. 302–314. Springer-Verlag, Berlin, Germany.

Bagga, A. and B. Baldwin (1998). Entity-based cross-document coreferencing using the vector space model. In *Proceedings of the 17th International Conference on Computational Linguistics*, Montreal, Canada.

Banko, M., M. Cafarella, S. Soderland, M. Broadhead, and O. Etzioni (2007). Open information extraction from the web. In *Proceedings of the Joint Conference on Artificial Intelligence (IJCAI-2007)*, Seattle, WA.

Bean, D. and E. Riloff (2004). Unsupervised learning of contextual role knowledge for coreference resolution. In *Proceedings of the Annual Meeting of the North American Chapter of the Association for Computational Linguistics (HLT/NAACL 2004)*, Boston, MA.

Bikel, D. M., R. Schwartz, and R. M. Weischedel (1999). An algorithm that learns what's in a name. *Machine Learning 34*(1), 211–231.

Brin, S. (1998). Extracting patterns and relations from the World Wide Web. In *WebDB Workshop at EDBT-98*, Valencia, Spain.

Bunescu, R. and R. Mooney (2004, July). Collective information extraction with relational Markov networks. In *Proceeding of the 42nd Annual Meeting of the Association for Computational Linguistics*, Barcelona, Spain, pp. 438–445.

Bunescu, R. and R. Mooney (2007). Learning to extract relations from the web using minimal supervision. In *Proceedings of the 45th Annual Meeting of the Association for Computational Linguistics*, Prague, Czech Republic.

Califf, M. and R. Mooney (1999). Relational learning of pattern-matching rules for information extraction. In *Proceedings of the 16th National Conference on Artificial Intelligence*, Stockholm, Sweden.

Califf, M. and R. Mooney (2003). Bottom-up relational learning of pattern matching rules for information extraction. *Journal of Machine Learning Research 4*, 177–210.

Cardie, C. and K. Wagstaff (1999). Noun phrase coreference as clustering. In *Proceedings of the Joint Conference on Empirical Methods in NLP and Very Large Corpora*, College Park, MD.

Chieu, H. and H. Ng (2002). A maximum entropy approach to information extraction from semi-structured and free text. In *Proceedings of the 18th National Conference on Artificial Intelligence*, Edmonton, Alberta, Canada.

Chieu, H., H. Ng, and Y. Lee (2003). Closing the gap: Learning-based information extraction rivaling knowledge-engineering methods. In *Proceedings of the 41th Annual Meeting of the Association for Computational Linguistics*, Sapporo, Japan.

Choi, Y., C. Cardie, E. Riloff, and S. Patwardhan (2005). Identifying sources of opinions with conditional random fields and extraction patterns. In *Proceedings of Human Language Technology Conference and Conference on Empirical Methods in Natural Language Processing*, Vancouver, Canada, pp. 355–362.

Ciravegna, F. (2001). Adaptive information extraction from text by rule induction and generalisation. In *Proceedings of the 17th International Joint Conference on Artificial Intelligence*, Seattle, WA.

Collins, M. and Y. Singer (1999). Unsupervised models for named entity classification. In *Proceedings of the Joint SIGDAT Conference on Empirical Methods in Natural Language Processing and Very Large Corpora (EMNLP/VLC-99)*, College Park, MD.

Croft, W. A. (1991). *Syntactic Categories and Grammatical Relations*. University of Chicago Press, Chicago, IL.

Cucerzan, S. and D. Yarowsky (1999). Language independent named entity recognition combining morphological and contextual evidence. In *Proceedings of the Joint SIGDAT Conference on Empirical Methods in Natural Language Processing and Very Large Corpora (EMNLP/VLC-99)*, College Park, MD.

Cunningham, H., D. Maynard, K. Bontcheva, and V. Tablan (2002). GATE: A framework and graphical development environment for robust nlp tools and applications. In *Proceedings of the 40th Annual Meeting of the Association for Computational Linguistics*, Philadelphia, PA.

Dagan, I. and A. Itai (1990). Automatic processing of large corpora for the resolution of anaphora references. In *Proceedings of the 13th International Conference on Computational Linguistics (COLING-90)*, Helsinki, Finland, pp. 330–332.

Etzioni, O., M. Cafarella, A. Popescu, T. Shaked, S. Soderland, D. Weld, and A. Yates (2005). Unsupervised named-entity extraction from the Web: An experimental study. *Artificial Intelligence 165*(1), 91–134.

Finkel, J., T. Grenager, and C. Manning (2005, June). Incorporating non-local information into information extraction systems by Gibbs sampling. In *Proceedings of the 43rd Annual Meeting of the Association for Computational Linguistics*, Ann Arbor, MI, pp. 363–370.

Finn, A. and N. Kushmerick (2004, September). Multi-level boundary classification for information extraction. In *Proceedings of the 15th European Conference on Machine Learning*, Pisa, Italy, pp. 111–122.

Fleischman, M. and E. Hovy (2002, August). Fine grained classification of named entities. In *Proceedings of the COLING Conference*, Taipei, Taiwan.

Fleischman, M., E. Hovy, and A. Echihabi (2003). Offline strategies for online question answering: Answering questions before they are asked. In *Proceedings of the 41th Annual Meeting of the Association for Computational Linguistics*, Sapporo, Japan.

Freitag, D. (1998a). Multistrategy learning for information extraction. In *Proceedings of the 15th International Conference on Machine Learning*, Madison, WI. Morgan Kaufmann Publishers.

Freitag, D. (1998b). Toward general-purpose learning for information extraction. In *Proceedings of the 36th Annual Meeting of the Association for Computational Linguistics*, Madison, WI.

Freitag, D. and A. McCallum (2000, August). Information extraction with HMM structures learned by stochastic optimization. In *Proceedings of the 17th National Conference on Artificial Intelligence*, Austin, TX, pp. 584–589.

Friedman, C. (1986). Automatic structuring of sublanguage information. *Analyzing Language in Restricted Domains: Sublanguage Description and Processing*. Lawrence Erlbaum Associates, Hillsdale, NJ.

Gooi, C. and J. Allan (2004). Cross-document coreference on a large scale corpus. In *Proceedings of the Annual Meeting of the North American Chapter of the Association for Computational Linguistics (HLT/NAACL 2004)*, Boston, MA.

Grishman, R., S. Huttunen, and R. Yangarber (2002). Real-time event extraction for infectious disease outbreaks. In *Proceedings of HLT 2002 (Human Language Technology Conference)*, San Diego, CA.

Gu, Z. and N. Cercone (2006, July). Segment-based hidden Markov models for information extraction. In *Proceedings of the 21st International Conference on Computational Linguistics and 44th Annual Meeting of the Association for Computational Linguistics*, Sydney, Australia, pp. 481–488.

Haghighi, A. and D. Klein (2007). Unsupervised coreference resolution in a nonparametric Bayesian model. In *Proceedings of the 45th Annual Meeting of the Association for Computational Linguistics*, Prague, Czech Republic.

Harabagiu, S., R. Bunescu, and S. Maiorana (2001). Text and knowledge mining for coreference resolution. In *Proceedings of the The Second Meeting of the North American Chapter of the Association for Computational Linguistics*, Pittsburgh, PA.

Hirschman, L., A. Yeh, C. Blaschke, and A. Valencia (2005, May). Overview of BioCreAtIvE: Critical assessment of information extraction for biology. *BMC Bioinformatics 6*(Suppl 1), S1.

Hobbs, J. R., D. E. Appelt, J. Bear, D. Israel, and M. Tyson (1992). FASTUS: A system for extracting information from natural-language text. SRI Technical Note 519, SRI International, Menlo Park, CA.

Hobbs, J. R., D. E. Appelt, J. Bear, D. Israel, M. Kameyama, M. Stickel, and M. Tyson (1997). FASTUS: A cascaded finite-state transducer for extracting information from natural-language text. In E. Roche and Y. Schabes (Eds.), *Finite State Devices for Natural Language Processing*, pp. 383–406. MIT Press, Cambridge, MA.

Huffman, S. (1996). Learning information extraction patterns from examples. In S. Wermter, E. Riloff, and G. Scheler (Eds.), *Connectionist, Statistical, and Symbolic Approaches to Learning for Natural Language Processing*, pp. 246–260. Springer-Verlag, Berlin, Germany.

Igo, S. and E. Riloff (2008). Learning to identify reduced passive verb phrases with a shallow parser. In *Proceedings of the 23rd National Conference on Artificial Intelligence*, Chicago, IL.

Joshi, A. K. (1996). A parser from antiquity: An early application of finite state transducers to natural language parsing. In *European Conference on Artificial Intelligence 96 Workshop on Extended Finite State Models of Language*, Budapest, Hungary, pp. 33–34.

Kehler, A. (1997). Probabilistic coreference in information extraction. In *Proceedings of the Second Conference on Empirical Methods in Natural Language Processing*, Providence, RI.

Kim, J. and D. Moldovan (1993). Acquisition of semantic patterns for information extraction from corpora. In *Proceedings of the Ninth IEEE Conference on Artificial Intelligence for Applications*, Los Alamitos, CA, pp. 171–176. IEEE Computer Society Press.

Lehnert, W., C. Cardie, D. Fisher, E. Riloff, and R. Williams (1991). University of Massachusetts: Description of the CIRCUS system as used for MUC-3. In *Proceedings of the Third Message Understanding Conference (MUC-3)*, San Mateo, CA, pp. 223–233. Morgan Kaufmann.

Lehnert, W., C. Cardie, D. Fisher, J. McCarthy, E. Riloff, and S. Soderland (1992). University of Massachusetts: Description of the CIRCUS system as used for MUC-4. In *Proceedings of the Fourth Message Understanding Conference (MUC-4)*, San Mateo, CA, pp. 282–288. Morgan Kaufmann.

Lewis, D. D. and J. Catlett (1994). Heterogeneous uncertainty sampling for supervised learning. In *Proceedings of the 11th International Conference on Machine Learning*, New Brunswick, MJ.

Li, Y., K. Bontcheva, and H. Cunningham (2005, June). Using uneven margins SVM and perceptron for information extraction. In *Proceedings of Ninth Conference on Computational Natural Language Learning*, Ann Arbor, MI, pp. 72–79.

Liere, R. and P. Tadepalli (1997). Active learning with committees for text categorization. In *Proceedings of the 14th National Conference on Artificial Intelligence*, Providence, RI.

Light, M., G. Mann, E. Riloff, and E. Breck (2001). Analyses for elucidating current question answering technology. *Journal for Natural Language Engineering 7*(4), 325–342.

Mann, G. and D. Yarowsky (2003). Unsupervised personal name disambiguation. In *Proceedings of the Seventh Conference on Natural Language Learning (CoNLL-2003)*, Edmonton, Canada.

Maslennikov, M. and T. Chua (2007). A multi-resolution framework for information extraction from free text. In *Proceedings of the 45th Annual Meeting of the Association for Computational Linguistics*, Prague, Czech Republic.

Mayfield, J., D. Alexander, B. Dorr, J. Eisner, T. Elsayed, T. Finin, C. Fink, M. Freedman, N. Garera, P. McNamee, S. Mohammad, D. Oard, C. Piatko, A. Sayeed, Z. Syed, R. Weischedel, T. Xu, and D. Yarowsky (2009). Cross-document coreference resolution: A key technology for learning by reading. In *Working Notes of the AAAI 2009 Spring Symposium on Learning by Reading and Learning to Read*, Stanford, CA.

McCallum, A. K. and K. Nigam (1998). Employing EM and pool-based active learning for text classification. In *Proceedings of the 15th International Conference on Machine Learning*, Madison, WI.

McCallum, A. and B. Wellner (2004). Conditional models of identity uncertainty with application to noun coreference. In *18th Annual Conference on Neural Information Processing Systems*, Whistler, Canada.

McCarthy, J. and W. Lehnert (1995). Using decision trees for coreference resolution. In *Proceedings of the Fourteenth International Joint Conference on Artificial Intelligence*, Denver, CO.

MUC-4 Proceedings (1992). *Proceedings of the Fourth Message Understanding Conference (MUC-4)*, Baltimore, MD. Morgan Kaufmann.

MUC-5 Proceedings (1993). *Proceedings of the Fifth Message Understanding Conference (MUC-5)*, San Francisco, CA.

MUC-6 Proceedings (1995). *Proceedings of the Sixth Message Understanding Conference (MUC-6)*, Columbia, MD.

MUC-7 Proceedings (1998). *Proceedings of the Seventh Message Understanding Conference (MUC-7)*, Fairfax, VA.

Ng, V. and C. Cardie (2002). Improving machine learning approaches to coreference resolution. In *Proceedings of the 40th Annual Meeting of the Association for Computational Linguistics*, Philadelphia, PA.

Niu, C., W. Li, and R. K. Srihari (2004). Weakly supervised learning for cross-document person name disambiguation supported by information extraction. In *Proceedings of the 42nd Annual Meeting of the Association for Computational Linguistics*, Barcelona, Spain.

Pasca, M. (2007). Weakly-supervised discovery of named entities using web search queries. In *Proceedings of the 16th ACM Conference on Information and Knowledge Management (CIKM-07)*, Lisbon, Portugal, pp. 683–690.

Pasca, M., D. Lin, J. Bigham, A. Lifchits, and A. Jain (2006). Names and similarities on the web: Fact extraction in the fast lane. In *Proceedings of the 21st International Conference on Computational Linguistics and 44th Annual Meeting of the Association for Computational Linguistics (COLING/ACL-06)*, Sydney, Australia, pp. 809–816.

Patwardhan, S. and E. Riloff (2007). Effective information extraction with semantic affinity patterns and relevant regions. In *Proceedings of 2007 the Conference on Empirical Methods in Natural Language Processing (EMNLP-2007)*, Prague, Czech Republic.

Peng, F. and A. McCallum (2004). Accurate information extraction from research papers using conditional random fields. In *Proceedings of the Annual Meeting of the North American Chapter of the Association for Computational Linguistics (HLT/NAACL 2004)*, Boston, MA.

Phillips, W. and E. Riloff (2007). Exploiting role-identifying nouns and expressions for information extraction. In *Proceedings of the 2007 International Conference on Recent Advances in Natural Language Processing (RANLP-07)*, Boroverts, Bulgaria, pp. 468–473.

Ravichandran, D. and E. Hovy (2002). Learning surface text patterns for a question answering system. In *Proceedings of the 40th Annual Meeting on Association for Computational Linguistics*, Philadelphia, PA.

Riloff, E. (1993). Automatically constructing a dictionary for information extraction tasks. In *Proceedings of the 11th National Conference on Artificial Intelligence*, Washington, DC.

Riloff, E. (1996a). An empirical study of automated dictionary construction for information extraction in three domains. *Artificial Intelligence 85*, 101–134.

Riloff, E. (1996b). Automatically generating extraction patterns from untagged text. In *Proceedings of the 13th National Conference on Artificial Intelligence*, Portland, OR pp. 1044–1049. The AAAI Press/MIT Press.

Riloff, E. and R. Jones (1999). Learning dictionaries for information extraction by multi-level bootstrapping. In *Proceedings of the 16th National Conference on Artificial Intelligence*, Orlando, FL.

Roth, D. and W. Yih (2001, August). Relational learning via propositional algorithms: An information extraction case study. In *Proceedings of the 17th International Joint Conference on Artificial Intelligence*, Seattle, WA, pp. 1257–1263.

Sang, E. F. T. K. and F. D. Meulder (2003). Introduction to the conll-2003 shared task: Language-independent named entity recognition. In *Proceedings of CoNLL-2003*, Edmonton, Canada, pp. 142–147.

Sekine, S. (2006). On-demand information extraction. In *Proceedings of Joint Conference of the International Committee on Computational Linguistics and the Association for Computational Linguistics (COLING/ACL-06)*, Edmonton, Canada.

Shinyama, Y. and S. Sekine (2006, June). Preemptive information extraction using unrestricted relation discovery. In *Proceedings of the Human Language Technology Conference of the North American Chapter of the Association for Computational Linguistics*, New York, pp. 304–311.

Soderland, S. (1999). Learning information extraction rules for semi-structured and free text. *Machine Learning*, 34, 233–272.

Soderland, S. and W. Lehnert (1994). Wrap-Up: A trainable discourse module for information extraction. *Journal of Artificial Intelligence Research 2*, 131–158.

Soderland, S., D. Fisher, J. Aseltine, and W. Lehnert (1995). CRYSTAL: Inducing a conceptual dictionary. In *Proceedings of the 14th International Joint Conference on Artificial Intelligence*, Montreal, Canada, pp. 1314–1319.

Soon, W., H. Ng, and D. Lim (2001). A machine learning approach to coreference of noun phrases. *Computational Linguistics 27*(4), 521–541.

Stevenson, M. and M. Greenwood (2005, June). A semantic approach to IE pattern induction. In *Proceedings of the 43rd Annual Meeting of the Association for Computational Linguistics*, Ann Arbor, MI, pp. 379–386.

Strassel, S., M. Przybocki, K. Peterson, Z. Song, and K. Maeda (2008). Linguistic resources and evaluation techniques for evaluation of cross-document automatic content extraction. In *Proceedings of the Sixth International Language Resources and Evaluation Conference (LREC-08)*, Marrakech, Morocco.

Subramaniam, L. V., S. Mukherjea, P. Kankar, B. Srivastava, V. S. Batra, P. V. Kamesam, and R. Kothari (2003). Information extraction from biomedical literature: Methodology, evaluation and an application. In *CIKM '03: Proceedings of the Twelfth International Conference on Information and Knowledge Management*, New Orleans, LA, pp. 410–417.

Sudo, K., S. Sekine, and R. Grishman (2003). An improved extraction pattern representation model for automatic IE pattern acquisition. In *Proceedings of the 41st Annual Meeting of the Association for Computational Linguistics (ACL-03)*, Edmonton, Canada.

Surdeanu, M., S. Harabagiu, J. Williams, and P. Aarseth (2003). Using predicate-argument structures for information extraction. In *Proceedings of the 41st Annual Meeting of the Association for Computational Linguistics*, Sapporo, Japan.

Thelen, M. and E. Riloff (2002). A bootstrapping method for learning semantic lexicons using extraction pattern contexts. In *Proceedings of the 2002 Conference on Empirical Methods in Natural Language Processing*, Philadelphia, PA, pp. 214–221.

Thompson, C. A., M. E. Califf, and R. J. Mooney (1999). Active learning for natural language parsing and information extraction. In *Proceedings of the Sixteenth International Conference on Machine Learning*, Bled, Slarnia.

Yakushiji, A., Y. Miyao, T. Ohta, J. Tateisi, and Y. Tsujii (2006). Automatic construction of predicate-argument structure patterns for biomedical information extraction. In *Proceedings of the 2006 Conference on Empirical Methods in Natural Language Processing*, Sydney, Australia.

Yang, X., J. Su, and C. L. Tan (2005). Improving pronoun resolution using statistics-based semantic compatibility information. In *Proceedings of the 43rd Annual Meeting of the Association for Computational Linguistics*, Ann Arbor, MI.

Yangarber, R. (2003). Counter-training in the discovery of semantic patterns. In *Proceedings of the 41st Annual Meeting of the Association for Computational Linguistics*, Sapporo, Japan.

Yangarber, R., R. Grishman, P. Tapanainen, and S. Huttunen (2000). Automatic acquisition of domain knowledge for information extraction. In *Proceedings of the Eighteenth International Conference on Computational Linguistics (COLING 2000)*, Saarbrucken, Germany.

Yu, K., G. Guan, and M. Zhou (2005, June). Resumé information extraction with cascaded hybrid model. In *Proceedings of the 43rd Annual Meeting of the Association for Computational Linguistics*, Ann Arbor, MI, pp. 499–506.

Zelenko, D., C. Aone, and A. Richardella (2003). Kernel methods for relation extraction. *Journal of Machine Learning Research 3*, 1083–1106.

Zhao, S. and R. Grishman (2005). Extracting relations with integrated information using kernel methods. In *Proceedings of the 43rd Annual Meeting of the Association for Computational Linguistics (ACL-05)*, Ann Arbor, MI, pp. 419–426.

22

Report Generation

Leo Wanner
*Institució Catalana de
Recerca i Estudis Avançats
and Universitat Pompeu
Fabra*

22.1 Introduction

The first sense of the term *report* in the *Longman Dictionary of Contemporary English* is "a written or spoken description of a situation or event, giving people the information they need." This is precisely what *report* has come to mean in NLP—with the restriction that it is, as a rule, written information.* *Report generation* (RG) thus stands for the automatic production of written material required by the users. Usually, this material is produced from structured data—numerical time series or a formal content representation; its length may range from one paragraph to several pages.

RG is a domain-specific application of Natural Language Generation (NLG). Since the early days of NLG, report generators have been developed for a number of different domains—among them labor market (Rösner, 1986; Iordanskaja et al., 1992), stock market (Kukich, 1983; Reiter and Dale, 2000), weather (Elhadad and Robin, 1996; Coch, 1998; Yao et al., 1998; Sripada et al., 2003), air quality (Busemann and Horacek, 1997; Wanner et al., 2007), patient histories (Bontcheva and Wilks, 2004), and team game commentaries (Robin, 1994). A number of report generators passed beyond the prototypical implementation; some of them reached an operational state; see, e.g., FoG (Goldberg et al., 1994),

---

* See for reference a definition of *report* in the context of NLP: "The most basic form of narration recounts events in their temporal order of occurrence. This occurs in a journal, record, account, or chronicle, collectively termed a report. Reports typically consist of the most important or salient events in some domain during one period of time (e.g., stock market report, weather report, news report, battle report). Sometimes reports focus on events and states involving one dimension of an agent as in a medical record, or a political record" (Maybury, 1990).

MultiMeteo (Coch, 1998), AutoText (Bohnet et al., 2001), and Narrative Engine (Harris, 2008). Nowadays, RG is commercially the most promising NLG application.

Each report generator can be characterized along the following eight dimensions which constitute the *leitmotif* of the chapter: (1) the domain covered by the generator, (2) the input data it takes, (3) language(s) it covers, (4) the kind of user model it uses (if at all), (5) the type of data preprocessing it does, (6) the text planning model it implements, (7) the linguistic model underlying it, and, (8) the linguistic realization (incl. sentence planning) tasks it carries out.

The structure of this chapter follows as much as possible the structure of Kittredge and Polguère's chapter in the first edition of the Handbook. However, given that since then the state of the art in RG advanced and new themes have come to the fore, it was necessary to restructure this chapter in order to reflect these advances. In particular, we felt that it is necessary to give more prominence to the individual tasks in RG—input and background data assessment and interpretation, user modeling, text planning, linguistic realization—and the evaluation of report generators. In Section 22.2, we discuss the features that make RG distinct from other NLG applications. Section 22.3 analyzes the types of data and knowledge resources that report generators tend to use as input and the preprocessing tasks that are carried out on the input prior to generation proper. Sections 22.4 and 22.5 discuss how the main NLG tasks, namely, text planning and sentence planning, are dealt with in RG. Section 22.6 presents a number of state-of-the-art report generators. In Section 22.7, the current evaluation techniques of report generators are briefly reviewed. Section 22.8, finally assesses the present and the future of RG.

22.2 What Makes Report Generation a Distinct Task?

With the advance of the state of the art in NLG, the horizon of RG widened as well. Thus, while some years ago, the objective single-view statement of fact was still an essential characteristic of RG (Kittredge and Polguère, 2000), in more recent applications, addressee-tailored reporting, which earlier used to be a feature of general discourse NLG, and even subjective reporting, is increasingly on demand. Let us discuss why it remains meaningful to make a clear distinction between RG and other applications of NLG.

22.2.1 What Makes a Text a Report?

If we cast the definition of *report* in the Longman dictionary into more formal and more precise terms (and restrict it to written material), we obtain the following three properties that can be assumed to underly any report generated by automatic means: (1) be informative, (2) imply the notion of relevance to the addressee in question, (3) target an event, a situation or, in general, a state of affairs that takes place in time.

A whole range of automatically generated material does not necessarily show some or all of these properties. Thus, automatically generated narrations (Kim et al., 2002; Cheong and Young, 2006; Szilas, 2007), poetry (Gervás, 2001), or humorous stories (Binsted and Ritchie, 1996) are not meant to inform the addressees, but rather to entertain them.

The notion of relevance implies a prior assessment of the input data with respect to the information needs of the addressee and, thus, indirectly, user-oriented content selection and, in some cases, also content summarization. Applications whose sole purpose is to render a given abstract representation into wording do not have this property, even if the produced information is judged useful to the addressee and is informative. Exclass (Caldwell and Korelsky, 1994), which generates job descriptions, and AlethGen (Coch, 1996), which generates replies to complaints of clients of a catalogue selling service, are examples of such applications.

Technical instructions (Rösner, 1994; Paris et al., 1995) and travel guides (Lu et al., 2000) are also informative. They may also involve user-tailored content selection and summarization: imagine the case where a tourist leaflet is tailored to an individual in his 50s interested in opera; obviously, this leaflet will not suppose to contain details on a night bar popular among teenagers. But they do not have the third of the properties of a report: they do not describe an event or a situation that is located on a temporal axis.

To these three properties, we may add a fourth property that is not definitial, but nonetheless characteristic of the majority of the reports, namely (4) describe a recurrent state of affairs. The recurrency criterion is of practical (rather than theoretical) nature: automatic RG becomes justified if the state of affairs in question occurs with a certain frequency.

As mentioned above, in the past, automatically generated reports were assigned a further property: reflection of an objective single-view statement. However, this property does not always apply. In the case of a gas turbine monitoring bulletin as produced, e.g., by SumTime-Turbine (Yu et al., 2007), indeed only one view is required: the view of the expert who has to judge whether there is a need for intervention or not. Similarly, in the case of the generation of weather forecasts for offshore oilrigs as done by SumTime-Mousam (Sripada et al., 2003), only the perspective of the workers stationed on the oilrigs is required. But in the case of air quality bulletins as produced by MARQUIS (Wanner et al., 2007), different views are clearly disirable: air quality information is relevant to joggers, individuals with weak health conditions, air quality experts, public administrations, etc.; each of them is interested in specific details that do not need to coincide with the details the others are interested in; nor is the presentation of the details in the bulletin the same for all of them.

22.2.2 Report as Text Genre

By its nature, any report draws on a state of affairs in a particular domain—be it stock market exchange, meteorology, air quality, soccer, or any other field. Each of these domains possesses its own language, in linguistics studied under the heading of *specialized discourse* (Gotti, 2003).* In NLP, specialized discourse is commonly referred to as *sublanguage* (Kittredge and Lehrberger, 1982).

The notion of sublanguage implies idiosyncrasy in layout, text structure, discourse structure, syntactic patterns, and vocabulary. Thus, **layout conventions** may require a header to be contrasted to the text body by particular typographical features (e.g., be in bold and/or in capitals), the use of a specific font for the main text, the placement of graphical illustrative material in a predefined place relatively to the text, predefined space between text paragraphs, etc. Thus, any weather or air quality bulletin contains a header with the date, time, the covered region, and time period. An additional label may specify the authoring agency.

Text structure conventions predetermine whether the text body is to be divided into several paragraphs and if yes which content is supposed to go into which paragraph and how the paragraphs are to be ordered. For instance, weather bulletins require a summary of the global atmospheric conditions that determine the weather to appear in the first paragraph, followed by the review of the weather in the recent past and the present, which is then followed by a forecast.

Discourse structure conventions predetermine the order of the messages within a paragraph and the discourse relations between the messages. For example, a soccer game commentary begins with the mention of the teams and the result of the game, of which then usually an elaboration is given.

Conventions on the syntactic patterns may require that several relative clauses and subordinate constructions be avoided in a single sentence (as, e.g., in the case of the generation of air quality bulletins); that no pronominalization be applied (as, e.g., in the case of invention summaries); etc.

Conventions on the vocabulary are the most prominent characteristics of specialized discourse. These conventions concern, on the one hand, the use of specific terms that are not common or have a different meaning in generalized discourse. For instance, *goal, corner, pass*, etc., have specific meanings in the soccer discourse; *drop, high, implied volatility*, etc., have specific meanings in the stock market discourse. On the other hand, they imply the use of domain-specific word combinatorics (or *collocations*) (Wanner, 1996), such as *cut [the] forecast* and *shares close [at]* in the stock market discourse, *shoot [a] goal* and

---

* The most prominent aspect of specialized discourse is *terminology*, which deals with the compilation, organization and use of specialized vocabulary (Cabré, 1998). In the context of RG, terminology is essential for the task of lexicalization; see below.

collect [*a*] *pass* in the soccer discourse, and *outbreak* [*of*] *rain* and *mist/fog thins* in the weather discourse. While in general NLG, the use of collocations can still be limited in order to avoid the problem of their codification and their motivated selection, in RG, collocations express "how it is being talked" in the domain in question. The problem of an adequate treatment of collocations is thus imminent.

The fact that RG deals with specialized discourse often has direct consequences for the architecture of the report generator and the approach to the individual tasks—especially if the discourse in question shows limited variation at the different stages of processing and thus does not require a strict modularization of the tasks or the use of a formal theoretical framework. However, we should be aware that for many domains the complexity of the linguistic style is higher than it appears at the first glance such that a thorough study of the requirements is advisable prior to making decisions concerning the architecture and processing strategies of the generator.

22.2.3 Characteristic Features of Report Generation

RG reveals the following characteristics, which are in accordance with the properties of a report and idiosyncrasies of specialized discourse discussed above:

(1) its input is composed of structured data: numerical data time series or an abstract content representation;
(2) it implies assessment and interpretation of the input data, which can involve summarization in accordance with some (possibly implicit) criteria of relevance;
(3) it takes the restrictions of the sublanguage of the field in question into account.

Report generators are typical "data-to-text" and "concept-to-text" applications. They take as input structured data (e.g., one or several numerical time series measured by external devices or an abstract content representation), which require, at least to a certain extent, assessment and interpretation. Guided by criteria of relevance to established norms or to the addressee, assessment and interpretation often involve summarization of the data/content.

Strictly speaking, data assessment and interpretation is not necessarily an RG task: it is needed for any content presentation mode—be it a text, a table, a curve, or a diagram. In AI, this task has often been attributed to *expert systems* (Giarratano and Riley, 2005). Therefore, in many advanced report generators, the data assessment and interpretation module is not considered part of the generator. However, some authors also argue for the inclusion of assessment and interpretation into the RG system architecture (Reiter, 2007).

While assessment converts data into content or makes inferences in a knowledge base, it does not include the selection of the content that is to be communicated in a report in order to satisfy the needs of the user. Content selection constitutes a separate task, which can be omitted if the content of the entire input structure is to be verbalized, as in the case of SEMTEX (Rösner, 1986), LFS (Iordanskaja et al., 1992), and FoG (Goldberg et al., 1994). In a few report generators, user profile or context criteria are taken into account to drive the selection; compare, for instance, MARQUIS and SumTime-Mousam. In TEMSIS (Busemann and Horacek, 1997), the user selects the content directly via an interactive interface.

From the discussion in Subsection 22.2.2 of the idiosyncrasies of sublanguages with which RG has to deal at all levels of the linguistic description, it is obvious that report generators need to take these idiosyncrasies into account in order to produce a naturally sounding text.

As far as the architecture of report generators is concerned, it is not different from the architecture common in general discourse NLG. Most often, this is a pipeline architecture (Reiter and Dale, 2000). The number of modules and the distribution of tasks among the modules varies (which is not different from general discourse NLG generators). However, as already indicated above, the nature of the tasks addressed by report generators is nearly always the same: (1) data assessment and interpretation, (2) content selection, (3) discourse planning, and (4) linguistic realization. In the following sections, we discuss what RG starts from and how the tasks (1) through (4) tend to be addressed in RG.

22.3 What Does Report Generation Start From?

RG uses a number of data and knowledge sources and implies certain preprocessing stages, notably some data preprocessing and data interpretation.

22.3.1 Data and Knowledge Sources

In general, RG draws upon three different data and knowledge sources: input data, background knowledge of the domain, and user models. However, not all generators use all three sources. Especially user models may be absent in simpler report generators.

22.3.1.1 Input Data

As pointed out above, the input to RG are structured data. The data format and the level of abstraction may be rather different. Thus, LFS (Iordanskaja et al., 1992), MARQUIS, TEMSIS, SumTime-Turbine (Yu et al., 2007), etc., take numerical time series; MIAKT (Bontcheva and Wilks, 2004) starts from a structure related to an ontology; PLANDOC (McKeown et al., 1995), BT-45 (Portet et al., 2009), etc., draw upon both numerical time series and ontologies. In contrast to general discourse NLG, RG hardly ever starts from linguistic, semantic, or syntactic structures.

Numerical time series are very common as input to report generators, which clearly lies in the nature of the task: numerical series monitored over time call for an interpretation, an assessment of relevance, and a summarized verbal presentation. Consider, for illustration, a sample of the input received by SumTime-Turbine in Figure 22.1. Analogous, although smaller, time series are used by FoG (Goldberg et al., 1994), MARQUIS and other time-series based generators.

The size of the series, i.e., the amount of data to be preprocessed by the assessment and interpretation module, may vary significantly. Thus, turbine monitoring series are much larger than, e.g., air pollutant series. However, the complexity of the assessment is not necessarily proportional to the size of the series. Thus, a major share of the assessment of any numerical series is a mathematical curve analysis in that it contains, e.g., (1) determination of the start and end values within the considered interval of the series, (2) detection of the significant relative and absolute minima and maxima; (3) identification of significant

Date	Time	TTXD-1	TTXD-2	TTXD-3	TTXD-4	TTXD-5	TTXD-6
27/11/1999	12:02:19	430.56	450.88	429.27	481.40	452.13	463.38
27/11/1999	12:02:20	430.98	451.15	429.27	481.68	451.99	463.93
27/11/1999	12:02:21	430.84	451.29	429.59	481.09	452.27	463.80
27/11/1999	12:02:22	431.12	451.15	429.27	481.40	452.27	464.21
27/11/1999	12:02:23	431.25	451.85	429.59	481.68	452.27	464.35
27/11/1999	12:02:24	431.53	452.40	429.00	481.40	451.85	464.07
27/11/1999	12:02:25	431.39	451.57	429.27	481.40	451.71	463.66
27/11/1999	12:02:26	431.25	451.57	429.41	481.26	451.99	463.52
27/11/1999	12:02:27	430.28	449.73	429.14	480.53	451.85	464.07
27/11/1999	12:02:28	430.00	449.59	429.73	480.81	452.54	464.07
27/11/1999	12:02:29	430.56	450.74	429.59	480.95	452.54	464.21
27/11/1999	12:02:30	430.56	450.74	429.41	481.68	452.40	463.80
27/11/1999	12:02:31	430.56	451.15	429.27	481.09	452.40	463.38
27/11/1999	12:02:32	431.25	451.85	429.41	481.82	452.27	463.52
27/11/1999	12:02:33	431.39	452.40	430.14	481.82	452.27	463.66
27/11/1999	12:02:34	431.25	452.13	430.28	481.82	452.82	464.80
27/11/1999	12:02:35	430.98	450.88	429.59	481.96	451.99	464.21
27/11/1999	12:02:36	430.28	450.15	429.00	481.82	452.13	463.38

FIGURE 22.1 Sample of the input as used by SumTime-Turbine. TTXD-*i* are temperatures (in °C) measured by the exhaust thermocouple *i*. (Reproduced from Yu, J. et al., *Nat. Lang. Eng.*, 13, 25, 2007.)

positive and negative gradients; (4) evaluation of the difference between the maxima/minima and the predefined thresholds within the considered interval, etc.

Conceptual structures instantiated from ontologies or inspired by ontology representation formalisms are other "natural" input structures in RG. Some report generators use ontologies, either already as initial input, as MIAKT or for intermediate structures, as BT-45.

22.3.1.2 Background Domain Knowledge

In addition to the dynamic input, most of the report generators draw upon some static background knowledge, which is either represented explicitly in terms of a knowlede base, lists or tables, or incorporated into the processing procedures. This knowledge may concern domain-specific content interpretation, static information to be included when certain contextual conditions are met and language conventions that are to be observed.

A typical example of static background information are legal notices in the air quality bulletins as produced by TEMSIS and MARQUIS: specific threshold pollutant concentrations are assigned legal notices, which must be included without modification into the report when these concentrations are reached. Refer to the following legal notice for the ozone threshold of 180 μg/m^3:

> Active children and adults, and people with respiratory disease, such as asthma, should avoid all outdoor exertion; everyone else, especially children, should limit prolonged or heavy exertion outdoors.

The language conventions concern all levels of RG; they can be domain-oriented or cultural. Thus, *domain communication knowledge* can be instrumental for the realization of the discourse structure (Rambow, 1990) and also influence the syntactic structures of the sentences in the report. However, most illustrative is the domain and culture dependency of the vocabulary. For instance, in the weather domain, the notion of 'hot' depends on the cultural perception (coined by the geographical location); in the air quality domain, the perception of air quality in general and of pollutant concentrations in particular varies from one region to another—which is even reflected in the environmental regulations of each country that associate air quality index scales with labels such as "good," "bad," "satisfactory," etc.

The interpretation and naming of the time intervals of a day is also cultural. For example, the Spanish *mañana* 'morning' extends more or less until 2:00 p.m. and the *tarde* 'afternoon' until 8:00 or 9:00 p.m. The German *Morgen* 'morning' can go until 12:00 p.m., and the *Nachmittag* 'afternoon' until 5:00 p.m. at the latest. The diverging interpretation is occasionally reflected by the vocabulary; for instance, in German, a special term for 'time before noon'—*Vormittag*—is available, while in English, French, etc., this is still *morning*.

22.3.1.3 User Models

Advanced RG is increasingly applied to domains that require a variation of the content and a language style in which this content is presented depending on the user model.

In general, a user model in NLG can be considered as being composed of the profile of the user and the history of generation. The profile captures the user's characteristic features that are relevant to generation; the history contains the information that has already been communicated to the user (either in the current or in the previous sessions). As a rule, report generators do not protocol the history. Therefore, we focus on the profile.

The profile of a user may have the following dimensions: (1) expertise, (2) need for specific information, (3) cultural background, and (4) interpersonal content bias, i.e., personal content interpretation preferences.

The expertise dimension is the most obvious and the oldest dimension in NLG; see, e.g., (Paris, 1993; Zukerman and Litman, 2001). The standard range is 'expert–intermediate–novice' or a more detailed variant thereof. In RG, instead of a clear range, other (domain-specific) typologies that are tailored to the different user types may be more appropriate. For instance, the MARQUIS user typology distinguishes in this respect between air quality experts, health professionals, public administrations, and average citizens.

The expertise dimension is, as a rule, used to guide content selection on the detail scale. Thus, a novice is contented with an overview while an expert requires details. On the other hand, an expert knows that between the concentration of ozone and the concentration of nitrogen dioxyde a reciproke correlation holds (and thus does not need an explicit mention of it), while an average citizen does not. The expertise dimension may also constrain lexicalization and influence the discourse structure. For instance, for an expert, the relation between the statement on the concentration of a pollutant and the statement that the air quality reached a health threatening level is appropriately realized as IMPLICATURE, while for an average citizen as ELABORATION.

The dimension that specifies the need for specific information is supposed to capture the distinct content aspects that are of relevance to different users. In MARQUIS, a jogger, an individual with weak heart conditions, and an individual with a respiratory disease will receive an air quality bulletin of the same degree of detail, but with deviating content. This is because ozone is especially critical to individuals with weak heart conditions (even if its concentration is only moderately elevated), fine dust particles (PM_{10}) are of particular relevance to patients with asthma, and a jogger must be made aware of high concentrations of ozone, carbon dioxyde, and PM_{10}. In SumTime-Mousam, the need for specific weather forecast information is correlated with the location of the oilrig on which the user is located.[*]

The dimension of cultural background may be rather important in report generators that address users from different cultural regions. For instance, in Spain, users are less sensitive to the topic of air quality than in Finland and users in Finland have a different perception of low temperatures than users in Spain. Such cultural idiosyncrasies must be considered in RG during content selection, discourse planning, and lexicalization.

The dimension of the interpersonal content bias is a dimension that can be dispensed with in "objective" reporting on, for instance, gas turbine monitoring, weather, stock market exchange, etc. However, it turned out to be essential for RG in domains that are *per se* subjective—as, e.g., game commentaries. Thus, experiments demonstrated that a soccer game commentary is judged by an addressee to be of higher quality if the content nuances and language are adapted to his personal preferences for a team—which confirms the work by Hovy in early non-report NLG (Hovy, 1988).

Traditionally, any user is assigned a predefined profile. However, when the diversity of information that can be communicated is rather high and/or the user profiles cannot be unambiguously assigned information preferences, the possibility of a personification of the profile by the users is important. For instance, in MARQUIS, a new user is first assigned a default profile, which can be personalized during the registration procedure.

22.3.2 Data Assessment and Interpretation

RG involves a data preprocessing stage that is ocassionally considered part of text planning (Kittredge and Polguère, 2000). However, as pointed out in Section 22.2.3, it is very different in nature from the other tasks related to text planning, and it could be even considered as being outside RG.

The first, basic, task in this stage that may be needed is the transformation of the input data format into a more convenient format or the relation of the input data to data already available to the generator. For instance, quantitative time series tables may be mapped onto equivalent XML-strucures (as, e.g., in AutoText (Bohnet et al., 2001) or MARQUIS). Strictly speaking, this task does not involve any assessment or interpretation.

The second task is the reinterpretation of the input data in terms of a different scale or with respect to a predefined reference date. For instance, in the weather domain, the numerical value of the speed of the wind in km/h may be mapped onto a qualitative scale ('light,' 'moderate,' 'strong,' . . .) or onto the

---

[*] SumTime-Mousam generated marine weather forecasts for offshore oilrigs, see also Section 22.6.

Beaufort scale—depending on the user. Similarly, in the air quality domain, the actual concentration of a pollutant substance (measured in μg/m^3) must be projected onto the corresponding index scale (ranging, for instance, from 1 to 6) and onto a qualitative scale ('low,' 'moderate,' ...). Furthermore, a given concentration, temperature, labor market figure, etc., is often compared to either a prominent figure detected in the past (as, e.g., the number of unemployed in SEMTEX (Rösner, 1986) and LFS (Iordanskaja et al., 1992)) or to a predefined reference (as, e.g., a legally fixed threshold concentration in TEMSIS and MARQUIS) and the result of the comparison is incorporated into the content.

The third task is the identification of patterns within the input data and the assignment of meaning to these patterns. Thus, ANA (Kukich, 1983) derives from a half-hourly price time series of a stock 'decrease' and 'increase' patterns. Similarly, in LFS the increase or decrease of the employment rate is determined via the evaluation of the numerical change between two consecutive months. MARQUIS's assessment module performs a mathematical curve analysis on the pollutant concentration time series in order to identify the decreases/increases and the gradients thereof, local maxima and minima, etc., and identifies semantic relations (such as 'cause,' 'part-of,' 'sequence,' etc.) between conceptual configurations—similar to BT-45, which also detects 'cause,' 'includes,' and 'associates' relations. In SumTime-Mousam, the input data are segmented in that linear intervals in the data are identified before the segmented data are mapped onto a conceptual representation. In the Streak generator (Robin, 1994; McKeown et al., 1995), no patterns are identified, but quantitative data are assigned conceptual *fact structures* that explicitly represent their meaning (e.g., that a given numeric score is a win or a loss).

The fourth task is the abstraction of patterns—as, e.g., in ANA, where from the elementary 'increase' and 'decrease' patterns of a number of stocks, such complex conceptual configurations as 'broadly based decline in the market' are derived. SumTime-Turbine contains several pattern abstraction algorithms along the temporal dimension.

The fifth task, which may be interrelated with the previous four, is the assessment of the relevance of the derived content to the users. In MARQUIS, the task consists in distilling all content that may be relevant to any of the users registered to the system. In BT-45, explicit importance ratings are assigned to the derived content.

22.4 Text Planning for Report Generation

Text planning in NLG traditionally involves content selection and discourse planning. This is not different in RG—although in the past, it has often been assumed that the report genre has a stereotype discourse structure, which is best captured in terms of text schemas (McKeown, 1985) that are rigid to a major extent and that reduce the task of text planning to the minimum. This is about to change.

Depending on the concrete report generator, both tasks are dealt with in separate (sub)modules or together in one single module; as a matter of fact, in most RG-systems, it is one module. The result of text planning is a *text plan*, which is usually already packaged sentence-wise, although its degree of detail depends on how elaborated the linguistic realization module is (see Section 22.5.1).

22.4.1 Content Selection

The task of content selection can be obsolete if the entire content structure obtained from the input data is communicated, as, e.g., in AutoText. However, in more advanced report generators, which deal with larger sets of input data or which serve several types of users, it assumes a prominent role.

Content selection is guided by content relevance criteria, which may be valid in general or be specific to the user, and by the personal preferences of the user. The content selection mechanisms usually operate on the output of the data assessment and interpretation task. If no such task is foreseen, they navigate directly on the content repository (e.g., ontology or knowledge base).

In BT-45 (Portet et al., 2009), the content selection algorithm selects from the content repository a number of "key events" that have received a sufficiently high relevance rating in the assessment stage. Along with a key event, events that are co-temporal with it or that are explicitly related to it by one of the predefined relations are selected. The algorithm is controlled by a set of parameters and a number of domain-specific rules that determine the relevance threshold for key events, the maximal number of messages that can be selected for communication, and so on. In MARQUIS, content selection is driven by domain criteria (such as, e.g., the relation of the measured or forecasted pollutant concentrations to legal or system-defined threshold concentrations, the values of the concentration increase or decrease gradients, the primacy of the individual pollutants in the given region, etc.) and by user preferences. MIAKT (Bontcheva and Wilks, 2004) starts from the description of the case of the patient encoded by a medical expert in RDF. In principle, the entire case description (enriched by concepts from a medical domain ontology) is to be verbalized, such that no content selection is involved. However, the case description may contain duplicated RDF-triples and pairs of inverse triples. The content selection task consists thus in removing repetitive and inverse triples.

22.4.2 Discourse Planning

The primary task of discourse planning in RG is *discourse structuring*, i.e., the determination of the order between the paragraphs as well as between the messages within the individual paragraphs. FoG, ANA, AutoText, and a number of other generators implement a rigid schema-oriented planning such that the order of the paragraphs in a report they produce and the order of the statements within each paragraph are predetermined. However, in applications where content selection is dynamic to a large extent, this strategy can be problematic. Therefore, in more recent report generators, more flexible structuring strategies are used. For instance, in BT-45, key events (see above) are always mentioned first. They are followed by events that are explicitly linked to the key event, which are in their turn followed by other co-temporal events. The messages on a key event with the messages on the events that are related to it form a paragraph in the report. The key event paragraphs are ordered by the start time of their respective key event. In LFS, statements are ordered according to their relative salience; a global salience assessment procedure ensures that statements on the most significant economic changes are moved to the beginning of the text plan. In MARQUIS, a mixture of schema-based planning at the paragraph level and top-down discourse structure based planning within the individual paragraphs is realized (Wanner et al., 2007)—which makes, as in TechDoc (Rösner and Stede, 1992), a prior (context- and user-tailored) identification of discourse relations that hold between statements necessary.

22.5 Linguistic Realization for Report Generation

The importance of the linguistic realization for RG is controversial. Thus, some report generators, such as TEMSIS, use templates, with gaps left open for words to be filled in. In SumTime-Mousam, SumTime-Turbine, and BT-45, linguistic realization plays a minor role; some attention is given only to lexicalization and aggregation. On the other side, we observe rather elaborate linguistic modules in Gossip (Iordanskaja et al., 1991), FoG (Goldberg et al., 1994), LFS (Iordanskaja et al., 1992), Project Reporter (Korelsky et al., 1993), PLANDOC, and MARQUIS. McDonald (McDonald, 1993) argues that realization is a relatively trivial task in generation. In reality, the importance and complexity of the linguistic realization decisively depends on a variety of criteria into which we cannot delve here. It suffices to cite (Reiter, 1995) that a thorough cost-benefit analysis is needed to decide upon the most adequate linguistic realization.

22.5.1 Input and Levels of Linguistic Representation

The nature and degree of concretization of the text plan that serves as input to the linguistic realization module depends on the linguistic framework that underlies a report generator. It can be more or less abstract. Consider in Figure 22.2 the input structure to Streak's (Robin, 1994; Elhadad and Robin, 1996) linguistic module that is based on *Systemic Functional Linguistics* (SFL) (Halliday and Matthiessen, 1999; Halliday and Matthiessen, 2004); PLANDOC, which is also based on SFL, deals with similar input structures.

The linguistic models of report generators that are based on the *Meaning-Text Theory*, MTT (Mel'čuk, 1988), among them Gossip, LFS, FoG, MultiMeteo, and MARQUIS, take as input either conceptual graphs in the sense of Sowa (Sowa, 2000) or semantic predicate-argument structures of the kind displayed in Figure 22.3.

Depending on the linguistic framework and the complexity of the linguistic phenomena of the domain, a message received as input to the linguistic realization module can undergo concretization in several stages. The number of stages (or levels of linguistic representation) varies. Thus, a number of generators (among them, e.g., TEMSIS and the SumTime generators) realize a direct projection of content structures to lexicalized syntactic structures. This does not exclude that the latter can be further modified, aggregated, or paraphrased—but the level of abstraction remains always the same. MTT distinguishes, apart from the semantic structure (SemS), a deep-syntactic (DSyntS), a surface-syntactic (SSyntS), a deep-morphological (DMorphS), and a surface-morphological structure (SMorphS). Often, a conceptual structure as an interface representation between content-oriented text plan codification and semantic message codification is added. Conceptual structures are language independent, while all the other structures are language-specific. But not all MTT-based generators use all of them. Thus, while MARQUIS uses indeed all, LFS unifies DMorphS and SMorphS, and FoG also skips SemS.

In order to facilitate the choice between semantically equivalent but syntactically and lexically deviating variants (see, e.g., *The high ozone concentration made the AQ index rise* vs. *The AQ index rose due to the high ozone concentration* in MARQUIS), some generators use the *information* (or, in the MTT terminology, *communicative*) structure. The information structure defines the distribution of information

```
(cat clause
 (process (type material) (effect-type creative) (lex "score") (tense past)
          (participants (agent (cat proper)
                               (head (cat person-name)
                                     (first-name (lex "Michael"))
                                     (last-name (lex "Jordan"))))
                        (created (cat np) (cardinal (value 36))
                                 (head (lex "point") (definite no)))))))
```

FIGURE 22.2 Lexicalized input structure to Streak. (From Elhadad, M. and Robin, J., An overview of SURGE: A reusable comprehensive syntactic realization component. Technical report, Ben Gurion University in the Negev, Beersheba, Israel, 1996. With permission.)

```
mean{sem = 'mean'
    1→index{sem = 'index'
            1→quality{sem = 'quality'
                      1→air{sem = 'air'}}
            2→6{sem = 'six'}}
    2→quality{sem = 'quality'
              1→air{sem = 'air'}
              2→poor{sem = 'poor'}}}
very{sem = 'very'
    1→poor}
```

FIGURE 22.3 Sample semantic structure for the message 'The air quality index is 6, which means that the air quality is very poor' produced by MARQUIS as input to the MTT-based linguistic module.

in a propositional structure in terms of oppositions such as Theme vs. Rheme, Given vs. New, etc. (Lambrecht, 1994; Mel'čuk, 2001). See (Iordanskaja et al., 1991) for the illustration of the use of the information structure in RG.

Current report generators that are not based on any formal linguistic framework tend to neglect the information structure, but keep track of the anaphoric structure that contains the co reference links between units in order to be able to generate appropriate referring expressions by pronominalizing, choosing the definite article, or a hyperonym.

22.5.2 Tasks of Linguistic Realization

In general discourse NLG, linguistic realization is often divided into the tasks of micro-(sentence) planning and surface realization. Microplanning deals with such tasks as sentence packaging, syntactic structure determination, aggregation, lexicalization, and referring expression generation. Surface realization is then a rather straightforward instantiation of the resulting structure of microplanning.

In RG, usually only a subset of the microplanning tasks is addressed. Most of sentence packaging is, as a rule, avoided in that each message is a priori considered a clause. Some generators use rule-based algorithms to merge either already available messages or clauses to obtain a more fluid text (as, e.g., BT-45). In Streak and PLANDOC, special attention is given to lexicalization.

22.5.2.1 Syntactic Structure Determination

A number of generators use syntactic structure templates on which the content structures are mapped directly—as, e.g., SumTime-Turbine. These templates can be rather abstract and formal (in the case of BT-45, in a HPSG-like format).

Most MTT-based generators (e.g., Gossip, LFS, MARQUIS) use the Theme/ Rheme distribution defined over the semantic (or conceptual) structures and the *dominant* or *entry* node of the latter to determine "deep-syntactic" structures. The dominant node, comparable to the key event in BT-45, becomes the root of the syntactic tree; a Theme/Rheme partition embedded into another Theme or Rheme partition becomes a subordinate or relative clause.

22.5.2.2 Aggregation

Aggregation, i.e., the fusion of partly overlapping structures with the purpose to avoid redundancies and achieve a more fluid text, can be carried out at different levels of a linguistic representation (as, e.g., in PLANDOC). Most often, however, it is done either prior to the linguistic realization proper at the message (content) level (as in BT-45) or during the transition between the semantic and syntactic levels (as in MARQUIS). However, it is important to be aware that aggregation can be semantic, syntactic, or lexical (Dalianis, 1999), and that for more complex RG, a differentiation might be needed.

22.5.2.3 Lexicalization

Lexicalization, i.e., the mapping of content or semantic units onto lexical units (LUs), is traditionally given a more prominent role in RG. This is, on the one hand, due to the prominent place of lexicalization in general discourse NLG, and, on the other hand, due to the idiosyncratic vocabulary of the sublanguages in report domains.

Four types of lexicalization need to be dealt with:

(1) Full LUs, i.e., content words that correspond to one or several units in a message that is to be lexicalized;

(2) Collocational units such as *heavy storm, dramatic loss, sharp rise,* etc., where the choice of one of the LUs is contingent on the other LU;

(3) Functional words whose introduction is controlled by either subcategorization or idiosyncratic lexical restrictions of an LU, as, e.g., *relevant to* (and not **relevant for*) and *at* [*a*] *a measuring station* (and not **in* [*a*] *measuring station*);

(4) Discourse markers that connect messages and make explicit temporal, causal, and other types of relations that hold between these messages.

The majority of the report generators focuses on the choice of full LUs. For instance, BT-45 maps messages onto case frame like representations with a verbal predication as the head and thematic roles as arguments. The lexicalization is straight-forwardly linked to the ontology. In SumTime-Mousam, the input to microplanning are tuples of the kind (0600, 8, 13, W, nil): time, wind speed lower range, wind speed higher range, wind direction, "modifier" (such as 'gust,' 'shower'); each element in the tuple has a number of lexicalized phrase templates associated with it. In MARQUIS, the *semantic dictionary* gives for each semanteme all its possible lexicalizations. For instance, the meaning 'cause' is mapped to the LUs CAUSE$_{[V]}$, CAUSE$_{[N]}$, RESULT$_{[V]}$, RESULT$_{[N]}$, DUE, BECAUSE, CONSEQUENCE, etc.

Most of the MTT generators use the advanced lexicalization instrument offered by the theory—the *lexical functions*, LFs (Mel'čuk, 1996). LFs are a formal means to encode idiosyncratic names and collocations in a generic way. In a functional notation, they are written as follows: Magn(*storm*) = *heavy*, Magn(*loss*) = *dramatic*, Oper$_1$(*concentration*) = *have*, IncepFunc$_2$(*concentration*) = *reach*, etc. The LFs of an LU may be referenced in the semantic dictionary for lexicalization (as in MARQUIS) or be chosen in a paraphrasing stage that follows the default lexicalization (as in LFS).

With a few exceptions, as, e.g., ANA (Kukich, 1983), other report generators that are not based on MTT do not deal with collocations. ANA encodes them in a *phrasal lexicon* (Becker, 1975). The problem of encoding phraseological information in a lexicon of this type is that it is hard to extend and maintain. That is, it might mean a rich variety of lexicalization in small domains (such as in stock market reports in the case of ANA), but can hardly sustain a large scale generator in an operational mode.

As the only report generator, Streak implements "reitified lexicalization": the revision of lexical choices based, for instance, on aggregation criteria. Thus, having planned on the first pass two separate sentence structures, which would result, e.g., in *Karl Malone scored 39 points* and *Karl Malone's 39 point performance is equal to his season high*, respectively, Streak would conflate them in order to obtain *Karl Malone tied his season high with 39 points*.

22.6 Sample Report Generators

As already pointed out in the Introduction, report generators have been built since the early days of NLG. An increasing number of them are built for operational use—even if by far not all are then put into service. The reasons for this "failure" are manifold (Reiter et al., 2003) and, unfortunately, it is beyond the scope of this chapter to go into details here. So, let us simply observe that in order to be accepted by the users, RG must, on the one hand, serve a clearly identified need, and, on the other hand, fulfill increasingly high quality standards.

In this section, we survey 10 report generators. These are generators that are either recent (and thus show the tendency in the field) or of which we believe that they influenced the research and the state of the art in RG. Seven of the ten generators come from two groups that are most active in the field of RG: Gossip, FoG, LFS, and Project Reporter stem from GoGenTex Inc., and SumTime-Mousam, SumTime-Turbine, and BT-45 from the Aberdeen Natural Language Generation Group. Note also that there is a certain overlap with the list of generators discussed in Kittredge and Polguère (2000), which shows that some earlier works already set the course in the field of RG.

Gossip Gossip (**G**enerating **O**perating **S**ystem **S**ummaries **i**n **P**rolog) (Iordanskaja and Polguère, 1988; Iordanskaja et al., 1991) provides computer operating system (OS) reports. The input to Gossip are OS

```
ee(martin, ttyp0, editor, [f1], 8:30:00,9:10:32,0:40:32,240)    The system was used
```
for 7 hours 32 minutes and 12 seconds. The users of the system ran compilers and
editors during this time. Compilers were run six times (the cpu-time equal to 46%
of the total cpu-time). Editors were run twelve times (the cpu-time equal to 53%
of the total cpu-time). Two users, Martin and Jessie, logged on to the system.
Martin used the system for 63% of the time in use. Jessie used the system for 40%
of the time in use.

FIGURE 22.4 Input and output of the Gossip system. (From Kittredge, R.I. and Polguère, A., The generation of reports from databases, in *Handbook of Natural Language Processing*, Dale, R., Moisl, H., and Somers, H. (eds.), Taylor & Francis, New York, 2000, 261–304.)

audit log records of the kind shown in the first line of Figure 22.4. Each input data record is composed of the parameter list of an elementary event 'ee': the user name (Martin), terminal ID (ttyp0), OS program execution command (editor), and its parameter list ([f1]), as well the time for the start, stop and duration of the execution of the program.

The input data record trails are processed by the *Text Structuring and Content Determination Module* (TSCDM) (Carcagno and Iordanskaja, 1992). The backbone of the TSCDM is the *Topic Tree* (TT)—a predefined hierarchical ordering of the potential topics in the domain of OS reports. For content selection, the TT is traversed and the individual topics are instantiated accessing the data trails (in the DB) and making inferences; if no information is available on the topic, the topic is dropped. The instantiated TT undergoes some further transformations before it is mapped onto *conceptual-communicative representations* (conceptual graphs a la Sowa (Sowa, 2000), enriched by the Theme/Rheme structure), which in their turn are mapped onto semantic representations (semantic structures enriched by Theme/Rheme structures) in the sense of the MTT. Semantic representations are then used as input to the linguistic realization module to generate reports of the type shown in Figure 22.4.

Gossip was one of the first report generators to use fully spelled out text planning and linguistic realization modules. In particular, it already uses the Theme/Rheme structure as a guidance criterion for choice at all levels of generation. It did not become operational—as its developers point out, due to the lack of a large enough user community.

FoG FoG (Forecast Generator) is one of the few operational report generators (Goldberg et al., 1994; Kittredge et al., 1986). It produces two types of bilingual (English and French) weather bulletins: *public* and *marine* forecasts. The input to FoG are meteorological data time series (such as wind direction and speed, precipitation (type) and temperature). The first processing stage of the input data is "space and time merging"—the segmentation of the individual data along the temporal and geographical axes (see also SumTime-Mousam below). For instance,[*] in the case of a continuous range of wind direction and wind speed in a specific time interval as in the case of (1100Z, 170, 4, 0, -22), (1200Z, 180, 5, 0, -21), (1300Z, 180, 4, 0, -21), where from 11:00 to 13:00 the wind direction is predicted to be between 170 and 180 (compass) degrees, with a wind speed between 4 and 5, the time merger would produce a tuple of the type: winds, (1 3 di s sp 4 5), where the first two elements of the tuple ('1' and '3') specify the time interval (in hours after the issue of the forecast), 'di' stands for "direction," 's' for "sourth," 'sp' for "speed," and the last two elements ('4' and '5') specify the wind speed. The merge of data for geographically continuous areas (space merging) is done in a similar way. The obtained tuples are passed to the text planner, which outputs a conceptual (language-independent) structure similar to the one produced in Gossip. The conceptual structure is then processed by the linguistic realization module, which is based on a simplified MTT-model. Refer to Figure 22.5 for a report produced by FoG for two merged areas, BELLE ISLE and NORTHEAST COAST.

---

[*] Data originally cited in (Kittredge and Polguère, 2000).

```
        BELLE ISLE

        NORTHEAST COAST.
        WINDS LIGHT INCREASING TO NORTHWEST 25 TO 30 KNOTS EARLY THIS
        AFTERNOON THEN DIMINISHING TO NORTHWEST 15 BY EVENING.
        WINDS DIMINISHING TO LIGHT WEDNESDAY AFTERNOON.
        SNOW BEGINNING EARLY THIS AFTERNOON THEN ENDING LATE THIS EVENING.
        VISIBILITY FAIR IN SNOW. MODERATE FREEZING SPRAY
        DEVELOPING NEAR DAWN THEN BECOMING SEVERE EARLY THIS EVENING.
        SEVERE FREEZING SPRAY ENDING WEDNESDAY MORNING
        TEMPERATURES MINUS 23 TO MINUS 19.
        OUTLOOK FOR THURSDAY ...LIGHT WINDS.
```

FIGURE 22.5 English report generated by FoG.

Based on the experience with FoG, GoGenTex developed the configurable toolkit MeteoCogent for the implementation, the customization, and the maintenance of weather forecast generators (Kittredge and Lavoie, 1998).

LFS LFS (Labor Force Statistics) (Iordanskaja et al., 1992) is one of the three bilingual (English, French) generators developed at CoGenTex in the early 1990s to produce summaries from Canadian economy statistics: LFS on labor force, RTS on retail trade, and CPIS on the consumer price index.

The input to LFS are employment statistics tables published monthly by Statistics Canada. The output are summaries on the labor market (of up to 3 pages in length) of the kind shown in Figure 22.6. The summaries may be accompanied by graphics.

LFS (as its two sister generators RTS and CPIS) comes with a graphical user interface that allows for the control of the data display, of the linguistic generation (such as length of the sentences), and of other output features.

LFS was successfully tested by analysts from Statistics Canada. However, for its practical use, the inclusion of additional types of statistical data had been requested.

PLANDOC PLANDOC has been developed for operational use at Bellcore by a team of Bellcore Research and Columbia University (McKeown et al., 1994, 1995). It generates summaries of the activities of telephone network planning engineers. As input, PLANDOC takes plan tracking information of the kind

```
COMMENTARY
Overview
Estimates for November 1989 from Statistics Canada's Labour Force Survey show that
the seasonally adjusted level of employment rose by 32000 and that the level of
unemployment increased by 30000. The unemployment rate increased by 0.2 to 7.6.

Employment
For the week ended November 3, 1989, the seasonally adjusted level of employment
was estimated at 12568000, up 32000 from October. The increase was concentrated
among women aged 25 and over. The employment/population ratio remained virtually
unchanged (62.1).

Employment among women aged 25 and over rose by 44000 and their
employment/population ratio increased by 0.5 to 52.3.
Employment among men aged 25 and over fell by 12000 and their
employment/population ratio decreased by 0.3 to 72.5.
...
Employment fell by 10000 in agriculture, by 12000 in transportation, communication
and other utilities and by 12000 in primary industries other than agriculture.
Employment rose by 68000 in servises and by 20000 in trade. It remained virtually
unchanged in the other sectors.

...
```

FIGURE 22.6 LFS output text fragment.

```
1. RUNID fiberall FIBER 6/19/93 act yes
2. FA 1301 2 1995
3. FA 1201 2 1995
4. FA 1401 2 1995
5. FA 1501 2 1995
6. ANF co 1103 2 1995 48
7. ANF 1201 1301 2 1995 24
8. ANF 1401 1501 2 1995 24
END. 856.0 670.2
RUN-ID: FIBERALL
```

This saved fiber refinement included all DLC changes in RUNID ALLDLC. RUNID FIBERALL demanded that PLAN activate fiber for CSAs 1201, 1301, 1401 and 1501 in 1995 Q2. It requested the placement of a 48-fiber cable from the CO to section 1103 and the placement of 24-fiber cables from section 1201 to section 1301 and from section 1401 to section 1501 in the second quarter of 1995. For this refinement, the resulting 20 year route PWE was $856.00K, a $64.11K savings over the BASE plan and the resulting 5 year IFC was $670.20K, a $60.55K savings over the BASE plan.

FIGURE 22.7 Input and output of PLANDOC. (From McKeown, K. et al., *Info. Process. Manage.*, 31, 703, 1995. With permission.)

displayed in the upper half of Figure 22.7 (originally cited in McKeown et al., 1995, p. 710). Lines 1–5 contain information on "fiber activation" (the site, the quarter of the year, and the year); lines 6–8 contain information on "cable placement" (cable starting site, cable ending site, the quarter, the year, and the number of fibers in the cable). The lower part of Figure 22.7 displays a sample PLANDOC summary.

As in ANA (Kukich, 1983), the input data in PLANDOC are passed to the *fact generator*, which maps them onto semantic feature structures (= facts) that do not contain any new information, but which are easier to handle by PLANDOC. The next module, the *ontologizer*, enriches each fact with further domain-specific knowledge. The enriched facts are then handed over to the discourse planner, which organizes the content and the overall structure of the summary. The text plan is processed by the lexicalizer and then by the surface generator SURGE (Elhadad and Robin, 1996).

Project Reporter Project Reporter is a commercial toolkit developed by CoGenTex for the generation of project management reports from standardized databases of commercial project management software such as, e.g., Microsoft Project. It runs as a plug-in to a Web server, integrating textual status summaries with tables and graphics. The summaries of the length of a few sentences each are supposed to highlight important information that is not easily conveyed by the graphics. Their generation is initiated by a mouse click on the item of interest (project, task, etc.) in the graphical display.

The linguistic model in Project Reporter is based on flexible sentence templates, called *Exemplars* (White and Caldwell, 1998). All more recent CoGenTex commercial generators use the Exemplars framework. The most recent of them is ARNS, which is now producing summaries of harbor conditions in 18 different U.S. ports, using real-time sensor data on tides, currents, winds, etc. The data are refreshed every 6 min; see Figure 22.8 for a sample output.

SumTime-Mousam SumTime-Mousam produces marine weather forecasts for offshore oilrigs from forecast data obtained from a numerical weather prediction model and edited by a human forecaster. In total, about 40 basic weather parameters are captured in a 3 h interval; the prediction extends over 72 h. The forecasters, i.e., domain experts, play an important role in that they intervene to tune the parameter settings of the system (see below), edit the input data (if needed twice, before the start of SumTime-Mousam and after an intermediate run), and post-edit the output of the generator to produce the final forecast.

Observations for Upper Chesapeake Bay 2009-04-19 13:39:07 EDT
```
Water levels are falling at Lewisetta, Reedy Point, and Solomons Island. Levels
are rising at Annapolis, Baltimore, and Washington-DC. Water level at Tolchester
Beach is 1.2 feet, with no trend data available.
Currents are flooding at Chesapeake Channel LBB '92' and Tolchester Front Range,
and slack at Cove Point LNG Pier and Potomac River Mid-channel Buoy B. Speeds are
between 0 and 0.6 knots.
Reported winds are generally from the east, between 2 and 15 knots with gusts to
18 knots.
Reported air temperatures range from the high 50s to the high 60s °F, and reported
water temperatures are in the low to mid 50s °F.
Barometric pressure is falling at Cape Henry, Chesapeake City, Cove Point LNG
Pier, Lewisetta, Rappahannock Lt. Front Range, Reedy Point, Solomons Island, and
Tolchester Beach. Pressure is rising at Baltimore and Francis Scott Key Bridge NE
Tower.

Air gap is 188.5 feet and increasing at Bay Bridge Air Gap, 143.3 feet and steady

at Chesapeake City Air Gap, and 140.3 feet and increasing at Reedy Point Air Gap.
```

FIGURE 22.8   Summaries generated by ARNS, a report generator based on the same technology as the Project Reporter.

```
2. FORECAST 6 - 24 GMT, Wed 12-Jun 2002
      WIND(KTS)
            10M: W 8-13 backing SW by mid afternoon and S 10-15 by midnight.
            50M: W 10-15 backing SW by mid afternoon and S 13-18 by midnight.
      WAVES(M)
            SIG HT:0.5-1.0 mainly SW swell.
            MAX HT: 1.0-1.5 mainly SW swell falling 1.0 or less mainly SSW swell
                    by afternoon, then rising 1.0-1.5 by midnight.
            PER(SEC)
                  WAVE PERIOD: Wind wave 2-4 mainly 6 second SW swell.
                  WINDWAVE PERIOD: 2-4.
                  SWELL PERIOD: 5-7.
      WEATHER: Mainly cloudy with light rain showers becoming overcast around
                    midnight.
      VIS(NM): Greater than 10.
      AIR TEMP(C): 8-10 rising 9-11 around midnight.
      CLOUD(OKTAS/FT): 4-6 ST/SC 400-600 lifting 6-8 ST/SC 700-900 around
                    midnight.
```

FIGURE 22.9   Report generated by SumTime-Mousam. (From Sripada, S., *Expert Update*, 6, 4, 2003.)

SumTime-Mousam tailors the forecasts to the preferences of the end users, or more precisely, to different contexts in which the end users can be situated (Williams et al., 2003). The preferences are controlled by forecasters and can thus be dynamically adjusted (also, for instance, with respect to the desired detail and style).

From the input data, SumTime-Mousam derives representations of the kind (0600, 8, 13, W, nil), (1500, 8, 13, SW, nil), (2400, 10, 15, S, nil)—with the first element of each tuple as time, the second and third as the forcasted wind range, the fourth as wind direction, and fifth as additional information of the type 'gust,' 'shower,' etc. Each tuple element is associated with a predefined phrase template that is instantiated with it. Figure 22.9 shows a sample report generated by SumTime-Mousam.

MIAKT   MIAKT (Medical Imaging and Advanced Knowledge Technologies) is one of the few report generators that generate information exclusively from an ontology (Bontcheva and Wilks, 2004). MIAKT generates medical reports of the type shown in Figure 22.10 from case descriptions written by attending physicians and a medical (background and history) ontology.

The case descriptions appear in RDF. First, the input RDF-statments are filtered to remove repetitions, which might occur due to inverse relations in the ontology or due to entailments of relations, and structured in accordance with a predefined recursive discourse schema. In the next stage, aggregation is

```
The 68 years old patient is involved in a triple assessment procedure. The triple
assessment procedure contains a mammography exam. The mammography exam is carried
out on the patient on 2 9 1995. The mammography exam produced a right CC image.
The right CC image contains an abnormality and the right CC image has a right
lateral side and a craniocaudal view. The abnormality has a mass, a probably
malignant assessment, a microlobulated margin, and a round shape.
```

FIGURE 22.10   Medical report as generated by MIAKT.

performed. Aggregation joins adjacent statements that have the same first element and the same property name, or if they are sub-properties of attribute or part-whole relations, as, e.g. (see also the consequences for verbalization in Figure 22.10):

```
ATTR(Abnormality: 01401_abnormality, Mass: 01401_mass)
ATTR(Abnormality: 01401_abnormality, Margin: inst_margin_microlob)
ATTR(Abnormality: 01401_abnormality, Shape: inst_shape_round)
ATTR(Abnormality: 01401_abnormality, Diagnose: inst_ass_prob_malig)
```

The structured and aggregated RDF-statements are transformed into conceptual graphs, which serve as input to the HYLITE+ linguistic realization module (Bontcheva, 1997).

MARQUIS: Generation of multilingual air quality reports   MARQUIS is another generator that is based on MTT (Wanner et al., 2007). MARQUIS produces user-tailored air quality information for five European regions in Catalan, English, Finnish, French, German, Polish, Portuguese, and Spanish. When appropriate, the reports contain tables and graphics to complement the text.

MARQUIS takes as input times series of the major air pollution substances delivered by regional air quality measurement networks. The size of the networks (and thus also the size of the time series) varies between 7 and 65 monitoring stations. The time series are interpreted by the Assessment and Interpretation Module (AIM), which identifies the global and local minima and maxima, the gradients of the changes of pollutant concentrations, the relation of the measured concentrations to predefined threshold concentrations, etc., and assesses the results of the analysis with respect to their relevance to any of the users captured in MARQUIS's user typology. The user typology in MARQUIS is rather detailed and can be further personalized by registered users (see Section 22.3.1.3).

The output of the AIM is an XML content structure, which is processed by the Document Planning Module (DPM). The DPM selects the content relevant to the addressee in question, chooses the mode of presentation for each chunk of content, and creates a text plan using a strategy that attempts to integrate the advantages of schema-based and dynamic planning. The text plan is mapped onto a conceptual graph structure, which serves as input to the linguistic realization module (Bohnet et al., 2007). Figure 22.11 shows an English report produced by MARQUIS.

```
The air quality index is 3, which means that the air quality is satisfactory.
This is due to the ozone concentration. The NO2 concentration and the PM10
concentration do not contribute to the index.
The current air quality index is the highest of the whole day. The lowest index
was 2 (at midnight). Between midnight and 9am, the air quality index remained
stable at 2, and between 10am and 3pm it remained stable at 3.
The ozone concentration (70µgr/m3) is relatively low. As a result, no
harmful effects to human health are expected. Between 4am and 10am, the ozone
concentration increased considerably from 22 to 76µgr/m3. The current ozone
concentration is close to the highest of 76µgr/m3.
```

FIGURE 22.11   English AQ report as produced by MARQUIS.

MARQUIS continues to be operational for the generation in Polish and in Finnish for the region of Silesia in Poland and for Finland, respectively.

SumTime-Turbine SumTime-Turbine is a prototype for the generation of summaries from gas turbine monitoring data time series (Yu et al., 2007). One of the distinctive features of SumTime-Turbine is certainly the size of the time series it has to handle: several hundreds of MB daily of data of the kind displayed in Figure 22.1. From such time series, SumTime-Turbine generates summaries illustrated in Figure 22.12.

Given the size of the time series, it is not surprising that the focus of the work in SumTime-Turbine has been on the assessment and interpretation of the data, which consists of three stages: (1) pattern recognition, (2) pattern abstraction, and (3) relevant pattern selection. Typical patterns (captured in an ontology) are spikes and oscillations. Aggregation is done at the level of patterns (rather than at the level of linguistic structures). The linguistic realization in SumTime-Turbine is template-based.

BT-45 BT-45 is the first prototype of the BabyTalk project, which targets the generation of textual summaries of neonatal clinical data time series for different purposes and different target users (Portet et al., 2009). Figure 22.13 shows a report generated by BT-45.

The purpose of BT-45 is to present information in a narrative form, highlighting aspects assessed to be salient. Compared to the two SumTime generators, BT-45 is considerably more advanced with respect to the assessment of data, document planning and linguistic realization. The assessment is divided into

```
[Background information]
Gas turbine: aylesford
Subsystem: exhaust temperature
Monitoring channels: TTXD-1, TTXD-2, TTXD-3, TTXD-4, TTXD-5 and TTXD-6
Turbine running state: part load
Time interval of these channels: from 12 to 15 on 27 Nov 99
[Overview information]
There were large erratic spikes in all channels at 12:59, 13:01, 13:41 and 14:40.
[Most significant patterns]
At 12:59, there were large erratic spikes in TTXD-1, TTXD-2, TTXD-3, TTXD-4,
TTXD-5 and TTXD-6. These patterns violated the pairs and follows check. In more
detail, there were dips with oscillatory recoveries in TTXD-3 and TTXD-4, followed
1s later by dips with oscillatory recoveries in TTXD-1, TTXD-2, TTXD-5, and
TTXD-6. This occurred between 12:59:17 and 12:59:54.
```

FIGURE 22.12 An example summary generated by SumTime-Turbine, from the data set displayed in Figure 22.1. (From Yu, J. *Nat. Lang. Eng.*, 13, 25, 2007.)

```
You saw the baby between 14:10 and 14:50. Heart Rate (HR) = 159. Core Temperature
(T1) = 37.7. Peripheral Temperature (T2) = 34.3. Transcutaneous Oxygen (TcPO2) =
5.8. Transcutaneous CO2 (TcPCO2) = 8.5. Oxygen Saturation (SaO2) = 89. Over
the next 30 minutes T1 gradually increased to 37.3. By 14:27 there had been 2
successive desaturations down to 56. As a result, Fraction of Inspired Oxygen
(FIO2) was set to 45%. Over the next 20 minutes T2 decreased to 32.9. A heel
prick was taken. Previously the spo2 sensor had been re-sited. At 14:31 FIO2 was
lowered to 25%. Previously TcPO2 had decreased to 8.4. Over the next 20 minutes HR
decreased to 153. By 14:40 there had been 2 successive desaturations down to 68.
Previously FIO2 had been raised to 32%. TcPO2 decreased to 5.0. T2 had suddenly
increased to 33.9. Previously the spo2 sensor had been re-sited. The temperature
sensor was re-sited.
```

FIGURE 22.13 A BT-45 text. (From Portet, F. et al., *Artif. Intell.*, 173, 789, 2009. With permission.)

two stages: (1) data analysis, pattern/event identification and computing of the importance of the events, and (2) data interpretation, which consists in detecting temporal, causal, and other relations between events. The DPM is responsible for the content selection (see Section 22.4.1 for BT-45's content selection strategy) and the construction of a discourse tree whose edges are annotated with rhetorical relations.

The messages in the discourse tree are mapped onto lexicalized event case frames. The relations between events detected during the data interpretation stage predetermine the syntactic structure of the sentences into which the interrelated case frames are casted.

The evaluation of BT-45 revealed some deficiences in data analysis and interpretation and, in particular, in discourse structure planning. As the authors point out, the main value of BT-45 is that it demonstrates that the generation of textual summaries from complex (clinical) data is possible.

22.7 Evaluation in Report Generation

Due to the ultimate purpose of any report generator—the operational use—the issue of evaluation becomes increasingly important in RG. To be evaluated is, on the one hand, the coverage of the relevant information communicated in reports produced by a generator, i.e., whether the information offered is relevant and whether relevant information has been ommitted, and, on the other hand, the (linguistic) quality of the presentation of the information. The most standard evaluation practice is the assessment of the produced summaries by domain and language experts with respect to criteria concerning usefulness and linguistic quality outlined in a questionnaire. Such a technique has been applied, e.g., in AutoText and MARQUIS. However, other, more purpose-oriented, evaluation techniques can also be applied. For instance, in SumTime-Mousam, the evaluation metrics has been the number of amendment edits of a professional weather forecaster (recall that SumTime-Mousam generates weather forecasts) in a SumTime-Mousam generated report. In the case of BT-45, the utility of the automatically generated reports for decision support making by medical personnel has been evaluated: the participants of the evaluation experiment were confronted with a number of different scenarios, written either by a human or generated by BT-45, and asked to choose the appropriate action from a number of offered options to respond to the situation described in the scenario. The choices made in connection with BT-45 summaries were compared with the reference choices and the choices made in connection with human written summaries.

A further evaluation technique is the use of metrics (such as BLEU) to compare the proximity of the automatically generated reports with human written reports from the same input data. However, in contrast to, e.g., Machine Translation, automatic metrics are not yet widely used in RG. This is likely to change. Recently, research of adequate evaluation methods in NLG became a prominent issue addressed in shared-task challenges and other events. Advances in this direction will without any doubt benefit RG.

22.8 Conclusions: The Present and the Future of RG

We discussed the tasks related to RG and presented a number of representative report generators. A look into Kittredge and Polguère's chapter in the first edition of the Handbook shows that within the last 8 years, the field of RG experienced some significant changes. First, the context of the work on RG shifted from thesis projects to multiple partner or commercial initiatives, with the participation of domain experts. This is a clear sign that the potential of RG has been recognized by the users. It is to expected that this trend will be further strengthened. Second, some tasks are about to receive a higher weight than it used to be in the past. This is especially the case for data assessment and interpretation and evaluation. In a sense, this is consistent with the first change since both tasks imply the participation of domain experts.

In a series of recent report generators, linguistic realization is given rather little attention, which automatically leads to limited fluency and variation of the generated summaries. However, disturbing repetition of both word choices and syntactic structures can be also observed in applications with more developed linguistic realization modules. We believe that this is a sign that RG needs more powerful sentence planning mechanisms than those that are used so far.

On the negative side of RG, it can be furthermore observed that currently RG is still dominated by English—although, for instance, AutoText generates German air quality summaries, the CoGenTex generators traditionally work with English and French, and some generators are multilingual (as, e.g., MultiMeteo, TEMSIS, and MARQUIS). In particular Asian report generators such as, for instance, (Yao et al., 1998) for weather report generation in Chinese, are still very rare. The situation will certainly change in the near future. Especially in Europe multilinguality is about to become a prominent issue, and with the society going multilingual, RG will need to react accordingly.

Acknowledgments

This chapter is a new version of Richard Kittredge and Alain Polguère's chapter in the first edition of the Handbook. (Kittredge and Polguère, 2000) was more than a blueprint; where possible, I followed its argumentation line and took over passages from it—which tremendously facilitated the writing. I would like to thank Robert Dale and Richard, who reviewed the first draft and provided many helpful comments and suggestions.

References

Becker, J.D. The phrasal Lexicon. In R.C. Schank and B.L. Nash-Webber, editors, *Theoretical Issues in Natural Language Processing* (TINLAP): *1*, pp. 70–73. Bolt, Cambridge, MA, 1975.

Binsted, K. and G. Ritchie. Speculations on story puns. In *Proceedings of the International Workshop on Computational Humour*, pp. 151–159, Enschede, NL, 1996.

Bohnet, B., F. Lareau, and L. Wanner. Automatic production of multilingual environmental information. In *Proceedings of the EnviroInfo Conference*, Warsaw, Poland, 2007.

Bohnet, B., L. Wanner, R. Ebel, B. Knoerzer, M. Tauber, W. Weiss and H. Scheu-Hachtel. Autotext-UIS: Automatische Produktion von Ozonkurzberichten im Umweltinformationssystem Baden-Württemberg. In *Proceedings of the Workshop Hypermedia und Umweltschutz*, Ulm, Germany, 2001.

Bontcheva, K. Generation of multilingual explanations from conceptual graphs. In *Recent Advances in Natural Language Processing*, pp. 365–376. Benjamins, Amsterdam, the Netherlands, 1997.

Bontcheva, K. and Y. Wilks. Automatic generation from ontologies: The MIAKT approach. In *Proceedings of the International Conference on Applications of Natural Language to Information Systems*, pp. 324–335, Salford, U.K., 2004.

Bouayad-Agha, N., L. Wanner, and D. Nicklaß. Discourse structuring of dynamic content. In *Proceedings of the Spanish Conference on Computational Linguistics (SEPLN)*, Zaragoza, Spain, 2006.

Busemann, S. and H. Horacek. Generating air-quality reports from environmental data. In *Proceedings of the DFKI Workshop on Natural Language Generation*, pp. 15–21, Saarbrücken, Germany, 1997.

Cabré, M.T. *Terminology. Theory, Methods and Applications*. Benjamins, Amsterdam, the Netherlands, 1998.

Caldwell, D. and T. Korelsky. Bilingual generation of job descriptions from quasiconceptual forms. In *Fourth Conference on Applied Natural Language Processing*, pp. 1–6, Stuttgart, Germany, 1994.

Carcagno, D. and I. Iordanskaja. Content determination and text structuring: Two interrelated processes. In H. Horacek and M. Zock, editors, *New Concepts in Natural Language Generation*, pp. 10–26. Pinter Publishers, London, U.K., 1992.

Cheong, Y.-G. and R.M. Young. A computational model of narrative generation for suspense. In *Proceedings of the AAAI 2006 Computational Aestetic Workshop*, Boston, MA, 2006.

Coch, C. Overview of ALETHGEN. In *Proceedings of the 8th International Workshop on Natural Language Generation*, Herstmonceux, Volume 2, pp. 25–28, Sussex, U.K., 1996.

Coch, J. Interactive generation and knowledge administration in MultiMeteo. In *Ninth International Workshop on Natural Language Generation*, pp. 300–303, Niagara-on-the-Lake, Canada, 1998.

Dalianis, H. Aggregation in natural language generation. *Computational Intelligence*, 15(4):384 – 414, 1999.

Elhadad, M. and J. Robin. An overview of SURGE: A reusable comprehensive syntactic realization component. Technical Report, Ben Gurion University in the Negev, Beersheba, Israel, 1996.

Gervás, P. Modeling literary style for semi-automatic generation of poetry. In *Proceedings of the 8th International Conference on User Modeling*, Sonthofen, Germany, 2001.

Giarratano, J. and G. Riley. *Expert Systems: Principles and Programming*. PWS Publishing Company, Boston, MA, 2005.

Goldberg, E., N. Driedger, and R. Kittredge. Using natural language processing to produce weather forecasts. *IEEE Expert*, 9:45–53, April 1994.

Gotti, M. *Specialized Discourse. Linguistic Features and Changing Conventions*. Peter Lang, Bern, Switzeland, 2003.

Halliday, M.A.K. and C.M.I.M. Matthiessen. *Construing Experience through Meaning: A Language-Based Approach to Cognition*. Continuum, London, U.K., 1999.

Halliday, M.A.K. and C.M.I.M. Matthiessen. *Introduction to Functional Grammar*. Oxford University Press, Oxford, U.K., 2004.

Harris, M.D. Building a large-scale commercial NLG system for an EMR. In *Proceedings of the International Natural Language Generation Conference*, pp. 157–160, Salt Fork, OH, 2008.

Hovy, E.H. *Generating Natural Language under Pragmatic Constraints*. Lawrence Erlbaum, Hillsdale, NJ, 1988.

Iordanskaja, L.N. and A. Polguère. Semantic processing for text generation. In *Proceedings of the International Computer Science Conference*, Hong Kong, 1988.

Iordanskaja, L.N., R. Kittredge, and A. Polguère. Lexical selection and paraphrase in a Meaning-Text generation model. In C.L. Paris, W.R. Swartout, and W.C. Mann, editors, *Natural Language Generation in Artificial Intelligence and Computational Linguistics*. Kluwer Academic Publishers, Dordrecht, the Netherlands, 1991.

Iordanskaja, L.N., M. Kim, R. Kittredge, B. Lavoie, and A. Polguère. Generation of extended bilingual statistical reports. In *COLING-92*, pp. 1019–1022, Nantes, France, 1992.

Kim, S., H. Alani, W. Hall, P. Lewis, D. Millard, N. Shadbolt, and M. Weal. Antequakt: Generating tailored biographies with automatically annotated fragments from the web. In *Proceedings of the Semantic Authoring, Annotation and Knowledge Markup Workshop at ECAI 2002*, Lyon, France, 2002.

Kittredge R. and J. Lehrberger, editors. *Sublanguage: Studies of Language in Restricted Semantic Domains*. de Gruyter, Berlin, Germany, 1982.

Kittredge, R. and B. Lavoie. MeteoCogent: A knowledge-based tool for generating weather forecast texts. In *Proceedings of the American Meteorological Society AI Conference (AMS-98)*, Phoenix, AZ, 1998.

Kittredge, R.I. and A. Polguère. The generation of reports from databases. In R. Dale, H. Moisl, and H. Somers, editors, *Handbook of Natural Language Processing*, pp. 261–304. Taylor & Francis, New York, 2000.

Kittredge, R., A. Polguère, and E. Goldberg. Synthesizing weather forecasts from formatted data. In *Proceedings of the Computational Linguistics Conference (COLING) '86*, pp. 563–565, Bonn, Germany, 1986.

Korelsky, T., D. McCullough, and O. Rambow. Knowledge requirements for the automatic generation of project management reports. In *Proceedings of the Eighth Knowledge-Based Software Engineering Conference*, Chicago, IL pp. 2–9. IEEE Computer Society Press, 1993.

Kukich, K. Knowledge-based report generation: A technique for automatically generating natural language reports from databases. In *Proceedings of the Sixth International ACM SIGIR Conference*, Washington D.C., 1983.

Lambrecht, K. *Information Structure and Sentence Form: Topic, Focus, and the Mental Representation of Discourse Referents*. Cambridge Studies in Linguistics 71. Cambridge University Press, Cambridge, U.K., 1994.

Lu, S., F. Paradis, C. Paris, S. Wan, R. Wilkinson, and M. Wu. Generating personal travel guides from discourse plans. In *Proceedings of the International Conference on Adaptive Hypermedia and Adaptive Web-based Systems*, Trento, Italy 2000.

Maybury, M. Using discourse focus, temporal focus, and spatial focus to generate multisentential text. In *Proceedings of the 5th International Workshop on Natural Language Generation*, pp. 70–78, Dawson, PA, 1990.

McDonald, D. Issues in the choice of a source for natural language generation. *Computational Linguistics*, 19:191–197, 1993.

McKeown, K. *Text Generation: Using Discourse Strategies and Focus Constraints to Generate Natural Language Text*. Cambridge University Press, Cambridge, U.K., 1985.

McKeown, K., K. Kukich, and J. Shaw. Practical issues in automatic documentation generation. In *Proceedings of the Fourth Conference on Applied Natural Language Processing*, pp. 7–14, Stuttgart, Germany, 1994.

McKeown, K., J. Robin, and K. Kukich. Generating concise natural language summaries. *Information Processing and Management*, 31:703–733, 1995.

Mel'čuk, I.A. *Dependency Syntax: Theory and Practice*. SUNY Press, Albany, NY, 1988.

Mel'čuk, I.A. Lexical Functions: A tool for the description of lexical relations in a lexicon. In L. Wanner, editor, *Lexical Functions in Lexicography and Natural Language Processing*, pages 37–102. Benjamins Academic Publishers, Amsterdam, the Netherlands, 1996.

Mel'čuk, I. A. *Communicative Organization in Natural Language (The Semantic-Communicative Structure of Sentences)*. Benjamins Academic Publishers, Amsterdam, the Netherlands, 2001.

Paris, C. *User Modelling in Text Generation*. Frances Pinter Publishers, London, U.K., 1993.

Paris, C., K. Vander Linden, M. Fischer, A. Hartley, L. Pemberton, R. Power, and D. Scott. A support tool for writing multilingual instructions. In *Proceedings of the Fourteenth International Joint Conference on Artificial Intelligence (IJCAI-95)*, Montreal, Canada, 1995.

Portet, F., E. Reiter, A. Gatt, J. Hunter, S. Sripada, Y. Freer, and C. Sykes. Automatic generation of textual summaries from neonatal intensive care data. *Artificial Intelligence*, 173(7–8):789–916, 2009.

Rambow, O. Domain communication knowledge. In *Proceedings of the 5th Natural Language Generation Workshop, June 1990*, pp. 87–94, Dawson, PA, 1990.

Reiter, E. NLG vs. Templates. In *Proceedings of the 5th European Workshop on Natural Language Generation*, pp. 95–104, Leiden, the Netherlands, 1995.

Reiter, E. An architecture for data-to-text systems. In *Proceedings of the 11th European Workshop on Natural Language Generation*, pp. 97–104, Schloss Dagstuhl, Germany, 2007.

Reiter, E. and R. Dale. *Building Natural Language Generation Systems*. Cambridge University Press, Cambridge, U.K., 2000.

Reiter, E., R. Robertson, and L. Osman. Lessons from a failure: Generating tailored smoking cessation letters. *Artificial Intelligence*, 144:41–58, 2003.

Robin, J. Revision-based generation of natural language summaries providing historical background. PhD thesis, Graduate School of Arts and Sciences, Columbia University, New York, 1994.

Rösner, D. Ein System zur Generierung von deutschen Texten aus semantischen Repräsentationen. PhD thesis, Institut für Informatik, Stuttgart University, Stuttgart, Germany, 1986.

Rösner, D. and M. Stede. Customizing RST for the automatic production of technical manuals. In R. Dale, E. Hovy, D. Rösner, and O. Stock, editors, *Aspects of Automated Natural Language Generation*. Springer Verlag, Berlin, Germany, 1992.

Rösner, D. and M. Stede. Generating multilingual documents from a knowledge base: The TechDoc project. In *Proceedings of COLING-94*, pp. 339–346, Kyoto, Japan, 1994.

Sowa, J. *Knowledge Representation*. Brooks Cole, Pacific Grove, CA, 2000.

Sripada, S., E. Reiter, and I. Davy. SumTime-Mousam: Configurable marine weather forecast generator. *Expert Update*, 6(3):4–10, 2003.

Szilas, N. A computational model of an intelligent narrator for interactive narratives. *Applied Artificial Intelligence*, 21(8):753–801, 2007.

Wanner, L. Lexical choice in text generation and machine translation. *Machine Translation*, 11(1–3):3-35, 1996.

Wanner, L., D. Nicklaß, B. Bohnet, N. Bouayad-Agha, J. Bronder, F. Ferreira, R. Friedrich, A. Karppinnen, F. Lareau, A. Lohmeyer, A. Panighi, S. Parisio, H. Scheu-Hachtel, and J. Serpa. From measurement data to environmental information: MARQUIS–A multimodal air quality information service for the general public. In A. Swayne and J. Hrebicek, editors, *Proceedings of the 6th International Symposium on Environmental Software Systems*, Prague, Czech Republic, 2007.

White, M. and T. Caldwell. EXEMPLARS: A practical, extensible framework for dynamic text generation. In *Proceedings of the Ninth International Natural Language Generation Workshop*, pp. 266–275, Niagara-on-the-Lake, Canada, 1998.

Williams, S., E. Reiter, and L. Osman. Experiments with discourse-level choices and readability. In *Proceedings of the 9th European Natural Language Generation Workshop at the 10th Conference of the EACL*, pp. 127–134, Budapest, Hungary, 2003.

Yao, T., D. Zhang, and Q. Wang. MLWFA: Multilingual weather forecasting system. In *Proceedings of the Ninth International Natural Language Generation Workshop*, pp. 296–299, Niagara-on-the-Lake, Canada, 1998.

Yu, J., E. Reiter, J. Hunter, and C. Mellish. Choosing the content of textual summaries of large time-series data sets. *Natural Language Engineering*, 13(1):25–49, 2007.

Zukerman, I. and D. Litman. Natural language processing and user modeling: Synergies and limitations. *User Modeling and User-Adapted Interaction*, 11:129–158, 2001.

23

Emerging Applications of Natural Language Generation in Information Visualization, Education, and Health Care

Barbara Di Eugenio
University of Illinois at Chicago

Nancy L. Green
University of North Carolina Greensboro

23.1 Introduction

In this chapter, we present applications of Natural Language Generation (NLG) that we believe are among the most novel and exciting of the last few years. In general, NLG endows a software application with the ability to present information to the user via natural language (NL). As for any task involving information presentation, two orthogonal dimensions need to be considered: the purpose for which the information is presented, and the way it is presented. To us, the most far reaching NLG applications of today try to help the user acquire information that is of high value to the individual, but also more in general, to society: hence, we focus on applications of NLG in education and health care. Across the world, and especially in the more industrialized countries, there is a keen interest in using technology to support both education and health care, and to assess whether and how technology can improve the outcomes of both. Technology is also seen as a tool to help level the playing field, addressing educational and health disparities in disadvantaged groups, and in a larger context, in poorer areas of the world. The type of system we will discuss has the potential to contribute to better learning and better health in actual users.

Clearly, whenever information is presented to a user, the question arises, regarding which modalities should be used to present that information. Whereas we focus on the generation of textual and verbal information in the education and health-care applications we will discuss, nowadays it is extremely rare that only language is used in an interface. While there are interactive systems that are purely textual, such as document search or document summarization, it has been shown over and over that different media have different affordances and can provide the user with different perspectives on the presented information, e.g., see (Oviatt 1999; Shneiderman and Plaisant 2004). Hence, we will describe what we call second-generation multimedia presentation systems, which generate text that summarizes information as a complement to visual displays. Some of these second-generation multimedia presentation systems are within the realm of education and health care themselves, although they may not affect user behavior directly (e.g., in Section 23.2, we present CLEF, that summarizes a patient's health history for the health-care provider). But even if they do not, it is easy to envision that this type of multimedia presentation will become more and more important in deploying systems that can effectively interact with users, where effectiveness is measured in concrete outcomes of learning and improved health.

The last point about effectiveness is not just made in the abstract. One common aspect across all the applications we will present is that they have been evaluated with users. In some cases the user studies are confined to paid subjects in the laboratory, while in others applications are evaluated with real users (e.g., in Section 23.4, we present STOP, which generates personalized letters to help people stop smoking). Evaluation with users distinguishes this type of research from much other research in NLP, where the evaluation is confined to testing the system on predefined test sets, very often considered standard by the community. Evaluating NLG systems with user studies owes much to Human Computer Interaction, which in turn owes this style of evaluation to the controlled experimental paradigm coming from cognitive psychology, or to the randomized clinical trial approach used in the health disciplines.

This chapter is organized as follows. We first discuss techniques used by second-generation multimedia presentation systems. Then, we turn to NL interfaces for Intelligent Tutoring Systems (ITSs), a specific type of educational application. Finally, we discuss the generation of argumentation addressed to the health-care consumer.

23.2 Multimedia Presentation Generation

Document planning, the first stage of generation in an idealized NLG pipeline architecture (Reiter and Dale 2000), includes content selection and document structuring tasks. Content selection (or content determination) is the selection of relevant information from a knowledge source. Interleaved with or following content selection, document structuring is the organization and ordering of the selected content.

In the 1980s and 1990s, the first generation of research on intelligent multimedia presentation generation focused mostly on document structuring, and specifically, on multimedia presentation planning, media allocation, generation of referring expressions, and media coordination. To summarize each of these issues, first, in research on multimedia presentation planning two contrasting approaches were explored: (1) use of presentation planning knowledge sources in which the structuring of content and its allocation to text or graphics is prespecified by system developers, and (2) generation of media-independent presentation plans whose parts can be realized as text or graphics. In the latter approach, a media allocation module is used to decide how best to allocate content in the presentation plan to a media-specific generator for realization. Another issue, the generation of referring expressions in a multimedia presentation must take into account not only the preceding text but also the visual context. Finally, spatial and temporal coordination issues include layout, sequencing of spoken language with the visual display, and the use of deictic gestures by embodied agents. First generation research published through the end of the 1990s is thoroughly surveyed in André (2000). Some of the application areas included the generation of written instructions and diagrams (Feiner and McKeown 1991; André et al. 1993), the generation of text and information graphics (Mittal et al. 1998; Fasciano and Lapalme 2000;

Green et al. 2004), and the generation of text and dynamic multimedia and animation (Dalal et al. 1996; Lester et al. 1999; Rickel and Johnson 1999).

Although document structuring in the context of multimedia presentations is still an important area of research, more recent research has focused on the content selection and the integration of text generation with information visualization, whereas standard NLG techniques tend to be used in subsequent stages of generation. Whereas most of the first generation systems performed content selection on output from another component of the same application (e.g., a planner), the second generation has used external data sources. A range of knowledge sources is represented in this work: numerical time-series data, medical records, images of bar charts published on the Web, and corpora of evaluative text. In fact, use of such knowledge sources has broadened the scope of content selection to include nonlinguistic techniques such as numerical data analysis. The goal of this research is to provide text that summarizes the knowledge source as an alternative or complement to visual displays. In the latter case, the text is generated as part of an information visualization architecture. Information visualization, from the field of human–computer interaction, addresses the presentation of information graphically to exploit human perceptual abilities and to facilitate data exploration. In the rest of this section, we survey this second generation multimedia presentation research.

The SumTime project has investigated the generation of textual summaries of numerical time-series data. Although the numerical data used in these systems could be displayed graphically, the researchers argue that generating textual summaries is advantageous to the intended audience. In both SumTime systems we will discuss (SumTime-Turbine and BT-45), data analysis techniques are employed to identify patterns in the data that are likely to be of interest to the user. SumTime-Turbine (Yu et al. 2007), generates short textual summaries of large (100 KB or more) datasets of turbine sensor data. In this case, the sheer volume of data makes a graphical display impractical for the user. Thus, the goal of that research was to summarize up to hundreds of KB of numerical data in a few sentences.

Figure 23.1 shows an example of a summary generated by SumTime-Turbine covering three hours of sensor readings at one-second intervals for six sensors. SumTime-Turbine was evaluated with two domain experts at both the component level and the system level. The authors summarize the evaluation results as follows (Yu et al. 2007, p. 47):

[Background information]

Gas turbine: aylesford
Subsystem: exhaust temperature
Monitoring channels: TTXD-1, TTXD-2, TTXD-3, TTXD-4, TTXD-5 and TTXD-6
Turbine running state: part load
Time interval of these channels: from 12 to 15 on 27 Nov 99

[Overview information]

There were large erratic spikes in all channels at 12:59, 13:01, 13:41 and 14:40.

[Most significant patterns]

At 12:59, there were large erratic spikes in TTXD-1, TTXD-2, TTXD-3, TTXD-4, TTXD-5 and TTXD-6. These patterns violated the pairs and follows check. In more detail, there were dips with oscillatory recoveries in TTXD-3 and TTXD-4, followed 1s later by dips with oscillatory recoveries in TTXD-1, TTXD-2, TTXD-5 and TTXD-6. This occurred between 12:59:17 and 12:59:54.

FIGURE 23.1   A summary generated by SumTime-Turbine. (Reproduced from Yu, J. et al., *Nat. Lang. Eng.*, 13, 25, 2006. With permission.)

they [the two domain experts] think SumTime-Turbine is doing a reasonable job, but they also think there is room for improvement.

Another SumTime system, BT-45 (Portet et al. 2008), generates textual summaries of 45 min of physiological signals and discrete events describing a patient in a neonatal intensive care unit. One motivation for developing BT-45 was a previous study that found that clinical decision-making was improved by the use of summaries written by human experts compared to graphical displays of the data ((Law et al. 2005), cited in (Portet et al. 2008)). In addition, BT-45 infers temporal and causal relationships between clinical events and the importance of the events to the audience. The BT-45 document planning component uses parameters such as importance thresholds and desired document length to perform an additional filtering of content. The bottom of Figure 23.2 shows a summary generated by BT-45 of the data displayed graphically at the top of Figure 23.2.

An evaluation of BT-45 involved 30 medical personnel (15 nurses and 15 doctors) having to take action in simulated scenarios, with the data presented via human-written summaries, or just the graphics, or the computer-written summaries. The subjects' actions were then judged by experts as appropriate,

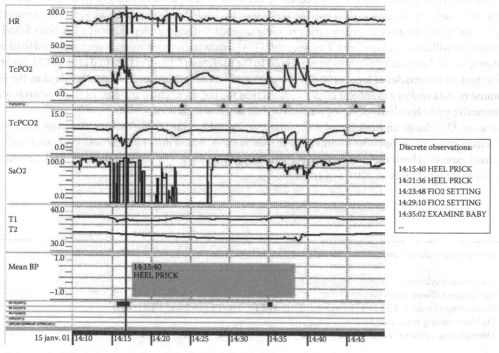

You saw the baby between 14:10 and 14:50. Heart Rate (HR) = 159. Core Temperature (T1) = 37.7. Peripheral Temperature (T2) = 34.3. Transcutaneous Oxygen (TcPO2) = 5.8. Transcutaneous CO2 (TcPCO2) = 8.5. Oxygen Saturation (SaO2) = 89.
Over the next 30 minutes T1 graduallly increased to 37.3.
By 14:27 there had been 2 successive desaturations down to 56. As a result, Fraction of Inspired Oxygen (FIO2) was set to 45%. Over the next 20 minutes T2 decreased to 32.9. A heel prick was taken. Previously the spo2 sensor had been re-sited.
At 14:31 FIO2 was lowered to 25%. Previously TcPO2 had decreased to 8.4. Over the next 20 minutes HR decreased to 153.
By 14:40 there had been 2 successive desaturations down to 68. Previously FIO2 had been raised to 32%. TcPO2 decreased to 5.0. T2 had suddenly
increased to 33.9. Previously the spo2 sensor had been re-sited. The temperature sensor was re-sited.

FIGURE 23.2 Bottom: Summary generated by BT-45 for the graphical data at the top. (Reprinted from Portet, F. et al., *Artif. Intell.*, 173, 791, 2009, Elsevier. With permission.)

inappropriate, or neutral. Subjects performed the best with human-written summaries, while performance with simple graphics or with computer-written summaries was not as good.

Bridging the first and second generations of intelligent multimedia presentation systems, AutoBrief generates presentations on transportation schedules in text and information graphics (Green et al. 2004). In addition to addressing first-generation issues in multimedia presentation planning and media allocation, AutoBrief exemplifies the second-generation theme of integrating text generation with an information visualization architecture. For example, after AutoBrief has generated a multimedia presentation, the user can drag elements of the generated information graphics (such as a bar in a bar chart) or highlighted elements in the generated text into a data visualization tool to explore the data underlying the selected element.

In the CLEF project, text generation is integrated with a visualization architecture used to enable clinicians to navigate cancer patients' medical histories (Hallett and Scott 2005; Hallett 2008). A medical history includes large amounts of numeric data from test results, chronological data such as the dates that tests were performed, and textual data such as reports. Information from each patient's medical history is aggregated into a semantic network, the chronical. A visual navigator displays events in the chronical along three parallel timelines showing diagnoses, treatments, and investigations. A user can zoom in and out to modify the graphical display, or request a report about a selected event on display. The generated text summarizes features of the event and its relationship to other events in the history. A key task of the document planner is to recognize important events in the chronical. As in BT-45, the selection of content from the chronical is constrained by parameters, in this case, the desired type and the length of the report to be generated. As far as we know, there are no published evaluation results for CLEF.

Another example of research integrating text generation with visualization, an interactive summarizer generates interactive multimedia summaries of large corpora of evaluative text such as product reviews (Carenini et al. 2006). As shown in Figure 23.3, the interface includes an interactive visualization of the data on the right, and a generated textual summary on the left. Users are expected to spend most of their time exploring the data via the visualization. The purpose of the textual summary is to orient the user before interacting with the visualization. Content selection tasks include determining features of an entity in the evaluative text, and then recognizing the strength and the polarity of the evaluation. Content selection creates a hierarchy of extracted features and aggregates the extracted information based upon the hierarchy, polarity and strength. After content selection, the summary is structured using a discourse strategy for evaluative summarization. Note that this work differs from other research on multi-document summarization; in that work, summaries are constructed directly from text extracted from documents rather than by NLG techniques. A formative evaluation study showed that users found the interface both intuitive and informative.

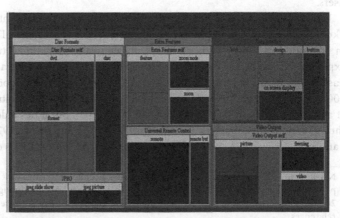

Summary of customer reviews for: Apex AD2600 progressive-scan DVD player

There was disagreement among the users about the Apex AD2600. Although some purchasers found the video output [1] to be very poor, customers had mixed opinions about the range of compatible disc formats [2,3]. Furthermore, there was disagreement among the users about the user interface [4,5]. However, users did agree on some things. Some purchasers thought the extra features [6] were poor, because some users found the supplied universal remote control [7] to be very poor.

FIGURE 23.3 Textual summaries to orient the user in information visualization.

The Caption Generation System, a first-generation research project, addressed generation of captions for information graphics automatically produced by an automated graphic design system (Mittal et al. 1998). Content selection included the analysis of aspects of a generated graphics design that might be difficult for a viewer to interpret. Greatly broadening the scope of content selection for caption generation, the SIGHT project (Elzer et al. 2006, 2007) has investigated the generation of text summarizing the main communicative goal of a bar chart appearing on the Web. The motivation for SIGHT is to provide an alternative means of access for visually impaired users. For example, if a user encounters a bar chart on a web page, he can invoke SIGHT, which would generate a summary such as *This bar chart titled 'The notebook spiral' shows that the dollar value of the average laptop prices fell from 2000 to 2003 and then falls more slowly until 2007* (Elzer et al. 2007). To produce such a summary, first, a visual extraction module creates a representation of a bar chart's visual elements (e.g., axes, bars, and labels). Given this input, SIGHT's content selection module uses Bayesian plan recognition to infer the main communicative goal of the bar chart. The evidence used for plan recognition includes the predicted relative effort for different perceptual tasks supported by the graphic, the relative salience of elements of the graphic, and the use of visual terminology in the graphic's accompanying text. Note that using perceptual task effort as evidence for the bar chart designer's communicative goal is motivated by an approach used in the multimedia presentation system mentioned above, AutoBrief (Green et al. 2004); there communicative goals in the document plan are mapped by the graphics generator to perceptual tasks that a graphic should facilitate in order to convey those goals. After SIGHT has inferred the main communicative goal of a bar chart, generation of the summary is template-based. However, corpus-derived heuristics are used to extract additional content from the accompanying text in order to generate adequate descriptions of the data displayed on the dependent axis of the bar chart (Demir et al. 2007). SIGHT was evaluated by two human evaluators, that judged the quality of summaries generated by SIGHT for 202 bar charts, randomly selected from 19 different newspapers and magazines. The texts generated by SIGHT were judged between good and very good, and significantly better than the texts generated by three competitive, and different, baselines (Demir et al. 2007).

23.3 Language Interfaces for Intelligent Tutoring Systems

Educational technology is an area of great significance for researchers interested in issues of human computer interaction in general and of conversational agents in particular, well beyond the purview of NLG. Educational applications that are supported by appropriate interactive user interfaces, are called Interactive Learning Environments (ILEs). For CL/NLP/HLT research, the question arises, what role language and language processing can play to support ILEs, and ultimately, to engender learning in their users.

Here we focus on one kind of ILEs, ITSs, software systems that provide individualized instruction, like human tutors do in one-on-one tutoring sessions.* Whereas ITSs have been shown to be effective in engendering learning, they still are not equivalent to human tutors. Hence, many researchers are exploring NL as the key to bridging the gap between human tutors and current ITSs. This area of inquiry has been flourishing in the last few years (Aleven et al. 2003a; Moore et al. 2004; Di Eugenio et al. 2005, 2008; Graesser et al. 2005; Zinn et al. 2005; Kumar et al. 2006; Litman and Forbes-Riley 2006; Litman et al. 2006; Pon-Barry et al. 2006; Fossati et al. 2008), but it has older roots: first, pioneering work from the 1970s and 1980s, such as (Carbonell 1970; Burton and Brown 1979); second, continuing research by a handful of researchers such as Martha Evens and colleagues (Evens et al. 1993; Evens and Michael 2006),

---

* Needless to say, the literature on ILEs is vast and we cannot do justice to it here. In particular, there are ILEs built as pedagogical agents (Lester et al. 1999), or ILEs that support learning through collaboration (Soller 2001; Kersey et al. 2009). Some of them do include language in their interfaces. Please refer to the Handbook Wiki for further discussion and references.

who did not abandon the enterprise like many others did, probably because of the brittleness of the NL components of the time.

Two crucial goals of this collective effort are (a) to ascertain whether an ITS that models *tutorial dialogue*, namely, one-on-one conversations between a human tutor and a student, does positively impact learning; and (b) to investigate which specific features of tutorial dialogues engender learning. The pursuit is both theoretical and practical. From a cognitive point of view, researchers in psychology, education, and computer science are investigating which features of dialogue are conducive to learning. From a practical point of view, full-fledged NL interaction with an ITS is not attainable yet. If only some specific features of human tutoring engender learning, then an ITS that only includes those would be easier to build, and more likely to be effective than an ITS that tries to address the full complexity of human dialogue. For example, several researchers have studied *prompts* (Chi et al. 1994; Pilkington 1999; Evens and Michael 2006; Cade et al. 2008). While definitions vary, a core component of a *prompt* is the tutor prodding the student along, either with a pump (a content-free question such as *And then?*), or a question proper (*How can TPR change?*), or a trailing statement (*If you divide 10 by 1, you get . . .*). If we discovered that, say, pumps but not contentful *questions* engender learning, obviously pumps would be much easier to implement. We note that fine-grained studies that compare the effectiveness of different features of tutoring dialogues have started to appear only in the very last few years (Litman and Forbes-Riley 2006; Lu et al. 2007; Ohlsson et al. 2007).

It is not by accident that we focused on moves on the part of the tutor, rather than on the part of the students, as examples of possible effective features of tutoring dialogues. Whereas language interaction with an ITS needs to address both components of a dialogue, the interpretation of the input from the student and providing feedback on the part of the ITS, much research has focused on the latter, perhaps because providing hints and feedback in the appropriate way is considered as a primary goal of ILEs (Aleven et al. 2003b); or perhaps because many studies of tutoring dialogues have shown that tutors do most of the talking, producing anywhere from 63% (Evens and Michael 2006), to 77% (Cade et al. 2008), to an astounding 93% of the total words (Fossati et al. 2008).

Before turning to the description of some representative systems and their interfaces, a few words on how these systems are evaluated. The most important thing to ascertain is whether they foster learning. Hence, they are often evaluated in terms of *learning gains*: did students who used the ITS show more learning that students in a competitive condition? *Learning gains* are most often a function of two scores obtained by the students on two tests: the pretest, a test taken before the treatment, and the posttest, a test taken after the treatment. The pre- and posttest are most often identical. To track persistence of learning, sometimes the posttest is (re)administered after a delay of days or weeks. The simplest version of learning gain is the difference between these two scores, sometimes normalized by the maximum possible gain. Finally, much research on educational technology talks about *effect size*: given a statistical difference between the various conditions, how much more effective is one condition with respect to the other? One common definition of effect size is Cohen's d, the difference between the two means of post- and pretest scores, divided by the standard deviation of either (Cohen 1988).*

As the reader will note after reading the rest of this section, evaluations of ITSs endowed with language interfaces provide a mixed picture. Specifically, it is still not clear whether ITSs that are able to engage in full-fledged dialogue interactions are more effective than ITSs endowed with simpler language interfaces, such as providing canned explanations to address students' misconceptions. However, these results are not necessarily disappointing from an NLG point of view. Even if it turns out that full-fledged dialogue interaction is not necessary, it is important to note that an interface that provides language feedback, even if not interactive, still appears to be the superior choice, as we hope to demonstrate by the end of this section.

---

* Cohen argued that the standard deviation of either group could be used when the variances of the two groups are homogeneous. Otherwise, a measure of *pooled standard deviation* can be employed.

23.3.1 CIRCSIM-Tutor

CIRCSIM-Tutor (http://www.cs.iit.edu/~circsim/) can be considered as the pioneer among the ITSs endowed with NL interfaces developed in the last 15–20 years. The book by Evens and Michael (2006) retraces its history and development. Since its inception, it was meant to help students learn about a specific kind of cardiovascular phenomenon, by simulating the interactions that two expert tutors in this domain had with their students in the physiology computer laboratory. The CIRCSIM-Tutor project has resulted in a wealth of data and analyses of that data, from tutor moves to students' answers. The CIRCSIM-Tutor project was also one of the first to use machine learning, specifically, decision tree learning, to uncover how human tutors make decisions. One part of the analysis that has been very influential on many other researchers engaged in modeling tutorial dialogues was the identification of *Directed Lines of Reasoning* (DRL). A DLR is a series of questions, prompts, and hints that tutors use to deliver information and to remedy misconceptions. Often it ends with the student uncovering a contradiction. The excerpt in Figure 23.4 shows this style of tutoring (it is taken from the data included on the CD accompanying the Evens and Michael (2006) book). These were keyboard–keyboard dialogues, and formatting and mistypings are from the original. The acronyms stand for: RAP, for Right Atrial Pressure; HR, for Heart rate; MAP, for Mean Arterial Pressure; TPR, for Total Pheriperal Resistance. The tutor's turns are labelled as K2-**tu**-16-1, and the student's, as K2-**st**-17-1.

DLRs are representative of an interactive and reactive tutoring style: the tutor is pursuing certain tutoring goals, decomposes them both according to tutoring strategies but also according to how the student reacts and takes part in the dialogue itself. This sort of interaction thus poses some requirements on the dialogue planner the ITS uses. The latest version of the CIRCSIM-TUTOR dialogue manager is built on top of APE (Freedman 1996). APE is a hierarchical task network planner, and as such it is particularly appropriate for hierarchically organized dialogues. APE supports single-turn and multi-turn teaching strategies. It uses simple template driven generation for realizing elementary plan steps. We will find APE used again below, in ATLAS-ANDES and WHY2-ATLAS.

Three versions of CIRCSIM-Tutor were evaluated, including the last Version 2.9. This version of CIRCSIM-TUTOR is able to understand the student's input via a parser that is composed by a cascade of finite state automata, which can also interpret "algebraic sentences" that mix English and mathematics. Subjects were medical students who were learning the material. The experiments show that CIRCSIM-Tutor did engender learning, and the learning effects were larger than simply reading text. However, no significant differences in learning were uncovered in an experiment that pitted CIRCSIM-TUTOR against

```
K2-tu-16-1: Is rap the first variable that would be affected by
            a suddenincrease in HR?
K2-st-17-1: No, I believe that map would first be affected
K2-tu-18-1: Could you write an equation that showed how HR and
            MAP wererelated?
K2-st-19-1: Map is not directly related to HR but is directly related
            to Co tpr
K2-tu-20-1: So then when HR goes up suddenly, what will be the
            next variableaffected and in what direction will it
            change?
K2-st-21-1: Tpr will increase
K2-tu-22-1: TPR is a neurally controlled variable.
K2-tu-22-2: We are in the DR period,before reflexes and neural
            firing rates change.
K2-tu-22-3: How can TPRchange?
K2-st-23-1: TPR can change by sympathetic action, therefore without
            this neuralresponse, the next variable to be affected
            would be the CO
K2-tu-24-1: Absolutely.
K2-tu-24-2: Now were on the right track.
```

FIGURE 23.4 An example of a Directed Line of Reasoning from the CIRCSIM dialogues.

CIRCSIM, a much simpler version of the system that does not include tutorial dialogue, but that provides feedback as authored mini-lessons (in the authors' words, *carefully edited relevant texts*).

23.3.2 AUTOTUTOR

AUTOTUTOR (http://www.autotutor.org/) is an ITS whose design is routed in a long tradition at the University of Memphis of studying learning by means of tutorial interactions (influential older papers by Graesser and collaborators include (Person et al. 1994; Graesser et al. 1995)). In its fuller incarnation, AutoTutor is embodied as an animated agent that engages in a conversation with the student, and interacts via spoken language, facial expressions, and gestures. The input from students is most often typed, not spoken. The AUTOTUTOR architecture has been applied to three domains, computer literacy, scientific reasoning, and qualitative Newtonian physics (for the latter, see below on WHY2-AUTOTUTOR) (Graesser et al. 2001, 2004, 2005).

AUTOTUTOR's dialogue management relies on curriculum scripts. AUTOTUTOR asks the student questions about certain topics, and conducts a dialogue until a good answer to that question has been obtained. Each script includes a main focal question, an ideal complete answer, expected good answers, and misconceptions. Latent Semantic Analysis (LSA) (Landauer and Dumais 1997; Foltz et al. 1999), an approach based on Singular Value Decomposition, is used to compare student contributions to expected answers, good and bad. A Dialog Advancer Network (DAN) manages the conversation. The DAN comprises a set of dialog paths linked to particular student speech act types, so that AutoTutor can adapt each dialog move to the preceding student turn and respond appropriately.

The DAN embeds different algorithms to choose the next move. One employs a set of 15 fuzzy production rules to select the next dialogue move for the tutoring system. Although these production rules have achieved good results for AUTOTUTOR, they are defined manually and only cover limited situations. Manual design of production rules (or of the plan operators in APE, for that matter) is resource- and time- consuming, hence, the field is moving toward more empirical approaches—for example, see the newly established area of Educational Data Mining (http://www.educationaldatamining.org/). Additionally, AUTOTUTOR's DAN does not allow for dialogue strategies that are multiturn or result in subdialogues.

23.3.3 ATLAS-ANDES, WHY2-ATLAS, and WHY2-AUTOTUTOR

The ANDES physics tutor from the University of Pittsburgh is an ITS designed to support students in learning Newtonian mechanics. ANDES presents students with quantitative problems to be solved within a graphical interface that tries to resemble a piece of paper as much as possible. Immediate feedback is presented via red or green highlighting, and hints are provided upon request. It has been used in classrooms at U.S. colleges (http://www.andestutor.org/).

In a first development toward adding language to ANDES, the group at the University of Pittsburgh developed ATLAS-ANDES. ANDES was endowed with a full dialogue planning approach, via the ATLAS dialogue manager, which in turn has the APE dialogue planner at its core, that we described above (Freedman 2000; VanLehn et al. 2000).

In a second more encompassing development, the ANDES research group moved to explore the following hypothesis: engaging students in *qualitative* physics problem solving, as opposed to quantitative, would engender more opportunities for tutoring them via natural dialogues, and as a consequence, would help them deepen their conceptual understanding. Two different ITSs emerged from this effort, WHY2-ATLAS and WHY2-AUTOTUTOR* (http://www.pitt.edu/~vanlehn/why2000.html). These two ITSs engage students in qualitative problems, such as *Suppose you are running at constant speed in a*

---

* The following description of the two ITSs is mainly adapted from VanLehn et al. (2007).

straight line. You throw a pumpkin straight up. Where will it land?. In response, students write an essay that is interpreted by the ITS; the ITS then engages the student in a dialogue to remedy misconceptions.

The two systems differ in the way the student essays are processed, and also somewhat in the purpose of the interaction: in WHY2-ATLAS, the ITS chooses one flaw from the ones the essay exhibited and engages the student in a dialogue to lead the student to correct it in writing in a dedicated subwindow, whereas WHY2-AUTOTUTOR directly uses hints and prompts to lead the student to correcting the flaw in the dialogue itself.

In WHY2-ATLAS, the system analyzes the flaw using a combination of knowledge-based and statistical techniques (Jordan et al. 2006). Interestingly, among those techniques is an abductive reasoner that analyzes the representation of the student's explanation for correctness and completeness. If the ITS finds that an essay has flaws, it picks one and discusses it with the student. The discussion is organized as a Knowledge Construction Dialogue (KCD), whose design, as the authors say, was strongly influenced by the Directed Line of Reasoning studied by Evens and colleagues. At the core of the dialogue manager we still find APE, described above; a compiler maps KCDs into plan operators, which are used by APE to combine KCDs into larger recursive automata, in this way supporting tutoring goals that develop over multiple turns of dialogue.

In WHY2-AUTOTUTOR, the general architecture is that of AUTOTUTOR, as described above (hence the name). Thus, the student essay is interpreted via LSA; and the ensuing dialogue is managed via the AUTOTUTOR dialogue manager. Additionally, the tutor is embodied as an animated conversational agent, and its turns are spoken via a text-to-speech synthesizer.

VanLehn et al. (2007) discusses an impressive battery of seven experiments where human tutoring and the two computer tutors are pitted against a variety of less interactive conditions: from reading from a textbook to reading canned text based on a general model of students' misconceptions, rather than on the specific misconceptions students show in their essays. The experiments were originally conceived as a way to verify the *Interaction Hypothesis*, i.e., that it is tutorial interaction that fosters learning in the tutee (Chi et al. 1989, 2001; Fox 1993). The expectation was that human tutors would be superior to computer tutors, which in turn would be superior to reading canned text and to reading a textbook. However, the results were mixed. In particular, interactive tutoring, whether by humans or by computers, was not the clear winner. Human and computer tutoring was better than reading from the textbook. As far as beating reading canned text, the hypothesis was verified only for novice students working with a human tutor when they were taught materials appropriate for intermediate students. From an NL interface point of view, it is interesting to note that no significant differences between WHY2-ATLAS and WHY2-AUTOTUTOR were found. It would be tempting to conclude that no matter what sort of interaction the system provides, students learn the same amount, and even more dramatically, that interaction is not crucial to learning. However, first, as VanLehn et al. (2007) mention, there may be alternative explanations, one of which—the lack of spoken interaction—is mentioned below, under ITSPOKE. Second, even if the interaction hypothesis were ultimately disproven, it is important to note that a language interface, even if not interactive, may still be the superior choice. In fact, the bar posed by the "canned text" condition was quite high: the texts the students read were carefully crafted, not just lifted out of a textbook, as in the experiment pitting CIRCSIM-Tutor against CIRCSIM we described earlier. NLG techniques could generate at least some of those texts on the fly, instead of humans preparing them in advance.

23.3.3.1 ITSPOKE

The research stemming from the original ANDES system spawned two more strands of inquiry that are worth mentioning. First, part of the reason why neither WHY2-ATLAS nor WHY2-AUTOTUTOR engendered as much learning as expected may be that the interaction between the ITS and the student is typed as opposed to spoken (in both, students type all their input, but in WHY2-AUTOTUTOR the output from the ITSs is spoken). There is evidence that using typed text may be detrimental. For example, Moreno (2006) shows that presenting text via speech in three different multimedia learning scenarios is more effective than presenting it in written form on the screen. Diane Litman and collaborators (http://www.cs.pitt.edu/~litman/itspoke.html) are precisely exploring this question: what are the consequences, if any, of adding spoken output to an ITS? ITSPOKE is a version of WHY2-ATLAS where the student still types the initial answer, and essay; however, the whole tutoring dialogue is spoken, by both the student and the ITS. Litman's research has resulted in a wealth of data and analyses of the differences between typed and spoken tutoring dialogues, with both human and software tutors. However, the jury is still out on whether speech is more effective than typed text in an ITS. Litman's results (Litman et al. 2006) are consistent with the initial hypothesis that tutored students learn more when the dialogue is spoken as opposed to typed. However, this holds only with human tutors. In fact, when ITSPOKE and WHY2-ATLAS were directly compared, there were no differences in learning. This could be due not so much to the different setting, but rather, to technological limitations. Students in ITSPOKE took significantly longer on average to complete their tasks, 97' with ITSPOKE but 68' with WHY2-ATLAS. The reverse holds with human tutors. The average length of spoken human–human dialogues was 166'; this length almost triples to 430' in typed human–human dialogues. The considerably longer dialogues with ITSPOKE are due to two factors. Extra utterances are generated by ITSPOKE due to speech recognition errors, as when ITSPOKE asks the student to repeat an utterance it did not understand. Additionally, students took longer to process ITSPOKE prompts, since they often first listened to them, and then read them: after the student and the tutor are finished speaking, the dialogue history window displays how ITSPOKE interpreted the student's input, and ITSPOKE's own turns.

23.3.3.2 TUTALK

Another offshoot of the ANDES research program is TuTalk (Jordan et al. 2001, 2007). In its authors' words, *TuTalk provides a dialogue system server and authoring tool that supports the rapid development of dialogue systems to be used in learning studies*. Its development was prompted by the realization that huge efforts are required to develop a dialogue manager for learning applications, and that researchers not versed in Computer Science would not be able to develop such a system at all. At the core of TuTalk are tools that support "Knowledge Construction Dialogues (KCDs)," inspired by the DLRs discussed under CIRCSIM-Tutor. In a KCD, the tutor tries to elicit a main line of reasoning from the student by a series of questions. The most basic dialogue that one can create with TuTalk corresponds to a finite state machine: each state contains a single tutor turn, and the arcs leaving the state correspond to all possible classifications of student turns. More complex dialogues can be created by nesting subdialogues; formally, TuTalk becomes a push-down automaton. The TuTalk dialogue manager is implemented using the reactive planner APE (Freedman 2000) that was discussed earlier, and decides what to express next and how to contextualize student responses. TuTalk also provides an authoring environment to author tutorial dialogues, meant for tutoring experts in the domain who are unlikely to be proficient at programming a dialogue manager. So far, TuTalk has been evaluated from the authoring point of view, but we are not aware of evaluation results for ITSs whose NL interfaces are built on top of TuTalk, other than (Kumar et al. 2006). However, various groups including (Kersey et al. 2009) are planning to conduct this sort of evaluation in the near future.

23.3.4 Briefly Noted

To conclude, we briefly note the work done by the following groups. We refer the reader to the Handbook Wiki for further information on all topics discussed in this section, and on the larger theme of marrying NLP and educational technology.

- Johanna Moore (University of Edinburgh) was one of the first investigators to explore the role of language in interfaces to ITSs, with a focus on the analysis and annotation of tutoring dialogues (Moser and Moore 1995, 1996), and on discourse planners that can deliver that feedback (Young et al. 1994; Moore et al. 1996; Zinn et al. 2002, 2005).

- Barbara Di Eugenio's group (University of Illinois at Chicago) has looked into how different features of feedback affect learning: from showing that providing more succinct and abstract feedback engenders more learning (Di Eugenio et al. 2005, 2008); to exploring the differences between expert and novice tutors (Di Eugenio et al. 2006; Lu et al. 2008); to modeling the role of positive and negative feedbacks in an ITS that tutors about linked lists, and that has started being evaluated in real classrooms (Ohlsson et al. 2007; Fossati et al. 2008).
- Much work on delivering explanations of mathematical proofs (Benzmüller et al. 2003; Fiedler and Tsovaltzi 2005) has been conducted at Saarland University in Saarbrücken, Germany.
- An interdisciplinary research group led by John Anderson and Ken Koedinger at Carnegie Mellon University has been extremely successful in developing a number of *Cognitive Tutors*, some of which have been adopted by hundreds if not thousands of schools (http://pact.cs.cmu.edu/). This group has explored many aspects of tutoring and learning, including the role of language (Heffernan and Koedinger 2002; Aleven et al. 2003a).

23.4 Argumentation for Health-Care Consumers

There has been a considerable amount of NLG research for health-care applications in general, as surveyed in Cawsey et al. (1997); Hüske-Kraus (2003); Bickmore and Giorgino (2006). The field includes research on the generation of argumentation addressed to the health-care consumer, which is the focus of this section. Argumentation is a social and verbal activity whose goal is to support or refute a position (van Eemeren et al. 1996). The scope of argumentation theory goes beyond the criteria of formal validity to acceptability in everyday discourse and in specialized fields such as law and science. Some argumentation theories consider contextual factors in the analysis of argumentative discourse, e.g., the analysis of an argument may include its implicit premises or assumptions. Some address the internal organization of arguments, the argumentation scheme that describes the relationship of a claim to its premises. Research on argument generation for health-care consumers can be characterized by its explicit or implicit basis in theories of argumentation (surveyed in (van Eemeren et al. 1996)) and/or theories from the social sciences (e.g., Prochaska and Clemente 1992). In most but not all of the work covered in this section the goal is to persuade the addressee to alter behavior in a way to promote good health, e.g., to adopt a healthy diet. The arguments may be expressed in written text or dialogue; dialogue may be delivered in text or spoken by an Embodied Conversational Agent (ECA). The main research focus in all of this work is on document planning (including content selection and document structuring) of arguments.

The STOP system (Reiter et al. 1999, 2003) generates personalized letters with the goal of encouraging the recipient to stop smoking. Using information acquired from a recipient's responses to a questionnaire, STOP classifies the recipient into one of seven categories of smoker. The recipient's classification is used to select from genre-specific document-planning schemas. The classification scheme is a refinement, suggested by domain experts, of the Stages of Change model used in health counseling (Prochaska and Clemente 1992). The schemas are also based upon knowledge acquired from domain experts. For example, a recipient who is classified as a Classic precontemplator, someone who is ambivalent about smoking but not currently planning to quit, would be given a letter emphasizing the disadvantages of smoking; whereas someone classified as Lacks confidence, i.e., someone who would like to stop smoking but doubts that he could, would be given a letter to increase his confidence. The effectiveness of letters generated by STOP was evaluated in a large-scale clinical trial to see if the recipients had quit smoking within six months of receiving the letter. However, the study found that recipients of letters generated by STOP were no more likely to quit than recipients of non-tailored letters. Reiter et al. (2003) speculates at length on why this may have been the case. Potential explanations range the gamut from the type of application (the important factor is to receive a letter from one's doctor encouraging a patient to stop smoking, as opposed to receiving a *tailored* letter); to tailoring being based on too little information, or being done incorrectly; to tailoring having an effect on heavy smokers, but the clinical trial being too small to provide statistically significant evidence of this.

Daphne (Grasso et al. 2000) is designed to engage in persuasive dialogue with a user to promote healthy nutrition. The design of Daphne's user model is based upon two complementary approaches from the field of health promotion. A user is characterized by his progress through the stages of the Stages of Change model. In addition, the Health Belief model (Becker 1974) is used to characterize the kinds of beliefs that impede behavior change. Daphne's dialogue generator employs a hierarchical planning process. The top-level goals are planned using operators that embody knowledge from the Stages of Change and Health Belief models. The next level of planning uses plan operators that embody argumentation schemas from the New Rhetoric (Perelman and Olbrechts-Tyteca 1969), a theory of informal argumentation that describes how people attempt to persuade an audience by use of premises that reflect the audience's preferences and values. Although the schemas of the New Rhetoric are not domain-specific, a study confirmed that the argumentative style used by actual nutritionists can be analyzed in terms of New Rhetoric schemas. To illustrate, Argumentation by dissociation makes a distinction that the audience may not have considered, such as *You said that people who are concerned about diet are self-centred but I prefer to consider them just responsible persons* (p. 1082). A schema in the category named Argumentation establishing the structure of reality uses an appeal to a model to promote an action, e.g., *Healthy people have fruit for breakfast* (p. 1082). In an evaluation of Daphne, 46 participants engaged in e-mail "dialogue" with Daphne. (Daphne's responses were translated into English by an experimenter.) Over half of the participants said that the system made them more conscious of their diet and led them to contemplate changing their diet (since there was only one experimental condition, it is not possible to ascertain the significance of these results).

A prototype ECA for nutrition counseling has been developed by de Rosis et al. (2006). As in Daphne, the system uses the Stages of Change model in dialogue planning. Represented with a dynamic Bayesian network (Nicholson and Brady 1994), the system's user model is updated after each dialogue move to infer the user's probable current Stage of Change and attitude toward the ECA. A related group of researchers (Mazzotta et al. 2007) developed Portia, the persuasion module for a dialogue system that has been implemented in the same domain. Again using Bayesian networks, Portia's user model infers the recipient's probable attitudes, values, and goals from knowledge of his personality traits and living habits. A Bayesian network is also used to represent rational and emotional argumentation strategies based upon schemes informally described by an argumentation theorist (Walton 1996), e.g., Appeal to Expert Opinion and Argument from Positive Consequences. When planning an argument, the inferred user attributes are used to predict the persuasiveness of different argumentation strategies, rational or emotional, that could be used. Portia may combine subarguments to increase the predicted persuasiveness. The arguments are translated into text or spoken dialogue by using canned text. For example, Portia can generate the following argument: *I'm surprised at you, John! You play sports and look after yourself with regular medical checkups, then you eat a lot of meat and carbohydrates, almost excluding vegetables from your diet! Perhaps you don't know the benefits that a diet rich in vegetables can have on your health. A dinner of fresh, tasty salads is easy to prepare and is an excellent way of having a good time with your friends* (Mazzotta et al. 2007, p. 48). Portia's design was partly based on the results of a formative experiment with 39 subjects; however, at the time of this writing, there are no published results on evaluating Portia itself with users.

The FitTrack system was developed to investigate the ability of an ECA exercise advisor to promote physical activity (Bickmore and Picard 2005; Bickmore et al. 2005a, 2005b). In contrast to the above research incorporating strategies from argumentation theories, the design of FitTrack was motivated by counseling theories and uses linguistic strategies for maintaining long-term social-emotional relationships with users, e.g., expressing empathy, use of social dialogue, self-disclosure, and talking about the relationship. In addition, FitTrack maintains a memory of the user's past interactions with the system to be referenced in future interactions. Dialogue management is controlled by an Augmented Transition Network (ATN). Generation of the ECA's utterances is template-based. In a later version of the system, to provide variability in dialogue, two simple approaches are followed. At each state of the dialogue, multiple utterances are provided and one is randomly selected. In addition, information stored from past dialogues with the user is used to select branches in the ATN and to fill in utterance template slots. One study compared the effectiveness of two versions of FitTrack. One version employed the linguistic strategies for maintaining long-term social–emotional relationships with users, as discussed above; the second version did not. Subjects interacted with the system almost daily for 30 days. The group interacting with the relational version showed a significant increase in a desire to continue using the system. Another study (Bickmore et al. 2005a) compared, over a 2 month period, subjects who used FitTrack to a control group who were given educational pamphlets. The intervention group performed significantly more walking during the experiment than the control group.

GenIE Assistant generates the first draft of genetic counseling letters, which typically contain arguments, e.g., justifying the diagnosis of a genetic condition (Green et al. 2009). Rather than generate arguments to persuade a recipient to change his behavior, the goal of this research is to generate normative arguments transparently so that the recipient can evaluate or challenge an argument or reevaluate it in light of new evidence. Transparency requires an argument's structure and components to be available to its audience. Arguments in a corpus of genetic counseling letters were analyzed in terms of their argument-theoretic components: data, claim, and warrant (Toulmin 1998). In addition, the domain content of the letters was analyzed in terms of a simplified quasi-causal conceptual model of genetics (Green 2005) that can be modeled in a Qualitative Probabilistic Network (QPN) formalism (Druzdzel and Henrion 1993). From the two analyses of the corpus, abstract non-domain-specific argumentation schemes, such as Effect to Cause, were described in terms of variables and formal properties of QPNs. For generation, GenIE Assistant uses the schemes to extract content from a QPN describing the genetic conditions to be covered in a letter. After an argument has been added to the discourse plan representing other parts of the letter (generated by a discourse grammar), the plan undergoes aggregation, pruning, and addition of discourse cues to promote argument transparency. The resulting plan is transformed to text by a linguistic realization component. The generated text is two to four paragraphs in length, depending upon the type of medical case. In an evaluation of letters generated by GenIE Assistant, domain experts found the writing quality of those letters to be about as good as that of letters on the same topic written by a genetic counselor, i.e., both the human-written and computer-generated letters received about the same amount of editing by the judges.

Acknowledgments

The authors are grateful to Nitin Indurkhya for all manners of encouragement and for helpful suggestions on the content and format of the chapter; to Giuseppe Carenini for his thoughtful review, and for providing us with Figure 23.3; and to Pamela Jordan for her help on the section on NLG for ITSs. Barbara Di Eugenio gratefully acknowledges the National Science Foundation (award ALT-0536968) and the Office of Naval Research (award N000140010640) for partial financial support. Nancy Green gratefully acknowledges the support of the National Science Foundation (award CAREER 0132821) during the period that this material was written.

References

Aleven, V., K. R. Koedinger, and O. Popescu (2003a, June). A tutorial dialog system to support self-explanation: Evaluation and open questions. In H. U. Hoppe, F. Verdejo, and J. Kay (Eds.), *AIED 03, Proceedings of the 11th International Conference on Artificial Intelligence in Education*, Biarritz, France, pp. 39–46. IOS Press.
Aleven, V., E. Stahl, S. Schworm, F. Fischer, and R. Wallace (2003b, Fall). Help seeking and help design in interactive learning environments. *Review of Educational Research 73*(3), 277–320.

André, E. (2000). The generation of multimedia presentations. In R. Dale, H. Moisl, and H. Somers (Eds.), *Handbook of Natural Language Processing* (1st ed.). Chapter 12, pp. 305–328. New York: Marcel Dekker, Inc.

André, E., W. Finkler, W. Graf, T. Rist, A. Schauder, and W. Wahlster (1993). WIP: The automatic synthesis of multimodal presentations. In M. T. Maybury (Ed.), *Intelligent Multimedia Interfaces*, pp. 75–93. Cambridge, MA: The MIT Press.

Becker, H. (1974). *The Health Belief Model and Personal Health Behavior.* Thorofare, NJ: C.B. Slack.

Benzmüller, C., A. Fiedler, M. Gabsdil, H. Horacek, I. Kruijff-Korbayová, D. Tsovaltzi, B. Q. Vo, and M. Wolska (2003). Discourse phenomena in tutorial dialogs on mathematical proofs. In I. Kruijff-Korbayová and C. Kosny (Eds.), *Proceedings of DiaBruck'03, the Seventh Workshop on the Semantics and Pragmatics of Language*, Wallerfangen, Germany, pp. 165–166.

Bickmore, T. and T. Giorgino (2006). Health dialog systems for patients and consumers. *Journal of Biomedical Informatics* 39(5), 556–571.

Bickmore, T. and R. Picard (2005). Establishing and maintaining long-term human–computer relationships. *ACM Transactions on Computer - Human Interaction* 12(2), 293–327.

Bickmore, T., L. Caruso, K. Clough-Gorr, and T. Hereen (2005a). 'It's just like you talk to a friend'— Relational agents for older adults. *Interacting with Computers* 17(6), 711–735.

Bickmore, T., A. Gruber, and R. Picard (2005b). Establishing the computer-patient working alliance in automated health behavior change interventions. *Patient Education and Counseling* 59(1), 21–30.

Burton, R. R. and J. S. Brown (1979). Toward a natural language capability for computer-assisted instruction. In H. O'Neill (Ed.), *Procedures for Instructional Systems Development*, pp. 272–313. New York: Academic Press.

Cade, W. L., J. L. Copeland, N. K. Person, and S. K. D'Mello (2008). Dialogue modes in expert tutoring. In *Intelligent Tutoring Systems, Lecture Notes in Computer Science* 5091:470–479. Berlin/Heidelberg: Springer.

Carbonell, J. (1970). AI in CAI: An artificial intelligence approach to computer-aided instruction. *IEEE Transactions on Man-Machine Systems* 11, 190–202.

Carenini, G., R. Ng, and A. Pauls (2006). Interactive multimedia summaries of evaluative text. In *IUI '06: Proceedings of the 10th International Conference on Intelligent User Interfaces*, New York, pp. 124–131. ACM.

Cawsey, A. J., B. L. Webber, and R. B. Jones (1997). Natural language generation in health care. *Journal of the American Medical Informatics Association* 4(6), 473–82.

Chi, M. T. H., M. Bassok, M. W. Lewis, P. Reimann, and R. Glaser (1989). Self-explanations: How students study and use examples in learning to solve problems. *Cognitive Science* 13(2), 145–182.

Chi, M. T. H., N. de Leeuw, M.-H. Chiu, and C. LaVancher (1994). Eliciting self-explanations improves understanding. *Cognitive Science* 18(3), 439–477.

Chi, M. T. H., S. A. Siler, T. Yamauchi, and R. G. Hausmann (2001). Learning from human tutoring. *Cognitive Science* 25, 471–533.

Cohen, J. (1988). *Statistical Power Analysis For the Behavioral Sciences* (2nd ed.). Hillsdale, NJ: Lawrence Earlbaum Associates.

Dalal, M., S. Feiner, K. McKeown, S. Pan, M. Zhou, T. Höllerer, J. Shaw, Y. Feng, and J. Fromer (1996). Negotiation for automated generation of temporal multimedia presentations. In *MULTIMEDIA '96: Proceedings of the Fourth ACM International Conference on Multimedia*, New York, pp. 55–64. ACM.

de Rosis, F., N. Novielli, V. Carofiglio, A. Cavalluzzi, and B. De Carolis (2006). User modeling and adaptation in health promotion dialogs with an animated character. *Journal of Biomedical Informatics* 39(5), 514–531.

Demir, S., S. Carberry, and S. Elzer (2007). Effectively realizing the inferred message of an information graphic. In *Proceedings of Recent Advances in Natural Language Processing (RANLP)*, Borovets, Bulgaria, pp. 150–156.

Di Eugenio, B., D. Fossati, D. Yu, S. Haller, and M. Glass (2005, June). Aggregation improves learning: Experiments in natural language generation for intelligent tutoring systems. In *ACL05, Proceedings of the 42nd Meeting of the Association for Computational Linguistics*, Ann Arbor, MI, pp. 50–57.

Di Eugenio, B., T. C. Kershaw, X. Lu, A. Corrigan-Halpern, and S. Ohlsson (2006). Toward a computational model of expert tutoring: A first report. In *FLAIRS06, the 19th International Florida AI Research Symposium*, Melbourne Beach, FL.

Di Eugenio, B., D. Fossati, S. Haller, D. Yu, and M. Glass (2008). Be brief, and they shall learn: Generating concise language feedback for a computer tutor. *International Journal of AI in Education* 18(4), 317–345.

Druzdzel, M. J. and M. Henrion (1993). Efficient reasoning in qualitative probabilistic networks. In *Proceedings of the 11th National Conference on Artificial Intelligence (AAAI-93)*, Washington, DC, pp. 548–553.

Elzer, S., N. Green, S. Carberry, and J. Hoffman (2006). A model of perceptual task effort for bar charts and its role in recognizing intention. *User Modeling and User-Adapted Interaction* 16(1), 1–30.

Elzer, S., E. Schwartz, S. Carberry, D. Chester, S. Demir, and P. Wu (2007). A browser extension for providing visually impaired users access to the content of bar charts on the web. In *Proceedings of Third International Conference on Web Information Systems and Technology (WebIST)* Barcelona, Spain.

Evens, M. W. and J. A. Michael (2006). *One-on-One Tutoring by Humans and Machines*. Mahwah, NJ: Lawrence Erlbaum Associates.

Evens, M. W., J. Spitkovsky, P. Boyle, J. A. Michael, and A. A. Rovick (1993). Synthesizing tutorial dialogues. In *Proceedings of the 15th Annual Conference of the Cognitive Science Society*, Hillsdale, NJ, pp. 137–140. Lawrence Erlbaum Associates.

Fasciano, M. and G. Lapalme (2000). Intentions in the coordinated generation of graphics and text from tabular data. *Knowledge and Information System* 2(3), 310–339.

Feiner, S. K. and K. R. McKeown (1991). Automating the generation of coordinated multimedia explanations. *Computer* 24(10), 33–41.

Fiedler, A. and D. Tsovaltzi (2005). Domain-knowledge manipulation for dialogue-adaptive hinting. In *Proceedings of the 12th International Conference on Artificial Intelligence in Education (AIED 2005)*, Amsterdam, the Netherlands, pp. 801–803.

Foltz, P. W., D. Laham, and T. K. Landauer (1999). The intelligent essay assessor: Applications to educational technology. *Interactive Multimedia Electronic Journal of Computer-Enhanced Learning* 1(2), http://imej.wfu.edu/articles/

Fossati, D., B. Di Eugenio, C. Brown, and S. Ohlsson (2008). Learning Linked Lists: Experiments with the iList System. In *ITS 2008, the Ninth International Conference on Intelligent Tutoring Systems*, Montreal, Canada.

Fox, B. A. (1993). *The Human Tutorial Dialogue Project: Issues in the Design of Instructional Systems*. Hillsdale, NJ: Lawrence Erlbaum Associates.

Freedman, R. K. (1996). Interaction of discourse planning, instructional planning and dialogue management in an interactive tutoring system. PhD thesis, Computer Science Department, Northwestern University, Evanston, IL.

Freedman, R. K. (2000, May). Plan-based dialogue management in a physics tutor. In *Proceedings of the Sixth Applied Natural Language Conference*, Seattle, WA.

Graesser, A. C., N. K. Person, and J. P. Magliano (1995). Collaborative dialogue patterns in naturalistic one-to-one tutoring. *Applied Cognitive Psychology* 9, 495–522.

Graesser, A. C., N. K. Person, D. Harter, and The Tutoring Research Group (2001). Teaching tactics and dialog in AutoTutor. *International Journal of Artificial Intelligence in Education* 12, 257–279.

Graesser, A. C., S. Lu, G. Jackson, H. Mitchell, M. Ventura, A. Olney, and M. Louwerse (2004). AutoTutor: A tutor with dialogue in natural language. *Behavioral Research Methods, Instruments, and Computers 36*, 180–193.

Graesser, A. C., N. Person, Z. Lu, M. Jeon, and B. McDaniel (2005). Learning while holding a conversation with a computer. In Brian L. Pytlik Zillig, M. Bodvarsson, and R. Brunin (Eds.), *Technology-Based Education: Bringing Researchers and Practitioners Together*. Greenwich, CN: Information Age Publishing.

Grasso, F., A. Cawsey, and R. Jones (2000). Dialectical argumentation to solve conflicts in advice giving: A case study in the promotion of healthy nutrition. *International Journal of Human - Computer Studies 53*(6), 1077–1115.

Green, N. (2005). A Bayesian network coding scheme for annotating biomedical information presented to genetic counseling clients. *Journal of Biomedical Informatics 38*(2), 130–144.

Green, N. L., G. Carenini, S. Kerpedjiev, J. Mattis, J. D. Moore, and S. F. Roth (2004). AutoBrief: An experimental system for the automatic generation of briefings in integrated text and information graphics. *International Journal of Human - Computer Studies 61*(1), 32–70.

Green, N., R. Dwight, K. Navoraphan, and B. Stadler (2009). Natural language generation of biomedical arguments for lay audiences. In preparation.

Hallett, C. (2008). Multi-modal presentation of medical histories. In *IUI '08: Proceedings of the 13th International Conference on Intelligent User Interfaces*, New York, pp. 80–89. ACM.

Hallett, C. and D. Scott (2005). Structural variation in generated health reports. In *Proceedings of the Third International Workshop on Paraphrasing (IWP2005)*, Jeju Island, Korea.

Heffernan, N. T. and K. R. Koedinger (2002). An intelligent tutoring system incorporating a model of an experienced human tutor. In *ITS02, International Conference on Intelligent Tutoring Systems*, Biarritz, France.

Hüske-Kraus, D. (2003). Text generation in clinical medicine—A review. *Methods of Information in Medicine 42*(1), 51–60.

Jordan, P. W., C. P. Rosé, and K. VanLehn (2001, May). Tools for authoring tutorial dialogue knowledge. In J. D. Moore, C. L. Redfield, and W. L. Johnson (Eds.), *Proceedings of the 10th International Conference on Artificial Intelligence in Education (AIED 2001)*, San Antonio, TX, pp. 222–233. IOS Press.

Jordan, P. W., M. Makatchev, U. Pappuswamy, K. VanLehn, and P. Albacete (2006). A natural language tutorial dialogue system for physics. In *FLAIRS06, the 19th International Florida AI Research Symposium*, Melbourne Beach, FL.

Jordan, P. W., B. Hall, M. Ringenberg, Y. Cui, and C. P. Rosé (2007). Tools for authoring a dialogue agent that participates in learning studies. In *Proceedings of the Thirteenth International Conference on Artificial Intelligence in Education (AIED 2007)*, Los Angeles, CA, pp. 43–50.

Kersey, C., B. Di Eugenio, P. W. Jordan, and S. Katz (2009, July). Knowledge co-construction and initiative in peer learning interactions. In *AIED 2009, the 14th International Conference on Artificial Intelligence in Education*, Brighton, U.K.

Kumar, R., C. P. Rosé, V. Aleven, A. Iglesias, and A. Robinson (2006, June). Evaluating the effectiveness of tutorial dialogue instruction in an exploratory learning context. In *Proceedings of the Seventh International Conference on Intelligent Tutoring Systems*, Jhongli, Taiwan.

Landauer, T. K. and S. Dumais (1997). A solution to Plato's problem: The latent semantic analysis theory of acquisition, induction, and representation of knowledge. *Psychological Review 104*, 211–240.

Law, A. S., Y. Freer, J. Hunter, R. H. Logie, N. McIntosh, and J. Quinn (2005). A comparison of graphical and textual presentations of time series data to support medical decision making in the neonatal intensive care unit. *Journal of Clinical Monitoring and Computing 19*(3), 183–194.

Lester, J. C., J. L. Voerman, S. G. Towns, and C. B. Callaway (1999). Deictic believability: Coordinated gesture, locomotion, and speech in lifelike pedagogical agents. *Applied Artificial Intelligence 13*(4–5), 383–414.

Litman, D. and K. Forbes-Riley (2006). Correlations between dialogue acts and learning in spoken tutoring dialogues. *Natural Language Engineering 12*(2), 161–176.

Litman, D. J., C. P. Rosé, K. Forbes-Riley, K. VanLehn, D. Bhembe, and S. Silliman (2006). Spoken versus typed human and computer dialogue tutoring. *International Journal of Artificial Intelligence in Education 16*, 145–170.

Lu, X., B. Di Eugenio, T. Kershaw, S. Ohlsson, and A. Corrigan-Halpern (2007). Expert vs. non-expert tutoring: Dialogue moves, interaction patterns and multi-utterance turns. In *CICLING07, Proceedings of the Eighth International Conference on Intelligent Text Processing and Computational Linguistics*, Mexico City, Mexico, pp. 456–467. Best Student Paper Award.

Lu, X., B. Di Eugenio, S. Ohlsson, and D. Fossati (2008). Simple but effective feedback generation to tutor abstract problem solving. In *INLG08, Proceedings of the Fifth International Natural Language Generation Conference*, Salt Fork, OH, pp. 104–112.

Mazzotta, I., F. de Rosis, and V. Carofiglio (2007). Portia: A user-adapted persuasion system in the healthy-eating domain. *IEEE Intelligent Systems 22*(6), 42–51.

Mittal, V. O., G. Carenini, J. D. Moore, and S. Roth (1998). Describing complex charts in natural language: A caption generation system. *Computational Linguistics 24*(3), 431–467.

Moore, J. D., B. Lemaire, and J. A. Rosenbloom (1996). Discourse generation for instructional applications: Identifying and exploiting relevant prior explanations. *Journal of the Learning Sciences 5*(1), 49–94.

Moore, J. D., K. Porayska-Pomsta, S. Varges, and C. Zinn (2004). Generating tutorial feedback with affect. In *FLAIRS04, Proceedings of the 17th International Florida Artificial Intelligence Research Society Conference*, Miami Beach, FL.

Moreno, R. (2006). Does the modality principle hold for different media? A test of the *method-affects-learning* hypothesis. *Journal of Computer Assisted Learning 22*(3), 149–158.

Moser, M. and J. D. Moore (1995). Investigating cue selection and placement in tutorial discourse. In *ACL95, Proceedings of the 33rd Meeting of the Association for Computational Linguistics*, Cambridge, MA, pp. 130–135.

Moser, M. and J. D. Moore (1996). Towards a synthesis of two accounts of discourse structure. *Computational Linguistics 22*(3), 409–419.

Nicholson, A. and J. Brady (1994). Dynamic belief networks for discrete monitoring. *IEEE Transactions on Systems, Man and Cybernetics 24*(11), 1593–1610.

Ohlsson, S., B. Di Eugenio, B. Chow, D. Fossati, X. Lu, and T. Kershaw (2007). Beyond the code-and-count analysis of tutoring dialogues. In *AIED 2007, the 13th International Conference on Artificial Intelligence in Education*, Marina del Rey, CA.

Oviatt, S. L. (1999, November). Ten myths of multimodal interaction. *Communications of the ACM 42*(11), 74–81.

Perelman, C. and L. Olbrechts-Tyteca (1969). *The New Rhetoric: A Treatise on Argumentation*. Notre Dame, IN: University of Notre Dame Press.

Person, N. K., A. C. Graesser, J. P. Magliano, and R. J. Kreuz (1994). Inferring what the student knows in one-to-one tutoring: The role of student questions and answers. *Learning and Individual Differences 6*(2), 205–229.

Pilkington, R. M. (1999). Analyzing educational dialogue: The DISCOUNT scheme (version 3). Technical Report 99/2, Computer Based Learning Unit, The University of Leeds, Leeds, U.K.

Pon-Barry, H., K. Schultz, E. O. Bratt, and S. Peters (2006). Responding to student uncertainty in spoken tutorial dialogue systems. *International Journal of Artificial Intelligence in Education 16*, 171–194.

Portet, F., E. Reiter, J. Hunter, S. Sripada, Y. Freer, and C. Sykes (2008). Automatic generation of textual summaries from neonatal intensive care data. *Artificial Intelligence 173*, 789–816.

Prochaska, J. and D. D. Clemente (1992). Stages of change in the modification of problem behaviors. *Progress in Behavior Modification 28*, 183–218.

Reiter, E. and R. Dale (2000). *Building Natural Language Generation Systems. Studies in Natural Language Processing.* Cambridge, U.K.: Cambridge University Press.

Reiter, E., R. Robertson, and L. Osman (1999). Types of knowledge required to personalise smoking cessation letters. In *AIMDM '99: Proceedings of the Joint European Conference on Artificial Intelligence in Medicine and Medical Decision Making,* London, U.K., pp. 389–399. Springer-Verlag.

Reiter, E., R. Robertson, and L. Osman (2003). Lessons from a failure: Generating tailored smoking cessation letters. *Artificial Intelligence 144*(1–2), 41–58.

Rickel, J. and W. L. Johnson (1999). Virtual humans for team training in virtual reality. In *Proceedings of the Ninth International Conference on AI in Education,* Le Mans, France, pp. 578–585. IOS Press.

Shneiderman, B. and C. Plaisant (2004). *Designing the User Interface: Strategies for Effective Human-Computer Interaction* (4th ed.). Reading, MA: Addison Wesley.

Soller, A. (2001). Supporting social interaction in an intelligent collaborative learning system. *International Journal of Artificial Intelligence in Education 12*, 40–42.

Toulmin, S. (1998). *The Uses of Argument* (9th ed.). Cambridge, U.K.: Cambridge University Press.

van Eemeren, F. H., R. Grootendorst, and F. S. Henkemans (1996). *Fundamentals of Argumentation Theory: A Handbook of Historical Backgrounds and Contemporary Developments.* Mahwah, NJ: Lawrence Erlbaum Associates.

VanLehn, K., R. Freedman, P. W. Jordan, C. Murray, C. Oran, M. Ringenberg, C. P. Rosé, K. Schultze, R. Shelby, D. Treacy, A. Weinstein, and M. Wintersgill (2000). Fading and deepening: The next steps for ANDES and other model-tracing tutors. In *Proceedings of the Intelligent Tutoring Systems Conference,* Montreal, Canada.

VanLehn, K., A. C. Graesser, G. T. Jackson, P. W. Jordan, A. Olney, and C. P. Rosé (2007). When are tutorial dialogues more effective than reading? *Cognitive Science 31*(1), 3–62.

Walton, D. (1996). *Argumentation Schemes for Presumptive Reasoning.* Mahwah, NJ: Lawrence Erlbaum Associates.

Young, R. M., M. E. Pollack, and J. D. Moore (1994). Decomposition and causality in partial order planning. In *Second International Conference on Artificial Intelligence and Planning Systems,* University of Chicago, Chicago, IL. Also Technical Report 94-1, Intelligent Systems Program, University of Pittsburgh, Pittsburgh, PA.

Yu, J., E. Reiter, J. Hunter, and C. Mellish (2007). Choosing the content of textual summaries of large time-series data sets. *Natural Language Engineering 13*(1), 25–49.

Zinn, C., J. D. Moore, and M. G. Core (2002). A 3-tier planning architecture for managing tutorial dialogue. In *ITS 2002, Sixth International Conference on Intelligent Tutoring Systems,* Biarritz, France, pp. 574–584.

Zinn, C., J. D. Moore, and M. G. Core (2005). Intelligent information presentation for tutoring systems. In M. Zancanaro and O. Stock (Eds.), *Multimodal Intelligent Information Presentation.* pp. 227–254. Dordrecht, the Netherlands: Kluwer Academic Publishers.

24

Ontology Construction

Philipp Cimiano
Delft University of Technology

Johanna Völker
University of Karlsruhe

Paul Buitelaar
National University of Ireland

24.1 Introduction

As humans, we base our decisions on our knowledge about the world, which we have acquired through education, reading, reflection, conversation, etc. We all have substantial commonsense knowledge as well as knowledge about how our world is structured, which guides us in our daily lives, helps us to take decisions, etc.

For example, due to basic knowledge of how European medieval cities are structured, we find it rather easy to find our way through them. European medieval cities typically have a church in the center, which, in many cases, has a tower we can see from a distance. As the marketplace of a medieval town is typically also in the center of a town, by following the church we will also find the marketplace. The towers are typically located on the western end of the churches, which gives us additional navigation help.

We know that there are different types of churches: basilicas, cathedrals, chapels, etc., originating from different centuries and having different styles: Romanesque, Gothic, Renaissance, etc. As we know the main characteristics of each of these styles, we can also (in many cases) recognize the corresponding styles. Romanesque churches are heavy and compact buildings with round-arched, small windows and feature-elaborated sculptures on the entrance portal. Gothic churches are taller and lighter (compared to Romanesque churches) and feature pointed arches.

This shows how much knowledge about our world we have as humans and it seems clear that making all this knowledge explicit (as we have attempted in a very sketchy and informal way above) is a very challenging endeavor. To some extent, this is exactly what our aim is when constructing *ontologies*. Ontologies aim at capturing knowledge about the world explicitly for a specific purpose or task. In most cases, ontologies are actually more modest and aim to capture the knowledge about a certain domain (e.g., medicine), a specific phenomenon (e.g., the function of the human heart), or even a certain situation or event (e.g., a football match). The essential purpose of an ontology is thus to encode knowledge about a certain reality in a declarative way, independently of any application and the way this knowledge might be used, such that somebody can reuse this knowledge and apply it in their own context. When encoding knowledge for machines, the purpose remains essentially the same, with the exception that the knowledge needs to be encoded in a formal language that machines can process and "understand." In fact, various languages, especially variants of (first-order) logic, have been used for the representation of and reasoning with knowledge in ontologies. We will come back to this issue in Section 24.2.

As mentioned in the ontology development guide by Noy and McGuinness (2001), at an abstract level, the reasons for developing an ontology are the following:

- To share a common understanding of the structure of information among people or software agents
- To enable the reuse of domain knowledge
- To make domain assumptions explicit
- To separate domain knowledge from operational knowledge
- To analyze domain knowledge

Ontologies can thus serve as artifacts for establishing a "common ground," thus fostering communication between people with different backgrounds by creating a shared understanding and consensus on how to understand the terminology in a certain domain. The above reasons, however, do not talk about the potential applications for ontologies. We cite only a few here:

- *Data integration*: The promise of ontologies is that they provide a unifying data schema bridging between the way different people have modeled their information, thus facilitating the integration of different sources of information at a higher level abstracting from these proprietary schemas (see Wache et al., 2001; Reynaud and Safar, 2002).
- *Content and functionality description at a "semantic level:"* By describing content (e.g., of Web sites) as well as functionality (e.g., of services or programs) at a semantic level, the matching of content to information needs or discovering appropriate services will be more effective compared to pure matching at a syntactic level (e.g., as done in current search engines to match content to information needs or relying mainly on method signatures for services). Describing resources (services, multimedia content, etc.) semantically is in fact the crucial aim of the Semantic Web (Berners-Lee et al., 2001). A semantic description of service functionality will also enable more complex tasks such as Web service composition into a workflow (McIlraith et al., 2001; Paolucci et al., 2001; Sirin et al., 2003).
- Providing relevant *background knowledge for knowledge-intensive tasks*: e.g., in *expert systems* (Russel and Norvig, 2003) that help users to take better decisions in specific domains specific domains as in the well-known MYCIN expert system (see Shortliffe, 2001). Natural language processing is another good example for this, where relevant background knowledge can help in disambiguation (lexical, syntactic, semantic, quantifier scope, etc.), discourse analysis (anaphora resolution, bridging reference resolution, inferring discourse relations), etc.

The remainder of this chapter is structured as follows. In Section 24.2 we discuss ontologies as such. We present the main definitions of an ontology, different types of ontologies as well as ontology representation languages, and the relation between ontologies and natural language. In Section 24.3 we deal with ontology engineering, in particular, describing different ontology engineering methods. In Section 24.4 we discuss automatic methods for ontology construction and present an overview of the different steps involved as specified by the so-called *ontology learning layer cake*. Finally, in Section 24.5 we briefly summarize the chapter.

Since the basic NLP and machine learning technologies needed for text-driven ontology construction are all described in this handbook, we do not describe them in detail here. Instead, we refer the reader to related chapters of this book, i.e., on (1) *lexical and phrase analysis* for term extraction (see Chapters 3, 10, and 12), (2) *multilingual processing* for multilingual term and translation extraction (see Chapter 16), (3) *similarity analysis* for synonym extraction (see Chapters 13 and 14), and (4) *parsing* for relation extraction and axiom analysis (see Chapter 4).

24.2 Ontology and Ontologies

While ontologies currently have the status of designed artifacts in computer science, *ontology* originally was a (philosophical) discipline concerned with the study of existence and the formal description of the structure of reality. According to Barry Smith, "*Ontology as a branch of philosophy is the science of what is, of the kinds and structures of objects, properties, events, processes and relations in every area of reality.*" (Smith, 2003, corresponding to Definition 1 in Guarino and Giaretta, 1995). According to this view, ontology is a universal discipline and deals with existence independent of any specific domains and of any belief systems.[*]

Aristotle (384–322 BC) can certainly be called the first ontologist as he fundamentally shaped the nature of ontologies as we understand them today (compare Sowa, 2000). Aristotle however never mentioned the word *ontology* in his works, which was introduced in the seventeenth century independently by two philosophers: Rudolf Göckel in his *Lexicon Philosophicum* (Göckel, 1613) and Jacob Lorhard in his *Ogdaes Scholasticas* Lorhard (1606) (compare Smith, 2003; Ohrstrom et al., 2005). Aristotle himself referred to the study of existence as "*first philosophy.*" In his works on *Categories*[†] he laid the foundations for (ontological) classification, developing a system for classification consisting of 10 basic categories: *substance, quantity, quality, relation, place, time, situation* (*or position*), *state* (*or condition*), *action, and affection* (*or passion*) (compare Studtmann, 2007). In the fundamental work described in the *Categories*, Aristotle introduced the basic ontological notions we today: *universals* (also known as classes or concepts) and *particulars* (also known as instances, individuals, or objects). Aristotle further established the basis for taxonomies as used in ontologies and knowledge representation nowadays. In order to come up with a taxonomical organization of things, Aristotle proposed a "method of division" according to which a general category (a *genus*) is specialized into several (*subgenera* or *species*) by means of *differentiae*, i.e., properties on which they differ from each other.

From the computer science point of view, *ontologies*[‡] can be defined as logical theories describing some aspect of reality. Typically, such logical theories describe a specific domain, i.e., some part of reality that is of relevance to a set of applications (compare the use of *domain of discourse* in database and information system design). For example, we could define an ontology for the domain of academia, such as the SWRC ontology (Sure et al., 2005), for medicine (Grenon et al., 2004), biochemistry (The Gene Ontology Consortium, 2000) etc. Such ontologies will be typically used for applications in which a declarative description of the domain is useful, for example, in order to infer implicit domain knowledge, for integrating different data sources, etc.

While there is no agreed-upon definition of ontology, there are a number of popular definitions of ontologies in computer science that are regularly cited by the community:[§]

1. "An explicit specification of a conceptualization" (Gruber, 1993)
2. "An explicit account or representation of [some part of] a conceptualization" (Uschold, 1996)

---

[*] This corresponds to the aim of "external metaphysics" of studying reality beyond any belief systems or cognitive biases. In fact, according to the realist's position, the objective of ontology is to reflect the physical reality (as studied by the physical and life sciences) as truthfully as possible. This is in contrast to the aims of internal metaphysicists studying the world by the way people perceive and talk about it.

[†] *The Categories* is part of the *Organon*: a collection of six works on logic.

[‡] Note the use of the plural "ontologies" here to distinguish this use from the upper case "Ontology" as a philosophical discipline. The use of the plural clearly denotes that there can be many ontologies, i.e., for different views of the world, different domains, different applications, etc. There can even be different ontologies for one and the same domain!

[§] Other possible interpretations of the term ontology can be found in Guarino and Giaretta (1995).

3. "A logical theory accounting for the *intended meaning* of a formal vocabulary, i.e., its *ontological commitment* to a particular *conceptualization* of the world" (Guarino, 1998a)

4. "A formal explicit description of concepts in a domain of discourse" (Noy and McGuinness, 2001)

5. "A formal, explicit specification of a shared conceptualization" (Studer et al., 1998)

Common to most of these definitions is the term *conceptualization* (Definitions 1, 2, 3, and 5) which "*is a world view; it corresponds to a way of thinking about some domain*" (Uschold, 1996) and can be seen as "*a set of informal rules that constrain the structure of a piece of reality*" (Guarino, 1997). Another common aspect of the definitions given above is that this conceptualization needs to be *explicit* (Definition 1 through 5),* i.e., in the sense that it is not just in someone's head but written down on a sheet of paper, stored in an electronic file, etc. Further, some of the definitions require an ontology to be *formal* (Definition 3 through 5, but also 1 according to the further descriptions in Gruber (1993)), i.e., in the sense that it should have a formal semantics and be machine readable as well as interpretable. Finally, some researchers (see Definition 5) require an ontology to be *shared* among different people.

In this chapter, we will not prefer any of the above definitions over the other. For our purposes, it suffices to understand ontologies as logical theories used to conceptualize a certain domain, i.e., to formalize an abstraction of some part of reality relevant to this domain.

24.2.1 Anatomy of an Ontology

In this section we give a brief overview of the prototypical axiomatic constructs found in ontologies. If we dissect a prototypical ontology (e.g., modeling information about medieval European cities) we might find the following:

- *Subclass axioms*: For example, Church is subclass of Building in the sense that all members of the class of churches are contained in the class of buildings. This is referred to as "extensional subsumption." Normally, we also say that "the class of buildings subsumes the class of churches."
- *Non-taxonomic relations*: For example, the relation between a church and its style, which can be modeled through the hasStyle relation for example.
- *Domain and range restrictions* (on relations): For a certain relation, i.e., hasStyle, the ontology might restrict which kind of entities can stand at the domain and range positions, respectively. At the range position we would expect, say, Architectonic_artefact, while at the range position we would expect some Architectonic_style.
- *Cardinality constraints*: We would for example like to say that each Basilica has at least one Apse. This can be done by attaching a cardinality constraint of "at least 1" to the corresponding relation in the ontology.
- *Part-of relations*: Have a special ontological status and have received special attention in the knowledge representation literature (Artale et al., 1996). While there are clearly different types of "part-of" relations, we will gloss over this aspect here (but see Artale et al., 1996 on this issue). We could for example specify that there can be a part-of relation between a Tower and the Church it belongs to.
- *Disjointness*: To further constrain the models of our logical theory, we might want to add also so-called disjointness axioms between classes which essentially state that the classes cannot have common elements. For instance, we would specify that the classes Style and Church are disjoint, i.e., there is no thing which is a style and a church at the same time. While such things look trivial for us as humans, for a machine processing our ontology there is in principle no reason why these two classes cannot share elements.

---

* Definition 3 talks about a "logical theory," which is trivially explicit.

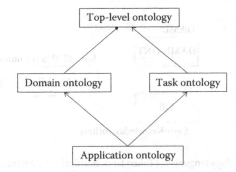

FIGURE 24.1 Ontology types according to Guarino (1998a). (Reproduced from Guarino, N., Formal ontology and information systems. In *Proceedings of Formal Ontology in Information Systems (FOIS)*, Trento, Italy, pp. 3–15, 1998.)

24.2.2 Types of Ontologies

Many researchers have attempted to provide a classification of ontologies according to type. Guarino (1998a), for example, distinguishes between the following types of ontologies (graphically depicted in terms of a specialization relation in Figure 24.1):

- *Top-level ontologies*: describing very general concepts related to time, space, matter, etc.
- *Domain ontologies*: describing the vocabulary in a specific domain.
- *Task ontologies*: describing the vocabulary of a generic task or activity, such as the task of *selling* something.
- *Application ontologies*: describing concepts that are often specializations of domain and task ontologies. Consider a domain ontology about books and a task ontology about selling, an online book retailer would specialize both ontologies to describe a book selling service for example.

These types appear in similar ways also in other classifications (compare Studer et al., 1998; Uschold, 1996, but also the orthogonal classification in Hovy, 2005). Further, Uschold (1996) has suggested a classification of ontologies according to the following dimensions:

- *Degree of formality*: ranging from *highly informal* (e.g., glossaries), *structured informal* over *semiformal* to *rigorously formal*.
- *Purpose*: mentioning different purposes such as (1) *communication between people*, (2) *interoperability* (between systems), where the ontology is used as an interchange format and (3) *knowledge reuse* across systems, as well as (in software engineering) (4) verification by *automated consistency checks* and assistance in the process of requirements specification.
- *Subject matter*: distinguishing (similarly to Guarino) between *domain ontologies, task, method or problem-solving ontologies*, and *meta-ontologies*, i.e., ontologies describing the vocabulary and semantics of a knowledge representation language.

Besides the different categories introduced by different researchers, the important message to bear in mind is that ontologies can be engineered for very different (but all legitimate) purposes.

24.2.3 Ontology Languages

As ontologies are in essence logical theories, we need logical formalisms to write such logical theories down (i.e., some syntax) as well as some specification of their formal semantics (i.e., a definition of logical consequence) in order to reason over the theory. For the purpose of formalizing ontologies, typically

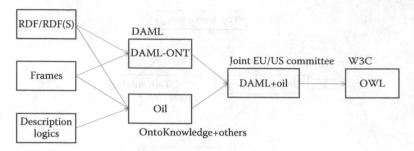

FIGURE 24.2   Evolution of ontology languages. (Taken from Bechhofer, S., An introduction to OWL. Tutorial slides for the Semantic Web Tutorial at ISWC'08, 2008. http://kmi.open.ac.uk/events/iswc08-semantic-web-intro/.)

variants of first-order logic with standard model-theoretic semantics are used (but also other non-first-order logics with non-monotonic properties have been proposed). Examples of older languages allowing to specify ontologies are KIF (Knowledge Interchange Format) (Genesereth and Fikes, 1992), but also DAML-ONT (McGuiness et al., 2002) or OIL (Ontology Inference Layer) (Fensel et al., 2001).

Figure 24.2 shows the evolution of various ontology languages into the nowadays widely known OWL language (Bechhofer et al., 2004). RDF (Lassila and Swick, 1999) and RDF(S) (Brickley and Guha, 2002) can be seen as a precursor to the DAML-ONT (McGuiness et al., 2002) language, which was developed in the context of the U.S. DAML Program.*

OIL was an ontology representation language developed in the context of European projects such as OntoKnowledge[†] and builds strongly on 'Description Logics' (Baader et al., 2003). The term 'description logics' actually refers to a family of languages for describing concepts as well as the subsumption relations between these.[‡] DAML-ONT (McGuiness et al., 2002) and OIL (Fensel et al., 2001) provided the basis for a new language called DAML+OIL (Conolly et al., 2001), developed by a joint initiative involving European and U.S. groups. DAML+OIL can be regarded as providing the foundations for OWL, which has been standardized by the W3C as "official" Web ontology language.[§] In what follows we briefly cite the main characteristics of the RDF, RDFS, and OWL languages, together with its dialects OWL Full, OWL DL, and OWL Lite. In general, for a more detailed discussion of OWL, its three dialects, the relation to other formalisms such as RDFS, DAML+OIL, to frame languages and to description logics, the interested reader is referred to the excellent overview by Horrocks et al. (2003).

- *RDF*: The Resource Description Framework essentially provides the vocabulary to express triples—i.e., constructs of the shape (subject,predicate,object)—which allow to provide elementary statements like the fact that Berlin is the capital of Germany, i.e., (Berlin,capitalOf,Germany). One of the important characteristics of RDF and which makes it especially suitable for the Web is that it relies on the crucial notion of a URI in the sense of a unique identifier allowing us to point to "things" (or "resources" as they are called in RDF). This is essential for a Web in which sites point to content (or things) on other sites, thus reflecting the true distributional architecture of the Web as we know it today. URIs thus provide the basis for talking about identity. However, it is not the case that RDF adopts the UNA (Unique Name Assumption), thus allowing different URIs to refer to the same thing (after all we cannot force people to use the same URIs, but only encourage it!).
- *RDF Schema*, abbreviated as RDFS, extends RDF in the sense of providing additional machinery for describing the vocabulary used in the triples in terms of their relation to other vocabulary

---

* http://www.daml.org/
[†] http://www.ontoknowledge.org/
[‡] For more details on DL, the interested reader is referred to the Description Logics Handbook (Baader et al., 2003).
[§] The Web Ontology Language is abbreviated OWL instead of WOL, see Hitzler et al. (2008) on this issue.

elements. RDF(S) allows one to introduce classes as well as to arrange them taxonomically via the `rdfs:subClassOf` property. In RDF Schema we could, for example, state that the class church is a subclass of building, i.e., (`Church,rdfs:subClassOf,Building`), thus specifying that all churches are buildings. An important feature in RDF(S) is that classes (and properties) arc themselves resources and thus "first class citizens" we can talk about. The expressivity of RDF Schema in terms of the logical repertoire that can be used to constrain the possible models is rather limited. This is the reason why more expressive ontology languages such as OWL (see below) were developed.

- *OWL Full* is the only dialect of OWL that is fully compatible with RDF(S), basically inheriting its semantics (with a few extensions). However, the way that OWL and RDF(S) have been merged together in OWL Full has lead to the fact that the latter is undecideable. In addition to allowing one to define subclasses (as in RDFS), OWL allows to define complex classes, i.e., the class of `Medieval Cities` as the intersection between the class `City` and `Medieval` (*MedievalCity* ≡ *Medieval* ⊓ *City* in OWL abstract syntax), or specify necessary conditions or a church, i.e., that it is subsumed by the class of things that are clerical buildings, have a specific style, and are located somewhere: *Church* ⊑ *ClericalBuilding* ⊓ ∃*hasStyle.Style* ⊓ ∃*hasLocation.Place*. Thus, OWL extends RDF by allowing to define more precisely the classes in terms of complex class descriptions like the above. It is clear that such descriptions allow more inferences as from the fact that something is a church we can infer that (1) it is a clerical building, (2) it has some style, and (3) it is located somewhere. OWL also allows to define classes by complements, i.e., the class of Non-Romanesque churches as *Church* ⊓ ¬∃*hasStyle.{Romanesque}*.* Further, OWL allows to state cardinality constraints on relations, e.g., specifying that elements of a certain class (e.g., a `Basilica`) needs to have at least one `Apse` (and similar for `at most` and specifications of exact cardinality). In OWL Full, there is essentially no restriction on the use of the OWL vocabulary.
- *OWL DL* is a member of the family of Description Logic Languages, corresponding to the language SHOIN(D) actually,[†] a language featuring a standard first-order model theoretic semantics (but less expressive than first order logic). OWL DL was designed in order to have a computationally decidable OWL fragment. It restricts OWL Full by fostering a clear separation between classes and individuals (no individual can be a class at the same time). The relation to RDF(S) is only an indirect one. First, OWL DL and RDF(S) have a different semantics. Further, there are OWL DL ontologies that are not valid RDF(S) ontologies and also the other way round. It is in this case that here is not direct relation between them other than that there is an RDF-based syntax to express OWL DL ontologies, where the constructs (axioms) defined in an OWL ontology are expressed as a set of RDF triples. While it might seem a rather awkward idea to use RDF (which is layered on top of XML in the sense that every RDF document is a valid XML document) to encode ontologies (RDF serializations of OWL ontologies look indeed like beasts!), it is important to mention that this was mainly done to allow for the publication and sharing of ontologies over the Web. As the Web inherently builds on standards such as XML and XHTML, this is an important move. The abstract syntax of an OWL ontology is certainly not something that lends itself to straightforward serialization in an ASCII document.
- *OWL Lite* is a subset of OWL DL removing several sources of complexity for practical reasoning algorithms, including (1) disjunction (in the form of class union in OWL), (2) complementation and disjointness of classes (both requiring negation), (3) constructs that implicitly introduce (in-) equalities, such as enumerated classes (realized by `oneOf` in OWL[‡]) and cardinality constraints

---

* Here we are using a special feature of the OWL abstract syntax to state that the style needs to be one of the elements in the set {Romanesque}, by which we essentially restrict the type to Romanesque. The detour over a set notation is necessary as OWL expects always a class at the range restriction for a role.

† See the description logic computational complexity navigator at http://www.cs.man.ac.uk/~ezolin/dl/

‡ Enumerated classes allow us to define a class extensionally, e.g., the class of continents as consisting exactly of Europe, Africa, Asia, North America, South America, Australia, and Antarctica.

on relations greater than "1." OWL DL allows only to restrict the cardinality of a property to "0" or "1" (an existential quantification in essence). This is enough to say that a `Basilica` has at least one `Apse`, but not to specify that a `Dog` has exactly four `legs` for instance.

24.2.4 Ontologies and Natural Language

There has been substantial debate over the relation between ontologies and lexica as well as between ontologies and natural language in general. We intend to shed light on this relation along the following lines: (1) the relation between ontologies and lexica, (2) the role of ambiguity in ontologies, and (3) a discussion of the issue whether the design of ontologies should be guided by linguistic distinctions.

24.2.4.1 Ontologies and Lexica

The main difference between an ontology and a lexicon, a lexical database or a thesaurus is that all of the latter are linguistic objects while ontologies are not (they are logical theories). In particular, while concepts and properties are defined on logical grounds (through necessary and sufficient conditions, expressed through axioms), words are organized in a lexicon with respect to lexical relations such as hypernymy (broader term), hyponymy (narrower term), meronymy/holonymy (part-of/has-part), antonymy (opposite term). These relations are not defined at a logical level, but rather defined linguistically, e.g., through so-called diagnostic frames (Cruse, 1986), i.e., by typical sentences describing the context in which a pair of words may or may not occur given a certain lexical relation among them. Thus, ontologically defined relations do not correspond directly to lexical relations, or citing (Hirst, 2004): *"lexical relationships between word senses mirror, perhaps imperfectly, certain relationships that hold between the categories themselves."* Hirst also emphasizes the fact that ontologies are not linguistic objects (in contrast to lexicons or lexical databases): *"An ontology, after all, is a set of categories of objects or ideas in the world, along with certain relationships among them: it is not a linguistic object. A lexicon, on the other hand, depends, by definition, on natural language and the word senses in it."*

For example, in the case of WordNet (Fellbaum, 1998), the basic unit of representation, the *synset*, can be understood as a *category* grouping together words according to similar meaning and which can be organized taxonomically according to the hypernymy/hyponymy relation. Nevertheless, synsets are still defined on the lexical level and as noted by Hirst (2004) do not correspond directly to concepts, which are defined extensionally and intensionally in the context of current KR representation paradigms. However, it has to be noted that for the kind of applications that WordNet was designed for, it probably does not matter what the semantics of a synset actually is. The semantics of a concept in an ontology on the other hand, and more particularly in description logics, is however clearly extensional, i.e., the model-theoretic interpretation of a concept C corresponds to a set of objects in the domain of discourse Δ. However, concepts also have an intensional dimension, axiomatized in terms of sufficient and necessary conditions, which, in many cases, is accompanied by a natural language definition, as many aspects of the concept definition are out of scope of logical formalization or it is simply not worth (in terms of a cost–benefit trade-off) capturing all aspects formally. The natural language definition thus basically serves as an interface to the human reader who requires a precise characterization of the intension of the concept in order to make sure that they are using it in the intended way.

24.2.4.2 Is There Ambiguity in Ontologies?

An important question concerning the interface of ontologies and language is that of ambiguity. Here we adhere to the position of Nirenburg and Raskin (2001) in the sense that, while language is inherently ambiguous, the question of ambiguity of concepts does simply not arise. Ontologies, as symbolic systems, rely on unique symbols to identify meaning through their logical connections to other symbols, such that according to this view concepts are simply uninterpreted symbols that can be manipulated according to some well-defined rules (a logical calculus typically). However, as people interact with an ontology through exploration, population, querying, etc., ontology concepts are typically assigned natural language "labels" and definitions for human consumption. As these labels and definitions are specified in natural language, they will be inherently ambiguous, but this concerns the label and/or natural language definition of a concept rather than the concept itself (as a symbol).

Obviously, concepts can be more or less precisely defined, thus leaving more or less room for interpretation. In this case, concepts are relatively vague, but clearly not ambiguous in the sense that they have completely different intensions (meanings). Sometimes it is simply the case that the logical repertoire at hand is not enough to capture the meaning of a concept as precisely as possible (and in many cases this is even not necessary, depending on the granularity that is required for a certain application). An extreme case of a vague concept is that which corresponds to a word such as *slim*, which is inherently vague in the sense that the boundaries of such a concept are not crisp and membership to the concept is clearly a matter of degree. But obviously, *slim* is not an ambiguous concept with completely different intensions.

24.2.4.3 The Role of Linguistic Distinctions in Ontology Design

Having clarified this, let us briefly turn to the question whether ontologies should mirror distinctions made in natural language (possibly across languages). As we saw above, ontologies mirror the structure of the world and thus are a priori independent of language. The question about "how" we learn about the structure of the world or a specific domain is a completely orthogonal one and it might well be the case that reading texts is the best way to learn about how the world is actually structured (we are not taking any strong position here!), but it does certainly not follow from this observation that an ontology should necessarily mirror distinctions made in natural language. As argued by Hirst (2004), on the one hand language makes distinctions that are not relevant from an ontological point of view and on the other hand there are for instance categories that are not necessarily lexicalized in a given language, but certainly exist (e.g., the class of objects that can be *ridden*). It does also not mean that an ontology should reflect the distinctions that a particular language makes. Ontologies should and can thus never be specific to a certain language as they are concerned with existence rather than lexicalization and existence is, in our view, language independent.

A good example for the differences that can exist between the lexicalizations of a concept in two languages is provided by Nirenburg and Raskin (2004): Given the complex lexicalization for the concept wall in Italian* (inside wall: *parete* vs. outside wall: *muro*) and the simple lexicalization in English (*wall* in both cases), one might be tempted to include the distinction between an inside and an outside wall into a "Italian ontology" but not into an "English ontology." Clearly, such artifacts as an English or Italian ontology do not exist. This conclusion is simply wrong. The only relevant decision is whether the existence of inside vs. outside walls is relevant for a certain domain or application. If yes, they will then be included in the ontology (possibly as subclasses of wall), otherwise not. The question whether there are direct lexicalizations of these concepts in different languages is an orthogonal issue and simply not relevant from the ontological point of view.

If the design of ontologies should not be based on linguistic distinctions, we certainly need a set of criteria that can guide the process of designing an ontology. We discuss such criteria as well as the main ontology design methodologies and paradigms in Section 24.3.

24.3 Ontology Engineering

The question of how to best develop an ontology is certainly a difficult one. Everyone who has tried to model an ontology even for a toy domain has faced the many design decisions that one has to take into account.[†] While there are clearly no definitive answers about how to best model a domain, a lot

---

* A similar distinction is made in Spanish, where *pared* refers to the inside wall and the word *muro* is used for the outside wall.

[†] In many cases we model intuitively and then discover the many modeling alternatives only later when rethinking the ontology.

of research has been done on meta-level issues concerning ontology engineering. Here we will discuss several of these, in particular: (1) Which principles should a good ontology follow? and (2) What does a good methodology for building an ontology look like? Further, we will discuss briefly (3) methodologies allowing to collaboratively design ontologies and (4) the important issue of ontology reuse as well as (5) different engineering paradigms to design ontologies.

24.3.1 Principles

Ontologies are engineered artifacts that, according to Gruber (1993), need to fulfill their purpose and provide the desired functionality. Gruber in fact formulated a number of principles that any ontology should follow:*

1. *Clarity*: An ontology should clearly state the meaning of the defined vocabulary. The definition should be objective and independent of computational aspects. Ontologies should be formal in the sense that definitions should be stated in the form of logical axioms (if possible), aiming for complete definitions in terms of necessary and sufficient conditions. All definitions in the ontology should be documented in natural language.
2. *Coherence*: On the one hand, ontologies should be coherent in the sense that the axioms contained therein should be logically consistent (i.e., the corresponding logical theory should be satisfiable). On the other hand, not everything can be axiomatized, such that the overall ontology should be consistent with respect to the natural language definitions.
3. *Extensibility*: An ontology should be designed in a general way such that it anticipates further usage that it was not conceived for. Thus, it should ideally be easily extensible and straightforwardly allow for the introduction of new concepts, relations, etc. This should be a monotonic process, i.e., it should not alter the structure developed so far.
4. *Minimal encoding bias*: The specification of the ontology should be as independent as possible of issues concerning its encoding in any particular ontology language.
5. *Minimal ontological commitment*: An ontology should make as few assumptions as necessary about the world being modeled, thus allowing other parties to reuse the ontology for their purposes.

As Gruber mentions, at the surface there seem to be some trade-offs between the above mentioned principles (e.g., between clarity and minimal ontological commitment), although the above principles are not in direct opposition. The interested reader is referred to Gruber (1993), for more details and two case studies illustrating how the above principles can be applied.

24.3.2 Methodologies

The task of building an ontology is certainly not a trivial one and requires guidance. Thus, research in the area of ontology engineering has developed methodologies to guide the process of building an ontology by describing some necessary steps to follow. Ontology engineering along these lines is a relatively new science. In fact, the first ontology engineering methodologies were proposed only in the early 1990s (compare Pinto and Martins, 2004), among which the one by Uschold and King (1995) has been the most influential, comprising of the following steps:

1. Identification of the **purpose** of the ontology
2. Building the ontology, consisting of the following substeps
    a. **Ontology capture** (at the so-called *knowledge level*)
    b. Ontology **coding**
    c. **Integration** of existing ontologies

---

* These principles have been reformulated here in our own words, trying to capture the original intent as faithfully as possible.

    3. Evaluation

    4. Documentation

The identification of the (intended) purpose of an ontology is a crucial step when building an ontology. For this, a variety of techniques can be used, such as defining competency questions (Uschold and King, 1995), carrying out interviews with domain experts, analyzing domain-specific texts, etc. (see Russel and Norvig, 2003). The development of competency questions is an integral part of many methodologies, e.g., in the unified methodology of Uschold (1996) and in the OntoKnowledge methodology by Sure et al. (2004). Competency questions clearly define the purpose and scope of the ontology by defining questions that the ontology should be able to answer.

The *ontology capture* step has the goal of producing an informal model of the ontology by compare Uschold and King (1995):

1. Identifying the **key concepts and relationships** in the domain
2. Precise and **unambiguous definitions** (in natural language) of the concepts and relationships
3. Identification of the **terms** that refer to these concepts and relations
4. **Agreeing** on all of the above

It is important to emphasize a few aspects of the ontology capture step as envisioned by Uschold and King. First, this step is targeted toward yielding agreement between a number of interested parties on the relevant concepts and relationships. Second, it is worth noticing that ambiguity is something that according to the above model has no place in the ontology, where meaning should be clearly specified, thus removing all ambiguities. Third, Uschold and King clearly distinguish between the concept level and the terms that are used to refer to these, thus clearly separating the ontological level from the linguistic level.

In the coding step, the informal model produced by the ontology building step is represented in some formal language. Thus, the methodology of Uschold and King clearly separates the task of developing the ontology from its representation in some formal language, thus modeling the ontology at the "knowledge level" (Newell, 1982) and inherently avoiding *encoding bias* as required by Gruber. Uschold and King acknowledge that reusing or integrating other ontologies is a nontrivial problem. However, they also stress that ontology reuse and integration is a central and crucial task in the complex process of designing an ontology. We discuss this issue further in Section 24.3.2.2.

The methodology by Uschold and King was later merged with the TOVE methodology by Grüninger and Fox (1995) to produce the *unified methodology* (Uschold, 1996) that is graphically depicted in Figure 24.3. After this seminal work, other proposals emerged, i.e., METHONTOLOGY by Corcho et al. (2005), OntoKnowledge by Sure et al. (2004), DOGMA by Spyns et al. (2008), and DILIGENT by Pinto et al., (2004).

The main lessons to be learned from all of the work on ontology engineering methodologies are the following:

- Defining the *purpose and scope* of an ontology beforehand is an important step of all methodologies, as emphasized, for example, by Uschold (1996) in the following: "*If you really cannot clearly identify your purpose, you should consider whether it is worth proceeding to build the ontology, for you may encounter problems later. For example, there will be no clear guidelines for determining the nature and content of the ontology, nor will it be clear by what criteria it can be evaluated.*"
- Every ontology engineering project should follow a clearly defined methodology. This decreases the risk of failure.
- Many methodologies are certainly "underspecified" in the sense that they do not spell out how to reach consensus or how to decide on certain modeling issues. Thus, while they support the overall process (macro-level), they certainly do not support the design at the micro-level. An exception is DILIGENT with a clear specification of how to reach consensus (see Section 24.3.2.1 below).

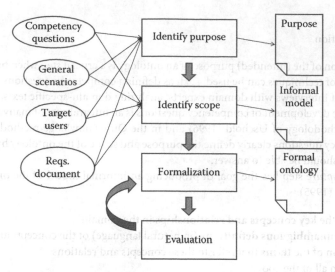

FIGURE 24.3 Unified methodology by Uschold and Gruninger, distilled from the descriptions in Uschold (1996). (From Uschold, M., Building ontologies: Towards a unified methodology, In *Proceedings of the 16th Annual Conference of the British Computer Specialist Group on Expert System*, Cambridge, U.K., 1996.)

Having described the main ontology engineering methodologies, we now discuss issues related to ontology engineering and orthogonal to the methodology adopted, i.e., the collaborative design of ontologies, issues related to ontology reuse as well as different *paradigms* for modeling ontologies.

24.3.2.1 Collaborative Aspects

Some definitions of ontologies state that they should describe a formalized and *shared* vocabulary.* For this reason, some researchers have worked on methodologies that are inherently collaborative in the sense that they support people (distributed parties in general) in the task of agreeing on certain modeling choices. Experiments have shown that without any rules or constraints, developing an ontology in a distributed fashion can be very inefficient (see Pinto and Tempich, 2004). As a solution to this, methodologies have been proposed that take into account the collaborative nature of ontology design. An example for this is the DILIGENT methodology (Pinto and Tempich, 2004; Tempich et al., 2005), which has provided a framework for collaborative design by way of a meta-ontology of—let us call them—"speech acts" that people can use to contribute to the discussion of an ongoing collaborative engineering project. The "speech acts" borrow heavily from the discourse relations defined in Rhetorical Structure Theory (Mann and Thompson, 1983) and in this sense represent a nice example of how work in linguistics has influenced ontology engineering methodologies. Participants in DILIGENT thus formulate their contributions according to primitives such as elaboration, contrast, counter-example, etc. A decision is then reached by consensus on the basis of the arguments raised during the structured discussion.

24.3.2.2 Ontology Reuse

Mentioned as a central step in the methodology of Uschold and King, integration is a crucial step within ontology engineering as one of the purposes of an ontology is to allow for the reuse of knowledge in different contexts. Pinto distinguishes between different types of "ontology reuse" (see Pinto et al., 1999; Pinto and Martins, 2000):

---

* It is a debatable issue whether the conceptualization, the ontology formulated at the knowledge level or the ontology formalized in a given language should be shared.

- **Fusion or Merging**: The process of unifying various ontologies (typically on similar or related domains) into a new ontology. Hereby, the contribution of each source ontology might not be clearly identifiable.
- **Composition or Integration**: The process of selecting parts of certain ontologies (typically on different domains) and integrating them into a new ontology in a modular fashion as clearly identifiable submodules drawn from other ontologies.

An essential prerequisite to merging or, more generally speaking, the reuse of ontological resources are methods for ontology alignment (for a good overview see Euzenat and Shvaiko, 2007). Ontology alignment is concerned with the development of methods for the alignment of ontology elements (classes, properties) from different ontologies, based on their semantic similarity. In general, three types of methods can be distinguished here: (1) structure-based methods that compute semantic similarity relative to the structure of the ontology (similar classes share similar parents, sisters, etc.); (2) instance-based methods that compute similarity based on the overlap in terms of instances for any given pair of classes (or properties); (3) lexical methods that build on string distance between the names of classes/properties or, in more sophisticated versions, on the similarity of linguistic contexts of class/property instances (which is only tractable if a semantically annotated textual data set is available, e.g., in the case of ontology-based information extraction). Once two ontologies have been aligned, they can be merged and queried in a really integrated way.

A different, and more recent strand of research in ontology reuse is concerned with identifying appropriate ontologies for reuse (merging, integration) from among the growing number of published ontologies. As these increase in number as well as quality, it will become much easier to *find* rather than to *construct* an appropriate ontology for a particular application. On the other hand, as more and more ontologies become available, the task of selecting an appropriate ontology becomes increasingly difficult. Originally, the solution to this problem was supposed to be handled by foundational ontology libraries as discussed by van Heijst et al. (1997). However, in recent years Web-based services like Swoogle,[*] Watson,[†] and OntoSelect[‡] have been developed that enable a more data-driven approach to ontology search and retrieval. An important aspect of these services is the ranking of retrieved ontologies relative to a keyword query for instance, or, as is the case of OntoSelect (Buitelaar and Eigner, 2008), a query document. A Web-based ontology, defined in RDFS or OWL, is in many respects just another Web document that can be indexed, stored, and retrieved. However, due to the fact that ontologies are structured objects, consisting of relations, possibly also pointing to other ontologies, structural criteria are needed to rank them. Along these lines, Alani et al. (2006) have defined, for example, ontology ranking measures exploiting the structure of the ontology, including measures of "class match," "density," "semantic similarity," "betweenness," etc. The last two measures are based on the assumption that ontologies (as structures) are well-balanced in the sense that the modeling granularity is homogeneous over the whole ontology. However, practical experience shows that this is not always the case, as some parts of the ontology will be modeled more in detail than others. Another set of measures or rather criteria for ontology selection has been proposed by Sabou et al. (2006). The focus here is more on the application of ranked/selected ontologies and therefore includes such criteria as "modularization" (Can retrieved ontologies be split up in useful modules?), "returning ontology combinations" (Can retrieved ontologies be used in combination?), and "dealing with instances" (Do retrieved ontologies include instances as well as classes/properties?) next to more standard measures such as coverage.

Several examples of "merged ontologies" can be found in the NLP literature. The design of language-neutral ontologies with application in machine translation (MT) was an important research topic in the SENSUS project (Knight and Luk, 1994), especially in the context of *interlingua MT systems*. Hovy and

---

[*] http://swoogle.umbc.edu/
[†] http://watson.kmi.open.ac.uk/WatsonWUI/
[‡] http://olp.dfki.de/ontoselect

Nirenburg (1992), however, argue that language independence is almost impossible to achieve in practice and propose a data-driven approach in which a language-independent interlingua is "approximated" by folding in various taxonomies for different languages into a target taxonomy that iteratively gets more and more *language-neutral.*" The approach proceeds by processing the taxonomies in a top-down fashion, merging different nodes as well as removing fine-granular distinctions proprietary to a given language. Other work along these lines involves merging linguistic knowledge sources such as WordNet (Fellbaum, 1998) and Mikrokosmos (Nirenburg and Raskin, 2004) into an ontology called Omega (Philpot et al., 2008). This has been accomplished by removing the top levels of WordNet and Mikrokosmos and aligning the remaining parts to a New Upper Level (NUL). The resulting and unlinked "taxonomic strands" (or "curtains" as the authors call them) are then cross-linked whereby the cross-linking is supported by an automatic approach suggesting some links to human users.

24.3.2.3 Engineering Paradigms

We have seen above that early methodologies for building ontologies emerged in the 1990s. Ontology engineering methodologies in essence describe the process of ontology engineering at a meta-level, describing which steps need to be carried out in order to actually build an ontology. In this sense they are the ontology engineer's companion, guiding them in the process of building an ontology. However, current methodologies do not provide any support for making decisions about whether to include a concept or not, to model something as a class vs. an individual (is Bordeaux wine a class or an instance?), as a property vs. a class (should we model colors as datatype property of objects or as a class?). Because of this, Hovy claims that there are currently no accepted methodologies for engineering ontologies (see Hovy, 2005). Still, there is no contradiction with what we have said so far in this chapter, because the notion of "ontology engineering methodology" in the knowledge representation literature is different from what Hovy calls an engineering methodology, i.e., a set of guidelines to follow when taking modeling decisions. This is different from the understanding of a methodology as a meta-description of the process of ontology engineering in terms of steps to follow. We will refer to Hovy's methodologies as *engineering paradigms.* In this sense there is indeed a lack of accepted ontology engineering paradigms. Hovy distinguishes between the following paradigms* that can be generally attributed to different schools of thought and disciplines:

- *The logico-philosophical/mathematical paradigm*: Borrowing directly from the ideas of Aristotle in the sense that the different properties (differentiae) of things are responsible for introducing ontological distinctions in terms of subclasses. As Hovy mentions, this paradigm features an unrivaled elegance and beauty but is more difficult to implement in practice as it introduces too many distinctions (leading to a combinatorial explosion) which we as humans would not always perceive as intuitive or cognitively plausible. Second, there are many things which we as humans perceive as different concepts but we would have a hard time specifying what the differentia actually are (e.g., what are the essential properties or features of *democracy*? to cite an example from Hovy). Nevertheless, this is an important ontology modeling paradigm that has most notably lead to the development of Formal Concept Analysis (Ganter and Wille, 1999) and influenced ontology engineering methodologies such as the one by Bouaud et al. (1995) and further elaborations thereof (Bachimont et al., 2002). A number of Italian researchers (among them the people behind DOLCE (Masolo et al., 2003)) have recently started a project of building a knowledge repository collaboratively relying on differentiating criteria drawn from formal ontology (the *Senso Comune* project[†]). They rely for this purpose on top-level distinctions such as whether something is countable or not, whether it has own identity criteria or not, etc.
- *The cognitive paradigm*: Making ontological distinctions on the basis of what is intuitively perceived as different without the need for an explicit and formal specification of the features on which classes

---

* We do not regard the "taxonomical clarity" as a distinct paradigm, because it is something that is pursued across paradigms, leading to the introduction of concepts or distinctions at a higher level to foster economy of representation.
† http://www.senso-comune.it/portale/

differ. Instead, in the cognitive paradigm, the meaning of classes can be captured through natural language definitions (as suggested by Gruber) delimiting the meaning of the class in question as close as possible and contrasting it indirectly to other concepts. We would not go as far as regarding this paradigm as "hopeless" as Hovy claims. In fact, we would claim that most of the ontologies out there are produced in this way. We agree though that this makes ontological engineering a highly subjective endeavor. But after all, everybody perceives the world differently and has different needs for engineering an ontology. Collaborative engineering methodologies (see Section 24.3.2.1) are clearly a step toward reducing this subjectivity and making people at least to agree on definitions.

- *The linguistic approach*: The linguistic approach typically assumes that an ontology needs to reflect linguistic distinctions. This is indeed problematic (see our "muro" vs. "parete" example above). An ontology engineered on the basis of linguistic distinctions needs to be language-specific (unless one tries to keep it language-neutral by an approach as pursued by Hovy and Nirenburg (1992)), such that distinctions like the count/mass distinction produce different ontologies in different languages (e.g., *"furniture"* being a mass noun in English while *"Möbel"* being countable in German, see again Hirst (2004)). While this approach has inherent problems as there are concepts for which there is no direct lexicalization (e.g., the so-called covert categories such as *"all the things that can be worn on the body,"* see Hirst (2004)) and on the other hand there are many linguistic distinctions that seem arbitrary and are not directly ontologically relevant (see again Hirst (2004) on this), the approach has been successfully applied in developing language-specific thesauri as well as lexical databases such as WordNet (Fellbaum, 1998) (with a clear cognitive influence though).
- *The computer science approach*: Here we certainly have different subparadigms. On the one hand, we have people modeling ontologies as a database schema, i.e., for describing data. Such data description ontologies are typically well-defined in scope and do not generate too much controversy (after all one models the data that is already there). Applications of such schema-oriented ontologies are important for data integration where data from different sources (e.g., databases) needs to be integrated in order to allow for uniform access. On the other hand, there are people modeling ontologies according to computational aspects (against Gruber's advice!), organizing knowledge so that reasoning can be accomplished efficiently.
- *The domain specialist approach*: In many domains, people model taxonomies reflecting their understanding of a certain area (such as the gene ontology (The Gene Ontology Consortium, 2001)). These ontologies are typically organized for browsing or classifying resources to facilitate retrieval. In such a context it does not matter at all if ontologies are philosophically adequate or logically consistent. In fact, in most cases the taxonomies modeled are so simple that the question of logical inconsistency does not even arise. Such lightweight ontologies (or should we rather call them vocabularies?) are so large and so dynamically evolving that it would be simply hopeless to apply any method of formal semantics to ensure their correctness.

While it seems inadequate to base ontology design decisions only on distinctions made in language (as argued above extensively), it is certainly the case that textual data can guide the development of an ontology. After all, texts deal with the world as perceived by people, thus reflecting reality (at least as it is perceived) and thus having the potential to guide the ontology engineering process. For this reason, some methodologies center on the (linguistic) analysis of text. For example, Aussenac-Gilles et al. (2000) have suggested to apply well-known techniques from NLP, such as term extraction, concordance extraction, clustering according to distributional similarity, etc., to the task of ontology engineering. Such a text-oriented approach to ontology engineering brings us finally to the topic of *ontology learning*, i.e., the question of how data-driven learning techniques (such as NLP techniques applied to a corpus of texts) can support the process of ontology engineering. We discuss this in more detail in Section 24.4.

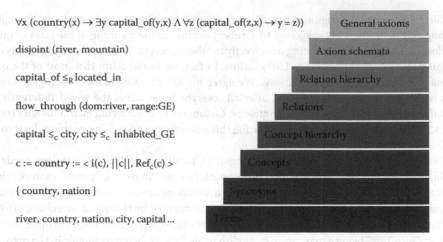

$\forall x \, (country(x) \rightarrow \exists y \, capital\_of(y,x) \land \forall z \, (capital\_of(z,x) \rightarrow y = z))$ General axioms

disjoint (river, mountain)   Axiom schemata

$capital\_of \leq_R located\_in$ Relation hierarchy

flow_through (dom:river, range:GE)   Relations

$capital \leq_c city, city \leq_c inhabited\_GE$ Concept hierarchy

$c := country := \, < i(c), ||c||, Ref_c(c) >$ Concepts

{ country, nation }   Synonyms

river, country, nation, city, capital ...   Terms

FIGURE 24.4   Ontology learning "layer cake." (Reproduced from Cimiano, P., *Ontology Learning and Population from Text: Algorithms, Evaluation and Application*, Springer-Verlag, New York, 2006.)

24.4 Ontology Learning

As ontologies are domain descriptions that tend to evolve rapidly over time and between different applications, there has been an increasing development in recent years toward learning or adapting ontologies dynamically, e.g., by analysis of a corresponding text collection. As human language is a primary mode of knowledge transfer, ontology learning from relevant text collections seems indeed a viable option. The term *"ontology learning,"* in its narrower sense meaning "ontology learning from text," has been coined by Mädche and Staab (2004) (see also Mädche, 2002) who proposed an initial set of tasks and methods for the automated generation of ontologies from natural language text—including term extraction, taxonomy induction, and relation learning.

All of these aspects of ontology development can be organized in a "layer cake" of increasingly complex subtasks (Cimiano, 2006). This layer cake, taking inspiration from the W3C's semantic Web technologies stack also known as *semantic web layer cake** has been proposed as a means for classifying approaches according to the fulfilled ontology learning tasks. As depicted by Figure 24.4, the most fundamental tasks in ontology learning are assumed to be the acquisition of lexical information about *terms* and their respective *synonymy* relationships. Atomic *concepts* (or classes) and associated labels constitute the third level of the cake, followed by *concept hierarchies*, non-taxonomic *relations* (or properties), and *relation hierarchies* represented by role inclusion axioms. The upper part of the stack comprises the instantiation of *axiom schemata* (including functional characteristics of properties and class disjointness) as well as the definition of *general axioms*.

Unavoidably, like any diagrammatic visualization or model, this layer cake represents a simplified view on the field of ontology learning. Since it has been tailored toward the requirements of ontology learning from text, it has a certain bias toward purely lexical approaches to ontology acquisition (e.g., starting with the acquisition of knowledge about terms and synonyms) without explicitly distinguishing between syntactic and semantic aspects of ontologies. Moreover, it does not commit to any particular ontology representation language and assumes an ideal, i.e., linear structure of the overall ontology learning process, without taking into account, e.g., the need for methodological ontology evaluation and engineering. However, from our point of view, the ontology learning layer cake is a respectable first

* http://www.w3.org/2001/sw/

attempt to classify ontology acquisition approaches as well as to give a structured overview of the field of ontology learning from text.

In Section 24.4.1, we will therefore adopt the layer cake as a basis for our state-of-the-art review, focusing on *open-domain* approaches to ontology learning from text. Note that nowadays more and more research aims at developing domain-specific ontology learning, e.g., in the field of bioinformatics (Alexopoulou et al., 2008). Since many of these approaches can draw upon large amounts of high-quality data or domain-specific heuristics, e.g., they often perform better than general purpose ontology learning methods.

24.4.1 State of the Art

24.4.1.1 Terms

Term extraction is a prerequisite for all other aspects of ontology learning from text. Terms are linguistic realizations of domain-specific concepts and hence a required input for all of the other layers higher up in the layer cake. The literature provides many examples of term extraction methods that could be used here. Most of these are based on information retrieval methods for term indexing (Salton and Buckley, 1998), but many also use methods from natural language processing (see Pearson, 1998; Frantzi and Ananiadou, 1999; Maynard and Ananiadou, 2001; Meyer, 2001; Ibekwe-SanJuan et al., 2007). Term extraction builds on syntactic and morphological analysis to identify and decompose complex nouns and noun phrases (compounds).

As such analysis tools are not always readily available for every language and technical domain or *sublanguage*, much of the research on term extraction for ontology learning has remained rather limited. State-of-the-art implementations mostly run a part-of-speech tagger over the domain corpus used for the ontology learning task and identifying terms over manually constructed ad hoc patterns. Additionally, and in order to identify only relevant term candidates, a statistical processing step will be included that compares the distribution of terms between corpora. The most widely used statistical measures for this include TFIDF (Salton, 1991), entropy (Gray, 1990), and C-value / NC-value (Frantzi et al., 1998), whereas the significance of term occurrences is determined by comparison with a reference corpus (Basili et al., 2001; Kilgarriff, 2001; Drouin, 2004) or by considering structural information that is provided by HTML or XML documents (Brunzel, 2008). For a good overview of term extraction methods, see Witschel (2005) and Jacquemin (2001). An ontology learning system that builds primarily on term extraction is TERMINAE (Biebow and Szulman, 1999).

24.4.1.2 Synonyms

The synonymy level addresses the acquisition of semantic variants, i.e., words as well as more complex terms that have similar meanings and can be mutually exchanged within semantically similar contexts. Synonymy can be defined within as well as between languages, where the latter in fact concerns the acquisition of term translations. Much of the work on synonymy acquisition has focused on the use of WordNet for English synonyms and EuroWordNet for multilingual synonyms and translations. An important aspect of this work is the identification of the appropriate sense of the word in question, which determines the set of synonyms that are to be extracted. Synonymy detection is therefore closely related to word sense disambiguation (cf. Lesk, 1986; Yarowsky, 1992) with some approaches directly applying sense disambiguation for synonymy acquisition (Turcato et al., 2000; Buitelaar and Sacaleanu, 2002). In the case of terms consisting of several words, ambiguity usually is a minor problem but the challenge here is to identify similarity across a set of terms with different lexical structures. Hamon and Nazarenko (2001) have for example developed a compositional projection approach in which they assume that complex terms are synonyms in case their components are the same or synonyms according to some given lexicon.

In contrast to all such approaches that are based on existing synonymy collections and therefore top-down, other, more bottom-up approaches have focused on algorithms for the dynamic acquisition of synonyms through clustering. Such algorithms are based primarily on Harris's distributional hypothesis, which states roughly that words are similar in meaning to the extent in which they share syntactic contexts, see Harris (1954, 1968) for seminal work as well as more recent work building on this assumption, e.g., Hindle (1990) and Lin and Pantel (2001b, 2002). Related work on Latent Semantic Indexing and similar algorithms (LSI, LSA, PLSI) emerged out of term indexing for information retrieval. LSI algorithms apply dimension reduction techniques to reveal inherent connections between words that may lead to group formation (Schütze, 1993; Landauer and Dumais, 1997). Given the growing importance of the Web in knowledge acquisition, such methods are now increasingly applied also to Web-based data sets (e.g., Turney, 2001; Baroni and Bisi, 2004).

24.4.1.3 Concepts

The extraction of concepts from text is controversial as it is not clear what exactly constitutes a concept. In our view, concept learning should provide an intensional definition of the concept, an extensional set of concept instances, and a set of linguistic realizations for the concept. Most of the research in concept learning addresses the question from a linguistic or textual perspective, regarding concepts as clusters of related terms. These approaches therefore overlap with those in term extraction and synonymy detection as discussed above.

Alternatively, researchers have approached the problem from an extensional point of view. Evans (2003), for example, derived concepts from hierarchies of named entities that were extracted from textual documents. In contrast, the KnowItAll system (Etzioni et al., 2004) aims at learning the extension of pre-defined concepts like movie actors as they appear in Web documents. In the approach of Evans the concepts as well as their extensions are derived simultaneously, whereas the KnowItAll system essentially populates existing concepts with instances. The population of existing concepts with instances is typically referred to as *ontology population*.

Finally, intensional concept learning includes the generation of formal and informal definitions. The generation of concept definitions can be based for example on the generation of a textual description in the form of a gloss. Research on this area is however quite rare. In fact the only work reported in this area is the OntoLearn system that derives glosses for domain-specific concepts from WordNet, text corpora and other Web resources (Velardi et al., 2005). Formal definition generation, in contrast, will be based on the extraction of relations and axioms as discussed in Sections 24.4.1.5 and 24.4.1.6.

24.4.1.4 Concept Hierarchy

The backbone of any ontology is constituted by a set of taxonomic relationships among classes. Each of the classes can be defined intensionally, e.g., by a descriptive label or its relationships to other classes, as well as extensionally by specifying a set of instances belonging to this class. Since the underlying taxonomy of an ontology, independently of the underlying ontology representation language, is of crucial importance for the use of ontologies as a means of abstraction, many ontology learning approaches have focused on the extraction of concept hierarchies. The vast majority of these approaches rely on lexico-syntactic patterns for hyponymy extraction, commonly known as *Hearst patterns*, named after Marti Hearst, who authored an influential and commonly cited paper on this topic (Hearst, 1992) (see also a description of the current state of the art in Auger and Barriere, 2008). The following examples are taken from Hearst's seminal publication:

- Such NP as {NP,}* {or | and} NP (e.g., *"religious buildings such as churches and mosques"*)
- NP {, NP}* {,} {and | or} other NP (e.g., *"senators, governors, and other politicians"*)
- NP {,} including {NP,}* {or | and} NP (e.g., *"green vegetables, including beans and spinach"*)
- NP {,} especially {NP,}* {or | and} NP (e.g., *"office furniture, especially desks and bookcases"*)

These patterns, essentially linguistic expressions encoding both lexical and syntactic constraints, have shown to be a helpful means to the acquisition of taxonomic knowledge such as hyponymy relationships or categories of named entities. Additional patterns such as the following have been proposed by Ogata and Collier (2004), Cimiano et al. (2004), Marhsman et al. (2002), and others:

- Exception: NP except for NP (e.g., "European *countries* except for *Spain*")
- Apposition: NP, the capital of NP (e.g., "*London*, the *capital* of England")
- Definites: the PN hotel (e.g., "the *Hilton hotel*")
- Copula: NP is a NP (e.g., "*Brazil* is a South American *country*")
- Doubly anchored hyponym patterns as suggested by Kozareva et al. (2008), (e.g., *presidents* such as *Clinton* and PN)

The latter kinds of patterns are called "doubly anchored" because they not only include the superclass or hyponym, i.e., "presidents" in the above example, but also an additional instance, subclass or, in linguistic terms, a hyponym, i.e., "Clinton" in the given example. The aim is to have more "focused" patterns yielding a higher precision, which in this case can be used to extract other presidents than Clinton. The above pattern would for example match an occurrence such as "presidents such as Clinton and Bush," where "Bush" would be extracted as a new instance of the class of presidents.

The performance of different patterns has been systematically investigated (e.g., Aussenac-Gilles and Jacques, 2008). Finally, a large body of work on dictionary parsing reaching back to the 1980s and 1990s (Cimiano, 2006, Chapter 6) as well as recent similar work on knowledge extraction from online glossaries (Hovy et al., 2003) and Wikipedia (Ruiz-Casado et al., 2005; Suh et al., 2006; Weber and Buitelaar, 2006) builds also on lexico-syntactic patterns.

Common to all pattern-based approaches to hyponymy extraction is the problem of data sparseness. Since occurrences of lexico-syntactic patterns are comparatively rare in naturally occurring text, most research nowadays concentrates on the use of search engines and therefore indirectly using the Web itself as a data set (Resnik and Smith, 2003; Cimiano et al., 2005; Blohm and Cimiano, 2007)—although the enormous syntactic and semantic heterogeneity of Web documents poses many new challenges. Additionally, approaches toward the automatic generation of lexico-syntactic patterns (Etzioni et al., 2004; Pantel and Pennacchiotti, 2006; Blohm et al., 2007; Brewster et al., 2007) also aim at increasing flexibility and effectiveness in hyponymy extraction.

A set of very different approaches rely instead on hierarchical clustering techniques in order to group terms with similar linguistic behavior into hierarchically arranged clusters (Caraballo, 1999; Faure and Nédellec, 1999; Cimiano et al., 2004). The clusters obtained by this kind of approach are assumed to represent classes, the meaning of which is constrained by a characterizing set of terms. Clustering techniques clearly have the advantage of yielding a higher recall than pattern-based approaches because they are less dependent on more or less explicit manifestations of hyponymy. On the other hand, the generated clusters, respectively classes, often lack meaningful labels, although several approaches to the automatic labeling of clusters have been proposed in recent years (Kashyap et al., 2005). Clustering-based taxonomy induction seems to yield only low precision, especially on small to medium size corpora, as here again data sparseness constitutes a serious challenge, e.g., Pantel and Pennacchiotti (2006) claim that clustering methods cannot work reliably on corpora with fewer than 100 million words.

24.4.1.5 Relation Extraction

Synonymy and concept hierarchies depend on the paradigmatic aspect of language, i.e., the extent in which words, terms, or more complex linguistic units can be exchanged across different contexts (sentences, paragraphs, or more extensive discourses). Relation extraction however, as discussed here, depends rather on the syntagmatic aspect of language, i.e., the extent in which more or less complex linguistic units are connected within a sentence, paragraph, or more extensive discourse. Syntagmatic relations are given by syntactic structure and have been, for example, exploited in the acquisition of non-taxonomic relations (or object properties) from text, specifically through the analysis of verbs and their arguments as defined lexically by subcategorization frames (see, e.g., Schutz and Buitelaar, 2005 on sports text and Ciaramita et al., 2005 on biomedical text). Relation extraction is therefore also very much related to the problem of acquiring selection restrictions for verb arguments as witnessed for instance by the ASIUM system that enables an integrated acquisition of relations and subcategorization frames for the verbs that underlie these relations (Faure and Poibeau, 2000). A major challenge in this is however the identification of the right level of abstraction in determining the most specific restrictions for the arguments (domain and range in RDF/OWL) of the extracted relation (see Cimiano et al., 2006 for some solutions).

Other methods for relation extraction include work based on association rules (Mädche and Staab, 2000; Antunes, 2007), in combination with shallow linguistic analysis on the level of part of speech and chunking, and collocations (Heyer et al., 2001). Such approaches require however a higher degree of user interaction as the generated relations lack any meaningful interpretation as well as naming or "labeling" of the relation (but see Kavalec and Svátek, 2005 for some relation labeling experiments).

Finally, as it is one of the most frequently used relations in ontology modeling, the extraction of part-of ("meronymy") relations is supported by many ontology learning frameworks, such as OntoLearn (Velardi et al., 2005) and TextToOnto (Mädche and Volz, 2001). Most of the approaches for meronymy extraction are again based on lexico-syntactic patterns (Girju et al., 2006; van Hage et al., 2006) as proposed originally by Berland and Charniak (1999).

24.4.1.6 Axiom Schemata and General Axioms

The task of learning general axioms and axiom schemata has not attracted much attention in the ontology learning community so far. Some early work includes the automatic generation of disjointness axioms (Haase and Völker, 2005; Völker et al., 2007) and complex class descriptions (Völker et al., 2007). In addition, semiautomatic approaches to taxonomy refinement (Völker and Rudolph, 2008b) and the acquisition of general domain-range restrictions (Völker and Rudolph, 2008a) based on Formal Concept Analysis have been proposed in recent years. Closely related is also work on learning paraphrases (Lin and Pantel, 2001a) and lexical entailments as well as on concept learning in Inductive Logic Programming (see, e.g., Cohen and Hirsh, 1994; Esposito et al., 2004; Fanizzi et al., 2004). Approaches to the automatic axiomatization of WordNet have been proposed, for example, by Navigli and Velardi (2006) as well as by Moldovan et al. (2007), who evaluated their approach in the context of a question answering application.

24.5 Summary

In this chapter we have provided an overview of the current *state of the art* in ontology construction with an emphasis on NLP-related issues such as text-driven ontology engineering and ontology learning methods. In order to put these methods into the broader perspective of knowledge engineering applications of this work, we also presented a discussion of ontology research itself, in its philosophical origins and historic background as well as in terms of methodologies in ontology engineering. We feel that a thorough discussion of these aspects of the research is needed in order to appreciate the underlying difficulties and challenges in the field of data (text)-driven ontology construction.

In essence, most of the techniques needed for text-driven ontology construction are already available and well-understood as discussed in Section 24.4. However, the most important challenge is to integrate these different techniques in such a way that effective (high performance) and efficient (robust and fast) ontology engineering systems can be designed, with the underlying NLP technique being seamlessly integrated and transparent to the domain knowledge engineer. However, as we are realistically still far away from such integrated systems, it is currently much more worthwhile to take stock of the different underlying technologies that are central to the integrated text-driven ontology construction task.

Acknowledgments

We would like to thank Nathalie Aussenac-Gilles and Eduard Hovy for their extensive and constructive reviewing, as well as Sofia Pinto and Sebastian Rudolph for providing further feedback, all of which helped in improving this chapter. However as always, any errors or shortcomings that remain are the sole responsibility of the authors.

The work presented in this paper has been funded in part by Science Foundation Ireland under Grant No. SFI/08/CE/I1380 for the Lion-2 project, the Multipla project sponsored by the German Research Foundation (DFG) under grant number 38457858 as well as by the European Commission under grant number IST-2005-027595 (NeOn project).

References

Alani, H., Ch. Brewster, and N. Shadbolt. Ranking ontologies with AKTiveRank. In *Proceedings of the Fifth International Semantic Web Conference (ISWC)*, Athens, GA, pp. 1–15, 2006.

Alexopoulou, D., T. Wächter, L. Pickersgill, C. Eyre, and M. Schroeder. Terminologies for text-mining; an experiment in the lipoprotein metabolism domain. *BMC Bioinformatics*, 9(Suppl 4):S2, April 2008.

Antunes, C. Mining rules in the Onto4AR framework for updating domain ontologies. In *Proceedings of the IADIS European Conference on Data Mining (IADIS-ECDM'07)*, Lisbon, Portugal, pp. 95–101. IADIS Press, 2007.

Artale, A., E. Franconi, N. Guarino, and L. Pazzi. Part-whole relations in object-centered systems: An overview. *Data Knowledge Engineering*, 20(3):347–383, 1996.

Auger, A. and C. Barriere. Pattern based approaches to semantic relation extraction: A state-of-the-art. *Terminology*, 14(1):1–19, 2008. (Special issue on Pattern-based approaches to semantic relation extraction.)

Aussenac-Gilles, N. and M.-P. Jacques. Designing and evaluating patterns for relation acquisition from texts with CAMALEON. *Terminology*, 14(1):45–73, 2008. (Special issue on Pattern-based approaches to semantic relation extraction.)

Aussenac-Gilles, N., B. Biebow, and S. Szulman. Revisiting ontology design: A methodology based on corpus analysis. In *Proceedings of the International Conference on Knowledge Engineering and Knowledge Management (EKAW)*, Juan-les-Pins, France, pp. 172–188, 2000.

Baader, F., D. Calvanese, D. McGuiness, D. Nardi, and P. Patel-Schneider, editors. *The Description Logic Handbook*. Cambridge University Press, Cambridge, U.K., 2003.

Bachimont, B., A. Isaac, and R. Troncy. Semantic commitment for designing ontologies: A proposal. In *Proceedings of the 13th International Conference on Knowledge Engineering and Knowledge Management (EKAW)*, Siguenza, Spain, pp. 114 – 121, 2002.

Baroni, M. and S. Bisi. Using cooccurrence statistics and the web to discover synonyms in a technical language. In *Proceedings of the Fourth International Conference on Language Resources and Evaluation (LREC)*, Lisbon, Portugal, pp. 1725–1728, 2004.

Basili, R., A. Moschitti, M.T. Pazienza, and F.M. Zanzotto. A contrastive approach to term extraction. In *Proceedings of the Fourth Terminology and Artificial Intelligence Conference (TIA)*, Nancy, France, 2001.

Bechhofer, S. An introduction to OWL. Tutorial slides for the Semantic Web Tutorial at ISWC'08, 2008. http://kmi.open.ac.uk/events/iswc08-semantic-web-intro/

Bechhofer, S., F. van Harmelen, J. Hendler, I. Horrocks, D.L. McGuinees, P.F. Patel-Schneider, and L.A. Stein. OWL Web Ontology Language Reference. http://www.w3.org/TR/owl-ref, 2004.

Berland, M. and E. Charniak. Finding parts in very large corpora. In *Proceedings of the 37th Annual Meeting of the Association for Computational Linguistics (ACL)*, College Park, MD, pp. 57–64, 1999.

Berners-Lee, T., J. Hendler, and O. Lassila. The Semantic Web. *Scientific American*, 284(5):34–43, 2001.

Biebow, B. and S. Szulman. TERMINAE: A linguistic-based tool for the building of a domain ontology. In *Proceedings of the 11th Workshop on Knowledge Acquisition, Modeling and Management (EKAW)*, Dagstuhl, Germany, pp. 49–66, 1999.

Blohm, S. and P. Cimiano. Using the web to reduce data sparseness in pattern-based information extraction. In *Proceedings of the 11th European Conference on Principles and Practice of Knowledge Discovery in Databases (PKDD)*, Warsaw, Poland, pp. 18–29, 2007.

Blohm, S., P. Cimiano, and E. Stemle. Harvesting relations from the web—Quantifiying the impact of filtering functions. In *Proceedings of the 22nd Conference on Artificial Intelligence (AAAI-07)*, Vancouver, Canada, pp. 1316–1323, 2007.

Bouaud, J., B. Bachimont, J. Charlet, and P. Zweigenbaum. Methodological principles for structuring an "ontology." In *Proceedings of the IJCAI'95 Workshop on Basic Ontological Issues in Knowledge Sharing*, Montreal, Canada, 1995.

Brewster, C., J. Iria, Z. Zhang, F. Ciravegna, L. Guthrie, and Y. Wilks. Dynamic iterative ontology learning. In *Proceedings of the International Conference on Recent Advances in Natural Language Processing (RANLP)*, Borovets, Bulgaria, September 2007.

Brickley, D. and R.V. Guha. RDF Vocabulary Description Language 1.0: RDF Schema. Technical report, W3C, 2002. W3C Working Draft. http://www.w3.org/TR/rdf-schema/.

Brunzel, M. The XTREEM methods for ontology learning from web documents. In P. Buitelaar and P. Cimiano, editors, *Ontology Learning and Population: Bridging the Gap between Text and Knowledge, Frontiers in Artificial Intelligence and Applications*, 167:3–26. IOS Press, Amsterdam, the Netherlands, 2008.

Buitelaar, P. and T. Eigner. Ontology search with the OntoSelect Ontology Library. In *Proceedings of the International Conference on Lexical Resources and Evaluation (LREC)*, Marrakech, Morocco, pp. 1030–1033. ELRA, 2008.

Buitelaar, P. and B. Sacaleanu. Extending synsets with medical terms. In *Proceedings of the First International WordNet Conference*, Mysore, India, January 21–25, 2002.

Caraballo, S.A. Automatic construction of a hypernym-labeled noun hierarchy from text. In *Proceedings of the 37th Annual Meeting of the Association for Computational Linguistics (ACL)*, College Park, MD, pp. 120–126, 1999.

Ciaramita, M., A. Gangemi, E. Ratsch, J. Saric, and I. Rojas. Unsupervised learning of semantic relations between concepts of a molecular biology ontology. In *Proceedings of the 19th International Joint Conference on Artificial Intelligence (IJCAI)*, Edinburg, U.K., pp. 659–664, 2005.

Cimiano, P. *Ontology Learning and Population from Text: Algorithms, Evaluation and Applications*. Springer Verlag, New York, 2006.

Cimiano, P., S. Handschuh, and S. Staab. Towards the self-annotating web. In *Proceedings of the 13th World Wide Web Conference (WWW)*, New York, pp. 462–471, 2004.

Cimiano, P., M. Hartung, and E. Ratsch. Finding the appropriate generalization level for binary relations extracted from the Genia corpus. In *Proceedings of the International Conference on Language Resources and Evaluation (LREC)*, Genoa, Italy, pp. 161–169, 2006.

Cimiano, P., A. Hotho, and S. Staab. Comparing conceptual, divisive and agglomerative clustering for learning taxonomies from text. In *Proceedings of the European Conference on Artificial Intelligence (ECAI)*, Valencia, Spain, pp. 435–439, 2004.

Cimiano, P., G. Ladwig, and S. Staab. Gimme' the context: Context-driven automatic semantic annotation with C-PANKOW. In *Proceedings of the 14th World Wide Web Conference (WWW)*, Chiba, Japan, pp. 332–341, 2005.

Cohen, W. and H. Hirsh. Learning the classic description logic: Theoretical and experimental results. In *Proceedings of the Fourth International Conference on Principles of Knowledge Representation and Reasoning (KR)*, Bonn, Germany, pp. 121–133. Morgan Kaufmann, 1994.

Conolly, D., F. van Harmelen, I. Horrocks, D.L. McGuiness, P.F. Patel-Schneider, and L.A. Stein. Daml+oil reference description. W3C Note, December 2001. Available at http://www.w3.org/TR/2001/NOTE-daml+oil-reference-20011218

Corcho, O., M. Fernández-López, A. Gómez-Pérez, and A. López-Cima. Building legal ontologies with METHONTOLOGY and WebODE. In R. Benjamins, P. Casanovas, A. Gangemi, and B. Selic, editors, *Law and the Semantic Web: Legal Ontologies, Methodologies, Legal Information Retrieval, and Applications*, volume 3369 of *Lecture Notes in Computer Science*. Springer, Berlin, Germany, pp. 142–157, 2005.

Cruse, D.A. *Lexical Semantics*. Cambridge University Press, Cambridge, U.K., 1986.

Drouin, P. Detection of domain specific terminology using corpora comparison. In *Proceedings of the Fourth International Conference on Language Resources and Evaluation (LREC)*, Lisbon, Portugal, pp. 79–82, 2004.

Esposito, F., N. Fanizzi, L. Iannone, I. Palmisano, and G. Semeraro. Knowledge-intensive induction of terminologies from metadata. In *Proceedings of the Third International Semantic Web Conference (ISWC)*, Hiroshima, Japan, volume 3298 of *Lecture Notes in Computer Science*, pp. 441–455. Springer, Berlin, Germany, 2004.

Etzioni, O., M. Cafarella, D. Downey, S. Kok, A.-M. Popescu, T. Shaked, S. Soderland, D.S. Weld, and A. Yates. Web-scale information extraction in KnowItAll (preliminary results). In *Proceedings of the 13th World Wide Web Conference (WWW)*, New York, pp. 100–109, 2004.

Euzenat, J. and P. Shvaiko. *Ontology Matching*. Springer, Heidelberg, Germany, 2007.

Evans, R. A framework for named entity recognition in the open domain. In *Proceedings of the International Conference on Recent Advances in Natural Language Processing (RANLP)*, Borovets, Bulgaria, pp. 137–144, 2003.

Fanizzi, N., L. Iannone, I. Palmisano, and G. Semeraro. Concept formation in expressive description logics. In *Proceedings of the 15th European Conference on Machine Learning (ECML)*, Pisa, Italy pp. 99–110. Springer Verlag, 2004.

Faure, D. and C. Nédellec. Knowledge acquisition of predicate argument structures from technical texts using machine learning: The system asium. In *Proceedings of the International Conference on Knowledge Engineering and Knowledge Management (EKAW)*, Dagstuhl Castle, Germany, *Lecture Notes in Computer Science*, 1621:329–334. Springer, 1999.

Faure, D. and T. Poibeau. First experiences of using semantic knowledge learned by ASIUM for information extraction task using INTEX. In S. Staab, A. Mädche, C. Nedellec, and P. Wiemer-Hastings, editors, *Proceedings of the First Workshop on Ontology Learning (OL) at the 14th European Conference on Artificial Intelligence (ECAI)*, Berlin, Germany, vol. 31 of *CEUR Workshop Proceedings*. CEUR-WS.org, 2000.

Fellbaum, C. *WordNet, an Electronic Lexical Database*. MIT Press, Cambridge, MA, 1998.

Fensel, D., F. van Harmelen, I. Horrocks, D.L. McGuiness, and P.F. Patel-Schneider. OIL: An ontology infrastructure for the semantic web. *IEEE Intelligent Systems*, 16(2):38–45, 2001.

Frantzi, K. and S. Ananiadou. The C-value / NC-value domain independent method for multi-word term extraction. *Journal of Natural Language Processing*, 6(3):145–179, 1999.

Frantzi, K., S. Ananiadou, and J. Tsuji. The C-value/NC-value method of automatic recognition for multi-word terms. In *Proceedings of the European Conference on Digital Libraries (ECDL)*, Heraklion, Crete, Greece, pp. 585–604, 1998.

Ganter, B. and R. Wille. *Formal Concept Analysis—Mathematical Foundations*. Springer Verlag, Heidelberg, Germany, 1999.

Genesereth, M.R. and R.E. Fikes. Knowledge interchange format version 3.0 reference manual. Technical Report Logic-92-1, Computer Science Department, Stanford University, Stanford, CA, 1992.

Girju, R., A. Badulescu, and D. Moldovan. Automatic discovery of part-whole relations. *Computational Linguistics*, 32(1):83–135, 2006.

Göckel, R. *Lexicon philosophicum, quo tanquam clave philosophicae fores aperiuntur*. Georg Olms Verlag, Hildesheim, Germany, 1613.

Gray, R.M. *Entropy and Information Theory*. Springer, New York, 1990.

Grenon, P., B. Smith, and L. Goldberg. Biodynamic ontology: Applying bfo in the biomedical domain. In D.M. Pisanelli, editor, *Ontologies in Medicine, Studies in Health Technology and Informatics*, 102:20–38. IOS Press, Amsterdam, the Netherlands, 2004.

Gruber, T.R. Toward principles for the design of ontologies used for knowledge sharing. In *Formal Analysis in Conceptual Analysis and Knowledge Representation.* Kluwer, Amsterdam, the Netherlands, 1993.

Grüninger, M. and M. Fox. The logic of enterprise modelling. In J. Brown and D. O'Sullivan, editors, *Reengineering the Enterprise.* Chapman & Hall, London, U.K., 1995.

Guarino, N. Understanding, building and using ontologies. *International Journal of Human Computer Studies,* 46(2):293–310, 1997.

Guarino, N. Formal ontology and information systems. In *Proceedings of Formal Ontology in Information Systems (FOIS),* Trento, Italy, pp. 3–15, 1998a.

Guarino, N. Some ontological principles for designing upper level lexical resources. In *Proceedings of First International Conference on Language Resources and Evaluation (LREC),* Granada, Spain, pp. 527–534, 1998b.

Guarino, N. and P. Giaretta. Ontologies and knowledge bases: Towards a terminological clarification. In N.J.I. Mars, editor, *Towards Very Large Knowledge Bases.* IOS Press, Amsterdam, the Netherlands, 1995.

Haase, P. and J. Völker. Ontology learning and reasoning—Dealing with uncertainty and inconsistency. In *Proceedings of the Workshop on Uncertainty Reasoning for the Semantic Web (URSW),* Galway, Ireland, pp. 45–55, 2005.

Hamon, T. and A. Nazarenko. Detection of synonymy links between terms: Experiments and results. In D. Bourigault, C. Jacquemin, and M.-C. L'Homme, editors, *Recent Advances in Computational Terminology,* Chapter 18, pp. 185–208. John Benjamins, Amsterdam, the Netherlands, 2001.

Harris, Z. Distributional structure. *Word,* 10(2/3):146–162, 1954.

Harris, Z. *Mathematical Structures of Language.* John Wiley & Sons, New York, 1968.

Hearst, M.A. Automatic acquisition of hyponyms from large text corpora. In *Proceedings of the 14th International Conference on Computational Linguistics (COLING),* Nantes, France, pp. 539–545, 1992.

Heyer, G., M. Läuter, U. Quasthoff, T. Wittig, and C. Wolff. Learning relations using collocations. In *Proceedings of the Second Workshop on Ontology Learning (OL) at the 17th International Conference on Artificial Intelligence (IJCAI),* Seattle, WA, 2001.

Hindle, D. Noun classification from predicate-argument structures. In *Proceedings of the Annual Meeting of the Association for Computational Linguistics (ACL),* Pittsburgh, PA, pp. 317–322, 1990.

Hirst, G. Ontology and the lexicon. In S. Staab and R. Studer, editors, *Handbook on Ontologies,* pp. 209–229. Springer Verlag, Berlin, Germany, 2004.

Hitzler, P., M. Krötzsch, S. Rudolph, and Y. Sure. *Semantic Web Grundlagen.* Examen.press, Springer, Berlin, Germany, 2008.

Horrocks, I., P.F. Patel-Schneider, and F. van Harmelen. From SHIQ and RDF to OWL: The making of a web ontology language. *Journal of Web Semantics,* 1(1):7–26, 2003.

Hovy, E. Methodologies for the reliable construction of ontological knowledge. In F. Dau, M.-L. Mugnier, and G. Stunmer, editors, *Proceedings of the International Conference on Conceptual Structures (ICCS),* Kassel, Germany, *Lecture Notes in Computer Sciences,* 3596:91–106, 2005.

Hovy, E. and S. Nirenburg. Approximating an interlingua in a principled way. In *Proceedings of the Workshop on Speech and Natural Language,* Harriman, NY, 1992.

Hovy, E., A. Philpot, J. Klavans, U. Germann, P. Davis, and S. Popper. Extending metadata definitions by automatically extracting and organizing glossary definitions. In *Proceedings of the Annual National Conference on Digital Government Research,* Boston, MA, pp. 1–6, 2003.

Ibekwe-SanJuan, F., A. Condamines, and M.T. Cabré, editors. *Application-Driven Terminology Engineering.* John Benjamins, Amsterdam, the Netherlands, 2007.

Jacquemin, C. *Spotting and Discovering Terms Through Natural Language Processing.* MIT Press, Cambridge, MA, 2001.

Kashyap, V., C. Ramakrishnan, C. Thomas, and A. Sheth. Taxaminer: An experimentation framework for automated taxonomy bootstrapping. *International Journal of Web and Grid Services*, 1(2):240–266, 2005.

Kavalec, M. and V. Svátek. A study on automated relation labelling in ontology learning. In P. Buitelaar, P. Cimiano, and B. Magnini, editors, *Ontology Learning from Text: Methods, Evaluation and Applications, Frontiers in Artificial Intelligence and Applications*, 123:44–58. IOS Press, Amsterdam, the Netherlands, 2005.

Kilgarriff, A. Comparing corpora. *International Journal of Corpus Linguistics*, 1(6):97–103, 2001.

Knight, K. and S. Luk. Building a large knowledge base for machine translation. In *Proceedings of the 12th National Conference on Artificial Intelligence (AAAI)*, Seattle, WA, pp. 773–778, 1994.

Kozareva, Z., E. Riloff, and E. Hovy. Semantic class learning from the web with hyponym pattern linkage graphs. In *Proceedings of the 46th Annual Meeting of the Association for Computational Linguistics (ACL) and the International Human Language Technology (HLT) Conference*, Columbus, OH, 2008.

Landauer, T.K. and S.T. Dumais. A solution to Plato's problem: The latent semantic analysis theory of acquisition, induction and representation of knowledge. *Psychological Review*, 104:211–240, 1997.

Lassila, O. and R. Swick. Resource description framework (RDF) model and syntax specification. Technical report, W3C, 1999. W3C Recommendation. http://www.w3.org/TR/REC-rdf-syntax

Lesk, M. Automatic sense disambiguation using machine readable dictionaries: How to tell a pine cone from an ice cream cone. In *Proceedings of the Fifth Annual International Conference on Systems Documentation*, Toronto, Canada, pp. 24–26, 1986.

Lin, D. and P. Pantel. DIRT—Discovery of Inference Rules from Text. In *Proceedings of the ACM SIGKDD International Conference on Knowledge Discovery and Data Mining*, San Francisco, CA, pp. 323–328, 2001a.

Lin, D. and P. Pantel. Induction of semantic classes from natural language text. In *Proceedings of the Seventh ACM SIGKDD International Conference on Knowledge Discovery and Data Mining*, San Francisco, CA, pp. 317–322, 2001b.

Lin, D. and P. Pantel. Concept discovery from text. In *Proceedings of the International Conference on Computational Linguistics (COLING)*, Taipei, Taiwan, pp. 1–7, 2002.

Lorhard, J. *Ogdoas Scholastica*. Saint Gallen, Switzerland, 1606.

Mädche, A. *Ontology Learning for the Semantic Web*. Kluwer Academic Publishers, Norwell, MA, 2002.

Mädche, A. and S. Staab. Discovering conceptual relations from text. In *Proceedings of the 14th European Conference on Artificial Intelligence (ECAI)*, Berlin, Germany, pp. 321–325. IOS Press, 2000.

Mädche, A. and S. Staab. Ontology learning. In Steffen Staab and Rudi Studer, editors, *Handbook on Ontologies, International Handbooks on Information Systems*, pp. 173–190. Springer, Berlin, Germany, 2004.

Mädche, A. and R. Volz. The Text-To-Onto ontology extraction and maintenance system. In *Proceedings of the ICDM Workshop on Integrating Data Mining and Knowledge Management*, San Jose, CA, 2001.

Mann, W.C. and S.A. Thompson. Rhetorical structure theory: Toward a functional theory of text organization. *Text*, 8(3):243–281, 1988.

Marhsman, E., T. Morgan, and I. Meyer. French patterns for expressing concept relations. *Terminology*, 8(1):1–30, 2002.

Masolo, C., S. Borgo, A. Gangemi, N. Guarino, and A. Oltramari. Ontology library (final). WonderWeb deliverable D18, December 2003. http://wonderweb.semanticweb.org/deliverables/documents/D18.pdf

Maynard, D. and S. Ananiadou. TRUCKS: A model for automatic term recognition. *Journal of Natural Language Processing*, 8(1):101–125, 2001.

McGuiness, D.L., R. Fikes, L.A. Stein, and J.A. Hendler. DAML-ONT: An ontology language for the semantic web. In D. Fensel, J. Hendler, H. Lieberman, and W. Wahlster, editors, *Spinning the Semantic Web: Bringing the World Wide Web to Its Full Potential*. MIT Press, Cambridge, MA, 2002.

McIlraith, S., T.C. Son, and H. Zeng. Semantic web services. *IEEE Intelligent Systems,* 16(2):46–53, March/April 2001.

Meyer, I. Extracting knowledge-rich contexts for terminography: A conceptual and methodological framework. *Recent Advances in Computational Terminology,* John Benjamins, Amsterdam, the Netherlands, pp. 279–302, 2001.

Moldovan, D., C. Clark, S.M. Harabagiu, and D. Hodges. Cogex: A semantically and contextually enriched logic prover for question answering. *Journal of Applied Logic,* 5(1):49–69, 2007.

Navigli, R. and P. Velardi. Ontology enrichment through automatic semantic annotation of on-line glossaries. In *Proceedings of the 15th International Conference on Knowledge Engineering and Knowledge Management (EKAW),* Prague, Czech Republic, *Lecture Notes in Computer Science,* 4248:126–140. Springer, 2006.

Newell, A. The knowledge level. *Artificial Intelligence,* 18(1), 87–127, 1982.

Nirenburg, S. and V. Raskin. Ontological semantics, formal ontology and ambiguity. In *Proceedings of Formal Ontology in Information Systems (FOIS),* Ogunquit, MI, pp. 151–161, 2001.

Nirenburg, S. and V. Raskin. *Ontological Semantics.* MIT Press, Cambridge, MA, 2004.

Noy, N.F. and D.L. McGuiness. Ontology development 101: A guide to creating your first ontology. Technical Report SMI-2001-0880, Stanford Medical Informatics, Stanford, CA, 2001.

Ogata, N. and N. Collier. Ontology express: Statistical and non-monotonic learning of domain ontologies from text. In *Proceedings of the Workshop on Ontology Learning and Population (OLP) at the 16th European Conference on Artificial Intelligence (ECAI),* Valencia, Spain, August 22–24, 2004.

Ohrstrom, O., J. Andersen, and H. Schärfe. What has happened to ontology. In F. Dau, M.-L. Mugnier, and G. Stumme, editors, *Conceptual Structures: Common Semantics for Sharing Knowledge, Proceedings of the 13th International Conference on Conceptual Structures (ICCS'05),* Kassel, Germany, pp. 425–438, 2005.

Pantel, P. and M. Pennacchiotti. Espresso: Leveraging generic patterns for automatically harvesting semantic relations. In *Proceedings of the 21st International Conference on Computational Linguistics (COLING) and 44th Annual Meeting of the Association for Computational Linguistics (ACL),* Sydney, Australia, 2006.

Paolucci, M., T. Kawamura, T.R. Payne, and K. Sycara. Semantic matching of web service capabilities. In *Proceedings of the First International Semantic Web Conference (ISWC),* Sardinia, Italy, pp. 333–347, 2001.

Pearson, J. *Terms in Context.* John Benjamins, Amsterdam, the Netherlands, 1998.

Philpot, A., E. Hovy, and P. Pantel. The Omega ontology. In C.-R. Huang, N. Calzolari, A. Gangemi, A. Lenci, A. Oltramari, and L. Prévot, editors, *Ontologies and Lexical Resources for Natural Language Processing,* Cambridge University Press, Cambridge, U.K., pp. 309–322, 2008.

Pinto, H.S., A. Gomez-Perez, and J.P. Martins. Some issues on ontology integration. In *Proceedings of the IJCAI99 Workshop on Ontologies and Problem Solving Methods,* Stockholm, Sweden, 1999.

Pinto, H.S. and J.P. Martins. Reusing ontologies. In *Proceedings of the AAAI Spring Symposium on Bringing Knowledge to Business Processes,* Stanford, CA, pp. 77–84, 2000.

Pinto, H.S. and J.P. Martins. Ontologies: How can they be built? *Knowledge and Information Systems,* 6(4):441–464, 2004.

Pinto, H.S. and C. Tempich. Diligent: Towards a fine-grained methodology for distributed, loosely-controlled and evolving engineering of ontologies. In *Proceedings of the European Conference on Artificial Intelligence (ECAI),* Valencia, Spain, pp. 393–397, 2004.

Pinto, H.S., S. Staab, and C. Tempich. DILIGENT: Towards a fine-grained methodology for distributed, loosely-controlled and evolving engineering of ontologies. In *Proceedings of the European Conference on Artificial Intelligence (ECAI),* Valencia, Spain, pp. 393–397, 2004.

Resnik, P. and N. Smith. The web as a parallel corpus. *Computational Linguistics,* 29(3):349–380, 2003.

Reynaud, C. and B. Safar. Representation of ontologies for information integration. In *Proceedings of the European Workshop on Knowledge Acquisition, Modeling and Management (EKAW)*, Siguenza, Spain, 2002.

Ruiz-Casado, M., E. Alfonseca, and P. Castells. Automatic extraction of semantic relationships for Word-Net by means of pattern learning from Wikipedia. In *Proceedings of the International Conference on Natural Language for Information Systems (NDLB)*, Alicante, Spain, *Lecture Notes in Computer Science*, 3513:67–79. Springer Verlag, New York, 2005.

Russel, S.J. and P. Norvig. *Artificial Intelligence: A Modern Approach*, chapter Knowledge Engineering. Prentice Hall, Upper Saddle River, NJ, 2003.

Sabou, M., V. Lopez, and E. Motta. Ontology selection on the real semantic web: How to cover the queens birthday dinner? In *Proceedings of the 15th International Conference on Knowledge Engineering and Knowledge Management (EKAW)*, Podebrady, Czech Republic, pp. 96–111, 2006.

Salton, G. Developments in automatic text retrieval. *Science*, 253:974–979, 1991.

Salton, G. and C. Buckley. Term-weighting approaches in automatic text retrieval. *Information Processing and Management*, 24(5):515–523, 1988.

Schutz, A. and P. Buitelaar. RelExt: A tool for relation extraction from text in ontology extension. In *Proceedings of the International Semantic Web Conference (ISWC)*, Sardinia, Italy, pp. 593–606, 2005.

Schütze, H. Word space. *Advances in Neural Information Processing Systems*, 5, 895–902, 1993.

Shortliffe, E. *Computer-Based Medical Consultations: MYCIN*. Elsevier, New York, 2001.

Sirin, E., J. Hendler, and B. Parsia. Semi-automatic composition of web services using semantic descriptions. In *Proceedings of the ICEIS Workshop on Web Services: Modeling, Architecture and Infrastructure*, Angers, France, 2003.

Smith, B. Ontology. In L. Floridi, editor, *Blackwell Guide to the Philosophy of Computing and Information*, Blackwell, Malden, MA, pp. 155–166, 2003.

Sowa, J.F. *Knowledge Representation: Logical, Philosophical and Computational Foundations*. Brooks/Cole, Pacific Grove, CA, 2000.

Spyns, P., Y. Tang, and R. Meersman. An ontology engineering methodology for DOGMA. *Applied Ontology*, 3(1-2):13–39, 2008.

Studer, R., V.R. Benjamins, and D. Fensel. Knowledge engineering: Principles and methods. *Data Knowledge Engineering*, 25(1-2):161–197, 1998.

Studtmann, P. Aristotle's categories. *Stanford Encyclopedia of Philosophy*, 2007. http://plato.stanford.edu/

Suh, S., H. Halpin, and E. Klein. Extracting common sense knowledge from Wikipedia. In *Proceedings of the Workshop on Web Content Mining with Human Language Technologies at ISWC'06*, Athens, GA, 2006.

Sure, Y., S. Bloehdorn, P. Haase, J. Hartmann, and D. Oberle. The SWRC ontology—Semantic web for research communities. In *Proceedings of the 12th Portuguese Conference on Artificial Intelligence—Progress in Artificial Intelligence (EPIA 2005)*, Corilha, Portugal, *Lecture Notes in Computer Science*, 3803:218–231, 2005.

Sure, Y., S. Staab, and R. Studer. On-To-Knowledge Methodology (OTKM). In S. Staab and R. Studer, editors, *Handbook of Ontologies, International Handbooks on Information Systems*. Springer Verlag, Berlin, Germany, 2004.

Tempich, C., H.S. Pinto, Y. Sure, and S. Staab. An argumentation ontology for distributed, loosely-controlled and evolving engineering processes of ontologies (DILIGENT). In *Proceedings of the European Semantic Web Conference (ESWC)*, Heraklion, Crete, Greece, pp. 241–256, 2005.

The Gene Ontology Consortium. Gene ontology: Tool for the unification of biology. *Nature Genetics*, 25:25–29, 2000.

The Gene Ontology Consortium. Creating the gene ontology resource: Design and implementation. *Genome Research*, (11):1425–1433, 2001.

Turcato, D., F. Popowich, J. Toole, D. Fass, D. Nicholson, and G. Tisher. Adapting a synonym database to specific domains. In *Proceedings of the ACL Workshop on Recent Advances in Natural Language Processing and Information Retrieval*, Hong Kong, China, 2000.

Turney, P.D. Mining the web for synonyms: PMI-IR versus LSA on TOEFL. In *Proceedings of the 12th European Conference on Machine Learning*, Freiburg, Germany, pp. 491–502, 2001.

Uschold, M. Building ontologies: Towards a unified methodology. In *Proceedings of the 16th Annual Conference of the British Computer Society Specialist Group on Expert Systems (Expert Systems '96)*, Cambridge, U.K., 1996.

Uschold, M. and M. King. Towards a methodology for building ontologies. In *Proceedings of the IJCAI Workshop on Basic Ontological Issues in Knowledge Sharing*, Montreal, Canada, 1995.

van Hage, W.R., H. Kolb, and G. Schreiber. A method for learning part-whole relations. In *Proceedings of the 5th International Semantic Web Conference (ISWC), Lecture Notes in Computer Science*, 4273:723–735. Springer, Athens, GA, 2006.

van Heijst, G., A.T. Schreiber, and B.J. Wielinga. Using explicit ontologies in KBS development. *International Journal of Human-Computer Studies*, 45:183–292, 1997.

Velardi, P., R. Navigli, A. Cucchiarelli, and F. Neri. Evaluation of OntoLearn, a methodology for automatic learning of domain ontologies. In P. Buitelaar and P. Cimiano, editors, *Ontology Learning from Text: Methods, Evaluation and Applications, Frontiers in Artificial Intelligence and Applications*, Vol. 123. IOS Press, Amsterdam, the Netherlands, 2005.

Völker, J., P. Hitzler, and P. Cimiano. Acquisition of OWL DL axioms from lexical resources. In *Proceedings of the Fourth European Semantic Web Conference (ESWC'07)*, Innsbruck, Austria, *Lecture Notes in Computer Science*, 4519:670–685. Springer, 2007.

Völker, J., and S. Rudolph. Fostering web intelligence by semi-automatic OWL ontology refinement. In *Proceedings of the Seventh International Conference on Web Intelligence (WI'08)*, Sydney, Australia, pp. 454–460, 2008a.

Völker, J. and S. Rudolph. Lexico-logical acquisition of OWL DL axioms—An integrated approach to ontology refinement. In *Proceedings of the Sixth International Conference on Formal Concept Analysis (ICFCA'08)*, Montreal, Canada, *Lecture Notes in Artificial Intelligence*, 4933:62–77. Springer, 2008b.

Völker, J., D. Vrandecic, Y. Sure, and A. Hotho. Learning disjointness. In *Proceedings of the Fourth European Semantic Web Conference (ESWC'07)*, Innsbruck, Austria, *Lecture Notes in Computer Science*, 4519:175–189. Springer, 2007.

Wache, H., T. Vögele, U. Visser, H. Stuckenschmidt, G. Schuster, H. Neumann, and S. Hubner. Ontology-based integration of information: A survey of existing approaches. In *Proceedings of the Workshop on Ontologies and Information Sharing, Collocated with the International Joint Conference on Artificial Intelligence (IJCAI)*, Seattle, WA, pp. 108–117, 2001.

Weber, N. and P. Buitelaar. Web-based ontology learning with ISOLDE. In *Proceedings of the ISWC Workshop on Web Content Mining with Human Language Technologies*, Athens, GA, 2006.

Witschel, H.-F. Terminology extraction and automatic indexing—Comparison and qualitative evaluation of methods. In *Proceedings of the Seventh International Conference on Terminology and Knowledge Engineering (TKE)*, Copenhagen, Denmark, 2005.

Yarowsky, D. Word-sense disambiguation using statistical models of Roget's categories trained on large corpora. In *Proceedings of the 14th International Conference on Computational Linguistics (COLING)*, Nantes, France, pp. 454–460, 1992.

25

BioNLP: Biomedical
Text Mining

K. Bretonnel Cohen
University of Colorado
Denver

25.1 Introduction

BioNLP, also known as biomedical language processing or biomedical text mining, is the application of
natural language processing techniques to biomedical data. The biomedical domain presents a number of
unique data types and tasks, but simultaneously has many aspects that are of interest to the "mainstream"
natural language processing community. Additionally, there are ethical issues in BioNLP that necessitate
an attention to software quality assurance beyond the normal attention (or lack thereof) that is paid to it
in the mainstream academic NLP community.

An embarrassing fact about BioNLP research to date is this: despite the fact that there has been a very large amount of work in the area, most deployed systems have been built not by people who self-identify as natural language processing specialists but by people who self-identify as biologists. At the end of this chapter, we will return to reasons why this might be so.

25.2 The Two Basic Domains of BioNLP: Medical and Biological

There are two basic user communities for BioNLP, and many different user types within those two communities. The two main communities are the clinical or medical community on the one hand, and the biological community on the other. (Additionally, there is much interest in the use of BioNLP for "translational research"—using basic biological research to inform clinical practice—but the two-way distinction mostly holds.)

25.2.1 Medical/Clinical NLP

Within the medical community, there are widely diverse user types. Clinicians are providers of medical care. They have many questions to ask over the course of a typical workday (Ely et al. 2000), they have very little time to answer them, and they are not necessarily sophisticated searchers (Hersh et al. 1999). Consumers, or patients, present a different set of challenges. They may be sophisticated searchers, but are typically not equipped to comprehend the vast body of publicly available biomedical literature. "Informationists" are professional information retrieval specialists. They typically have a library science background, and may work in a library or directly with a clinical team. Finally, hospital administrators have to cope with tasks that can be aided by NLP, ranging from billing to internal process quality assurance.

25.2.2 Biological/Genomic NLP

Within the biological community, there is an equivalently wide range of user types. They include high-throughput experimentalists, bench scientists, and model organism database curators. We will return to these later in this chapter.

Although there is a long history of research in clinical NLP, most BioNLP work in recent years has focussed on the biological domain. This is probably due to a fundamental difference in the two fields: biologically oriented texts are massively and freely available, while clinical data has been prohibitively difficult to obtain, and only recently has a free, publicly available collection of patient records become available (Pestian et al. 2007). Although we will discuss medical language processing when applicable, the majority of this chapter will focus on biological, primarily genomic, NLP.

25.2.2.1 High-Throughput Data Interpretation

One user type within the biological community is the high-throughput experimentalist. The past decade has seen a radical shift in the way that molecular biologists do science. Where 15 years ago a scientist might have been familiar with half a dozen proteins and would have been familiar with experimental methods that let him or her get data on one protein at a time, today there are assays available that make it possible to get data on as many as 30,000 genes in 12 subjects at a time at an economical and rapidly falling cost (under $500 for the basic materials at the time of writing). This flood of data has required the development of whole new ways of doing biological science. For example, familiar statistics are not applicable when this many cross-comparisons are possible, necessitating the development of ways of applying nonparametric significance tests to biological data. In addition, these high-throughput methodologies have led to a tremendous increase in our knowledge about genes, causing an exponential growth in the number of biomedical publications in recent years (Hunter and Cohen 2006). For example, it used to be thought that about 50 genes were involved in sporulation in yeast, one of the classic model organisms—through high-throughput assays, we now know from a single experiment of 500 genes that are involved in this fundamental process (Shatkay et al. 2000, citing Chu et al. 1998).

An experiment that can generate data on 30,000 genes may easily return a list of 200 or more genes that behave in a way that is statistically significantly different from the other genes in a sample. A biologist that is faced with a list of 200 genes immediately has a basic question: what do these hundreds of genes do? This is an area where natural language processing has been proposed as a useful tool. Given enough personnel resources, a scientist might send a postdoctoral researcher off to do a literature search on all 200 genes and sort the resulting papers in a way that makes sense given the interests of the individual researcher. Automatic approaches to both parts of this task have been proposed—doing the large-scale literature search, and then categorizing the papers, either in a knowledge-free way based on simple clustering, or in a knowledge-based way that takes into account the concerns and categories of researchers in a particular field. One example of the latter type of system is MedMiner (Tanabe et al. 1999). This system does a set of literature searches for a list of genes combined with different keywords related to particular themes that are known to be salient in a molecular biologist's mental model of the domain and, for each gene, returns the results grouped according to the category of keywords that retrieved it. A similar system has been built for researchers on the genetics of alcoholism, based on a different mental model.

Another approach is to look for prominent themes in the publications about the genes in the list. This approach contrasts with the more common approach of clustering genes and assuming that clustered genes share similar functions. Shatkay et al. (2000) describe one such approach. It centers on the intuition that documents that are about genes with similar functions will be associated with similar sets of documents. Thus, it is document-centric, rather than gene-centric. The method relies on there existing one representative document for every gene that is to be analyzed. For each representative document, the probabilistic algorithm retrieves a set of similar documents. Genes whose documents lead to the retrieval of similar sets of documents are then assumed to share similar functions. In the interpretive step, a Bernoulli process is used to generate a list of terms that represents the themes of each shared set of documents.

A very different approach to applying text mining to the high throughput data problem is to use publications about the genes in a list as primary data in interpreting the list. For example, one approach to dealing with a long list of genes is to categorize the genes themselves. In this situation, it can be useful to retrieve the publications about the genes in the list and cluster genes based on a model of the literature that describes them. Another application is to use text mining to build ad hoc networks of associations between genes based on published information in the literature. An excellent example of such a system is Chilibot (Chen and Sharp 2004).

25.2.2.2 Database Construction

Another common proposed use of BioNLP is in the construction of databases about particular phenomena. For example, a researcher might want to build a database that lists all known proteins and, for each protein, lists all proteins that it is known to interact with. Much of this data was initially reported in scientific publications. This is a classic problem for information extraction as that term is classically defined—that is, using NLP to extract assertions about a semantically restricted kind of relation from text. Many systems have been built for the specific problem of protein–protein interactions; an early one that actually saw use in the field was the PreBIND system (Donaldson et al. 2003). Systems have also been constructed in order to assist in the construction of databases about mutations in specific types of proteins (Horn et al. 2004) and post-translational modifications (changes to proteins after they are made) (Shah et al. 2005).

25.2.3 Model Organism Databases, and the Database Curator as a Canonical User

Although high throughput experimentation and phenomenon-based database construction are both possible use cases for BioNLP, the most extensively explored use case has been model organism database construction.

"Model organisms" are species that are used as experimental surrogates for humans. They are of importance to biomedical research because we share most of our genes with most living species, and because we cannot experiment on humans. A variety of common model organisms exist, with various experimental advantages to each. For example, the roundworm *Caenorhabditis elegans* is useful for studying cellular differentiation because the typical mature adult only has 959 cells, and the lineage of each one is known.

One of the fundamental enabling tools of modern genomic science has been the construction of databases containing information about all or most of the genes in various model organisms (and humans). To see a typical database entry for a gene, go to the Mouse Genome Informatics database at www.informatics.jax.org and search for *brca1*. The entry for this gene includes a unique identifier (MGI:104537) that is used as a primary key in the database, but rarely appears in free text. It also includes an official name* for the gene—*breast cancer 1*—and an official symbol: *Brca1*. (As will be seen in Section 25.4.2, the term "official" is something of a misnomer.) The wide range of types of data that are included in the database entry for *Brca1* include phenotypes (physical and behavioral characteristics) associated with it and with mutations in it, which in this case range from embryonic death to kinky tails, male infertility, and increased incidence of tumors; information on tissues in which the gene is expressed (is actively converted to a protein); biological processes that it takes part in; molecular functions that it has; and cellular components in which it is found. What is notable about this mass of information is that none of it is entered in the database based solely on an expert's knowledge of the gene: every piece of information on this gene in this database is indexed with a specific journal article from which it can be asserted. In the case of *Brca1*, 144 articles were consulted. Multiply that by the approximately 30,000 genes found in a mouse (or a human), and you begin to understand why the model organism database curator community has been an enthusiastic supporter of and participant in text mining research. Modeling studies on the growth of information in the model organism databases suggest a stark fact: at the current rates of manual extraction of this kind of information from text, it will be years, and in some cases decades, before the model organism databases are populated (Baumgartner et al. 2007).

25.2.4 BioNLP in the Context of Natural Language Processing and Computational Linguistics

From the perspective of the mainstream NLP practitioner, there are a number of reasons to be interested in BioNLP. Some of these are the same as the characteristics that make any problem in NLP interesting: it is difficult, but it might actually be tractable; aspects of the language of the domain might actually make it harder than newswire text, despite the fact that it is semantically more restricted; yet, resources, lexical and otherwise, exist that might make it more tractable than newswire text. These resources include

1. A variety of lexical resources. Some of these are smaller, on the order of 20,000 concepts, but have been extensively crafted and reworked by entire communities of researchers, so that they are essentially free of individual idiosyncrasies of representation and have been carefully vetted for errors of all sorts. The Gene Ontology is an example of such a resource (The Gene Ontology Consortium 2000). Other resources are less carefully constructed but are exceptionally large and have both broad coverage and some associated tools. An example of such a resource is the Unified Medical Language System (UMLS) (Lindberg et al. 1993), which currently comprises 900,000 concepts with 2,000,000 names and 12 million relations between those concepts.

2. A stunning amount of free text. At the time of writing, this includes 18 million abstracts of scientific journal articles in the PubMed/MEDLINE database and associated retrieval tools; as (Hunter and Cohen 2006) have shown, the size of this data collection is growing exponentially. There are an additional 1.4 million full-text journal articles available in the PubMedCentral database, with more

---

* Every gene has a name and a symbol. The two terms are generally used interchangeably.

coming all the time due to government pressure to make the products of federally funded research publicly available.

3. A wide variety of annotated corpora and classified document collections. Corpora and document collections are available with both linguistic annotations—sentence boundaries, tokenization, part of speech, word senses, coreference, etc.—and semantic annotations, such as named entities and relations. The majority of these are publicly available at no cost. Some of the more famous ones, including GENIA and the BioCreative gene mention (GM) corpus, are discussed below.

4. A wide variety of domain-specialized tools, including sentence segmenters, tokenizers (a notoriously difficult task for biomedical text), named entity recognition systems, and semantic concept normalizers.

As will be seen, the biomedical domain differs from newswire text on practically every level, ranging from tokenization to named entity recognition to corpus construction to semantic representation. Solving these problems for biomedical text has the potential to feed advances back to the newswire domain that can push work in that area forward, as well.

Beyond these reasons, BioNLP offers the researcher an opportunity to make a clear contribution to relieving the preventable pain and suffering of his or her fellow humans. This is not something found in most areas of NLP.

25.3 Just Enough Biology

Figure 25.1, from Wattarujeekrit et al. (2004), encapsulates in a single schematic diagram how biologists view the world. An immmediately salient point of the diagram is that the biologist's worldview is

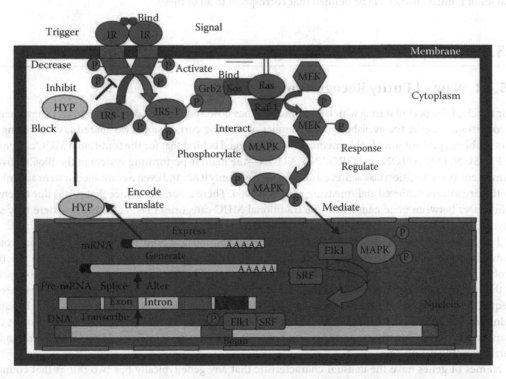

FIGURE 25.1 A biologist's view of the world, with linguistic correlates. (From Wattarujeekrit, T. et al., *BMC Info.*, 5, 155, 2004.)

fundamentally on a cellular level, and in particular primarily concerns itself with processes that take place inside the cell. The top part of the diagram illustrates the fact that these processes primarily take place involving state-changing interactions between proteins within networks of proteins. The diagram also illustrates two ways in which biology relates to language: on the one hand, via the names of these proteins, and on the other, via predicates that describe the relations between those proteins (as well as other things with which they interact—small molecules, cellular components, and other entities).

The bottom part of the diagram illustrates what is known as the Central Dogma of biology: that proteins are created via instructions that are encoded in genes. At the risk of a great deal of simplification, we can say that for every protein there is a corresponding gene. This correspondence leads to an enormous amount of metonymy in which genes are referred to by the names of the corresponding proteins and proteins are referred to by the names of the corresponding genes. The interface between the top and bottom parts of the diagram illustrates the fundamental fact that what proteins a particular cell produces is controlled by communication between the main body of the cell and its nucleus, and sometimes ultimately by messages that are transmitted from outside of the cell to the interior of the cell and eventually to the nucleus.

Understanding this worldview helps the NLP practitioner to make sense of two general trends in BioNLP. One of these is the fundamental importance of named entity recognition for a far larger class of entities than is common in working with newswire text. The other is that information extraction focussed on relations between these named entities, both in terms of pairwise interactions and in terms of the reconstruction of entire networks, is an important class of problems in the field.

Biology is a frustratingly holistic science (Hunter 1993), and entities at many levels other than that of the cell are entirely relevant to BioNLP tasks. These range from the smallest molecules, to tissues, to organs, and to organisms. For organisms, we may refer to relatively specific high-level constructs such as genotypes (complete configurations of genes in an organism) and to much-harder-to-define constellations of attributes known as phenotypes (physical and behavioral manifestations of genetic make-up). Semantic classes of named entities can be defined that correspond to all of these.

25.4 Biomedical Text Mining

25.4.1 Named Entity Recognition

For much of the period during which genomic NLP has flowered, a major concern has been named entity recognition. Despite the availability of a number of training corpora and two shared tasks focusing on this problem, performance for biomedical NER has lagged behind that for the traditional MUC categories of PERSON, LOCATION, and ORGANIZATION—the highest-performing system in the BioCreative II named entity recognition task achieved an F-measure of only 0.87, and even a combined system assembled by the organizers achieved an F-measure of only 0.9066. There is some evidence that this is due to length differences between gene names and the traditional MUC categories (Yeh et al. 2005). There may also have been inconsistencies in labeling early training data sets.

The most common named entity that is targetted by biomedical NER systems is the gene or protein name. (Genes and proteins are very distinct biological entities, but in practice there is often no practical problem with lumping them together for NER applications. Genes and proteins are related biologically in that the purpose of genes is to hold the genetic code for proteins, and in the genomic literature there is frequent metonymy, with gene names being used to refer to the corresponding protein and protein names being used to refer to the corresponding gene. Typically, though not always, a gene and the protein that it encodes have the same name. In the context of NER, I will use the term "gene" to refer to a gene and its corresponding products.)

Names of genes have the unusual characteristic that any gene typically has two things that count as names for NER purposes. One of these is the gene name per se. The other is a shorter form, known as its gene symbol. The mouse gene *breast cancer 1* and its symbol *Brca1* mentioned earlier are a typical example. From an NER perspective these are equivalent. It is often the case that both will appear in the same document. Often the "full" name is used on the first occurrence, along with an appositioned symbol in parentheses, and then subsequently the symbol is used. (This pattern is often exploited by good NER systems to disambiguate gene symbols.)

The form of gene names can vary widely depending on the community that studies the particular organism in which a gene was first discovered or is currently being studied. Mouse and human genes are often named by their function. For example, a typical human gene name would be *melanocortin 1 receptor* (GeneID 4157). This gene has the same name in the mouse (GeneID 17199). The community of *Drosophila melanogaster* (fruit fly) researchers has a very different tradition in naming genes. They originally named genes by the physical appearance of flies when the gene in question is mutated. For example, the first gene discovered in *D. melanogaster* was named *white* (symbol *w*) because flies have white eyes when this gene is mutated, rather than their normal red eyes. Another gene in fruit flies is called *wrinkled*; it is so named because flies with a mutation in this gene have wrinkled wings. The symbol for wrinkled is *W*; this illustrates an important point, which is that there are a variety of conditions in which the case of a gene name or symbol can be "phonemic" in the biomedical literature. The implications for BioNLP systems in this domain are obvious, since many text mining systems apply case normalization as an early processing step.

One of the first papers in the modern genomic BioNLP era (Fukuda et al. 1998) was on a gene name NER system. It is discussed below. In recent years, research on gene NER has taken place primarily within a shared task called BioCreative or subsequent to it using the BioCreative data. In BioCreative, gene NER was called the GM task, and we will refer to it in that way from here on. As noted above, one possible source of the lag in performance on GM as opposed to NER for the MUC categories has been lack of consistency in labeling gene names in training data sets. This lack of consistency has been seen in two areas: deciding what counts as a mention of a gene or a protein (e.g., should related gene products, such as RNAs, be included in the category?), and deciding what counts as the borders of a GM. For example, given a string like *human leptin receptor gene* (PMID 9537324), should *human* be included in the text span of the gene name? Should the word *gene* be included? Different annotation projects have come up with different answers to these questions, and some projects have applied their rules inconsistently in this area. The BioCreative organizers have attempted to give the annotation process a principled way of dealing with these varying interpretations by developing gold standards that allow for variant forms, so that *human leptin receptor gene*, *human leptin receptor*, and *leptin receptor gene* might all count as correct system outputs.

One interesting result of the BioCreative GM evaluations has been the finding that enhancing a rule-based or learning-based system with a lexical resource such as a canonical list of gene names typically does not enhance the performance of the system. (Even prior to BioCreative, it was known that gazetteer-based approaches to GM are not typically successful, although it has since been shown that very sophisticated gazeteer-based approaches can be successful, at the cost of about as much effort as building a good rule-based or learning-based system (Hanisch et al. 2005).) Figure 25.2 shows the results for the GM task for the first BioCreative event. As can be seen from Figure 25.2, systems did not benefit appreciably from using a lexical resource unless their performance without it was abysmal (the rightmost system in the figure).

In general, systems do benefit from any approach that helps in locating the left and right edges of a gene name, and in particular from approaches that help to extend them to the right and left. Approaches to doing this have included using shallow parsing and using the Schwartz and Hearst algorithm to map gene symbols to the full corresponding name (see below). Typical learning-based systems use both orthographic features—a much richer set than is applicable to MUC named entity categories—and contextual features. The top-performing BioCreative II system used a semisupervised learning-based system in which the provided training data was supplemented by unannotated PubMed/MEDLINE abstracts. It included the combination of two separate noun group chunkers, one operating left-to-right and the other right-to-left (Ando 2008). However, rule-based systems, as well as systems that combine machine learning and

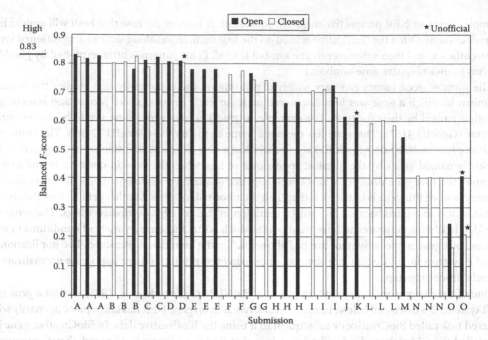

FIGURE 25.2 Results from the first BioCreative shared task on GM recognition. Closed systems did not use external lexical resources; open systems were allowed to use external lexical resources. (From Yeh, A. et al., *BMC Info.*, 6, S2, 2005.)

rules, can perform well on this task as well, and the top-performing system in the previous BioCreative combined both.

25.4.2 Named Entity Normalization

One of the unique but important problems in genomic BioNLP over the past few years has been what is known as the gene normalization problem. Gene normalization (GN) is the task of relating mentions of a gene name in text to some specific gene in a database of genes. Work on the GM task has long tended to define the problem as simply finding the boundaries and classes of gene names in text. However, such text spans are of little use in some (but not all) practical applications, where the more pressing need is to determine exactly which gene in the set of genes in some organism that text string refers to. One of the problems is massive ambiguity, both of names and symbols, although perhaps more so in the case of symbols. A perhaps larger issue is that authors exercise no notion of a standard gene name or symbol; different communities may have different names for the same gene, and authors may make up ad hoc symbols. The *Brca1* gene, for instance, has been referred to in print by at least seven different symbols—*IRIS, PSCP, BRCAI, BRCC1, RNF53, BROVA1*, and *Brca1*. Only the yeast community has been an exception to this.

GN can be thought of as occupying a midpoint on the continuum between targetted word sense disambiguation, which it is not, and all-words word sense disambiguation; the task is to disambiguate all gene names, but only all gene names.

As an example, consider TRP1. Just within humans alone, this can refer to five different genes. The names of four of them are *transient receptor potential channel 1* (GeneID 7220), *transfer RNA proline 1* (GeneID 7217), *transformation-related protein 2* [sic] (GeneID 5903), and *trypsinogen 1* (GeneID 5644). This symbol also illustrates the hazards of ignoring minor typographical differences: if you search the Entrez Gene database (see below under Resources) for *TRP-1* (with a hyphen), you get just a single hit—*tyrosinase-related protein 1* (GeneID 7306), the fifth human gene that shares this symbol and one that is not retrieved if the search is done without the hyphen. It bears emphasizing that in naturally occurring texts, any of these five genes may be referred to by the symbol with (TRP-1) or without (TRP1) the hyphen, as well as with a space before the numeral (TRP 1), and with any combination of letter cases, e.g., TRP1, Trp1, trp1, TRP-1, Trp-1, etc. Furthermore, the same kinds of variability can exist for the full name, so that for the gene with ID 5903 one may see *transformation-related protein 1*, *transformation related protein 1*, *transformation-related protein-1*, *Transformation Related Protein 1*, etc.

The BioCreative shared tasks—an MUC-like evaluation of BioNLP—has thus far always included a GN task, and the BioCreative definition of the task has had great influence. As defined by BioCreative, the input is an abstract of a journal article, and the output is a list of unique identifiers of genes mentioned in the text. This means that systems must be able to both recognize when two gene mentions in the text refer to the same gene and to recognize when two mentions in the text refer to separate genes.

Figure 25.3 shows the performance of systems in the first and second BioCreative events. In both shared tasks, participants were provided with a set of abstracts and a database to relate them to. For BioCreative I, three sets of abstracts were distributed, one for each of three species: yeast, mouse, and fly. For BioCreative II, a single set of abstracts was distributed, comprising only human genes.

The GN problem was first raised by Cohen et al. (2002) in the context of using official database identifiers to determine what differences between gene names could safely be ignored and what differences were likely to indicate that separate genes were being referred to. Using a model from descriptive linguistics in which minimally differing pairs of gene names or symbols indicated "phonemic" differences, this paper looked at hyphenation, letter case, parenthesized material, and edge effects, finding that (despite the difficult examples shown in this chapter) hyphenation, case, and parenthesized material could generally be safely normalized. Subsequent work on the problem of GN in text has tended to assume the findings of this paper, explicitly or implicitly.

Successful systems often approach this as a word sense disambiguation task and apply some combination of Lesk-like approaches (see (Lesk 1986) and Chapter 14 in this volume). They may differ by what they use as a surrogate for the definition—the full gene name, descriptions of gene function from a database, or the contents of literature references—and in where they look for words from the surrogate definition: within

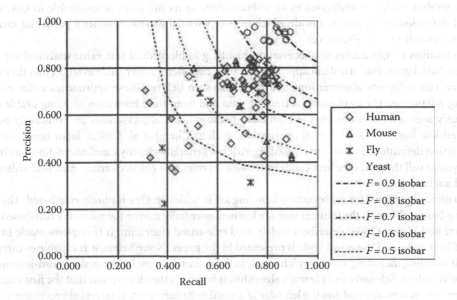

FIGURE 25.3 Results from the first BioCreative (yeast, mouse, and fly) and second BioCreative (human) shared tasks on GN. (From Morgan et al., *Genome Biol.*, 9(Suppl. 2), S3, 2008.)

abbreviation definitions (see below), in an N-word window around a name or symbol, within the local sentence, or within the entire abstract. See Baumgartner et al. (2008) for a representative approach. The top-scoring team in the BioCreative II task (Hakenberg et al. 2008) enhanced this approach by trimming the target set of names in the database, both by using *tf*idf* to recognize highly nonspecific terms and by using a rule-based approach that referred to tissues, functions, and some other domain-specific semantic classes. In a sophisticated additional step, it applied a tool for recognizing Gene Ontology terms (see below) in the abstract and matched those against Gene Ontology terms that were known to have been associated with the gene. (These were included in the database.)

Under the influence of the BioCreative GN task, GN systems have tended to assume that the species in which the gene is found is a given. However, this is a tremendous oversimplification, and for practical systems, it is important to be able to determine the species, as well. This is a nontrivial task in and of itself. Systems were required to do this for the BioCreative II protein–protein interaction task (Krallinger et al. 2008), although it is difficult to assess GN performance in that context because scores also involved carrying out an information extraction task. We have only recently begun to see research on the specific problem of combining species identification with the GN task (Wang and Matthews 2008).

25.4.3 Abbreviation Disambiguation

One area in which considerable progress has been achieved is handling abbreviations in biomedical text. This is important in part because abbreviations are extremely common in biomedical text, with one study finding that 22% of biomedical abbreviations are ambiguous and that there are an average of 4.61 definitions per abbreviation (Chang et al. 2002). The "one domain, one sense" assumption definitely does not hold. An example is the abbreviation *PDA* in cardiology texts. Just within cardiology, it has two common definitions: *posterior descending artery* and *patent ductus arteriosus*, the former being the name of a blood vessel and the latter being a congenital defect.

In addition to abbreviations as that term is commonly understood, there is a similar phenomenon that is quite common in scientific abstracts: pairing a gene symbol (see named entity recognition) with the full name of the gene.

Abbreviation handling has been found useful in multiple applications. One is GN; the ability to map a gene symbol, which is analogous to an abbreviation, to its full form is invaluable in GN, with the symbol definition being used to decide which of two potential database entries a particular mention in text corresponds to (see GN, above).

Two families of approaches to abbreviation-handling in biomedical text exist: statistical approaches, and rule-based ones. Bad statistical approaches train a classifier for every abbreviation that they can find and then run it for any abbreviations that they have seen before. These approaches suffer both from a strong reliance on the availability of training data and from their limitation to being usable only for previously seen abbreviations; this is a problem because novel abbreviations are constantly published on an ad hoc basis. Good statistical approaches, such as Chang et al. (2002), learn how to recognize abbreviation definitions in text. Rule-based approaches generally identify candidate definitions in text. A good system will then pick the best candidate, based on rules that enforce certain matches, ordering, and limited anchoring.

Two main algorithms for abbreviation-handling are in wide use. One is purely rule-based. The other is learning-based, although the features that are learned essentially mirror the rules in a rule-based system. Schwartz and Hearst (2003) describe a widely used rule-based algorithm. It is implementable in about a page of Java code, and the actual code is presented in the paper. Nonetheless, it is capable of carrying out difficult matches, including ones in which words in the definition must be skipped or word-internal letters must be matched. Schwartz and Hearst's algorithm is based on the observation that the first character of an abbreviation typically matches the left edge of a word in its definition. It targets abbreviation/definition pairs in which the definition appears first, followed by the abbreviation in parentheses. Its first step is to extract the abbreviation and a set of words to its left from the input text. The algorithm then begins from the right edge of the abbreviation and of the definition. It iterates from right to left through both strings, looking for a character in the potential definition words that matches each character in the abbreviation; as matches to the abbreviation characters are found, the iteration proceeds to the next leftward character. In a final step, the algorithm looks for the beginning of the first word of the potential definition. This algorithm achieves a precision of 95%–96% and a recall of 82% on two separate test collections and has the advantage of not requiring training data. It has been successfully incorporated into systems that carry out a variety of tasks, ranging from GM identification to summarization.

The other commonly used algorithm is that of Chang et al. (op. cit.). It is based on machine learning. Its primary advantage is that it is made available via a server to which inputs can be submitted.

25.5 Getting Up to Speed: Ten Papers and Resources That Will Let You Read Most Other Work in BioNLP

There are about 10 papers and resources that, if you are familiar with them, will allow you to catch the references in many publications in the BioNLP field. They are reviewed briefly here. These papers, supplemented by the latest BioCreative publications, will serve as an adequate introduction to the field of BioNLP, particularly from the genomics perspective.

25.5.1 Named Entity Recognition 1: KeX

Fukuda et al. (1998) is the first named entity recognition paper of the modern era in BioNLP. It was a ruled-based system. Its approach was simple:

1. Find a string of text that looks like a symbol for a yeast gene (e.g., *ABC1*)
2. Extend the name to the left (e.g., *yeast ABC1*)
3. Extend the name to the right (e.g., *ABC1 protein*)

The paper reported an *F*-measure in the 90s. This result has never been replicated. Part of the reported success may be due to the fact that the system was evaluated on documents about yeast; yeast genes are especially easy to recognize in text. The yeast community is the only one in which editors have insisted that authors adhere to a specific nomenclature for referring to genes, and they always make use of a symbol, which is highly restricted with respect to its possible shape.

25.5.2 Named Entity Recognition 2: Collier, Nobata, and GENIA

Nobata et al. (1999) and Collier et al. (2000) were the first papers to describe learning-based approaches to GM NER. They compared Naive Bayes, decision trees, and HMM-based solutions. Nobata et al. (1999) made innovative use of a gazetteer, using it to derive a list of words that, when they appear as head nouns in a putative entity name, are strong indicators that the candidate is, in fact, a named entity. These nouns included words like *protein, antigen, promoter, motif,* and *mRNA*. The work was also notable for the complexity of the ontology of named entity types that it assumed; in this case, the system targeted four classes that have been found to be very difficult even for humans to differentiate (Hatzivassiloglou et al. 2001): source, protein, DNA, and RNA. Collier et al. (2000) experimented with using an HMM to identify biologically relevant classes of named entities. The work was notable for the large number of semantic classes that it attempted to identify—10, which was much more than the MUC classes; for the large number of features that it found to be relevant for the biological domain, many of which have been adopted by subsequent researchers in this area; and for the high performance that it achieved with only a small amount of training data. These papers set the stage for a considerable amount of later work on machine-learning-based approaches to biological/genomic named entity recognition.

25.5.3 Information Extraction 1: Blaschke et al. (1999)

Blaschke et al. (1999) is the canonical paper on rule-based information extraction systems in BioNLP, particularly for extracting information about protein–protein interactions. The system described in the paper was unusual in that it had no linguistic processing per se—not even part of speech tagging. The system assumed manual GM NER and centered around a number of keywords that indicate protein–protein interactions. It then used distance between protein names (since the task is PPI and the target was network reconstruction) as an absolute filter, with pairs whose names were more than a maximum threshold of words apart being discarded. The system was evaluated on a set of text fragments that between them allowed the reconstruction of a particular signaling pathway if all interacting pairs were correctly extracted. (This data set has since been converted into a corpus with standoff annotation—(Johnson et al. 2007a).) Besides being the first paper on a rule-based system for this domain, this paper was important in that it showed what could be accomplished in the limiting case of an information extraction system that worked purely on the basis of surface lexical features, with no linguistic information per se used at all.

25.5.4 Information Extraction 2: Craven and Kumlein (1999)

Published the same year, Craven and Kumlein (1999) described the first machine-learning-based system for genomic information extraction. The system tackled three types of pairwise relations—protein/protein, protein/disease, and protein/subcellular location—although only one of these (subcellular localization) was investigated in detail in the paper. The first step of the system was to identify pairs of entities by simple string-matching. The second step of the system was to use a naive Bayes classifier to classify sentences that contained two entities as to whether or not they actually posited a relation between them. The features were a bag of words. Besides being the first paper on learning-based approaches to information extraction in this domain, the paper was also important in that it described a methodology for using "weakly labeled" training data; rather than constructing a manually judged gold standard data set, the authors reverse-engineered what is still the largest set of biomedical training data of its kind from three databases.

25.5.5 Information Extraction 3: MedLEE, BioMedLEE, and GENIES

Finally, the set of information extraction tools based on the MedLEE system (Friedman 2000) rounds out the well-known BioNLP IE tools. An early clinical information extraction system called MedLEE was extended to produce the BioMedLEE and GENIES systems (Friedman et al. 2001). These latter versions were meant to operate in the genomics domain. They used an unusual approach to GM named entity recognition (since abandoned) in which they mapped the input text and a set of all known gene names to faux amino acid sequences and then applied the BLAST algorithm to locate stretches of text in the input that had a high likelihood of being gene names. In many ways the MedLEE family of systems was much more sophisticated than any of its competitors for many years, incorporating a rich semantic representation and making heavy use of syntactic information. It was also the first information extraction system in this domain to be evaluated on the full text of journal articles, rather than abstracts.

25.5.6 Corpora 1: PubMed/MEDLINE

PubMed/MEDLINE is the primary source for input documents in genomic BioNLP. It is not a corpus, nor even really a text collection, since it is not static, but rather grows. (In fact, it is growing exponentially, as demonstrated by Hunter and Cohen (2006).) It is maintained by the National Library of Medicine. MEDLINE itself is a database of abstracts, which contains over 18 million abstracts at the time of writing. Each abstract has a moderate amount of metadata associated with it, including a PubMed ID (PMID), a unique identifier. PubMed is the search engine interface to MEDLINE. It returns documents in reverse order of publication date; this has often been questioned by natural language processing specialists, and there have been attempts to popularize versions of PubMed with relevance ranking. Other alternative interfaces to MEDLINE include GoPubMed, a search application that returns a set of Gene Ontology annotations for each abstract (Doms and Schroeder 2005), and the FABLE system (Fang et al. 2006), which is optimized for searches on human genes. (The unusual naming characteristics of genes, described above, can make searches for them difficult, and there is no easy way to limit literature searches to a specific species.)

All PubMed/MEDLINE contents are in ASCII and are available free. For serious BioNLP research, it is useful to maintain a local copy to avoid the considerable latency associated with frequent downloads (as well as National Library of Medicine limitations on how often their servers can be hit). A code base for maintaining a local copy in a relational database is available from the BioText project at http://biotext.berkeley.edu/software.html.

25.5.7 Corpora 2: GENIA

The most influential true corpus in the linguistic sense of that word is known as GENIA (Ohta et al. 2002; Kim et al. 2003; Erjavec et al. 2003). It is a fully annotated corpus, containing both linguistic and semantic mark-ups. It contains 2,000 abstracts and 432,560 words of text. It is currently annotated with sentence boundaries, token boundaries, part of speech, and named entities, and part of the corpus has been treebanked. Future versions will include event annotation and coreference. GENIA has demonstrably been the most heavily used corpus in BioNLP (Cohen et al. 2005). It is freely distributed at the GENIA project Web site. In recent years, another linguistically and semantically annotated corpus, known as PennBioIE, has become publicly available. It has already seen some use in linguistic and text processing works (Cohen et al. 2008b), although unlike GENIA, it is not freely available and it remains to be seen what its impact will be.

25.5.8 Lexical Resources 1: The Gene Ontology

The Gene Ontology is a three-part ontology that was originally built (and is still maintained) by biologists for classifying the function of genes. The three parts of the ontology are concerned with molecular functions (e.g., *chaperone regulator activity*), biological processes (e.g., *establishment of localization*), and cellular components. The basic building blocks of the ontology are terms and their associated definitions; these are linked to each other by the two relations is-a and part-of. The current version of the ontology contains about 23,000 concepts (versus the 147,000 in WordNet). Although the Gene Ontology is an interesting linguistic artifact and as such has been the subject of descriptive work that has had an impact on the maintenance of the ontology itself (Ogren et al. 2004, 2005; Mungall 2004), the Gene Ontology has been used less as a lexical resource than as a target for language processing applications. The GO has been used extensively by biologists to annotate genes in biological databases (see above on model organism databases), and a considerable amount of text mining work has had the goal of automatically assigning Gene Ontology classes to genes (known in the biological curation world as "annotation") based on textual inputs. The task is quite difficult, being complicated by a variety of factors that includes the necessity of being able to carry out good GN, the normal difficulties present in any information extraction task (where in this case relations must be found between genes and Gene Ontology concepts), and the very large difficulty in recognizing Gene Ontology terms in text themselves—typical leaf nodes include *acyl binding*, *flagellin-based flagellum basal body*, *structural constituent of cytoskeleton*, *cell growth*, and *circadian regulation of gene expression*. It will be obvious that there are many possible linguistic realizations for all of these concepts in unrestricted scientific text.

25.5.9 Lexical Resources 2: Entrez Gene

Entrez Gene (formerly LocusLink) is the premier database of genes in the world, currently containing over 5 million entries covering almost 6,000 species. It is maintained by the National Library of Medicine and is publicly available. Alongside its wealth of purely biological information (such as links to sequence data), Entrez Gene also contains a considerable amount of information that can be used as lexical resources. This includes gene names, symbols, known synonyms, protein products (which function as another source of synonym due to the rampant gene/protein metonymy that we have mentioned before), summaries of gene function, and Gene References Into Function (GeneRIFs). Many aspects of Entrez Gene entries have been used or targetted in BioNLP. For the GN task, Entrez Gene entries are the targetted database identifier. Its summaries of gene function were used to great success by Sehgal and Srinivasan (2006) in a gene symbol disambiguation task in an information retrieval context. Gene References Into Function are short, <255 character statements about the functions of a gene, broadly construed. They were initially used, with limited success, as relevance judgments in an ad hoc information retrieval task (Hersh and Bhupatiraju 2003). Sehgal and Srinivasan (2006) showed that this was due to the small number of them available at that time, and that they can now be used with success as relevance judgments. Since then, there has been a small body of work on the automatic extraction of GeneRIFs, modeling them as extractive, low compression ratio, focussed summaries (Lu et al. 2006, 2007).

25.5.10 Lexical Resources 3: Unified Medical Language System

The Unified Medical Language System is a large set of lexical resources that is primarily associated with the clinical domain. Its main components are the UMLS Metathesaurus and the Semantic Network. The UMLS Metathesaurus is an aggregation of an exceptionally large number of independent vocabularies; it now contains more than 8 million concepts. The Semantic Network is a hierarchy of semantic relations, ranging from very general ones such as *is-associated-with* to much more specific ones such as *treats*. It is primarily applied in the research of the Lister Hill Center for Biomedical Communications. One common interface to the UMLS is via the MetaMap system, described below.

25.6 Tools

There is currently a relatively broad set of preprocessing tools publicly available for BioNLP, particularly in the genomics domain. Whatever your needs, there is likely to be something available; however, there is generally room for improvement in these tools, particularly if your application is very task-specific. Tool-building has been a fruitful area of contribution for NLP specialists in BioNLP.

25.6.1 Tokenization

Tokenization of biomedical text is notoriously difficult. The following abstract is reasonably representative for the chemical domain:

> A series of mono and di-*N*-2,3-epoxypropyl *N*-phenylhydrazones have been prepared on a large scale by reaction of the corresponding *N*-phenylhydrazones of 9-ethyl-3-carbazolecarbaldehyde, 9-ethyl-3,6-carbazoledicarbaldehyde, 4-dimethyl-amino-, 4-diethylamino-, 4-benzylethylamino-, 4-(diphenylamino)-, 4-(4,4-4′-dimethyl-diphenylamino)-, 4-(4-formyldiphenylamino)- and 4-(4-formyl-4′-methyldiphenyl-amino)benzaldehyde with epichlorohydrin in the presence of KOH and anhydrous Na(2)SO(4).

PMID 17962747

Note that commas sometimes indicate word-boundaries and sometimes do not, and that the crucial conjunct is a word subsegment that is not separated either by whitespace or by a hyphen from the last conjunct preceding it, i.e., *benzaldehyde* in *4-(4-formyl-4′-methyldiphenyl-amino)benzaldehyde*.

A number of NER systems perform their own tokenization step, and those may be adequate for later processing needs. A system that works well for chemical names such as the difficult cases shown here is the OSCAR3 system (Corbett et al. 2007), available via an API. The KeX system's tokenizer generally works well, and is useful for Perl-based processing. For building one's own pipeline, the LingPipe API is increasingly popular. (LingPipe also provides a sentence segmenter that is optimized for PubMed/MEDLINE text.) Jiang and Zhai (2007) provide a tokenizer that is optimized for the needs of information retrieval.

25.6.2 Named Entity Recognition (Genes/Proteins)

Named entity recognition systems for genes and proteins are developed so frequently that any listing of them would likely be out of date before publication. However, one application deserves special mention because it illustrates an interesting principle in the sociology of NLP.

ABNER (A Biomedical Named Entity Recognizer) (Settles 2005) is a Conditional-Random-Field-based application that takes plain text as input and returns the text with SGML tags inserted or in IOB format for gene/protein names, cell lines, and cell types. (The exact set of named entities varies depending on the model on which it is trained.) It is packaged with models for two well-known data sets and can also be retrained with other corpora.

ABNER illustrates an important principle in the sociology of NLP, which is that achieving the highest-reported performance on some data set is not the only route to high citation rates and impact. ABNER's performance is not particularly high on the BioCreative set, which has rapidly become the standard for assessing GM systems, achieving an F-measure of 69.9. Nonetheless, ABNER is widely used in BioNLP systems that target the genomics domain. This is almost certainly due to the fact that it is nicely engineered—it is distributed as a Java .jar file, it has a very clean interface, and it is robust in the face of various operating systems and other architectural vagaries. ABNER provides an object lesson of the fact that good engineering can be a road to academic success.

25.6.3 Named Entity Recognition (Medical Concepts)

MetaMap/MMTx (Aronson 2001) is the only widely used medical NER system. Unlike NER systems that target only a restricted range of semantic types, MetaMap/MMTx labels any UMLS concept that it finds in text; this is an extraordinarily diverse and large set of concepts. It first carries out a shallow parse, and then attempts to map any noun phrase to some UMLS concept. It can be run from the command line, but is perhaps more often accessed via its flexible API. Although it was developed with medical applications in mind, it has also been shown to work well for genomics-domain texts (Aronson et al. 2004, 2005, Demner-Fushman et al. 2006, 2007).

25.6.4 Full Parsers

Full parsers that are optimized for biomedical text have only recently become available. Many of the problems that are pervasive when dealing with biomedical text raise their heads in the area of parsing. Tokenization is an obvious one—even shallow parsers often fail on the tokenization issues that come up in this domain. Another is the paradox that parsing is helpful for named entity recognition, but it is useful to do named entity recognition before parsing to avoid needless parsing of full gene names, such as *breast cancer associated 1*. Various papers have looked at the effectiveness of off-the-shelf parsers and their default models for biomedical text (Clegg and Shepherd 2005, 2007). Optimized parsers are now available, including the Enju structural parser with a GENIA-trained model (Miyao and Tsujii 2008). Pyysalo et al. have made a genomics dependency parser available (Pyysalo et al. 2006).

25.7 Special Considerations in BioNLP

Compared to many other application areas, and to academic NLP in general, BioNLP carries with it an unusual opportunity and an unusual burden. Much of the impetus for research in this area comes from the users themselves, and well-made BioNLP applications do actually get used. But, a poorly built BioNLP application cannot be relied on to do no more harm than a missed web page from an Internet search or a bad classification: a poor application may have harmful consequences for real people with real diseases. Therefore, good software engineering practices are an essential part of the practice of BioNLP.

25.7.1 Code Coverage, Testing, and Corpora

The BioNLP community differs from the mainstream NLP community in that many of its software products are developed with the stated goal of providing solutions to researchers and clinical personnel, rather than necessarily advancing the state of theoretical knowledge in NLP or linguistics. This brings a special burden to exercise good software engineering practices, and in particular to do industrial-quality software testing. Unfortunately, this has not necessarily been a widespread practice in the community: one survey of biomedical text-mining tools found that 7/20 Web sites disseminating BioNLP functionality could not pass a simple software test commonly executed by professional software testers (Cohen and Hunter, unpublished data). There have been various attempts to promulgate software testing within the BioNLP community. Cohen et al. (2004) presented a test suite generator for GM systems, and Johnson et al. (2007b) presented a fault model for testing ontology mapping, alignment, and linking systems. However, the impact of this work has been low so far. Cohen et al. (2008a) compared the efficacy of standard software testing approaches against running a huge corpus through a system, and found that higher code coverage was achievable in very short times by using manually constructed test suites than by using even very large corpora. They also noted that monitoring coverage was an effective method for steering a testing project, and that attempts to increase it quickly led to the discovery of previously unknown showstopper bugs. Cookbook-style introductions to software testing are widely available today, including a growing literature on using JUnit to do whitebox testing of Java code and a number of good books on black-box functional testing, such as Kaner et al. (1999).

25.7.2 User Interface Design

User interface design has received little attention in the BioNLP field. In fact, one study comparing academic and commercial BioNLP tools found that although the commercial tools demonstrated no advances in language processing abilities over academic systems, and in fact often lagged behind the academic systems in the area of named entity recognition, the commercial systems provided user interfaces that were far superior to anything available through the academic community.

The best-executed work on user interface evaluation to date was carried out in the context of Berkeley's BioText project, and the best of it can function as a tutorial on user interface evaluation. The project focussed on information retrieval. One such study evaluated the efficacy of searching figure captions in full-text journal articles (Hearst et al. 2007). The group implemented a search tool for figure captions, motivated by the observation that biomedical researchers tend to approach an article by first scanning its title, abstract, figures, and figure captions. Other tools, most notably PubMed/MEDLINE, already enable searching via words in the title and abstract, and Google Scholar enables searching words in the full text body; this was the first tool to specifically allow searching figure captions. They then performed a usability study, evaluating whether or not users found the caption search and the display of associated figures to be useful, and if they did, which of two layout formats worked best. The format of the study was that users were told that they were participating in an evaluation of a search interface, although they were not told that the researchers had in fact built that interface. They were shown two formats for result display, in varying orders of presentation. Users then executed queries of their own design for 10 minutes, and then completed a survey answering several questions about their reaction to the system. Seven out of eight users returned scores indicating that they liked the system and would be likely to use it, and users showed a preference for one display strategy over the other. Crucially, the study resulted in a number of design improvements, including additions to the types of links in the display, changes in the workflow, and different sorting strategies.

A very small body of related work has looked at usability and the impact of text-mining tools on curation workflows. Karamanis et al. (2007) looked at the effect of iterative usability testing of a text-mining tool interface and found that good usability tests were able to bring about a decrease in the time that it took model organism database curators to carry out a curation task. Alex et al. (2008) looked at several aspects of their text-mining tool using both measurements of curation time and surveys and found their curators had a preference for high recall over high precision. They also noted interesting inconsistencies between curation times and user preferences as reflected in the surveys; curators sometimes preferred features that actually led to slower curation times.

25.7.3 Portability

One of the persistent (and mostly unaddressed by the academic community) problems in BioNLP has been the creation of systems that can be ported to new domains by the system users. Many machine-learning-based systems can be retrained on new data, but this requires the possession of sometimes significant computational skills. Systems that can be adapted by a researcher or a clinician to their problem have not been seen outside of the industrial community. The user portability problem is a fruitful area for future research.

25.7.4 Proposition Banks and Semantic Role Labeling in BioNLP

As yet, there has not been a large proposition bank created in the BioNLP domain. However, there has been a small pilot project (Wattarujeekrit et al. 2004) that has stimulated fruitful research in the area of argument structure in the biomedical domain. It seems to be the case that semantic representations in this domain have fewer adjunctive arguments and make greater use of core arguments than is the case in General English (Cohen and Hunter 2006). This has repercussions for corpus construction, for semantic role labeling, and for the acceptance by biologists of claims about biomedical predicate semantics: biologists are likely to insist that information that would be in adjuncts in a PropBank-like representation are essential to interpreting the predicate and must be considered core arguments.

25.7.5 The Difference between an Application That Will Relieve Pain and Suffering and an Application That Will Get You Published at ACL

At the beginning of this chapter we pointed out a fact that should hold some embarrassment for the NLP community: most fielded BioNLP systems have been built not by NLP people but by biologists. Why might this be the case? One likely cause is that the community in which NLP practitioners publish rewards system construction less than it does increased performance on some metric for some task. In contrast, biological publications will publish papers on implemented systems as basic science. The NLP community will reward (with publication) work on increasing performance on processing tasks, e.g., part of speech tagging or parsing, and NLP people have certainly made a contribution to the progression of BioNLP by building better tools. However, it has mainly been biologists that have taken these tools and incorporated them into actual, functioning systems. Our publishing practices are perhaps contributing to our missing an opportunity to make novel contributions to the work of clinicians and biological researchers.

Acknowledgments

The author gratefully acknowledges input from Karin Verspoor to an NAACL tutorial on which this chapter was based. Sophia Ananiadou and Robert Futrelle kindly provided comments on a draft of the chapter.

References

Alex, B., C. Grover, B. Haddow, M. Kabadjov, E. Klein, M. Matthews, S. Roebuck, R. Tobin, and X. Wang (2008). Assisted curation: Does text mining really help? In *Pacific Symposium on Biocomputing*, Kohala Coast, HI, pp. 556–567.

Ando, R. (2008). BioCreative II gene mention tagging system at IBM Watson. In *Proceedings of the Second BioCreative Challenge Evaluation Workshop*, Spain, pp. 101–103.

Aronson, A. (2001). Effective mapping of biomedical text to the UMLS Metathesaurus: The MetaMap program. In *Proceedings of the AMIA 2001*, Bethesda, MD, pp. 17–21.

Aronson, A. R., D. Demner-Fushman, S. Humphrey, N. C. Ide, W. Kim, R. Loane, J. G. Mork, L. H. Smith, L. K. Tanabe, W. J. Wilbur, and N. Xie (2004). Knowledge-intensive and statistical approaches to the retrieval and annotation of genomics medline citations. In *The 13th Text Retrieval Conference, TREC 2004*, Gaithersburg, MD. National Institute of Standards and Technology.

Aronson, A., D. Demner-Fushman, S. Humphrey, J. Lin, H. Liu, P. Ruch, M. Ruiz, L. Smith, L. Tanabe, and W. Wilbur (2005). Fusion of knowledge-intensive and statistical approaches for retrieving and annotating textual genomics documents. In *Proceedings of the TREC 2005*, Gaithersburg, MD, pp. 36–45.

Baumgartner Jr., W. A., K. B. Cohen, L. Fox, G. K. Acquaah-Mensah, and L. Hunter (2007). Manual curation is not sufficient for annotation of genomic databases. *Bioinformatics 23*, i41–i48.

Baumgartner Jr., W. A., Z. Lu, H. L. Johnson, J. G. Caporaso, J. Paquette, A. Lindemann, E. K. White, O. Medvedeva, K. B. Cohen, and L. Hunter (2008). Concept recognition for extracting protein interaction relations from biomedical text. *Genome Biology, 9*(Suppl. 2), S9.

Blaschke, C., M. A. Andrade, C. Ouzounis, and A. Valencia (1999). Automatic extraction of biological information from scientific text: Protein-protein interactions. In *Intelligent Systems for Molecular Biology, 7*, 60–67.

Chang, J. T., H. Schütze, and R. B. Altman (2002). Creating an online dictionary of abbreviations from MEDLINE. *Journal of American Medical Informatics Association 9*(6), 612–620.

Chen, H. and B. M. Sharp (2004). Content-rich biological network constructed by mining PubMed abstracts. *BMC Bioinformatics 5*, 1471–2105.

Clegg, A. B. and A. J. Shepherd (2005). Evaluating and integrating treebank parsers on a biomedical corpus. In *Proceedings of the ACL Workshop on Software*, Ann Arbor, MI.

Clegg, A. B. and A. J. Shepherd (2007). Benchmarking natural-language parsers for biological applications using dependency graphs. *BMC Bioinformatics 8*(24).

Cohen, K. B. and L. Hunter (2006). A critical review of PASBio's argument structures for biomedical verbs. *BMC Bioinformatics 7*(Suppl. 3), S25.

Cohen, K. B., A. Dolbey, G. Acquaah-Mensah, and L. Hunter (2002). Contrast and variability in gene names. In *Natural Language Processing in the Biomedical Domain*, Philadelphia, PA, pp. 14–20. Association for Computational Linguistics.

Cohen, K. B., L. Tanabe, S. Kinoshita, and L. Hunter (2004). A resource for constructing customized test suites for molecular biology entity identification systems. In *HLT-NAACL 2004 Workshop: BioLINK 2004, Linking Biological Literature, Ontologies and Databases*, Boston, MA, pp. 1–8. Association for Computational Linguistics.

Cohen, K. B., L. Fox, P. V. Ogren, and L. Hunter (2005). Corpus design for biomedical natural language processing. In *Proceedings of the ACL-ISMB Workshop on Linking Biological Literature, Ontologies and Databases*, Detroit, MI, pp. 38–45. Association for Computational Linguistics.

Cohen, K. B., W. A. Baumgartner Jr., and L. Hunter (2008a). Software testing and the naturally occurring data assumption in natural language processing. In *Software Engineering, Testing, and Quality Assurance for Natural Language Processing*, Columbus, OH, pp. 23–30. Association for Computational Linguistics.

Cohen, K. B., M. Palmer, and L. Hunter (2008b). Nominalization and alternations in biomedical language. *PLoS ONE* 3(9), e3158.

Collier, N., C. Nobata, and J. Tsujii (2000). Extracting the names of genes and gene products with a hidden Markov model. In *Proceedings of COLING 2000*, Saarbrucken, Germany, pp. 201–207.

Corbett, P., C. Batchelor, and S. Teufel (2007, June). Annotation of chemical named entities. In *Biological, Translational, and Clinical Language Processing*, Prague, Czech Republic, pp. 57–64. Association for Computational Linguistics.

Craven, M. and J. Kumlein (1999). Constructing biological knowledge bases by extracting information from text sources. In *Intelligent Systems for Molecular Biology*, Heidelberg, Germany, pp. 77–86.

Demner-Fushman, D., S. Humphrey, N. Ide, R. Loane, P. Ruch, M. Ruiz, L. Smith, L. Tanabe, W. Wilbur, and A. Aronson (2006). Finding relevant passages in scientific articles: Fusion of automatic approaches vs. an interactive team effort. In *Proceedings of TREC 2006*, Gaithersburg, MD, pp. 569–576.

Demner-Fushman, D., S. Humphrey, N. Ide, R. Loane, J. Mork, P. Ruch, M. Ruiz, L. Smith, W. Wilbur, and A. Aronson (2007). Combining resources to find answers to biomedical questions. In *Proceedings of TREC 2007*, pp. 205–214.

Doms, A. and M. Schroeder (2005). GoPubMed: exploring PubMed with the Gene Ontology. *Nucleic Acids Research* 33, 783–786.

Donaldson, I., J. Martin, B. de Bruijn, C. Wolting, V. Lay, B. Tuekam, S. Zhang, B. Baskin, G. Bader, K. Michalickova, T. Pawson, and C. Hogue (2003). PreBIND and Textomy–mining the biomedical literature for protein-protein interactions using a support vector machine. *BMC Bioinformatics* 4(1), 11.

Ely, J. W., J. A. Osheroff, M. H. Ebell, G. R. Bergus, B. T. Levy, M. L. Chambliss, and E. R. Evans (2000). Analysis of questions asked by family physicians regarding patient care. *Western Journal of Medicine* 172(5), 315–319.

Erjavec, T., Y. Tateisi, J. Kim, T. Ohta, and J. Tsujii (2003). Encoding biomedical resources in TEI: The case of the GENIA corpus. In *Proceedings of the ACL 2003 Workshop on Natural Language Processing in Biomedicine*, Vol. 13, Sapporo, Japan, pp. 97–104. Association for Computational Linguistics.

Fang, H., K. Murphy, Y. Jin, J. Kim, and P. White (2006). Human gene name normalization using text matching with automatically extracted synonym dictionaries. In *Linking Natural Language Processing and Biology: Towards Deeper Biological Literature Analysis*, New York, pp. 41–48. Association for Computational Linguistics.

Friedman, C. (2000). A broad-coverage natural language processing system. In *Proceedings of the AMIA Symposium*, Los Angeles, CA, pp. 270–274.

Friedman, C., P. Kra, H. Yu, M. Krauthammer, and A. Rzhetsky (2001). GENIES: A natural-language processing system for the extraction of molecular pathways from journal articles. *Bioinformatics* 17(Suppl. 1), S74–S82.

Fukuda, K., A. Tamura, T. Tsunoda, and T. Takagi (1998). Toward information extraction: Identi-
       fying protein names from biological papers. In *Pacific Symposium on Biocomputing*, Maui, HI,
       pp. 707–718.
Hakenberg, J., C. Plake, L. Royer, H. Strobelt, U. Leser, and M. Schroeder (2008). Gene mention
       normalization and interaction extraction with context models and sentence motifs. *Genome Biology*
       9(Suppl. 2), S14.
Hanisch, D., K. Fundel, H.-T. Mevissen, R. Zimmer, and J. Fluck (2005). ProMiner: Rule-based protein
       and gene entity recognition. *BMC Bioinformatics* 6(Suppl. 1), S14.
Hatzivassiloglou, V., P. A. Duboué, and A. Rzhetsky (2001). Disambiguating proteins, genes, and RNA
       in text: A machine learning approach. *Bioinformatics* 17, S97–S106.
Hearst, M., A. Divoli, Y. Jerry, and M. Wooldridge (2007, June). Exploring the efficacy of caption
       search for bioscience journal search interfaces. In *Biological, Translational, and Clinical Language
       Processing*, Prague, Czech Republic, pp. 73–80. Association for Computational Linguistics.
Hersh, W. and R. T. Bhupatiraju (2003). TREC genomics track overview. In *The 12th Text Retrieval
       Conference—2003*, Gaithersburg, MD, pp. 14–23.
Hersh, W., S. Price, D. Kraemer, B. Chan, L. Sacherek, and D. Olson (1999). System and user
       attributes associated with successful searching. In *Advances in Digital Libraries '99*, Baltimore, MD,
       pp. 60–70.
Horn, F., A. L. Lau, and F. E. Cohen (2004). Automated extraction of mutation data from the lit-
       erature: Application of MuteXt to G protein-coupled receptors and nuclear hormone receptors.
       Bioinformatics 20(4), 557–568.
Hunter, L. (1993). *Molecular Biology for Computer Scientists*, Chapter 1, pp. 1–46. AAAI, Cambridge, MA.
Hunter, L. and K. B. Cohen (2006). Biomedical language processing: What's beyond PubMed? *Molecular
       Cell* 21(5), 589–594.
Jiang, J. and C. Zhai (2007). An empirical study of tokenization strategies for biomedical information
       retrieval. *Information Retrieval* 10, 341–363.
Johnson, H. L., W. A. Baumgartner Jr., M. Krallinger, K. B. Cohen, and L. Hunter (2007a). Corpus
       refactoring: A feasibility study. *Journal of Biomedical Discovery and Collaboration*.
Johnson, H. L., K. B. Cohen, and L. Hunter (2007b). A fault model for ontology mapping, alignment, and
       linking systems. In *Pacific Symposium on Biocomputing*, Maui, HI, pp. 233–244. World Scientific
       Publishing Company.
Kaner, C., H. Q. Nguyen, and J. Falk (1999). *Testing Computer Software*, 2nd edition. John Wiley & Sons,
       New York.
Karamanis, N., I. Lewin, R. Seal, R. Drysdale, and E. J. Briscoe (2007). Integrating natural language
       processing with FlyBase curation. In *Pacific Symposium on Biocomputing*, Maui, HI, pp. 245–256.
Kim, J.-D., T. Ohta, Y. Tateisi, and J. Tsujii (2003). Genia corpus—a semantically annotated corpus for
       bio-textmining. *Bioinformatics* 19(Suppl. 1), 180–182.
Krallinger, M., F. Leitner, C. Rodriguez-Penagos, and A. Valencia (2008). Overview of the protein-protein
       interaction annotation extraction task of BioCreative II. *Genome Biology* 9(Suppl. 2), S4.
Lesk, M. (1986). Automatic sense disambiguation using machine readable dictionaries: how to tell a
       pine cone from an ice cream cone. In *SIGDOC '86: Proceedings of the Fifth Annual International
       Conference on Systems Documentation*, New York, pp. 24–26. ACM Press.
Lindberg, D., B. Humphreys, and A. McCray (1993). The unified medical language system. *Methods of
       Information in Medicine* 32(4), 281–291.
Lu, Z., K. B. Cohen, and L. Hunter (2006). Finding GeneRIFs via Gene Ontology annotations. In *Pacific
       Symposium on Biocomputing 2006*, Maui, HI, pp. 52–63.
Lu, Z., K. B. Cohen, and L. Hunter (2007). GeneRIF quality assurance as summary revision. In *Pacific
       Symposium on Biocomputing*, Maui, HI, pp. 269–280.
Miyao, Y. and J. Tsujii (2008). Feature forest models for probabilistic HPSG parsing. *Computational
       Linguistics* 34(1), 35–80.

Morgan, A. A. et al. (2008). Overview of BioCreative II gene normalization. *Genome Biology* 9(Suppl. 2), S3.

Mungall, C. J. (2004, August). Obol: Integrating language and meaning in bio-ontologies. *Comparative and Functional Genomics* 5(6–7), 509–520.

Nobata, C., N. Collier, and J. Tsujii (1999). Automatic term identification and classification in biology texts. In *Proceedings of the Fifth Natural Language Processing Pacific Rim Symposium (NLPRS)*, Beijing, China, pp. 369–374.

Ogren, P. V., K. B. Cohen, G. K. Acquaah-Mensah, J. Eberlein, and L. Hunter (2004). The compositional structure of Gene Ontology terms. *Pacific Symposium on Biocomputing*, Boulder, CO, pp. 214–225.

Ogren, P., K. Cohen, and L. Hunter (2005). Implications of compositionality in the Gene Ontology for its curation and usage. In *Pacific Symposium on Biocomputing*, Big Island, HI, pp. 174–185.

Ohta, T., Y. Tateisi, J.-D. Kim, H. Mima, and J. Tsujii (2002). The GENIA corpus: An annotated corpus in molecular biology. In *Proceedings of the Human Language Technology Conference*, San Diego, CA.

Pestian, J. P., C. Brew, P. Matykiewicz, D. Hovermale, N. Johnson, K. B. Cohen, and W. Duch (2007). A shared task involving multi-label classification of clinical free text. In *Proceedings of BioNLP 2007*, Prague, Czech Republic. Association for Computational Linguistics.

Pyysalo, S., T. Salakoski, S. Aubin, and A. Nazarenko (2006). Lexical adaptation of link grammar to the biomedical sublanguage: A comparative evaluation of three approaches. *BMC Bioinformatics* 7(Suppl. 3), S2.

Schwartz, A. and M. Hearst (2003). A simple algorithm for identifying abbreviation definitions in biomedical text. In *Pacific Symposium on Biocomputing*, Vol. 8, Lihue, HI, pp. 451–462.

Sehgal, A. and P. Srinivasan (2006). Retrieval with gene queries. *BMC Bioinformatics* 7, 220.

Settles, B. (2005). Abner: An open source tool for automatically tagging genes, proteins and other entity names in text. *Bioinformatics* 21(14), 3191–3192.

Shah, P. K., L. J. Jensen, S. Boué, and P. Bork (2005). Extraction of transcript diversity from scientific literature. *PLoS Computational Biology* 1(1), 67–73.

Shatkay, H., S. Edwards, W. Wilbur, and M. Boguski (2000). Genes, themes and microarrays: Using information retrieval for large-scale gene analysis. In *Intelligent Systems for Molecular Biology*, La Jolla/San Diego, CA, pp. 317–328.

Tanabe, L., U. Scherf, L. Smith, J. Lee, L. Hunter, and J. Weinstein (1999). MedMiner: An Internet text-mining tool for biomedical information, with application to gene expression profiling. *Biotechniques* 27(6), 1216–1217.

The Gene Ontology Consortium (2000). Gene Ontology: Tool for the unification of biology. *Nature Genetics* 25(1), 25–29.

Wang, X. and M. Matthews (2008). Species disambiguation for biomedical term identification. In *Current Trends in Biomedical Natural Language Processing: BioNLP 2008*, Columbus, OH, pp. 71–79.

Wattarujeekrit, T., P. K. Shah, and N. Collier (2004). PASBio: Predicate-argument structures for event extraction in molecular biology. *BMC Bioinformatics* 5, 155.

Yeh, A., A. Morgan, M. Colosimo, and L. Hirschman (2005). BioCreative task 1A: Gene mention finding evaluation. *BMC Bioinformatics* 6(Suppl. 1), S2.

26

Sentiment Analysis and Subjectivity

Bing Liu
*University of Illinois at
Chicago*

Textual information in the world can be broadly categorized into two main types: *facts* and *opinions*. Facts are objective expressions about entities, events, and their properties. Opinions are usually subjective expressions that describe people's sentiments, appraisals, or feelings toward entities, events, and their properties. The concept of opinion is very broad. In this chapter, we only focus on opinion expressions that convey people's positive or negative sentiments. Much of the existing research on textual information processing has been focused on the mining and retrieval of factual information, e.g., information retrieval (IR), Web search, text classification, text clustering, and many other text mining and natural language processing tasks. Little work had been done on the processing of opinions until only recently. Yet, opinions are so important that whenever we need to make a decision we want to hear others' opinions. This is not only true for individuals but also true for organizations.

One of the main reasons for the lack of study on opinions is the fact that there was little opinionated text available before the World Wide Web. Before the Web, when an individual needed to make a decision, he or she typically asked for opinions from friends and families. When an organization wanted to find the opinions or sentiments of the general public about its products and services, it conducted opinion polls, surveys, and focus groups. However, with the Web, especially with the explosive growth of the user-generated content on the Web in the past few years, the world has been transformed.

The Web has dramatically changed the way that people express their views and opinions. They can now post reviews of products at merchant sites and express their views on almost anything in Internet forums, discussion groups, and blogs, which are collectively called the *user-generated content*. This online word-of-mouth behavior represents new and measurable sources of information with many practical applications. Now if one wants to buy a product, he or she is no longer limited to asking his or her friends and families because there are many product reviews on the Web that give opinions of existing users of the product. For a company, it may no longer be necessary to conduct surveys, organize focus groups, or employ external consultants in order to find consumer opinions about its products and those of its competitors because the user-generated content on the Web can already give them such information.

However, finding opinion sources and monitoring them on the Web can still be a formidable task because there are a large number of diverse sources, and each source may also have a huge volume of *opinionated text* (text with opinions or sentiments). In many cases, opinions are hidden in long forum posts and blogs. It is difficult for a human reader to find relevant sources, extract related sentences with opinions, read them, summarize them, and organize them into usable forms. Thus, automated opinion discovery and summarization systems are needed. *Sentiment analysis*, also known as *opinion mining*, grows out of this need. It is a challenging natural language processing or text-mining problem. Due to its tremendous value for practical applications, there has been an explosive growth of both research in academia and applications in the industry. There are now at least 20–30 companies that offer sentiment analysis services in the United States alone. This chapter introduces this research field. It focuses on the following topics:

1. *The problem of sentiment analysis*: As for any scientific problem, before solving it we need to define or to formalize the problem. The formulation will introduce the basic definitions, core concepts and issues, subproblems, and target objectives. It also serves as a common framework to unify different research directions. From an application point of view, it tells practitioners what the main tasks are, their inputs and outputs, and how the resulting outputs may be used in practice.

2. *Sentiment and subjectivity classification*: This is the area that has been researched the most in academia. It treats sentiment analysis as a text classification problem. Two subtopics that have been extensively studied are: (1) classifying an opinionated document as expressing a positive or negative opinion, and (2) classifying a sentence or a clause of the sentence as subjective or objective, and for a subjective sentence or clause classifying it as expressing a positive, negative, or neutral opinion. The first topic, commonly known as *sentiment classification* or *document-level sentiment classification*, aims to find the general sentiment of the author in an opinionated text. For example, given a product review, it determines whether the reviewer is positive or negative about the product. The second topic goes to individual sentences to determine whether a sentence expresses an opinion or not (often called *subjectivity classification*), and if so, whether the opinion is positive or negative (called *sentence-level sentiment classification*).

3. *Feature-based sentiment analysis*: This model first discovers the targets on which opinions have been expressed in a sentence, and then determines whether the opinions are positive, negative, or neutral. The targets are objects, and their components, attributes and features. An object can be a product, service, individual, organization, event, topic, etc. For instance, in a product review sentence, it identifies product features that have been commented on by the reviewer and determines whether the comments are positive or negative. For example, in the sentence, "*The battery life of this camera is too short*," the comment is on "battery life" of the camera object and the opinion is negative. Many real-life applications require this level of detailed analysis because in order to make product improvements one needs to know what components and/or features of the product are liked and disliked by consumers. Such information is not discovered by sentiment and subjectivity classification.

4. *Sentiment analysis of comparative sentences*: The evaluation of an object can be done in two main ways, direct appraisal and comparison. Direct appraisal, called *direct opinion*, gives positive or negative opinions about the object without mentioning any other similar objects. Comparison means to compare the object with some other similar objects (e.g., competing products). For example, "*The picture quality of this camera is poor*," expresses a direct opinion, while "*The picture*

quality of Camera-x is better than that of Camera-y." expresses a comparison. Clearly, it is useful to identify such sentences, extract comparative opinions expressed in them, and determine which objects are preferred by the sentence authors (in the above example, Camera-x is preferred with respect to the picture quality).

5. *Opinion search and retrieval*: Since the general Web search has been so successful in many aspects, it is not hard to imagine that opinion search will be very useful as well. For example, given a keyword query "gay marriage," one wants to find positive and negative opinions on the issue from an opinion search engine. For such a query, two tasks need to be performed: (1) retrieving documents or sentences that are relevant to the query, and (2) identifying and ranking opinionated documents or sentences from those retrieved. Opinion search is thus a combination of IR and sentiment analysis.

6. *Opinion spam and utility of opinions*: As opinions on the Web are important for many applications, it is no surprise that people have started to game the system. Opinion spam refers to fake or bogus opinions that try to deliberately mislead readers or automated systems by giving undeserving positive opinions to some target objects in order to promote the objects and/or by giving malicious negative opinions to some other objects in order to damage their reputations. Detecting such spam is very important for applications. The utility of opinions refers to the usefulness or quality of opinions. Automatically assigning utility values to opinions is useful as opinions can then be ranked based on their utility values. With the ranking, the reader can focus on those quality opinions. We should note, however, that spam and utility are different concepts, as we will see later.

Pang and Lee (2008) wrote a comprehensive survey of the sentiment analysis and opinion mining research. This chapter is not meant to be another such survey, but instead to introduce the field for teaching and learning. It focuses on the core topics of the research that are also essential for practical applications. It introduces the topics in sufficient detail so that the reader can have a good understanding of the main ideas without referring to the original papers. Another key characteristic of this chapter is that it takes a structured approach to exploring the problem. In non-NLP literature, natural language documents are regarded as unstructured data, while the data in relational databases are referred to as structured data. The structured approach means to turn unstructured text to structured data, which enables traditional data management tools to be applied to slice, dice, and visualize the results in many ways. This is extremely important for applications because it allows the user to gain insights through both qualitative and quantitative analyses.

26.1 The Problem of Sentiment Analysis

Sentiment analysis or opinion mining is the computational study of opinions, sentiments, and emotions expressed in text. We use the following review segment on iPhone to introduce the problem (a number is associated with each sentence for easy reference):

(1) *I bought an iPhone a few days ago.* (2) *It was such a nice phone.* (3) *The touch screen was really cool.* (4) *The voice quality was clear too.* (5) *Although the battery life was not long, that is ok for me.* (6) *However, my mother was mad with me as I did not tell her before I bought it.* (7) *She also thought the phone was too expensive, and wanted me to return it to the shop. ....*

The question is: what do we want to mine or extract from this review? The first thing that we may notice is that there are several opinions in this review. Sentences (2), (3), and (4) express positive opinions, while sentences (5), (6) and (7) express negative opinions or emotions. Then, we also notice that the opinions all have some targets or objects on which the opinions are expressed. The opinion in sentence (2) is on the iPhone as a whole, and the opinions in sentences (3), (4), and (5) are on the "touch screen," "voice quality," and "battery life" of the iPhone respectively. The opinion in sentence (7) is on the price of the iPhone, but the opinion/emotion in sentence (6) is on "me," not iPhone. This is an important point. In an application, the user may be interested in opinions on certain targets or objects, but not on all (e.g., unlikely on "me"). Finally, we may also notice the sources or holders of opinions. The source or holder of the opinions in sentences (2), (3), (4), and (5) is the author of the review ("I"), but in sentences (6) and (7) is "my mother." With this example in mind, we now formally define the sentiment analysis or opinion mining problem. We start with the opinion target.

In general, opinions can be expressed on anything, e.g., a product, a service, an individual, an organization, an event, or a topic. We use the term *object* to denote the target entity that has been commented on. An object can have a set of *components* (or *parts*) and a set of *attributes* (or *properties*). Each component may have its own subcomponents and its set of attributes, and so on. Thus, an object can be hierarchically decomposed based on the *part-of* relation. Formally, we have the following (Liu 2006):

Definition (object) *An object o is an entity that can be a product, person, event, organization, or topic. It is associated with a pair, o: (T, A), where T is a hierarchy of components (or parts), subcomponents, and so on, and A is a set of attributes of o. Each component has its own set of subcomponents and attributes.*

Example 26.1

A particular brand of cellular phone is an object. It has a set of components, e.g., *battery*, and *screen*, and also a set of attributes, e.g., *voice quality*, *size*, and *weight*. The battery component also has its set of attributes, e.g., *battery life* and *battery size*.

Based on this definition, an object can be represented as a tree, hierarchy, or taxonomy. The root of the tree is the object itself. Each non-root node is a component or subcomponent of the object. Each link is a *part-of* relation. Each node is also associated with a set of attributes or properties. An opinion can be expressed on any node and any attribute of the node.

Example 26.2

Following Example 26.1, one can express an opinion on the cellular phone itself (the root node), e.g., "*I do not like this phone,*" or on one of its attributes, e.g., "*The voice quality of this phone is lousy.*" Likewise, one can also express an opinion on any one of the phone's components or any attribute of the component.

In practice, it is often useful to simplify this definition due to two reasons: First, natural language processing is a difficult task. To effectively study the text at an arbitrary level of detail as described in the definition is extremely challenging. Second, for an ordinary user, it is probably too complex to use a hierarchical representation of an object and opinions on the object. Thus, we flatten the tree to omit the hierarchy and use the term *features* to represent both components and attributes. In this simplification, the object itself can also be seen as a feature (but a special feature), which is the root of the original tree. An opinionated comment on the object itself is called a *general opinion* on the object (e.g., "*I like iPhone*"). An opinionated comment on any specific feature is called a *specific opinion* on a feature of the object, e.g., "*The touch screen of iPhone is really cool,*" where "touch screen" is a feature of iPhone.

Using features for an object is quite common in the product domain as people often use the term *product features*. However, when the objects are events and topics, the term *feature* may not sound natural. Indeed in some other domains, researchers also use the term *topic* (Kim and Hovy 2004) or *aspect* (Kobayashi et al. 2007; Snyder and Barzilay 2007) to mean *feature*. In this chapter, we choose to use the term *feature* along with the term *object*. We should note that both terms are needed because in most applications the primary concern of the user is a set of objects of interest (e.g., a set of competing products). Then we need to know each feature talked about in an opinion document belonging to which object. One issue with the term feature is that it can confuse with the term feature used in machine learning, where a feature means a data attribute. To avoid the confusion, we will use the term *object feature* to mean feature of an object whenever such confusion may arise.

Let an *opinionated document* be *d*, which can be a product review, a forum post, or a blog that evaluates a set of objects. In the most general case, *d* consists of a sequence of sentences $d = \langle s_1, s_2, \ldots, s_m \rangle$.

Definition (opinion passage on a feature) *An opinion passage on a feature f of an object o evaluated in d is a group of consecutive sentences in d that expresses a positive or negative opinion on f.*

It is possible that a sequence of sentences (at least one) in an opinionated document together expresses an opinion on an object or a feature of the object. It is also possible that a single sentence expresses opinions on more than one feature, e.g., "*The voice quality of this phone is good, but the battery life is short.*"

Much of the current research focuses on sentences, that is, each passage consisting of a single sentence. In the subsequent discussion, we also treat each sentence as the basic information unit.

Definition (explicit and implicit feature) *If a feature f or any of its synonyms appears in a sentence s, f is called an explicit feature in s. If neither f nor any of its synonyms appear in s but f is implied, then f is called an implicit feature in s.*

Example 26.3

"Battery Life" in the Following Sentence is an Explicit Feature
"The battery life of this phone is too short."
Size is an implicit feature in the following sentence as it does not appear in the sentence but it is implied:
"This phone is too large."
Here, "large," which is not a synonym of *size*, is called a *feature indicator.* Many feature indicators are adjectives or adverbs. Some adjectives and adverbs are general and can be used to modify anything, e.g., *good, bad,* and *great,* but many actually indicate the types of features that they are likely to modify, e.g., *beautiful* (appearance), and *reliably* (reliability). Thus, such feature indicators may be directly mapped to their underlying features. We will discuss this again in Section 26.3.1.2.

Definition (opinion holder) *The holder of an opinion is the person or organization that expresses the opinion.*

Opinion holders are also called *opinion sources* (Wiebe et al. 2005). In the case of product reviews and blogs, opinion holders are usually the authors of the posts. Opinion holders are more important in news articles because they often explicitly state the person or organization that holds a particular opinion (Bethard et al. 2004; Choi et al. 2005; Kim and Hovy 2004). For example, the opinion holder in the sentence "*John expressed his disagreement on the treaty*" is "John."

Definition (opinion) *An opinion on a feature f is a positive or negative view, attitude, emotion, or appraisal on f from an opinion holder.*

Definition (opinion orientation) *The orientation of an opinion on a feature f indicates whether the opinion is positive, negative, or neutral.*

Opinion orientation is also known as *sentiment orientation, polarity of opinion,* or *semantic orientation.* We now put everything together to define a model of an object, a model of an opinionated text, and the mining objective, which are collectively called the *feature-based sentiment analysis model* (Hu and Liu 2004; Liu 2006; Liu et al. 2005).

Model of an object: An object *o* is represented with a finite set of features, $F = \{f_1, f_2, \ldots, f_n\}$, which includes the object itself as a special feature. Each feature $f_i \in F$ can be expressed with any one of a finite set of words or phrases $W_i = \{w_{i1}, w_{i2}, \ldots, w_{im}\}$, which are *synonyms* of the feature, or indicated by any one of a finite set of indicators $I_i = \{i_{i1}, i_{i2}, \ldots, i_{iq}\}$ of the feature.

Model of an opinionated document: A general opinionated document d contains opinions on a set of objects $\{o_1, o_2, \ldots, o_r\}$ from a set of opinion holders $\{h_1, h_2, \ldots, h_p\}$. The opinions on each object o_j are expressed on a subset F_j of features of o_j. An opinion can be any one of the following two types:

1. *Direct opinion*: A direct opinion is a quintuple $(o_j, f_{jk}, oo_{ijkl}, h_i, t_l)$, where o_j is an object, f_{jk} is a feature of the object o_j, oo_{ijkl} is the orientation or polarity of the opinion on feature f_{jk} of object o_j, h_i is the opinion holder and t_l is the time when the opinion is expressed by h_i. The opinion orientation oo_{ijkl} can be positive, negative, or neutral (or measured based on a more granular scale to express different strengths of opinions (Wilson et al. 2004)). For feature f_{jk} that opinion holder h_i comments on, he or she chooses a word or phrase from the corresponding synonym set W_{jk}, or a word or phrase from the corresponding feature indicator set I_{jk} to describe the feature, and then expresses a positive, negative, or neutral opinion on the feature.

2. *Comparative opinion*: A comparative opinion expresses a relation of similarities or differences between two or more objects, and/or object preferences of the opinion holder based on some of the shared features of the objects. A comparative opinion is usually expressed using the *comparative* or *superlative* form of an adjective or an adverb, although not always. More detailed discussions will be given in Section 26.4. The discussion below focuses only on direct opinions.

This opinionated text model covers the essential but not all the interesting information or all possible cases. For example, it does not cover the situation described in the following sentence: *"The view-finder and the lens of this camera are too close,"* which expresses a negative opinion on the distance of the two components. We will follow this simplified model in the rest of this chapter as it is often sufficient for practical applications.

On direct opinions, there are in fact two main subtypes. In the first subtype, opinions are directly expressed on object or some features of an object, e.g., *"The voice quality of this phone is great."* In the second subtype, opinions on an object are expressed based on its effect on some other objects. This subtype often occurs in the medical domain when patients express opinions on drugs or describe their side effects. For example, the sentence *"After taking this drug, my left knee felt great"* describes a desirable effect of the drug on the knee, and thus implies a positive opinion on the drug. We call both types direct opinions in this chapter for the sake of simplicity and to distinguish them from comparative opinions.

Before going further, let us also have some more discussions about the strength of an opinion (oo_{ijkl}). Opinions come in different strengths (Wilson et al. 2004). Some are very strong, e.g., *"This phone is a piece of junk"* and some are weak, e.g., *"I think this phone is fine."* Hence, the strength of opinions can be interpreted as scaled. For example, a positive opinion may express a feeling of *contented, happy, joyous,* or *ecstatic,* from the low intensity value of *contented* to the maximally high intensity value of *ecstatic* (Martin and White 2005). In a practical application, we can choose the number of strength values or levels depending on the application need. For example, for positive opinions, we may only need two levels, i.e., grouping *contented* and *happy* into one level, and *joyous* and *ecstatic* into the other level. This discussion in fact touches the concept of emotions.

Definition (emotion) *Emotions are our subjective feelings and thoughts.*

Emotions have been studied in many fields, e.g., psychology, philosophy, sociology, biology, etc. However, there is still not a set of agreed basic emotions of people among researchers. Based on (Parrott 2001), people have six types of primary emotions, i.e., *love, joy, surprise, anger, sadness* and *fear*, which can be subdivided into many secondary and tertiary emotions. Each emotion can also have different intensities. The strengths of opinions are closely related to the intensities of certain emotions, e.g., joy and anger. However, the concepts of emotions and opinions are not equivalent although they have a large intersection.

When discussing subjective feelings of emotions or opinions, it is useful to distinguish two different notions: people's mental states (or feelings) and language expressions used to describe the mental states. Although there are only six types of emotions, there are a large number of language expressions that can be used to express them. Similarly, there are also a large (seemly unlimited) number of opinion expressions that describe positive or negative sentiments. Sentiment analysis or opinion mining essentially tries to infer people's sentiments based on their language expressions.

We now describe the objective of sentiment analysis or opinion mining, which not only aims to infer positive or negative opinions/sentiments from text, but also to discover the other pieces of associated information which are important for practical applications of the opinions.

Objective of mining direct opinions: Given an opinionated document d,

1. Discover all opinion quintuples $(o_j, f_{jk}, oo_{ijkl}, h_i, t_l)$ in d
2. Identify all synonyms (W_{jk}) and feature indicators I_{jk} of each feature f_{jk} in d

Some remarks about this feature-based sentiment analysis or opinion mining model are as follows:

1. It should be stressed that the five pieces of information in the quintuple need to correspond to one another. That is, the opinion oo_{ijkl} must be given by opinion holder h_i on feature f_{jk} of object o_j at time t_l. This requirement gives some clue why sentiment analysis is such a challenging problem because even identifying each piece of information itself is already very difficult, let alone finding all five and match them. To make matters worse, a sentence may not explicitly mention some pieces of information, but they are implied due to pronouns, language conventions, and the context. Let us see an example blog (the number before each sentence is added as the sentence id to facilitate the discussion below):

Example 26.4

"(1) This past Saturday, I bought a Nokia phone and my girlfriend bought a Motorola phone. (2) We called each other when we got home. (3) The voice on my phone was not so clear, worse than my previous phone. (4) The camera was good. (5) My girlfriend was quite happy with her phone. (6) I wanted a phone with good voice quality. (7) So my purchase was a real disappointment. (8) I returned the phone yesterday."

The objects to be discovered in this blog are "Motorola phone" and "Nokia phone," which are by no means easy to identify in practice. To figure out what is "my phone" and what is "her phone" in sentences (3) and (5) is even more challenging. Sentence (4) does not mention any phone and does not have a pronoun. Then the question is which phone "the camera" belongs to. Sentence (6) seemingly expresses a positive opinion about a phone and its voice quality, but of course that is not the case. In sentences (7) and (8), it is hard to know what "my purchase" is and what "the phone" is. The opinion holder of all the opinions is the author of the blog except sentence (5) whose opinion holder is "my girlfriend."

2. In practice not all five pieces of information in the quintuple needs to be discovered for every application because some of them may be known or not needed. For example, in the context of product reviews, the object (product) evaluated in each review, the time when the review is submitted, and the opinion holder are all known as a review site typically records and displays such information. Of course, one still needs to extract such information from the Web page, which is usually a structured data extraction problem (see Chapter 9 of (Liu 2006)).

Example 26.4 above revealed another issue, namely, *subjectivity*, which is related to opinions. That is, in a typical document (even an opinionated document), some sentences express opinions and some do not. For example, sentences (1), (2), (6), and (8) do not express any opinions. The issue of subjectivity has been extensively studied in the literature (Hatzivassiloglou and McKeown 2006; Hatzivassiloglou and Wiebe 2000; Riloff et al. 2006; Riloff and Wiebe 2003; Turney 2002; Wiebe 2000; Wiebe and Mihalcea 2006; Wiebe and Wilson 2002; Wiebe et al. 2004; Wilson et al. 2004; 2005).

Definition (sentence subjectivity) *An objective sentence presents some factual information about the world, while a subjective sentence expresses some personal feelings or beliefs.*

For example, in Example 26.4, sentences (1), (2), and (8) are objective sentences, while all other sentences are subjective sentences. Subjective expressions come in many forms, e.g., opinions, allegations, desires, beliefs, suspicions, and speculations (Riloff et al. 2006; Wiebe 2000). Thus, a subjective sentence may not contain an opinion. For example, sentence (6) in Example 26.4 is subjective but it does not express a positive or negative opinion on any specific phone. Similarly, we should also note that not every objective sentence contains no opinion as the second sentence in Example 26.5 below shows.

Definition (explicit and implicit opinion) *An explicit opinion on feature f is a positive or negative opinion explicitly expressed on f in a subjective sentence. An implicit opinion on feature f is an opinion on f implied in an objective sentence.*

Example 26.5

The following sentence expresses an explicit positive opinion:
   "The voice quality of this phone is amazing."
The following sentence expresses an implicit negative opinion:
   "The earphone broke in two days."
Although this sentence states an objective fact, it implicitly indicates a negative opinion on the earphone. In fact, sentence (8) in Example 26.4 can also be said to imply a negative opinion. In general, objective sentences that imply positive or negative opinions often state the reasons for the opinions.

Definition (opinionated sentence) *An opinionated sentence is a sentence that expresses explicit or implicit positive or negative opinions. It can be a subjective or objective sentence.*

As we can see, the concepts of subjective sentences and opinionated sentences are not the same, although opinionated sentences are most often a subset of subjective sentences. The approaches for identifying them are similar. Thus for the simplicity of presentation, this chapter uses the two terms interchangeably. The task of determining whether a sentence is subjective or objective is called *subjectivity classification*.

Clearly, the idea of opinionated can also be applied to documents. So far we have taken opinionated documents for granted in the above definitions. In practice, they may also need to be identified. For example, many forum posts are questions and answers with no opinions. It is reasonable to say that whether a document is opinionated depends entirely on whether some of its sentences are opinionated. Thus, we may define a document to be opinionated if any of its sentences is opinionated. This definition, however, may not be suitable in all cases. For example, an objective news report may quote someone's opinion. It does not make good sense to say that the report is subjective or opinionated. It is perhaps more appropriate to say that the report contains some opinions. A more fair definition may be one that is based on the author's intention, that is, whether he or she intends to express opinions on something using the text. Product reviews fit this definition, that is, they are opinionated. Whether a sentence is opinionated or not is more clear-cut. In a typical document, some sentences are opinionated and some are not.

With the abstract model and mining objectives defined, let us now see how the mining results may be presented to the user in applications. Although this step is not so much of academic research, it is crucial for applications. It also gives us some gleams of how an industrial user wants to see the results, which in turn motivates our research. What we discuss below has already been used in the industry.

To start, we should note that for most opinion-based applications, it is important to study a collection of opinions rather than only one because one opinion only represents the subjective view of a single person, which is usually not significant for action. This clearly indicates that some form of summary of the mining results is needed because it does not make sense to list all quintuples (opinions) to the user. Below, we use product reviews as an example to present some ideas.

Recall we mentioned at the beginning of the chapter that we wanted to turn unstructured natural language texts to structured data. The quintuple output does exactly that. All the discovered quintuples can be easily stored in database tables. A whole suite of database and visualization tools can then be

Cellular phone 1:
PHONE:
    Positive: 125   <individual review sentences>
    Negative: 7   <individual review sentences>
Feature: **voice quality**
    Positive: 120   <individual review sentences>
    Negative: 8   <individual review sentences>
Feature: size
    Positive: 80   <individual review sentences>
    Negative: 12   <individual review sentences>
. . .

FIGURE 26.1 An example of a feature-based summary of opinions.

applied to view the results in all kinds of ways to gain insights of consumer opinions, which are usually called *structured summaries* and are visualized as bar charts and/or pie charts.

Structured opinion summary: A simple way to use the results is to produce a *feature-based summary* of opinions on an object or multiple competing objects (Hu and Liu 2004; Liu et al. 2005).

Example 26.6

Assume we summarize the reviews of a particular cellular phone, *cellular phone* 1. The summary looks like that in Figure 26.1, which was proposed by Hu and Liu (2004). In the figure, "PHONE" represents the phone itself (the root node of the object hierarchy). Positive opinions on the phone were expressed by 125 reviews and 7 reviews expressed negative opinions on the phone. "Voice quality" and "size" are two product features. Positive opinions on the voice quality were expressed by 120 reviews, and only 8 reviews expressed negative opinions. The <individual review sentences> link points to the specific sentences and/or the whole reviews that give positive or negative comments about the feature. With such a summary, the user can easily see how existing customers feel about the cellular phone. If he or she is interested in a particular feature, he or she can drill down by following the <individual review sentences> link to see why existing customers like it and/or what they are not satisfied with.

Such a summary can also be visualized easily using a bar chart (Liu et al. 2005). Figure 26.2a shows the summary of opinions in a set of reviews of a cellular phone. In the figure, each bar above the X-axis in the middle shows the number of positive opinions on a feature (given at the top), and the bar below the X-axis shows the number of negative opinions on the same feature. Obviously, other similar visualizations are also possible. For example, we may only show the percent of positive opinions (the percent of negative opinions is just one minus the percent of positive opinions) for each feature. To see the actual review sentences behind each bar, the bar can be programmed in such a way that clicking on the bar will show all the review sentences in a pop-up window.

Comparing opinion summaries of a few competing products is even more interesting (Liu et al. 2005). Figure 26.2b shows a visual comparison of consumer opinions on two competing phones. We can clearly see how consumers view different features of each product. Cellular phone 1 is definitely superior to cellular phone 2. Most customers have negative opinions about the voice quality, the battery, and the camera of cellular phone 2. However, on the same three features, customers are mostly positive about cellular phone 1. Regarding the size and the weight, customers have similar opinions about both phones. For the phone itself ("PHONE"), most people are positive about cellular phone 1, but negative about cellular phone 2. Hence, the visualization enables users to see how the phones compare with each other along different feature dimensions.

Clearly, many other types of visualizations are possible, see Pang and Lee (2008) for a survey of other techniques. Incidentally, opinion summary of product reviews in Microsoft Bing search uses a bar chart similar to the one in Figure 26.2a. At the time when this chapter was written, it did not provide the facility for side-by-side opinion comparison of different products as in Figure 26.2b.

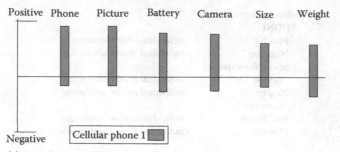

(a) Visualization of feature-based summary of opinions on a cellular phone

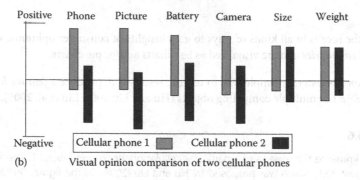

(b)   Visual opinion comparison of two cellular phones

FIGURE 26.2   Visualization of feature-based summaries of opinions.

In fact, many types of summaries without opinions are also useful. We give some examples below.

Feature buzz summary: This summary shows the relative frequency of feature mentions. It can tell a company what their customers really care about. For example, in an online banking study, the most mentioned feature may be the transaction security.

Object buzz summary: This summary shows the frequency of mentions of different competing products. This is useful because it tells the popularity of different products or brands in the market place.

Since the time of the opinion is recorded in each quintuple, we can easily monitor changes of every aspect using trend tracking.

Trend tracking: If the time dimension is added to the above summaries, we get their trend reports. These reports can be extremely helpful in practice because the user always wants to know how things change over time (Tong 2001).

All these summaries can be produced and visualized easily as they are just the results of some database queries with no additional mining. This shows the power of the structured output of opinion quintuples.

Finally, we note that researchers have also studied the summarization of opinions in the traditional fashion, e.g., producing a short textual summary based on multiple reviews or even a single review (Beineke et al. 2004; Carenini et al. 2006; Ku et al. 2006; Seki et al. 2006; Stoyanov and Cardie 2006). Such a summary gives the reader a quick overview of what people think about a product or service. However, one weakness of such a text-based summary is that it is often not quantitative but only qualitative, which is not suitable for analytical purposes, although it may be suitable for human reading. For example, a traditional text summary may say "*Most people do not like this product.*" However, a quantitative summary may say that 60% of the people do not like this product and 40% of them like it. In most opinion analysis applications, the quantitative aspect is crucial just like in the traditional survey research (in fact, reviews can be seen as open-ended surveys). In the survey research, structured summaries displayed as bar charts and/or pie charts are the most common approaches because they give the user a concise, quantitative, and visual view.

Note that instead of generating a text summary directly from input reviews, it is also possible to generate a text summary based on the mining results as displayed in Figures 26.1 and 26.2. For example, it is easy to generate some natural language summary sentences based on what is shown on the bar chart using predefined templates. For instance, the first two bars in Figure 26.2b can be summarized as "*Most people are positive about cellular phone 1 and negative about cellular phone 2.*"

26.2 Sentiment and Subjectivity Classification

We now discuss some key research topics of sentiment analysis. *Sentiment classification* is perhaps the most widely studied topic (Aue and Gamon 2005; Blitzer et al. 2007; Breck et al. 2007; Chesley et al. 2006; Choi et al. 2006; Das and Chen 2007; Dave et al. 2003; Devitt and Ahmad 2007; Gamon 2004; Gamon et al. 2005; Godbole et al. 2007; Hatzivassiloglou and McKeown 2006; Hatzivassiloglou and Wiebe 2000; Kanayama and Nasukawa 2006; Kennedy and Inkpen 2006; McDonald et al. 2007; Mihalcea et al. 2007; Nasukawa and Yi 2003; Ng et al. 2006; Ni et al. 2007; Pang and Lee 2002, 2004, 2005; Riloff et al. 2006; Riloff and Wiebe 2003; Stepinski and Mittal 2007; Thomas et al. 2006; Turney 2002; Wan 2008; Wiebe 2000; Wiebe et al. 1999, 2004, 2005; Wiebe and Mihalcea 2006; Wiebe and Wilson 2002; Wilson et al. 2004, 2005; Yang et al. 2006; Yi et al. 2003; Zhang et al. 2006). It classifies an opinionated document (e.g., a product review) as expressing a positive or a negative opinion. The task is also commonly known as the *document-level sentiment classification* because it considers the whole document as the basic information unit. The existing research assumes that the document is known to be opinionated. Naturally the same sentiment classification can also be applied to individual sentences. However, here each sentence is not assumed to be opinionated in the literature. The task of classifying a sentence as opinionated or not opinionated is called *subjectivity classification*. The resulting opinionated sentences are also classified as expressing positive or negative opinions, which is called the *sentence-level sentiment classification*.

26.2.1 Document-Level Sentiment Classification

Given a set of opinionated documents D, it determines whether each document $d \in D$ expresses a positive or negative opinion (or sentiment) on an object. Formally:

Task: Given an opinionated document d that comments on an object o, determine the orientation oo of the opinion expressed on o, that is, discover the opinion orientation oo on feature f in the quintuple (o, f, so, h, t), where $f = o$ and h, t, o are assumed to be known or irrelevant.

The existing research on sentiment classification makes the following assumption:

Assumption: The opinionated document d (e.g., a product review) expresses opinions on a single object o and the opinions are from a single opinion holder h.

This assumption holds for customer reviews of products and services. However, it may not hold for a forum and blog post because in such a post the author may express opinions on multiple products and compare them using comparative and superlative sentences.

Most existing techniques for document-level sentiment classification are based on supervised learning, although there are also some unsupervised methods. We give an introduction to them below.

26.2.1.1 Classification Based on Supervised Learning

Sentiment classification can obviously be formulated as a supervised learning problem with two class labels (positive and negative). Training and testing data used in the existing research are mostly product reviews, which is not surprising due to the above assumption. Since each review at a typical review site already has a reviewer-assigned rating (e.g., 1–5 stars), training and testing data are readily available. Typically, a review with 4–5 stars is considered a positive review (thumbs-up), and a review with 1–2 stars is considered a negative review (thumbs-down).

Sentiment classification is similar to but also different from classic topic-based text classification, which classifies documents into predefined topic classes, e.g., politics, sciences, sports, etc. In topic-based classification, topic related words are important. However, in sentiment classification, topic-related words are unimportant. Instead, sentiment or opinion words that indicate positive or negative opinions are important, e.g., *great, excellent, amazing, horrible, bad, worst*, etc.

Existing supervised learning methods can be readily applied to sentiment classification, e.g., naïve Bayesian, and support vector machines (SVM), etc. Pang et al. (2002) took this approach to classify movie reviews into two classes, positive and negative. It was shown that using unigrams (a bag of individual words) as features in classification performed well with either naïve Bayesian or SVM. Neutral reviews were not used in this work, which made the problem easier. Note that features here are data attributes used in machine learning, not object features refereed to in the previous section.

Subsequent research used many more kinds of features and techniques in learning. As most learning applications, the main task of sentiment classification is to engineer a suitable set of features. Some of the example features used in research and possibly in practice are listed below. For a more comprehensive survey of features used, please refer to Pang and Lee (2008).

Terms and their frequency: These features are individual words or word n-grams and their frequency counts. In some cases, word positions may also be considered. The TF–IDF weighting scheme from IR may be applied too. Note that these features are also commonly used in traditional topic-based text classification. They have been shown quite effective in sentiment classification as well.

Part of speech tags: It was found in many early researches that adjectives are important indicators of subjectivities and opinions. Thus, adjectives have been treated as special features.

Opinion words and phrases: *Opinion words* are words that are commonly used to express positive or negative sentiments. For example, *beautiful, wonderful, good*, and *amazing* are positive opinion words, and *bad, poor*, and *terrible* are negative opinion words. Although many opinion words are adjectives and adverbs, nouns (e.g., *rubbish, junk*, and *crap*), and verbs (e.g., *hate* and *like*) can also indicate opinions. Apart from individual words, there are also opinion phrases and idioms, e.g., *cost someone an arm and a leg*. Opinion words and phrases are instrumental to sentiment analysis for obvious reasons. We will discuss them further later in this section.

Syntactic dependency: Words dependency-based features generated from parsing or dependency trees are also tried by several researchers.

Negation: Clearly negation words are important because their appearances often change the opinion orientation. For example, the sentence "*I don't like this camera*" is negative. However, negation words must be handled with care because not all occurrences of such words mean negation. For example, "not" in "*not only ... but also*" does not change the orientation direction. We will discuss these issues again in Section 26.3.2.

Apart from the classification or prediction of positive or negative sentiments, research has also been done on predicting the rating scores (e.g., 1–5 stars) of reviews (Pang and Lee 2005). In this case, the problem is formulated as a regression problem since the rating scores are ordinal. Another interesting research direction that has been investigated is the transfer learning or domain adaptation as it has been shown that sentiment classification is highly sensitive to the domain from which the training data are extracted. A classifier trained using opinionated texts from one domain often performs poorly when it is applied or tested on opinionated texts from another domain. The reason is that words and even language constructs used in different domains for expressing opinions can be substantially different. To make matters worse, the same word in one domain may mean positive, but in another domain may mean negative. For example, as observed in Turney (2002), the adjective *unpredictable* may have a negative

TABLE 26.1 Patterns of POS Tags for Extracting Two-Word Phrases

	First Word	Second Word	Third Word (Not Extracted)
1.	JJ	NN or NNS	Anything
2.	RB, RBR, or RBS	JJ	Not NN nor NNS
3.	JJ	JJ	Not NN nor NNS
4.	NN or NNS	JJ	Not NN nor NNS
5.	RB, RBR, or RBS	VB, VBD, VBN, or VBG	Anything

orientation in a car review (e.g., "unpredictable steering"), but it could have a positive orientation in a movie review (e.g., "unpredictable plot"). Thus, domain adaptation is needed. Existing research has used labeled data from one domain and unlabeled data from the target domain and general opinion words as features for adaptation (Aue and Gamon 2005; Blitzer et al. 2007; Yang et al. 2006).

26.2.1.2 Classification Based on Unsupervised Learning

It is not hard to imagine that opinion words and phrases are the dominating indicators for sentiment classification. Thus, using unsupervised learning based on such words and phrases would be quite natural. The method in Turney (2002) is such a technique. It performs classification based on some fixed syntactic phrases that are likely to be used to express opinions. The algorithm consists of three steps:

Step 1: It extracts phrases containing adjectives or adverbs. The reason for doing this is that research has shown that adjectives and adverbs are good indicators of subjectivity and opinions. However, although an isolated adjective may indicate subjectivity, there may be an insufficient context to determine its opinion orientation. Therefore, the algorithm extracts two consecutive words, where one member of the pair is an adjective/adverb and the other is a context word. Two consecutive words are extracted if their POS tags conform to any of the patterns in Table 26.1. For example, the pattern in line 2 means that two consecutive words are extracted if the first word is an adverb and the second word is an adjective, but the third word (which is not extracted) cannot be a noun.

Example 26.7

In the sentence, *"This camera produces beautiful pictures,"* "beautiful pictures" will be extracted as it satisfies the first pattern.

Step 2: It estimates the orientation of the extracted phrases using the *pointwise mutual information* (PMI) measure given in Equation 26.1:

$$\text{PMI}(\text{term}_1, \text{term}_2) = \log_2 \left(\frac{\Pr(\text{term}_1 \wedge \text{term}_2)}{\Pr(\text{term}_1)\,\Pr(\text{term}_2)} \right). \tag{26.1}$$

Here, $\Pr(\text{term}_1 \wedge \text{term}_2)$ is the co-occurrence probability of term_1 and term_2, and $\Pr(\text{term}_1)\Pr(\text{term}_2)$ gives the probability that the two terms co-occur if they are statistically independent. The ratio between $\Pr(\text{term}_1 \wedge \text{term}_2)$ and $\Pr(\text{term}_1)\Pr(\text{term}_2)$ is thus a measure of the degree of statistical dependence between them. The log of this ratio is the amount of information that we acquire about the presence of one of the words when we observe the other. The opinion orientation (oo) of a phrase is computed based on its association with the positive reference word "excellent" and its association with the negative reference word "poor":

$$oo(\text{phrase}) = \text{PMI}(\text{phrase}, \text{"excellent"}) - \text{PMI}(\text{phrase}, \text{"poor"}). \tag{26.2}$$

The probabilities are calculated by issuing queries to a search engine and collecting the number of *hits*. For each search query, a search engine usually gives the number of relevant documents to the query, which is the number of hits. Thus, by searching the two terms together and separately, we can estimate the probabilities in Equation 26.1. Turney (2002) used the AltaVista search engine because it has a NEAR operator, which constrains the search to documents that contain the words within ten words of one another, in either order. Let *hits(query)* be the number of hits returned. Equation 26.2 can be rewritten as

$$so(phrase) = \log_2 \left(\frac{\text{hits(phrase NEAR "excellent")hits("poor")}}{\text{hits(phrase NEAR "poor")hits("excellent")}} \right). \qquad (26.3)$$

Step 3: Given a review, the algorithm computes the average *oo* of all phrases in the review, and classifies the review as recommended if the average *oo* is positive, not recommended otherwise.

Apart from this method many other unsupervised methods exist. See Dave et al. (2003) for another example.

26.2.2 Sentence-Level Subjectivity and Sentiment Classification

We now move to the sentence-level to perform the similar task (Hatzivassiloglou and Wiebe 2000; Riloff et al. 2006; Riloff and Wiebe 2003; Wiebe et al. 1999; Wilson et al. 2004, 2005; Yu and Hatzivassiloglou 2003).

Task: Given a sentence *s*, two subtasks are performed:

1. *Subjectivity classification*: Determine whether *s* is a subjective sentence or an objective sentence,
2. *Sentence-level sentiment classification*: If *s* is subjective, determine whether it expresses a positive or negative opinion.

Notice that the quintuple (*o, f, oo, h, t*) is not used in defining the task here because the sentence-level classification is often an intermediate step. In most applications, one needs to know what object or features of the object the opinions are on. However, the two subtasks of the sentence-level classification are still very important because (1) it filters out those sentences that contain no opinion, and (2) after we know what objects and features of the objects are talked about in a sentence, this step helps to determine whether the opinions on the objects and their features are positive or negative.

Most existing researches study both problems, although some of them only focus on one. Both problems are classification problems. Thus, traditional supervised learning methods are again applicable. For example, one of the early works reported by Wiebe et al. (1999) performed subjectivity classification using the naïve Bayesian classifier. Subsequent research also used other learning algorithms (Hatzivassiloglou and Wiebe 2000; Riloff and Wiebe 2003; Wilson et al. 2004; Yu and Hatzivassiloglou 2003).

One of the bottlenecks in applying supervised learning is the manual effort involved in annotating a large number of training examples. To save the manual labeling effort, a bootstrapping approach to label training data automatically is reported in Riloff and Wiebe (2003); Riloff et al. (2003). The algorithm works by first using two high-precision classifiers (HP-Subj and HP-Obj) to automatically identify some subjective and objective sentences. The high-precision classifiers use lists of lexical items (single words or *n*-grams) that are good subjectivity clues. HP-Subj classifies a sentence as subjective if it contains two or more strong subjective clues. HP-Obj classifies a sentence as objective if there are no strongly subjective clues. These classifiers will give very high precision but low recall. The extracted sentences are then added to the training data to learn patterns. The patterns (which form the subjectivity classifiers in the next iteration) are then used to automatically identify more subjective and objective sentences, which are then added to the training set, and the next iteration of the algorithm begins.

For pattern learning, a set of syntactic templates are provided to restrict the kinds of patterns to be learned. Some example syntactic templates and example patterns are shown below.

Syntactic Template	Example Pattern
<subj> passive-verb	<subj> was satisfied
<subj> active-verb	<subj> complained
active-verb <dobj>	endorsed <dobj>
noun aux <dobj>	fact is <dobj>
passive-verb prep <np>	was worried about <np>

Before discussing algorithms that also perform the sentiment classification of subjective sentences, let us point out an assumption made in much of the research on the topic.

Assumption of sentence-level sentiment classification: The sentence expresses a single opinion from a single opinion holder.

This assumption is only appropriate for simple sentences with a single opinion, e.g., "*The picture quality of this camera is amazing.*" However, for compound sentences, a single sentence may express more than one opinion. For example, the sentence, "*The picture quality of this camera is amazing and so is the battery life, but the viewfinder is too small for such a great camera,*" expresses both positive and negative opinions (one may say that it has a mixed opinion). For "picture quality" and "battery life," the sentence is positive, but for "viewfinder," it is negative. It is also positive for the camera as a whole.

Yu and Hatzivassiloglou (2003) reported a study that tries to classify subjective sentences and also determine their opinion orientations. For subjective or opinionated sentence identification, it applied supervised learning. Three learning methods were evaluated: sentence similarity, naïve Bayesian classification, and multiple naïve Bayesian classification. For the sentiment classification of each identified subjective sentence, it used a similar method to the method in Turney (2002), but with many more seed words (rather than only two used in Turney (2002), and the score function was log-likelihood ratio. The same problem is studied in Hatzivassiloglou and Wiebe (2000) considering gradable adjectives. In Gamon et al. (2005), a semi-supervised learning method is applied, and in Kim and Hovy (2004), the decision is made by simply summing up opinion words in a sentence. Kim and Hovy (2006, 2007); Kim et al. (2006) build models to identify some specific types of opinions in reviews.

As we mentioned earlier, sentence-level classification is not suitable for compound sentences. Wilson et al. (2004) pointed out that not only a single sentence may contain multiple opinions, but also both subjective and factual clauses. It is useful to pinpoint such clauses. It is also important to identify the strength of opinions. A study of automatic sentiment classification was presented to classify clauses of every sentence by the *strength* of the opinions being expressed in individual clauses, down to four levels deep (*neutral*, *low*, *medium*, and *high*). The strength of *neutral* indicates the absence of opinion or subjectivity. Strength classification thus subsumes the task of classifying language as subjective versus objective. In Wilson et al. (2005), the problem is studied further using supervised learning by considering contextual sentiment influencers such as negation (e.g., *not* and *never*) and contrary (e.g., *but* and *however*). A list of influencers can be found in Polanyi and Zaenen (2004).

Finally, as mentioned in Section 26.1, we should bear in mind that subjective sentences are only a subset of opinionated sentences, and many objective sentences can also imply opinions. Thus, to mine opinions from text one needs to mine them from both types of sentences.

26.2.3 Opinion Lexicon Generation

In preceding sections, we mentioned that opinion words are employed in many sentiment classification tasks. We now discuss how such words are generated. In the research literature, opinion words are also known as *polar words*, *opinion-bearing words*, and *sentiment words*. Positive opinion words are used to express desired states while negative opinion words are used to express undesired states. Examples of positive opinion words are *beautiful*, *wonderful*, *good*, and *amazing*. Examples of negative opinion words are *bad*, *poor*, and *terrible*. Apart from individual words, there are also opinion phrases and idioms, e.g., *cost someone an arm and a leg.* Collectively, they are called the *opinion lexicon.* They are instrumental for sentiment analysis for obvious reasons.

Opinion words can, in fact, be divided into two types, the *base type* and the *comparative type.* All the examples above are of the base type. Opinion words of the comparative type are used to express comparative and superlative opinions. Examples of such words are *better, worse, best, worst,* etc, which are comparative and superlative forms of their base adjectives or adverbs, e.g., *good* and *bad.* Unlike opinion words of the base type, the words of the comparative type do not express a direction opinion/sentiment on an object, but a comparative opinion/sentiment on more than one object, e.g., "*Car-x is better than Car-y.*" This sentence tells something quite interesting. It does not express an opinion that any of the two cars is good or bad. It just says that compared to Car-y, Car-x is better, and compared to Car-x, Car-y is worse. Thus, although we still can assign a comparative word as positive or negative based on whether it represents a desirable or undesirable state, we cannot use it in the same way as an opinion word of the base type. We will discuss this issue further when we study sentiment analysis of comparative sentences. This section focuses on opinion words of the base type.

To compile or collect the opinion word list, three main approaches have been investigated: the manual approach, the dictionary-based approach, and the corpus-based approach. The manual approach is very time consuming (Das and Chen 2007; Morinaga et al. 2002; Tong 2001; Yi et al. 2003) and thus it is not usually used alone, but combined with automated approaches as the final check because automated methods make mistakes. Below, we discuss the two automated approaches.

Dictionary-based approach: One of the simple techniques in this approach is based on bootstrapping using a small set of seed opinion words and an online dictionary, e.g., WordNet (Fellbaum 1998). The strategy is to first collect a small set of opinion words manually with known orientations, and then to grow this set by searching in the WordNet for their synonyms and antonyms. The newly found words are added to the seed list. The next iteration starts. The iterative process stops when no more new words are found. This approach is used in Hu and Liu (2004); Kim and Hovy (2004). After the process completes, manual inspection can be carried out to remove and/or correct errors. Researchers have also used additional information (e.g., glosses) in WordNet and additional techniques (e.g., machine learning) to generate better lists (Andreevskaia and Bergler 2006; Esuli and Sebastiani 2005, 2006, 2007; Kamps et al. 2004). So far, several opinion word lists have been generated (Ding et al. 2008; Esuli and Sebastiani 2006; Hu and Liu 2004; Stone 1966; Wiebe et al. 1999).

The dictionary-based approach and the opinion words collected from it have a major shortcoming. The approach is unable to find opinion words with domain specific orientations, which is quite common. For example, for a speakerphone, if it is quiet, it is usually negative. However, for a car, if it is quiet, it is positive. The corpus-based approach can help to deal with this problem.

Corpus-based approach and sentiment consistency: The methods in the corpus-based approach rely on syntactic or co-occurrence patterns and also a seed list of opinion words to find other opinion words in a large corpus. One of the key ideas is the one proposed by Hatzivassiloglou and McKeown (2006). The technique starts with a list of seed opinion adjective words, and uses them and a set of linguistic constraints or conventions on connectives to identify additional adjective opinion words and their orientations. One of the constraints is about the conjunction AND, which says that conjoined adjectives usually have the same orientation. For example, in the sentence, "*This car is beautiful and spacious,*" if "beautiful" is known to be positive, it can be inferred that "spacious" is also positive. This is so because people usually express the same opinion on both sides of a conjunction. The following sentence is rather unnatural, "*This car is beautiful and difficult to drive.*" If it is changed to "*This car is beautiful but difficult to drive,*" it becomes acceptable. Rules or constraints are also designed for other connectives, OR, BUT, EITHER–OR, and NEITHER–NOR. We call this idea *sentiment consistency.* Of course, in practice it is not always consistent. Learning to use the log-linear model is applied to a large corpus to determine if two conjoined adjectives are of the same or different orientations. Same- and different-orientation links between adjectives forms a graph. Finally, clustering is performed on the graph to produce two sets of words: positive and negative.

Kanayama and Nasukawa (2006) expanded this approach by introducing the idea of intra-sentential (within a sentence) and inter-sentential (between neighboring sentences) sentiment consistency (called *coherency* in (Kanayama and Nasukawa 2006)). The intra-sentential consistency is similar to that in Hatzivassiloglou and McKeown (2006). Inter-sentential consistency applies the idea to neighboring sentences. That is, the same opinion orientation (positive or negative) is usually expressed in a few consecutive sentences. Opinion changes are indicated by adversative expressions such as *but* and *however*. Some criteria to determine whether to add a word to the positive or negative lexicon are also proposed. This study was based on Japanese text. Other related works include Kaji and Kitsuregawa (2007); Wiebe and Wilson (2002).

Qiu et al. (2009), proposed another method to extract domain specific sentiment words from reviews using also some seed opinion words. The main idea is to exploit certain syntactic relations of opinion words and object features for extraction. They showed that opinion words are almost always associated with object features in some ways. Thus, opinion words can be recognized by identified features, and features can be identified by known opinion words (no seed feature is needed). The extracted opinion words and features are utilized to identify new opinion words and new features, which are used again to extract more opinion words and features. This propagation or bootstrapping process ends when no more opinion words or features can be found. As the process involves propagation through both opinion words and features, the method is called *double propagation*. The extraction rules are designed based on different relations between opinion words and features, and also opinion words and features themselves. Dependency grammar (Tesnière 1959) was adopted to describe these relations.

Using the corpus-based approach alone to identify all opinion words, however, is not as effective as the dictionary-based approach because it is hard to prepare a huge corpus to cover all English words. However, as we mentioned above, this approach has a major advantage that the dictionary-based approach does not have. It can help to find domain-specific opinion words and their orientations if a corpus from only the specific domain is used in the discovery process.

In Ding et al. (2008), Ding and Liu explores the idea of intra-sentential and inter-sentential sentiment consistency further. Instead of finding domain dependent opinion words, they showed that the same word might have different orientations in different contexts even in the same domain. For example, in the digital camera domain, the word *long* expresses different opinions in the two sentences: "*The battery life is **long**"* (positive) and *"The time taken to focus is **long**"* (negative). Thus, finding domain dependent opinion words is still insufficient. They then proposed to consider both opinion words and object features together, and use the pair (*object_feature, opinion_word*) as the *opinion context*. Their method thus determines opinion words and their orientations together with the object features that they modify. The above rules about connectives were still applied. The work in Ganapathibhotla and Liu (2008) adopts the same context definition but used it for the sentiment analysis of comparative sentences. In fact, the method in Takamura et al. (2007); Turney (2002) can also be considered as a method for finding context specific opinions. However, it does not use the sentiment consistency idea. Its opinion context is based on syntactic POS patterns rather than object features and opinion words that modify them. Breck et al. (2007), went further to study the problem of extracting any opinion expressions, which can have any number of words. The conditional random fields (CRF) method (Lafferty et al. 2001) was used as the sequence learning technique for extraction.

Finally, we should note that populating an opinion lexicon (domain dependent or not) is different from determining whether a word or phrase is actually expressing an opinion and what its orientation is in a particular sentence. Just because a word or phrase is listed in an opinion lexicon does not mean that it actually is expressing an opinion in a sentence. For example, in the sentence, "*I am looking for a good health insurance for my family*," "good" here does not express either a positive or negative opinion on any particular insurance. And the same is true for polarity/opinion orientation. We should also realize that opinion words and phrases are not the only expressions that bear opinions. There are many others as we will see in Section 26.3.3 when we discuss rules of opinions.

26.3 Feature-Based Sentiment Analysis

Although classifying opinionated texts at the document level or at the sentence level is useful in many cases, they do not provide the necessary detail needed for some other applications. A positive opinionated document on a particular object does not mean that the author has positive opinions on all aspects or features of the object. Likewise, a negative opinionated document does not mean that the author dislikes everything. In a typical opinionated text, the author writes both positive and negative aspects of the object, although the general sentiment on the object may be positive or negative. Document-level and sentence-level classifications do not provide such information. To obtain such details, we need to go to the object feature level, which means we need the full model of Section 26.1. Recall, at the feature level, the mining task is to discover every quintuple $(o_j, f_{jk}, oo_{ijkl}, h_i, t_l)$ and identify all the synonyms (W_{jk}) and feature indicators I_{jk} of feature f_{jk}. In this section, we mainly focus on two key mining tasks:

1. Identify *object features* that have been commented on. For instance, in the sentence, "*The picture quality of this camera is amazing*," the object feature is "picture quality."
2. Determine whether the opinions on the features are positive, negative, or neutral. In the above sentence, the opinion on the feature "picture quality" is positive.

Opinion holder, object, and time extraction: In some applications, it is useful to identify and extract opinion holders, i.e., persons or organizations that expressed certain opinions. As we mentioned earlier, opinion holders are more useful for news articles or other types of formal documents, in which the persons or organizations who expressed opinions are stated explicitly in the text. Such holders need to be identified by the system (Bethard et al. 2004; Choi et al. 2005; Kim and Hovy 2004). In the case of the user-generated content on the Web, the opinion holders are often the authors of the discussion posts, bloggers, or reviewers, whose login ids are known although their true identities in the real world may be unknown.

However, object name extraction is needed for discussion posts, blogs, and also reviews. Note that although a review focuses on evaluating a particular object, it may compare it with other competing objects. Time extraction is also needed in the Web context. Since each Web site usually displays the time when every post is submitted. So, the extraction is easy. However, in news and other types of documents time extraction is also an issue. All these three extraction tasks are collectively known as the Named Entity Recognition (NER) in the information extraction community. They have been studied extensively. See a comprehensive survey of information-extraction tasks and algorithms in Sarawagi (2008). Chapter 21 also deals with information extraction.

Coreference resolution: In product reviews, the reviewed objects are usually known. However, this is not the case for opinions expressed in blogs and discussion posts. For example, in the post, "*I have a Canon S50 camera purchased from Amazon. It takes great photos*," two interesting questions can be asked: (1) what object does the post praise and (2) what "it" means in the second sentence? Clearly, we humans know that the post praises "Canon S50 camera," which is the problem of object extraction discussed above, and we also know that "it" here means "Canon S50 camera," which is the problem of coreference resolution. Coreference resolution has been studied extensively in NLP. However, it is still a major challenge. We will not discuss it here. A study in the sentiment analysis context is reported in Stoyanov and Cardie (2006).

In the next two subsections, we focus on the two tasks listed above.

26.3.1 Feature Extraction

Current research on object feature extraction is mainly carried out in online product reviews. We thus also focus on such reviews here. There are two common review formats on the Web. Different formats may need different techniques to perform the feature extraction task (Liu 2006; Liu et al. 2005).

My SLR is on the shelf
by camerafun4. Aug 09 '04
Pros: Great photos, easy to use, very small
Cons: Battery usage; included memory is stingy.
I had never used a digital camera prior to purchasing this Canon A70. I have always used a SLR . . . **Read the full review**

FIGURE 26.3 An example review of Format 1.

GREAT Camera., Jun 3, 2004
Reviewer: **jprice174** from Atlanta, Ga.
I did a lot of research last year before I bought this camera . . . It kinda hurt to leave behind my beloved nikon 35 mm SLR, but I was going to Italy, and I needed something smaller, and digital.
The pictures coming out of this camera are amazing. The 'auto' feature takes great pictures most of the time. And with digital, you're not wasting film if the picture doesn't come out. . . .

FIGURE 26.4 An example review of Format 2.

> *Format 1—Pros, cons, and the detailed review*: The reviewer is asked to describe pros and cons separately and also write a detailed/full review. An example of such a review is given in Figure 26.3.
>
> *Format 2—Free format*: The reviewer can write freely, i.e., no separation of pros and cons. An example of such a review is given in Figure 26.4.

26.3.1.1 Feature Extraction from Pros and Cons of Format 1

We describe a supervised pattern learning approach to extracting product features from pros and cons in reviews of Format 1 (not the detailed review, which is the same as that in Format 2). The key observation is that pros and cons are usually very brief, consisting of short phrases or sentence segments. Each sentence segment contains only one feature, and sentence segments are separated by commas, periods, semicolons, hyphens, *&*, *and*, *but*, etc.

Example 26.8

Pros in Figure 26.3 can be separated into three segments:

Great photos	⟨photo⟩
Easy to use	⟨use⟩
Very small	⟨small⟩ ⇒ ⟨size⟩.

Cons in Figure 26.3 can be separated into two segments:

Battery usage	⟨battery⟩
Included memory is stingy	⟨memory⟩

We can see that each segment describes a product feature, which is given within ⟨ ⟩. Notice that ⟨small⟩ is a feature indicator for feature ⟨size⟩. Clearly, many methods can be used to extract features, e.g., CRF (Lafferty et al. 2001). Here, we describe a sequential rule-based method (Liu et al. 2005).

The rules are called *label sequential rules* (LSR), which are generated from sequential patterns in data mining. An LSR is of the following form, $X \rightarrow Y$, where Y is a sequence and X is a sequence produced from Y by replacing some of its items with wildcards. A wildcard, denoted by a "*," can match any item.

The learning process is as follows: Each segment is first converted to a sequence. Each sequence element is a word, which is represented by both the word itself and its POS tag in a set. In the training data, all object features are manually labeled and replaced by the label $feature. An object feature can be expressed with a noun, adjective, verb, or adverb. Thus, they represent both explicit features and implicit feature indicators. The labels and their POS tags used in mining LSRs are {$feature, NN}, {$feature, JJ}, {$feature, VB}, and {$feature, RB}; where $feature denotes a feature to be extracted, and NN stands for noun, JJ for adjective, VB for verb, and RB for adverb. Note that to simplify the presentation, we use NN and VB to represent all forms of nouns and verbs respectively.

For example, the sentence segment, "*Included memory is stingy,*" is turned into the sequence

$$\langle\{\text{included, VB}\}\{\text{memory, NN}\}\{\text{is, VB}\}\{\text{stingy, JJ}\}\rangle.$$

After labeling, it becomes ("memory" is an object feature):

$$\langle\{\text{included, VB}\}\{\text{\$feature, NN}\}\{\text{is, VB}\}\{\text{stingy, JJ}\}\rangle,$$

All the resulting sequences are then used to mine LSRs. An example rule is

$$\langle\{\text{easy, JJ}\}\{\text{to}\}\{^{*}, \text{VB}\}\rangle \rightarrow \langle\{\text{easy, JJ}\}\{\text{to}\}\{\text{\$feature, VB}\}\rangle \text{ confidence} = 90\%$$

where the *confidence* is the conditional probability, $\Pr(Y|X)$, which measures the accuracy of the rule.

Feature extraction is performed by matching the patterns with each sentence segment in a new review to extract object features. That is, the word in the sentence segment that matches $feature in a pattern is extracted. In the pattern match, only the right-hand side of each rule is used. In rule generation, both the right- and the left-hand sides are needed to compute the conditional probability or confidence. Details of sequential pattern mining and LSR mining can be found in Liu (2006).

26.3.1.2 Feature Extraction from Reviews of Format 2

Pros and Cons of Format 1 mainly consist of short phrases and incomplete sentences. The reviews of Format 2 usually use complete sentences. To extract features from such reviews, the above algorithm can also be applied. However, experiments show that it is not effective because complete sentences are more complex and contain a large amount of noise. Below, we describe some unsupervised methods for finding explicit features that are nouns and noun phrases. The first method is due to Hu and Liu (2004). The method requires a large number of reviews, and consists of two steps:

1. Finding frequent nouns and noun phrases. Nouns and noun phrases (or groups) are identified by using a POS tagger. Their occurrence frequencies are counted, and only the frequent ones are kept. A frequency threshold can be decided experimentally. The reason for using this approach is that when people comment on product features, the vocabulary that they use usually converges, and most product features are nouns. Thus, those nouns that are frequently talked about are usually genuine and important features. Irrelevant contents in reviews are often diverse and thus infrequent, i.e., they are quite different in different reviews. Hence, those nouns that are infrequent are likely to be non-features or less important features.

2. Finding infrequent features by making use of opinion words. The idea is as follows: The same opinion word can be used to describe different object features. Opinion words that modify frequent features can also modify infrequent features, and thus can be used to extract infrequent features. For example, "picture" is found to be a frequent feature, and we have the sentence,

   "The pictures are absolutely amazing."

   If we know that "amazing" is a positive opinion word, then "software" can also be extracted as a feature from the following sentence,

   "The software is amazing."

   because the two sentences follow the same pattern and "software" in the sentence is also a noun.

The precision of step 1 of the above algorithm was improved by Popescu and Etzioni (2005). Their algorithm tries to remove those noun phrases that may not be product features. It evaluates each noun phrase by computing a PMI score between the phrase and some *meronymy discriminators* associated with the product class, e.g., a scanner class. The meronymy discriminators for the scanner class are, "of scanner," "scanner has," "scanner comes with," etc., which are used to find components or parts of scanners by searching on the Web. The PMI measure is a simplified version of the measure in (Turney 2002) (also see Section 26.2.1.2)

$$\text{PMI}(f, d) = \frac{\text{hits}(f \wedge d)}{\text{hits}(f)\text{hits}(d)}, \qquad (26.4)$$

where

    f is a candidate feature identified in step 1
    d is a discriminator

Web search is used to find the number of hits of individuals and also their co-occurrences. The idea of this approach is clear. If the PMI value of a candidate feature is too low, it may not be a component of the product because f and d do not co-occur frequently. The algorithm also distinguishes components/parts from attributes/properties using WordNet's *is-a* hierarchy (which enumerates different kinds of properties) and morphological cues (e.g., "-iness," "-ity" suffixes).

The double propagation method in Qiu et al. (2009), which has been described in Section 26.2.3, can also be used to extract features. It in fact exploits and extends the idea in step 2 above (without using step 1), and starts with only a set of seed opinion words (no seed features are required). That is, it utilizes the association or the dependency relations of opinion words and features, i.e., opinion words always modify features. The associations are described using the dependency grammar (Tesnière 1959), which results in a set of syntactic rules for the extraction of both opinion words and object features in an iterative fashion.

Other related works on feature extraction mainly use the ideas of topic modeling and clustering to capture topics/features in reviews (Liu et al. 2007; Lu and Zhai 2008; Mei et al. 2007; Su et al. 2008; Titov and McDonald 2008; Yi et al. 2003). For example, Mei et al. (2007) proposed a probabilistic model called *topic-sentiment mixture* to capture the mixture of features and sentiments simultaneously. One topic model and two sentiment models were defined based on language models to capture the probabilistic distribution of words in different topics/features with their associated opinion orientations. Su et al. (2008) also proposed a clustering-based method with mutual reinforcement to identify implicit features. In (Ghani et al. 2006), a semi-supervised learning method was presented for feature extraction as well.

After the extraction of object features, two additional problems need to be solved.

Group synonyms: It is common that people use different words or phrases to describe the same feature. For example, *photo* and *picture* refer to the same feature in digital camera reviews. Identifying and grouping synonyms is essential for applications. Although WordNet (Fellbaum 1998) and other thesaurus dictionaries help to some extent, they are far from sufficient due to the fact that many synonyms are domain dependent. For example, *picture* and *movie* are synonyms in movie reviews, but they are not synonyms in digital camera reviews as *picture* is more related to *photo* while *movie* refers to *video*. Carenini et al. (2005) proposed a method based on several similarity metrics similar to those in information integration (Liu 2006). It requires a taxonomy of features to be given for a particular domain. The algorithm merges each discovered feature to a feature node in the taxonomy. The similarity metrics are defined based on string similarity, synonyms, and other distances measured using WordNet. Experiments based on digital camera and DVD reviews show promising results.

Mapping to implicit features: Feature extraction may discover many feature indicators. Adjectives and adverbs are perhaps the most common types of feature indicators. It is known that many adjectives and adverbs modify or describe some specific attributes or properties of objects. This step maps such feature indicators to features. For example, the adjective *heavy* usually describes the *weight* of an object, and thus should be mapped to the *weight* feature. *Beautiful* is usually used to describe the *appearance* of an object, and thus should be mapped to the *appearance* feature. However, this needs to be done with care as the usage of many adjectives can be quite versatile. Their exact meaning may be domain/context dependent. For example, "heavy" in the sentence "*The traffic is heavy*" does not describe the *weight* of the traffic. One way to map indicator words to (implicit) features is to manually compile a list of such mappings during training data annotation, which can then be used in the same domain in the future. However, it is not clear whether this is an effective approach as little research has been done.

26.3.2 Opinion Orientation Identification

We now discuss how to identify the orientation of opinions expressed on an object feature in a sentence. Clearly, the sentence-level and clause-level sentiment classification methods discussed in Section 26.2 are applicable here. That is, they can be applied to each sentence or clause that contains object features, and the features in it will take its opinion orientation. Here, we only describe a *lexicon-based approach* to solving the problem (Ding et al. 2008; Hu and Liu 2004). See a more complex method based on relaxation labeling in Popescu and Etzioni (2005).

The lexicon-based approach basically uses *opinion words* and *phrases* in a sentence to determine the orientation of the opinion. Apart from the opinion lexicon, negations and *but*-clauses in a sentence are also crucial and need to be handled. The approach works as follows (Hu and Liu 2004; Ding et al. 2008):

1. *Identifying opinion words and phrases*: Given a sentence that contains an object feature, this step identifies all opinion words and phrases. Each positive word is assigned the opinion score of $+1$, each negative word is assigned the opinion score of -1, and each context dependent word is assigned the opinion score of 0. For example, we have the sentence, "*The picture quality of this camera is not great, but the battery life is long.*" After this step, the sentence is turned into "The *picture quality* of this camera is not **great**[+1], but the *battery life* is **long**[0]" because "great" is a positive opinion word and "long" is context dependent. The object features are italicized.

2. *Handling negations*: Negation words and phrases are used to revise the opinion scores obtained in step 1, based on some negation handling rules. After this step, the above sentence is turned into "The *picture quality* of this camera is not **great**[−1], but the *battery life* is **long**[0]" due to the negation word "not." We note that not every "not" means negation, e.g., "not only ... but also." Such *non-negation phrases containing negation words* need to be considered separately.

3. *But-clauses*: In English, *but* means *contrary*. A sentence containing *but* is handled by applying the following rule: the opinion orientation before *but* and after *but* are opposite to each other. After this step, the above sentence is turned into "The *picture quality* of this camera is not **great**[−1], but the *battery life* is **long**[+1]" due to "but." Apart from *but*, phrases such as "*with the exception of*," "*except that*," and "*except for*" behave similarly to *but* and are handled in the same way. As in the case of negation, not every *but* means contrary, e.g., "*not only ... but also.*" Such *non-but phrases containing "but"* also need to be considered separately.

4. *Aggregating opinions*: This step applies an opinion aggregation function to the resulting opinion scores to determine the final orientation of the opinion on each object feature in the sentence. Let the sentence be s, which contains a set of object features $\{f_1, \ldots, f_m\}$ and a set of opinion words or phrases $\{op_1, \ldots, op_n\}$ with their opinion scores obtained from steps 1, 2, and 3. The opinion orientation on each feature f_i in s is determined by the following opinion aggregation function:

$$\text{score}(f_i, s) = \sum_{op_j \in s} \frac{op_j \cdot oo}{d(op_j, f_i)}, \quad (26.5)$$

where

    op_j is an opinion word in s

    $d(op_j, f_i)$ is the distance between feature f_i and opinion word op_j in s

    $op_j \cdot oo$ is the orientation or opinion score of op_j

The multiplicative inverse in the formula is used to give low weights to opinion words that are far away from feature f_i. If the final score is positive, then the opinion on feature f_i in s is positive. If the final score is negative, then the opinion on the feature is negative. It is neutral otherwise.

This simple algorithm is useful but not sufficient in many cases. One major shortcoming is that opinion words and phrases do not cover all types of expressions that convey or imply opinions. There are in fact many others. Below, we present basic rules of opinions.

26.3.3 Basic Rules of Opinions

A rule of opinion is an implication with an expression on the left and an implied opinion on the right. The expression is a conceptual one as it represents a concept, which can be expressed in many ways in an actual sentence. The application of opinion words/phrases above can be represented as such rules. Let Neg be a negative opinion word/phrase and Pos be a positive opinion word/phrase. The rules for applying opinion words/phrases in a sentence are as follow:

1. Neg → Negative
2. Pos → Positive

These rules say that Neg implies a negative opinion (denoted by *Negative*) and Pos implies a positive opinion (denoted by *Positive*) in a sentence. The effect of negations can be represented as well:

3. Negation Neg → Positive
4. Negation Pos → Negative

The rules state that negated opinion words/phrases take their opposite orientations in a sentence. Note that the above use of "*but*" is not considered an opinion rule but a language convention that people often use to indicate a possible opinion change. We now describe some additional rules of opinions.

Deviation from the norm or some desired value range: In some domains, an object feature may have an expected or desired value range or norm. If it is above and/or below the normal range, it is negative, e.g., "*This drug causes low (or high) blood pressure.*" We then have the following rules.

5. Desired value range → Positive
6. Below or above the desired value range → Negative

Decreased and increased quantities of opinionated items: This set of rules is similar to the negation rules above. Decreasing or increasing the quantities associated with some opinionated items may change the orientations of the opinions. For example, "*This drug reduced my pain significantly.*" Here, "pain" is a negative opinion word, and the reduction of "pain" indicates a desirable effect of the drug. Hence, the decreased pain implies a positive opinion on the drug. The concept of "decreasing" also extends to "removal" or "disappearance", e.g., "*My pain has disappeared after taking the drug.*"

7. Decreased Neg → Positive
8. Decreased Pos → Negative
9. Increased Neg → Negative
10. Increased Pos → Positive

The last two rules may not be needed as there is no change of opinion orientations.

Producing and consuming resources and wastes: If an object produces resources, it is positive. If it consumes resources, especially a large quantity of them, it is negative. For example, "money" is a resource. The sentence, "*Company-x charges a lot of money*" gives a negative opinion on "Company-x". Likewise, if an object produces wastes, it is negative. If it consumes wastes, it is positive. These give us the following rules:

11. Consume resource → Negative
12. Produce resource → Positive
13. Consume waste → Positive
14. Produce waste → Negative

These basic rules can also be combined to produce compound rules, e.g., "Consume decreased waste → Negative" which is a combination of rules 7 and 13. To build a practical system, all these rules and their combinations need to be considered.

As noted above, these are conceptual rules. They can be expressed in many ways using different words and phrases in an actual text, and in different domains they may also manifest differently. By no means, we claim these are the only basic rules that govern expressions of positive and negative opinions. With further research, additional new rules may be discovered and the current rules may be refined or revised. We also do not claim that any manifestation of such rules imply opinions in a sentence. Like opinion words and phrases, just because a rule is satisfied in a sentence does not mean that it actually is expressing an opinion, which makes sentiment analysis a very challenging task.

26.4 Sentiment Analysis of Comparative Sentences

Directly expressing positive or negative opinions on an object and its features is only one form of evaluation. Comparing the object with some other similar objects is another. Comparisons are related to but are also quite different from direct opinions. They not only have different semantic meanings, but also different syntactic forms. For example, a typical direct opinion sentence is "*The picture quality of this camera is great.*" A typical comparison sentence is "*The picture quality of camera-x is better than that of camera-y.*" This section first defines the problem, and then presents some existing methods for their analysis (Ganapathibhotla and Liu 2008; Jindal and Liu 2006a,b).

26.4.1 Problem Definition

In general, a comparative sentence expresses a relation based on similarities or differences of more than one object. The comparison is usually conveyed using the *comparative* or *superlative* form of an adjective or adverb. A comparative is used to state that one object has more of a certain quantity than another object. A superlative is used to state that one object has the most or least of a certain quantity. In general, a comparison can be between two or more objects, groups of objects, and one object and the rest of the objects. It can also be between an object and its previous or future versions.

Two types of comparatives: In English, comparatives are usually formed by adding the suffix "*-er*" and superlatives are formed by adding the suffix "*-est*" to their *base adjectives* and *adverbs*. For example, in "*The battery life of Camera-x is longer than that of Camera-y,*" "longer" is the comparative form of the adjective "*long.*" In "*The battery life of this camera is the longest,*" "longest" is the superlative form of the adjective "long." We call this type of comparatives and superlatives *Type 1 comparatives* and *superlatives*. For simplicity, we will use Type 1 comparatives to mean both from now on.

Adjectives and adverbs with two syllables or more and not ending in *y* do not form comparatives or superlatives by adding "*-er*" or "*-est.*" Instead, *more, most, less,* and *least* are used before such words, e.g., *more beautiful*. We call this type of comparatives and superlatives *Type 2 comparatives* and *Type 2 superlatives*. Both Type 1 and Type 2 are called *regular comparatives* and *superlatives*.

In English, there are also some *irregular comparatives* and *superlatives*, which do not follow the above rules, i.e., *more, most, less, least, better, best, worse, worst, further/farther*, and *furthest/farthest*. They behave similarly to Type 1 comparatives and superlatives and thus are grouped under Type 1.

Apart from these standard comparatives and superlatives, many other words can also be used to express comparisons, e.g., *prefer* and *superior*. For example, the sentence, "*Camera-x's quality is superior to Camera-y*," says that "Camera-x" is preferred. Jindal and Liu (2006) identified a list of such words. Since these words behave similarly to Type 1 comparatives, they are also grouped under Type 1.

Further analysis also shows that comparatives can be grouped into two categories according to whether they express increased or decreased values, which are useful in sentiment analysis.

> *Increasing comparatives*: Such a comparative expresses an increased value of a quantity, e.g., *more* and *longer*.
> *Decreasing comparatives*: Such a comparative expresses a decreased value of a quantity, e.g., *less* and *fewer*.

Types of comparative relations: Comparative relations can be grouped into four main types. The first three types are called *gradable comparisons* and the last one is called the *non-gradable comparison*.

1. *Non-equal gradable comparisons*: Relations of the type *greater* or *less than* that express an ordering of some objects with regard to some of their features, e.g., "*The Intel chip is faster than that of AMD*." This type also includes user preferences, e.g., "*I prefer Intel to AMD*."
2. *Equative comparisons*: Relations of the type *equal to* that state two objects are equal with respect to some of their features, e.g., "*The picture quality of Camera-x is as good as that of Camera-y*."
3. *Superlative comparisons*: Relations of the type greater or less than all others that rank one object over all others, e.g., "*The Intel chip is the fastest*."
4. *Non-gradable comparisons*: Relations that compare features of two or more objects, but do not grade them. There are three main subtypes:
   - Object A is similar to or different from object B with regard to some features, e.g., "*Coke tastes differently from Pepsi*"
   - Object A has feature f_1, and object B has feature f_2 (f_1 and f_2 are usually substitutable), e.g., "*Desktop PCs use external speakers but laptops use internal speakers*."
   - Object A has feature f, but object B does not have, e.g., "*Phone-x has an earphone, but Phone-y does not have*."

Mining objective: Given an opinionated document d, *comparison mining* consists of two tasks:

1. Identify comparative sentences in d, and classify the identified comparative sentences into different types or classes.
2. Extract comparative opinions from the identified sentences. A *comparative opinion* in a comparative sentence is expressed with

$$(O_1, O_2, F, PO, h, t)$$

where
> O_1 and O_2 are the object sets being compared based on their shared features F (objects in O_1 appear before objects in O_2 in the sentence)
> PO is the preferred object set of the opinion holder h
> t is the time when the comparative opinion is expressed

As for direct opinions, not every piece of information is needed in an application. In many cases, h and t may not be required by applications.

Example 26.9

Consider the comparative sentence *"Canon's optics is better than those of Sony and Nikon."* written by John on May 1, 2009. The extracted comparative opinion is

({Canon}, {Sony, Nikon}, {optics}, *preferred*:{Canon}, John, May-1-2009).

The object set O_1 is {Canon}, the object set O_2 is {Sony, Nikon}, their shared feature set F being compared is {optics}, the preferred object set is {Canon}, the opinion holder h is John and the time t when this comparative opinion was written is May-1-2009.

Below, we study the problem of identifying comparative sentences and mining comparative opinions.

26.4.2 Comparative Sentence Identification

Although most comparative sentences contain comparative adjectives and comparative adverbs, e.g., *better*, and *longer*, many sentences that contain such words are not comparatives, e.g., *"I cannot agree with you more."* Similarly, many sentences that do not contain such indicators are comparative sentences (usually non-gradable), e.g., *"Cellphone-x has Bluetooth, but Cellphone-y does not have."*

An interesting phenomenon about comparative sentences is that such a sentence usually has a keyword or a key phrase indicating comparison. It is shown in Jindal and Liu (2006) that using a set of 83 keywords and key phrases, 98% of the comparative sentences (recall = 98%) can be identified with a precision of 32% using the authors' data set. The keywords and key phrases are

1. Comparative adjectives (JJR) and comparative adverbs (RBR), e.g., *more, less, better*, and words ending with *-er*.
2. Superlative adjectives (JJS) and superlative adverbs (RBS), e.g., *most, least, best*, and words ending with *-est*.
3. Other indicative words such as *same, similar, differ, as well as, favor, beat, win, exceed, outperform, prefer, ahead, than, superior, inferior, number one, up against*, etc.

Since keywords alone are able to achieve a high recall, the set of keywords can be used to filter out those sentences that are unlikely to be comparative sentences. We can then improve the precision of the remaining set of sentences.

It is also observed that comparative sentences have strong patterns involving comparative keywords, which is not surprising. These patterns can be used as features in machine learning. To discover these patterns, class sequential rule (CSR) mining is used in Jindal and Liu (2006). CSR mining is a sequential pattern mining method from data mining. Each training example used for mining CSRs is a pair (s_i, y_i), where s_i is a sequence and y_i is a class, e.g., $y_i \in \{comparative, non\text{-}comparative\}$. The sequence is generated from a sentence. Instead of using each full sentence, only words near a comparative keyword are used to generate each sequence. Each sequence is also labeled with a class indicating whether the sentence is a comparative sentence or not. Using the training data, CSRs can be generated. Details of the mining algorithm can be found in Jindal and Liu (2006); Liu (2006).

For classification model building, the left-hand side sequence patterns of the rules with high conditional probabilities are used as data features in Jindal and Liu (2006). If the sentence matches a pattern, the corresponding feature value for the pattern is 1, and otherwise it is 0. Bayesian classification is employed for model building.

Classify comparative sentences into three types: This step classifies comparative sentences obtained from the last step into one of the three types, *non-equal gradable, equative*, and *superlative* (non-gradable may also be added). For this task, keywords alone are already sufficient. That is, the set of keywords is used as data features for machine learning. It is shown in Jindal and Liu (2006) that SVM gives the best results.

26.4.3 Object and Feature Extraction

To extract objects and object features being compared, many information extraction methods can be applied, e.g., CRF, Hidden Markov Models (HMM), and others. For a survey of information extraction techniques, see Sarawagi (2008). Jindal and Liu (2006) used LSR and CRF to perform the extraction. The algorithm makes the following assumptions:

1. There is only one comparative relation in a sentence. In practice, this is violated only in a very small number of cases.
2. Objects or their features are nouns (includes nouns, plural nouns, and proper nouns) and pronouns. These cover most cases. However, a feature can sometimes be a noun used in its verb form or some action described as a verb (e.g., "*Intel costs more*"; "costs" is a verb and an object feature). These are adverbial comparisons and are not considered in Jindal and Liu (2006).

Bos and Nissim (2006) also proposed a method to extract some useful items from superlative sentences.

26.4.4 Preferred Object Identification

Similar to the sentiment analysis of normal sentences, the sentiment analysis of comparative sentences also needs to determine whether a comparative sentence is opinionated or not. However, unlike normal sentences, it does not make good sense to apply sentiment classification to comparative sentences because an opinionated comparative sentence does not express a direct positive or negative opinion. Instead, it compares multiple objects by ranking the objects based on their shared features to give a *comparative opinion*. In other words, it presents a preference order of the objects based on the comparison of some of their shared features. Since most comparative sentences compare only two sets of objects, the analysis of an opinionated comparative sentence means to identify the preferred object set. Since little research has been done on classifying whether a comparative sentence is opinionated or not, below we only briefly describe a method (Ganapathibhotla and Liu 2008) for identifying the preferred objects.

The approach bears some resemblance to the lexicon-based approach to identifying opinion orientations on object features. Thus, it needs opinion words used for comparisons. Similar to normal opinion words, these words can also be divided into two categories.

1. *Comparative opinion words*: For Type 1 comparatives, this category includes words such as *better*, *worse*, etc., which have explicit and domain independent opinions. In sentences involving such words, it is normally easy to determine which object set is the preferred one of the sentence author.

    In the case of Type 2 comparatives, formed by adding *more*, *less*, *most*, and *least* before adjectives/adverbs, the preferred object set is determined by both words. The following rules are useful:

    <Increasing Comparative> Negative → Negative Comparative Opinion

    <Increasing Comparative> Positive → Positive Comparative Opinion

    <Decreasing Comparative> Negative → Positive Comparative Opinion

    <Decreasing Comparative> Positive → Negative Comparative Opinion

    The first rule says that the combination of an increasing comparative (e.g., *more*) and a negative opinion word (e.g., *awful*) implies a negative Type 2 comparative. The other rules are similar. Note that the positive (or negative) opinion word is of the base type, while the positive (or negative) comparative opinion is of the comparative type.

2. *Context-dependent comparative opinion words*: In the case of Type 1 comparatives, such words include *higher*, *lower*, etc. For example, "*Car-x has higher mileage per gallon than Car-y*" carries a positive sentiment on "Car-x" and a negative sentiment on "Car-y" comparatively, i.e., "Car-x" is preferred. However, without domain knowledge it is hard to know whether "higher" is positive

or negative. The combination of "higher" and "mileage" with the domain knowledge tells us that "higher mileage" is desirable.

In the case of Type 2 comparatives, the situation is similar. However, in this case, the comparative word (*more*, *most*, *less*, or *least*), the adjective/adverb and the object feature are all important in determining the opinion or preference. If we know whether the comparative word is increasing or decreasing (which is easy since there are only four of them), then the opinion can be determined by applying the four rules in (1) above.

As discussed in Section 26.2.3, the pair (*object_feature*, *opinion_word*) forms an opinion context. To determine whether a pair is positive or negative, the algorithm in Ganapathibhotla and Liu (2008) resorts to external information, i.e., a large corpus of pros and cons from product reviews. It basically determines whether the object_feature and the opinion_word are more associated with each other in pros or in cons. If they are more associated in pros, it is positive. Otherwise, it is negative. Using pros and cons is natural because they are short phrases and thus have little noise, and their opinion orientations are also known.

To obtain comparative opinion words, due to the observation below we can simply convert opinion adjectives/adverbs to their comparative forms, which can be done automatically based on the English comparative formation rules described above and the WordNet.

Observation: If an adjective or adverb is positive (or negative), then its comparative or superlative form is also positive (or negative), e.g., *good*, *better*, and *best*.

After the conversion, these words are manually categorized into increasing and decreasing comparatives.

Once all the information is available, determining which object set is preferred is relatively simple. Without negation, if the comparative is positive (or negative), then the objects before (or after) *than* is preferred. Otherwise, the objects after (or before) *than* are preferred. Additional details can be found in Ganapathibhotla and Liu (2008). Fiszman et al. (2007) studied the problem of identifying which object has more of certain features in comparative sentences in biomedical texts, but it does not analyze opinions.

26.5 Opinion Search and Retrieval

As Web search has proven to be very important, it is not hard to imagine that opinion search will also be of great use. One can crawl the user-generated content on the Web and enable people to search for opinions on any subject matter. Two typical kinds of opinion search queries may be issued:

1. Find public opinions on a particular object or a feature of the object, e.g., find customer opinions on a digital camera or the picture quality of the camera, and find public opinions on a political topic. Recall that an object can be a product, an organization, an event, or a topic.
2. Find opinions of a person or organization (i.e., opinion holder) on a particular object or a feature of the object, e.g., find Barack Obama's opinion on abortion. This type of search is particularly relevant to news articles, where individuals or organizations who express opinions are explicitly stated.

For the first type of queries, the user may simply give the name of the object or the name of the feature and the name of the object. For the second type of queries, the user may give the name of the opinion holder and the name of the object.

Similar to traditional Web search, opinion search also has two major tasks: (1) retrieving relevant documents/sentences to the user query, and (2) ranking the retrieved documents/sentences. However, there are also major differences. On retrieval, opinion search needs to perform two subtasks:

1. Find documents or sentences that are relevant to the query topic. This is the only task performed in the traditional Web search or IR.
2. Determine whether the documents or sentences express opinions and whether the opinions are positive or negative. This is the task of sentiment analysis. Traditional search does not perform this subtask. It is this subtask that makes the opinion search more complex than traditional search.

As for ranking, traditional Web search engines rank Web pages based on authority and relevance scores (Liu 2006). The basic premise is that the top ranked pages (ideally the first page) contain sufficient information to satisfy the user's information need. This paradigm is adequate for factual information search because *one fact equals to any number of the same fact.* That is, if the first page contains the required information, there is no need to see the rest of the relevant pages. For opinion search, this paradigm is fine for the second type of queries because the opinion holder usually has only one opinion on a particular object or topic, and the opinion is contained in a single document or page. However, for the first type of opinion queries, this paradigm needs to be modified because ranking in opinion search has two objectives. First, it needs to rank those opinionated documents or sentences with high utilities or information contents at the top (see Section 26.6.2). Second, it also needs to reflect the natural distribution of positive and negative opinions. This second objective is important because in most practical applications, the actual proportions of positive and negative opinions are the most important pieces of information as in traditional opinion surveys. Only reading the top-ranked results as in the traditional search is problematic because *one opinion does not equal to multiple opinions.* The top result only represents the opinion of a single person or organization. Thus, ranking in opinion search needs to capture the natural distribution of the positive and negative sentiments of the whole population. One simple solution is to produce two rankings, one for positive opinions and one for negative opinions. The numbers of positive and negative opinions indicate the distribution.

Providing a feature-based summary for each opinion search will be even better. However, it is an extremely challenging problem as we have seen that feature extraction, feature grouping, and associating objects to its features are all very difficult problems. Like opinion search, comparison search will be useful too. For example, when one wants to register for a free e-mail account, one most probably wants to know which e-mail system is the best for him/her, e.g., hotmail, gmail, or *Yahoo!* mail. Would not it be nice if one can find comparisons of features of these e-mail systems from existing users by issuing a search query "hotmail vs. gmail vs. yahoo mail"? So far, little research has been done in this direction although the work in (Ganapathibhotla and Liu 2008; Jindal and Liu 2006a,b) can be of use in this context.

To give a favor of what an opinion search system looks like, we present an example system (Zhang and Yu 2007), which is the winner of the blog track in the 2007 TREC evaluation (http://trec.nist.gov/). The task of this track is exactly opinion search (or retrieval). This system has two components. The first component is for retrieving relevant documents for each query. The second component is for classifying the retrieved documents as opinionated or not-opinionated (subjectivity classification). The opinionated documents are further classified into positive, negative, or mixed (containing both positive and negative opinions).

Retrieval component: This component performs the traditional IR task. Unlike a normal IR system, which is based on keyword match, this component considers both keywords and concepts. Concepts are named entities (e.g., names of people or organizations) or various types of phrases from dictionaries and other sources (e.g., Wikipedia entries). The strategy for processing a user query is as follows (Zhang et al. 2008; Zhang and Yu 2007): It first recognizes and disambiguates the concepts within the user query. It then broadens the search query with its synonyms. After that, it recognizes concepts in the retrieved documents, and also performs pseudo-feedback to automatically extract relevant words from the top-ranked documents to expand the query. Finally, it computes a similarity (or relevance score) of each document with the expanded query using both concepts and keywords.

Opinion classification component: This component performs two tasks: (1) classifying each document into one of the two categories, opinionated and not-opinionated, and (2) classifying each opinionated document as expressing a positive, negative, or mixed opinion. For both tasks, the system uses supervised learning. For the first task, it obtains a large amount of opinionated (subjective) training data from review sites such as rateitall.com and epinion.com. The data are also collected from different domains involving consumer goods and services as well as government policies and political viewpoints. The not-opinionated training data are obtained from sites that give objective information such as Wikipedia. From these training data, a SVM classifier is constructed.

This classifier is then applied to each retrieved document as follows: The document is first partitioned into sentences. The SVM classifier then classifies a sentence as opinionated or not opinionated. If a sentence is classified to be opinionated, its strength as determined by SVM is also noted. A document is regarded opinionated if there is at least one sentence that is classified as opinionated. To ensure that the opinion of the sentence is directed to the query topic, the system requires that enough query concepts/words are found in its vicinity. The totality of the opinionated sentences and their strengths in a document together with the document's similarity with the query is used to rank the document relative to other documents.

To determine whether an opinionated document expresses a positive, negative, or mixed opinion, the second classifier is constructed. The training data are reviews from review sites containing review ratings (e.g., rateitall.com). A low rating indicates a negative opinion while a high rating indicates a positive opinion. Using positive and negative reviews as training data, a sentiment classifier is built to classify each document as expressing positive, negative, or mixed opinions.

There are many other approaches for opinion retrieval. The readers are encouraged to read the papers at the TREC site (http://trec.nist.gov/pubs/trec16/t16_proceedings.html), and the overview paper of 2007 TREC blog track (MacDonald et al. 2007). Other related work includes Eguchi and Lavrenko (2006(; Gamon (2004); Nasukawa and Yi (2003).

26.6 Opinion Spam and Utility of Opinions

E-mail spam and Web spam are quite familiar to most people. E-mail spam refers to unsolicited commercial e-mails selling products and services, while Web spam refers to the use of "illegitimate means" to boost the search rank positions of target Web pages. The reason for spam is mainly due to economics. For example, in the Web context, the economic and/or publicity value of the rank position of a page returned by a search engine is of great importance. If someone searches for a product that your Web site sells, but the product page of your site is ranked very low (e.g., beyond the top 20) by a search engine, then the chance that the person will go to your page is extremely low, let alone to buy the product from your site. This is certainly bad for the business. There are now many companies that are in the business of helping others improve their page ranking by exploiting the characteristics and weaknesses of current search ranking algorithms. These companies are called *Search Engine Optimization* (SEO) companies. Some SEO activities are ethical and some, which generate spam, are not. For more information on Web spam, please refer to (Liu 2006).

In the context of opinions, we have a similar spam problem (Jindal and Liu 2007, 2008). Due to the explosive growth of the user-generated content, it has become a common practice for people to find and to read opinions on the Web for many purposes. For example, a person plans to buy a camera. Most probably, he or she will go to a merchant or review site (e.g., amazon.com) to read the reviews of some cameras. If he or she finds that most reviews are positive about a camera, he or she is very likely to buy the camera. However, if most reviews are negative, he or she will almost certainly choose another camera. Positive opinions can result in significant financial gains and/or fames for organizations and individuals. This, unfortunately, also gives good incentives for *opinion spam*, which refers to human activities (e.g., writing spam reviews) that try to deliberately mislead readers or automated opinion mining systems by giving undeserving positive opinions to some target objects in order to promote the objects and/or by giving unjust or false negative opinions to some other objects to damage their reputations. Such opinions are also called *fake opinions* or *bogus opinions*. They have become an intense discussion topic in blogs and forums, and also in press (e.g., http://travel.nytimes.com/2006/02/07/business/07guides.html), which show that the review spam has become a problem. We can predict that as opinions on the Web are increasingly used in practice by consumers and organizations, the problem of detecting spam opinions will become more and more critical.

A related problem that has also been studied in the past few years is the determination of the usefulness, helpfulness, or utility of a review (Ghose and Ipeirotis 2007; Kim et al. 2006; Liu et al. 2007; Zhang and Varadarajan 2006). The idea is to determine how helpful a review is to a user. This is a useful task as it is desirable to rank reviews based on utilities or qualities when showing the reviews to the user, with the most useful reviews at the top. In fact, many review aggregation sites have been practicing this for years. They obtain the helpfulness or utility score of each review by asking readers to provide helpfulness feedbacks to each review. For example, in amazon.com, the reader can indicate whether he or she finds a review helpful by responding to the question *"Was the review helpful to you?"* just below each review. The feedback results from all those responded are then aggregated and displayed right before each review, e.g., *"15 of 16 people found the following review helpful."* Although most review sites already provide the service, automatically determining the quality or the usefulness of a review is still useful because many reviews have few or no feedbacks. This is especially true for new reviews and reviews of products that are not very popular.

This section uses customer reviews of products as an example to study opinion spam and utility of opinions. However, most of the analyses are also applicable to opinions expressed in other forms of the user-generated content, e.g., forum posts and blogs.

26.6.1 Opinion Spam

There are generally three types of spam reviews as defined by Jindal and Liu (2007, 2008).

- *Type 1 (untruthful opinions)*: These are reviews that deliberately mislead readers or opinion mining systems by giving undeserving positive opinions to some target objects in order to promote the objects and/or by giving unjust or malicious negative opinions to some other objects in order to damage their reputation. Untruthful reviews are also commonly known as fake reviews or bogus reviews as we mentioned earlier.
- *Type 2 (opinions on brands only)*: These are reviews that do not comment on the specific products that they are supposed to review, but only comment on the brands, the manufacturers, or the sellers of the products. Although they may be useful, they are considered as spam because they are not targeted at the specific products and are often biased. For example, in a review for a HP printer, the reviewer only wrote *"I hate HP. I never buy any of their products."*
- *Type 3 (non-opinions)*: These are not reviews or opinionated although they appear as reviews. There are two main subtypes: (1) advertisements, and (2) other irrelevant texts containing no opinions (e.g., questions, answers, and random texts).

In general, spam detection can be formulated as a classification problem with two classes, *spam* and *non-spam*. Due to the specific nature of the different types of spam, they need to be dealt with differently. For spam reviews of type 2 and type 3, they can be detected based on traditional classification learning using manually labeled spam and non-spam reviews because these two types of spam reviews are easily recognizable manually. The main task is to find a set of effective data features for model building. Note again that here the features refer to features in machine learning not object features used in feature-based

TABLE 26.2 Spam Reviews vs. Product Quality

	Positive Spam Review	Negative Spam Review
Good quality product	1	2
Bad quality product	3	4
Average quality product	5	6

sentiment analysis. In (Jindal and Liu 2007; Jindal and Liu 2008), three sets of features were identified for learning:

Review centric features: These are features about the content of each review. Example features are the actual text of the review, the number of times that brand names are mentioned, the percentage of opinion words, the review length, and the number of helpful feedbacks.

Reviewer centric features: These are features about a reviewer. Example features are the average rating given by the reviewer; the standard deviation in rating; the ratio of the number of reviews that the reviewer wrote, which were the first reviews of the products to the total number of reviews that he or she wrote; and the ratio of the number of cases in which he or she was the only reviewer.

Product centric features: These are features about each product. Example features are price of the product, sales rank of the product (amazon.com assigns sales rank to "now selling products" according to their sales volumes), average rating, and standard deviation in ratings of the reviews on the product.

Logistic regression was used in learning. Experimental results based on a large number of amazon.com reviews showed that type 2 and types 3 spam reviews are fairly easy to detect.

However, this cannot be said about type 1 spam, untruthful opinions, or fake reviews. In fact, it is very difficult to detect such reviews because manually labeling training data is very hard, if not impossible. The problem is that identifying spam reviews by simply reading the reviews is extremely difficult because a spammer can carefully craft a spam review that is just like any innocent review.

In order to detect such spam, let us analyze fake reviews in greater detail. As indicated above, there are two main objectives for spam:

- Write undeserving positive reviews for some target objects in order to promote them. We call such spam reviews *hype spam*.
- Write unfair or malicious negative reviews for some target objects to damage their reputations. We call such spam reviews *defaming spam*.

In certain cases, the spammer may want to achieve both objectives, while in others, he or she only aims to achieve one of them because either he or she does not have an object to promote or there is no competition.

We now discuss what kinds of reviews are harmful and are likely to be spammed. Table 26.2 gives a simple view of type 1 spam. Spam reviews in regions 1, 3, and 5 are typically written by manufacturers of the product or persons with direct economic or other interests in the product. Their goal is to promote the product. Although opinions expressed in region 1 may be true, reviewers do not announce their conflict of interests. Note that good, bad, and average products can be defined based on average review ratings given to the product. Spam reviews in regions 2, 4, and 6 are likely to be written by competitors. Although opinions in reviews of region 4 may be true, reviewers do not announce their conflict of interests and have malicious intentions. Clearly, spam reviews in regions 1 and 4 are not so damaging, while spam reviews in regions 2, 3, 5, and 6 are very harmful. Thus, spam detection techniques should focus on identifying reviews in these regions. One important observation from this table is that harmful fake reviews are often outlier reviews. In other words, deviating from the norm is the necessary condition for harmful spam reviews, but not sufficient because many outlier reviews may be truthful.

Since manually labeling training data is extremely difficult, other ways have to be explored in order to find training examples for detecting possible type 1 spam. In Jindal and Liu (2008), it exploits duplicate reviews.

In their study of 5.8 million reviews, 2.14 million reviewers and 6.7 million products from amazon.com, they found a large number of duplicate and near-duplicate reviews, which indicates that review spam is widespread. These duplicates (which include near-duplicates) can be divided into four groups:

1. Duplicates from the same userid on the same product.
2. Duplicates from different userids on the same product.
3. Duplicates from the same userid on different products.
4. Duplicates from different userids on different products.

The first type of duplicates can be the results of reviewers mistakenly clicking the submit button multiple times (which of course can be detected based on the submission dates and times), or the same reviewers coming back to write updated reviews after using the product for some time. However, the last three kinds of duplicates are almost certainly type 1 spam reviews. Further sanity check was performed on these duplicate reviews because amazon.com cross-posts reviews to different formats of the same product, e.g., hardcover and paperback of the same book. Manually checking a large number of duplicate reviews showed that only a small percentage of them falls into this category. One reason for the low percentage could be because the reviews being studied were all from manufactured products, which perhaps have fewer formats of the same product (unlike books).

In the work reported in Jindal and Liu (2008), these three types of duplicates and near duplicates are treated as type 1 spam reviews, and the rest of the reviews are treated as non-spam reviews. Logistic regression is used to build a classification model. The experiments show some tentative but interesting results.

- Negative outlier reviews (whose ratings have significant negative deviations from the average rating) tend to be heavily spammed. The reason for such spam is quite intuitive. Positive outlier reviews are not badly spammed.
- Those reviews that are the only reviews of some products are likely to be spammed. This can be explained by the tendency of promoting an unpopular product by writing a spam review.
- Top-ranked reviewers are more likely to be spammers. Amazon.com gives a rank to each member/reviewer based on the frequency that he or she gets helpful feedback on his or her reviews. Additional analysis shows that top-ranked reviewers generally write a large number of reviews. People who wrote a large number of reviews are natural suspects. Some top reviewers wrote thousands or even tens of thousands of reviews, which is unlikely for an ordinary consumer.
- Spam reviews can get good helpful feedbacks and non-spam reviews can get bad feedbacks. This is important as it shows that if the usefulness or quality of a review is defined based on the helpful feedbacks that the review gets, people can be readily fooled by spam reviews. Note that the number of helpful feedbacks can be spammed too.
- Products of lower sale ranks are more likely to be spammed. This is good news because spam activities seem to be limited to low selling products, which is actually quite intuitive as it is difficult to damage the reputation of a popular product by writing a spam review.

Finally, it should be noted again that these results are only tentative because (1) it is not confirmed that the three types of duplicates are absolutely spam reviews, and (2) many spam reviews are not duplicated and they are not considered as spam in model building but are treated as non-spam due to the difficulty of manual labeling. For additional analysis and more spam detection strategies, please refer to Jindal and Liu (2008). This research is still at its infancy. Much work needs to be done. As we mentioned at the beginning of the section, with more and more people and organizations relying on opinions on the Web, devising good techniques to detect opinion spam is urgently needed. We do not want to wait until the day when the opinions on the Web are so heavily spammed that they become completely useless.

26.6.2 Utility of Reviews

Determining the utility of reviews is usually formulated as a regression problem. The learned model then assigns a utility value to each review, which can be used in review ranking. In this area of research, the ground truth data used for both training and testing are usually the user-helpfulness feedbacks given to each review, which as we discussed above are provided for each review at many review aggregation sites. So, unlike fake review detection, the training and testing data here is not an issue.

Researchers have used many types of data features for model building (Ghose and Ipeirotis 2007; Kim et al. 2006; Zhang and Varadarajan 2006). Example features include review length, review ratings (the number of stars), counts of some specific POS tags, opinion words, tf-idf weighting scores, wh-words, product attribute mentions, product brands, comparison with product specifications, and comparison with editorial reviews, and many more. Subjectivity classification is also applied in Ghose and Ipeirotis (2007). Liu et al. (2007) formulated the problem slightly differently, as a binary classification problem. Instead of using the original helpfulness feedbacks as the classification target or dependent variable, they performed manual annotation based on whether a review comments on many product attributes/features or not.

Finally, we note again that review utility regression/classification and review spam detections are different concepts. Not-helpful or low quality reviews are not necessarily fake reviews or spam, and helpful reviews may not be non-spam. A user often determines whether a review is helpful or not based on whether the review expresses opinions on many attributes/features of the product. A spammer can satisfy this requirement by carefully crafting a review that is just like a normal helpful review. Using the number of helpful feedbacks to define review quality is also problematic because user feedbacks can be spammed too. Feedback spam is a subproblem of click fraud in search advertising, where a person or robot clicks on some online advertisements to give the impression of real customer clicks. Here, a robot or a human spammer can also click on helpful feedback button to increase the helpfulness of a review. Another important point is that a low quality review is still a valid review and should not be discarded, but a spam review is untruthful and/or malicious and should be removed once detected.

26.7 Conclusions

This chapter gave an introduction to sentiment analysis and subjectivity (or opinion mining). Due to many challenging research problems and a wide variety of practical applications, it has been a very active research area in recent years. In fact, it has spread from computer science to management science (Archak et al. 2006; Chen and Xie 2008; Dellarocas et al. 2007; Ghose et al. 2007; Hu et al. 2006; Liu et al. 2007; Park et al. 2007). This chapter first presented an abstract model of sentiment analysis, which formulates the problem and provides a common framework to unify different research directions. It then discussed the most widely studied topic of sentiment and subjectivity classification, which determines whether a document or sentence is opinionated, and if so whether it carries a positive or negative opinion. We then described feature-based sentiment analysis that exploits the full power of the abstract model. After that, we discussed the problem of analyzing comparative and superlative sentences. Such sentences represent a different type of evaluation from direct opinions that have been the focus of the current research. The topic of opinion search or retrieval was introduced as well, as a parallel to the general Web search. Last but not least, we discussed opinion spam, which is increasingly becoming an important issue as more and more people are relying on opinions on the Web for decision making. This gives more and more incentive for spam. There is still no effective technique to combat opinion spam.

Finally, we conclude the chapter by saying that all the sentiment analysis tasks are very challenging. Our understanding and knowledge of the problem and its solution are still very limited. The main reason is that it is a natural language processing task, and natural language processing has no easy problems. Another reason may be due to our popular ways of doing research. We probably relied too much on machine learning algorithms. Some of the most effective machine learning algorithms, e.g., support vector machines and CRF, produce no human understandable results such that although they may achieve improved accuracy, we know little about how and why apart from some superficial knowledge gained in the manual feature engineering process. However, that being said, we have indeed made significant progresses over the past few years. This is evident from the large number of start-up companies that offer sentiment analysis or opinion mining services. There is a real and huge need in the industry for such services because every company wants to know how consumers perceive their products and services and those of their competitors. The same can also be said about consumers because whenever one wants to buy something, one wants to know the opinions of existing users. These practical needs and the technical challenges will keep the field vibrant and lively for years to come.

Acknowledgments

I am very grateful to Theresa Wilson for her insightful and detailed comments and suggestions, which have helped me improve the chapter significantly. I thank my former and current students for working with me on this fascinating topic: Xiaowen Ding, Murthy Ganapathibhotla, Minqing Hu, Nitin Jindal, Guang Qiu (visiting student from Zhejiang University), and Lei Zhang. I would also like to express my gratitude to Birgit König (McKinsey & Company) for many valuable discussions that have helped shape my understanding of the practical side of sentiment analysis and its related issues.

References

A. Andreevskaia and S. Bergler, Mining WordNet for a fuzzy sentiment: Sentiment tag extraction from WordNet glosses, *Proceedings of the European Chapter of the Association for Computational Linguistics (EACL)*, Trento, Italy, 2006.

N. Archak, A. Ghose, and P. Ipeirotis, Show me the money! Deriving the pricing power of product features by mining consumer reviews, *Proceedings of the ACM SIGKDD Conference on Knowledge Discovery and Data Mining (KDD)*, San Jose, CA, 2007.

A. Aue and M. Gamon, Customizing sentiment classifiers to new domains: A case study, *Proceedings of Recent Advances in Natural Language Processing (RANLP)*, Borovets, Bulgaria, 2005.

P. Beineke, T. Hastie, C. Manning, and S. Vaithyanathan, Exploring sentiment summarization, *Proceedings of the AAAI Spring Symposium on Exploring Attitude and Affect in Text*, Stanford, CA, AAAI Technical Report SS-04-07, 2004.

S. Bethard, H. Yu, A. Thornton, V. Hatzivassiloglou, and D. Jurafsky, Automatic extraction of opinion propositions and their holders, *Proceedings of the AAAI Spring Symposium on Exploring Attitude and Affect in Text*, Stanford, CA, 2004.

J. Blitzer, M. Dredze, and F. Pereira, Biographies, Bollywood, boom-boxes and blenders: Domain adaptation for sentiment classification, *Proceedings of the Association for Computational Linguistics (ACL)*, Prague, Czech Republic, 2007.

J. Bos and M. Nissim, An empirical approach to the interpretation of superlatives, *Proceedings of the Conference on Empirical Methods in Natural Language Processing (EMNLP)*, Sydney, Australia, 2006.

E. Breck, Y. Choi, and C. Cardie, Identifying expressions of opinion in context, *Proceedings of the International Joint Conference on Artificial Intelligence (IJCAI)*, Hyderabad, India, 2007.

G. Carenini, R. Ng, and A. Pauls, Multi-document summarization of evaluative text, *Proceedings of the European Chapter of the Association for Computational Linguistics (EACL)*, Trento, Italy, pp. 305–312, 2006.

G. Carenini, R. T. Ng, and E. Zwart, Extracting knowledge from evaluative text, *Proceedings of International Conference on Knowledge Capture (K-CAP)*, Banff, Canada, pp. 11–18, 2005.

Y. Chen and J. Xie, Online consumer review: Word-of-mouth as a new element of marketing communication mix, *Management Science*, 54, 477–491, 2008.

P. Chesley, B. Vincent, L. Xu, and R. Srihari, Using verbs and adjectives to automatically classify blog sentiment, *AAAI Symposium on Computational Approaches to Analysing Weblogs (AAAI-CAAW)*, Stanford, CA, pp. 27–29, 2006.

Y. Choi, E. Breck, and C. Cardie, Joint extraction of entities and relations for opinion recognition, *Proceedings of the Conference on Empirical Methods in Natural Language Processing (EMNLP)*, Sydney, Australia, 2006.

Y. Choi, C. Cardie, E. Riloff, and S. Patwardhan, Identifying sources of opinions with conditional random fields and extraction patterns, *Proceedings of the Human Language Technology Conference and the Conference on Empirical Methods in Natural Language Processing (HLT/EMNLP)*, Vancouver, Canada, 2005.

S. R. Das and M. Y. Chen, Yahoo! for Amazon: Sentiment extraction from small talk on the Web, *Management Science*, 53, 1375–1388, 2007.

K. Dave, S. Lawrence, and D. M. Pennock, Mining the peanut gallery: Opinion extraction and semantic classification of product reviews, *Proceedings of WWW*, Budapest, Hungary, pp. 519–528, 2003.

C. Dellarocas, X. Zhang, and N. F. Awad, Exploring the value of online product ratings in revenue forecasting: The case of motion pictures, *Journal of Interactive Marketing*, 21, 23–45, 2007.

A. Devitt and K. Ahmad, Sentiment analysis in financial news: A cohesion based approach, *Proceedings of the Association for Computational Linguistics (ACL)*, Prague, Czech Republic, pp. 984–991, 2007.

X. Ding, B. Liu, and P. S. Yu, A holistic lexicon-based approach to opinion mining, *Proceedings of the Conference on Web Search and Web Data Mining (WSDM)*, Stanford, CA, 2008.

K. Eguchi and V. Lavrenko, Sentiment retrieval using generative models, *Proceedings of the Conference on Empirical Methods in Natural Language Processing (EMNLP)*, Sydney, Australia, pp. 345–354, 2006.

A. Esuli and F. Sebastiani, Determining the semantic orientation of terms through gloss analysis, *Proceedings of the ACM Conference on Information and Knowledge Management (CIKM)*, Bremen, Germany, 2005.

A. Esuli and F. Sebastiani, Determining term subjectivity and term orientation for opinion mining, *Proceedings of the European Chapter of the Association for Computational Linguistics (EACL)*, Sydney, Australia, 2006.

A. Esuli and F. Sebastiani, SentiWordNet: A publicly available lexical resource for opinion mining, *Proceedings of Language Resources and Evaluation (LREC)*, Genoa, Italy, 2006.

A. Esuli and F. Sebastiani, PageRanking WordNet synsets: An application to opinion mining, *Proceedings of the Association for Computational Linguistics (ACL)*, Prague, Czech Republic, 2007.

C. Fellbaum, ed., *Wordnet: An Electronic Lexical Database*. MIT Press, Cambridge, MA, 1998.

M. Fiszman, D. Demner-Fushman, F. Lang, P. Goetz, and T. Rindflesch, Interpreting comparative constructions in biomedical text, *BioNLP*, Prague, Czech Republic, 2007.

M. Gamon, Sentiment classification on customer feedback data: Noisy data, large feature vectors, and the role of linguistic analysis, *Proceedings of the International Conference on Computational Linguistics (COLING)*, Geneva, Switzerland, 2004.

M. Gamon, A. Aue, S. Corston-Oliver, and E. Ringger, Pulse: Mining customer opinions from free text, *Proceedings of the International Symposium on Intelligent Data Analysis (IDA)*, Madrid, Spain, pp. 121–132, 2005.

G. Ganapathibhotla and B. Liu, Identifying preferred entities in comparative sentences, *Proceedings of the International Conference on Computational Linguistics, COLING*, Manchester, U.K., 2008.

R. Ghani, K. Probst, Y. Liu, M. Krema, and A. Fano, Text mining for product attribute extraction, *SIGKDD Explorations Newsletter*, 8, 41–48, 2006.

A. Ghose and P. G. Ipeirotis, Designing novel review ranking systems: Predicting usefulness and impact of reviews, *Proceedings of the International Conference on Electronic Commerce (ICEC)*, Minneapolis, MN, 2007.

A. Ghose, P. G. Ipeirotis, and A. Sundararajan, Opinion mining using econometrics: A case study on reputation systems, *Proceedings of the Association for Computational Linguistics (ACL)*, Prague, Czech Republic, 2007.

N. Godbole, M. Srinivasaiah, and S. Skiena, Large-scale sentiment analysis for news and blogs, *Proceedings of the International Conference on Weblogs and Social Media (ICWSM)*, Boulder, CO, 2007.

V. Hatzivassiloglou and K. McKeown, Predicting the semantic orientation of adjectives, *Proceedings of the Joint ACL/EACL Conference*, Toulouse, France, pp. 174–181, 1997.

V. Hatzivassiloglou and J. Wiebe, Effects of adjective orientation and gradability on sentence subjectivity, *Proceedings of the International Conference on Computational Linguistics (COLING)*, Saarbrücken, Germany, 2000.

M. Hu and B. Liu, Mining and summarizing customer reviews, *Proceedings of the ACM SIGKDD Conference on Knowledge Discovery and Data Mining (KDD)*, Seattle, WA, pp. 168–177, 2004.

N. Hu, P. A. Pavlou, and J. Zhang, Can online reviews reveal a product's true quality?: Empirical findings and analytical modeling of online word-of-mouth communication, *Proceedings of Electronic Commerce (EC)*, Ann Arbor, MI, pp. 324–330. ACM, New York, 2006.

N. Jindal and B. Liu, Identifying comparative sentences in text documents, *Proceedings of the ACM Special Interest Group on Information Retrieval (SIGIR)*, Seattle, WA, 2006a.

N. Jindal and B. Liu, Mining comparative sentences and relations, *Proceedings of AAAI*, Boston, MA, 2006b.

N. Jindal and B. Liu, Review spam detection, *Proceedings of WWW*, Banff, AB, 2007. (Poster paper).

N. Jindal and B. Liu, Opinion spam and analysis, *Proceedings of the Conference on Web Search and Web Data Mining (WSDM)*, Stanford, CA, pp. 219–230, 2008.

N. Kaji and M. Kitsuregawa, Building lexicon for sentiment analysis from massive collection of HTML documents, *Proceedings of the Joint Conference on Empirical Methods in Natural Language Processing and Computational Natural Language Learning (EMNLP-CoNLL)*, Prague, Czech Republic, pp. 1075–1083, 2007.

J. Kamps, M. Marx, R. J. Mokken, and M. de Rijke, Using WordNet to measure semantic orientation of adjectives, *Proceedings of the LREC'04*, Lisbon, Portugal, pp. 1115–1118, 2004.

H. Kanayama and T. Nasukawa, Fully automatic lexicon expansion for domain-oriented sentiment analysis, *Proceedings of the Conference on Empirical Methods in Natural Language Processing (EMNLP)*, Sydney, Australia, pp. 355–363, July 2006.

A. Kennedy and D. Inkpen, Sentiment classification of movie reviews using contextual valence shifters, *Computational Intelligence*, 22, 110–125, 2006.

S.-M. Kim and E. Hovy, Determining the sentiment of opinions, *Proceedings of the International Conference on Computational Linguistics (COLING)*, Geneva, Switzerland, 2004.

S.-M. Kim and E. Hovy, Automatic identification of pro and con reasons in online reviews, *Proceedings of the COLING/ACL Main Conference Poster Sessions*, Sydney, Australia, pp. 483–490, 2006.

S.-M. Kim and E. Hovy, Crystal: Analyzing predictive opinions on the web, *Proceedings of the Joint Conference on Empirical Methods in Natural Language Processing and Computational Natural Language Learning (EMNLP/CoNLL)*, Prague, Czech Republic, 2007.

S.-M. Kim, P. Pantel, T. Chklovski, and M. Pennacchiotti, Automatically assessing review helpfulness, *Proceedings of the Conference on Empirical Methods in Natural Language Processing (EMNLP)*, Sydney, Australia, pp. 423–430, 2006.

N. Kobayashi, K. Inui, and Y. Matsumoto, Extracting aspect-evaluation and aspect-of relations in opinion mining, *Proceedings of the 2007 Joint Conference on Empirical Methods in Natural Language Processing and Computational Natural Language Learning*, Prague, Czech Republic, pp. 1065–1074, 2007.

N. Kobayashi, K. Inui, Y. Matsumoto, K. Tateishi, and T. Fukushima, Collecting evaluative expressions for opinion extraction, *Proceedings of the First International Joint Conference on Natural Language Processing (IJCNLP)*, Hainan Island, China, pp. 584–589, 2004.

L.-W. Ku, Y.-T. Liang, and H.-H. Chen, Opinion extraction, summarization and tracking in news and blog corpora, *AAAI Symposium on Computational Approaches to Analysing Weblogs (AAAI-CAAW)*, Stanford, CA, pp. 100–107, 2006.

L.-W. Ku, Y.-T. Liang, and H.-H. Chen, Novel relationship discovery using opinions mined from the web, *National Conference on Artificial Intelligence (AAAI)*, Boston, MA, 2006.

J. Lafferty, A. McCallum, and F. Pereira, Conditional random fields: Probabilistic models for segmenting and labeling sequence data, *Proceedings of ICML*, Williamstown, MA, pp. 282–289, 2001.

B. Liu, *Web Data Mining: Exploring Hyperlinks, Contents, and Usage Data*. Springer-Verlag, Berlin, Germany, 2006.

B. Liu, M. Hu, and J. Cheng, Opinion observer: Analyzing and comparing opinions on the web, *Proceedings of WWW*, Chiba, Japan, 2005.

J. Liu, Y. Cao, C.-Y. Lin, Y. Huang, and M. Zhou, Low-quality product review detection in opinion summarization, *Proceedings of the Joint Conference on Empirical Methods in Natural Language Processing and Computational Natural Language Learning (EMNLP-CoNLL)*, Prague, Czech Republic, pp. 334–342, 2007. (Poster paper).

Y. Liu, J. Huang, A. An, and X. Yu, ARSA: A sentiment-aware model for predicting sales performance using blogs, *Proceedings of the ACM Special Interest Group on Information Retrieval (SIGIR)*, Amsterdam, the Netherlands, 2007.

Y. Lu and C. X. Zhai, Opinion integration through semi-supervised topic modeling, *Proceedings of 2008 International WWW Conference (WWW'08)*, Beijing, China, pp. 121–130, 2008.

C. MacDonald, I. Ounis, and I. Soboroff, Overview of the TREC2007 Blog Track, 2007. http://trec.nist.gov/pubs/trec16/papers/BLOG.OVERVIEW16.pdf

J. Martin and P. White, *The Language of Evaluation, Appraisal in English*. Palgrave Macmillan, London/New York, 2005.

R. McDonald, K. Hannan, T. Neylon, M. Wells, and J. Reynar, Structured models for fine-to-coarse sentiment analysis, *Proceedings of the Association for Computational Linguistics (ACL)*, Prague, Czech Republic, pp. 432–439, 2007.

Q. Mei, X. Ling, M. Wondra, H. Su, and C. X. Zhai, Topic sentiment mixture: Modeling facets and opinions in weblogs, *Proceedings of WWW*, Banff, Canada, pp. 171–180, 2007.

R. Mihalcea, C. Banea, and J. Wiebe, Learning multilingual subjective language via cross-lingual projections, *Proceedings of the Association for Computational Linguistics (ACL)*, Prague, Czech Republic, pp. 976–983, 2007.

S. Morinaga, K. Yamanishi, K. Tateishi, and T. Fukushima, Mining product reputations on the Web, *Proceedings of the ACM SIGKDD Conference on Knowledge Discovery and Data Mining (KDD)*, Edmonton, Canada, pp. 341–349, 2002. (Industry track).

T. Nasukawa and J. Yi, Sentiment analysis: Capturing favorability using natural language processing, *Proceedings of the Conference on Knowledge Capture (K-CAP)*, Sanibel Island, FL, 2003.

V. Ng, S. Dasgupta, and S. M. N. Arifin, Examining the role of linguistic knowledge sources in the automatic identification and classification of reviews, *Proceedings of the COLING/ACL Main Conference Poster Sessions*, Sydney, Australia, pp. 611–618, 2006.

X. Ni, G.-R. Xue, X. Ling, Y. Yu, and Q. Yang, Exploring in the weblog space by detecting informative and affective articles, *Proceedings of WWW*, Banff, Canada, 2007.

K. Nigam and M. Hurst, Towards a robust metric of polarity, in *Computing Attitude and Affect in Text: Theories and Applications*, Vol. 20, *The Information Retrieval Series*, J. G. Shanahan, Y. Qu, and J. Wiebe, (eds.), Springer-Verlag, Berlin, Germany, 2006.

B. Pang and L. Lee, A sentimental education: Sentiment analysis using subjectivity summarization based on minimum cuts, *Proceedings of the Association for Computational Linguistics (ACL)*, Prague, Czech Republic, pp. 271–278, 2004.

B. Pang and L. Lee, Seeing stars: Exploiting class relationships for sentiment categorization with respect to rating scales, *Proceedings of the Association for Computational Linguistics (ACL)*, Ann Arbor, MI, pp. 115–124, 2005.

B. Pang and L. Lee, Opinion mining and sentiment analysis, *Foundations and Trends in Information Retrieval*, 2(1–2), 1–135, 2008.

B. Pang, L. Lee, and S. Vaithyanathan, Thumbs up? Sentiment classification using machine learning techniques, *Proceedings of the Conference on Empirical Methods in Natural Language Processing (EMNLP)*, Philadelphia, PA, pp. 79–86, 2002.

D.-H. Park, J. Lee, and I. Han, The effect of on-line consumer reviews on consumer purchasing intention: The moderating role of involvement, *International Journal of Electronic Commerce*, 11, 125–148, 2007.

W. Parrott, *Emotions in Social Psychology*. Psychology Press, Philadelphia, PA, 2001.

L. Polanyi and A. Zaenen, Contextual lexical valence shifters, *Proceedings of the AAAI Spring Symposium on Exploring Attitude and Affect in Text*, Stanford, CA, 2004.

A.-M. Popescu and O. Etzioni, Extracting product features and opinions from reviews, *Proceedings of the Human Language Technology Conference and the Conference on Empirical Methods in Natural Language Processing (HLT/EMNLP)*, Vancouver, Canada, 2005.

G. Qiu, B. Liu, J. Bu, and C. Chen, Expanding domain sentiment lexicon through double propagation, *International Joint Conference on Artificial Intelligence (IJCAI-09)*, Pasadena, CA, 2009.

E. Riloff, S. Patwardhan, and J. Wiebe, Feature subsumption for opinion analysis, *Proceedings of the Conference on Empirical Methods in Natural Language Processing (EMNLP)*, Sydney, Australia, 2006.

E. Riloff and J. Wiebe, Learning extraction patterns for subjective expressions, *Proceedings of the Conference on Empirical Methods in Natural Language Processing (EMNLP)*, Sappora, Japan, 2003.

E. Riloff, J. Wiebe, and T. Wilson, Learning subjective nouns using extraction pattern bootstrapping, *Proceedings of the Conference on Natural Language Learning (CoNLL)*, Edmonton, Canada, pp. 25–32, 2003.

S. Sarawagi, Information extraction, *Foundations and Trends in Databases*, 1(3), 261–377, 2008.

Y. Seki, K. Eguchi, N. Kando, and M. Aono, Opinion-focused summarization and its analysis at DUC 2006, *Proceedings of the Document Understanding Conference (DUC)*, New York, pp. 122–130, 2006.

B. Snyder and R. Barzilay, Multiple aspect ranking using the good grief algorithm, *Proceedings of Human Language Technology Conference of the North American Chapter of the Association of Computational Linguistics, HLT-NAACL 2007*, Rochester, NY, pp. 300–307.

X. Song, Y. Chi, K. Hino, and B. Tseng, Identifying opinion leaders in the blogosphere, *Proceedings of the Conference on Information and Knowledge Management (CIKM)*, Lisbon, Portugal, pp. 971–974, 2007.

A. Stepinski and V. Mittal, A fact/opinion classifier for news articles, *Proceedings of the ACM Special Interest Group on Information Retrieval (SIGIR)*, Amsterdam, the Netherlands, pp. 807–808, 2007.

P. J. Stone. *The General Inquirer: A Computer Approach to Content Analysis*. MIT Press, Cambridge, MA, 1966.

V. Stoyanov and C. Cardie, Partially supervised coreference resolution for opinion summarization through structured rule learning, *Proceedings of the Conference on Empirical Methods in Natural Language Processing (EMNLP)*, Sydney, Australia, pp. 336–344, 2006.

Q. Su, X. Xu, H. Guo, X. Wu, X. Zhang, B. Swen, and Z. Su. Hidden Sentiment Association in Chinese Web Opinion Mining, *Proceedings of WWW'08*, Beijing, China, pp. 959–968, 2008.

H. Takamura, T. Inui, and M. Okumura, Extracting semantic orientations of phrases from dictionary, *Proceedings of the Joint Human Language Technology/North American Chapter of the ACL Conference (HLT-NAACL)*, Rochester, NY, 2007.

L. Tesnière, éléments de syntaxe structurale, Klincksieck, Paris, 1959.

M. Thomas, B. Pang, and L. Lee, Get out the vote: Determining support or opposition from congressional floor-debate transcripts, *Proceedings of the Conference on Empirical Methods in Natural Language Processing (EMNLP)*, Sydney, Australia, pp. 327–335, 2006.

I. Titov and R. McDonald, A joint model of text and aspect ratings for sentiment summarization, *Proceedings of 46th Annual Meeting of the Association for Computational Linguistics (ACL'08)*, Columbus, OH, 2008.

R. M. Tong, An operational system for detecting and tracking opinions in on-line discussion, *Proceedings of the Workshop on Operational Text Classification (OTC)*, New Orleans, LO, 2001.

P. Turney, Thumbs up or thumbs down? Semantic orientation applied to unsupervised classification of reviews, *Proceedings of the Association for Computational Linguistics (ACL)*, Philadelphia, PA, pp. 417–424, 2002.

X. Wan, Using bilingual knowledge and ensemble techniques for unsupervised Chinese sentiment analysis, *Proceedings of EMNLP08*, Honolulu, HI, pp. 553–561, 2008.

J. Wiebe, Learning subjective adjectives from corpora, *Proceedings of AAAI*, Austin, TX, 2000.

J. Wiebe, R. F. Bruce, and T. P. O'Hara, Development and use of a gold standard data set for subjectivity classifications, *Proceedings of the Association for Computational Linguistics (ACL)*, College Park, MD, pp. 246–253, 1999.

J. Wiebe and R. Mihalcea, Word sense and subjectivity, *Proceedings of the Conference on Computational Linguistics/Association for Computational Linguistics (COLING/ACL)*, Sydney, Australia, pp. 1065–1072, 2006.

J. Wiebe and T. Wilson, Learning to disambiguate potentially subjective expressions, *Proceedings of the Conference on Natural Language Learning (CoNLL)*, Taipei, Taiwan, pp. 112–118, 2002.

J. Wiebe, T. Wilson, and C. Cardie, Annotating expressions of opinions and emotions in language, *Language Resources and Evaluation*, 1(2), 165–210, 2005.

J. Wiebe, T. Wilson, R. Bruce, M. Bell, and M. Martin, Learning subjective language, *Computational Linguistics*, 30, 277–308, 2004.

T. Wilson, J. Wiebe, and R. Hwa, Just how mad are you? Finding strong and weak opinion clauses, *Proceedings of AAAI*, San Jose, CA, pp. 761–769, 2004.

T. Wilson, J. Wiebe, and P. Hoffmann, Recognizing contextual polarity in phrase-level sentiment analysis, *Proceedings of the Human Language Technology Conference and the Conference on Empirical Methods in Natural Language Processing (HLT/EMNLP)*, Vancouver, Canada, pp. 347–354, 2005.

H. Yang, L. Si, and J. Callan, Knowledge transfer and opinion detection in the TREC2006 blog track, *Proceedings of TREC*, Gaithersburg, MD, 2006.

J. Yi, T. Nasukawa, R. Bunescu, and W. Niblack, Sentiment analyzer: Extracting sentiments about a given topic using natural language processing techniques, *Proceedings of the IEEE International Conference on Data Mining (ICDM)*, Melbourne, FL, 2003.

H. Yu and V. Hatzivassiloglou, Towards answering opinion questions: Separating facts from opinions and identifying the polarity of opinion sentences, *Proceedings of the Conference on Empirical Methods in Natural Language Processing (EMNLP)*, Sapporo, Japan, 2003.

W. Zhang, L. Jia, C. Yu, and W. Meng, Improve the effectiveness of the opinion retrieval and opinion polarity classification. *ACM 17th Conference on Information and Knowledge Management (CIKM)*, Nap Valley, CA, 2008.

W. Zhang and C. Yu, UIC at TREC 2007 Blog Report, 2007. http://trec.nist.gov/pubs/trec16/papers/uic-zhang.blog.final.pdf

Z. Zhang and B. Varadarajan, Utility scoring of product reviews, *Proceedings of the ACM Conference on Information and Knowledge Management (CIKM)*, Arlington, VA, pp. 51–57, 2006.

L. Zhuang, F. Jing, X.-Y. Zhu, and L. Zhang, Movie review mining and summarization, *Proceedings of the ACM Conference on Information and Knowledge Management (CIKM)*, Arlington, VA, 2006.

Index

9781420085921